PROGRAMMING IN C++: LESSONS AND APPLICATIONS

Timothy B. D'Orazio
San Francisco State University

Boston Burr Ridge, IL Dubuque, IA Madison, WI New York San Francisco St. Louis
Bangkok Bogotá Caracas Kuala Lumpur Lisbon London Madrid Mexico City
Milan Montreal New Delhi Santiago Seoul Singapore Sydney Taipei Toronto

The McGraw·Hill Companies

Higher Education

PROGRAMMING IN C++: LESSONS AND APPLICATIONS

Published by McGraw-Hill, a business unit of The McGraw-Hill Companies, Inc., 1221 Avenue of the Americas, New York, NY 10020.

This book is printed on acid-free paper.

International 1 2 3 4 5 6 7 8 9 0 DOC/DOC 0 9 8 7 6 5 4 3
Domestic 1 2 3 4 5 6 7 8 9 0 DOC/DOC 0 9 8 7 6 5 4 3

ISBN 0–07–242412–5
ISBN 0–07–119453–3 (ISE)

Publisher: *Elizabeth A. Jones*
Sponsoring editor: *Kelly Lowery*
Developmental editor: *Melinda Dougharty*
Marketing manager: *Dawn R. Bercier*
Project manager: *Jane Mohr*
Production supervisor: *Sherry L. Kane*
Senior media project manager: *Stacy A. Patch*
Senior media technology producer: *Phillip Meek*
Designer: *David W. Hash*
Cover/interior designer: *Scan Communications Group, Inc.*
Compositor: *Interactive Composition Corporation*
Typeface: *10/12 Times Roman*
Printer: *R. R. Donnelley Crawfordsville, IN*

Library of Congress Cataloging-in-Publication Data

D'Orazio, T. B.
Programming in C++ : lessons and applications / Timothy B. D'Orazio.—1st ed.
p. cm.
ISBN 0–07–242412–5—ISBN 0–07–119453–3 (ISE)
1. C++ (Computer program language). I. Title.

QA76.73.C153D66 2004
005.13'3—dc21 2003046446
CIP

INTERNATIONAL EDITION ISBN 0–07–119453–3

www.mhhe.com

DEDICATION

To Elizabeth, Ashlyn, and Adlae

BRIEF CONTENTS

CONTENTS

PREFACE

This book teaches the C++ language and object-oriented design to students with no previous programming experience. The text is intended for first or second year students. A background in high school mathematics, physics, and chemistry is beneficial but not required.

FEATURES

The following features distinguish this book from others.

- *More than 35 case studies.* These application examples illustrate how to solve practical problems from many fields of practice.
- *Multilevel approach to get students involved in reading and understanding source code.* Each lesson uses a number of techniques (code annotations, questions, topic list, and exercises) to make students engaged in the code.
- *Early introduction to debugging.* At the end of Chapter 2, students are presented with a methodology for finding bugs and developing their first programs.
- *Detailed description of tracing and debugging loops.* A method for developing and checking the reliability of both simple and complex loops is included in several chapters.
- *Numerous figures.* Figures are generously used to illustrate many of the difficult C++ concepts.
- *Simple to complex application examples.* The application examples span a range of difficulty levels so that beginning to more advanced students are appropriately challenged.
- *Step-by-step methodology for program development.* Each of the application examples illustrates a structured approach to developing programs.
- *Early introduction to classes and objects.* Classes and objects are introduced in Chapter 8. However, the text structure allows instructors to postpone the coverage until Chapter 14, if so desired.
- *Numerical method examples.* The application examples include illustrations of some fundamental numerical methods and how to code them.
- *Modification exercises.* These exercises are good for courses with a two- or three-hour lab. Students can prepare for the lab by reading a particular application example. If they have done this, many of these exercises can be done in a two- or three-hour time frame.

- *Introduction to the UML.* Students are presented with a description of the basics of the UML and are shown how to convert some UML diagrams into C++ code.
- *Simple, straightforward introduction to the C++ Standard Template Library.* The purpose of this coverage is to give students the ability to use the Standard Template Library as soon as possible. The terminology is made nonintimidating, so students can quickly use the basic parts of the library.

BOOK STRUCTURE

Each chapter of the book is divided into two parts—Lessons and Application Examples. The Lessons teach C++ language elements and simple programming techniques, and the Application Examples teach program design.

Lessons

The Lessons are designed to teach aspects of the C++ language and to make students aware of what is available to them in writing programs. This includes basic syntax, how to get input and output, what the operators mean, what library functions are available, and how to create classes and use objects. The Lessons also teach such basic programming manipulations as finding a maximum in a group, summing array values, and working with random numbers.

Each Lesson focuses on a single example program and has the following sections and pedagogical concepts in order.

Section	Pedagogical Concept
Topics—a list of the topics to be covered.	Alerts students to what they will learn.
Introduction—a brief introduction giving background to the topics.	Informs students of the importance of what is being covered and prepares them to read the source code.
Questions—a few questions asked of the students about the program.	Encourages students to attempt to interpret the code on their own before it is explained to them.
Annotated source code with output—the example program with output that demonstrates the topics of the lesson.	The code demonstrates the techniques being taught, and the annotations focus students' attention on the details that are important in the new programming topics. Annotations in text boxes have been used because they stand out more than "in code" comments, and allow for more detail to be given. If a student reads nothing but the source code for a lesson, he or she learns at least the basics of the lesson.

Description—describes what the example program demonstrates and how the techniques can be applied to other programs. Illustrations, tables, and lists of C++ language aspects are presented.	The Description language is deliberately conversational to create a soft environment for learning detailed technical material. Illustrations are used to give students visual images of concepts and actions. Tables and lists of C++ language aspects are presented for later reference.
Lesson exercises (at end of chapter)—true/false, short answer, and basic program assignments.	These exercises highlight the important points shown in the lessons. The questions are meant to be relatively simple, so students willingly test themselves at the end of each lesson. This reinforces the material. The program assignments are reasonably straightforward. Instructors can assign them when they are interested only in focusing on language elements and not problem solving.
Lesson exercise solutions (at end of chapter)—answers to the true/false and short answer questions.	The solutions are readily available to give students instant feedback.

Overall, the different sections in the Lessons encourage students to read and understand the C++ code. The goal is to develop strong skills in students for comprehending programs written by others. Upon completion of the Lessons, students are fluent in the C++ language because they have been required (and guided) to read and understand C++ code written throughout the text.

Application Examples

Because it is not enough that students simply know how the language works and simple programming manipulations, the Application Examples demonstrate program design and how to solve practical problems.

A structured multistep method is used to develop each Application Example. Students can follow the same method to create their own programs. Much emphasis is placed on the thought processes used to design practical programs. There are no multiple page programs with little explanation.

The Application Examples have the following sections and pedagogical concepts.

Section	Pedagogical Concept
Problem statement—describes problem specifications with input and output requirements.	The problem is designed to highlight particular skills and illustrate why they are needed in solving problems with programming, for instance, using compound operators in practical problems. Because the book is meant for freshman/sophomore level, the mathematics deliberately is not advanced.

Solution: relevant equations—describes technical aspects of the problem including the use of the equations needed.	Gives students insight into how to manipulate equations to get a form that is applicable for a computer solution. For problems that may go slightly beyond some students' background, further description of the concepts is given here.
Solution: specific example—hand calculation example using specific input data. Numeric result is obtained.	Shows how to use the relevant equations and the steps needed to obtain a numeric result.
Solution: classes and objects—discussion of classes and objects and object-oriented design features needed for the program. Used only in programs that emphasize classes and objects.	Illustrates thought processes and methodology in developing classes.
Solution: algorithms and code segments—lists steps needed in solution and shows code for the steps (for complex example programs).	Illustrates how steps can be converted into source code. The classes and objects are integrated into this section for examples illustrating object-oriented design.
Solution: source code—source code with annotations that solves the problem.	This illustrates how well-conceived designs (and algorithms) translate into complete working code.
Comments—describes implications of the source code with regard to developing other programs in a similar vein. Points out shortcomings of code shown.	This section is meant to take students beyond the program written. It points out how changes can be made to make the program more powerful and what problems can arise in certain circumstances.
Modification exercises—assignments that can be done by making changes to the given source code.	The purpose here is to get students to work with the code of others. Some are reasonably simple changes. Others require more effort. In all cases, students need an understanding of the code to make the changes. These exercises are good for courses with a two- or three-hour lab. Students can prepare for the lab by reading a particular application example. If they have done this, many of these exercises can be done in a two- or three-hour time frame.

Application exercises (at end of chapter)—these are technically oriented programming assignments.	These exercises are meant to be one- to three-week-long home assignments where students must write a program from scratch. They can be developed using the techniques learned in the application examples. It is believed that most instructors using the book's assignments will use these or a modification of these problems.

The purpose of this approach is to get students to follow a consistent methodology for program design. Even if an instructor has a different approach, they realize from reading the text that programs are not developed in a haphazard manner.

The Application Examples show in detail the thought processes in working with such things as complex loops, arrays, classes, and pointers.

ACKNOWLEDGMENTS

I would like to thank Tom Casson, Kelly Lowery, and Melinda Dougharty of McGraw-Hill for their interest, support, encouragement, and insightful comments in the development of this book. I have enjoyed working with them very much. Jane Mohr, David Hash, and Jill Barrie were also very helpful and effective in bringing about the book's production.

We also had a number of very thoughtful reviewers who made quite useful comments that definitely contributed to improving the book's quality:

Drue Coles, Boston University

Nurgun Erdol, Florida Atlantic University

Juan Gilbert, Auburn University

Linda J. Hayes, University of Texas

Glenn Heinrichs, Oakton Community College

Timothy Henry, University of Rhode Island

Mark Jones, Virginia Tech

Robert A. Rouse, Washington University

Ruth Ungar, University of Connecticut

I would like to thank my first computing instructor, Professor Raymond Canale at the University of Michigan, my Ph.D. advisor, Professor J. Michael Duncan of Virginia Tech (formerly of the University of California, Berkeley), and my postdoctoral supervisor, Dr. Suzanne Lacasse, director of the Norwegian Geotechnical Institute, for inspiring me to tackle challenging programming assignments. I would also like to thank Eric Munson, formerly of McGraw-Hill, for supporting the creation of this text.

Most importantly, I would like to thank my family. My wife Elizabeth and daughters Ashlyn and Adlae have been very supportive and understanding through many long nights and early mornings.

TO THE INSTRUCTOR

The book is set up for a 15-week course with one or two chapters covered each week. The text can be followed in the order presented or in an order described next.

Reordering the Coverage

If an instructor wishes to cover classes later, reduce or eliminate the coverage of pointers, and/or reduce or eliminate the coverage of strings, the order of coverage can be changed according to this list:

1. Late class coverage.
   Chapters 1–7 (all)
   Chapter 9 (9.1–9.4)
   Chapter 10 (all)
   Chapter 11 (11.1–11.2, 11.5–11.8)
   Chapters 12–13 (all)
   Chapter 8 (all)
   Chapter 9 (9.5–9.6)
   Chapter 11 (11.3–11.4)
   Chapters 14–18 (all)
2. Reduced pointer coverage.
   Chapters 1–10 (all)
   Chapter 11 (11.1–11.2)
   Chapters 12–13 (all)
   Chapter 11 (11.3–11.5)
   Chapter 14 (14.1–14.5)
   Chapter 15 (15.1–15.4)
   Chapter 17 (17.1–17.3)
   Chapter 18 (all)
3. Reduced string coverage.
   Chapters 1–11 (all)
   Chapter 12 (12.1)
   Chapters 14–18 (all)
4. Late class coverage with reduced pointer and string coverage.
   Chapters 1–7 (all)
   Chapter 9 (9.1–9.4)
   Chapter 10 (all)
   Chapter 11 (11.1–11.2)
   Chapter 12 (12.1)
   Chapter 8 (all)
   Chapter 9 (9.5–9.6)
   Chapter 11 (11.3–11.5)
   Chapter 14 (14.1–14.5)
   Chapter 15 (15.1–15.4)
   Chapter 17 (17.1–17.3)
   Chapter 18 (all)
5. Late and reduced class coverage (eliminated pointer and string coverage).
   Chapters 1–7 (all)
   Chapter 9 (9.1–9.4)
   Chapter 10 (all)
   Chapter 8 (all)

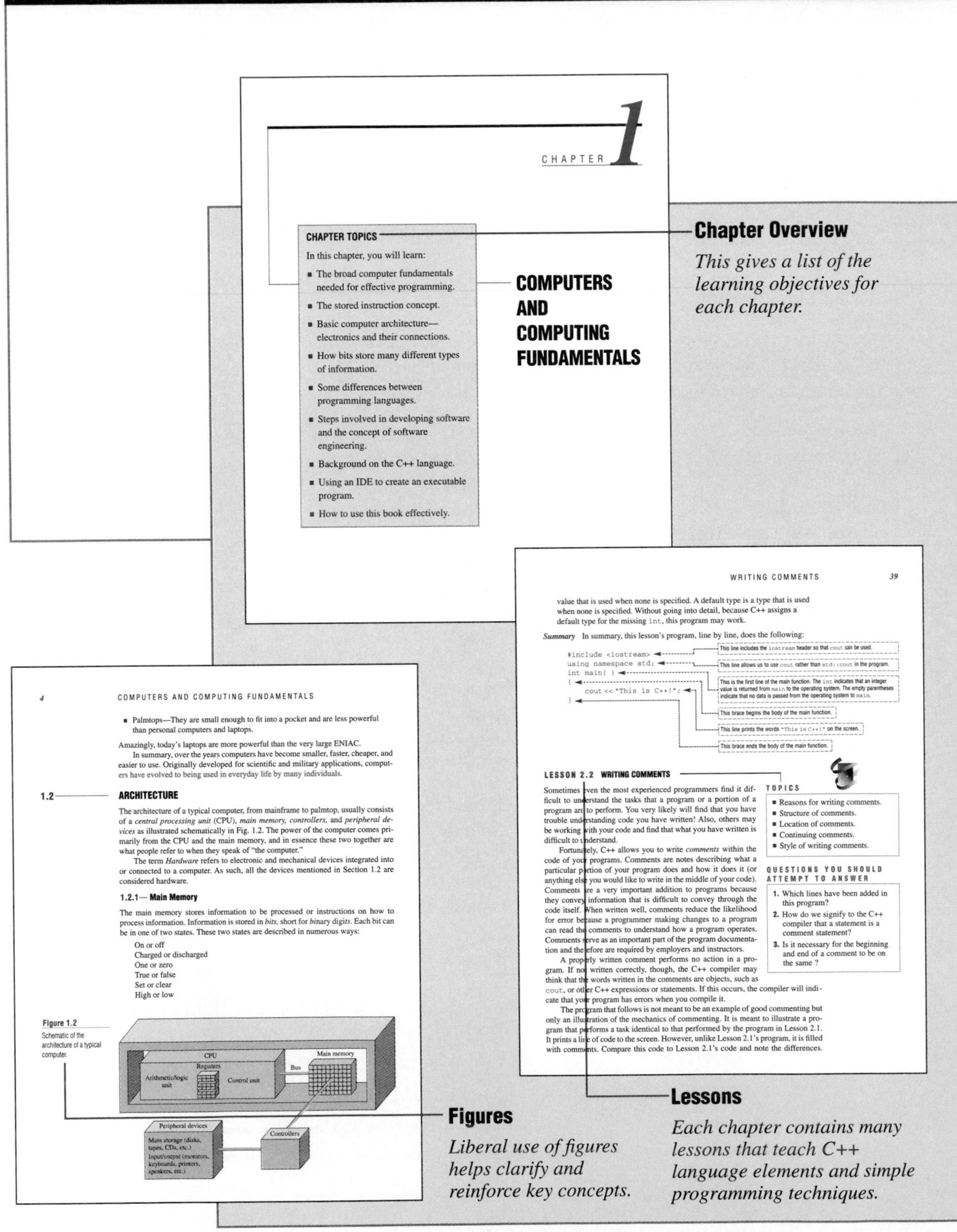

CHAPTER 1
CHAPTER TOPICS
In this chapter, you will learn:
The broad computer fundamentals needed for effective programming.
The stored instruction concept.
Basic computer architecture—electronics and their connections.
How bits store many different types of information.
Some differences between programming languages.
Steps involved in developing software and the concept of software engineering.
Background on the C++ language.
Using an IDE to create an executable program.
How to use this book effectively.
COMPUTERS AND COMPUTING FUNDAMENTALS
Chapter Overview
This gives a list of the learning objectives for each chapter.
WRITING COMMENTS 39
value that is used when none is specified. A default type is a type that is used when none is specified. Without going into detail, because C++ assigns a default type for the missing int, this program may work.
Summary In summary, this lesson's program, line by line, does the following:
#include <iostream>
using namespace std;
int main( )
{
cout << "This is C++!";
}
This line includes the iostream header so that cout can be used.
This line allows us to use cout rather than std::cout in the program.
This is the first line of the main function. The int indicates that an integer value is returned from main to the operating system. The empty parentheses indicate that no data is passed from the operating system to main.
This brace begins the body of the main function.
This line prints the words "This is C++!" on the screen.
This brace ends the body of the main function.
LESSON 2.2 WRITING COMMENTS
Sometimes even the most experienced programmers find it difficult to understand the tasks that a program or a portion of a program are to perform. You very likely will find that you have trouble understanding code you have written! Also, others may be working with your code and find that what you have written is difficult to understand.
Fortunately, C++ allows you to write comments within the code of your programs. Comments are notes describing what a particular portion of your program does and how it does it (or anything else you would like to write in the middle of your code). Comments are a very important addition to programs because they convey information that is difficult to convey through the code itself. When written well, comments reduce the likelihood for error because a programmer making changes to a program can read the comments to understand how a program operates. Comments serve as an important part of the program documentation and therefore are required by employers and instructors.
A properly written comment performs no action in a program. If not written correctly, though, the C++ compiler may think that the words written in the comments are objects, such as cout, or other C++ expressions or statements. If this occurs, the compiler will indicate that your program has errors when you compile it.
The program that follows is not meant to be an example of good commenting but only an illustration of the mechanics of commenting. It is meant to illustrate a program that performs a task identical to that performed by the program in Lesson 2.1. It prints a line of code to the screen. However, unlike Lesson 2.1's program, it is filled with comments. Compare this code to Lesson 2.1's code and note the differences.
TOPICS
Reasons for writing comments.
Structure of comments.
Location of comments.
Continuing comments.
Style of writing comments.
QUESTIONS YOU SHOULD ATTEMPT TO ANSWER
1. Which lines have been added in this program?
2. How do we signify to the C++ compiler that a statement is a comment statement?
3. Is it necessary for the beginning and end of a comment to be on the same ?
4 COMPUTERS AND COMPUTING FUNDAMENTALS
Palmtops—They are small enough to fit into a pocket and are less powerful than personal computers and laptops.
Amazingly, today's laptops are more powerful than the very large ENIAC.
In summary, over the years computers have become smaller, faster, cheaper, and easier to use. Originally developed for scientific and military applications, computers have evolved to being used in everyday life by many individuals.
1.2 ARCHITECTURE
The architecture of a typical computer, from mainframe to palmtop, usually consists of a central processing unit (CPU), main memory, controllers, and peripheral devices as illustrated schematically in Fig. 1.2. The power of the computer comes primarily from the CPU and the main memory, and in essence these two together are what people refer to when they speak of "the computer."
The term Hardware refers to electronic and mechanical devices integrated into or connected to a computer. As such, all the devices mentioned in Section 1.2 are considered hardware.
1.2.1— Main Memory
The main memory stores information to be processed or instructions on how to process information. Information is stored in bits, short for binary digits. Each bit can be in one of two states. These two states are described in numerous ways:
On or off
Charged or discharged
One or zero
True or false
Set or clear
High or low
Figure 1.2
Schematic of the architecture of a typical computer.
CPU
Registers
Arithmetic/logic unit
Control unit
Bus
Main memory
Peripheral devices
Mass storage (disks, tapes, CDs, etc.)
Input/output (monitors, keyboards, printers, speakers, etc.)
Controllers
Figures
Liberal use of figures helps clarify and reinforce key concepts.
Lessons
Each chapter contains many lessons that teach C++ language elements and simple programming techniques.

WALK THROUGH

32 GETTING STARTED

The only way to learn programming is to write programs. You will find that the more time you spend at a computer, the more you will learn. In this chapter we show a number of programs that illustrate the basic form and structure of a C++ program. You should begin programming by imitating what we show and then customizing your program to meet your needs.

This chapter's lessons show you how to create simple text output and how to add documentation (in the form of comments) to a program. The application examples illustrate how to print neat tabular headings and how to detect program errors. In themselves, the example programs described in this chapter have limited practical use. However, portions of these programs form integral pieces of many valuable C++ programs.

LESSON 2.1 **BASIC STRUCTURE**

TOPICS

- Writing a simple C++ program.
- Using the `cout` object to display text on the screen.
- Structure of a simple C++ program.
- Basic rules for writing a C++ program.

QUESTION YOU SHOULD ATTEMPT TO ANSWER

1. If you wanted to display the statement "I am learning a programming language," how would you write the `cout` statement?

The program that follows illustrates the basic structure of a C++ program. When you execute the program, the statement

This is C++!

appears on the screen and remains there until other tasks eliminate it.

Examine the program and the output carefully before you read the description. The program is written in what is called *code*. You may understand why it is called code because it looks cryptic. Since at this point you know nothing about C++, you probably will find the first few lessons difficult. As you learn more, though, you will find that indeed you can interpret much of the code yourself (assisted by the boxed annotations) before we explain it fully to you.

Read the source code line by line, and follow the boxed annotations.

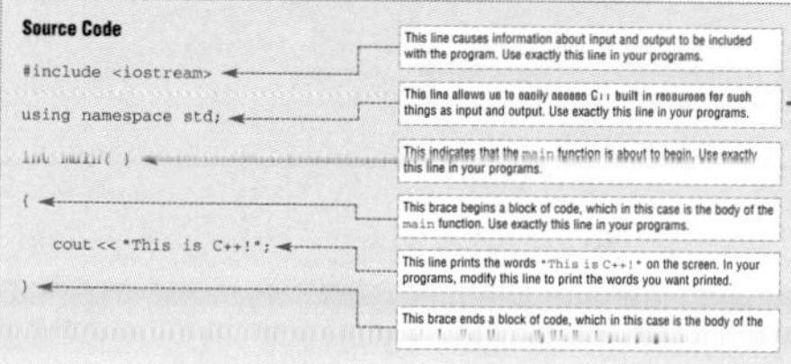

Source Code

```
#include <iostream>

using namespace std;

int main( )

{

   cout << "This is C++!";

}
```

This line causes information about input and output to be included with the program. Use exactly this line in your programs.
This line allows us to easily access C++ built in resources for such things as input and output. Use exactly this line in your programs.
This indicates that the main function is about to begin. Use exactly this line in your programs.
This brace begins a block of code, which in this case is the body of the main function. Use exactly this line in your programs.
This line prints the words "This is C++!" on the screen. In your programs, modify this line to print the words you want printed.
This brace ends a block of code, which in this case is the body of the

Source Code

Code annotations, questions, topic lists, and exercises get students involved in reading and understanding source code.

122 VARIABLES AND ARITHMETIC OPERATIONS

Comments

The user can look at the output and decide the correct letter order. For DRAE, the English word can be DARE, DEAR, or READ.

If a dictionary type database were available, the anagram list could be compared to the dictionary and a list containing only the correct possibilities could be created.

Using this same form, a program for solving a five-letter anagram could be created. A total of 120 `cout` statements would be needed for such a program. When we cover loops and arrays, we will see that we can write such a program with far fewer `cout` statements.

You can see that as anagrams become longer, the number of possible combinations becomes quite great, since the number is *n* factorial. A 12-letter anagram has 12! = 479,001,600 combinations! Having a human read such a number is unwieldy. [illegible]

When humans do anagrams by hand, they mentally look for common letter orders to reduce the number of possibilities. For instance, in the anagram "TRAB," the order BT at the beginning of the word is not possible. Recognizing this eliminates a number of possibilities. However, BR is a likely combination and leads to one possible solution "BRAT."

Modification Exercises

1. Modify the program to solve the anagram "OWDR."
2. Modify the program to solve just a three-letter anagram.
3. Modify the program to solve a five-letter anagram.

LESSON EXERCISES

LESSON 3.1 EXERCISES

1. True or false:
   a. The following `int` type variable names are legal:
      `1cat, 2dogs, 3pears, %area`
   b. The following `double` variable names are legal:
      `cat, dogs2, pears3, cat_number`
   c. We can print more than one variable value with a single `cout` statement.
   d. We cannot print both `double` and `int` type variable values with a single `cout` statement.
   e. The two statements that follow are identical:
      ```
      int ABC, DEF;
      int abc, def;
      ```
2. Which of the following are incorrect C++ variable names and why?
   `enum, ENUM, lotus123, A+B23, A(b)c, AaBbCc, Else, abx, pi, p`

Lesson Exercises

Lesson exercises allow students to test their understanding of material covered in each lesson.

46 GETTING STARTED

TABLE 2.1 — Character escape sequences

Escape sequence	Meaning	Result
`\0`	Null character	Terminates a character string
`\a`	Alert/bell	Generates an audible or visible alert
`\b`	Backspace	Moves the active position (e.g., for the console, this is the current cursor location) back one space on the current line
`\f`	Form feed	Moves the active position to the initial position at the start of the next logical page (e.g., ejects printer page)
`\n`	New line	Linefeeds to the initial position of the next line
`\r`	Carriage return	Moves the active position to the initial position of the current line
`\t`	Horizontal tab	Moves the active position to the next horizontal tabulation position on the current line
`\v`	Vertical tab	Moves the active position to the initial position of the next vertical tabulation position
`\0ddd`	Octal constant	Represents an integer constant using base 8 where ddd represents a sequence of digits 0–7 only
`\xddd` `\Xddd`	Hexadecimal constant	Represents an integer constant using base 16, where ddd represents a sequence of the decimal digits, and the letters a–f or A–F represent values of 10 through 15 respectively
`\\`	Backslash	Displays a backslash
`\'`	Single quote	Displays a single quote
`\"`	Double quote	Displays a double quote
`\%`	Percent	Displays a percent character
`\?`	Question mark	Prevents the misinterpretation of trigraph-like character sequences; e.g., trigraph sequence `??=` will display the character `#`, but `\?\?=` will display `??=`

APPLICATION EXAMPLE 2.1 **CREATING LOGO AND TABLE HEADINGS**

TOPIC

- Using `cout`

Problem Statement

Neatly displayed output is essential for effectively communicating results. Properly written table headings are extremely useful because program output is frequently displayed in the form of a table. Write a program that creates a logo and two sets of table headings for a monthly bank statement. The logo is for Harrison Bank in the form:

```
HARRISON
HH      H
HH      H
HARRISON
HARRISON
IIII    II
HH      H
HARRISON
```

The title of the document is "MONTHLY BANK STATEMENT." The first set of table headings should consist of five columns: Account Name, Interest Rate, Number of Transactions, Beginning Balance, and Ending Balance. The number of spaces for each column is 20, 12, 12, 15, and 15, respectively. The second set of table headings should consist of three columns repeated once: Check Number, Date Paid, and Amount. The number of spaces for each column is 12, 9, and 10, respectively.

Application Examples

These allow students to apply the features of the lessons and solve practical problems from many different disciplines.

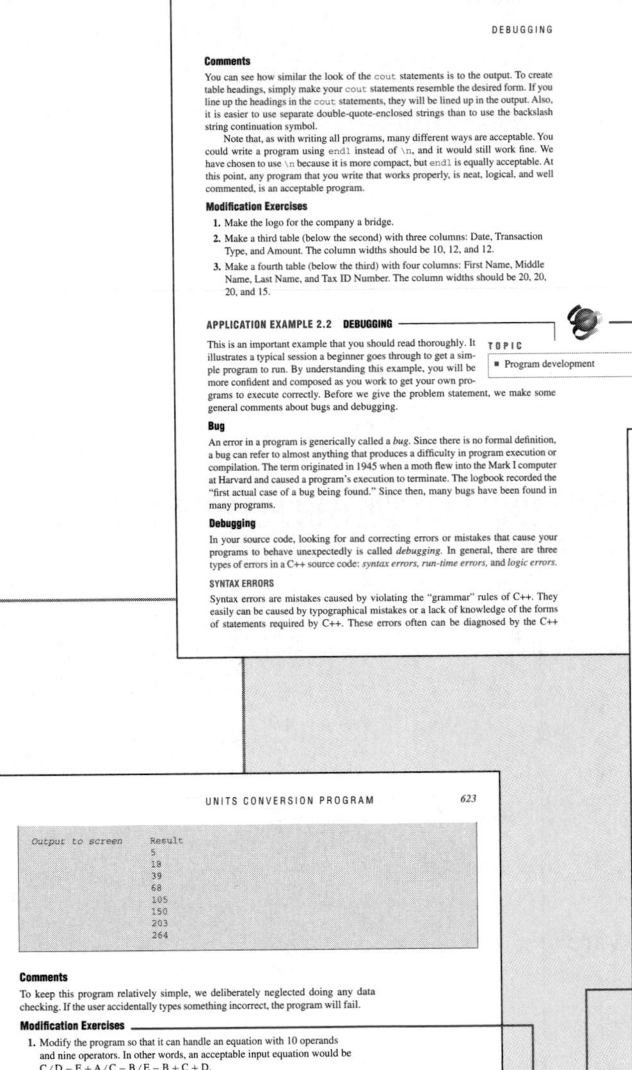

DEBUGGING 49

Comments

You can see how similar the look of the `cout` statements is to the output. To create table headings, simply make your `cout` statements resemble the desired form. If you line up the headings in the `cout` statements, they will be lined up in the output. Also, it is easier to use separate double-quote-enclosed strings than to use the backslash string continuation symbol.

Note that, as with writing all programs, many different ways are acceptable. You could write a program using `endl` instead of `\n`, and it would still work fine. We have chosen to use `\n` because it is more compact, but `endl` is equally acceptable. At this point, any program that you write that works properly, is neat, logical, and well commented, is an acceptable program.

Modification Exercises

1. Make the logo for the company a bridge.
2. Make a third table (below the second) with three columns: Date, Transaction Type, and Amount. The column widths should be 10, 12, and 12.
3. Make a fourth table (below the third) with four columns: First Name, Middle Name, Last Name, and Tax ID Number. The column widths should be 20, 20, 20, and 15.

APPLICATION EXAMPLE 2.2 DEBUGGING

TOPIC
- Program development

This is an important example that you should read thoroughly. It illustrates a typical session a beginner goes through to get a simple program to run. By understanding this example, you will be more confident and composed as you work to get your own programs to execute correctly. Before we give the problem statement, we make some general comments about bugs and debugging.

Bug

An error in a program is generically called a *bug*. Since there is no formal definition, a bug can refer to almost anything that produces a difficulty in program execution or compilation. The term originated in 1945 when a moth flew into the Mark I computer at Harvard and caused a program's execution to terminate. The logbook recorded the "first actual case of a bug being found." Since then, many bugs have been found in many programs.

Debugging

In your source code, looking for and correcting errors or mistakes that cause your programs to behave unexpectedly is called *debugging*. In general, there are three types of errors in a C++ source code: *syntax errors*, *run-time errors*, and *logic errors*.

SYNTAX ERRORS

Syntax errors are mistakes caused by violating the "grammar" rules of C++. They easily can be caused by typographical mistakes or a lack of knowledge of the forms of statements required by C++. These errors often can be diagnosed by the C++

Debugging

At the end of Chapter 2, students are shown a methodology for finding bugs, and a detailed description of tracing and debugging loops is included in several chapters.

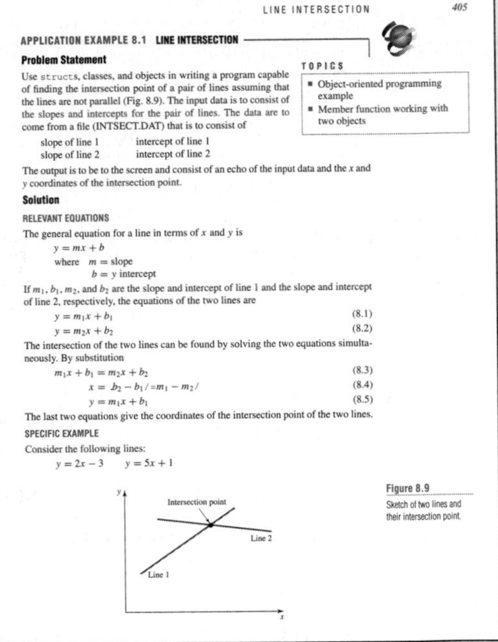

LINE INTERSECTION 405

APPLICATION EXAMPLE 8.1 LINE INTERSECTION

TOPICS
- Object-oriented programming example
- Member function working with two objects

Problem Statement

Use `structs`, classes, and objects in writing a program capable of finding the intersection point of a pair of lines assuming that the lines are not parallel (Fig. 8.9). The input data is to consist of the slopes and intercepts for the pair of lines. The data are to come from a file (INTSECT.DAT) that is to consist of

slope of line 1 intercept of line 1
slope of line 2 intercept of line 2

The output is to be to the screen and consist of an echo of the input data and the x and y coordinates of the intersection point.

Solution

RELEVANT EQUATIONS

The general equation for a line in terms of x and y is

$y = mx + b$

where m = slope
b = y intercept

If m_1, b_1, m_2, and b_2 are the slope and intercept of line 1 and the slope and intercept of line 2, respectively, the equations of the two lines are

$$y = m_1x + b_1 \qquad (8.1)$$
$$y = m_2x + b_2 \qquad (8.2)$$

The intersection of the two lines can be found by solving the two equations simultaneously. By substitution

$$m_1x + b_1 = m_2x + b_2 \qquad (8.3)$$
$$x = (b_2 - b_1)/(m_1 - m_2) \qquad (8.4)$$
$$y = m_1x + b_1 \qquad (8.5)$$

The last two equations give the coordinates of the intersection point of the two lines.

SPECIFIC EXAMPLE

Consider the following lines:

$y = 2x - 3 \qquad y = 5x + 1$

Figure 8.9 Sketch of two lines and their intersection point.

UNITS CONVERSION PROGRAM 623

```
Output to screen     Result
                     5
                     18
                     39
                     68
                     105
                     150
                     203
                     264
```

Comments

To keep this program relatively simple, we deliberately neglected doing any data checking. If the user accidentally types something incorrect, the program will fail.

Modification Exercises

1. Modify the program so that it can handle an equation with 10 operands and nine operators. In other words, an acceptable input equation would be C / D − E + A / C − B / E − B + C + D.
2. Modify the program so that it can handle an input table with 10 columns (A–J). Change the input file so that it has 10 columns. Have the program accept 10 operands and nine operators.
3. Modify the program so that it can use a variable number of operands. Have the program automatically determine the number of operands entered.
4. Modify the program so that it prints an error message if an unacceptable operand or operator has been typed. Make sure that the program does not stop executing. Allow the user to type in a new equation. Repeat the process until the user types in an acceptable equation.
5. Modify the program so that it can handle one set of parentheses. In other words, an acceptable equation would be A * (B + C + D − E). Although this sounds simple, it does involve a fair amount of rewriting of the program.

APPLICATION EXAMPLE 12.2 UNITS CONVERSION PROGRAM

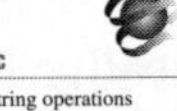

TOPIC
- C string operations

Problem Statement

Write a program that converts measurements of length or weight in one set of units to another set of units. Input should be typed in from the keyboard in the form of (for example)

```
5.2 cm to inches
```

Output should be to the screen giving the original measurement and the measurement in the new units. For example,

```
5.2 cm is 2.047 inches
```

Step-by-Step Methodology for Program Development

Each of the Application Examples illustrates a structured approach to developing programs.

Modification Exercises

These challenge students to apply what they've learned in a particular Application Example. They are useful for courses with labs or for self-study.

CHAPTER 1

COMPUTERS AND COMPUTING FUNDAMENTALS

CHAPTER TOPICS

In this chapter, you will learn:

- The broad computer fundamentals needed for effective programming
- The stored instruction concept
- Basic computer architecture—electronics and their connections
- How bits store many different types of information
- Some differences between programming languages
- Steps involved in developing software and the concept of software engineering
- Background on the C++ language
- Using an IDE to create an executable program
- How to use this book effectively

1.1 HISTORY OF ELECTRONIC COMPUTERS

Electronic computers have a relatively short history. The Atanasoff-Berry computer (ABC) was developed in the 1930s at Iowa State University for the sole purpose of solving large numbers of simultaneous equations. The ENIAC (electronic numeric integrator and calculator) was a military computer built shortly thereafter for general computations, but the wiring had to be reconfigured, in a manner similar to an old-time switchboard, each time a new task was performed. For both of these computers, once the electronic wiring was set, only the data (that is, numbers to be added or other information with which to work) were input to the computer's memory.

Mathematician John von Neumann made a major advance in computing theory when he proposed an alternative to the process of reconfiguring the wiring. He introduced the concept of storing a computer's instructions in its own memory. The instructions, among other things, would dictate the directions and locations to which electronic pulses would flow in much the same way that wires dictated the flow. For computers built on von Neumann's concept, both the data and the computer's instructions were input to the computer's memory.

Figure 1.1a schematically illustrates a computer with direct wiring. Data stored in cells A–F is directly connected to the output cells. This figure shows A, B, and C going to X and D, and E, and F going to Y. This gives X = A + B + C and Y = D + E + F. If we wanted to create the equations X = A + C + E and Y = B + D + F, we would have to rewire the computer.

In contrast, Fig. 1.1b shows input cells for both data and instructions and wiring going to both X and Y from each input cell. One can envision that it would be easy to compute all the X and Y calculations given in the previous paragraph by simply using the correct instructions. Only the instructions need to be changed to solve new problems for the computer of Fig. 1.1b. Thus, the computer illustrated in Fig. 1.1b is superior to the one shown in Fig. 1.1a. Fig. 1.1b represents a modern computer, in that both instructions and data are supplied to the computer. This text shows you how to write computer instructions in the C++ language. Writing computer instructions is called *programming*.

Figure 1.1

Conceptual drawing of hardwired computer and computer with stored instructions.

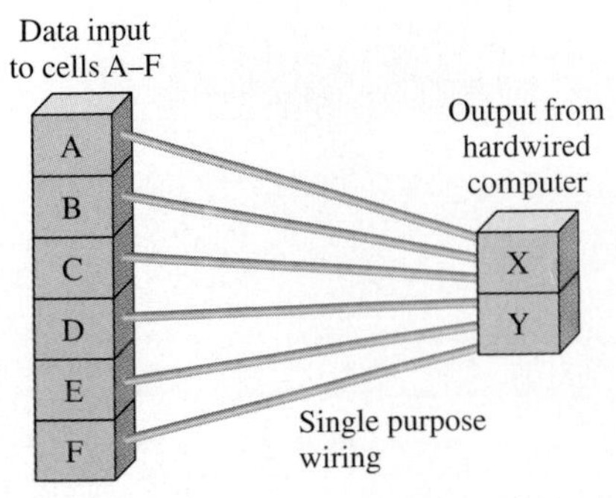

(a) Hardwired schematic with X = A + B + C and Y = D + E + F.

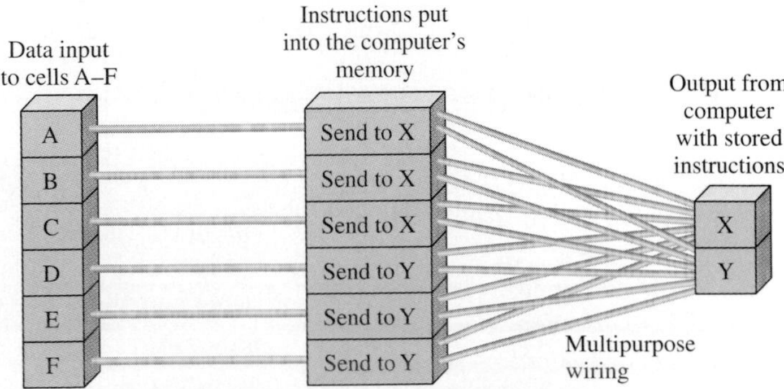

(b) Schematic showing output from computer using stored instructions with X = A + B + C and Y = D + E + F.

The stored program concept led to the development of multipurpose computers because only the instructions needed to be changed to change the type of problem to be solved. It was found that each instruction input, although simple in itself, when combined correctly with other simple instructions could solve complex problems. For instance, one set of instructions could be put into the computer's memory to get the computer to perform long division, and another set of instructions could be put in to get the computer to perform square root calculations. Then many of these sets of instructions could be combined to solve more difficult problems. As computers have become more complicated, developing computer instructions has become a science.

Electronics have changed significantly since the early days of computing. Vacuum tubes were used in the ABC and ENIAC. In the late 1950s, large transistors were the primary logic units for computers. In the middle 1960s, integrated circuits were developed. Integrated circuits actually contain large numbers of very small transistors, resistors, diodes, and capacitors. Today, integrated circuits on silicon chips form the heart of most computers. Technology improvements in materials and manufacturing processes have made the electronics smaller and faster. Today, the processing power of a room full of 1950s computing equipment can be put into a microprocessor chip the size of a small coin.

In addition, advances have been made in the way that people communicate with computers. Manually moving wires, punching holes in cards, and typing on keyboards were some of the first methods used. Mice, pens, and voice are more recent developments.

Unlike in the early days, today many different categories of computers exist. Although the boundaries between the categories are not always distinct, some of the computers in use today include:

- Supercomputers—Supercomputers, the largest and fastest of all computers, are used primarily for large scientific or military calculations. Like the computers of old, they occupy one or more rooms. Due to the expense of supercomputers, universities do not own a single supercomputer but instead share the use of one, possibly located in another state or city. In your advanced studies, you may use a supercomputer.
- Mainframe computers—These computers are not as fast or as large as supercomputers. Most universities own one or more mainframe computers. They usually take up a portion of a room and can be accessed from remote locations on campus.
- Workstations—Workstations are small enough to fit on a tabletop or next to a desk. Pricewise, they are suitable for small to medium-size businesses. They are more powerful than personal computers.
- Personal computers—They can fit on a desktop and are meant to be inexpensive enough for individuals, even students, to own. They have also been called *microcomputers*.
- Laptops—They can fit into a briefcase and are nearly as powerful as personal computers.

- Palmtops—They are small enough to fit into a pocket and are less powerful than personal computers and laptops.

Amazingly, today's laptops are more powerful than the very large ENIAC.

In summary, over the years computers have become smaller, faster, cheaper, and easier to use. Originally developed for scientific and military applications, computers have evolved to being used in everyday life by many individuals.

1.2 ARCHITECTURE

The architecture of a typical computer, from mainframe to palmtop, usually consists of a *central processing unit* (CPU), *main memory, controllers,* and *peripheral devices* as illustrated schematically in Fig. 1.2. The power of the computer comes primarily from the CPU and the main memory, and in essence these two together are what people refer to when they speak of "the computer."

The term *hardware* refers to electronic and mechanical devices integrated into or connected to a computer. As such, all the devices mentioned in section 1.2 are considered hardware.

1.2.1 — Main Memory

The main memory stores information to be processed or instructions on how to process information. Information is stored in *bits,* short for *bi*nary digi*ts*. Each bit can be in one of two states. These two states are described in numerous ways:

On or off
Charged or discharged
One or zero
True or false
Set or clear
High or low

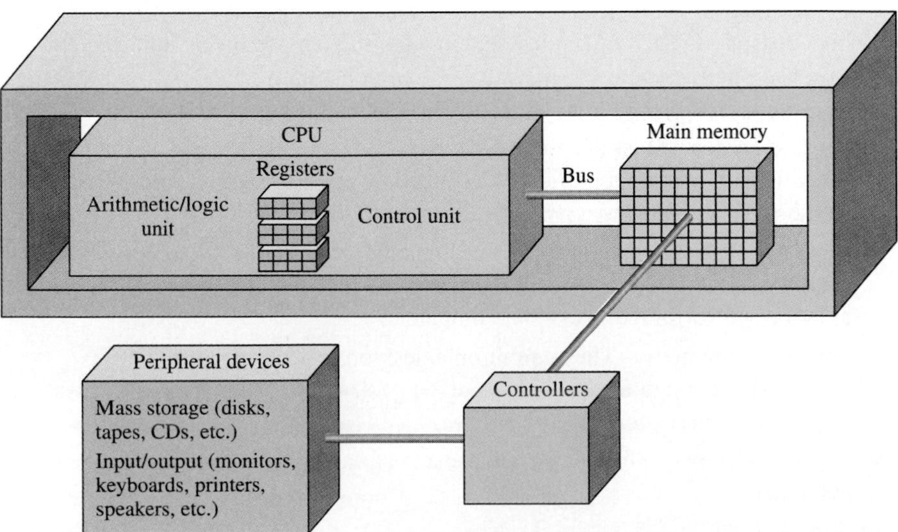

Figure 1.2
Schematic of the architecture of a typical computer.

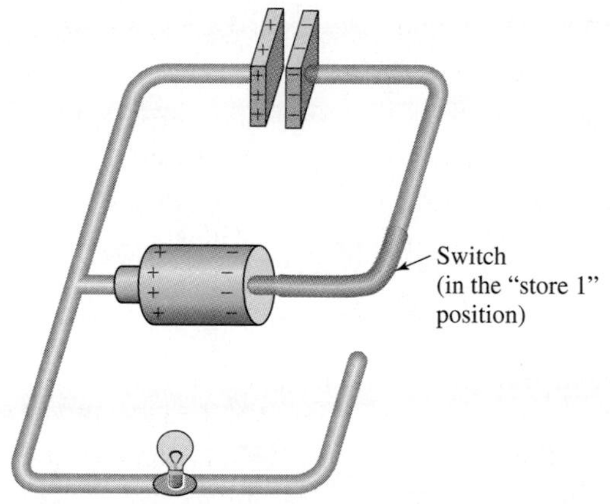

(a) Switch connected to battery, charging capacitor—analogous to storing 1 as a bit in a cell.

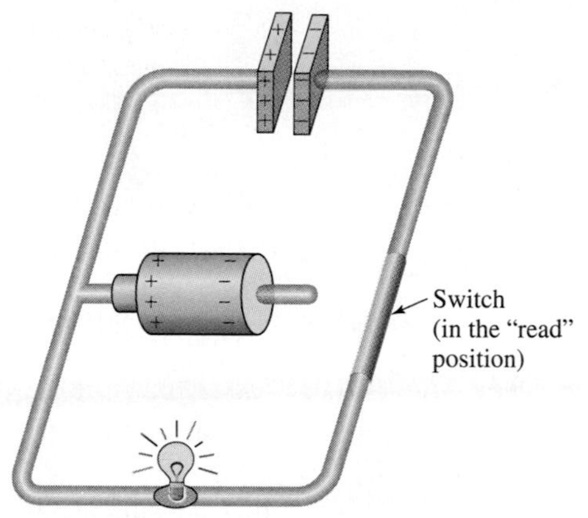

(b) Switch connected to bulb with the capacitor having been charged. Bulb lights—analogous to reading the bit value 1.

Figure 1.3

Conceptual illustration of storing to and reading from memory. The capacitor represents one bit of a cell. The bit has a value of 1.

In this text we will describe the state of a bit as 1 or 0. Why is a two-state bit used in computers? Primarily because it is easy to create one of two states electronically. Figure 1.3 illustrates how an on/off circuit can be created. The capacitor (the two charged parallel plates) represents a single bit of computer memory. (Note: this is not a perfect analogy, so if you do not understand what a capacitor is or what it does, simply skip this figure.) The position of the switch in the figure determines whether a value is to be stored (charging or not charging the capacitor) or whether the memory is to be read (discharging the capacitor). The figure is not meant to represent a duplicate of what is used in a computer. It simply illustrates how two different states can be created and read using a simple circuit.

In Fig. 1.3, on the left, the value 1 is put into the bit location because the switch is set into the position that causes the capacitor to be charged. When we move the switch into the read position (on the right), we know that the capacitor had been previously charged because the capacitor discharges and lights the bulb momentarily. We interpret the illuminated light as meaning that the bit had the value 1. This contrasts with Fig. 1.4. On the left, the switch is in the neutral position, not charging the capacitor. After moving the switch to the read position (on the right), the light does not illuminate, meaning this bit has the value 0.

In memory bits are typically grouped into packets called *cells* or *words*. Very large numbers of cells form the memory. In Fig. 1.5 each cell has 8 bits (8 bits is typically called 1 *byte*). Each cell has its own address that serves a function much the same as your home's address. Your home's address indicates where letters are to be sent; a cell's address indicates where in memory a bit pattern is to be sent.

The bit patterns in each of the cells are a type of code that is explained in section 1.4 of this chapter. As a brief example, though, in one type of computer code the capital letter G is represented by the bits 01000111. You can see that cell B5 in Fig. 1.5 contains the code for G. When all the bits of this cell are read, the letter G is interpreted. We shall see that symbols such as commas, dollar signs, and numbers also can be stored in a code represented by bit patterns.

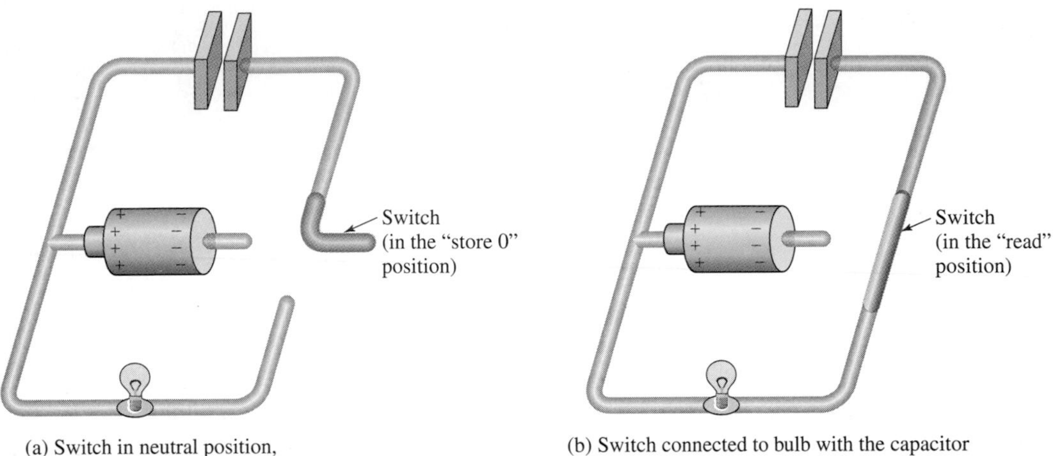

Figure 1.4

Conceptual illustration of storing to and reading from memory. The capacitor represents one bit of a cell. The bit has a value of 0.

Also capable of being stored in memory are instructions, which, like letters and numbers, are represented by a type of code. For instance, a certain bit pattern stored in cell C3 may say to take the contents of cells C4 and C5 and add them together. Should a code be needed that is more than 8 bits long, it is possible to use two or more consecutive cells.

The size of memory often is given in terms of *megabytes* (MB) or *gigabytes* (GB). As we will see when we look at bit representations, the power of 2 is fundamental. Although *mega* normally means exactly 1 million, when referring to memory it is actually 2^{20}, which is 1,048,576. Therefore, 300 MB of memory means $300 \times 1{,}048{,}576 = 314{,}572{,}800$ bytes of storage. Similarly, *giga* is not exactly 1 billion but 2^{30}, which is 1,073,741,824.

Figure 1.5

Conceptual image of cells and addresses.

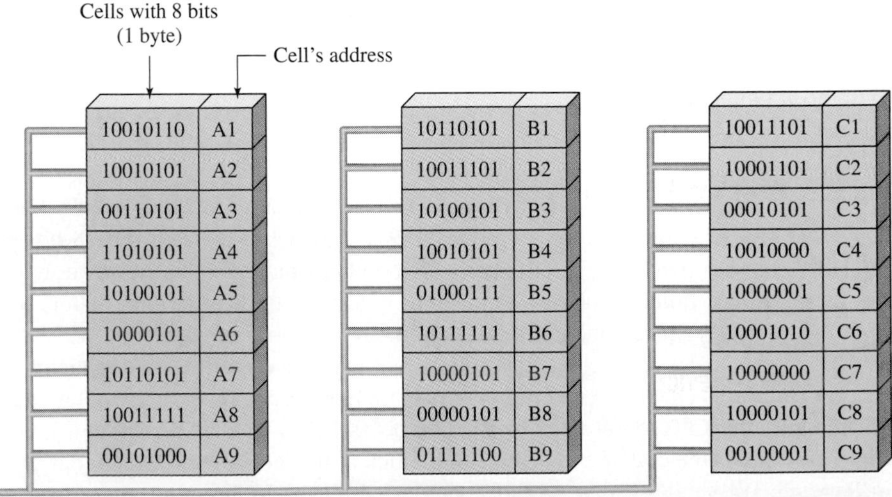

A *bus* connects the main memory to the CPU. Conceptually, a bus is a group of wires with one wire connected to each bit of memory. *Random access memory* (RAM) allows access to each of the cells in no particular order. It contrasts with *serial access,* which indicates a sequence of cells that must be followed to extract the desired information. *Read-only memory* (ROM) represents bits of information that are permanent in memory, meaning the bits cannot be modified by the user because they have been set during the manufacturing process. ROM usually contains instructions and information considered to be fundamental to the computer's performance.

1.2.2 — Central Processing Unit

The central processing unit consists of *registers,* a *control unit* (CU), and an *arithmetic-logic unit* (ALU). Each of these is described here.

REGISTERS

Registers are memory cells within the central processing unit. They allow rapid access of information by the control unit and the arithmetic-logic unit.

CONTROL UNIT

The control unit controls the activities of the CPU. It copies both data and instructions from memory, then decodes the instructions and obeys them. In other words, the control unit copies information of interest from the main memory and puts that information into the registers. The unit communicates with the arithmetic-logic unit, informing it which cells contain the information and which cells should contain the results of any manipulations performed on the information. The control unit, acting on instructions received from memory, directs which circuitry should be utilized within the arithmetic-logic unit for operations to be performed. The control unit under normal conditions reads instructions from memory cells sequentially; however, it can jump to different cells when it receives instructions to do so.

ARITHMETIC-LOGIC UNIT

The arithmetic-logic unit contains the circuitry for performing fundamental data manipulations. In addition to the fundamental arithmetic operations of addition, subtraction, multiplication, and division, it can handle so-called *logical operations.* Without explaining them in detail, these include the operations of COMPARE, AND, OR, SHIFT, and ROTATE.

1.2.3 — Peripheral Devices

You probably are familiar with peripheral devices, as you see, touch, and hear many of these when you use a computer. Peripheral devices can be divided into two categories: *mass storage* (also called *secondary storage* or *secondary memory*) and *input-output (I/O).*

MASS STORAGE DEVICES

Simply put, mass storage devices store information. They include units that operate tapes, hard disks, floppy disks, CDs, and DVDs: the media on which the information actually is stored. The devices that rotate, write to, or read from the disks or tapes are called *drives:* tape drives, hard disk drives, floppy disk drives, CD-ROM drives, or DVD drives.

Information is stored on either disks or tape in a series of "on-off" markings. The on-off may be represented by magnetic spots, where a spot on a disk (for hard disks or floppy disks) or tape is either magnetized or not magnetized. On CDs, the on-off is represented by either a pit or a smooth area. These markings are put onto disks in the same type of code briefly described in the section on main memory. The computer can read and write this code, making these mass storage devices useful for holding information.

Like mass storage devices, main memory also stores information; however, four major differences exist between mass storage devices and main memory:

1. Accessing information in mass storage is slower than accessing information in main memory. This is because the information from mass storage must be transferred into main memory before it can be processed. Also, mass storage devices typically require mechanical motion, which slows the access of information considerably.
2. The media of mass storage devices (disks, tapes, etc.) can be portable and therefore used as a means of conveying information to other computers.
3. Mass storage devices usually have a greater capacity than main memory and serve the function of holding large amounts of information.
4. The information stored on mass storage devices remains even after power is cut off from the computer.

INPUT-OUTPUT (I/O) DEVICES

Many different input and output devices can be used by computers. For instance, a small computer in a microwave oven may have a temperature sensor as an input device and the on-off switch of the oven as its output device—causing the oven to turn off when the temperature reaches a certain value. For a standard computer devoted to manipulation of information, the most common input devices are keyboards, scanners, microphones, and pointing devices such as mice. The most common output devices are monitors, printers, and speakers.

1.2.4 — Controllers and Communication to Peripheral Devices

Controllers actually are miniature computers within themselves. They coordinate the actions of the peripheral devices connected to them with the actions of the computer.

One particular design for the connection of computers to peripheral equipment is illustrated schematically in Fig. 1.2. Here, the central processing unit communicates with peripheral devices through controllers via the main memory. With this design, a controller can act very much like a CPU. For instance, the CPU can write a large amount of information into memory and then instruct that it be sent to a printer. Then the controller can take over and extract the information as needed from the memory and send it to the printer. This process also can work in reverse when, for instance, information is extracted from a disk. Based on instructions it has received from the CPU, the controller can take information from the disk and put it into the main memory.

Information constantly flows back and forth between the peripheral equipment and the controller. Why? There are many reasons. One is that the controller needs to know roughly what the peripheral equipment is doing. For example, a typical printer cannot print information as rapidly as it receives it. When the printer falls behind it must signal this to the controller so that the information can be saved and the flow of information to the printer can be slowed if necessary. Because the usefulness of a computer depends on its ability to coordinate peripheral devices, controllers are an important part of the computer system.

NETWORKS — 1.3

We include a very short discussion of *networks* here because you likely will be using a network in your class work. Networks are groups of individual computers and peripheral devices linked together to share information and resources. They can be broken down into two categories: *wide area networks* (WANs) and *local area networks* (LANs).

The Internet is an example of a wide area network because it spans a vast geographical region, linking machines throughout the world. Because of the large number of resources and area encompassed by the Internet, a variety of machines exist within it. Part of the challenge of getting the Internet to work well involves getting diverse machines to communicate efficiently with each other. Much of the shared information is sent over telephone lines. When you access a site on the World Wide Web, you may be receiving information from a mass storage device located in another part of the world. Should you so desire, you may have the information transferred to your own mass storage device for use at a later time.

Your university or the company you work for most likely has a local area network. It may be closed, in that it is meant to allow communication primarily among the computers within your organization (although one of the shared devices that may be on the LAN is a modem for communicating with other networks). Often, the equipment within a LAN is of a similar type. This simplifies communication between the machines. Since communication usually is not done over long telephone lines and the connections are much simpler, the response is much faster than for the Internet. Within a small company, a LAN is very useful for sharing printers, scanners, mass storage, and other devices that are expensive but not used continuously by a single user. Shared machines in a network appear devoted to a single user. A network server is a computer on the network that holds much of the network software and controls shared devices. For instance, network software on the server handles such things as setting the queue (pronounced "cue," it is a sequential list of users) for the printer. The server allows each user to use the printer one after another. It also handles electronic mail and the sharing of mass storage devices.

Networks can be connected in various ways (called *topologies*). A few popular types, such as tree, ring, irregular, and bus, are shown in Fig. 1.6. The Internet is an example of a network with irregular topology. Local area networks may have other types of topologies.

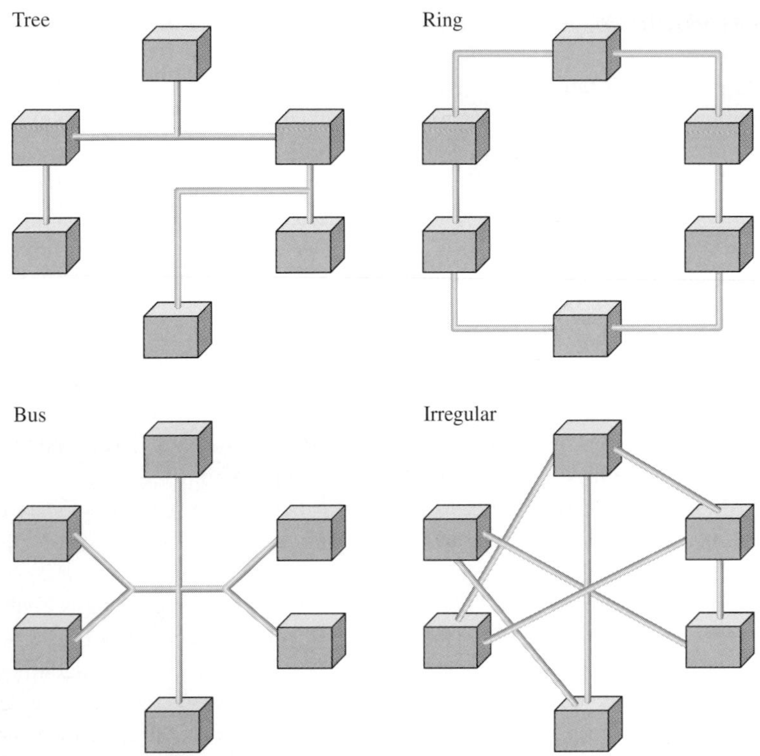

Figure 1.6

Some computer network topologies.

1.4 USING BITS TO REPRESENT CHARACTERS AND SYMBOLS, INTEGERS, REAL NUMBERS, ADDRESSES, AND INSTRUCTIONS

1.4.1 — Characters and Symbols

In the early days of data transmission, Morse code used dashes and dots to represent characters and symbols. The advent of computers led to the development of more complex codes that serve essentially the same function. Instead of dashes and dots, however, the customary notation for computers is 0 and 1. *ASCII* (pronounced "ask-ee," for American standard code for information interchange) is the code most commonly used for representing characters and symbols. Table 1.1 lists the codes for the capital letters A–F and a few symbols (a listing of the standard characters for ASCII code is given in Table 3.5). Note that each of the characters and symbols is represented by 8 bits, which we will refer to as 1 byte.

1.4.2 — Integers

Integers are represented in memory by a type of a binary or base 2 system. Base 2 is used because only 1s and 0s are needed to represent digits, and this fits in well with our bit representation of information. The binary system contrasts with our everyday number system, which is decimal or base 10. In base 10, recall that each placeholder represents a power of 10 with the rightmost placeholder representing 10^0 (which is 1). Each

TABLE 1.1 — Code samples

Symbol	ASCII code
A	01000001
B	01000010
C	01000011
D	01000100
E	01000101
F	01000110
?	00111111
+	01001110
(	01001101

succeeding placeholder to the left represents a successively greater power of 10. For example, the five-digit number 78,326 is interpreted as $(7 \times 10^4) + (8 \times 10^3) + (3 \times 10^2) + (2 \times 10^1) + (6 \times 10^0)$.

In a standard binary scheme, placeholders all represent powers of 2. The rightmost placeholder represents 2^0 (which is 1), and each succeeding placeholder to the left represents a successively greater power of 2 as illustrated:

Base 2 placeholders	2^7	2^6	2^5	2^4	2^3	2^2	2^1	2^0
Decimal value of placeholders	128	64	32	16	8	4	2	1

EXAMPLE: Determine the base 10 representation of the 8-bit base 2 number 10010110.

Solution: Using the preceding table of placeholders, the value can be calculated by

Base 2 placeholders	2^7	2^6	2^5	2^4	2^3	2^2	2^1	2^0
Decimal value of placeholders	128	64	32	16	8	4	2	1
Binary digits	1	0	0	1	0	1	1	0
Binary digit times decimal value	128	0	0	16	0	4	2	0

The base 10 representation then is the sum of all of the numbers in the last row, which is $128 + 16 + 4 + 2 = 150$.

EXAMPLE: Using the previously described representation of binary numbers, determine the largest and smallest values that can be represented by an 8-bit cell.

Solution: The largest number is with all the digits being 1, and the smallest is with all the digits being 0. Therefore the largest number is $128 + 64 + 32 + 16 + 8 + 4 + 2 + 1 = 255$ (which is also $2^8 - 1$). The smallest number is 0. Note that negative numbers cannot be represented with this scheme.

Suppose we wanted to represent an equal number of negative and positive integers with 8 bits. How might it be done? One method would be to let one of the bits be a sign bit so that each bit would represent

Sign 2^6 2^5 2^4 2^3 2^2 2^1 2^0

We could set the convention so that 1 in the sign bit would indicate a negative number (0 would be positive). If so, the following range of numbers could be represented:

largest $= 01111111 = +(64 + 32 + 16 + 8 + 4 + 2 + 1) = 127$
smallest $= 11111111 = -(64 + 32 + 16 + 8 + 4 + 2 + 1) = -127$

The effect of using the sign bit is to shift the numbers represented from all positive to half positive and half negative.

Sometimes it is necessary to determine the binary representation from the decimal representation as illustrated in the next example.

EXAMPLE: Determine the 8-bit binary representation of the decimal number 87.

Solution: This problem can be solved by repeated comparisons of a decimal number to the line of powers of 2 (64 32 16 8 4 2 1). Follow the table below from left to right, line by line.

	STEP 1—Compare the value in column 1 to the numbers in the line below, which are all powers of 2. Put the value 1 into the location for the power of 2, which is just less than or equal to the compare value (put 0 into unfilled places to the left).								Decimal value of the current binary number.	STEP 2—Get the new compare value by subtracting the original number from the current number.
	Sign	**64**	**32**	**16**	**8**	**4**	**2**	**1**		
Compare **87**	0	1	—	—	—	—	—	—	= 64	87 − 64 = 23
Compare **23**	0	1	0	1	—	—	—	—	= 80	87 − 80 = 7
Compare **7**	0	1	0	1	0	1	—	—	= 84	87 − 84 = 3
Compare **3**	0	1	0	1	0	1	1	—	= 86	87 − 86 = 1
Compare **1**	0	1	0	1	0	1	1	1	= 87	87 − 87 = 0

The final result is that decimal 87 is equal to binary 01010111.

A problem with this signed binary scheme occurs when the operation of addition is performed (see Appendix A). As a result, most applications use a scheme called *two's complement*. This scheme is described in more detail in Appendix A.

The problem of exceeding the largest or smallest number that can be represented is called *overflow* and must be avoided to assure that the computer gives the correct result. Using a greater number of bits is one way to reduce the likelihood of overflow occurring. For instance, the range for 16 bits is:

$$2^{15} - 1 = 32767$$
$$-2^{15} = -32768$$

And for 32 bits is:

$$2^{31} - 1 = 2147483647$$
$$-2^{31} = -2147483648$$

Clearly, using a greater number of bits increases the range substantially; however, no matter how many bits are used overflow is still a possibility. Overflow is a problem that you must be cognizant of when writing your computer programs.

In summary, integers are most commonly stored in memory with a two's complement representation. Arithmetic operations can be readily performed with this scheme. The number of bits controls the size of the integers that can be represented. Overflow is a problem that can occur regardless of the number of bits used. Even with a two's complement representation, a sign takes up a bit. An unsigned scheme creates a different range of numbers represented. We will see that with the C++ language, we can specify, somewhat, the number of bits we want to use for integers (thereby controlling the size of the integer that we may use) and whether or not we want to use a sign in one of the bits.

1.4.3 — Real Numbers

Real numbers are stored in binary format just like integers, characters, and symbols. The binary code for real numbers, though, is different from that used for integers.

The method for converting between binary and decimal for real numbers is very similar to that for integers. The placeholders to the right of the decimal point (called the *radix point* for bases other than base 10) are powers of 2 in the following order:

Base 2 placeholders	2^{-1}	2^{-2}	2^{-3}	2^{-4}	2^{-5}	2^{-6}	2^{-7}	**etc.**
Decimal value of placeholders	0.5	0.25	0.125	0.0625	0.03125	0.015625	0.0078125	

The next example illustrates the conversions.

EXAMPLE: Determine the base 10 representation of the 8-bit base 2 number 100.10110.

Solution: Using the preceding table of placeholders, the value can be calculated by

Base 2 placeholders	2^2	2^1	2^0	2^{-1}	2^{-2}	2^{-3}	2^{-4}	2^{-5}
Decimal value of placeholders	4	2	1	0.5	0.25	0.125	0.0625	0.03125
Binary digits	1	0	0	1	0	1	1	0
Binary digit times decimal value	4	0	0	0.5	0	0.125	0.0625	0

The answer is the sum of the numbers in the bottom line, which is $4 + 0.5 + 0.125 + 0.0625 = 4.6875$.

To make efficient use of computer memory, though, real numbers are stored in a form of scientific notation. You may recall that in decimal, for example, 15,230,000 is represented in scientific notation as 1.523×10^7. The 1.523 is called the *mantissa,* 10 is called the *base,* and 7 is called the *exponent.*

We also can use scientific notation in binary. For example,

$$101.01100 = 1.0101100 \times 2^2$$
$$-0.0001011101 = -1.011101 \times 2^{-4}$$

We will not go into the details of exactly how real numbers typically are stored. However, from these simple examples we can see that to store real numbers we must

- Store both the mantissa and the exponent (we need not store the base since it is always 2).
- Have space in memory for a sign for both the mantissa and the exponent.

Unlike integers, where the number of bits used to store the integer restricts only the integer size, with real numbers the number of bits restricts both the size and *precision* (that is, the number of digits after the decimal point) of the numbers that can be stored. This is because, in storing real numbers, the total number of bits allowed must be apportioned between the mantissa and exponent.

1.4.4 — Hexadecimal and Octal Notation

At times, humans must write bit patterns using a pencil and paper or some other form. While a computer, in general, has no difficulty in dealing with a large number of 1s and 0s, humans find large numbers of 1s and 0s cumbersome. For instance the 32-bit representation of 635,163,077 is 00100101110110111101000111000101. If you had to deal with these long strings of numbers on a daily basis, you would find your work quite tedious and you easily could err. Also, the lack of direct correspondence between decimal number and binary number representations makes decimal numbers difficult to work with when dealing with bits and cells. As a result, *hexadecimal* (or base 16) and *octal* (or base 8) notation can be used as a human shorthand for representing large strings of bits. Table 1.2 shows decimal, hexadecimal, octal, and bit patterns.

Note that capital letters are used in hexadecimal to represent 10 to 15 (decimal) because it is necessary to have a single symbol as a placeholder. The table can be

TABLE 1.2 — Comparison of notations

Decimal	Hexadecimal	Octal	Bit pattern
0	0	0	0000
1	1	1	0001
2	2	2	0010
3	3	3	0011
4	4	4	0100
5	5	5	0101
6	6	6	0110
7	7	7	0111
8	8		1000
9	9		1001
10	A		1010
11	B		1011
12	C		1100
13	D		1101
14	E		1110
15	F		1111

used to create the octal and hexadecimal representations of long bit strings. The octal digits (0–7) are used to represent 3-bit groups (ignoring the left-most 0 of the bit pattern of Table 1.2), and the hexadecimal digits (0–F) are used to represent 4-bit groups. For instance, the bit pattern 101001100110011000111011 is represented in octal as 51463073, as shown:

Bit pattern	**101**	**001**	**100**	**110**	**011**	**000**	**111**	**011**
Octal digit	5	1	4	6	3	0	7	3

And 00100101110110111101000111000101 is represented in hexadecimal as 25DBD1C5, as shown:

Bit pattern	**0010**	**0101**	**1101**	**1011**	**1101**	**0001**	**1100**	**0101**
Hexadecimal	2	5	D	B	D	1	C	5

You can see that both the octal and hexadecimal representations clearly are more wieldy than the long binary bit patterns.

1.4.5 — Addresses

As we have seen to this point, information that can be coded in binary can be stored in a memory cell. Each memory cell has an address associated with it as shown in Fig. 1.7. Although we have not been precise in the way we have indicated the addresses (or in a two-dimensional illustration of memory when a one-dimensional image or list is more representative), the concept is that a binary code can represent the address of a cell. For instance, one can assume that the addresses listed in the

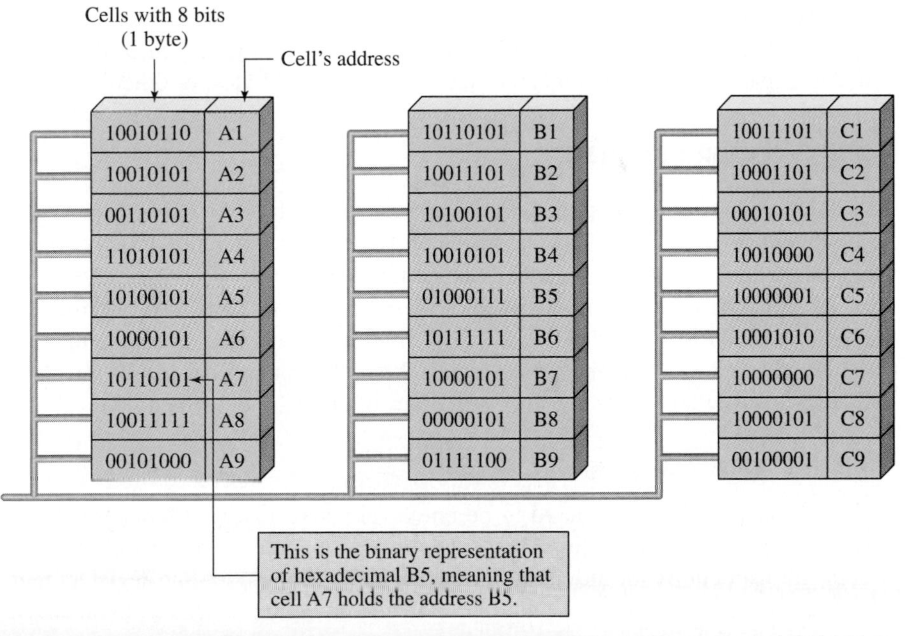

Figure 1.7
Conceptual image of cells and addresses.

figure are hexadecimal. One easily could convert these to binary. Then, one memory cell could hold the address of another memory cell. In this figure, the address B5 is contained in cell A7.

1.4.6 — Instructions

Instructions must be stored in a code, too. In this book we will not go into the details. However, you should be aware that the instructions you write in the C++ language must be converted into a binary-type code and stored in memory. This binary code is referred to as *machine language*. Section 1.7 describes how you will convert your C++ instructions to machine language.

1.4.7 — Comment

As described, all these can be stored in memory cells:

Characters and symbols
Integers
Real numbers
Addresses
Instructions

All are stored in a binary code, but the code used for each one is different. Therefore, for the computer to interpret the information in a cell correctly, it must know what type of information is in the cell. In other words, if a cell contains an integer, the computer must somehow know or be told that an integer is in that cell. Otherwise, it would not know whether to treat the binary code as a real number, an instruction, an address, or whatever. In your C++ programs, you will indicate to the computer the type of information you will store in each cell.

In addition, the computer must know whether or not the information spills over into more than one cell. For instance, in your C++ programs, you will indicate whether a real number should be represented by 4 bytes, 8 bytes, or other.

1.5 PROGRAMMING LANGUAGES

Machine language was mentioned briefly in Section 1.4. It is the only language that a computer can understand. The language consists of instructions in binary code (or hexadecimal, for shorthand) specific to the particular computer processor. Every step that the computer takes must be written in these instructions. Because machine language is so cumbersome and tedious to write, most programs are written in other languages and translated into machine language. Many languages that can be translated into machine language have been written. Some of them are described here.

1.5.1— Assembly Language

Assembly language is considered to be one level above machine language. In assembly language, all the machine language instruction steps are necessary. In other words, all instructions for moving information between memory and registers must be included to successfully write a program in assembly language. The main advantage of assembly language over machine language is that instructions in assembly language are not in a binary code but in English words. The words are translated into machine language code with a language translating program. Assembly language is also cumbersome to write (although less so than machine language) because each fundamental instruction must be given.

1.5.2 — High-Level Languages

High-level languages are meant to further simplify commands written by human programmers. For instance, to add two numbers in machine language, multiple steps are required to transfer information from one memory cell to another. A simplified method might be to write a + b, and after the language has been translated, the series of instructions necessary to add two values would be written in machine language and stored in memory. Unlike machine language, high-level languages allow programmers to write programs with far less concern about the internal design of the machine on which the program will be used. It is necessary, however, that the translator be compatible with the computer, so programs can be portable. If you write a program in a high-level language on your home computer, you should be able to use that program on your university's mainframe, provided that the university has a translator for the language you use.

High-level languages have rules that must be followed to get an accurate translation into machine language. Such languages are designed to simplify the writing of programs to solve particular types of problems. For instance, some languages are made to write programs that solve scientific problems while others deal with such things as business accounting.

Languages (summarized in Table 1.3) can be broken down into four types:

Procedural (or imperative)
Functional
Declarative
Object oriented

At this point, what you should know about the languages in Table 1.3 is that C++ is an object-oriented language while C is a procedural language. C is a subset of the C++ language (even though C is a procedural language and C++ is an object-oriented language). This means that a program written in C also follows the acceptable rules

TABLE 1. 3 — A summary of some high-level languages

Language name	Language type	When developed
Fortran	Procedural	middle 1950s
Basic	Procedural	middle 1960s
Lisp	Functional	late 1950s
Prolog	Declarative	early 1970s
Ada	Procedural	middle 1970s
Smalltalk	Object oriented	middle 1970s
Pascal	Procedural	early 1970s
C	Procedural	middle 1970s
Java	Object oriented	middle 1990s
C++	Object oriented	middle 1980s

of C++, although a C program does not utilize the most powerful features of C++. However, a program written in C++ does not necessarily follow the rules of C.

1.6 SOFTWARE

Recall that hardware is the name for the tangible equipment involved in a computer's operations. *Software* is not tangible. Software is a set of instructions that (after being translated into machine code, if necessary) can be read into a computer's memory and later executed on demand.

Software can be broken down into two categories: system software and application software. The vast majority of software on the market is application software, and this is the type of software that you will learn to write from this text. However, to write application software, you will need to use system software. Therefore, you should be familiar with some of the fundamentals of system software. Software categories are shown in Fig. 1.8. The relationship between users and the different categories of software is illustrated in Fig. 1.9.

1.6.1 — System Software

System software includes *operating systems, utility programs,* and *language translators.*

OPERATING SYSTEMS

The operating system is software (that is, a set of instructions) written into memory upon startup of a computer. The operating system instructs the computer to "watch for" and respond to messages given to it from the keyboard, mouse, or other input

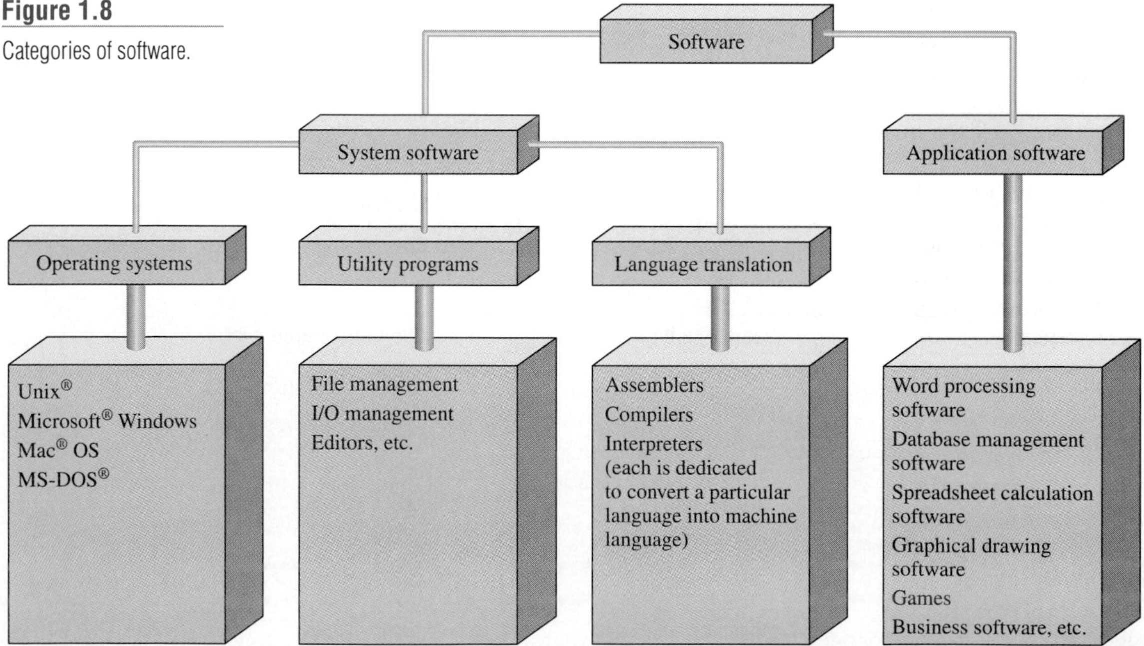

Figure 1.8

Categories of software.

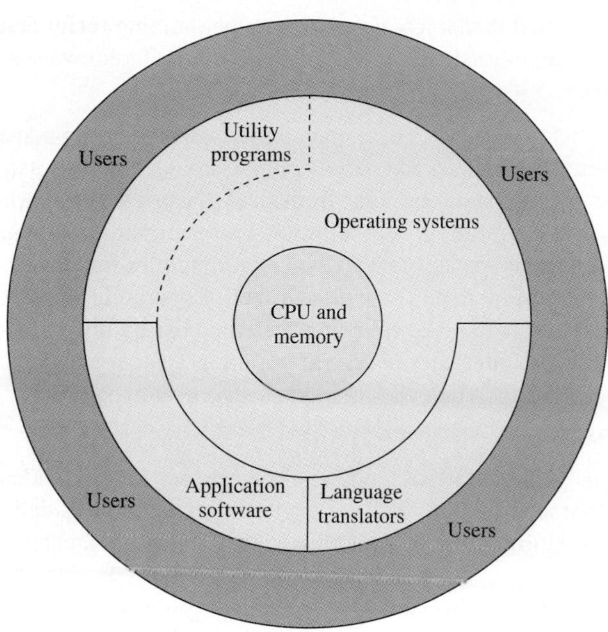

Figure 1.9

Onion-skin-type diagram illustrating the relationship between users, software, and CPU. For instance, a user interacts with application software which interacts with the operating system which interacts with the CPU and memory.

device. An operating system establishes the instructions for utilizing peripherals, memory, and registers, thereby freeing users and many programmers from worrying about certain details in dealing with these devices. The operating system creates the look and feel of the computer for the user. Usually the user deals with the operating system when he or she begins a session on a computer.

Because the operating system is the fundamental software used on a computer, there must be a match between a computer's circuitry and its operating system. In other words, one type of computer may or may not be capable of using a particular operating system.

Operating systems can be broken down into two categories: those for multiple-user computers and those for single-user computers. The names of operating systems are well-known among users and in the computing industry. Here are a few:

UNIX—multiple user.
Microsoft Windows—single user.
Macintosh operating system—single user.
MS-DOS—single user.

Multiple-user operating systems. Large numbers of users can be connected simultaneously to supercomputers and mainframes. For these devices, users compete for use of the CPU, printers, and other peripherals. The operating system coordinates the computer's activities with all its users, in such a way as to satisfy the needs of each user—not making one wait too long before his or her commands are executed. Typically, an operating system will share the CPU among users by executing at least a portion of each user's instructions before moving to the next user. By doing this, no one user monopolizes the entire computer's resources. This procedure does not work for sharing printers, for example, because it would make no sense to print a few pages for one user and then a few pages for another, mixing them all up. Therefore, the operating system must share different resources in different ways and do so in an efficient manner.

Single-user operating systems. These operating systems focus on managing just one computer's memory, registers, and peripherals. Although only one user may be on a computer, input to the system can come from disks, the printer, the keyboard, or other input devices. The operating system allocates space in main memory for files read from disk. It also keeps track of information regarding files in mass storage.

Much has been said about the look and feel of operating systems for personal computers. The trend is to make computers easier to use by making interfaces more user friendly. Popular interfaces in current use are graphical user interfaces such as those used by Microsoft Windows and Macintosh operating systems.

UTILITY PROGRAMS

Utility programs perform the basic operations necessary for the fundamental performance of the computer system, such as creating, copying, saving, deleting, merging, and sorting files. Utility programs commonly are included in a package with an operating system.

Utility programs encapsulated with operating systems are becoming more sophisticated, so much so that the boundary between utility and application software is becoming less distinct. So, you may find that a piece of software classified as utility software in one text is classified as application software in another.

Editors are an example of such software. An editor enables a user to create and modify the contents of a text file. Early editors were very simple. They allowed a user to put information into a file but had limited capabilities for moving around in the file, copying sections of files, and exchanging data between files. Today, however, such programs can have a variety of features that make them very versatile. Thus, although editors perform fundamental computer tasks, they can still be considered application software.

LANGUAGE TRANSLATORS

Language translators convert programmer-made instructions into machine-language instructions (or *object code*). Three types of language translators exist: *assemblers, interpreters,* and *compilers.*

Assemblers convert programs written in assembly language to object code. Since assembly language parallels machine language very closely, assemblers are less complicated in nature than interpreters and compilers.

Interpreters are used for high-level languages. Interpreters contrast with compilers in that they translate and execute instructions one after another. In other words, an interpreter takes an instruction given in a high-level language, converts it to a machine-language instruction, and executes it. Then the interpreter moves on to the next instruction and repeats the process until all the instructions have been executed.

Compilers take an entire program written in a high-level language and convert it to machine instructions. Your computer programs written in the C++ language will be translated into machine language using a compiler.

Working hand-in-hand with a compiler is a linker program, which is capable of linking together different translated modules. By linking numerous modules, one large program can be made out of many small ones. The complete translated machine-language file is commonly longer than the C++ language file. One reason for this is that each instruction given in a high-level language represents many machine-language instructions.

In the conversion process, errors in the C++ code may be detected by the compiler. The compiler looks for violations of established language rules such as improper punctuation or conflicting declarations. You need to modify your program sufficiently to satisfy the compiler. After doing this, you will execute and test your program to ensure that it performs the tasks it is intended to perform. If your program does not perform correctly, you will need to modify, add to, or delete some of your C++ language instructions; compile the program again; and execute it. You will repeat this process until you get satisfactory performance from your program.

Repeated execution and modification of a program is a normal and essential process in developing correct programs. Sometimes, beginning programmers are under the mistaken assumption that a program that compiles correctly is one that gives correct answers. However, a program that compiles with no error messages given by the compiler is much like an English paper written with no grammatical mistakes. It may conform to certain rules, but it does not necessarily make sense.

You should be aware that the word *compiler* is sometimes used in an imprecise manner. If you go to a software outlet and ask for a C++ compiler, you will be given a package that contains more than a compiler—likely an *Integrated Development Environment* (IDE) which includes a compiler and other tools for developing software (such as a text editor and a debugging tool, which we talk about later). In this text, we will sometimes refer to the C++ compiler in the general sense (but only when it is not important to specify which part of the IDE is being used).

Numerous C++ IDEs (or, generally said, compilers) are on the market. Most likely your university will have one. Your professor will give you instructions for it, which will tell you how to translate your C++ code into object code and how to operate other features of the IDE.

1.6.2 — Application Software

Almost innumerable types of application software exist. The most commonly used types of application software involve word processing, database management, drawing, graphing, and games. Specialty software for business, science, government, and education is developed every day. An organization that you work for may ask you to write application software for its internal use or to sell on the open market.

In this text, you will learn to write application programs. Through examples, this book illustrates how to write reliable, understandable, and efficient programs using the C++ language to solve practical problems. In writing large application programs, it is necessary to follow a rigorous software design procedure to assure that the finished product lives up to expectations.

SOFTWARE ENGINEERING, THE C++ LANGUAGE, AND C++ COMPILERS — 1.7

The term *software engineering* describes the process of software development. It indicates that software is not meant to be created haphazardly, but thoroughly thought out, planned, constructed, and tested. The term reflects the parallel between creating software and creating machines, buildings, and other such things traditionally thought of as engineered.

For instance, in the development of a large building, first, the functional requirements of the building must be established. Is the building meant to be used for office space, warehousing material, individual residences, hospital facilities, or maybe a combination of these? Once the purpose or purposes of the building have been established, the shape and layout of the building can be sketched out. At this stage, the expected users, the building's owner, architects, and engineers all can comment on the plans. Modifications can be made to satisfy all the participants. After the general outline has been agreed to, the individual components of the structure can be addressed. Columns, beams, and walls can be designed in some detail, giving the sizes and exact placement of each individual member. Once as many details as possible have been laid out, construction can begin. However, the design process is not finished. Unexpected changes always need to be made, because as construction proceeds it becomes obvious that certain units do not perform as they are intended.

Modifications to the initial design are implemented. Modifications to the design do not stop until a trial period has been completed, and the occupants are satisfied. Note that all modifications are thoroughly thought out and detailed so that they fit efficiently and functionally in the building. Engineering drawings are maintained for reference should information about the building be needed to efficiently use the building or make future modifications.

Developing software is a similar process. The function of the software is defined first. An initial sketch of the layout is developed and input from all the parties (users, owners, programmers, and others) is solicited. Modifications are made, and the design of individual components is addressed. It is recognized in the design that all the components must fit together properly. Then, like a building, piece by piece, the software is constructed. Modifications are planned out and made as the software is assembled and tested for functionality. After completion, the software is comprehensively tested and modified as necessary. Documentation about the software is maintained carefully so that the software can be used efficiently or modified in the future. Along the way, cost and time estimates for each step are made to keep the project economically feasible and on schedule.

Thus, software development is a process that involves many steps and continues throughout the life of the software. In other words, a piece of software does not stop being developed after it is on the market. It continues to be developed and improved until it is found no longer useful.

Many of the steps involved in development of software are illustrated in Fig. 1.10. From this figure it is important to note the "loops" shown. The loops are the steps repeated, that is, the testing and modifying steps. These are important because software continually undergoes testing and modification.

1.7.1 — Program Organization and Design in C++

To discuss program organization and design in C++, it is necessary to understand a bit about the history of program development. Over the last 40 years computer programs have become increasingly complex, so much so that they can push the

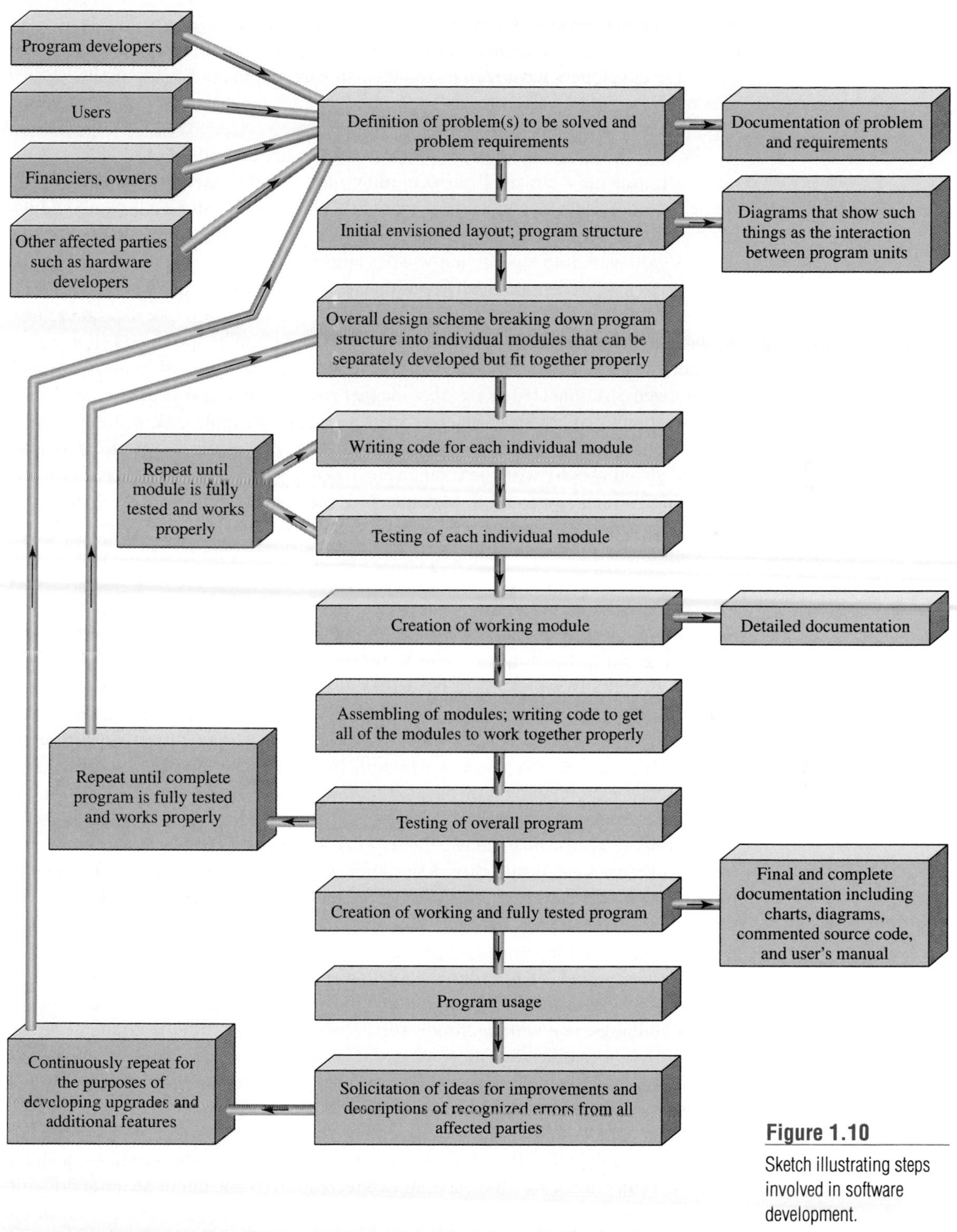

Figure 1.10

Sketch illustrating steps involved in software development.

limits of human understanding. Human understanding of programs is essential because ultimately it is humans that modify or extend programs over their lifetime. Language developers have recognized this, so each language has an organizational philosophy to make programs written in the language concise, comprehensible, and appropriate for the type of tasks they are to perform.

Programs written in C, the predecessor to C++, are composed of *functions*. Simply stated, functions are small programming units. Many functions together form a single program. Consider an analogy that will help you understand a little about how C programs are organized. If you can imagine a fully automated or serviced house, where if you walk into the kitchen you are automatically fed or if you walk into the living room you are automatically entertained, then the rooms in the house are similar to functions in a C program, and the people in the house are like data in the program. In this analogy, the people (data) are operated upon by the rooms (functions). An individual room not connected to any other room has limited value, but many rooms together, connected in a proper manner results in a useful structure. Similarly, each function in a C program may perform a relatively simple task, but many functions together, when connected in a proper manner can result in a useful program. The design philosophy with the C language, roughly speaking, is to get each function to operate correctly first and then connect all the functions to have a valuable program. This philosophy has worked well to produce many useful programs.

Continuing the house analogy, modifying a program with functions can be a little like remodeling a house. For instance, if you add a member to your family, it may be simple to add a bedroom to your house. If you add three or four members, you may find that you need a larger living room, kitchen, and more bedrooms, meaning that each room in the house may need redesigning. And different connections between rooms (hallways) may be needed to avoid congestion and confusion for the people traveling in the house.

Programs with functions are similar. Adding a few new features to a C program with functions may be simply done with little modification to existing functions. But, adding many new features may necessitate modifying many existing functions and their connections and significantly redesigning the entire program. This, of course, is not desirable because it is considerable work (meaning expensive) and can cause errors to be introduced into programs. Thus, it has been seen that when programs become very large and need to be maintained and improved over many years, C programming with functions has some limitations.

C++ also uses functions, but the primary units in C++ are *objects*. Using the structure analogy, a C++ program is more like a family compound than a house. One can envision a family compound, that may not be entirely practical, but consists of several buildings, one with bedrooms for sleeping, another with the kitchen and eating rooms, and another for showering and bathing. As more family members are added, each individual building can be reasonably modified because each building is somewhat independent and the connections between buildings are not complex. It is a relatively simple task to add to this living complex an exercise room and game room. A building including these rooms can be easily added. This contrasts with the single structure house to which adding two recreation rooms might be quite difficult.

The compound is like a C++ program, and the buildings in the compound are like C++ objects. Each building (object) has rooms (functions) that have people

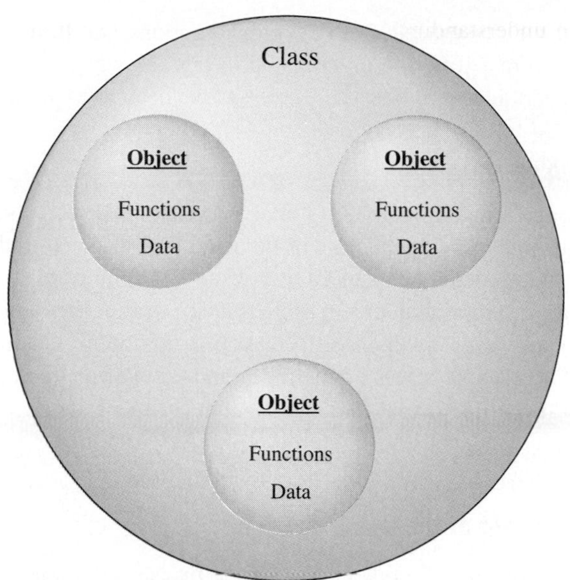

Figure 1.11
Schematic illustration of relationship between classes, objects, functions, and data.

(data) traveling between them. C++ also has *classes* that serve to group objects. For instance, a large compound might be one that has many buildings devoted to recreation, one with an indoor swimming pool, another with a small movie theater, and another with a basketball court. All these buildings (objects) would belong to the same class (recreation). See Fig. 1.11 for an illustration. While this analogy does not hold if studied too closely, the concept is that C++ programs have different fundamental units than C programs. However, the fundamental unit of the C program (the function) plays an important role in C++ programs.

The impact of this on learning C++ is that functions and C style programming must be somewhat learned before objects and classes can be learned. In this text, we describe some aspects of C style *structured programming* before we fully introduce you to C++ style *object-oriented programming* (OOP).

STRUCTURED PROGRAMMING

A top-down design scheme, which is commonly used, begins by defining all the tasks that a program is to perform. Then functions are developed, which are parts of the whole. Each part is less complex than the whole and can be designed separately but with the requirement that each of the parts fit together properly.

Functions are primarily of two types: library functions and programmer-defined functions. Library functions are modules that already have been developed and are included with the C or C++ development environment. They perform things like standard mathematical operations, such as the sine function, which is capable of finding the sine of an angle. That these functions are available saves the user from developing the specific instructions for performing many standard operations.

Programmer-defined functions are functions that are custom-made by a programmer. These functions perform tasks that are not available from the function library of the development environment. An important aspect of both C and C++ programming is developing functions.

In this text, we illustrate how to develop functions and how to connect them together so they form a cohesive organized program. However, we do not dwell on this aspect of program design because, for C++, we need to explain object-oriented programming.

OBJECT-ORIENTED PROGRAMMING

The object-oriented capabilities of C++ make the language very powerful. At this point in your programming career, it will be difficult for you to understand classes and objects, which form the heart of OOP in C++. To think of a class as a generalization of similar objects and an object as a grouping of functions and data as we described earlier is probably good enough for you at this point. It is not worth going into more detail here about object-oriented design because you do not have the background to understand it. However, we can say that a C++ programmer poses a question that is different from the C programmer's. A C++ programmer is concerned with developing classes and getting the classes to interact properly.

1.7.2 — Development of the C++ Language

The C++ language was developed in the middle 1980s at Bell Laboratories by Bjarne Stroustrup. The language was developed as an improvement upon the C language also developed at Bell Laboratories. Its object-oriented nature makes it far more powerful than C. C++ is a high-level language yet capable of controlling low-level operations. It is a highly portable and machine-independent language.

In 1997, a committee of the American National Standards Institute (ANSI) and the International Standards Organization (ISO) approved a version of C++ that is meant as a standard for the computing community. In this text, we refer to it as *standard C++*. The intent is that developers of C++ compilers make their compilers capable of correctly handling all programs written in standard C++ code. Thus, a program you write in standard C++ should be capable of being compiled and executed on any machine with a compiler that is standard C++ compatible. In this text, we follow the C++ standard. Wherever we show anything that varies from it, we make a notation.

1.7.3 — C++ Development Environment

The primary goal in writing the programs we discuss in this text is to create what is called an *executable file*. An executable file contains a set of machine language instructions (in binary form) that is ready to be executed by a user. When you buy commercial software, you purchase the executable file (among other things) that you load onto the hard disk of your computer. Once there, you can run it when you need it. You will need to create executable files from the programs that you produce through reading this book. Once you have created these executable files, you can store them on your hard disk and use them when you need them, just like commercial software.

Most of this text is devoted to showing you how you can create your source code. This, generally speaking, is the most difficult part of the process. The process of converting correct source code into an executable file, in general, is much simpler than writing the source code itself because the development environment does most of the work in converting and grouping C++ statements to a single machine language file. The steps involved in converting a correct source code into an executable file are shown in Fig. 1.12.

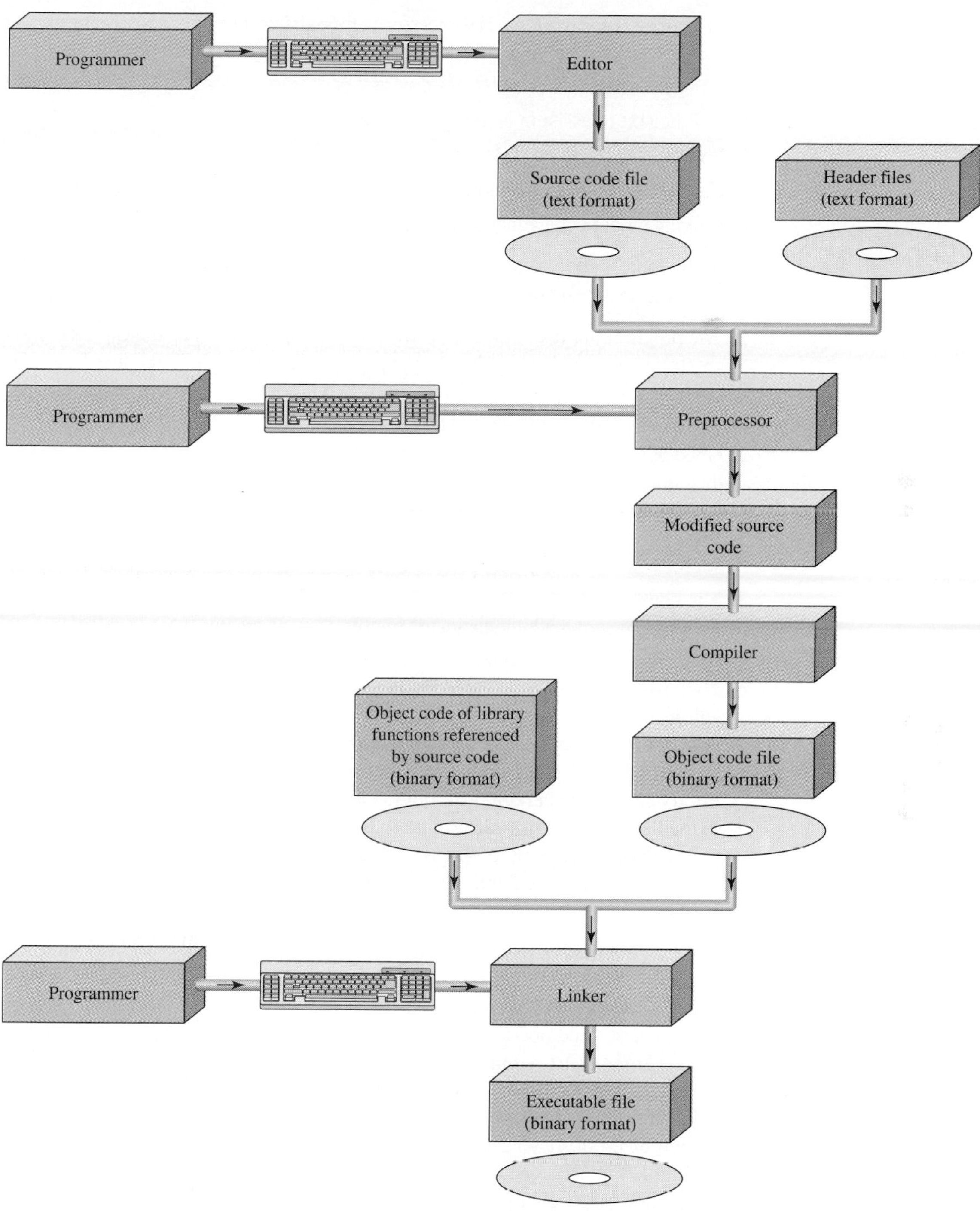

Figure 1.12

Steps involved for a programmer to create an executable file. Not all IDEs work exactly as shown. However, most follow this general procedure. Linking is often performed automatically, without explicit direction from the programmer.

In general, modern C++ IDEs perform four different types of operations (for specifics, please consult your IDE documentation or ask your instructor for details on the IDE made available to you):

1. Editing text to assist in creating source code.
2. Preprocessing source code.
3. Compiling source code and code attached by the preprocessor.
4. Linking object code generated in step 3 with other object code.

These four operations are indicated by rectangles in Fig. 1.12.

To generate an executable file,

1. The programmer uses an editor (often, a particular portion of the C++ IDE) to create a source code file. The programmer can simply type in the text from the keyboard. This text is written according to the rules described in this book. You will spend many hours learning how to write this C++ code properly.
2. Once this code is properly written, the programmer can direct the IDE to begin the compilation process. The first step is preprocessing, which is accomplished by different IDEs in different ways. A common type of preprocessor attaches source code that has been previously written and contained in the IDE to the source code written by the programmer.
3. The compiler takes the source code passed to it by the preprocessor and translates it into machine language instructions. It creates what is called *object code* and stores this object code in another file.
4. Then the programmer calls on the linker portion of the IDE (or the IDE does it automatically) to complete the machine language instructions and to make sure that all the instructions are assembled in the proper manner. In most cases, the source code written by the programmer will call on information in the C++ library to perform certain operations. This information is stored in binary form in the library. The linker determines what information is needed and attaches it to the object code created in step 3. Once the linker has finished, the process is complete and an executable file has been generated. This file is stored on the hard disk.

IDEs on the market have different characteristics. Some have editors built into them, making it very simple for you to create your source code and perform the necessary steps for you to create your executable file. Some of them automatically perform all the described operations with just a single keystroke command or click of the mouse. Some IDEs require more effort, and there may be times when you may want to manually get them to go through all the steps. Because of the number of C++ IDEs available and publishing constraints on this text, space does not permit a description of them. If you have purchased an IDE to get started with this book, please refer to the user manual for information on

Naming source code files.
Creating source code files (perhaps with a built-in editor).
Preprocessing, compiling, and linking files.
Executing programs (also known as *running* programs).

ABOUT THIS TEXTBOOK AND HOW TO GET THE MOST OUT OF IT 1.8

Each chapter of this book is divided into two parts: the lessons (approximately 10 per chapter) and the application examples (approximately 3 per chapter). The lessons come first and are meant to familiarize you with characteristics of the C++ language. Upon completion of the lessons, you should know the syntax or form of the C++ features described in the chapter. You are then ready to learn how to apply the features and solve practical problems. Each application example illustrates a practical type problem. The entire example lays out the steps and thought processes needed to develop a program that solves the problem. You can apply the techniques learned from the application examples to write programs to solve your own problems.

1.8.1 — The Lessons

Each lesson has a single complete example program (with output) that demonstrates the concepts taught in the lesson. To benefit most from the lessons in this book, you should follow this step-by-step procedure:

1. Read the introduction to each lesson to get an understanding of what you are about to learn. Read the source code *line by line* and follow the annotations. It is important that you read the code for each program carefully even though you probably will not understand it fully the first time through. The annotations will help you decipher some of the meaning of the code initially.
2. Read the lesson's *Description* portion to gain further insight into programming and to clarify points that may have been confusing in step 1. During this step, you should frequently refer back to the lesson's source code. It is important that you read and interpret as much C++ code as you can. You should be able to understand each and every line after you complete the lesson. Remember, reading code is not like reading a novel. You need to realize the action of each statement. Each statement is an instruction, and you need to determine what each instruction does to fully understand the lesson's program. After finishing this book you should be "fluent" in the C++ language—unafraid of facing many pages of pure C++ code given to you by your instructor or employer. In this section, when describing general forms of C++ structures, we use the bold Courier font (**`this is bold Courier`**) to indicate C++ code that you should use without modification. We use italics Courier (*`this is italics Courier`*) to indicate the portions that you need to change to fit your own program. The use of this convention will become more apparent as you progress through the book.
3. Do the exercises for the lesson (at the end of the chapter) and satisfy yourself that you've learned the concepts sufficiently well to prepare yourself for the next lesson.

1.8.2 — The Application Examples

In reading the application examples pay close attention to the methodology used. In illustrating the development of the programs, we utilize a multistep procedure. Prior to illustrating object-oriented concepts the procedure is (beginning in Chapter 3):

1. Assemble the relevant equations and/or give background information.
2. Do a hand calculation of a specific example problem.
3. Write an algorithm (which is a list of steps for solving the problem) that uses the equations and follows the pattern of the hand calculation.
4. Use the algorithm to write the actual source code.

As object-oriented programming is introduced the programs become more complex, and we add steps for such things as developing classes and objects. Although we recommend that you follow our procedure in writing your own programs, we recognize that as you become more adept at programming, you may be able to skip some of the steps, develop a method that suits your own style better, or use a method preferred by your instructor. While it is not necessarily important whose methodology you follow, it is very important that you follow a formal procedure rather than develop programs haphazardly.

EXERCISES

1. Convert the following binary numbers to decimal: 1001001001, 101010.101010, 1111100000.
2. Convert the following hexadecimal integers to decimal integers: F8, 3D5, A5BE.
3. Convert the following octal integers to hexadecimal integers: 12, 345, 7654.
4. Convert the following octal integers to bit patterns: 12, 345, 7654.
5. Convert the following hexadecimal integers to octal integers: F8, 3D5, A5BE.
6. Convert the following hexadecimal integers to bit patterns: F8, 3D5, A5BE.
7. List the ASCII codes for the three capital letters—A, B, and C—using binary and decimal integers.
8. Convert 53, −17, and −29 to two's complement binary (use Appendix A).
9. Add the two's complement values (Appendix A) and convert the result to decimal. Convert the original values to decimal. Is the addition done properly?

   a. 10100101, 00110111

   b. 01111001, 11100011

   c. 00011001, 11011011
10. Read your IDE documentation. Write a few paragraphs on how to create, compile, link, and execute a program with it.
11. See if your IDE has a debugger. Write a paragraph on how you can access it (not use it).

CHAPTER 2

GETTING STARTED—PROGRAM STRUCTURE, SCREEN OUTPUT, AND COMMENTS

CHAPTER TOPICS

In this chapter, you will learn how to:

- Write simple C++ programs
- Display keyboard symbols on the screen
- Write program comments
- Display table headings
- Debug your first programs

The only way to learn programming is to write programs. You will find that the more time you spend at a computer, the more you will learn. In this chapter we show a number of programs that illustrate the basic form and structure of a C++ program. You should begin programming by imitating what we show and then customizing your program to meet your needs.

This chapter's lessons show you how to create simple text output and how to add documentation (in the form of comments) to a program. The application examples illustrate how to print neat tabular headings and how to detect program errors. In themselves, the example programs described in this chapter have limited practical use. However, portions of these programs form integral pieces of many valuable C++ programs.

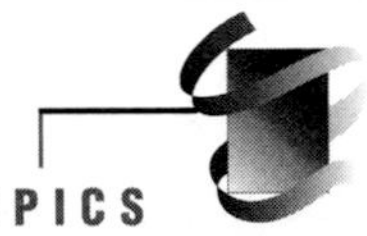

LESSON 2.1 BASIC STRUCTURE

TOPICS

- Writing a simple C++ program.
- Using the `cout` object to display text on the screen.
- Structure of a simple C++ program.
- Basic rules for writing a C++ program.

QUESTION YOU SHOULD ATTEMPT TO ANSWER

1. If you wanted to display the statement "I am learning a programming language," how would you write the `cout` statement?

The program that follows illustrates the basic structure of a C++ program. When you execute the program, the statement

```
This is C++!
```

appears on the screen and remains there until other tasks eliminate it.

Examine the program and the output carefully before you read the description. The program is written in what is called *code.* You may understand why it is called code because it looks cryptic. Since at this point you know nothing about C++, you probably will find the first few lessons difficult. As you learn more, though, you will find that indeed you can interpret much of the code yourself (assisted by the boxed annotations) before we explain it fully to you.

Read the source code line by line, and follow the boxed annotations.

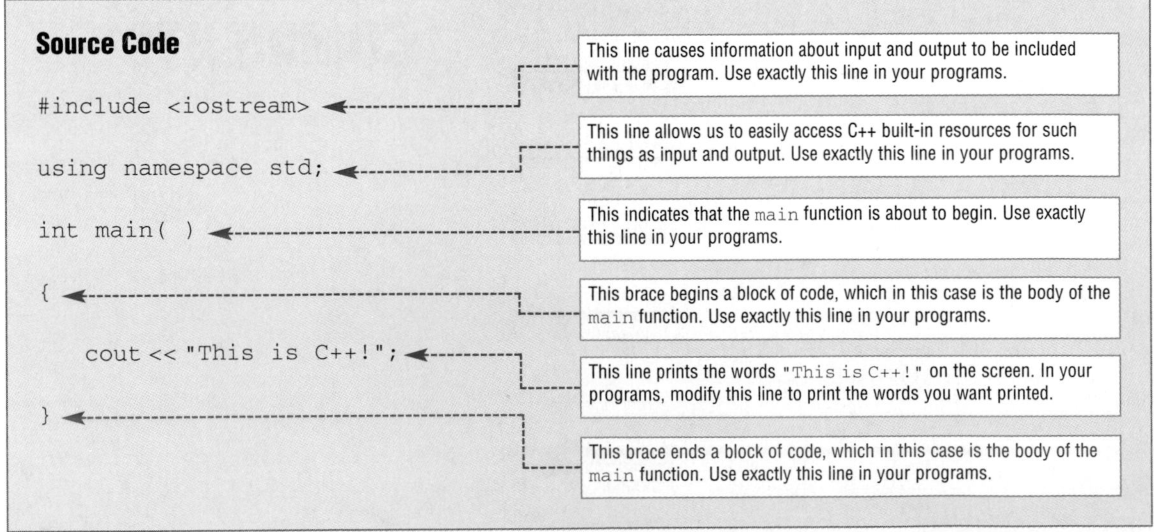

Source Code

```
#include <iostream>

using namespace std;

int main( )

{

    cout << "This is C++!";

}
```

Output

(Displayed on the screen after the source code has been compiled and the program has been executed.)

```
This is C++!
```

Description

Headers C++ has many built-in features; too many to be automatically included in every program. In this lesson's program, we need the C++ output system. Therefore, we have the line

```
#include <iostream>
```

This causes the C++ preprocessor to take code existing in a file (associated with the name `iostream` that is already in the C++ system) and group it with our program. All the code (that is, our code and the `iostream` code) is compiled to produce a single package of binary instructions. With this particular line, our program is allowed access to C++ I/O (input/output) features. For this program it allows us to easily print output to the screen using `cout` in the program body. In almost all programs in this text, exactly this line is needed.

The C++ preprocessor is the part of the IDE that performs actions prior to the translation of the code into machine language instructions. What the preprocessor does with *headers* (also called header files) is shown conceptually in Fig. 2.1. This figure illustrates the C++ preprocessor grouping existing code with our code. Not all

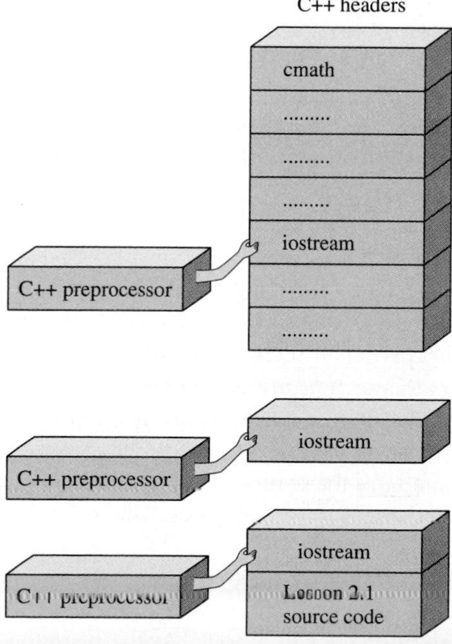

Figure 2.1

Conceptual illustration of the action performed by the C++ preprocessor caused by the line of code `#include <iostream>`. After this action, the code can be successfully translated into machine language because it has enough information to allow the use of `cout` for screen output.

C++ preprocessors work exactly as this figure illustrates, but the effect is the same—that using a statement that begins with `#include` gives a program additional information that allows it to access built-in features of C++.

We will find that when we want to use standard C++ math functions such as `sin` or `cos` in the program body that we need to use the `cmath` header with the line

```
#include <cmath>
```

We can use a number of headers in C++, and we describe these in other chapters. However, for most of the programs in this book, we include only two to four standard C++ headers per program, and therefore this is not a major part of the programming process.

A complete list of headers is

```
algorithm    cstdlib      iostream    set
bitset       cstring      iterator    sstream
cassert      ctime        limits      stack
cctype       deque        list        stdexcept
cfloat       fstream      locale      string
climits      functional   map         typeinfo
cmath        exception    memory      utility
cstdio       iomanip      queue       vector
```

We use many of these headers in this text. You do not need to understand them now. Throughout the text we tell you when you need each header and why. You will find that if you do not include the proper header, the C++ compiler will send you an error message when you attempt to compile your program, and your program will not compile successfully.

Namespaces A *namespace* is somewhat like the name (or number) of a chapter in a book. The name or number of the chapter uniquely indicates a particular region of the book where, for instance, certain terms are defined. If, at another point in the book, we want to refer to some terms that are defined in that chapter, we need to indicate the chapter name each time we refer to material in that chapter to be perfectly clear. If we make many references to terms in that chapter we would need many statements indicating the chapter name. You could imagine that although this could be done, writing and reading the text could be very tedious because of the repetition of the chapter references.

An alternative to constantly referring to the chapter would be to state at the beginning of the section which chapter is being referred to. For instance, if we were referring to Chapter 5 in a particular section, we could say at the beginning of the section something like, "In this section, terms not defined here are defined in Chapter 5." With this statement it is no longer necessary to mention Chapter 5 for every reference. A very abbreviated way to state this would be to have the statement, "Using Chapter 5" at the beginning of the section. This is more cryptic than the longer statement, but it is understandable if it were an agreed upon convention for making references to other chapters.

C++ has such a convention for making references. C++ has something called the *standard namespace* which is abbreviated `std`. The standard namespace is somewhat like a different chapter in a book. At the beginning of our program we use the statement

```
using namespace std;
```

which indicates that certain terms not defined in the program are defined in the standard namespace (which is invisible to the reader of our program's source code but is built into C++).

In this particular program, `cout` is within the standard namespace. A typical program in this textbook uses `cout` many times. Without the `using namespace std;` statement, we would need to refer to the standard namespace each time we use `cout` in the following way (for example, for the statement in this lesson's program):

```
std :: cout << "This is C++";
```

This statement explicitly indicates that `cout` is in the standard namespace. By having the `using namespace std;` statement in the program, we do not need to explicitly state that `cout` is in the standard namespace each time we use it. We can simply write:

```
cout << "This is C++";
```

In all the programs in this book, we have the `using namespace std;` statement and do not need to concern ourselves with namespaces beyond this. At this point, we do not need to go into more detail with namespaces.

The* `main` *function Typical C++ programs are composed of classes, objects, and functions among others things. C++ not only allows you to use functions in its library (such as `sin` or `cos`), it allows you to write your own functions. Every C++ program has a primary function that must be assigned the name `main`. The name `main` is mandatory and cannot be altered by you, the programmer. In other words, even if your program had the purpose of printing your address to the screen you could not name the primary function `printmyaddress`. The function must be called `main`. The C++ compiler searches for the function named `main` and compiles the program in a manner to ensure that `main` is the first function executed.

The first line of the `main` function in this lesson's program is

```
int main( )
```

This line gives the name of the function (`main`) and information about what goes into and out of the function. The `int` indicates that `main` returns an integer value to the operating system (which is considered to be the unit that calls the function `main`) when `main` finishes execution. In standard C++, the value 0 is automatically returned to the operating system upon successful execution of `main`. The empty parentheses indicate that no information is passed from the operating system to `main`. We will not go into more detail here. For now, you should simply memorize the form of this line because you will use it in all your programs.

After the line that contains the function name is the function body. The function body has the following features:

- It begins with an opening brace `{`.
- It ends with a closing brace `}`.

- The pair of braces, `{}`, are used to enclose what is called a *block* of code. We use braces quite frequently to form blocks of code. Sometimes we use blocks within blocks. In this case, the braces enclose the block of code that is the function body.
- The function body consists of C++ declaration(s) and statement(s). The structure of a simple C++ `main` function is as follows:

```
int main( )
{  <------------------------------- Begin function body.
   declaration 1;  ┐
   declaration 2;  │
   statement 1;    ├----------- Program declarations and statements.
   statement 2;    ┘
}  <------------------------------- End function body.
```

In this chapter, we discuss some statements you can use. In Chapter 3, we discuss declarations.

The `cout` object In this lesson's program, we have only one executable statement

```
cout << "This is C++!";
```

It uses the `cout` *object* and the *insertion operator,* `<<`, to print the characters enclosed in double quotes to the screen. An object is a region of storage in memory, and in C++ programs, the `cout` region of memory is linked to the standard output device (usually the screen). The line enclosed in double quotes, `"This is C++!"` is called a *string constant* or *string literal.* The string constant is stored in another region of memory when the program is executed. The insertion operator is called that because it inserts a copy of information into the `cout` region of memory. In this case, a copy of the string constant `"This is C++!"` is inserted into `cout` and then is transferred to the screen. This is illustrated schematically in Fig. 2.2.

We will use `cout` in most of the programs in this book. You should become adept at using `cout` in your programs. We discuss `cout` in detail in Chapters 2 and 3.

C++ syntax C++ has rules for writing statements. These are called *syntax* rules. The syntax rules must be followed strictly by a programmer. Most programmer syntax errors will be detected by the compiler at compile time (that is, when you compile the program). Application Program 2.2 describes in detail how to correct syntax errors. Here, we describe some syntax rules. Throughout the text we describe the syntax rules for each C++ feature introduced.

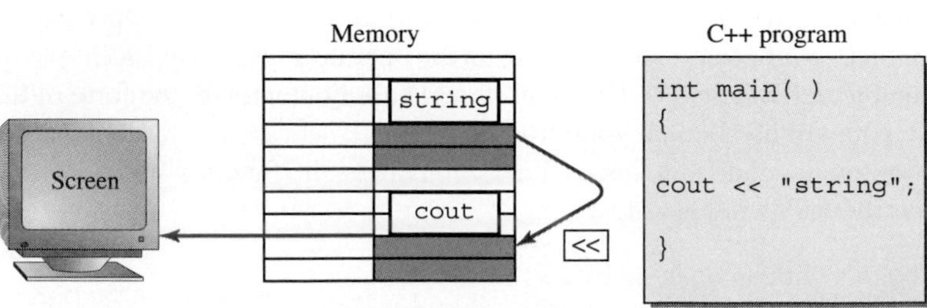

Figure 2.2

Schematic of action of a `cout` statement to print a string to the screen. The insertion operator (`<<`) copies the string to `cout`. Then the string is passed to the screen.

- *Semicolons*—The line `cout << "This is C++!";` is an executable C++ statement. Executable C++ statements appear in the body of functions and must be terminated by a semicolon. The semicolon at the end of a C++ statement acts much like a period at the end of a sentence. It serves as a statement terminator. A typical program has many C++ statements, each terminated with a semicolon. Some (but not all) other types of statements also require semicolons. The `using namespace std;` statement is an example of another type of statement that requires a semicolon. Throughout this book, we indicate where semicolons are required and not required.
- *Case sensitivity*—The C++ language distinguishes between lower- and uppercase letters. Thus, `cout` is different from `COUT`, `Cout`, or `CoUt`. It is said, therefore, that C++ is considered to be case sensitive. In this lesson, all letters except those between the double quotes must be written in lowercase letters. When you begin naming your own variables and functions, you may use whatever case you consider appropriate. However, C++ traditionally is written primarily in lowercase letters. We describe situations when other than lowercase letters commonly are used, as the need arises.
- *Blank spaces*—C++ code consists of a number of *tokens*. A C++ token is the smallest element that the C++ compiler does not break down into smaller parts. A token can be a function name (e.g., `main`), an object name (e.g., `cout`), or a C++ reserved word, which we discuss in Lesson 3.1. All C++ words should be written continuously. For example, the line

  ```
  int ma in( )
  ```

  is not legal because no blank characters are allowed between the characters `a` and `i` in the word `main`.

  Between tokens, extra *white-space characters* (white-space characters are blank, tab, and the carriage return "Enter") can be inserted, but this is optional. For example, the line

  ```
  int main( )
  ```

  is equivalent to

  ```
  int main (     )
  ```

  or

  ```
  int   main   ( )
  ```

  In general, it is acceptable to add blanks between tokens, but not acceptable to add blanks within tokens.
- *Spacing*—A white-space type character is created when you press the Enter key. In most cases, when extra spaces are used between tokens, they are invisible to the C++ compiler. Therefore, you have the freedom to write most of your C++ code at any row or column you like. The C++ compiler, for example, allows you to rewrite and pack this lesson's program into two lines

  ```
  #include <iostream>
  using namespace std;int main(){cout<<"This is C++!";}
  ```

or rewrite it as

```
#include<iostream>

using

namespace std; int
main(        )  {
 cout<<
"This is C++!" ;    }
```

However, these styles will make your program more difficult to understand and should not be used.

There is no required form for spacing within your program. However, your instructor or employer may want you to adhere to certain standard accepted styles. Our example programs are meant to illustrate acceptable style; however, at times, publishing constraints do not allow us to follow any one accepted style rigorously. Indentation and spacing (both within a line and between lines) are considered important for the look of a program, even though they do not affect performance.

Within a line, many programmers like to put a space before and after operators (which we discuss in more detail in Chapter 3). For instance, the `<<` in a `cout` statement is an operator, and many programmers put a space before and after it.

In general, to make your programs readable, do such things as write one statement per line, line up your braces, and add blank lines and spaces where there are natural breaks in code instructions. Remember, the look of a program is important because programs continually undergo change. A program that is neat and organized is easier to understand and therefore easier to modify. As a result, the likelihood for error is reduced in programs that follow a certain visual and organizational style compared to those that do not.

- *Accepted modifications*—Each C++ IDE (also called *implementation*) is somewhat different. Some are more lenient than standard C++ and allow some statements to be omitted. For instance, the following program may compile and work like this lesson's program.

```
using namespace std;
main()
{
    cout << "This is C++!";
}
```

The reason it may work is that

1. The `iostream` header is used so frequently in C++ that, for some IDEs, it is included automatically to programs despite no specific direction to do this.
2. Even though we have not written `int` before `main`, C++ assigns a *default* type for this. The word default is used commonly in computing. A default value is a

value that is used when none is specified. A default type is a type that is used when none is specified. Without going into detail, because C++ assigns a default type for the missing `int`, this program may work.

Summary In summary, this lesson's program, line by line, does the following:

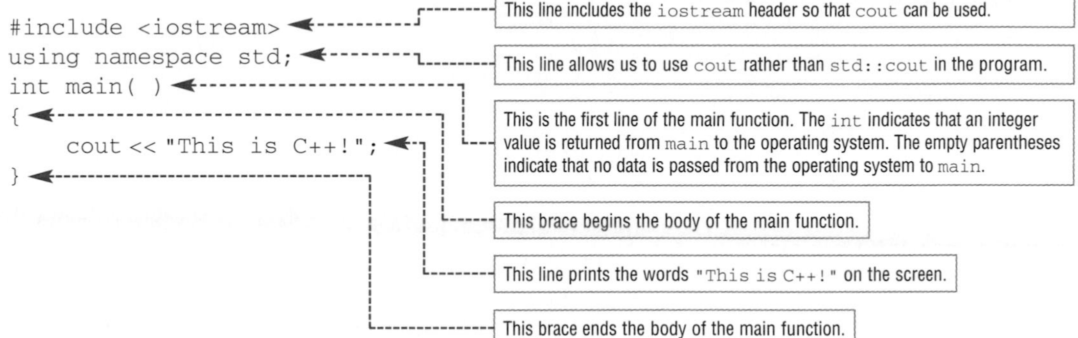

LESSON 2.2 WRITING COMMENTS

TOPICS

- Reasons for writing comments.
- Structure of comments.
- Location of comments.
- Continuing comments.
- Style of writing comments.

QUESTIONS YOU SHOULD ATTEMPT TO ANSWER

1. Which lines have been added in this program?
2. How do we signify to the C++ compiler that a statement is a comment statement?
3. Is it necessary for the beginning and end of a comment to be on the same ?

Sometimes even the most experienced programmers find it difficult to understand the tasks that a program or a portion of a program are to perform. You very likely will find that you have trouble understanding code you have written! Also, others may be working with your code and find that what you have written is difficult to understand.

Fortunately, C++ allows you to write *comments* within the code of your programs. Comments are notes describing what a particular portion of your program does and how it does it (or anything else you would like to write in the middle of your code). Comments are a very important addition to programs because they convey information that is difficult to convey through the code itself. When written well, comments reduce the likelihood for error because a programmer making changes to a program can read the comments to understand how a program operates. Comments serve as an important part of the program documentation and therefore are required by employers and instructors.

A properly written comment performs no action in a program. If not written correctly, though, the C++ compiler may think that the words written in the comments are objects, such as `cout`, or other C++ expressions or statements. If this occurs, the compiler will indicate that your program has errors when you compile it.

The program that follows is not meant to be an example of good commenting but only an illustration of the mechanics of commenting. It is meant to illustrate a program that performs a task identical to that performed by the program in Lesson 2.1. It prints a line of code to the screen. However, unlike Lesson 2.1's program, it is filled with comments. Compare this code to Lesson 2.1's code and note the differences.

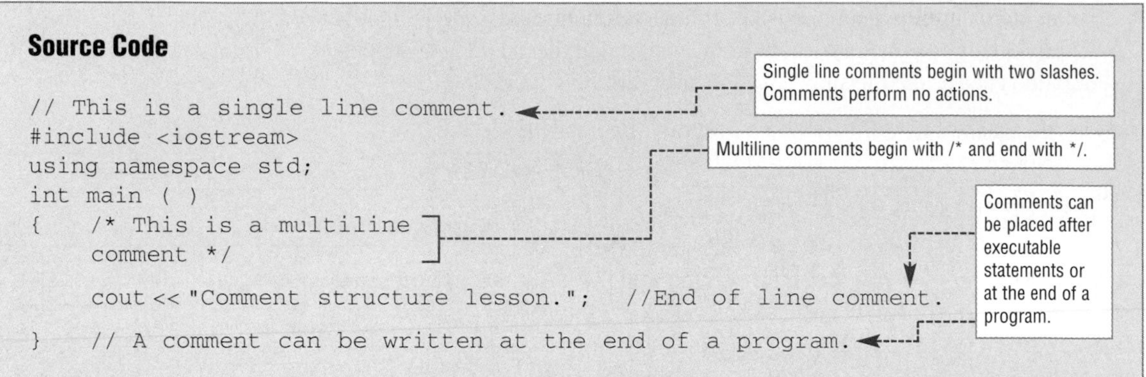

Source Code

```
// This is a single line comment.
#include <iostream>
using namespace std;
int main ( )
{    /* This is a multiline
     comment */

     cout << "Comment structure lesson.";   //End of line comment.

}    // A comment can be written at the end of a program.
```

Single line comments begin with two slashes. Comments perform no actions.
Multiline comments begin with /* and end with */.
Comments can be placed after executable statements or at the end of a program.

Output

```
Comment structure lesson.
```

Description

Single line comment structure The structure of a single line comment is

```
// comments
```

where there should be no blanks between the two slashes. All the `comments` must be on a single line and consist of acceptable C++ symbols (listed in Table 3.5). A comment causes no action to take place. It simply is a message to a reader of the source code.

A comment does not necessarily need to be alone on the line. It can be placed after a C++ statement. For instance,

```
cout << "Comment structure lesson.";   //End of line comment.
```

puts a comment on the same line but after the `cout` statement. Note that we cannot place the comment before the `cout` statement like this

```
//End of line comment. cout << "Comment structure lesson.";
```

because the `cout` portion would be regarded as part of the comment and not an executable statement.

Multiline comment structure The structure of a multiline comment is

```
/* comments */
```

where there should be no blanks between the `/` and `*`. The `/*` and `*/` are called comment *delimiters.*

The `/*` and `*/` must form a couple, but they need not be on the same line. Therefore, such a comment may occupy more than one line. A multiline comment starts with `/*`, followed by multiple lines of text consisting of numbers, characters, or symbols. The multiline comment terminates with `*/`. For example,

```
/* This is a multiline
      comment */
```

These are examples of incorrect multiline comments:

```
/* Wrong comment 1, no
end asterisk and slash

/* Wrong
comment 2,          no end slash *

/ *Wrong comment 3, there is
                    a space between /and * */
```

Comment locations A comment line can be written on the very first line, very last line, or in the middle of a program. The C++ compiler treats comments like a single white-space character. Therefore, comments can appear anywhere a white-space character is allowed. This means that comments may be placed on any line. Within a line, a comment can appear between tokens, but not within a token. (Note: a string constant is a token.)

Usage of comments Be wise in your use of comments. Remember that comments enhance the understandability of your programs. Make them pleasing to the eye and clear. With practice, you can develop a clear style of writing comments. In this text, we do not use many comments because we have the ability to write boxed annotations that stand out more clearly than comments do. Your programs should use comments far more frequently than we use them.

We recommend that you avoid writing comments on the same line as other C++ code unless you can clearly distinguish the comments from the code by using many tabs.

There is no standard for writing comments, but we like a style that highlights comments and separates them from other C++ text. The reason is, if not highlighted, comments tend to blend in with the rest of the code and make following the logic of the code confusing. In other words, do not hide your comments. Make them stand out—they are there to help you and others. You can make your comments stand out by using repeating stars (*) or some other symbol that is easily distinguished from the rest of the code.

We strongly recommend that you add a banner at the beginning of your program. A banner is a set of comments that describe such things as the name, parameters used, history, author, purpose, and date of the program. A better look for the program for this lesson is with a banner as follows:

```
//*****************************************************
// Name: Lesson 2.2
// Purpose: Learning how to write comments in C++
// Date: Written on 11/22/2005
// Author: Joe Kelly
// Reference: None
//*****************************************************

#include <iostream>
using namespace std;
int main ( )
{
  cout << "Comment structure lesson";
}
```

The disadvantage of making comments stand out is that it takes time to type them in this way. When you are in a hurry, you will tend to skip the comments. Do not let this style of programming continue for very long. Plan ahead to set aside half an hour or so each day to do nothing but write comments. In the long run, the time that you spend writing comments will save you considerable frustration in finding errors in your programs. As you gain experience with programming, you will become aware of how many and what types of comments are useful.

Take writing comments seriously. You will be regarded as a better programmer and your programs will have fewer errors if you write comments properly. Your coworkers and employer will appreciate a good commenting style.

Nested comments Comment statements cannot be nested (meaning that we cannot write a comment within a comment) in C++. For example,

```
/*/* This is an illegal comment because it is */ nested */
```

is not legal.

"Commenting out" code We would never find a need to deliberately write a nested comment, but it is very easy to create one accidentally. A common technique for isolating operations of source code is to "comment them out," that is, remove some of the operations temporarily by converting them into comments to see the effect on the program's performance. For instance, suppose we were working with this lesson's program (meaning we were modifying and running it repeatedly to create a new program). We could prevent the `cout` statement from executing by putting comment delimiters `/*` and `*/` before and after it to give

```
/*
cout << "Comment structure lesson";
*/
```

If we compile and run the program with the code like this, the compiler will think that the `cout` statement is a comment and not convert it into machine language instructions.

It then is a simple task to later recreate the line of code by removing the comment delimiters. In other words, if you had deleted the line of code to prevent its execution, you would have had to retype it to get it back. Commenting the line out saves you typing and easily gives you exactly what you had before. For this program, such action would not help us very much, but for other programs, you will find this technique quite useful for finding errors in your programs.

However, if we make a mistake in where we put our comment delimiters, we accidentally could enclose a comment with the statements we want to comment out. For instance, suppose we wanted to comment out a large number of lines, and these many lines included a comment that we did not see. A convenient way of commenting out a large number of lines is to simply put comment delimiters on the lines above and below the section of code we are commenting out as shown here.

```
/*
executable statement 1
executable statement 2
executable statement 3
```

```
/* comment */
executable statement 4
executable statement 5
*/
```

An error would have been generated during compilation because we would have accidentally created a comment within a comment, which is illegal. Remember, if you comment out code while you are modifying your programs, make sure you do not accidentally create a nested comment.

LESSON 2.3 CREATING NEW LINES IN OUTPUT

TOPICS

- Formatting output.
- Line feeding.
- Connecting strings.
- Other escape sequences.

QUESTIONS YOU SHOULD ATTEMPT TO ANSWER

1. What are the differences between the double quote enclosed strings in the `cout` statements and the printed output?
2. Why is there no space between "`is`" and "`C++`" in the output?

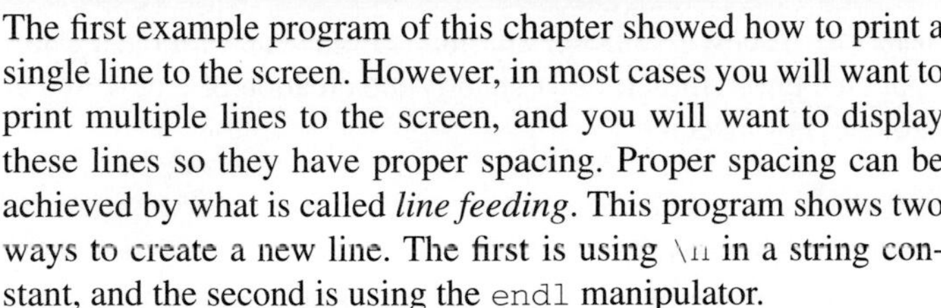

The first example program of this chapter showed how to print a single line to the screen. However, in most cases you will want to print multiple lines to the screen, and you will want to display these lines so they have proper spacing. Proper spacing can be achieved by what is called *line feeding*. This program shows two ways to create a new line. The first is using `\n` in a string constant, and the second is using the `endl` manipulator.

Included in the Description, but not shown in this lesson's program, are other output formatting features. For instance, we can use a `\` in a string constant to connect a string constant part on one line with another string constant part on another line. Also, we can insert symbols in string constants to do such things as indent a tab or backspace. We do not describe all the possibilities but list them in a table.

Read the code to see how to create new lines, and read the Description to see how to connect string constants.

Source Code

```
#include <iostream>
using namespace std;
int main ( )
{
        cout << "This is";
        cout << "C++!";

        cout << "\nWe can\njump\n\ntwo lines.";

        cout << endl;
        cout << "Here, we show 2 ways to\ncreate a new line." << endl;
}
```

Look at the output for these two statements. Even though these statements are on two lines, the output is on one line. Also note that the output shows no space between "`is`" and "`C++`".

Look at the output for this statement. The "`\n`" is not printed. Wherever a "`\n`" appears in the string constant, a new line is created in the output.

The word `endl` has no double quotes around it and is not printed out. A new line is created in the output where `endl` appears.

Output

```
This isC++!
We can
jump

two lines.
Here, we show 2 ways to
create a new line.
```

Description

Creating a new line with `\n` A new line is *not* automatically created for each `cout` statement executed. You, the programmer, must specify the creation of a new line at each location you need one. For instance,

```
cout << "This is";
cout << "C++!";
```

prints "`This isC++!`" on one line not two. In fact there is no space between "`is`" and "`C++!`" because no space is contained between these words and the double quotes.

A new line can be created using the linefeed symbol, `\n`, in the string constant. The symbol `\n` consists of two characters, `\` (backslash, not to be confused with slash, `/`) and `n`, with no blank in between. In C++, the two character symbol `\n` is one of many character *escape sequences.* The C++ compiler considers an escape sequence within a string constant as one character (not two). The importance of this will be seen in Lesson 3.3. The escape sequence `\n` causes the cursor to move to the next line and will not be displayed on the screen. Any data behind this symbol is written at the beginning of the next line. You can use `\n` at any location in the string constant. The number of `\n` can be more than one. For example, in the statement

```
cout << "\nWe can\njump\n\ntwo lines.";
```

the program uses the first `\n` to move the cursor to a new line, displays "`We can`", uses the second `\n` to jump to a new line, prints "`jump`", uses the next two `\n` to jump another two lines, and prints "`two lines.`".

Creating a new line with `endl` We can also use the `endl` *manipulator* to create a new line. The statement

```
cout << endl;
```

performs the single action of creating a new line, and the statement

```
cout << "Here, we show 2 ways to\ncreate a new line." << endl;
```

creates a new line between "`to`" and "`create`" using `\n` and a new line after "`line.`" using `endl`. Each `endl` in a `cout` statement must be alone between the `<<` operators. Some forms for using `endl` are:

```
cout << endl << endl << endl;
cout << endl << "string constant" << endl;
```

where *string constant* is any text. Whether to use `\n` or `endl` to create a new line is primarily a matter of preference (although there are some small differences between the mechanics of `\n` and `endl`, which we will not discuss here) for a programmer. Generally if many new lines are to be created within a string, `\n` is more convenient. Otherwise, `endl` is usually easier to write.

Connecting strings Here, we illustrate two methods for connecting strings (not shown in this lesson's program). In method 1, we use a backslash at the end of a line to indicate that a string constant in the source code has not finished and continues on the next line. For example, the statement

```
cout << "We can connect \
strings on two lines." << endl << endl;
```

is equivalent to

```
cout << "We can connect strings on two lines." << endl << endl;
```

Since the C++ compiler disregards all blank characters behind a statement, the connection to the next line starts at the end of the preceding statement. If you want to include blank characters in a string constant that occupies two lines, either place them before the backslash in the first line or at the beginning of the second line. In method 2, we enclose each unfinished string constant in double quotes; for example, the statement

```
cout << "We can " "use "
   "separate" " strings.\n";
```

is equivalent to the statement

```
cout << "We can use separate strings.\n";
```

Other escape sequences Not shown in this lesson's program are other escape sequences that are used less frequently than `\n`. Here is one example. Others are listed in Table 2.1.

- *Printing double quotes.* Because double quotes are special symbols that could be misinterpreted if used alone within a string constant, we must put a backslash immediately in front of them to display them on the screen. No space is allowed between the backslash and the double quotes following it. Thus, the statement

  ```
  cout << "Print 3 double quotes    -\" \" \" \n";
  ```

  produces the following output:

  ```
  Print 3 double quotes    -" " "
  ```

- *List of escape sequences.* Character escape sequences consist of a backslash followed by a letter, symbol, or a combination of digits. Each represents a character that has special meaning or specifies an action. (Note: Table 2.1 is a complete list of escape sequences that you can use as a reference later. At this point you do not need to understand the meanings of all of them.)

TABLE 2.1 — Character escape sequences

Escape sequence	Meaning	Result
`\0`	Null character	Terminates a character string
`\a`	Alert/bell	Generates an audible or visible alert
`\b`	Backspace	Moves the active position (e.g., for the console, this is the current cursor location) back one space on the current line
`\f`	Form feed	Moves the active position to the initial position at the start of the next logical page (e.g., ejects printer page)
`\n`	New line	Linefeeds to the initial position of the next line
`\r`	Carriage return	Moves the active position to the initial position of the current line
`\t`	Horizontal tab	Moves the active position to the next horizontal tabulation position on the current line
`\v`	Vertical tab	Moves the active position to the initial position of the next vertical tabulation position
`\0ddd`	Octal constant	Represents an integer constant using base 8 where ddd represents a sequence of digits 0–7 only
`\xddd` `\Xddd`	Hexadecimal constant	Represents an integer constant using base 16, where ddd represents a sequence of the decimal digits, and the letters a–f or A–F represent values of 10 through 15 respectively
`\\`	Backslash	Displays a backslash
`\'`	Single quote	Displays a single quote
`\"`	Double quote	Displays a double quote
`\%`	Percent	Displays a percent character
`\?`	Question mark	Prevents the misinterpretation of trigraph-like character sequences; e.g., trigraph sequence `??=` will display the character `#`, but `\?\?=` will display `??=`

TOPIC

- Using `cout`

APPLICATION EXAMPLE 2.1 CREATING LOGO AND TABLE HEADINGS

Problem Statement

Neatly displayed output is essential for effectively communicating results. Properly written table headings are extremely useful because program output is frequently displayed in the form of a table. Write a program that creates a logo and two sets of table headings for a monthly bank statement. The logo is for Harrison Bank in the form:

```
HARRISON
HH      H
HH      H
HARRISON
HARRISON
HH      H
HH      H
HARRISON
```

The title of the document is "MONTHLY BANK STATEMENT." The first set of table headings should consist of five columns: Account Name, Interest Rate, Number of Transactions, Beginning Balance, and Ending Balance. The number of spaces for each column is 20, 12, 12, 15, and 15, respectively. The second set of table headings should consist of three columns repeated once: Check Number, Date Paid, and Amount. The number of spaces for each column is 12, 9, and 10, respectively.

Solution

Because this particular program is not very complicated, we need not do much planning. (Beginning in Chapter 3, we follow our formal procedure for developing programs.) We can immediately start writing on paper or on the computer. In either case, you should begin writing your programs with the lines of code that you need for most of your programs. You can immediately write the following:

```
#include<iostream>
using namespace std;

int main ( )
{

}
```

Memorize this form so you can write it within a few seconds of sitting down to write your source code!

For this program, the next step is to write the `cout` statements. One difficulty in this program is that the number of spaces allocated for many columns is insufficient for a one-line column heading. Therefore, many column headings must be put on two lines of the `cout` statements. We show the statements in the source code. Look at the source code and make sure that you understand exactly what all the symbols do. We finish the program by writing a short comment banner at the beginning of the code.

Source Code

```
//*********************************************
// Name:          Application 2.1
// Purpose:       Harrison Bank Statement Form
// Date:          Written on 5/2/2006
// Author:        Mary Smith
// References:    None
//*********************************************

#include <iostream>
using namespace std;

int main ( )
{

    cout << "\n"
    "          HARRISON    \n"
    "          HH        H   \n"
    "          HH        H   \n"
    "          HARRISON    \n"
    "          HARRISON    \n"
    "          HH        H   \n"
    "          HH        H   \n"
    "          HARRISON    \n";
```

Comment banner.

You should memorize these three lines exactly.

Our `cout` statements can look very similar to the output.

```
    cout << "\n"
    "MONTHLY BANK STATEMENT  \n"
    "\n"
    "Account        Interest  Number of      Beginning  Ending   \n"
    "Name           Rate      Transactions   Balance    Balance \n"
    "\n"
    "\n"
    "\n"
    "\n"
    "\n";

    cout << "\n"
    "Check         Date   Amount    Check    Date    Amount    \n"
    "Number        Paid             Number   Paid              \n"
    "\n"
    "\n"
    "\n";
}
```

Each `cout` statement line is a double-quote-enclosed string ending in `\n`.

Output

```
    HARRISON
    HH      H
    HH      H
    HARRISON
    HARRISON
    HH      H
    HH      H
    HARRISON

MONTHLY BANK STATEMENT

Account                 Interest  Number of      Beginning  Ending
Name                    Rate      Transactions   Balance    Balance





Check                Date   Amount    Check    Date    Amount
Number               Paid             Number   Paid
```

Comments

You can see how similar the look of the `cout` statements is to the output. To create table headings, simply make your `cout` statements resemble the desired form. If you line up the headings in the `cout` statements, they will be lined up in the output. Also, it is easier to use separate double-quote-enclosed strings than to use the backslash string continuation symbol.

Note that, as with writing all programs, many different ways are acceptable. You could write a program using `endl` instead of `\n`, and it would still work fine. We have chosen to use `\n` because it is more compact, but `endl` is equally acceptable. At this point, any program that you write that works properly, is neat, logical, and well commented, is an acceptable program.

Modification Exercises

1. Make the logo for the company a bridge.
2. Make a third table (below the second) with three columns: Date, Transaction Type, and Amount. The column widths should be 10, 12, and 12.
3. Make a fourth table (below the third) with four columns: First Name, Middle Name, Last Name, and Tax ID Number. The column widths should be 20, 20, 20, and 15.

APPLICATION EXAMPLE 2.2 DEBUGGING

TOPIC

- Program development

This is an important example that you should read thoroughly. It illustrates a typical session a beginner goes through to get a simple program to run. By understanding this example, you will be more confident and composed as you work to get your own programs to execute correctly. Before we give the problem statement, we make some general comments about bugs and debugging.

Bug

An error in a program is generically called a *bug.* Since there is no formal definition, a bug can refer to almost anything that produces a difficulty in program execution or compilation. The term originated in 1945 when a moth flew into the Mark I computer at Harvard and caused a program's execution to terminate. The logbook recorded the "first actual case of a bug being found." Since then, many bugs have been found in many programs.

Debugging

In your source code, looking for and correcting errors or mistakes that cause your programs to behave unexpectedly is called *debugging.* In general, there are three types of errors in a C++ source code: *syntax errors, run-time errors,* and *logic errors.*

SYNTAX ERRORS

Syntax errors are mistakes caused by violating the "grammar" rules of C++. They easily can be caused by typographical mistakes or a lack of knowledge of the forms of statements required by C++. These errors often can be diagnosed by the C++

compiler as it compiles the program. If your compiler indicates errors when you try to compile a program, it will not translate your code into machine instructions. You must fix the errors before the compiler will translate your code. Therefore, when you have syntax errors you will not generate any output, even if your syntax errors are very minor and located in the very last lines of code.

RUN-TIME ERRORS

Run-time errors, also called *semantic* errors or *smart* errors, are caused by violation of the rules during execution of your program. The compiler does not recognize them during compilation. However, the computer displays a message during execution that something has gone wrong and (usually) that execution is terminated. If a run-time error occurs near the end of execution, you may get some of your results. The error message given by the computer may help you locate the source of error in your code.

LOGIC ERRORS

Logic errors are the most difficult errors to recognize and correct because the computer does not indicate that there are errors in your program as it does with syntax and run-time errors. It is up to you to identify that there is a problem at all. It is up to you to look at your output and decide that it is incorrect. In other words, your program may have appeared to have executed successfully, perhaps giving very reasonable results. However, the answers may be completely wrong. You must recognize that they are wrong and correct the code in the program. (Be careful, though. We will see, as we go further in this book, that the problem may be your input data. Many hours have been spent looking for bugs in programs only to find out that the program is correct, but the input data is incorrect.)

Defending Against Bugs

To reduce the number of bugs in your programs, you need to make sure that you develop good programming habits. This includes such things as

Writing your programs neatly.
Adding blank lines at natural locations.
Lining up your opening and closing braces.
Adding comments properly.

Following these steps will get you started in avoiding bugs. In essence, you should try to work in an organized and structured manner. Remember, a computer is not forgiving. Any error that you make will not be ignored by the computer. Throughout this text, we will note common errors to keep you aware of certain issues so that you can focus on these issues and avoid bugs.

First Steps in Debugging

If your program does not run, do not get frustrated. Realize that debugging is a part of programming. When you are debugging at this stage in your programming career, look at the whole program, and ask yourself:

Did I type anything wrong? For example, was `cout` typed `cut`?
Did I use and follow C++ punctuation properly? For example, `int main ()` being typed `int main ();`.
Are my parentheses and braces in pairs?

In other words, look for obvious things first—the common errors. Then, like looking for problems with your car when it is not working, identify the performance problem and use it as a guide to find the source. For instance, if your car's windshield wipers do not work, you do not look for the source in the rear of the car. Instead, you look at the windshield wiper motor and wiring. With a computer program, if a certain calculation is not performing correctly you look at the portion of code where that calculation is performed and the portions of code that connect to that calculation.

Although the C++ compiler can help you find some errors, do not expect it to pinpoint all the errors and give you instructions on how to correct them. For example, you may just miss the closing `"*/"` in one of your multiline comments at the beginning of your program. If this is the case, the C++ compiler may think the rest of your program is simply a part of an unfinished comment. This minor error may generate 30 error messages. Do not be alarmed. Remember that the typical C++ compiler is not particularly sophisticated in identifying syntax errors. You may be able to eliminate 100 error messages by modifying a single character in your source code.

Problem Statement

This problem is meant to illustrate the debugging that is needed in the process of developing a required program. Here, the goal is to create a program that can print the following to the screen:

```
DEBUGGING EXAMPLE:

This is an example of debugging. By following the step-by-step procedure
that we describe in this application example, you will begin to develop the
skills you need for successful and efficient debugging.
```

Envision that you have written the following program as a first attempt to print this statement (note that we have included line numbers for this program so that we can reference them in the description of the errors):

Line number

```
1  #<include iostream>;
2  using namespace std;
3  int main ( );
4  (
5       cout << 'DEBUGGING EXAMPLE:';
6       cout << "This is an example of debugging.\;
7       By following the step-by-step procedure";
8       cout << "that we describe in this application example,
9       you will begin to develop the;
10      cout << "skills you need for successful and efficient
          debugging.";
11 }
```

Use the compiler to help you modify the code. Follow the step-by-step procedure outlined in the following methodology.

Methodology

First, we outline the steps involved in debugging. Then, we use the steps to guide us to debug the preceding program. The procedure we describe is not the only one that can be used. Your instructor may have other suggestions that you will find helpful. However, at this point in your programming career, follow these steps to correct your program errors:

1. Compile your source code.
2. Look at the location in your source code that is indicated by the first error message. At this point, do not try to understand what the error message means. Only the location indicated is important to us right now.
3. Examine approximately five statements at this location—two or three statements above the indicated location, the statement at the location, and two or three statements below the indicated location.
4. Use this text and your reference books to check your syntax (that is, "grammar, notation, punctuation, and form") for all the lines in the region indicated by step 3.
5. Correct the syntax error(s) you see. At this point, do not attempt to correct your program for every error the C++ compiler has printed out. Fix only the first one.
6. Repeat steps 1–5. Note that each time you compile your program you will likely get a set of error messages that are completely different from the ones the compiler printed previously. This is one reason why we fix only one error at a time. Remember, just one error may cause 100 error messages to be printed. There is no need to read and try to interpret all 100 messages! Fix only the first one and then recompile your program.

   You may need to repeat steps 1–5, even 10 or 15 times. Do not get discouraged, this is not unusual. Eventually, you will fix all these errors (which are syntax errors) indicated by your compiler, and your program will begin executing when you try to run it. However, even after you have fixed all the syntax errors, your program still may have run-time or logic errors.
7. Now that all the syntax errors are corrected, execute your program again and look at the output. Does the output have statements printed that are not like any you have used in your `cout` statements? You may see such words as *overflow* or *execution terminated.* If you have these, then these are run-time errors. From this message, you may get an idea of the location in your program where the run-time error occurred. Also, your program may have printed some of your `cout` statements before the run-time error is printed. This means that the run-time error is located after these `cout` statements in your program. Go back to your source code and look at the statements in the region indicated by the run-time error. Correcting run-time errors is somewhat similar to correcting logic errors. We describe correcting both of these in step 8.

8. You can identify logic errors in your program by noticing that the output is not what you want or expect. In other words, suppose you were expecting the output

```
This is my output.
```

but the program printed

```
This is myoutput.
```

From this you know which `cout` statement has an error, and you must go back to the code and modify it.

Sometimes the location and cause of the error is not as obvious as in this example. You often can get an idea of the location of the error, though, by looking at your output. For instance, suppose your program has 10 `cout` statements in it. If your program produces errors after the first five have been printed correctly, then the error is located in your source code after the fifth `cout` statement.

As we did for syntax errors, look at five or six statements in the region where you feel that the error has occurred. Do not look at just one statement, even if you are sure that execution stopped at that statement. At this point you should ask yourself, "Why is the program not doing what I am trying to tell it to do?" If you cannot see the necessary correction initially, you can make small adjustments to the statements in the error region and see the effect on the output. You should make adjustments and rerun the program repeatedly. This is how you get experience programming—change something and see its effect. It is a major part of the learning process. Do not get discouraged by the computer telling you that you have made errors. Do not make changes blindly, though. Think about what you are doing and what effect you expect the changes will have. Throughout this book, we discuss techniques for helping recognize the source of logic errors and the changes to correct them.

9. After running, making changes, and rerunning your program repeatedly you will have developed a working program. Congratulations! However, before you put this program in your program library, make sure that it is well commented so that you can understand it later or others can easily interpret what you have done. If you have not commented it well, go back at this point and put in comments before you forget what you have done, and then create whatever other documentation is necessary. Resist the temptation to quit and celebrate. You will thank yourself later for spending a relatively small amount of time at this point to properly document your program. A summary of debugging is presented in Fig. 2.3.

Debugging the Given Program

1. We begin by compiling the program in the problem statement. Each compiler gives slightly different error messages, so your compiler may not give exactly what we show here. When we compile the program, our compiler lists eight error messages. The first message points to line 1 of the code and says "Unknown preprocessor directive." As stated in the methodology, we will not worry about what this means but simply look at the line indicated and a few

Figure 2.3

Debugging in a Nutshell.

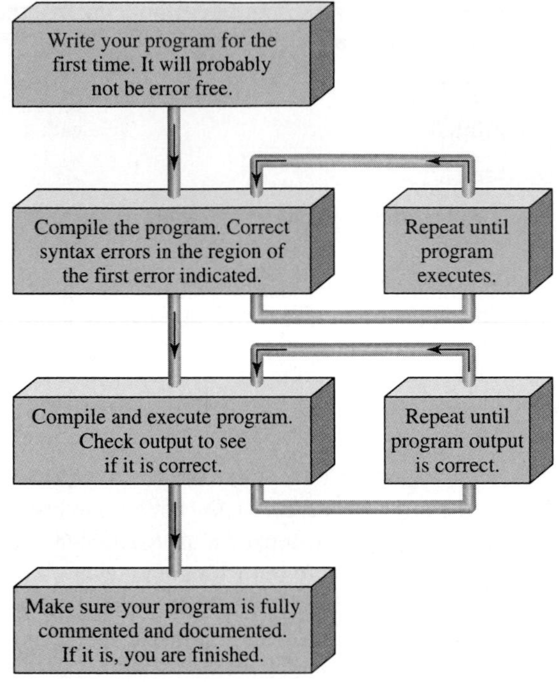

Write your program for the first time. It will probably not be error free.
Compile the program. Correct syntax errors in the region of the first error indicated.
Repeat until program executes.
Compile and execute program. Check output to see if it is correct.
Repeat until program output is correct.
Make sure your program is fully commented and documented. If it is, you are finished.

lines above and below for an error. Since line 1 is the first line of code, we focus on this line. When we do this, we see that we typed:

```
#<include iostream>;
```

when we should have typed:

```
#include <iostream>
```

Note that we had two errors in this statement: the < was in the wrong location, and we had a semicolon at the end of the line. At this point we ignore the other seven errors, correct just this one line and recompile the program. Also, refer to Table 2.2, Table 2.3 and Fig. 2.4 for a summary of all the errors we describe here.

2. On compiling the next time, we get an error indicated at the first `cout` statement (line 5) with the message, ") expected", which is read "Right parenthesis expected." Again, we do not try to determine why this message is being given. Instead, we look a few lines above our location and see that we typed:

   ```
   int main ( );
   ```

   when we should not have put a semicolon at the end of this line. Thus, we remove the semicolon and recompile the program. Note that the compiler indicated the error was at line 5, but the error was really at line 3.

3. We now recompile the program and get one warning and seven errors. Warnings are not fatal errors. In other words, your program can execute correctly and completely with many warnings being given by the compiler. Warnings are exactly those: messages from the compiler to the programmer to

TABLE 2.2 — Syntax error correction summary

Step	Total number of errors indicated by compiler	First line to which the compiler points indicating a syntax error	First error message	First line with a syntax error	Action required to correct the syntax error
1	8	1	Unknown preprocessor directive	1	change #<include iostream>; to #include <iostream>
2	7	5	Character constant too long	3	change int main( ); to int main ( )
3	7	5	Comma expected	4	change (to {
4	17	5	Character constant too long in function main	5	change 'DEBUGGING EXAMPLE:' to "DEBUGGING EXAMPLE:"
5	16	6	Unterminated string or character constant in function main	6	change debugging.\; to debugging.\
6	7	8	Unterminated string or character constant in function main	8	change example, to example,"
7	6	8	Undefined symbol 'you' in function main	9	change you to "you

Note: The error messages are dependent upon the IDE used.

TABLE 2.3 — Logic error correction summary

Step	Indication of error	Action required to correct the logic error
8	Output spacing is incorrect	add \n after EXAMPLE: after procedure after develop the
9	Output spacing is incorrect	1. add another \n after EXAMPLE: 2. replace \ after debugging. with " 3. add " before By

indicate that something unusual is happening, and an error may be caused by this. While you are still trying to locate syntax errors in your programs, we recommend that you ignore warnings and focus on the errors. (It also may be helpful to read the first warning. If you can understand it and it indicates a simple problem, you can correct it quickly. Otherwise, pass it by. When your program begins to execute, read and evaluate all the warning messages given.)

The first error message is ", expected", which is read "Comma expected." The location indicated is again the first cout statement in the program (line 5).

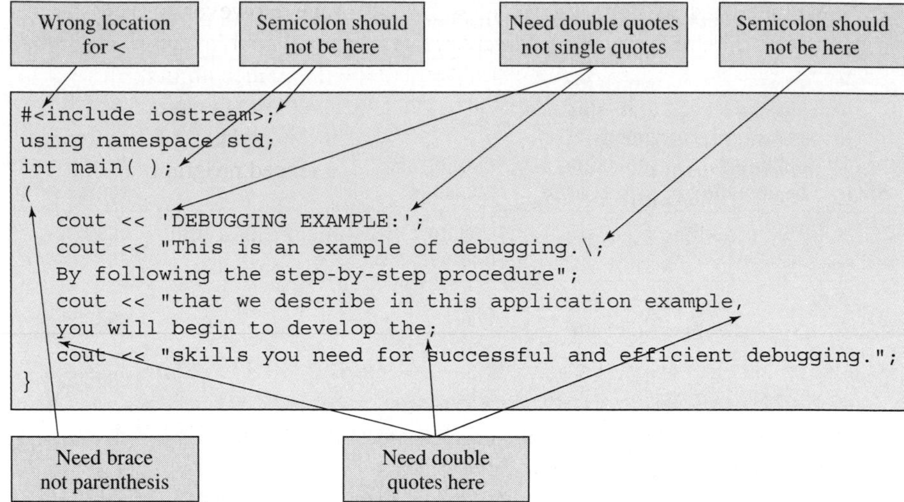

Figure 2.4

Summary of syntax errors in Application Example 2.2.

Again, we look above this location and see that line 4 has a left parenthesis, (, instead of a left brace, {. So we change the parenthesis to a brace and recompile the program.

4. On recompiling we find that the number of errors is not reduced, instead it increases to 17 errors! We should not be alarmed by this. Instead, we simply work with the first message that reads, "Character constant too long in function main." The location indicated by this message is once more the first `cout` statement (line 5). Since we thought we fixed the errors prior to this statement, we look at this statement and realize that we have used single quotes and not double quotes. We, therefore, change the single quotes to double quotes and recompile the program.

5. Our compiler now gives 16 error messages. The first one is indicated by the compiler to be on the second `cout` statement (line 6) in the program and says, "Unterminated string or character constant in function main." We look at this `cout` statement and see that we should not have used a semicolon at the end of the line. So we remove it and recompile.

6. We now get seven error messages. The first one points to the third `cout` statement (line 8) and says, "Unterminated string or character constant in function main." At this point we can describe some of the rationale behind the error messages. We note that the written description of the error for step 5 is the same as that for step 6. Our string constants are enclosed in double quotes. The error message says that we have an "unterminated string constant." Remember, spacing is significant in string constants. The compiler says that because it is looking for a second pair of double quotes or a continuation character, `\`, on the same line as our third `cout` statement and does not find it, it thinks the string is unterminated. Of course, we meant to terminate it on the next line, but this does not work. Therefore, we add `"` to the end of the third `cout` line (line 8) to terminate the string.

Note that step 5 gave us the same error message. However, in that case our action was to remove a semicolon rather than add double quotes. C++ interpreted the semicolon to mean the end of the line. Since no matching double quote was at the end of the line, C++ believed that the string was unterminated. As you get more experience, you will be able to make some use of the actual error messages. However, even experienced programmers often find the messages not particularly helpful because they do not necessarily point out the immediate problem. Rather than spend time trying to interpret the message, it is frequently more efficient to simply focus on the syntax in the region of the error.

We now recompile the program.

7. We get six errors with the first being, "Undefined symbol 'you' in function main" at line 9. We realize that this line was meant to be part of the `cout` string constant, and we put quotes at the start and end of this line. We recompile the program.

8. We get no errors and therefore attempt to run the program. The program executes completely! However, the output is

```
DEBUGGING EXAMPLE:This is an example of debugging a program. By following the
step-by-step procedure that we describe in this application example, you will be
gin to develop theskills you need for successful and efficient debugging.
```

Our program executes but is incorrect because the spacing is wrong. Because the compiler sent no error message, we find that we do not have any run-time errors in this program. However, we have logic errors that now must be addressed. At this point, the compiler can no longer aid us in finding or correcting our errors. We must do it completely on our own by looking at the source code and the output and figuring out what is incorrect and changing it. In your own programs, if you are completely stumped at this point, before you ask for help, make small changes in your code and recompile and run the program. By doing this, you will understand the effect changes make, and it may inspire you to find the source of your error.

In this example, we must get the spacing correct. We add `\n` after `EXAMPLE:`, after `procedure`, and after `develop the`. We make these changes from the knowledge we developed reading this chapter.

9. After having made the changes indicated in step 8 and rerunning the program we find that the resulting output is

```
DEBUGGING EXAMPLE:
This is an example of debugging.      By following the step-by-step procedure
that we describe in this application example, you will begin to develop the
skills you need for successful and efficient debugging.
```

This is still not quite correct because we want double space after `DEBUGGING EXAMPLE:` and because we have too much space before the word `By`. So, we add another `\n` after `DEBUGGING EXAMPLE:`. Eliminating the space before `By` is more difficult. We have extra space because the continuation character, `\`, on the `cout` line above `By` causes the indentation in the source code to be interpreted as extra space. Therefore, we choose to eliminate the continuation character, replace it with double quotes, and put double quotes before `By`.

10. After having made these changes, we get the correct result when we execute the program. However, we are not finished because we must comment our program. Had our program been longer, we would have written comments earlier. However, for this short program now is a good time to write comments. Our end product is

```
//*********************************************************
// Name: Application 2.2
// Purpose: Learning debugging skills.
// Date: Written on 3/7/2002
// Author: John Jones
// Reference: None
//*********************************************************
#include <iostream>
using namespace std;
int main ()
{
     cout << "DEBUGGING EXAMPLE:\n\n");
     cout << "This is an example of debugging."
     "By following the step-by-step procedure\n");
     cout << "that we describe in this application example,"
     "you will begin to develop the\n");
     cout << "skills you need for successful and efficient
       debugging.\n");
}
```

11. We run our program after commenting it to make sure that it still works. If this were a larger program, we would need to write supplementary documentation as well. However, for this program we are now finished.

Comments

You should notice the following from Tables 2.2 and 2.3:

1. The line indicated by the compiler may not be the line with the error. You must look above and below that line to find the error.
2. The error messages given by the compiler may or may not be helpful. As you gain experience, you will be able to use the error messages more effectively.
3. When you recompile the program after having corrected an error, the number of error messages indicated by the compiler may actually increase. This does not mean that the program is becoming more incorrect.
4. The compiler does not indicate logic errors. You must observe that logic errors have occurred on your own. Then you must correct them without help from the compiler.

Even though the procedure we have described here is valuable, we cannot guarantee that if you follow it you will definitely eliminate all your errors. For instance, the method does not work if you were to simply forget the terminating / on a multiline comment. Try doing this. You will find that the compiler indicates an error on the very last line of the program when the error is really located much earlier! Therefore, looking only a few lines above and below the indicated error location would not uncover the error. Although the method we presented does not work in this situation, we believe that you will find the method helpful for locating many of your programming errors. As we go further in this book, we describe other techniques for recognizing and correcting errors. The method described here simply is to get you started in the process of debugging.

We urge you to learn the debugging feature of your IDE. Right now you may have difficulty understanding it, but, by the end of Chapter 3, you should have made an effort at learning how to use it. See your IDE's documentation or ask your instructor about how to use it. Learning to use the debugger will save you many hours of programming frustration. We will not discuss it more as each IDE's debugger is different. We simply encourage you to learn this device on your own.

Also, be as independent as you can be, and be selective in your attempts at getting help. In general, try not to rely on others to debug your programs for you. Start by trying to work through any problems on your own. After you have made an effort to solve your own problem and still have not solved it, seek help. As painful as it may be, you will learn the most and become a better programmer by solving problems relying just on your books and computer.

LESSON EXERCISES

LESSON 2.1 EXERCISES

1. True or false:

a. In general, C++ statements are case sensitive.

b. By default, any C++ statement is location sensitive.

c. A C++ statement must be terminated with a period.

d. The name of the primary function of a C++ program must be `Main`.

e. `#include iostream` is a complete and correct C++ statement.

f. `cout` and `main` are C++ tokens.

2. Find the error(s), if any, in each of these statements:

a. `int main ();`

b. `cout ("Do we need parentheses here?");`

c. `#include (iostream)`

d. `using namespace std`

3. Type, compile, and run this program:

```
main(          )
{ cout << "There is no class tomorrow!"   ;  }
```

Correct any errors you may find.

4. Type, compile, and run this program:

```
ma in() COUT *, ('What is wrong?' }
```

Correct any errors you may find.

5. Modify this lesson's program so that it prints your name and address to the screen.

Solutions

1. a. (true); b. (false); c. (false); d. (false); e. (false); f. (true)
2. a. `int main ()`
   b. `cout << "Do we need parentheses here?";`
   c. `#include <iostream>`
   d. `using namespace std;`

LESSON 2.2 EXERCISES

1. True or false:

   a. A C++ comment line may appear on the first line of a program.

   b. A C++ comment line may not appear on the last line of a program.

   c. We may write a comment at the end of a C++ statement.

   d. We may write a comment line that contains 5000 characters.

   e. C++ allows us to write nested comments.

2. Compile and run this program (file LE2_2_2.CPP) that executes correctly but is not good style:

```
//Comment before main
#include <iostream>
using namespace std;
void main /* We learn how to write comments*/ (void)
{ cout<< /*This is not a nested*/ /*comment*/
  "Let's fly to Paris";
} // Comment after the program is OK
```

3. Correct, rewrite the program neatly, and then compile and run the program file LE2_2_3.CPP:

```
#include <iostream>
using namespace std;
void ma/* This comment is illegal */ in()
{cout << "Let's fly to Paris";
/*This /* is a nested*/ comment */ }
/ This comment is missing a '/'
```

4. Modify this lesson's program so that it has a banner reflecting you as the programmer and other pertinent information.

Solutions

1. a. (true); b. (false); c. (true); d. (true); e. (false)

LESSON 2.3 EXERCISES

1. True or false:

a. The statement `cout << endl,endl,endl<<;` will create 3 blank lines.

b. The statement `cout << "/n/n/n";` will create 3 blank lines.

c. The statement `cout << "\n\n\n";` will create 3 blank lines.

d. The statement `cout << endl << "\n" << endl;` will create 3 blank lines.

e. The statement `cout << "\ n" << "\ n" << "\ n";` will create 3 blank lines.

f. The escape sequence `\n` represents two characters.

2. Find the errors, if any, in each of these statements:

a. `cout << "I \n Come from \n California \n";`

b. `cout << "I \ n Come from \ n California \ n";`

c. `cout << I Come from << endl << New York;`

3. Compile and run the program file LE2_3_3.CPP:

```
#include <iostream>
using namespace std;
int main ()
{cout << "I \n Come from \n California \n");
 cout << "I \ n Come from \ n California \ n";
 cout << "I n Come from n California n";
}
```

How can you correct this program to have the output make sense?

4. Write a program to display a 10-line story on your screen.

5. Modify this lesson's program so that it

a. Prints all of the text on just two lines.

b. Prints the following output:

```
This is C++! We
can jump
two lines.
```

We can print on one line.

c. Prints the following output using just two `cout` statements:

```
This is C++! We can jump
two lines. We can jump
one line.
```

Solutions

1. a. (false); b. (false); c. (true); d. (truc); c. (false); f. (false)

2. a. No error

b. No error but will not linefeed, character `n` also will be displayed

c. `cout << "I Come from" << endl << "New York";`

LESSON 2.4 EXERCISES

1. True or false:

a. The statement `cout << "ABC\a\a";` will display ABC and generate two beeps.

b. The statement `cout << "ABC\b\b";` will display ABC only.

c. The statement `cout << "ABC\r\r";` will display A only.

d. The statement `cout << "ABC\t\t";` will display ABC.

2. Compile and run the program file LE2_4_2.C. What do you expect to see on the screen?

```
#include <iostream>
using namespace std;
int main ()
{
    cout << "\n1. I come from \a\a\a California \n";
    cout << "\n2. I come from \b\b\b Chicago \n";
    cout << "\n3. I come from \r\r\r Hawaii \n";
    cout << "\n3. I come from \t\t\t Nevada \n";
}
```

Solutions

1. a. (true); b. (false); c. (false); d. (true)

APPLICATION EXERCISES

1. Write a program capable of displaying your name and address and a border on the screen.

2. Design your own logo. Write a program that will display that logo on the screen.

3. Write a program that can print out the first four letters of your first name in this form:

```
NNNN   NN        A        MM       MM    EEEEE
NN NN  NN       A A       M M     M M    E
NN  NN NN      AAAAA      M  M   M  M    EEEEE
NN    NNN     A     A     M   M M   M    E
NN     NN    A       A    M    M    M    EEEEE
```

4. Write a program that can print this shape using `%` and `"`. Note that some compilers may allow you to use `%` without using the escape sequence shown in Table 2.1.

```
                      """"
                       """""""
%%%%%%%%%%%%%%%%%%%%%%%%"""""""""
%%%%%%%%%%%%%%%%%%%%%%%%"""""'""""""
                        """""""""
                       """""""
                      """"
```

5. Write a program that can display this following shape using \:

```
\\\                                   \\\
\\\\\\\\\\                     \\\\\\\\\\
\\\\\\\\\\\\\\\\\\\\\\\\\\\\\\\\\\\\\\\\\
\\\\\\\\\\                     \\\\\\\\\\
\\\                                   \\\
```

6. Debug the following program using the method described in Application Example 2.2. Correct the program until it produces this output:

```
/// This is a program to help you practice "debugging".\\\
///There are a few errors in this program. You should be
  able to fix them.\\\
```

Make your output neat and orderly.

```
**********************************************
** Comments are valuable additions to programs
**********************************************
#include<istream>
int main ()
{cout<<"/// This is a program to help you practice
  "debugging"\\\");
cout<<"///There are a few errors in this program\n
you should be able to fix them.\\\"
cut<<"Make your output neat and orderly")}
```

7. Debug the program until it produces the following output.

```
This program has a large number of errors.
Use the method we
described to fix it.
As you program more and more, you will
get better at debugging.
```

```
/****************************************
** Put a banner on your programs
****************************************
#include(iostream)
using namespace std
void<main>void
[
cout<<"This program has a \n large number of errors.\n';
cout<<"\nUse the method we \
described to fix it.";
cot (As you program more and more, you will \\
get better at debugging.)
]
```

8. Debug the program shown until it produces the following output.

```
As you program more, you will
realize that you are spending a
considerable amount of time
```

```
debugging programs.
You will be able to do it
more quickly as you
get more experience.
```

```
/*********************************
** Put your own comment here
*********************************
#include<iosteam>
using namespace std;
void(main)void
Cout<<'As you program more, you will';
cout>>"realize that you are spending a\n
"considerable amount of time
debugging programs.\n";
cout<<"You will be able to do it"
"more quickly as you"
"get more experience.";
```

9. Debug the program shown until it produces the following output.

```
This program, as it is shown,
executes without syntax errors!
However, it does not produce
the output desired.
```

```
/*********************************
** Another debugging challenge
*********************************
include<iostream>
using namespace std;
{int main ()
cout<<"This program, as it is shown,
executes without syntax errors!");
cout{"However, it does \n not produce \
the output desired.'
}*/
```

10. Debug the program shown until it produces the following output.

```
If you have successfully debugged all
of the programs in this lesson, you
are ready to move on to Chapter 3.
```

```
/*******************************************
** You should feel comfortable with debugging.
*******************************************/
#include iostream
using namespace std;
{int main ()
{
cout<<"If you have successfully debugged all"
cout<<"of the programs in this lesson, you;
cout<<'are ready to move on to Chapter 3.;
}
```

11. Write a program that creates a form for an energy bill. Design your own logo. Make table headings. The columns are Date From, Date To, Energy Type, Units, Cost per Unit, and Total Cost. The column widths are 8, 8, 9, 8, 8, and 9, respectively.

12. Write a program that creates a form that reports the results of a baseball game. Make your own team logo. The columns are Player Name, At Bats, Hits, Bases on Balls, Runs Batted In, and Runs. The column widths are 20, 6, 6, 6, 8, and 5 respectively.

CHAPTER 3

VARIABLES AND ARITHMETIC OPERATIONS

CHAPTER TOPICS

In this chapter, you will learn how to:

- Work with variables
- Perform arithmetic calculations
- Use mathematical functions

To get your programs to solve practical problems, you need to know how to create and manipulate variables. The variables can be used in math functions like sin, cos, and log (that are built into C++) as well as with ordinary operators such as +. However, C++ has strict rules on how arithmetic operations are carried out. For instance, in an arithmetic statement involving addition and multiplication, the multiplication is performed first. This chapter describes these types of rules and illustrates how to create programs that solve some basic problems.

LESSON 3.1 VARIABLES (1): NAMING, DECLARING, ASSIGNING, AND PRINTING VALUES

TOPICS

- Naming variables
- Declaring variables
- Displaying variable values
- Elementary assignment statements

Variables are crucial to virtually all C++ programs. You have learned about variables in algebra, and you will find that in C++ variables are used in much the same manner.

Suppose, for instance, you want to calculate the area of many triangles, all of different sizes. And suppose that the given information is

1. The length of each of the three sides.
2. The size of each of the three angles.

To write an algebraic equation to determine the area, you need to make up your own variable names. You might choose as variable names

1. Lengths: a, b, c
2. Angles: α, β, γ

Or you could name the variables

1. Lengths: l_1, l_2, l_3
2. Angles: θ_1, θ_2, θ_3

Or you could name the variables something completely different. It is entirely up to you what to name them, and you most likely would choose variable names that are descriptive to you and others or conventionally used in a particular context.

For programming in C++, the situation is quite similar. *You* choose the variable names, and it is best to choose names that are descriptive to you and others or conventionally used in a particular context. A major difference between typical C++ programs and typical algebraic expressions is that the variables in most algebraic expressions consist of just one or two characters, maybe with a subscript or superscript. Variables in C++ programs often consist of entire words rather than single characters. Why? Because, as you will find, programs can get quite long, and there simply are not enough single characters to represent all the necessary variables. Also, you will find that it will be easier for you and others to understand your programs if you have given very descriptive names to each variable.

For instance, for the triangle area program you may use the variable names

1. Lengths: `length1`, `length2`, `length3`
2. Angles: `angle1`, `angle2`, `angle3`

Or, if you wanted to be even more descriptive, you could name your variables

1. Lengths: `side_length1`, `side_length2`, `side_length3`
2. Lengths: `SideLength1`, `SideLength2`, `SideLength3`
3. Angles: `angle_opposite_side1`, `angle_opposite_side2`, `angle_opposite_side3`
4. Angles: `AngleOppositeSide1`, `AngleOppositeSide2`, `AngleOppositeSide3`

These variable names are much less ambiguous than their algebraic counterparts. Unfortunately, expressions using these variable names look much more cumbersome than the ones using simple algebraic notation. However, this is a disadvantage with which we simply must live. Check with your instructor or employer regarding the preferred form for naming variables. Some organizations use forms 1 and 3 while others use forms 2 and 4.

C++ has rules you must follow in dealing with variables. For instance, you must *declare* all your variable names in your programs, which means to list your variables and indicate what type they are. Variables can be integers or reals (as well as other types) and must be declared to be of the desired type in your programs. Also, older C++ compilers do not allow you to use more than 31 characters for one variable name, while current standard C++ compilers have no practical limit on the number of characters. These and other rules will be discussed in the lesson.

We can give numeric values to the variables using assignment statements. Assignment statements have a single variable name followed by an = sign and an expression.

QUESTIONS YOU SHOULD ATTEMPT TO ANSWER

1. What type of variable is `tank_id`?
2. What type of variable are `diameter` and `pressure`?

The program for this lesson works with variables associated with an industrial facility. At this facility are a number of tanks. Each tank has an identification number (variable `tank_id`), diameter (variable `diameter`) and pressure (variable `pressure`). The program assigns numeric values to these variables and prints them out along with text. Read the source code and pay particular attention to the declarations, assignment statements, and the `cout` statements used to print the variable values.

Source Code

```
#include <iostream>
using namespace std;
int main ( )
{
        int tank_id;
        double diameter, pressure;

        tank_id = 12;
        diameter = 111.1;
        pressure = 100.  ;
```

Declaring variable (`tank_id`) to be an integer using the keyword `int`.

Declaring variables (`diameter` and `pressure`) to be real using the keyword `double`.

Assignment statements using the = sign store numerical values in the memory cells for the declared variables.

```
        cout << "Tank_id=" << tank_id << ",  Diameter=" << diameter << endl;

        tank_id = 11;
        diameter = 82.1;

        cout << "Tank_id=" << tank_id
             << ", Diameter=" << diameter
             << ", Pressure=" << pressure << "\n";
}
```

Variable *names* (without double quotes) after insertion operators in `cout` statements cause the variable *values* to be printed.

Assignment statements cause the values previously stored in variable memory cells to be overwritten.

This `cout` statement prints the values of the variables `tank_id`, `diameter`, and `pressure` after the last two assignment statements have been executed.

Output

```
Tank_id=12, Diameter=111.1
Tank_id=11, Diameter=82.1, Pressure=100
```

The variable *values* are printed at the locations where the variable *names* have been used in the `cout` statements.

Description

Actions in memory as a program executes. As a program executes, conceptually, a table is created internally. This table contains variable names, types, addresses, and values. The names, types, and addresses are first established during compilation; then as execution takes place space is reserved in memory, and the variable values are put into the memory cells reserved for the variables at the locations indicated by the addresses. In this lesson's program, we declared three variables and after assigning values to them, the table looks like:

Variable name	Variable type	Memory cell address	Variable value
tank_id	int	FFE0	12
diameter	double	FFFE	111.1
pressure	double	FFF6	100.

Later in the program, we assign new values to the variables and the table changes. It becomes

Variable name	Variable type	Memory cell address	Variable value
tank_id	int	FFE0	11
diameter	double	FFFE	82.1
pressure	double	FFF6	100.

Comparing the two tables, we can see that the memory cell addresses do not change, but the variable values do change. You will find that your programs continually change the variable values in the table. (Note: The memory cell addresses are written in hexadecimal notation—we use hexadecimal notation for memory cell addresses throughout the remainder of this text. You need not be concerned about the memory cell addresses at this point. The addresses are automatically set by the computer when you compile and execute your programs.) Next, we describe how to properly set up such a table by naming, declaring, and assigning values to variables.

Naming variables. Variables in C++ programs are identified by name. Remember, you choose the variable names for your programs. Variable names are classified as *identifiers*. Therefore, when naming variables you must obey the rules used for identifiers. For instance, the first character of an identifier cannot be numeric, and the other characters must be a–z, A–Z, _, or 0–9. Table 3.1 lists the constraints on creating valid identifiers. Read this table to understand the rules for identifiers.

TABLE 3.1 — Some constraints on identifiers

Topic	Comment
The first character in identifier	Must be letters (a–z, A–Z) or _
Other characters in identifier	Must be letters (a–z, A–Z) _, or digits 0–9
The maximum number of characters in an internal identifier (i.e., identifier within a function)	Standard C++ does not restrict the number of characters; however older compilers have a limit of 31 (which is more than enough for most programs)
Use of all uppercase characters	Allowed; however, many programmers use all uppercase for constant names
Use of mixed cases or underscores	Allowed and commonly used when variables need long descriptive names. For example, `AngleOppositeSide1` or `angle_opposite_side1` are preferred over `angleoppositeside1`

Use of C++ keywords (also called *reserved words*) and alternative representations of certain operators and punctuators as identifiers	Not allowed; do not use these as identifiers:
	`asm` `bitand` `bitor`
	`auto` `break` `case`
	`bool` `catch` `class`
	`char` `const` `continue`
	`compl` `not` `not_eq`
	`const_cast` `delete` `dynamic_cast`
	`default` `do` `double`
	`else` `enum` `extern`
	`explicit` `false` `friend`
	`float` `for` `goto`
	`if` `int` `long`
	`inline` `mutable` `namespace`
	`new` `operator` `private`
	`or` `or_eq` `xor`
	`protected` `public` `reinterpret_cast`
	`register` `return` `short`
	`signed` `sizeof` `static`
	`static_cast` `template` `this`
	`struct` `switch` `typedef`
	`throw` `true` `try`
	`typeid` `typename` `using`
	`union` `unsigned` `void`
	`virtual` `wchar_t` `and`
	`volatile` `while` `and_eq`
	`xor_eq`

Use of standard identifiers such as `main`	Standard identifiers, such as `main`, can be used as variable names. However, their use is not recommended because it leads to confusion.
Use of blank within an identifier	Not allowed, because an identifier is a token

Here are some examples of illegal variable names:

`1apple`	(illegal because it begins with a number)
`interest_rate%`	(illegal because it has `%` in it)
`float`	(illegal because it is a keyword)
`In come`	(illegal because it has a space)
`one'two`	(illegal because it has a quote in it)

and examples of legal variable names:

```
apple1    interest_rate    xfloat    Income    one_two
```

Keywords. A *keyword* is an identifier type token for which C++ has a defined purpose (Table 3.1). Keywords used in this lesson's program are `using`, `namespace`, `int`, and `double`. Because these have special meanings in C++, we cannot use them as variable names.

You do not need to memorize the keywords in this table; however, it is very important that you recognize the keywords in a program you read. If you do not know the keywords, you may confuse a keyword with a variable name, function name, or other identifier. As you read this book you will learn how to use many of the keywords listed in Table 3.1, and they will naturally become part of your C++ vocabulary.

Declaring variables. Variable names in C++ must be declared. The statement

```
int tank_id;
```

declares the variable `tank_id` to be of the `int` (which must be typed in lowercase letters and means *integer*) type.

Variables of the same type may be declared in the same statement. However, each must be separated from the others by a comma; for example, the statement

```
double diameter, pressure;
```

declares the variables `diameter` and `pressure` to be of the `double` (which must be typed in lower case) type (see Fig. 3.1).

The type `double` is one of C++'s real data types. Variables declared to be `double` have their values stored using the binary method partially described in Chapter 1 for real numbers. Variables declared to be `double` can hold values that contain digits after the decimal point.

Declaring variables causes the C++ compiler to know that space is to be reserved in memory for storing the values of the variables. By stating a variable's type, the C++ compiler knows how much space in memory is to be set aside. Although not explicitly set by the C++ standard, the standard implies (because C++ is a superset of C) the minimum number of bits to be used for each variable type. For instance, C++ requires that

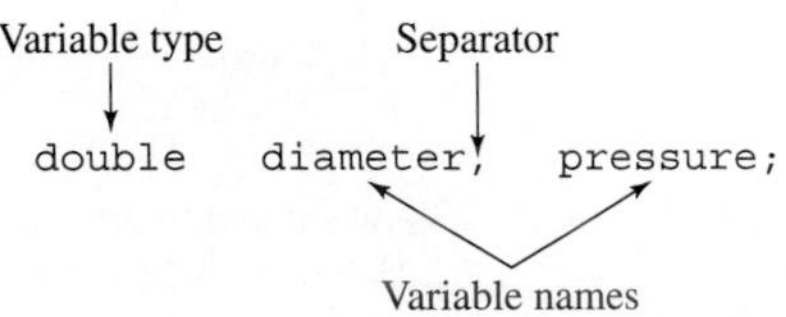

Figure 3.1
Declaring variables.

type `int` be capable of storing at least a range of values between −32768 and 32767. This requires 16 bits or 2 bytes of memory. Therefore, declaring the variable `tank_id` as `int` indicates that at least 16 bits or 2 bytes of memory is reserved for this variable's value. On the other hand, a `double` type value occupies a minimum of 8 bytes or 64 bits. Therefore, declaring a variable to be a `double` requires at least 8 bytes of memory to be reserved.

Remember, as we described in Chapter 1, C++ uses different types of binary codes for integers and reals. This means that, for example, the bit pattern for 87 stored as an `int` is completely different from the bit pattern for storing 87 as a `double`. It is important that we keep this in mind. Forgetting this fact will lead to errors as we will see when we begin working more with variables.

Many implementations of C++ (that is, many C++ IDEs) exceed the minimums required by standard C++. Such implementations often have an `int` occupying 4 bytes or 32 bits. The range for a 32 bit `int` is −2,147,483,648 to 2,147,483,647. In this book, we will assume and work with the minimum ranges. However, you should be aware that your implementation may reserve more memory than what we show.

Assignment statements and using variables. An assignment statement assigns a value to a variable, which means an assignment statement causes a value to be stored in the variable's memory cell. For example, the statement

```
tank_id = 12;
```

assigns the integer value 12 to `int` type variable `tank_id`. It causes 12, written in two's complement binary type of notation, to be stored in the `tank_id` memory cell (Fig. 3.2).

In C++, a simple assignment statement takes the form of

```
variable_name = value;
```

where this statement stores the *`value`* on the right side of the equal sign in the memory cell reserved for the *`variable_name`* on the left side of the equal sign. The binary representation of the value is stored in the variable's memory cell after the assignment has taken place. The *`value`* can be a constant, a variable with a known value, or other, such as a function or an expression that returns a value (see the next few lessons for more details). Note that the equal sign in an assignment statement does not really mean equal. It simply indicates that a value is to be stored in the variable's memory cells.

The following forms are *not* allowed:

```
value = variable_name;
```

or

```
12 = tank_id;
```

Although you learned in algebra that $x = 5$ and $5 = x$ are equivalent, C++ does not allow a value to appear on the left side of an assignment statement. Also, a single variable name should appear on the left.

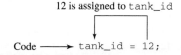

12 is assigned to `tank_id`

Code ——→ `tank_id = 12;`

Figure 3.2

Assignment statement. This assignment statement causes the bit pattern representing 12 (in binary type representation) to be stored in the memory cell reserved for the variable `tank_id`.

Variables *must* be declared before they are assigned values! In other words, we could not have written the beginning of this lesson's program:

```
#include <iostream>
using namespace std;
int main ( )
{
        tank_id = 12 ;
        diameter = 111.1;
        pressure = 100. ;

        int tank_id;
        double diameter, pressure;
```

The variables are assigned values.

The variables are declared.

because the variables were assigned values before being declared. Remember, C++ processes the statements one after another. If you try to assign a value to a variable before declaring it, no memory exists for that variable, and therefore no value can be placed in memory. An error will be indicated during compilation if you either do not declare a variable or declare a variable after it has been used.

C++ does not require that variable declarations be the first lines of the body of the program or function. In other words, we could have written the beginning of this lesson's program as:

```
#include <iostream>
using namespace std;
int main ( )
{
        int tank_id;
        tank_id = 12 ;

        double diameter, pressure;
        diameter = 111.1;
        pressure = 100.;
```

Variable declared.

Variable assigned value.

Variables declared.

Variables assigned values.

because each variable is declared before it is used.

In most places in this textbook, we will declare our variables at the beginning of each function. You may see some programmers declaring their variables immediately before they are used. You should check with your instructor or employer on which method is preferred. We recommend that you follow a method consistently throughout your programs so that others can easily follow your code.

You may also see a line of the type:

```
double diameter = 111.1;
```

This both declares the variable `diameter` to be type `double` and *initializes* it (that is, gives the variable its first value) to be 111.1. Such a line does not need to appear at the beginning of a function.

When we study functions more thoroughly in Chapter 7, we will see that there are other rules for when we declare variables outside the body of any function.

Displaying the value of a variable or constant on the screen. The `cout` object can be used to display the value of a variable or constant on the screen. The syntax is

```
cout << variable_name;
```

where *`variable_name`* is a variable that has been declared and assigned a value. This simple form will display the variable value only and contain no explanatory text. To add explanatory text and advance the cursor to the next line, the following form can be used:

```
cout << "explanatory_text" << variable_name
     << "explanatory_text" << endl;
```

where *`explanatory_text`* is any text information as described in Chapter 2. Only one *`variable_name`* can be used between stream insertion operators (<<). To print more than one variable value with one `cout` statement use a form such as:

```
cout << variable_name << "explanatory_text"
     << variable_name << "explanatory_text" << endl;
```

LESSON 3.2 VARIABLES (2): CREATING CONSTANT QUALIFIED VARIABLES AND MORE ABOUT PRINTING VARIABLE VALUES

TOPICS

- Creating constant qualified variables with the `const` qualifier.
- Setting the after decimal point precision for printing.
- Controlling the space used for printing.
- Scientific notation.
- Left justifying values.

You will find sometimes that you need to use values in your programs that do not change. For instance, we know that π is approximately 3.14159. For a program that involves areas of circles, it is convenient to simply write the characters `PI` in the equations rather than the digits 3.14159. This can be done by using the `const` qualifier in the declaration. Once the `const` qualifier has been used in declaring a variable, the value of the variable cannot be modified later in the program.

Sometimes you will want to display your values in special ways rather than in the C++ default manner. For instance, to display a table neatly you may want to use 20 spaces for each value no matter how many digits a number may have. C++ allows you to set the width in your `cout` statements. Also, you may want to display fewer digits after the decimal point than a number actually has. This is particularly important when dealing with dollar calculations where only two digits after the decimal should be displayed. In this lesson's program we show how to perform these manipulations with `cout` statements.

QUESTIONS YOU SHOULD ATTEMPT TO ANSWER

1. What do you think `setw` does? (Look at the second line of the output.)
2. What do you think `setprecision` does? (Look at the third line of the output.)
3. What do you think `setfill` does? (Look at the fourth line of the output.)
4. What do you think `setiosflags` does? (Look at the fifth line of the output.)

When working with very large or very small numbers, scientific notation is convenient. For example, to represent 57,650,000, the scientific notation would be 5.765×10^7, which in C++ would be 5.765e+007 or 5.765E+007. In other words, we can use scientific notation in our source code. For instance, we could use the following declaration and assignment statement in a program:

```
double x;
x = 5.63e+009;
```

C++ accepts and properly interprets this notation in source code.

We can also display scientific notation in our output as we show in this program. By specifying scientific notation in our `cout` statements, C++ decides the value of the exponent, and thus it is possible to display an extremely large number in a small number of spaces. The programmer need decide only on the number of significant digits to display.

This program creates one constant qualified variable, `PI`. It prints the numerical value of this variable in a number of formats. Read the program and notations and look at the output.

Source Code

```
#include <iostream>
#include <iomanip>
using namespace std;

int main( )
{
    const double PI = 3.14159;
    cout << "1.  PI=[[" << PI << "]]" << endl;
    cout << "2.  PI=[[" << setw(15) << PI << "]]" << endl;
    cout << "3.  PI=[[" << setprecision(2) << PI << "]]" << endl  ;
    cout << "4.  PI=[[" << setw(20) << setfill('*') << PI << "]]" << endl;
    cout << "5.  PI=[[" << setiosflags(ios::left) << setw(20) << PI << "]]"
        << endl;

    cout << setprecision(4);
    cout << "6.  PI=[[" << setiosflags(ios::scientific) << PI << "]]" << endl;
    cout << "7.  PI=[[" << setiosflags(ios::left | ios::scientific)
        << setw(20) << PI << "]]" << endl;
}
```

The `iomanip` header is needed to enable formatting of the output.

The use of the `const` qualifier, declaration, and assignment of the value of `PI` are all done in one line of code. C++ will not allow us to use `PI` on the left side of an assignment statement later in the program. Note that the variable name `PI` is written in all capital letters.

This `cout` statement prints the value of `PI` between a set of double brackets.

These `cout` statements print the value of `PI` between double brackets in various formats. Note the use of the manipulators `setw`, `setprecision`, `setfill`, and `setiosflags`.

We can even print scientific notation with a specified precision and left justification with `cout`. Note the use of `ios::left` and `ios::scientific`.

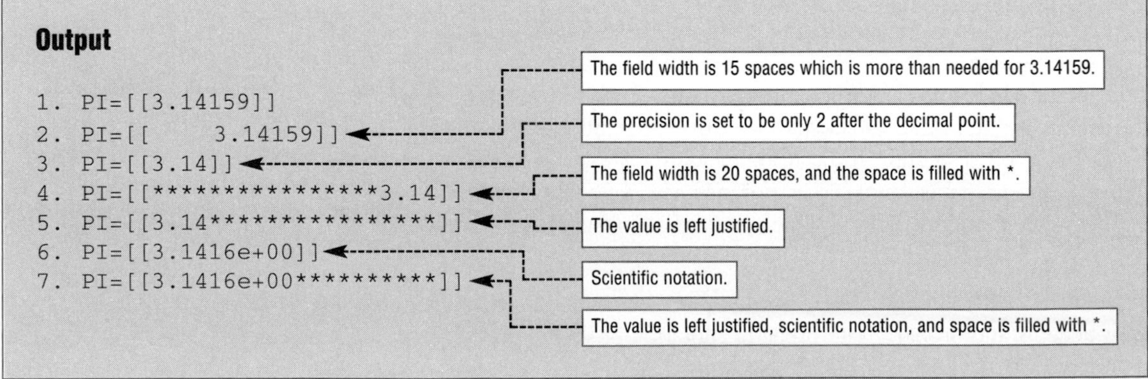
Output
1. PI=[[3.14159]]
2. PI=[[3.14159]]
3. PI=[[3.14]]
4. PI=[[****************3.14]]
5. PI=[[3.14****************]]
6. PI=[[3.1416e+00]]
7. PI=[[3.1416e+00**********]]
The field width is 15 spaces which is more than needed for 3.14159.
The precision is set to be only 2 after the decimal point.
The field width is 20 spaces, and the space is filled with *.
The value is left justified.
Scientific notation.
The value is left justified, scientific notation, and space is filled with *.

Description

Constant qualified variables. We use the `const` qualifier (`const` is a keyword) and assign a value in the declaration (which is required) to create constant qualified variables. For example, the line

```
const double PI = 3.14159;
```

assigns the value of 3.14159 to `PI` and qualifies it so that it cannot be modified later in the program. An error would have been generated during compilation if we had used an assignment statement later in the program of the sort:

```
PI = 3.1415926;
```

because C++ does not allow us to use a constant qualified variable on the left side of an assignment statement after it has been initialized.

We will find a number of uses for the `const` qualifier. The `const` qualifier helps us write better code because it can assure us that we do not accidentally modify something that should not be modified. As we go through the text, we will point out the uses of the `const` qualifier when appropriate. For now, we will create constant qualified variables when we use such things as conversion factors (for instance, the number of centimeters per inch is 2.54) or fixed numbers (for instance, the number of days in a week is 7).

Many C++ programmers use all uppercase characters to name constant qualified variables (as in this lesson's program with `PI`). Lowercase characters are used to name ordinary variables (with underscores and some uppercase characters possibly mixed in). This book follows this convention in most cases. The value of following this convention is that it is easier for others to understand your code and for you to understand others' code. Check with your employer or instructor if another convention is to be used.

Formatting output using manipulators. In the program for Lesson 3.1, the C++ compiler decided how many digits would be displayed for a number on output and how much space a number would occupy. There will be times when you will want to decide how a number will be displayed rather than leaving it to the compiler (for instance, when you want to print a table neatly). To do this, we insert *I/O manipulators* called *parameterized manipulators,* into `cout` statements that we use to print variable values. The parameterized manipulators are declared in the header `iomanip`. You must include this header with the statement:

```
#include <iomanip>
```

to use parameterized manipulators in your `cout` statements.

In its most basic form, a parameterized manipulator can be inserted into a `cout` statement like this:

```
cout << manipulator(parameter);
```

where *`manipulator`* is any standard C++ parameterized manipulator and *`parameter`* is what the manipulator uses to modify output. We can also use parameterized manipulators between << operators in our `cout` statements as we have done in this

TABLE 3.2 — The C++ I/O parameterized manipulators

Manipulator	Action	Example
`setfill (int f)`	Set the fill character to `f`	`setfill ('*')`
`setprecision(int p)`	Set the precision of a floating-point number to `p`	`setprecision(2)`
`setw(int w)`	Set the field width to `w`	`setw(20)`
`setiosflags(long f)`	Set the format flag specified by `f`	`setiosflags(ios::left)`
`resetiosflags(long f)`	Return to default for the flag specified by `f`	`resetiosflags(ios::left)`
`setbase(int b)`	Set the base of numbers output to be `b` (must be 8, 10, or 16)	`setbase(16)`

lesson's program. Table 3.2 lists the C++ I/O parameterized manipulators. The most important of these at this time are used in this lesson's program and are described here.

- *setw.* We can make empty space appear on the left side of a displayed number by setting the *field width* (that is, the number of text spaces that a printed number occupies) much larger than the number needs by inserting the parameterized manipulator `setw` into the `cout` statement. For example, the statement

  ```
  cout << "2. PI=[[" << setw(15) << PI << "]]" << endl;
  ```

  uses the manipulator `setw` to change the field width to 15. The output for this lesson's program shows that this statement prints:

  ```
  2. PI=[[        3.14159]]
  ```

  which illustrates 15 spaces between the double brackets. Observe that the number is *right justified* within the 15 spaces, meaning that the number is pushed to the right edge of the field. C++ does this automatically.

  If the `cout` statement does not specify the field width, as we did in Lesson 3.1, C++ decides how large the field width should be. When integers are printed, C++ makes the field width equal to the number of digits in the integer, meaning that no empty text space is displayed on either side of the integer. However, if we use `setw(4)` to print the number 549382, C++ will automatically expand the width to accommodate all the digits. For instance, if we have the statements:

  ```
  i = 549382;
  cout << setw(4) << i;
  ```

  the output will be:

  ```
  549382
  ```

  not `5493`. In other words, you need not worry about accidentally specifying the width to be smaller than what is actually required.

- *setprecision.* The manipulator `setprecision()` sets the number of digits after the decimal point to be printed. For instance, in this lesson's program, we use `setprecision` with the line:

  ```
  cout << "3. PI = [[" << setprecision(2) << PI << "]]" << endl ;
  ```

This causes the output to show only two digits after the decimal point for PI, making the output:

```
3. PI = [[3.14]]
```

Even though only two digits are displayed, all the digits are retained in memory so that later in the program one can use setprecision(4) and still have four digits correctly printed.

Once the precision is set in a cout statement, this precision may or may not be used until another statement changes it. It depends on your compiler as standard C++ does not require that all compilers work this way. Some compilers may need the precision to be specified with each cout statement (or the default will be used). Check the manual of your compiler to see how setprecision is implemented. For our compiler, in this lesson's program, the statement:

```
cout << setprecision(4);
```

sets the precision to 4 for all the cout statements after it in the program.

- *setfill.* The manipulator setfill() specifies the character for filling blank space in a field. For instance:

```
cout << "4.  PI=[[" << setw(20) << setfill('*') << PI << "]]"
     << endl;
```

creates a field width of 20 (with setw(20)) and fills the portion of the field not containing digits with the character * (with setfill('*')). Observe that single quotes (not double quotes) are required around the character enclosed in parentheses. The output from this statement is:

```
4. PI=[[***************3.14]]
```

Note that the precision is 2 (two digits after the decimal point) even though the precision is not specified in this cout statement. Because the precision was previously specified to be 2, cout (with the compiler we have used) retains that precision until a new precision is specified. Depending on your compiler, this filler may appear until changed by another cout statement.

- *setiosflags.* The manipulator setiosflags can perform a number of different actions. In this lesson's program, we use it to left justify the value of PI by using setiosflags(ios::left) in the line:

```
cout << "5.  PI=[[" << setiosflags(ios::left) << setw(20)
     << PI << "]]" << endl;
```

which produces the output:

```
5. PI=[[3.14***************]]
```

For the time being, simply remember to use ios followed by two colons and then left to left justify. (Actually, left is considered to be a flag of the ios class. For now, you do not need to know the details of what this means.) Observe that we used setw(20) to make the field width 20. Unlike setprecision(), we need setw() for each cout statement if the field width is to be something other than the default.

TABLE 3.3 — Flags and their uses

Type	Flag	Usage
Format	`left`	Left-adjust output
	`internal`	Left-adjust sign or base, right-adjust numerical value
	`right`	Right-adjust output
	`dec`	Display number as decimal value equivalent
	`hex`	Display number as hexadecimal value equivalent
	`oct`	Display number as octal value equivalent
	`fixed`	Specifies nonscientific notation for a floating point number
	`scientific`	Specifies scientific notation for a floating point number
	`showpoint`	Show decimal point
	`showbase`	Show base for numerical values
	`showpos`	Show '+' sign for a positive number
	`uppercase`	Print letters in uppercase
	`skipws`	Skip leading whitespace on input
	`unitbuf`	Flush output after each output operation
	`boolalpha`	Insert and extract `bool` type in alphabetic format
Format constant	`adjustfield`	Used with `left`, `right`, or `internal` for `setiosflags`
	`basefield`	Used with `dec`, `hex`, or `oct` for `setiosflags`
	`floatfield`	Used with `fixed` or `scientific` for `setiosflags`
I/O state	`badbit`	Bit indicating loss of integrity of input or output
	`eofbit`	Bit indicating end of file has been encountered
	`failbit`	Bit indicating failed input or output (generally no data loss)
Open mode	`app`	Move position indicator to end before each write
	`ate`	Open and move position indicator to end immediately after opening
	`binary`	Perform input and output in binary (rather than text) mode
	`in`	Open for input
	`out`	Open for output
	`trunc`	Truncate an existing stream when opening
Seek directions	`beg`	Move position indicator relative to beginning (for input or output)
	`cur`	Move position indicator relative to current location (for input or output)
	`end`	Move position indicator relative to end (for input or output)

In this lesson's program, we used `setiosflags(ios::scientific)` to display a number in scientific notation. Look at the output from the program to see the effect of this.

We can use `setiosflags()` with more than one flag by combining the flags with the symbol `|`. For example, the manipulator `setiosflags()` in the statement:

```
cout << "7. PI=[[" << setiosflags(ios::left | ios::scientific)
     << setw(20) << PI << "]]" << endl;
```

uses the `|` symbol to combine the `left` and `scientific` flags to produce the output:

```
7. PI=[[3.1416e+00**********]]
```

You can use other flags to perform other tasks. Other flags and what they do are shown in Table 3.3. You do not need to understand all of this table at this time. We will highlight what is important as we go along. You can use this table later as a reference when you do more advanced programming.

- *endl.* Some stream manipulators do not require parameters. In fact, `endl` is classified as a standard manipulator that does not require parameters. Table 3.4 lists other standard manipulators and what they do. Again, you do not need to know and understand these at this time. We simply present them here for later reference.

Printing in "dollar" format. To print output in "dollar" format (meaning two digits after a decimal point), it is necessary to use I/O manipulators. For instance, the statement

```
cout << setprecision(2) << setiosflags(ios:fixed | ios:showpoint)
     << "Income=$" << income;
```

uses the manipulator `setprecision(2)` to indicate two digits after the decimal point, and `setiosflags(ios:fixed | ios:showpoint)` to assure the decimal point will be displayed in fixed notation with the decimal point shown. For the variable income having the value 7842, the output produced by this `cout` statement is:

```
Income = $7842.00
```

TABLE 3.4 — Standard manipulators

Manipulator	Action	Use
`dec`	Display or interpret numbers as base 10	I/O
`oct`	Display or interpret numbers as base 8	I/O
`hex`	Display or interpret numbers as base 16	I/O
`endl`	Output new line and flush the stream	Output
`ends`	Output a null	Output
`flush`	Flush the stream	Output
`ws`	Skip any leading white space	Input

LESSON 3.3 VARIABLES (3): ASSIGNING AND PRINTING SINGLE CHARACTER DATA

TOPICS

- The set of characters
- Single character output

QUESTION YOU SHOULD ATTEMPT TO ANSWER

1. What is the effect on the output in printing `c3`?

The single character type, `char`, can be utilized somewhat similarly to the numeric types, `int` and `double`.

The term *character* refers to more than just lowercase and uppercase letters. There are graphic characters such as `!`, `#`, and `^`. Even "space" (hitting the space bar) is considered a character. Escape sequences (like `\n` and `\r`) also are regarded as single characters.

The numbers 0–9 can be treated as characters as well. We may find this helpful when we want to store such things as telephone numbers. Telephone numbers have no arithmetic manipulations on them (it makes no sense to add two of them together). Because of this, a telephone number may be more difficult to manipulate if it is stored as an integer. Therefore, we may find it convenient to store numbers that do not require arithmetic operations as characters.

This program assigns and prints characters. We use the `static_cast` operator to print the decimal integer equivalent of each of the characters and show the effect of using characters in addition statements. Read the code and annotations.

Source Code

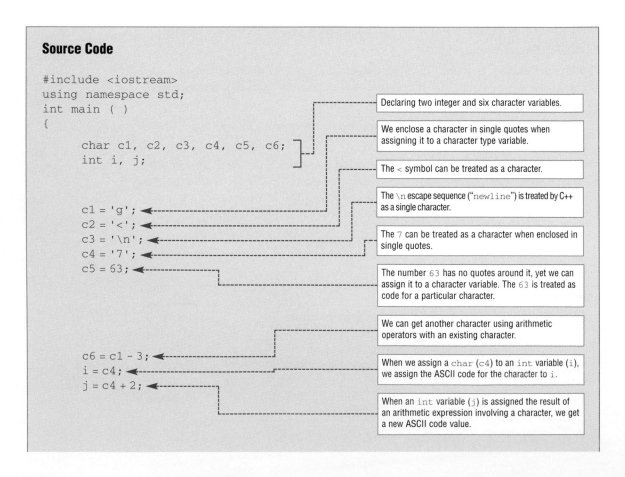

```
#include <iostream>
using namespace std;
int main ( )
{
     char c1, c2, c3, c4, c5, c6;
     int i, j;

     c1 = 'g';
     c2 = '<';
     c3 = '\n';
     c4 = '7';
     c5 = 63;

     c6 = c1 - 3;
     i = c4;
     j = c4 + 2;
```

- `char c1, ... int i, j;` — Declaring two integer and six character variables.
- `c1 = 'g';` — We enclose a character in single quotes when assigning it to a character type variable.
- `c2 = '<';` — The < symbol can be treated as a character.
- `c3 = '\n';` — The `\n` escape sequence ("`newline`") is treated by C++ as a single character.
- `c4 = '7';` — The `7` can be treated as a character when enclosed in single quotes.
- `c5 = 63;` — The number `63` has no quotes around it, yet we can assign it to a character variable. The `63` is treated as code for a particular character.
- `c6 = c1 - 3;` — We can get another character using arithmetic operators with an existing character.
- `i = c4;` — When we assign a `char` (`c4`) to an `int` variable (`i`), we assign the ASCII code for the character to `i`.
- `j = c4 + 2;` — When an `int` variable (`j`) is assigned the result of an arithmetic expression involving a character, we get a new ASCII code value.

```
        cout << "c1=" << c1 << "  c2=" << c2 << "  c3=" << c3 << "c4=" << c4
             << "  c5=" << c5 << "  c6=" << c6 << "  i=" << i << "  j=" << j << endl;
}
```

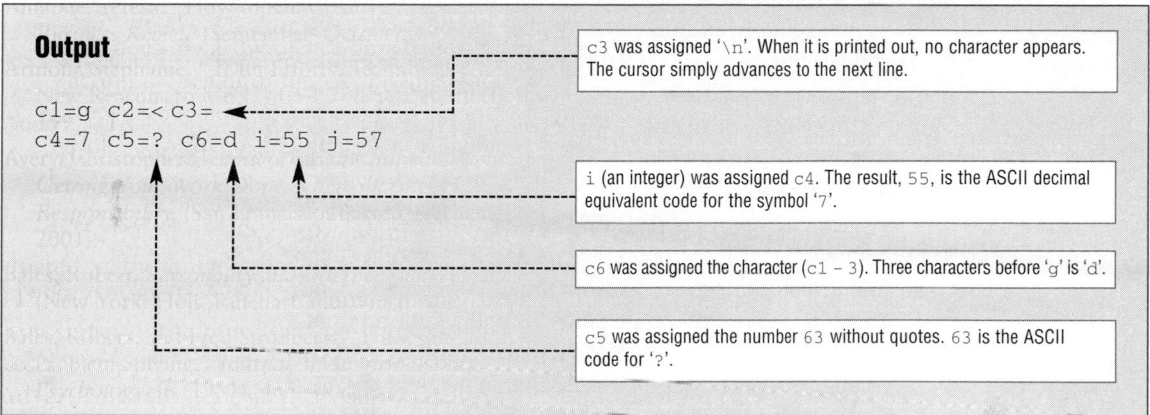
Output
c1=g c2=< c3=
c4=7 c5=? c6=d i=55 j=57
c3 was assigned '\n'. When it is printed out, no character appears. The cursor simply advances to the next line.
i (an integer) was assigned c4. The result, 55, is the ASCII decimal equivalent code for the symbol '7'.
c6 was assigned the character (c1 - 3). Three characters before 'g' is 'd'.
c5 was assigned the number 63 without quotes. 63 is the ASCII code for '?'.

Description

Declaring character variables. Character variables are declared with the keyword `char`. The form is

```
char variable1, variable2, variable3, . . . ;
```

For example, the declaration in this lesson's program:

```
char c1, c2, c3, c4, c5, c6;
```

declares `c1`, `c2`, `c3`, `c4`, `c5`, and `c6` to be of character type.

Assigning characters to character variables. To assign a character constant to a character variable, it is necessary to enclose the constant in single quotes, `''`(not double quotes, `" "`). For instance, the assignment statement

```
c1 = 'g';
```

assigns the symbol `g` to variable `c1`. Using single quotes, we can assign a "less than" symbol with:

```
c2 = '<';
```

and treat the number 7 as a symbol with:

```
c4 = '7';
```

Because the escape sequences are treated as a single symbol, the assignment statement

```
c3 = '\n';
```

makes `c3` represent "newline."

When we print these out with `cout` statements, the `g`, `<`, and `7` symbols are printed out directly. The "newline" character does not appear; it simply causes the cursor to advance to the next line. The output from this lesson's program illustrates this. If we choose to print a different escape sequence such as tab (`\t`), a tab takes place with no symbol printed out. Other escape sequences behave similarly.

If we assign a number to a `char` variable without using single quotes as we did with the statement

```
c5 = 63;
```

we are actually assigning the symbol with the ASCII (for most personal computers) code decimal equivalent value of 63. From the list of ASCII code decimal equivalent values shown in Table 3.5, we see that this represents the symbol `?`. (A complete list with decimal, octal, and hexadecimal equivalents is given in Appendix D.) Therefore, when we print out `c5` using `cout` as we did in this lesson's program, we print the `?` symbol.

Only computers that use the ASCII encoding scheme (which is most personal computers) will interpret `63` as meaning `?`. Another encoding scheme, EBCDIC (not in our table) interprets `63` as being a nonprintable control character. Thus, different computers give different results. To make your programs portable from computer to computer, we recommend you replace `c5 = 63;` with `c5 = '?';`. (Note: As stated in Chapter 1, we restrict our discussion in this text to ASCII.)

If we add or subtract from a character, we get a different ASCII code value and a different symbol. For instance, the statement

```
c6 = c1 - 3;
```

subtracts 3 from the ASCII code value for `c1` (which is 103 for the symbol `g`) and arrives at 100. Thus, this statement is equivalent to

```
c6 = 'd';
```

When we print `c6`, we print `d` as shown in this lesson's output.

Standard C++ does not support all the ASCII symbol set. Therefore, you will notice that the given list in Table 3.5 does not include a symbol such as `$`. The result of this is that the following statement:

```
c9 = '$';
```

may or may not compile with your compiler. Compilers that go beyond the C++ standard may be able to compile and execute this statement properly. C++ has methods for using even more symbols, but a description of this goes beyond the scope of this book.

Assigning characters to `int` variables. If we assign a character to an `int` variable, C++ assigns the ASCII code value for the `char` to the `int`. For instance, the statement

```
i = c4;
```

in this lesson's program assigns the ASCII code value for the symbol `7` (which is 00110111 and this interprets to `55` in decimal as shown in Table 3.5) to `i`. Note that it does not assign the value 7! In fact, if we take `c4 + 2` as we did in the assignment statement

```
j = c4 + 2;
```

TABLE 3.5 — Standard C++ characters and their ASCII codes/values (in decimal)

Character	ASCII decimal equivalent	Character	ASCII decimal equivalent	Character	ASCII decimal equivalent
`\a`	7	`<`	60	`_`	95
`\b`	8	`=`	61	`` ` ``	96
`\t`	9	`>`	62	`a`	97
`\n`	10	`?`	63	`b`	98
`\v`	11	`A`	65	`c`	99
`\f`	12	`B`	66	`d`	100
`\r`	13	`C`	67	`e`	101
`space`	32	`D`	68	`f`	102
`!`	33	`E`	69	`g`	103
`"`	34	`F`	70	`h`	104
`#`	35	`G`	71	`i`	105
`%`	37	`H`	72	`j`	106
`&`	38	`I`	73	`k`	107
`'`	39	`J`	74	`l`	108
`(`	40	`K`	75	`m`	109
`)`	41	`L`	76	`n`	110
`*`	42	`M`	77	`o`	111
`+`	43	`N`	78	`p`	112
`,`	44	`O`	79	`q`	113
`-`	45	`P`	80	`r`	114
`.`	46	`Q`	81	`s`	115
`/`	47	`R`	82	`t`	116
`0`	48	`S`	83	`u`	117
`1`	49	`T`	84	`v`	118
`2`	50	`U`	85	`w`	119
`3`	51	`V`	86	`x`	120
`4`	52	`W`	87	`y`	121
`5`	53	`X`	88	`z`	122
`6`	54	`Y`	89	`{`	123
`7`	55	`Z`	90	`|`	124
`8`	56	`[`	91	`}`	125
`9`	57	`\`	92	`~`	126
`:`	58	`]`	93		
`;`	59	`^`	94		

we get `57` not `9`. This also is shown in this lesson's output. Remember, when we treat numbers as characters, C++ works with the ASCII code value not with the numeric value.

One benefit of working with characters this way is that we can sort or alphabetize since ASCII code values increase by one for each letter progressed in the alphabet (see Table 3.5). Using techniques described later, we can arrange characters in alphabetic order using this property.

LESSON 3.4 ARITHMETIC OPERATIONS (1): ARITHMETIC OPERATORS AND EXPRESSIONS

TOPICS

- Utilizing variables
- Operands
- Arithmetic operators and their properties
- Arithmetic expressions
- Exceeding the integer range
- Overflow errors

QUESTIONS YOU SHOULD ATTEMPT TO ANSWER

1. What is the symbol used for multiplication?
2. What is the symbol used for division?
3. What does `i = i + 1;` do to the value of `i`? (Hint: Recall what we said about assignment statements causing the value on the right side of the assignment statement to be computed and then put into the memory cell of the variable on the left side of the assignment statement.)
4. Look at the output for Section 2 of the program. What do you think the `%` operator does? (Hint: It has something to do with division.)

Arithmetic expressions in C++ look much like algebraic expressions that you write. In this program we show how to use expressions to perform arithmetic operations, save the results in memory, and avoid errors. We show the different C++ arithmetic operators and what they mean. The program is separated into two sections with `cout` statements indicating the section. Different arithmetic operations are performed in each section.

We noted in the description of the `int` variable type that a minimum range of values allowed was −32768 to 32767. You might wonder what happens if we attempt to assign a value outside this range. In this program, we make such an assignment and print the assigned value in the output.

Sometimes you will attempt to execute your programs, and you will get an *abnormal termination* (meaning that the program terminates before each statement is executed properly). You may get a message that uses the word *overflow* when this happens. You will need to trace the source of the overflow error and modify your code if this occurs. In this program we do not show code that produces an overflow error, but in the description we discuss a common cause of overflow problems and how to correct them.

Read the program and annotations, and pay special attention to the operators used in the assignment statements. Note that in this and the next few lessons, we use one-letter variable names. We do this simply because we are only demonstrating arithmetic operations, not writing real programs. In the application examples, we use descriptive variable names. Remember, when writing your programs make sure your variable names are long enough to convey the meaning of what they represent.

Source Code

```
#include <iostream>
using namespace std;
int main ( )
{
        int i, j, k, p, m, n;
        double a, b, c, d, e, f, g, h, x, y, z;

        i = 5;
        j = 5;
        k = 11;
        p = 3;
        x = 3.0;
        y = 4.0;
```

Initializing six different variables.

```
    cout << "---------- Section 1 output"
         "-------------" << endl << endl;
    a = x + y;
    b = x - y;
    c = x * y;
    d = x / y;
    e = d + 3.0 ;
    f = d + 3;
    i = i + 1;
    j = j + 1;
    cout << "a=" << a << "\t b=" << b << "\t c=" << c << "\t d=" << d << endl;
    cout << "e=" << e << "\t f=" << f << "\t i=" << i << "\t j=" << j << endl;
    cout << "\n\n---------- Section 2 output"
         "-------------" << endl << endl;
    m = k % p;
    n = p % k;
    i++;
    ++j;
    e--;
    --f;
    cout << "m=" << m << "\t n=" << n << "\t i=" << i << "\t j=" << j << endl;
    cout << "e=" << e << "\t f=" << f << endl << endl;

    x = y + z;

    cout << "With z not initialized, x = y+z = " << x << endl << endl;

    i = 32770;
    cout << "i=" << i << endl;
}
```

Begin Section 1 output.

The variables x and y have been initialized and therefore can be used on the right side of assignment statements.

The variable d has been initialized as being x/y in the previous assignment statement. It can now be used in this assignment statement.

Observe that all the variables on the right side of these assignment statements have been initialized in previous assignment statements.

Begin Section 2 output.

Special C++ arithmetic operators are %, ++ and --.

The variable z has not been initialized, but we have used it on the right side of an assignment statement to compute x.

We assign a value that is out of the range for int variables.

The value of x is printed out.

The value of i is printed out. Look at the output, and see that the assigned value is not what is printed.

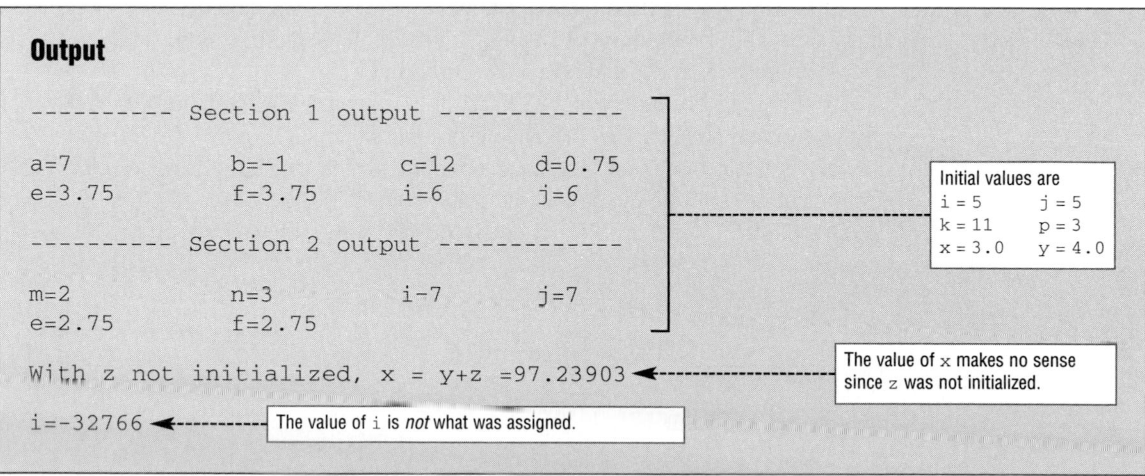
Output

```
---------- Section 1 output -------------

a=7          b=-1        c=12       d=0.75
e=3.75       f=3.75      i=6        j=6

---------- Section 2 output -------------

m=2          n=3         i=7        j=7
e=2.75       f=2.75

With z not initialized, x = y+z =97.23903

i=-32766
```

Initial values are
i = 5 j = 5
k = 11 p = 3
x = 3.0 y = 4.0
The value of x makes no sense since z was not initialized.
The value of i is *not* what was assigned.

Description

Utilizing variables. Before we utilize a variable by putting it on the right side of an assignment statement, we must initialize it. In this lesson's program, the variables `i`, `j`, `k`, `p`, `x`, and `y` are initialized in the first six assignment statements.

```
i = 5;          j = 5;
k = 11;         p = 3;
x = 3.0;        y = 4.0;
```

After this they are put on the *right* side of the next assignment statements, for example:

```
a = x + y;
i = i + 1;
j = j + 1;
```

Notice that you can take your hand calculator (or use your head) to calculate a numerical value for each arithmetic expression shown here on the right side of the `=` sign because all the variables have been initialized. For all your programs, no matter how complex, you can (although it may be very tedious and time consuming) use your hand calculator or do hand arithmetic and perform the same computations that your source code instructs the computer to do. In theory, you could go from the beginning to the end of the program line by line using your hand calculator and arrive at the same results as the program.

Remember, your programs execute one line at a time in order from the top of your code to the bottom (although we will see in Chapter 5 that we can modify this). You *must* make sure that each variable that appears on the right side of an assignment statement has been given the correct numerical value in a line of code that has been previously executed!

Arithmetic expressions, operands, and operators. An arithmetic expression is a formula for computing a value. For example, the expression `x + y` computes `x` plus `y`, `x - y` computes `x` minus `y`, `x * y` computes `x` times `y`, and `x / y` computes `x` divided by `y`. Often, arithmetic expressions appear on the right side of assignment statements.

An arithmetic expression consists of a sequence of operand(s) and operator(s) that specify the computation of a value. For example, the expression, `-x + y`, consists of two operands `x` and `y` and two operators `+` and `-`.

An operand can be a variable, such as `x` or `y`, or a constant, such as 3.1416, or anything that represents a value, such as a function (see Chapter 7 for details).

The operator `++` is an increment operator, which can be placed before or after (but not both) a variable. The operator increases the value of the variable by 1. For example, assuming a variable `i` is equal to 1, then after the statement

```
i++;
```

or

```
++i;
```

is executed, the value of `i` is 2 (`i++` is not exactly the same as `++i`, see Lesson 3.5

for details). Note that the C++ statement

```
i++;
```

or

```
++i;
```

can be understood as the statement

```
i = i + 1;
```

which also causes the value of the variable `i` to increase by 1. Similarly, the operator -- is a decrement operator, which decreases the value of a variable by 1. The statement

```
i--;
```

or

```
--i;
```

can be understood as the statement

```
i = i - 1;
```

The operator `%` is a remainder operator, meaning that it calculates the remainder of a division operation. The `%` operator must be placed between two *integer* variables or constants. Assuming `k` and `p` are two integer variables, the meaning of `k % p` is the remainder of `k` divided by `p`. For example, if `k` is 11 and `p` is 3, then `k % p` is equivalent to `11 % 3`, which is equal to 2 (because 3 goes into 11 three times with a remainder of 2). The operator `%` is pronounced "mod." So this example would be `k` mod `p`. Standard C++ states that if either operand is negative, the sign of the result of the `%` operation is implementation defined; that is, it is free for the C++ compiler designer to decide. For example, depending on the compiler you use, the results of `-50 % 6` and `50 % (-6)` may be `2` or `-2`.

Arithmetic expressions and assignment statements. An arithmetic expression is not a complete C++ statement, but only a component of a statement. The value obtained from the expression may be stored in a variable using an assignment statement. For example, the arithmetic expression `x / y` is part of the C++ assignment statement

```
d = x / y;
```

The statement assigns the value obtained from the arithmetic expression on the right to the variable on the left. Thus, the assignment statement

```
i = i + 1;
```

although not looking correct algebraically, is a valid C++ assignment statement. The arithmetic expression `i + 1` creates a new value that is 1 greater than the current value of `i`. The assignment statement then gives `i` this new value.

Note that we cannot write these two assignment statements as

```
x / y = d;
i + 1 = i;
```

because on the left side of assignment statements we can have only single variables, not expressions. Single variables are allowed to be *lvalues* (pronounced ell-values), meaning they are allowed to be on the left side of assignment statements. Expressions are *rvalues* (pronounced are-values) because they are allowed on the right side of assignment statements.

A single variable located alone on the right side of an assignment statement is considered an expression. We will see other times when a single variable is considered an expression.

Uninitialized variables. Note that if an *uninitialized* variable is used in an expression on the right side of an assignment statement no error may be indicated at compile time! The C++ compiler is incapable of recognizing this type of error. This means that if the programmer does not observe the error, the program will be executed with an error.

In fact, a program may execute completely without a run-time error even if uninitialized variables appear on the right side of assignment statements! However, the results will be incorrect. It is up to you, the programmer, to recognize that the results are incorrect and to change the program. Sometimes a program will be obviously incorrect and can be easily modified by a programmer. At other times it is not so obvious, and it takes an astute programmer to detect the error. The moral is that you must look closely at your results and test your programs thoroughly before concluding that they are correct.

Just to demonstrate the effect of not initializing a variable, in this lesson's program we have not initialized the variable `z`, used the assignment statement

```
x = y + z;
```

and printed out the value of `x` with a succeeding `cout` statement. The value of `x` is shown in the output line

```
With z not initialized, x = y + z = 97.23903
```

Observe that `x` makes no sense and has nothing to do with the values used in this program, yet the program ran without indicating an error! The variable `z` was assigned a value of 93.23903 by the computer since we did not assign a value to `z` ourselves. Without a close examination of the output, one might think that the printed value of `x` is correct.

Why was `z` assigned a value of 93.23903 by the computer? It was not deliberate. Remember, because `z` is declared a `double`, 8 bytes (minimum) is reserved in memory for `z`. The address of this memory is set during compilation, and during execution this memory is reserved. However, when the memory is reserved, the bits are not set to specific values. When we use `z` on the right side of an assignment statement, the computer simply reads the memory cells at the address reserved for `z`. Whatever is there is read and interpreted using the binary scheme for `double` type variables. Other computer activities may have used the same memory cells, and what is left behind is being read when `z` is used. It just so happened on this particular execution of the program that bits that are interpreted to be 93.23903 were left in the memory cells for `z`. This program may have a different number for `z` each time it is executed since it is dependent upon activities of the computer *before* the program is run. In fact, if you run this program you will almost certainly not get `x = 97.23903`. You will get whatever is in the memory cells for `z` plus 4.0 (which is the value assigned to `y`). Clearly, this type of behavior for a program is unacceptable.

It is not unusual that a programmer forgets to initialize a variable before using it. You will likely do it during your programming. You must be able to recognize that you have not initialized a variable, so you can correct it. One hint that you may have made this mistake is that sometimes bits interpreted to be very large numbers are stored in the memory cells for uninitialized variables. Therefore, if you see numbers printed out that are displayed in scientific notation with large exponents, look for uninitialized variables in your program. Also, if you get different results with the same input each time you run your program, an uninitialized variable may be the problem. We cannot give a method that will always work for recognizing this type of error in your programs. You simply must be meticulous, look at your output carefully, and test your programs thoroughly to assure that your programs are reliable.

Exceeding integer range. We noted in our description of the `int` type that the range of possible integer values is −32768 to 32767 due to the use of two bytes of memory for an integer (for the minimum allowable C++ implementation). In this lesson's program we have shown what happens if an integer variable is assigned a value outside this range by assigning a value of 32770 to `i`. Without going into the details of the values of each bit (see Appendix A for more information), we show how you can determine the assigned value when the range is exceeded in Fig. 3.3. It operates somewhat like a clock. At the top of the clock is 0, the right side has the range of positive values, and the left side has the range of the negative values. The large negative and positive numbers meet at the bottom of the clock.

To determine the assigned value for 32770, which exceeds the range by 3, one can think of the hand of the clock continuing to rotate in the clockwise direction, as shown in the figure. Going 3 past 32767 (which is 32770) takes the hand of the clock to −32766, and this is the value assigned to `i` in this lesson's program. Similarly, if we exceed the value in the negative direction by 3 (that is, a value of −32771), the value assigned would be 32765.

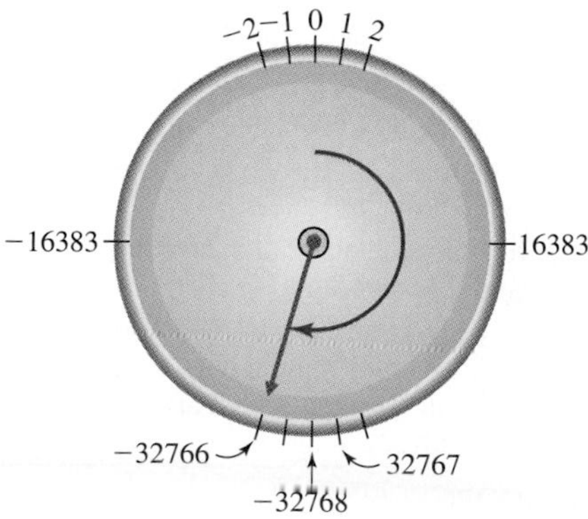

Figure 3.3

Conceptual illustration of an integer "clock." When the value 32770 is assigned to `i` in this lesson's program, the hand of the clock goes clockwise three places past 32767 and arrives at −32766.

Note that if you make an error of this type in one of your programs, it will not necessarily crash! Because an assignment is made, your program may execute completely, but it is likely that your answers will be incorrect. Luckily, for many programs, integers are used mainly for counting and 32767 is usually more than enough. (Also, a 4-byte integer C++ implementation gives even greater integer values. If an even greater integer value is needed we can use a `long int` integer data type that we describe in Lesson 3.6.) But if you accidentally exceed the allowed integer value, it is up to you to recognize that the program is faulty and to change it. The computer may not help you at all with this type of error. Remember, you must be careful not to exceed the integer range, and you need to look closely at your results in all cases because there are many types of errors that the computer will not detect.

Division by zero and overflow errors. If we accidentally attempt to divide a number by zero in a program, in general, a run-time error and termination of execution will take place. The computer displays an error message that commonly uses the word *overflow*. So, unlike the uninitialized variable problem and exceeding the integer range, division by zero is recognized by the computer. The word overflow is used because division by 0 or a number close to 0 produces a very large number. The number, too large to store in the allocated memory, causes an interpretation of an overflow problem.

If you get an overflow error in your program, you need to use some of the debugging techniques described in Chapter 2 to find the statement(s) that are the source of the problem, and this may not be simple (Table 3.6 summarizes this process). For instance, say we have in a program:

```
b = c / ( x - y );
```

with `x` and `y` being equal values before this statement is executed. This statement will cause a run-time error on execution (because the denominator is zero). However, by

TABLE 3.6 — Finding the source of an overflow error

1. Look at your output. You know the error has been caused by a statement after the last `cout` statement that produced the last line of the output.
2. If no `cout` statement has been executed prior to the overflow error, add `cout` statements to your program for the sole purpose of helping you find the location of the error.
3. Rerun the program (even though you know that the program will crash).
4. Use the `cout` statements executed to locate the error within a few lines.
5. Look at the source code in the region of the lines causing the error.
6. Add more `cout` statements to print out the values of the variables in these statements. Rerun the program.
7. Use your hand calculator to check the equations used in your program, so you can see exactly which statement caused an overflow.
8. At this point, we cannot tell you exactly how to modify your program to correct the error. However, performing these steps should have given you enough insight into your problem to make it easier for you to recognize errors in your equations or other methods for avoiding overflow errors.

simply looking at the code, it is not possible to immediately say that this statement is the source of the problem because nothing is inherently wrong with the statement itself.

Therefore, in your programs, if you get an overflow error message caused by division by zero, the first thing you need to do is to find the statement in your program at which the division by 0 has taken place. To do this, observe from the output which `cout` statements have already executed before the error message saying overflow is printed. This tells you that the division by 0 was caused by a statement executed after the `cout` statements were executed. This is a first step in finding the problem statement.

If no `cout` statements were executed prior to the error occurring, then one method for finding the statement with the error is simply to put `cout` statements in the source code at a number of locations for the sole purpose of finding the error causing location. For instance, statements such as

```
cout << " Execution has taken place to statement 5  \n";
cout << " Execution has taken place to statement 10  \n";
```

can be repeated throughout your program. After writing a large number of these, you can execute your program again (even though you know that it will get an overflow error). On rerunning it, you see which `cout` statements were executed. If you have spread these throughout your program, then you know that the division by 0 has been caused by a statement shortly after the last `cout` statement executed.

Once the approximate location of the statement causing the error is known, examine your source code and focus on the statements in the region following the last correct `cout` statement. Look for divisions that have taken place, paying particular attention to such things as the variables in denominators. Take all the variables and write a `cout` statement to have their values printed out. Put that `cout` statement immediately after the last `cout` statement executed on the previous run.

Rerun your program again, even though you know that it will still encounter an overflow error. Look at the values of the variables printed out. Use your calculator to perform hand calculations with these variables. Look at your source code and the equations you wrote in the region of the error. By plugging the numbers in your calculator, you should find that one of the denominators in this region calculates to be 0 or nearly 0. It may not work out to be exactly 0 because the computer may be working with numbers slightly different from those that are printed out (one reason is that the computer may be working with 30 digits when you have printed only 6 and use only 6 in your calculator). By doing this you have now narrowed the problem down to one statement, and you should understand exactly how the computer is beginning to divide by 0.

The method for correcting the problem depends on the overall purpose of your computer program. However, in many cases, you will find that the process you have gone through to find the source of the error has made you aware of an error you have made in programming. For instance, maybe you used a subtraction sign where you should have used an addition sign, or you put the wrong variable in the denominator. Recognizing these sorts of things and making the appropriate changes normally will solve your problem. However, you need to address this on a case-by-case basis.

An easier way to locate the error is to learn how to use your compiler's debugger (see the manual). It will save you from writing all the `cout` statements. However, if you do not learn the debugger, you should become proficient enough to write all the `cout` statements that you need quickly and easily.

LESSON 3.5 ARITHMETIC OPERATIONS (2): MIXED TYPE ARITHMETIC, COMPOUND ASSIGNMENT, OPERATOR PRECEDENCE, AND TYPE CASTING

TOPICS

- Precedence of arithmetic operations
- Pitfalls in arithmetic statements
- Mixing integers and reals in arithmetic expressions
- Type casting
- Side effects

QUESTION YOU SHOULD ATTEMPT TO ANSWER

1. What do you think the `+=` operator does?

When we use numbers in our source code, the way we write the numbers influences how C++ treats the numbers. For instance, if we write the number 4 (without a decimal point), C++ treats the number as an `int`. If we write the number 4. or 4.0 (with a decimal point) C++ treats the number as a `double`. As we see in this program, we must be aware of the types we use when performing arithmetic calculations.

This program is broken into four sections separated by `cout` statements. They illustrate:

Section 1	The difference between using `++` before and after a variable.
Section 2	The effect of using both `double` and `int` variables in a single arithmetic expression, and using integers in division operations.
Section 3	The compound operators.
Section 4	The precedence of arithmetic operators (meaning which operator is executed first).

As you read the source code, use your calculator to compute the values of the variables on the right sides of the assignment statements.

Source Code

```
#include <iostream>
using namespace std;
int main ( )
{
     int   i = 1, j = 1,
           k1 = 10, k2 = 20, k3 = 30, k4 = 40, k5 = 50,
           k, h, m, n;

     double a = 7, b = 6, c = 5, d = 4,
            e, p, q, x, y, z;
```

Note that `i` and `j` are initialized to `1`. The `k` variables are initialized to 10 to 50.

```
cout << "************ Section 1 ***************" << endl;
cout << "Before increment, i=" << i << ", j=" << j << endl;

k = i++;
h = ++j;

cout << "After increment, i=" << i << ", j=" << j
     << ", k=" << k << ", h=" << h << endl << endl;

cout << "************ Section 2 ***************" << endl;

m = 6 / 4;
p = 6 / 4;
n = 6 / 4.0;
q = 6 / 4.0;

cout << "m=" << m << ", p=" << p << ", n=" << n << ", q=" << q << endl << endl;

cout << "************ Section 3 ***************" << endl;
cout << "Original k1=" << k1 << ", k2=" << k2 << ", k3=" << k3
     << ", k4=" << k4 << ", k5=" << k5 << endl;

k1 += 2;
k2 -= i;
k3 *= (8/4);
k4 /= 2.0;
k5 %= 2;

cout << "New    k1=" << k1 << ", k2=" << k2 << ", k3=" << k3 << ", k4=" << k4
     << ", k5=" << k5 << endl << endl;

cout << "************ Section 4 ***************" << endl;

e = 3;
x = a + b - c / d * e;
y = a + (b - c) / d * e;
z = ((a + b) - c / d) * e;

cout << "a=" << a << ", b=" << b << ", c=" << c << ", d=" << d << ", e=" << e
     << endl << endl;

cout << "x= a + b - c / d  * e = " << x << endl
     << "y= a + (b - c) / d  * e = " << y << endl
     << "z= ((a + b) - c / d) * e = " << z << endl;
}
```

Begin Section 1 of the program.

Post-increment operator. (k = i++;)

Pre-increment operator. (h = ++j;)

Pre- and post-increment operators on the right side of assignment statements produce different results for `k` and `h` (`i` and `j` are the same). After execution, `i` and `j` are 2 but `k` is 1 and `h` is 2 (see the output).

Begin Section 2 of the program.

Right sides of assignment statements have both `int` and `double`. Left sides of assignment statements also have both `int` and `double`. C++ has rules for handling these situations. See the output for the values computed.

Begin Section 3 of the program.

Compound assignment operators cause the variable on the left side to be operated upon by the value on the right.

Begin Section 4 of the program.

C++ has precedence rules for operators, meaning that some operations in an expression are performed before others. Parentheses are used to control the order of execution of the expressions.

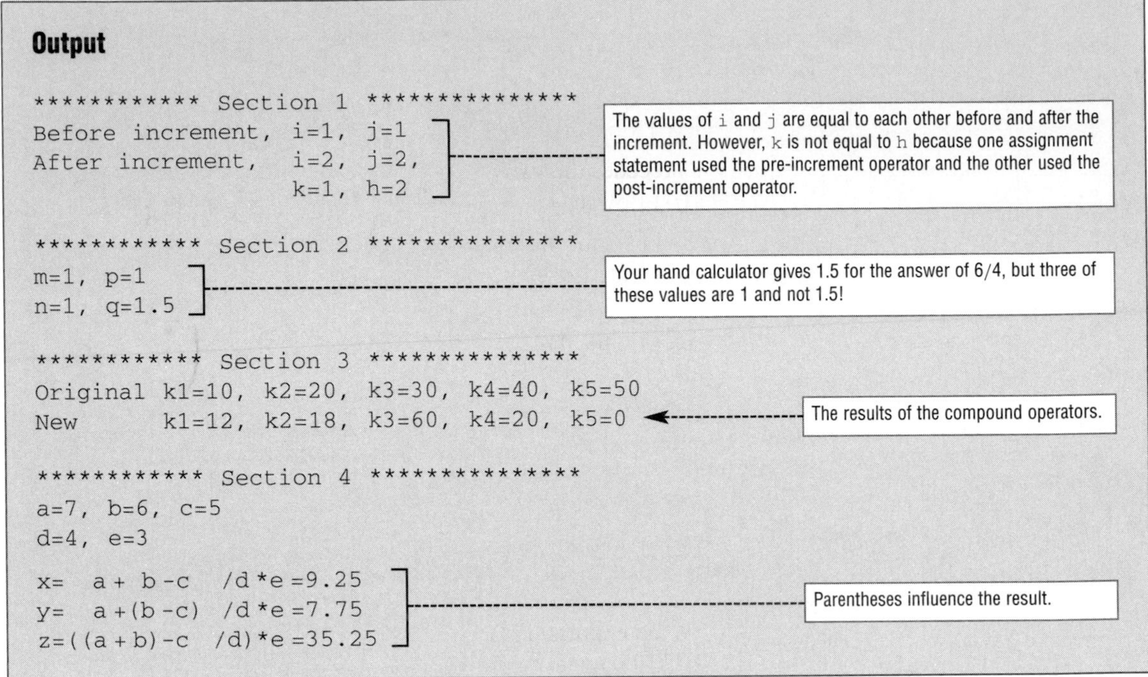

Output

```
************ Section 1 ***************
Before increment, i=1, j=1
After increment,  i=2, j=2,
                  k=1, h=2

************ Section 2 ***************
m=1, p=1
n=1, q=1.5

************ Section 3 ***************
Original k1=10, k2=20, k3=30, k4=40, k5=50
New      k1=12, k2=18, k3=60, k4=20, k5=0

************ Section 4 ***************
a=7, b=6, c=5
d=4, e=3

x=  a + b -c   /d *e =9.25
y=  a +(b -c)  /d *e =7.75
z=((a +b)-c   /d)*e =35.25
```

The values of i and j are equal to each other before and after the increment. However, k is not equal to h because one assignment statement used the pre-increment operator and the other used the post-increment operator.

Your hand calculator gives 1.5 for the answer of 6/4, but three of these values are 1 and not 1.5!

The results of the compound operators.

Parentheses influence the result.

Description

Pre- and post-increment operators used in assignment statements. In this lesson's program, we initialized both i and j to 1 and used the assignment statements:

```
k = i++;
h = ++j;
```

These statements illustrate the difference in the post-increment (as in i++) and pre-increment (as in ++j) operators when used in assignment statements. In the first statement, the value of i is assigned to the variable k *before* the value of i is incremented. After the assignment, the variable i is incremented by the post-increment operator ++ from 1 to 2. Therefore, after executing

```
k = i++;
```

i = 2 and k = 1. In other words, the statement **k = i++;** is equivalent to the statements

```
k = i;
i = i + 1;
```

However, for h = ++j, the value of j is incremented by the pre-increment operator ++ from 1 to 2. *After* the increment, the new j value, which is 2, is assigned to the variable h. Therefore, after executing

```
h = ++j;
```

j = 2 and h = 2. In other words, the statement **h = ++j;** is equivalent to statements

```
j = j + 1;
h = j;
```

The decrement operator (--) works similarly. These are the rules for such operators:

1. If the increment or decrement operator precedes the variable, the variable is first incremented; then the assignment takes place.
2. If the increment or decrement operator follows the variable, the assignment takes place first; then the variable is incremented or decremented.

You must memorize these two rules.

When more complex expressions are used with the ++ and -- operators, the same rules apply. For instance:

```
i = 2;
j = 3 * ( i++ ) - 2;
```

gives j a value of 4, whereas

```
i = 2;
j = 3 * ( ++i ) - 2;
```

gives j a value of 7 because in the first case the expression is evaluated with i = 2 (before the increment) and in the second case the expression is evaluated with i = 3 (after the increment).

In this text, we normally use the ++ and -- operators in lone standing statements because, as you can see, some confusion is caused when they are used in more complex statements. We recommend that you do the same. However, you still need to know the rules because you may see them used in complex statements in programs written by others.

Same type and mixed type arithmetic. The calculation of 6.0/4.0 is considered to be same type arithmetic since both these values are real (both 6.0 and 4.0 have a decimal point as shown). The result is 1.5. This operation is illustrated schematically at the top left of Fig. 3.4. Because both operands are real (like the double type), the result is real.

By contrast, when we calculate 6/4, we have an integer divided by an integer (because neither 6 nor 4 have a decimal point). When this occurs, if both operands are negative or positive, the fractional part of the quotient is discarded. Therefore, using C++, 6/4 is not equal to 1.5. It is equal to 1! This is illustrated at the top right of Fig. 3.4.

Using a negative integer in an integer division operation (such as −6/5) produces a result that is *implementation defined*. This means that standard C++ has no hard and fast rule; therefore, the result depends on the compiler you use. Check your compiler; for −6/5 it should give either −1 or −2 as a result. Note that the "correct" answer is −1.2. The compiler therefore has a choice of rounding up or down.

It is considered mixed type arithmetic when we calculate 6/4.0. For this operation, one operand is a real type and the other operand is an integer type. When this occurs, C++ converts the integer to a real type temporarily (meaning that 6 is

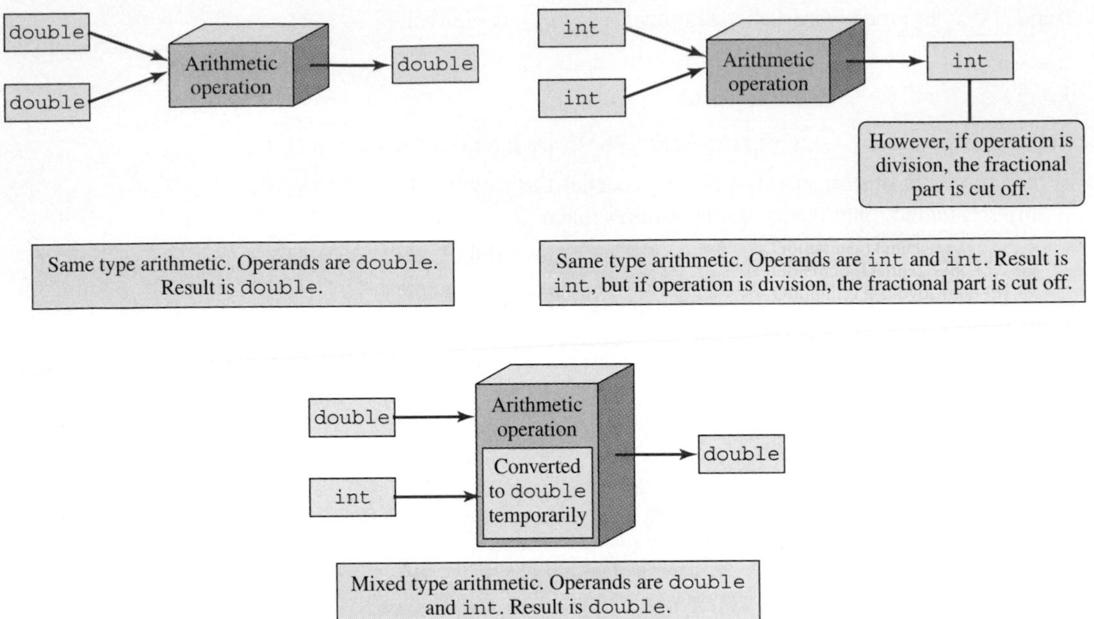

Figure 3.4

Mixed type and same type arithmetic operations.

converted to 6.0), then performs the operation, and the result is a real type. Thus, 6/4.0 gives the result 1.5. This procedure is illustrated at the bottom of Fig. 3.4.

Assigning real values to `int` variables. If we try to assign a real type value to a variable that has been declared to be `int`, C++ cuts off the fractional part of the real value, converts the remaining part to `int`, and stores the result in two's complement binary form in the memory cells for the variable. For instance, the statement in this lesson's program

```
n = 6 / 4.0;
```

takes the real value (6/4.0, which is 1.5), cuts off the 0.5 to give 1.0, converts this to 1 (without a decimal point, meaning it is in two's complement binary form), and stores this in the memory cell for the `int` variable `n`. The assignment statements for `m`, `p`, and `q` are described in Fig. 3.5.

Assigning `int` values to real variables. When assigning `int` values to real variables, C++ puts a decimal point at the end, converts the method of storage to exponential binary form, and stores the result in the variable's memory cell. Thus,

```
p = 6 / 4;
```

takes the integer value (6/4, which becomes 1 due to the cutting off of the fractional part), converts this to 1.0 (with a decimal point meaning it is in exponential binary form), and stores this in the memory cell for the variable `p`.

Modifying the way C++ uses types in arithmetic operations. We have not shown it in this lesson's program, but C++ has *cast* operators. Cast operators can change the type of an expression (recall that a single variable can be regarded as an expression). Thus, we can use cast operators on the right side of an assignment statement to modify the

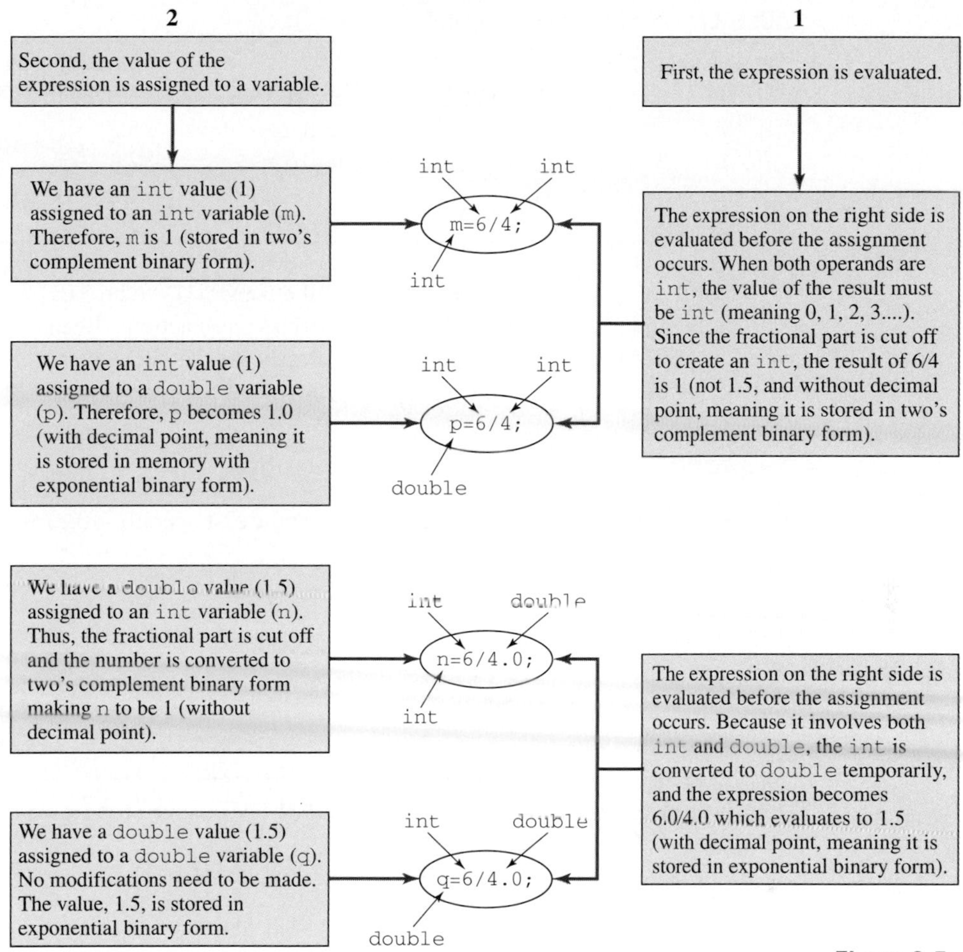

2
1
Second, the value of the expression is assigned to a variable.
First, the expression is evaluated.
We have an int value (1) assigned to an int variable (m). Therefore, m is 1 (stored in two's complement binary form).
int
int
m=6/4;
int
The expression on the right side is evaluated before the assignment occurs. When both operands are int, the value of the result must be int (meaning 0, 1, 2, 3....). Since the fractional part is cut off to create an int, the result of 6/4 is 1 (not 1.5, and without decimal point, meaning it is stored in two's complement binary form).
We have an int value (1) assigned to a double variable (p). Therefore, p becomes 1.0 (with decimal point, meaning it is stored in memory with exponential binary form).
int
int
p=6/4;
double
We have a double value (1.5) assigned to an int variable (n). Thus, the fractional part is cut off and the number is converted to two's complement binary form making n to be 1 (without decimal point).
int
double
n=6/4.0;
int
The expression on the right side is evaluated before the assignment occurs. Because it involves both int and double, the int is converted to double temporarily, and the expression becomes 6.0/4.0 which evaluates to 1.5 (with decimal point, meaning it is stored in exponential binary form).
We have a double value (1.5) assigned to a double variable (q). No modifications need to be made. The value, 1.5, is stored in exponential binary form.
int
double
q=6/4.0;
double

Figure 3.5

Same type and mixed type arithmetic operations. Assigning real values to `int` variables and integer values to `double` variables. Read the right column of boxes first and the left column second.

type of an arithmetic expression's result. Here, we describe the `static_cast` operator. It consists of the keyword `static_cast` followed by a type enclosed in angle brackets. The operand should be enclosed in parentheses.

For instance, if we have declared the variables

```
int aa = 5, bb = 2, cc;
double xx, yy = 12.3, zz = 18.8;
```

then the `static_cast` operator can be used in the following way:

```
xx = (static_cast < double > (aa)) / (static_cast < double > (bb));
cc = static_cast < int > (yy) + static_cast < int > (zz);
```

To understand how the operations in these statements are to take place, realize that in performing arithmetic operations C++ makes copies of the variable values and works with the copies. After the operation has been completed using the copies, a final result for the expression is obtained. If the expression is on the right side of an assignment statement, the assignment then takes place.

TABLE 3.7 — Actions by cast operators

Variable name and type	Initial value	Cast operation	Value of copy used in arithmetic operation
`int aa`	5	`<double> 5`	5.0
`int bb`	2	`<double> 2`	2.0
`double yy`	12.3	`<int> 12.3`	12
`double zz`	18.8	`<int> 18.8`	18

Thus, the static_cast operator causes the copy of aa to be 5.0, bb to be 2.0, yy to be 12, and zz to be 18. Table 3.7 summarizes these actions. Because the operations are performed with the copies, we can clearly see that the values stored for the variables on the left sides of the assignment statements are

```
xx = 5.0 / 2.0 = 2.5
cc = 12 + 18 = 30
```

Had the program statements been written without the cast operators, the results would have been

Expression without cast operators	Stored result
`xx = aa/bb;`	`xx = 5/2 = 2.0` (because xx is a double while the operands are int)
`cc = yy + zz;`	`cc = 12.3 + 18.8 = 31` (because cc is an int while the operands are double)

Thus, we can see that the static_cast operator has changed the results stored for the variables xx and cc.

The general form for use of the static_cast operator is

```
static_cast < type > (expression)
```

where the keyword static_cast uses the underscore symbol, and *expression* is the expression for which a temporary copy is to be made of type *type*. The *type* can be any valid C++ data type. We will learn of more valid C++ data types later in this text.

Note that the use of static_cast will make such things as the right sides of assignment statements look very complicated. Do not be deterred from using static_cast because of this. Use static_cast whenever it is necessary to get the correct numerical results.

Also, C++ has an old form of cast operators that looks less complicated. The form is

```
(type) expression
```

For instance

```
(double) aa
```

While such a form is simpler, the static_cast form is recommended.

Compound assignment operators. The operators +=, -=, *=, /=, and %= are compound assignment operators. Each performs an arithmetic operation and an assignment operation. These operators require two operands: The left operand must be a variable; the right one can be a constant, a variable, or an arithmetic expression. In general, the two operands can be of integer or real data type. However, the `%=` operator requires that its two operands be of integer type.

For instance, the meaning of

```
k1 += 2;
```

(not `k1 =+ 2;`) can be understood to be similar to the statement

```
k1 = k1 + 2;
```

If the original value of `k1` is equal to 20, the new value will be 20 + 2 or 22. Similarly, these statements also are valid if we replace the arithmetic operator `+` with operator `-`, `*`, `/`, or `%`. For example,

```
k1 *= 2;
```

is similar to

```
k1 = k1 * 2;
```

With `k1` initially 20, the new value for `k1` is 40.

Summary of arithmetic operators. Table 3.8 shows the operators along with their properties that can be used in an arithmetic expression. The number of operands is

TABLE 3.8 — Arithmetic operators

Operator	Name	Number of operands	Position	Associativity	Precedence
(	parentheses	unary	prefix	L to R	1
)	parentheses	unary	postfix	L to R	1
++	post-increment	unary	postfix	L to R	2
--	post-decrement	unary	postfix	L to R	2
++	pre-increment	unary	prefix	R to L	3
--	pre-decrement	unary	prefix	R to L	3
+	positive sign	unary	prefix	R to L	3
-	negative sign	unary	prefix	R to L	3
static_cast	cast	unary	prefix	R to L	4
%	remainder	binary	infix	L to R	5
*	multiplication	binary	infix	L to R	5
/	division	binary	infix	L to R	5
+	addition	binary	infix	L to R	6
-	subtraction	binary	infix	L to R	6
+=	addition and assignment	binary	infix	R to L	7
-=	subtraction and assignment	binary	infix	R to L	7
*=	multiplication and assignment	binary	infix	R to L	7
/=	division and assignment	binary	infix	R to L	7
%=	remainder and assignment	binary	infix	R to L	7
=	assignment	binary	infix	R to L	7

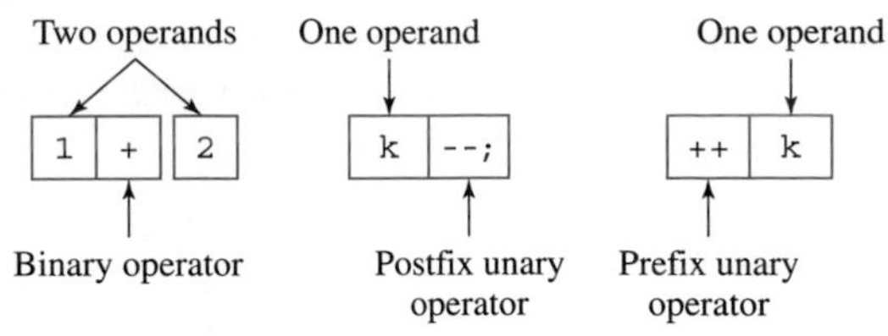

Figure 3.6
Unary and binary operators.

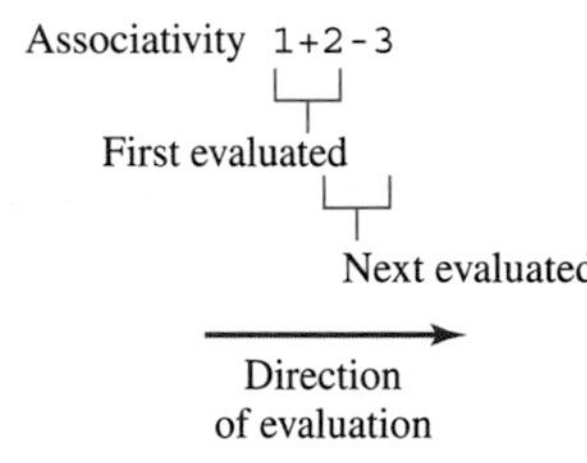

Figure 3.7
Concept of associativity.

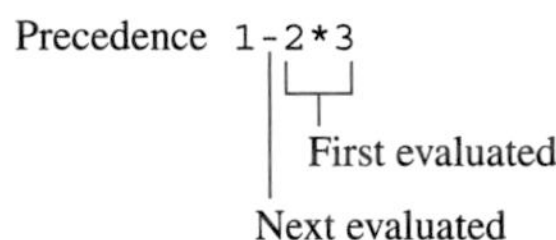

Figure 3.8
Concept of precedence.

the number of operands required by an operator. A binary operator, such as `/`, requires two operands while a unary operator, such as `++`, needs only one. Fig. 3.6 shows the concepts of these two types of operators.

The position is the location of an operator with respect to its operands. For a unary operator, its position is prefix if the operator is placed before its operand and postfix if it is placed after its operand; for a binary operator, the position is infix because it is always placed between its two operands. For example, the negation operator in `-x` is prefix, the post-increment operator in `y++` is postfix, and the remainder operator in `a % b` is infix.

The associativity specifies the direction of evaluation of the operators with the same precedence. For example, the operators `+` and `-` have the same level of precedence and both associate from left to right, so `1 + 2 - 3` is evaluated in the order of `(1 + 2) - 3` rather than `1 + (2 - 3)`. This concept is shown in Fig. 3.7.

The precedence specifies the order of evaluation of operators with their operands. Operators with higher precedence are evaluated first. For example, the operator `*` has higher precedence than `-`, so `1 - 2 * 3` is evaluated as `1 - (2 * 3)` rather than `(1 - 2) * 3`. Note that in this example the `-` indicates subtraction and is a binary operator with precedence 4. The `-` also can be used as a negative sign, which is a unary operator with precedence 2. For example, `-2 + 3 * 4` is evaluated as `(-2) + (3 * 4)` rather than `-(2 + (3 * 4))`. This concept is shown in Fig. 3.8.

Note from Table 3.8 that the assignment operator has the lowest precedence. This means that in an assignment statement, the other operators are executed and then the assignment takes place. This, of course, is the desired intent. Also, the assignment operator associates from right to left. This means the expression on the right side of the assignment operator is assigned to the variable on the left (again, the desired action).

Using parentheses. Parentheses can control the order of operation in arithmetic expressions. Arithmetic operators located within the parentheses always are executed prior to any outside the parentheses. When an arithmetic expression contains more than one pair of parentheses, the operators located in the innermost pair of parentheses are executed first. For example, the `+` operator in the statement

```
z = ((a + b) - c / d);
```

will be executed before the `-` or `/` operator and `a + b` will be evaluated first.

We cannot use two consecutive arithmetic operators in an arithmetic statement unless parentheses are used. For example, `x/-y` is not permissible, but `x/(-y)` is permissible.

To illustrate how to use the precedence table in deciding where parentheses are important, consider the `static_cast` operator. Because the `static_cast` operator has higher precedence (4) than the arithmetic operators (5) parentheses may not be needed in some cases. For instance, with the declarations

```
int a, b;
double x;
```

the statement

```
x = (static_cast <double> (a)) / (static_cast <double> (b));
```

is equivalent to

```
x = static_cast <double> (a) / static_cast <double> (b);
```

because the cast operation is performed before the division operation. In addition, the effect of C++'s arithmetic operation rules is that sometimes you may not need to use a large number of cast operators in an expression. For instance, the previous assignment statement could be written as

```
x = static_cast <double> (a) / b;
```

and give the same result. This works because (as we described for mixed type arithmetic) dividing a `double` by an `int` is done in C++ by copying the `int` in `double` form and dividing the two as `double` variables as illustrated in Fig. 3.4.

Side effects. The primary effect of evaluating an expression is arriving at a value for that expression. Anything else that occurs during the evaluation of the expression is considered a *side effect*. For instance, the primary effect of the C++ statement (assuming `i` originally is 7)

```
j = i++;
```

is that the expression on the right side of the assignment statement is found to have a value of 7 (and then the assignment is made). The side effect of this statement is that the value of `i` is incremented by 1 (to make `i` equal to 8).

Consider the following C++ statement:

```
j = (i = 4) + (k = 3) - (m = 2);
```

Its primary effect is to arrive at the value of the expression on the right side of the assignment statement (which is 5 obtained from $4 + 3 - 2$). Three side effects occur during the evaluation of the expression:

1. i is set equal to 4.
2. k is set equal to 3.
3. m is set equal to 2.

At times, side effects can be confusing. For the statement

```
k = (k = 4) * (j = 3);
```

the result of k will be 12 instead of 4. It is best not to use side effects except in their simplest form, such as

```
i = j++;
```

or

```
i = j = k = 5;
```

Note that because the associativity of the assignment operator is from right to left, multiple assignment statements such as the preceding one can be written. The order of operation is

1. k = 5
2. j = k
3. i = j

Also, an expression

```
i = j = k = 2 + n + 1;
```

is evaluated in this order:

1. k = 2 + n + 1;
2. j = k;
3. i = j;

because the addition operation has a higher precedence than the assignment operator.

Programming with C++ style arithmetic. All this may sound confusing, but when writing arithmetic statements in your programs you need only to keep in mind a few things to handle most cases:

- When you have a division operation, make sure it does not involve two integer type variables or constants unless you really want the fractional part cut off. Remember, check your variable types before you write a division operation.
- When you are writing your code and a double or floating type variable is on the left side of an assignment statement, to be safe, use decimal points for any constants on the right side of the assignment statement. You may get the correct result without using decimal points, but we recommend that you use decimal points until you feel comfortable with mixed type arithmetic.

- When an `int` type variable is on the left side of an assignment statement, you must make sure that the arithmetic expression on the right side of the assignment statement creates an integer value. If you observe that it creates a real value, you must realize that the fractional part will be lost when the assignment is made.

Programming with C++ precedence rules. The most important precedence rule for you to remember is that multiplication and division occur before addition and subtraction. Knowing and using this fact will make your arithmetic expressions easy to write without the need for many parentheses. If you feel confident using the precedence table and have it handy while you are programming, you can use it to write statements involving other operators. However, when you do not have the table available or are in doubt, use parentheses to write your equations and control the order of operation. As you develop experience, you will be able to avoid parentheses in some cases.

It is not necessary to memorize the precedence list in Table 3.8 (and as we learn more operators, the precedence list becomes even longer). In this text we will indicate the importance of parentheses when introducing new operators. For now though, to be safe, use parentheses whenever you are uncertain about the precedence rules.

LESSON 3.6 ARITHMETIC OPERATIONS (3): MATH LIBRARY FUNCTIONS AND DATA TYPES

TOPICS

- Using the standard math header
- Contrasting the `double` and `float` data types
- Other data types

QUESTIONS YOU SHOULD ATTEMPT TO ANSWER

1. What header is needed for math functions?
2. Use your calculator to compute `sin(x)` (with x = 3.0 as given in the program). Does your result agree with the output?
3. What kind of logarithm does the `log` function take?
4. What do you think the `pow` function does?
5. Why do you think `c` and `g` are not equal as shown in the output?
6. What function names do you recognize?

Your calculator makes it very easy for you to perform such operations as sin, log, and square root by having single buttons for them. Similarly, the C++ compiler makes it easy for you to perform these operations by providing mathematical library functions that you can call from your program. This lesson illustrates the use of some of these library functions. Without going into unnecessary detail at this point, know that to call a function we need to write the function name followed by parentheses. Enclosed in the parentheses may be variables or values which serve as *arguments* (meaning values that are transferred to the function being called). The functions in this lesson's program operate on the argument values and return other values.

In this lesson we also introduce other real and integer data types (including the real data type `float`). Read the program with your calculator in hand, and see if you can deduce what is returned by each function and the difference between the `float` and `double` data types.

Source Code

```
#include <cmath>
#include <iostream>
#include <iomanip>
using namespace std;
int main ( )
{         double x = 3.0,  y = 4.0;
          double a, b, c, d, e, f;
          float g;

          a = sin(x);
          b = exp(x);
          c = log(x);

          d = sqrt(x);
          e = pow(x,y);
          f = sin(y) + exp(y) - log10(y) * sqrt(y) / pow(3.2,4.4);
          g = log(x);

          cout << setprecision(9)
              << "x=" << x << "  y=" << y << endl << endl
              << "a=sin(x) = " << a
              << "\n" "b=exp(x) = " << b
              << "\n" "c=log(x) = " << c
              << "\n\n" "d=sqrt(x) = " << d
              << "\n" "e=pow(x,y) = " << e
              << "\n" "f=sin(y)+exp(y)log10(y)*sqrt(y)/pow(3.2,4.4)= " << f
              << "\n\n" "g=log(x) = " << g << "\n";
}
```

Including the header for math functions.

Variable `g` is the real data type called `float`. The other variables are `double` type.

Both `c` and `g` are assigned `log(x)`, but the output shows the two are different.

A comma separates the two values 3.2 and 4.4.

Standard C++ math functions used in expressions. Arguments are enclosed in parentheses.

Output

```
x=3    y=4
a=sin(x)  = 0.141120008
b=exp(x)  = 20.085536923
c=log(x)  = 1.098612289

d=sqrt(x) = 1.732050808
e=pow(x,y) = 81
f=sin(y)+exp(y)log10(y)*sqrt(y)/pow(3.2,4.4)= 53.834136299

g=log(x)  = 1.098612309
```

Use your calculator to decide which of `c` or `g` is more reliable.

Description

Real data types. The `float` data type is one of C++'s floating-point (real) data types. The `float` type usually occupies half the memory (4 bytes minimum) of the `double` type (8 bytes minimum). The amount of memory used influences the range or the number of significant digits. Because of the extra precision given by `double` types, in this text we will use `double` rather than `float` to represent real numbers. However, we show you `float` because you may see it in other programs, and we want to illustrate the effect of using a smaller amount of memory to store numbers.

We already have observed that real data types like `double` and `float` types cause values to be stored in exponential binary form and that the `double` data type occupies more memory than the `float` data type. When is it a good idea to use the extra memory and make sure that we carry a greater number of digits? Carrying a greater number of digits may be important when a large number of calculations are to be done. The drawback in declaring all variables as being of the `double` data type is that more memory is required to store `double` type variables than `float` type variables.

Consider the following example, which illustrates the effect of the number of digits carried in a calculation. You should try this on your calculator. Suppose you are multiplying a number by π, 100 times. You essentially will be computing π^{100}. The influence on the number of significant digits used for π is the following. Using five significant digits (similar to `float`) for π gives

$$(3.1416)^{100} = 5.189061599 * 10^{49}$$

while using eight significant digits (similar to `double`) for π gives

$$(3.1415926)^{100} = 5.1897839464 * 10^{49}$$

Here, it can be seen that while the first estimate of π has five significant digits, $(3.1416)^{100}$ is accurate only for the first four digits. This illustrates that accuracy is reduced after numerous arithmetic operations. Since one computer program easily can do one million operations, one can begin to understand the need for initially carrying many digits.

We can even see a difference in the values calculated for `log(3)` for this lesson's program. With `double` we get the natural log to be

```
c = log(3)  = 1.098612289
```

whereas with `float` we get

```
g = log(3)  = 1.098612309
```

If you compare these with your calculator, you will find that the `double` result is more accurate. You should be aware that your calculator probably carries 12 or more digits, whereas `float` minimally carries only 6 digits. Therefore, you should not use `float` if you want to be at least as accurate as your calculator.

In addition to the `float` and `double` data types is `long double`. The `long double` type occupies even more memory than `double`. This means that `long double` carries more digits, is capable of storing larger numbers, and is more accurate for calculations than `float` and `double`.

TABLE 3.9 — Real data types, common sizes and ranges, and precision

Item	float	double	long double
Minimum memory used	4 bytes = 32 bits	8 bytes = 64 bits	10 bytes = 80 bits
Range of values	1.1754944E−38 to 3.4028235E+38	2.2250738E−308 to 1.7976935E+308	Approximately 1.0E−4931 to 1.0E+4932
Precision (digits)	6	15	19

TABLE 3.10 — Integer data types and common sizes and ranges

Item	int signed int short int signed short int	unsigned int unsigned short int	long int signed long int	unsigned long int
Memory used	2 bytes = 16 bits	2 bytes = 16 bits	4 bytes = 32 bits	4 bytes = 32 bits
Range of values	−32768 to 32767	0 to 65535	−2147483648 to 2147483647	0 to 4294967295

The real data types, `float`, `double`, and `long double`, are compared in Table 3.9. The C++ standard does not state absolutely how much memory each of the types should occupy. So the table lists just the minimums. Check your compiler for the actual amount of memory it uses for each of these data types.

Integer data types. The different integer data types are compared in Table 3.10, again with minimal sizes that are sometimes used. Note that the range of possible values for the integer data types is considerably smaller than the range for the real data types. Also note that C++ has a number of synonyms for the same data type. In other words, `int`, `signed int`, `short int`, and `signed short int` are all the same. Most programmers simply use `int` for this type. However, you may see old programs that use one of the other names for `int`.

Note that `long int` and `unsigned long int` have a greater range than `int`. Using one of these types may eliminate a problem with exceeding the integer range in one of your programs as described in Lesson 3.4. In Lesson 7.2 we give an example of a program that needs an `unsigned long int`.

Math functions. The meanings of all the C++ mathematical library functions are shown in Table 3.11. It is very important that you notice that the argument for the `sin` function (as well as the `tan`, `cos`, and other functions that use angles as input) must be in radians, not degrees! So, if you want to use the sin of 30 degrees in one of your programs, you must manually write source code that converts degrees to radians by multiplying by $\pi/180$. For instance, this code might be

```
angle = 30.;
x = angle * 3.141592654/180.;
y = sin(x);
```

You should carry a large number of digits for π to maintain accuracy.

You should read Table 3.11 to get an idea of what is available. You do not need to memorize the table. You can simply refer to it later when you need to use any of the functions.

TABLE 3.11 — Math library functions

Function	Example	Description
abs(x)	y=abs(x);	Gets the absolute value of an integer type argument, x and y are integers (Note: this function needs #include <cstdlib> not <cmath>)
fabs(x)	y=fabs(x);	Gets the absolute value of a real type argument, x and y are real (Note: this function needs #include <cmath> not <cstdlib>)
sin(x)	y=sin(x);	Calculates the sine of an angle in radians, x and y are real
sinh(x)	y=sinh(x);	Calculates the hyperbolic sine of x, x and y are real
asin(x)	y=asin(x)	Calculates the arc sine of x, x must be between −1 and 1, y is in radians
cos(x)	y=cos(x);	Calculates the cosine of an angle in radians, x and y are real
cosh(x)	y=cosh(x);	Calculates the hyperbolic cosine of x, x and y are real
acos(x)	y=acos(x)	Calculates the arc cosine of x, x must be between −1 and 1, y is in radians
tan(x)	y=tan(x);	Calculates the tangent of an angle in radians, x and y are real
tanh(x)	y=tanh(x);	Calculates the hyperbolic tangent of x, x and y are real
atan(x)	y=atan(x)	Calculates the arc tangent of x, x must be between −1 and 1, y is in radians
atan2(x1,x2)	y=atan(x1,x2)	Calculates the arc tangent of x1/x2, y is in radians, the argument signs determine the quadrant of the result. x1, x2, and y are real.
exp(x)	y=exp(x)	Calculates e^x, x and y are real
frexp(x1,x2)	y=frexp(x1,x2)	Calculates the mantissa (assigned to y) for x1 such that $x1 = y*2^p$. The argument x2 is a pointer variable (a topic not yet covered in this text) that can be used to get the exponent p.
ldexp(x1,x2)	y=ldexp(x1,x2)	Calculates $x1*2^{x2}$.
modf(x1,x2)	y=modf(x1,x2)	Calculates fractional part (assigned to y) of x1. For example, if x1 = 2.56, y = 0.56. The argument x2 is a pointer variable (a topic not yet covered in this text) that can be used to get the integer part, 2.
fmod(x1,x2)	y=fmod(x1,x2)	Calculates the remainder of x1/x2. x1, x2, and y are real.
sqrt(x)	y=sqrt(x)	Calculates the square root of x. x must be positive (a run-time error occurs if it is not), y is real.
pow(x,z)	y=pow(x,z)	Calculates x^z. x and z can be real or int. y is real. Remember, we cannot do such things as take the square root (using z = 0.5) of negative numbers ($x < 0$). Thus, run-time errors can occur when $z < 1$ and $x < 0$.
floor(x)	y=floor(x)	Calculates the largest integer less than or equal to x. For example if x = 25.9, y = 25.0, if x = −12.1, y = −13.0. x and y are real.
ceil(x)	y=ceil(x)	Calculates the smallest integer greater than or equal to x. For example if x = 25.9, y = 26.0, if x = −12.1, y = −12.0. x and y are real.
log(x)	y=log(x);	Evaluates the natural logarithm of x, x and y are real
log10(x)	y=log10(x);	Evaluates the base 10 logarithm of x, x and y are real

Another important point is that the log function calculates the natural logarithm. To calculate the base 10 logarithm use the log10 function.

To use C++ math functions, you need the cmath or cstdlib headers. Make sure your programs have:

```
#include <cmath>
```

or

#include <cstdlib> for using the abs function.

APPLICATION EXAMPLE 3.1 PATTERN RECOGNITION

TOPICS

- Compound operators
- Program development

This application is not meant to be practical but simply an illustration of how to recognize patterns and develop a program based on those patterns. In addition, this program illustrates one of the program development methodologies described in Chapter 1 without introducing new theory that can distract from the focus on patterns and methodology. This example is deliberately simple in concept. Its function is to introduce you to the logic of writing programs that perform arithmetic calculations.

Problem Statement

Write a program that computes the areas of four right triangles. Three of the triangles are shown in Fig. 3.9. You should deduce the dimensions of the fourth triangle from the pattern exhibited by the first three. Use the pattern in writing your program.

Solution

We use the first procedure listed at the end of Chapter 1 in developing this application program because we do not want to focus on object-oriented design in this example. We are more interested in simply getting each individual statement to perform the intended tasks. Remember, in developing your own programs it is important that you follow a formal procedure rather than develop your programs haphazardly. If you choose not to follow the methodology we describe, please follow one recommended by your instructor.

RELEVANT EQUATIONS

We begin by creating the equations needed to solve the problem. Remember, you cannot begin by writing source code. You must first analyze the problem.

Initially, note that there is a pattern to the length of the legs. The lengths of the horizontal legs are 5, $5 + 1 = 6$, $6 + 1 = 7$, and the vertical legs are 7, $7/2 = 3.5$, $3.5/2 = 1.75$. Thus, we can see that the fourth triangle has a horizontal leg length of $7 + 1 = 8$ and a vertical leg length of $1.75/2 = 0.875$.

The horizontal leg length can be computed from the following equations:

$$L_{h2} = L_{h1} + 1$$
$$L_{h3} = L_{h2} + 1$$
$$L_{h4} = L_{h3} + 1$$

where L_{h1} = horizontal leg length of the first triangle = 5.0
L_{h2} = horizontal leg length of the second triangle
L_{h3} = horizontal leg length of the third triangle
L_{h4} = horizontal leg length of the fourth triangle

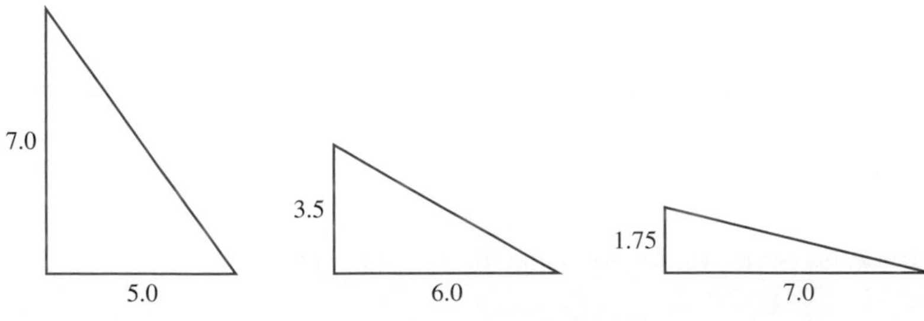

Figure 3.9
Triangles for the problem.

Also the vertical leg length is

$$L_{v2} = L_{v1}/2$$
$$L_{v3} = L_{v2}/2$$
$$L_{v4} = L_{v3}/2$$

where L_{v1} = vertical leg length of the first triangle
L_{v2} = vertical leg length of the second triangle
L_{v3} = vertical leg length of the third triangle
L_{v4} = vertical leg length of the fourth triangle

Note that the area of a right triangle is

$$A = 0.5 L_v L_h$$

SPECIFIC EXAMPLE

For this particular program, the results easily can be found using a hand calculator. For most real programs, this is not practical because of the very large number of calculations that are performed. The calculations that follow show the lengths and the areas.

Triangle 1

$$L_{h1} = 5$$
$$L_{v1} = 7$$
$$A_1 = (0.5)(5)(7) = 17.50$$

Triangle 2

$$L_{h2} = 5 + 1 = 6$$
$$L_{v2} = 7/2 = 3.5$$
$$A_2 = (0.5)(6)(3.5) = 10.50$$

Triangle 3

$$L_{h3} = 6 + 1 = 7$$
$$L_{v3} = 3.5/2 = 1.75$$
$$A_3 = (0.5)(7)(1.75) = 6.125$$

Triangle 4

$$L_{h1} = 7 + 1 = 8$$
$$L_{v1} = 1.75/2 = 0.875$$
$$A_1 = (0.5)(8)(0.875) = 3.50$$

ALGORITHM

One purpose of performing a sample calculation is to clearly outline all the steps needed to arrive at a correct and complete result. The sample calculation has been used as a guide to writing the algorithm:

Begin

Declare variables

Initialize horizontal leg length of first triangle
Initialize vertical leg length of first triangle
Calculate area of first triangle

Calculate horizontal leg length of second triangle
Calculate vertical leg length of second triangle
Calculate area of second triangle

Calculate horizontal leg length of third triangle
Calculate vertical leg length of third triangle
Calculate area of third triangle

Calculate horizontal leg length of fourth triangle
Calculate vertical leg length of fourth triangle
Calculate area of fourth triangle

Print results onto the screen

End

Source Code

The source code has been written directly from the algorithm. Look at each line and make sure that you understand exactly what each is doing. You can compare the code with the algorithm line by line to guide you. Note that we have used compound operators in the calculations.

```
#include <iostream>
using namespace std;
int main ( )
{
      double horizleg, vertleg, area1, area2, area3, area4;

      horizleg = 5.0;
      vertleg  = 7.0;
      area1    = 0.5 * horizleg * vertleg;

      horizleg += 1.0;
      vertleg  /= 2.0;
      area2     = 0.5 * horizleg * vertleg;

      horizleg += 1.0;
      vertleg  /= 2.0;
      area3     = 0.5 * horizleg * vertleg;

      horizleg += 1.0;
      vertleg  /= 2.0;
      area4     = 0.5 * horizleg * vertleg;

      cout << endl
           << "First triangle area = " << area1 << endl
           << "Second triangle area = " << area2 << endl
           << "Third triangle area = " << area3 << endl
           << "Fourth triangle area = " << area4 << endl;
}
```

Declaring leg length and area variables to be doubles.

Initializing the leg lengths.

Calculating the first area.

Using compound operators and the recognized patterns to calculate new lengths.

Calculating a new area from the new lengths.

Repeating the form of the previous statements.

Printing the results.

Output

```
First  triangle area = 17.50
Second triangle area = 10.50
Third  triangle area =  6.13
Fourth triangle area =  3.50
```

Comments

This program illustrates how patterns are used in programming. As you can see, the same group of three statements is used repeatedly. One can imagine that it would be very simple to write a program similar to this one that computes the areas of 50 triangles that follow the same pattern by simply repeating the same three statements 50 times. As we illustrate more programming techniques, you will see that you can write such a program with very few statements.

This particular example is somewhat contrived, in that it is deliberately set up to have a pattern to it. You will find, though, that real problems also have patterns and that part of the skill in writing application programs is in recognizing patterns and writing efficient code to take advantage of the patterns.

Modification Exercises

Modify the preceding program to

1. Calculate the areas of 10 triangles following the same pattern.
2. Use only three variables (`horizleg`, `vertleg`, and `area`), yet produce the same output.
3. Make each vertical leg length double instead of half each time through the sets of equations.

APPLICATION EXAMPLE 3.2 TEMPERATURE UNITS CONVERSION

TOPICS

- Compound operators
- Program development

Problem Statement

Write a program that creates a table of degrees Celsius with the corresponding degrees Fahrenheit. Begin at 0°C and proceed to 100°C in 20°C increments. Use no more than two variables in your program.

Solution

RELEVANT EQUATIONS

First, assemble the relevant equations. The equation converting degrees Celsius to degrees Fahrenheit is

$$F = (9/5)C + 32$$

where C = degrees Celsius
F = degrees Fahrenheit

SPECIFIC EXAMPLE

Once again, for this simple program, all the calculations can be done by hand.

$$C = 0$$
$$F = C\left(\frac{9}{5}\right) + 32 = 32$$
$$C = 20$$
$$F = C\left(\frac{9}{5}\right) + 32 = 68$$
$$C = 40$$
$$F = C\left(\frac{9}{5}\right) + 32 = 104$$
$$C = 60$$
$$F = C\left(\frac{9}{5}\right) + 32 = 140$$
$$C = 80$$
$$F = C\left(\frac{9}{5}\right) + 32 = 176$$
$$C = 100$$
$$F = C\left(\frac{9}{5}\right) + 32 = 212$$

ALGORITHM

We use the specific example to guide us in writing the algorithm. We add to it the printing of the headings and the results.

Begin
Declare variables
Print headings of table
  Set C = 0
  Calculate F
  Print C and F

  Set C = 20
  Calculate F
  Print C and F

  Set C = 40
  Calculate F
  Print C and F

  Set C = 60
  Calculate F
  Print C and F

  Set C = 80
  Calculate F
  Print C and F

Set C = 100
Calculate F
Print C and F

End

Source Code

This source code has been written from the algorithm. Note that this code has used the fact that the values of degrees Celsius are in increments of 20. Again, read this code line by line and make sure that you understand exactly how the program operates.

```
#include <iostream>
#include <iomanip>
using namespace std;
int main ( )
{
      double degC, degF;

      cout << "Table of Celsius and Fahrenheit degrees\n\n"
                 "        Degrees              Degrees  \n"
                 "        Celsius              Fahrenheit \n";

      degC  = 0.;
      degF  = degC * 9./5. + 32.;
      cout << setw(16) << degC << setw(20) << degF << endl;

      degC  += 20.;
      degF  = degC * 9./5. + 32.;
      cout << setw(16) << degC << setw(20) << degF << endl;

      degC  += 20.;
      degF  = degC * 9./5. + 32.;
      cout << setw(16) << degC << setw(20) << degF << endl;

      degC  += 20.;
      degF  = degC * 9./5. + 32.;
      cout << setw(16) << degC << setw(20) << degF << endl;

      degC  += 20.;
      degF  = degC * 9./5. + 32.;
      cout << setw(16)<< degC << setw(20) << degF << endl;

      degC  += 20.;
      degF  = degC * 9./5. + 32.;
      cout << setw(16) << degC << setw(20) << degF << endl;
}
```

To make a neat table, we need to use I/O manipulators and therefore need to include the `iomanip` header.

Declaring just two variables.

Printing the table heading. You will find that when you print your results in the form of a table, you must print the table headings before anything else is printed.

Following the algorithm line by line.

Output

```
Table of Celsius and Fahrenheit degrees

       Degrees          Degrees
       Celsius          Fahrenheit
         0.00             32.00
        20.00             68.00
        40.00            104.00
        60.00            140.00
        80.00            176.00
       100.00            212.00
```

Comments

First, we can see immediately that this program has the same three statements written repeatedly. Had we wanted to display the results for every single degree between 0 and 100 instead of every 20th degree, the program would have been extremely long but with the same three statements written over and over again. Chapter 6 has more advanced programming techniques to allow us to write a program that can accomplish the same task but with many fewer statements.

Second, we could have used the programming technique illustrated in the previous application program, which had a single `cout` statement at the end of the program instead of one immediately after each calculation of `degF`. However, this would have necessitated the use of more variables.

For instance, the program could have been

```
#include <iostream>
#include <iomanip>
using namespace std;
int main ( )
{

     double degC1, degC2, degC3, degC4, degC5, degC6,
            degF1, degF2, degF3, degF4, degF5, degF6;

     cout << "Table of Celsius and Fahrenheit degrees\n\n"
              "        Degrees            Degrees \n"
              "        Celsius            Fahrenheit \n";
```

Declaring many Celsius and Fahrenheit variables.

```
        degC1   = 0.;
        degF1   = degC1 * 9./5. + 32.;

        degC2   = 20.;
        degF2   = degC2 * 9./5. + 32.;

        degC3   = 40.;
        degF3   = degC3 * 9./5. + 32.;

        degC4   = 60.;
        degF4   = degC4 * 9./5. + 32.;

        degC5   = 80.;
        degF5   = degC5 * 9./5. + 32.;

        degC6   = 100.;
        degF6   = degC6 * 9./5. + 32.;

        cout << setw(16) << degC1 << setw(20) << degF1 << endl
             << setw(16) << degC2 << setw(20) << degF2 << endl
             << setw(16) << degC3 << setw(20) << degF3 << endl
             << setw(16) << degC4 << setw(20) << degF4 << endl
             << setw(16) << degC5 << setw(20) << degF5 << endl
             << setw(16) << degC6 << setw(20) << degF6 << endl;
}
```

Because there are many variables, no `cout` statement is needed after each calculation. Also, the same statements are not repeated as they were in the previous source code.

A single `cout` statement can now be used to print all the variable values.

With this program 12 variables have been used instead of just 2. Variables take up space in the memory of the computer, so the program with 12 variables would occupy more memory than the program with just 2 variables. Efficient programming, in part, means to write a program that takes as little memory as possible. For this very small program, either programming technique could be used on today's computers. However, for very large programs, the memory needed by the program may be very important. So, it is good to develop efficient programming habits while you are learning programming. Reducing memory size is only a part of developing efficient programs. Comments on other ways to make your programs efficient will be made throughout this book.

Also note that it is necessary to make your program understandable to someone other than you, the reason being that it is common for programs to be developed by teams of people and then undergo several revisions. This means that someone who has never seen a particular program may be responsible for modifying it. Your program is more valuable if it is easily understood.

Sometimes you will find a conflict between understandability and efficiency. In other words, efficient programs may not be understandable and understandable programs may not be efficient. Should you write code that is efficient but confusing, make sure that you comment it extremely well. Such comments can go a long way in making the code both efficient and understandable. If you run into a conflict, though, you should consult your employer or your course instructor for guidance in determining the more important characteristic for your particular program.

Note that the division is specified to be 9./5. (using decimal points) not 9/5 (no decimal points). The decimal points are required to prevent integer division, which causes a truncation of the decimal portion. Remember, when doing division of real numbers use decimal points to assure that you get a real number as a result.

You can begin to see that there are many ways to write even the simplest of programs. One can argue that there is no right or wrong way, provided the program gives the correct result. However, it is best to write code that is efficient and understandable.

Modification Exercises

Modify the program to

1. Calculate the degree conversions every 5 degrees rather than every 20 degrees.
2. Do the conversions between –100 and 0 degrees in 20 degree increments.

APPLICATION EXAMPLE 3.3 ANAGRAM SOLUTION

TOPICS

- Character variables
- Pattern combinations
- Program development

Problem Statement

Write a program to solve the anagram "DRAE." Print out all possible letter arrangements. Have the user decide the correct solution by examining the output.

Solution

RELEVANT EQUATIONS AND BACKGROUND INFORMATION

An anagram is a group of letters that can be reordered to form readable text. Computers are well suited to solving anagrams because they are capable of evaluating a large number of reordered combinations easily. In this problem, we are asked to solve a four-letter anagram. We first describe solving two-letter and three-letter anagrams. Then we extend the solution to four letters.

TWO-LETTER ANAGRAM

Consider the anagram:

si

There are only two possibilities:

si and **is**

For this case, the solved anagram (in English) is "is."

It is somewhat easier to use place holding numbers to evaluate anagrams objectively. We can think of a generic two-letter anagram as:

12

Then the two possibilities are:

12 and **21**

THREE-LETTER ANAGRAM

A three-letter anagram can be represented as

123

The possibilities for this anagram are all the possibilities for the two-letter anagram (12 and 21) with a 3 located in the first, second, and third locations.

312 321 (two-letter combinations with 3 in the first location)
132 231 (two-letter combinations with 3 in the second location)
123 213 (two-letter combinations with 3 in the third location)

Note that the number of possible combinations are $3 \times 2 = 6$, which can be considered to be 3 rows of 2 (as shown) or 3! (3 factorial).

FOUR-LETTER ANAGRAM

A four-letter anagram can be represented as

1234

The possibilities for this anagram are all the possibilities for the three-letter anagram (312, 321, 132, 231, 123, and 213) with a 4 in the first, second, third, and fourth place. That is, the possible combinations are:

4312	**4321**	**4132**	**4231**	**4123**	**4213**	(three-letter combinations with 4 in first place)
3412	**3421**	**1432**	**2431**	**1423**	**2413**	(three-letter combinations with 4 in second place)
3142	**3241**	**1342**	**2341**	**1243**	**2143**	(three-letter combinations with 4 in third place)
3124	**3214**	**1324**	**2314**	**1234**	**2134**	(three-letter combinations with 4 in fourth place)

Note that the number of possible combinations are $4 \times 6 = 24$, which can be considered to be 4 rows of 6 (as shown) or 4! (4 factorial).

FIVE-LETTER ANAGRAM

We do not concern ourselves with five-letter anagrams in this program, but the method we have demonstrated can easily be extended to five letters. The five-letter anagram

12345

can have all the possible combinations of the four-letter anagram with 5 inserted in the first, second, third, fourth, and fifth places. Therefore, the number of combinations is $5 \times 24 = 120$ (or 5!). In general, for an n-letter anagram, the number of possible combinations is n factorial ($n!$).

SPECIFIC EXAMPLE

For simplicity here we show a three-letter anagram. The anagram is "wot," which we number 1 = w, 2 = o, 3 = t. The possibilities are

312	**321**
two	**tow**
132	**231**
wto	**otw**
123	**213**
wot	**owt**

By observation we see that "two" and "tow" are possible solutions.

ALGORITHM

The steps involved are:

- Declare `char` variables `letter1`, `letter2`, `letter3`, and `letter4`.
- Assign values to these variables.
- Write 24 `cout` statements with the variables printed in the order combinations.

These steps are shown in the source code. The `cout` statements have all the combinations in the list.

Source Code

```
#include <iostream>
using namespace std;

int main()
{
        char letter1, letter2, letter3, letter4;

        letter1 = 'D';
        letter2 = 'R';
        letter3 = 'A';
        letter4 = 'E';
```

Initializing the letters.

```
        cout << letter1 << letter2 << letter3 << letter4 << "  ";
        cout << letter1 << letter2 << letter4 << letter3 << "  ";

        cout << letter1 << letter3 << letter2 << letter4 << "  ";
        cout << letter1 << letter3 << letter4 << letter2 << "  ";

        cout << letter1 << letter4 << letter2 << letter3 << "  ";
        cout << letter1 << letter4 << letter3 << letter2 << endl;

        cout << letter2 << letter1 << letter3 << letter4 << "  ";
        cout << letter2 << letter1 << letter4 << letter3 << "  ";

        cout << letter2 << letter3 << letter1 << letter4 << "  ";
        cout << letter2 << letter3 << letter4 << letter1 << "  ";

        cout << letter2 << letter4 << letter1 << letter3 << "  ";
        cout << letter2 << letter4 << letter3 << letter1 << endl;

        cout << letter3 << letter1 << letter2 << letter4 << "  ";
        cout << letter3 << letter1 << letter4 << letter2 << "  ";

        cout << letter3 << letter2 << letter1 << letter4 << "  ";
        cout << letter3 << letter2 << letter4 << letter1 << "  ";

        cout << letter3 << letter4 << letter1 << letter2 << "  ";
        cout << letter3 << letter4 << letter2 << letter1 << endl;

        cout << letter4 << letter1 << letter2 << letter3 << "  ";
        cout << letter4 << letter1 << letter3 << letter2 << "  ";

        cout << letter4 << letter2 << letter1 << letter3 << "  ";
        cout << letter4 << letter2 << letter3 << letter1 << "  ";

        cout << letter4 << letter3 << letter1 << letter2 << "  ";
        cout << letter4 << letter3 << letter2 << letter1 << endl;
}
```

Printing out the letters in different order.

Output

```
DRAE  DREA  DARE  DAER  DERA  DEAR
RDAE  RDEA  RADE  RAED  REDA  READ
ADRE  ADER  ARDE  ARED  AEDR  AERD
EDRA  EDAR  ERDA  ERAD  EADR  EARD
```

Comments

The user can look at the output and decide the correct letter order. For DRAE, the English word can be DARE, DEAR, or READ.

If a dictionary type database were available, the anagram list could be compared to the dictionary and a list containing only the correct possibilities could be created.

Using this same form, a program for solving a five-letter anagram could be created. A total of 120 `cout` statements would be needed for such a program. When we cover loops and arrays, we will see that we can write such a program with far fewer `cout` statements.

You can see that as anagrams become longer, the number of possible combinations becomes quite great, since the number is n factorial. A 12-letter anagram has $12! = 479{,}001{,}600$ combinations! Having a human read such a number is unwieldy. In such a case, comparing the result list to a dictionary is imperative.

When humans do anagrams by hand, they mentally look for common letter orders to reduce the number of possibilities. For instance, in the anagram "TRAB," the order BT at the beginning of the word is not possible. Recognizing this eliminates a number of possibilities. However, BR is a likely combination and leads to one possible solution "BRAT."

Modification Exercises

1. Modify the program to solve the anagram "OWDR."
2. Modify the program to solve just a three-letter anagram.
3. Modify the program to solve a five-letter anagram.

LESSON EXERCISES

LESSON 3.1 EXERCISES

1. True or false:

   a. The following `int` type variable names are legal:

      `1cat, 2dogs, 3pears, %area`

   b. The following `double` variable names are legal:

      `cat, dogs2, pears3, cat_number`

   c. We can print more than one variable value with a single `cout` statement.

   d. We cannot print both `double` and `int` type variable values with a single `cout` statement.

   e. The two statements that follow are identical:

```
int ABC, DEF;
int abc, def;
```

2. Which of the following are incorrect C++ variable names and why?

   `enum, ENUM, lotus123, A+B23, A(b)c, AaBbCc, Else, abx, pi, p`

3. Find error(s), if any, in the following statements.

   a. `year = 1967`

   b. `1967 = oldyear;`

   c. `day = 24 hours;`

   d. `while = 32;`

4. Find error(s), if any, in the following statements.

```
cout < "My salary in 2012 will be " << salary << endl;
cout << "In year << year << , my salary will be" >> salary
     << endl;
cout << "My salary in" << year << will be << salary << "\n";
cout << "My" << salary << "in" << year << "will be" << "salary"
     << endl;
```

5. The price of an apple is 50 cents, a pear is 35 cents, and a melon is 2 dollars. Write a program to display the prices as follows:

```
***** ON SALE *****
Fruit type    Price
Apple         $ 0.50
Pear          $ 0.35
Melon         $ 2.00
```

Solutions

1. a. false
   b. true
   c. true
   d. false
   e. false
2. `enum` is a keyword, `A+B23` uses the `+` operator, `A(b)c` uses parentheses.
3. a. `year = 1967;`
   b. `oldyear = 1967;`
   c. `day = 24;`
   d. `minutes = 32;`
4. a. `cout << "My salary in 2012 will be " << salary << endl;`
   b. `cout << "In year " << year << ", my salary will be " >> salary << endl;`
   c. `cout << "My salary in " << year << "will be " << salary << "\n";`
   d. No syntax error, but output is nonsense.

LESSON 3.2 EXERCISES

1. Given the declarations

```
const int X = 123;
const double Y = 12.345678;
```

determine whether the following statements are true or false

a. The statement `cout >> X;` displays 123.

b. The statement `cout << X;` displays 123.

c. The statement `cout << setw(5) | setfill('&') << X;` displays &&123.

d. The statement `cout << setprecision(4) << Y;` displays 12.34.

e. The statement `cout << setiosflags(ios:left) << setw(8) << setfill(%) << X` displays 123%%%%%.

2. Find error(s), if any, in these statements:

a. `const int PI = 3.1416`

b. `const PI = 3.1416;`

c. `const double PI = 3.14, MoreAccuratePI = 3.1416;`

d. `cout << 123.4567;`

e. `#include iomanip`

3. Write a program to declare and initialize the variables:

```
int          aa=123;
double       bb=3.141592;
```

and display them on the screen as follows:

```
123456789012345678901234567890123456789012345678901234567890
int        123                        +123******
double     3.141592                   3.14e+00**
```

4. Write a program to display the following output:

```
1234567890123456789012345678901234 5
income      expense     Name
+111.1      -999.99     Tom
+222.2      -888.88     Dennis
+333.3      -777.77     Jerry
```

5. Use four different flags but the same field width and precision, four different field widths but the same flag and precision, and four different precisions but the same flag and field width (i.e., a total of 12 format specifications) to display an `int` type variable A and a `float` type variable B, where A = 12345 and B = 9876.54321.

Solutions

1. a. false
b. true
c. false—use << instead of |
d. false—displays 12.3456
e. false—need two colons

2. a. `const double PI = 3.1416;`
b. `const double PI = 3.1416;`
c. No error; we can have two constants in one declarative statement.

d. No error.
e. `#include <iomanip >`

LESSON 3.3 EXERCISES

1. True or false, assuming

```
char c1, c2, c3, c4;
```

a. The statement `c1 = g;` assigns `g` to character `c1`.

b. The statement `cout << c1;` causes the character assigned to `c1` to be printed to the screen.

c. The statement `cout << 'c4';` prints `c4`.

d. The statement `c2 = 9;` gives `c2` the numeric value of 9, and `cout << c2;` prints the number 9.

e. The statements `c3 = 57;` and `cout << c3;` print the number 9 to the screen.

2. Write a program that prints all of the ASCII symbols supported by C++.

Solutions

1. True or false:
a. false, should be `c1 = 'g';`
b. true
c. false
d. false, in ASCII the number 9 represents tab. The `cout` statement prints a tab.
e. true

LESSON 3.4 EXERCISES

1. True or false:

a. The term `a + b` is a correct arithmetic expression.

b. The term `x = a + b;` is a complete C++ statement.

c. If `a = 5`, then `a` is equal to `6` after `a++;` is executed, but (with `a = 5`) `a` is still equal to `5` after `++a;` is executed.

d. The term `5 % 3` is equal to 2, and `3 % 5` is equal to 3.

e. The operands of the `%` operator must have integer type.

f. The meaning of the equal sign, =, in the statement

```
a = x + y;
```

is equal; that is, `a` is equal to `x + y`.

2. Supposing `a`, `b`, and `c` are `int` variables and `x`, `y`, and `z` are `double` variables, decide whether each of the following is a valid or invalid C++ statement.

a. `a + b = c;`

b. `a + x = y;`

c. `c = a % b;`

d. `a / b = x + y;`

e. `x = a * 3;`

f. `z = x + y;`

3. Write a program to calculate your expected average GPA in the current semester and display your output on the screen.

Solutions

1. a. true
b. true
c. false
d. true
e. true
f. false

2. a. invalid, `c = a + b`
b. invalid, `y = a + x`
c. valid
d. invalid, `a = b * (x + y)`
e. valid
f. valid

LESSON 3.5 EXERCISES

1. Based on

```
int i = 10, j = 20, k, m, n;
double a, b, c, d, e = 12.0;
```

Determine whether each of the following statements is true or false:

a. The statement `i =+ 2;` is a valid C++ statement.

b. The statement `i %= e;` is a valid C++ statement.

c. The statement `i *= (i + j * e / 123.45);` is a valid C++ statement.

d. When `k = i / j;` k is equal to 0.5.

e. When `i += j;` i is equal to 30 and j is equal to 20.

f. The term `k = 1 / 3 + 1 / 3 + 1 / 3;` is equal to 1.

g. The term `d = 1 / 3. + 1.0 / 3 + 1.0 / 3.0` is equal to 1.0.

h. The term `a = 1 / 3 + 1 / 3 + 1 / 3` is equal to 1.0.

i. The term `a = 1. / 3 + 1 / 3. + 1.0 / 3.0` is equal to 1.0.

j. The term `i + 2 / 3 * 3 / 2` is equal to 11.

k. The term `i + 3 / 2 * 2 / 3` is equal to 10.

l. The term `++i = j;` i is equal to 21;.

m. The term `++i++;` i is equal to 31;.

2. Convert each of the following formulas to a C++ arithmetic expression:

$1 + \frac{1}{3} + \frac{1}{5} + \frac{1}{7}$

$1 + \frac{1}{2.0} + \frac{1}{3.0} + \frac{1}{4.0}$

$$\pi R^2$$

$$\frac{(a+b)^2}{(a-b)^3}$$

$$\frac{a + \dfrac{\dfrac{b}{c}}{d + \dfrac{e}{f}}}{gh^2}$$

3. Assume a, b, and c are int variables and have the following values: a = 10, b = 20, c = 30. Find the values of a, b, and c at the end of each list of statements:

a.	b.	c.	d.
`a = c;`	`a = c++;`	`a = ++c;`	`a += c;`
`b = a;`	`b = a++;`	`b = ++a;`	`b *= a;`
`c = b;`	`c = b++;`	`c = ++b;`	`c %= b;`

4. Suppose that a, b, and c are variables as just defined, write a program to rotate the value of a, b, and c so that a has the value of c, b has the value of a, and c has the value of b.

5. Hand calculate the values of x, y, and z in the following program and run the program to check your results:

```
#include <iostream>

using namespace std;
int main ( )
{
    double a = 2.5, b = 2, c = 3, d = 4, e = 5, x, y, z;
    x = a * b - c + d / e ;
    y = a * (b - c) + d / e ;
    z = a * (b - (c + d) / e);
    cout << x << "  " << y << "  " << z << endl;
}
```

6. Calculate the value of each of the following arithmetic expressions:
13 / 36, 36 / 4.5, 3.1 * 4, 3 – 2.6, 12 % 5, 32 % 7

Solutions

1. a. false
   b. false
   c. true
   d. false
   e. true
   f. false
   g. false
   h. false
   i. true
   j. false

k. true
l. false
m. false

3. a. a = 30, b = 30, c = 30
   b. a = 31, b = 31, c = 31
   c. a = 32, b = 33, c = 33
   d. a = 40, b = 800, c = 30

LESSON 3.6 EXERCISES

1. True or false:

   a. The term `#include <Math>` is a correct C++ preprocessor directive.

   b. The `#include <cmath>` header must be placed at the first line of a C++ program using math functions.

   c. In C++, the value of `sin(30)` is equal to 0.5.

   d. In C++, the value of `log(100)` is equal to 2.0.

2. The following program can be compiled and linked without error, but you get an error message when you run it. Why?

```
#include <cmath>
int main ( )
{
  float x = -111.11, y = 0.5, z;
  z = pow(x,y);
  cout << "x=" << x
       << "y=" << y
       << "z=" << z << endl;
}
```

3. Write a program to calculate these unknown values:

Alpha(degree)	Alpha(radian)	sin(2*Alpha)
30.0	?	?
45.0	?	?

Solutions

1. a. false
   b. false, does not need to be the first line
   c. false, sin uses radians not degrees
   d. false, log10 gives the base 10 log

APPLICATION EXERCISES

1. Write a program that creates a table of Olympic competition running distances in meters, kilometers, yards, and miles. The following distances should be used:

   100 m
   200 m
   400 m
   800 m

Use the pattern exhibited in these distances to write your program. (Note: 1 m = 0.001 km = 1.094 yd = 0.0006215 mi.)

Input specifications. No external input (meaning no data input from the keyboard or file). All distances are real numbers.

Output specifications. Print the results to the screen in the following manner:

Table of Olympic running distances

Meters	Kilometers	Yards	Miles
100	____	____	____
200	____	____	____
400	____	____	____
800	____	____	____

Right-justify the numbers in the table.

2. Write a program that computes the length of the hypotenuse of four right triangles based on the lengths of the two legs. The lengths are:

Triangle 1 5.4, 8.7
Triangle 2 3.1, 12.6
Triangle 3 23.7, 5.8
Triangle 4 1.56e + 8, 2.37e + 6

Output specifications. Print the result to the screen with the following format:

Hypotenuse lengths of five triangles

Triangle number	Leg 1 length	Leg 2 length	Hypotenuse length
1	____	____	____
2	____	____	____
3	____	____	____
4	____	____	____

Right-justify the numbers in the table.

3. Write a program that computes the values of the two acute angles of a right triangle given the lengths of the two legs. Use the input data given in problem 3.2.

Output specifications. The output results should be in degrees, not radians. In your program, make sure that you convert from radians to degrees.

The output should go to file `ANGLE.OUT` and have the following format:

Acute angles of five triangles

Triangle number	Acute angle 1	Acute angle 2
1	____	____
2	____	____
3	____	____
4	____	____
5	____	____

4. The distance that a car (undergoing constant acceleration) will travel is given by the expression

$$s = V_0 t + 0.5at^2$$

where s = distance traveled
V_0 = initial velocity
t = time of travel
a = acceleration

Write a program that computes this distance given V_0, t, and a.

Output specifications. Print the results to the screen and complete the following table:

Car under constant acceleration

Initial velocity	Time	Acceleration	Distance
10	5	3	—
		4	—
		5	—
		6	—
		7	—
10	10	3	—
		4	—
		5	—
		6	—
		7	—

5. The general gas law for an ideal gas is given by

$$\frac{PV}{T} = \text{constant}$$

where $P =$ pressure
$V =$ volume
$T =$ temperature (Rankine or Kelvin)

which leads to the equation

$$\frac{P_1 V_1}{T_1} = \frac{P_2 V_2}{T_2}$$

for a given mass of gas.

Write a computer program that computes the temperature of a gas that is originally at

$P_1 = 5$ atmospheres
$V_1 = 30$ liters
$T_1 = 273$ degrees Kelvin

Output specifications. Your output should be to the screen and should complete the following table.

The below-listed pressure, volume, and temperature conditions can occur for a given mass of an ideal gas which is originally at $P = 5$ atm, $V = 30$ liters, and $T = 273$ K.

Case	P(atm)	V(l)	T(K)
1	2	40	—
2	3	80	—
3	6	50	—
4	1	15	—
5	2	70	—

6. Ohm's law for a steady electrical current can be written as

$$V = IR$$

where $V =$ potential difference across a conductor
$I =$ current in the conductor
$R =$ resistance of the conductor

Write a program capable of filling in the blanks in the following table:

Case	V (Volts)	I (Amps)	R (Ohms)
1	10	2	—
2	—	5	7
3	3	—	4

Output specifications. Print the completed table to the screen.

7. Write a program that is capable of displaying the distances from the sun to the four planets closest to the sun in centimeters and inches given the kilometer distances as follows:

Planet	Distance from the sun (million km)
Mercury	58
Venus	108.2
Earth	149.5
Mars	227.8

Input specifications. No external input is needed. These distances can be initialized in the source code.

Output specifications. Print the results to the screen in the form of the following table:

	Distance from the sun		
Planet	(million km)	(cm)	(inches)
Mercury	58.0	—	—
Venus	108.2	—	—
Earth	149.5	—	—
Mars	227.8	—	—

Note: To fit the numbers properly in the table, you must use scientific notation. Use constants where appropriate.

CHAPTER 4

BASIC INPUT/OUTPUT

CHAPTER TOPICS

In this chapter, you will learn how to:

- Read input from the keyboard
- Write output to a file
- Read data from a file
- Read and work with character data

This chapter shows how to make a program read from the keyboard, read from a file, write to a file, and handle single character type input data.

LESSON 4.1 READING DATA FROM THE KEYBOARD

TOPICS

- Inputting data from the keyboard using the `cin` object
- Prompting input

QUESTION YOU SHOULD ATTEMPT TO ANSWER

1. Why is the `iomanip` header needed?

Most commonly, your programs will have both input and output. Previous programs in this text had only output, and for them, the output device was always the screen (or monitor). No previous programs in this text had input. This lesson's program illustrates keyboard input during execution.

Your program can instruct the computer to retrieve data from various input devices. Input devices include

Keyboard
Mouse
Hard disk drive
Floppy disk drive

to name a few. Keyboard input uses the `cin` object. The `cin` object is simply a region of memory identified with the name `cin` (recall that in C++ an object is described as a "region of memory"). When you run this program you will see that execution stops when the program executes a statement using the `cin` object (which we call a `cin` statement). The program waits for the user to type information (and press "Enter") at the keyboard. It takes that information typed at the keyboard, uses it, and continues executing line by line until the next `cin` statement is encountered. It continues in this manner until all the statements have been executed.

Programs that have input from the keyboard usually create a dialogue between the program and the user during execution of the program by using a sequence of `cout` and `cin` statements. A `cout` statement immediately before a `cin` statement is used to indicate to a user what to enter at the keyboard. This `cout` statement is called a *prompt*.

Read the program, identify the prompts, and look at the form of the `cin` statements.

Source Code

```
#include <iostream>
#include <iomanip>
using namespace std;
int main ( )
{
        double income, expense;
        int month;

        cout << "What month is it?" << endl;
        cin >> month;
        cout << "You have entered month=" << month << endl;

        cout << "Please enter your income and expenses" << endl;
        cin >> income >> expense;
```

Each `cin` statement needs a prompting `cout` statement.

This `cin` statement reads a value from the keyboard.

This `cin` statement reads two values from the keyboard.

```
        cout << setprecision(2)
             << setiosflags(ios:fixed | ios:showpoint)
             << "Entered income=$" << income
             << ",expenses=$" << expense << endl;
}
```

We need manipulators to show output in the dollar format of a decimal point and two digits.

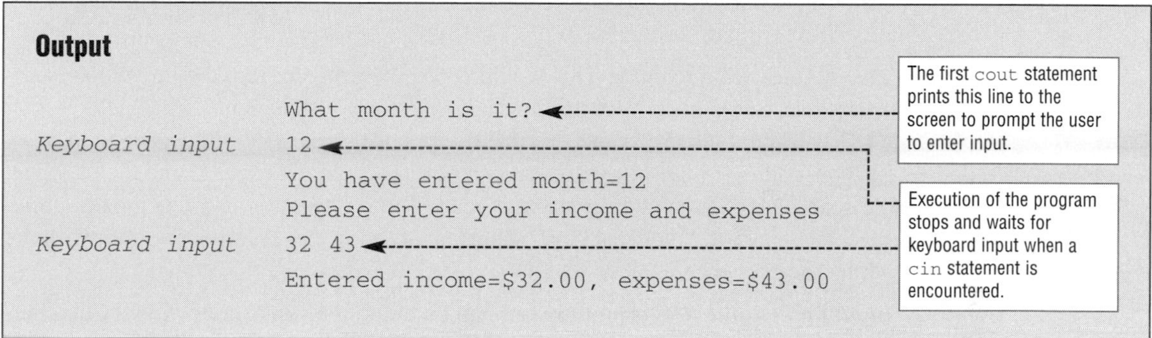
Output
What month is it?
Keyboard input 12
You have entered month=12
Please enter your income and expenses
Keyboard input 32 43
Entered income=$32.00, expenses=$43.00
The first cout statement prints this line to the screen to prompt the user to enter input.
Execution of the program stops and waits for keyboard input when a cin statement is encountered.

Description

Keyboard input. To stop program execution and allow a user to input a value from the keyboard, we use the `cin` object, `>>` operator, and a variable name. The syntax is

```
cin >> variable;
```

In this statement, *`variable`* is the name of the variable given the value typed by the user at the keyboard. In this lesson's program, the statement:

```
cin >> month;
```

causes execution of the program to stop and wait for the user input. The user types 12 and "Enter." Execution resumes when "Enter" is typed, and the value 12 is inserted into the memory cell reserved for the variable `month`.

The `>>` symbol is called the *extraction operator* (also sometimes called the *input stream operator*). The statement

```
cin >> income >> expense;
```

uses the extraction operator twice to send the values typed at the keyboard (separated by whitespace) to the memory cells reserved for the variables `income` and `expense`. The first value typed (32 for this lesson's program) automatically goes to the memory cells reserved for `income`, and the second value typed (43 for this lesson's program) automatically goes to the memory cells reserved for `expense`.

To assure that a user knows the variables for which input is needed, a program must prompt the user. A prompt is a message sent from the program to the screen (using `cout` in this program) asking the user to enter information. In this lesson's program we used two prompts, one to ask for the `month` and the other to ask for `income` and `expense`. It is necessary to precede each `cin` statement with a prompt. If no prompt were given, the program would stop execution at the `cin` statement, and the user would

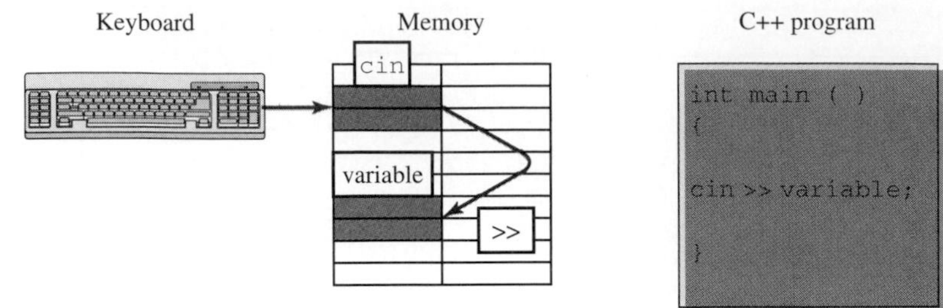

Figure 4.1

Illustration of `cin` and >> for input. The value typed is sent to `cin`, and the extraction operator moves it to the memory location reserved for the variable.

have no idea what to enter. This would cause the program to hang up, which is unacceptable. Remember, write prompts before your `cin` statements.

You should also be aware that the >> operator skips over whitespace to look for an input value. If in response to a prompt, a user enters five spaces and then a value, the spaces are passed and the value is read. The >> operator also recognizes whitespace as separating numeric input values (as it did in this lesson's program with the whitespace between 32 and 43).

Input and output streams. Streams can be thought of as a series of bytes in a particular sequence that flow from device to device (for instance, from the keyboard to memory). Objects are regions of storage (memory cells) in memory. The object used with the stream determines the device to which or from which the bytes flow. For instance, using the `cin` object indicates that the bytes flow from the keyboard to the `cin` object, and using the `cout` object indicates that the bytes flow from the `cout` object to the screen. Other objects can be used with streams as we will see later. We can manipulate the contents of the streams with the stream manipulators. Using the objects and the stream manipulators, streams can be created or interpreted. In C++, this I/O concept allows us to read or fill the streams without regard to what device is connected to them. Thus, communicating with a keyboard or a disk drive is similar from the programmer's point of view.

The concept is illustrated schematically in Fig. 4.1 (you should compare this figure to Fig. 2.2 which illustrates the `cout` object). When a `cin` statement is executed, values are transferred from the keyboard to the `cin` memory cells. They are copied to the variable memory cells using the extraction (>>) operator.

Both `cout` and `cin` are identifiers for objects (defined by `iostream`) that by default refer to the standard output stream (connected to the screen usually) and standard input stream (connected to the keyboard usually), respectively. These streams are automatically opened when a C++ program is executed and are therefore available for our use in any program that we write.

LESSON 4.2 WRITING OUTPUT TO A FILE

TOPICS

- Opening files for output
- Closing a file
- Writing data to a file

Previous programs have displayed all their output on the screen. This may be convenient at times; however, once the screen scrolls or clears, the output is lost.

In most cases, you will want a more permanent record of your output, which can be obtained by writing your output to a file instead of to the screen. Once the output is in a file, you can use a file editor to view it. You can use the editor to print the result on a printer, too.

The program for this lesson illustrates how to print output to a file. A program that prints to an output file should make sure the file

1. Has an acceptable file name.
2. Is opened before it is used.
3. Is closed after it is used.

Writing output to a file is similar to writing output to the screen. With the C++ stream input system, we simply use an object that is connected to an output file rather than the screen. Read the program to see how we create an object connected to a file. Once this is done, observe how similar to using `cout` it is to use this object.

QUESTION YOU SHOULD ATTEMPT TO ANSWER

1. How do we close the output file?

Source Code

```
#include <iostream>
#include <fstream>
using namespace std;
int main ( )
{
        double income = 123.45, expenses = 987.65;
        int week = 7, year = 2006;

        ofstream outfile("C:\\L4_2.OUT");

        outfile << "Week=" << week << endl << "Year="
              << year << endl;
        outfile << "Income=" << income << endl
              << "Expenses=" << expenses << endl;
        outfile.close();
}
```

We use the `fstream` header for both file input and output.

Because we have used the `fstream` header, we can declare objects of the `ofstream` class. Here, we declare `outfile` to be an object of the `ofstream` class.

When we declare `ofstream` objects, we put the name of the file we want to open after the object name and enclose it in double quotes and parentheses.

We can now use the `outfile` object like we used the `cout` object.

We close the file by calling the `close` function using a period to separate the object (`outfile`) and function name (`close`). Parentheses follow the function name. For the `close` function, the parentheses should be empty.

Output File L4_2.OUT

```
Week=7
Year=2006
Income=123.45
Expenses=987.65
```

Description

Opening a file for output. For file output we need the `fstream` header. The line

```
#include <fstream>
```

is required.

To open a file for writing, we declare an object of the `ofstream` class in a manner very similar to declaring a variable of `int` or `double` type. Because we have included the header `fstream`, we can declare `ofstream` objects. The declaration

```
ofstream outfile("C:\\L4_2.OUT");
```

declares `outfile` to be an object of the class `ofstream`. In addition, this declaration also calls a *constructor function* to open the file `L4_2.OUT` and associate it with the `outfile` object. You do not have to be concerned about classes and how constructor functions work at this time. For now, just learn that the form for opening an output file is

```
ofstream object_name ("file_name");
```

You choose the *`object_name`* in the same way that you choose your variable names. For this program, we have chosen the name `outfile`. You also choose the *`file_name`*. It must correspond to the name of the file in which the output is to be stored. For this program, we have chosen the name `L4_2.OUT`. In this case, the file is located on the C hard disk of a personal computer, so we used "`C:\\L4_2.OUT`." Two backslashes are required rather than just one (recall the rules given in Table 2.1 for escape sequences in string constants where two backslashes are equivalent to one) to indicate the root or main directory. If the root directory (C:) is not available for students, you can use a path to an accessible directory.

Writing to a file. We use our `ofstream` object to write to a file as we used `cout` to print to the screen. For instance,

```
outfile << "Week=" << week << endl << "Year=" << year << endl;
```

in this lesson's program writes the values of `week` and `year` in the file along with text making the first two lines of the file

Week=7
Year=2006

The next line of code

```
outfile << "Income=" << income << endl << "Expenses=" << expenses
        << endl;
```

writes the values of `income` and `expenses` along with text after the location of the last information written.

Note that a new statement for writing to the `outfile` file does *not* cause writing to begin again at the start of the file. The C++ I/O system is smart enough to know where in the file it stopped writing previously and continues writing from that point.

Closing an output file. We use the C++ library function `close` which is available for use with `ofstream` objects to close a file after it has been written to. Like the `sin` and `log` functions, C++ has standard functions in its library that are capable of performing operations such as closing files. Unlike the `sin` and `log` functions, these must be associated with an object. To use these functions, we must use both the object and function names. We use the object name, a period, and then the function name. In some cases we will also need to send other information to the function such as values of variables. This is done by putting variable names enclosed in parentheses after the function name.

In this lesson's program,

```
outfile.close( );
```

uses the `outfile` object of the `ofstream` class (as we declared it to be) to call the `close` library function. The parentheses after the function name are empty because the `close` function does not need additional information to close the file associated with `outfile`.

The general form for closing an output file is

```
object_name.close( );
```

where *object_name* is the name of the object associated with the output file. You need not understand all the details at this time. We will be making use of many C++ library functions throughout this text and will describe each of them as we use them. In Chapter 7, we discuss functions in detail. For now, just use the form shown to close files that you opened.

It is good practice to close files after they have been used as we have done in this lesson's program. However, C++ will automatically close all open files after execution is completed.

LESSON 4.3 READING DATA FROM A FILE

TOPICS

- Opening a file for input
- Reading data from a file
- Reading with the wrong type

QUESTIONS YOU SHOULD ATTEMPT TO ANSWER

1. Why do you think we use the lines `infile1.close();` and `infile2.close();`?
2. Why is the last value of `x` printed in the output equal to 0.3 and not 89.01?

If your input data is lengthy and you are planning to execute your program many times, it is not convenient to input your data from the keyboard. This is true especially if you want to make only minor changes to the input data each time you execute the program.

For instance, if your income is the same every month and only your expenses change, it is cumbersome to repeatedly type the same number for each month. It is more convenient to set up a file that has your income and expenses. Your program can read that file during execution instead of receiving the input from the keyboard. If you want to rerun the program with different input data, you can simply edit the input file first and then execute the program.

This lesson's program illustrates how to read data from two different input files. In the program, the file names specified are `L4_3A.DAT` and `L4_3B.DAT`. You must remember that when you create your input file using your editor that you give that file the same name you have specified in the code for your program. When you execute your program, the computer searches for a file of that name and reads it. If that file does not exist, your program will not execute.

To read the values correctly, you need to make sure that a match exists between the number and types of values in the file and the number and types specified in the source code. If these do not match, you may get an error that is not detected by the computer. In this program, we illustrate such an error.

Read the source code and look at the way input files are opened and read from.

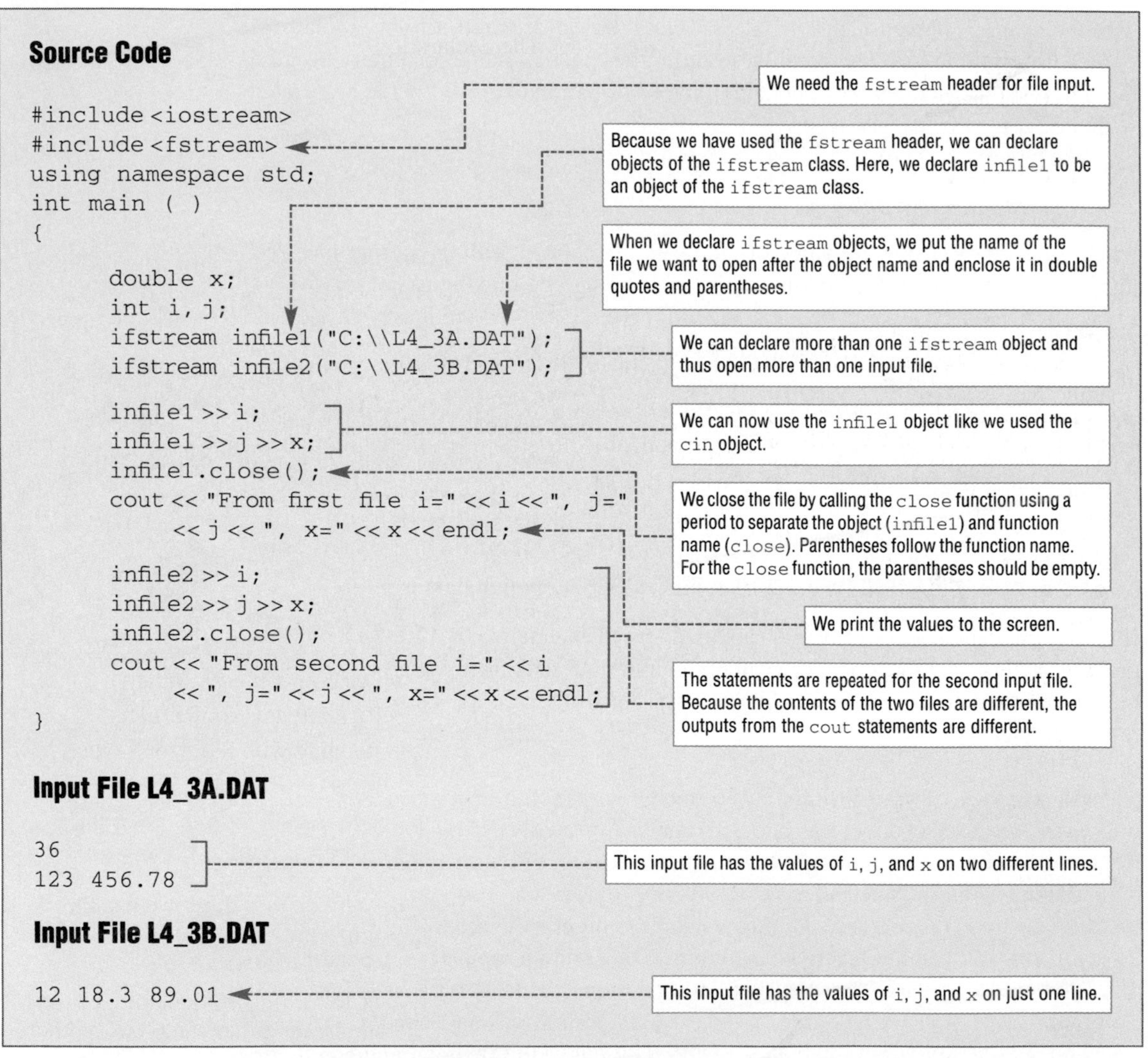

Source Code

```
#include <iostream>
#include <fstream>
using namespace std;
int main ( )
{
      double x;
      int i, j;
      ifstream infile1("C:\\L4_3A.DAT");
      ifstream infile2("C:\\L4_3B.DAT");
      infile1 >> i;
      infile1 >> j >> x;
      infile1.close();
      cout << "From first file i=" << i << ", j="
           << j << ", x=" << x << endl;
      infile2 >> i;
      infile2 >> j >> x;
      infile2.close();
      cout << "From second file i=" << i
           << ", j=" << j << ", x=" << x << endl;
}
```

Input File L4_3A.DAT

```
36
123 456.78
```

Input File L4_3B.DAT

```
12 18.3 89.01
```

We need the fstream header for file input.
Because we have used the fstream header, we can declare objects of the ifstream class. Here, we declare infile1 to be an object of the ifstream class.
When we declare ifstream objects, we put the name of the file we want to open after the object name and enclose it in double quotes and parentheses.
We can declare more than one ifstream object and thus open more than one input file.
We can now use the infile1 object like we used the cin object.
We close the file by calling the close function using a period to separate the object (infile1) and function name (close). Parentheses follow the function name. For the close function, the parentheses should be empty.
We print the values to the screen.
The statements are repeated for the second input file. Because the contents of the two files are different, the outputs from the cout statements are different.
This input file has the values of i, j, and x on two different lines.
This input file has the values of i, j, and x on just one line.

Output

```
From first file i=36, j=123, x=456.78
From second file i=12, j=18, x=0.3
```

The second input file had 18.3 for j, but only 18 is printed out here. The value of x is 0.3. These are errors because we want j=18.3 and x=89.01.

Description

Opening a file for input. For file input we need the `fstream` header as we did for file output. The line

```
#include <fstream>
```

is required.

To open a file for reading we declare an object of the `ifstream` class, which is allowed because we have included the header `fstream`. The declaration

```
ifstream infile1("C:\\L4_3A.DAT");
```

declares `infile1` to be an object of the class `ifstream`. In addition, this declaration also calls a constructor function to open the file `L4_3A.DAT` and associate it with the `infile1` object. The form for opening an input file is

```
ifstream object_name ("file_name");
```

As with opening an output file, you choose the *`object_name`* and the *`file_name`*. The *`file_name`* must correspond to the name of the file in which the input data is stored. For this program, we have chosen the name `L4_3A.DAT`. In this case, the file is located on the C hard disk of a personal computer, so we used "`C:\\L4_3A.DAT`." Remember, two backslashes are required rather than just one because of the rules for escape sequences in string constants. Use an accessible directory if the root directory is unavailable for student use.

Make sure you have created and filled the file with data or numbers (with, for instance, a word processor, saving the result as plain text, or an ordinary editor) prior to running the program. If the file does not exist or not enough data is in the file, an error will be indicated during program execution.

Reading a file. We use our `ifstream` object to read a file as we used `cin` to read input from a keyboard. For instance,

```
infile1 >> i;
```

in this lesson's program reads the first number in the file and stores it in the memory cells reserved for the variable `i`. The statement

```
infile1 >> j >> k;
```

reads the next two numbers in the file and stores the first of the two in the memory cells reserved for `j` and the second of the two in the memory cells reserved for `k`. Note that a new statement reading from the `infile1` file does *not* cause reading to begin again at the start of the file. The C++ I/O system is smart enough to know where in the file it stopped reading from the previous read statement and continues from that point with the new read statement. Proceeding in this manner, we never read the same data twice.

It is not necessary to put each number on a different line of the file for it to be read properly. The C++ stream I/O system looks for whitespace between numbers. The newline character is treated as whitespace. Separation between numbers with a new line or simple space are treated the same. We illustrate the effect of different types of separation in this lesson's program with the two different input files:

Input file L3_8A.DAT

```
36
123 456.78
```

Input file L3_8B.DAT

```
12 18.3 89.01
```

Even though the first file has data on two lines while the second file has data on just one line, the same read statements can be used to read them. For instance, if we had the following read statement and file (not used in this lesson's program):

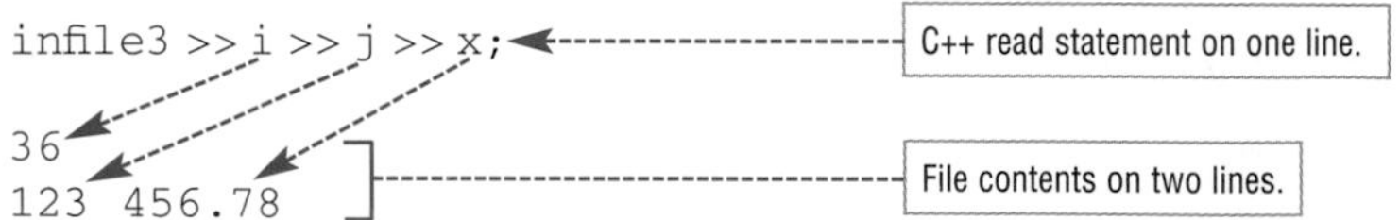

after executing this read statement, the value of the variables would be `i` = 36, `j` = 123 and `x` = 456.78 because of the correspondence between variable names and order in the file as illustrated by the arrows.

Effect of types not matching. If a variable is an integer and the corresponding file value is real, an error may occur. For instance, in this lesson's program the correspondence in reading from `infile2` is meant to be

However, because `j` is declared as `int`, it is not capable of storing 18.3 only 18. The 0.3 gets stored as the `x` value. The correspondence actually is

meaning `i` = 12, `j` = 18, and `x` = 0.3. The value 89.01 is neither read nor stored, and C++ does *not* indicate that an error has occurred! The lesson is that a real number cannot be read using an `int` type variable. (We can, though, read an integer with a `double` type variable—it will simply be stored in real format.) You need to recognize this error yourself when it occurs and correct it by either changing the data file or the variable type. This type of error can also occur when using `cin` for keyboard input.

Closing a file. As we did with output files, we use the C++ library function `close` which is available for use with `ifstream` objects to close a file after it has been read. The line

```
infile1.close( );
```

closes the input file associated with the object `infile1`.

LESSON 4.4 READING CHARACTERS FROM THE KEYBOARD

TOPICS

- Reading characters from the keyboard
- Effect of typing errors by a user

QUESTION YOU SHOULD ATTEMPT TO ANSWER

1. Whitespace is needed to separate input numbers. Is whitespace needed to separate input characters?

This program simply reads characters typed by a user at the keyboard and prints them. We show three different outputs for this program. The outputs are different because each keyboard input is different. In the program, we prompt the user to enter three characters with the first `cin` statement. In the first output, the user did enter three characters. In the second output, the user entered four characters even though the prompt said to enter only three, and in the third output, the user entered only two characters even though three were asked for. The outputs illustrate what can happen when an incorrect number of characters is entered. We examine this occurrence because reliable software should be able to accommodate the mistakes of the user without crashing (that is, terminating unintentionally).

Look at the output and note the following:

1. Output #1 shows three characters (`ALD`) typed as keyboard input for the first `cin` statement.
2. Output #1 shows that the program works as expected for the correct input.
3. Output #2 shows two characters (`AL`) initially typed as keyboard input for the first `cin` statement.
4. Output #2 shows that the program waits for a third character (D) to be typed at the keyboard.
5. Output #3 shows four characters (`ALDT`) typed as keyboard input for the first `cin` statement.
6. Output #3 shows that the fourth character is read by the subsequent `cin` statement.

Source Code

```
#include <iostream>
using namespace std ;
int main ( )
{
     char c1, c2, c3, c4;

     cout << "Enter your first, middle and last initials" << endl;
     cin >> c1 >> c2 >> c3;
     cout << "You entered" << c1 << c2 << c3 << endl;

     cout << "Enter 1 more character" << endl;
     cin >> c4;
     cout << "You entered" << c4 << endl;
}
```

Prompting keyboard input.

Reading three characters from the keyboard.

Echoing the input.

Prompting, reading, and echoing one more character.

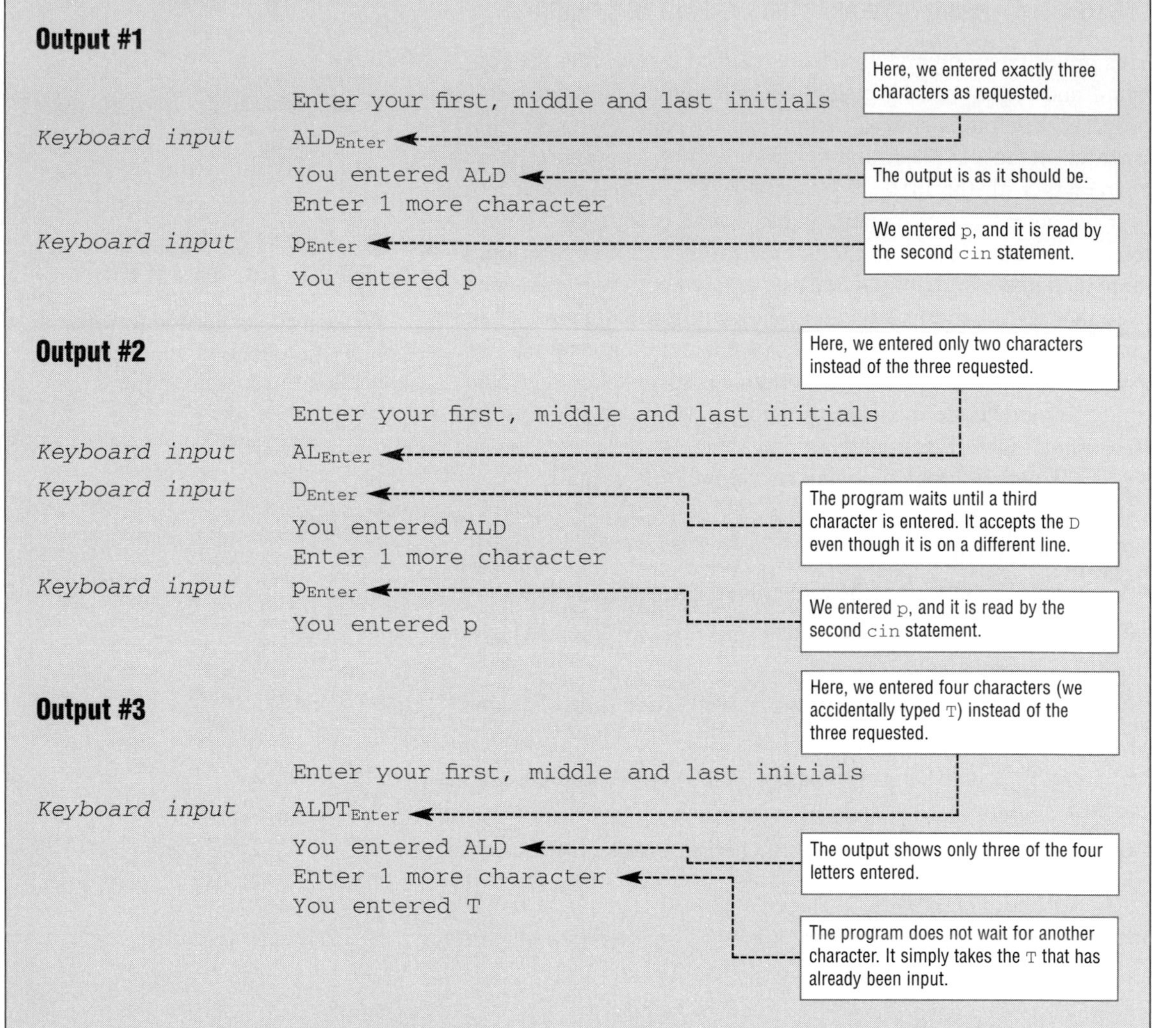

Description

Reading character data. To read character data typed in at the keyboard, we can use `cin` in a manner similar to the way we did for reading numeric data. For instance, the statement:

```
cin >> c1 >> c2 >> c3;
```

reads the next three characters typed at the keyboard and stores them in the memory cells reserved for the `c1`, `c2`, and `c3` variables, respectively. Unlike numeric data though, whitespace is not needed for separating character data using `cin`. Whitespace can be used to separate characters if desired, but the whitespace is ignored. In other words, we cannot input the characters "`A`", "`space`", "`L`", to make `c1`='`A`', `c2`='`space`', and `c3`='`L`' by typing "`A L`" as keyboard input. You can try this. If you do, you will find that `c1` is assigned '`A`' correctly, but `c2` is assigned '`L`'. This is done because the whitespace between A and L is ignored. Because cin ignores whitespace, endline, tab, and space cannot be input as characters in this manner.

In this lesson's program the next cin statement is

```
cin >> c4;
```

This statement reads another character. However, as we analyze each of the three outputs, we see that the value given c4 may not be correct if a user accidentally types too many characters in response to the first cin statement.

Output #1 description In typing ALD, as was done for Output #1, A is assigned to c1, L to c2, and D to c3. In this case the user has entered three characters correctly as directed, and the character variables are assigned the correct values. This is followed by typing p in response to the second cin statement, and p is assigned to c4.

Output #2 description In typing AL_{Enter}, as was done for Output #2, A is assigned to c1, L is assigned to c2, but the "Enter" is ignored (because it is considered whitespace) and not assigned to c3. It is not until we type another nonwhitespace character that the assignment for c3 is made. When "D" is typed after "Enter," D is assigned to c3. In this case the user has entered only two characters when three were requested, and this causes the program to hang up and wait for another letter (D). This is followed by typing p in response to the second cin statement, and p is assigned to c4.

Output #3 description In typing $\text{ALDT}_{\text{Enter}}$, four characters were accidentally typed instead of three. For this, A is assigned to c1, L to c2, and D to c3, which is correct. What happens to the T? When the second cin statement is executed, it automatically takes the T without waiting for input from the keyboard! We are not given the opportunity to type in the letter p as we did in Output #1. The end result is that the error in typing causes the input to be incorrect for the second cin statement.

Role of operating system input buffer. The mechanics of the way C++ handles character input with cin can be explained by describing the input *buffer*. A buffer is a region of memory used for the temporary storage of information being transferred between two devices. It is memory that is accessed sequentially meaning that one memory cell after another (in sequence) is read. A position indicator keeps track of the point to which information has been read. Upon reading a cell, the position indicator advances one cell so that the next cell can be read.

Output #1 description The first keys pressed were:

$\textbf{ALD}_{\textbf{Enter}}$

This transfers four symbols to the buffer (because Enter is considered a symbol). The cin input system reads three characters from the buffer with the statement:

```
cin >> c1 >> c2 >> c3;
```

assigns c1 = A, c2 = L, c3 = D, and advances the position indicator past the D and Enter as shown here:

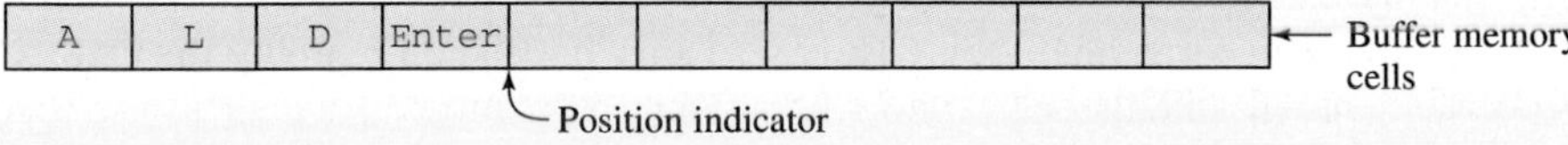

When the second `cin` statement (`cin >> c4;`) is executed (for which the user entered `p`), the `p` is read and assigned to `c4`, and the buffer and position indicator are:

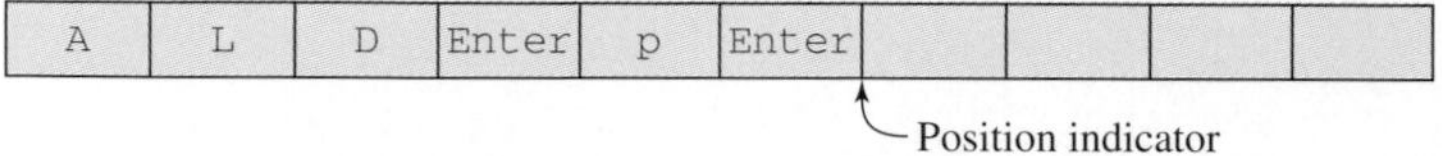

Since the user has entered the correct number of characters as instructed, the correct assignments using `cin` have been made.

Output #2 description Output #2 illustrates what happens if the user enters only two characters instead of the three that the first `cin` statement attempts to read. The buffer and position indicator after partially executing the first `cin` statement are:

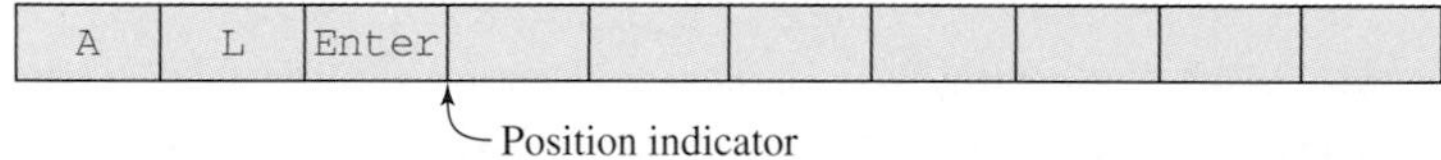

Because the `cin` statement wants three characters (remember Enter is not recognized as a character by `cin`) and only two are entered, the `cin` input system causes the program to wait for a third character to be entered. Pressing the Enter key without a new character will not cause execution to advance. Another character must be entered, so the user enters D. In Output #2, the buffer after completely executing the first `cin` statement is:

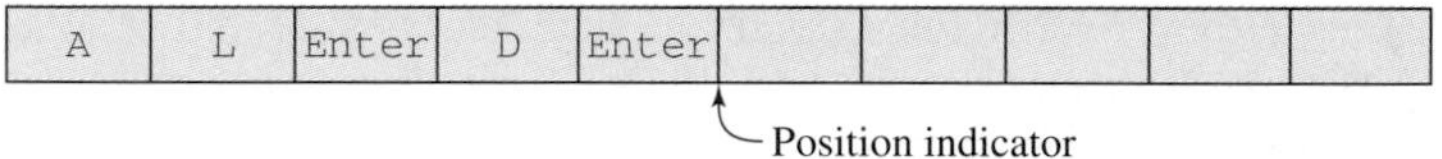

The second `cin` statement is then executed and the character `p` is read with the buffer being:

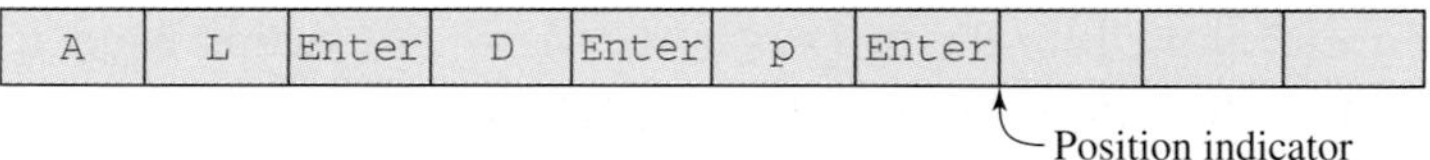

The correct assignments (`c1 = A`, `c2 = L`, `c3 = D`, and `c4 = D`) have been made even though the user has not followed the instructions perfectly.

Output #3 description Output #3 shows the effect of entering four characters instead of the three that the first `cin` statement reads. In this case, the buffer after executing the first `cin` statement is:

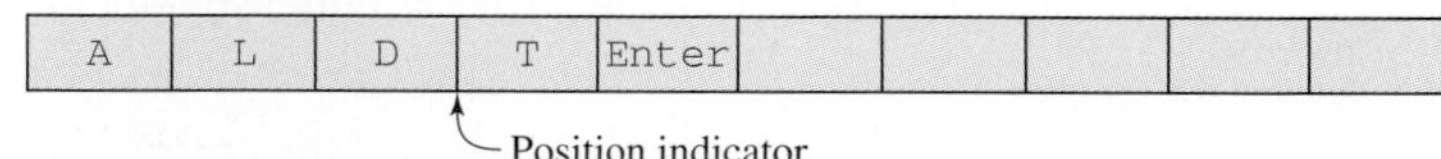

Note that the character `T` is in the buffer but has not yet been read. When the second `cin` statement is executed, the `cin` input system simply takes the `T` from the buffer and does not wait for further input! The user never has the opportunity to enter the p character. The buffer and position indicator after executing the second cin statement are:

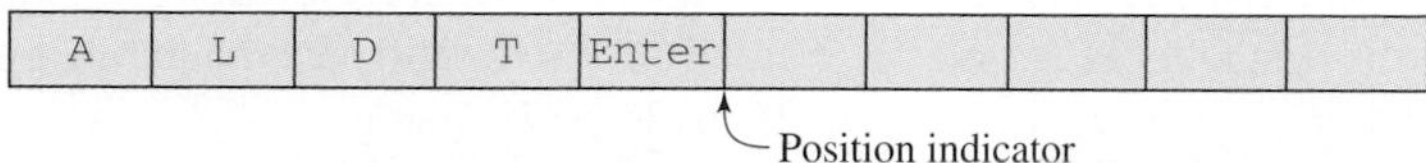

In this case, the assignments are incorrect (c1 = A, c2 = L, c3 = D, but c4 = T) because the user has not followed the instructions properly.

We illustrate these types of occurrences because reliable software should be able to handle errors by the user.

As you learn more, you will be able to allow users a second chance to input the data correctly if the first attempt fails.

Comment. There is more to learn about character data in C++. Right here we have just touched the surface of handling characters. For instance, C++ has library functions that can be used for input of single characters that eliminate some of the problems caused by cin. In addition, in C++ we can deal with groups of characters (as in words or sentences) called *strings* which is more practical in many cases. We cover these features in Chapters 12 and 13. In this lesson, we have chosen to cover some basics (without going into a lot of detail) with a technique that you already know, so you can successfully perform some manipulations with characters.

APPLICATION EXAMPLE 4.1 CAESAR CIPHER

Problem Statement

Write a program that will encrypt and decipher a 10-letter word. Have the user enter an ordinary English 10-letter word at the keyboard. Make the program encrypt this word using a Caesar cipher, then reverse the process and print the original message.

TOPICS

- Keyboard input
- Compound operators
- Program development
- Simple encryption/decryption

Solution

RELEVANT EQUATIONS AND BACKGROUND INFORMATION

Julius Caesar is credited with developing one of the first encryption methods. In writing a confidential message, he simply replaced each letter with the letter three places later in the alphabet. In other words, instead of writing "A" he wrote "D," and instead of "B," he wrote "E." For letters late in the alphabet, like "Z," he would circle back to the beginning and write "C." The message

```
ET TU BRUT
```

would have been written as

```
HY YX EUXY
```

The number 3 does not need to be an offset to make a valid Caesar type code. Any integer offset from 1 to 26 can be used with the English alphabet (using 27 as an offset is equivalent to using a 1 offset). However, the receiver of the message must know the offset to easily decipher the message. Forms of encryption that involve this simple offset are now known as *Caesar ciphers*.

The ASCII code scheme is easily utilized to make a simple Caesar cipher (see Lesson 3.3 and Table 3.5). Because C++ treats characters as integers, we can add the offset to create the encoded letter. For instance, if we use the variable `letter1` to represent the first letter in our message and `offset` to represent the number of letters after our letter of interest, we can encode the letter by using

```
letter1 += offset;
```

Repeating this for each letter in a word encodes the word.

To decode an encrypted message, we simply do the reverse. Therefore

```
letter1 -= offset;
```

returns us the original letter.

SPECIFIC EXAMPLE

With an offset of 4, encrypting the word

developing

makes

hizipstmrk

ALGORITHM

We need to realize that our program needs 10 letters and an offset for variables. The algorithm is

Begin
Declare variables.

Prompt user to enter original word.
Read original word.
Echo input.

Prompt user to enter offset.
Read offset.

Compute all 10 coded letters
Print encrypted form.

Decode coded letters.
Print original word.

The source code follows the algorithm.

Source Code

```
#include <iostream>
using namespace std;

int main()
{
```

```
          char letter1, letter2, letter3, letter4, letter5;
          char letter6, letter7, letter8, letter9, letter10;
          int offset;

          cout << "Enter a 10 letter word (no spaces)." << endl;
          cin >> letter1 >> letter2 >> letter3 >> letter4 >> letter5
             >> letter6 >> letter7 >> letter8 >> letter9 >> letter10;
          cout << "You wrote:" << endl << letter1 << letter2 << letter3
              << letter4 << letter5 << letter6 << letter7 << letter8
              << letter9 << letter10 << endl;

          cout << "Enter the offset." << endl;
          cin >> offset;

          letter1 += offset;
          letter2 += offset;
          letter3 += offset;
          letter4 += offset;
          letter5 += offset;
          letter6 += offset;
          letter7 += offset;
          letter8 += offset;
          letter9 += offset;
          letter10 += offset;

          cout << "The encrypted message is" << endl << letter1
              << letter2 << letter3 << letter4 << letter5
              << letter6 << letter7 << letter8 << letter9
              << letter10 << endl;

          letter1 -= offset;
          letter2 -= offset;
          letter3 -= offset;
          letter4 -= offset;
          letter5 -= offset;
          letter6 -= offset;
          letter7 -= offset;
          letter8 -= offset;
          letter9 -= offset;
          letter10 -= offset;

          cout << "The deciphered message is" << endl << letter1
              << letter2 << letter3 << letter4 << letter5 << letter6
              << letter7 << letter8 << letter9 << letter10
              << endl << endl;
}
```

Declaring a different variable for each letter and an integer for the offset.

Prompting the user to enter input.

Reading the word one letter at a time, and echoing the input one letter at a time.

Prompting for and reading the offset.

Calculating new letters from the offset.

Printing the encrypted message.

Decoding the letters.

Printing the decoded message.

Output

```
                   Enter a 10 letter word (no spaces).
Keyboard input    developing
                  You wrote:
                   developing
                  Enter the offset
Keyboard input     4
                  The encrypted message is
                  hizipstmrk
                  The deciphered message is
                  developing
```

Comments

This is not a pure Caesar cipher because the letters late in the alphabet do not circle back to the beginning. That is, for an offset of 4, the letters w, x, y, and z do not code to be `a`, `b`, `c`, and `d` as they would for a true Caesar cipher. In this code, these letters simply advance to the ASCII code symbols `{`, `|`, `}`, and `~`.

Since there are only 26 possible offsets, it is reasonably easy to decode a Caesar cipher even without knowing the offset. We could simply write a program that tries all the possible offsets. More difficult codes to crack are those that require more possible trials to arrive at the original message.

Modification Exercises

Modify the code to:

1. Read the input from a file.
2. Print the output to a file.
3. Use 15 letters instead of 10.

APPLICATION EXAMPLE 4.2 LANDSLIDE ANALYSIS

Problem Statement

TOPICS

- Keyboard input
- Working with variables
- Line-circle intersection
- Program development

Write a program that determines the boundaries of a potential landslide by calculating the coordinates of the beginning and end points of the slip surface (see Figs. 4.2 and 4.3). Have a user enter the center (x_0, y_0) and radius (r) of the circle that describes the slip surface and the slope (m) and intercept (k) of the line that defines the hillside. The intersection points of the line and circle define the landslide boundaries. Print the coordinates of the intersection points to the screen. Assume all data are in the first quadrant of an x–y plot and that the circle and line intersect at two points.

Solution

RELEVANT EQUATIONS AND BACKGROUND INFORMATION

Analyzing the problem and developing the solution equations is part of the programming process. In this particular case, we must develop the equations for the intersection of a line and circle as described next.

The line and circle involved are shown in Fig. 4.3.

By knowing the boundaries of the potential landslide region, the area that needs to be reinforced can be determined. The endpoints (x_1, y_1) and (x_2, y_2) are found from the intersection of the equations of the hillside line and the slip surface circle. If we define the line and circle with the formulas, respectively:

$$y = mx + k \tag{4.1}$$

$$(x - x_0)^2 + (y - y_0)^2 = r^2 \tag{4.2}$$

we can find the intersection points by substituting Eqn. 4.1 into Eqn. 4.2. This leads to:

$$(x - x_0)^2 + (mx + k - y_0)^2 = r^2$$

Expanding and grouping terms, this becomes:

$$(1 + m^2)x^2 + (2km - 2y_0m - 2x_0)x + (x_0 + y_0 + k^2 - 2y_0k - r^2) = 0 \tag{4.3}$$

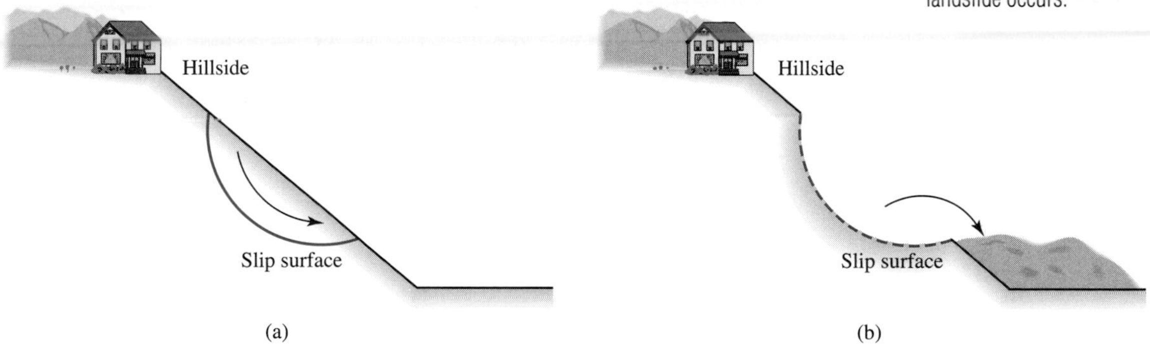

Figure 4.2

Illustration of landslide. (a) Region defined before landslide occurs. (b) After landslide occurs.

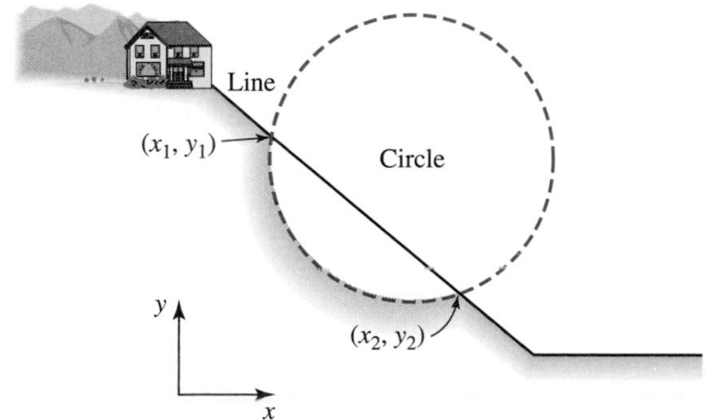

Figure 4.3

Illustration of line and circle that define the landslide.

This equation is in the form of

$$ax^2 + bx + c = 0$$

$$\text{where} \quad a = (1 + m^2) \tag{4.4}$$

$$b = (2km - 2y_0m - 2x_0) \tag{4.5}$$

$$c = \left(x_0^2 + y_0^2 + k^2 - 2y_0k - r^2\right) \tag{4.6}$$

Using the solution to the quadratic equation we get

$$x_1 = \frac{-b + \sqrt{b^2 - 4ac}}{2a} \tag{4.7}$$

$$x_2 = \frac{-b - \sqrt{b^2 - 4ac}}{2a} \tag{4.8}$$

$$y_1 = mx_1 + k \tag{4.9}$$

$$y_2 = mx_2 + k \tag{4.10}$$

The last four equations give the coordinates of the endpoints of the landslide.

SPECIFIC EXAMPLE

Consider a circle with center at (5, 8) and radius of 3. If the hillside is defined by the line $y = -0.5x + 9$, then $x_0 = 5$, $y_0 = 8$, $r = 3$, $m = -0.5$, and $k = 9$.

Using Eqns. 4.4 to 4.6

$$a = (1 + (-0.5)^2) = 1.25$$

$$b = (2(9)(-0.5) - 2(8)(-0.5) - 2(5)) = -11$$

$$c = (5^2 + 8^2 + 9^2 - 2(8)(9) - 3^2) = 17$$

Then using Eqns. 4.7 to 4.10

$$x_1 = \frac{-(-11) + \sqrt{(-11)^2 - 4(1.25)(17)}}{2(1.25)} = 6.8$$

and

$$x_2 = \frac{-(-11) - \sqrt{(-11)^2 - 4(1.25)(17)}}{2(1.25)} = 2$$

$$y_1 = -0.5(6.8) + 9 = 5.6$$

$$y_2 = -0.5(2) + 9 = 8$$

Thus, the coordinates of the two intersection points are (6.8, 5.6) and (2, 8).

ALGORITHM

We use the specific example to guide us in writing the algorithm. We also read the data and print the results.

Begin
Declare variables.
Prompt user for input.
Read keyboard input.
Solve for a, b, and c.
Solve for x_1, x_2, y_1, and y_2.
Print the results.

Source Code

```
#include <iostream>
#include <cmath>
using namespace std;

int main()
{
        double a, b, c;
        double x1, x2, y1, y2;
        double x0, y0, r;
        double m, k;

        cout << "Enter the center coordinates and radius of the slip circle."
            << endl;
        cin >> x0 >> y0 >> r;

        cout << "Enter the slope and intercept of the hillside line."
            << endl;
        cin >> m >> k;

        a = 1.+ m * m;
        b = 2.* k * m - 2.* y0 * m - 2.* x0;
        c = x0 * x0 + y0 * y0 + k * k - 2.* y0 * k - r * r;

        x1 = (-b + sqrt(b * b - 4.* a * c))/(2.* a);
        x2 = (-b - sqrt(b * b - 4.* a * c))/(2.* a);

        y1 = m * x1 + k;
        y2 = m * x2 + k;

        cout << "The coordinates of the landslide boundaries are:" << endl;
        cout << "(x1, y1) = (" << x1 << ",  " << y1 << ")" << endl;
        cout << "(x2, y2) = (" << x2 << ",  " << y2 << ")" << endl;
}
```

Declaring the variables.

Reading the input data.

Using Eqns. 4.4–4.10.

Printing the results.

Output

```
                  Enter the center coordinates and radius of the slip circle.
Keyboard input    5 8 3
                  Enter the slope and intercept of the hillside line.
Keyboard input    -0.5 9
                  The coordinates of the landslide boundaries are:
                  (x1, y1) = (6.8,  5.6)
                  (x2, y2) = (2,  8)
```

Comments

As indicated in the problem statement, this program assumes there are two intersection points. If a user enters data for a circle and line that do not intersect, the program will crash. The program cannot handle the possibility that the solution to the quadratic equation has imaginary numbers, as occurs when there are no intersection points. In Application Example 5.1, we illustrate how to handle imaginary solutions to the quadratic equation.

We could have written the program and Eqns. 4.4–4.10 without using the variables `a`, `b`, and `c`. While this would save memory, the equations written without `a`, `b`, and `c` are clumsy looking. Therefore, we elect to use the memory and simplify the look of the program. This also makes the program more understandable.

It is usually not good practice to use single letter variable names because single letters are often not very descriptive. However, in this case, single letters are acceptable because the quadratic equation and the standard equations for a line and circle use single letters. If you have such a situation in a program you write, you can use single letters. However, you should make sure the documentation (comments or other supplemental text) describes the meaning of the variables.

Note that the quadratic equation never appears in the source code. Only the *solution* to the equation is translated into code. In general, you will need to develop solution equations for your problems and put the solution equations into the program. Developing the solution equations is considered to be part of the programming process.

Modification Exercises

Modify the program to

1. Read the input data from a file called `LANDSL.DAT`.
2. Print the result to a file called `LANDSL.OUT`.
3. Perform the calculations without using the variables `a`, `b`, and `c`.

APPLICATION EXAMPLE 4.3 BLOCK ON FRICTIONLESS SURFACE

TOPICS

- Arithmetic operators
- File input

Problem Statement

Write a program that computes the number of people required to push a large rectangular block from rest to a specified velocity (Fig. 4.4). The surface is frictionless, and the pushing distance is specified. Assume that one person can push with the force of 800 N. Consider three different blocks. The specifications for each block are:

Material	Height (m)	Width (m)	Length (m)	Density (kg/m^3)	Distance to push (m)	Velocity to achieve (m/sec)
Concrete	3	6	5	2500	20	0.55
Wood	4.2	8.1	3.4	1200	12.4	0.81
Steel	5.9	3.2	2.5	5200	18.6	0.43

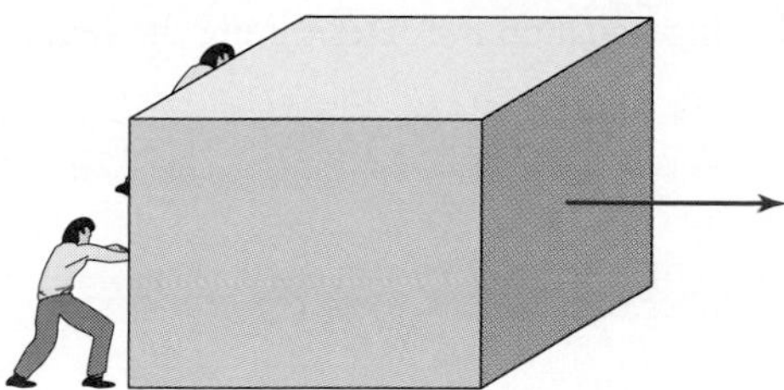

Figure 4.4

Block being pushed.

INPUT SPECIFICATIONS

The input should come from the file `BLOCK.DAT` and consist of (in the order given here) the height, width, length, mass density, distance to push, and velocity to achieve for three different blocks (on different lines, meaning that there are three lines in the file). All input should be in the standard metric units of m, kg, sec.

OUTPUT SPECIFICATIONS

The output should be to the screen and consist of an echo of the input and the number of people required for each of the three cases.

Solution

RELEVANT EQUATIONS

You have probably learned how to solve this problem in your physics class. First, the mass of a rectangular block can be computed from its dimensions and density with the following equation:

$$m = hwld \tag{4.11}$$

where h = block height
w = block width
l = block length
d = block density

The kinetic energy of an object in motion is expressed as:

$$K = \frac{1}{2}mv^2$$

where K = kinetic energy of object
m = mass of object
v = velocity of object

The work done by a constant force pushing on an object in the direction of the object's motion is:

$$W = Fs$$

where W = work done by the force
F = force on object
s = distance traveled by the object during the time the object is pushed

For an object pushed horizontally from rest on a frictionless surface, $W = K$ so that:

$$Fs = \frac{1}{2}\,mv^2$$

This leads to the following equation for determining the required force to move an object:

$$F = \frac{mv^2}{2s} \tag{4.12}$$

We can compute the number of people to push the block with

$$N = \frac{F}{800} \tag{4.13}$$

where N = number of people
800 = force per person (800 N/person)

SPECIFIC EXAMPLE

In many cases you will have to make up the example problem yourself, which means that you will need to create the information that goes into the input file. In this case, we will take the concrete block of dimensions $3 \times 6 \times 5$ m in height, width, and length and want to determine the number of people to push the block to a velocity of 0.55 m/sec from rest in 20 m distance. The density of concrete is approximately 2500 kg/m^3.

Using Eqns. 4.11, 4.12, and 4.13 we get

$$m = (3)(6)(5)(2500) = 225{,}000 \text{ kg}$$

$$F = \frac{(225{,}000)(0.55)^2}{2(20)} = 1701.5625N$$

$$N = \frac{1701.5625}{800} = 2.126953 = 3 \text{ people}$$

Notice that the calculation gives 2.12 people, but the correct answer is 3 people since 2 people will not be able to do the job. Our program must be capable of rounding up the value calculated to get the right answer. In C++, this is done using the `ceil` function described in Lesson 3.6.

Developing test cases and test input data is an important part of programming. The process becomes more difficult as programs become more complex. For now, when you test your programs, you should enter a variety of input data that can cover a range of possibilities. Large, small, medium, negative (where appropriate), and positive numbers should be used. Numbers like 1 or 0 (where appropriate) can be input but only if other more general cases have been studied. The appropriateness of negative numbers or 0 should be examined based on the nature of the problem being solved. For this example, a negative or 0 distance is not appropriate (in fact, 0 would likely crash the program because Eqn. 4.12 shows division by the distance, s).

ALGORITHM

We show this application example to illustrate that sometimes even a problem that sounds difficult can be boiled down to a relatively simple algorithm and program. It becomes more obvious that the program is simple after assembling the relevant equations and doing a specific example problem. If we write an algorithm that follows the specific example we get the three simple steps:

Compute *M*
Compute *F*
Compute *N* with rounding upward

To write a complete algorithm, we need to include reading the input, printing the results, and other things that a program must do. The steps are:

Include headers
Declare variables
Open the input data file
Print table headings

Read first block information
Compute *M*
Compute *F*
Compute *N* with rounding upward
Print *N*

Read second block information
Compute *M*
Compute *F*
Compute *N* with rounding upward
Print *N*

Read third block information
Compute *M*
Compute *F*
Compute *N* with rounding upward
Print *N*

close the input file

With this complete algorithm, we can write the source code line by line.

Source Code

Go through each line of this program and make sure you understand how it was developed from the algorithm.

```
#include <iostream>
#include <iomanip>
#include <fstream>
#include <cmath>
using namespace std ;

int main ( )
{
```

These four headers are needed.

```
    double height, width, length, density, distance, velocity, mass, force;
    int number ;
    const double force_per_person = 800.;
    ifstream infile("C:\\BLOCK.DAT");

    cout << "Block height  Width  Length  Density  "
      "Distance  Velocity  Mass  Force  Number people" << endl;

    infile >> height >> width >> length >> density >> distance
        >> velocity;
    mass = height * width * length * density;
    force = (mass * velocity * velocity) / (2. * distance);
    number = ceil(force / force_per_person);
    cout << setw(12) << height << setw(8) << width
        <<setw(11) << length
        << setw(10) << density << setw(11) << distance
        << setw(10) << velocity << setw(9) << mass
        << setw(11) << force << setw(19) << number << endl;

    infile >> height >> width >> length >> density >> distance
        >> velocity;
    mass = height * width * length * density;
    force = (mass * velocity * velocity) / (2.* distance);
    number = ceil(force / force_per_person);
    cout << setw(12) << height << setw(8) << width
        << setw(11) << length
        << setw(10) << density << setw(11) << distance
        << setw(10) << velocity << setw(9) << mass
        << setw(11) << force << setw(19) << number << endl;

    infile >> height >> width >> length >> density >> distance
        >> velocity;
    mass = height * width * length * density;
    force = (mass * velocity * velocity) / (2.* distance);
    number = ceil(force / force_per_person);
    cout << setw(12) << height << setw(8) << width
        << setw(11) << length
        << setw(10) << density << setw(11) << distance
        << setw(10) << velocity << setw(9) << mass
        << setw(11) << force << setw(19) << number << endl;

    infile.close();
}
```

Declaring `force_per_person` as a variable having a constant value.

The `ceil` function is used to round upward.

Following the algorithm for one block.

Following the algorithm for one block.

Following the algorithm for one block.

Input File BLOCK.DAT

```
3 6 5 2500 20 0.55
4.2 8.1 3.4 1200 12.4 0.81
5.9 3.2 2.5 5200 18.6 0.43
```

Output

Block height	Width	Length	Density	Distance	Velocity	Mass	Force	Number of people
3	6	5	2500	20	0.65	225000	1702.6	3
4.2	8.1	3.4	1200	12.4	0.81	138802	3672.1	5
5.9	3.2	2.5	5200	18.6	0.43	245440	1219.9	2

Comments

Use your calculator to check these results. Note that once again several statements have been repeated. Also note that every program can be written many ways. Do you have any ideas on how to change this program to fit your own personal style of programming?

Observe that the `ceil` function (Table 3.11) has been used to round up the number of people. Its complement function, `floor`, can be used to round downward.

Also, we have declared `force_per_person` to be a constant valued variable and initialized it to 800. With this method, the number 800 appears only once in the code. If in the future we wish to change the code to accommodate a different `force_per_person`, we need to change only one line. Had we used 800 in the denominator of the force equation for each block, it would have appeared three times, meaning we would have had to change three lines of code. This does not sound like much of a difference, but in large programs such a value can be used in many more lines necessitating many more changes. Writing code to reduce the number of changes reduces errors and is better programming. Using a constant also means that the value cannot be inadvertently modified in the code by a programmer. Another advantage of using the named `const` variable `force_per_person` is that a reader of the program can clearly see the meaning of the number 800. If 800 appears alone in a program, its purpose may be confusing.

The units are specified in the problem statement to be metric. Units are frequently an issue in programs. This particular program will not work correctly if other units are used as the basis for the numbers in the input file because the 800 in the code is in newtons. If the input data is in feet and pounds, the program will execute completely, but the results will be entirely incorrect! A programmer, through documentation, should clearly indicate to a user the type and importance of inputting the correct units. Automatically converting units in programs is a topic illustrated in Application Example 12.1.

Note that the first read statement reads the first line of the data file. When the second read statement is executed the program automatically begins reading in the file at the end of the first line. It reads to the end of the second line. When the third read statement is executed the program automatically begins reading at the end of the second line. Remember, the C++ input system is smart enough to know where it stopped reading in a file and uses this information the next time it reads the file.

It is also necessary that the file input data be listed in the order height, width, length, density, distance, and velocity. If the input is accidentally put in a different order the answers will be incorrect. Beware of this in working with your own programs. Sometimes your program is correct, but your input file is incorrect. Many hours can be spent looking for program bugs when in reality it is the input that is the problem. Remember, before debugging your programs check your input for errors first.

Modification Exercises

Modify the program to

1. Calculate the number of people required to push hollow blocks (read the thickness of the block from input data file; you must develop your own equations for the mass of the block).
2. Read all the input data prior to performing any calculations, which means you will have to create different variables.
3. Print the result to a file called `BLOCK.OUT`.

LESSON EXERCISES

LESSON 4.1 EXERCISES

1. True or false:

   a. The statement

      `cin << a << b;`

      will store the first and second keyboard input data to variables `a` and `b`.

   b. The statement

      `cin >> "a" >> "b";`

      will store the first and second keyboard input data to variables `a` and `b`.

   c. The statement

      `cin >> a >> b;`

      will store the first and second keyboard input data to variables `a` and `b`.

2. Write a program to input all your grades in the last semester from the keyboard and then display your input and the average GPA on the screen.

Solutions

1. a. false
   b. false
   c. true

LESSON 4.2 EXERCISES

1. True or false:

   a. We use the `cout` object to write output to an external file.

   b. We declare an `ostream` object to open an external file.

   c. We need the `ofstream` header to write output to an external file.

   d. It is good practice to close an output file once you no longer need it.

   e. The C++ I/O system is smart enough to know where in a file it last wrote.

2. Find error(s), if any, in each statement:

   a. #include <ofstream>

   b. ostream outfile("XX.OUT");

   c. outfile >> x;

   d. using namespace std

   e. close(myfile);

3. Write a program to input all your grades in the last semester from the keyboard, compute your average GPA, and write all the input and average GPA on the screen and in a report file named MYGRADE.REP.

Solutions

1. a. false
   b. false, we use an ofstream object
   c. false, need fstream header
   d. true
   e. true
2. a. #include <fstream>
   b. ofstream outfile("XX.OUT");
   c. outfile << x;
   d. using namespace std;
   e. myfile.close;

LESSON 4.3 EXERCISES

1. True or false:

   a. We use the infile function to read input from the keyboard.

   b. We use the infile function to read input from a file.

   c. You must create a link between an external disk file and an ifstream object before you can read your input data.

   d. It is good practice to close an input file when you need no further access to the file.

   e. It is not possible to make input errors with the sophisticated C++ I/O system.

2. Find error(s), if any, in each statement:

   a. #include <ifstream>

   b. istream myfile(IN.DAT);

   c. ifstream >> i;

   d. ifstream infile("IN.DAT");
      infile << i;

   e. ifstream infile("IN.DAT");
      infile.close("IN.DAT");

3. Write a program to read your grades from last semester from an input file named GRADE.REP, which has one line of data consisting of four grades only

(no characters); for example,

```
4.0 3.3 2.7 3.7
```

Compute your average GPA, and write all the input data and average GPA on the screen.

Solutions

1. a. false
   b. false
   c. true
   d. true
   e. false
2. a. #include <iostream>
   b. ifstream myfile("IN.DAT");
   c. ifstream infile("IN.DAT");
      infile >> i;
   d. ifstream infile("IN.DAT");
      infile >> i;
   e. ifstream infile("IN.DAT");
      infile.close();

LESSON 4.4 EXERCISES

1. True or false, assuming

```
char c1, c2, c3, c4;
```

   a. Space (ASCII value 32) can be treated as a char.
   b. We must put space between characters when we type them in at the keyboard.
   c. If we have cin >> c1 >> c2 >> c3 >> c4; and type in only three characters, our program will crash.
   d. All computers recognize ASCII code.

2. Write a program to read the following sequence of characters:

```
&gt 891><
-rew {[]}
```

   Print them out as

```
{98we[-gt] -&r1<>}
```

3. Write a program to display the following output:

```
A B C D E
 B C D E
  C D E
   D E
    E
```

4. Write a program to ask a user to enter five integers between 0 and 255 from the keyboard and convert them to characters. Display both the number and the characters on the screen.

Solutions

1. a. true
   b. false
   c. false (the program will hang up, waiting for the fourth character to be typed)
   d. false

APPLICATION EXERCISES

1. Write the program described in Application Exercise 3.1 with the output going to a file called `OLYM.OUT`. Left-justify the numbers in the table.

2. Write a program that computes the length of the hypotenuse of five right triangles based on the lengths of the two legs.

   Input specifications. Read the input data from the keyboard by prompting the user in the following way:

Screen output	`Input the values of the leg lengths for five right triangles`
Keyboard input	`leg1 leg2`
Keyboard input	`leg1 leg2`
Keyboard input	`leg1 leg2`
Keyboard input	`leg1 leg2`

   All input values are real numbers.

   Output specifications. Print the result to the file `HYPLENG.OUT` with the following format:

   ```
           Hypotenuse lengths of five triangles

     Triangle     Leg 1       Leg 2       Hypotenuse
     number       length      length      length
     1            —           —           —
     2            —           —           —
     3            —           —           —
     4            —           —           —
   ```

   Right-justify all the numbers in the table.

3. Write a program that computes the values of the two acute angles of a right triangle given the lengths of the two legs. Create the input data file `ANGLE.DAT` before executing your program.

   Input specifications. Input should come from data file `ANGLE.DAT` with the following form:

line 1	`leg1  leg2`
line 2	`leg1  leg2`
line 3	`leg1  leg2`
line 4	`leg1  leg2`
line 5	`leg1  leg2`

   All the values are real numbers.

Output specifications. The output results should be in degrees, not radians. Make sure that in your program you convert from radians to degrees. The output should go to file `ANGLE.OUT` and have the following format:

```
      Acute angles of five triangles
Triangle         Acute          Acute
number           angle 1        angle 2
  1                —              —
  2                —              —
  3                —              —
  4                —              —
  5                —              —
```

4. The distance that a car (undergoing constant acceleration) will travel is given by the expression

$$s = V_0 t + 0.5at^2$$

where s = distance traveled
V_0 = initial velocity
t = time of travel
a = acceleration

Write a program that computes this distance given V_0, t, and a.

Input specifications. The input should come from the file DISTANCE.DAT with the following format:

line 1 v_0 t
line 2 a_1
line 3 a_2
line 4 a_3
line 5 a_4
line 6 a_5
line 7 v_0 t
line 8 a_1
line 9 a_2
line 10 a_3
line 11 a_4
line 12 a_5

All the above numbers are real numbers. An example data file is

```
10 5                 10 10
3                    3
4                    4
5                    5
6                    6
7                    7
```

Output specifications. Print the results to the file `DISTANCE.OUT` in the following form:

Car under constant acceleration

Initial velocity	Time	Acceleration	Distance
10	5	3	—
		4	—
		5	—
		6	—
		7	—
10	10	3	—
		4	—
		5	—
		6	—
		7	—

5. The general gas law for an ideal gas is given by

$$\frac{PV}{T} = \text{constant}$$

where $P =$ pressure
$V =$ volume
$T =$ temperature (Rankine or Kelvin)

which leads to the equation

$$\frac{P_1 V_1}{T_1} = \frac{P_2 V_2}{T_2}$$

for a given mass of gas.

Write a computer program that computes the temperature of a gas that is originally at

$P_1 = 5$ atmospheres
$V_1 = 30$ liters
$T_1 = 273$ Kelvins

Input specifications. The input data should come from the file `TEMPER.DAT` and consist of five lines:

line 1 P_2 V_2
line 2 P_3 V_3
line 3 P_4 V_4
line 4 P_5 V_5
line 5 P_6 V_6

A sample data file is

```
2 40
3 80
6 50
1 15
2 70
```

All these values are real.

Output specifications. Your output should be to the screen and consist of the following table:

The below-listed pressure, volume, and temperature conditions can occur for a given mass of an ideal gas which is originally at P = 5 atm, V = 30 l, and T = 273 K

Case	P(atm)	V(l)	T(K)
1	2	40	—
2	3	80	—
3	6	50	—
4	1	15	—
5	2	70	—

6. Ohm's law for a steady electrical current can be written as

$$V = IR$$

where V = potential difference across a conductor
I = current in the conductor
R = resistance of the conductor

Write a program capable of filling in the blanks in the following table:

Case	V (Volts)	I (Amps)	R (Ohms)
1	10	2	—
2	—	5	7
3	3	—	4

Input specifications. The input data should come from the keyboard and be treated as real numbers. You should prompt the user in the following manner:

"For case 1, enter the voltage and current."
"For case 2, enter the current and resistance."
"For case 3, enter the voltage and resistance."

Output specifications. Print the completed table to the screen.

7. The pressure at depth in water is given by

$$P = h\gamma_w$$

where P = pressure
h = depth
γ_w = weight density of water

Write a program that determines the pressure at five different depths. Use metric units ($\gamma_w = 9.8$ kN/m^2).

Input specifications. Create a data file called `PRESS.DAT` with your editor. In the data file, list the five depths on one line:

```
depth1  depth2  depth3  depth4  depth5
```

An example data file is

```
10.  15.  828.  1547.  431.2
```

All the data are real.

Output specifications. Print the results to file `PRESS.OUT` in the following form:

```
Depth        Pressure
(m)          (kPa)
_____        ________
 –            –
 –            –
 –            –
 –            –
 –            –
```

8. The period of one swing of a simple pendulum is given by

$$T = 2\pi\sqrt{\frac{l}{g}}$$

where (in metric units) T = period (sec)
l = length of pendulum (m)
g = gravitational acceleration = 9.81 m/sec^2

Write a program capable of completing the following table:

```
Length           Period
 (m)             (sec)
 0.5               –
 1.0               –
  –               10.
  –               20.
0.32               –
```

Input specifications. Prompt the user to input the data from the keyboard.

Output specifications. Print the completed table to the screen.

9. Review Application Program 4.3 for this problem. The kinetic energy of an object in motion is expressed as

$$K = \frac{1}{2}mv^2$$

where $K =$ kinetic energy of object
$m =$ mass of object
$v =$ velocity of object

The work done by a force pushing on an object in the direction of the object's motion is

$$W = Fs$$

where $W =$ work done by the force
$F =$ force on object
$s =$ distance traveled by the object during the time the object is pushed

For an object pushed horizontally from rest on a frictionless surface, $K = W$, so that

$$Fs = 0.5\ mv^2$$

Assume that one person can push with the force of 0.8 kN and that we have a car of $m = 1000$ kg. Write a program that can complete the following table:

Distance pushed (m)	Final velocity (m/sec)	Number of people required to push
5	10	—
—	10	15
20	—	8

Input specifications. Prompt the user to enter the data from the keyboard.
Output specifications. Print the completed table to the screen.

10. Write a program that uses a modified Caesar cipher to encrypt and decipher a 10-letter word. Use an offset of three for the first letter, four for the second letter, five for the third letter, and so on for all 10 letters. Have the user enter the 10-letter word from the keyboard.

11. Write a program that determines the intersection point of two straight lines. The input is the slope and intercept of the two lines (m_1, m_2, b_1, and b_2). Use an input file. Assume the lines are not parallel.

12. Assume that a straight line and parabola intersect at two points. Use $y = mx + k$ for the line, and $y = ax^2 + bx + c$ for the parabola. Write a program that calculates the two intersection points.

13. Write a program that solves a 2 × 2 set of equations. Use:

$$ax + by = c$$
$$dx + cy = f$$

The input file should contain a, b, c, d, e, and f. Solve for x and y.

CHAPTER 5

DECISION MAKING

CHAPTER TOPICS

In this chapter, you will learn how to:

- Create `if` and `if-else` structures
- Use logical operators and relational expressions
- Make `switch` structures
- Use the `bool` data type
- Write programs with decision making

You will find as you continue learning to program that you will want your programs to make decisions regarding which calculations to perform. For instance, suppose you want to write a program that computes your income tax. Suppose that the percentage of tax is based on your income in the following way:

Income	Percent tax
0–$50,000	20%
$50,000–100,000	30%
>$100,000	40%

For your program to correctly compute your tax, it must be able to decide which percent tax applies to your income. In this chapter you will learn how to get your programs to make decisions of this sort.

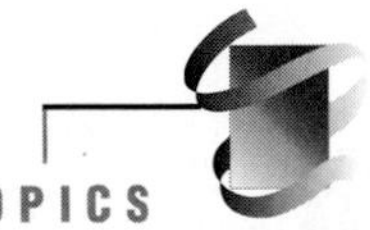

LESSON 5.1 if CONTROL STRUCTURE (1)—BASICS

TOPICS

- Simple if statements
- Block if statements
- Controlling program flow
- Relational operators
- Relational expressions

QUESTIONS YOU SHOULD ATTEMPT TO ANSWER

1. What do you think the different relational operators mean?
2. If the user types two values of pcode_entered that are greater than the pcode value, which statements are executed?

The if statement or if control structure is capable of making decisions in C++. The form of the if statement is fairly simple. A relational expression (meaning an expression that compares the values of two variables, for instance) is contained in the if statement; if the relational expression is true, then the statements within the "true" group are executed. If the relational expression is false, then the statements are not executed.

The program for this lesson has four if statements. This program checks a pass code entered by a user. If the pass code is correct, the user must enter it one more time to verify it. If the pass code is incorrect, the user is given a second opportunity to enter it. If it is incorrect a second time, the user is notified that access is denied. The correct pass code is built into the program to be 8765. Because a user of the program does not normally see the source code, the pass code is unknown to an invalid user.

Unlike the other programs we have studied, not all the statements in this program are executed (because the if control structure causes some of them to be skipped over). Do your best to trace the actions of the code line by line and see which statements are executed and which are not. Look at the keyboard input to help you follow the flow.

The purpose of this program is to show basic if structures and different operators commonly used with them.

Source Code

```
#include <iostream>
using namespace std;
int main ( )
```

```
{
     int i, pcode_entered;
     const int pcode = 8765;

     cout << "Enter your pass code." << endl;
     cin >> pcode_entered;

     if (pcode_entered < pcode) cout << " Incorrect code "
           "(too small). Enter it again." << endl;

     if (pcode_entered > pcode) cout << " Incorrect code "
           "(too large). Enter it again." << endl;

     if (pcode == pcode_entered) cout << " Verify your "
           "code by entering it again." << endl;

     cin >> pcode_entered;

     if (pcode_entered == pcode)
           {
           cout << "Access approved." << endl;
           cout << "Welcome!" << endl;
           }

     if (pcode_entered != pcode) cout << "Access denied." << endl;
}
```

The pass code is 8765.

Prompting the user to enter his or her pass code.

Reading the value typed by the user and assigning it to the variable `pcode_entered`.

Relational expression. The result of a relational expression can be regarded as being only true or false. Each relational expression in this program compares the values of `pcode_entered` and `pcode`.

These are all simple `if` statements. The `cout` statement is executed if the relational expression is true.

The equality relational operator has *two* equal signs.

This is a block `if` statement. The statements in the block are executed if the relational expression is true.

This expression uses another relational operator.

Output

```
                    Enter your pass code.
Keyboard input      8766
                    Incorrect code (too large). Enter it again.
Keyboard input      8765
                    Access approved.
                    Welcome!
```

Description

Relational expressions. The expression

`pcode_entered < pcode`

is a relational expression that compares the values of two arithmetic expressions. A relational expression is a type of logical expression and produces a result of either true or false. Here, it checks whether the value of the variable pcode_entered is less than the value of the variable pcode. Its general syntax is

```
left_operand   relational_operator   right_operand
```

where the *left_operand* and *right_operand* can be variables, such as pcode_entered in this lesson's program or any arithmetic expression. The *relational_operator* is used to compare the values of two operands. C++ contains six relational operators:

Relational operator	**Meaning**
<	Less than
<=	Less than or equal to
==	Equal to
>	Greater than
>=	Greater than or equal to
!=	Not equal to

Observe in the table the meaning of !=. No ↑ symbol is found on the keyboard, so C++ uses !=.

Simple* if *statements. A simple if statement can be generalized as

```
if (expression) statement;
```

where *expression*, represents a logical expression and *statement*, is an executable statement. For instance

```
if (pcode_entered < pcode) cout << "Incorrect code (too small). "
      "Enter it again." << endl;
```

uses pcode_entered < pcode as the *expression* and cout << "Incorrect code (too small). Enter it again." << endl; as the *statement*. Note that any executable statement can be used as the *statement*, including if and other control statements. A logical *expression* produces a result of either true or false. If the logical *expression* is true, the *statement* is executed. If the logical *expression* is false, the *statement* is not executed. The logical *expression* within an if statement is called a *condition* or *test expression*.

Make sure that you do not put a semicolon immediately after the parentheses enclosing the expression. In other words, if you write

```
if (expression);   statement;
```

then you will have created two independent statements. The first uses an if conditional that does nothing whether the *expression* is true or false. The second is a *statement* that will always be executed (because the if conditional has no effect on it. This is clearly not what you want. Remember, do not put a semicolon separating the test expression from the executable statements.

Block* if *statements. The statement

```
if (pcode_entered == pcode)      {statements...}
```

is called a block `if` statement. If the logical expression (between the two parentheses) is true, the statements in the "true" block (between the two braces) are executed. Otherwise, the entire true block of statements is ignored. The general form of a block `if` statement is

```
if (expression)
   {
   executable statement 1;
   executable statement 2;
   ...
   }
```

The code block should be indented one tab (at least three spaces) in from the keyword, `if`. We will see as we go further in this book that indentation is an important way of making your program understandable to others. Although there are no absolute rules on indentation (it is not required by standard C++), it has become common practice in programming.

Comparing the equality of two integer values. The equality relational operator `==` (with 2 not 1 = signs) is capable of comparing two values. If the two values are equal, the relational expression using `==` has the value true. If the two values are not equal, the relational expression using `==` has the value false. The equality relational operator is commonly used in test expressions for `if` control structures.

The `==` operator works very well for integer type comparisons (with integer values on both sides of `==`). However, a major error can occur if you mistakenly use `=` rather than `==`. For instance, in this lesson's program, we could have mistakenly written just one equal sign and the expression in the form:

```
if (pcode_entered = pcode) cout << "Verify your code by "
      "entering it again." << endl;
```

The result is that `pcode_entered` is *assigned* the value of `pcode`, and the `cout` statement is executed (for a reason we will see in the next lesson)! This type of error is very difficult to find in a large program. The compiler does not help because it accepts the single equal sign. Consequently, you must find this error on your own.

If the comparison is to a constant, then this form of writing the comparison works well:

```
if (2 == x)
```

because the compiler will not accept

```
if (2 = x)
```

if we accidentally type just one instead of two equal signs. Consequently, the compiler has helped us find the single equal sign problem. In this lesson's program, the constant is on the left side of the expression in

```
if (pcode == pcode_entered) cout << "Verify your code by "
      "entering it again." << endl;
```

because pcode is declared to be const int. If we had accidentally typed (with =)

```
if (pcode = pcode_entered) cout << "Verify your code by "
    "entering it again." << endl;
```

the compiler would have indicated an error for us. In general, be very careful when you use ==. Make sure you do not use just one =.

Comparing the equality of two real values. It is not recommended to use == to compare the values of double, long double, or float type variables in most cases, although the C++ compiler will not indicate an error if it is done.

The reason why it is not recommended for real number comparisons is that a typical C++ compiler carries a large number of significant digits for the real variable types (the number depends on the number of bytes used to store the type). If two doubles are compared with == and they differ in only the last significant digit, then the result of a comparison with == is false. For instance, if a = 12.3456789123456789 and b = 12.3456789123456788, then the result of a == b is false although they differ by only 10^{-16}. Often in real programs, we perform calculations using slightly approximate values and compare them with other approximate values. In many cases, we are interested only if the numbers are nearly or very nearly equal. Therefore, we want a comparison to evaluate to true when the values are very nearly equal. Because == does not do this, we do not use it.

Also, although we lacked the space to describe it in detail in Chapter 1, the binary representation of decimal numbers often requires an approximation. For instance, we need many binary bits to represent the simple decimal number 5.3 exactly. Because of this characteristic, numbers that we calculate to be exact with decimal arithmetic may not be exact using binary arithmetic with a limited number of bits. In other words, a calculation that you believe is exact using a hand calculation in decimal may not be exact using binary with a limited number of bits. We avoid the comparison problems caused by this effect by not using == for real type variables.

If we do not use == to compare real numbers, what do we do? One way to compare real values is to use the fabs function and <. For instance, to compare the double values of a and b as listed previously, the following statement would evaluate to true:

```
if (fabs (a - b) < 1.0e - 10)
```

Here, we have somewhat arbitrarily selected the constant 1.0e – 10 as a very small number. In writing your own programs, you must decide how small that number should be based on what you require for your problem.

Comment. The following cout statements were not executed in this lesson's program for the given input data:

```
cout << "Incorrect code (too small). Enter it again." << endl;
cout << "Verify your code by entering it again." << endl;
cout << "Access denied." << endl;
```

because the relational expressions preceding these cout statements all evaluated to false.

Note that an inefficiency in this lesson's program is that five relational expressions are executed. Fewer relational expressions (and therefore, fewer comparisons, which is more efficient) are needed when we use if-else control structures. We cover these next, in Lesson 5.2.

LESSON 5.2 if CONTROL STRUCTURE (2)—SIMPLE if-else

TOPICS

- Simple if-else control structures
- The conditional ? : operator

QUESTIONS YOU SHOULD ATTEMPT TO ANSWER

1. Which block of code is executed if the entered revenue is greater than the entered expenses?
2. Which block of code is executed if the entered revenue is less than the entered expenses?

Another form of the if statement is the if-else form. It is used when a group of statements is to be executed if the logical expression is false.

The program in this lesson computes whether or not a company is profitable. The program prompts for revenue and expenses and computes either the profit or loss. An if-else control structure is used to decide which calculations to perform.

In this lesson we introduce the ? : operator. It is the only operator in C++ that is a *ternary* operator, meaning that three operands are needed for it to be used properly. In this program, we have used all three operands on the right side of an assignment statement. A colon separates two of the operands. We use the ? : operator to help determine the interest on the company's debt if it is operating at a loss.

Read the source code line by line along with the keyboard input portion of the output section. Determine which statements are executed and which are not executed.

Source Code

```
#include <cmath>
#include <iostream>
#include <iomanip>
using namespace std;
int main ( )
{
      double revenue = 0, expenses = 0, profit = 0, loss = 0, interest = 0;

      cout << setprecision(2) << setiosflags(ios :: showpoint);
      cout << "Enter the company's revenue and expenses:" << endl;
      cin >> revenue >> expenses;
      cout << endl << endl;
```

Declaring and initializing 5 variables.

Setting a format for printing dollar values.

Prompting for and reading revenue and expenses.

```
    if  (revenue > expenses)
            {
            profit = revenue - expenses;
            cout << "The company is profitable.\n"
                 << "The company's profit for this month "
                    "is: $" << profit << endl;
            }
    else
            {
            loss = expenses - revenue;
            cout << "The company is running a loss.\n"
                 << "The company's loss for this month "
                    "is : $" << loss << endl;
            }

    interest = (loss > 0.0) ? (0.05 * loss) : (0.0);
    cout << "The interest the company owes on its debt is $"
         << interest << endl;

}
```


Output

```
                  Enter the company's revenue and expenses
Keyboard input    350000 450000
                  The company is running a loss
                  The company's loss this month is : $100000.00
                  The interest the company owes on its debt is $5000.00
```

Description

Simple `if-else` control structure. The syntax of a simple C++ `if-else` control structure is

```
if (expression)
  {
  executable statement 1a;
  executable statement 1b;
  ...
  }
else
 {
 executable statement 2a;
 executable statement 2b;
 ...
 }
```

Executable statements 1a, 1b, . . . are part of the "true" block, whereas executable statements 2a, 2b, . . . are part of the "false" block. If the expression is true, statements in the true block are executed. If the expression is false, control is transferred to the false block. If the statement block (either true or false) contains more than one statement, the block must be bounded by a pair of braces; otherwise, braces are optional. For example,

```
if (test >= 0)
   {
   true block statements...
   }
else
   a single statement;
```

where the true block contains more than one statement and therefore must be bounded by a pair of braces. However, the false block contains only one statement, so the braces are optional.

If no statements are to be executed in the false block, then the false block may be omitted. The syntax without the false block is as given in Lesson 5.1.

```
if (expression)
   {
   executable statement 1a;
   executable statement 1b;
   ...
   }
```

Note that the impact of using such a control structure is to cause the execution of one block while bypassing another.

The ? : conditional operator. The ? : operator requires three operands. Its form is the following:

```
expression1 ? expression2 : expression3
```

If *expression1* is true, *expression2* is evaluated. If *expression1* is false, *expression3* is evaluated. The value of the entire ? : expression becomes equal to the value of the expression evaluated (either *expression2* or *expression3*).

For this lesson's program, *expression1*, loss > 0.0 is true. Therefore, *expression2*, 0.05 * loss is evaluated, and the value of the right side of the assignment becomes equal to the value of *expression2*. Thus, interest becomes equal to 0.05 * loss.

As another example, the ? : operator can be used to find the smaller of two numbers. The statement

```
x = (y < z) ? y : z;
```

assigns x the value of the smaller of y and z.

Statements using the ? : operator are good shorthand for longer if-else type control structures. Note that for the unevaluated expression no side effects occur.

LESSON 5.3 `if` CONTROL STRUCTURE (3)—NESTED `if-else`

TOPIC

- Nested `if-else` control structures

`if-else` control structures can be nested, meaning an `if-else` control structure can be contained within another `if-else` control structure.

Suppose you are a civil engineer managing a construction project. You may be interested in writing a program that tells you what should be done during a phase of a project during the week at a particular time.

Say that the following 24-hour, 7-day schedule is needed to complete the phase of the project in a timely manner:

Weekdays
(Days 1–5)

0:00–9:00	Drive piles
9:00–24:00	Construct formwork

Weekends
(Days 6–7)

0:00–8:00	Maintain equipment
8:00–24:00	Pour concrete

This schedule can be used to produce the following algorithm, which illustrates the logic that you would use to respond to a question about what would be done on a particular day at a particular time:

QUESTION YOU SHOULD ATTEMPT TO ANSWER

1. What activity should be performed when day = 2 and time = 10.00?

```
If day = weekday (1-5), then
    if time = 0:00-9:00 Drive piles
    if time = 9:00-24:00 Construct formwork
If day = weekend (6-7), then
    if time = 0:00-8:00  Maintain equipment
    if time = 8:00-24:00  Pour concrete
```

A computer program written in C++ can duplicate the logic of this algorithm. Examine the source code to see how `if-else` statements can be used to mimic this. Note that these `if-else` statements are said to be nested.

Source Code

```
#include <iostream>
using namespace std;
int main ( )
{
         int day;
         double time;

         cout << "Type the day and time of interest" << endl;
         cin >> day >> time;

     if (day <= 5)
```

```
        {
        if (time <= 9.00)
                cout << "Drive piles" << endl;
        else
                cout << "Construct formwork" << endl;
        }
    else
        {
        if (time <= 8.00)
                cout << "Maintain equipment" << endl;
        else
                cout << "Pour concrete" << endl;
        }
}
```

if-else control structures contained within an if-else control structure.

Output

```
                      Type the day and time of interest
Keyboard input        3 10.00
                      Construct formwork
```

Description

Nested `if-else` control structures. In C++, different levels of `if-else` control structures can be nested. One can trace which statement blocks are executed by closely following the code. For example, follow these nested structures:

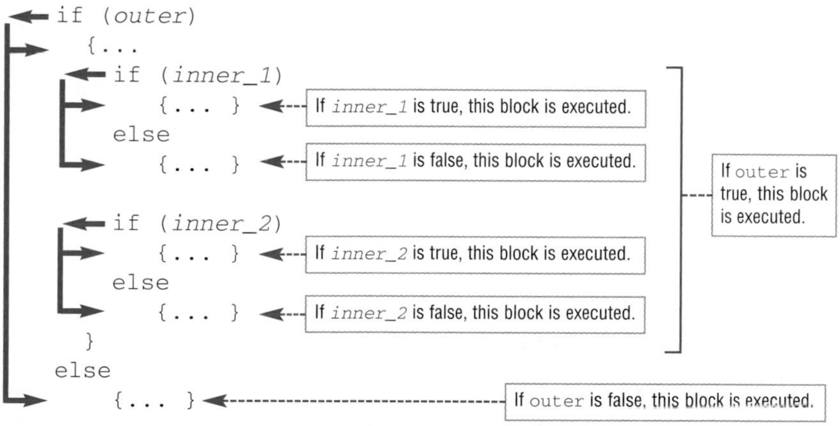

```
if (outer)
  {...
    if (inner_1)
        {... }     <--- If inner_1 is true, this block is executed.
    else
        {... }     <--- If inner_1 is false, this block is executed.

    if (inner_2)
        {... }     <--- If inner_2 is true, this block is executed.
    else
        {... }     <--- If inner_2 is false, this block is executed.
  }
else
    {... }  <--- If outer is false, this block is executed.
```

If outer is true, this block is executed.

Each nested loop that you create or examine in someone else's code must be evaluated on a case-by-case basis. A conceptual illustration of the nested `if-else` control structure used in this lesson is given in Fig. 5.1. Note the branching that is produced by the nesting.

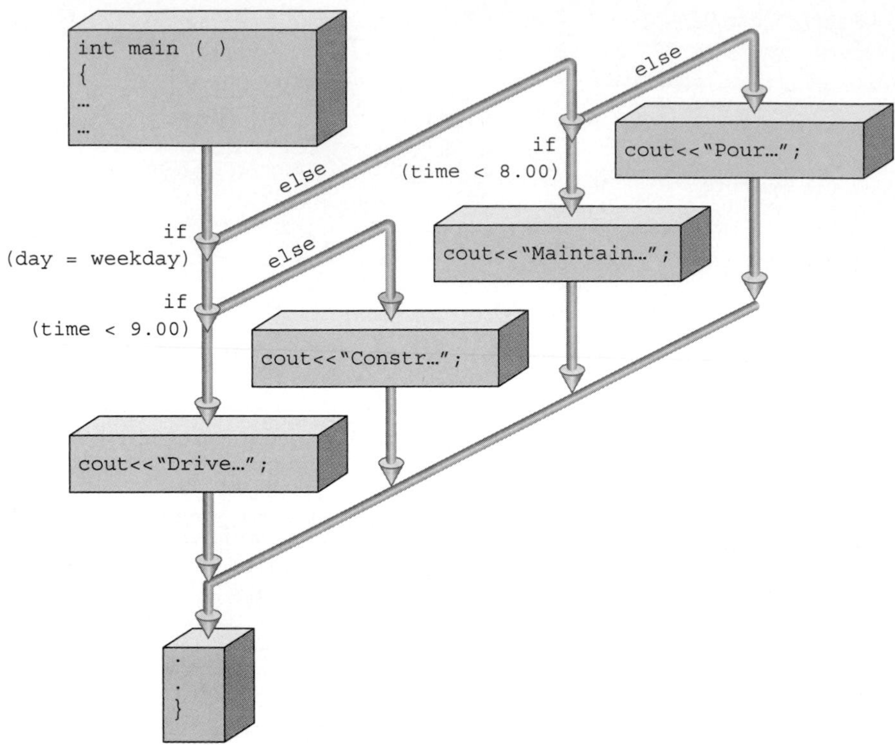

Figure 5.1
Illustration of nested `if-else` control structure for Lesson 5.3's program.

In nested `if-else` statements, the total number of "ifs" can be greater than or equal to, but not less than the total number of "elses." By default, an `else` clause is associated with the closest previous `if` statement that has no other `else` statement. Handdrawn arrows can be used to clarify the pairing of "if" and "else" clauses as shown at the beginning of this lesson's description. The arrows should not cross in properly written nested `if-else` statements. If arrows do cross, you must rewrite your `if` statements so they do not cross.

As `if-else` control structures become nested, the flow of programs becomes more difficult to trace. Making the program more readable can improve the ease at which it can be followed. The traditional way to make a program readable is to use indentation. We recommend that you indent each pair of `if-else` statements so that the inner `else` is paired with the inner `if` and the outer `else` is paired with the outer `if`. An example of this is shown in the indentation of this lesson's program.

LESSON 5.4 LOGICAL OPERATIONS (1)—LOGICAL OPERATORS

TOPICS

- Using logical operators
- Using logical expressions

Logical operators can be used to connect two relational expressions. For example, the following

```
if (x == 0 && y == 0)
```

is read, "If x is equal to 0 *and* y is equal to 0."

Here, the logical operator is `&&` which is read "and." It connects the two relational expressions, `x == 0` and `y == 0`. The other two logical operators in C++ are `||` and `!`. These are used in this lesson's program. Read the source code and follow the flow of the program line by line. This program performs no useful task; it simply illustrates logical operators.

QUESTIONS YOU SHOULD ATTEMPT TO ANSWER

1. What does the `||` operator mean?
2. What does the `!` operator do?

Source Code

```
#include <iostream>
using namespace std;
int main ( )
{
         int x = 5, y = 0;
         cout << "x=" << x << ", y=" << y << endl;

         if (x > 0 && y >= 0)
                  cout << "x is greater than 0 and "
                         "y is greater than or equal to 0" << endl;

         if (x == 0 || y == 0)
                  cout << "x equals 0 or y equals 0" << endl;

         if (! (x == y))
                   cout << "x is not equal to y" << endl;
}
```

x is 5 and y is 0.

Logical expression with *AND* operator.

Logical expression with *OR* operator.

Logical expression with *NOT* operator.

Output

```
x=5, y=0
x is greater than 0 and y is greater than or equal to 0
x equals 0 or y equals 0
x is not equal to y
```

All the `cout` statements are executed.

Description

Logical operators. C++ has three logical operators, `&&`, `||`, and `!`. The `&&` and `||` operators are binary operators because they appear between two relational expression operands. The `!` operator is unary because it precedes a single relational operand. The formal meanings of these operators follow:

Operator	Name	Operation	Operator type
!	Logical NOT	Negation	Unary
&&	Logical AND	Conjunction	Binary
||	Logical OR	Inclusive disjunction	Binary

The logical NOT operator reverses the result of a relational expression. For instance, if x is 5 and y is 0, x is not equal to y, and the expression x == y is false. The logical NOT operator can be used to reverse the false value. Therefore,

```
! (x == y)
```

is true.

The logical AND and logical OR operators perform much the same way the words "and" and "or" were used in your very early mathematics classes. The C++ statement

```
if (x > 0 && y >= 0)
```

is read, "If x is greater than 0 and y is greater than or equal to 0," meaning that the logical expression enclosed in parentheses is true when both x > 0 and y >= 0 are true. On the other hand,

```
if (x == 0 || y == 0)
```

is read, "If x equals 0 or y equals 0." For the logical expression between the parentheses to be true in this case, only one of

```
x == 0     y == 0
```

need be true.

In the table that follows, we have indicated relational expressions with the symbols A and B. You can use this table to determine the result of a logical expression that includes the two relational expressions. For example, suppose again that x is 5 and y is 0. For a relational expression A being x > 0 and a relational expression B being y >= 0, the relational expression A is true, and the relational expression B is true. This means that we use line 1 in the table. Therefore, A && B is equivalent to true && true and the logical result is true. Looking again at line 1, we can determine the logical result of A || B, !A, and !B.

Similarly, for the relational expressions A being x == 0 and B being y == 0, we have A is false and B is true. This leads us to line 3 of the table. Reading across this line, we get A || B being true. We also can look at it as false || true, which results in true.

Finally, consider relational expression A being x == y (which is false) and relational expression B being ! (x == y) (which is equivalent to !(false), which results in true). This also leads us again to line 3 of the table. This line indicates A && B is false. Otherwise, looking at this, A && B is true && false, which is false.

The results of other combinations of relational expressions within logical expressions can be discerned from the table.

A	B	A && B	A || B	!A	!B
true	true	true	true	false	false
true	false	false	true	false	true
false	true	false	true	true	false
false	false	false	false	true	true

One way to remember the table is to realize that for two expressions being operated on,

1. For &&, if one of the relational expressions is false then the result is false.
2. For ||, if one of the relational expressions is true then the result is true.

LESSON 5.5 LOGICAL OPERATIONS (2)—VALUES OF RELATIONAL EXPRESSIONS AND PRECEDENCE OF RELATIONAL AND LOGICAL OPERATORS

TOPICS

- Precedence of logical operators
- Finding the result of a logical expression

QUESTIONS YOU SHOULD ATTEMPT TO ANSWER

1. Without looking at the output, which `cout` statements do you expect will be printed?
2. Looking at the output, which logical operators have the greatest precedence?

To this point, we have not mentioned that C++ gives relational expressions numerical values just as it gives arithmetic expressions numerical values. If a relational expression is false, C++ gives it a value of 0. If it is true, C++ gives it a value of 1 (which you should recognize as being nonzero). The C++ compiler also operates in the reverse manner. If the value of a relational expression is 0, then it knows the result is false; and if the value of a relational expression is not 0, then the result is true.

Something similar can be done with variables. If the value of a variable is 0, then it can be treated as false; and if the value of a variable is not 0, then it can be treated as true. This works this way because (you will recall) that a single variable can be considered to be an expression.

We saw earlier that C++ has an established order of precedence for arithmetic operators. Similarly, C++ has an established order of precedence for relational and logical operators. In this lesson's program, we illustrate the precedence of relational and logical operators. Read and follow the source code and annotations. Use the output to help you determine how the program operates.

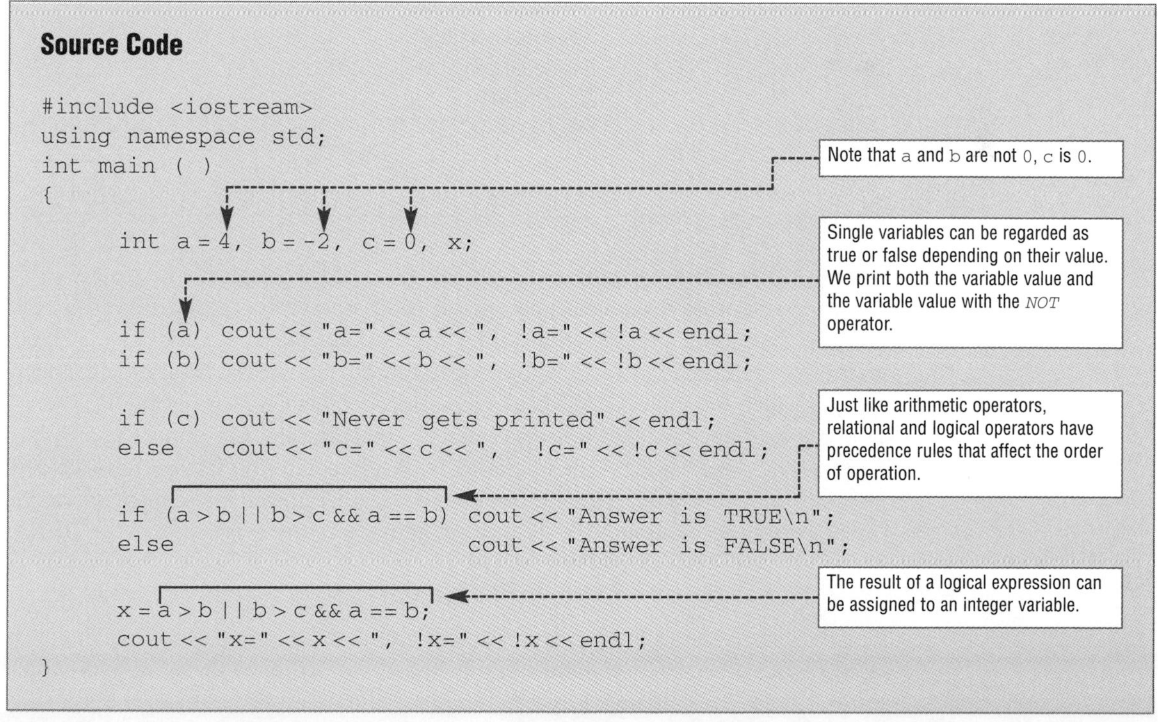

Source Code

```
#include <iostream>
using namespace std;
int main ( )
{
     int a = 4, b = -2, c = 0, x;

     if (a) cout << "a=" << a << ", !a=" << !a << endl;
     if (b) cout << "b=" << b << ", !b=" << !b << endl;

     if (c) cout << "Never gets printed" << endl;
     else   cout << "c=" << c << ",  !c=" << !c << endl;

     if (a > b || b > c && a == b) cout << "Answer is TRUE\n";
     else                          cout << "Answer is FALSE\n";

     x = a > b || b > c && a == b;
     cout << "x=" << x << ", !x=" << !x << endl;
}
```

Note that a and b are not 0, c is 0.
Single variables can be regarded as true or false depending on their value. We print both the variable value and the variable value with the NOT operator.
Just like arithmetic operators, relational and logical operators have precedence rules that affect the order of operation.
The result of a logical expression can be assigned to an integer variable.

Output

```
a=4,  !a=0
b=-2, !b=0
c=0,  !c=1

Answer is TRUE
x=1, !x=0
```

Description

Precedence and associativity of logical, relational, and arithmetic operators. The precedence and associativity of the logical, relational, and arithmetic operators follow:

Operator	Name	Associativity	Precedence
()	Parentheses	L to R	1 (highest)
++, --	Postincrement	L to R	2
++, --	Preincrement	R to L	3
!	Logical NOT	L to R	3
+, -	Positive, negative sign	L to R	3
*, /, %	Multiplication, division	L to R	4
+, -	Addition, subtraction	L to R	5
<=, >=, >, <	Relational operator	L to R	6
==, !=	Relational operator	L to R	7
&&	Logical AND	L to R	8
||	Logical OR	L to R	9
+=, -=, *=, /=, %=	Compound assignment	R to L	10
=	Assignment	R to L	10 (lowest)

This table shows that parentheses have the highest order of precedence, followed by unary increment or decrement and logical NOT operators. In general, arithmetic operators, including multiplication, division, addition, and subtraction, have a higher order of precedence than any relational operator. Then come the binary logical operators, in which the logical AND has higher precedence than the logical OR. The assignment operator has the lowest precedence (meaning the assignment takes place after the other operations). The operators work (associativity) left to right—except the preincrement or predecrement, compound assignment, and assignment operators.

For example, assuming a $= 4$, b $= -2$, and c $= 0$, the expression

```
x = (a > b || b > c && a == b)
```

is equivalent to the following expressions (note that the sequence of evaluation is based on the precedence level of each operator; we add parentheses at appropriate

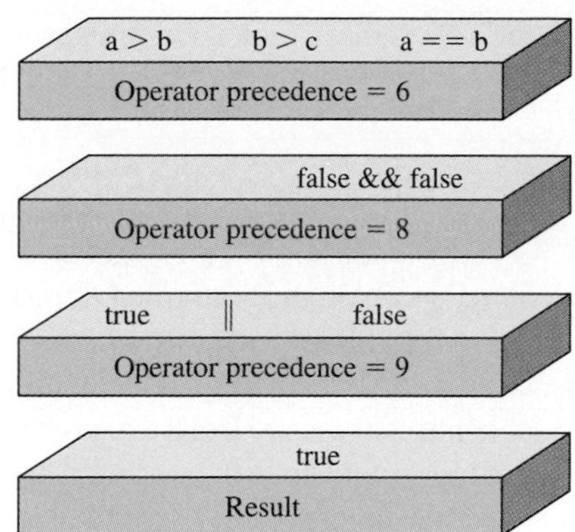

Figure 5.2

Operation of compound logical expression `a > b || b > c && a == b`, from this lesson's program.

locations so that the expression can be grouped and evaluated):

```
x = (a > b || b > c && a == b)
x = ((a > b) || (b > c) && (a == b))
x = ((4 > -2) || (-2 > 0) && (4 == -2))
x = (TRUE || FALSE && FALSE)
x = (TRUE || FALSE)
x = (TRUE)
```

which results in true. The value of `x` becomes 1 (true). If `x` is true, `!x` is false, and `!x` is printed as 0 in this lesson's program.

The effect of the different precedences of the relational and logical operators on the relational expressions in this lesson's program is illustrated in Fig. 5.2.

Although not shown in this lesson's program, a relational expression of the sort $a > b == c$ is evaluated from left to right since all the operators have equal precedence. For instance, if `a` $= 4$, `b` $= -2$, and `c` $= 5$, this expression evaluates to false. The steps in evaluation are

`a > b` is true, giving this expression a value of 1
`1 == c` is false.

Logical value of a single variable. The logical value of a single variable is false if the variable has a value of 0 and true if the value is nonzero. This is illustrated in Fig. 5.3a. For example, in this lesson, the logical value of `c` is false, since `c` is equal to 0, but the logical values of `a` and `b` are true, since `a` (which is 4) and `b` (which

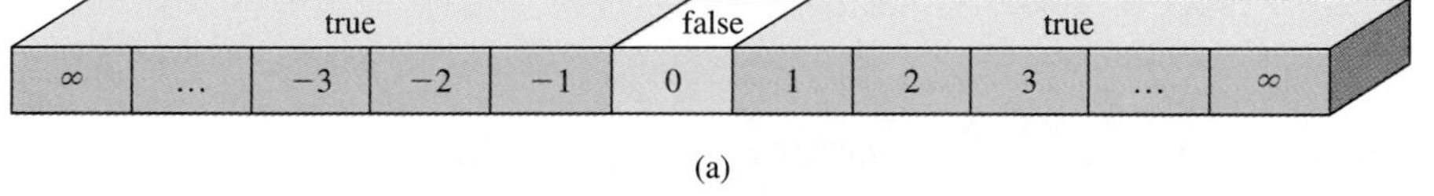

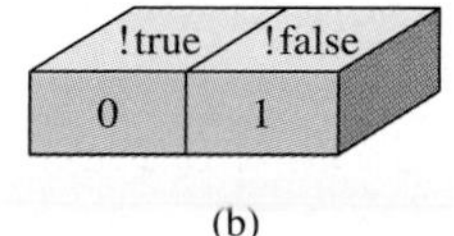

Figure 5.3

(a) True or false result of integer values. (b) Integer values for `!true` and `!false`.

is −2) are nonzero. Also, the values of `!a` and `!b` are false and therefore printed out as 0, whereas the value of `!c` is printed out as 1. This is shown in Fig. 5.3b.

LESSON 5.6 if-else-if AND switch CONTROL STRUCTURES

TOPICS

- Using `if-else-if` control structures
- Using `switch` statements
- Comparing `if-else-if` and `switch` control structures

QUESTION YOU SHOULD ATTEMPT TO ANSWER

1. If `option` is typed in to be 2, which statements are executed (without looking at the output)?

The `if-else` control structure executes one of two statement blocks. Frequently in programming, though, we want to execute one of a number (three, four, or more) of statement blocks. This is usually most conveniently done with an `if-else-if` or a `switch` control structure. Both these structures contain multiple statement blocks and have the feature that when one of the blocks is executed, the others are bypassed.

Two source codes are given for this lesson. They perform the same tasks but in different ways. The first source code uses an `if-else-if` control structure, and the second source code uses a `switch` control structure. Read and follow the flow of both codes using the output as a guide.

Source Code 1

```
#include <iostream>
using namespace std;
int main ( )
{
  int option;

    cout << "Please type 1, 2, or 3\n"
    cin >> option ;

   if (option == 1)
             {
             cout << "Attend meeting\n";
             }
   else if (option == 2)
             {
             cout << "Debug program\n";
             }
   else if (option == 3)
             {
             cout << "Write documentation\n";
             }
   else
             {
             cout << "Do nothing\n";
             }
}
```

The value of `option` is read from the keyboard.

`if-else-if` control structure. Only one of the statement blocks (enclosed in braces) is executed.

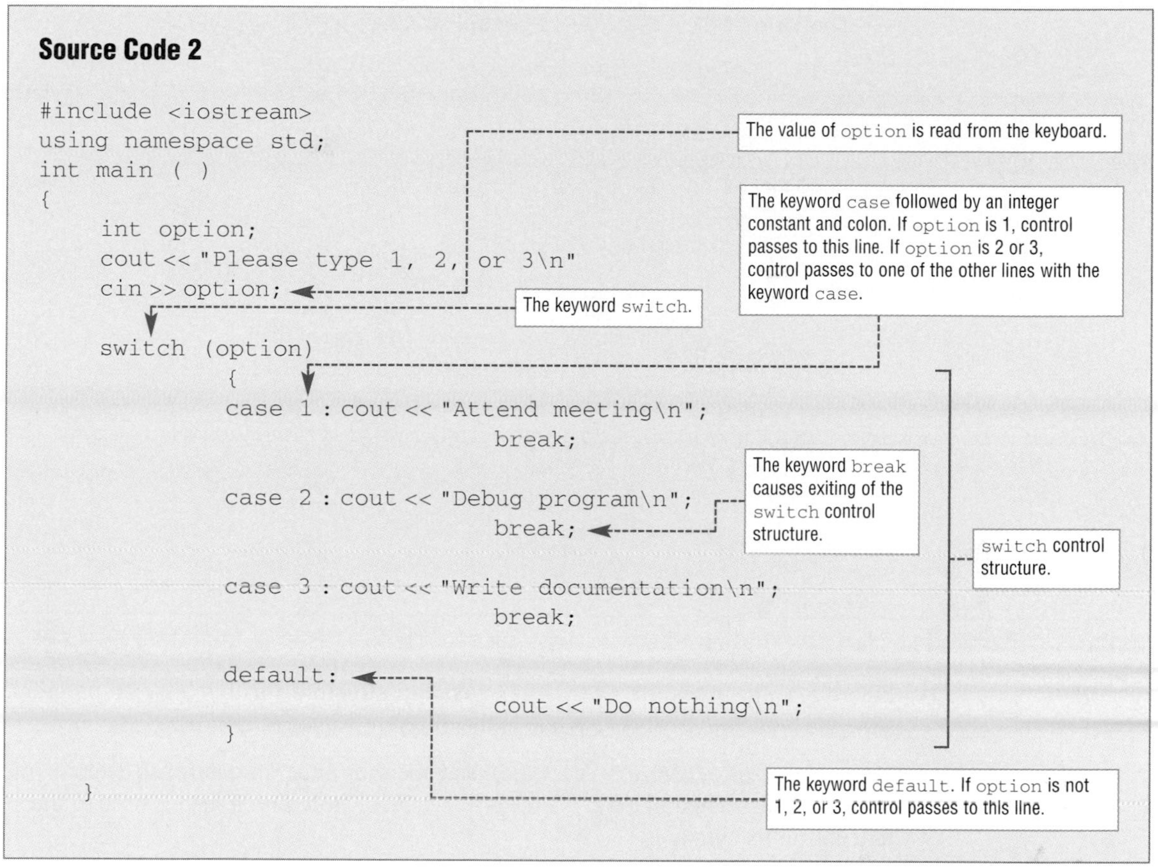

The value of option is read from the keyboard.
The keyword case followed by an integer constant and colon. If option is 1, control passes to this line. If option is 2 or 3, control passes to one of the other lines with the keyword case.
The keyword switch.
The keyword break causes exiting of the switch control structure.
switch control structure.
The keyword default. If option is not 1, 2, or 3, control passes to this line.

Source Code 2

```
#include <iostream>
using namespace std;
int main ( )
{
     int option;
     cout << "Please type 1, 2, or 3\n"
     cin >> option;

     switch (option)
             {
             case 1 : cout << "Attend meeting\n";
                             break;

             case 2 : cout << "Debug program\n";
                             break;

             case 3 : cout << "Write documentation\n";
                             break;

             default:
                             cout << "Do nothing\n";
             }
   }
```

Output from Both Source Codes

```
                   Please type 1, 2, or 3
Keyboard input     2
                   Debug program
```

Description

***if-else-if* control structure.** An if-else-if control structure shifts program control, step by step, through a series of statement blocks. Control stops at the relational expression that is true and executes the corresponding statement block. After execution of that statement block, control shifts to the end of the control structure. If none of the relational expressions is true, the final statement block is executed. In this lesson's program the value of option was read in to be 2, so the first statement block was not executed. Because the relational expression option == 2 was true, the second statement block was executed. The third and fourth statement blocks were bypassed, and control transferred to the end of the control structure.

The form of the `if-else-if` control structure is

```
if (relational_expression_1)
      {
      statement_block_1
      }
else if (relational_expression_2)
      {
      statement_block_2
      }
.
.
.
.
.
else if (relational_expression_n-1)
         {
         statement_block_n-1
         }
else
         {
         statement_block n
         }
```

Figure 5.4 illustrates the `if-else-if` control structure for this lesson's program. Note the branching that occurs due to the different values of `option`.

`switch` control structure. A `switch` statement or `switch` control structure commonly is constructed like the `if-else-if` control structure. It also is used to transfer control. Its syntax is

```
switch (expression)
       {
       case constant1:
          statement1a
          statement1b
          ...
       case constant2:
          statement2a
          statement2b
          ...
          ...
       default:
          statements
       }
```

where the *`expression`* must be enclosed in a pair of parentheses and must result in an integer type value when the program flow enters the `switch` block. A `switch` block must be bounded by a pair of braces. The terms *`constant1`*, *`constant2`*, and so on are integer type constant expressions. Note that all constant expressions are followed by colons. All the constant expressions must be unique, meaning that none can have the same value as another constant expression. Although not required, it is

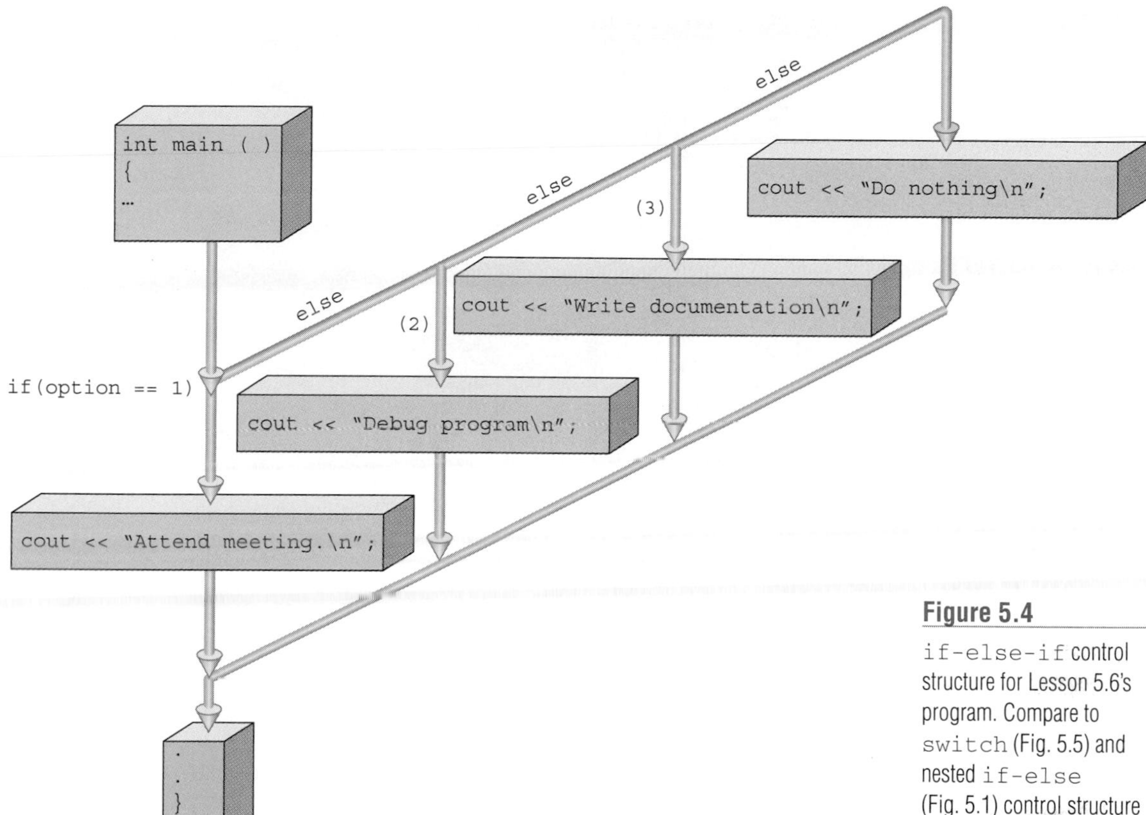

Figure 5.4

if-else-if control structure for Lesson 5.6's program. Compare to switch (Fig. 5.5) and nested if-else (Fig. 5.1) control structure illustrations.

common that the last case type line is the keyword default. If no constant matches the value of the *expression*, the statements in the default case are executed. The default case is optional. If no default case is given and no constant expression matches the *expression* value, the entire switch block is ignored.

Figure 5.5 shows the switch control structure for this lesson's program. Compare this figure to Figs. 5.1 and 5.4. Note the similarities between the if-else-if, nested if-else, and switch control structures. In all the cases illustrated, the control structure has chosen a single block of code to execute and bypassed the others.

The keyword case can be used only in a switch control structure. It is used to form a label called a case label. A case label is a constant followed by a colon. The label does not affect the execution of the statement that follows it. In switch control structures, C++ looks for a match between the switch expression and the expression in a case label. C++ then executes the statement sequence following the matching case label. For instance, for the form shown previously, if the value of the switch expression matches *constant1*, then the program flow is transferred to case *constant1* and *statement1a*, *statement1b*, and so forth are executed. Because the switch control structure can search only for equality, it differs from the if-else-if control structure, which can use other relational operators.

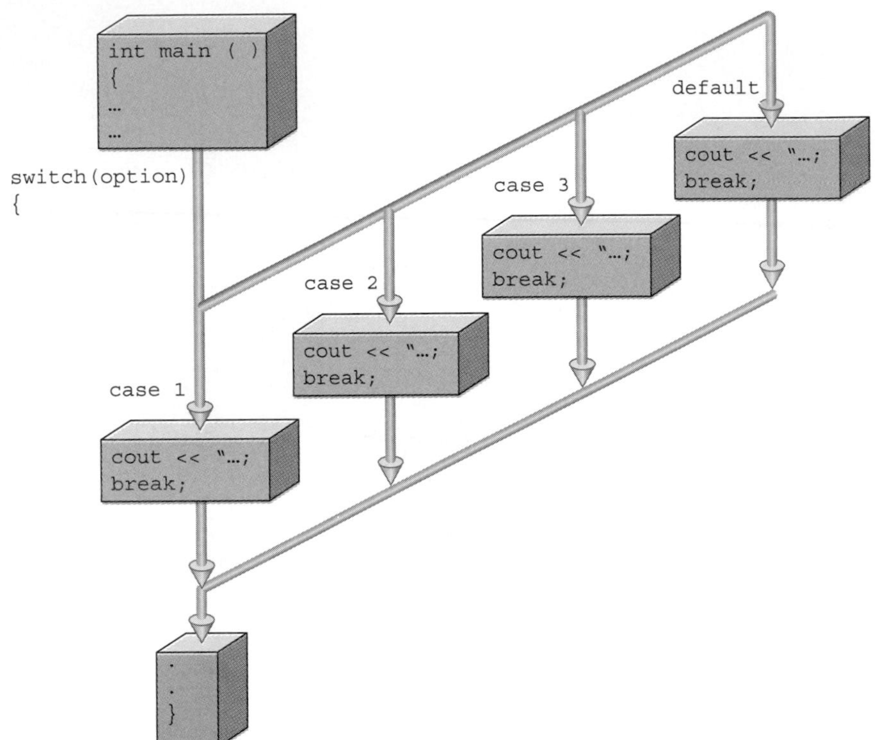

Figure 5.5
switch control structure for Lesson 5.6's program. Note the importance of the break statement in controlling program flow for the switch control structure. Compare to if-else-if (Fig. 5.4) and nested if-else (Fig. 5.1) control structure illustrations.

A break statement in a switch control structure terminates execution of the smallest enclosing switch statement. The keyword break terminates (which means to send control to the point of the closing brace) the switch structure. We will see that break statements have other uses, which operate similarly in that they cause control to pass to a closing brace.

Often the last statement for each case is the break statement because it terminates the process and exits switch. If no break statement is used, then the statements in the next case are executed. For example, in the following code,

```
switch (option)
{
 case (1): cout << "Entering case 1\n";
           break;
 case (2): cout << "Entering case 2\n";

 case (3): cout << "Entering case 3\n";
           break;
}
```

if option is 1, then "Entering case 1" will be displayed on the screen. If option is 3, "Entering case 3" will be displayed. However, if option is 2, both "Entering case 2" and "Entering case 3" will be displayed because C++ first finds a match between the switch expression and a case label. Execution then continues, line by line, until a break or the end of the block (indicated by a closing brace) is encountered. This is because a statement label has no effect on the statement

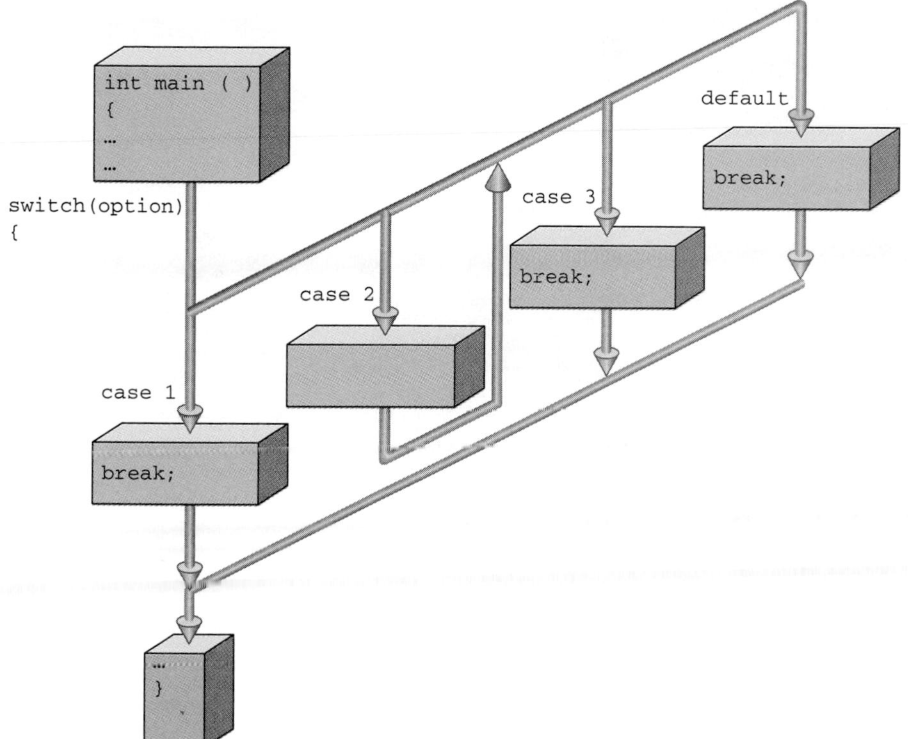

Figure 5.6

Flow of program control for the switch control structure of Lesson 5.6's program if no break statement were given for the case 2 block. Observe that the break statement causes control to exit the switch structure. With no break statement, control passes directly to the next block.

that follows it. A case statement label serves only as a marker to which control can be sent. The program flow when a break statement is missing is shown in Fig. 5.6.

The keyword default is a special label used only for switch control structures. In the event that none of the case label constants agrees with the switch expression, control passes to the default labeled statement sequence. Because the label default is a keyword, it is not considered to be a user-defined label.

Nested switch control structures. We can nest switch control structures. A nested switch control structure could take the following form:

```
switch (outer_expression)
        {
         case constant_outer1:
                  switch (inner_expression)
                         {
                         case constant_inner1:
                                  statement inner_1a
                                  statement inner_1b
                                  ..
                                  ..
                         case constant_inner2:
                                  statement inner_2a
                                  statement inner_2b
                                  ..
                                  ..
                         }
```

Figure 5.7

Nested `switch` control structure with `break` statements.

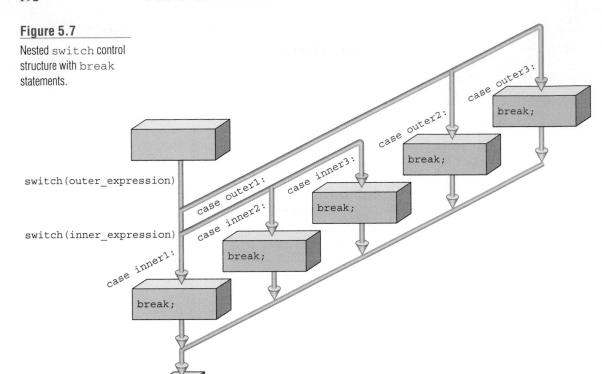

```
case constant_outer2:
          statement outer_2a
          statement outer_2b
          ..
          ..
case constant_outer3:
          statement outer_3a
          statement outer_3b
          ..
          ..
}
```

An illustration of a nested `switch` structure is given in Fig. 5.7.

LESSON 5.7 THE `bool` DATA TYPE

TOPICS

- Using the `bool` data type
- Input and output for `bool` data

C++ supports another data type that we have not yet discussed—the `bool` data type, named after mathematician George Boole who worked in the area of logic. Unlike an `int` variable that can hold any integer value (within memory limits), a variable declared to be `bool` can contain one of only two values which are most conveniently regarded as 0 or 1. The 0 or 1 value of a bool variable can be interpreted to mean false or true, fail or pass, off or on, or any two states we are interested in. This type of representation can be useful for storing such information as the results of material testing among other things. For instance, if a steel piece has met the requirements for use in a machine a bool variable can be used to represent pass/fail for the test results.

In this lesson's program, we illustrate how bool variables can help represent water quality. In this case, we want to indicate whether the water is salty, hard, acidic, has a good taste, and whether the user receives home service for this water. A bool type variable is useful because there are only two states for each of these. In other words, we classify the water as being salty or not salty, hard or not hard, acidic or not acidic, having a good taste or not a good taste, and a user receives the water or does not receive it. In the program, we create bool variables salty, hard, acidic, good_taste, and have_service. For instance, if we set the value of hard to be 0 (meaning false) then the water is not hard; if we set hard to 1 (meaning true) then the water is hard.

For the variables salty, hard, and acidic there are scientific tests that determine which state the water is in. If the sodium level is greater than 4000 mg/l, the water can be considered salty. If the calcium is greater than 40 mg/l and the magnesium is greater than 20 mg/l, the water can be considered hard. If the pH is less than 7, the water is acidic. As a result, we have double type variables in the program that represent the sodium, calcium, magnesium, and pH levels of the water. By checking the values of these variables, we can determine in which state each of the bool variables should be. This means we can assign the result of a relational expression to a bool type variable, and the bool variable indicates the state. Read the program to see how we do this.

QUESTIONS YOU SHOULD ATTEMPT TO ANSWER

1. The bool variable good_taste is input as 1. What is the printed value?
2. Why is good_taste not printed as 1?

Source Code

```
#include <iostream>
#include <fstream>
#include <iomanip>
using namespace std;
int main ( )
{
     bool salty, hard, acidic, good_taste, have_service;
     double sodium, Ca, Mg, pH;

     ifstream infile("C:\\water.dat");
     infile >> sodium >> Ca >> Mg >> pH;

     salty = (sodium > 4000);
     hard = (Ca > 40 && Mg > 20);
     acidic = (pH < 7);
```

Five bool type variables that represent water characteristics.

These double variables represent numerical values of quantities representing water chemistry.

The numerical values are read from a data file.

The logical expressions on the right side are evaluated to be true or false. The results are assigned to the bool variables. A true result assigns 1 to the bool variable and a false result assigns 0.

```
    cout << "Water composition"
         << "  salty " << salty << "  hard " << hard << "  acidic " << acidic;

    cout << boolalpha << "Water composition"
         << "  salty " << salty << "  hard "
         << hard << "  acidic " << acidic;

    cout << "You believe that this water tastes good "
            "(Enter zero for no or nonzero for yes);
         << endl << cin >> good_taste;

    cout << "Service of this water is provided to "
            "your home (enter true or false);
         << endl << cin >> boolalpha >> have_service;

    cout << boolalpha << "tastes good - " << good_taste
         << "have service - " << have_service;
}
```

The bool values are printed as 0 or 1 using cout without manipulation.

The bool values are printed as true or false using the boolalpha manipulator.

The user is prompted to enter zero or nonzero to indicate the water's taste.

The user is prompted to enter true or false to indicate whether they have service because the boolalpha manipulator is used with cin.

The boolalpha manipulator is used to print the keyboard entered values.

Input File

```
3500 60 50 7.3
```

Sodium, Ca, Mg, and pH.

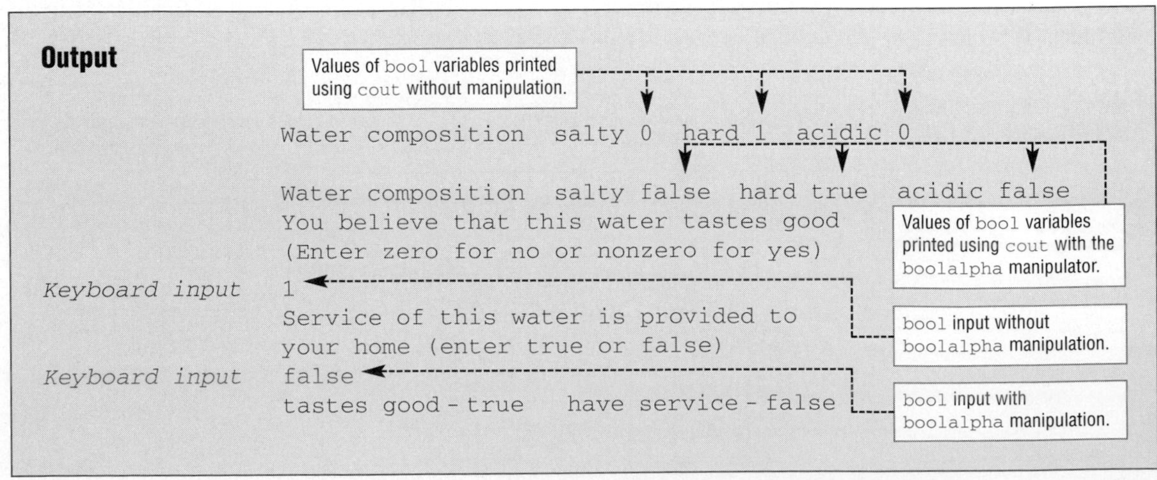
Output
Values of bool variables printed using cout without manipulation.
Water composition salty 0 hard 1 acidic 0
Water composition salty false hard true acidic false
You believe that this water tastes good
(Enter zero for no or nonzero for yes)
Keyboard input 1
Service of this water is provided to
your home (enter true or false)
Keyboard input false
tastes good - true have service - false
Values of bool variables printed using cout with the boolalpha manipulator.
bool input without boolalpha manipulation.
bool input with boolalpha manipulation.

Description

bool data type. The bool data type is a C++ data type that can be used to represent quantities that can have one of two states. To declare variables to be type bool, we use the keyword bool followed by a comma separated list of variable names in a manner similar to declaring int or double variables. For instance, to declare the variables salty, hard, and acidic to be bool, the following declaration is used:

```
bool salty, hard, acidic;
```

The states of a bool variable are most conveniently thought of as being 1 or 0, where 1 is equivalent to true and 0 is equivalent to false. Commonly, bool type variables occupy one byte of memory.

Uses for bool variables.

- As we showed in this lesson's program, bool variables can represent characteristics of materials. We have declared bool variables salty, hard, acidic, and good_taste to represent characteristics of water. Two states are appropriate for each of these variables because the water can be thought to be salty or not salty, hard or soft, acidic or basic, good tasting or bad tasting. This means that the variables are ideally suited to being bool type.
- The current status of events can be represented with bool type variables when a state can be considered to be either existent or not existent. For instance, in this lesson's program, we have used the bool variable have_service. Having service is an event that either exists or not. When this variable has a value of true, the user has service. When it is false, the user does not have service. Other events that either exist or not, such as a switch being on or off, can also be represented by bool variables.
- In general, bool variables can be used for any quantity that can be described by one of two states.

Assigning values to bool variables.

- One way to assign a value to a bool variable is to write a logical expression on the right side of an assignment statement. For instance, in this lesson's program we used:

  ```
  salty = (sodium > 4000);
  hard = (Ca > 40 && Mg > 20);
  acidic = (pH < 7);
  ```

  In each case, if the logical expression is true, the value 1 is assigned to the bool variable. On the other hand, if the logical expression is false, the value 0 is assigned to the bool variable. This is illustrated in Fig. 5.8.
- We can also assign integer values to bool variables. Although not shown in this lesson's program, we could have used the assignment statements:

  `good_taste = 15;` (the nonzero value, 15, indicates true and causes the value 1 to be assigned to good_taste)

Figure 5.8

Assigning values to bool variables.

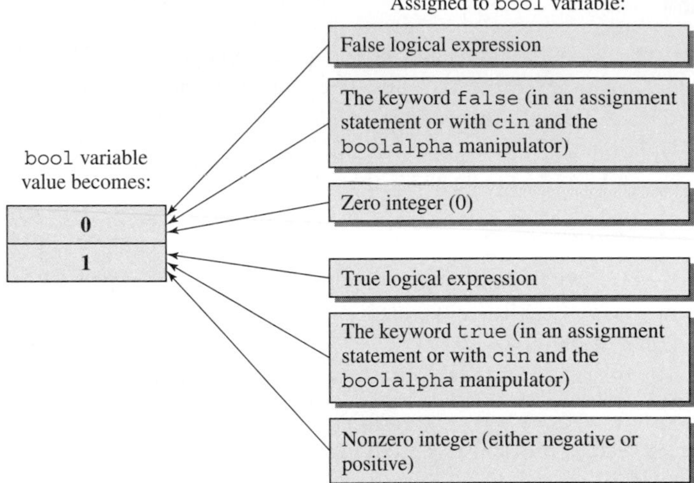

or

good_taste = 0; (the zero value indicates false)

In the first of these, a nonzero integer has been assigned to a bool variable, which is equivalent to assigning a true logical expression. Any nonzero integer (negative or positive) produces the result of assigning a value of 1 to the bool variable even if the nonzero integer is not 1! In the second of these, zero has been assigned to a bool variable, which is equivalent to assigning a false logical expression. Only zero assigns a value of 0 to a bool variable.

In addition to using assignment statements to accomplish this, we can use cin statements as we have done in this lesson's program with

```
cin >> good_taste;
```

The user in our example entered the integer 1 (although any nonzero value would have been equivalent) for the value of good_taste. Again, this is the same as assigning a true logical expression to the good_taste variable. Had the user entered 0, it would have been the same as assigning a false logical expression to the variable good_taste. This is also illustrated in Fig. 5.8.

- We can also assign the keywords true or false to bool variables. Although not shown in this lesson's program, we could have used the assignment statement:

```
good_taste = true;
```

or

```
good_taste = false;
```

Similarly a user can enter the words true or false in response to a cin statement as we did in this lesson's program in response to

```
cin >> boolalpha >> have_service;
```

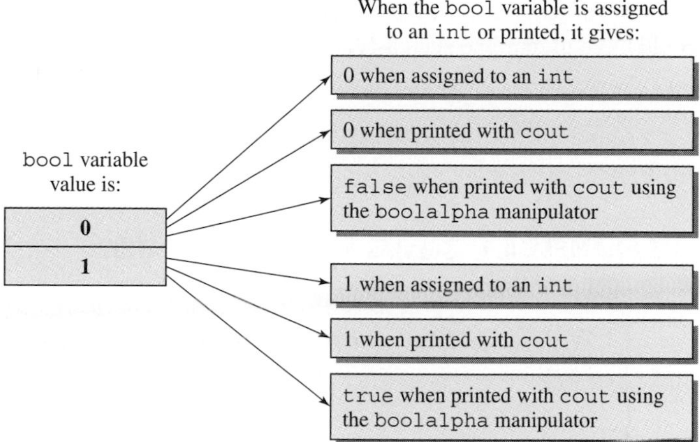

Figure 5.9

Assigning bool variable values to int types or printing bool variables.

to assign a value to the variable have_service. Note that the boolalpha manipulator is needed for C++ to properly interpret the true or false word input as shown in Fig. 5.8.

Assigning bools to int variables. We could have used in this lesson's program code of the sort:

```
int i;
i = salty;
```

after the variable salty had been initialized. Because salty is false (sodium < 4000) it has a value of 0. The int variable i then gets the value 0. Had salty been true, i would have been given a value of 1. This is illustrated in Fig. 5.9.

Printing the values of bool variables. In using cout to print bool variable values, we can choose to use the boolalpha manipulator or not. If we do not use boolalpha, bool variable values are printed as 1 (for true) or 0 (for false). For instance,

```
cout << "Water composition"
     << "   salty " << salty << "   hard " << hard << "   acidic "
     << acidic;
```

prints the line

```
Water composition   salty 0   hard 1   acidic 0
```

If we use the boolalpha manipulator, the values are printed as "true" or "false." For instance,

```
cout << boolalpha << "Water composition"
     << "   salty " << salty << "   hard " << hard << "   acidic "
     << acidic;
```

prints the line

```
Water composition  salty false  hard true  acidic false
```

These are illustrated in Fig. 5.9.

Using `bool` variables with `if` statements. Although not shown in this lesson's program, we could have used a line such as:

```
if (salty) cout << "The water is salty";
```

The output is printed only if the `bool` variable `salty` is 1 (true). This is another common way to use `bool` variables.

APPLICATION EXAMPLE 5.1 SOLVING A QUADRATIC EQUATION

TOPICS

- `if-else` control structure
- Numerical method example

Problem Statement

Write a computer program capable of solving the quadratic equation

$$ax^2 + bx + c = 0$$

The input data is to consist of the values of *a*, *b*, and *c* and is to come from the keyboard. The output is to consist of the values of *x* and go to the screen.

Solution

RELEVANT EQUATIONS

The quadratic equation has two solutions:

$$x_1 = \frac{-b + \sqrt{b^2 - 4ac}}{2a} \tag{5.1}$$

and

$$x_2 = \frac{-b - \sqrt{b^2 - 4ac}}{2a} \tag{5.2}$$

Having been assigned to write a computer program, you must do a thorough and correct job. Consider all the possibilities. In the case of the quadratic equation, no real solution may exist, and your computer program must account for this possibility. If $b^2 - 4ac$ is positive, then Eqns. 5.1 and 5.2 can be used directly to find the solutions x_1 and x_2. However, if $b^2 - 4ac$ is negative, the solutions become:

$$x_1 = -\frac{b}{2a} + \frac{\sqrt{-(b^2 - 4ac)}}{2a} i \tag{5.3}$$

and

$$x_2 = -\frac{b}{2a} - \frac{\sqrt{-(b^2 - 4ac)}}{2a} i \tag{5.4}$$

where $i = \sqrt{-1}$

SPECIFIC EXAMPLE

Consider the following equation:

2x² + 8x + 3 = 0

For this case

```
a = 2
b = 8
c = 3
```

and $b^2 - 4ac = 40$, which is positive. The two solutions are:

$$x_1 = \frac{-8 + \sqrt{8^2 - 4(2)(3)}}{2(2)} = -0.41886$$

and

$$x_2 = \frac{-8 - \sqrt{8^2 - 4(2)(3)}}{2(2)} = -3.58114$$

Consider also the equation:

```
15x² - 2x + 3 = 0
```

For this case

```
a = 15
b = -2
c = 3
```

and $b^2 - 4ac = -176$, which is negative. The two solutions from Eqns. 5.3 and 5.4 are:

$$x_1 = \frac{-(-2)}{2(15)} + \frac{\sqrt{-((-2)^2 - 4(15)(3))}}{2(15)}i = -0.06667 + 0.44222i$$

and

$$x_2 = \frac{-(-2)}{2(15)} - \frac{\sqrt{-((-2)^2 - 4(15)(3))}}{2(15)}i = -0.06667 - 0.44222i$$

Just like your calculator, the computer indicates an error and stops executing when it tries to take the square root of a negative number. For this program to execute properly, it should calculate the real and imaginary parts (in this example the real part is −0.06667 and the imaginary part is 0.44222) separately. To calculate the imaginary part, it is necessary to reverse the negative number under the square root to a positive one and then take the square root.

ALGORITHM

Equations 5.1 through 5.4 have been written such that only a single variable appears on the left-hand side of the equations. This form is useful because it fits the form of assignment statements in C++ code. As you write equations for programs, you should get your equations into this form so that you can easily write the source code.

The algorithm (including equations) and a check for taking the square roots of negative numbers is given below.

1. Read the values of *a*, *b*, and *c* from the keyboard.
2. Compute the value of $b^2 - 4ac$.
3. If $b^2 - 4ac$ is positive then

$$x_1 = \frac{-b + \sqrt{b^2 - 4ac}}{2a}$$

and

$$x_2 = \frac{-b - \sqrt{b^2 - 4ac}}{2a}$$

4. Print x_1 and x_2 to the screen.
5. If $b^2 - 4ac$ is negative then the real part is

$$\text{real} = -\frac{b}{2a}$$

and

$$\text{imaginary} = \frac{\sqrt{-(b^2 - 4ac)}}{2a}$$

6. Print the real and imaginary parts in the form real + imaginary * i and real – imaginary * i.

Source Code

The source code below has been written from the preceding algorithm.

```
#include <cmath>
#include <iostream>
using namespace std;
int main ( )
{
    double i, a, b, c, x1, x2, test, real, imag;

    cout << "Enter the values of a, b, and c (each separated\n"
          "by a space) then press return\n";

    cin >> a >> b >> c;

    test = b * b - 4 * a * c;

    if (test >= 0)
             {
             x1 = (-b + sqrt(test)) / (2 * a);
             x2 = (-b - sqrt(test)) / (2 * a);
             cout << "Real result:\n x1=" << x1 << "\n x2=" << x2 << "\n\n";
             }

    else

             {
             real = -b / (2 * a);
             imag = sqrt(-test) / (2 * a);
             cout << "Imaginary result:\ n"
                   "x1=" << real << "+" << imag << "i\nx2=" << real
                        << -imag << "i\n";
             }
}
```

Calculating the test value.

Calculating the two values of *x* if the test value is greater than zero.

Calculating real and imaginary values if test is less than zero.

Output

```
                    Enter the values of a, b, and c (each separated
                    by a space) then press return
Keyboard input      15 -2 3
                    Imaginary result:
                       x1=    0.06667 +    0.44222 i
                       x2=    0.06667 -    0.44222 i
```

Comments

One can see that the quadratic equation itself never appears in the source code, only the solution to the quadratic equation. In general, you will need to solve your equation or equations before you can begin writing your algorithm or source code. This is considered part of the programming process and is integral to developing a reliable, efficient program. If you solve your equations incorrectly, then your program will give incorrect results even though it is capable of executing without terminating abnormally.

Your program also must be able to handle all possibilities. In this program it was necessary to handle cases where the result is imaginary. Your responsibility as a programmer is to envision all the possibilities and write a program to handle them.

Note that the variable `test` was used in the source code. This variable was used only for convenience and to simplify the look of the program. It was not necessary for this variable to be used. However, we recommend that you also use variables for convenience and to simplify the look of your programs.

Note also that the directive `#include <cmath>` is necessary for this program because the function `sqrt` is used.

Modification Exercises

Modify the program to

1. Handle the input of five different equations. Have the user type in five lines when prompted. Each line should contain three coefficients.
2. Read the input from a data file.
3. Read five equations from a data file and print the results to a data file.

APPLICATION EXAMPLE 5.2 LOAD-DEFORMATION OF STRUCTURAL MEMBER

TOPICS

- `switch` and `if-else-if` control structures
- Compound relational expressions
- Representing an *x-y* relationship

Problem Statement

Mathematically modeling curves or relationships in *x-y* space is commonly done in programming. The load-deformation of a structural member can be represented roughly with a discontinuous curve (as shown in the Fig. 5.10). This curve illustrates that

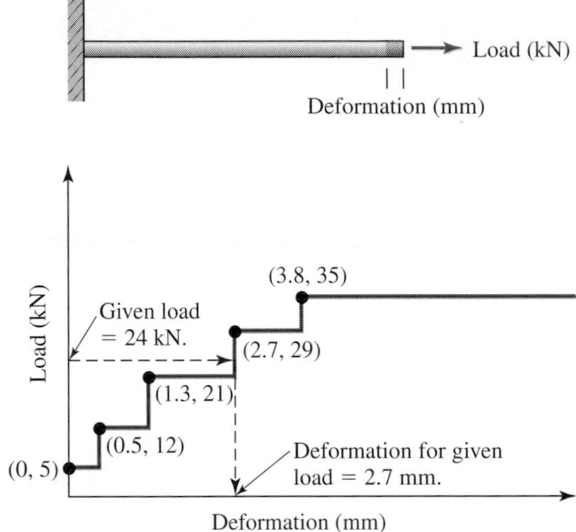

Figure 5.10

The x-y relationship of load vs deformation. Here, this relationship is discontinous.

as the tensile load on a structural member increases, the deformation (stretching) increases. Write a program that can model this curve. Read the x-y coordinates of the five points (shown as dark dots in the figure) that describe the curve from the file LOADDEF.DAT. Ask a user to input a load from the keyboard. Compute the corresponding deformation and print it to the screen. Assume that the user's input data does not land on a point of discontinuity.

Solution

RELEVANT EQUATIONS

The data points can be represented by the variables (shown for the values in Fig. 5.10)

`def1` = 0	`load1` = 5	`load_range` = 1
`def2` = 0.5	`load2` = 12	`load_range` = 2
`def3` = 1.3	`load3` = 21	`load_range` = 3
`def4` = 2.7	`load4` = 29	`load_range` = 4
`def5` = 3.8	`load5` = 35	`load_range` = 5

According to the figure, if the input load is less than `load1`, the deformation is `def1` (which must be 0). If the input load is between `load1` and `load2`, the deformation is `def2`. If the input load is between `load2` and `load3`, the deformation is `def3`. Extending this pattern to the rest of the loads, we can determine the deformation for any given load less than `load5`. If the load is greater than `load5`, the member fails and the deformation is very large.

SPECIFIC EXAMPLE

With the given data points, consider an input load of 24 kN. This value is between `load3` and `load4`, which means the deformation is `def4`. This is 2.7 mm.

ALGORITHM

Determining the correct load range is the key to solving the problem. The steps are:

1. Read the data file
2. Prompt for and read keyboard input of load
3. Determine the load range
4. Print the deformation to the screen

SOURCE CODE

We have written the source code for this example twice. Source code 1 has `if` statements with compound relational expressions and a `switch` statement. Source code 2 illustrates the use of `if-else-if` control structures. Read the codes; compare and contrast them.

Source Code 1

```
#include <iostream>
#include <fstream>
using namespace std;
int main ( )
{
   int load_range;
   double load, deformation;
   double def1, def2, def3, def4, def5;
   double load1, load2, load3, load4, load5;
   ifstream infile("C:\\LOADDEF.DAT");

   infile >> def1 >> load1 >> def2 >> load2 >> def3
         >> load3 >> def4 >> load4 >> def5 >> load5;

   cout << "Enter the load applied to the structural "
          "member:\n";
   cin >> load;

   if (load < load1) load_range = 1;
   if (load1 < load && load < load2) load_range = 2;
   if (load2 < load && load < load3) load_range = 3;
   if (load3 < load && load < load4) load_range = 4;
   if (load4 < load && load < load5) load_range = 5;
   if (load > load5) load_range = 6;

   switch (load_range)
```

Reading the data file to assign values that match those shown in Fig. 5.10.

Reading the load entered by the user.

Series of `if` statements to define the load range.

```
  {
  case 1: deformation = def1;
          break;
  case 2: deformation = def2;
          break;
  case 3: deformation = def3;
          break;
  case 4: deformation = def4;
          break;
  case 5: deformation = def5;
          break;
  case 6: deformation = 1000.;
          break;
  default:break;
  }

cout << "The deformation is  " << deformation << endl;

}
```

The `switch` structure is used to determine the deformation.

Source Code 2

```
#include <iostream>
#include <fstream>
using namespace std;
int main ( )
{
   double load, deformation;
   double def1, def2, def3, def4, def5;
   double load1, load2, load3, load4, load5;
   ifstream infile("C:\\LOADDEF.DAT");

   infile >> def1 >> load1 >> def2 >> load2 >> def3 >> load3 >> def4 >> load4
        >> def5 >> load5;

   cout << "Enter the load applied to the structural member:\n";
   cin >> load;

   if (load < load1) deformation = def1;
   else if (load1 < load && load < load2) deformation = def2;
   else if (load2 < load && load < load3) deformation = def3;
   else if (load3 < load && load < load4) deformation = def4;
   else if (load4 < load && load < load5) deformation = def5;
   else if (load > load5) deformation = 1000.;

   cout << "The deformation is " << deformation << " mm." << endl;

}
```

`if-else-if` structure to define the load range and calculate the deformation.

Output

```
                    Enter the load applied to the structural member:
Keyboard input      24
                    The deformation is 2.7 mm.
```

Comments

The first source code is somewhat less efficient than the second because it involves more comparisons in the decision-making process. One way to assess the efficiencies of algorithms and code is to look at the number of comparisons. An algorithm that performs the same task with fewer comparisons often is more efficient.

Note that the compound relational expressions within the `if` statements in this program have been written with a form that corresponds to the typical mathematical form. For instance, to express that the variable load is between load2 and load3 the mathematical form is

```
load2 < load < load3
```

and an equivalent C++ relational expression is

```
(load2 < load && load < load3)
```

This is not the only form that will work in C++; however, we recommend this form because it corresponds to the mathematical form.

With this program, we have effectively modeled a discontinuous curve with decision-making control structures. If we use more data points in a figure similar to Fig. 5.10, then we can make the load deformation relationship appear smoother and therefore more like a continuous curve. It is common when using measured data to be confronted with the question of how many data points to use in a computer analysis. In general, more data points are better, but using millions of points, for instance, may increase memory usage and slow execution time. You may need to choose a number of data points that balances the reliability of the curve and the needed program performance.

Modification Exercises

Modify the programs to

1. Put a cap on the total amount of deformation to be 3 mm. Run the program with the same input file and a load of 30 kN to check your result.
2. Have the program accept three loads from the keyboard, and print the deformation for each.
3. Have the program read 10 loads from a file, and print the results to the screen for all 10 loads in the form of a table with two headings: Load and Deformation.

APPLICATION EXAMPLE 5.3 SCHEDULING A MEETING

TOPICS

- `if-else-if` control structures
- Compound relational expressions
- File input
- Finding max and min of 2

Problem Statement

Write a program that can assist you in scheduling a meeting of the four members of your project group. Have each member enter his or her available morning and afternoon times in 24-hour decimal notation (that is, 8:30 AM is represented by 8.5 and 3:30 PM is represented by 15.5) into an input file. Make the program determine the range of time that all members have free in both the morning and afternoon. Allow the user to specify a preference for selecting the longest meeting time, the morning meeting time, or the afternoon meeting time. If the morning time is specified as a preference but none is available, have the program state it and print the afternoon meeting time. If the afternoon time is specified as a preference but none is available, have the program state it and print the morning meeting time. To conserve memory, reduce the number of variables you need by performing operations with the input after reading the second, third, and fourth member data.

Solution

RELEVANT EQUATIONS AND BACKGROUND INFORMATION

You have probably experienced the problem of trying to choose a time for a meeting or a party with a group of friends. The organizer usually asks each person when he or she is available. If there is a large number of people involved, it can be quite confusing to look at a list of times and visualize when everyone can meet.

Sketching a simple diagram is useful. For instance, Fig. 5.11 shows how to determine the mutually free time of two people by "lining out" the beginning and ending times of each person's availability. This figure shows Member 1 available from 8:30 to 11:00 in the morning and 1:30 to 8:30 in the afternoon, and Member 2 available from 10:00 to 12:00 in the morning and 3:00 to 7:00 in the afternoon. The possible meeting times are those that both members have lined out. Visually, we simply look for the "overlapped" region, and we see that the possible meeting times are 10:00 to 11:00 in the morning and 15:00 to 19:00 (3:00 PM to 7:00 PM) in the afternoon. These are shown in the third line of the figure.

Using such a figure is straightforward, but to program the method we must describe our logic more precisely. As we think it through, we realize that we determined the "overlapping" time by comparing the two beginning free times and the two ending free times. The time available for a meeting is between the greater of the two beginning times and the lesser of the two ending times. For instance, in Fig. 5.11, the greater of the two beginning morning times (8:30 and 10:00) is 10:00, and the lesser

Figure 5.11

Using the available times for two group members to determine possible meeting times.

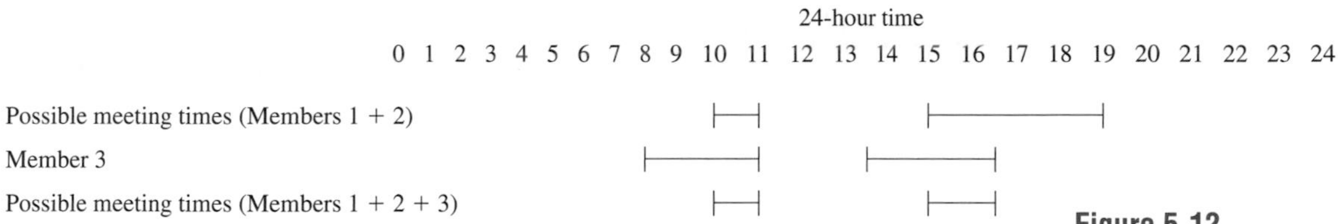

Figure 5.12

Using the possible meeting times for two group members and the third member's availability to determine possible meeting times for all three members.

of the two ending morning times (11:00 and 12:00) is 11:00. Therefore, a possible meeting time is between 10:00 and 11:00. Similarly, the greater of the two beginning afternoon times (13:30 and 15:00) is 15:00, and the lesser of the two ending afternoon times (20:30 and 19:00) is 19:00. Therefore, a possible meeting time is 15:00 to 19:00.

We see that this method works well for two people; how can we consider a third person? Fig. 5.12 shows that putting the possible meeting times for the first two people on the top line and the third member's availability on the second line, we get the possible meeting times for all three people on the third line using the previously described method.

We can continue this process to accommodate a fourth member as shown in Fig. 5.13. Note, in this figure, there is no overlap in the morning times. Therefore, no morning time is available for a meeting. We can recognize this by using the first two lines to see that the greater of the two morning beginnings is 10:00 and the lesser of the two morning endings is 9:30. No meeting time is available because the ending time minus the beginning time (9:30 − 10:00) is a negative number. Therefore in our program we need to check the meeting length (ending time − beginning time). If it is negative, we indicate that no meeting is possible.

The problem statement also asks us to allow a user to specify a preference in deciding the meeting time. Two choices are available. The program is to select the longest meeting time (L), the morning meeting time (M) if there is one, or the afternoon meeting time (A) if there is one.

SPECIFIC EXAMPLE

Table 5.1 shows the available meeting times for all the members. The preference is for the longest meeting.

We use the rows for members 1 and 2. We choose the latest beginning times and earliest ending times. This leads to the row "1 and 2" in Table 5.2.

Again, we choose the latest beginning times and earliest ending times for rows "1 and 2" and row 3 in Table 5.2. This leads to the row "1, 2, and 3" in Table 5.3.

Repeating the procedure for the last two lines of Table 5.3 gives Table 5.4.

Figure 5.13

Using the possible meeting times for three group members and the fourth member's availability to determine possible meeting times for all four members. Note that no meeting is possible in the morning.

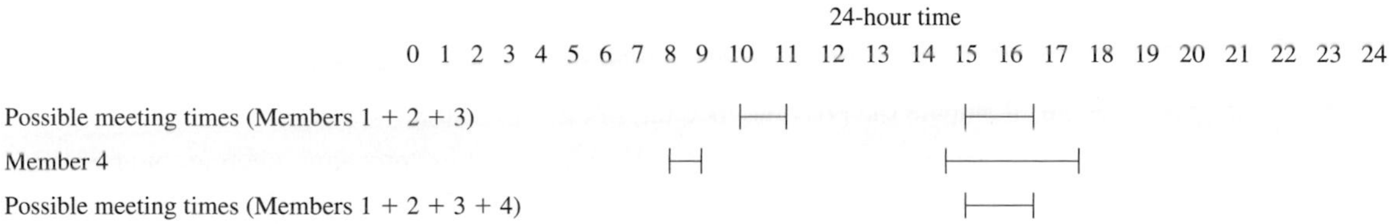

TABLE 5.1 — Meeting times for members

Member	Morning beg time	Morning end time	Afternoon beg time	Afternoon end time
1	5.5	11.3	12.7	17.2
2	8.3	11.1	14.5	18.0
3	9.5	10.3	14.3	19.4
4	9.2	11.1	15.2	20.3

TABLE 5.2 — Meeting times after comparing members 1 and 2

Member	Morning beg time	Morning end time	Afternoon beg time	Afternoon end time
1 and 2	8.3	11.1	14.5	17.2
3	9.5	10.3	14.3	19.4
4	9.2	11.1	15.2	20.3

TABLE 5.3 — Meeting times after comparing members 1, 2, and 3

Member	Morning beg time	Morning end time	Afternoon beg time	Afternoon end time
1, 2, and 3	9.5	10.3	14.5	17.2
4	9.2	11.1	15.2	20.3

TABLE 5.4 — Meeting times after comparing all members

Member	Morning beg time	Morning end time	Afternoon beg time	Afternoon end time
1, 2, 3, and 4	9.5	10.3	15.2	17.2

To find the longest meeting time, we calculate the meeting lengths:

Morning meeting length $= 10.3 - 9.5 = 0.8$ hrs

Afternoon meeting length $= 17.2 - 15.2 = 2$ hrs

Therefore, the meeting begins at 15.2 and ends at 17.2.

ALGORITHM AND CODE SEGMENTS

The steps are:

1. Read the available meeting times for the first two members.
2. Compute the possible meeting times for these two.
3. Read the available meeting times for the third member.
4. Compute the possible meeting times for the first three members.
5. Read the available meeting times for the fourth member.
6. Compute the possible meeting times for all four members.
7. Read the user's preference for longest meeting, morning meeting, or afternoon meeting.
8. Print the meeting time based on the user's preference.

Steps 1, 2, 4, and 8 are described. The other steps are straightforward or can easily be deduced from the explanations and the source code.

STEP 1—READ THE AVAILABLE MEETING TIMES FOR THE FIRST TWO MEMBERS

The code:

```
infile >> possible_morn_beg_time >> possible_morn_end_time;
infile >> possible_aft_beg_time >> possible_aft_end_time;
```

reads the *available* time for the first member, but since these are also the first possible meeting times, we use the *possible* name prefix. The code:

```
infile >> available_morn_beg_time >> available_morn_end_time;
infile >> available_aft_beg_time >> available_aft_end_time;
```

reads the available time for the second member.

STEP 2—COMPUTE THE POSSIBLE MEETING TIMES FOR THESE TWO

We can use the `? :` operator to find the greater or lesser of two meeting times. For instance, the code

```
possible_morn_beg_time = available_morn_beg_time >
  possible_morn_beg_time ? available_morn_beg_time :
  possible_morn_beg_time;
```

makes the possible morning beginning time equal to the greater of the *available* morning beginning time (from member 2) and the *possible* morning beginning time (from member 1). (Remember how the `? :` operator works in assignment statements. First, the relational expression before the `?` is evaluated. If this expression is true, the value before the colon is assigned to the far left variable. If this expression is false, the value after the colon is assigned to the far left variable.)

Similar assignment statements establish the possible morning ending time and afternoon beginning and ending times. These statements are:

```
possible_morn_end_time = available_morn_end_time
  < possible_morn_end_time ? available_morn_end_time :
  possible_morn_end_time;

possible_aft_beg_time = available_aft_beg_time
  > possible_aft_beg_time ? available_aft_beg_time :
  possible_aft_beg_time;

possible_aft_end_time = available_aft_end_time
  < possible_aft_end_time ? available_aft_end_time :
  possible_aft_end_time;
```

STEP 4—COMPUTE THE POSSIBLE MEETING TIMES FOR THE FIRST THREE MEMBERS

By reading in the third member's available times with

```
infile >> available_morn_beg_time >> available_morn_end_time;
infile >> available_aft_beg_time >> available_aft_end_time;
```

We can use exactly the same statements shown for step 2 for this step. This works because we have created the possible meeting times using both Member 1 and 2 available meeting times.

STEP 8—PRINT THE MEETING TIME BASED ON THE USER'S PREFERENCE

First, we need to evaluate if any meeting is possible. We calculate the morning and afternoon meeting lengths. If a meeting length is negative (meaning that the possible ending time is before the possible beginning time) then it is not possible. The meeting lengths are calculated by subtracting the beginning time from the ending time with:

```
morning_meeting_length = possible_morn_end_time
  - possible_morn_beg_time;
afternoon_meeting_length = possible_aft_end_time
  - possible_aft_beg_time;
```

Then they are checked with the `if` control structure to see if both morning and afternoon meetings have negative lengths:

```
if (morning_meeting_length <= 0 &&
  afternoon_meeting_length <= 0)
          {
          cout << "There is no possible meeting "
                  "time" << endl;
          }
```

- *Morning preference* We create an `if-else-if` type structure with the previous `if` structure as the `if` part. We put an `if-else` structure within the `if-else-if` structure to check if the morning meeting has a negative length. If so, we state that no morning meeting is possible. Otherwise, we print the morning meeting time. This structure does it:

```
else if (preference == 'M')        <-- If the preference is for a morning meeting.
          {
          if (morning_meeting_length <= 0)   <-- If a morning meeting is not possible.

                  {
                  cout << "No morning meeting time "
                          "is available." << endl;
                  cout << "The available afternoon "
                          "meeting is:" << endl;
                  cout << possible_aft_beg_time
                      << " to " << possible_aft_end_time
                      << endl;
                  }
                  [Print that no morning meeting time is possible.]

          else
                  {
                  cout << "Begin the meeting at:"
                      << possible_morn_beg_time
                      << endl;
                  cout << "End the meeting at:"
                      << possible_morn_end_time
                      << endl;
                  }
                  [Print the morning meeting time.]
          }
```

- *Afternoon preference* The afternoon preference structure is identical in form to the morning preference structure, so we do not describe it further.
- *Longest meeting preference* If none of the previous preferences are specified, then the preference is for the longest meeting. This means this is the final `else` in the `if-else-if` structure. In this structure we simply compare the meeting lengths and choose the longer of the two. This structure does it.

```
else
       {
       if (morning_meeting_length
         >= afternoon_meeting_length)
               {
               cout << "Begin the meeting at:"
                    << possible_morn_beg_time << endl;
               cout << "End the meeting at:"
                    << possible_morn_end_time << endl;
               }
       else
               {
               cout << "Begin the meeting at:"
                    << possible_aft_beg_time << endl;
               cout << "End the meeting at:"
                    << possible_aft_end_time << endl;
               }
       }
```

If the other preferences are not chosen, the preference is for the longest meeting.

If a morning meeting is longest.

Print the morning meeting time.

Print the afternoon meeting time.

The complete source code shows how the complete `if-else` structure looks.

Source Code

```
#include <iostream.h>
#include <fstream.h>
using namespace std;

int main()
{
        double possible_morn_beg_time, possible_morn_end_time;
        double available_morn_beg_time, available_morn_end_time;
        double possible_aft_beg_time, possible_aft_end_time;
        double available_aft_beg_time, available_aft_end_time;
        double morning_meeting_length, afternoon_meeting_length;
        ifstream infile("C:\\MEETING.DAT");
        char preference;

        infile >> possible_morn_beg_time >> possible_morn_end_time;
        infile >> possible_aft_beg_time >> possible_aft_end_time;

        infile >> available_morn_beg_time >> available_morn_end_time;
        infile >> available_aft_beg_time >> available_aft_end_time;
```

Declaring the variables and opening the input file.

Reading the times for the first two members.

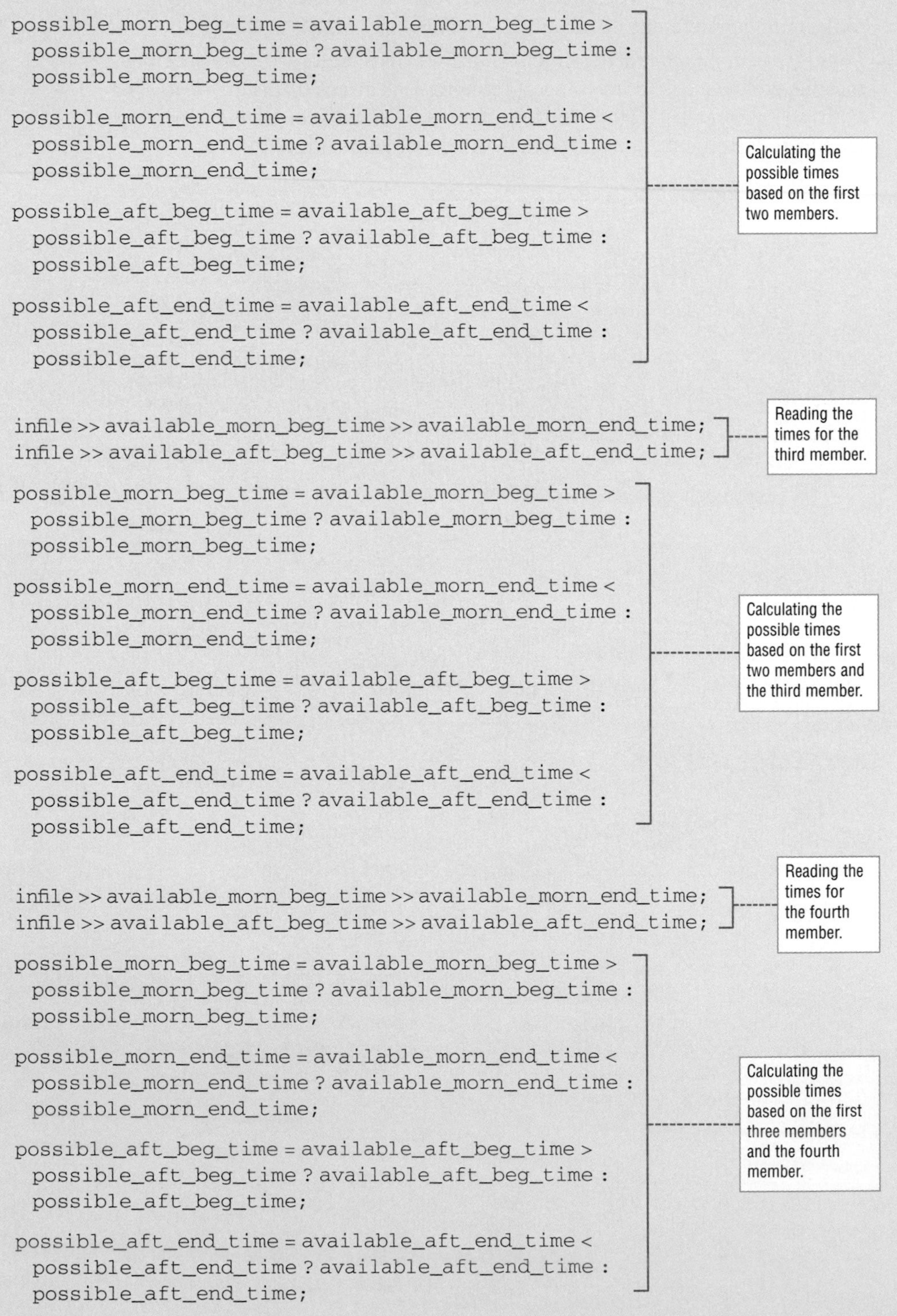

```
possible_morn_beg_time = available_morn_beg_time >
  possible_morn_beg_time ? available_morn_beg_time :
  possible_morn_beg_time;

possible_morn_end_time = available_morn_end_time <
  possible_morn_end_time ? available_morn_end_time :
  possible_morn_end_time;

possible_aft_beg_time = available_aft_beg_time >
  possible_aft_beg_time ? available_aft_beg_time :
  possible_aft_beg_time;

possible_aft_end_time = available_aft_end_time <
  possible_aft_end_time ? available_aft_end_time :
  possible_aft_end_time;

infile >> available_morn_beg_time >> available_morn_end_time;
infile >> available_aft_beg_time >> available_aft_end_time;

possible_morn_beg_time = available_morn_beg_time >
  possible_morn_beg_time ? available_morn_beg_time :
  possible_morn_beg_time;

possible_morn_end_time = available_morn_end_time <
  possible_morn_end_time ? available_morn_end_time :
  possible_morn_end_time;

possible_aft_beg_time = available_aft_beg_time >
  possible_aft_beg_time ? available_aft_beg_time :
  possible_aft_beg_time;

possible_aft_end_time = available_aft_end_time <
  possible_aft_end_time ? available_aft_end_time :
  possible_aft_end_time;

infile >> available_morn_beg_time >> available_morn_end_time;
infile >> available_aft_beg_time >> available_aft_end_time;

possible_morn_beg_time = available_morn_beg_time >
  possible_morn_beg_time ? available_morn_beg_time :
  possible_morn_beg_time;

possible_morn_end_time = available_morn_end_time <
  possible_morn_end_time ? available_morn_end_time :
  possible_morn_end_time;

possible_aft_beg_time = available_aft_beg_time >
  possible_aft_beg_time ? available_aft_beg_time :
  possible_aft_beg_time;

possible_aft_end_time = available_aft_end_time <
  possible_aft_end_time ? available_aft_end_time :
  possible_aft_end_time;
```

Calculating the possible times based on the first two members.
Reading the times for the third member.
Calculating the possible times based on the first two members and the third member.
Reading the times for the fourth member.
Calculating the possible times based on the first three members and the fourth member.

```
infile >> preference;
morning_meeting_length = possible_morn_end_time
  - possible_morn_beg_time;
afternoon_meeting_length = possible_aft_end_time
  - possible_aft_beg_time;

if (morning_meeting_length <= 0 && afternoon_meeting_length <= 0)
        {
        cout << "There is no possible meeting time" << endl;
        }
else if (preference == 'M')
         {
         if (morning_meeting_length <= 0)
                 {
                 cout << "No morning meeting time is "
                       "available. " << endl;
                 cout << "The available afternoon "
                       "meeting is:" << endl;
                 cout << possible_aft_beg_time << " to"
                     << possible_aft_end_time << endl;
                 }
         else
                 {
                 cout << "Begin the meeting at: "
                     << possible_morn_beg_time << endl;
                 cout << "End the meeting at: "
                     << possible_morn_end_time << endl;
                 }
         }
else if (preference == 'A')
          {
          if (afternoon_meeting_length <= 0)
                  {
                  cout << "No afternoon meeting time is "
                        "available." << endl;
                  cout << "The available morning meeting "
                        "is: " << endl;
                  cout << possible_morn_beg_time << " to "
                      << possible_morn_end_time << endl;
                  }
          else
                  {
                  cout << "Begin the meeting at: "
                      << possible_aft_beg_time << endl;
                  cout << "End the meeting at:"
                      << possible_aft_end_time << endl;
                  }
          }
```

Reading the preference.

Calculating the meeting lengths.

If no meeting is possible.

Morning preference.

Afternoon preference.

```
      else
                {
                if (morning_meeting_length >=
                  afternoon_meeting_length)
                      {
                      cout << "Begin the meeting at: "
                           << possible_morn_beg_time << endl;
                      cout << "End the meeting at:"
                           << possible_morn_end_time << endl;
                      }
               else
                      {
                      cout << "Begin the meeting at: "
                           << possible_aft_beg_time << endl;
                      cout << "End the meeting at: "
                           << possible_aft_end_time << endl;
                      }
               }

}
```

Longest meeting preference.

Input File

```
5.5 11.3 12.7 17.2
8.3 11.1 14.5 18.0
9.5 10.3 14.3 19.4
9.2 11.1 15.2 20.3
L
```

Output

```
Begin the meeting at: 15.2
End the meeting at:  17.2
```

Comments

If we were not asked to conserve memory, we could have read all the input data and searched for the latest beginning times and earliest ending times. For instance, in Fig. 5.14, we show all four members' data on one diagram. The possible meeting times are simply those that have all four members' lined-out region overlapping. The latest morning beginning time is 10:00, and the earliest ending time is 9:30. This gives a negative meeting length, which means that there is no possible morning meeting. The latest afternoon beginning time is 15:00, and the earliest ending time is 16:30. This means the afternoon meeting length is 1 hour and 30 minutes. Programming the

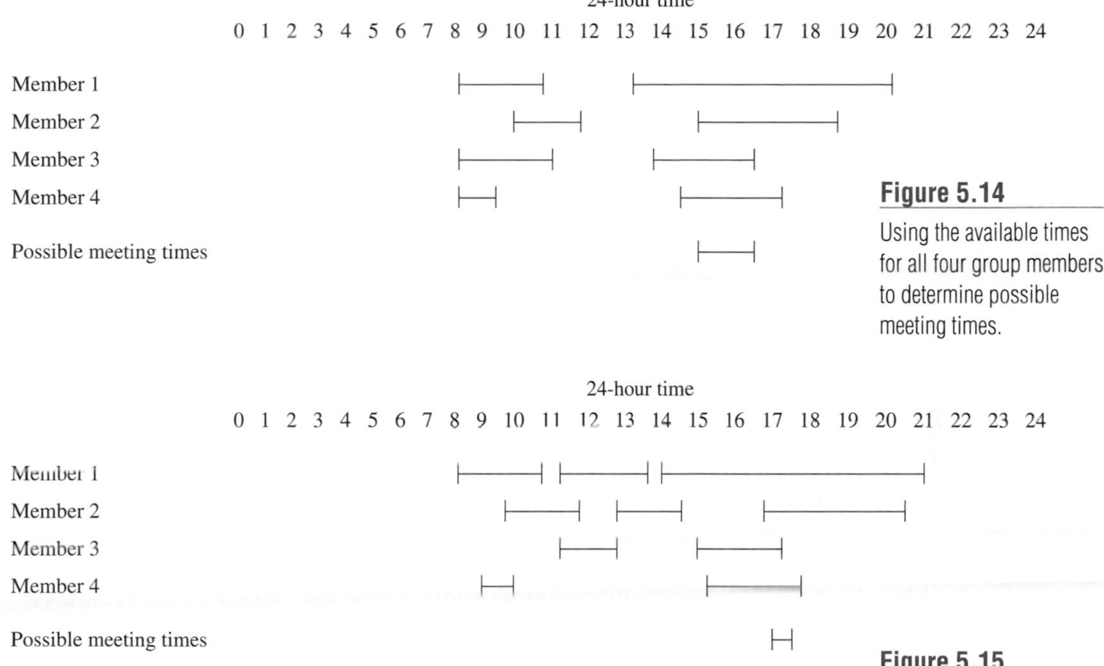

Figure 5.14

Using the available times for all four group members to determine possible meeting times.

Figure 5.15

Members with variable numbers of possible meeting times.

method shown in Fig. 5.14 requires four variables for each member. Then we simply compare the values one after another to find the greatest or least.

The approach can be easily extended to accommodate more members. In the program shown, we need only to repeat the two `infile` statements and the subsequent four assignment statements for each additional group member.

The program becomes more complicated if we allow each member to input a variable number of acceptable time regions. For instance, in Fig. 5.15, we show Members 1 and 2 inputting three regions while Members 3 and 4 input only two.

Modification Exercises

1. Modify the program to accommodate six members.
2. Modify the program to allow a preference for the shortest positive meeting length.
3. Ignore the memory reduction interest. Modify the program to read all the data first, and then create the possible meeting times.

LESSON EXERCISES

LESSON 5.1 EXERCISES

1. Find the error(s), if any, in each of these statements:

   a. `if (today = 7) cout<<"Go to the park";`

   b. `if (today = 7);`

c. `if (today == 7);`

d. `if (today == 7) if (Money>100) cout<<"Dine out!";`

e. `if (today == 7) j=i;`

f.
```
if (Today == 7)
{
  j=i+1; k=100/j;
}
```

2. Write the following text in C++:

   a. if $b^2 - 4ac$ is less than 0, skip a block of code

   b. if n is equal to 0, assign 100 to x

   c. if n is not equal to 0, calculate $1.0/n$

3. Write a program to input your grades from the keyboard and average your GPA. If your GPA is less than 2.0, output a 20 line warning message on the screen. If it is higher than 3.9, then produce a beep 10 times to celebrate.

Solutions

1. a. `if (today == 7) cout<<"Go to the park";`
   b. `if (today == 7);`
   c. No error, but statement does not do anything.
   d. No error. The expression can be an `if` statement.
   e. No error.
   f. No error.

LESSON 5.2 EXERCISES

1. Find the error(s), if any, in each of these statements:

   a.
```
if (today = 7) cout<<"Go to the park";
else cout << "Go to work";
```

   b. `if (today == 7) ; else  cout<<"Go to work";`

   c. `y = ? z > x :a w;`

2. Write a program to input a number `x` from the keyboard. If the number is larger than 0, find its square root. Otherwise, calculate `x*x`.

Solutions

1. a.
```
if (today == 7) cout<<"Go to the park";
else            cout<<"Go to work";
```
   b. No error. When today!=7, it displays `"Go to work"`. When today == 7, nothing will be executed.
   c. `y = z > x ? a : w;`

LESSON 5.3 EXERCISES

1. Find the error(s), if any, in each of these statements:

   a.
```
if (i > 100) cout<<"Hot\n";
else         cout<<"Warm\n";
else         cout<<"Cool\n";
```

b.
```
if (i > 100)   cout<<"Hot\n";
if (i == 100)  cout<<"Warm\n";
else           cout<<"Cool\n";
```

2. Write a program to input these 10 revenues from a file:

```
 1 187
 2 2768
 3 1974
 4 373
 5 66733
 6 437892
 7 593
 8 8091
 9 48903
10 1839
```

and then calculate the tax on each revenue based on the following assumptions:

a. If revenue < 1000, no tax.

b. If 1000 <= revenue < 2000, tax rate = 25 percent.

c. If revenue >= 2000, tax rate = 500 + 30 percent above 2000.

Solutions

1. a. Too many elses.
   b. No error. But when i > 100, the program will display both `Hot` and `Cool`.

LESSON 5.4 EXERCISES

1. Given `x` = 200 and `y` = −400, determine whether each of these logical expressions is true or false. Note that, for a and b, it is necessary only to evaluate the first of the expressions to determine whether the result is true or false. Why?

   a. `(x < y && x != y)`

   b. `(x > y || x == y)`

   c. `!(x > y)`

2. Write the following statements in C++:

   a. If $(a/b) > 100$ and $a < b$

   b. If $(a + b)$ is not equal to 200 and $b >= 300$

   c. If $(a + b) <= 2200$ or $(a - b) \times 4$ is equal to 500

3. Suppose the yearly demand, D, and supply, S, for C++ programmers in a given area are defined as follows:

   $S = 1000 + 50 * (Y - 2005)$ $(2005 <= Y <= 2050)$
   $D = 1200$ $(2005 <= Y <= 2025)$
   $D = 1200 + 60 * (Y - 2000)$ $(2025 <= Y <= 2050)$

Write a program to

a. Print the yearly demand and supply of C++ programmers from 2005 to 2050.

b. Find the years in which there are not enough C++ programmers for that area.

c. Find the total number of unemployed C++ programmers between 2005 and 2050.

Solutions

1. a. False (because the first expression is false and the operator is `&&`, the result is false no matter what the second expression is).
   b. True (because the first expression is true and the operator is `||`, the result is true no matter what the second expression is).
   c. false
2. a. `if ((a/b)>100 && a<b)`
   b. `if ((a+b)!=200 && b>=300)`
   c. `if ((a+b)<=2200 || (a-b)*4==500)`

LESSON 5.5 EXERCISES

1. Assuming `a` is 100, determine whether each logical expression that follows is true or false.

   a. `a==100 && a>100 && !a`

   b. `a==100 || a>100 && !a`

   c. `a==100 && a>100 || !a`

   d. `a==100 || a>100 || !a`

2. Find the error(s), if any, in these statements, assuming `a` is 1, `b` is 2, `c` is 3, and `d` is 4:

   a.
   ```
   if (a>b)
   cout<<"This is an arithmetic if_statement\n"
   ```

   b.
   ```
   if (a>b)
   {
   cout<<"This is a block if_statement\n";
   other_statements...
   }
   ```

   c.
   ```
   if (a>b == c)
     cout<<"This is a block if-else statement\n";
     other_statements...
   }
   else
   {
   cout<<"This is a block if_else statement\n";
   other_statements...
   }
   ```

   d.
   ```
   if (a>b) if (c>d)
   cout<<"This is a nested if_statement\n";
   ```

e.
```
if (a);
   {
     cout<<"if and else are matched";
     other_statements...
   }
   else
     if(b>a)
     {
     cout<<"if and else are matched";
       other_statements...
     }
     else
     {
      cout<<"if and else are matched";
        other_statements...
      }
```

f.
```
if (a>b)
   if (c<d)
   {
    cout<<"More if than else");
    other_statements...
   }
   else
   {
    cout<<"This else is associated with the last if";
    other_statements...
   }
```

g.
```
if (a>b)
   {
    if (c<d)
     {
      cout<<"More if than else";
        other_statements...
     };
    };
     else
     {
     cout<<"This else is associated with the 1st if";
     cout<<"since we use braces to block the last if";
     };
```

Solutions

1. a. true && false && false = false
   b. true || false && false = true
   c. true && false || false = false
   d. true || false || false = true

2. a. Needs semicolon at end of `cout` statement.
   b. No error.
   c. Needs opening brace, `{`, before first `cout` statement. Expression is evaluated from left to right.
   d. No error. This is a nested `if` statement.
   e. Should not have semicolon after `if` (a).
   f. No error.
   g. Should not have semicolons after the three closing braces.

LESSON 5.6 EXERCISES

1. True or false:

   a. The `case` constants within a `switch` statement must be arranged in sequence, such as 101, 102, 103, and so forth.

   b. A `switch` statement can be replaced by an `if-else-if` control structure.

   c. A `switch` statement must contain a `default` section.

2. Find the error(s), if any, in the following statements (assume `a` and `b` are `int` and `a` is 1 and `b` is 2):

   a. `default:`

   b. `switch (a);`

   c. `case 123;`

   d. `switch {a+b}`

   e. `switch (a): {case 1: b=a+2; break;}`

3. Use an `if-else-if` structure to write a program to calculate the tax based on the following tax code:

   income < 1000, tax = income × 20 percent
   1000 <= income < 2000, tax = income × 30 percent
   income >= 2000, tax = income × 40 percent

4. Use a `switch` structure to program Problem 3. (Hint: Introduce an `int` variable `a = income/1000`, and use it as a `switch` variable.)

Solutions

1. a. false
   b. true
   c. false
2. a. No error.
   b. `switch (a)`
   c. `case 123:`
   d. `switch (a+b)`
   e. `switch (a) {case 1: b=a+2; break;}`

LESSON 5.7 EXERCISES

1. True or false:

   a. Integer values cannot be assigned to `bool` variables.

   b. If `x` is a `bool` variable and we use the assignment statement `x=-1;`, then this is equivalent to `x= false;`.

c. Using the `boolalpha` manipulator, we can print `true` or `false` for the values of `bool` variables.

d. We cannot use `boolalpha` with `cin`, only with `cout`.

e. We can use `bool` variables to represent material characteristics.

2. Find errors, if any, in the following statements assuming the declarations

```
bool completed, begun, over_budget;
int i, j, k;
```

a. `completed = i;`

b. `i = completed;`

c. `if (begun) cout >> "Project has begun";`

d. `if (begun = over_budget) cout << "Project has begun and is over budget";`

e. `begun == false;`

3. Write a program that uses `bool` variables to print warnings to the screen if the following conditions exist:

settlement > 5cm (indicates cracking)
load > 60 MN (indicates yielding)
strength < 700 kPa (indicates failure)

Read the input data from a file.

Solutions

1. a. false
b. false, all nonzero values (which includes negative numbers) are interpreted as true.
c. true
d. false
e. true

2. a. No error.
b. No error, `i` is given the value 1 if `completed` is true, 0 if `completed` is false.
c. `if (begun) cout << "Project has begun";`
d. `if (begun == over_budget) cout << "Project has begun and is over budget";` although an equally valid output for this case would be `"Project has not begun and is not over budget";`
e. `begun = false;`

APPLICATION EXERCISES

1. Write a program that can compute the deformation of a structural member given the force in that member and a bilinear load-deformation curve. The first line should pass through the origin as shown in the figure. The second line begins at point (x_b, y_b). Have a user enter the slope of the first line, the slope and intercept of the second line, and the value of x_b. Then ask the user to enter a value of load. The program should print out the deformation corresponding to that load. Assume all numbers are positive.

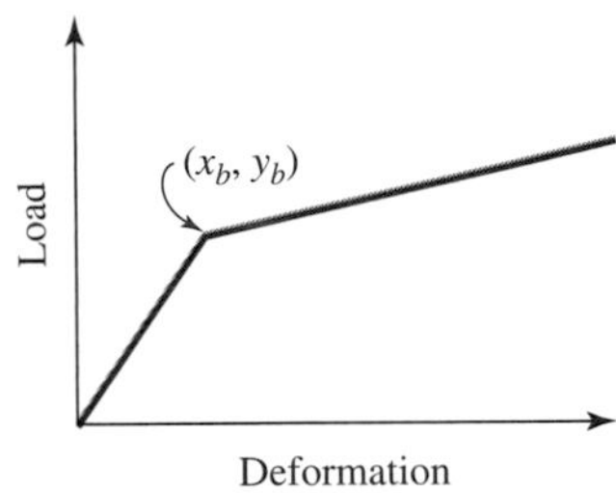

2. Write a program that can compute the pressure in a fluid. Make the program capable of handling both liquids and gases. Compute the pressure in a liquid from the depth of the point in the liquid considered and the weight density of the liquid, using the equation $P = dD$ (where d = depth and D = density). Compute the pressure in a gas, assuming a constant temperature and the equation $P_2 = P_1V_1/V_2$ (where P_2 = final pressure, P_1 = original pressure, V_1 = original volume, V_2 = final volume). Have a user enter 1 for a liquid and 2 for a gas. Then ask a user to input the information on the right side of the correct equation and print the result.

3. Write a program that prints out the quadrant in which an angle lies. Ask a user to input an angle in degrees and print the quadrant number to the screen. Assume angles in increments of 90 degrees are located in the lower quadrant number of the bordering quadrants.

4. A block is to be pushed horizontally on a horizontal surface. Write a program that computes the frictional resistance considering both static and kinetic conditions. First compute the static frictional resistance using $F = u_sW$ (where u_s = static friction coefficient and W = block weight). If the applied force exceeds this value of F, then compute the kinetic frictional resistance using $F = u_kW$ (where u_k = kinetic friction coefficient). Have a user enter u_s, u_k, and W. Then ask for the applied force (**P**). Print the frictional resistance to the screen, and indicate whether or not the block is moving.

5. A moving car is being braked at constant acceleration. Compute whether or not the car has come to a complete halt. Read v_0 (the initial velocity), a (the acceleration which is negative to represent braking), and t (the amount of braking time) from the keyboard. If the quantity a times t is greater in absolute value than v_0, the car has come to a complete stop; otherwise the final velocity is $v_0 + at$. Print the final velocity or the statement "The car has come to a complete stop."

6. A bicycle accelerates at a constant rate from a stationary position. The gear in which the bicycle is in depends on the velocity in the following manner:

Velocity (km/hr)	Gear
0–3	1
3–5	2
5–7	3
7–10	4
10–12	5
12–15	6
15–17	7
17–21	8
21–24	9
24–28	10
28–35	11
35–40	12
40–48	13
48–55	14
55–100	15

Have a user input an acceleration and the riding time. Determine which gear the bicycle is in at that time. Print the velocity and the gear number to the screen. Limit the maximum velocity to 100 km/hr. For any velocities that are on the border of a gear change, use the lower gear.

7. Write a program that can find possible meeting times for a group of four people. Each person should input free time in the periods 8:00–12:00, 12:00–18:00, and 18:00–23:00.

8. A rectangle in x–y space can be defined with the (x, y) coordinates of the lower left and upper right corners. Write a program to determine if two rectangles overlap. Have a user input the corners of the two rectangles (a total of four x–y pairs). Print out whether or not the rectangles overlap.

9. Write the program described in Application Exercise 5.8 and print out the coordinates of the corners of the overlapping region.

10. Write the program described in Application Exercise 5.8 with three rectangles instead of just two.

CHAPTER 6

ITERATION

CHAPTER TOPICS

In this chapter, you will learn how to:

- Create `while`, `do-while` and `for` loops
- Trace and debug loops
- Use loops to solve problems

You have probably heard of computer programs performing millions or billions of calculations. Such programs can be considered extremely powerful because so many calculations could not have been done in human history prior to the advent of computers. With the skills you have developed so far you could write a program that can perform a billion calculations, but you would need to write about a billion lines of code to do so! This is not particularly useful because it may be as tedious to write such code as it is to perform so many calculations. So, how do you write a program that can perform many calculations? Usually, you need to use the process of *iteration,* which can be performed with a built in structure in C++.

Iteration is the repeated execution of a statement or group of statements. To do useful iteration, we usually must make a change in one or more variable values prior to, or in the process of, executing the statement group. This assures that the exact calculations are not simply repeated. The intent with iteration commonly is to repeat similar calculations.

Previously in this text, we illustrated programs for which an iteration control structure would be appropriate. You may recall Application Examples 3.1, 3.2, and 4.2 (if not, look at them now). These programs illustrated cases where it was necessary to write the same few statements numerous times to perform a calculation repeatedly. In this chapter we describe how to repeat calculations (iteration) in C++ without writing the statements over and over. Application Examples 6.1, 6.2, and 6.3 show how to rewrite Application Examples 3.1 and 3.2 using iteration.

The control structure for performing iteration is called a *loop*. C++ has three primary types of loops: `while` loops, `do-while` loops, and `for` loops. All these loop types are described in this chapter.

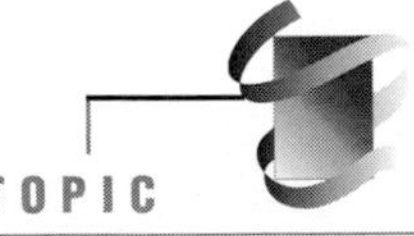

LESSON 6.1 `while` LOOP (1)

TOPIC

- Using `while` loops

QUESTIONS YOU SHOULD ATTEMPT TO ANSWER

1. How many times is the code block executed?
2. Why is it executed this many times?

C++ provides for a number of iterative control structures, known as loops. Loops involve the repeated execution of one or more statements. The programmer controls how many times the statements are to be executed and the values that will change with each repetition or iteration. A generic illustration of the effect of looping and the repeated execution of a block of statements is shown in Fig. 6.1.

The C++ language provides several methods for looping. The simplest one is the `while` loop. The code for a `while` loop contains just two parts: code that is the test expression part and code that is the loop body. When a program reaches the keyword `while`, the test expression is checked. If the expression is true, the loop body is executed and continued to be executed until the test expression becomes false. When the test expression becomes false, the loop body is bypassed, and program control is transferred to a point after the end of the `while` loop. Read the program, and look at the output to see how a `while` loop works.

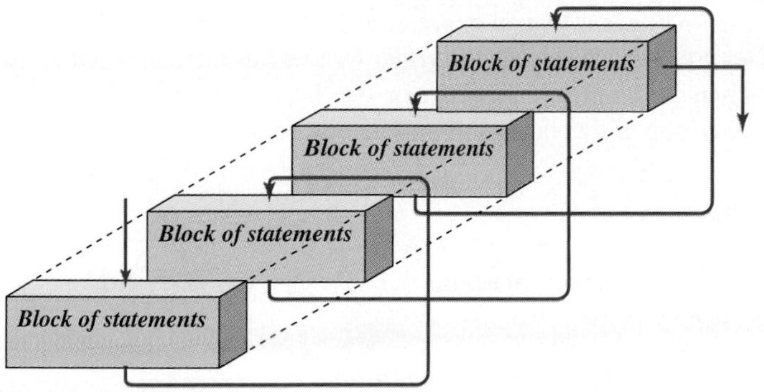

Figure 6.1

Illustration of repeated execution of a block of statements caused by looping.

Source Code

```
#include <iostream>
using namespace std;
int main ( )
{
     int i;
     i = 1;
     while (i <= 5)
        {
        cout << "Loop number " << i << " in the while loop\n";
        i++;
        }
}
```

The keyword `while` is followed by a logical expression. The logical expression serves as a test expression. Initially, the logical expression is true which means the loop body is entered.

The loop body, enclosed in brackets, is repeatedly executed until the test expression becomes false.

Incrementing the counter variable. Each time through the loop, the value of `i` is incremented. After five times through the loop, the logical expression becomes false, and the loop body is bypassed.

Output

```
Loop number 1 in the while loop
Loop number 2 in the while loop
Loop number 3 in the while loop
Loop number 4 in the while loop
Loop number 5 in the while loop
```

The printed value of `i` changes each time through the loop. The maximum value of `i` for which the text expression is true is 5.

Description

while loops. In general, the structure of a C++ `while` loop is

```
while (expression)
   {
   statement1
   statement2
   ...
   }
```

where `expression` is a logical expression (`expression` may be a variable or an arithmetic expression) that results in either true or false. If the result is true, the loop body, which is the statements between the braces, is executed. Braces are not required if the loop body consists of only one statement.

The meaning of

```
while (i <= 5)
    {
    cout << "Loop number " << i << " in the while loop\n";
    i++;
    }
```

is that, while the variable `i` is less than or equal to 5, the statements between the braces are executed repeatedly. If the variable `i` becomes greater than 5, the statements between the braces are not executed, and control passes to the next statement after the loop. The `i` value is increased by 1 for each loop cycle by the statement

```
i++;
```

The loop is executed five times, when `i` = 1, 2, 3, 4, and 5. The loop is bypassed when `i` = 6.

Figure 6.2 shows the two parts of a `while` loop, the test expression and the body. The test expression is always evaluated one more time than the body. When the test expression becomes false, the body is bypassed and the looping stops.

A* `while` *loop body that never executes. If a `while` loop's test expression is false initially, the `while` loop body is never executed. For example, the `cout` statement in this `while` loop

```
while (100 < 50) cout << "This will never be displayed\n";
```

will never be executed because 100 < 50 is false.

A* `while` *loop body that executes an infinite number of times. When constructing `while` loops, make sure that at least one variable in the test expression changes value

Figure 6.2

The two parts of a `while` loop. When the test expression becomes false, the body is bypassed and looping stops.

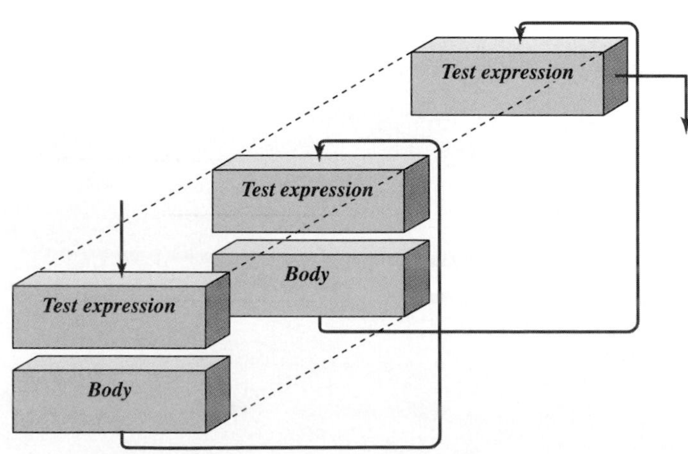

in the loop (we accomplished this in this lesson's program with the statement `i++;`). If the value of the test expression is always true, the loop will execute an infinite (in theory) number of times, and your program will get stuck or hang up. We discuss this situation in more detail in Lesson 6.2.

LESSON 6.2 while LOOP (2)

TOPICS

- One variable test expressions
- Creating a sum of a range of numbers
- The effect of using `break` in a loop
- Avoiding creating an infinite loop
- Early termination of a `while` loop

QUESTION YOU SHOULD ATTEMPT TO ANSWER

1. Will the second loop ever terminate? Why or why not?

The test expression for a `while` loop does not necessarily have to be a relational expression; it can be a single variable. A variable can be treated like a relational expression with a zero value treated as false and a nonzero value treated as true. When we use a single variable as a test expression, the `while` loop is executed as long as the variable is nonzero. As soon as the variable is zero, the loop is exited. Since we always want the loop to be exited at some point, the value of the variable must change within the loop. In this lesson's program we have created two such loops.

If the variable never becomes zero the loop is never exited. This means that the loop body is executed over and over, in theory, an infinite number of times. If this happens in one of your programs, the program will never stop executing. This obviously is not acceptable. In this lesson, we show how one of these loops can be accidentally created and describe how to avoid creating one.

Read the source code, and pay particular attention to the loops. See if you can deduce how many times each loop should execute, and then look at the output to see if you are correct. We show the second loop to illustrate a problem that can be caused by writing a loop improperly. It is an example of poor loop design.

Source Code

```
#include <iostream>
using namespace std;

int main ( )
{
    int i = 4, k = 1, sum = 0;    ◄--- The sum variable is initialized to zero.

    while (i)    ◄--- Single variable acts as test expression.
      {
      cout << "old i= " << i;
      sum += i;    ◄--- Summing the numbers from 1 to i.
      i--;
      cout << ", new i= " << i << ", sum= " << sum << endl;
      }
    cout << endl;
```

```
     while (k)
        {
        k++;
        cout << "k=  " << k << endl;
        }
}
```

We have created an infinite loop because the value of `k` never becomes false (0). This is an example of what you should not do. Do *not* accidentally create an infinite loop.

Output

```
old i= 4, new i= 3, sum= 4
old i= 3, new i= 2, sum= 7
old i= 2, new i= 1, sum= 9
old i= 1, new i= 0, sum=10

k= 2
k= 3
k= 4
k= 5
k= 6
...
```

`sum` is initially zero. The value of `sum` increases by the amount of old `i` each time through the loop.

The value of `k` increases by 1 each time through the loop and never reaches the value 0.

Description

First loop in program. In this lesson's program, the first `while` loop is

```
while (i)
        {
        statements
        }
```

This loop means during the time the variable `i` is not equal to 0, the statements between the braces are executed. The variable `i` is initialized to 4 in the program, and the loop body is executed when `i` = 4, 3, 2, and 1 and terminated when `i` = 0. The value of `sum` is zero initially. Therefore, the values of `i` are summed by the statement in the loop body

```
sum += i;
```

This effectively sums the numbers $(4 + 3 + 2 + 1)$ because the value of `i` is decreased by one for each loop cycle by the expression

```
i--;
```

Alternative body statements. A shorthand for the two body statements is

```
sum += i--;
```

(Please review Lesson 3.4 if you do not understand the shorthand.) You may see this shorthand if you review programs written by others. We will never use this shorthand in this text. Note that in this shorthand the -- occurs *after* the variable on the right-hand side. This is because the value of i is to be decremented after it is to be summed.

Alternative test expression. An alternative but equivalent test expression for the first loop is

```
while (i != 0)
```

This form is much clearer in its intent than simply while(i). However, we show while(i) because you are likely to see it in programs written by others.

Second loop in program. This loop begins

```
while (k)
```

The variable k is initialized to 1 in the program, and the value of k is increased by one for each loop cycle by the expression

```
k++;
```

Thus k = 1, 2, 3, 4, 5, . . . each time through the loop. Because 0 is false and nonzero is true, the value of k is repeatedly found to be true. In fact as execution proceeds, k never becomes equal to 0, and therefore the loop is never exited! Try to run this program, and you will see that it never stops because this loop goes on and on. Such a loop is called an *infinite* loop because, in theory, it would execute an infinite number of times. An infinite loop in a program is unacceptable.

Note that the test expression could also be written while (k != 0).

Infinite loops. It can be beneficial to create a counter variable that can be used to prevent the accidental creation of an infinite loop. The counter variable keeps track of the number of times that the loop has been executed. For example, in the following code:

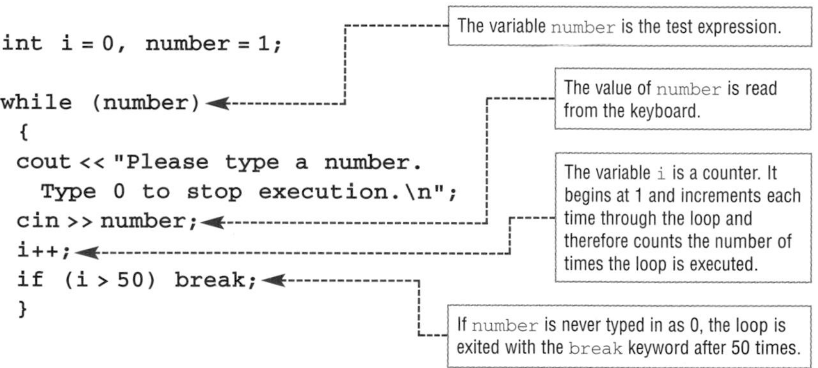
```
int i = 0, number = 1;

while (number)
 {
 cout << "Please type a number.
   Type 0 to stop execution.\n";
 cin >> number;
 i++;
 if (i > 50) break;
 }
```


the variable i is the counter. In this case, the loop automatically stops after 50 times because the break keyword causes control to pass to the statement after the braces. If the counter were not used and number never became 0, then the loop would go on indefinitely.

The variable number is the test expression.
The value of number is read from the keyboard.
The variable i is a counter. It begins at 1 and increments each time through the loop and therefore counts the number of times the loop is executed.
If number is never typed in as 0, the loop is exited with the break keyword after 50 times.

A break statement can occur only in a switch or loop body. The C++ standard says that it "terminates execution of the smallest enclosing switch or iteration statement." The line

```
if (i > 50) break;
```

causes control to transfer out of the loop when the relational expression is true. If the counter variable i is larger than 50, the loop will be stopped by the break statement. A C++ break statement alone is a complete C++ statement, but usually it is used as part of a control statement to terminate a process.

One way to correct the infinite loop in this lesson's program is to create a counter variable. The counter variable is i in the loop that follows. It causes the loop to terminate after it has been executed 30 times.

```
i = 0;
while (k)
   {
   k++;
   i++;
   cout << "k = " << k << endl;
   if (i >= 30) break;
   }
```

We can rewrite this lesson's while loop using no break statement by using a compound relational expression as the test expression. The following loop avoids a break statement.

```
i = 0;
while (k && i <= 30)
   {
   k++;

   cout << "k = " << k << endl;
   i++;
   }
```

Note that the body of the loop is executed with i = 30. The loop is executed only when both conditions are met, being k not equal to zero and i <= 30. If one of these is not true then the loop terminates.

In general, it is better to avoid using break statements in loops wherever possible. break statements make programs less structured because they make program control more difficult to follow. However, if you need to break out of the middle (that is, in the midst of a number of calculations) of a loop, a break statement may be required.

LESSON 6.3 do-while LOOP

TOPICS

- Using do-while loops
- Differences between do-while loops and while loops

QUESTION YOU SHOULD ATTEMPT TO ANSWER

1. What is the value of i that terminates the first loop?

A second type of loop exists in C++: the do-while loop. do-while loops are a slight variation of while loops. They begin with the keyword do and end with the keyword while and test expression. Between these is the loop body. Because the test expression is at the end instead of at the beginning, the loop body is always executed at least once. This is unlike while loop bodies which are not executed at all if the test expression first evaluates to false. Follow the loops in the source code line by line.

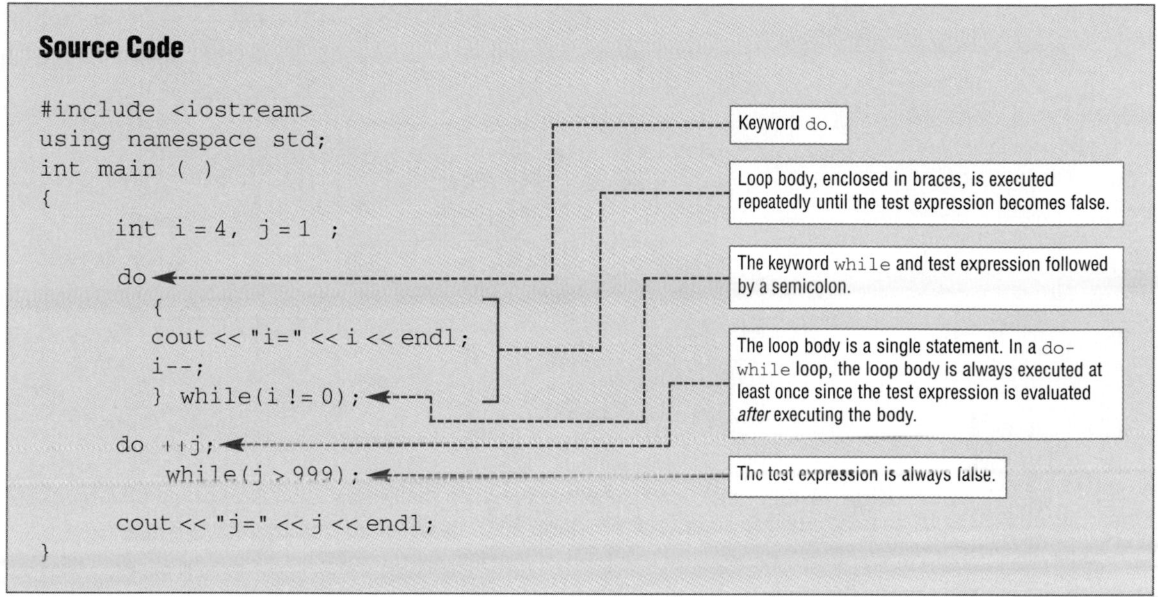

Source Code

```
#include <iostream>
using namespace std;
int main ( )
{
     int i = 4, j = 1 ;

     do
        {
        cout << "i=" << i << endl;
        i--;
        } while(i != 0);

     do ++j;
        while(j > 999);

     cout << "j=" << j << endl;
}
```

Keyword do.
Loop body, enclosed in braces, is executed repeatedly until the test expression becomes false.
The keyword while and test expression followed by a semicolon.
The loop body is a single statement. In a do-while loop, the loop body is always executed at least once since the test expression is evaluated *after* executing the body.
The test expression is always false.

Output

```
i=4
i=3
i=2
i=1
j=2
```

The body of the second loop is executed only once because the test expression is false the first time it is executed.

Description

***do-while* loops.** Where there is only one statement in the body of a `do-while` loop, the loop can be written

```
do statement;
   while (expression);
```

If the loop body consists of more than one statement, the structure of a C++ `do-while` loop is

```
do
   {
   statement1;
   statement2;
   . . .
   } while (expression);
```

where the *statements* between the braces represent the loop body. The *expression*, which is a logical expression (including a variable, an arithmetic expression, or a relational expression) that results in either true or false, is evaluated.

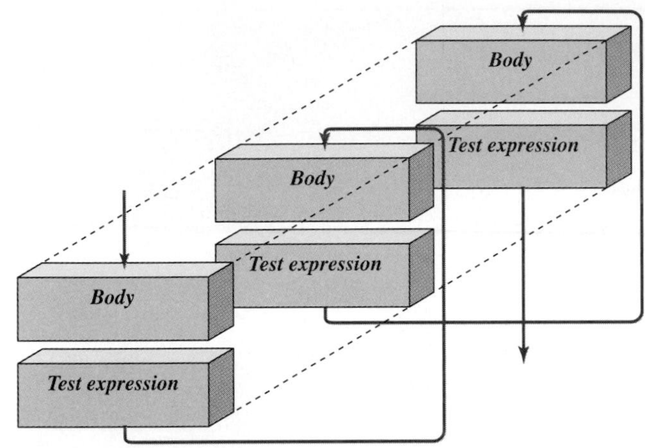

Figure 6.3

The two parts of a `do-while` loop. The body and test expression are evaluated the same number of times. When the test expression becomes false, the looping stops.

If the result is true, the statements between the braces again are executed. Braces are not required if the `do-while` loop body consists of only one statement.

In the first `do-while` loop of this lesson, the loop body statements are executed when `i` = 4, 3, 2, and 1. When `i` = 0, the test expression becomes false, so the loop is terminated.

In the second `do-while` loop, the loop body statements are executed once. The test expression `j > 999` is false the first time it is evaluated because the `j` value is 2. This terminates the loop.

Remember that within the statement portion of the `do-while` loop, it is necessary to increment or modify the variable(s) involved in the test expression to assure that an infinite loop is not produced.

Differences between `while` loops and `do-while` loops. `while` loops and `do-while` loops are similar. You may be able to use a `while` loop to replace a `do-while` loop and vice versa; however, it may take some adjustment in the statements of the loop body to do so. The primary difference between the two loops is that in a `while` loop, the test expression is evaluated first, whereas in a `do-while` loop, the test expression is evaluated last. Figure 6.3 illustrates the structure. Compare this figure to Fig. 6.2.

In a `do-while` loop, the loop body always is executed once. After that, the test expression is evaluated; if the test result is false, the loop body is not executed again.

Also, observe that a semicolon is required at the end of a `do-while` loop (after the closing parentheses). No semicolon is required at the end of `while` loops.

LESSON 6.4 `for` LOOP

TOPICS

- The `for` loop control structure
- Form of a simple `for` loop
- Difference between `for` loops and `while` loops
- Tracing and debugging loops

This lesson illustrates another looping structure: the `for` loop control structure. A `for` loop is very appropriate when you know how many times the operation needs to be repeated. For instance, if an operation is to be performed once for each day of the week, then you know that the operation is to be performed seven times. Or if your program involves some sort of countdown from 10 to 0, then you know that the operation is to be performed 11 times. A for loop is ideally suited to performing operations under these circumstances. Later in this book, we show other situations appropriate for for loops.

A typical way to write a for loop is with a variable that is initialized, tested, and incremented. for loops are easy to follow because all these operations are listed in one place and not hidden in other parts of the code or the loop body. Read this lesson's program, and examine the two for loops. Note that none of the variables is initialized in the declarations.

QUESTIONS YOU SHOULD ATTEMPT TO ANSWER

1. What is the test expression for the second for loop?
2. What is the increment expression for the second for loop?

Source Code

```
#include <iostream>
using namespace std;
int main ( )
{

    int day, hour, minutes;

      for (day = 1; day <= 3; day++)
         cout << "Day= " << day << endl;

      for (hour = 5; hour > 2; hour--)
         {
         minutes = 60 * hour;
         cout << "Hour = " << hour << ", Minutes=" << minutes << endl;
         }
}
```

Keyword for.
Initialization.
Test expression.
Increment expression.
Body of for loop.
Body of for loop.

Output

```
Day= 1
Day= 2
Day= 3
Hour = 5, Minutes=300
Hour = 4, Minutes=240
Hour = 3, Minutes=180
```

Description

for loops. A for loop is another iterative control structure. For example, the statements

```
for (day = 1; day <= 3; day++)
      cout << "Day=" << day << endl;
```

causes `cout` to display the value of `day` three times, that is, from `day` equals 1 to `day` equals 3. The simplest `for` loop takes the following form:

```
for (loop_expressions)
      single_statement_for_loop_body;
```

where the *`loop expressions`*, such as `day = 1; day <= 3; day++`, are separated from each other by semicolons (not commas, a common error); are enclosed by a pair of parentheses with no semicolon at the end; and must consist of three parts that typically can be described as

1. An initialization expression that initializes the `for` loop control variable (or counter) and tells the program where to start the loop. For example, `day = 1;` initializes control variable `day` to 1 and starts the loop at `day` = 1.
2. A loop repetition condition. This serves as a test expression. If the test expression is false, the loop is terminated. For example, `day <= 3;` tests whether control variable `day` is less than or equal to 3; if `day` is greater than 3, the loop is terminated.
3. An increment expression that increases or decreases the control variable. The increment can be in the positive direction (increment) or negative direction (decrement). The increment of the control variable can be achieved by using an increment operator such as `++`. For each loop, the `++` will add 1 to the control variable. Similarly, the decrement operator, `--`, will subtract 1 from the control variable.

In addition, the counter variable can be `int`, `double`, or other type of variable. Its value can be positive, negative, or 0. To avoid round-off error, we recommend that you use integer type variables as counter variables. Figure 6.4 schematically displays the structure of a `for` loop. In this figure, observe that at the beginning of the loop, the initialization expression is executed. After that, the order of operation is condition, body, and increment. In other words, the increment expression is evaluated *after* the loop body even though in the source code text, the increment expression appears *before* the loop body. As we look at more complicated `for` loops, this fact is important to remember.

What we have described here is a typical loop in a way that we will commonly use in this book and that you will commonly see in practice. However, be aware that the three loop expressions can be used in other ways. Later in this book, we use `for` loops in ways that differ somewhat from this description.

In general, the `for` loop takes the form of

```
for (loop_expressions)
    {
    for_loop_body
    }
```

where the *`for_loop_body`* consists of the statements between the two braces. The *`for_loop_body`* describes all the processes to be executed repeatedly in the loop. For example, the *`for_loop_body`*

```
{
minutes = 60 * hour;
cout << "Hour = " << hour << ", Minutes = " << minutes << endl;
}
```

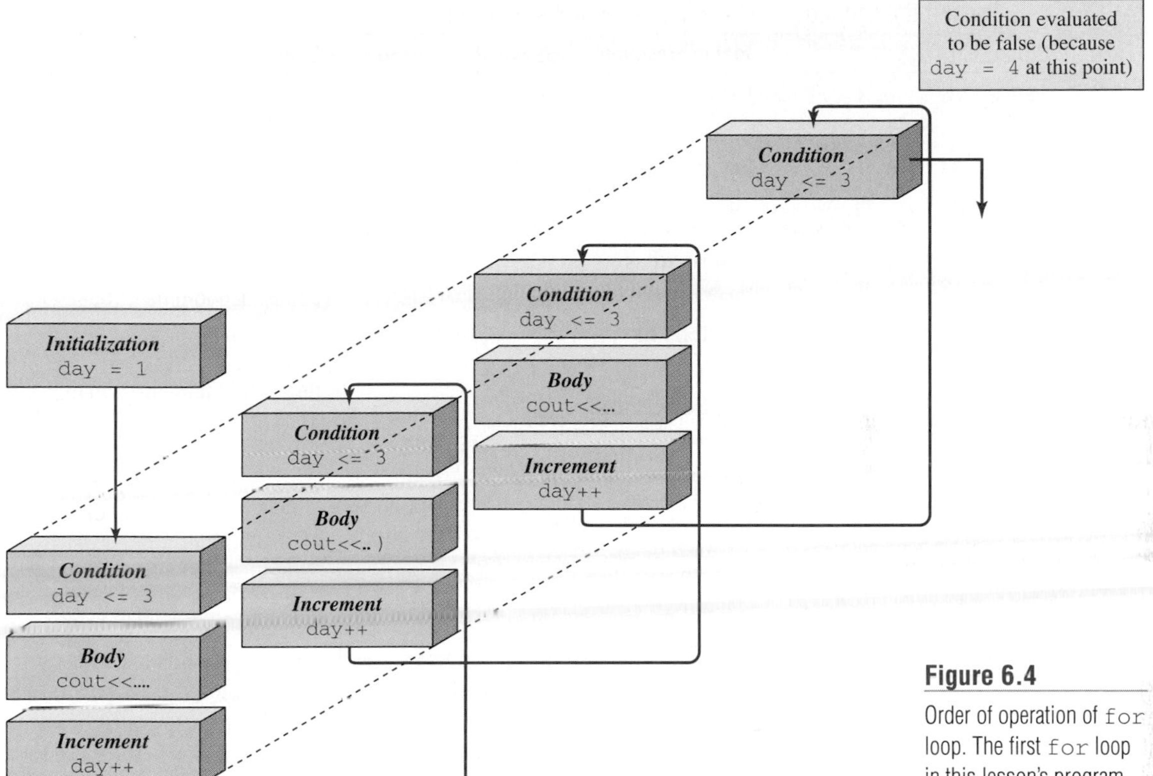

Figure 6.4

Order of operation of `for` loop. The first `for` loop in this lesson's program is used as an example. Observe that the first time through the loop, the initialization statement is the first executed. Subsequent times through, the increment statement is the first executed. For each iteration, the condition is executed before the body. If the condition is false, the body is not executed.

contains an arithmetic statement and a `cout` statement. In this lesson, both statements are executed three times, when `hour` is equal to 5, 4, and 3.

Note that the general structure of the `for` loop is different from the simplest structure. The general structure must be used when the `for` loop body contains more than one C++ statement. As we saw with the `if` control structure, the braces create a block of code. To create a code block, simply enclose a group of statements with braces. If the `for` loop body is to contain only one C++ statement, then the simplest `for` loop structure can be used.

Tracing and debugging `for` loops. As you write loops in your own programs, you will need to debug them. To do this, you will need to trace the actions of a loop step by step. We show tracing loops here because `for` loops are somewhat trickier than the other types of loops. With `for` loops, it is not obvious when the increment and test expressions are evaluated. For this reason, we show Table 6.1 that has each statement in the order executed for the second `for` loop in this lesson's program. Each value in the column is the value of the variable or test expression *after* the statement in the row has been executed. Only variable values that change due to the statement's actions are shown in that row.

For instance, first the initialization takes place in row 2, and `hour` is assigned the value 5 (this is indicated in column 5). Then the loop begins because row 3 tests for `hour` being greater than 2 (which is true, as shown in column 3). The value of `hour`

TABLE 6.1 — Tracing the second `for` loop in Lesson 6.4's program

Row	Statement	Test expression	`minutes`	`hour`	Comment
1	*Before loop*		----	----	No values are initialized before the loop
2	`hour = 5;`			5	Initialization
3	`hour > 2;`	true			Begin first time through loop
4	`minutes = 60 * hour;`		300		
5	`hour--;`			4	
6	`hour > 2;`	true			Begin second time through loop
7	`minutes = 60 * hour;`		240		
8	`hour--;`			3	
9	`hour > 2;`	true			Begin third time through loop
10	`minutes = 60 * hour;`		180		
11	`hour--;`			2	
12	`hour > 2;`	false			Begin fourth time through loop. End loop—hour is not greater than 2.

remains 5 until it is changed so that in row 4, `minutes` is calculated to be 60 * 5 which is 300 (column 4). Then `hour` is decremented in row 5, and `hour` becomes 4 (column 5). This value of `hour` is used the next time through the loop, making `minutes` = 240 (which is 4 times 60, row 7, column 4). This process continues until `hour` becomes 2, the test expression becomes false (row 12, column 3), and the loop is terminated.

We go through this much detail to emphasize two things. First, the order of operation of a `for` loop is test expression, body, increment expression. And second, we want to illustrate a method for creating a table that you can use to trace and debug your own loops as they become more complex.

The method is as follows. Create a table with the first two columns labeled *Statement* and *Test Expression*. The other columns are all the variable names used in the loop. (The columns labeled *Row* and *Comment* are not needed; we show them only for clarification.) The first row of the table should be labeled *Before loop* and should indicate the variable values before the loop is begun. (For the loops in this lesson's program, this row is not important, but for other loops it may be important.) The second row of the table should be the initialization statement. After that the rows should be ordered *test expression, loop body, increment expression*. Then fill in the variable values in the table line by line. Each time a statement changes a variable value, write the new value in the line. Remember, the values in the table are the variable values *after* the statement in the row is executed. To calculate a variable's value, use the *last previous* values listed for the other variables in the statement and perform the calculation.

By creating such a table, we are doing the same actions the computer does when executing the loop. Going through the process of creating this table gives you insight into how the loop is working. Loops that execute a large number of times need not be completely followed. By going through a few iterations you can usually see how the loop will finish and whether it will be correct. Your compiler's debugger or `cout` statements can help you create such a table if you do not do it by hand.

TABLE 6.2 — Form for tracing a `for` loop

Statement	Test expression	Variable 1	Variable 2	Variable 3	Variable 4
Before loop					
Initialization expression					
Test expression					
Body					
Increment expression					
Test expression					
Body					
Increment expression					
Test expression					

To create your own table for your loops, follow the form in Table 6.2.

In this table, Variable 1, Variable 2, Variable 3, and Variable 4 represent the variables used in the loop you are debugging. Repeat the pattern shown in the table appropriate for your own loop. Fill in the values of the table until you have confidence that you understand how the loop is operating.

Also, to help you debug your program with loops, it can be useful to clarify where your `for` loops start and end in a print-out of your code. You can sketch open brackets as we have done in the left portion of this lesson's source code to indicate the starting and ending points. This is especially useful when you have many `for` loops in your program. One purpose of doing this is to make sure that none of the brackets cross. As with `if` control structures, we cannot have loop control structures that cross.

Differences between `while` loops and `for` loops. In general, `while` loops and `for` loops are similar in their order of execution. You can use a `for` loop to replace a `while` loop, but you must realize that the bodies of the loops must be different. You should note the similarity in structure of a `for` loop and a `while` loop (compare Figs. 6.2 and 6.4). If you compare these two, you will see the similarity of the placement of the test expression for both the `while` and `for` loops. However, in a `for` loop, the increment expression is forced to be the last expression executed each time through the loop, whereas in a `while` loop, the increment expression can be embedded in the loop body. Also, a `for` loop sometimes is easier to follow in a code than a `while` or a `do-while` loop because, in a `for` loop all three expressions used in a looping structure are in one location.

The differences between the `for` and `while` loops are illustrated in Table 6.3.

Changing the counter variable. It is not recommended to change the value of the counter variable in the body of a `for` loop, although it is allowed. A counter variable is used to control the loop, so its value should be changed in the increment expression, not in the loop body. You may cause errors if you change the value of the counter variable in both the increment expression and the loop body. For example, the following loop is "correct." However, it is an infinite loop and never ends. For

TABLE 6.3 — Comparison between `for` and `while` loops

Item	`for` loop	`while` loop
Initialization expression	Is one of the loop expressions	Must be given prior to the loop
Test expression	Is one of the loop expressions	Is one of the loop expressions
Increment expression	Is one of the loop expressions	Must be in the loop body
When number of iterations is known	Is very convenient and clear to use	Is less convenient and clear
When number of iterations is unknown	Less convenient and clear	May be more convenient than for loop

each loop, the increment expression increases the counter variable, `k`, by 1, but the loop body always restores it back to 1:

```
for (k = 1;   k < 3;   k++) k = 1;
```

Remember, check your loops carefully to avoid creating infinite loops.

`for` loops and `break` statements. Be aware that there are different schools of thought regarding using `for` loops that require `break` statements in the loop body. Some programmers feel that doing so violates the rules of structured programming and that it is acceptable only to break out of `while` or `do-while` loops. Others feel that it is acceptable to break out of `for` loops as well. In this book, we occasionally break out of `for` loops as we feel you may see it in practice. However, before you use a `break` statement in a `for` loop in your programs, you should check with your instructor or employer.

Multiple expressions for initialization and increment. We have not shown it in this lesson's program, but C++ allows multiple expressions (using a comma separated list) for the initialization and increment portions of a `for` loop. For example:

```
for (i = 1,  j = 2;   i < 10;   i++,  j++)
```

initializes and increments *both* `i` and `j`. The body of the loop can then contain other expressions involving these variables. This form is convenient when multiple variables are changing with each loop iteration.

LESSON 6.5 NESTED `for` LOOPS

TOPICS

- Using the `+=` type operator in an increment expression
- Nested `for` loops

QUESTIONS YOU SHOULD ATTEMPT TO ANSWER

1. Why is `i` equal to 1 for the first four lines of output?
2. Why are there 12 lines of output?

The loops in this program are *nested,* meaning that there is a loop within a loop. Roughly speaking, a nested loop is executed from the inside out. In other words, roughly speaking, the inner loop is executed multiple times, and then the outer loop is executed once. The inner loop is executed multiple times again, and the outer loop is executed a second time. This continues until the outer loop has gone completely through its cycle. Look at the program and the output. See if you can trace the flow of the program line by line.

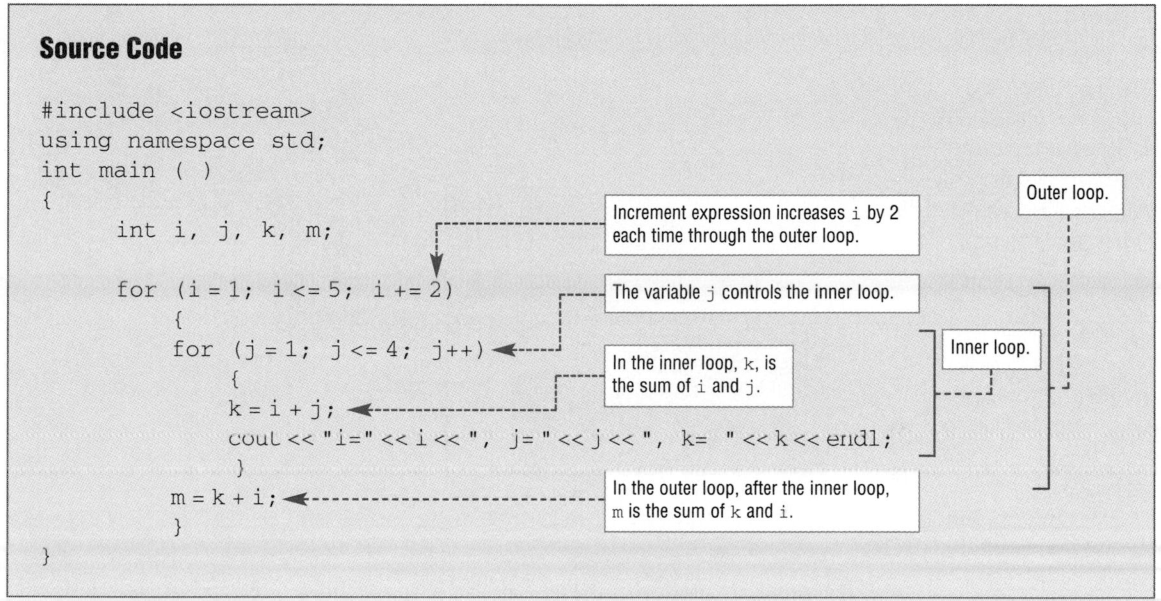
Source Code
#include <iostream>
using namespace std;
int main ( )
{
int i, j, k, m;
for (i = 1; i <= 5; i += 2)
{
for (j = 1; j <= 4; j++)
{
k = i + j;
cout << "i=" << i << ", j= " << j << ", k= " << k << endl;
}
m = k + i;
}
}
Increment expression increases i by 2 each time through the outer loop.
The variable j controls the inner loop.
In the inner loop, k, is the sum of i and j.
In the outer loop, after the inner loop, m is the sum of k and i.
Outer loop.
Inner loop.

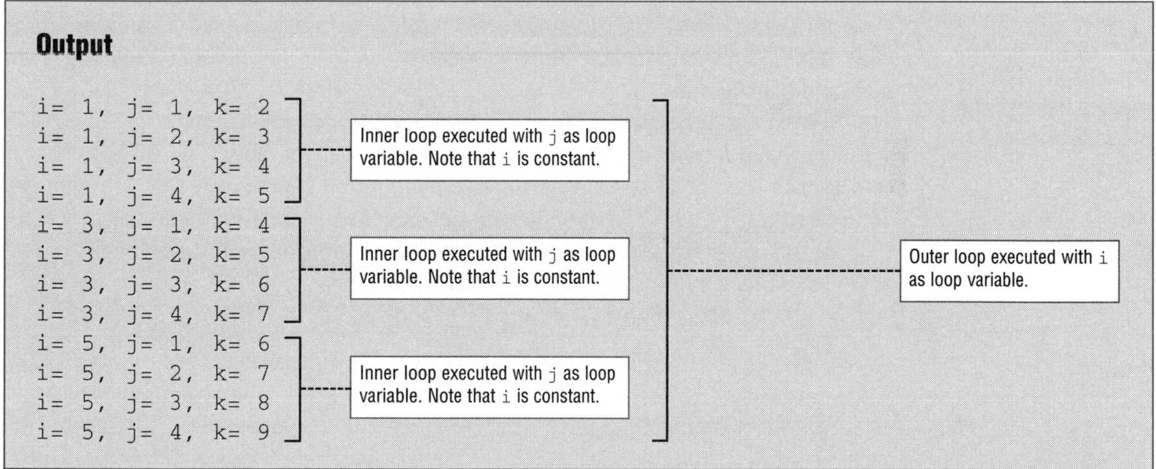
Output
i= 1, j= 1, k= 2
i= 1, j= 2, k= 3
i= 1, j= 3, k= 4
i= 1, j= 4, k= 5
i= 3, j= 1, k= 4
i= 3, j= 2, k= 5
i= 3, j= 3, k= 6
i= 3, j= 4, k= 7
i= 5, j= 1, k= 6
i= 5, j= 2, k= 7
i= 5, j= 3, k= 8
i= 5, j= 4, k= 9
Inner loop executed with j as loop variable. Note that i is constant.
Inner loop executed with j as loop variable. Note that i is constant.
Inner loop executed with j as loop variable. Note that i is constant.
Outer loop executed with i as loop variable.

Description

Nested `for` loops. A nested `for` loop has at least one loop within a loop. Each loop is like a layer and has its own counter variable, its own loop expressions, and its own loop body. In a nested loop, for each value of the outermost counter variable, the inner loop body is executed multiple times. This means that the inner loop body will be executed more frequently than the outer loop body. The example in this lesson has two counter variables, `i` and `j`, where `i` is the outer loop counter and `j` is the inner loop counter. The outer loop body is executed three times, when `i` = 1, 3, and 5. For each `i` value, the inner loop body is executed four times (for `j` = 1, 2, 3, and 4). Thus, the total number of times that the inner loop body is executed is 3 * 4 or 12 times.

Figure 6.5

Conceptual illustration of nested `for` loop for Lesson 6.5's program. The unlabeled numbers are the values of `j`. For simplicity, the test expressions and their proper locations are not shown. First, the outer loop initialization is executed, then the code before the inner loop is executed, then the inner loop is executed four times, then the code after the inner loop (`m = k + i`) is executed. This completes one pass through the nested loop. Two additional passes through the nested loop are shown in the figure. Note that the inner loop is executed repeatedly for each execution of the outer loop.

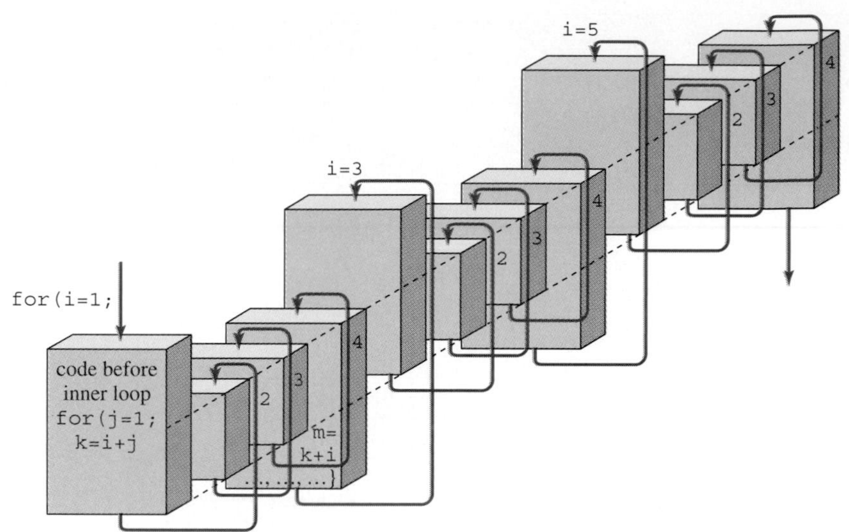

A conceptual illustration of the nested `for` loop for this lesson's program is shown in Fig. 6.5. Observe from this figure how the value of `j` changes each time through the inner loop, and how `i` does not change until many complete passes through the inner loop. This figure demonstrates how control flows from the outer loop to the inner loop and back again.

Note that in a nested `for` loop, if either loop body contains more than one C++ statement, that loop body must be enclosed with a pair of braces. Arrowhead brackets for each loop body (such as those displayed in the source code that follows) can be used to clarify which loop body belongs to which loop. The braces for any inner loop must be within the brace pair for its outer loop. For all cases, hand drawn arrowhead brackets for different loops must not cross.

In general, the syntax of a nested `for` loop is

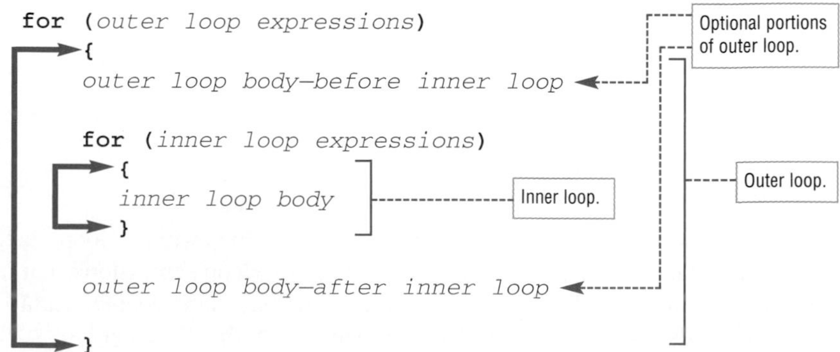

The pattern of nested loops can be anything, provided that the loops do not cross (meaning that the arrowhead brackets do not cross). The sketches in Fig. 6.6 illustrate some of the many possibilities. The way the loops are nested is determined primarily by the problem to be solved by the program.

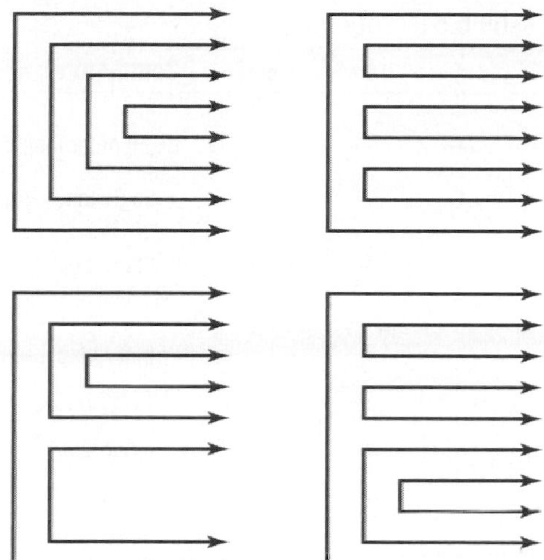

Figure 6.6

Some possible patterns for nested loops. Note that none of the brackets cross.

Nested `for` loops should use indentation to make them more readable. Remember, indentation is not necessary and has no effect on the code's performance; however, it is considered standard practice. We recommend you use the following style at this point in your programming career when writing nested `for` loops:

```
for (...)
          {
          ......
          ......
          for (...)
                  {
                  ......
                  ......
                  }
          ......
          ......
          }
```

The advantage of the indentation is that even in the absence of drawn arrows, one can discern the nesting of loops and program flow. In many instances in this text, we would like to have shown more indentation than is illustrated in the source codes; however, publishing restrictions preclude us from doing so.

Tracing and debugging nested loops. We have created a table (Table 6.4) to trace the nested loops of this lesson's program. This table was created using the method described in Lesson 6.4. Follow the table line by line to see how the values change in the loops. Note that the table shows that after the inner loop executes multiple times, the outer loop statements are executed once.

To create your own table for debugging nested loops, use the form in Table 6.5. Repeat the pattern shown in the table appropriate for your own loop. Fill in the values of the table until you have confidence that you understand how the loop is operating.

TABLE 6.4 — Tracing the nested loop from Lesson 6.5's program

Statement	Test expression	i	j	k	m	Comment
Before loop		—	—	—	—	
`i = 1;`		1	—	—	—	Begin outer loop
`i <= 5`	true					Outer loop
`j = 1;`			1	—	—	Begin inner loop
`j <= 4`	true					
`k = i + j;`				2	—	Inner loop
`j++;`			2			
`j <= 4`	true					
`k = i + j;`				3		Inner loop
`j++;`			3			
`j <= 4`	true					
`k = i + j;`				4		Inner loop
`j++;`			4			
`j <= 4`	true					
`k = i + j;`				5		Inner loop
`j++;`			5			
`j <= 4`	false					End inner loop (j is greater than 4)
`m = k + i;`					6	Outer loop
`i += 2;`		3				Outer loop
`i <= 5`	true					Outer loop
`j = 1;`			1			Begin inner loop
`j <= 4`	true					
`k = i + j;`				4		Inner loop
`j++;`			2			
`j <= 4`	true					
`k = i + j;`				5		Inner loop
`j++;`			3			
`j <= 4`	true					
`k = i + j;`				6		Inner loop
`j++;`			4			
`j <= 4`	true					
`k = i + j;`				7		Inner loop
`j++;`			5			
`j <= 4`	false					End inner loop (j is greater than 4)
`m = k + i;`					10	Outer loop
`i += 2;`		5				Outer loop
`i <= 5`	true					Outer loop
`j = 1;`			1			Begin inner loop
`j <= 4`	true					
`k = i + j;`				6		Inner loop
`j++;`			2			
`j <= 4`	true					
`k = i + j;`				7		Inner loop
`j++;`			3			
`j <= 4`	true					
`k = i + j;`				8		Inner loop
`j++;`			4			
`j <= 4`	true					
`k = i + j;`				9		Inner loop
`j++;`			5			
`j <= 4`	false					End inner loop (j is greater than 4)
`m = k + i;`					14	Outer loop
`i += 2;`		7				Outer loop
`i <= 5`	false					End outer loop (i is greater than 5)

TABLE 6.5 — Form for tracing nested `for` loop

Statement	Test expression	Variable 1	Variable 2	Variable 3	Variable 4
Before loop					
Initialization outer					
Body outer (before inner)					
Initialization inner					
Test expression inner					
Body inner					
Increment inner					
Test expression inner					
Body inner					
Increment inner					
Test expression inner					
Body outer (after inner)					
Increment outer					
Test expression outer					
Body outer (before inner)					
Initialization inner					
Test expression inner					
Body inner					
Increment inner					
Test expression inner					
Body inner					
Increment inner					
Test expression inner					
Body outer (after inner)					
Increment outer					
Test expression outer					

Making a table like this is helpful when you initially write the code and when you are debugging the code. You usually can make a first attempt at writing a nested loop, and then make a table and write in the values as shown here. You gain confidence that you have written the loops correctly if the values in the table are what you expect.

When debugging code that you have already written, you can write `cout` statements within the loops to print the variables and counters on each step. If you put `cout` statements both within and outside the nests, you can see the variables change as they are printed out. These `cout` statements should be written so that a table similar to the one here is displayed.

Your compiler's debugging option is extremely useful in tracing loops. You can set markers causing the program execution to pause at various locations within the loops. During the pause you can check the values of variables and counters. If any of these have unexpected values, you can rewrite the code of the loops.

Realize that although the loops we have shown here are relatively straightforward, loops can be very tricky. Even experienced programmers need to carefully evaluate loops to make sure they are correct. The method of tracing loops using a table will get you on your way to writing effective and correct loops.

Looping and decision making. Figure 6.7 illustrates looping and decision making together in one program. We have not shown the code that corresponds to this figure; however, from what you know at this point, you could create one that does. Of

Figure 6.7

Flow of program with mix of loops and `if` control structures.

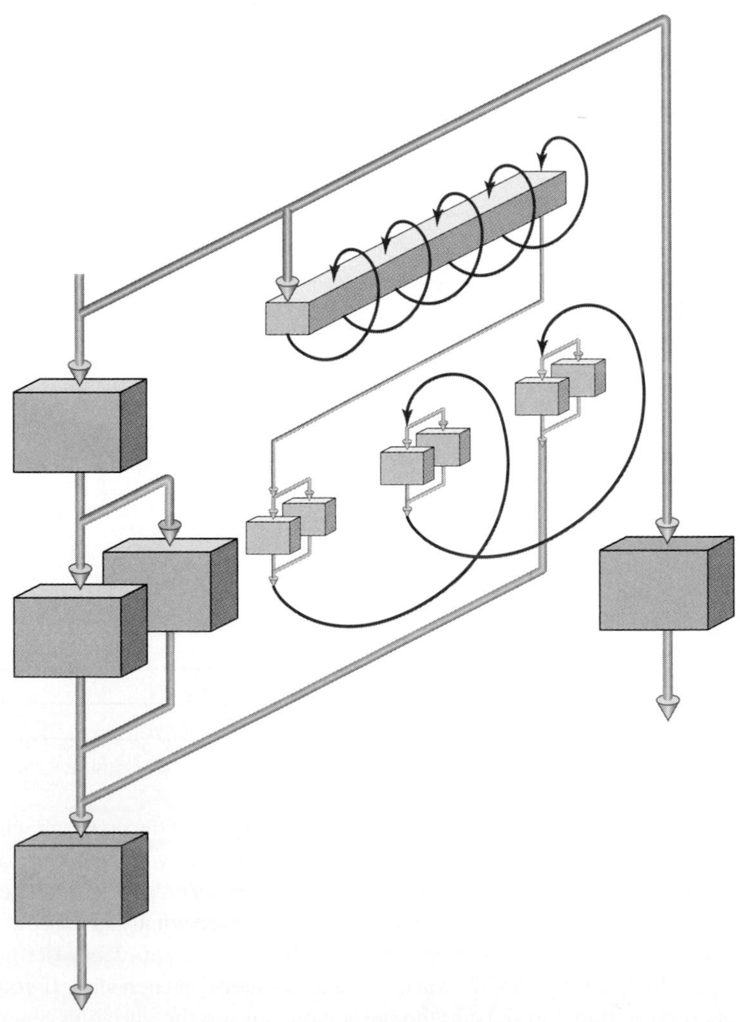

course, the actual problem to be solved dictates how control should flow. We will illustrate this in the application examples.

APPLICATION EXAMPLE 6.1 AREA CALCULATION (1)

TOPIC

- `for` loop

As illustrated, `for` loops can be used to repeat execution of C++ statements. As such, they can be used in programs that perform the same tasks as those done by many of the application programs in previous chapters.

Problem Statement

Write a program that uses a `for` loop to perform the same task as Application Example 3.1. Use the triangle leg length pattern in the `for` loop to compute the area for each triangle.

Solution

RELEVANT EQUATIONS

Please look at Application Example 3.1 for the development of the relevant equations.

SPECIFIC EXAMPLE

See also Application Example 3.1 for the specific example.

ALGORITHM

When you design your `for` loops, you must remember to make sure that all variables are initialized properly for the first time through the loop. For this program, this means that the leg lengths must be initialized before the loop is entered (that is, making the horizontal leg length 5 and the vertical leg length 7). Within the loop, the area must be calculated first because this must be done before the leg lengths are changed. The result can then be printed. Then each time through the loop, the leg lengths are calculated from the previous leg lengths. The algorithm is given here.

1. Declare variables
2. Create table headings
3. Initialize horizontal leg length of first triangle
4. Initialize vertical leg length of first triangle
5. Begin for loop (looping from 1 to 4, because there are 4 triangles)
   a. Calculate area of triangle from leg lengths
   b. Print leg lengths and area
   c. Calculate new horizontal leg length from previous horizontal leg length
   d. Calculate new vertical leg length from previous vertical leg length
6. End

The source code is written directly from the algorithm.

Source Code

```
#include <iostream>
#include <iomanip>
using namespace std;
int main( )
{
   int    i;
   double horizleg, vertleg, area;

   cout << "Triangle number         Area" << endl << endl;

   horizleg = 5.0;
   vertleg  = 7.0;

   for (i = 1; i <= 4; i++)
      {
      area = 0.5 * horizleg * vertleg;
      cout << setw(15) << i << setw(10) << area << endl;

      horizleg += 1.0;
      vertleg /= 2.0;
     }
}
```

Creating table headings.

Initializing the variables.

Using a `for` loop to calculate four areas.

Modifying the leg lengths each time through the loop.

Output

```
Triangle number         Area
              1         17.5
              2         10.5
              3        6.125
              4          3.5
```

Comments

Compare the source code for Application Example 3.1 with this one. Closely follow the flow of both source codes, statement by statement.

Pay particular attention to the way the variables `horizleg` and `vertleg` are used. You can see that they are initialized before the `for` loop. Once in the `for` loop, the `area` is first calculated and then printed. Then new values of `horizleg` and `vertleg` are calculated. Note that these new values of `horizleg` and `vertleg` are retained and used to calculate the `area` the second time through the loop. The values of `horizleg` and `vertleg` calculated during the second time through the loop are retained and used for calculating the `area` during the third time through the loop.

TABLE 6.6 — Form for tracing the program's loop

Statement	Test expression	i	area	horizleg	vertleg
Before loop					
i = 1;					
i <= 4;					
Other statements					

And the `area` on the fourth time through the loop is obtained from the values of `horizleg` and `vertleg` calculated during the third time through the loop. Note that the values of `horizleg` and `vertleg` calculated during the fourth time through the loop are not used.

This program is much shorter than Application Example 3.1. In addition, unlike Application Example 3.1 it easily can be changed to calculate the areas of 50 triangles that follow the same pattern of leg lengths.

Modification Exercises

Modify the program to

1. Calculate the areas of 30 triangles following the same pattern. Note how small the values become. How can you print out at least four significant digits?
2. Calculate the areas of 10 triangles with the vertical leg length doubling instead of halving each time through the loop.
3. Calculate the areas of 40 rectangles with the horizontal leg length reduced by 5 percent each time through the loop and the vertical leg length increased by 3 percent.
4. Calculate the areas of 20 trapezoids. Read in the height, bottom length, and top length. Invent your own variable names. Make this pattern: The bottom length is reduced by 3 percent each time through the loop, the top length is increased by 8 percent, and the height is increased by 2 percent.

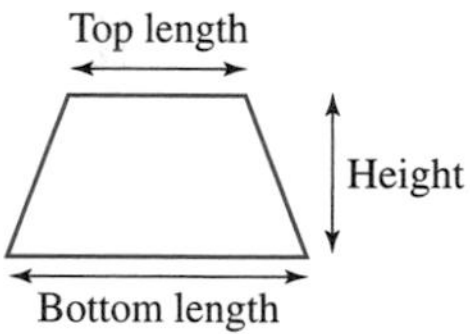

Tracing Exercise

1. Use your calculator and the loop in the program to expand and complete Table 6.6 in accordance with Table 6.1.

APPLICATION EXAMPLE 6.2 AREA CALCULATION (2)

TOPICS

- `for` loop
- Equation development

Problem Statement

Write Application Example 3.1 another way. Use the loop counting variable `n` to create new equations.

Solution

RELEVANT EQUATIONS

We can develop independent equations representing the values of the lengths of the legs of the triangles by looking again at the pattern exhibited by the lengths. Recall that the lengths of the legs are

Triangle number	Horizontal leg length	Vertical leg length
1	5	7
2	$5 + 1 = 6$	$7/2 = 3.5$
3	$5 + 2 = 7$	$7/4 = 1.75$
4	$5 + 3 = 8$	$7/8 = 0.875$

If the triangle number is `n`, then the horizontal leg length is

$$\text{Horizontal leg length} = 5 + (n - 1) \tag{6.1}$$

And the vertical leg length is

$$\text{Vertical leg length} = 7/2^{(n-1)} \tag{6.2}$$

We can use these equations in our C++ program. Note that it is up to us to recognize the patterns and write the equations that represent the patterns. Recognizing patterns and writing the necessary equations are parts of programming.

SPECIFIC EXAMPLE

Using equations (6.1) and (6.2), we get

n	Horizontal leg length	Vertical leg length	Area
1	$5 + (1 - 1) = 5$	$7/2^{(1-1)} = 7.0$	0.5 * 5 * 7 = 17.5
2	$5 + (2 - 1) = 6$	$7/2^{(2-1)} = 3.5$	0.5 * 6 * 3.5 = 10.5
3	$5 + (3 - 1) = 7$	$7/2^{(3-1)} = 1.75$	0.5 * 7 * 1.75 = 6.125
4	$5 + (4 - 1) = 8$	$7/2^{(4-1)} = 0.875$	0.5 * 8 * 0.875 = 3.5

ALGORITHM

From the specific example we see that we can put Eqns. 6.1 and 6.2 into a loop with `n` going from 1 to 4. Therefore, the algorithm becomes

1. Include headers
2. Declare variables
3. Create the table headings
4. Loop n from 1 to 4
   a. Calculate horizontal leg length using equation (4.1)
   b. Calculate vertical leg length using equation (4.2)
   c. Calculate area as 0.5 * horizleg * vertleg
   d. Print results

Source Code

This source code follows the algorithm step by step.

```
#include <cmath>
#include <iostream>
#include <iomanip>
```

```
using namespace std;
int main( )
{
    int     n;
    double nminus1, horizleg, vertleg, area;

    cout << "Triangle number    Area"<< endl <<endl;

    for (n = 1; n <= 4; n++)
        {
        nminus1  = n - 1;
        horizleg = 5.0 + nminus1;
        vertleg  = 7.0 / pow(2,nminus1);
        area     = 0.5 * horizleg * vertleg;
        cout << setw(15) << i << setw(10) << area << endl;
        }
}
```

Creating the table headings.

Using the counter variable `n` in the calculation in the `for` loop body.

Eqn. 6.1.

Eqn. 6.2.

Output

```
Triangle number         Area
              3         17.5
              4         10.5
              3        6.125
              4          3.5
```

Comments

As you write more programs, you will find that often it is convenient to use the counter variable in calculating the values of other variables within a `for` loop. Just remember that you have to be clever in writing the equations that use the counter variable, and you must be cautious about mixed type arithmetic.

Notice that we created a new variable, `nminus1`. It was not absolutely necessary to create this variable. It was created only for convenience and to improve the look of the program. You will find that as you write programs, you often will create variables for these two reasons. To make your programs as understandable as possible, we recommend that you choose names that are very descriptive of what the variables represent.

Notice also that in the calculation of `nminus1`, the expression on the right side of the assignment statement is `int` type. By assigning this to a `double` variable (`nminus1`), a `double` is placed in the memory cell for `nminus1`. Thus, we have done no mixed type arithmetic in this code.

Also observe that we included `cmath` because we used the `pow` function. Remember this function. You likely will use it in your programs.

TABLE 6.7 — Form for tracing the program's loop

Statement	Test expression	n	nminus1	horizleg	vertleg	area
Before loop						
`n = 1;`						
`n <= 4;`						
Other statements						

Modification Exercises

Modify the program to

1. Calculate the result for 10 triangles following the same pattern.
2. Calculate the result for four triangles, with each one having the vertical leg length shrink by one-third rather than one-half each time through the loop.

Tracing Exercise

1. Use your calculator and the loop in the program to expand and complete Table 6.7 in accordance with Table 6.1.

TOPIC

- `for` loop

APPLICATION EXAMPLE 6.3 TEMPERATURE UNIT CONVERSIONS

Problem Statement

Write a program that creates a table of degrees Celsius with the corresponding degrees Fahrenheit. Begin at 0°C and proceed to 100°C in 20°C increments using a `for` loop. In other words, rewrite Application Example 3.2 using a `for` loop.

Solution

RELEVANT EQUATIONS

The equation developed in Application Example 3.2 is

$$F = C * (9/5) + 32$$

where F is Fahrenheit, in degrees, and C is Celsius, in degrees.

SPECIFIC EXAMPLE

A specific example was given in Application Example 3.2, so it will not be repeated here. We note, though, that we print out six values of degrees, at $C = 0, 20, 40, 60, 80$, and 100.

ALGORITHM

Again, before the loop, there are activities that the program must perform. For this program, because we want to print the results in the form of a table, we must print the headings of the table before we begin the loop. Also, we must make sure that variables used in the loop are properly initialized before the loop, if necessary. Therefore, the algorithm becomes

1. Include headers
2. Declare variables
3. Print headings for table

4. Initialize Centigrade degrees
5. Loop from 1 to 6
    a. Calculate new value of Centigrade degrees
    b. Calculate corresponding value of Fahrenheit degrees
    c. Print values for table

The source code follows this algorithm step by step. Read the program to see how it is done. Once again, follow through the `for` loop carefully to understand how it is executed.

Source Code

```
#include <iostream>
#include <iomanip>
using namespace std;
int main( )
{
        int i;
        double degC, degF;

        cout << " \nTable of Celsius and Fahrenheit degrees \n\n"
                        " Degrees                Degrees \n"
                        " Celsius                Fahrenheit \n";

        degC = -20.;

        for (i = 1; i <= 6; i++)
                {
                degC += 20.;
                degF = degC * 9. / 5. + 32.;
                cout << setw(12) << degC << setw(19) << degF << endl;
                }
}
```

Before the loop, we print the table headings.

Also before the loop, we initialize variables that need initializing. In this case, we initialize `degC`. We need not initialize `degF` because it is calculated directly from `degC` in the loop.

Loop for calculating `degF`.

Output

```
Table of Celsius and Fahrenheit degrees
       Degrees           Degrees
       Celsius           Fahrenheit
         0.00              32.00
        20.00              68.00
        40.00             104.00
        60.00             140.00
        80.00             176.00
       100.00             212.00
```

TABLE 6.8 — Form for tracing the program's loop

Statement	Test expression	i	degC	degF
Before loop				
`i = 1;`				
`i <= 6;`				
Other statements				

Comments

You can see that the variable `i` has no real function except to serve as a counter for the `for` loop. Since it is not used anywhere within the `for` loop, it is called a *dummy* variable. You often will need to create dummy variables in your programs.

Note that a slightly different approach (from that of Application Example 6.1) is taken in this program for initializing the variables used in the `for` loop. First, the variable `degC` is set to −20 rather than the first value of interest which is 0. Then the first statement in the `for` loop increments the value of `degC` to 0. In other words, another method for initializing variables before loops is to initialize them to values other than the first ones of interest. Then, the first statements in the loop must modify these variables to be what are needed.

An alternative to this approach is to have the statement `degC=0;` before the `for` loop and then increment `degC` after `degF` is calculated and after the `cout` statement within the `for` loop. This type of approach was used in Application Example 6.1 for calculating the triangle areas.

Modification Exercises

Modify the program to

1. Create a table of values that go from C = 0 to C = 100 in increments of one degree.
2. Create a table with F in the left column and F incrementing by five degrees from −50 to +300.
3. Create a table including Rankine degrees.

Tracing Exercise

1. Use your calculator and the loop in the program to expand and complete Table 6.8 in accordance with Table 6.1.

TOPIC

- Nested `for` loops

APPLICATION EXAMPLE 6.4 INTEREST CALCULATION

Problem Statement

Write a program capable of computing the value of the money in a bank account at the end of each month for a period of five years. The account will start with $5,000 and have neither deposits nor withdrawals. The interest will be compounded monthly. The annual interest rate is to be input from the keyboard. The output will be to a file (MONEY.OUT) and consist of a table listing the year, month, and new principal (balance).

Solution

Relevant equations. If the annual interest rate is i, then the monthly interest rate is $i/12$. And the amount of interest for one month is

$$I = P_0\left(\frac{i}{12}\right) \tag{6.3}$$

where $I =$ interest for the month
$P_0 =$ principal at the beginning of the month
$i =$ annual interest rate

The principal at the end of the month (which is the principal for the beginning of the succeeding month) is:

$$P_f = P_0 + I = P_0 + P_0\left(\frac{i}{12}\right) = P_0\left(1 + \frac{i}{12}\right) \tag{6.4}$$

where P_f is the principal at the end of the month.

SPECIFIC CALCULATION

For a starting principal of \$5,000 and an annual interest rate of 6 percent, the principal at the end of the first month, using Eqn. 6.4, is:

$$P_0 = 5000$$
$$i = 0.06$$
$$P_f = 5000\left(1 + \frac{0.06}{12}\right) = 5025.00$$

This calculation can be done for four months of the first year:

$i = 0.06$
year $= 1$

beginning of month 1	$P_0 = 5000.0$
end of month 1	$P_f = 5000\left(1 + \frac{0.06}{12}\right) = 5025.00$
beginning of month 2	$P_0 = 5025.0$
end of month 2	$P_f = 5025\left(1 + \frac{0.06}{12}\right) = 5050.13$
beginning of month 3	$P_0 = 5050.13$
end of month 3	$P_f = 5050.13\left(1 + \frac{0.06}{12}\right) = 5075.38$
beginning of month 4	$P_0 = 5075.38$
end of month 4	$P_f = 5075.38\left(1 + \frac{0.06}{12}\right) = 5100.75$

ALGORITHM

One can begin by writing an algorithm for the main portion of the program directly from this specific calculation. The specific calculation illustrates that the same equations are used repeatedly, which means that it is ideally suited for looping in a program. We do 12 calculations per year for five years. A nested `for` loop with the inner nest going from 1 to 12 and the outer nest from 1 to 5 would work. The algorithm is

1. Read annual interest rate, i
2. Open output file
3. $P_0 = 5000$
4. Loop on year = 1 to 5
   a. Loop on month = 1 to 12
      i. $P_f = P_0 * (1 + i/12)$
      ii. Print year, month, P_f
      iii. $P_0 = P_f$

However, we can simplify the algorithm even further because we know that the equation

$$P_f = P_0 * (1 + i/12)$$

means

$$P_{(\text{new value})} = P_{(\text{old value})} * (1 + i/12)$$

which can be written in code as

```
P = P * (1 + i/12);
```

With a compound operator, this statement is

```
P *= (1 + i/12);
```

Consider the following algorithm and follow the flow of the source code, paying particular attention to the value of P:

1. Read annual interest rate, i
2. Open output file
3. $P = 5000$
4. Loop on year = 1 to 5
   a. Loop on month = 1 to 12
      i. $P* = (1 + i/12)$
      ii. Print year, month, P

Source Code

This source code can be written using the preceding algorithm as a guide.

```
#include <iostream>
#include <fstream>
#include <iomanip>
```

```
using namespace std;
int main( )
{
     int month, year;
     double i, p;
     ofstream outfile("C:\\MONEY.OUT");
     outfile << " Year Month Balance" << endl << endl;

     cout << "Enter the annual interest rate" << endl;
     cin >> i;

     p = 5000.;
     for (year = 1; year <= 5; year++)
            {
            for (month = 1; month <= 12; month++)
                   {
                   p *= (1 + i / 12);

                   outfile << setprecision(2)
                          << setiosflags(ios::
                     showpoint | ios::fixed);
                   outfile << setw(5) << year << setw(10) << month
                          << setw(10) << p1 << endl;
                   }
            }
     outfile.close();
}
```

Creating the table headings.

Prompting the user for the interest rate.

Looping on the year from 1 to 5.

Looping on the month from 1 to 12.

Computing the new principal.

Manipulators for printing money values.

Nested loop that corresponds to the algorithm.

Output to Screen

```
                 Enter the annual interest rate
Keyboard input   0.06
```

Output File MONEY.OUT

```
Year      Month     Balance

  1         1       5025.00
  1         2       5050.12
  1         3       5075.38
  1         4       5100.75
  1         5       5126.26

and so forth for five years.
```

TABLE 6.9 — Form for tracing the program's loops

Statement	Test expression	`year`	`month`	`i`	`p`
Before loop					
Initialization outer					
Initialization inner					
Test expression					
Body					
Increment					

Comments

Note that if we had hand drawn arrowhead brackets for the inner and outer loops, the brackets would not have crossed.

Modification Exercises

Modify the program to

1. Compound the interest not once per month but once every two weeks.
2. Compound the interest once per week.
3. Carry out the calculation for 10 years.
4. Begin with a principal of $10,000, an interest rate of 5 percent, and interest compounded once per week for eight years. Print the result only every six months.

Tracing Exercise

1. To check the loop, expand and fill in Table 6.9 for two years.

APPLICATION EXAMPLE 6.5 MATHEMATICAL SERIES

TOPICS

- `for` loop
- `do-while` loop
- `if-else` control structure
- Translating summation equations to code
- Numerical method example

Problem Statement

Write a program capable of calculating tan $h^{-1}(x)$ using an infinite series. Read the value of x from the keyboard and print the result to the screen.

Solution

RELEVANT EQUATIONS

As you solve more advanced problems in mathematics, science, or engineering, you may find you need to write programs capable of solving advanced equations, such as those that involve series representations. You often will find that a `for` loop or a `while` loop is ideally suited to simulating the series.

For instance the tan $h^{-1}(x)$ function can be represented by the infinite series:

$$\tan h^{-1}(x) = x + \frac{x^3}{3} + \frac{x^5}{5} + \frac{x^7}{7} + \cdots \qquad (6.5)$$

where $|x| < 1.0$

This infinite series can be written in summation form as follows:

$$\tan h^{-1}(x) = \sum_{n=1}^{n=\infty} \frac{x^{(2n-1)}}{(2n-1)} \tag{6.6}$$

Recall that one characteristic of some (but not all) converging infinite series is that each successive term of the series decreases in value. In other words, the first term of the series is the largest. The second term of the series is smaller than the first but larger than the third. In general, the 50th term in this type of series is considerably smaller than the first term (this, of course, depends on the behavior of the particular series considered). The impact of this is that if you were going to calculate a value from the series representation, you could take a finite number of terms (for instance, the first 50) and ignore the rest yet get a reliable value for use in practical applications. A question that arises, though, is, How many terms are necessary to get a reliable value?

The answer is when the values of the terms get small enough, they can be ignored. For instance, if you are interested in calculating the value of a number represented by a series to six decimal places, then when the value of the sum of the remaining terms becomes less than 0.000001, the remaining terms can be ignored. Knowledge of the convergence of the particular series to be calculated is necessary to guarantee a reliable result. However, from a practical standpoint, it may be possible to terminate a series when a particular term becomes substantially smaller than the desired accuracy. For example, if you are interested in calculating the value of a number represented by a series accurately to six decimal places and the series converges in the manner just described, then it might be possible to say that when the value of a single term becomes smaller than 0.0000000000001, it is likely that the value of the number has reached the desired accuracy. (Please consult a mathematics text for further understanding of the convergence of infinite series.)

With the material in this chapter, you learned enough to write a program that can calculate a large number of terms in a series and decide whether the terms are small enough to be ignored.

SPECIFIC CALCULATION

Suppose we wanted to find $\tan h^{-1}(0.5)$ using the series representation in Eqn. 6.6. Then,

$$x = 0.5$$

and Eqn. 6.6 becomes

$$\tan h^{-1}(0.5) = \sum_{n=1}^{n=\infty} \frac{0.5^{(2n-1)}}{(2n-1)}$$

The first 14 terms of the series are

Term number (n)	Term value
1	$(0.5)^1/(1) = 0.500000000$
2	$(0.5)^3/(3) = 0.041666667$
3	$(0.5)^5/(5) = 0.006250000$
4	$(0.5)^7/(7) = 0.001116071$
5	$(0.5)^9/(9) = 0.000217014$

(continued)

Term number (n)	Term value
6	$(0.5)^{11}/(11) = 0.000044389$
7	$(0.5)^{13}/(13) = 0.000009390$
8	$(0.5)^{15}/(15) = 0.000002035$
9	$(0.5)^{17}/(17) = 0.000000449$
10	$(0.5)^{19}/(19) = 0.000000100$
11	$(0.5)^{21}/(21) = 0.000000023$
12	$(0.5)^{23}/(23) = 0.000000005$
13	$(0.5)^{25}/(25) = 0.000000001$
14	$(0.5)^{27}/(27) = 0.0000000003$
	$\Sigma = 0.5493061443$

As can be seen, the 14th term is considerably smaller than the first. If you have the tan h^{-1} function on your calculator, you can check the result shown. Unfortunately, the C++ compiler does not have this function built in (like it has sin, cos, tan, etc.). So, if you need to use the tan h^{-1} function in a program, you need to calculate its value from the series representation.

ALGORITHM

Clearly, an infinite number of terms cannot be used in the series. Generally, we need to:

1. Set a fixed number of terms to be used in the series.
2. Set a criteria by which the loop can be terminated.

An algorithm that utilizes a `for` loop follows:

1. Prompt the user to input a value of x
2. Read the value of x
3. If x is not between -1 and 1
   a. Write a message to the screen
   b. Stop execution
4. If x is between -1 and 1
5. For loop with a counter going from 1 to 500
   a. Calculate an individual term in the series
   b. Add the term to the rest of the series
   c. Exit the loop if an individual term absolute value is less than 0.0000000001
6. Print the result to the screen

An algorithm that utilizes a `do-while` loop follows:

1. Prompt the user to input a value of x
2. Read the value of x
3. If x is not between -1 and 1
   a. Write a message to the screen
   b. Stop execution
4. If x is between -1 and 1

5. `do-while` loop (exit the loop when an individual term absolute value is less than 0.0000000001 or when the value of the counter is greater than 500)
   a. Calculate an individual term in the series
   b. Add the term to the rest of the series
   c. Increment the counter
6. Print the result to the screen

The `for` loop is easily written from the summation equation. First, we create a variable to represent the sum and set it to zero before the loop. This is required before we sum any list of numbers. For example:

```
series_sum = 0;
```

The summation portion of the equation:

$$\sum_{n=1}^{n=\infty}$$

is represented by:

```
for (n = 1; n <= large_number; n++)
```

where `n` is our loop control variable and `large_number` is a finite value chosen to assure a sufficient number of terms are carried.

Then we translate the single term into C++ code. The single term:

$$\frac{x^{(2n-1)}}{(2n-1)}$$

is written in C++ as:

```
single_term = (pow (x,  (2.* (n - 1.))) / (2.* n - 1.);
```

We sum each single term with the assignment statement:

```
series_sum += single_term;
```

The entire loop is:

```
series_sum = 0;
for (n = 1; n <= 500; n++)
   {
   single_term = (pow (x,  (2.* n - 1.))) / (2.* n - 1.);
   series_sum += single_term;
   if (single_term < 0.0000000001) break;
   }
```

Note that we break out of the loop before 500 iterations if a single term is sufficiently small.

Source Code

Source codes using both a `for` loop and a `do-while` loop follow. They are based on the two algorithms and, therefore, check for the value of x between −1 and 1 and make sure that an infinite loop is not produced by stopping at 500 terms.

Source Code with `for` Loop

```
#include <iostream>
#include <iomanip>
#include <cmath>
using namespace std;
int main( )
{
    int n;
    double x, single_term, series_sum ;

    cout << "Input value of x (where -1 < x < 1) \n";
    cin >> x;

    if (x < -1. || x > 1.)
       {
       cout << "\n"
                 "You have entered an invalid value of x.\n"
                 "Program execution has halted\n";
       }
    else

       {
        series_sum = 0.0 ;

        for (n = 1; n <= 500; n++)
            {
            single_term = (pow(x, (2.* n - 1.))) / (2.* n - 1.);
            series_sum += single_term;
            if (single_term < 0.0000000001) break;
            }

        cout << "x = " << x << "     tanh-1(x) = "
            << setprecision(9) << series_sum << endl;
        }
}
```

If `x` is not between −1 and 1, no more calculations are performed.

The variable used to hold the sum (`series_sum`) must be initialized to zero before the loop is begun.

The loop will execute 500 times unless it is exited early.

The `single_term` is calculated from the counter, `n`.

The sum of the series terms is calculated using the compound assignment operator `+=`.

The loop is exited when the `single_term` is very small.

Source Code with `do-while` Loop

```
#include <iostream>
#include <iomanip>
#include <cmath>
using namespace std;
int main( )
{
    int n;
    double x, single_term, series_sum;
```

```
    cout << "Input value of x (where -1 < x <1) \n";
    cin >> x;

    if (x < -1. || x > 1.)
     {
     cout << "\n"
                  "You have entered an invalid value of x.\n"
                  "Program execution has halted\n";
     }
    else
     {
       n = 1;
       series_sum = 0.0;

       do
          {
          single_term = (pow(x, (2.* n - 1.)))/(2.* n - 1.);
          series_sum += single_term;
          n++;
          }
       while (single_term > 0.0000000001 && n <= 500);
     cout << "x = " << x << "    tanh-1(x) = "
          << setprecision(9) << series_sum << endl;
     }
}
```

The conditional in this `do while` loop checks both the `single_term` value and the number of iterations.

Output

```
                    Input value of x (where -1 < x < 1)
Keyboard input      0.5
                    x = 0.500000
                    tanh-1(x) = 0.549306144
```

Comments

Either of these source codes is acceptable; however, the `do-while` loop is more structured because it has no break statement. We can also write the `for` loop with no break statement if we use a compound relational expression with a logical operator as a test expression as we did with the `do-while` loop. For instance, the `for` loop

```
single_term = 1.0;
for (n = 1; n <= 500 && (fabs(single_term) > 0.0000000001); n++)
     {
     single_term = (pow(x, (2.* n - 1.)))/(2. * n - 1.);
     series_sum += single_term;
     }
```

accomplishes the same task as the `for` loop shown in the original source code. Here, we do not need the `break` statement because we have used a more complex test expression. Notice that we have arbitrarily initialized `single_term` to be 1.0. This has no effect on the calculation of `series_sum`. It simply assures us of initially entering the `for` loop because it makes `fabs(single_term)` greater than 0.0000000001.

Remember, to write code equivalent to a summation equation, you should:

1. Create a variable for storing the sum and initialize it to zero before the loop (for this description, we simply call it `sum`).
2. Make a `for` loop (or other type) with the control variable (here, we call it `n`) representing the variable below the capital sigma in the summation equation. The control variable, `n`, should initially be the value below the capital sigma and progress to the value at the top of the capital sigma.
3. Translate the single term (to the right of the capital sigma) to C++ code. For convenience, you can create a variable to store the single term value each time through the loop (which we will call `single_term`).
4. Within the loop write:

```
sum += single_term;
```

5. Break out of the loop after a limited number of terms, if necessary, to prevent creating an infinite loop.

From this application example and description, you should observe how easy it is to develop a loop from an equation written in summation form (Eqn. 6.6). In your assignments, if you express your equations in summation form prior to writing your source code (whenever possible), you will find it easy to write your source code.

Also, the include directive

```
#include <cmath>
```

is needed for this program because the `pow()` and `fabs()` functions are used.

If you use your calculator to find the value of tan h^{-1} (0.50), you will see that it agrees with the value listed in the output. However, if you were to use `float` instead of `double` for the type of real variables in this program, the result would not agree with your calculator (assuming `float` is 2 bytes). The comparison follows for both 0.50 and 0.35:

x	tan h^{-1} (x) (from program using double)	tan h^{-1} (x) (from program using float instead of double)
0.50	0.549306144	0.549306273
0.35	0.365443754	0.365443736

This may seem like a minor difference, but because many calculations may be done with this number if it were to be used in other programs, this difference could have a significant effect on output results. Remember, use `double` or `long double` in your programs, not `float`.

TABLE 6.10 — Form for tracing the program's loop

Statement	Test expression	n	single_term	series_sum
Before loop				
n = 1;				
n <= 500;				
Other statements				

Modification Exercises

Modify the program to

1. Use `float` instead of `double`. Use the input values 0.1, 0.3, 0.7, and 0.9. Compare the printed results with results from your calculator. Are the program results satisfactory?
2. Calculate the natural log of 2 using the series $\ln 2 = 1 - 1/2 + 1/3 - 1/4 + 1/5 \ldots$ to eight significant digits.
3. Calculate $\pi^2/6 = 1/1^2 + 1/2^2 + 1/3^2 + 1/4^2 + \ldots$. Then calculate π to five significant digits.
4. Calculate $0.5 = [1/(1 * 3)] + [1/(3 * 5)] + [1/(5 * 7)] + [1/(7 * 9)] + [1/(9 * 11)] + \ldots$ to seven significant digits.
5. Calculate $0.75 = [1/(1 * 3)] + [1/(2 * 4)] + [1/(3 * 5)] + [1/(4 * 6)] + [1/(5 * 7)] + \ldots$ to seven significant digits.
6. Calculate $\pi^2/12 = 1/1^2 - 1/2^2 + 1/3^2 - 1/4^2 + \ldots$. Then calculate π to six significant digits.

Tracing Exercises

1. Use your calculator and the `for` loop in the program to expand and complete Table 6.10 in accordance with Table 6.1.
2. Use the same table format to trace the `do-while` loop.

APPLICATION EXAMPLE 6.6 ENCRYPTING AND ANALYZING A MESSAGE

Problem Statement

TOPICS

- `if-else` control structure
- `for` loop
- File input
- File output
- Binary search

Write a program capable of encrypting an ordinary text message using a substitution cipher and counting the number of times each letter in the alphabet appears in the message. Use a binary search technique in the program to substitute each letter. The text message should have only lowercase letters and use periods in place of spaces between words. Use the example message:

```
this.message.is.encrypted.with.a.substitution.cipher.
we.can.evaluate.the.frequency.content.of.the.letters.
to.assist.us.with.deciphering.the.message.
the.described.method.works.better.with.longer.text.
```

Solution

RELEVANT EQUATIONS AND BACKGROUND INFORMATION

In sending and receiving a secure message, we require a program that encrypts the message at the sending location and a program that deciphers the message at the receiving location (Fig. 6.8). In doing so, we assume that someone intercepts the message with the intention of deciphering it (also shown in Fig. 6.8). The intended receiver knows the algorithm for deciphering the message, whereas the interceptor does not. Therefore, the two deciphering programs are different.

In this application example, we illustrate elements of the encrypting program and an interceptor's deciphering program. We could write this program more easily than what we show in this example if we use more advanced programming methods. However, it is still possible to write this program using just a loop and `if` control structures.

For the encrypting program, we use the process of substitution. In its simplest form, substitution is represented by the alphabet with the substitution letters below each letter (Table 6.11).

For the letter substitution in Table 6.11, the encrypted word "hello" would be written as "exyya."

For the deciphering program, we show how to count the letters in the encrypted message. While this does not decode the message, it is useful because English letters do not appear in equal numbers in typical text. For example, e, t, a, i, and s are the most commonly used English letters (not counting the "space" character). By counting the letters of a long encrypted message, we can begin deciphering the message by

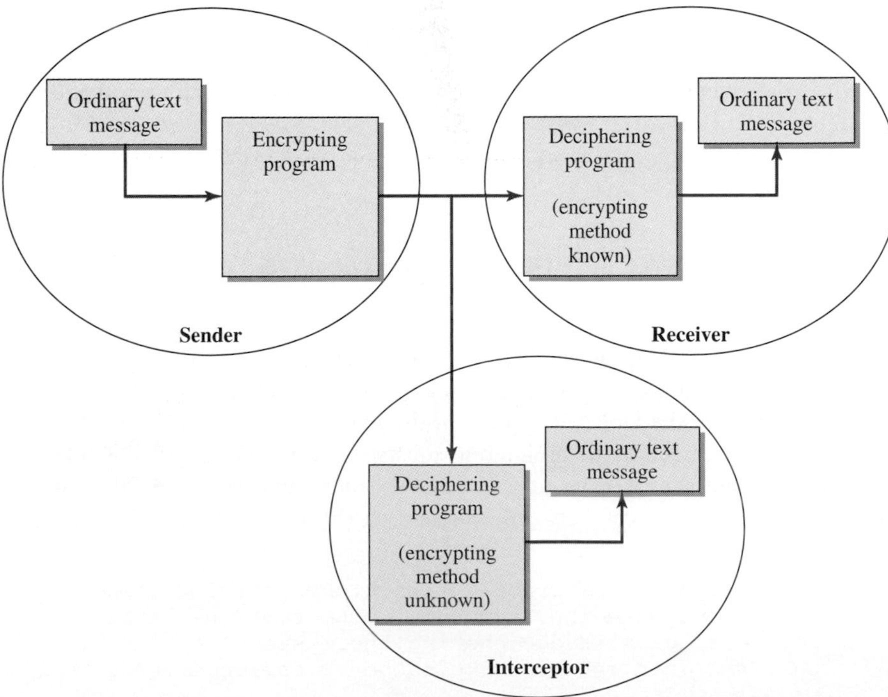

Figure 6.8

The process of sending, receiving, and intercepting an encrypted message.

TABLE 6.11 — Substitution cipher

a	b	c	d	e	f	g	h	i	j	k	l	m	n	o	p	q	r	s	t	u	v	w	x	y	z	.
s	u	v	w	x	z	.	e	n	c	r	y	p	t	a	b	d	f	g	h	i	j	k	l	m	o	q

The top row is the alphabet. The bottom row has the substitution letters.

TABLE 6.12 — Frequencies of original and encrypted letters

Original message	d	e	c	i	p	h	r	.	t	i	s
Encrypted message	w	x	v	n	b	e	f	q	h	n	g
Number of occurrences	1	2	1	1	1	2	1	1	1	1	1

substituting the most common letters in English for the most common letters in the encrypted message. Therefore, a first step in deciphering a message coded with a substitution cipher is counting the number of times each letter appears in the message.

SPECIFIC EXAMPLE

For the message:

```
d e c i p h e r . t h i s
```

the encrypted message is:

```
w x v n b e x f q h e n g
```

Note that the "space" symbol (.) is represented by the letter q in the encrypted message. This makes the encrypted message look spaceless. The number of letters (for both the original and encrypted message) is shown in Table 6.12.

This message is too short to reliably apply letter frequency methods. However, the original message does have the letters e and h (which are two of the most commonly used English letters) present more than the others.

ALGORITHM AND CODE SEGMENTS

Because we have not yet learned how to use arrays (Chapter 9), we need to read one character at a time from the input file, figure out what letter it is, count it, and print the substitute letter. To do so, we need to save a count for each letter and the space indicator (.). Therefore, we need 27 counting variables, which we will call `counta`, `countb`, `countc`, and so on for all the letters.

The steps for the program are:

1. Declare a single char.
2. Declare 27 integers as counting variables.
3. Open input and output files.
4. Repeat for each character in the message:
   a. Read a single character from the input file.
   b. Determine which letter it is using a binary search.
   c. Increase the count for that letter.
   d. Print the substitute letter to the output file.
5. Print the counts for all the letters.

Here, we describe steps 4b and 4d. The other steps are easily done.

STEP 4B—DETERMINE WHICH LETTER IS READ USING A BINARY SEARCH

We describe a binary search by first comparing it to a linear search. In a linear search, we would read a letter with the statement:

```
infile >> ltr;
```

and increase the count and print the substitute letter with a long `if-else-if` control structure of the form:

```
if  (ltr == 'a')
         {
         counta++;
         outfile << "s";
         }
else if  (ltr == 'b')
         {
         countb++;
         outfile << "u";
         }
else if  (ltr == 'c')
         {
         countc++;
         outfile << "v";
         }
```

We could simply have 27 of these structures.

One way to choose an algorithm or program form is to evaluate the number of comparisons (like `ltr == 'a'`) needed during execution. Fewer comparisons usually means faster execution because comparisons take execution time. With the `if-else-if` structure shown, if the letter read is ‘a’, only one comparison is done and we exit the structure. If the letter read is ‘b’, two comparisons are done before we exit the structure. Therefore, we see that if a letter is at the beginning of the alphabet, the `if-else-if` control structure executes quickly because few comparisons are needed. However, if the letter is ‘z’, we do 26 comparisons. Therefore, while this `if-else-if` control structure works, the number of comparisons is dependent upon the content of the message, and therefore the performance of the structure can be somewhat unpredictable.

If we can develop a method that is more predictable and keeps the number of comparisons low, we should probably use it because such a method will give a more reliable performance and have a reasonably fast execution speed. In this example, we choose to illustrate a binary search technique. With this technique, we can reduce the maximum number of comparisons per letter to only five. We use the fact that C++ treats characters as integers with their ASCII code value (for ASCII systems). (Recall that the letter b is one greater numerically than the letter a using the ASCII code.)

Figure 6.9 shows how we can repeatedly break the possibilities into two groups. Using this figure, the binary search method is to start at the top and move down the branches until we arrive at a letter. We always check the range in our location’s left branching box. If the letter is in the left branching box range, we go to the left branching box. If it is not, we go to the right branching box. We continue until we reach the bottom.

For example, suppose the letter we are considering is ‘z’ (but we do not know it). We start at the top (box “Letter”). We compare the unknown letter to the range a–m (the left branching box). We get that it is not in this range, so we go to the right (n–z) box. Then we check the range n–s (the left branching box) and find it is not in this

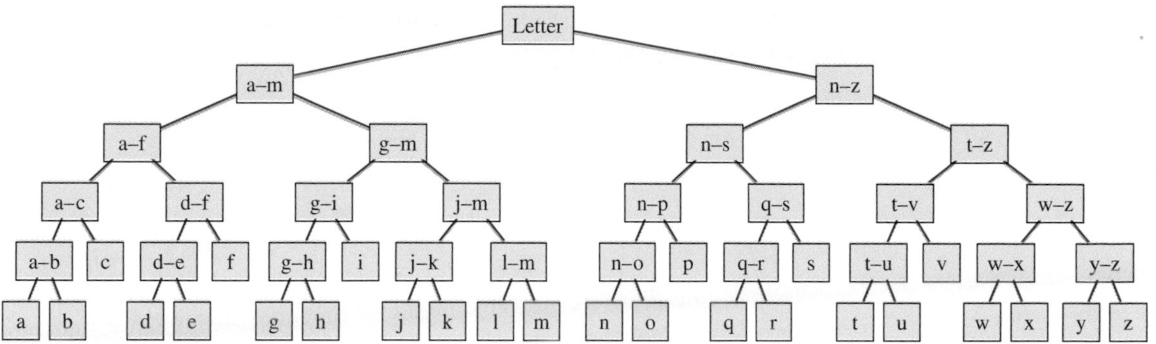

Figure 6.9

Tree used for finding a letter.

range, so we go to the right (t–z) box. We then check if it is in the t–v range (the left branching box), and it is not so we go to the right (w–z) box. We check the w–x range (the left branching box), get no, and go to the right (y–z) box. We then check y (the left branching box) and find that it is not y, so we go to the right and the letter is z. We are at the bottom and are done.

Note that by following the Fig. 6.9 chart, we have found our letter using a total of only five comparisons! This is substantially better than the 26 comparisons we would use for a straight comparison with each letter. Therefore, we get a more consistent performance with the Fig. 6.9 decision tree.

To program such a tree, it is somewhat easier to start at the bottom of the tree and move upward. Here, we will simply illustrate the logic in programming the a–f subtree and the process of increasing the count for each letter. The source code shows the entire tree.

First, we need to remember that we only check the left branching box and go to the right branching box if the comparison is false. This leads to an `if-else` control structure. For instance, if we are in the a–b box (Fig. 6.9), the `if-else` structure is straightforward. It is:

a–b structure:

```
if (ltr == 'a')
          {
          counta++;
          }
else
          {
          countb++;
          }
```

And, if we are in the d–e box, the `if-else` structure is:

d–e structure:

```
if (ltr == 'd')
          {
          countd++;
          }
else
          {
          counte++;
          }
```

However, if we are in the a–c box, we need to have the a–b structure (the left branching box) as our true block. We could write:

a–c structure:

```
if ('a' <= ltr && ltr <= 'b')
          {
          a-b structure
          }
else
          {
          countc++;
          }
```

However, since we are already in the a–m portion of the tree, we know that `'a' <= ltr`, so we do not need that comparison and write:

a–c structure:

```
if (ltr <= 'b')
          {
          a-b structure
          }
else
          {
          countc++;
          }
```

And, if we are in the d–f box, we need to have the d–e structure as our true block. The d–f structure could be written:

d–f structure:

```
if ('d' <= ltr && ltr <= 'e')
          {
          d-e structure
          }
else
          {
          countf++;
          }
```

Again, because we already know that `'d' <= ltr` we can eliminate that comparison and write:

d–f structure:

```
if (ltr <= 'e')
          {
          d-e structure
          }
else
          {
          countf++;
          }
```

Lastly, if we are in the a–f box, we have the a–c structure in our true block and the d–f structure in our false block. The a–f structure is: (Using that we know already that `'a' <= ltr`.)

a–f structure:

```
if (ltr <= 'f')
          {
          a-c structure
          }
else
          {
          d-f structure
          }
```

We see that the final a–f structure contains a number of other structures. These are easily combined, but we must remember that indentation is important, so we indent each embedded structure one tab. The source code shows all the structures together.

STEP 4D—PRINTING THE SUBSTITUTION LETTER

Each time we determine an original message letter and increment the count for that letter, we print the encrypted letter to the output file. For instance, when we determine a letter is a, the code

```
if (ltr == 'a')
          {
          counta++;
          outfile << "s";
          }
```

increases the count for a and prints the encoded letter s.

Look at the source code and see the entire structure. Then look at the output and see the strange looking encrypted message.

Source Code

```
#include <iostream>
#include <fstream>
using namespace std;

int main()
{
      char ltr;
      int i;
      int counta=0, countb=0, countc=0, countd=0, counte=0, countf=0, countg=0;
      int counth=0, counti=0, countj=0, countk=0, countl=0, countm=0, countn=0;
      int counto=0, countp=0, countq=0, countr=0, counts=0, countt=0, countu=0;
      int countv=0, countw=0, countx=0, county=0, countz=0, count_period=0;

      ifstream infile("C:\\A7_2.DAT");
      ofstream outfile("C:\\A7_2.OUT");

      outfile << "Encrypted message:" << endl;

      for (i = 0; i < 199; i++)
            {
            infile >> ltr;
            if (i == 53 || i == 106 || i == 148) outfile << endl;
```

Initializing all the counts to zero.

Opening the input and output files.

Looping over all the characters in the file.

Reading a letter and creating a new line in the output, occasionally.

```
if (ltr <= 'm')
     {
     if (ltr <= 'f')
          {
          if (ltr <= 'c')
               {
               if (ltr <= 'b')
                    {
                    if ('a' == ltr)
                         {
                         counta++;
                         outfile << 's';
                         }
                    else
                         {
                         countb++;
                         outfile << 'u';
                         }
                    }
               else
                    {
                    countc++;
                    outfile << 'v';
                    }
               }
          else
               {
               if (ltr <= 'e')
                    {
                    if ('d' == ltr)
                         {
                         countd++;
                         outfile << 'w';
                         }
                    else
                         {
                         counte++;
                         outfile << 'x';
                         }
                    }
               else
                    {
                    countf++;
                    outfile << 'z';
                    }
               }
          }
```

```
else
    {
    if (ltr<='i')
        {
        if (ltr<='h')
            {
            if ('g'==ltr)
                {
                countg++;
                outfile<<'.';
                }
            else
                {
                counth++;
                outfile<<'e';
                }
            }
        else
            {
            counti++;
            outfile<<'n';
            }
        }
    else
        {
        if (ltr<='k')
            {
            if ('j'==ltr)
                {
                countj++;
                outfile<<'c';
                }
            else
                {
                countk++;
                outfile<<'r';
                }
            }
        else
            {
            if ('l'==ltr)
                {
                countl++;
                outfile<<'y';
                }
            else
                {
                countm++;
                outfile<<'p';
                }
            }
        }
    }
}
```

The letter is g.

The letter is h.

True block of g–h.

The letter is i.

True block of g–i.

The letter is j.

The letter is k.

True block of j–k.

The letter is l.

The letter is m.

False block of j–k.

False block of g–i.

False block of a–f.

```
else
    {  <------------------------------------------------- Begin false block of a–m.
    if (ltr <= 's')
        {
        if (ltr <= 'p')
            {
            if (ltr <= 'o')
                {
                if ('n' == ltr)
                    {
                    countn++;
                    outfile << 't';
                    }
                else
                    {
                    counto++;
                    outfile << 'a';
                    }
                }
            else
                {
                countp++;
                outfile << 'b';
                }
            }
        else
            {
            if (ltr <= 'r')
                {
                if ('q' == ltr)
                    {
                    countq++;
                    outfile << 'd';
                    }
                else
                    {
                    countr++;
                    outfile << 'f';
                    }
                }
            else
                {
                counts++;
                outfile << 'g';
                }
            }
        }
```

```
else
    {
    if (ltr <= 'v')
        {
        if (ltr <= 'u')
            {
            if ('t' == ltr)
                {
                countt++;
                outfile << 'h';
                }
            else
                {
                countu++;
                outfile << 'i';
                }
            }
        else
            {
            countv++;
            outfile << 'j';
            }
        }
    else
        {
        if (ltr <= 'x')
            {
            if ('w' == ltr)
                {
                countw++;
                outfile << 'k';
                }
            else
                {
                countx++;
                outfile << 'l';
                }
            }
        else
            {
            if ('y' == ltr)
                {
                county++;
                outfile << 'm';
                }
            else
                {
                if (ltr == 'z')
                    {
                    countz++;
                    outfile << 'o';
                    }
                else
                    {
                    count_period++;
                    outfile << 'q';
                    }
                }
            }
        }
    }
```

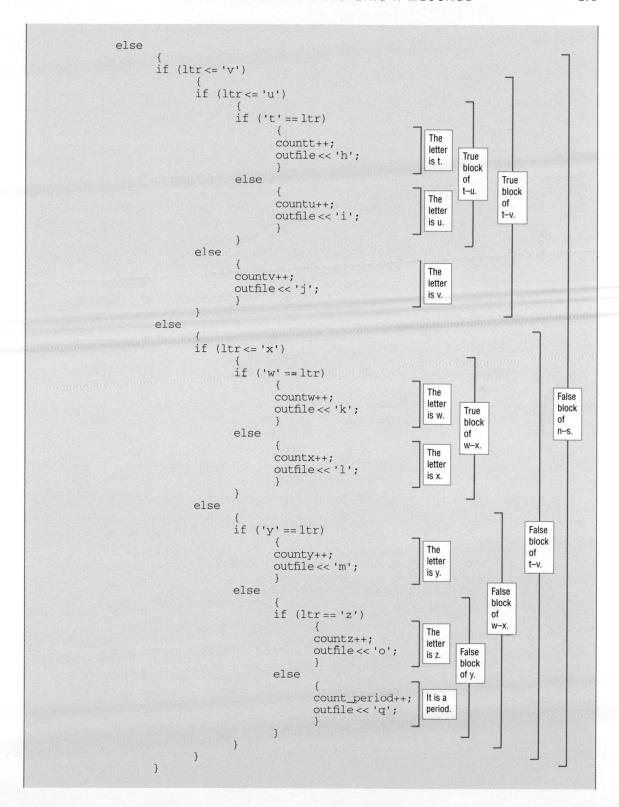

```
                }
        }
        outfile << endl << endl;

        outfile << "Original message frequency evaluation:" << endl;
        outfile << "a freq = " << counta << "   " << "b freq = " << countb << "  ";
        outfile << "c freq = " << countc << "   " << "d freq = " << countd << endl;
        outfile << "e freq = " << counte << "   " << "f freq = " << countf << "  ";
        outfile << "g freq = " << countg << "   " << "h freq = " << counth << endl;
        outfile << "i freq = " << counti << "   " << "j freq = " << countj << "  ";
        outfile << "k freq = " << countk << "   " << "l freq = " << countl << endl;
        outfile << "m freq = " << countm << "   " << "n freq = " << countn << "  ";
        outfile << "o freq = " << counto << "   " << "p freq = " << countp << endl;
        outfile << "q freq = " << countq << "   " << "r freq = " << countr << "  ";
        outfile << "s freq = " << counts << "   " << "t freq = " << countt << endl;
        outfile << "u freq = " << countu << "   " << "v freq = " << countv << "  ";
        outfile << "w freq = " << countw << "   " << "x freq = " << countx << endl;
        outfile << "y freq = " << county << "   " << "z freq = " << countz << "  ";
        outfile << "period freq = " << count_period << endl;
        outfile << endl << endl;
}
```

Printing all the counts.

Input File (Contains Original Message)

```
this.message.is.encrypted.with.a.substitution.cipher.
we.can.evaluate.the.frequency.content.of.the.letters.
to.assist.us.with.deciphering.the.message.
the.described.method.works.better.with.longer.text.
```

Output

```
Encrypted message:
hengqpxggs.xqngqxtvfmbhxwqknheqsqgiughnhihnatqvnbexfq
kxqvstqxjsyishxqhexqzfxdixtvmqvathxthqazqhexqyxhhxfgq
haqsggnghqigqknheqwxvnbexfnt.qhexqpxggs.xq
hexqwxgvfnuxwqpxheawqkafrgquxhhxfqknheqyat.xfqhxlhq

Original message frequency evaluation:
a freq = 7   b freq = 3   c freq = 7   d freq = 5
e freq = 28   f freq = 2   g freq = 4   h freq = 11
i freq = 12   j freq = 0   k freq = 1   l freq = 3
m freq = 3   n freq = 8   o freq = 7   p freq = 3
q freq = 1   r freq = 9   s freq = 15   t freq = 24
u freq = 5   v freq = 1   w freq = 5   x freq = 1
y freq = 2   z freq = 0   period freq = 32
```

Comments

The encrypted message is definitely mysterious looking. There are no spaces because the letter q represents "space" (the period in the original message). The frequency content evaluation of the original message shows that period is the most common character (32 times). Because the encoded message comes directly from the original, an evaluation of the letter frequencies of the encoded message would reveal that q is present 32 times. If we were decoding the encrypted message without knowing the encoding scheme, we could begin by concluding that q is the "space" symbol because "space" is the most common symbol in a typical text.

After that, the most common letter in the original message is e, which occurs 28 times and is represented by the letter x (which occurs 28 times in the encrypted message). Since e is the most common letter in English usage, a next reasonable step in decoding the encrypted message might be to conclude that x is the letter e.

This technique of substituting the most common English letters for the most common ones found in the encrypted message does not work flawlessly. We see that the next most common letter in the original message is t (represented by h in the coded message). However, a is the next most common in English. If we look at the encrypted message and conclude that h is a, we would be wrong.

In this message, the 10 most common letters are e, t, s, i, h, r, n, a, c, and o. These also happen to be the 10 most commonly used English language letters. Therefore, even for this short message, letter frequency analysis can be quite useful. To get further, we would need to look at the frequencies of letter combinations (such as "th" and "er") and one- and two-letter words (which are likely to be I, a, is, as, of, if, on, in, and others).

You may have noticed that the substitution key of Table 6.11 has the word "encrypt" in the lower row. After the t in encrypt is the alphabet (a–z and period) in order, except for the letters e, n, c, r, y, p, and t. The letter e in encrypt is offset eight letters from the beginning of the alphabet. Such a scheme makes it easy for the sender and receiver to communicate the substitution key of Table 6.11. Simply indicating the word "encrypt" with an 8 offset allows the receiver to reproduce Table 6.11, and therefore, to easily decode the message.

Note that we have used the `if-else` form of the `if` control structures. This has fewer comparisons than an equivalent `if-if` form. For instance, we wrote

```
if (ltr == 'a')
          {
          counta++;
          }
else
          {
          countb++;
          }
```

but we could have written

```
if (ltr == 'a')
          {
          counta++;
          }
```

```
if (ltr == 'b')
            {
            countb++;
            }
```

and accomplished the same task. However, the second form compares `ltr` to both 'a' and 'b', whereas the first compares `ltr` only to 'a'. Because there are fewer comparisons, the `if-else` form is superior to the `if-if` form. Therefore, in our program we use the `if-else` form.

Modification Exercises

1. Write your own ordinary message of one paragraph in a data file. Modify the loop in the program and have it read and work with your data file. Create your own letter substitution in the program.
2. Perform Exercise 1. Use the output file as input for another execution of the program to analyze the letter frequencies of your coded message.
3. Perform Exercises 1 and 2. Partner with a friend in class who has also performed these exercises. Exchange encrypted messages and letter frequencies. Try to decipher each other's messages. Use this order of letter frequencies to assist your analysis.

   Space, e, a, t, i, s, h, r, o, n, c.
4. Write a two-page ordinary message and perform Exercises 1–3.
5. Write a five-page ordinary message and perform Exercises 1–3. Is it easier to determine the letter decoding of the longer messages?
6. For the given substitution cipher of Table 6.11, write a receiver's program (Fig. 6.8) that deciphers the coded message in the output of the program shown.

LESSON EXERCISES

LESSON 6.1 EXERCISES

1. Find error(s), if any, in the following statements (assume `a` is `int` and `a = 1`):

   a. `while (a < 5): {cout << "a=" << a); a++;`

   b. `while (a < 5)   {cout << "a=" << a; a--;}`

2. Write a program that uses a `while` loop to create the following table (`x` is `double` type):

```
x        x*x        x+x
1.0      1.00       2.00
1.5      2.25       3.00
2.0      4.00       4.00
...
10.0     100.00     20.00
```

3. Use a `while` loop to show that the following series converges to 2:

$$1 + \frac{1}{2} + \frac{1}{4} + \frac{1}{8} + \frac{1}{16} + \cdots$$

4. Use `if` and other C++ statements to determine if a given integer, N, is a prime number or not. (Hint: use an `if` statement to test if N can be divided by 2 or any odd integer $<= N/2$.)

Solutions

1. a. `while (a < 5) {cout << "a=" << a; a++;}`
b. No error, but the loop will be executed forever because `a` never becomes greater than or equal to 5.

LESSON 6.2 EXERCISES

1. Find error(s), if any, in the following statements (assume `a` is `int` and `a` = 1):

a. `while (5) cout << "Good morning\n";`

b. `while (5<a): cout << "a="<<a<<endl; a++;}`

c. `while (5+1==7) {cout << "a=" << a << endl; break;}`

2. Use a `while` loop to calculate 8 factorial.

Solutions

1. a. No error, but it is an infinite loop. It will print `Good morning` an infinite number of times because the constant 5 represents true.
b. `while (5 < a) {cout << "a=" << a << endl; a++;}`
c. No error, but the loop will not be executed.

LESSON 6.3 EXERCISES

1. Find error(s), if any, in the following statements (assume `a` is `int` and `a` = 1):

a. `do cout << "Good morning\n"; while(5);`

b. `do (cout << "a=" << a; a++;) while (a < 5):`

c. `Do {cout << "a=" << a); break;} while (a > 5)`

2. Use a `do-while` loop to make the following table (`x` is `double` type):

```
x        x*x        x+x

1.0      1.00       2.00
1.5      2.25       3.00
2.0      4.00       4.00
...
10.0     100.00     20.00
```

3. Use a `do-while` loop to calculate 8 factorial.

4. Use a `do-while` loop and the following formula to calculate the value of π. Discuss the accuracy and the rate of convergence:

$$1 - \frac{1}{3} + \frac{1}{5} - \frac{1}{7} + \cdots = \frac{\pi}{4}$$

Solutions

1. a. No error, but it is an infinite loop (meaning that `Good morning` will be printed an infinite number of times on execution of the program).
   b. `do {cout << "a=\n" << a; a++;} while (a < 5);`
   c. `do {cout << "a=\n" << a; break;} while (a > 5);`

LESSON 6.4 EXERCISES

1. True or false:

   a. In a `for` loop expression, the starting counter value must be smaller than the ending counter value.

   b. The three loop expressions used in `for` loops must be separated by commas.

   c. Some programmers do not break out of `for` loops.

   d. `While` loops can be used to replace `for` loops without changing the loop body.

2. Find the error(s), if any, in each of these statements:

   a. `for  day = 1,3,1`

   b. `for (day = 1, day < 3, day++)`

   c. `for (day = 10;day<=20;day++);`

   d. `for (day = 10;day<5;day++)`

   e. `for (day = 100;day<100;day--)`

   f. `for (day = 10;day>100;day--)`

   g. `for (i = 20; i > 10; i--) i=i*3;`

3. Use a `for` loop and this formula to find the value of π. The result should at least be as accurate as 3.1416:

$$\frac{\pi}{2} = \frac{2}{1} * \frac{2}{3} * \frac{4}{3} * \frac{4}{5} * \frac{6}{5} * \frac{6}{7} \cdots$$

4. Use a `for` loop to construct this conversion table:

```
Inch      Feet        Meter
1         0.0833      0.0254
2         0.1667      0.0762
3         0.2500      0.0762
...
100       8.3333      2.5400
```

Solutions

1. a. false
   b. false
   c. true
   d. false
2. a. `for (day = 1; day <= 3; day++)`
   b. `for (day = 1; day < 3; day++)`

c. No error, the do nothing statement, `;` , will be executed 10 times.
d. No error, but its loop body will not be executed.
e. No error, but its loop body will not be executed.
f. No error; its loop body will be executed once.
g. No error, but the loop is an infinite loop.

LESSON 6.5 EXERCISES

1. True or false:

a. In C++, `day *= 5` may be used as a third expression in a `for` loop.

b. In C++, `day =+ 5` is similar to `day = day + 5`.

2. Find the error(s), if any, in each of these statements:

a. `for (i = 1; i < 3; i++) i = i + 100;`

b.
```
for (i = 1; i < 3; i++)
for (j = 100; j > 10; j /= 5) k = i + j;
```

c.
```
for (i = 1; i < 3; i++)   k = i + 10;
for (j = 100; j > 10; j /= 5) k = i + j;
```

3. Hand-calculate the final value of `c` in this program. Create a table of all of the values. After doing this, add `cout` statements and run the program to check your results:

```
#include <iostream>
using namespace std;
int main ( )
{
   int a,b,c;
   for (a = 1;a < 3;a++)
      {
        c = a;
        for (b = 1;b < 3;b++) c += a + b;
        c += 10;
        }
}
```

4. Write a program to calculate the mean, variance, and standard deviation of the first 10 positive integers. The mean, *m*, variance, *v*, and standard deviation, *s*, are defined as follows:

$$m = \sum_{i=1}^{n} \frac{x_i}{n}$$

$$s = \sqrt{v}$$

5. Run the following program and discuss the effect of using different types of variables as counter variables. Remember that it is recommended that you use only integers as your counter variables.

```
#include <iostream>
using namespace std;
```

```
int main ( )
{
    int i, isum1 = 0, isum2 = 0, N = 9999;
    float f, x, sum1 = 0.0, sum2 = 0.0;

    x = 1.0 / N;
    cout << "x = " << x << endl;

    for (i = 1; i <= N; i++) {sum1 += x; isum1 += 1;}
    cout << "sum1=" << sum1 << ", isum1=" << isum1 << endl;

    for (f = x;f <= 1.0;f += x) {sum2 += x; isum2 += 1;}
    cout << "sum2=" << sum2 <<", isum2="<< isum2 << endl;
}
```

Solutions

1. a. true
   b. false
2. a. No error, but it is not recommended to modify the counter variable `i` in its loop body.
   b. No error. This is a nested loop. Division of integer by integer would cause the fractional part to be lost if the test expression had a smaller comparison value.
   c. No error. This is not a nested loop.

APPLICATION EXERCISES

1. Rewrite Application Exercise 3.1 using a `for` loop.
2. Rewrite Application Exercise 3.1 using a `while` loop.
3. Rewrite Application Exercise 3.1 using a `do-while` loop.
4. Rewrite Application Exercise 3.4 using `for` loops.
5. Rewrite Application Exercise 3.4 using `while` loops.
6. Rewrite Application Exercise 3.4 using `do-while` loops.
7. Rewrite Application Exercise 4.7 using a `for` loop.
8. Rewrite Application Exercise 4.7 using a `while` loop.
9. Rewrite Application Exercise 4.7 using a `do-while` loop.
10. Rewrite Application Exercise 4.5 using a `do-while` loop.
11. Rewrite Application Exercise 4.3 using a `while` loop.
12. Rewrite Application Exercise 4.1 using a `for` loop.
13. The equation of a parabola is $y = ax^2 + bx + c$. Use a `for` loop and `if` statements in a program capable of finding the maximum or minimum of four different parabolas. As input, the program is to read the data consisting of *a*, *b*, and *c* for the four parabolas from a file called PARA.DAT, which consists of four lines:

    line1 a_1 b_1 c_1 (coefficients for parabola 1)
    line2 a_2 b_2 c_2 (coefficients for parabola 2)
    line3 a_3 b_3 c_3 (coefficients for parabola 3)
    line4 a_4 b_4 c_4 (coefficients for parabola 4)

An example data file is

```
1.1    -2     1
-1.3   1      15
-0.7   15      18.3
1.5    15.5    14.2
```

As output, print your result to file PARA.OUT in the following form:

Parabola number	Equation	(x, y) coordinates of minimum or maximum
1	y = 1.1x * x - 2x + 1	(0.909,0.0909) min
2	y = 21.3x * x + 1x + 15	—
3	y = 20.7x * x + 15x + 18.3	—
4	y = 1.5x * x + 15.5x + 14.2	—

14. The binomial theorem can be written as

$$(a+b)^n = a^n + na^{n-1}b + \frac{n(n-1)}{2!}a^{n-2}b^2 + \frac{n(n-1)(n-2)}{3!}a^{n-3}b^3 + \cdots$$

Write a program for which $a = 1$ and $0 < b < 1$ that uses the binomial theorem to calculate $(a+b)^n$ accurately to eight decimal places. Your program also should calculate $(a+b)^n$ using the `pow()` function. Make sure that your program checks for b being between 0 and 1. (Note: This is a converging series.)

Input data from file BINO.DAT: The first line of the file consists of the number of values (`m`). Then, `m` lines of data follow, each consisting of one value of `b` and one value of `n`. (Here, `b` is real, `m` and `n` are `int`.)

BINO.DAT

line 1 m
line 2 b n
line 3 b n
line 4 b n
...
...
...
line m + 1 b n

An example data file is

```
5
0.5  8
0.2  10
0.33 5
0.08 6
0.45 15
```

Show on the output:

```
Binomial theorem and pow() output
a = 1            b = ...           n = ...
(a+b)_n                            (a+b)_n
From the pow() function            From the binomial theorem
...                                ...
...                                ...
...                                ...
...                                ...
```

15. Write a program capable of using the month and day of a given date to calculate the number of days from January 1 that it represents. Make the program capable of computing values for as many as 20 dates.

Data should be input from a data file called DAYS.DAT. The data file should have the following format:

line 1	`n`	(number of dates to be computed)
line 2	`month`	`day`
line 3	`month`	`day`
line $n + 1$	`month`	`day` (all data are integers)

An example data file is

```
5
12   7
8    5
1    27
4    18
7    22
```

Print your results to file DAYS.OUT in the following format:

```
Table of dates and days from January 1
Date                 Days from Jan. 1
December 7           ...
August 5             ...
January 27           ...
April 18             ...
July 22              ...
```

Note that you must display the month in words and not numbers.

16. Write a program that computes the sum of all the negative integers in a list of integers. As input, the program is to read the data from the data file SUMNEG.DAT. The data file has the following format:

line 1	`n`	(number of integers in list)
line 2	`int1`	
line 3	`int2`	
line 4	`int3`	
...		
...		
...		

Write the output to the screen in the following manner:

```
The sum of the negative integers is:
...
The list of integers is:
...
...
...
...
```

17. The grading structure for a class is the following:

90–100	A
80–89	B
70–79	C
60–69	D
< 60	F

Write a program that prints the grades for 10 different numerical scores. As input, the program is to read the 10 scores (all integers) from the data file GRADE.DAT. The contents are line 1 score1 score2 score3 ....score10.

Print the results to file GRADE.OUT in the following table:

```
Numerical score          Grade
       ...                ...
       ...                ...
       ...                ...
       ...                ...
```

18. Write a program that is capable of finding the two largest and two smallest integers in a list of 20 integers. As input, the program is to read the data from the data file TWOMM.DAT. This data file consists of

line 1	`int1`	`int2`	`int3`	`... int10`
line 2	`int11`	`int12`	`int13`	`... int20`

Write the output to the screen in the form:

```
The two largest values in the list are:
...        ...
The two largest values in the list are:
...        ...
```

19. The constant percentage method of computing depreciation of an asset is based on the assumption that the depreciation charge at the end of each year is a fixed percentage of the book value of the asset at the beginning of the year. This assumption leads to the following relationship:

$$S = C(1 - d)^n$$

where C = original cost of asset
d = depreciation rate per year
n = number of years
S = book value at the end of n years

Write a program to compute the number of years of useful life of an asset given the original cost, depreciation rate, and book value at the end of its useful life (called *scrap value*).

As input, the program is to read the data from the keyboard. Prompt the user to enter the data in the following way:

```
Enter the original cost and depreciation rate:
...       ...
Enter the book value at the end of the useful life of an
  asset:
...       ...
```

Print the result to the screen as follows:

```
The useful life of the asset is:   ...years
```

20. Write a program that creates a substitution cipher when the original message contains both lower- and uppercase letters. Make the program operate similar to Application Example 6.6. Use periods for spaces.

21. Use the statement `cout << "*";` and loops and `if` control structures as needed to print the form of stars:

```
******
*    *
*    *
*    *
******
```

22. Use the statement `cout << "*";` and loops and `if` control structures as needed to print the form of stars:

```
    *
   * *
  *   *
 *     *
*********
```

23. Use the statement `cout << "*";` and loops and `if` control structures as needed to print the form of stars:

```
**********
*        *
*  ****  *
*  *  *  *
*  ****  *
*        *
**********
```

CHAPTER 7

FUNCTIONS

CHAPTER TOPICS

In this chapter, you will learn how to:

- Define and call functions
- Overload functions
- Use pointers and references

Functions form integral parts of C++ programs. If we continue the analogy, begun in Chapter 1, between building a structure and creating a program, we will gain further insight into the value of functions in programming.

Suppose you were given the task of constructing a footbridge across a river. One way to do it would be to find a very large tree that is tall enough to span the river and wide enough to handle foot traffic (Fig. 7.1). You could chop down that tree, cut it so it is just long enough to reach from one side of the river to the other, and then carve the tree so it is flat and suitable to walk across. Such an approach could be taken, but it is difficult and usually not practical because of the awkwardness in working with a single large entity.

Another way to construct the bridge would be to cut down many small trees and make a number of boards from each of them to use as girders for the bridge. Then you could use bolts for connectors and assemble the bridge girder by girder. This approach is usually more practical because each tree is lighter and smaller and easier to work with than the one large tree. However, in such a design, connections and planning are very important because each individual part must work with all the other parts.

Creating a large C++ program with just one function, `main`, is somewhat similar to building a bridge with a single tree. It is cumbersome and unwieldy because of the many lines of code. Creating a large C++ program with many functions (and, as we shall see, objects and classes) is similar to building a bridge with many girders. It involves putting many pieces together and making sure that they all work correctly with each other. In the same way that it is unwise, impractical, and maybe

Figure 7.1

Analogy between building a bridge and writing a program with functions.

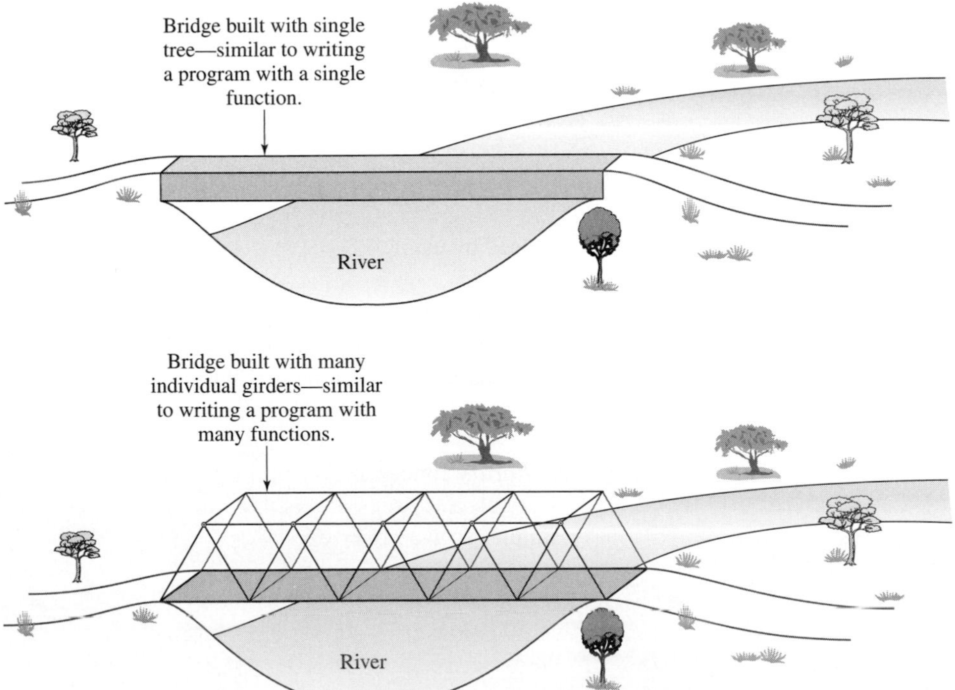
Bridge built with single tree—similar to writing a program with a single function.
River
Bridge built with many individual girders—similar to writing a program with many functions.
River

impossible to build a large bridge out of a single tree, it is unwise, impractical, and maybe impossible to create a large C++ program with a single function.

In addition, your programs become more powerful with functions you have created. For instance if your program repeatedly needs to use factorials, you could write a function named `fact` (as we do in Lesson 7.2) and use it like the C++ library functions `sin` or `cos` every time a factorial is needed. Each time the `fact` function is used (we say that the function is *called* or *invoked*), data goes into and out of the function. For instance, if we want to calculate the factorial of 4, we would call or invoke the function using `fact(4)`. Doing so causes data to pass to and return from the function `fact`. The value 4 goes to `fact`, and `fact` returns the number 24 (the factorial of 4). As you write functions, you will find it is important to correctly transfer data to and from functions. Not transferring data correctly is the source of many errors for beginning programmers.

Even if your program does not repeatedly perform a particular task, it is good programming practice to put separate tasks in separate functions. A well-written function can be saved and reused in another program that needs a similar task performed. For instance, our factorial function can be used in another program that needs factorials.

A typical professional program consists of many functions each named by the programmer for the task it performs. In writing functions for your programs, planning becomes very important. It is necessary to lay out exactly how the functions are to be connected together (meaning what information will be transferred into and out of the functions).

We can refer to a function's *specification* and *design*. Its specification refers to what goes into and out of a function and its design refers to the function's tasks. When working with a library function, the function's specification is very important because a user's responsibility is to correctly transfer data to the function and correctly use data returned from the function. In developing your own functions the design is also very important because you must write the function's code.

As you are beginning to learn how to write programs with many functions, you probably will become frustrated because of the added complexity and want to write your program with no functions other than `main`. Do not succumb to this temptation. Write your programs with functions, even if they are not completely necessary, so that you can learn how to overcome the issues raised by using functions. In this text, we illustrate programs with functions in many cases. However, because sometimes we want to focus on issues different from those that are raised by using functions, we do not use functions in all the programs in which we could have. You will see that using functions sometimes adds length to your programs. This is fine in practice; however, here we have publishing constraints and have tried to keep the programs as short as possible.

Functions can be broken into two groups, *library* functions and *programmer-defined* functions (Fig. 7.2). We have already described the use of some library functions. Using library functions is reasonably simple, so we cover each function as needed throughout this text. This chapter focuses on the more difficult process of creating programmer-defined functions. These functions are further separated into three categories—functions that return no value, functions that return a single value, and functions that are "pass by reference." We describe these three categories in Lessons 7.1, 7.2, and 7.3, respectively.

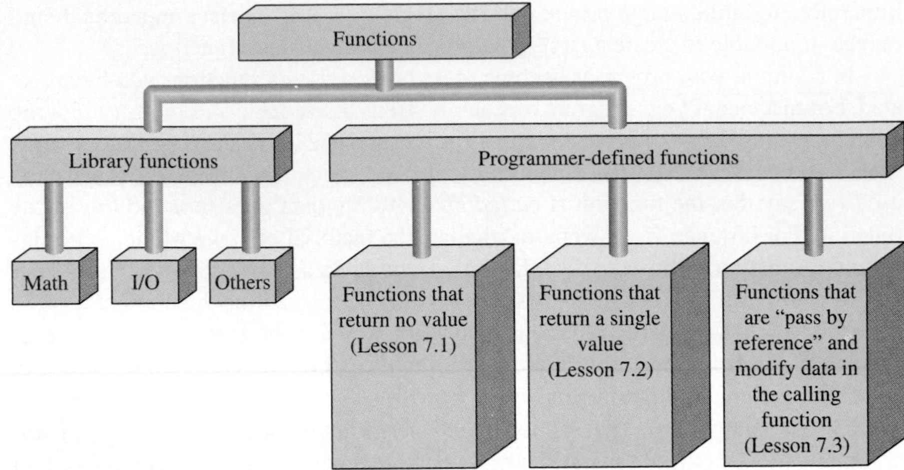

Figure 7.2

Categories of functions.

LESSON 7.1 FUNCTION BASICS

TOPICS

- Function calls
- Function declarations
- Function definitions
- Transferring values to functions
- Types of functions

We need three things to make use of a function in a program:

1. A function declaration
2. A function call
3. A function definition

A *declaration* (also called *prototype*) for a function is like a declaration for a variable. A function declaration indicates that a function of a particular name (which is chosen by the programmer, and must follow the rules for identifiers that we described for variables) exists and tells other information about the function. Like variables, functions must be declared prior to their use in a program.

A function *call* (also called *invocation*) is a statement that causes control to transfer from one function (for instance, `main`) to another function. The call statement may transfer data values to the function.

A function *definition* consists of a header line (which is similar in form to the function declaration) followed by the function body enclosed in braces. The function body is composed of executable statements such as `cout` statements, loops, and `if` control structures that perform the desired actions.

In this lesson we describe the development of two functions (which we name `potential_energy` and `kinetic_energy`) that are called from `main`. These functions calculate the potential and kinetic energy of groups of kilogram-sized blocks. Figure 7.3 illustrates the effect of calling `potential_energy` from `main`. This figure illustrates that when the function call is executed in `main`, the next statements executed are in `potential_energy`. When `potential_energy` is done executing, control returns to `main` at the same line `potential_energy` was called or invoked from (and the next statements executed are in `main`).

QUESTION YOU SHOULD ATTEMPT TO ANSWER

1. What are the numerical values passed to function `kinetic_energy()`?

We say that we *pass* data values to a function and *return* data values from a function. In this lesson, we cover functions that do

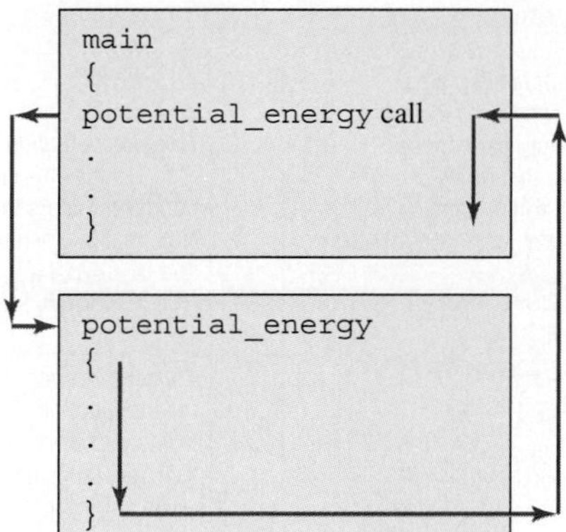

Figure 7.3

Direction of program flow when `potential_energy` is called.

not return any values, so no values are returned from either `potential_energy` or `kinetic_energy`. We do not pass any values to `potential_energy` but pass two values to `kinetic_energy`.

Read the program and look for the calls, declarations, and definitions for the two functions. Also, trace the flow of the program using the source code and the output. Recognize that when a function is invoked, control passes to the function and the function body is executed. Also note that data values are passed to `kinetic_energy`.

Source Code

```
#include <iostream>
using namespace std;

void potential_energy();
void kinetic_energy (int, double);

int main ( )
{
    int mass = 15;
    double velocity = 308.24;

    cout << "The value of mass in main "
            "is mass=" << mass << endl;

    potential_energy( );
    kinetic_energy (mass, velocity);

    cout << "The value of mass in main is still mass=" << mass << endl;
}
```

Function declarations. These indicate the number and types of arguments and the type of return value. The `void` preceding the function names indicates that no values are returned from the functions. Items enclosed in parentheses indicate the *number, order,* and *type* of data to be passed to the function when it is called. For `potential_energy`, the empty parentheses mean no data is passed to `potential_energy` when it is called. For `kinetic_energy`, two values are passed, an `int` and a `double`. The `int` is the first value in the list, and the `double` is the second.

Function calls. These lines are calls to `potential_energy` and `kinetic_energy`. These statements cause control to pass to `potential_energy` first then to `kinetic_energy`. There are no arguments for `potential_energy` (empty parentheses). There are two arguments for `kinetic_energy` (these are enclosed in parentheses). The arguments for `kinetic_energy` are `mass` and `velocity`. Note that `mass` is an `int` and `velocity` is a `double`. The number of arguments (2), order (`int` first and `double` second) and type (`int` and `double`) match what is listed for `kinetic_energy` in its declaration. The function call causes the *values* of `mass` and `velocity` to be passed from `main` to `kinetic_energy`.

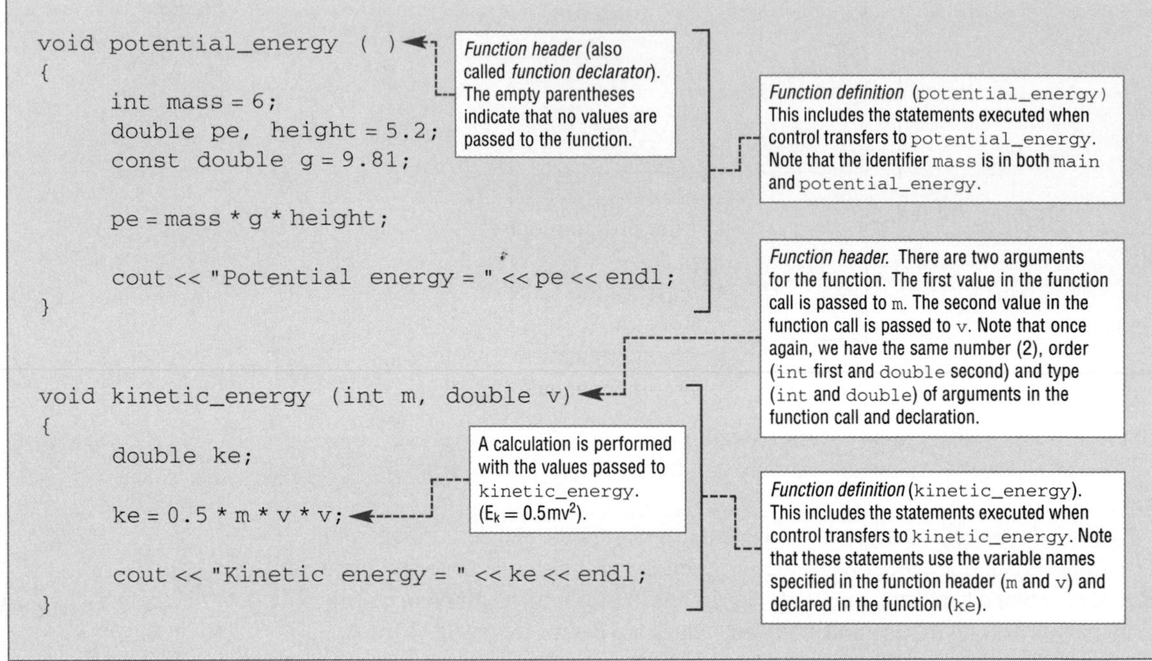

```
void potential_energy ( )
{
     int mass = 6;
     double pe, height = 5.2;
     const double g = 9.81;

     pe = mass * g * height;

     cout << "Potential energy = " << pe << endl;
}


void kinetic_energy (int m, double v)
{
     double ke;

     ke = 0.5 * m * v * v;

     cout << "Kinetic energy = " << ke << endl;
}
```


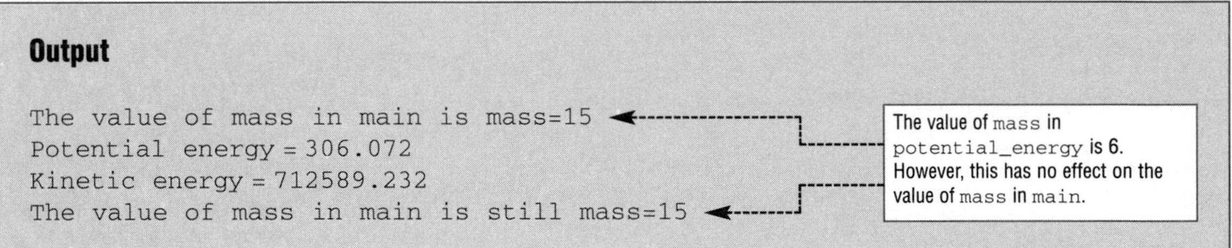

Output

```
The value of mass in main is mass=15
Potential energy = 306.072
Kinetic energy = 712589.232
The value of mass in main is still mass=15
```

The value of mass in potential_energy is 6. However, this has no effect on the value of mass in main.

Description

Function declaration. A function declaration indicates the function name, return type and types of values passed to the function. For example, the declaration for `kinetic_energy` is

```
void kinetic_energy (int, double);
```

Looking only at the function declaration, we see that `kinetic_energy` returns no value because it is of type `void`, and it has two arguments. The first argument is an `int`, and the second argument is a `double`. This means that `kinetic_energy` is passed (or receives) an `int` value and a `double` value when it is called.

The function declaration indicates information about the function *specification* (what goes into and out of the function). However, it does not tell the entire story because we need to know the meaning of the value returned and the meanings of the variables in the argument list to properly call a function. Therefore, you cannot properly use a function in a program by examining only its declaration.

The general form of a function declaration for a function with two values in its argument list is:

```
ftype fname (atype, atype);
```

where *ftype* is the function return type, *fname* is the function name, and *atype* is the argument type (not necessarily both the same).

Note the need for the semicolon at the end of the function declaration. A function declaration is typically placed at the start of the program outside the body of `main`. It is required to be located prior to the function call. In this lesson, we cover only `void` type functions, meaning no value is returned from the function. In Lesson 7.2, we cover returning values from a function.

If we wanted, we could have given the argument names in our function declaration. Standard C++ does not require that the argument names be given. It allows them but does not use them. This leads to an acceptable form of a function declaration to be

```
ftype fname (atype aname, atype aname);
```

where the *aname*s are the argument names (not the same). So, an equally acceptable function declaration for `kinetic_energy` is

```
void kinetic_energy (int m, double v);
```

This form of the declaration is the same as the function header except it has a terminating semicolon.

Should more than two arguments be needed for a function, more types can be enclosed in parentheses, each separated by a comma. Check with your instructor or employer about the preferred form for function declarations. In this text, we will normally use the form without argument names.

Function call. A function call transfers program control to the function. In this lesson's program, after executing the line

```
potential_energy ();
```

in the `main` function, control goes to `potential_energy` and the next lines of code executed are

```
int mass = 6;
double pe, height = 5.2;
const double g = 9.81;
pe = mass * g * height;
cout << "Potential energy = " << pe << endl;
```

which are within the body of `potential_energy`. This is illustrated schematically in Fig. 7.3.

We have not passed any information from `main` to `potential_energy`. We can see this because the call to `potential_energy` has no variables or expressions enclosed in the parentheses. Thus, no values are passed from `main` to `potential_energy`. We have done this because `potential_energy` needs no values from `main`. All its values are created within the function.

After `potential_energy` has finished executing, control goes back to the location of the call (Fig. 7.3) to `potential_energy` in `main`. That means the next line executed is

```
kinetic_energy (mass, velocity);
```

which is a call to kinetic_energy. This call causes the values of mass and velocity to be passed from main to kinetic_energy and causes control to pass to kinetic_energy.

In general, a function call consists of a function name (which is an identifier) followed by an *argument list,* which is a comma separated list of expressions enclosed in parentheses. The arguments represent values that are transferred between the call and the function. The form for calling a function with two arguments is

```
fname (exp1, exp2)
```

where *fname* is the function name, *exp1* and *exp2* are arguments that are expressions that can be, and commonly are, single variables or constants, and (*exp1*, *exp2*) is called the argument list.

Function definition. A function definition includes the function's executable statements. For instance, the definition of kinetic_energy is:

Function return type. Function name. Function argument declarations.

```
void kinetic_energy(int m, double v)
{
    double ke;

    ke = 0.5 * m * v * v;

    cout << "Kinetic energy = " << ke << endl;
}
```

Function body.

Observe that a function definition includes the return type, name, argument declarations, and the entire function body. The combination of the function return type, name, and argument declarations represents what is called the function *signature.*

A definition for a function that has two arguments has the following form:

```
ftype fname (atype aname, atype aname)
{
        ...
        ...
        ...
 }
```

Where *ftype* is the function return type (void means no return value), *fname* is the function name, *atype* is the argument type (int, double, or other), and *aname* is the argument name. The programmer needs to develop the function body. In this lesson's program, potential_energy calculates $E_p = mgh$, and prints it. The function kinetic_energy calculates $E_k = 0.5\,mv^2$ and prints it.

The argument lists in the function call and function header must coordinate. In general, to successfully transfer values to a function, we must make the *number, order,* and *type* of parameters in the argument list of a function call match the number, order, and type in the argument list in the function header. This is sometimes referred to by the acronym NOT (number, order, type). In other words, if the function header has two arguments then the function call must have two arguments. If the types are `int` and `double` in the header, then the types in the function call should be `int` and `double`, in that order.

For example, for `kinetic_energy` we have

```
kinetic_energy (mass, velocity);          <---- Function call in main.
void kinetic_energy (int m, double v)     <---- Function header.
```

This transfers the value of `mass` in `main` to `m` in `kinetic_energy` and the value of `velocity` in `main` to `v` in `kinetic_energy`. This transfer, illustrated in Fig. 7.4, is equivalent to the assignment statements `m = mass` and `v = velocity`. For both the call and header:

- The number of the arguments is two.
- The order of arguments is the first represents mass, and the second represents velocity.
- The types of arguments are `int` and `double`.

Therefore, we have met the number, order, and type (NOT) requirements because all three match in the call and header.

In `main`, at the location of the call to `kinetic_energy`, the value of `mass` is 15 and the value of `velocity` is 308.24. So, `kinetic_energy` receives the values 15 and 308.24. Because of the correspondence, `m` receives the value of 15, and `v` receives the value of 308.24. In this program, we used `m` and `v` to calculate the value of `ke` with the statement

```
ke = 0.5 * m * v * v;
```

This is equivalent to

```
ke = 0.5 * 15 * 308.24 * 308.24;
```

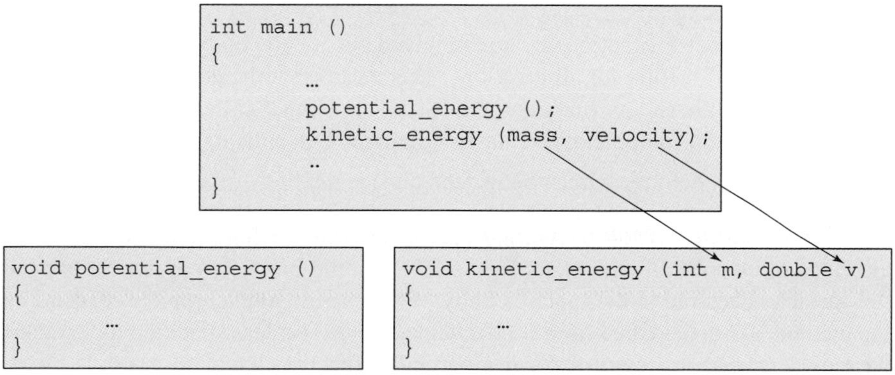

```
int main ()
{
        ...
        potential_energy ();
        kinetic_energy (mass, velocity);
        ..
}
```

```
void potential_energy ()
{
        ...
}
```

```
void kinetic_energy (int m, double v)
{
        ...
}
```

Figure 7.4

Relationship between functions in Lesson 7.1's program. Values are passed from `main` to `kinetic_energy`. No values are passed to `potential_energy`.

Arrangement within programs.

- It is not necessary for the first function listed to be `main`. For the program in this lesson, it would be perfectly acceptable to write the program as

```
#include <iostream>
using namespace std;

void kinetic_energy (int m, double v)
{
     function body
}

void potential_energy ( )
{
     function body
}

int main ( )
{
     function body
}
```

  Here, `potential_energy` and `kinetic_energy` appear in the listing before `main`. This is perfectly acceptable as C++ searches through the listing for `main` to begin execution.

  In this particular listing we have actually eliminated the need for the function declarations. This is because the function definitions are given in the code before the functions are called. Because of the similarity between the first line of the function definition and the function declaration, C++ allows the programmer to skip the declaration provided the function definition appears before the function call. In most cases in this text, we use declarations for functions.

- A function declaration can be written in a function body rather than outside the body of all functions. However, a function declaration given in a function body serves as a declaration only for the function in which it is declared. This means that the declared function can be called only from the body of the function where the declaration exists.

  In contrast, a function declaration given outside the body of all functions declares the function for all functions. This means that the declared function can be called from any function in the program. Note that the function declaration must appear before the first function that calls it.

- The function definition must be located outside the body of any other function.

Variable storage in memory. During execution, when a function is called, C++ allocates space within memory for the variables in the function's argument list and the variables declared in the function body. When the function completes execution, the memory is freed up, and the variable values are lost (unless specified to do otherwise as described in Lesson 7.5). If a particular function is called multiple times, memory is allocated and freed repeatedly for it.

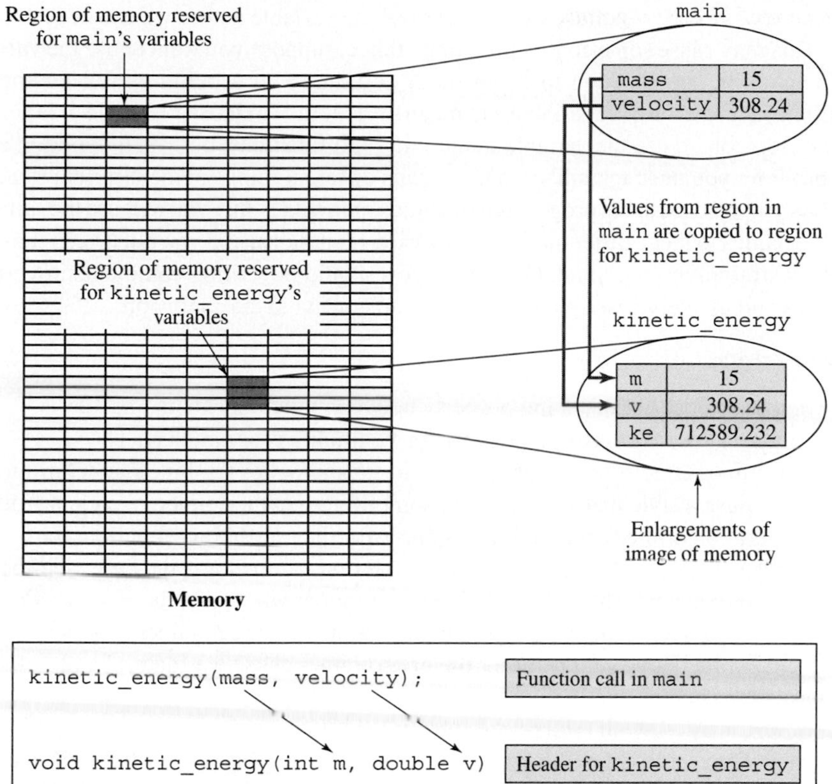

Figure 7.5

Illustration of actions taking place in memory when `kinetic_energy` is called in `main`. Note that values in `main`'s memory region are copied to `kinetic_energy`'s memory region. For Lesson 7.1's program, the two regions of memory may be adjacent to each other rather than separated as we have shown in the figure.

Each function's variables occupy a different region of memory. In Fig. 7.5, we show a representation of function variables being stored. It can be seen in this figure that the variables of `main` occupy a different region than the variables of `kinetic_energy`. Because of the correspondence in the function call and header, `m` and `v` in `kinetic_energy` are *copies* of the values of `mass` and `velocity` in `main`, respectively. Because they are copies, we can work with `m` and `v` in `kinetic_energy` and have no effect on `mass` and `velocity` in `main`.

Call by value or pass by value. As shown in Fig. 7.5, a *copy* of the values of `mass` and `velocity` in `main` are stored in the variable locations for `m` and `v` in `kinetic_energy`. Therefore, it is said that function `kinetic_energy` uses "call by value" or "pass by value." We will see in Lesson 7.3 that the alternative to "pass by value" is "pass by reference." For now, you should just realize that a function (working in the manner we have shown here) receives a copy of the value of each argument. This allows the function to modify the value of any argument without causing a change in the value of the original variable in the function call. In other words, function `kinetic_energy` can modify the values of `m` and `v`, but this will not affect the values of `mass` and `velocity`.

Variable names. Variable names are declared for each function. As a result, we are allowed to use the same variable name in different functions without having any connection between those variables (such as we have in this lesson's with `mass` in `main` and `mass` in `potential_energy`).

As we write each function, we must choose the variable names we use in each of them. This may cause some confusion. For instance, suppose you want to use the variable name `x` in one function to mean the x coordinate of a point, and in another function you want to use the variable `x` to mean the length of a side of a triangle. It is perfectly acceptable to use the variable name `x` in both functions, but when you look at your program you must remember that `x` means different things in the different functions! As you work with big programs it becomes more likely that you will use the same variable names to mean different things in various functions, and you must keep these variables straight in your mind. Of course, you should be writing comments in your programs and use very descriptive names to help you avoid the confusion.

Avoiding errors.

- Argument order not matching properly between function call and header is a common source of error, especially for beginning programmers. The programmer establishes the order when he or she writes the function definition. You can use a style that you like, and sometimes a natural order is evident from the operation of the function. For instance, for the `pow` library function, the order is `pow(x,y)` which calculates x^y. The first parameter is the base, and the second parameter is the exponent. The programmer who wrote the `pow` function easily could have written the function definition with the arguments in the reverse order. However, the order the programmer chose was natural and makes it easier for another programmer to call the function.

  One way to avoid errors caused by order is to make your variable names clearly representative of the quantities they are portraying. For instance, if you had written the `pow` function as a programmer defined function, you could have used in your definition (and declaration) the names `base` and `exponent` (instead of `x` and `y`). When you later write a call in your program to that function, you can simply look at the header to refresh your memory on the order of the parameters. With these descriptive names, you clearly know that the first argument in the call represents the base and the second argument the exponent. If the names `x` and `y` are used in the function header, one must study the function's code to determine whether the function calculates x^y or y^x.

  Another way to avoid errors caused by order is to use good commenting. Good commenting in your code, using a banner at the top of each function and clearly describing the meaning of each argument, is helpful in reducing the likelihood of error caused by incorrect order.

  Remember, if you have an incorrect order, your program may execute completely. Do not be fooled. This does not mean your answers are correct. If you find your answers are incorrect, you can check your parameters by inserting `cout` statements displaying the parameters just before the function call and at the very beginning of the function body. These `cout` statements should display values that you expect to see. If not, you may find that the order is incorrect.

- Types not matching may or may not produce errors. Suppose we had called `kinetic_energy` from `main` with two integers in the parameter list instead of an integer and a `double`. Because `kinetic_energy` needs to work with an integer and a `double`, the second integer would have been converted to a double automatically by C++. Converting an integer into a double usually does not cause errors. Therefore, even though the types do not match exactly, a successful execution can still take place. However, it is best to code your programs so that the types do match exactly.

A worse situation would have occurred if we had called kinetic_energy with two doubles in the parameter list instead of an integer and a double. This type of situation is more likely to cause errors. This is because the first double would have been converted into an integer for kinetic_energy, which usually causes truncating the fractional part of the value.

For instance, consider the following short program. Look at the call to kinetic_energy and the kinetic_energy declaration. The call is with doubles even though kinetic_energy is declared to have int arguments. Look at the output. The values of mass and velocity are truncated in being passed to m and v in kinetic_energy and printed to be only 12 and 2, losing a large number of digits.

The source code is

```
#include <iostream>
using namespace std;

void kinetic_energy (int, int);
int main ()
{
        double mass = 12.34985, velocity = 2.5678;
        kinetic_energy (mass, velocity);
        cout << "mass= " << mass << ", velocity= " << velocity;
}

void kinetic_energy (int m, int v)
{
      cout << "m= "<< m <<", v= " << v;
}
```

The variables, mass and velocity, are doubles. However, the function declaration states that the arguments should be int.

When mass and velocity are passed, copies are made, and the fractional part of the double values is cut off from them. This type of loss of information may cause errors in your programs. Note that because copies are made, the values of mass and velocity remain unchanged.

The output is

```
m= 12  v= 2
mass= 12.34985, velocity= 2.5678
```

Be careful; do not make this kind of error in calling your functions. Again, your best approach is to match the types in the argument list for the function declaration and the function call.

- We pass no more to a function than the information it needs because if there is an error in a function, it will affect only the information to which the function has access. This helps control the extent of errors.

  Beginning programmers sometimes struggle with determining what information should be passed to a function and how to pass it correctly. To determine what information a function needs, we must clearly define the activities a function is to have. This requires considerable advance planning. In this book, we focus on the aspect of planning in the application examples at the end of the chapter, where we illustrate practical programs. In the lessons, we focus on the mechanics of how to correctly pass information between functions.

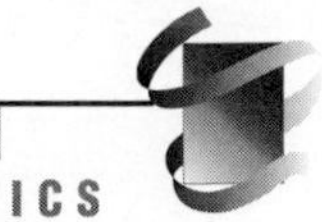

LESSON 7.2 RETURNING A VALUE FROM A FUNCTION

TOPICS

- Returning a value from a function
- Considerations about return value types

QUESTION YOU SHOULD ATTEMPT TO ANSWER

1. What is the reason the user is asked to enter a number no greater than 12?

We already have learned how to make use of library functions that accept one value and return another. An example of one of these is the `log` function from C++'s function library. For instance, if we write

```
y = log(x);
```

the value of `x` is passed to the `log` function, and the `log` function returns the value of the natural logarithm of `x`. The assignment statement gives `y` the value of `log(x)`.

You can utilize functions that you define in a similar manner. Suppose, for instance, that you need to compute the factorial of an integer n (written $n!$). You could check the function library and find out that C++ has no function that computes factorials like it does log, sin, tan, and others. Therefore, if you want to use a factorial in a calculation you need to write your own function. Then, you can call your function in the same way that you call a library function.

In this lesson's program, we have written a function named `fact`. Recall that the factorial of n is $n * (n - 1) * (n - 2) * (n - 3) \ldots * (2) * (1)$. In the discussion, we show line by line how this function calculates a factorial. After `fact` computes $n!$, the `main` function computes $1/n!$ and prints the value.

Read the code and annotations to observe other features of programming that we illustrate in this lesson.

Source Code

```
#include <iostream>
#include <iomanip>
using namespace std;

unsigned long int fact (int);

int main()
{

     int fact_argument;
     unsigned long int fact_value;
     double one_over_fact_value;

     cout << "Enter a positive integer less "
             "than or equal to 12:" << endl;
     cin >> fact_argument;
     fact_value = fact (fact_argument);
     one_over_fact_value = 1.0 / fact_value;
```

Function declaration. The function name is `fact`. It has one argument that is of type `int`. Instead of `void`, `double`, or `int`, it uses `unsigned long int` as its return type. We use `unsigned long int` because all factorial values are positive, and factorials are very large, so we want the maximum possible positive range.

Declaring the variable, `fact_value`, as type `unsigned long int`.

This statement both calls `fact` and assigns the return value to `fact_value`. Note that both the return value for `fact` and `fact_value` are the same type, `unsigned long int`. The value of `fact_argument` is passed from `main` to `fact`.

```
cout << "1/" << fact_argument << "! =" << setiosflags(ios :: scientific)
    << one_over_fact_value << endl;
    return (0);  <---- We have returned an integer (0) from main to the operating system.
}

unsigned long int fact (int arg)  <---- Function header. The variable, arg, contains the value of fact_argument which was passed from main.
{
    int i;
    unsigned long int factorial_of_arg;  <---- Declaring the variable, factorial_of_arg, as type unsigned long int. It serves as the variable returned by fact.

    factorial_of_arg = 1;
    for (i = arg; i >= 1; i--)
          {
          factorial_of_arg *= i;      <---- Loop for calculating the factorial of arg.
          }
    return (factorial_of_arg);
}
                                  Function definition. Definition of fact.
```

Output

```
                 Enter a positive integer less than or equal to 12:
Keyboard input   9
                 1/9! = 2.755732e-06
```

Description

Returning a value from a function. Two things are needed to return a value from a function—an appropriate return type for the function and a `return` statement in the function.

1. In its declaration and definition, a function that returns a value must have a type that reflects the type of value returned. For instance,

   ```
   unsigned long int fact(int);
   ```

   declares the function `fact` to return a value that is of type `unsigned long int`. The first line of the definition

   ```
   unsigned long int fact(int arg)
   ```

   also indicates that an `unsigned long int` is returned from the function.
2. In addition, a return statement must appear in the body of the function. For the function `fact` in this lesson's program, the value of `factorial_of_arg` is

the return value with the statement

```
return (factorial_of_arg);
```

The form of the return statement is

```
return expression;
```

Some programmers put parentheses around the *expression* (which does not change the expression's value) to give a form of

```
return (expression);
```

In this lesson's program, the transfer of information between the function call and the function is shown here. The value of `fact_argument` in `main` goes to `arg` in `fact`. Then the return value of `factorial_of_arg` returns to the location of the function call (which is the right side of the assignment statement).

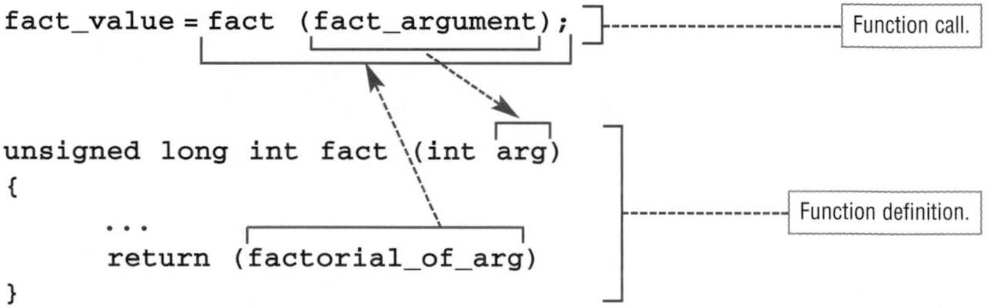

For instance, if we were finding the factorial of 4 (which is 24), the value of `factorial_of_arg` (24) is returned to the location of the function call. The assignment statement in `main` would be equivalent to:

```
fact_value = 24;
```

Thus, on execution of this assignment statement, the variable `fact_value` acquires the value 24.

A return statement can appear anywhere in the function body, and more than one return statement can appear in a function. A common structure for returning a value is

```
if (expression)
        {
        return (a);
        }
else
        {
        return (b);
        }
```

For this, if *expression* is true, the value of `a` is returned. If *expression* is false, the value of `b` is returned.

We learned in Lesson 7.1 that `void` type functions do not return values. However, we can use a `return` statement in a `void` function, but we must not use an expression with it. In a `void` function, we can use a `return` statement with the following form

```
return;
```

If we do not include a return statement in a `void` function, control transfers back to the calling function automatically. The C++ standard states that "reaching the } that terminates a function is equivalent to executing a `return` statement without an expression." Return statements are needed in `void` functions if there is to be more than one exit point or if a function is to be exited at a point other than the end. Because a `void` function does not return a value, a call to a `void` function cannot appear on the right side of an assignment statement.

C++ considers a `return` statement to be a jump statement because it causes execution to transfer unconditionally to another location. Another jump statement we have learned to this point is the `break` statement.

Returning a value from `main`. The calling "function" for `main` is the operating system. By using

```
int main ()
```

we indicate that we are returning an integer from `main` to the operating system. With the line

```
return (0);
```

we return the value 0 to the operating system. The operating system typically interprets the integer 0 as meaning that the program has terminated normally. Operating systems are different; therefore, you should examine your operating system's documentation for information on sending other types of termination messages from `main`. If `return(0)` is not included in `main`, C++ automatically returns 0 to the operating system. Therefore, in most programs in this text we do not use `return(0)`.

Mechanics of the `fact` function. We can trace the actions of the loop in the `fact` function:

```
for (i = arg; i >= 1; i--)
          {
          factorial_of_arg *= i;
          }
```

line by line to see that it does indeed compute the factorial of a number. As we did in Chapter 6, we create a table with the first column being the statement and the other columns being the test expression and variables. Here is the table:

Statement	Test expression	arg	i	factorial_of_arg
Before the loop		9	—	1
`i = arg;`			9	
`i >= 1;`	True			
`factorial_of_arg *= i`				9 * 1 = 9
`i--;`			8	
`i >= 1;`	True			
`factorial_of_arg *= i`				8 * 9 = 72
`i--;`			7	

(continued)

Statement	Test expression	arg	i	factorial_of_arg
i >= 1;	True			
factorial_of_arg *= i				7 * 72 = 504
i--;			6	
i >= 1;	True			
factorial_of_arg *= i				6 * 504 = 3024
i--;			5	
i >= 1;	True			
factorial_of_arg *= i				5 * 3024 = 15,120
i--;			4	
i >= 1;	True			
factorial_of_arg *= i				4 * 15120 = 60,480
i--;			3	
i >= 1;	True			
factorial_of_arg *= i				3 * 60480 = 181,144
i--;			2	
i >= 1;	True			
factorial_of_arg *= i				2 * 181144 = 362,880
i--;			1	
i >= 1;	True			
factorial_of_arg *= i				1 * 362880 = 362,880
i--;			0	
i >= 1;	False			

The last column of the table illustrates that the value of `factorial_of_arg` does indeed become the factorial.

Note that before the loop, `factorial_of_arg` is initialized to 1. This is necessary to make the loop work properly. If we had initialized `factorial_of_arg` to 0, the loop would have given an incorrect result! (The result would have been 0.) Remember, to create accurate loops, you may need to initialize some variables to certain values *before* the loop begins.

Also, as we can see from the table, numbers in a factorial calculation become big very quickly. For instance 13! is 6,227,020,800. To make the function capable of handling as big an integer as possible, we have designated the data type for `fact` to be an `unsigned long int` (also called `unsigned long`), which is required by standard C++ to be at least 4 bytes. This means that the largest possible integer the function can correctly handle is 4,294,967,295 unless the compiler exceeds standard C++. Since 13! is greater than what standard C++ specifies for `unsigned long int`, we restricted the input value `n` to be 12 or less. Should we want to calculate greater values, we would need to use `double` or `long double`. (But these would likely lead to truncating of the result, which may be acceptable or unacceptable. With an integer type, there is no truncating.)

Note that library functions have similar restrictions on values received and returned. Consider the natural log function, `log(x)`. You cannot use a value of `x` less than or equal to 0. If you call the `log` function with a value less than 0, your program will stop executing and a run-time error (usually indicating something about the function domain) will occur. If this happens, it is up to you to determine why the value has become negative. Finding the reason why a function is called incorrectly is considered part of the debugging process.

LESSON 7.3 PASS BY REFERENCE

TOPICS

- Calling functions with references
- The symbol &

QUESTION YOU SHOULD ATTEMPT TO ANSWER

1. How would you return three values from a function?

The previous lessons in this chapter have illustrated how each function has its own variables and region of memory. They have also shown how to use the argument list to copy values from the calling function memory region to the called (or invoked) function memory region. This is how values are transferred from the calling function *to* the called function. To transfer a single value *back* from the called function to the calling function we used the `return` statement.

However, this lesson's program has a function that calculates both the volume and surface area of a cube. How can we communicate *two* values back to the calling function? We can do this by using the argument list to indicate two arguments with which the called function can work directly (rather than with a copy). By working directly with the calling function's variables, the called function is effectively able to transfer back more than one value.

In this lesson, we describe how to use the argument list to allow a function to directly use a calling function's values (rather than use a copy).

Examine the source code and note the use (or lack of use) of & in the function declaration, call, and header.

Source Code

Function declaration. We put & after the variable type in the function declaration to indicate that the function is allowed to work directly with (and therefore modify) the calling function value. Here, we indicate that function `cube_vol_area()` is allowed to modify the values of the fifth and sixth variables in the argument list.

Function call. We do not use & before the variable names in the function call. Because `a` and `v` are in the fifth and sixth argument spots, we are allowing `cube_vol_area()` to modify the values of `a` and `v`.

```
#include <iostream>
using namespace std;


void cube_vol_area (int, double, double, double, double&, double&);

int main()
{
        int id = 5;
        double a, v;
        double x = 6.3, y = 7.2, z = 1.5;

        cube_vol_area (id, x, y, z, a, v);

        cout << "cube surface area = " << a << " cube volume = " << v << endl;

}
```

```
void cube_vol_area (int id, double width, double length, double height,
  double& surface_area, double& volume)
{
        cout << "For cube id = " << id << endl;

        surface_area = 2 * width * height +
          2 * length * height + 2 * width * length;
        volume = width * length * height;
}
```

Function header. We use & after the variable type for the fifth and sixth variables in the function header. In this program, we are indicating that the variables surface_area and volume in cube_vol_area() are alias names for a and v in main. This means that modifying surface_area and volume in cube_vol_area modifies a and v in main.

Because cube_vol_area is a void type function, no return statement is needed. Despite this, the values calculated for surface_area and volume are effectively transferred to a and v in main.

Output

```
For cube id = 5
cube surface area = 131.22 cube volume = 68.04
```

The output shows that the values calculated in cube_vol_area are effectively transferred to a and v in main.

Description

References. The reference symbol, &, is required in a function declaration to indicate arguments that will have their values modified by the function. For function cube_vol_area(), this is

```
void cube_vol_area (int, double, double, double,
  double&, double&)
```

which indicates that the fifth and sixth arguments are double references. This means that cube_vol_area() can modify the fifth and sixth arguments in a function call.

The function call

```
cube_vol_area (id, x, y, z, a, v);
```

has the values of a and v (double type variables and the fifth and sixth arguments) in the argument locations that allow cube_vol_area() to modify their values. Variables in the first to fourth locations (id, x, y, and z) cannot be modified by cube_vol_area(). Note that no & symbol is used in the argument list in the function call.

The header in the definition for cube_vol_area() does indicate the references using & in the fifth and sixth variable locations

```
void cube_vol_area (int id, double width, double length,
  double height, double& surface_area, double& volume)
```

Here, variable names are given (surface_area and volume), and these are the names of the variables used in the function. The values of surface_area and volume computed in `cube_vol_area()` replace the values of `a` and `v` in `main`, respectively. However, as we saw in Lessons 7.1 and 7.2, the values of variables without references (`id`, `width`, `length`, and `height`) computed in a function (`cube_vol_area`) do *not* replace the values of their corresponding variables (`id`, `x`, `y`, and `z`) in the calling function (`main`).

Remember, use `&` in the function declaration and header (on the variables to be transferred back to the calling function). Do not use `&` in the function call.

When we use references in this manner we are creating new names or *aliases* for the original variable names. In other words, we have made `surface_area` an alias (second name) for `a` and `volume` an alias (second name) for `v`. When we use `surface_area` in `cube_vol_area` we are actually *referring* (and, hence, the name reference) to `a`, and when we use `volume` in `cube_vol_area` we are actually referring to `v`. In fact, no storage is necessary for `surface_area` and `volume` in `cube_vol_area`'s memory region! This is schematically illustrated in Fig. 7.6.

Figure 7.6

Schematic illustration of actions taking place in memory as `cube_vol_area()` is executed. Since `surface_area` and `volume` are references for `a` and `v`, no memory for `surface_area` and `volume` is created in `cube_vol_area`'s memory region.

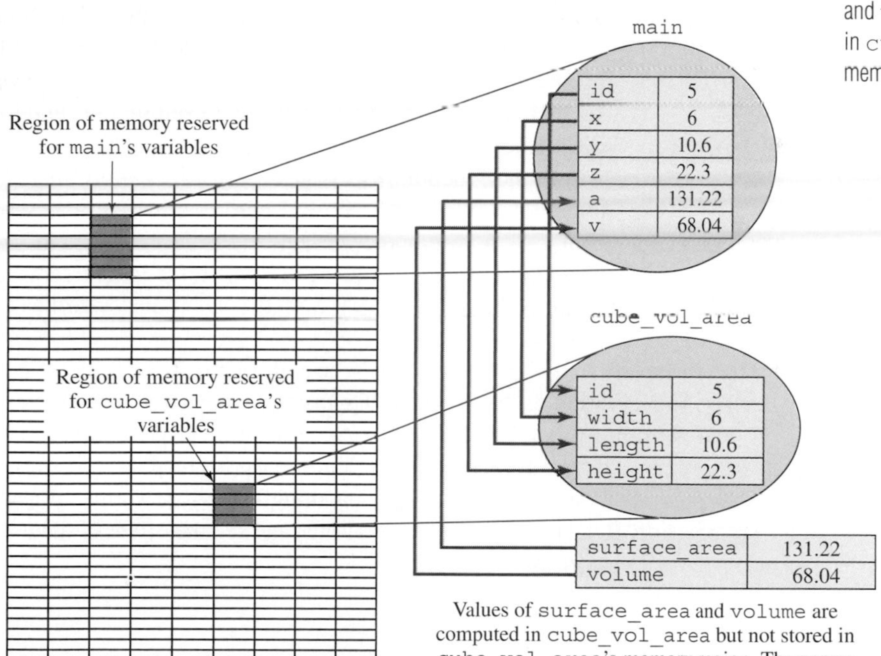

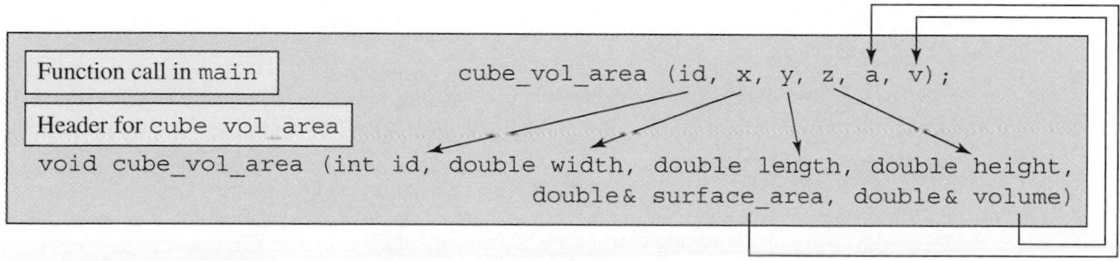

The purpose of this lesson is to illustrate how functions can transfer more than one value back to the calling function using references. The method is simple. We have deliberately not explained the exact mechanics of the process so that we can focus only on the method. In Chapter 13 we describe the mechanics.

At this point, you should remember that references create aliases. In essence, when using a reference in an argument list, we are transferring the argument's *identifier* to the function. The function simply creates a new identifier that represents the same memory cells. You can effectively work with references if you envision an identifier transfer from one function to another.

LESSON 7.4 SCOPE

TOPICS

- File scope
- Function scope
- Block scope

QUESTION YOU SHOULD ATTEMPT TO ANSWER

1. Why is `days_in_month` not declared in function `april()`?

We must be careful *where* we put variable declarations in our programs. Declaring a variable outside the body of any function means something completely different from declaring a variable within a function. The effect is illustrated in this lesson's program.

The variable `days_in_month` is declared outside the body of any function, which gives `days_in_month` *file scope*. File scope means that the variable can be used in any function in the file without passing it through the argument list or declaring it within the function (this is generally a procedure that should be avoided; however we show it here to illustrate the scope concept). As a result, the variable `days_in_month` in `main` and `days_in_month` in `april()` both refer to the same memory cells. Modifying the value of `days_in_month` in `april()`, also modifies the value of `days_in_month` in `main`.

The variables `friends_birthdays` are declared within both `main` and `april()`. These variables have *function scope* because they are declared within `main` and within `april()` separately. As a result, `friends_birthdays` in `april()` refers to different memory cells than `friends_birthdays` in `main`.

This program does not perform any meaningful task. It simply illustrates the concept of scope. Read the code and annotations, and see the effect of the declaration location on the behavior of variables.

Source Code

```
#include <iostream>
using namespace std;

int days_in_month = 31;

void april ( );
```

The declaration for `days_in_month` is outside the body of any function. This makes `days_in_month` have file scope.

Declaration for function `april()`. It has no arguments and does not return a value.

```
int main( )
{
        int friends_birthdays = 0;

        cout << "Before call to april()" << endl;
        cout << "days_in_month = "<< days_in_month << endl
             << "friends_birthdays = "<< friends_birthdays << endl << endl;

        april ();

        cout << "After call to april()" << endl;
        cout << "days_in_month = " << days_in_month << endl
             << "friends_birthdays = "<< friends_birthdays << endl << endl;
}

void april ( )
{
        int friends_birthdays = 2;
        days_in_month = 30;
}
```

The variable, `friends_birthdays`, has function scope because it is declared within a function (in this case, `main`).

The variable values are printed before and after the call to `april()`.

Call to `april()`.

The variable, `friends_birthdays`, has function scope because it is declared within a function (in this case, `april`).

Note that `days_in_month` is *not* declared in function `april()`. This is allowed because `days_in_month` is declared outside the body of any function.

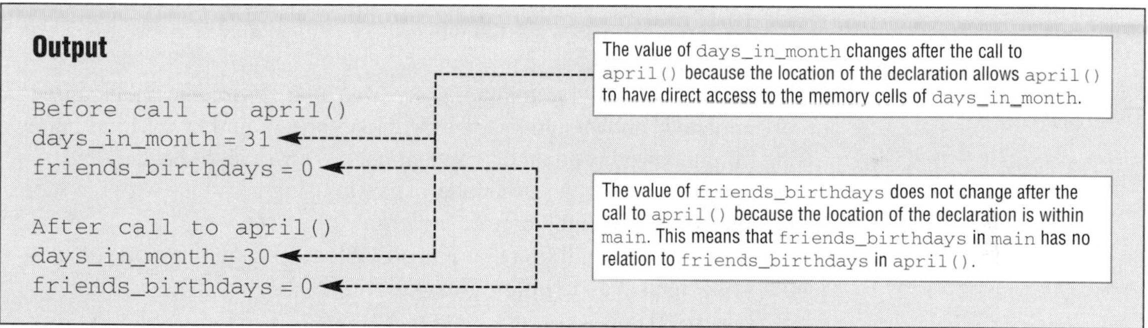
Output
Before call to april()
days_in_month = 31
friends_birthdays = 0
After call to april()
days_in_month = 30
friends_birthdays = 0
The value of days_in_month changes after the call to april() because the location of the declaration allows april() to have direct access to the memory cells of days_in_month.
The value of friends_birthdays does not change after the call to april() because the location of the declaration is within main. This means that friends_birthdays in main has no relation to friends_birthdays in april().

Description

Scope. Scope refers to the region in which a declaration is active. In C++, three kinds of scope are *block, function,* and *file*. Scope for an identifier is determined by the location of the identifier's declaration. A conceptual image of active regions for variables in this lesson's program is shown in Fig. 7.7.

- *Function scope.* The variables `friends_birthdays` in this lesson's program are said to have function scope, which means that a value assigned to `friends_birthdays` is valid only within the function in which it is defined. For example, `friends_birthdays` was declared in `main` and was assigned the value of 0. This assignment pertains only to the function `main` because `friends_birthdays` was declared in `main`. The `friends_birthdays`

Figure 7.7

Illustration of region in which Lesson 7.4's program's variables are active. The variable `days_in_month` is active in all functions in the file because its declaration is outside the body of any function. One `friends_birthdays` variable is active in `main`, and the other `friends_birthdays` variable is active in `april`.

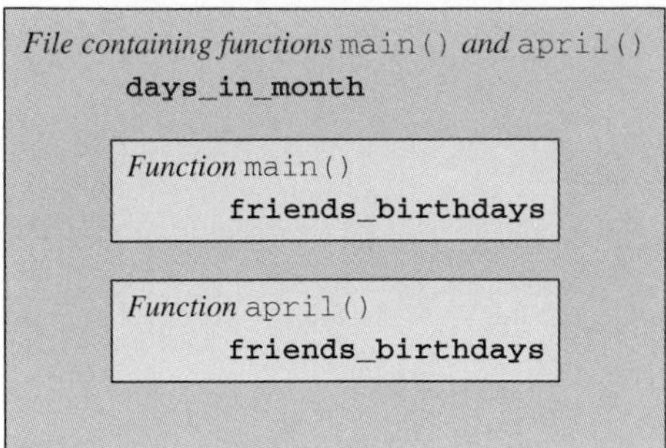

that was declared in `april()` has no relation to the `friends_birthdays` in `main` because its scope is only within `april()`. We assigned `friends_birthdays` a value of 2 in `april()`, and the output clearly shows that the `friends_birthdays` in `main` remains 0 while the `friends_birthdays` in `april()` is 2.

- *File scope.* On the other hand, the variable `days_in_month` has file scope because it was declared outside and before the body of any function. Its active region begins at its declaration point and extends to the end of the source code file. Note that `days_in_month` was not declared within the body of either of the functions yet was used by both `main` and `april()`. As a consequence, when `days_in_month` was modified in `april()`, the value of `days_in_month` in `main` also was modified.

  To follow good programming practice, this type of variable declaration is not recommended and should be avoided. Good programming style has values passing to functions through the argument lists. We will also see that object-oriented programming gives us an alternative to using variables with file scope that is more structured and therefore preferable.

  In Lesson 7.5, we will find that it is possible to expand the scope of an identifier to extend even to different files.

- *Block scope.* Recall that a block of code begins with a left brace (`{`) and ends with a right brace (`}`). An identifier declared within a block limits its active region to be within that block. Consider statement labels, such as those used in `switch` control structures. They have block scope, meaning that a statement label can be used in a different `switch` structure in the same function.

  Also, creating variables with block scope is sometimes done to assure that certain loop variables are only valid within the loop. We did not show it in this lesson's program, but we could have used the following function:

```
void function2 (int a, int b, int c, int d)
{
     int i;
     for (i = 1; i < 3; i++)
```

```
                {
                int n;
                n += a + b + c + d;
                cout << "In function2 n="<< n << endl;
                }
        cout << "In function2 n="<< n << endl;

}
```

The variable, n, has block scope because it is declared within the for loop block. The variable n can be used only within the for loop.

The reference to n in this statement is valid because it is within the loop.

The reference to n in this statement causes a compilation error because it is outside the loop.

This function will not compile because of the reference to n outside the for loop.

Block scope can be accidentally created for a variable if you declare your variables later than the beginning of a function. If you inadvertently declare a variable within a loop or if-else control structure and attempt to use that same variable later in the function, you will get a compilation error. To be safe, we recommend that you declare your variables at the beginning of your functions unless you deliberately want to create variables with block scope.

Identical variable names. C++ allows variables of different scope to have the same name. When choosing which declared variable a named variable represents, C++ chooses the one with the smallest scope. For instance, if april() in this lesson's program had the declaration and the executable statements

```
int days_in_month = 28;
days_in_month += 2;
cout << days_in_month;
```

the value of days_in_month would be calculated using the function scope days_in_month value (28) not the file scope days_in_month value of 31. Thus, the printed value of days_in_month is 30 not 33.

If a third days_in_month were declared in a separate block in april(), that days_in_month would be used over the one with function scope.

While C++ accepts this type of name repetition, it is not recommended that it be used except in the most simple and obvious circumstances. It becomes very confusing for someone looking at your code to see the same variable names meaning different things.

Distinguishing declarations. As you get familiar with C++, you should be able to look at a declaration and clearly understand what is being declared. Declarations for functions and file scope variables can be confused sometimes. For instance, of the two declarations (not shown in this lesson's program)

```
int x;
double y ( );
```

the first declares an integer variable named x, and the second declares a function named y which has no arguments and returns a double. The primary difference in the declarations is the parentheses. Remember (with some exceptions that are described later in the text), *when an identifier is followed immediately by a left parenthesis, the identifier represents a function.* Knowing this allows you to clarify confusing declarations.

Local and global variables. *Local* and *global* are not terms defined by the C++ standard but generic terms commonly used by programmers. Loosely speaking, global variables are variables with file scope, and local variables are variables with function scope. For example, in this lesson's program, `days_in_month` is a global variable while `friends_birthdays` is a local variable. Remember, global variables (variables with file scope) should be avoided. Use local variables and transfer them through argument lists from function to function.

Formal and actual parameters. These are other terms not defined by the C++ standard. Commonly, *formal* parameters refer to the parameters listed in the function definition and function declaration (if any). *Actual* parameters are parameters in the parameter list of the function call.

LESSON 7.5 STORAGE CLASSES

TOPICS

- Modifying C++ scope and storage
- `static` variables
- Global variables in multifile programs
- Passing `ifstream` references
- Finding the maximum value in a list

C++ allows us to manually modify the scope and storage rules by stating a variable's *storage class* in its declaration. The storage class for a variable refers to both a variable's scope and the length of time (in terms of execution of the program) during which memory is reserved for a variable.

There are four storage class specifiers in C++: `register`, `auto`, `static`, and `extern`.

We can indicate our desire (but not command) that a variable's value be stored in the registers by using the keyword `register` in the declaration. For instance:

```
register double x;
```

may make access to the value more rapid and may improve program performance by requesting that `x` be stored in the registers. However, today's compilers are often sophisticated enough to identify frequently used variables and automatically assign storage for them in the registers, so we will not concern ourselves further with the `register` storage class specifier in this text.

Variables declared in functions, by default, are `auto` (meaning when the function finishes executing the memory is freed), so `auto` is rarely used. Consequently, we will not concern ourselves further with the `auto` storage class specifier in this text.

We illustrate the other two storage class specifiers in the two source codes for this lesson. Both source codes perform the same tasks. The first code illustrates the use of `static`, and the second illustrates the use of `extern`.

Source code 1. Should we want the memory for a particular variable to persist and retain its value even after a function has completed execution, we can declare it `static`. For example, if we wanted to use a function to keep track of the maximum value as we read a list of numbers, we can use a variable declared as `static`. Each time the function is called, the maximum value from the previous function call is preserved and can be used to create a new maximum, if necessary, as the list is read. The source code shows how the `static` variable `max` in function `max_of_2` can be used to find the maximum value in a list of eight numbers.

This program also shows how to open a file in `main` and read it in a function. To do so, we need to pass an `ifstream` reference to the function. Since the reference creates an alias for the `ifstream` object, we can access the `ifstream` object directly in the function.

QUESTION YOU SHOULD ATTEMPT TO ANSWER

1. Why is `max` assigned such a small initial value?

Source code 2. This code is given in two files with `main` in one file and `max_of_2` in the other. A global variable, which by default has file scope, is used for `max`. We can make the scope for `max` extend to other files with the keyword `extern`. We need to declare `max` as a global variable in each file. However in all but one file, the keyword `extern` is needed.

Compare and contrast the two codes and see how to change the storage class of variables.

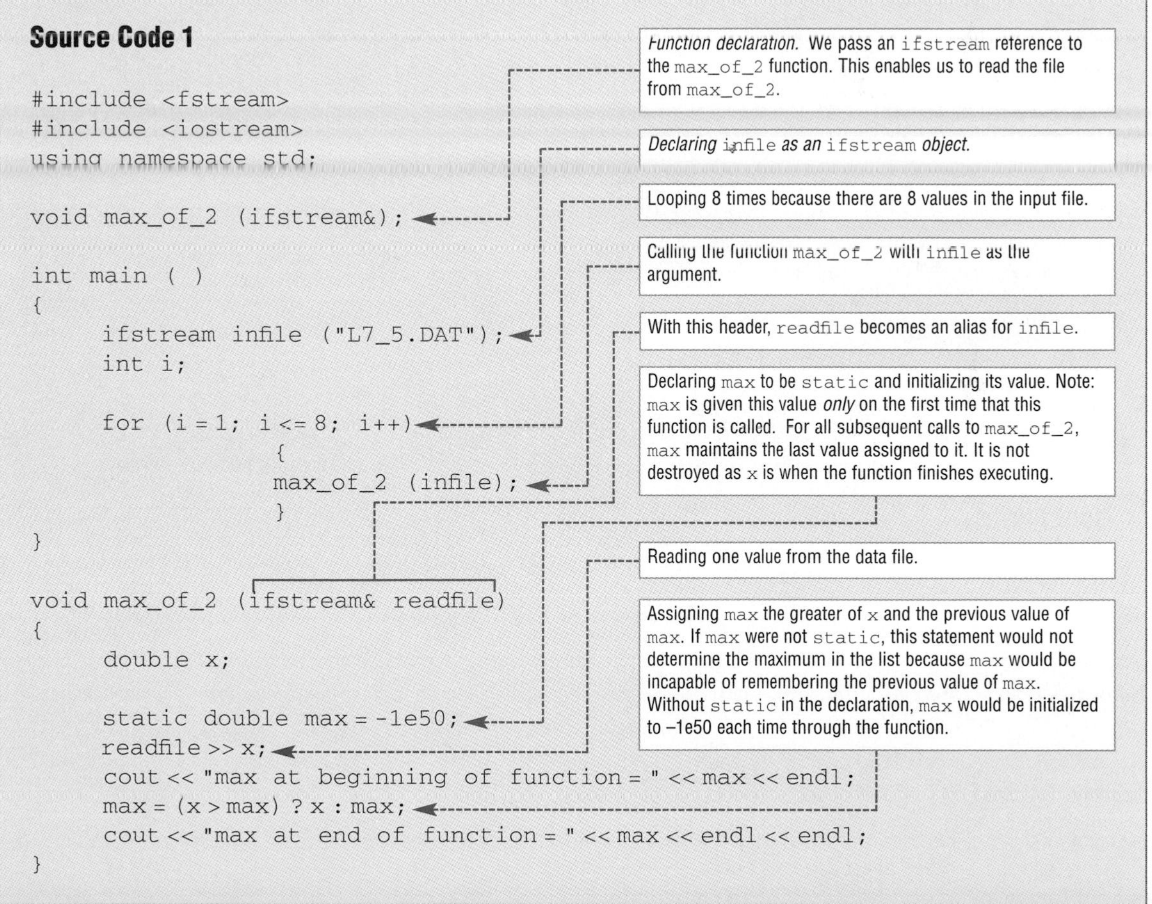
Source Code 1
#include <fstream>
#include <iostream>
using namespace std;
void max_of_2 (ifstream&);
int main ( )
{
ifstream infile ("L7_5.DAT");
int i;
for (i = 1; i <= 8; i++)
{
max_of_2 (infile);
}
}
void max_of_2 (ifstream& readfile)
{
double x;
static double max = -1e50;
readfile >> x;
cout << "max at beginning of function = " << max << endl;
max = (x > max) ? x : max;
cout << "max at end of function = " << max << endl << endl;
}
Function declaration. We pass an ifstream reference to the max_of_2 function. This enables us to read the file from max_of_2.
Declaring infile as an ifstream object.
Looping 8 times because there are 8 values in the input file.
Calling the function max_of_2 with infile as the argument.
With this header, readfile becomes an alias for infile.
Declaring max to be static and initializing its value. Note: max is given this value only on the first time that this function is called. For all subsequent calls to max_of_2, max maintains the last value assigned to it. It is not destroyed as x is when the function finishes executing.
Reading one value from the data file.
Assigning max the greater of x and the previous value of max. If max were not static, this statement would not determine the maximum in the list because max would be incapable of remembering the previous value of max. Without static in the declaration, max would be initialized to –1e50 each time through the function.

Source Code 2

File 1

```
#include <fstream>
#include <iostream>
using namespace std;

void max_of_2 (ifstream&);
double max = -1e50;

int main ( )
{
     ifstream infile ("L7_5.DAT");
     int i;

     for (i = 1; i <= 8; i++)
                {
                max_of_2 (infile);
                }
}
```

In this program, max is a global variable.

This main function is identical to the previous one.

File 2

```
extern double max;

void max_of_2 (ifstream& readfile)
{
    double x;

    readfile >> x;
    cout << "max at beginning of function = " << max << endl;
    max = (x > max) ? x : max;
    cout << "max at end of function = " << max << endl << endl;
}
```

The keyword extern indicates that max has been declared in another file. This means that max has been given more than file scope.

There is no need for declaring max in this function since it is a global variable.

These are the same executable statements as those used in the previous max_of_2 function.

Input File

```
12.4   -38.3   87.5   13.2   -76.1   98.4   76.2   -34.2
```

The maximum value in this list is 98.4.

Output

```
max at beginning of function = -1e+50
max at end of function = 12.4

max at beginning of function = 12.4
max at end of function = 12.4
```

The first value is what was given to max in its declaration as a static variable in max_of_2 or as a global variable.

```
max at beginning of function = 12.4
max at end of function = 87.5

max at beginning of function = 87.5
max at end of function = 87.5

max at beginning of function = 87.5
max at end of function = 87.5

max at beginning of function = 87.5
max at end of function = 98.4

max at beginning of function = 98.4
max at end of function = 98.4

max at beginning of function = 98.4
max at end of function = 98.4
```

The value 12.4 is the maximum in the list until 87.5 is encountered.

The value 87.5 is the maximum in the list until 98.4 is encountered.

The value 98.4 is the maximum in the list.

Description

Multiple file programs. The source codes for large programs are frequently put into multiple files. Multiple smaller files are usually easier and more efficient to work with than one large file when developing programs.

The process is roughly this: a programmer compiles and saves the object code for portions of a program that are correct and complete in multiple separate files. The source code for the part of the program still under development is stored in another file. This source code is compiled separately and then all the object codes are linked together to create an executable file. (A more complete explanation is given in Lesson 18.2.)

This process is more efficient for several reasons. It saves compilation time since only the modified portion of the program need be compiled each time a modification is to be tested. It more easily allows multiple programmers to work on a single program. Also, moving around in a small file is much simpler than in a large file. And, with separate files, one is less likely to accidentally move to a location in the file with correct code and modify it. These are some reasons why multiple files improve the program development process.

The `extern` storage class specifier. C++ requires the use of the `extern` storage class specifier for global variables when programs are in multiple files. In one of the files, the global variable is declared without a storage class specifier. In the other files, the keyword `extern` is used before the variable type. The general form is

```
extern type variable;
```

where *type* is any valid data type and *variable* is a legal identifier. For this program, the `extern` declaration is:

```
extern double max;
```

A typical declaration indicates a variable's type and name *and* reserves memory for the variable. A declaration with `extern` is a declaration in the purest sense in that it simply indicates a variable's type and name. It does not reserve memory for the variable because the memory is already reserved with its declaration in another file. This declaration simply allows the use of `max` in the file in which it is given.

Functions themselves need not be declared with `extern`. A function declared and defined in one file is available to be called in a second file without even an `extern` declaration in the second file.

The `static` storage class specifier. When the `static` storage class specifier is used in the declaration of a variable, that variable maintains its storage space and value even after the function finishes executing. This contrasts with automatic (`auto`) variables (the default storage class) which are destroyed when a function completes execution. If a function is called a number of times in a program, memory space for automatic variables is reserved when the function is called and freed up when the function completes execution. By contrast, memory for `static` variables is reserved and initialized only once, the first time the function is called. Any value in the memory cells for a `static` variable is retained even after the function has finished executing, and the value used the next time the function is called.

In general, the form for declaring a variable `static` is

```
static type variable;
```

where *type* is a legal data type and *variable* is a legal identifier.

A `static` variable can also be initialized in the declaration. This assigns the `static` variable a value the first time its function is executed but does *not* assign it that value on subsequent executions of the function. On each subsequent function execution, the value is the last value that the variable had on the previous function execution. For instance, in this lesson's program, `max` is made `static` and initialized with the declaration

```
static double max = -1e50;
```

The *first* time the function is executed, `max` is assigned −1e50. Upon reading the value 12.4 for `x`, comparing `x` and `max`, and assigning `max` the greater of the two, `max` becomes 12.4. The next time the function is executed, `max` is not reset to −1e50. It is still 12.4! This allows us to compare the next value of `x` to 12.4 and gives us the ability to go number by number in the list to determine the overall maximum. We follow the code step by step later in this lesson. Remember, for a `static` variable, the value initialization (when it is in the declaration) occurs only on the first execution of the function.

If not initialized in their declarations, C++ initializes `static` variables to zero. This contrasts with ordinary automatic variables that are not initialized by C++.

Another use for `static` is when we may want to assure that a global variable in one file is not accidentally declared as `extern` and used in another file. Although not shown in this lesson's program, `static` can be used with a global variable to restrict the variable to being used only by functions contained in the same file.

Similarly for functions, should we want to assure that a function is called only in the file in which it is declared, the function can be declared with the `static` storage class specifier.

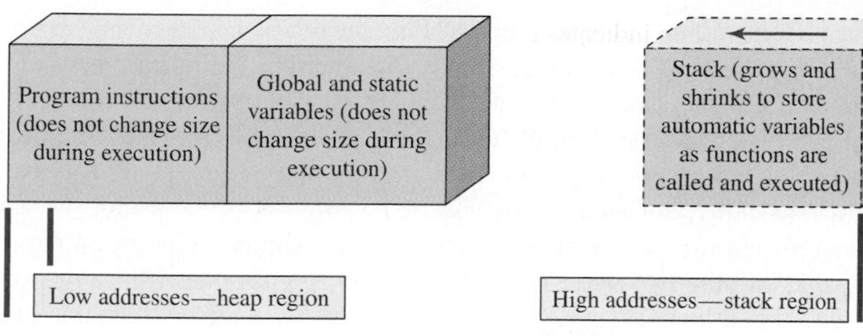

Figure 7.8

Conceptual image of regions of memory.

Comparing global and `static` variables. It can be seen from this lesson's program that similar effects can be achieved using global and `static` variables. You often will have a choice between the two if you need such data while programming. You can choose wisely between them by knowing their similarities and differences.

One similarity between global and `static` variables is that so called permanent storage is created for both of them. This storage is created during execution and remains for the life of the program. This is conceptually illustrated in Fig. 7.8. The program instructions, global variables, and `static` variables are stored on what is known as the *heap* (located at the low addresses of memory). This occupied region of memory does not change size during execution of this lesson's program. (On the other hand, the *stack* portion of memory, located at the high addresses of memory, grows and shrinks as functions are called and executed, and memory is reserved and freed for the functions' automatic variables. The memory region between the stack and heap is available memory.)

A major difference between global and `static` variables is that `static` variables can be accessed only from the function in which they are declared. Attempts to access a `static` variable outside the function cause compilation errors. By contrast, global variables can be accessed from any function, and, when `extern` is used, any file. With multiple developers, each working with a different file, global variable values may be changed unpredictably. As a result, the superior choice is `static` variables rather than global variables. Also, using `static` variables leads to a more structured program because access to `static` variables is more limited than access to global variables.

Finding the maximum value in a list of numbers. To find a maximum value in a list, it is first necessary to create a variable for the sole purpose of storing the maximum value. In this program, we created `max` and initialized `max` to a value smaller than any in the list. (Another method is to initialize the value to the first in the list, but this is not shown in this lesson's program.) Then the first value in the list is compared to `max`, and the larger of the two becomes the new value of `max`. Since `max` is initially smaller than the first value, the first value becomes `max` after the first comparison.

One by one, each value in the list is compared to `max`. If a value is greater than `max`, `max` takes its value. After all the values have been compared, the last value of `max` is the maximum in the list.

Only two lines of code in a loop are needed to read the values and change the value of `max`, as needed. They are

```
readfile >> x;
max = (x > max) ? x : max;
```

Remember how the `?:` operator works? First the relational expression (`x > max`) before the `?` is evaluated. If this expression is true, then the entire right-hand side of the assignment statement becomes equal to `x` (the variable before the colon). If the relational expression is false, the right side takes the value of `max` (the variable after the colon, which represents the previous maximum value). The assignment operator (`=`) then assigns either `x` or `max` to `max`.

We can trace how the program determines the maximum value by creating our loop table that lists the two statements in one column eight times. (Since the loop is straightforward and just executes from i = 1 to i = 8, we simplify the table and do not include the test expression and increment expression.) The variables are `x` and `max`. Remember, in these columns are the values of `x` and `max` *after* the given statement in the row has been executed. Follow the values in the table line by line and verify that the columns of `x` and `max` are correct:

Function execution	Statement	x	max
Before function executed		—	−1e50
1 (First time executed)	`readfile >> x;`	12.4	
	`max = (x > max) ? x : max;`		12.4
2	`readfile >> x;`	−38.3	
	`max = (x > max) ? x : max;`		12.4
3	`readfile >> x;`	87.5	
	`max = (x > max) ? x : max;`		87.5
4	`readfile >> x;`	13.2	
	`max = (x > max) ? x : max;`		87.5
5	`readfile >> x;`	−76.1	
	`max = (x > max) ? x : max;`		87.5
6	`readfile >> x;`	98.4	
	`max = (x > max) ? x : max;`		98.4
7	`readfile >> x;`	76.2	
	`max = (x > max) ? x : max;`		98.4
8	`readfile >> x;`	−34.2	
	`max = (x > max) ? x : max;`		98.4

The end result is that `max` is 98.4, which is the maximum value in the list.

LESSON 7.6 FUNCTIONS WITH DEFAULT ARGUMENTS

TOPICS

- Initializing default arguments
- Calling a function with default arguments

We previously described the underlying principle of transferring information to functions using matching NOT (number, order, type) in the function call and declaration. However, C++ allows violations to this when default arguments are used. A *default argument* is an argument that is assigned a particular value when an argument is omitted in the function call. It is convenient to use a default argument when that argument commonly (but not always) has a particular value.

For instance, a traffic engineer may want to compute commute times to the nearest major city from a new suburban development. The commute distance and the number of traffic lights encountered would be the same on most days, but the average speed at which commuters drive may vary depending on traffic conditions. A function to compute the commute time could use default values for the distance and the number of traffic lights. This lesson's program shows such a function (called `commute_time`) and illustrates how to call the function using the default values, and how to call it using values that override the defaults. Read the program and observe how the function is declared and called.

QUESTION YOU SHOULD ATTEMPT TO ANSWER

1. Which function argument does not have a default value?

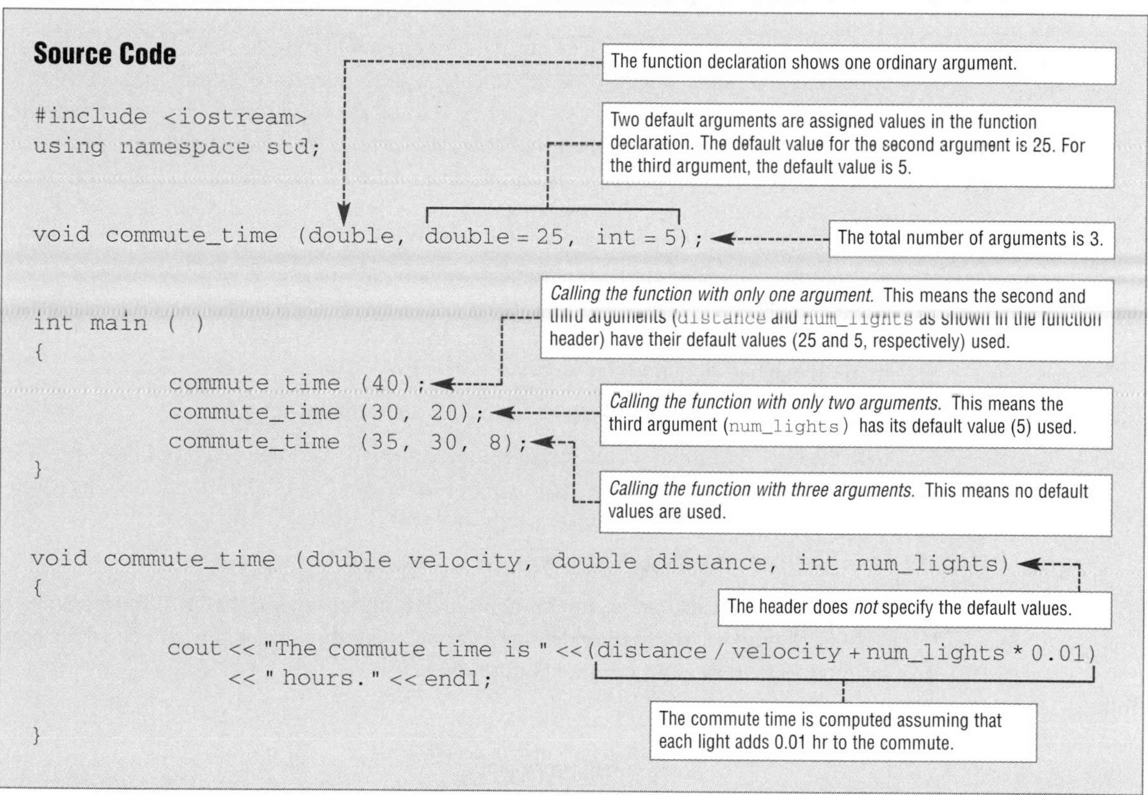
Source Code
#include <iostream>
using namespace std;
void commute_time (double, double = 25, int = 5);
int main ( )
{
commute_time (40);
commute_time (30, 20);
commute_time (35, 30, 8);
}
void commute_time (double velocity, double distance, int num_lights)
{
cout << "The commute time is " << (distance / velocity + num_lights * 0.01)
<< " hours." << endl;
}
The function declaration shows one ordinary argument.
Two default arguments are assigned values in the function declaration. The default value for the second argument is 25. For the third argument, the default value is 5.
The total number of arguments is 3.
Calling the function with only one argument. This means the second and third arguments (distance and num_lights as shown in the function header) have their default values (25 and 5, respectively) used.
Calling the function with only two arguments. This means the third argument (num_lights) has its default value (5) used.
Calling the function with three arguments. This means no default values are used.
The header does not specify the default values.
The commute time is computed assuming that each light adds 0.01 hr to the commute.

Output

```
The commute time is 0.675 hours.
The commute time is 0.716667 hours.
The commute time is 0.937143 hours.
```

Description

Declaring a function with default arguments. The default argument values need to be specified in the declaration for a function with default arguments. For instance, the declaration

```
void commute_time (double, double = 25, int = 5);
```

declares the function `commute_time` to have three arguments. The first argument is an ordinary `double` type argument. The second argument is a `double` with a default value of 25, and the third is an `int` with a default value of 5. An `=` sign is required to set the default value. Some programmers like to use the argument names (although they are not required) giving an acceptable declaration of

```
void commute_time (double, double distance = 25,
  int num_lights = 5);
```

C++ has a strict rule regarding which arguments may be selected to be default arguments. We may select some arguments as default arguments and the rest as ordinary arguments. However, they cannot be written randomly in the argument list. The rule is that no ordinary argument may be listed after any default argument. The result of this is that all the ordinary arguments are written first, and this is followed by all the default arguments. Otherwise stated, if we want to use the `n`th argument as a default argument, then all arguments after the `n`th argument also must be default arguments. This concept is illustrated schematically in Fig. 7.9.

For example, in the function, `commute_time`, we selected the second argument (`distance`) as a default argument; then the third is *required* to be a default argument. If we had declared the function `commute_time` as

```
void commute_time (double = 60, double, int);
```

then the C++ compiler would have generated an error message on compilation because the first argument is a default argument but the second and the third are ordinary arguments. The following function declaration also is illegal

```
void commute_time (double, double = 25, int);
```

because with the second argument being a default argument, the third must also be a default argument. You will understand the need for this rule when you consider how a function with default arguments is called.

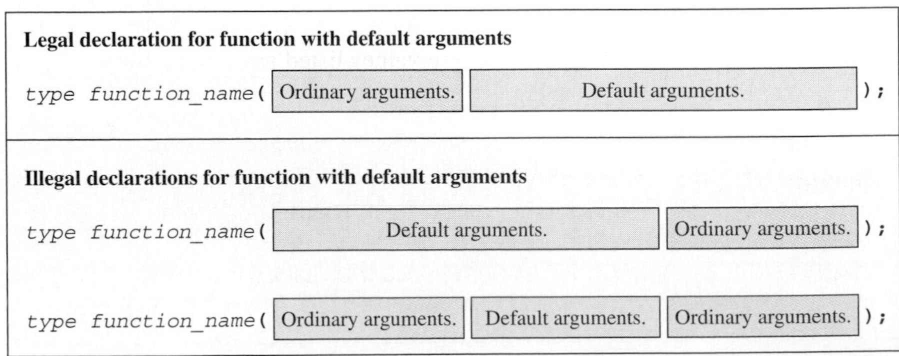

Figure 7.9

Schematic illustration of legal and illegal declarations for functions with default arguments. Legal declarations have all the default arguments after the ordinary arguments. The illegal declarations have ordinary arguments listed after default arguments.

We have not shown it in this lesson's program, but we can use default values when we have a function for which we pass values by reference. For instance, if we made modifications to this lesson's program and made `commute_time` use references, its declaration with default values would be:

```
void commute_time (double&, double& = 25, int& = 5);
```

where a space is required between `&` and `=` (otherwise C++ thinks that `&=` is some sort of operator). Another acceptable declaration is

```
void commute_time (double&, double& distance = 25,
  int& num_lights = 5);
```

Here, the argument names are used.

Calling a function with default arguments. To call a function and make use of the default values for the arguments, it is necessary to use fewer than the total number of arguments in the argument list. However, the function must be called with at least the number of ordinary arguments included in the list. The declaration for the function `commute_time` has one ordinary argument and three total arguments. Therefore, we must call the function using at least one argument. If we call the function using one or two arguments (meaning less than three arguments), then default values are used in the execution. For instance, the call with just one argument

```
commute_time (40);
```

uses the default values for the second and third arguments and assigns the value of 40 to the first argument. The call

```
commute_time (30, 20);
```

explicitly assigns 30 and 20 to the first two arguments and uses the default value for the third argument. And the call

```
commute_time (35, 30, 8);
```

overrides all the default values and assigns 35, 30, and 8 to the first, second, and third arguments, respectively.

Note that there is no way to use the default value for the second argument without the default value also being used for the third argument. This is because if two arguments are used in the function call, the first is the value for the first argument and the second is the value for the second argument, automatically. Only the third argument uses the default value. In general, when fewer than the total number of arguments is used in the call, the values listed are assigned in the order first, second, third on up in the argument list with no intermediate default values used.

Using functions with default arguments. As mentioned in the introduction to this lesson, a typical usage of default arguments is for a function that commonly is called with the same values.

Another usage is when a function is modified from its original definition. For instance, suppose we have the following program with a function `add` that adds two numbers together.

```
#include <iostream>
using namespace std;
double add (double, double);
int main ( )
{
    cout << add (15,39) << endl;
}

double add (double a, double b)
{
    return (a + b);
}
```

Declaring a function with two ordinary arguments.

Calling the function with two arguments.

Defining the function to add just two numbers.

And suppose we want to modify it to add three numbers. If we use a default argument for the new argument needed, then the existing function call in `main` need not be modified. The new program would be

The modified declaration has three arguments with the third being a default argument. The default value is zero.

```
#include <iostream>
using namespace std;
double add (double, double, double=0);
int main ( )
{
    cout << add (15,39) << endl;
    cout << add (57,87,1230) << endl;
}

double add (double a, double b, double c)
{
    return (a + b + c);
}
```

This function call is still valid. It uses the default value of 0 for `c`.

Defining the function to add three numbers.

For this simple program, the benefit of not modifying old function calls is not great since there is only one of them. However, with large programs a function may be called many times. Not having to modify every function call saves time and reduces errors. Thus, when you need to modify an existing function in a working program, you may be able to use default arguments.

Be careful when using default arguments, however. The default values that you choose must be such that the function works under all circumstances. They should not cause your program to crash.

Also, the power that C++ gives you in allowing default arguments means that you must be extra careful in calling your functions. Do not forget the number, order, type (NOT) principle. It still applies to the arguments that are used in a function call. If you violate the NOT principal with a function that uses default arguments, it is less likely that the C++ compiler will catch the error than it is with functions that do not use default arguments. This is especially true if you call a function with the wrong number of arguments. For instance, if a function has 10 arguments and you call it with only 9 when you mean to call it with 10, the function will simply use the default value for the tenth argument and not necessarily indicate any sort of error.

LESSON 7.7 FUNCTION OVERLOADING

TOPICS

- Overloading functions
- Distinguishing between overloaded functions

Function overloading is a bit of a strange term that in C++ simply means to define two or more functions with the same name. These functions typically perform different (but often similar) tasks even though their names are identical. Although you might think that having two functions with the same name would cause a compilation error, or that the call to such a function would cause the program to crash, if done properly, overloading a function causes neither of these things to occur.

Why would you want to create two functions of the same name? We have seen the number-order-type requirement for C++ functions, and sometimes we find this constrictive. For instance, suppose we are interested in *rotating* a number of values between variables. In other words, if we have four variables with values

```
a = 1    b = 2    c = 3    d = 4
```

and we rotate them (using one method of rotation); then their values become

```
a = 2    b = 3    c = 4    d = 1
```

Note that rotating has caused the first value to be transferred to the last variable and the other values to be shifted up one place. We could write a function called `rotate` that does this, but the NOT requirement means that our function would work only with four arguments. If we wanted to perform the same task with three arguments we could write another function, but it would need a different name. If we wanted to use just two arguments, we would need another function with a third name. The different names for similar tasks become confusing to a programmer wanting to call those functions.

Instead, overloading the functions (giving them all the same name) makes programming easier because a programmer does not need to remember all the different names. With function overloading in this lesson's program, we make several functions all with the same name, `rotate`. Each function takes a different number of arguments. We simply call `rotate` with different numbers of arguments, and C++ is smart enough to know which function we are calling by counting the number of arguments.

Another reason to overload functions is to accommodate different types of arguments. For instance, if we wanted to rotate the following

```
x = 1.5    y = 2.5    z = 3.5
```

QUESTION YOU SHOULD ATTEMPT TO ANSWER

1. What is the purpose of the variable `temp` in each function?

we would need to call the `rotate` function with 3 `double` type arguments rather than 3 `int`. Without function overloading, we would need a different name for such a function to accommodate the `double` arguments. But, since C++ allows function overloading, we can simply define another function with the name `rotate` and make it accommodate 3 `double` arguments. C++ is smart enough to not confuse this function with the `rotate` version that has 3 `int` arguments by simply looking at the types of arguments in the function call. (Note: For this particular example, we could write `rotate` with `double` arguments only and use C++'s automatic type conversions in calling it with `int` arguments, but for the sake of this discussion, we will use function overloading to account for different argument types.)

Read this lesson's program and note the different declarations, calls, and definitions for function `rotate`. In the description, we indicate how the code for each function rotates values and how to trace and debug the code.

Source Code

```
#include <iostream>
using namespace std;
void rotate (int&, int&);
void rotate (int&, int&, int&);
void rotate (int&, int&, int&, int&);
void rotate (double&, double&, double&);

int main ( )
{
        int a, b, c, d;
        double x, y, z;

        a = 1; b = 2;
        rotate (a, b);
        cout << "a=" << a << ", b=" << b << endl;

        a = 1; b = 2; c = 3;
        rotate (a, b, c);
        cout << "a=" << a << ", b=" << b << ", c=" << c << endl;

        a = 1; b = 2; c = 3; d = 4;
        rotate (a, b, c, d);
        cout << "a=" << a << ", b=" << b << ", c=" << c << ", d=" << d << endl;

        x = 1.5; y = 2.5; z = 3.5;
        rotate (x, y, z);
        cout << "x=" << x << ", y=" << y << ", z=" << z << endl;

}

void rotate (int& aa, int& bb)
{
        int temp;

        temp = aa;
        aa = bb;
        bb = temp;
}
```

Declaring `rotate` with 2, 3, and 4 `int&` arguments.

Declaring `rotate` with 3 `double&` arguments.

Calling `rotate` with 2 `int` arguments.

Calling `rotate` with 3 `int` arguments.

Calling `rotate` with 4 `int` arguments.

Calling `rotate` with 3 `double` arguments.

Defining `rotate` with 2 `int&` arguments.

```
void rotate (int& aa, int& bb, int& cc)
{
        int temp;

        temp = aa;
        aa = bb;
        bb = cc;
        cc = temp;
}
```

Defining `rotate` with 3 `int&` arguments.

```
void rotate (int& aa, int& bb, int& cc, int& dd)
{
        int temp;

        temp = aa;
        aa = bb;
        bb = cc;
        cc = dd;
        dd = temp;
}
```

Defining `rotate` with 4 `int&` arguments.

```
void rotate (double& aa, double& bb, double& cc)
{
       double temp;

       temp = aa;
       aa = bb;
       bb = cc;
       cc = temp;
}
```

Defining `rotate` with 3 `double&` arguments.

Output

```
a=2, b=1
a=2, b=3, c=1
a=2, b=3, c=4, d=1
x=2.5, y=3.5, z=1.5
```

With only 2 values, rotating is equivalent to *exchanging* or *swapping*.
Three int values have been rotated.
Four int values have been rotated.
Three double values have been rotated.

Description

Overloaded functions with different numbers of arguments. C++ allows us to give different functions the same name if they all have different numbers of arguments. Nothing special need be done with the declarations. For instance,

```
void rotate (int&, int&);
void rotate (int&, int&, int&);
void rotate (int&, int&, int&, int&);
```

declares three different functions, all with the same name but with different numbers of arguments. C++ knows which function is being called by counting the number of arguments used. For example,

```
rotate (a, b);
rotate (a, b, c);
rotate (a, b, c, d);
```

call the 2, 3, and 4 argument versions of `rotate`, respectively. A different definition is required for each function as shown in this lesson's program.

Overloaded functions with different types of arguments. C++ also allows us to overload functions if the functions have different types of arguments. A fourth version of function `rotate`, one that takes `double` arguments instead of `int` arguments, is declared with the line

```
void rotate (double&, double&, double&);
```

and called with the line

```
rotate (x, y, z);
```

C++ recognizes that the call has 3 `double` arguments rather than 3 `int` arguments and, therefore, knows which version of `rotate` is being called.

Comments on function overloading.

- There is no requirement that overloaded functions perform similar tasks. It is permissible to have two functions of the same name performing completely different operations, but this style of programming is not recommended. For instance, it is allowable to have the 3-argument version of `rotate` perform rotation and the 2-argument version of `rotate` perform addition. However, doing so would confuse the programming process rather than simplify it. One of the benefits of overloading functions is to make it easier for a programmer to use the functions. Therefore, it is recommended that overloaded functions perform similar tasks.
- It is imperative that there be no ambiguity in which function is being called when overloaded functions are used. If you use both function overloading and default arguments, ambiguity easily can be created. For instance, if we had declared (and defined) in this lesson's program a function

  ```
  void rotate (int&, int&, int&, int&, int& = 5);
  ```

  which indicates 5 arguments with the fifth having a default value of 5, and used the function call

  ```
  rotate (a, b, c, d);
  ```

  the compiler will not know which version of `rotate` is being called. This call could represent a call to the 4-argument version of `rotate` or the 5-argument version with the default value being used. Because of this ambiguity, an error during compilation would be generated.

- Ambiguity could also have been created if we had declared two functions

```
void rotate (int&, int&);
void rotate (int, int);
```

because the call

```
rotate (a, b)
```

does not clearly indicate which version of `rotate` is being called (because having integers as arguments in the function call could indicate that they are passed by reference or value).

- Be also aware of the automatic type conversions that C++ uses on function calls. Before we even discussed function overloading, we noted that when an `int` type argument is used to call a function that specifies `double` for that argument, C++ automatically converts the `int` to `double` and proceeds with the function operation. When using function overloading, C++ first looks for an exact match between the argument types. If no exact match exists, automatic type conversions may occur and the function called. For instance, had we used the function call

```
rotate (1.0, 2.0);
```

in this lesson's program, the 2-argument `int` version of `rotate` would have been called even though the arguments are `double`.

  If in the process of doing automatic type conversions, ambiguity occurs, a compilation error will be indicated. For instance, if we had used the call

```
rotate (x, b, c);
```

in this lesson's program, no clear cut version of `rotate` is being called. An error would be indicated on compilation because the call has both `double` and `int` arguments. Automatic type conversions do not know whether to transfer `x` as an `int` and call the `int` version of `rotate`, or transfer `b` and `c` as `double`s and call the `double` version of `rotate`.

- Changing only the return type of a function does not constitute function overloading. For example, if we had declared two functions

```
void rotate (int&, int&);
int  rotate (int&, int&);
```

we would not have properly overloaded the `rotate` function, and a compilation error would have been indicated. This is because a function call such as

```
rotate (a, b);
```

cannot indicate which 2-argument version of `rotate` to call.

- Remember that, in general, C++ treats numerical constants written in the source code without decimal points as `int`s and with decimal points as `double`s. (More precisely stated, `int`s and `double`s are used unless their range is exceeded, whereupon C++ automatically uses `long int`, `unsigned long int`, or `long double`, as needed.) If we had used in this lesson's program the call

```
rotate (1, 2, 3);
```

the version of `rotate` with 3 `int` arguments would have been called because there are no decimal points with the numerical constants. If we had used

```
rotate (1., 2., 3.)
```

the version of `rotate` with 3 `double` arguments would have been called because there are decimal points with the arguments.

Should we desire, we can explicitly specify the type of a constant by adding a suffix to the number. The letter L should be added to make a number a `long int` or `long double`. For instance, 5L would store the number 5 as a `long int`, and 5.L would store the number 5 as a `long double`. This table summarizes suffixes for constants.

Table of suffixes for constants

Suffix	Meaning	Example
L	Specifies `long int` or `long double`	37L indicates `long int` 37.L indicates `long double` 3.145e15L indicates `long double`
U	Specifies `unsigned long int`	125U
F	Specifies `float`	458F

Simply to complete this discussion, we note that we can change the base of a constant by using a prefix. To use hexadecimal notation in a source code, the prefix 0x is needed. For instance, 0xFFD4 represents hexadecimal FFD4. The prefix is 0 for octal notation. To represent 567 octal, use 0567. Remember, do not accidentally use 0 before any of your integers. If you do you will create a base 8 rather than base 10 integer.

- At times you may have a choice between overloading a function and using default arguments. In the description of Lesson 7.6, we illustrated an `add` function and described how a third default argument of 0 could be used to allow calls to `add` using both 2 and 3 arguments. Had we chosen to, we could have overloaded the `add` function to accommodate both 2 and 3 arguments. If you are faced with the option of choosing overloaded functions or default arguments, there is no clear cut rule that works in all cases. Begin by looking at your code closely and use the one that makes your code most understandable and least likely to produce errors. Expected future modifications in a program should also be considered when making a decision on which to use. However, this generalization is simply a guide. You need to consider each situation on a case-by-case basis.

Rotating values—tracing and debugging code. Again, we can create a table to assist us in tracing and debugging code. In this case, there is no loop, so the table is simple to construct. The first column has the statements, and the other columns are the variables. The first row should be the variable values before the portion of code is executed.

For instance, consider the 2-argument version of `rotate`. Rotating with just two values is called swapping or exchanging values. To program swap, a temporary storage space must be created for a value (using a variable most commonly called `temp`). By copying one of the two values to `temp`, the swap can be made. The 2-argument version of `rotate` then has three variables, `temp`, `aa`, and `bb`. This table shows the values stored in each variable *after* executing the statement shown in the first column.

Statement	`temp`	`aa`	`bb`
At beginning of the function	—	1	2
`temp = aa;`	1		
`aa = bb;`		2	
`bb = temp;`			1

As can be seen, first `temp` takes the value of `aa`, and then `aa` takes the `bb` value, and then `bb` takes the value of `temp`. At the end, the value of `aa` is 2 and `bb` is 1, and the values have been swapped.

When rotating more than two values, still only one temporary value need be created. For the 3-argument version of `rotate`, the following table gives the values.

Statement	`temp`	`aa`	`bb`	`cc`
At beginning of the function	—	1	2	3
`temp = aa;`	1			
`aa = bb;`		2		
`bb = cc;`			3	
`cc = temp;`				1

Again, the end result, after executing all the lines of code, is that the values of `aa`, `bb`, and `cc` have been rotated from their original values. Their values are 2, 3, and 1 (the last values of each in the table), respectively.

LESSON 7.8 GENERATING RANDOM NUMBERS

TOPICS

- The `rand()` function
- The `srand()` function
- The `time()` function
- Creating random numbers within a specified range

In this program, we illustrate generating random numbers. Generating random numbers is useful for such things as performing what are called Monte Carlo methods of analysis. They go beyond the scope of this book, so we will not describe them here. A simpler application of random numbers is for games of chance such as those involving dice or cards. Many of today's sophisticated computer games make substantial use of random numbers to create unpredictable events. In short, random numbers are used frequently in programming, so we include them in this chapter.

To create a random number within a small defined range, we need three functions and an operator. They are

1. The `rand()` function, which is a C++ library function that returns a pseudorandom (meaning that it is random but dependent upon an input value) integer in the range 0 to 32767 (or greater depending on your implementation).

2. The `srand()` library function, which is designed to operate with the `rand()` function using a global variable that is invisible to a programmer.
3. The `time()` library function that returns the number of seconds from midnight on the system's clock, and
4. The mod (`%`) operator, which computes the remainder of an integer division operation.

QUESTION YOU SHOULD ATTEMPT TO ANSWER

1. How can the `rand()` and `srand()` functions work together when there is no apparent connection between them?

In this program we demonstrate how to use these functions and operator to generate random numbers within the range `min_pass_code` to `max_pass_code` (both entered by a user).

If you try running this program yourself, you will see that your output is different from what we show and different each time you run the program. Do not spend a significant amount of time trying to figure out how this program operates right now. Read the program and annotations, then read the Description to learn how to generate random numbers in your programs.

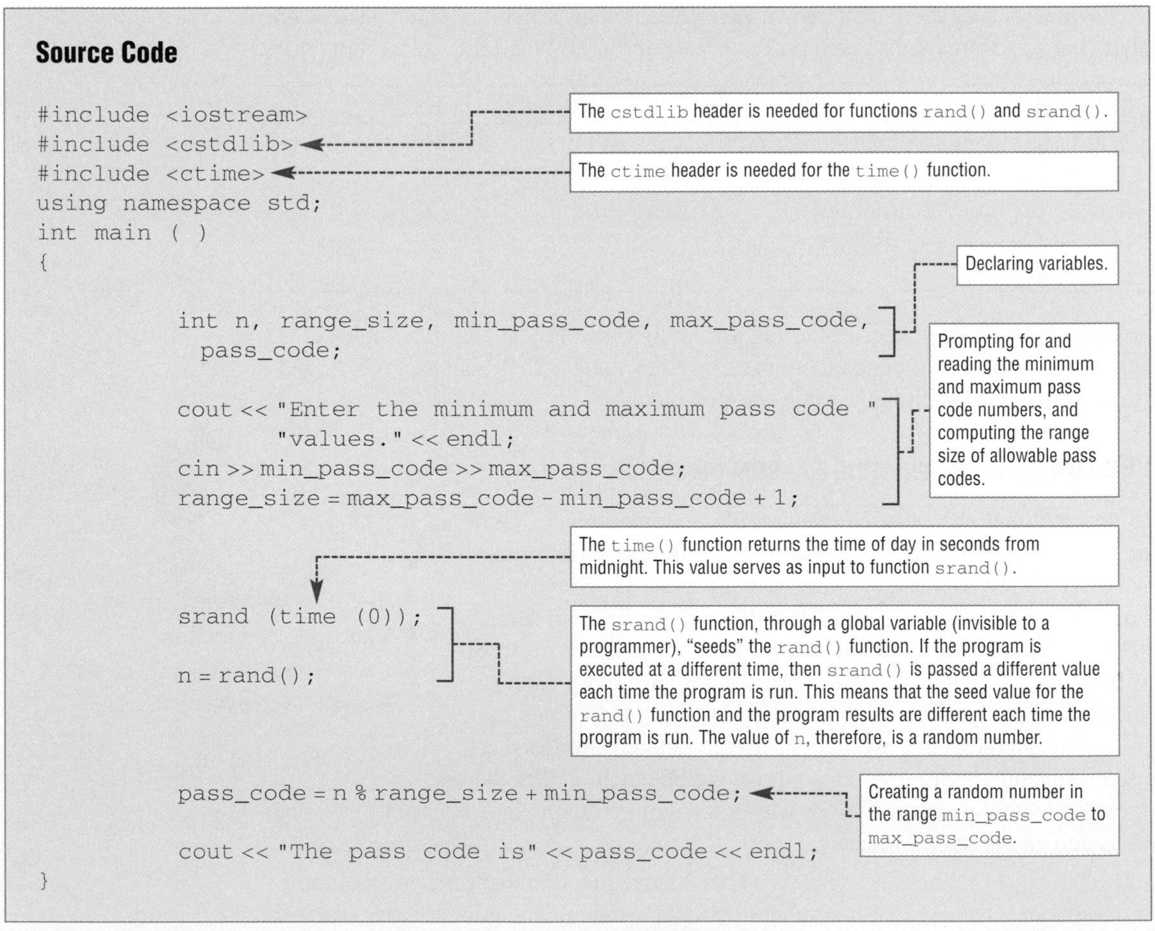
Source Code

```
#include <iostream>
#include <cstdlib>
#include <ctime>
using namespace std;
int main ( )
{

        int n, range_size, min_pass_code, max_pass_code,
          pass_code;

        cout << "Enter the minimum and maximum pass code "
              "values." << endl;
        cin >> min_pass_code >> max_pass_code;
        range_size = max_pass_code - min_pass_code + 1;

        srand (time (0));

        n = rand();

        pass_code = n % range_size + min_pass_code;

        cout << "The pass code is" << pass_code << endl;
}
```

The cstdlib header is needed for functions rand() and srand().
The ctime header is needed for the time() function.
Declaring variables.
Prompting for and reading the minimum and maximum pass code numbers, and computing the range size of allowable pass codes.
The time() function returns the time of day in seconds from midnight. This value serves as input to function srand().
The srand() function, through a global variable (invisible to a programmer), "seeds" the rand() function. If the program is executed at a different time, then srand() is passed a different value each time the program is run. This means that the seed value for the rand() function and the program results are different each time the program is run. The value of n, therefore, is a random number.
Creating a random number in the range min_pass_code to max_pass_code.

Output

```
Enter the minimum and maximum pass code values
1000 9999
The pass code is 3237
```

Description

The* `rand()`, `srand()`, *and* `time()` *functions. The function `rand()` can return a random integer that is different each time we use the program if we use it properly with the `srand()` and `time()` functions. The theory of random number generation is complex, so we will not go through the details here; however, `rand()` working alone returns only a pseudo-random number. To get a more nearly true random number, we need all three functions.

First, the `rand()` and `srand()` functions are designed to work together in a way that is very unusual in C++. The function `srand()` automatically "seeds" the function `rand()` by giving `rand()` a value to begin its calculation. The functions `rand()` and `srand()` are linked together through a global variable that is invisible to a programmer (and therefore, the functions appear to be completely unconnected in this lesson's program). The function `srand()` modifies this global variable and `rand()` uses the global variable in calculating its number.

If the value of the global variable is the same each time `rand()` is called, then the number returned by `rand()` is unpredictable, but it is the same each time the program is run. However, if the global variable is different each time `rand()` is called, then unrelated and nearly random numbers are returned by `rand()`. Therefore, the challenge in getting `rand()` to work randomly is to get the global variable to be different. To do this we use the `time()` function.

The C++ `time()` function cannot be guaranteed to return a different number each time the program is run but will likely give such a number. The function `time()`, when called with the argument 0, returns the single integer time of day in seconds by reading the computer's clock. Unless you execute a program at precisely the same time every day, the function `time()` returns a different value each time you run the program. Because of this feature, the `time` function is well suited for use in creating a different integer each time the program is run and can be used with function `srand()` to create a new global variable for `rand()`, which means `rand()` then returns a nearly random number. Thus,

```
srand (time (0));
```

creates a new global variable each time `srand()` is called. We then can call `rand()` with no argument using

```
rand ()
```

to create a random number.

Note that rand() and srand() require the <cstlib> header and time() requires <ctime>.

Generating random numbers within a specified range. We can use the mod operator to create an integer in a specified range. For instance, for any integer n, the value of n % 25 is a number from 0 to 24. Similarly, n % 90 is a number from 0 to 89.

If we want to simulate the roll of a single die (where the result is an integer from 1 to 6) an action such as (n % 6) + 1 works because n % 6 is a number from 0 to 5, and adding 1 to this gives a minimum of 1 and a maximum of 6 (which is what we want). If rand() returns a random number, then the following pair of statements simulates a roll of the die:

```
n = rand ( );
roll = (n % 6) + 1;
```

where roll is an integer representing the value of the roll.

Similarly, if we want to create a random number in the range 10 to 99 inclusive, then (n % 90) + 10 would do it. The 90 in this expression is computed from the maximum value (99) minus the minimum value (10) plus 1 (that is $90 = 99 - 10 + 1$). In general, the range size is computed from

```
range_size = max - min + 1;
```

And, the random number in the range min to max (inclusive) is computed from

```
{n % range_size) + min
```

Putting this together, we see that in this lesson's program, the statements

```
n = rand ( );
pass_code = (n % range_size) + min_pass_code;
```

produce a pass code in the region min_pass_code to max_pass_code inclusive.

Summary. To summarize, rand() and srand() are functions that are unusual in C++ in the manner that they are connected. In this lesson's program the calls to these functions appear to be unrelated. However, their connection through an invisible global variable and the use of the time function enables rand() to create a random number. With a random number and the mod (%) operator, we can create a random number within a specified range.

APPLICATION EXAMPLE 7.1 INTEGRATION WITH THE TRAPEZOIDAL RULE

Problem Statement

TOPICS

- Returning a value from a function
- Numerical method example

Write a program that can integrate a third-order polynomial function using the trapezoidal rule. The input should come from the keyboard and consist of

1. The number of trapezoids to be used.
2. The limits of integration.
3. The coefficients a, b, c, and d of the polynomial $ax^3 + bx^2 + cx + d$.

The output should be to the screen and consist of the area under the polynomial between the limits of integration given.

Solution

RELEVANT EQUATIONS

You may have learned the trapezoidal rule in your calculus class. If not, we review it here. The trapezoidal rule states that the area under a curve can be approximated by calculating the area of a number of trapezoids formed by connecting individual points on the curve. This is illustrated in Fig. 7.10.

This figure shows that, in some regions of the curve, a trapezoid is a good representation of the area. In other regions, a trapezoid is not particularly representative of the true area. Clearly, as more (and therefore narrower) trapezoids are used between the same limits, the approximation improves. When using the trapezoidal rule, we decide the number of trapezoids to be represented. Since we are writing a computer program to do the calculations, there is little penalty for choosing a large number.

We first decide the number of trapezoids to be used, n. Then, with the given left and right limits of integration, the value of h is computed to be (term definitions in Fig. 7.10)

$$h = (x_{\text{right limit}} - x_{\text{left limit}})/n \tag{7.1}$$

We can get the left and right x values for the first trapezoid using

$$x_1 = x_{\text{left limit}}$$
$$x_2 = x_{\text{left limit}} + h$$

and for subsequent trapezoids

$$\begin{aligned} x_1 &= x_{2\text{previous}} \\ x_2 &= x_1 + h \end{aligned} \tag{7.2}$$

In each case, we get the corresponding y values using

$$y_1 = ax_1^3 + bx_1^2 + cx_1 + d \tag{7.3}$$
$$y_2 = ax_2^3 + bx_2^2 + cx_2 + d \tag{7.4}$$

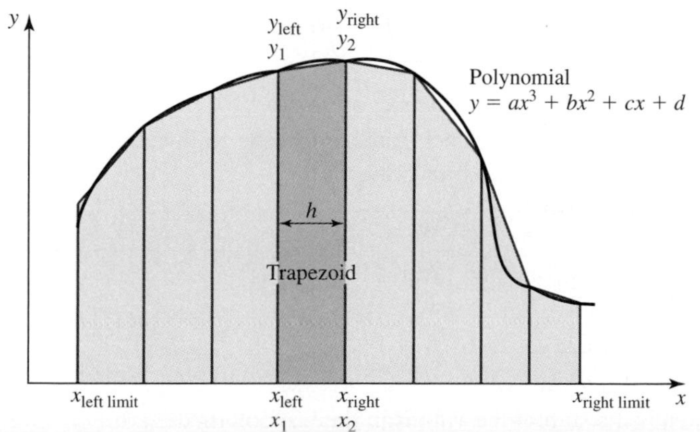

Figure 7.10

Illustration of a trapezoid in the trapezoidal rule. Note that the area of the trapezoid approximates the area beneath the curve between x_1 and x_2. In this figure the number of trapezoids (n) is 8.

With h, y_1, and y_2, we can get the area of each trapezoid. For instance, the area of the shaded trapezoid shown in Fig. 7.10 is

$$A_i = h\frac{y_1 + y_2}{2} \tag{7.5}$$

where A_i = area of a single trapezoid, y_1 is the y value of the left edge of a single trapezoid (also y_{left}), and y_2 is the y value of the right edge of a single trapezoid (also y_{right}). The total area is the sum of the areas of the individual trapezoids:

$$A_{\text{total}} = \sum_{i=1}^{n} A_i \tag{7.6}$$

Note that we have written the equation in summation form. This form is easily translated into source code. In our case, we will use a function to calculate the area of a single trapezoid (A_i) and put the call to the function in a loop (that goes from $i = 1$ to $i = n$).

SPECIFIC CALCULATION

Suppose we want to determine the area beneath the curve:

$$y = -2x^3 + 3x^2 + x - 4$$

between $x = 1$ and $x = 5$. For illustration purposes, we will use four trapezoids to do this (for a real problem you would choose many more). This gives us a value of h using Eqn. 7.1:

$$h = (5 - 1)/4 = 1$$

For each trapezoid, we get the following using Eqns. 7.2, 7.3, 7.4, and 7.5. For trapezoid 1,

$$x_1 = 1$$
$$x_2 = 1 + 1 = 2$$
$$y_1 = -2(1)^3 + 3(1)^2 + (1) - 4 = -2$$
$$y_2 = -2(2)^3 + 3(2)^2 + (2) - 4 = -6$$
$$A = (-2 - 6)(1)/2 = -4$$

For trapezoid 2,

$$x_1 = x_2 \text{ from the first trapezoid} = 2$$
$$x_2 = x_1 + h = 3$$
$$y_1 = -2(2)^3 + 3(2)^2 + (2) - 4 = -6$$
$$y_2 = -2(3)^3 + 3(3)^2 + (3) - 4 = -28$$
$$A = (-6 - 28)(1)/2 = -17$$

and so on (repeat the steps for each trapezoid). The following table of results summarizes the calculations for all four trapezoids:

Trapezoid	x_1	x_2	y_1	y_2	A
1	1	2	−2	−6	−4
2	2	3	−6	−28	−17
3	3	4	−28	−80	−54
4	4	5	−80	−174	−127

The total area is the sum of the values in the last column:

$$A_{\text{tot}} = -4 - 17 - 54 - 127 = -202$$

Note that the exact value of the integral is

$$A = -192$$

Clearly, our trapezoid answer is approximate. We would do better with more trapezoids. For instance, with 100 trapezoids we get $A = -192.016000$, which is much closer to the correct result.

ALGORITHM

We choose to put the calculation of the area of each trapezoid into a function called `trapezoid`. This gives us the *data flow diagram* in Fig. 7.11. A data flow diagram, loosely speaking, is a sketch of the relationship between functions in a program. It shows how the functions call other functions in a program and the information that passes between functions. In this text, we do not dwell on data flow diagrams because they are primarily a procedural programming tool, and C++ is an object-oriented language.

For this program, the data flow diagram illustrates that `main` passes the values of $h, x_1, x_2, a, b, c,$ and d to function `trapezoid`. These are all the data values needed to calculate the area of a single trapezoid, and this is the reason this particular data was chosen to be passed to the function. Since we need only a single value (the area) to be calculated by the function, we make the function have a return value (we do not need to use references). The area is a real number, so we choose to return a `double`.

This general algorithm for this program can be written from the specific calculation and the data flow diagram.

1. Prompt the user to enter the number of trapezoids, left limit, right limit.
2. Read the number of trapezoids, left limit, right limit.
3. Prompt the user to enter the coefficients of the polynomial.
4. Read the coefficients of the polynomial.
5. Calculate h.
6. Calculate x_1 (left point).
7. Calculate x_2 (right point) from the left point.
8. Calculate y_1.
9. Calculate y_2.
10. Calculate A.
11. Accumulate A's from each trapezoid.
12. Print the total A.

Function trapezoid. (steps 8–10)

Repeat for each trapezoid. (steps 6–12)

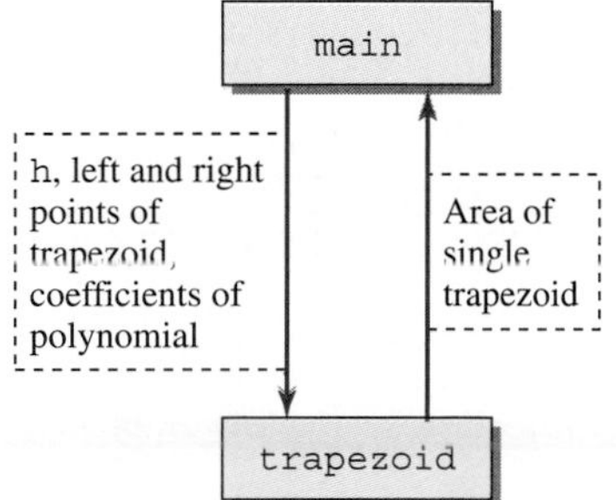

Figure 7.11 Data flow diagram for integration using the trapezoidal rule.

Source Code

This source code can be written from the algorithm and the data flow diagram:

```
#include <iostream>
#include <cmath>
using namespace std;
double trapezoid (double, double, double, double,
                  double, double, double);
void main (void)
{
        double left_point, right_point, a, b, c, d, h, area;
        int n, i;

        cout << "Enter n, left point, right point\n";
        cin >> n >> left_point >> right_point;
        cout << "Enter a, b, c, d\n";
        cin >> a >> b >> c >> d;

        area = 0.0;
        h = (right_point - left_point) / n;

        for (i = 1; i <= n; i++)
            {
            right_point = left_point + h;
            area += trapezoid (h, left_point,
              right_point, a,b,c,d);
            left_point = right_point;
            }

        cout << "Area = " << area << endl;
}

double trapezoid (double h, double x1, double x2, double a,
                 double b, double c, double d)
{
        double y1, y2, area_of_trapezoid;
        y1 = a * x1 * x1 * x1 + b * x1 * x1 + c * x1 + d;
        y2 = a * x2 * x2 * x2 + b * x2 * x2 + c * x2 + d;
        area_of_trapezoid = (y1 + y2 * h/2.;
        return (area_of_trapezoid);
}
```

Declaring the function to receive 7 `double`s and return a `double`. The function name is `trapezoid`.

Reading the input values.

We must initialize `area` to 0.0 before the loop because we will use it to accumulate a sum.

Calculating the distance between points, `h`. In this statement, `right_point` means the farthest right point. After `h` has been calculated, we no longer need to store the farthest right point.

Since we no longer need the farthest right point, we use `right_point` here to represent the right point of each individual trapezoid.

Looping over the number of intervals, n.

Calling `trapezoid` to calculate the area of a single trapezoid. The compound assignment operator causes `area` to be the sum of all of the areas of the individual trapezoids.

For the first time through the loop, `left_point` is set to be the farthest left point (before the loop is entered). After that, the `left_point` for each individual trapezoid is set to be the `right_point` for the previous trapezoid.

Function header. Because none of the arguments has `&`, `trapezoid` does not modify any of the variables in `main`.

Calculating the area of a single trapezoid.

Returning the area of a single trapezoid.

Output

```
                  Enter n, left point, right point
Keyboard input    100 1 5
                  Enter a, b, c, d
Keyboard input    -2 3 1 -4
                  Area = -192.016000
```

Comments

This is a straightforward example of the use of a function that returns a single value. It illustrates a numerical technique of the sort commonly used in programs. While the trapezoidal rule is effective and direct, to get a reliable result, a large number of trapezoids may be needed, requiring a large number of computations. As you learn more about numerical methods, you will learn other techniques for evaluating integrals that require fewer computations to achieve the same reliability, and thus are more efficient.

Modification Exercises

1. Modify the program so that it can integrate a fourth-order polynomial.
2. Modify the program so that it can integrate a fifth-order polynomial.
3. Rewrite a portion of the program so that a function is used to accumulate the area. Give this function the name `area` and have it call the function `trapezoid`.

Tracing Exercise

1. Trace the loop by filling in (and expanding) the following table for a few times through the loop. (Note: Since this is a simple loop from 1 to `n`, we do not need to include the loop test and increment expressions.)

Statement	a	b	c	d	h	right_point	left_point	area
Before the loop	–2	3	1	–4			1	0

`right_point = left_point + h;`
`area += trapezoid (h, left_point,`
`  right_point, a,b,c,d);`
`left_point = right_point;`								

`right_point = left_point + h;`
`area += trapezoid (h, left_point,`
`  right_point, a,b,c,d);`
`left_point = right_point;`								

APPLICATION EXAMPLE 7.2 WORKING WITH GRIDS

TOPICS

- Logic
- Complex looping
- Functions

A programmer often is faced with the task of working with a grid or a mesh. A grid may be used to analyze stresses in a plate or temperature distribution in a solid object, by subdividing the region of interest into smaller, more manageable parts. Then, each individual part can be evaluated.

The application program for this lesson is intended to help you develop logic skills in dealing with grids, using functions, and writing loops. Pay close attention to how the function, many loops, and `if` control structures are combined to produce the desired result.

Problem Statement

A chessboard has eight rows and eight columns. If you are familiar with chess, then you know that a knight can move from its location (i, j) in the k direction (as shown in Fig. 7.12) one or two squares and in the m direction one or two squares (where k and m are measured from the initial location of the knight indicated by the clear circle on the board). A knight near the center of the chessboard has eight possible moves as illustrated in Fig. 7.12 (shaded circles) and listed in the table in the left part of the figure.

However, a knight located in the corner has only two possible moves because of the presence of the edges of the chessboard, as illustrated in Fig. 7.13 and shown in the table in the upper left part of the figure.

For this application, write a program that can compute the number of possible moves for a knight located at any location on the chessboard. There is no input information. The output is to be to the screen in the form of a grid-like pattern, showing the chessboard with the number of possible moves as a numeral in each chessboard location.

Solution

With a grid problem, it is necessary first to number the grid locations. For the chessboard, we recommend using a two number sequence (i, j) to label the board.

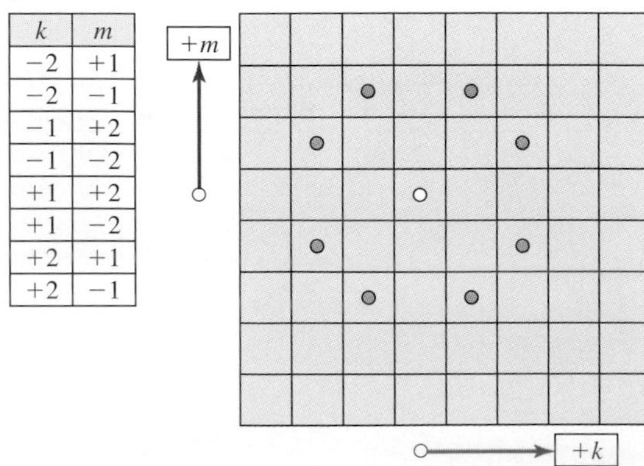

k	m
−2	+1
−2	−1
−1	+2
−1	−2
+1	+2
+1	−2
+2	+1
+2	−1

Figure 7.12

Figure illustrating possible movement locations (shaded circles) of a knight (clear circle) in the center of a chessboard.

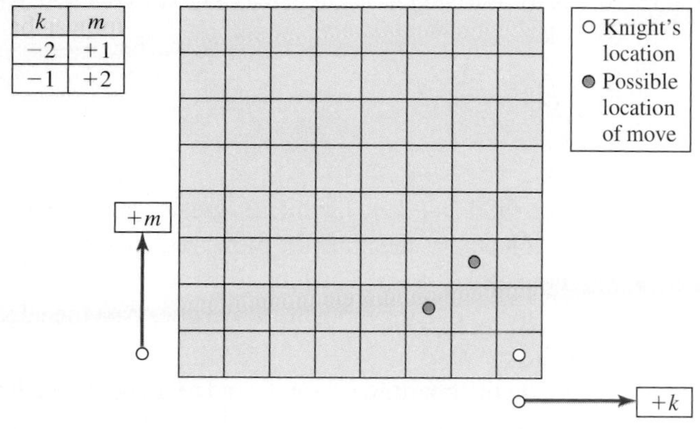

Figure 7.13

Figure illustrating possible movement locations (shaded circles) of a knight (clear circle) located in the corner of a chessboard.

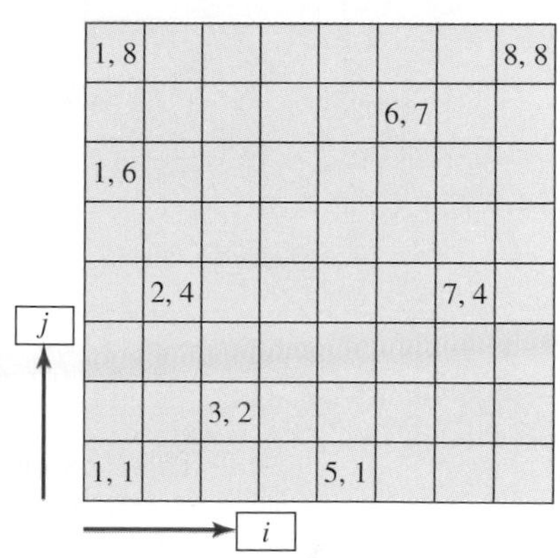

Figure 7.14

Figure illustrating the i, j coordinates of the chessboard grid.

Figure 7.14 shows some grid locations. The values of i and j increase from left to right and down to up, respectively. You should be able to deduce the values not shown from the ones shown.

RELEVANT EQUATIONS

If the initial knight location is (i, j), then we will call the new location $(i + k, j + m)$. To be legal, a move must meet the following criteria

$$1 \leq (i + k) \leq 8 \tag{7.7}$$

and

$$1 \leq (j + m) \leq 8 \tag{7.8}$$

because there are eight squares in each direction on a chessboard.

A list of all possible combinations of k and m are given in the table of Fig. 7.12. We must check a location (i, j) on the chessboard for the possible combinations of k and m to see if they are feasible. If a move is found to be feasible, then we will count it. All unfeasible moves simply will not be counted. Since there are eight possible combinations of k and m, the maximum possible number of moves for a knight beginning at a particular square is eight.

We need to check each of the 64 (i, j) locations on the chessboard, which means we will check $8 * 64 = 512$ possible moves. (For this particular problem we will not use the symmetry of the board to reduce the number of operations.)

SPECIFIC CALCULATION

Consider the location (7, 4) on the chessboard ($i = 7$ and $j = 4$). We list all the possible moves and check to see if the moves fall within the chessboard and not outside the edges. Using the values of k and m from the table in Fig. 7.12 and Eqns. 7.7

and 7.8, the possible moves are in the order $(i + k, j + m)$:

$(7 - 2, 4 + 1) = (5, 5)$ ok ($i + k$ and $j + m$ are in the range 1 to 8, inclusive)
$(7 - 2, 4 - 1) = (5, 3)$ ok
$(7 - 1, 4 + 2) = (6, 6)$ ok
$(7 - 1, 4 - 2) = (6, 2)$ ok
$(7 + 1, 4 + 2) = (8, 6)$ ok
$(7 + 1, 4 - 2) = (8, 2)$ ok
$(7 + 2, 4 + 1) = (9, 5)$ not valid ($i + k$ is 9, which is greater than the 8 allowable, meaning the move goes past the edge)
$(7 + 2, 4 - 1) = (9, 3)$ not valid ($i + k$ is 9, which is greater than the 8 allowable, meaning the move goes past the edge)

This location, therefore, has six valid moves.

To find a solution at each point on the board, we would need to do the preceding calculation for i from 1 to 8 and j from 1 to 8.

ALGORITHM AND CODE SEGMENTS

We can break our program into two distinct parts:

1. Creating the values of i and j that correspond to each point on the chessboard.
2. Checking a single point (i, j) for the number of permissible moves.

We create a function, `check_point`, to do the second part, and we do the first part in `main`. This leads to the data flow diagram in Fig. 7.15.

FUNCTION `check_point`

To check an individual point, we must write code that does what is illustrated in the specific calculation. We realize that we must write a number of loops to accomplish this. We first focus on how we can create the combinations of `k` and `m` within a loop.

We note in the list of possible `k` (in the table in the left part of Fig. 7.12) that `k` goes from −2 to 2 excluding 0. This implies a `for` loop of the sort

```
for (k = -2; k <= 2; k++)
        {
        if (k != 0);
                {
                ...
                }
        }
```


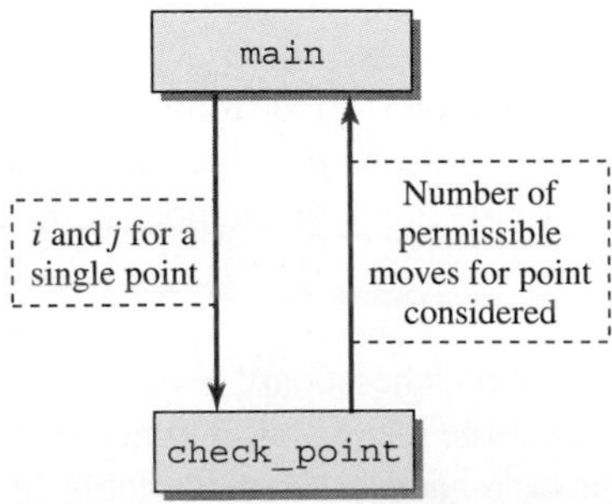

Figure 7.15
Data flow diagram for knight moves program.

Note that with this loop structure we create four iterations (for k = −2, −1, 1, and 2). At this point, we have created k correctly, and we now need to create m. From the table of Fig. 7.12, we see that we need to create two values of m for each value of k. We can calculate m from the value of k if we note that

$$|k| + |m| = 3$$

where $|k|$ is absolute value of k and $|m|$ is absolute value of m. Therefore,

$$|m| = 3 - |k|$$

which can be stated as

$$m = (3 - |k|)$$

and

$$m = -(3 - |k|)$$

So, we need to create a loop that executes twice within the loop that goes from −2 to 2. The first time through the loop, $m = (3 - |k|)$, and the second time through the loop $m = -(3 - |k|)$. We can do this with the following:

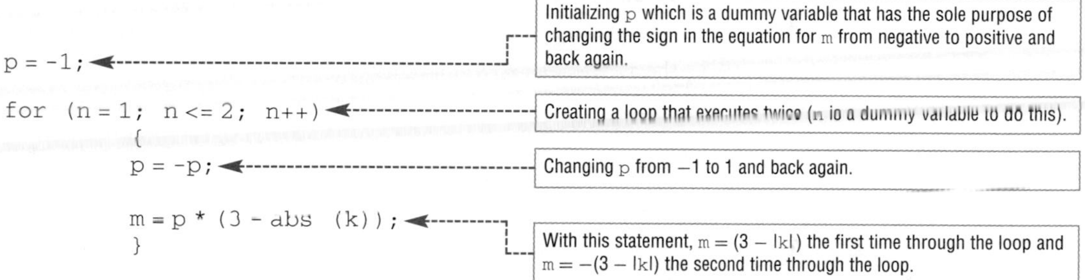

Putting this into the loop for k gives

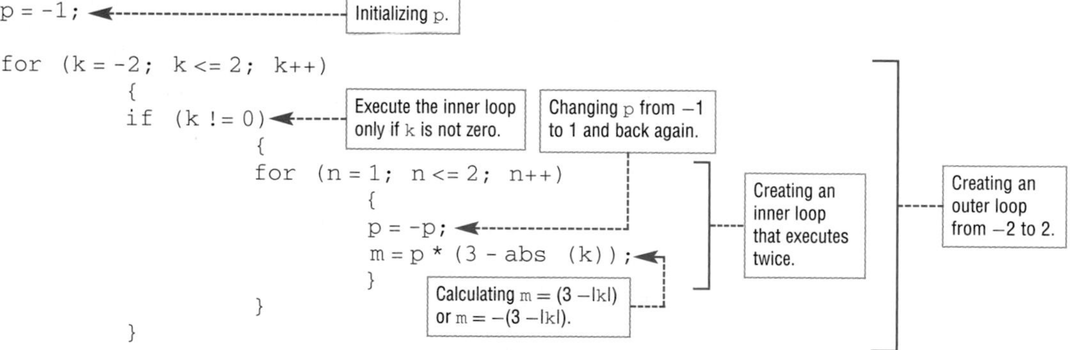

We can check this complex loop by making our table. Here it is for some iterations:

Statement	Test expression	p	k	n	m
Before the loop		−1			
`k = -2;`			−2		
`k <= 2;`	True				
`k != 0`	True				

(continued)

Statement	Test expression	p	k	n	m	
n = 1;				1		
n <= 2;	True					
p = -p;		1				
m = p * (3 - abs (k));					1	At this point in the loop, k = −2 and m = 1.
n++;				2		
n <= 2;	True					
p = -p;		−1				
m = p * (3 - abs (k));					−1	At this point in the loop, k = −2 and m = −1.
n++;				3		
n <= 2;	False					
k++;			−1			Inner loop.
k <= 2;	True					
k != 0;	True					
n = 1;				1		
n <= 2;	True					
p = -p;		1				
m = p * (3 - abs (k));					2	At this point in the loop, k = −1 and m = 2.
n++;				2		
n <= 2;	True					
p = -p;		−1				
m = p * (3 - abs (k));					−2	At this point in the loop, k = −1 and m = −2.
n++;				3		
n <= 2;	False					
k++;			0			

The boxed annotations indicate the points in the loop at which *k* and *m* are equal to our desired values according to the table in Fig. 7.12. Therefore, at those locations in the loop, we next insert a check on our values of *k* and *m*. With a given combination of *i* and *j*, we can use each of these combinations of *k* and *m* to check whether we have a valid move for the knight. If we have a valid move, then we should add 1 to the count that keeps track of the number of valid moves.

If we call the counter `icount`, then we should add 1 to `icount` when a move is valid. This indicates that we need an `if` statement and a condition to evaluate. The condition was stated earlier to be

$$1 \leq (i + k) \leq 8$$

and

$$1 \leq (j + m) \leq 8$$

This conditional and the addition to `icount` (if the conditional is true) can be written in C++ form as

```
if (1 <= (i + k) && (i + k) <= 8    &&
    1 <= (j + m) && (j + m) <= 8) icount++;
```

This statement goes into the inner loop immediately after the location noted in the previous table where *k* and *m* were the desired values. We put all this code in the function `check_point`. Values passed to `check_point` are `i` and `j`. The function returns the value of `icount`. The function is this:

```
int check_point (int i, int j)
{
     int icount, p, k, n, m;

     icount = 0;
     p = -1;

     for (k = -2; k <= 2; k++)
            {
            if (k != 0)
                     {
                     for (n = 1; n <= 2; n++)
                              {
                              p = -p;
                              m = p * (3 - abs (k));
                              if (1 <= (i + k) && (i + k) <= 8 &&
                                   1 <= (j + m) && (j + m) <= 8)
                                        icount++;
                              }
                     }

     return (icount);
}
```

The function is passed the values of `i` and `j`, and returns an integer.

Conditional that assesses whether the move is legal and adds to the count if it is. This conditional is at a location in the loop where `k` and `m` have the desired values.

Inner loop.

Outer loop.

FUNCTION `main`

Within `main` we need to make loops that create combinations of `i` and `j` that represent each point on the chessboard. This is an easier structure to create than what we did for function `check_point`. The following nested loop gives it to us:

```
for (j = 1; j <= 8; j++)
         {
         for (i = 1; i <= 8; i++)
                  {
                  ...
                  ...
                  }
         }
```

This nested loop creates a combination of `i` and `j` that covers all 64 points.

j

i

Using this nested loop, we create a combination of `i` and `j` for each square on the chessboard. This is shown in abbreviated form in the table that follows:

j	i
1	1 through 8
2	1 through 8
3	1 through 8
4	1 through 8
5	1 through 8
6	1 through 8
7	1 through 8
8	1 through 0

This loop indeed creates the values of i and j that cover the entire chessboard. For each combination of i and j, we then check all the possible combinations of k and m within function check_point. This leads to the following for main:

```
int main ()
{
        int n, i, j, icount;
        cout << "Number of possible moves for a knight "
             " on a chess board \n\n";
        for (j = 1; j <= 8; j++)
             {
             for (i = 1; i <= 8; i++)
                  {
                  icount = check_point (i, j);
                  cout << setwidth (5) << icount;
                  }
             cout << endl;
             }
}
```

Function check_point returns the number of valid moves.

We print the number of valid moves.

To get the table correct, we advance a line after completing an entire inner loop.

Combining main and check_point leads to the complete source code.

Source Code

```
#include <iostream>
#include <iomanip>
#include <cmath>
using namespace std;

int check_point(int, int);

int main ( )
{
        int n, i, j, icount;
        cout << "Number of possible moves for a knight "
             "on a chess board \n\n";
        for (j = 1; j <= 8; j++)
             {
             for (i = 1; i <= 8; i++)
                  {
                  icount = check_point (i, j);
                  cout << setwidth (5) << icount;
                  }
             cout << endl;
             }
}

int check_point (int i, int j)
{
        int icount, p, k, n, m;
```

The number of valid moves is assigned to icount.

Nested loop that creates i and j for each point.

Calling check_point to calculate the number of valid moves for each point.

```
            icount = 0;
            p = -1;
            for (k = -2; k <= 2; k++)
                   {
                   if (k != 0)
                          {
                          for (n = 1; n <= 2; n++)
                                 {
                                 p = -p;
                                 m = p * (3 - abs (k));
                                 if (1 <= (i + k) && (i + k) <= 8 &&
                                    1 <= (j + m) && (j + m) <= 8) icount++;
                                 }
                          }
                   }
            return (icount);
}
```

The loop and the `if` statement create only valid values of `k`.

Calculating a value of `m` from a value of `k`.

If the combination of `i`, `j`, `k`, and `m` make a valid move, add to the count of valid moves.

Return the number of valid moves for the values of `i` and `j` considered.

Output

```
Number of possible moves for a knight on a chess board.
2     3     4     4     4     4     3     2
3     4     6     6     6     6     4     3
4     6     8     8     8     8     6     4
4     6     8     8     8     8     6     4
4     6     8     8     8     8     6     4
4     6     8     8     8     8     6     4
3     4     6     6     6     6     4     3
2     3     4     4     4     4     3     2
```

Comments

Note that the output table shows that knights located in the corners have only two possible moves. Knights on the edges have three or four moves, and those near the center have eight possible moves.

Because we used a function for `check_point`, the code for `main` is reasonably simple. Separating such activities in a program makes it easier to read and understand. This feature leads to better code and reduced likelihood for errors.

You should also learn from this example how loops and `if` control structures are combined to create the calculations you want. As you can see, it is not necessarily simple. Use handwritten tables to help you follow the loops. The process of following loops like this will help you gain insight in developing complex loops.

To keep this program reasonably simple and directly related to a chessboard, we have not used constants for such things as the number of squares in the *i* and *j* directions.

Also, function `check_point` was written for a knight. One could imagine a different function for each chess piece and create a program that could determine the number of options for any piece.

Modification Exercises

1. Modify the program to handle a board that is 10 by 10 rather than 8 by 8.
2. Modify the program to handle a board that is 15 by 23 rather than 8 by 8.
3. Write a new function for the program that is capable of handling a rook's moves.
4. Write a new function for the program that is capable of handling a bishop's moves.

APPLICATION EXAMPLE 7.3 BOARD GAME SIMULATION

TOPICS

- Functions calling functions
- Pass by reference
- Using random numbers

Problem Statement

Write a program that simulates the board game shown in Fig. 7.16. Allow two players to compete. The goal is to be first to space 90 by rolling the dice and moving forward the number shown on the roll. Spaces 10, 30, 40, 60, 70, and 80 have special instructions as shown in the figure. Use functions to simulate rolling the dice, picking a card, spinning the wheel, choosing between picking a card and spinning the wheel, and checking the location of a player. The spinning wheel commands are shown

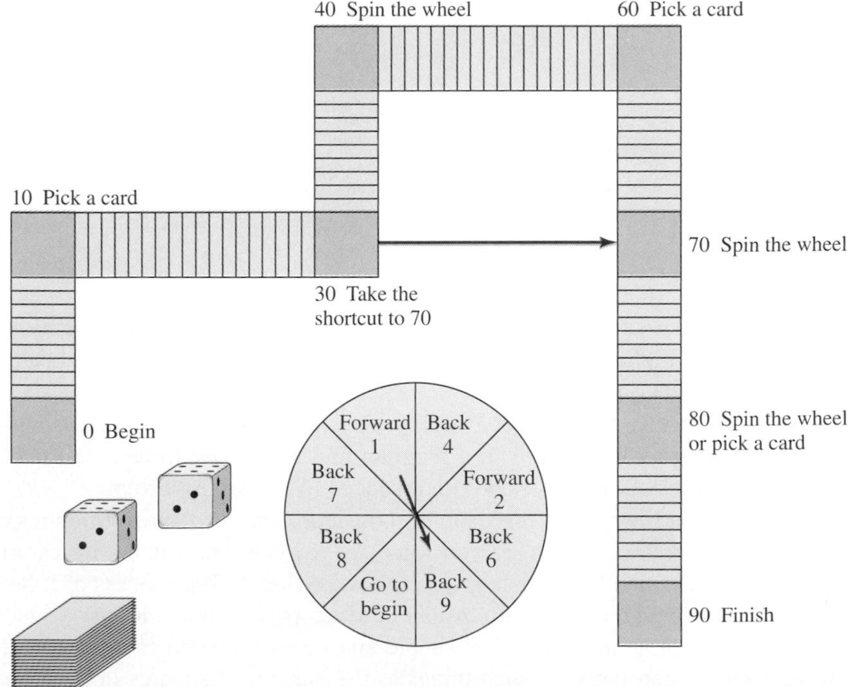

Figure 7.16

Board game with dice, spinning wheel, and deck of cards. Players begin at 0 and end at 90. The first to 90 wins.

on the wheel in the figure. Use 10 cards with the following instructions. The cards should remain in the order given.

The order of the cards is predetermined to be:

1. Go back 9 spaces.
2. Go to the beginning.
3. Go back 3 spaces.
4. Go back 8 spaces.
5. Go forward 2 spaces.
6. Go forward 1 space.
7. Go forward 3 spaces.
8. Go to the beginning.
9. Go back 4 spaces.
10. Go forward 6 spaces.

Interact with the user by printing to the screen, and save a permanent record of the game by printing to a file.

Solution

RELEVANT EQUATIONS AND BACKGROUND INFORMATION

Many of you have played board games involving dice and moving a piece from space to space. This game is explained in the figure. A player moves his or her piece forward the number of spaces shown on the dice. If a piece lands on a special instruction space, the user follows the special instructions. The first player to reach the end (space 90) wins. The `rand()` function should be used to roll the dice (to obtain a number from 2 to 12) and to spin the wheel (to obtain a number from 1 to 8).

ALGORITHM AND CODE SEGMENTS

Fundamentally, we need to roll the dice and check if a player has moved to a special instruction location. We create functions for these and call them from `main` (first `roll_the_dice` and then `check_the_location`) as shown in the data flow diagram of Fig. 7.17. If a player has landed on a special spot, we call a function that performs the necessary action (either `pick_a_card`, `spin_the_wheel`, or `choose_card_or_wheel`). Otherwise, the program should simply proceed and allow the next player to roll the dice. Within the program, we need to keep track of the location of each player and the card number at the top of the deck.

The steps in the program are

1. Initialize both Player 1 and Player 2 spots to be 0.
2. Player 1 rolls the dice, and the roll amount is added to Player 1's spot.
3. Check the location of Player 1's spot. Call a special instruction function if necessary, or declare Player 1 the winner.
4. Player 2 rolls the dice, and the roll amount is added to Player 2's spot.
5. Check the location of Player 2's spot. Call a special instruction function if necessary, or declare Player 2 the winner.

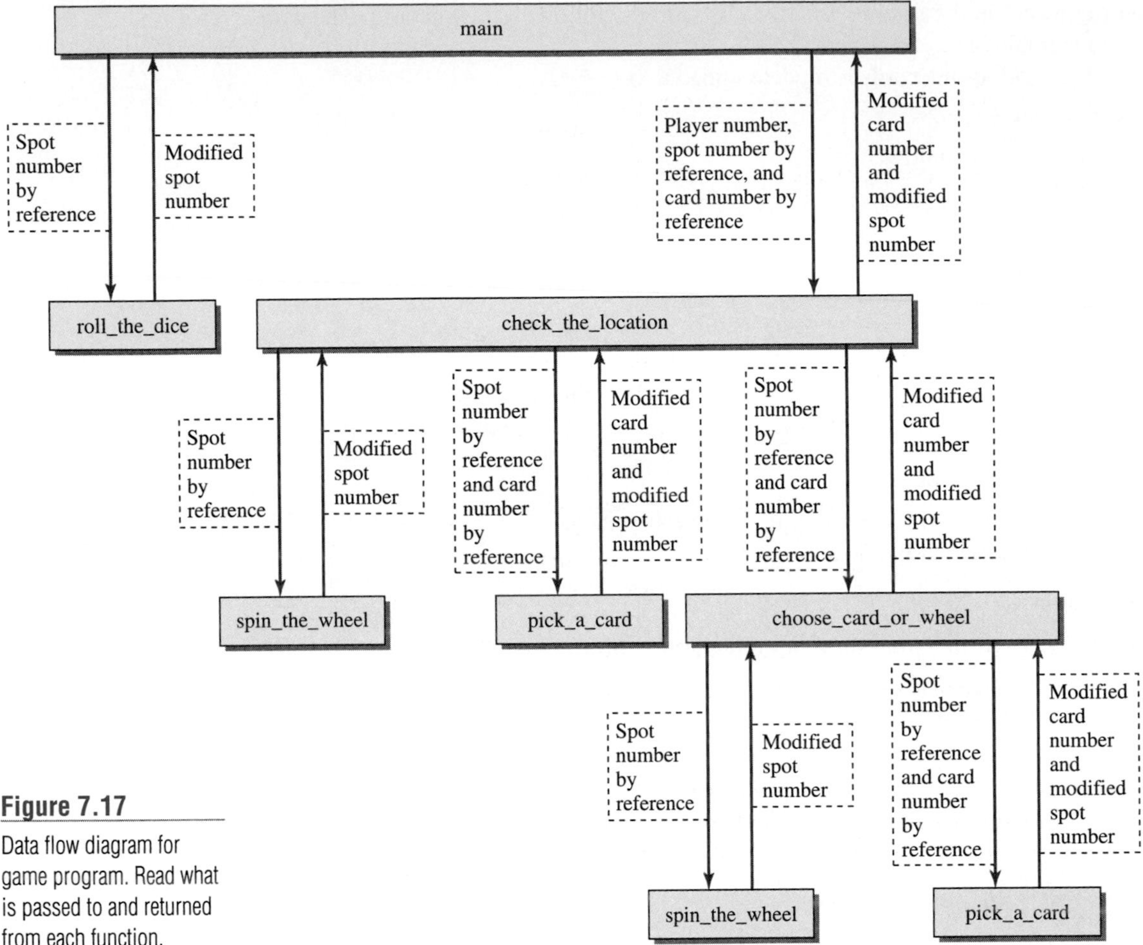

Figure 7.17

Data flow diagram for game program. Read what is passed to and returned from each function.

Steps 2 to 5 should be repeated until either Player 1's spot or Player 2's spot is 90 or more. This loop in `main` performs these steps.

```
int player1_spot = 0, player2_spot = 0;
int player, card_num;

do
        {
        cout << "\nPlayer 1 - Enter 1 to roll the dice."
             << endl;
        cin >> player;
        roll_the_dice (player1_spot);
        check_the_location (player, player1_spot,
             card_num);
        if (player1_spot >= 90) break;

        cout << "\nPlayer 2 - Enter 2 to roll the dice."
             << endl;
        cin >> player;
```

The players begin at spot 0. The `player` is either 1 or 2. We keep track of which card is on top with `card_num`.

Player 1 rolls the dice by entering his or her player number (1).

First the `roll_the_dice` function is called and then the location is checked.

We break out of the loop if player 1 wins by reaching 90.

Player 2 rolls the dice by entering his or her player number (2).

```
roll_the_dice (player2_spot);
check_the_location (player, player2_spot,
        card_num);

}
while (player2_spot < 90);
```

Player 2 rolls the dice, and then the location is checked.

The loop also ends when player 2 gets to spot 90 or beyond.

Note that, in theory we do not need each player to enter his or her player number to roll the dice. We ask to input a number to keep the player involved in the game. The `roll_the_dice()` and `check_the_location()` functions are described next.

FUNCTION `roll_the_dice()`

We want this function to obtain a random number from 2 to 12 and to add that to the player's spot. Therefore, we must pass the spot by reference to the function, so the function can modify it. Note that if we pass by value, the function cannot modify the player's spot because doing so allows the function to work with just a copy of the spot value, not the spot value itself. The function is:

```
void roll_the_dice (int& spot)
{
        int roll;
        roll = rand () % 11 + 2;
        spot += roll;
        cout << "You rolled " << roll << endl;
        }
```

The integer spot is passed by reference.

The value of roll is a random number from 2 to 12.

We increase the spot by the amount of the roll.

Printing the roll to the screen.

FUNCTION `check_the_location()`

This function checks to see if the player is on a special instruction spot. If the player is on a special spot; the function calls the appropriate specialty function. Since it calls all the specialty functions, it must be passed the information needed by all the specialty functions. This means it needs the spot and card number by reference. In addition, the function uses the player number to print the name of the winner. Since the function does not modify the player number, the player number is passed by value. The function is:

```
void check_the_location (int player, int& spot,
    int& card_num)
{
    int choose;

    cout << "You landed on spot " << spot << endl;

    if (spot == 30)
            {
            cout << "You get the shortcut "
                    "to 70." << endl;
            spot = 70;
            }

    if (spot == 10 || spot == 60)
            {
            pick_a_card (spot, card_num);
            }
    else if (spot == 40 || spot == 70)
            {
            spin_the_wheel (spot);
            }
```

The function is passed the player number by value, the spot by reference, and the card number by reference.

The 30 spot has the shortcut to the 70 spot, so we make the spot 70.

The 10 and 60 spots are for picking a card, so we call the `pick_a_card()` function.

The 40 and 70 spots are for spinning the wheel, so we call the `spin_the_wheel()` function.

```
            else if (spot == 80)
                    {
                    choose_card_or_wheel (spot, card_num);
                    }
            else if (spot >= 90)
                    {
                    cout << "Player " << player
                         << " wins! " << endl;
                    }
            else
                    {
                    cout << "Keep playing." << endl;
                    }
            return;
    }
```

The 80 spot is for choosing between picking a card or spinning the wheel, so we call the `choose_card_or_wheel()` function.

The 90 spot indicates a winner.

If none of the special spots are hit, keep playing.

A description of the special instruction functions follows.

FUNCTION `choose_card_or_wheel()`

This function asks the user to choose to pick a card or spin the wheel and calls the appropriate function. The function needs the information needed by the `spin_the_wheel()` and `pick_a_card()` functions. The function is:

```
    void choose_card_or_wheel (int& spot, int& card_num)
    {
            int choice;

            cout << "Enter 1 to spin the wheel or "
                 " 2 to pick a card." << endl;
            cin >> choice;
            if (choice == 1)
                    {
                    spin_the_wheel (spot);
                    }
            else
                    {
                    pick_a_card (spot, card_num);
                    }
            return;
    }
```

Prompting the user to choose.

Reading the choice entered by the user.

Calling the chosen function.

FUNCTION `pick_a_card()`

We want this function to select the first unused card and follow the card instructions. We assume a constant order for the cards. This means that we must keep track of the top card number. Therefore, we pass the top card number (`card_num`) to the function. In addition, we change the player's spot, so we pass the spot (`spot`) to the function also.

Initially, the top card number is 0. Each time the function is entered, we increase the card number by 1. Then we follow the instructions indicated by the card. (Note: If the card number is 11, we reset the card number to be 1, meaning we go back to the top of the deck.) A portion of the function is:

```
void pick_a_card (int& spot, int& card_num)
{

        cout << "You get to pick a card!" << endl;

        card_num ++;
        if (card_num == 11) card_num = 1;

        if (card_num == 1)
                {
                spot -= 9;
                cout << "Go back 9. You are at "
                  "spot" << spot << endl;
                }
        else if (card_num == 2)
                {
                spot = 0;
                cout << "Go back to the beginning. "
                        "You are at spot" << spot << endl;
                }
        .
        .
        return;
}
```

Both the player's spot and top card number are passed by reference.

Increasing the top card number by 1 (that is, drawing the card).

If the card number is 11, go back to the top of the deck by making the card number equal to 1.

Following the instructions for each card as described in the problem statement. The entire source code has all ten cards.

FUNCTION `spin_the_wheel()`

We want this function to select a random number in the range 1 to 8 and perform the instructions shown on the wheel in Fig. 7.16. To do this, we need to pass the player's spot by reference to the function. A portion of the function is:

```
void spin_the_wheel (int& spot)
{
        int spin;
        cout << "You get to spin the wheel!" << endl;
        spin = rand () % 8 + 1;
        if (spin == 1)
                {
                spot -= 4;
                cout << "Go back 4. You are at spot"
                     << spot << endl;
                }
        else if (spin == 2)
                {
                spot += 2;
                cout << "Go forward 2. You are at "
                        "spot" << spot << endl;
                }
        .
        .
        .
        return;
}
```

The player's spot is passed to the function by reference.

Creating a random number from 1 to 8.

Following the instructions for each wheel number as described in Fig. 7.16. The entire source code has all eight numbers.

The entire source code shows all the functions put together. We have created a permanent record of the game by adding statements that print to a file. It also shows seeding of the `rand()` function using `srand()`.

Source Code

```
#include <iostream>
#include <ctime>
#include <cstdlib>
#include <fstream>
using namespace std;

void pick_a_card (int&, int&);
void spin_the_wheel (int&);
void choose_card_or_wheel (int&, int&);
void check_the_location (int, int&, int&);
void roll_the_dice (int&);
ofstream outfile ("C:\\BDGAME.OUT");

int main ( )
{
        int player1_spot=0, player2_spot=0;
        int player, card_num;

        srand (time (0));

        do
                {
                outfile << "\nPlayer 1 - Enter 1 to roll the dice." << endl;
                cout << "\nPlayer 1 - Enter 1 to roll the dice." << endl;
                cin >> player;
                roll_the_dice (player1_spot);
                check_the_location (player, player1_spot, card_num);
                if (player1_spot >= 90) break;

                outfile << "\nPlayer 2 - Enter 2 to roll the dice." << endl;
                cout << "\nPlayer 2 - Enter 2 to roll the dice." << endl;
                cin >> player;
                roll_the_dice (player2_spot);
                check_the_location (player, player2_spot, card_num);

                }
                while (player2_spot < 90);
}
```

These are the headers needed for the `rand` function, `time` function, and file output.

Function declarations.

We create a "`cout`-like" output file by opening the output file outside all functions. This means all the functions can print to the output file.

Seeding the `rand()` function with `srand()`.

This is the primary loop that controls the program execution.

```
void roll_the_dice (int& spot)
{
        int roll;
        roll = rand () % 11 + 2;
        spot += roll;
        outfile << "You rolled " << roll << endl;
        cout << "You rolled " << roll << endl;
}
```

Function roll_the_dice().

```
void check_the_location (int player, int& spot, int& card_num)
{
        int choose;

        outfile << "You landed on spot " << spot << endl;
        cout << "You landed on spot " << spot << endl;
        if (spot == 30)
                {
                outfile << "You get the shortcut to 70." << endl;
                cout << "You get the shortcut to 70." << endl;
                spot = 70;
                }
       if (spot == 10 || spot == 60)
                {
                pick_a_card (spot, card_num);
                }
       else if (spot == 40 || spot == 70)
                {
                spin_the_wheel (spot);
                }
       else if (spot == 80)
                {
                choose_card_or_wheel (spot, card_num);
                }
       else if (spot >= 90)
                {
                outfile << "Player " << player << " wins!" << endl;
                cout << "Player " << player << " wins!" << endl;
                }
       else
                {
                outfile << "Keep playing." << endl;
                cout << "Keep playing." << endl;
                }
       return;
}
```

Function check_the_location.

```
void choose_card_or_wheel (int& spot, int& card_num)
{
        int choice;

        outfile << "Enter 1 to spin the wheel or 2 to pick a card." << endl;
        cout << "Enter 1 to spin the wheel or 2 to pick a card." << endl;
        cin >> choice;
        if (choice == 1)
                 {
                 spin_the_wheel (spot);
                 }
        else
                 {
                 pick_a_card (spot, card_num);
                 }

        return;
}

void spin_the_wheel (int& spot)
{
         int spin;
         outfile << "You get to spin the wheel!" << endl;
         cout << "You get to spin the wheel!" << endl;
         spin = rand () % 8 + 1;
         if (spin == 1)
                  {
                  spot -= 4;
                  outfile << "Go back 4. You are at spot " << spot << endl;
                  cout << "Go back 4. You are at spot " << spot << endl;
                  }
         else if (spin == 2)
                  {
                  spot += 2;
                  outfile << "Go forward 2. You are at spot " << spot << endl;
                  cout << "Go forward 2. You are at spot " << spot << endl;
                  }
         else if (spin == 3)
                  {
                  spot -= 6;
                  outfile << "Go back 6. You are at spot " << spot << endl;
                  cout << "Go back 6. You are at spot " << spot << endl;
                  }
         else if (spin == 4)
                  {
                  spot -= 9;
                  outfile << "Go back 9. You are at spot " << spot << endl;
                  cout << "Go back 9. You are at spot " << spot << endl;
                  }
```

Function `choose_card_or_wheel`.

Begin function `spin_the_wheel()`.

```
        else if (spin == 5)
                {
                spot = 0;
                outfile << "Go back to the beginning. You are at spot "
                      << spot << endl;
                cout << "Go back to the beginning. You are at spot "
                    << spot << endl;
                }
        else if (spin == 6)
                {
                spot -= 8;
                outfile << "Go back 8. You are at spot " << spot << endl;
                cout << "Go back 8. You are at spot " << spot << endl;
                }
        else if (spin == 7)
                {
                spot -= 7;
                outfile << "Go back 7. You are at spot " << spot << endl;
                cout << "Go back 7. You are at spot " << spot << endl;
                }
        else
                {
                spot += 1;
                outfile << "Go forward 1. You are at spot " << spot << endl;
                cout << "Go forward 1. You are at spot " << spot << endl;
                }

        return;
}

void pick_a_card (int& spot, int& card_num)
{

        cout << "You get to pick a card!" << endl;
        outfile << "You get to pick a card!" << endl;

        card_num ++;
        if (card_num == 11) card_num = 1;
        if (card_num == 1)
                {
                spot -= 9;
                outfile << "Go back 9. You are at spot " << spot << endl;
                cout << "Go back 9. You are at spot " << spot << endl;
                }
        else if (card_num == 2)
                {
                spot = 0;
                outfile << "Go back to the beginning. You are at spot "
                      << spot << endl;
```

Begin function `pick_a_card()`.

```
            cout << "Go back to the beginning. You are at spot "
                 << spot << endl;
            }
else if (card_num == 3)
            {
            spot -= 3;
            outfile << "Go back 3. You are at spot " << spot << endl;
            cout << "Go back 3. You are at spot " << spot << endl;
            }
else if (card_num == 4)
            {
            spot -= 8;
            outfile << "Go back 8. You are at spot " << spot << endl;
            cout << "Go back 8. You are at spot " << spot << endl;
            }
else if (card_num == 5)
            {
            spot += 2;
            outfile << "Go forward 2. You are at spot " << spot << endl;
            cout << "Go forward 2. You are at spot " << spot << endl;
            }
else if (card_num == 6)
            {
            spot -= 8;
            outfile << "Go back 8. You are at spot " << spot << endl;
            cout << "Go back 8. You are at spot " << spot << endl;
            }
else if (card_num == 7)
            {
            spot += 1;
            outfile << "Go forward 1. You are at spot " << spot << endl;
            cout << "Go forward 1. You are at spot " << spot << endl;
            }
else if (card_num == 8)
            {
            spot += 3;
            outfile << "Go forward 3. You are at spot " << spot << endl;
            cout << "Go forward 3. You are at spot " << spot << endl;
            }
else if (card_num == 9)
             {
             spot = 0;
             outfile << "Go back to the beginning. You are at spot "
                    << spot << endl;
             cout << "Go back to the beginning. You are at spot "
                  << spot << endl;
             }
```

```
        else if (card_num == 10)
                {
                spot -= 4;
                outfile << "Go back 4. You are at spot " << spot << endl;
                cout << "Go back 4. You are at spot " << spot << endl;
                }
        else
                {
                spot += 6;
                outfile << "Go forward 6. You are at spot  " << spot << endl;
                cout << "Go forward 6. You are at spot  " << spot << endl;
                }

        return;
}
```

Output (Partial)

```
Player 1 - Enter 1 to roll the dice.
You rolled 5
You landed on spot 5
Keep playing.

Player 2 - Enter 2 to roll the dice.
You rolled 3
You landed on spot 3
Keep playing.
.
.
.
Player 1 - Enter 1 to roll the dice.
You rolled 2
You landed on spot 30.  You get the shortcut to 70.
You landed on spot 70
You get to spin the wheel!
Go forward 2. You are at spot 72

Player 2 - Enter 2 to roll the dice.
You rolled 4
You landed on spot 63
Keep playing.
.
.
.
```

```
Player 1 - Enter 1 to roll the dice.
You rolled 7
You landed on spot 86
Keep playing.

Player 2 - Enter 2 to roll the dice.
You rolled 12
You landed on spot 80
Enter 1 to spin the wheel or 2 to pick a card.
You get to pick a card!
Go back 9. You are at spot 71

Player 1 - Enter 1 to roll the dice.
You rolled 8
You landed on spot 94
Player 1 wins!
```

Comments

A number of different complications can be added to this game. Ones commonly included in this sort of game are Lose a turn, Double your roll, Send your opponent back, and Stay put until you roll a certain number. We could also change the number of spaces or add branching to reach the desired location. We could require the last spot to be landed on exactly. The primary purpose of this program is to give the user entertainment. Therefore, any modifications to the program that add chance or skill requirements will likely make using the program more enjoyable.

Modification Exercises

1. Add "choose card or wheel" to spaces 20 and 50.
2. Make the game go to space 150. Make a special instruction space every 10 spaces.
3. Add "Lose a turn" to the `spin_the_wheel` function.
4. Add your favorite board game devices and make the game as much fun as you can.

LESSON EXERCISES

LESSON 7.1 EXERCISES

1. True or false:

   a. One reason for defining a function is to avoid writing the same group of C++ statements over and over again.

   b. A programmer-defined function may be written before the `main` function.

   c. A programmer-defined function may be written after the `main` function.

   d. A programmer-defined function may be written within the `main` function.

e. A function body must be enclosed within a pair of braces.

f. A programmer-defined function must be called at least once; otherwise, you will get a warning message from the C++ compiler.

g. In general, you write a programmer-defined function if and only if no such function is in the C++ library. The reason is that the C++ library functions were written by professional programmers and have been used and tested many times. Therefore, they are more reliable, more efficient, and more portable than the functions you can write.

h. If needed, keywords such as `for`, `double`, and `while` can be used as function names.

2. Find the errors, if any, in the following function declarations:

a. `void (function1) void;`

b. `void function2 (void)`

c. `void function (n, x, a, b);`

d. `void function1 (int, double, float, long int, char);`

e. `void function2 (int n, double y, float, long int a, char);`

f. `void function1 (int, a, double, b, float,c);`

3. Given the following function declarations and variable declarations, find errors in the function calls:

```
void function1 (void);
void function2 (int n, double x);
void function3 (double, int, double, int);
void function4 (int a, int n, int b, int c);
int main ()
{
      int a, b, c, d, e;
      double r, s, t, u, v;
...
}
```

a. `function1 (a, b);`

b. `function2 (a, b);`

c. `function3 (r,a,s,b);`

d. `function4 (a,b,c,d,e);`

e. `function1 ();`

f. `function2 (r, a);`

g. `function3 (r, a, r, a);`

h. `function4 (r, s, t, u);`

4. What will be the output from this program?

```
#include <iostream>
using namespace std;
void function1 (int a, double x);
int main ()
{
        int a = 1, b = 2, c = 3, d = 4;
        double r = 3.2, s = 4.3, t = 5.4, u = 6.5;
        function1 (a,b);
        function1 (r,s);
}
void function1(int a, double x)
{
        cout << "a = " << a << ",   x = " << x << endl;
}
```

Solutions

1. a. true
   b. true
   c. true
   d. false
   e. true
   f. false
   g. true
   h. false

2. a. `void function1 (void);`
   b. `void function2 (void);`
   c. `void function (int n, double x, int a, int b);`
   d. No error, argument names are not required.
   e. No error but not a good form; argument names should be either all given or not given.
   f. `void function1 (int a, double b, float c);`

3. a. `function1();`
   b. No error detected by C++, but the value of `b` will be transferred in double form.
   c. No error.
   d. `function4 (a,b,c,d);`
   e. No error.
   f. No error detected by C++, but the value of `r` will be transferred in integer form.
   g. No error; we can pass the same value to many arguments.
   h. No error detected by C++, but the values of `r`, `s`, `t`, and `u` will be transferred in integer form.

4.
```
a = 1, x = 2.000000
a = 3, x = 4.300000
```
Note that because the types in the function call and function declaration do not match, `b` has been converted to 2.000000 and `r` has been converted to 3. This sort of conversion may cause errors in your programs.

LESSON 7.2 EXERCISES

1. True or false:

a. A correctly written `int` type function will return an `int` type value to the calling function.

b. Only a function with a `void` return type is allowed to have an argument.

c. The arguments for an `int` type function need not conform to the number, order, and type agreement requirement.

d. The call to an `int` or `double` type function must appear on the right side of an assignment statement.

2. Given the following function declarations and variable declarations, find errors in the statements using the function calls:

```
double function1(void);
int function2(int n, double x);
double function3 (double, int, double, int);
double function4 (int a, int n, int b, int c);
int main ()
{
      int a, b, c, d, e;
      double r, s, t, u, v;
      ...
}
```

a. `a = function1 ();`

b. `b = function2 (a, b);`

c. `r = function3 (r,a,s,b);`

d. `s = function4 (a,b,c,d,e);`

e. `u = function1 ();`

f. `c = d + function2 (r, s);`

g. `t = s * function3 (r, a, r, a);`

h. `a = v + function4 (r, s, t, u);`

Solutions

1. a. true
b. false
c. false
d. false

2. a. No error detected by C++, but the `double` value returned by `function1` will be stored in an `int`.
b. No error detected by C++, but `b` will be transferred to `function2` in `double` form.
c. No error.
d. `s = function4 (a, b, c, d);`
e. No error.
f. No error detected by C++, but `r` will be transferred to `function2` as an `int`.
g. No error.
h. No error detected by C++, but `r`, `s`, `t`, and `u` will be transferred to `function4` as `int`. Also, there are two `double`s on the right side of the assignment statement but an `int` variable on the left side of the statement.

LESSON 7.3 EXERCISES

A C++ program contains the following statements:

```
void plus(int, long int&);
int main ( )
{
     int x=100;
     long int y=9999;

     plus(x+200, y);
. . . . . .
}
void plus(int a, long int& b)
{
...
}
```

1. Determine whether each of the following statements is true or false:

   a. The `plus` function is of `void` type; therefore, it can never be used to return a value to the `main` function.

   b. The integer variable `a` in the function `plus` can be used to transfer a value from `plus` to the `main` function.

   c. Without using a `return` statement, the `plus` function can return a value to the `main` function.

   d. The symbol `&` in the plus function declaration is wrong; it should be `*`, not `&`.

   e. The value of `y` can be modified by the `plus` function.

   f. The value of `x` can be modified by the `plus` function.

2. Write a program that calls a `void` type function to find the maximum of three given integer numbers.

3. Write a program without calling a function to exchange the values of two long type integers.

4. Write a program that calls a function to exchange the values of two long type integers.

Solutions

1. a. false
   b. false
   c. true
   d. false
   e. true
   f. false

LESSON 7.4 EXERCISES

1. True or false:

   a. In general, we should use global variables (i.e., variables with file scope) as often as we can.

b. The argument types of a function must be the same as the function type.

c. You may alter the value of a variable, `n`, by calling a function that uses `n` as its argument and changes its value within the function.

d. The memory reserved for the variables of other functions is the same as the memory reserved for the variables of `main`.

e. Memory is reserved when a function is called.

f. When variable values are passed to functions, a copy is made and put into the memory reserved for the functions' variables.

Solutions

1. a. false
b. false
c. false
d. false
e. true
f. true

LESSON 7.5 EXERCISES

1. True or false:

a. We can often replace global variables with static variables.

b. Given a choice between global and static variables, global variables are usually better to use.

c. The keyword `extern` gives file scope to a variable.

d. Using `extern` with a global variable does not create a true declaration.

e. Ordinary automatic variables are destroyed when a program completes execution.

f. The keyword `static` in a declaration means that a variable's value cannot change at any time during program execution.

g. We can pass `ifstream` references to functions.

Solutions

1. a. true
b. false
c. false
d. false
e. false
f. false
g. true

LESSON 7.6 EXERCISES

1. Use default arguments to write a program that

a. Creates the following default output:

```
ABCD CORPORATION
Project ____     Contract No. 3815-A   File No. ______
Designed: JKR    Checked __________    Date _____/2008
```

b. Gets input from the user on Project, File No., Checked, and Date data.

c. Generates a nondefault output as follows:

```
ABCD CORPORATION
Project USA-OIL-1   Contract No.3815-A   File No. OIL-A12345
Designed: JKR       Checked John & Ken   Date 12/13/2008
```

2. Use default arguments to write a program that

a. Reads the data in a file called "INPUT.DAT." The file always has four columns of data representing the point number, X, Y, and Z coordinate. The number of rows may vary. Use the following data for input:

```
No.        X          Y          Z
1          755.0      221.9      696.4
2          744.4      204.3      698.6
3          743.1      206.8      689.9
4          734.8      225.4      701.3
```

b. Ask the user to input two point numbers; for example, if the user enters 3 4, then calculate the distance between points 3 and 4. However, if the user only presses the return key, calculate the distances between points 1 and 2, 2 and 3, 3 and 4, and 4 and 1.

c. Generate neat screen output.

LESSON 7.7 EXERCISES

1. True or false:

a. C++ does not allow two functions to have the same name.

b. The C++ automatic type conversions are not used with overloaded functions.

c. If there is ambiguity in a function call, the program will not compile.

d. It is permissible to use constants in the argument list to call an overloaded function.

e. C++ always uses `double` for real constants and `int` for integer constants.

2. Use overloaded functions to write a program that can find the maximum of 3, 4, or 5 numbers.

3. Use overloaded functions to write a program that can add

a. 4 integers

b. 5 `doubles`

Solutions

1. a. false
   b. false
   c. true
   d. true
   e. false

APPLICATION EXERCISES

Use at least one function other than `main` for each of these programs. The problems indicated by * are ones that require more background knowledge than the others.

1. The ancient Greek mathematician Euclid developed a method for finding the greatest common divisor of two integers, A and B. His method is

a. If the remainder of A/B is 0, then B is the greatest common divisor.

b. If it is not 0, then find the remainder of A/B and assign B to A and the remainder to B.

c. Return to step a and repeat the process.

Write a program that uses a function to perform this procedure. Display the two integers and the greatest common divisor.

2. Cost analysis is an important part of project work. When you are in practice, you may be asked to write programs to determine the minimum cost for a number of different potential circumstances. Your programs can be used as decision-making tools for a project.

Consider building an airport with the runway built on landfill. The contractor has two dump trucks, one with a capacity of 8 tons and the other with a capacity of 12 tons. The contractor uses the trucks to haul fill from a remote site to the airport location. The operating cost per trip for the 8 and 12 ton trucks is \$14.57 and \$16.26, respectively. One truck cannot make more than 60 percent of the total trips.

Write a program that develops the minimum cost for a given number of tons. Prompt the user to enter the total number of tons. Display the number of trips required for each truck and the total cost.

3. The strength of an earthquake can be measured by its magnitude. In 1935, Charles F. Richter developed a scale, commonly known as the Richter scale, for determining an earthquake's magnitude. The amount of energy released in an earthquake, the length of an earthquake's fault rupture, and the number of worldwide earthquakes all have been correlated with magnitude. The following approximate equations relating these have been developed:

$$\log_{10} \mathrm{E} = 11.8 + 1.5\mathrm{M}$$
$$\log_{10} \mathrm{L} = 1.02\mathrm{M} - 5.77$$
$$\log_{10} \mathrm{N} = 7.7 - 0.9\mathrm{M}$$

where M = Richter magnitude ($0 < \mathrm{M} < 8.2$)
E = Energy released in ergs
L = Length of the fault rupture in kilometers
N = Number of worldwide earthquakes in a 100 year period

Variation from the equations can be ±20 percent. Write a program that accepts values of E and L and computes the possible ranges of magnitude for this earthquake. Tell the user if the input data is totally incompatible. Determine the most likely numbers of earthquakes of these magnitudes.

***4.** A block is resting on a horizontal plane and is intended to be pulled with a force acting at an angle θ to the horizontal. The block weighs 30 kN and has a coefficient of friction of 0.2. Write a program that uses a function to calculate the magnitude of the force, F, needed to pull the block for $\theta = 0$, 5, 10, 20, 30, 40, 50, 60, 70, and 80 degrees.

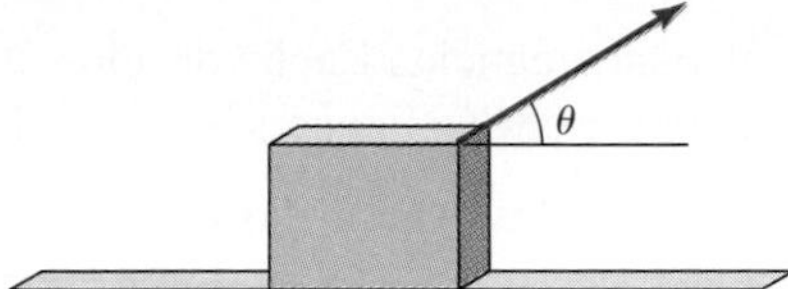

***5.** For the same block as in Problem 6, write a program that considers the effect of the plane being at an angle to the horizontal:

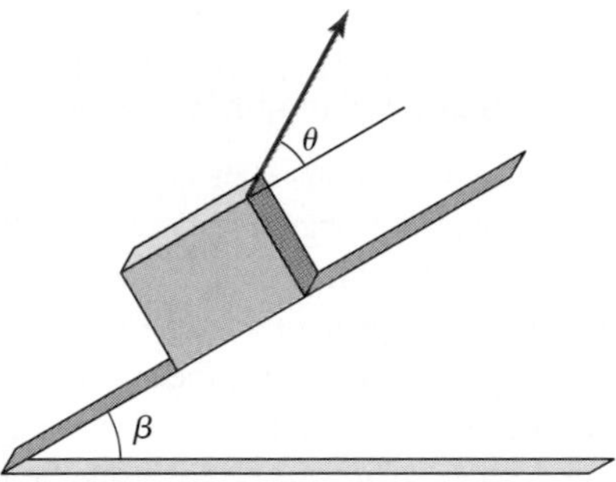

Solve the problem for the values of θ and β being 0, 10, 20, 30, 40, 50, 60, 70, and 80 degrees, but with the sum of θ and β being less than 90 degrees.

***6.** Solve Problem 5 with the coefficient of friction being 0.1, 0.2, 0.3, and 0.4.

***7.** Write a program that computes the forces at the supports, A and B, of the following beam for the distance x being 0, 0.25L, 0.5L, 0.75L and L and F being 100, 200, 300, 400, and 500 kN.

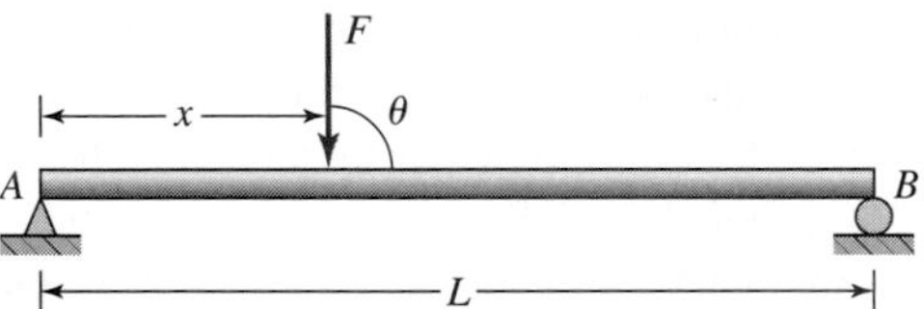

***8.** Write a program that can solve Problem 7 with θ being 0, 30, 60, and 90 degrees.

***9.** Write a program to calculate the necessary forces in cables used to tow a car if it takes a total of 3 kN in the rolling direction of the car to get it moving with no net force component perpendicular to the rolling direction of the car. Consider the values of θ and β being 0, 10, 20, 30, 40, 50, 60, 70, and 80 degrees, but with the sum of θ and β being less than 140 degrees.

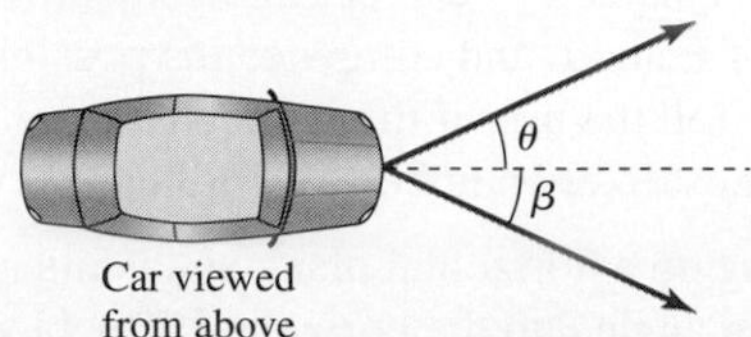

*10. Two vehicles collide and remain locked together after impact. Write a program that computes the direction (indicated by β) and speed (v_3) of these collided vehicles after contact takes place:

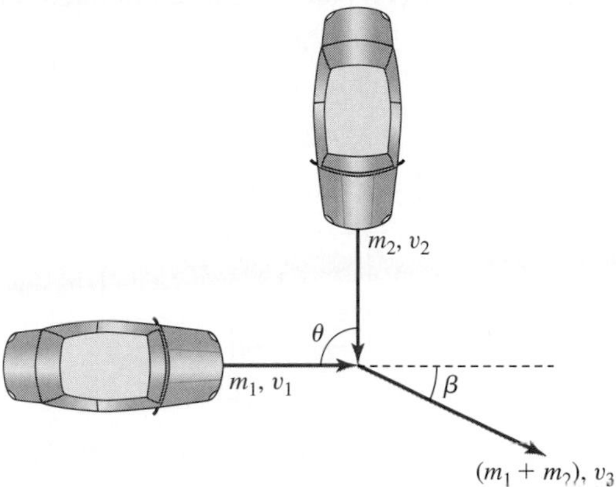

Use the following input data: $m_1 = 1000$ kg, $m_2 = 3000$ kg, $v_1 = 30$ m/sec, $v_2 = 10$, 20, 30, 40, 50, 60, 70, and 80 m/sec.

*11. Write a program for solving Problem 10, but with the following variations: $\theta = 10$, 20, 30, 40, 50, 60, 70, 80, and 90 degrees; $m_1 = 1000$, 2000, and 3000 kg, and $m_2 = 2000$, 4000, and 6000 kg.

*12. Write a program for solving Problem 10, but with the following variations: $\theta = 10$, 20, 30, 40, 50, 60, 70, 80, and 90 degrees; $v_1 = 10$, 20, and 30 m/sec; and $v_2 = 20$, 40, and 60 m/sec.

*13. Write a program that can calculate the tensile force in a cable for holding down this submerged buoy:

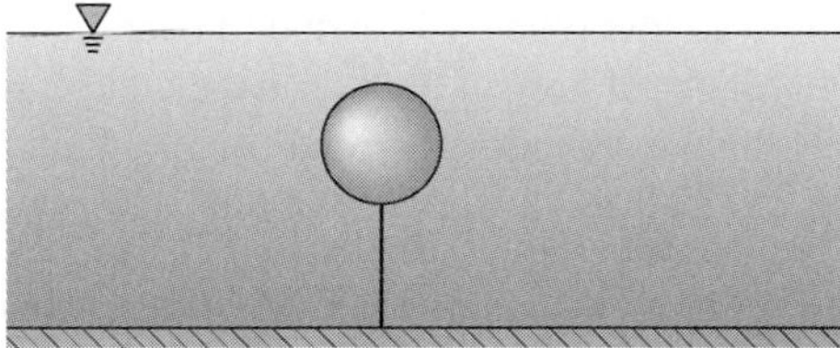

The buoy is filled with air. The water can be assumed to have a density of 9.8 kN/m^3. The program should compute the tensile force in the cable for a buoy radius of 1, 2, 3, 4, and 5 m.

*14. Write a program that can compute the cable tension for this partially submerged buoy:

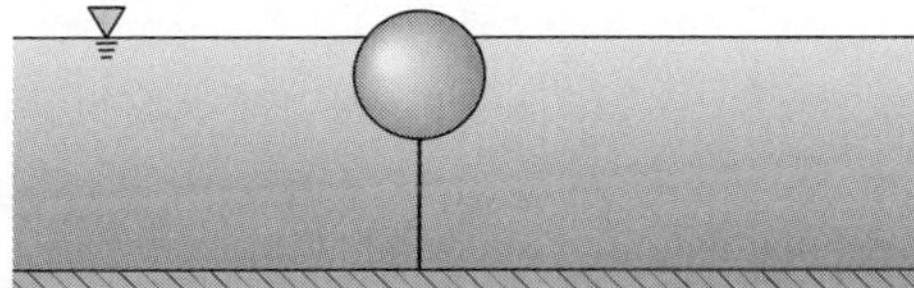

Consider the variations of the buoy being 0.25, 0.5, 0.75, and fully submerged. Consider both fresh water (density of 9.8 kN/m^3) and salt water (density of 10.05 kN/m^3). The program should compute the tensile force in the cable for a buoy radius of 1, 2, 3, 4, and 5 m.

***15.** Write a program that can compute the current through each resistor for this circuit:

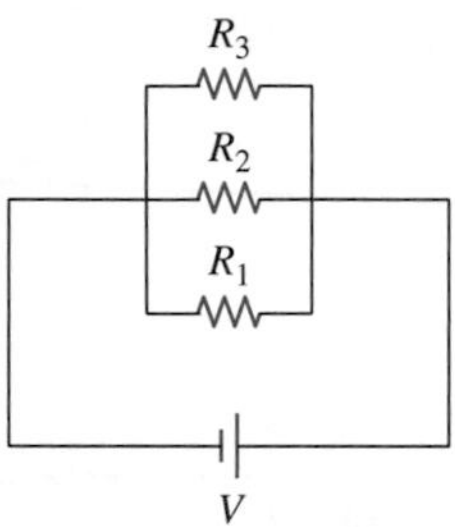

Take the voltage, V, equal to 30 volts. Use $R_1 = 10$, 20, and 30 ohms; $R_2 =$ 40, 60, and 80 ohms; and $R_3 = 100$, 120, and 130 ohms.

***16.** Repeat Problem 15 with the number of resistors varying from one to five; with $R_4 = 50$, 70, and 90 ohms; and $R_5 = 140$, 160, and 180 ohms.

17. The flow of water through porous media is normally laminar (fluid flows in parallel layers without mixing) and therefore follows the Darcy (a French engineer) equation:

$Q = kiA$

where $Q =$ the flow rate (volume/time, cm^3/sec)
$k =$ the coefficient of permeability (volume/time/area, cm/sec)
$i =$ the hydraulic gradient (head loss per unit of length, no units, $i = H/L$)
$H =$ head loss (energy loss due to friction, cm)
$L =$ length of flow in the porous media (cm)
$A =$ the cross-sectional area through which flow occurs

A steel pipe that has an internal diameter of $D = 10$ cm and length of $L = 200$ cm is filled with sand; the permeability of sand is $k = 0.1$ cm/sec. The head loss is maintained at $H = 50$ cm. Write a program to calculate the rate of flow through the pipe. The input specifications are as follows. No external input from the keyboard or file. However, the program shall declare Q, k, i, H, L, A, and D as `double` type variables. The flow is calculated by calling a function named `flow_rate()` from the main function. Its declaration is

```
void flow_rate(double D, double L, double k, double H);
```

The output specifications are as follows. The output shall display the following data on the screen:

```
All raw data D, L, k, and H
Calculated values of i and k
Flow rate, Q
```

18. During a rainstorm, water collected from a given area is guided to ditches or road culverts. To size the ditch or culvert, hydraulic engineers use what is called the rational method to calculate the peak rate of runoff water. The formula is

$$Q = CiA$$

where Q = peak rate of runoff (ft^3/sec)
C = weighted average runoff coefficient (no units)
i = average precipitation intensity (in/hour)
A = watershed (area of rainfall) tributary to the point of interest (acres)

Note that the value of C depends on the type of surface. In rural areas, the values of C are as follows:

Type of surface	Average runoff coefficient, C
Concrete	0.9
Bare earth	0.6
Cultivated fields	0.3
Forested areas	0.2

If the watershed area consists of different types of surfaces, C shall be calculated using the weighted average method. For example, if the area is 20 percent covered by concrete, 30 percent by bare earth, 50 percent by forest, the weighted average C is

$$C = [(0.9 * 20\%) + (0.6 * 30\%) + (0.2 * 50\%)] = 0.46$$

Write a program to determine the peak runoff in a given area based on the following. The input specifications are these. Call a function named `read_data ()` to read an input file similar to this table (the third column is used for explanation only; it is not part of the input file):

6.9		The first line only contains the rainfall intensity $i = 6.9$ in/sec
100	0.9	The first column is the size of subarea in acres (100) that is covered by $C = 0.9$ type surface
200	0.6	The first column is the size of subarea in acres (200) that is covered by $C = 0.6$ type surface
300	0.3	The first column is the size of subarea in acres (300) that is covered by $C = 0.3$ type surface
150	0.2	The first column is the size of subarea in acres (150) that is covered by $C = 0.2$ type surface

The declaration of `read_data()` is as follows:

```
double read_data (double &i, double &A);
```

The function shall:

Calculate the total watershed area, A (A should be $= 100 + 200 + 300 + 150 = 750$ acres).

Calculate the weighted average runoff coefficient C and return this value to the `main()` function.

In the `main ()` function, calculate $Q = CiA$.

The output specifications are these. The output shall display the following data on the screen:

Raw data i, and size of each subarea and its runoff coefficient.
Size of total watershed area, A, and the weighted average runoff coefficient, C.
Peak rate of runoff, Q.

19. Redo Problem 18; however, the declaration of `read_data ()` is changed to:

```
void read_data (double &i, double &A, double &C);
```

20. This table shows the coefficient of permeability, k, for various types of soils:

Soil type	Range of coefficient of permeability (cm/sec)
Clay	1.0E−10 to 1.0E−8
Silt	1.0E−8 to 1.0E−4
Sand	1.0E−4 to 1.0
Gravel	1.0 to 100.0

Given the coefficient of permeability of a soil, write a program to determine its type. The input specifications are these: Call a function named `soil_type ()` to:

Read the coefficient of permeability from the keyboard
Find the range of the input k value
Determine the soil type

The function declaration is

```
void soil_type (void);
```

The output shall display the following data on the screen:

```
The coefficient of permeability entered by the user
                  The soil type
```

21. The power consumed by a heater can be calculated by the equation

$p = vi$

where p = power (watts)
v = voltage (volts)
i = current (amperes)

Write a program to calculate the power consumed by various types of heaters. The input specifications are these: Read the voltage, v (first column), and the current, i (second column), from this file.

```
110          5.5
220         23.5
90          13.6
370         44.4
```

The output specifications are these: The output shall display the following data on the screen:

The input values of v and i

The power

For example, after reading the first line of input data, you should display the following on the screen:

```
Input voltage = 110.0 volts, current = 5.5 amperes
Power consumed by the heater = 605.0 watts
```

22. Redo Problem 21, but display the resistance value, R ($R = v/i$, ohms) of each heater. The output for the first line of input data shall be

```
Input voltage = 110.0 volts, current = 5.5 amperes
Power consumed by the heater = 605.0 watts
Heater resistance = 20.0 ohms
```

CHAPTER 8

INTRODUCTION TO CLASSES AND OBJECTS

CHAPTER TOPICS

In this chapter, you will learn how to:

- Define a class
- Use an object
- Select class data members
- Select class function members
- Create a constructor function

At this point, you have learned how to use both data and functions in your programs. You can now begin to understand the concept of *encapsulation* and how data and functions can be linked together in the form of an *object*. The manner in which the data and functions are linked are defined within a *class*.

In this chapter, we show you how to form your programs using classes and implement the classes with objects. Programming with classes (that is, linked functions and data) is considerably different than programming with just functions. There are a number of advantages of using objects (object-oriented programming) over using just functions (procedural programming). Among them are:

1. Classes form a tightly knit group of functions. The programming rules (with classes) create more distinct boundaries and reduce complexities in data flow (compared to procedural programming).
2. The distinct program boundaries make it easier to coordinate multiple programmers. Programmers can work somewhat independently constructing and debugging their own program segment.
3. By assembling thoroughly tested and debugged program segments, more reliable large programs can be created.
4. Classes created by independent vendors may be readily incorporated into a new program. This sometimes reduces the amount of programming that must be done "from scratch."

These are some of the reasons that object-oriented programming has become so popular. We do not say any more here. In Lesson 8.3, after you have seen what a class and object are, we describe more object-oriented concepts. For now, just recognize that many very powerful programs have been developed using object-oriented technology. This chapter covers a number of the fundamentals, so it is an important one. Study the chapter closely to understand the basics of object-oriented programming.

LESSON 8.1 FUNDAMENTALS OF A `struct`—A GROUPING OF DATA

TOPICS

- Defining a `struct`
- Declaring and using `struct` variables

C++ allows us to create a data type that is a grouping of other data types (such as `int` or `double`). Such a data type is called a `struct`. Because it is defined by a programmer, it is called a *derived data type*. For example, we may create a `struct` that has an `int` and two `double`s as *data members* of the `struct`. When we declare a variable to be of our `struct` type, space is reserved in memory for all the data members (in this example, an `int` and two `double`s). If we define a `struct` to have a large number of data members, then the storage space required for a single variable of the `struct` type could be substantial.

Why would we want to create our own types that contain data members? Suppose we want to write a program that works with the temperature, density, and velocity of fluids. We could create a `struct` called `Fluid` (which is the name of our data type) that has three `double` type members (one each for temperature, density, and velocity) and a `char` to represent the first initial of the fluid type. This is illustrated in Fig. 8.1 where we show `struct` type groupings of data representing `water`,

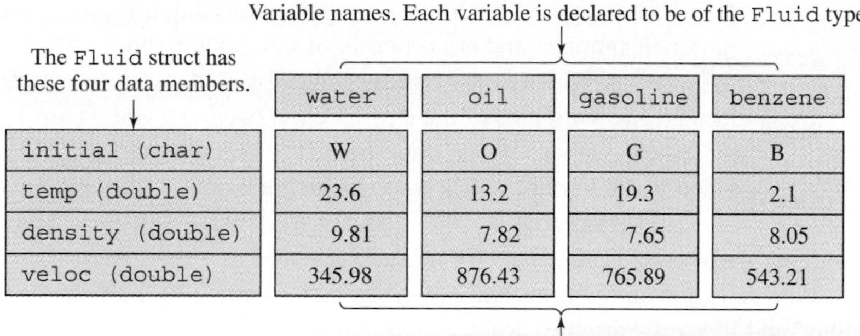

Figure 8.1
Conceptual illustration of `struct` type variables.

`oil`, `gasoline`, and `benzene`. All these are of the `struct` data type `Fluid`. The meanings are:

`initial`—for the first initial of the fluid type (`char`)
`temp`—for the fluid temperature (`double`)
`density`—for the fluid density (`double`)
`veloc`—for the fluid velocity (`double`)

When we declare a variable to be type `Fluid`, we reserve space for a `char` and three `doubles`. Such a variable has all these members linked together and can be regarded as a group. Such a grouping can be very useful to do such things as arrange or sort the variables according to different members. For instance, we can sort and print the variables in alphabetical order according to the fluid's first initial. This is shown at the top of Fig. 8.2. When the variables are sorted, all the members remain grouped. Similarly, we can sort and print the variables according to temperature. The members remain grouped, but the variables are in a different order as shown at the bottom of Fig. 8.2. This type of operation is one that is easily performed using `struct` type variables.

In this lesson's program, we create two `structs`, `Fluid` and `Solid`. For `Fluid`, the data members represent the `struct` variable's first initial, temperature, density, and velocity. The `Solid struct` has data members representing the variable's first initial, temperature, density, and stiffness. Notice that the difference between our `Fluid` and `Solid structs` is that the `Fluid struct` has velocity as a member (because fluids can flow), whereas the `Solid struct` has stiffness as a member (because stiffness,

Figure 8.2
Variables arranged in different orders.

Variables arranged in alphabetical order from left to right.

initial (char)	B	G	O	W
temp (double)	2.1	19.3	13.2	23.6
density (double)	8.05	7.65	7.82	9.81
veloc (double)	543.21	765.89	876.43	345.98

Variables arranged in order of increasing temperature from left to right.

initial (char)	B	O	G	W
temp (double)	2.1	13.2	19.3	23.6
density (double)	8.05	7.82	7.65	9.81
veloc (double)	543.21	876.43	765.89	345.98

QUESTION YOU SHOULD ATTEMPT TO ANSWER

1. Why have we made the class names (Fluid and Solid) begin with an uppercase letter?

which is a property similar to a spring constant, is represented by a single number, and is a property of solid materials).

We create two variables of the Fluid class (water and oil) and two variables of the Solid class (steel2 and steel6). We assign values to the data members for the water, oil, and steel2 variables. Then we make the steel6 variable have the same properties as the steel2 variable using an assignment statement, and print out all the values for all the variables.

Read the code and annotations and pay particular attention to the way structs are defined and struct variables are declared and used.

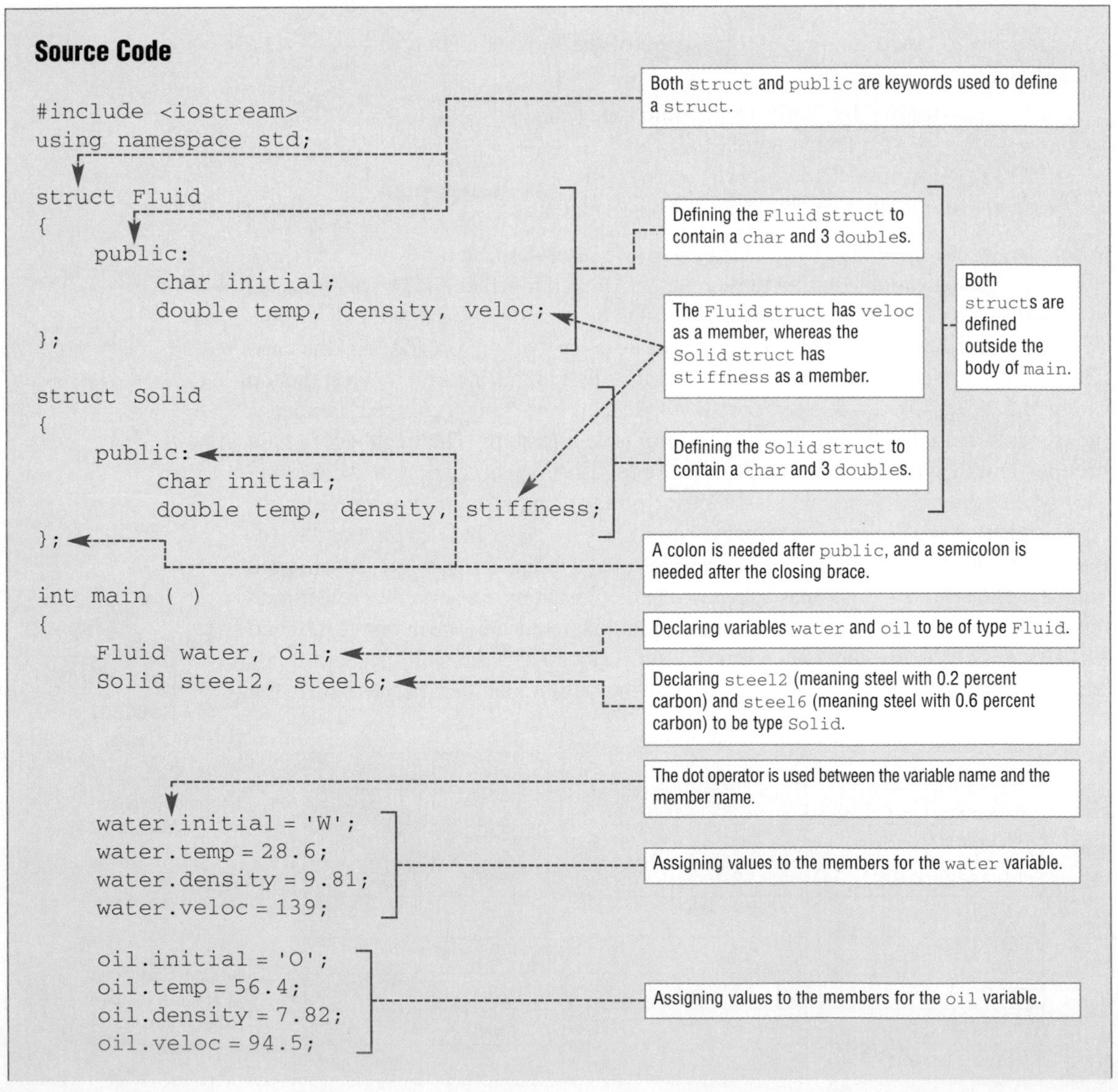

Source Code
Both struct and public are keywords used to define a struct.
Defining the Fluid struct to contain a char and 3 doubles.
The Fluid struct has veloc as a member, whereas the Solid struct has stiffness as a member.
Both structs are defined outside the body of main.
Defining the Solid struct to contain a char and 3 doubles.
A colon is needed after public, and a semicolon is needed after the closing brace.
Declaring variables water and oil to be of type Fluid.
Declaring steel2 (meaning steel with 0.2 percent carbon) and steel6 (meaning steel with 0.6 percent carbon) to be type Solid.
The dot operator is used between the variable name and the member name.
Assigning values to the members for the water variable.
Assigning values to the members for the oil variable.


```
#include <iostream>
using namespace std;

struct Fluid
{
    public:
        char initial;
        double temp, density, veloc;
};

struct Solid
{
    public:
        char initial;
        double temp, density, stiffness;
};

int main ( )
{
    Fluid water, oil;
    Solid steel2, steel6;

    water.initial = 'W';
    water.temp = 28.6;
    water.density = 9.81;
    water.veloc = 139;

    oil.initial = 'O';
    oil.temp = 56.4;
    oil.density = 7.82;
    oil.veloc = 94.5;
```

```
    steel2.initial = 'S';
    steel2.temp = 25.2;
    steel2.density = 7850;
    steel2.stiffness = 200000;

    steel6 = steel2;

    cout << "Water information " << water.initial << "\ntemp="
        << water.temp << "\ndensity=" << water.density << "\nveloc="
        << water.veloc << endl << endl;

    cout << "Oil information " << oil.initial << "\ntemp="
        << oil.temp << "\ndensity=" << oil.density << "\nveloc="
        << oil.veloc << endl << endl;

    cout << "Steel2 information " << steel2.initial << "\ntemp="
        << steel2.temp << "\ndensity=" << steel2.density
        << "\nstiffness=" << steel2.stiffness << endl << endl;

    cout << "Steel6 information " << steel6.initial << "\ntemp="
        << steel6.temp << "\ndensity=" << steel6.density
        << "\nstiffness=" << steel6.stiffness << endl << endl;

}
```

Assigning values to the members for the `steel2` variable.

With this single assignment statement, we assign *all* the member values for `steel2` to `steel6`. This is appropriate because steel with 0.2 percent and 0.6 percent carbon have the same first initial, density, and stiffness.

Printing all the values.

Output

```
Water information W
temp=28.6
density=9.81
veloc=139

Oil information O
temp=56.4
density=7.82
veloc=94.5

Steel2 information S
temp=25.2
density=7850
stiffness=200000

Steel6 information S
temp=25.2
density=7850
stiffness=200000
```

The numeric values of the data members for `steel2` and `steel6` are equal.

Description

***Defining a* `struct`.** Although a `struct` can be more, for now we can think of it as a type we define that is actually a grouping of other types.

To define a `struct`, we start with the keyword `struct` which must be written completely in lowercase letters. This is followed by the name of the `struct`, a left brace (`{`), the keyword `public`, colon, the types and names of the members, a right brace (`}`), and a semicolon. The general form is:

```
struct Struct_name
{
        public:
                type member_name1;
                type member_name2;
};
```

where *`Struct_name`* is the programmer chosen name for the `struct` (using the C++ rules for identifiers), *`type`* is any valid data type, and *`member_name1`* and *`member_name2`* are programmer chosen data member names. These elements are illustrated in Fig. 8.3 for the `Fluid struct` in this lesson's program.

Note that it is not required that the first letter of a `struct` name be in uppercase. However, one convention is to make the first letter uppercase. Some programmers use all lowercase. Check with your instructor or employer whether you should use all lowercase or a leading uppercase letter. In this text, we use a leading uppercase letter in most cases.

Also, the keyword `public` is not required, but we show it for clarity. We will see in Lesson 8.2 that there is also a keyword `private`. For now, just realize that the `public` designation of the data members indicates that all functions can access the data members using the variable name, dot operator, and data member name. The meanings of `public` and `private` will become clear after Lesson 8.2.

We should define our `struct`s outside the body of `main`. This means the scope rules allow any function to use the `struct` data type.

Choosing data members. The data members for a `struct` should represent the characteristics of the `struct`. In this lesson's program, we can consider temperature, density, and velocity to be fluid characteristics. Fluids can be considered to have other characteristics such as pressure, viscosity, and other things. Depending on the problem to be solved, these characteristics can be added to the `struct`.

Figure 8.3

Defining a C++ `struct` with public data members.

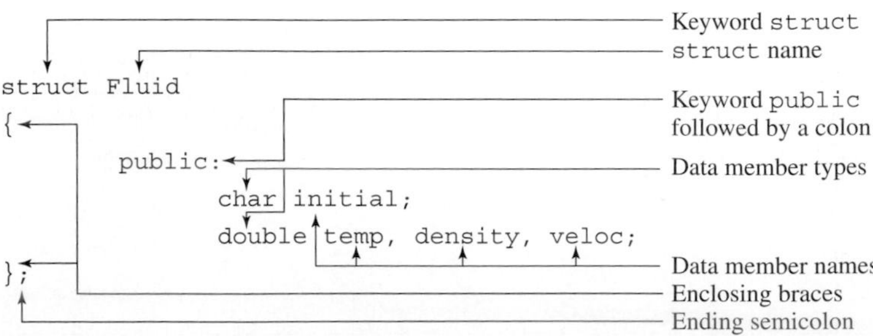

As another example, we can consider a circle struct. Recall the equation for a circle is

$$(x - x_{\text{cent}})^2 + (y - y_{\text{cent}})^2 = r^2$$

where $(x_{\text{cent}}, y_{\text{cent}})$ are the x and y coordinates of the center and r is the radius. If we were to define a circle struct, then a definition could be:

```
struct Circle
{
          public:
                    double x_center, y_center, radius;
};
```

Even more can be included in a circle struct definition, such as color or area, depending on the problem to be solved.

In general, you can select the data members for your structs by evaluating what characteristics describe or represent the struct you are creating.

Declaring struct variables. By declaring a variable to be of a particular struct type, we specify what types of information can be stored in the region of memory reserved for the variable.

To declare variables to be types of a struct, we use the struct name and follow it with the names of the variables. For instance,

```
Fluid water, oil;
```

declares water and oil to be variables of type Fluid.

This declaration causes memory to be reserved for all the data members of the Fluid struct for each variable. In other words, for this lesson's program, memory for one character and three doubles (all the data members of the Fluid struct) is reserved for each variable (water and oil). This is illustrated in Table 8.1.

Assigning values to data members. To access and store values in the memory cells reserved for a struct variable, we use the variable name, dot operator, and the data

TABLE 8.1 — Table illustrating concept of struct variables

Name	Type		Address	Value
water	Fluid			
	initial	char	FFDE	W
	temp	double	FFDD	28.6
	density	double	FFE5	9.81
	veloc	double	FFED	139
oil	Fluid			
	initial	char	FFC2	0
	temp	double	FFC3	56.4
	density	double	FFCD	7.82
	veloc	double	FFD3	94.5

member name to access the memory cells. For example,

```
water.density
```

refers to the cells reserved for the data member `density` for the variable `water`. In general, the form for accessing `public` data members of a `struct` is:

```
variable.data_member
```

where *`variable`* is a `struct` variable name and *`data_member`* is a data member name. We can store a value in the memory cells reserved for a data member using an assignment statement of the sort

```
water.density = 9.81;
```

This assignment statement causes the numerical value 9.81 to be stored in the memory cells reserved for the `density` member for the `water` variable.

We can copy the values of all the data members from one `struct` variable to another with a single assignment statement. For instance, in this lesson's program, the statement

```
steel6 = steel2;
```

copies the values of each member for the `steel2` variable to the members for the `steel6` variable. Observe that it is not necessary to copy the values member by member. In other words, if we are copying all the member values, we need not write (although we can):

```
steel6.initial = steel2.initial;
steel6.temp = steel2.temp;
steel6.density = steel2.density;
steel6.stiffness = steel2.stiffness;
```

Printing data member values. To print the values of all the data members for a `struct` variable, we must specify each member individually using the dot operator. We cannot print the values of all the data members using the name of the variable alone. For instance, to print all the members for the `water` variable we use

```
cout << "Water information " << water.initial << "\ntemp="
     << water.temp << "\ndensity=" << water.density
     << "\nveloc=" << water.veloc << endl << endl;
```

where `water.initial`, `water.temp`, `water.density`, and `water.veloc` are each specified.

Comparison between `struct` and `class`. A `struct` as it is commonly used is powerful because it groups data together. A `class` is even more powerful because it groups both data and functions. We will go into more detail in Lesson 8.2. At this point, we just want to point out that this lesson's program could have been written with a `class` instead of a `struct`. The only change is that the keyword `struct` is replaced by the keyword `class`. The program is:

```
#include <iostream>
using namespace std;
```

The keyword `class` replaces the keyword `struct` in the definition. The rest of the program is identical to the program using `struct`.

```
class Fluid
{
    public:
        char initial;
        double temp, density, veloc;
};

class Solid
{
    public:
        char initial;
        double temp, density, stiffness;
};

int main ( )
{
    Fluid water, oil;
    Solid steel2, steel6;

    water.initial = 'W';
    water.temp = 28.6;
    water.density = 9.81;
    water.veloc = 139;

    oil.initial = 'O';
    oil.temp = 56.4;
    oil.density = 7.82;
    oil.veloc = 94.5;

    steel2.initial = 'S';
    steel2.temp = 25.2;
    steel2.density = 7850;
    steel2.stiffness = 200000;

    steel6 = steel2;

    cout << "Water information " << water.initial << "\ntemp="
         << water.temp << "\ndensity=" << water.density
         << "\nveloc=" << water.veloc << endl << endl;

    cout << "Oil information " << oil.initial << "\ntemp="
         << oil.temp << "\ndensity=" << oil.density << "\nveloc="
         << oil.veloc << endl << endl;

    cout << "Steel2 information " << steel2.initial << "\ntemp="
         << steel2.temp << "\ndensity=" << steel2.density
         << "\nstiffness=" << steel2.stiffness << endl << endl;
```

```
        cout << "Steel6 information " << steel6.initial "\ntemp="
             << steel6.temp << "\ndensity=" << steel6.density
             << "\nstiffness=" << steel6.stiffness << endl << endl;

}
```

In other words, the form of the definitions for classes is the same as that for `struct`s, the dot operator works the same for classes and `struct`s, and the declaration form is the same for classes and `struct`s.

The terminology for classes is different from that for `struct`s. The equivalent of a `struct` variable with classes is an *object*. This is the object that is being referred to in the term *object-oriented programming* (OOP) or *object-oriented design* (OOD). Therefore, we would speak of the `water` object or the `oil` object in this lesson's program written with classes.

We will not say any more at this time. Read the next lesson to see the effect of grouping both data and functions.

LESSON 8.2 FUNDAMENTALS OF A CLASS—A GROUPING OF DATA AND FUNCTIONS

TOPICS

- Concept of encapsulation
- Keywords `public` and `private`
- Class function members
- Accessing `private` data members

As stated in the C++ standard, "An object is a region of storage" in memory. By defining a class and declaring an object to be of that class, we specify what types of information can be stored in the region of memory reserved for the object.

As we indicated in Lesson 8.1, classes can have both data members (also called *member data*) and function members (also called *member functions*). We will see that the *function* members are used to store and manipulate the *data* members. Also, we will see that there is a strong relationship between the data and function members of a class.

In Lesson 8.1, we learned that `public` data members of a class are accessed using an object name, dot operator, and data member name in sequence. In other words, the data members of a class are associated with a declared object. Similarly, we call `public` function members of a class with an object name, dot operator, and function name sequence. This means that function calls are also associated with declared objects.

When a member function is called with the object name, the data members of the object are automatically passed to the function (by reference) *without* being given in the argument list! The function can use each data member by name and modify the object's data member values directly. This feature provides a very clean and orderly way of working with data and is a core aspect of object-oriented programming.

In the previous lesson, we used the keyword `public` in the class definitions of `Fluid` and `Solid`. The `public` indicated that the data members of the class could be accessed from any function. For object-oriented programming, typically, we do not want every function to be able to access the data members of the class. We generally restrict access to the data members by using the keyword `private` in the class declaration. Making the access `private` means that only a class's function members can access a class's data members. This fact complicates the life of beginning programmers considerably because it means that since the `main` function is not a member of any class, we cannot access any class member data directly in `main`. Any time we want to do something as simple as printing out a data member value, we must use a member function.

We also need member functions to read the data, initialize the data, and do arithmetic operations on the data. In short, the program becomes filled with functions, some of which perform very small tasks. This increases the program length and, for a beginning programmer, makes it more difficult to understand; however, we will see the value of using member data and functions as we go along in this chapter.

Because the data members are `private`, it is not necessary to use the object name and dot operator to access the data. When we call the member function, we have already given the object name, so C++ knows which object's data members are being accessed. In a member function, the data member names may be used directly.

In this lesson's program, we find the area beneath a parabola. To do so, we create a class called `Parabola`. A parabola is described with the equation $y = ax^2 + bx + c$. Therefore, the values of the coefficients a, b, and c define a parabola. A simple `Parabola` class then has `a`, `b`, and `c` as data members. We could add other parabola attributes or characteristics of the data members, but for this introductory lesson we choose to use the fewest data members.

QUESTION YOU SHOULD ATTEMPT TO ANSWER

1. What other data members might you use as attributes of a parabola?

In addition to data members, a class needs function members. As mentioned, we need function members to perform even the simplest tasks. Therefore, we need a function to read the values of `a`, `b`, and `c` from the keyboard. We call this function `read_coeffs`. Also, we need a function to calculate the parabola area, and we call this function `calc_area`. We could add more functions to this class such as a function to print the coefficients (which we could call `show_coeffs`), but we have deliberately set up this program to demonstrate a number of features of classes and objects rather than a complete standard design.

Read the code and pay particular attention to the class and function definitions and how the data members are accessed in the member functions.

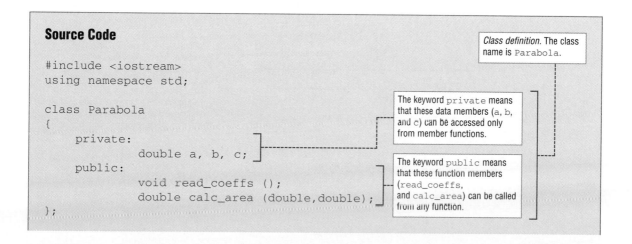

Source Code

```
#include <iostream>
using namespace std;

class Parabola
{
    private:
            double a, b, c;
    public:
            void read_coeffs ();
            double calc_area (double,double);
};
```

Class definition. The class name is `Parabola`.

The keyword `private` means that these data members (`a`, `b`, and `c`) can be accessed only from member functions.

The keyword `public` means that these function members (`read_coeffs`, and `calc_area`) can be called from any function.

```
void Parabola :: read_coeffs ()
{
    cout << "Enter the a, b, and c parabola coefficients." << endl;
    cin >> a >> b >> c;
}
```

The class name (Parabola) and scope resolution operator (::) must precede the function name (read_coeffs).

Definition of function read_coeffs.

Since read_coeffs is a member function, the data members, a, b, and c can be accessed directly. There is no need to use an object name and dot operator with the variables.

The function return type is double.

The class name (Parabola) and scope resolution operator (::) must precede the function name (calc_area).

Two double values are passed to the function.

```
double Parabola :: calc_area (double x1, double x2)
{
    double integral_result;
    integral_result = (a * x2 * x2 * x2/3 + b * x2 * x2/2 + c * x2) -
                      (a * x1 * x1 * x1/3 + b * x1 * x1/2 + c * x1);
    return (integral_result);
}
```

Definition of function calc_area.

Since calc_area is a member function, the data members, a, b, and c can be accessed directly without the need for an object name and dot operator. Note that to get the integral of the parabola $ax^2 + bx + c$ we evaluate $ax^3/3 + bx^2/2 + cx$ at the left and right limits of integration (x1 and x2, respectively).

```
int main ( )
{
     double left_limit, right_limit, area;
     Parabola p1, p2;

     p1.read_coeffs ();
     cout << "Enter left and right limits of integration." << endl;
     cin >> left_limit >> right_limit;

     area = p1.calc_area(left_limit, right_limit);
     cout << "The parabola area is "
          << area << endl << endl;

     p2.read_coeffs ();
     cout << "Enter left and right limits of integration." << endl;
     cin >> left_limit >> right_limit;
     area = p2.calc_area (left_limit, right_limit);
     cout << "The parabola area is " << area << endl << endl;

}
```

Declaring two objects (p1 and p2) to be type Parabola. This means we are working with two parabolas.

Calling read_coeffs with object p1. We must use an object name and dot operator to access public member functions from a nonmember function like main. With this call, function read_coeffs initializes the values of a, b, and c for object p1.

Calling calc_area with object p1. Because calc_area is a member function, it automatically has access to p1's data members. Also, left_limit and right_limit are passed through the argument list. The return value for the function is the result of the integral.

The actions are repeated for object p2.

Output

```
                  Enter the a, b, and c parabola coefficients.
Keyboard input    8.5  -3.2  12.6
                  Enter left and right limits of integration.
Keyboard input    -17.9  39.4
                  The parabola area is 188296.1085

                  Enter the a, b, and c parabola coefficients.
Keyboard input    -2.4  5.2  -9.2
                  Enter left and right limits of integration.
Keyboard input    6.4  54.8
                  The parabola area is -124187.4304
```

Description

Classes. Quoting from the C++ standard, "A class is a type." It is a type that consists of an aggregation of both data and functions.

Class definitions.

- *Form*—As we saw in Lesson 8.1 a class is defined with the keyword `class`, the class name, and the class members enclosed in brackets. In the brackets, the keywords `public` and `private` followed by colons are used to specify the accessibility of the members. The form is:

  ```
  class Class_name
  {
          private:
                  private_members;
          public:
                  public_members;
  };
  ```

  where `Class_name` is a programmer chosen valid identifier for a class, `public_members` represents declarations for members given public access, and `private_members` represents declarations for members given private access. The entire class definition is terminated with a semicolon. The detailed class components for the `Parabola` class are shown in Fig. 8.4.

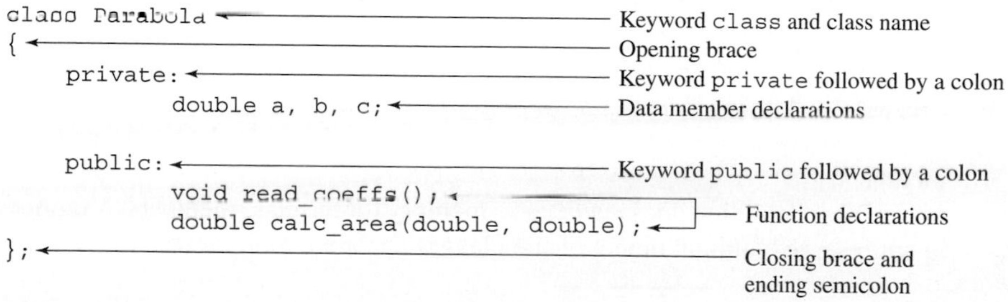

```
class Parabola                                    ← Keyword class and class name
{                                                 ← Opening brace
    private:                                      ← Keyword private followed by a colon
          double a, b, c;                         ← Data member declarations

    public:                                       ← Keyword public followed by a colon
          void read_coeffs();                     ┐
          double calc_area(double, double);       ┘← Function declarations
};                                                ← Closing brace and ending semicolon
```

Figure 8.4

Defining a C++ class with private data members and public function members.

Members not specifically given an access are made private by default, so an equivalent class definition is:

```
class Class_name
{
                private_members;
        public:
                public_members;
};
```

In this text, we explicitly specify `private` to enhance clarity although it is not required. Also, the specifiers can be used more than once in a class definition in the form of

```
class Class_name
{
        private:
                private_members;
        public:
                public_members;
        private:
                private_members;
        public:
                public_members;
};
```

However, in most cases, it is preferable to group all the `private` members together and all the `public` members together. Typically, the function members are made `public` and the data members are made `private`. This ensures encapsulation, which is described later in this lesson.

- *Class members*—The class members are listed as they are in ordinary declarations. We list the data members using type and identifier in sequence. For instance for this lesson's program

  ```
  double a, b, c;
  ```

  indicates that `a`, `b`, and `c` are `double` type data members for class `Parabola`.

  Similarly, functions are declared in the class definition in the form we have already studied. For instance,

  ```
  void read_coeffs ( );
  double calc_area (double, double);
  ```

  declare member function `read_coeffs` to have no arguments and no return value, and member function `calc_area` to have two `double` arguments and a `double` return value.

  Note that a *function has parentheses following the identifier* in the declaration. A *data member has no parentheses following the variable name*. You need to be aware of this in order to distinguish between data and function members.

  A class definition does not reserve memory for the class members. Memory is not reserved until an object of the class is declared. Some texts have a terminology that calls a class definition a declaration (since it *does not* reserve memory) and an object declaration a definition (because it *does* reserve memory). However, the C++ standard does not make such a distinction, so neither do we here. Just remember, a class definition does not reserve memory but an object declaration does.

We are allowed to have `static` data members, but not allowed to use the storage class specifiers `auto`, `extern`, or `register`. Nonstatic data members cannot be initialized in the class definition. Data members can also be objects of other classes, but we are not allowed to have data members that are objects of the class being defined. The implications of these allowances and restrictions are covered throughout this chapter.

- *Access specifiers*—Specifying `private` access for the data members restricts access of the data to member functions. This means that member data cannot be accessed directly from `main` (a nonmember function). Restricting data access to member functions is not a form of security but more a method of reducing errors. It is less likely that data members will be corrupted when only specific functions can access them.

  Specifying `public` access for functions allows a member function to be called from `main` or any other function in the program. This allows us to, in a sense, access the data members from any function by first calling a member function. Even the simplest actions must use a member function, so it is necessary to call a member function to do even the simplest actions like reading and printing the data member values.

- *Location in program*—Class definitions are normally located at the beginning of a program and outside the body of any function. Such a location assures that an object of the class can be declared in any program function. After a class has been defined it can be referenced, so a class definition should appear in the program before it is used (although there may be times when this is not possible, and C++ has a method for getting around this requirement).

Member function definitions. Member function definitions (when not included inside the class definition) require the class name and scope resolution operator (`::`) to immediately precede the function name (see Fig. 8.5). The function return type is the

Figure 8.5

Defining a C++ member function.

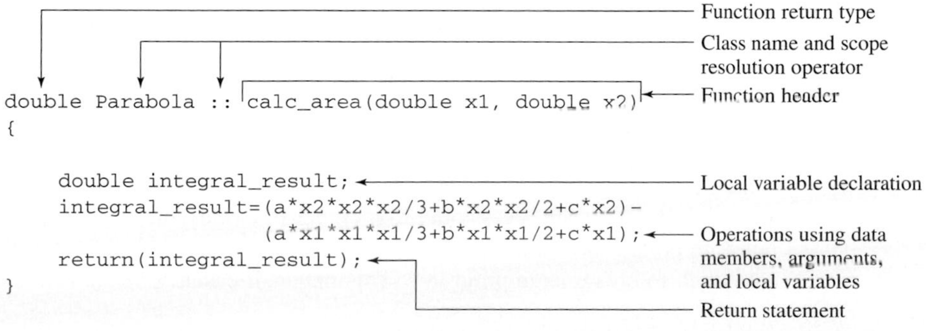

```
double Parabola :: calc_area(double x1, double x2)
{

    double integral_result;
    integral_result=(a*x2*x2*x2/3+b*x2*x2/2+c*x2)-
                    (a*x1*x1*x1/3+b*x1*x1/2+c*x1);
    return(integral_result);
}
```

- Function return type
- Class name and scope resolution operator
- Function header
- Local variable declaration
- Operations using data members, arguments, and local variables
- Return statement

first item in the line. For example

```
void Parabola :: read_coeffs ( )
{
        cout << "Enter the a, b, and c parabola "
                "coefficients." << endl;
        cin >> a >> b >> c;
}
```

indicates that the function return type is `void`, the function name is `read_coeffs`, and the class of which the function is a member is `Parabola`. The name of the class is needed because the same function name may be used for many classes.

Each member function automatically has access to all the data members. This means that some functions have no arguments in their argument list since they work only with data members, as does `read_coeffs`. When a member function works with a data member, it can modify the actual value of the data member. Because `read_coeffs` has full access to data members `a`, `b`, and `c`, the `cin` statement is capable of storing values for these data members. These data member values can be used later by other member functions.

Nonmember data needed by a member function should be passed through the argument list. For instance,

```
double Parabola :: calc_area (double x1, double x2)
{
        double integral_result;
        integral_result = (a * x2 * x2 * x2 / 3 + b * x2 * x2 / 2 + c* x2) -
                          (a * x1 * x1 * x1 / 3 + b * x1 * x1 / 2 + c * x1);
        return (integral_result);
}
```

has nonmember data passed through the function call to `x1` and `x2` (the left and right limits of integration). Within the function, `x1` and `x2` are used normally. Also, a new local variable `integral_result` has been declared, and the data members `a`, `b`, and `c` have been used in the function.

Objects. When an object is declared, new memory is reserved for each of the data members of the class to which the object belongs. If three objects are declared, then three different regions of memory are reserved, one region for each object. However, only one copy of the memory needed for the function members (that is, the instructions in binary that represent the actions of the functions) of the class is reserved, and the objects share this memory. This is illustrated conceptually in Fig. 8.6.

Encapsulation is a term that describes the link between the data and functions of an object. The dashed lines in Fig. 8.6 represent the concept of encapsulation. The result of encapsulation is that data access is restricted to member functions which is sometimes called *data hiding*. Encapsulation is a cornerstone of object-oriented design. By allowing data access only to member functions, the classes create programming units that have distinct boundaries. The programming units (classes) can be combined to create large programs. This makes it easier to make reliable software.

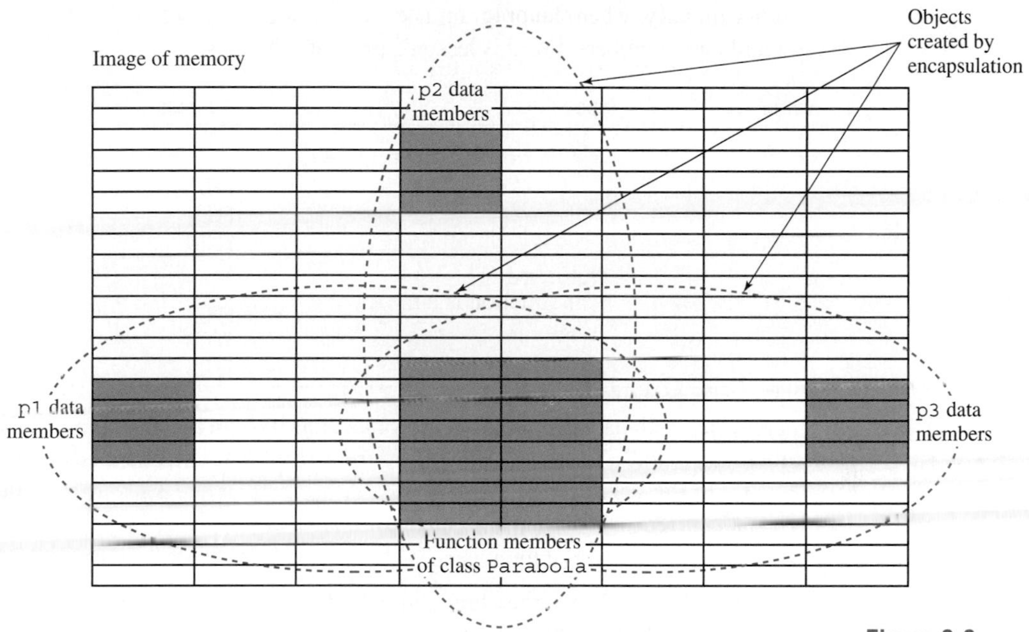

Figure 8.6

An image of memory that illustrates the concept of objects and encapsulation. Here, three objects are shown, `p1`, `p2`, and `p3`. The memory for the data members of each object are separate and unique. However, the memory needed for the function members (that is, the function instructions) is shared among the objects in a class. The data members are linked with the function members in an object.

For instance, programmers can be assigned to work on separate classes and to design and debug them. Then many classes can be combined in a single program. Encapsulation makes the combining process reasonably straightforward. We will see examples of combining classes in Chapter 14.

Since a class forms a new type, objects declared of a particular class are considered *instances* of the class. The word "instance" leads to saying that an object is *instantiated* when it is declared. When an object is declared or instantiated, memory is reserved for each of the members. We will see in later lessons that other actions can also occur when an object is declared or instantiated. In this text, we will use both declare and instantiate to represent the process of creating an object.

To declare an object, use the class name followed by a comma separated list of object names. For example

```
Parabola p1, p2;
```

declares `p1` and `p2` to be objects of class `Parabola`. This declaration reserves memory for data members `a`, `b`, and `c` for both `p1` and `p2`, meaning memory for a total of six `double` values is reserved. Remember, each object has its own data members. There is no connection between variables `a`, `b`, and `c` for object `p1` and `a`, `b`, and `c` for object `p2`.

When your classes are defined at the beginning of the source code and outside the body of any function, you can declare an object in any function. It is allowable to declare an object for one class (or variable for a `struct`) in another class's member function. We illustrate this in Application Example 8.1.

Conceptually, when the program is executed, a table is created with the object, class, and data members. For this lesson's program the table is

Name	Type		Address	Value
p1	Parabola			
	a	double	FFDD	8.5
	b	double	FFE5	−3.2
	c	double	FFED	12.6
p2	Parabola			
	a	double	FFC3	−2.4
	b	double	FFCD	5.2
	c	double	FFD3	−9.2

Note that each data member for each object has its own address. Clearly, the data members `a`, `b`, and `c` for object `p1` are different from data members `a`, `b`, and `c` for object `p2`. In the definitions for functions `read_coeffs` and `calc_area`, though, only the identifiers `a`, `b`, and `c` are given. How then does C++ know which object's data members, `p1` or `p2`, are being referred to? The answer lies in the function call.

Function calls. Each member function called must be associated with an object. A `public` member function being called from a nonmember function (such as `read_coeffs` being called from `main`) needs an object name, dot operator, and function name. For example

```
p1 . read_coeffs ( );
```

calls the `read_coeff` function with object `p1`. Here, `p1` is called the *invoking object*. This means that on this execution of `read_coeffs`, the identifiers `a`, `b`, and `c` refer to the data members for object `p1`. Similarly, the call

```
p2 . read_coeffs ();
```

makes `a`, `b`, and `c` (in `read_coeffs`) refer to the data members for object `p2`. Here, `p2` is the invoking object.

We use the argument list to transfer nonmember data to a function. The call and function header

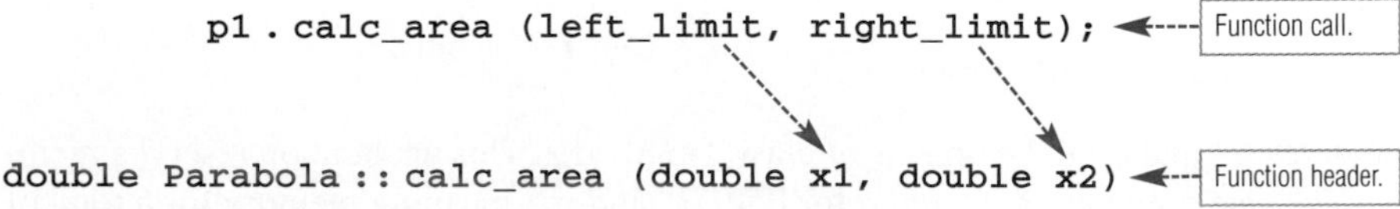
p1 . calc_area (left_limit, right_limit);
Function call.
double Parabola :: calc_area (double x1, double x2)
Function header.

pass the values of local variables `left_limit` and `right_limit` in `main` to local variables `x1` and `x2` in `calc_area`. On this execution of `calc_area`, the variables `a`, `b`, and `c` in the body of `calc_area` refer to the data members for object `p1`.

The call and function header

```
        p2 . calc_area (left_limit, right_limit);      <---- Function call.

double Parabola :: calc_area (double x1, double x2)    <---- Function header.
```

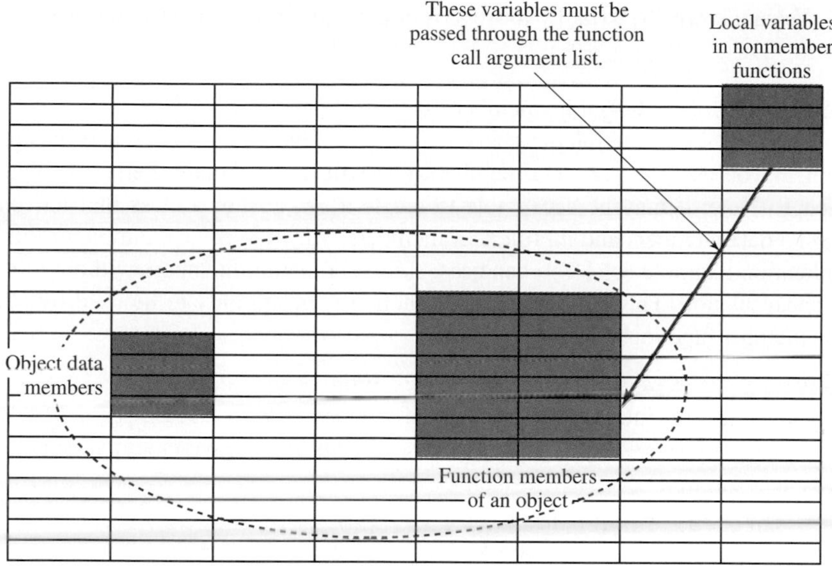

Figure 8.7

Conceptual illustration of the fact that function members of an object have direct accessibility to the data members of the object as indicated by the dashed ellipse. However, local variables in nonmember functions must be passed through an argument list.

again pass the values of local variables `left_limit` and `right_limit` in `main` to local variables `x1` and `x2` in `calc_area`. However, on this execution of `calc_area`, the variables `a`, `b`, and `c` in the body of `calc_area` refer to the data members for object `p2`. The concept of data members being linked to a member function, while nonmember data is passed through the argument list is illustrated in Fig. 8.7.

Like ordinary functions, member functions can return values. Function `calc_area` returns the `double` value of the area beneath a parabola. When called as `p1.calc_area`, it returns the area beneath the `p1` parabola. This value is assigned to the local variable in `main`, `area`, with the assignment statement

```
area = p1 . calc_area (left_limit, right_limit);
```

Similarly, the area beneath the `p2` parabola is assigned to `area` with the statement

```
area = p2 . calc_area (left_limit, right_limit);
```

Consequence of using `private` data members and `public` function members. Note that because the data members are `private`, we cannot do such things as read the values of the data members directly in `main`. In other words, we cannot use the line:

```
cin >> p1.a >> p1.b >> p1.c;
```

within `main`. If we try to do so, the program will not compile. The reason is that `main` is not a member function of the `Parabola` class. Only member functions have access to the `private` data. Remember, within `main` (or any other nonmember function) we cannot write:

```
object . data
```

where *`object`* is the object name, *`data`* is the private data member name, and the dot operator separates the two.

We can, however, write (within `main` or any other nonmember function):

```
object . function
```

where *`function`* is the public member function name.

Using `public` function members and `private` data members creates encapsulation. If you use `public` data members you will likely violate the encapsulation concept. (Note: it may be acceptable to create a `struct` or a class that has only `public` data members and *no* function members. We will see an example of this in Application Example 8.1.) You can use `private` function members without violating encapsulation. This is done when a function is meant only to be used by other class member functions.

Calculating the area beneath a parabola. From your calculus class, you most likely know that the integral from x_1 to x_2 of $y = ax^2 + bx + c$ is $[ax_2^3/3 + bx_2^2/2 + cx_2] - [ax_1^3/3 + bx_1^2/2 + cx_1]$. This is used directly in the assignment statement in function `calc_area`:

```
integral_result = (a * x2 * x2 * x2 / 3 + b * x2 * x2 / 2 + c * x2) -
                  (a * x1 * x1 * x1 / 3 + b * x1 * x1 / 2 + c * x1);
```

All the variables on the right side of the assignment statement are known since `x1` and `x2` are passed through the argument list and `a`, `b`, and `c` are data members of the class `Parabola`. Thus, it is reasonably simple to program the calculation of such an integral.

LESSON 8.3 CONSTRUCTOR FUNCTIONS (1)—NO ARGUMENTS

TOPICS

- Declaring a constructor function
- Defining a constructor function

At this point, you know what classes and objects are. Now you can begin to understand how to design programs with them. Sound design means properly constructing individual classes as well as the interaction between classes. This chapter is devoted to constructing individual classes. Chapter 14 focuses on the interactions between classes.

We could have given such a discussion earlier in this chapter, but you would likely have found the subject matter difficult to follow. You are prepared now because you have seen programs that use classes and objects.

Let us begin with a discussion of classes. A class should have a clear goal. It should be kept relatively simple. If it becomes too complicated, it may need to be broken into several classes. A large class should not have more than 30 or so function members.

To design a class, you must analyze the problem thoroughly. Choosing the appropriate data and function members is important. Within a problem statement, it is sometimes said that the nouns represent the classes, the characteristics of the nouns are the data members, and the verbs associated with the nouns are the function members. For instance, if a problem statement were to write a program that "calculates the cross product of two matrices of integers," the class would be `Matrix`, the data members would be integer type, and a member function would be `calc_cross_product()`, at least as a beginning of the program design.

Determining the best classes to use for a complex problem is not simple. Everyone involved in the process should be consulted, as described in Chapter 1. For instance, for designing a program that analyzes or controls the pipe network for a refinery, the owners, operators, technicians, and engineers should be consulted. Then, classes such as `Fluid`, `Pipe`, `Tank`, `Pump`, and others can be created. As we saw with the `Fluid struct` in Lesson 8.1, the characteristics of a fluid such as density, velocity, pressure, or temperature would be data members. The verbs associated with fluid such as flow or evaporate can guide us to using member functions such as `calc_flow_rate` or `calc_evaporation_rate`. Each refinery may have many different types of fluids, and sizes of pipes and tanks, and sizes and types of pumps. These are represented with objects of the classes.

How can we understand the object concept? A commonly used analogy is that a class is a mold and an object a figurine cast in the mold. That is, the mold determines the size and shape of each figurine, but not all the characteristics. For instance, one figurine could be made of wax and another ceramic. One can be painted red and another blue. So while all figurines come from the same mold, each can be quite unique.

Similarly, while many objects may be of the same class, each object can be quite unique. For example, the `Tank` class for the refinery problem could have one object representing a 50 m diameter tank and another object representing a 10 m diameter tank. All objects are tanks, but they have different characteristics.

One can talk about how an object behaves. The values of the data members perhaps cause certain member functions to be called and the object to behave in a certain manner. For instance, with the `Fluid` class, when we declare objects like `water` and `oil`, we have created materials that can take on certain behaviors. Water and oil have distinct properties and act in particular manners (for instance, have viscosities that control their velocities in some situations). A particular viscosity may trigger a lubrication function to be called for a particular object. Therefore, the value of the data member, viscosity, has affected the behavior of an object within a program.

In illustrating objects in this book, sometimes we use the image shown in Fig. 8.6 (with functions shared among objects), and sometimes we use the image shown in Fig. 8.8 (with each object containing its own functions). Although objects of the same class share function members, in many situations it is better to envision that each object contains its own separate function members (Fig. 8.8). This makes it clear that an object must be associated with each function call and that a member function has direct access to only one object's data members. In most cases, we have private data members and public function members.

We should also comment about problem descriptions. In this text, we explicitly define the problem. However, in practice, preparing such a definition is part of the program development process. Creating a detailed problem statement is sometimes called the *analysis phase*. Complex programs will have *use cases* where the type of input and type of output can vary. For instance, a program that controls a banking machine would have one use case where a person withdraws money and another use case where a person deposits money. The end result is that a particular program may solve many different types of problems. In this text, we will not cover the analysis phase.

The rest of this chapter is considered to be only an introduction to classes and objects. Read each program and see a number of different classes. As you do so,

Figure 8.8

Illustration showing how objects are sometimes represented in this text.

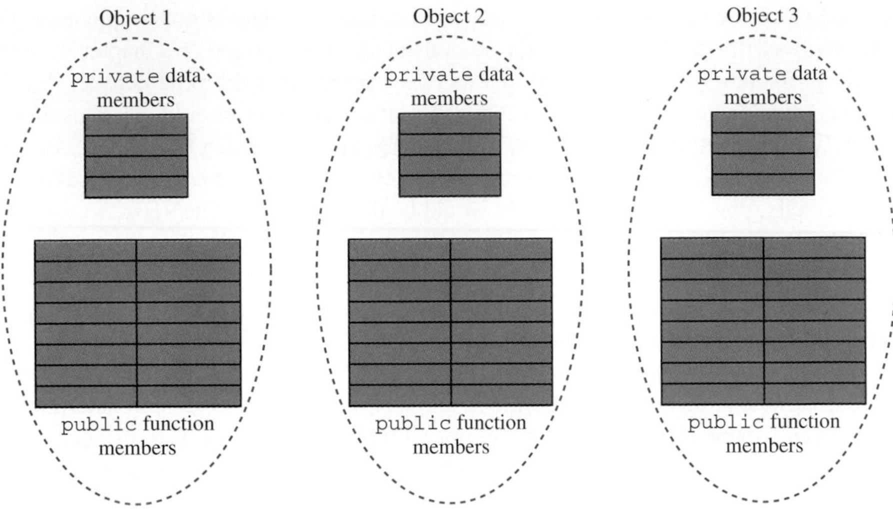

make note of the types of data and function members. Each data member should be a characteristic or attribute of the class. Each function member should perform a useful task dedicated to the class. As you are exposed to more and more classes, you will develop a greater understanding of what to put into your own classes.

Details on constructing individual classes for particular problems are given in the application examples. In the rest of the lessons in this chapter, we discuss some of the tools you need to make robust single classes. In this lesson, we cover constructor functions.

A *constructor function* (or constructor) is a class member function that is executed automatically upon declaration of an object. Constructor functions are frequently used to initialize values of data members. In this program, we have created a `Ventilator` class with a single data member, `fan_speed`. Look at the source code and read the annotations and output to see how the constructor initializes the value of `fan_speed`. Observe from the output that the constructor function is executed before the member function `print_fan_speed()`.

QUESTION YOU SHOULD ATTEMPT TO ANSWER

1. How do you name a constructor function?

Source Code

```
#include <iostream>
using namespace std;

class Ventilator
{
        private:
                int fan_speed;
        public:
                Ventilator ();
                void print_fan_speed ();
};
```

The class definition includes a member function, `Ventilator()`, that has no return type and a name that is identical to the class name, `Ventilator`. This is the constructor function.

```
Ventilator :: Ventilator ()
{
        fan_speed = 4;
        cout << "Constructor  executed" << endl;
}

void Ventilator :: print_fan_speed ()
{
        cout << "fan_speed=" << fan_speed << endl;
}

int main ( )
{
        Ventilator ventilator1;
        ventilator1.print_fan_speed ();
}
```

The header for the constructor function contains the name of the class twice: once for the name of the class and once for the name of the function.

The data member fan_speed is initialized in the constructor.

The value of fan_speed is printed in function print_fan_speed.

This declaration both reserves memory for the object, ventilator1, and calls the constructor function.

This calls function print_fan_speed() with object ventilator1.

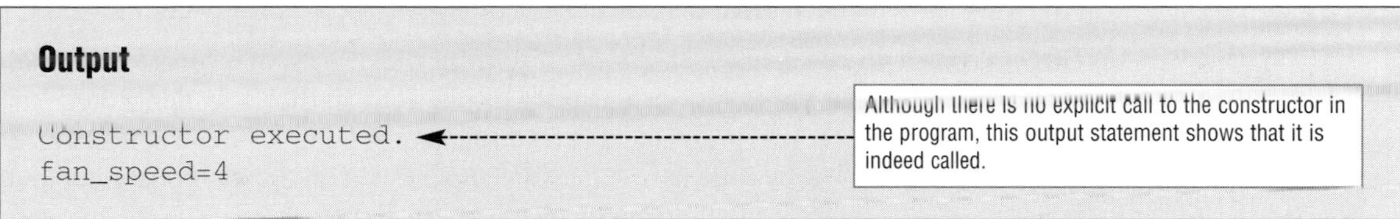

Output

```
Constructor  executed.
fan_speed=4
```

Although there is no explicit call to the constructor in the program, this output statement shows that it is indeed called.

Description

Constructor characteristics. Constructor functions have the following characteristics:

1. The function name is identical to the class name.
2. The function does not return a value (even the explicit type `void` cannot be used for the function).
3. The function has `public` access. (This means that an object can be declared in any function. Private access is not common but can be used for one or more overloaded constructor functions. These are described in Lesson 8.5.)
4. The function may or may not have arguments.

Note that the `Ventilator` constructor has no arguments (the parentheses are empty).

Constructor function form. In general, a constructor function can be declared and defined in the following way:

```
class Name
{
        private:
                type data_member;
        public:
                Name ();
                type function_member ();
};
```

The class name and constructor function name are identical.

Class definition.

```
Name :: Name()
{
        data_member = value;
}
```

The first *Name* refers to the class and the second *Name* refers to the function.
Constructor function definition.

where `Name` is the class name, `type` refers to the types of the data and function members, `data_member` is a data member name, `function_member` is a function member name, and `value` is the initial value of the data member. We will see in Lesson 8.4 that there is an alternative form to initializing the values in the constructor function. However, what is shown here will work for initializing ordinary data members.

Activities of a constructor. Although a programmer can make a constructor perform most any operation, a constructor typically initializes the data members and performs other tasks associated with creating an object. In this lesson's program, the `Ventilator` constructor initializes the data member `fan_speed`.

Had we created two objects with the declaration

```
Ventilator ventilator1, ventilator2;
```

the constructor would have been called twice, once for `ventilator1` and once for `ventilator2`. In each case, the object's data member `fan_speed` is initialized.

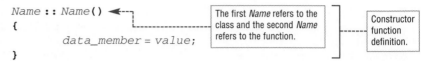

Tracing code with constructor functions. To trace the actions of a source code with objects requires that you look for constructor functions in the class definition. You must do this because there is no clue that a constructor is being called when an object is declared. Therefore, as you are tracing code and see that an object is declared, look at the class definition for a constructor. If a constructor exists, next go to the constructor function and follow the code line by line. For instance, in this lesson's program, after executing the line:

```
Ventilator ventilator1;
```

the next line of code executed is not `ventilator1.print_fan_speed();`, which is the line following it in `main`. Instead, control goes to the `Ventilator` constructor function, and the lines

```
fan_speed = 4;
cout<<"Constructor executed"<<endl;
```

are executed! Because constructors are so commonly used in classes, you must remember that the declaration of an object will likely call a function. To understand what a program is doing you must follow the code to that function. You can find the constructor function because it has the same name as the class and does not have a return value.

LESSON 8.4 CONSTRUCTOR FUNCTIONS (2)—ARGUMENTS

TOPICS

- Passing values to constructor functions
- Initializing data members with passed values
- Explicitly calling constructors

Although a constructor function cannot return a value, it can receive a value through its argument list. The function can assign this value to a data member. One purpose of doing so is to create different data member values for different objects. This means that a programmer is not restricted to initializing each object the same, that is, using the same values each time the constructor is called.

For instance, suppose we are analyzing data from weather stations. One weather station might have its wind speed initialized to 5 km/hr while another might be initialized to 20 km/hr. By passing a value to the constructor, we can initialize each station to its desired value, as we do in this lesson's program.

Remember we do not call a constructor like we do other functions. Since we call a constructor in the declaration, it is in the declaration that we pass the values. Read the program and see how to pass a value to a constructor function.

Also note that, as we indicated in the previous lesson, we do not necessarily initialize the data members in the constructor body. Observe in the program the syntax for initializing values in an initialization list, which is outside the body of the constructor.

QUESTION YOU SHOULD ATTEMPT TO ANSWER

1. How do you think we can initialize two data members in a constructor?

Source Code

```
#include <iostream>
using namespace std;

class Weather_station
{
      private:
             int wind_speed;
      public:
             Weather_station (int);
             void print_wind_speed ();
};

Weather_station :: Weather_station (int wind_speed_var)
              : wind_speed  (wind_speed_var)
{
      cout << "Constructor executed" << endl;
}

void Weather_station :: print_wind_speed ()
{
      cout << "wind_speed=" << wind_speed << endl;
}

int main ( )
{
      Weather_station  station1 (5), station2 (20);
      station1.print_wind_speed ();
      station2.print_wind_speed ();
}
```

The constructor function has one argument of type `int`. This type matches the type of the data member `wind_speed`.

Class name. Function name. Argument list.

Single colon followed by a data member and variable enclosed in parentheses. This initializes the data member `wind_speed` to the value passed through the argument list (which goes to `wind_speed_var`).

The function body does *not* do the initialization.

The value 5 is passed to the constructor for object `station1`, and 20 is passed to the constructor for object `station2`. These values are passed to `wind_speed_var`, and then they are assigned to `wind_speed`.

Output

```
Constructor executed
Constructor executed
wind_speed=5
wind_speed=20
```

The output shows that the data members for each object are initialized.

Description

Passing a value to a constructor. To pass a single value to a constructor, the class definition must indicate that the constructor has an argument. In this lesson's program, the `Weather_station` class definition has the constructor function declared as

```
Weather_station (int);
```

This means that a single integer is passed to the `Weather_station` constructor. This constructor is called from `main` with the declaration of the object `station1`. Such a declaration passes the value 5 to the constructor function as shown here.

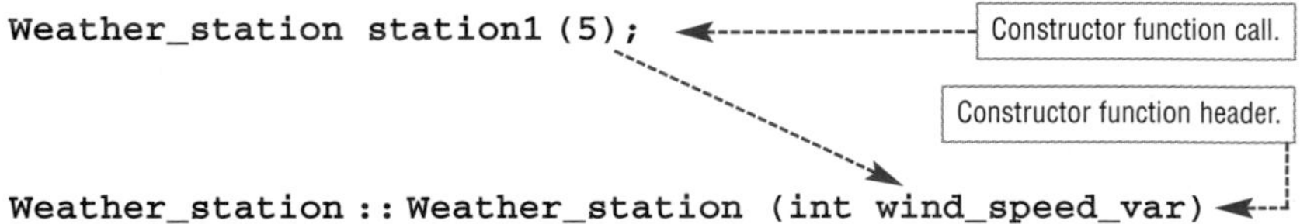

This illustrates that the value 5 is passed to the variable `wind_speed_var`, which acts as a temporary storage variable for the wind speed value.

Initializing a data member with the constructor. This lesson's initialization form is different from that of Lesson 8.3. This lesson's form uses an initialization list which follows a single colon written after the header. The data member name and temporary storage variable name (enclosed in parentheses) form the initialization list. For instance, in

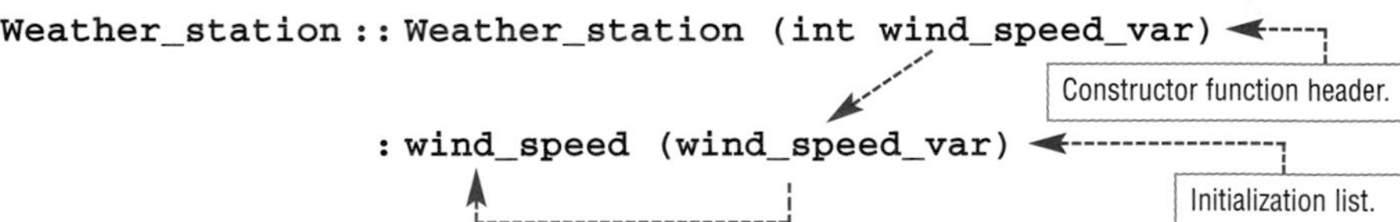

the value of `wind_speed_var` is given to the data member `wind_speed` automatically. The arrows show the transfer of information. Therefore, the value 5 used in declaring the `station1` object is passed to `wind_speed_var` and is then passed to the data member `wind_speed`.

The general form for initializing a data member in a constructor is

```
Class :: Class (type dummy)
        : data_member (dummy)
```

where *`Class`* is the class name, *`type`* is the data member type, *`dummy`* is the temporary storage variable name, and *`data_member`* is the data member name. In this form, *`data_member`* is set equal to the value passed to *`dummy`*.

Initializing more than one data member. If a class has more than one data member, a comma separated list following the single colon is used to initialize all the data members. For instance, if the class `Weather_station` has two `double` type data members (`wind_speed` and `temperature`), and both data members are initialized in the constructor, as in the class definition:

```
class Weather_station
{
      private:
             double wind_speed, temperature;
      public:
             Weather_station (double, double);
             void print_data ();
};
```

Constructor function declaration. This function has two double type arguments.

then the object declaration and constructor function would be, for example,

```
                       Weather_station station1 (5, 27);
Weather_station :: Weather_station (double wind_speed_var, double temperature_var)
                 : wind_speed (wind_speed_var), temperature (temperature_var)
{
     cout<<"Constructor executed"<<endl;
}
```

Object declaration

Constructor function definition.

The arrows show the transfer of information. These lines pass the value 5 to `wind_speed_var` and 27 to `temperature_var` in the constructor. Then `wind_speed` takes on the value of `wind_speed_var`, and `temperature` takes on the value of `temperature_var`.

This lesson's initialization form works well when a simple value is assigned to a data member. It does not work when steps of calculations are needed to create an initialization value. In such cases, the Lesson 8.3 form is appropriate. Overall, though, this lesson's initialization form is the preferred form, and should be used when possible.

Explicitly calling a constructor function. We cannot explicitly call a constructor function like we call other member functions. In other words, we cannot use an object name, dot operator, and function name to call the constructor. For this lesson's program, we cannot use the statement

```
station1 . Weather_station (10);
```

to assign 10 to the data member `wind_speed`.

However, suppose an object has been declared and the constructor called. We can call the constructor a second time for that object using an assignment statement. For this lesson's program, if we wanted to change the `wind_speed` to 10 for `station1`, we could have used:

```
station1 = Weather_station (10);
```

The right side creates a *nameless* object that is assigned to `station1`. (Remember from Lesson 8.1 that assigning objects causes the data members to be copied one by one from one object to the other).

This form can also be used for declaring an object the first time. In this lesson's program, the declaration line could have been

```
Weather_station station1 = Weather_station (5),
                station2 = Weather_station (20);
```

With this declaration, two nameless objects have been created and their data member values assigned to `station1` and `station2`.

Syntax. With the introduction of constructors with arguments, you must learn new and sometimes confusing syntax.

- First, contrast the two declarations:

  ```
  Weather_station station1 (5);
  Weather_station station1 (int);
  ```

  The first is a declaration for a `station1` object, and the value 5 is passed to the `Weather_station` constructor. The second is a declaration for a function called `station1` that has an integer argument and returns an object of type `Weather_station`! Note how similar these declarations are (one has a constant, and the other has a data type enclosed in parentheses). These are confusing because prior to this point in the text, whenever an identifier was followed by parentheses, the identifier was a *function* name (except for the `sizeof` operator). Now, you should be aware that *object* names may be followed by parentheses.
- Second, the syntax for initializing data members is unusual because it uses a *data member* name followed by parentheses. For instance:

  ```
  Weather_station :: Weather_station (int wind_speed_var)
                   : wind_speed (wind_speed_var)
  ```

  has the data member `wind_speed` followed by parentheses. In addition, this syntax is even more difficult when it is all written in a single line (as some programmers write it) because it is a long sequence of identifiers, colons, and parentheses. We recommend that you memorize the location of the single colon and the way that the dummy variable appears twice. It is easier to see if you line up the colons vertically and use more than one line.
- The third unusual syntax in this lesson is in the explicit call to a constructor. It uses a *class name* followed by parentheses. In the statement

  ```
  station1 = Weather_station (10);
  ```

  `Weather_station` refers to the constructor function, which, of course, has the same name as the class. Remember, following a class name with parentheses calls the constructor *and* creates a nameless object.

In summary, be aware that objects, data members, and class names (not just functions) can be followed by parentheses. Such syntax usually indicates something involved with the activities of a constructor function.

LESSON 8.5 CONSTRUCTOR FUNCTIONS (3)—OVERLOADING AND DEFAULT COPY CONSTRUCTOR

TOPICS

- Overloading a constructor function
- Default copy constructor

QUESTION YOU SHOULD ATTEMPT TO ANSWER

1. What operator is used in calling the default copy constructor?

It is quite common to want to initialize objects in different ways. Luckily, C++ allows constructor function overloading, which means that we can have two or more constructor functions in our class definition. The constructor functions can be designed to fit our needs for different objects. In addition, C++ has a built in *copy* constructor called the *default copy constructor*. This constructor is automatically executed when one object is declared to be identical to another object.

This lesson's source code defines three constructors: a no-argument constructor, a one-argument constructor, and a two-argument constructor. The code declares objects using each of the three constructors and the default copy constructor.

In the code, we have a `Microwave_instruction` class. Its data members (`time` and `power_level`) represent attributes of automatic cooking instructions (called programs) for a microwave oven. Four program objects are declared. Read the source code and see how the constructors are overloaded. Look closely at the object declarations, and observe how each object calls a different constructor.

Source Code

```
#include <iostream>
using namespace std;

class Microwave_instruction
{
        private:
                int time, power_level;
        public:
                Microwave_instruction ();
                Microwave_instruction (int);
                Microwave_instruction (int, int);
                void show_data();
};

Microwave_instruction :: Microwave_instruction ( )
                        : time (60), power_level (10)
{
      cout << "No argument constructor executed." << endl;
}

Microwave_instruction :: Microwave_instruction (int time_var)
                        : time (time_var), power_level (10)
{
      cout << "One argument constructor executed." << endl;
}
```

Three constructors. The first has no arguments, the second has one argument, and the third has two arguments.

No-argument constructor (initializes `time` to 60 and `power_level` to 10).

One-argument constructor (initializes `time` to the argument and `power_level` to 10).

```
Microwave_instruction :: Microwave_instruction (int time_var, int power_level_var)
                    : time (time_var), power_level (power_level_var)
{
      cout << "Two argument constructor executed." << endl;
}

void Microwave_instruction :: show_data ()
{
      cout << "time = " << time << " power level = " << power_level << endl;
}

int main()
{
      Microwave_instruction program1, program2 (30), program3 (45,6),
                            program4 = program3;

      program1.show_data ();
      program2.show_data ();
      program3.show_data ();
      program4.show_data ();
}
```

Two-argument constructor (initializes `time` and `power_level` to the arguments).

Calls no-argument constructor.

Calls one-argument constructor.

Calls two-argument constructor.

Calls default copy constructor.

Printing the data for each object.

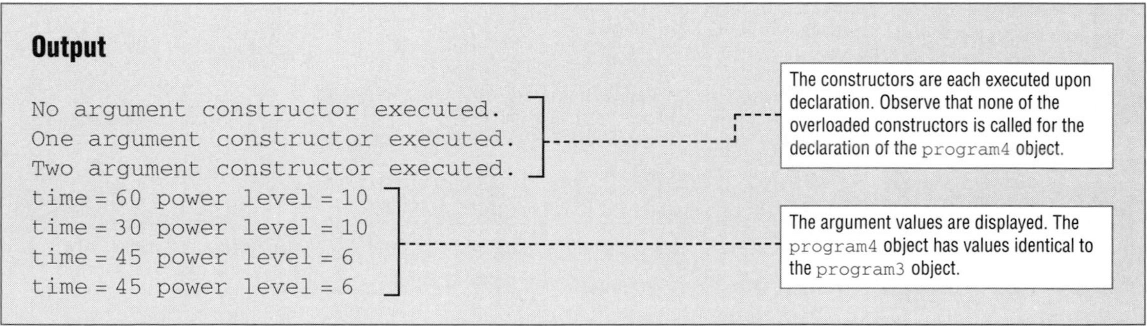
Output
No argument constructor executed.
One argument constructor executed.
Two argument constructor executed.
time = 60 power level = 10
time = 30 power level = 10
time = 45 power level = 6
time = 45 power level = 6
The constructors are each executed upon declaration. Observe that none of the overloaded constructors is called for the declaration of the program4 object.
The argument values are displayed. The program4 object has values identical to the program3 object.

Description

Class definition for constructor overloading. In the class definition, all the constructors are given the name of the class. However, each constructor is distinguishable in terms of number or type of arguments in a manner described in Lesson 7.7 about function overloading. For instance, the declarations:

```
Microwave_instruction ( );
Microwave_instruction (int);
Microwave_instruction (int, int);
```

all have different numbers of arguments (0, 1, and 2). Therefore, the compiler can distinguish between the constructors listed in the class definition.

Constructor function definition for constructor overloading. All constructor functions are defined separately. When fewer than the total number of data members are used as arguments, a constructor will typically assign default values to the other data members. For instance, the no-argument constructor:

```
Microwave_instruction :: Microwave_instruction ( )
                        : time (60), power_level (10)
{
        cout << "No argument constructor executed." << endl;
}
```

makes time = 60 and power_level = 10. A no-argument constructor is typically referred to as a default constructor because it is used when no other constructor is explicitly indicated.

The one-argument constructor

```
Microwave_instruction :: Microwave_instruction (int time_var)

                        : time (time_var), power_level (10)
{
        cout << "One argument constructor executed." << endl;
}
```

makes power_level = 10. It also initializes time to be equal to the argument value (passed through time_var).

The two-argument constructor:

```
Microwave_instruction :: Microwave_instruction (int time_var, int power_level_var)

                    :time (time_var), power_level (power_level_var)
{
     cout << "Two argument constructor executed." << endl;
}
```

initializes both data members through the argument list.

In general, overloading constructors is similar to overloading other functions. The compiler uses the methods described in Lesson 7.7 to distinguish between functions. If any ambiguity occurs, the program will not work.

Note from the declarations of the objects:

```
Microwave_instruction program1, program2 (30),
                      program3 (45, 6);
```

the object that calls the no-argument constructor (program1) does not have parentheses (even empty parentheses) following it, and it is an error to have them included. However, if you were to call the no-argument constructor explicitly, then empty parentheses would be used. In other words,

```
program1 = Microwave_instruction ();
```

creates a nameless object using the no-argument constructor, and assigns the nameless object to program1.

Note also that if you have not defined a no-argument constructor, but have other constructors, you *must* have arguments with your objects when they are declared. You can use no arguments in declaring your objects only if you have defined no constructors at all, or you have defined a no-argument constructor.

Since you will most commonly have constructors with your classes, we recommend creating a no-argument constructor (which becomes a default constructor) to reduce the likelihood of error. We did not indicate it earlier, but if you have defined no constructors at all, C++ automatically calls a do-nothing (default) constructor for each object you declare.

Default copy constructor. The default *copy* constructor is used to initialize objects with other objects. The values of the data members are copied one by one from one object to another. For instance, the `Microwave_instruction` class has two integer data members. The values of these data members are copied from `program3` to `program4` using the default copy constructor with the declaration

```
Microwave_instruction program4 = program3;
```

This declaration can also be written

```
Microwave_instruction program4 (program3);
```

For both declarations, none of the programmer defined constructor functions is called. The C++ compiler recognizes that an object is initialized with another object and calls its own constructor.

The C++ default copy constructor works well for classes that have ordinary built-in data types as data members such as `int` or `double`. However, when pointers (Chapter 13) or abstract data types are data members, the member-by-member copy may not be the desired result. In such cases a programmer-defined copy constructor function, as described in Chapter 14, may be needed.

Default arguments for constructors. C++ allows default arguments for constructor functions. The method is described in Lesson 7.6 and will not be repeated here. Remember, though, if both default arguments and function overloading are used in your constructor functions, you run the risk of creating ambiguity as described in Lesson 7.7. To avoid this issue altogether, we recommend you use overloading instead of default arguments for your constructors.

Constructors and arrays of objects. We have not shown it in this lesson's program, but if an array of objects were declared, the constructor would have been called once for each array member (see Chapter 9 to fully understand this subject). For instance, if the declaration in `main` were

```
Microwave_instruction program1[3];
```

then each element of the array would have been initialized with the data members `time` = 60 and `power_level` = 10. The output created by this declaration is:

```
No argument constructor executed.
No argument constructor executed.
No argument constructor executed.
```

indicating that the constructor has been called once for each array element.

APPLICATION EXAMPLE 8.1 LINE INTERSECTION

Problem Statement

Use `structs`, classes, and objects in writing a program capable of finding the intersection point of a pair of lines assuming that the lines are not parallel (Fig. 8.9). The input data is to consist of the slopes and intercepts for the pair of lines. The data are to come from a file (INTSECT.DAT) that is to consist of

TOPICS

- Object-oriented programming example
- Member function working with two objects

slope of line 1	intercept of line 1
slope of line 2	intercept of line 2

The output is to be to the screen and consist of an echo of the input data and the x and y coordinates of the intersection point.

Solution

RELEVANT EQUATIONS

The general equation for a line in terms of x and y is

$$y = mx + b$$

where m = slope
b = y intercept

If m_1, b_1, m_2, and b_2 are the slope and intercept of line 1 and the slope and intercept of line 2, respectively, the equations of the two lines are

$$y = m_1x + b_1 \tag{8.1}$$

$$y = m_2x + b_2 \tag{8.2}$$

The intersection of the two lines can be found by solving the two equations simultaneously. By substitution

$$m_1x + b_1 = m_2x + b_2 \tag{8.3}$$

$$x = (b_2 - b_1)/(m_1 - m_2) \tag{8.4}$$

$$y = m_1x + b_1 \tag{8.5}$$

The last two equations give the coordinates of the intersection point of the two lines.

SPECIFIC EXAMPLE

Consider the following lines:

$$y = 2x - 3 \qquad y = 5x + 1$$

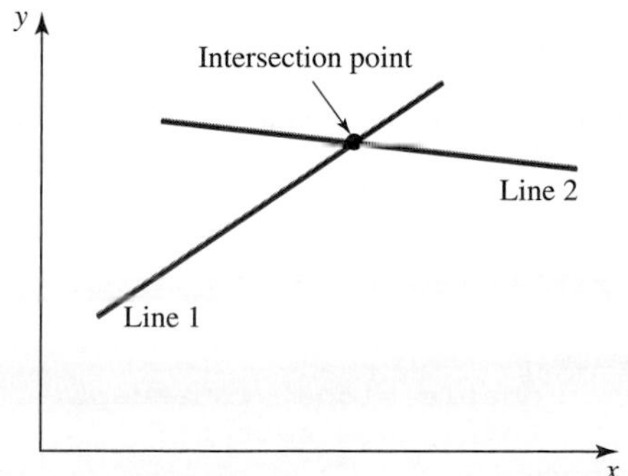

Figure 8.9
Sketch of two lines and their intersection point.

For these lines

$$m_1 = 2$$
$$b_1 = -3$$
$$m_2 = 5$$
$$b_2 = 1$$

From Eqns. 8.4 and 8.5,

$$x = (1 - (-3))/(2 - 5) = -1.333333$$
$$y = 2(1.333333) + (-3) = -5.666666$$

which are the coordinates of the intersection point.

CLASSES AND OBJECTS

Before we can write code, we need to have a plan that includes the `struct`s, classes, and objects we are to create. For this program, we can use a `Point` `struct` and a `Line` class.

POINT

A point's attributes are the x and y coordinates of the point. This leads to the following `struct`:

```
struct Point
{
          public:
                    double x_coord, y_coord;
};
```

Because there are no function members, using this `struct` (with `public` data members) does not violate the concept of encapsulation.

LINE

The attributes that characterize a line that is considered to possess an intersection point are:

1. The slope
2. The intercept
3. The intersection point

The operations needed to be performed for lines are to:

1. Read the line data
2. Print the line data
3. Calculate an intersection point between the given line and another line

The attributes and operations lead to the following class (a constructor is included):

```
class Line
{
          private:
                    double slope, intercept;
                    Point intersect_pt;
```

```
        public:
                Line ();
                void read_line_data (ifstream&);
                void show_line_data ();
                void calc_intersect_pt (Line);
};
```

Observe that the `slope` and `intercept` data members are type `double` and the `intersect_pt` data member is type `Point` (meaning it has *x* and *y* coordinates like the data members for the `Point struct`), which is what we want. For our problem, we have only two lines, so we need only one intersection point. However, by giving each line an intersection point, we can later expand the program to have more lines and intersection points.

We declare two objects for the `Line` class, `line1` and `line2`, to represent the two intersecting lines. These are declared as:

```
Line line1, line2;
```

We will say more about the member functions when we describe their activities in the Algorithm section.

ALGORITHM

The algorithm to be performed in `main` is:

1. Declare 2 `Line` objects and open an input file.
2. Read the values of `slope` and `intercept` for each object.
3. Echo the input data.
4. Calculate and print the values of `x_coord` and `y_coord` (intersection point).

The actual operations for steps 2–4 should be performed in member functions and are described next.

STEP 2—READ THE VALUES OF THE SLOPE AND INTERCEPT FOR EACH OBJECT

With the input file opened in `main`, we need to pass an `ifstream` object (by reference) to the member function to be able to read the data. We use a `Line` object to call the function. The function call using the `line1` object, and the function definition are:

```
line1 . read_line_data (infile);

void Line :: read_line_data (ifstream& readfile)
{
        readfile >> slope >> intercept;
}
```

Calling the function using the `line1` object.

Because the function call uses the `line1` object, the slope and intercept variables (for this call) represent the data members for the `line1` object.

Note that if we call the `read_line_data()` function with the `line2` object, we read the `slope` and `intercept` for the `line2` object.

STEP 3—ECHO THE INPUT DATA

The input data can be displayed by simply printing the values of the data members for an object. The function call

```
line1 . show_line_data ( );
```

displays the member data for object `line1`. The function definition is:

```
void Line :: show_line_data ( )
{
     cout << "Slope = " << slope << ", Intercept = " << intercept << endl;
}
```

Note that nothing is passed to or returned from the function. No variables are declared in the function because the data members (`slope` and `intercept`) are automatically available to member functions such as `show_line_data()`. Because the `line1` object is given in the function call, it is the data members for the `line1` object that are printed.

STEP 4—CALCULATE AND PRINT THE VALUES OF `x_coord` AND `y_coord` (INTERSECTION POINT)

We need to use *two* line objects (not just one) to calculate an intersection point. To handle this situation, which we have not seen before, we use one object to call the function and pass the other object through the argument list. To perform the calculation properly, we must pay attention to the way we refer to data members for invoking objects and data members for argument list objects. The function call and definition shown next (with arrows) point out the data members for the argument list object.

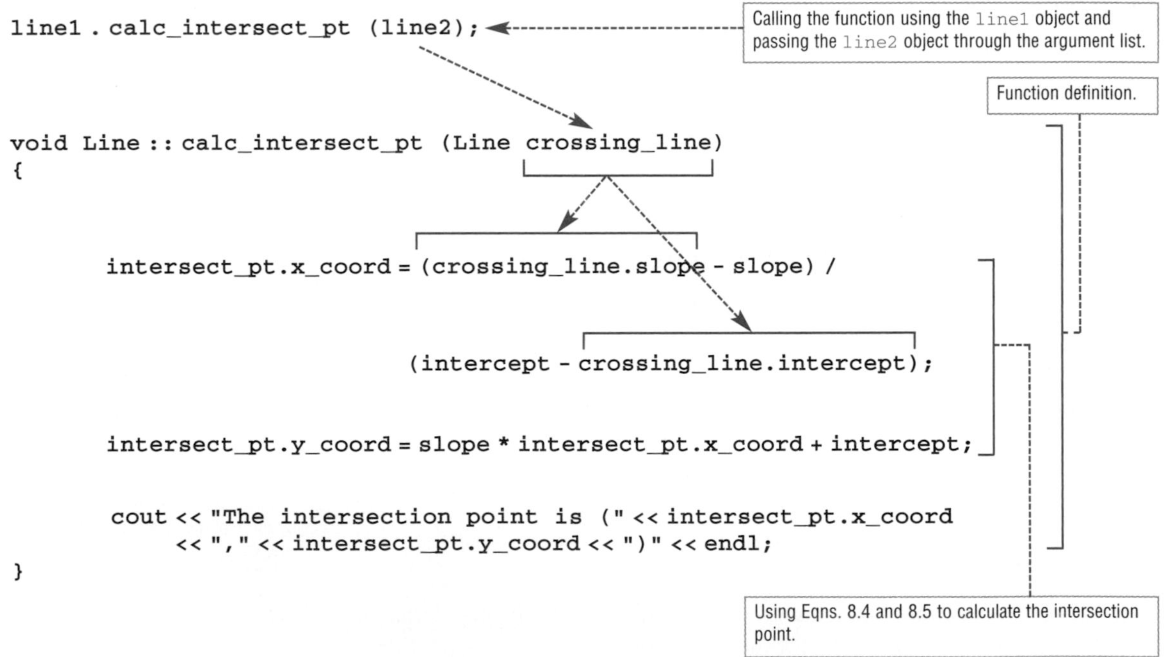

Note that the object name and dot operator are required for referring to the argument list object's member data (this is permissible because `calc_intersect_pt` is a member function). Also, note that the argument type in the function header is `Line`. This means we transfer a `Line` object to the function.

We repeat the function call and definition with arrows indicating the invoking object's data members.

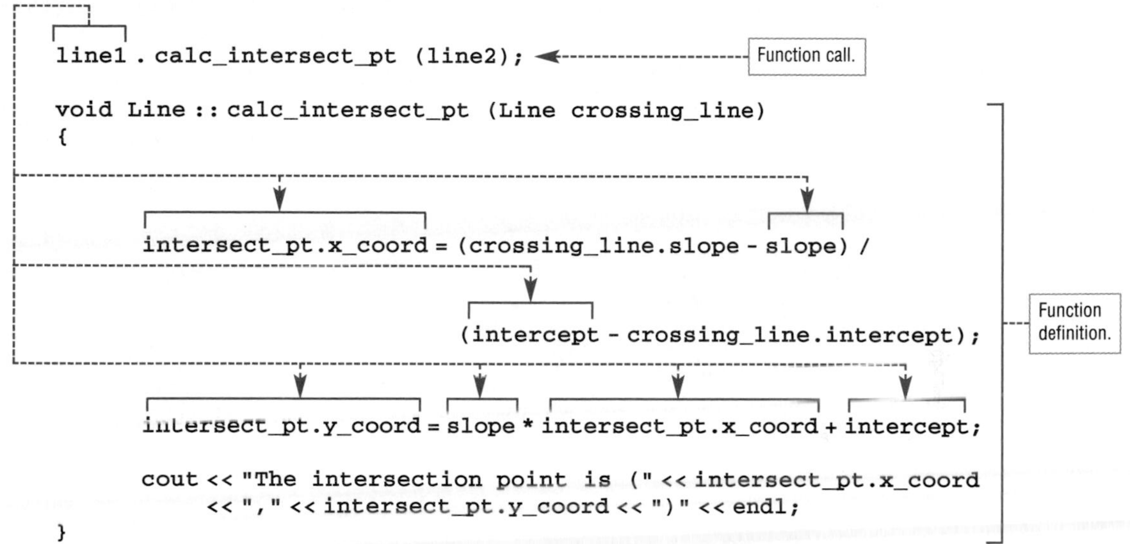

As shown with the arrows, the identifiers `slope` and `intercept` refer to the invoking object's (`line1`) data members. This is because the rules state that within the body of a member function, data member names indicate the invoking object's data members.

Also, `intersect_pt` is a data member of the `Line` class. Therefore, references to `intersect_pt` within the function refer to the invoking object's value of `intersect_pt`. Because `intersect_pt` is a `struct` within the `Line` class, we use `intersect_pt.x_coord` and `intersect_pt.y_coord`.

Because of the way that we have called the function, the correspondence between the variables in Eqns. 8.4 and 8.5 and the variables in the function is:

Variables in equations	Variables in function
m_1	`slope`
b_1	`intercept`
m_2	`crossing_line.slope`
b_2	`crossing_line.intercept`
x	`intersect_pt.x_coord`
y	`intersect_pt.y_coord`

Overall, remember that when you need to use more than one object in a member function, one object is the invoking object, and the other objects are passed through the argument list. Be aware that you must be consistent in your code and use the object's data members properly in the function body to get your program to work.

Putting all this together leads to the following source code.

Source Code

```
#include <fstream.h>
#include <iostream.h>

struct Point
{
        public:
                double x_coord, y_coord;
};

class Line
{
        private:
                double slope, intercept;
                Point intersect_pt;
        public:
                Line();
                void read_line_data (ifstream&);
                void show_line_data ();
                void calc_intersect_pt (Line);
};

Line :: Line ()
     : slope (0), intercept (0)
{
}

void Line :: read_line_data (ifstream& readfile)
{
         readfile >> slope >> intercept;
}

void Line :: show_line_data ()
{
         cout << "Slope = " << slope << ", Intercept = " << intercept << endl;
}

void Line :: calc_intersect_pt (Line crossing_line)
{
         intersect_pt.x_coord = (crossing_line.slope - slope) /
                                (intercept - crossing_line.intercept);
         intersect_pt.y_coord = slope * intersect_pt.x_coord + intercept;

         cout << "The intersection point is (" << intersect_pt.x_coord
              << "," << intersect_pt.y_coord << ")" << endl;
}
```

The Point struct with x and y coordinate members.

The Line class with data members of slope, intercept and intersect_pt, and function members including a constructor and three other functions.

Line constructor. This initializes the data members to zero.

Reading one line of the input file.

Printing the line data members.

Calculating the x and y coordinates using Eqns. 8.4 and 8.5.

```
int main ()
{
        Line line1, line2;

        ifstream infile ("C:\\INTSECT.DAT");

        line1.read_line_data (infile);
        line2.read_line_data (infile);

        line1.show_line_data ();
        line2.show_line_data ();

        line1.calc_intersect_pt (line2);
}
```

Declaring two objects of the `Line` class.

Opening the input file.

Calling a member function to read the data for each object.

Calling a member function to print the input data.

Two line objects are needed to calculate an intersection point. The first line object is used to call the function; the other line object is passed through the argument list

Input File INTSECT.DAT

```
2 -3
5 1
```

Output

```
Slope=2,   Intercept=-3
Slope=5,   Intercept=1
The intersection point is (-1.333333,-5.666667)
```

Comments

The classes and objects for this program were reasonably obvious. In Application Example 8.2, we describe in more detail the thought processes needed for developing the classes.

For this program, we were not required to account for the possibility that the two lines would be parallel. However, had the input file contained two lines with the same slope (`line1.slope=line2.slope`) our program would have crashed. Try changing the input file to have equal slope lines and observe that an overflow error occurs! We described overflow errors earlier and how to trace them. If you were to apply the tracing techniques to this program, you would find that the assignment statement in `calc_intersect_pt()` is the source of the error.

A division by zero takes place because the denominator in the expression is zero (the two slopes are equal). When we described how to correct overflow errors earlier, we indicated that likely an expression is in error. In this case, the expression is clearly correct! How then do we avoid the overflow error? You can get your program to jump over the asssignment statement that causes the problem and print a message saying that the two lines are parallel and have no intersection point using an `if-else` control structure. This is another method you may need to use to correct overflow errors. Remember, for commercial software, it is unacceptable for your program to crash. You must design your programs to accommodate all possible input and still execute completely, and we will find that there are a number of techniques for doing this.

Modification Exercises

1. Modify the program so that the input comes in from the keyboard.
2. Modify the program so that the output goes to a file.
3. Since we know that two points define a line, have the user input four points and create two lines from the four points. Then find the intersection point of the two lines.

APPLICATION EXAMPLE 8.2 AREA OF PARALLELOGRAM, VOLUME OF PARALLELEPIPED

TOPICS

- Object-oriented programming example
- Function returning an object
- Member function working with two objects
- Numerical method example

Problem Statement

Write a program that can calculate the area of a parallelogram defined by two vectors and the volume of a parallelepiped defined by three vectors (Fig. 8.10). Input the **i**, **j**, and **k** components of each of the three vectors from the keyboard and print the result to the screen. Use an object-oriented design.

Solution

RELEVANT EQUATIONS

You may have learned in your math classes that the area of a parallelogram defined by the vectors

$$\mathbf{A} = a_1\mathbf{i} + a_2\mathbf{j} + a_3\mathbf{k}$$
$$\mathbf{B} = b_1\mathbf{i} + b_2\mathbf{j} + b_3\mathbf{k}$$

is the length of the vector created by the cross product of the two vectors. This is indicated in equation form as

$$\text{Area} = |\mathbf{A}\ \mathrm{X}\ \mathbf{B}| \tag{8.6}$$

where the || symbol indicates the length of the vector and X is the cross product.

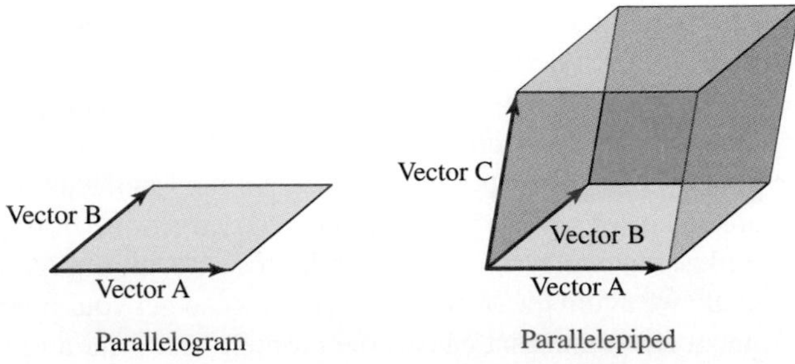

Figure 8.10
Parallelogram formed by two vectors and parallelepiped formed by three vectors.

Recall that the cross product of the two vectors **A X B** is given by the following determinant:

$$\mathbf{A\,X\,B} = \begin{vmatrix} \mathbf{i} & \mathbf{j} & \mathbf{k} \\ a_1 & a_2 & a_3 \\ b_1 & b_2 & b_3 \end{vmatrix}$$

$$= (a_2b_3 - a_3b_2)\,\mathbf{i} - (a_1b_3 - a_3b_1)\,\mathbf{j} + (a_1b_2 - a_2b_1)\,\mathbf{k} \tag{8.7}$$

and that the length of a vector is given by the square root of the sum of the squares of the components. In equation form, this is the following. For a vector **G**,

$$\mathbf{G} = g_1\mathbf{i} + g_2\mathbf{j} + g_3\mathbf{k}$$

The length of **G** is

$$|\mathbf{G}| = \left(g_1^2 + g_2^2 + g_3^2\right)^{0.5} \tag{8.8}$$

Equations 8.7 and 8.8 are used in equation 8.6 to give the area. You also may have learned that the volume of the parallelepiped defined by the three vectors

$$\mathbf{A} = a_1\mathbf{i} + a_2\mathbf{j} + a_3\mathbf{k}$$
$$\mathbf{B} = b_1\mathbf{i} + b_2\mathbf{j} + b_3\mathbf{k}$$
$$\mathbf{C} = c_1\mathbf{i} + c_2\mathbf{j} + c_3\mathbf{k}$$

is

$$\text{Volume} = \text{abs}\,[\mathbf{A} \bullet (\mathbf{B\,X\,C})] \tag{8.9}$$

where the dot product (represented by •) of two vectors **G** and **H**:

$$\mathbf{G} = g_1\mathbf{i} + g_2\mathbf{j} + g_3\mathbf{k}$$
$$\mathbf{H} = h_1\mathbf{i} + h_2\mathbf{j} + h_3\mathbf{k}$$

is

$$\mathbf{G} \bullet \mathbf{H} = g_1h_1 + g_2h_2 + g_3h_3 \tag{8.10}$$

Equations 8.7 (using **B X C**) and 8.10 are used in equation 8.9 to give the volume.

SPECIFIC CALCULATION

Consider the following vectors:

$$\mathbf{A} = 3\mathbf{i} + 2\mathbf{j} + 2\mathbf{k}$$
$$\mathbf{B} = 4\mathbf{i} + 3\mathbf{j} + 1\mathbf{k}$$
$$\mathbf{C} = 8\mathbf{i} + 2\mathbf{j} + 7\mathbf{k}$$

The area of the parallelogram is

$$\mathbf{A\,X\,B} = \begin{vmatrix} \mathbf{i} & \mathbf{j} & \mathbf{k} \\ 3 & 2 & 2 \\ 4 & 3 & 1 \end{vmatrix}$$

$$= [(2 * 1) - (2 * 3)]\mathbf{i} - [(3 * 1) - (2 * 4)]\mathbf{j} + [(3 * 3) - (2 * 4)]\mathbf{k}$$

which gives

$$\mathbf{A\,X\,B} = -4\mathbf{i} + 5\mathbf{j} + \mathbf{k}$$

The length of this vector is

$$|\mathbf{A\,X\,B}| = [(-4)^2 + (5)^2 + (1)^2]^{0.5} = 6.48074$$

Therefore, the area of the parallelogram is 6.48074. To get the volume,

$$\mathbf{B} \text{ X } \mathbf{C} = \begin{vmatrix} \mathbf{i} & \mathbf{j} & \mathbf{k} \\ 4 & 3 & 1 \\ 8 & 2 & 7 \end{vmatrix}$$
$$= [(3 * 7) - (1 * 2)]\mathbf{i} - [(4 * 7) - (1 * 8)]\mathbf{j} + [(4 * 2) - (8 * 3)]\mathbf{k}$$

which gives

$$\mathbf{B} \text{ X } \mathbf{C} = 19\mathbf{i} - 20\mathbf{j} - 16\mathbf{k}$$
$$\mathbf{A} \bullet (\mathbf{B} \text{ X } \mathbf{C}) = (3\mathbf{i} + 2\mathbf{j} + 2\mathbf{k}) \bullet (19\mathbf{i} - 20\mathbf{j} - 16\mathbf{k})$$
$$= (3 * 19) + [2 * (-20)] + [2 * (-16)] = -15.0$$

The absolute value of -15.0 is 15.0. Therefore, the volume of the parallelepiped is 15.0.

CLASSES AND OBJECTS

In this section, we describe some of the logic used in creating the classes and objects for this program. You can imitate some of the thought processes and figures in creating classes and objects for your own programs. We are not demonstrating a rigorous object-oriented design procedure in this example. We are simply illustrating some of the thought processes. In Chapter 14 we show a more formal design methodology.

In this particular program, we are dealing with three entities: vectors, parallelograms, and parallelepipeds. The relationship between these entities is shown in Fig. 8.11. This figure shows that three components form a vector, two vectors form a parallelogram, and three vectors form a parallelepiped. Given these relationships, we realize it is wise to create a class for each entity that we call `Vector`, `Paragram`, and `Parapiped` (the last two shortened for simplicity). We can think of the function members as the verbs that describe what can be done by or to an object.

To determine the data members of each class, we consider what defines an object of the class (upper circles in Fig. 8.11) and what attributes we need an object to have. We can sometimes think of the data members as the nouns that define and describe an object.

To determine the function members of the class we consider what actions need to be performed on an object (boxes in Fig. 8.11). With vectors, we want to calculate magnitudes, dot products, and cross products. With parallelograms we want to

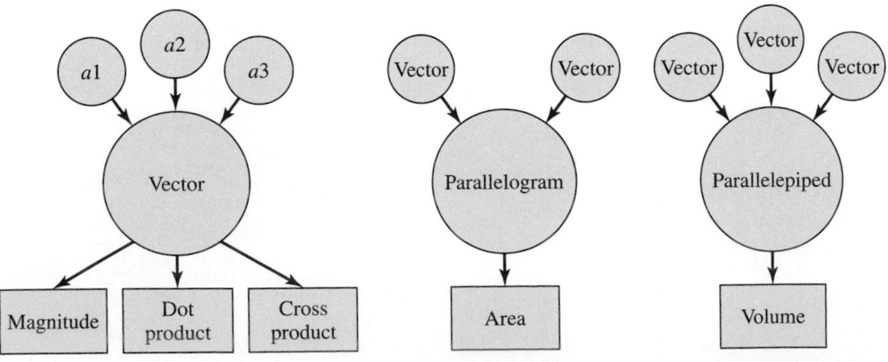

Figure 8.11

Relationship between entities for this program. The upper circles indicate what defines the entity. The bottom blocks indicate what we want to calculate from the entity. Such a sketch can help us create our classes. We create data members for the upper circles and function members to calculate the bottom boxes.

calculate areas, and with parallelepipeds, we want to calculate volumes. In addition, we typically need functions for performing ordinary programming tasks on an object such as initializing (by such things as reading from the keyboard) and displaying on the screen or writing to a file.

CLASS `Vector`

Vectors are defined by the coefficients of `i`, `j`, and `k` that we have called a_1, a_2, and a_3. Therefore, we use `a1`, `a2`, and `a3` as the data members for the `Vector` class.

Actions we need to perform with vectors are shown in the bottom boxes in Fig. 8.11. Therefore, we create functions that we call `magnitude`, `dot`, and `cross`. The ordinary programming task that we need for this program is reading the vector components from the keyboard. We call this function `set_components`.

We need to decide the return types for each of the four functions. Since the result of a cross product is a vector, we make the return type for function `cross` to be `Vector`. The results of magnitude and dot product calculations are both real numbers (scalars not vectors); therefore we make the functions `magnitude` and `dot` have the return type `double`. When we define a vector we simply store values in the `a1`, `a2`, and `a3` data members for the `Vector` object, so nothing need be returned from the function `set_components` meaning we make the return type `void`.

We also need to decide on the argument lists for the four functions. In making the argument list we need to remember that all the data members for the object that calls the function automatically are accessible by the function. So there is no need to transfer the data member values. This means that function `magnitude` has an empty argument list because to compute the magnitude of a single vector, only the components of the vector are needed, and these are accessible by the function automatically. Similarly, `set_components` needs no arguments because it simply sets the components of the object that calls the function directly from the keyboard. However, the functions `dot` and `cross` need two vectors not one because both dot and cross products involve operating on two vectors. Since one of the vectors is the `Vector` object that calls the function, the other vector must be passed through the argument list. Therefore, `dot` and `cross` have single `Vector` objects in their argument lists.

Here is the `Vector` class definition:

```
class Vector
{
    private:
            double a1, a2, a3;
    public:
            void set_components ();
            double magnitude ();
            double dot (Vector);
            Vector cross (Vector);
};
```

CLASS `Paragram`

Parallelograms are defined by the vectors **A** and **B.** In addition, we are interested in the area of a parallelogram. Therefore, our data members are the `area` and the vectors `A` and `B`.

The primary action that we want to perform on a parallelogram is to calculate the area, so we create a function `calc_area`. In addition, we need to perform ordinary programming tasks such as initializing a parallelogram with its vectors using a function we call `set_vectors`, and print the area to the screen with `show_area`.

The return types for all these functions is `void` meaning that nothing is returned from any of the functions. This works because `set_vectors` and `calc_area` simply assign values to the data members `A`, `B`, and `area`. The function `show_area` need not return anything because it simply prints the area to the screen.

The argument list for `set_vectors` contains the two vectors that are read from the keyboard. Once this function is executed, the parallelogram is defined by the data members `A` and `B`. As a result, we can calculate the area with `calc_area` without passing any values through the argument list. Also, `show_area` needs only the area of the parallelogram from the data members, so it has an empty argument list also.

Here is the `Paragram` class definition:

```
class Paragram
{
private:
          Vector A,B;
          double area;
public:
          void set_vectors (Vector,Vector);
          void calc_area ();
          void show_area ();
};
```

CLASS `Parapiped`

Parallelepipeds are defined by the vectors **A, B,** and **C.** In addition, we are interested in the volume of a parallelepiped. Therefore, our data members are the `volume` and the vectors `A`, `B`, and `C`. The primary action that we want to perform on a parallelepiped is to calculate the volume, so we create a function `calc_volume`. In addition, we need to perform ordinary programming tasks such as initializing a parallelepiped with its vectors using a `set_vectors` function, and print the volume to the screen with `show_volume`.

The return types for all these functions are `void`, meaning that nothing is returned from any of the functions. This works because `set_vectors` and `calc_volume` simply assign values to the data members `A`, `B`, `C`, and `volume`. The function `show_volume` need not return anything because it simply prints the volume to the screen.

The argument list for `set_vectors` contains the three vectors that are read from the keyboard. Once this function is executed, the parallelepiped is defined by the data members `A`, `B`, and `C`. As a result, we can calculate the volume with `calc_volume` without passing any values through the argument list. Also, `show_volume` needs only the volume of the parallelepiped from the data members, so it has an empty argument list also.

Here is the `Parapiped` class definition:

```
class Parapiped
{
    private:
            Vector A,B,C;
            double volume;
    public:
            void set_vectors (Vector,Vector,Vector);
            void calc_volume ();
            void show_volume ();
};
```

FUNCTION ALGORITHMS AND CODE

The overall algorithm for the program is this:

1. Declare 3 `Vector` objects.
2. Declare 1 `Paragram` object.
3. Declare 1 `Parapiped` object.
4. Read the vector components for the 3 vectors by calling `set_components` with all 3 `Vector` objects.
5. Assign the first 2 `Vector` objects as data members for the `Paragram` object.
6. Calculate the parallelogram area calling `calc_area` with the `Paragram` object.
7. Display the parallelogram area calling `show_area` with the `Paragram` object.
8. Assign all 3 `Vector` objects as data members for the `Parapiped` object.
9. Calculate the parallelepiped volume by calling `calc_volume` with the `Parapiped` object.
10. Display the parallelepiped volume by calling `show_volume` with the `Parapiped` object.

Source Code

Read the source code by beginning with `main` (which is at the end of the code). Then read the class definitions and member function definitions. Note how the functions use the data members, and how the `calc_area` and `calc_volume` functions call the `cross` and `dot` functions.

This source code is commented partially. Read the comments to get a feeling for what information is useful in comments.

```
//*********************************************************************
//    Application program to calculate
//    area of parallelogram and volume of
//    parallelepiped defined by vectors A, B and C
//    area = length of (A cross B)
//    volume = abs value of (A dot (B cross C))
//
```

```
//    Programmer names   Revision dates
//
//
//
//
//
//   Class Vector
//         Data
//                  a1, a2, a3 = coeffs. of i,j,k for vector
//         Functions
//                  set_components sets a1,a2,a3 by prompting
//                    the user to enter them at the keyboard
//
//                  magnitude calculates vector length from a1,a2,a3
//
//                  dot returns the dot product of 2 vectors. The first vector
//                    is from the object that calls the function. The second
//                    vector is passed through the argument list.
//
//                  cross returns the cross product of 2 vectors. The first
//                    vector is from the object that calls the function.
//                    The second vector is passed through the argument list.
//
//
//   Class Paragram (which is short for parallelogram)
//         Data
//                  A, B = vectors that form the parallelogram
//                  area = area of parallelogram
//         Functions
//                  set_vectors sets the A,B vectors through the argument list
//
//                  calc_area computes the parallelogram area
//                    using area = length of (A cross B)
//
//                  show_area displays the area on the screen
//
//
//   Class Parapiped (which is short for parallelepiped)
//         Data
//                  A, B, C = vectors that form the parallelepiped
//                  volume = volume of parallelepiped
//         Functions
//                  set_vectors sets the A,B,C vectors through the
//                    argument list
//
//                  calc_volume computes the parallelepiped volume
//                    using volume = abs value of (A dot (B cross C))
//
```

```
//                       show_volume displays the volume on the screen
//
//***************************************************************************

#include <iostream>
#include <cmath>
using namespace std;

class Vector
{
    private:
            double a1, a2, a3;
    public:
            void set_components ();
            double magnitude ();
            double dot (Vector);
            Vector cross (Vector);
};


class Paragram
{
    private:
            Vector A,B;
            double area;
    public:
            void set_vectors (Vector,Vector);
            void calc_area ();
            void show_area ();
};


class Parapiped
{
    private:
            Vector A,B,C;
            double volume;
    public:
            void set_vectors (Vector,Vector,Vector);
            void calc_volume ();
            void show_volume ();
};

//***************************************************************************
//
//  Class Vector functions
//
//***************************************************************************
```

The vector components define a vector.

The functions initialize the vector components and perform operations on vectors.

Two vectors define a parallelogram. Area is an attribute of a parallelogram.

These functions initialize the vectors that define a parallelogram, calculate the area, and display the area.

Three vectors define a parallelepiped. Volume is an attribute of a parallelepiped.

These functions initialize the vectors that define a parallelepiped, calculate the volume, and display the volume.

```
void Vector :: set_components ()
{
    cout << "Enter vector (a1 a2 a3 - the coeffs of i,j,k):" << endl;
    cin >> a1 >> a2 >> a3;
}

double Vector :: magnitude ()
{
    return(sqrt(a1*a1+a2*a2+a3*a3));
}

double Vector :: dot (Vector v2)
{
    return(a1*v2.a1+a2*v2.a2+a3*v2.a3);
}

Vector Vector :: cross (Vector v2)
{
    Vector v3;
    v3.a1 = a2 * v2.a3 - a3 * v2.a2;
    v3.a2 = - (a1 * v2.a3 - a3 * v2.a1);
    v3.a3 = a1 * v2.a2 - a2 * v2.a1;
    return (v3);
}

//**********************************************************************
//
//  Class Paragram functions
//
//**********************************************************************

void Paragram :: set_vectors (Vector v1, Vector v2)
{
    A = v1;
    B = v2;
}

void Paragram :: calc_area ()
{
    Vector v3;
    v3 = A.cross (B);
    area = v3.magnitude ();
}

void Paragram :: show_area ()
{
    cout << "The parallelogram area is "
         << area << endl;
}
```

Note that there is no need to declare the variables `a1`, `a2`, or `a3` in any of the vector functions. These variables are data members of the class `Vector`, and therefore are automatically associated with the object that calls the function. The statements in these functions come directly from the Relevant Equations section.

Computing the dot and cross products involves two vectors. One vector is the vector object that calls the function; the other vector is passed through the argument list as `v2`. Because `v2` is in the argument list, in the function we need to use `v2.a1`, `v2.a2`, and `v2.a3` to represent the data components of `v2`.

The result of the cross product of two vectors is a third vector. This third vector (`v3`) is declared in the function and returned. Because `v3` is declared in the function, we must use the notation `v3.a1`, `v3.a2`, and `v3.a3`.

The vectors in the argument list are assigned to A and B for the `paragram` object that calls the `set_vectors` function.

There is no need to declare the variables A, B, (which are `vectors`) or `area` in any of the `paragram` functions. These variables are data members of the class `paragram`, and therefore are automatically associated with the object that calls the function. The assignment statements in these functions come directly from the Relevant Equations section.

The `cross` function is called using the `A` vector object, so the call is written `A.cross`. This means that within `cross` for this function call, the variables `a1`, `a2`, and `a3` refer to the data members for the A object. The B vector is passed through `cross`'s argument list so `A.cross(B)` computes AxB. Also, `cross` returns a vector, so it is assigned to vector `v3`.

Because we want to find the magnitude of `v3`, we use `v3.magnitude()`. This means that within `magnitude` for this function call, `a1`, `a2`, and `a3` refer to the data members for the `v3` object.

```
//*************************************************************************
//
//  Class Parapiped functions
//
//*************************************************************************
void Parapiped :: set_vectors (Vector v1,
  Vector v2, Vector v3)
{
     A = v1;
     B = v2;
     C = v3;
}

void Parapiped :: calc_volume ()
{
     Vector v4;
     v4 = B.cross (C);
     volume = fabs (A.dot (v4));
}

void Parapiped :: show_volume ()
{
     cout << "The parallelepiped volume "
             "is " << volume << endl;
}

//*************************************************************************
//
//  main
//
//*************************************************************************

int main ()
{
      Vector A, B, C;
      Paragram pg1;
      Parapiped pp1;

      A.set_components ();
      B.set_components ();
      C.set_components ();

      pg1.set_vectors (A, B);
      pg1.calc_area ();
      pg1.show_area ();

      pp1.set_vectors (A,B,C);
      pp1.calc_volume ();
      pp1.show_volume ();
}
```

The vectors in the argument list are assigned to A, B, and C for the `Parapiped` object that calls the function.

There is no need to declare the variables A, B, C, (which are vectors) or volume in any of the `Parapiped` functions. These variables are data members of the class `Parapiped`, and therefore are automatically associated with the object that calls the function. The assignment statements in these functions come directly from the Relevant Equations section.

The `cross` function is called using the B vector, so the call is written `B.cross`. This means that within `cross` for this function call, the variables `a1`, `a2`, and `a3` refer to the data members for the B object. The C vector is passed through cross's argument list so `B.cross(C)` computes BxC. Also, `cross` returns a vector, so it is assigned to vector `v4` (which is declared in the function for the sole purpose of storing the return vector).

The `dot` function is called using the A vector, so the call is written `A.dot`. This means that within `dot` for this function call, the variables `a1`, `a2`, and `a3` refer to the data members for the A object. The second vector is passed through dot's argument list, so `A.dot(v4)` computes A • v4. Also, `dot` returns a `double`, so it is assigned to `volume` (which is another data item for the object).

We need 3 vector, 1 parallelogram, and 1 parallelepiped objects.

These set the components for the `A`, `B`, and `C` vectors.

The `pg1` object becomes defined by A and B with this function call.

Calculating and displaying the area for `pg1`.

The `pp1` object becomes defined by A, B, and C with this function call.

Calculating and displaying the volume for `pp1`.

Output

```
Enter vector (a1 a2 a3 - the coeffs of i,j,k):
3 2 2
Enter vector (a1 a2 a3 - the coeffs of i,j,k):
4 3 1
Enter vector (a1 a2 a3 - the coeffs of i,j,k):
8 2 7
The parallelogram area is 6.480741
The parallelepiped volume is 15
```

Comments

The classes that we formed did not have all the possible members. For instance, vectors have attributes such as direction cosines. We did not include such attributes in our data members nor functions to calculate them in our function members because we were not interested in them. A complete Vector class would have them.

In the `main` function, we declare objects, call functions and little more. This is a typical `main` function for many programs in that not many calculations are performed in `main`. By looking at `main` for this program, you immediately get a general impression of the program's operations. The `main` function for your object-oriented programs should be similar.

We can construct a type of data flow diagram for functions `calc_volume` and `calc_area`. These are shown in Fig. 8.12. This figure illustrates how some information passes to `cross`, `dot`, and `magnitude` through the argument list, and some passes to `cross` through encapsulation with the object that calls the function.

Remember, it is only possible to access private data members through member functions. This means that we need to use functions for even the simplest tasks like printing or reading data.

In this program, the comments were put at the beginning of the program enclosed in a banner of *s. One of the reasons for using the *s is to clearly distinguish comments from code. If commenting is not done properly, when you try to debug code, the comments can "get in the way" and make it difficult to follow the logic. We have found that using *s at the top and bottom of code blocks works well for separating out comments. This does not work very well, however, when it is necessary to write comments at the end of a line of code. There is no standard commenting scheme. We recommend that you follow your instructor's or employer's requirements in writing comments.

As you can see, making an object-oriented design and including proper comments adds considerably to the length of a program. Do not let this bother you. The benefits of having an object-oriented design and clear comments outweigh the disadvantages of added length. In this book, though, it is not efficient for us to use object-oriented design techniques in every example because we also are trying to teach you elements of the C++ language, such as looping and control structures. Therefore, we will show only a few complete object-oriented, commented programs. Because so

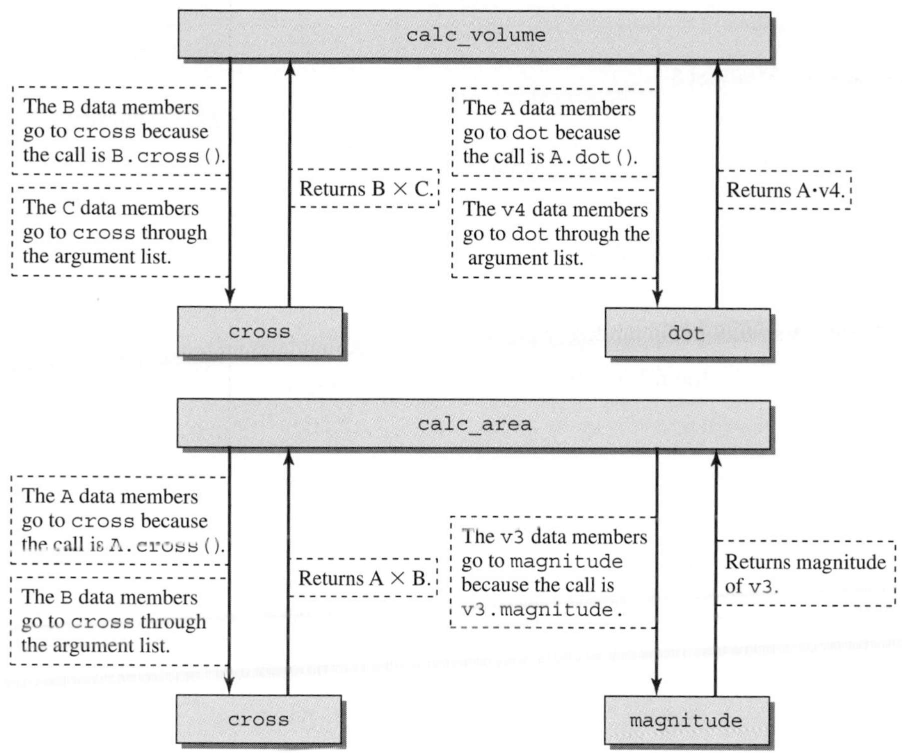

Figure 8.12

Data flow type diagrams for `calc_volume` and `calc_area`. This illustrates how some information passes to `cross`, `dot`, and `magnitude` through the argument list, and some passes to `cross` through encapsulation with the object that calls the function.

many programs in this text are not written that way, please do not get the impression that we advocate not using an object-oriented design or comments. We strongly endorse using both.

Clearly, a much simpler program could have been written to accomplish the same tasks as the program shown here. However, had the requirement been to work with a group of people to create the program, then each could write the functions for a different class. This type of approach improves the creation of large programs. As you become accustomed to object-oriented design, you will be able to produce very powerful, reliable programs.

Modification Exercises

Use the Vector class in this program to create programs that are capable of evaluating the following expressions (with **A, B, C,** and **D** being vectors expressed in the form **i, j,** and **k**):

1. **A** X (**B** X **C**)
2. (**A** X **B**) • (**C** X **D**)
3. (**A** X **B**) X (**C** X **D**)
4. **B**(**A** • **C**) – **A**(**B** • **C**)
5. **B**(**A** • **C**) – **C**(**A** • **B**)

LESSON EXERCISES

LESSON 8.1 EXERCISES

1. True or false:

a. A `struct` must contain all like type data.

b. A `struct` creates a new data type.

c. To print all the data members of a `struct`, we do not need to use the dot operator.

d. A semicolon is needed to end a `struct` definition.

e. A semicolon follows the keyword public in a `struct` definition.

2. Find the syntax errors in the following `struct` definition:

```
Struct gas:
{
        public.
                temp;
                pressure;
}
```

Solutions

1. a. false
b. true
c. false
d. true
e. false

2.
```
struct gas:
{
        public:
                double temp;
                double pressure;
};
```

LESSON 8.2 EXERCISES

1. True or false:

a. Defining a class reserves memory for the class's data members.

b. Declaring an object reserves memory for the data members of the object's class.

c. An object of a class (with the class defined at the beginning of a program outside the body of any function) can be declared only in member functions.

d. Only private member functions can access private member data.

e. Only public member functions can access public member data.

2. Write a program that creates a `Cubic` class and integrates a third-order polynomial.

Solutions

1. a. false
   b. true
   c. false
   d. talse
   e. false

LESSON 8.3 EXERCISES

1. True or false:

   a. Constructor functions can be given any name.

   b. All classes must contain a constructor function.

   c. A constructor function is called automatically when an object is declared.

   d. It is usually useful for a class to have a constructor.

2. Find the syntax errors in the following class and function definition.

```
Class class1
{
            private
                        int data;
            public
                        class1 : class1 ();
                        double function1 ();
}

Class : class1()
{
            data = 5;
}
```

3. Write a program that creates a `Bicycle` class. Create a constructor that initializes the wheel size and number of gears.

Solutions

1. a. false
   b. false
   c. true
   d. true
2.
```
class class1
{
            private:
                        int data;
            public:
                        class1 ();
                        double function1 ();
};

class1 :: class1 ()
{
      data = 5;
}
```

LESSON 8.4 EXERCISES

1. True or false:

a. Constructor functions cannot return values.

b. Constructor functions can receive values.

c. We pass a value to a constructor in a declaration.

d. A function name is the only identifier that can be followed by parentheses.

e. We can call a constructor function for an object only once in a program.

2. Find the errors in the following:

a. `Weather_station :: Weather_station (int wind_speed_var) : wind_speed_var (wind_speed)`

b. `Weather_station :: Weather_station (int wind_speed_var) :: wind_speed (wind_speed_var)`

c. `Weather_station = station1(10);`

3. Write a program that creates three `Weather_station` objects. At each weather station, the wind speed, temperature, and humidity are recorded. Use a constructor to initialize the values. Print out the data.

Solutions

1. a. true
b. true
c. true
d. false
e. false

2. a. `Weather_station :: Weather_station (int wind_speed_var) : wind_speed (wind_speed_var)`
b. `Weather_station :: Weather_station (int wind_speed_var) : wind_speed (wind_speed_var)`
c. `station1 = Weather_station (10);`

LESSON 8.5 EXERCISES

1. True or false:

a. C++ requires that a programmer define a constructor function for each class it defines.

b. Overloading constructors is useful and commonly done.

c. If C++ is not able to distinguish between constructor functions, it chooses the first in the class definition.

d. C++ uses the number and type of arguments to distinguish between constructor functions.

e. Arrays of objects cannot be used when constructor functions are used.

2. Find the errors:

```
class Microwave_instruction
{
        private:
                int time, power_level
        public:
                Microwave_instruction;
                Microwave_instruction (int, int);
                Microwave_instruction (int, int);
                void show_data ();
};
```

3. Write a program that creates a `Bus` class. Create a constructor that initializes the number of passengers and number of seats. Declare four objects. Use the default copy constructor to initialize two of the objects.

Solutions

1. a. false
   b. true
   c. false
   d. true
   e. false
2. Missing semicolon after `power_level`. Missing parentheses after the name of the first constructor function. Two constructors with `(int, int)` arguments.

APPLICATION EXERCISES

1. The data from a land survey contain the *x* and *y* coordinates of a number of control points. Based on the given data, you are asked to write a program to calculate the perimeter length indicated by the points. The *x-y* coordinate control points are as follows:

100.0	100.0
100.0	200.0
200.0	100.0
600.0	100.0
300.0	700.0
400.0	900.0
800.0	100.0

The program should contain a class named `Land_survey`. A `Land_survey` object should be able to read the input file as shown above and calculate the length of the perimeter.

2. Given three sides of a triangle *a, b,* and *c,* its area can be calculated using the formula

$$\text{Area} = \sqrt{s(s-a)(s-b)(s-c)}$$

where *s* is the perimeter of the triangle. Write a program that contains a class named `Tri_area`. The class should contain a function member that accepts *a, b,* and *c* as arguments and another that calculates the area of the triangle. Given two points in 3-D space, (x_1, y_1, z_1) and (x_2, y_2, z_2), the equation of the plane perpendicular to the line formed by the two points and passing through (x_1, y_1, z_1) is $(x_2 - x_1)(x - x_1) + (y_2 - y_1)(y - y_1) + (z_2 - z_1)(z - z_1) = 0$.

Write a computer program capable of creating the equation of such a plane. You will find the coordinates of the two points (x_1, y_1, z_1) and (x_2, y_2, z_2) by solving

$$\begin{bmatrix} a_{11} & a_{12} & a_{13} \\ a_{21} & a_{22} & a_{23} \\ a_{31} & a_{32} & a_{33} \end{bmatrix} \begin{bmatrix} x_1 \\ y_1 \\ z_1 \end{bmatrix} = \begin{bmatrix} b_1 \\ b_2 \\ b_3 \end{bmatrix}$$

and

$$\begin{bmatrix} c_{11} & c_{12} & c_{13} \\ c_{21} & c_{22} & c_{23} \\ c_{31} & c_{32} & c_{33} \end{bmatrix} \begin{bmatrix} x_2 \\ y_2 \\ z_2 \end{bmatrix} = \begin{bmatrix} d_1 \\ d_2 \\ d_3 \end{bmatrix}$$

Use Cramer's rule to solve the equations. Cramer's rule, to solve for x_1, for instance, is written as:

$$x_1 = \frac{\begin{vmatrix} b_1 & a_{12} & a_{13} \\ b_2 & a_{22} & a_{23} \\ b_3 & a_{32} & a_{33} \end{vmatrix}}{\begin{vmatrix} a_{11} & a_{12} & a_{13} \\ a_{21} & a_{22} & a_{23} \\ a_{31} & a_{32} & a_{33} \end{vmatrix}}$$

To solve for x_2, the denominator is the same, but the *b* column in the numerator replaces the second column in the matrix. And for x_3, the *b* column replaces the third column in the numerator matrix. The input data will be in the text file plane.dat. It consists of six lines:

$$\begin{matrix} a_{11} & a_{12} & a_{13} & b_1 \\ a_{21} & a_{22} & a_{23} & b_2 \\ a_{31} & a_{32} & a_{33} & b_3 \\ c_{11} & c_{12} & c_{13} & d_1 \\ c_{21} & c_{22} & c_{23} & d_2 \\ c_{31} & c_{32} & c_{33} & d_3 \end{matrix}$$

An example data file is:

```
2 -12 3 55
-1 1 4 -65
-15 4 5 -51
5 -1 1 24
10 20 100 -60
0.01 0.1 0.01 0.44
```

Create a matrix class that calculates determinants and solves equations using Cramer's rule.

3. Write a program capable of finding the enclosed area of three "C" shaped regions in the first quadrant of a Cartesian coordinate system.

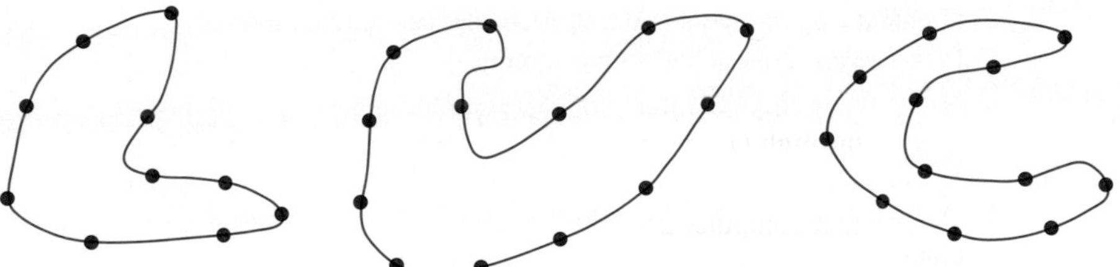

Use the trapezoidal rule with the data point coordinates given as input data. The data file called carea.dat consists of

```
i
x1 y1
x2 y2
...
xi yi
j
x1 y1
x2 y2
...
xj yj
k
x1 y1
x2 y2
...
xk yk
```

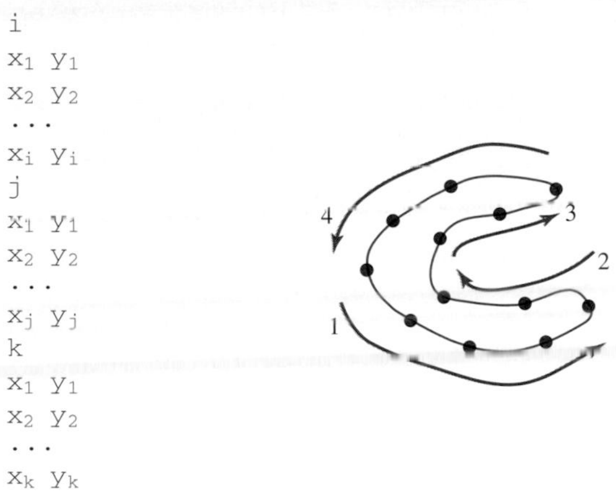

where i, j, and k are the number of data points in the first, second, and third C areas, respectively. The x and y are the point coordinates on the lines forming the C. The first point given for each area is the leftmost point. The other points are given in the order shown in the trace indicated by 1, 2, 3, and 4 in the figure. To compute the enclosed C area, the trapezoidal rule area for stretches 1 and 3 should be negative and for 2 and 4 should be positive. Summing all the areas gives the C area. A sample data for one C is:

```
16
3 5.5
5 2.4
6 1.8
9 1.3
12 1.5
16 4.2
17 5.5
15 6.2
11 5.6
9 6.8
11 8.6
13 9.3
15 11.2
13 11.8
9 11.2
5 9.3
```

Create a `Point` struct and a `C_shape` class. Create three `C_shape` objects. Print the area of each *C* to the screen.

4. Write a program to solve Application Exercise 7.3 using an `Earthquake` class.
5. Write a program to solve Application Exercise 7.5 using a `Sliding block` class.
6. Write a program to solve Application Exercise 7.7 using a `Beam` class.
7. Write a program to solve Application Exercise 7.9 using a `Car` class.
8. Write a program to solve Application Exercise 7.10 using a `Collision` class.
9. Write a program to solve Application Exercise 7.13 using a `Cable` class.
10. Write a program to solve Application Exercise 7.15 using a `Current` class.
11. Write a program to solve Application Exercise 7.17 using a `Flow` class.
12. Write a program to solve Application Exercise 7.21 using a `Heater` class.

CHAPTER 9

ONE-DIMENSIONAL NUMERIC ARRAYS

CHAPTER TOPICS

In this chapter, you will learn how to:

- Create and manipulate arrays
- Trace and debug loops that manipulate arrays
- Reserve memory during program execution
- Use arrays to solve problems

An array is a data structure in C++. It is a grouping of like-type data. In its simplest form, an array can represent a list of numbers, for instance, a list of the temperatures recorded every hour at a particular weather station for one year. In this case, all the numbers in the list represent temperatures and therefore are like-type data.

Another use of arrays might be in denoting the x and y coordinates of a number of data points. If there are 10,000 data points, then there are 10,000 x coordinates and 10,000 y coordinates. For this, we could create two arrays, one for x and another for y. In C++, arrays are indicated with brackets containing a positive integer constant or expression following an identifier. For instance, the x coordinate of a data point might be represented as `x[129]` or `x[4976]` (anything from 0 to 9999 is acceptable in the brackets for an array of 10,000 points).

This is a convenient representation for like-type data because we easily can write expressions for calculating and manipulating this data. The value enclosed in brackets is called a *subscript* or *index*. It can be used much as subscripts are used in algebraic expressions. For instance, to find the slope, m_1, of a line connecting two points indicated by the coordinates (x_1, y_1) and (x_2, y_2) we can use the following algebraic expression:

$$m_1 = (y_2 - y_1)/(x_2 - x_1)$$

With C++'s array structure, we can write this as an assignment statement:

```
m[1] = (y[2] - y[1])/(x[2] - x[1]);
```

Note the direct correspondence between the algebraic expression and the assignment statement. The subscripts in the algebraic expression match the bracketed values in the array expression.

If we wanted to calculate the slope for many different pairs of points we could put the array in a loop, such as

```
for (i = 0; i < 9999; i++)      <------ Loop over all the data points.
          {
          m[i] = (y[i + 1] - y[i]) / (x[i + 1] - x[i]);   <------ Calculate the slope of lines connecting data points i and i + 1.
          }
```

At this point, you need not understand this loop completely, but let us just say that these few lines can be used to calculate all the slopes of the lines connecting all 10,000 data points! We cannot do a calculation of this type so simply without arrays. So, we find arrays to be very useful.

Loops are commonly used for numeric array manipulations because loops are very efficient in handling the large numbers of elements in arrays. Typically, with each iteration of a loop, the subscripts in the array expressions change, as you can see if you study the previous loop. Sometimes the subscript manipulations can be complex and confusing; however, understanding subscript manipulation in loops is crucial to successfully working with arrays. Even experienced programmers sometimes need to slowly think through the process and trace their loops carefully to make sure that a loop is properly manipulating array elements.

Therefore, in this chapter, we frequently use our table format, with the loop expressions in the first column and the variable names in the first row, to illustrate tracing a loop with arrays. We start with some simple loops at the beginning of the chapter and progress to more complex loops at the end of the chapter. You should go through the tables carefully and follow step by step how the values in each row are obtained. We will highlight the important observations for each loop as we go along.

The Lesson portion of the chapter covers basic array operations, such as initializing, reading, and printing array contents. These topics are relatively straightforward and are covered in the Lessons reasonably quickly. Some of the explanations of array actions are given in the annotations and not elaborated upon in the Descriptions.

However, using arrays in practical programs is more difficult, so we have several application examples that focus primarily on the logical steps needed to solve real problems with arrays. You should pay close attention to the way arrays are manipulated in these examples so you can perform similar manipulations in your own programs.

LESSON 9.1 INTRODUCTION

TOPICS

- Definition of arrays
- Characteristics of an array
- Sizing arrays
- Printing array elements

QUESTION YOU SHOULD ATTEMPT TO ANSWER

1. What types of values are enclosed in brackets?

Like ordinary variables, arrays must be declared before they can be used in a program. An array declaration indicates the array name and reserves space for **all** the elements of the array. In other words, a declaration for an array of 10,000 doubles reserves space in memory for 10,000 real numbers. The *programmer* determines the number of array elements (by writing the declaration), but a *user* fills only the array elements he or she needs.

For instance, a programmer may write a general program for analyzing 10,000 data points (by declaring size 10,000 arrays), but a user may have only 500 data points to analyze. In such a case, memory is wasted because only a fraction of the reserved memory is used. This is not efficient, but it is an acceptable situation. An unacceptable situation is when the opposite occurs. Another user may have 50,000 data points. When he or she tries to use the program, serious problems can occur because access may be attempted beyond what is reserved. In this lesson we illustrate what may happen when an array is declared to be smaller than the attempted access.

Values can be assigned to array elements using assignment statements. This lesson's program declares two one-dimensional arrays, `a[]` and `b[]`, initializes some of the elements of the arrays, and prints them out.

Read the program and observe how arrays are declared and initialized. Also see what happens when we try to access array elements beyond those declared.

Source Code

```
#include <iostream>
using namespace std;

int main ( )
{
     const int N = 10;
     int a[2];
     double b[N];
```

A `const int` is defined and used to size the `b[]` array. It is frequently good programming practice to use declared constant variables to size arrays.

Array declarations. The value enclosed in brackets indicates the total number of array elements for which space is to be reserved. Array `a[]` has 2 elements and array `b[]` has 10 elements.

```
    a[0] = 11;
    a[1] = 22;

    b[3] = 777.7;
    b[6] = 888.8;

    cout << "a[0] = " << a[0] << ", a[1] = " << a[1] << endl;
    cout << "b[3] = " << b[3] << ", b[6] = " << b[6] << endl;
    cout << "b[2] = " << b[2] << endl;
    cout << "a[3] = " << a[3] << endl;
    return 0;
}
```

These statements fill all the elements of the a[] array. Note that the first element has the subscript 0 not 1! This means that the available elements for a[] are a[0] and a[1], not a[1] and a[2]. In C++, the first array element is always subscript 0 not 1.

We initialize only 2 of the 10 elements of b[]. The available elements for b[] are b[0] to b[9], not b[1] to b[10].

Printing the two initialized element values for a[] and b[].

We have printed an element of b[] that has not been initialized. No error has been indicated during execution.

The array a[] has been declared to have only two elements, yet we have printed an element, a[3], that goes beyond the two allowed. No error was indicated during compilation or execution!

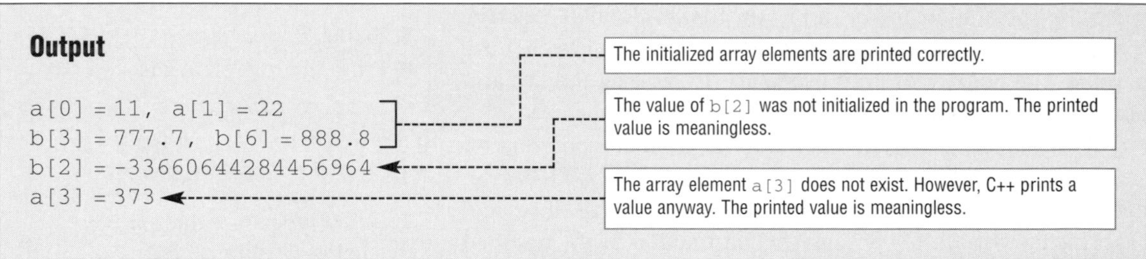
Output
a[0] = 11, a[1] = 22
b[3] = 777.7, b[6] = 888.8
b[2] = -33660644284456964
a[3] = 373
The initialized array elements are printed correctly.
The value of b[2] was not initialized in the program. The printed value is meaningless.
The array element a[3] does not exist. However, C++ prints a value anyway. The printed value is meaningless.

Description

One-dimensional arrays. A one-dimensional array is a collection of the same type of variables (standard C++ calls an array an aggregate type variable) stored in contiguous and increasing memory locations (see Fig. 9.1). It is identified by its name, type, dimension, and number of elements.

For example, as illustrated in Fig. 9.2, the statement

```
int a[2];
```

declares that:

The name of the array is a.
The type of the array elements is int.
The dimension is 1 (it has only one pair of brackets [ ]).
The number of elements or size is 2 (meaning that memory for two elements is reserved).

In general, the syntax for a 1-D array declaration is

```
type name[num_elements];
```

where *type* specifies the type of the array's elements, such as int, float, double, or any other valid C++ data type, except void; *name* is the name of the array; and

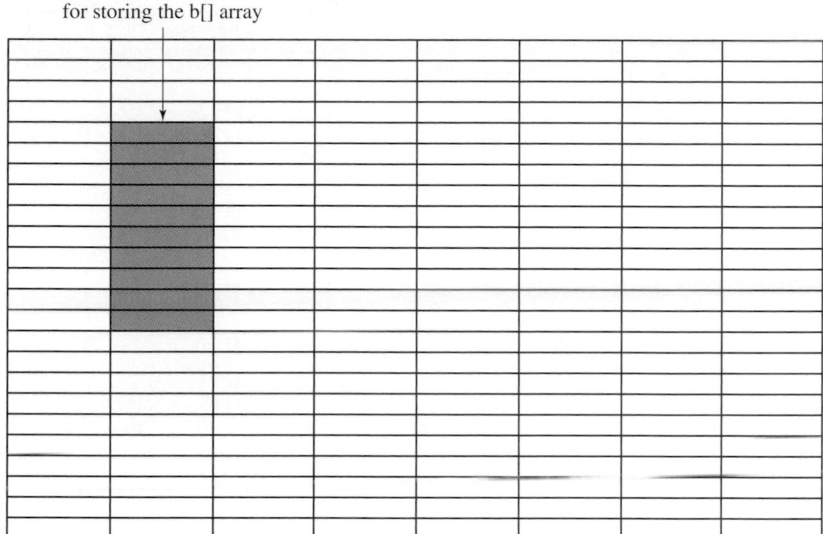

Figure 9.1

Image of memory with 10 adjacent memory cells. These cells can store the `b[]` array used in this lesson's program.

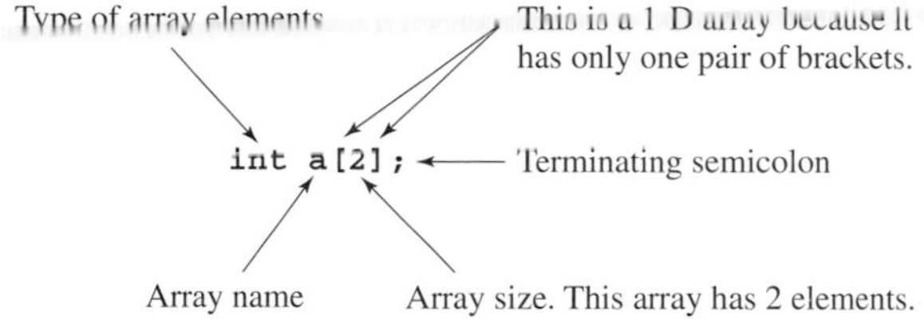

Figure 9.2

Components of an array declaration.

`num_elements` specifies the maximum number of elements that can be stored in the array. The value of *`num_elements`* must be a positive integer constant.

The memory arrangement for the `a[]` and `b[]` arrays of this lesson's program are shown in Table 9.1. The addresses in this table illustrate that the array elements are contiguous (with each `int` occupying 4 bytes and each `double` occupying 8 bytes for this implementation). Both elements of the `a[]` array are initialized, whereas only two of the ten elements of the `b[]` array are initialized.

Array names are classified as identifiers. Therefore, the name of an array must follow the rules used for naming identifiers.

Array length. It is up to the programmer to set the length (also called size or maximum number of elements) of an array, based on the needs of that particular program. The length of a 1-D array is determined by the result of the expression enclosed in brackets in the declaration. The length must be an integer constant greater than 0. The length of a 1-D array can be defined explicitly, such as:

```
int a[2], c[20], g[100];
```

Another common way to size arrays is to use a `const int` type variable, such as in this lesson's program, which uses:

```
const int N = 10;
double b[N];
```

TABLE 9.1 — Array elements for Lesson 9.1's program

Name	Type		Address	Value
a	Array of `int` (2 elements)			
	a[0]	int	FFF2	11
	a[1]	int	FFF6	22
b	Array of `double` (10 elements)			
	b[0]	double	FF60	—
	b[1]	double	FF70	—
	b[2]	double	FF80	—
	b[3]	double	FF90	777.7
	b[4]	double	FFA0	—
	b[5]	double	FFB0	—
	b[6]	double	FFC0	888.8
	b[7]	double	FFD0	—
	b[8]	double	FFE0	—
	b[9]	double	FFF0	—

Only integer type variables such as `int` and `char` with their modifiers `signed`, `unsigned`, `short`, and `long` can be used as index variables. Since integer expressions are allowed, the following declarations also would be valid (used together with `const int N = 10;`):

```
int c[100 + N], d[50 * N];
```

Using a `const int` type variable in sizing arrays makes a program more flexible and less prone for errors when modified. For example, if you have 100 1-D arrays that all have the size of 9, that is, a1[9], a2[9], . . . , a100[9], and you want to change the size from 9 to 25, you have to change 9 to 25 a total of 100 times. The effort involved in making this change and the likelihood of error is reduced by using a `const int` type variable in declaring the array length; for example, a1[N], a2[N], . . . , a100[N] with N defined as a `const int`. To increase the size from 9 to 25, all that is necessary is to change the value of N from 9 to 25 in the declaration for N. In general, where possible, use a `const int` to size your arrays.

Note that you may declare arrays and single variables in the same line. For instance,

```
double b[N], f, g, h;
```

is legal. The C++ compiler knows that `b` is an array because it is followed by brackets and that the others are single variables because they are not.

The following are array declarations with invalid numbers of elements:

```
int  c[-25], b[32.5]
```

These declarations are illegal because the numbers in brackets are not positive integers.

Memory requirements. By multiplying the number of elements expressed in the declaration and the amount of memory for each element, we can determine the amount of memory reserved by an array declaration. For instance, if an `int` occupies 2 bytes, then the `int` array `a[]` that has a length of 2 occupies $2 \times 2 = 4$ bytes. Similarly, the double array `b[]` with a length of 10 (with type `double` occupying 8 bytes each) occupies $10 * 8 = 80$ bytes.

Array subscripts. In C++, by default, the first index or subscript is 0. This usually leads to confusion and error by students and even some experienced programmers who forget that C++ begins at 0 and not 1 (as some other languages do). For instance, in this lesson's program we declared

```
int a[2];
```

This means that there are two elements of the array `a[]`. Since C++ begins at 0, the two elements that are used in the program body are `a[0]`, and `a[1]` with the lines

```
a[0] = 11;
a[1] = 22;
```

Observe that we did *not* use `a[2]` in the executable statements of the program body. This is because `a[2]` in the declaration means something completely different from `a[2]` in an executable statement! In an executable statement, `a[2]` means the third element of the array `a[]`. Since only two elements are declared for `a[]`, we should *not* use `a[2]` in an executable statement.

If `a[2]` were used in an executable statement C++ would not have indicated an error! C++ does not check to see if you try to access an array outside its range. If `a[2]` were specified in the program, C++ actually would go to the memory location after `a[1]` and extract a value from that location. With this value, the program may execute completely and give answers (which very likely will be wrong).

In programs you write, it is up to you to recognize that your answers are wrong and find the source of the errors. With many arrays in your programs and many complicated control structures, it may be very difficult to find which array at which location causes the array size to be exceeded. If nothing meaningful is in that memory location, you very likely will get a run-time error, which may also be difficult to trace. Therefore, when writing your programs, be very careful to not exceed the size of your arrays. Remember your arrays begin at 0 and end at one less than the number of elements.

For illustration only, in this lesson's program we printed out `a[3]`, which very clearly is outside the range specified in the declaration for `a[]`. However, neither during compilation nor execution was any error indicated. (Try it yourself.) The integer 373 (which has absolutely no meaning in the context of this program) was found in the memory cell indicated by `a[3]`. We chose to simply print this value using the last `cout` statement in the program; however, we easily could have performed calculations with `a[3]` being on the right side of an assignment statement or even stored a new value in `a[3]`! Because it is outside the range specified in the declaration, doing anything with `a[3]` probably would have caused chaos in our program. This is because the value stored in `a[3]` is unpredictable (if you run this program on your computer, you probably will get something other than 373), and if we tried to store something into `a[3]`, we probably would overwrite a value in another variable's memory cell that is supposed to be there. In summary, be careful. If you find that you are getting nonsensical answers from your programs, check whether you are exceeding the specified range for any of your arrays.

In this program, we assigned values for `b[3]` and `b[6]`. However, `b[]` has been declared to have ten elements. What is stored in the other elements of the `b[]` array?

No meaningful values are stored in the memory locations for these elements. The statement

```
cout << "b[2] = " << b[2] << endl;
```

has printed the value of `b[2]`. The value of −33660644284456964 simply is representative of the miscellaneous bits currently in the memory location reserved for `b[2]`. Should you run this program, you probably would get a different value for `b[2]`. Therefore, as we saw with ordinary variables, array elements must be initialized before using them. Note that this program ran with no errors being indicated during compilation or execution; however, the result for `b[2]` was nonsensical. So, if you find that you are getting nonsensical answers from your programs, check whether you have initialized all the elements of your arrays. The next lesson illustrates various ways of initializing array elements.

***Printing array elements using* cout.** For printing, we treat an array element much like we treat a single variable. For instance, the statements

```
cout << "a[0] = " << a[0] << ",  a[1] = " << a[1] << endl;
cout << "b[3] = " << b[3] << ",  b[6] = " << b[6] << endl;
```

cause the values of `a[0]`, `a[1]`, `b[3]`, and `b[6]` to be printed.

Note that we must print array elements one at a time. We cannot simply use the variable name without subscripts and expect the entire array to be printed. For instance,

```
cout << a << endl;
```

will not print the elements of the `a[]` array. In the next lessons we will find that looping can be used to print all the element values of an array.

Distinguishing between 1-, 2-, and 3-D arrays. A one-dimensional array has only one pair of brackets following its name. A two-dimensional array has two pairs of brackets, and a three-dimensional array has three pairs of brackets, such as in this declaration:

```
         2-D array     3-D array
int      b[2][4],      c[6][9][5];
```

In this chapter we restrict our discussion to 1-D arrays.

LESSON 9.2 INITIALIZATION

TOPICS

- Methods for initializing array elements in declarations
- Initializing array elements using `cin`
- Initializing array elements using assignment statements in loops

In Lesson 9.1, we saw the importance of assigning values to the array elements used in our programs. We assigned values one element at a time.

In Chapter 3, we illustrated initializing the values of simple variables in their declarations. We did this by writing an assignment type statement within the declaration. We can do something similar for arrays. That is, we can initialize arrays in declarations. However, with arrays the situation is somewhat different because arrays have many elements and, if we want to initialize the values of many elements in a declaration, we need to list many values in the declaration. In

C++, we do this using braces { } to enclose the values of the array elements we are initializing. In this program we show the details of initializing an array in the declaration.

We can use `cin` statements to enter array element values one by one from the keyboard. We can also use loops to help us calculate array element values.

Read this program and see different ways to initialize arrays.

QUESTIONS YOU SHOULD ATTEMPT TO ANSWER

1. How many elements does `b[]` have?
2. How many times is the `for` loop executed?
3. What does the `for` loop initialize the `y[]` values to be?

Source Code

```
#include <iostream>
using namespace std;

int main ( )
{
     int a[3] = {11,22}, b[] = {44, 55, 66}, i;
     double x[2], y[10];

     cout << "a[0]=" << a[0] << ", a[1]=" << a[1] << ", a[2]=" << a[2] << endl
          << "b[0]=" << b[0] << ", b[1]=" << b[1] << ", b[2]=" << b[2] << endl;

     cout << "Please enter two real numbers" << endl;
     cin >> x[0] >> x[1];
     cout << "x[0] = " << x[0] << "  x[1] = " << x[1] << endl << endl;

     for (i = 0; i < 10; i++)
          {
          y[i] = i * 100.0;
          cout << "y[" << i << "]=" << y[i] << endl;
          }
}
```

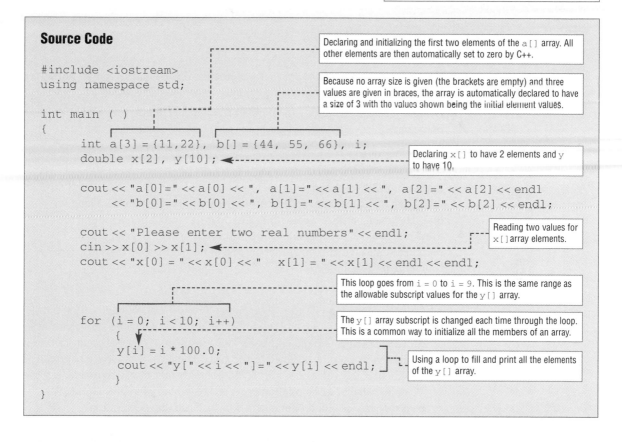

Declaring and initializing the first two elements of the `a[]` array. All other elements are then automatically set to zero by C++.

Because no array size is given (the brackets are empty) and three values are given in braces, the array is automatically declared to have a size of 3 with the values shown being the initial element values.

Declaring `x[]` to have 2 elements and `y` to have 10.

Reading two values for `x[]` array elements.

This loop goes from `i = 0` to `i = 9`. This is the same range as the allowable subscript values for the `y[]` array.

The `y[]` array subscript is changed each time through the loop. This is a common way to initialize all the members of an array.

Using a loop to fill and print all the elements of the `y[]` array.

Output

```
                   a[0]=11, a[1]=22, a[2]=0
                   b[0]=44, b[1]=55, b[2]=66

                   Please enter two real numbers
Keyboard input     77.0 88.0
                   x[0] = 77    x[1] = 88
```

The value of `a[2]` is 0 even though it was never explicitly initialized in the declaration.

```
y[0]=0
y[1]=100
y[2]=200
y[3]=300
y[4]=400
y[5]=500
y[6]=600
y[7]=700
y[8]=800
y[9]=900
```

Description

Initializing arrays in a declaration. The elements of a 1-D array can be initialized in a declaration using either of the following two methods (Fig. 9.3):

1. Declare the array, including the number of elements in brackets, and immediately list values of at least some of the array elements enclosed in braces. For example, the declaration

   ```
   int a[3] = {11, 22};
   ```

   initializes `a[0]` to 11 and `a[1]` to 22. With this statement we have explicitly initialized only the first two elements of the array `a[]`, which has a length of 3. However, because we use this particular method of initialization, the third element, `a[2]`, is automatically initialized to be 0. In general, to initialize some elements and to set the rest of the elements to 0, we use the following form:

   ```
   type name[num_elements] = {value, value,....... value};
   ```

   where *type* is the type of array elements, *name* is the array name, *num_elements* is the maximum number of array elements, *value* is an array element value, and the number of *value*s is *num_elements* or less. The values in braces are assigned to the array elements in sequence beginning with element 0. All values not initialized in braces are set equal to zero.

   C++ will detect a compilation error if the number of values in braces exceeds the size specified in brackets. For instance, the declaration

   ```
   int b[2] = {44, 55, 66};
   ```

   would cause an error in C++ because we stated that `b[]` has only two elements, but we listed three. Although C++ will not detect out-of-range errors with arrays, it will detect this error.

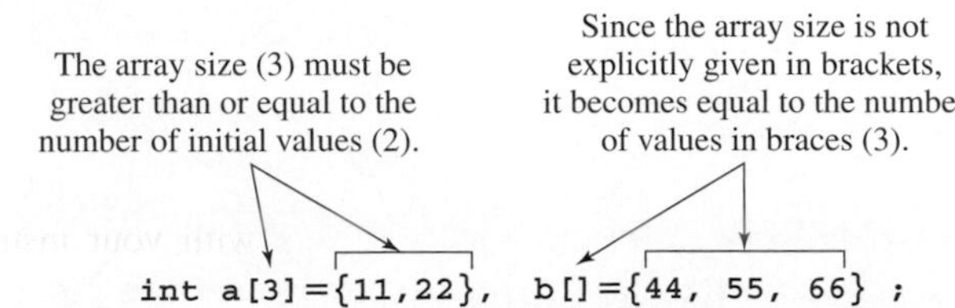
The array size (3) must be greater than or equal to the number of initial values (2).
Since the array size is not explicitly given in brackets, it becomes equal to the number of values in braces (3).
int a[3]={11,22}, b[]={44, 55, 66} ;

Figure 9.3

Initializing an array in its declaration.

2. Declare the array without including the number of elements in brackets and immediately list values of the array elements in braces. For example, the declaration

```
int b[] = {44, 55, 66};
```

automatically declares the size of `b[]` to be three elements (`b[0]`, `b[1]`, and `b[2]`) because three values are listed in braces. In this case, if we try to access `b[3]`, we would be exceeding the range of `b[]`. In general, the form of this type of declaration is

```
type name[ ] = {value, value,...... value};
```

where the terms are given in the method 1 description.

This form initializes all elements of the array. The number of elements in the array is equal to the number of *value*s in the braces.

Two advantages of this type of declaration and initialization are that it is unnecessary to count the number of array elements, and, should more elements be added to the array during program modification, it is unnecessary to change the declared number of elements (since it is not included in the declaration). A disadvantage is that it is not readily apparent to a programmer how many elements are in the array. This can lead to out-of-range errors. Therefore, in this text, when initializing arrays in a declaration, we will use primarily the first method described.

Other methods of initializing arrays. We can declare an array first, and then read the array element values from the keyboard. For example, the statements

```
double x[2];
cin >> x[0] >> x[1];
```

initialize the array elements `x[0]` and `x[1]` with the values entered by the user.

We also can declare the array first, and then use an assignment statement to initialize the array elements one by one in a loop. For example, the statements

```
double y[10];
for (i = 0; i < 10, i++)
     {
     y[i] = i * 100.0;
     }
```

initialize array elements `y[0]` through `y[9]` to be 0.00 through 900.00 in increments of 100.00. Note that, in this `for` loop, the array subscript (`i`) has gone from 0 to 9 (because when `i` = 10, the conditional `i < 10` is false). This is a simple example of array subscript manipulation in a loop. By changing the subscript, we assign a value to a different array element each time through the loop.

Another way to write this `for` loop is

```
for (i = 0; i <= 9, i++)

     {
     y[i] = i * 100.0;
     }
```

Here, the test expression is `i <= 9` not `i < 10`. Check with your instructor for the preferred method for writing these loops. Some programmers prefer the second method because it clearly shows that only 0–9 are valid array indices. Despite this shortcoming, for most cases we use the first method for writing for loops. However, we recommend that you not forget that the largest valid array index is one less than the declared size.

Remember, in C++ we must initialize each element of an array individually. Also, if we want to modify an entire array, we must modify it element by element. It is common to use loops to initialize and modify arrays.

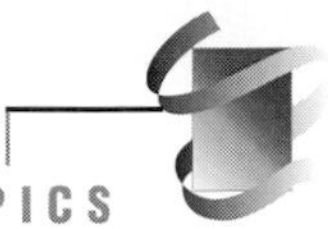

LESSON 9.3 INPUT/OUTPUT AND CALCULATIONS

TOPICS

- Reading arrays from files
- Printing arrays in a neat table
- The `eof()` function
- Using arrays in arithmetic statements
- Using arrays in loops

QUESTIONS YOU SHOULD ATTEMPT TO ANSWER

1. Why is `eof()` called using `infile1.eof()`?
2. How many times does the first `for` loop execute?
3. Why must `sum_x` be initialized to 0 and `prod_y` be initialized to 1?

For many practical problems, arrays have very large numbers of elements. Therefore, most commonly, array values come from files not the keyboard. In this lesson, we illustrate how to read arrays from files and perform some simple array calculations. The program is broken into three sections.

Section 1—Reading from file, number of elements unknown. Sometimes only array element values and nothing else are contained in a file. When we write a program, we usually do not know how many array values are in the file we want to read. Typically, we will want to read the entire array, but not crash the program by attempting to read past the end of the file. C++ helps a programmer do this by providing a function called `eof()` which gets its name from the end-of-file initials. This function returns 0 if the end of file has not yet been encountered and 1 if it has been. In Section 1 of this program we call `eof()` while we are reading a file and stop attempting to read the file when `eof()` returns 1. The loop control variable (`i`) counts the number of times we attempt to read the file and when the loop is finished we use the value of `i` to compute the number of elements (`num_elem`) in the array. Once `num_elem` has a value, we use it to print the array (we could also use it to perform other array manipulations).

Section 2—Reading from file, number of elements included. Other times, a file has information about the array within it. The first value of our second input file is the number of values in the file's arrays. In Section 2 of this program, the first value is read and stored in `num_elem`, and then `num_elem` is used in reading and printing the arrays and performing array calculations. In essence, a program needs to know the number of values in an array in order to work efficiently with the array. Two ways a program determines the number of array values are illustrated in Sections 1 and 2 of this program. A third way is presented in the Description.

Section 3—Simple array calculations. We perform two simple array calculations in Section 3. The first is summing the array elements and the second is finding the total product of the array elements. Both are performed in a loop over the number of elements, and both require a value being initialized before the loop.

Read the program, and observe how `eof()` is used in Section 1, how the number of elements is read and used in Section 2, and how the elements are summed and multiplied in Section 3.

Source Code

```
#include <iostream>
#include <fstream>
#include <iomanip>
using namespace std;

int main ( )
{
        int i, k, num_elem;
        double sum_x, prod_y, x[20], y[20];
        ifstream infile1 ("C:\\L9_3A.DAT");
        ifstream infile2 ("C:\\L9_3B.DAT");

        cout << "**********************************************" << endl;
        cout << "Section 1 - Reading from file, number of elements unknown" << endl;
        cout << "**********************************************" << endl;

        k = infile1.eof();
        cout << "k=" << k << endl;
        cout << " x[i]  y[i]" << endl;

        for (i = 0; !infile1.eof (); i++)
            {
            infile1 >> x[i];
            infile1 >> y[i];
            }

        num_elem = i - 1;

        for (i = 0; i < num_elem; i++)
            {
            cout << setw (6) << x[i]<< setw (7)<< y[i]<< endl;
            }

        k = infile1.eof ();
        cout << "k=" << k << endl;
```

Declaring two arrays of `double`s. The size (20) is set by the programmer to be greater than the number of lines in the file. It is better to use a `const int` type value to size this array. For simplicity we have used an ordinary integer constant.

Opening two input files. The first file contains two arrays with an unknown number of elements. The second file contains the number of elements and the arrays.

Begin Section 1.

We can call the `eof()` (meaning end-of-file) function using the `infile1` object and dot operator. The empty parentheses mean that no arguments are passed to the function. The function returns 0 (false), meaning the end of file has not been encountered at this point. The value of `k` is printed as 0.

Arrays are typically printed in table style. The table headings should be printed before the loop that prints the array values.

The loop test expression. The `eof()` function returns 1 when the end of file is encountered (note that !1 is 0 which terminates the loop).

Reading two array values from the file.

We can calculate the number of array elements using the last value of `i` from the `for` loop. We can then use the number of array elements in the test expression in a `for` loop that prints the array values or does other array calculations.

Printing the array in a neat table. The `setw` manipulators are needed to make the spacing correct.

The value of `k` is now printed to be 1 (true) because the end of file has been encountered since all the array has been read.

```
        cout << "***********************************************" << endl;
        cout << "Section 2 - Reading from file, number of elements "
                "included" << endl;
        cout << "***********************************************" << endl;
        cout << "  x[i]    y[i]" << endl;

        infile2 >> num_elem;
        for (i = 0; i < num_elem; i++)
                {
                infile2 >> x[i];
                infile2 >> y[i];
                }

        for (i = 0; i < num_elem; i++)
                {
                cout << setw (6) << x[i] << setw (7) << y[i] << endl;
                }
        cout << "******************************" << endl;
        cout << "Section 3 - Simple array calculations" << endl;
        cout << "******************************" << endl;

        sum_x = 0;
        prod_y = 1;

        for (i = 0; i < num_elem; i++)
                {
                sum_x += x [i];
                prod_y *= y[i];
                }

        cout << "The sum of all x = " << sum_x << endl;
        cout << "The product of all y = " << prod_y << endl;

        infile1.close ();
        infile2.close ();
}
```

Begin Section 2.

The first number in the second file is the number of array elements. We read that number with a separate statement. Then we use the number in a `for` loop to read the rest of the file.

Reading and printing the array elements. Since `x[]` and `y[]` are the array names, we are reading in values that overwrite the previous values.

Begin Section 3.

To sum all the elements of an array, we start by initializing a variable to 0.

To find the product of all the elements of an array, we start by initializing a variable to 1.

The `sum_x` variable begins at 0. Each time through the loop, the value of an array element is added to `sum_x`. When the loop ends, `sum_x` holds the sum of all the elements.

The `prod_y` variable begins at 1. Each time through the loop, the value of an array element is multiplied by `prod_y`. When the loop ends, `prod_y` holds the product of all the elements.

Closing the input files.

Input File L9_3A.DAT

```
3 4
6 8
9 12
```

This input file has only the values of the array elements. The first value in each row is `x` and the second is `y`.

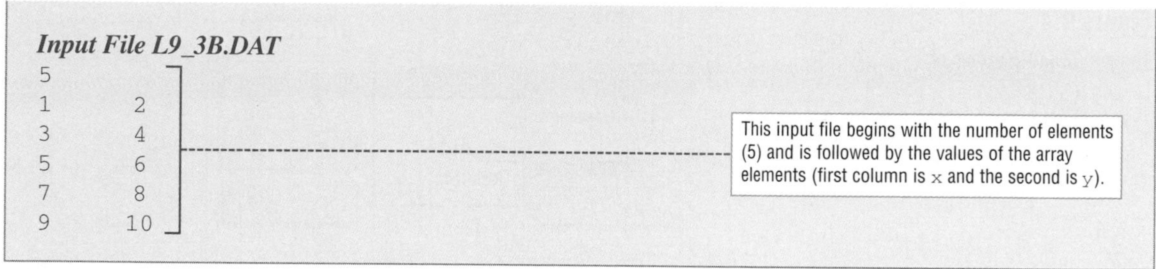

Input File L9_3B.DAT

```
5
1    2
3    4
5    6
7    8
9    10
```

This input file begins with the number of elements (5) and is followed by the values of the array elements (first column is `x` and the second is `y`).

Output

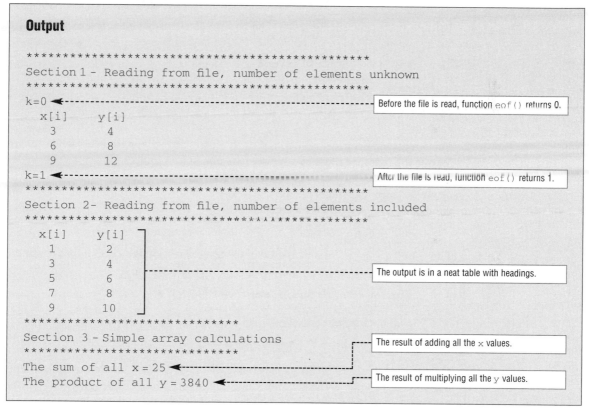

```
**********************************************
Section 1 - Reading from file, number of elements unknown
**********************************************
k=0
  x[i]    y[i]
    3       4
    6       8
    9      12
k=1
**********************************************
Section 2- Reading from file, number of elements included
**********************************************
  x[i]    y[i]
    1       2
    3       4
    5       6
    7       8
    9      10
****************************
Section 3 - Simple array calculations
****************************
The sum of all x = 25
The product of all y = 3840
```

Before the file is read, function `eof()` returns 0.

After the file is read, function `eof()` returns 1.

The output is in a neat table with headings.

The result of adding all the `x` values.

The result of multiplying all the `y` values.

Description

File input—number of array elements unknown. When we do not know the number of array elements in a file (but can assume that it is more than one less than the declared array size), we simply keep reading the file in a loop until the end of file is encountered. This is determined with the `eof()` function which is a member of the `ios` class. Since it is a member function, it must be called using an object and a dot operator. For instance,

```
infile1.eof ();
```

calls `eof()` to determine if the file associated with object `infile1` has been completely read. The `eof()` function returns 0 (false—end of file not encountered) or

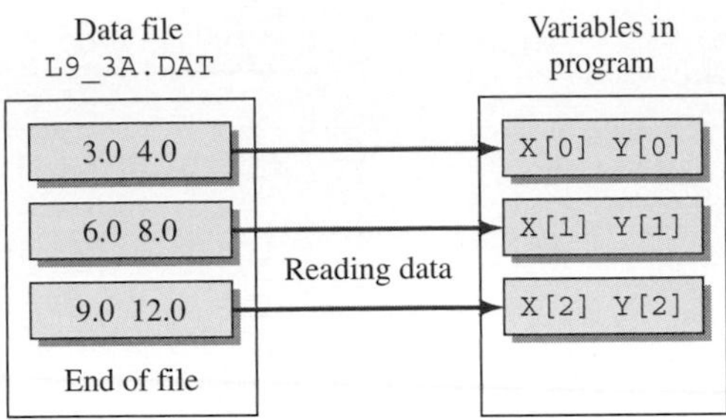

Figure 9.4

The first x and y arrays of Lesson 9.3's program.

1 (true—end of file encountered). The return value is used in the test expression for the for loop

```
for (i = 0; !infile1.eof (); i++)
        {
        infile1 >> x[i];
        infile1 >> y[i];
        }
```

The not (!) operator reverses the return result so that the loop executes while eof() returns 0. Figure 9.4 illustrates how data is transferred from the file.

After executing this loop, the value of i is one more than the number of array elements since it attempts to read x[] and encounters the end of file. As a result the number of array elements is computed with

```
num_elem = i - 1;
```

The value of num_elem is then used in the test expression for a for loop to print the array elements:

```
for (i = 0; i < num_elem; i++)
        {
        cout << setw (6) << x[i] << setw (7) << y[i] << endl;
        }
```

File input—number of array elements included. If the first line of the file contains the number of array elements, this value can be used to read the array without the need for eof(). The first line of the file is read separately, and the value is stored in the variable num_elem and used in the loop test expression:

```
infile2 >> num_elem;
for (i = 0; i < num_elem; i++)
        {
        infile2 >> x[i];
        infile2 >> y[i];
        }
```

The value of num_elem is also used in the test expression for the loop that prints the array, as shown in this lesson's program.

Finding the sum and product of all the array elements. When summing all the elements of an array, a variable (called sum_x for this lesson's program) is initialized to 0. This variable is used to store the sum, as the sum is calculated element by

TABLE 9.2 — Tracing the calculation loop in Lesson 9.3's program

Statement	i	x[i]	y[i]	sum_x	prod_y
Before loop	—	x[] = 1,3,5,7,9	y[] = 2,4,6,8,10	0	1
sum_x += x[i];	0	x[0] = 1		0 + 1 = 1	
prod_y *= y[i];			y[0] = 2		1 * 2 = 2
sum_x += x[i];	1	x[1] = 3		1 + 3 = 4	
prod_y *= y[i];			y[1] = 4		2 * 4 = 8
sum_x += x[i];	2	x[2] = 5		4 + 5 = 9	
prod_y *= y[i];			y[2] = 6		8 * 6 = 48
sum_x += x[i];	3	x[3] = 7		9 + 7 = 16	
prod_y *= y[i];			y[3] = 8		48 * 8 = 384
sum_x += x[i];	4	x[4] = 9		16 + 9 = 25	
prod_y *= y[i];			y[4] = 10		384 * 10 = 3840

element. When finding the product of all the elements of an array, a variable (called prod_y for this lesson's program) is initialized to 1. This variable is used to store the product, as the product is calculated element by element.

A loop over the number of elements calculates the sum and product. The code is given in the lesson's program. We can trace the code line by line as we have done earlier with a table (Table 9.2) that has the statements in the first column (repeated five times because the loop executes five times) and the variable values *after* the statement has been executed in the other columns. Because it is a simple loop, we have omitted the test and increment expressions from the table and have only the loop body. To understand the loop, follow the table line by line and reason out how sum_x and prod_y are calculated. Note that the subscript i increments each time through the loop. Therefore, the x[i] and y[i] also change each time through the loop. Recall that sum_x += x[i] is the same as sum_x = sum_x + x[i], and prod_y *= y[i] is the same as prod_y = prod_y * y[i]. This means that the value of sum_x from the previous loop iteration is used to calculate sum_x for the current iteration, and prod_y from the previous iteration is used to calculate prod_y on the current iteration.

After executing the loop, it can be seen that sum_x and prod_y are indeed the sum and products of the x[] and y[] array elements, respectively. In this table, we explicitly write out x[0]=, x[1]=, and the other x and y values to emphasize that to follow the table, you must change the subscripts on the array elements x[i] and y[i] each time through the loop. We also show the values used to calculate sum_x and prod_y. On future tables, we do not show such explicit detail. We show only numbers in the table to keep the look of the table clean. Remember, the array subscript value determines which array element is being referenced. When you examine this type of table, pay close attention to the array subscript values.

File input—sentinel value separating data groups. Not shown in this lesson's program, is the situation of a particular predefined value contained in a file that indicates the end of the data group. The value is predefined to be significantly different from all the others in the data. For instance, consider data whose values represent the number of vehicles passing through an intersection each day. A good value indicating the end of a group is −1 because all the other array values must be positive (it makes no sense to have a negative number of vehicles passing through an intersection). A file containing such data may look like:

```
230 349 76 -1
```

This data indicates that three days of information are included. The last value in the file is the value indicating no more data. The purpose of the sentinel is to stop the loop execution.

Sometimes several data groups can be together in a file each separated by a sentinel. For instance, this list has three data groups of different length each ended by −1

```
230 349 76 -1 237 748 26 39 7 -1 43 58 -1
```

Here, each data group may represent a different intersection.

How do we read such a list of arrays? As we read the data value by value, we check to see if a value is −1. If it is, we stop reading for that group. Each group can be stored in a different array (for instance the first group is `x[]` and the second is `y[]`).

For example, assume that before reading a data file all elements of all arrays in a particular program are initialized to 0, and that all arrays are declared to have a more than adequate size. You might think that the following loop, which is similar to other loops we have written, would read the values and store them in the first array

```
for (i = 0; vehicles_per_day[i] != -1; i++)
          {
          infile >> vehicles_per_day[i];
          }
```

However, if we trace the loop in a table, we can see that it does not! Table 9.3 traces the loop. We have included the test and increment expressions in the table because it is not a simple loop.

Note that the test expression is always true because the value of `vehicles_per_day[i]` (from the previous loop iteration) is 0 when the test expression is evaluated. Rather than stopping at the −1 sentinel value, this loop continues reading the 237 which is into the next array. We do not want this. We want the loop to stop executing when it encounters the −1.

Why is the test expression true each time it is tested? Recall how `for` loops execute (see Chapter 6). First the test expression is evaluated, second the loop body is executed, and third the increment expression is executed. The sequence for this loop then is:

```
vehicles_per_day[i] != -1;             Test expression
infile >> vehicles_per_day[i];         Loop body
i++;                                   Increment expression
```

The reason the loop reads into the second array is that the test expression is evaluated in the loop *before* the new array value is read. So, the test expression evaluates the *initialized* array values (which are all 0) and not the *file* array values. This causes the

TABLE 9.3 — Using a `for` loop to read this data from a file: 230 349 76 −1 237 748 26 39 7 −1 43 58 −1

Statement	Test expression	i	vehicles_per_day[i]
Before loop		—	vehicles_per_day[0 to 10] = 0
i = 0;		0	0

vehicles_per_day[i] != -1;
infile >> vehicles_per_day[i];
i++;
	vehicles_per_day[0] = 0, therefore True	1	vehicles_per_day[0] = 230
			0

vehicles_per_day[i] != -1;
infile >> vehicles_per_day[i];
i++;
	vehicles_per_day[1] = 0, therefore True	2	vehicles_per_day[1] = 349
			0

vehicles_per_day[i] != -1;
infile >> vehicles_per_day[i];
i++;
	vehicles_per_day[2] = 0, therefore True	3	vehicles_per_day[2] = 76
			0

vehicles_per_day[i] != -1;
infile >> vehicles_per_day[i];
i++;
	vehicles_per_day[3] = 0, therefore True	4	vehicles_per_day[3] = -1
			0

vehicles_per_day[i] != -1;
infile >> vehicles_per_day[i];
i++;
	vehicles_per_day[4] = 0, therefore True	5	vehicles_per_day[4] = 237
			0

test expression to be true each iteration. We want the test expression to be false on the iteration that the program reads −1.

To correct the situation and evaluate the test expression immediately after reading the file, we could use a `do-while` loop. Such a loop would be

```
i = 0;
do
        {
        infile >> vehicles_per_day[i];
        }
        while (vehicles_per_day[i++] != -1);
```

This works because the test expression is evaluated immediately after the file is read. Remember that the use of `i++` in the test expression is equivalent to the following two statements

```
vehicles_per_day[i] != -1;
i++;
```

because when `++` is after (not before) `i`, first the expression is evaluated using `i`, and then `i` is incremented.

Table 9.4 traces the `do-while` loop. Note that the test expression becomes false and the loop is terminated when the −1 is read. This is the desired behavior.

Note that reading the sentinel value of −1 causes the loop to terminate. This is the correct behavior for this loop.

In summary, loops are used frequently with arrays. However, loops can be tricky. You must trace your loops carefully to make sure they do what you want them to do.

TABLE 9.4 — `do-while` loop that can read data with sentinels separating the data groups

Statement	Test expression	i	`vehicles_per_day[i]`
Before loop		—	`vehicles_per_day[`0 to 10`]` = 0
`i = 0;`		0	0
`infile >> vehicles_per_day[i];`			230
`vehicles_per_day[i] != -1;`	True		
`i++;`		1	0
`infile >> vehicles_per_day[i];`			349
`vehicles_per_day[i] != -1;`	True		
`i++;`		2	0
`infile >> vehicles_per_day[i];`			76
`vehicles_per_day[i] != -1;`	True		
`i++;`		3	0
`infile >> vehicles_per_day[i];`			−1
`vehicles_per_day[i] != -1;`	False – loop terminates		

LESSON 9.4 1-D ARRAYS AND FUNCTIONS

TOPICS

- Passing array addresses to functions
- Passing array addresses to functions with a restriction

QUESTION YOU SHOULD ATTEMPT TO ANSWER

1. Why are we able to print out the values of the `c[ ]` array in `function3`?

For large arrays, if we were to pass each value to a function, we would use a considerable amount of memory. Why? Because, as you may recall, each function has its own region of memory for storing its own values. If we were to pass array values to functions, each function that uses a large array would store a copy of that array, which is wasteful.

Rather than passing array *values* to a function, we pass the *address* of the first element of an array (which we will refer to as the *address of the array*) to a function. Consequently, the region of memory holding a function's values does not have an entire array. It has only a single value, an address.

Function declaration. In a function declaration the syntax for an array address is somewhat odd looking. It consists of a data type and empty brackets. For instance, `double[]` means address of an array of `double` values, and `int[]` means the address of an array of `int` values.

Function call. In a function call an array address is represented quite simply. It consists of the array name with no brackets. For instance, `x` means the address of an array `x[ ]`, and `y` means the address of an array `y[ ]`.

Function header. In a function header, an array address is a combination of the two previous. It consists of the data type, name, and empty brackets. For instance, `double a[ ]` means that within the function we use `a[0]` to represent the first element of an array of `double` and `a[1]` to represent the second element.

Read the program and note the syntax used for passing array addresses to functions. Also note that we can pass an array address with the `const` restriction.

Source Code

```
#include <iostream>
using namespace std;

void function2 (double[], int);
void function3 (const double[], int);

int main ( )
{
     double c[5] = {2.,4.,6.,8.,10.};

     function2(c,5);
     function3(c,5);
}

void function2 (double b[], int num_elem)
{
     int i;
     for (i = 0; i < num_elem; i++) b[i]*= 10.;
}

double function3 (const double d[], int num_elem)
{
     int i;
     cout << "c[ ] is ";
     for (i = 0; i < num_elem; i++) cout << d[i] << " ";
}
```

This indicates that the first argument passed to `function2` is the address of a 1-D array of `double` values.

The `const` means that even though `function3` receives the address of the array, it cannot use that address to modify the contents of the array.

The arguments, `c` without brackets, represent the address of the first element of the `c[ ]` array. The second argument, 5, represents the number of elements of the `c[ ]` array.

In the header, we use `double b[ ]` not just `double[]`. Because the address of `c` was passed to `b`, `b[0]` represents `c[0]` and `b[1]` represents `c[1]` and so forth throughout the array.

This loop modifies each element of the `c[]` array!

In this function, the `const` qualifier for `d[]` in the header means that we cannot modify the array contents. In other words, we cannot use `d[]` on the left side of an assignment statement in this function. This means that the `c[]` array is guaranteed to remain intact after executing this function. This makes this function safe to call if we do not want `c[]` to be accidentally modified.

Output

```
c[ ] is 20 40 60 80 100
```

Description

Passing array information to a function. C++ needs three pieces of information to manipulate array data within a function:

1. The size of a single array element (indicated by the data type—`int`, `double`, or other—followed by brackets in the function declaration).
2. The address of the array (indicated by an array name in the function call).
3. A location to store the array address (indicated by an identifier followed by brackets in the function header).

With this knowledge, C++ can move element to element within memory. For instance, the declaration, call, and header for `function2` in this lesson's program are:

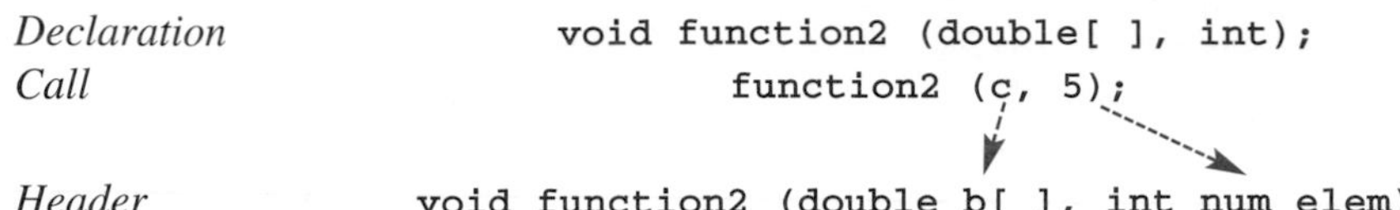

Declaration void function2 (double[ ], int);
Call function2 (c, 5);
Header void function2 (double b[ ], int num_elem)

The function declaration indicates the array data type is `double`. The function call indicates the array name is `c` (saying that the address of `c[]` in `main` is passed to `function2`). The function header indicates that within `function2`, the identifier `b` is used to work with the array elements.

That is all that C++ needs to work with an array in a function. However, a programmer needs one more piece of information, and that is the number of elements in the array. C++ does not need this because it, unfortunately, moves happily past the end of an array. So, if we want to make sure that C++ does not do this, we need another argument, the number of array elements. Therefore, the second argument in `function2` is the integer `num_elem` which is passed the value 5 in the function call.

The table of values for `main` and `function2` for this lesson's program is shown in Fig. 9.5. Note that the memory region for `function2` does *not* contain an array! The actual element values are contained in `main`'s memory region. In `function2` is only the address of the beginning of that region (FFF2) transferred from `c` to `b`. Within `function2`, C++ allows us to access memory cells beyond FFF2 using 1-D array notation (that is, using brackets after the identifier `b`) because we have used

```
double b[]
```

in the `function2` header. Remember to use empty brackets in your function declarations and headers when passing array information to functions.

Also remember to pass the number of array elements as a separate argument. It is not meaningful to put the number of elements in the brackets adjacent to the array

Figure 9.5

Table of values showing transfer of address from `main` to `function2`.

In `main`

Name	Type	Address	Value
`c`	Array of `double`, size = 5	FFF2	2
			4
			6
			8
			10

In `function2`

Name	Type	Address	Value
`b`	Address of `double`	FFDE	FFF2
`num_elem`	`int`	FFCE	5
`i`	`int`	FFBE	0

name. In other words, we cannot transfer the information that function2 is to receive five elements by writing the header as

```
void function2 (double b[5])
```

C++ will not indicate an error if this is done, but it will *not* pass the information to function2 that b[] has only five elements.

We do not need to use the "address of" (&) operator to pass the address of an array to a function (like &c in the function calls for this lesson's program). This is because, in C++, the address of the first element of an array is indicated by the array name with no brackets following it. Therefore, the symbol, c, alone indicates the address of the first element of the c[] array. We put this in the function call.

In general, the form for a declaration, call, and header for a function working with a 1-D array is:

```
Declaration        rtype function (type [ ], int);
Call               function (array, num);

Header       rtype function (type b[ ], int num_elem)
```

where *rtype* is the function return type, *function* is the function name, *type* is the type of values stored in the array, *array* is the array name in the calling function, *num* is the number of array elements, *b* is the identifier used to represent the array within the function, and *num_elem* is used to represent the number of array elements in the function. Note that the second argument is type int. For very large arrays, this may need to be long int or unsigned long int. Also, C++ does allow the variable *b* to be used in the function declaration in the form *type b[ ]*. Using this form is simply a matter of preference.

The const qualifier is used to preserve the contents of the array. It is inserted prior to the array data type. The form is:

```
Declaration        rtype function (const type[ ], int);
Call               function (array, num);

Header       rtype function (const type b[ ], int num_elem)
```

In this lesson's program, function3 used the const qualifier. This was appropriate because the function simply printed the array values; it did not modify them. If we use const and attempt to modify an array's contents either through assignment statements or reading input values, C++ will indicate an error on compilation. Although a function can execute successfully without const, it is good practice to use const whenever a function does not have the purpose of modifying an array.

C++ also allows the pointer notation * (not discussed yet in this text) to be used in place of brackets. So another acceptable form is:

```
Declaration        rtype function (type*, int);
Call               function (array, num);

Header       rtype function (type* b, int num_elem)
```

Using such notation does not change the function body. In other words, brackets can still be used in a function body even though the transfer of address information in the argument list is done with * and not brackets [ ]. (C++ allows this, and we describe the process in more detail in Chapter 11.) Note that using *type** indicates that b represents an address. In this text, we use brackets for numeric arrays (Chapters 9 and 10), and * for character arrays (Chapter 12). These are the common usages.

Manipulating arrays within a function. Within a function, we use array notation (brackets) to operate element by element on arrays in loops, and use the number of elements to control the loops. For instance, in function1, the body

```
for (i = 0;   i < num_elem;   i++) b [i] *= 10.;
```

uses array notation with b to access each element of the c[ ] array (because the address of c[ ] was passed to b in the function call). It also uses num_elem in the test expression to control the loop.

The body of function3 has a similar loop to print the c[ ] array values:

```
for (i = 0; i < num_elem; i++) cout << d[i] << "  ";
```

Again, because the const d[] is used in the header for function3, we cannot put d[] on the left side of an assignment statement in function3. If we try, the compiler will indicate an error.

LESSON 9.5 CLASSES WITH ARRAYS AS DATA MEMBERS

TOPICS

- Declaring an array as a data member
- Sizing member arrays

QUESTION YOU SHOULD ATTEMPT TO ANSWER

1. What is the keyword used in creating a size for a data member array?

When arrays are used as private data members of classes, they are automatically made accessible to public class member functions. The public member functions can modify the arrays when necessary.

To size an array and keep everything contained within the class requires special treatment. In this lesson, we show the use of the keyword enum to assist us.

This lesson's program uses a 1-D array (elevation[]) as a data member of a class called Seabed. Each value in the array represents the elevation at a point located on the seabed at a distance from shore as shown in Fig. 9.6. This array, therefore, contains a portion of the topography of the seafloor. In this program, we also illustrate a simple programming technique for finding the minimum value in a 1-D array. The program finds the minimum elevation of the seabed along the line of points.

Read the code and observe that the function members in the class perform all the operations needed on the data members. The main function simply calls all the member functions using the line1 object.

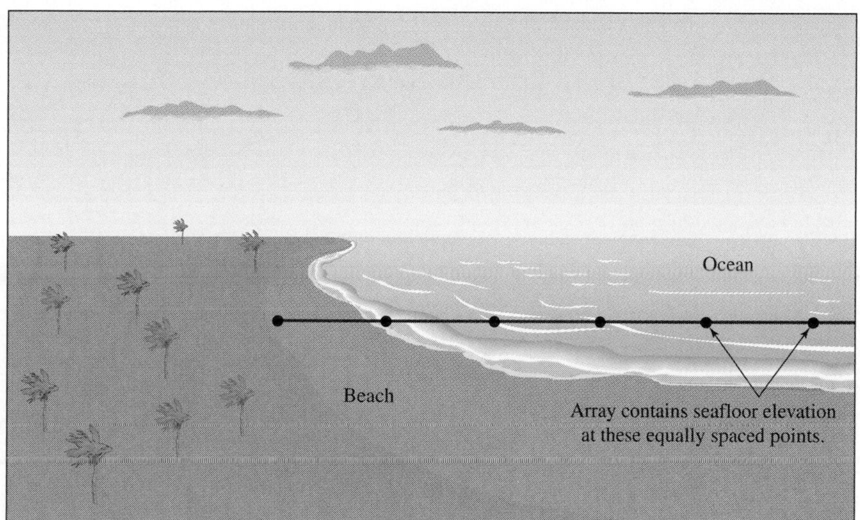
Ocean
Beach
Array contains seafloor elevation at these equally spaced points.

Figure 9.6

Line covering the seabed. The elevation at each of the points is placed in the `elevation[]` array.

Source Code

```
#include <iostream>
#include <fstream>
using namespace std;

class Seabed
{
      private:
            enum {MAX_NUM_PTS = 25};
            double elevation[MAX_NUM_PTS], min_elev;
      public:
            void read_data();
            void calc_min_elev();
            void show_min_elev();
};

void Seabed::read_data()
{
      int i,j;
      ifstream infile("C:\\L9_5.DAT");

      for (i = 0; i < MAX_NUM_PTS; i++)
            {
            infile >> elevation[i];
            }
}
```

The array `elevation[]` is a member of class `Seabed`. The variable `MAX_NUM_PTS` is an enumeration. We are allowed to give an enumeration (within a class definition) a value. In this case, we have given `MAX_NUM_PTS` the value 25.

The minimum elevation is a data member of the class.

Function members of the class. None of the functions need arguments because they work only with data members of the class.

Return type.

Class name and two colons.

Function name.

Using a loop and file input to fill the `elevation[]` array with values. The array is not declared within the function because the function is a member function. All member functions have automatic access to all array data members.

```
void Seabed :: calc_min_elev()
{
      int i,j;
      min_elev = elevation[0];
      for  (i = 0;  i < MAX_NUM_PTS;  i++)
            {
            if  (elevation[i] <= min_elev)   min_elev = elevation[i];
            }
}

void Seabed :: show_min_elev()
{
      cout << "The minimum elevation is:  " << min_elev << endl;
}

int main ( )
{
      Seabed line1;
      line1.read_data();
      line1.calc_min_elev();
      line1.show_min_elev();
}
```

Using a loop to search the array for the minimum value.

Even the simple act of printing the result must be done in a member function because only member functions can access private data members.

Declaring an object of the `Seabed` class.

Using that object to call each member function.

Input file L9_5.DAT

```
-300. -400. -225. -300. -448.
-876. -384. -298. -348. -123.
-789. -487. -109. -564. -626.
-389. -132. -897. -938. -547.
-876. -556. -788. -764. -863.
```

These are 25 elevations stored in the `elevation[]` array.

Output

```
The minimum elevation is: -938
```

Description

Sizing a data member array. Previously we described using `const int` global variables to size arrays. However, we do not want to use global variables with classes because such a variable is outside the class and, therefore, violates encapsulation. C++ does not allow us to assign a value to a `const int` within the class definition. Consequently, we use an enumeration. First, we give a general description of enumerations; then we show how to use an enumeration to size data member arrays.

An enumeration is a comma-separated list of identifiers. Each identifier is automatically assigned a constant integer value. The value assigned depends on the order in which an identifier appears in the enumeration list. The keyword enum and a left brace begin the enumeration. For example:

```
enum {sunday = 1, monday, tuesday, wednesday, thursday,
  friday, saturday};
```

This definition assigns the integer constants 1 to identifier sunday, 2 to monday, 3 to tuesday, and so on through all the days. The first identifier, sunday, is explicitly assigned 1, and the others are given successive integers in the order they appear in the list.

Such a list can make code more readable. For instance, we could declare an integer day and assign day = friday, in our code. This has the effect of assigning 6 to day but is much more readable than the assignment day = 6.

In our program, rather than use an entire list, we have a single value:

```
enum {MAX_NUM_PTS = 25};
```

This serves our purpose because we want to assign a single value not an entire list. Such a definition allows us to use MAX_NUM_PTS anywhere in our class, and it is quite convenient for controlling loops in our member functions. Should we decide to change the array size, we need to change only a single number and not all the loop control variables.

Note that C++ does not allow us to use

```
const int MAX_NUM_PTS = 25;
```

in our class definition because assignment of values to ordinary data should take place within the member functions. Therefore, we need to use an enumeration to create MAX_NUM_PTS.

This is not meant to be a complete description of enumerations; however, it serves our purposes for the time being. One other comment should be made. The late 1990s update of the C++ standard does allow the form

```
static const int MAX_NUM_PTS = 25;
```

in a class definition. However, a number of compilers still do not accept this form; therefore, we show the enumeration for sizing arrays. You can check your compiler. If it accepts the static const int form, you should use it.

Finding the minimum in the array. The function calc_min_elev() is used to find the minimum elevation value in the array. The calculation begins by assigning the value of the first array element to the variable min_elev. This variable keeps track of the minimum elevation.

```
min_elev = elevation[0];
```

Note that elevation[0] is not necessarily the smallest value in the array. Making this assignment simply begins the process of searching for the mininum.

A loop looks at every value in the array and compares it to min_elev. Any value that is less than min_elev becomes the new minimum. Here is the comparison statement:

```
if (elevation [i]<= min_elev) min_elev = elevation [i];
```

Each array value is compared to the minimum using this statement in a loop. If the current `elevation[]` value is less than the `min_elev`, the current `elevation[]` becomes the new `min_elev`. After executing the loop, `min_elev` holds the minimum elevation in the array.

LESSON 9.6 ARRAYS OF OBJECTS

TOPICS

- Declaring arrays of objects
- Calling functions with an array element

QUESTION YOU SHOULD ATTEMPT TO ANSWER

1. What is the initial velocity for the second object?

We can create arrays of objects in a manner similar to creating arrays of `int` or `double`. This lesson's program defines a `Vehicle` class and calculates the distance a vehicle would travel given an initial velocity, acceleration, and travel time period using the familiar equation from physics $s = v_0 t + 0.5at^2$ (where $s =$ distance travelled, $v_0 =$ initial velocity, $a =$ acceleration, $t =$ time).

An array of three objects of the `Vehicle` class is declared. This array represents three vehicles. Read the program and see how arrays of objects are used. Note, in particular, how the member functions are called from the `main` function.

Source Code

```
#include <iostream>
using namespace std;

class Vehicle
{
      private:
            double vo, a, t, distance;
      public:
            void set_data(double, double, double);
            void calc_distance();
            void show_distance();
};

void Vehicle :: set_data(double veloc, double accel, double time)
{
      vo = veloc;
      a = accel;
      t = time;
}

void Vehicle :: calc_distance()
{
      distance = vo * t + 0.5 * a * t * t;
}
```

Each vehicle has the characteristics of initial velocity, acceleration, travel time, and distance. Therefore, these are all private data members.

The `set_data` function initializes three data members (all except `distance`, which is calculated by function `calc_distance`).

We have member functions for basic operations. Here, `calc_distance` and `show_distance` calculate and display the distance traveled by a vehicle.

Three data members are initialized with values passed through the argument list.

A standard physics equation is used to calculate the travel distance.

```
void Vehicle :: show_distance()
{
      cout << "The distance is " << distance << endl;   <---- The distance is displayed.
}

int main ( )
{
      int i;
      Vehicle truck[3];   <---- Declaring an array of three objects.

      truck[0].set_data(50,2,3);
      truck[1].set_data(30,1,1);
      truck[2].set_data(20,4,5);
```

We call the `set_data()` function using an array element and the dot operator. The arguments serve as initial values for data members.

```
      for(i = 0; i < 3; i++)
            {
            truck[i].calc_distance();
            truck[i].show_distance();
            }
}
```

A loop can be used to call the function members. Each time through the loop, a different object is used to call the functions and, therefore, different data is manipulated.

Output

```
The distance is 159.
The distance is 30.5.
The distance is 150.
```

Description

Creating arrays of objects. An array of objects is declared using the class name, object name, and brackets enclosing an integer constant. For instance, in this lesson's program, the declaration

```
Vehicle truck[3];
```

declares an array of three objects, `truck[0]`, `truck[1]`, and `truck[2]` of class `Vehicle`. Each of these objects holds all the data members. The table created, in concept, by C++ is shown in Fig. 9.7.

To call a member function with an object that is part of an array, we need to use the object, dot operator, and function name. For example,

```
truck[0] . set_data (50, 2, 3);
```

calls the `set_data()` function with the `truck[0]` object. This function initializes

Figure 9.7

Table illustrating array of objects.

Name	Type		Address	Value
b	Array of Vehicle			
truck[0]	vo	double	FFDE	50
	a	double	FFDD	2
	t	double	FFE5	3
	distance	double	FFED	
truck[1]	vo	double	FFCE	30
	a	double	FFCD	1
	t	double	FFD5	1
	distance	double	FFDD	
truck[2]	vo	double	FFBE	20
	a	double	FFBD	4
	t	double	FFC5	5
	distance	double	FFCD	

the vo, a, and t data members. Calling the function with the truck[0] object, initializes the vo, a, and t data members for that object.

Creating arrays of objects makes it easy to use loops to perform manipulations. For instance, the loop

```
for (i = 0; i < 3; i++)
        {
        truck[i].calc_distance ();
        truck[i].show_distance ();
        }
```

calls the calc_distance() and show_distance() functions for each of the three objects in the truck[] array.

Uses of arrays of objects. Arrays of objects are superior to arrays of int or double when multiple pieces of information are linked. For instance, suppose we have measured the water pressure in a long pipe at various distances from a base station, and the following distance-pressure measurements are in a file (with the first column being distance and the second column being pressure):

```
12        87
7         43
10        22
5         56
29        89
3         34
0         10
14        3
8         65
```

Note that the data are in the file in random order. Envision that our goal is to rearrange and print these values in order of increasing distance (column 1).

A very efficient way to do this is to create a class with data members of distance and pressure:

```
class Pipe_pressure
{
        private:
                double distance, pressure;
        public:
                ...
}
```

Then an array of objects could be declared:

```
Pipe_pressure measurement[9];
```

In doing so we create an array of connected members that can be illustrated as shown in Fig. 9.8.

We can rearrange the data (using a sorting method described in Application Example 9.4) in increasing order according to the distance. The array is modified as shown in Fig. 9.9.

You should notice that in rearranging the first column of the array, the second column of the array is rearranged also, maintaining the correspondence between the

measurement [i]	distance (m)	pressure (kPa)
i = 0	12	87
1	7	43
2	10	22
3	5	56
4	29	89
5	3	34
6	0	10
7	14	3
8	8	65

Figure 9.8

Array of objects with two data members.

measurement [i]	distance (m)	pressure (kPa)
i = 0	0	10
1	3	34
2	5	56
3	7	43
4	8	65
5	10	22
6	12	87
7	14	3
8	29	89

Figure 9.9

The array of objects from Fig. 9.8 rearranged.

distance and pressure data. This would not have happened had we not used an array of objects.

For instance, if we had put the distance into an ordinary `double` array, `distance[9]`, and the pressure into another ordinary `double` array, `pressure[9]`, then upon rearranging the `distance[ ]` array, we would not have automatically rearranged the `pressure[ ]` array. This would eliminate the distance-pressure correspondence. Of course, we could write code to rearrange the `pressure[ ]` array, however it is clearly much more efficient to use an array of objects and have it done automatically.

Another useful example of using arrays of objects is the storage of an address book. Names, addresses, and telephone numbers of clients can be stored in an array of objects of a `Client` class. Then if we need to perform manipulations like rearranging the objects according to alphabetical by name, the addresses and telephone numbers are automatically also rearranged. (Note: to create such an array requires the storage and manipulation of character strings that are covered in Chapter 12).

In Chapter 14, we will see other examples of arrays of objects.

Copying object array elements. We can copy the data members of one object array element to another using an assignment statement. For instance, if the following statement were used in this lesson's program

```
truck[1] = truck[0];
```

all the data member values of `truck[0]` would be copied into the memory reserved for `truck[1]`.

APPLICATION EXAMPLE 9.1 EVALUATING VOLTAGE MEASUREMENT DATA

TOPICS

- 1-D array manipulation
- Linear interpolation
- Numerical method example

Problem Statement

Voltage measurements have been made for an electronic circuit in sequence at various times. However, after collecting the data, it is desired to know the voltage at a time that is different from the times at which the data were collected. Write a program that will read the collected voltage data, the corresponding times, and the time at which the voltage is desired. Make the program compute the desired voltage based on a linear interpolation using the nearest measured values. Have the program read the time and voltage data from a file, the desired time from the keyboard, and print the interpolated voltage to the screen.

Solution

RELEVANT EQUATIONS

Interpolating linearly between two given points, (x_1, y_1) and (x_2, y_2), means drawing a straight line connecting the points and obtaining a y value on that line for a given x value (between the x values of the two endpoints). Figure 9.10 illustrates this.

The slope of the line, m, is:

$$m = \frac{(y_2 - y_1)}{(x_2 - x_1)} \tag{9.1}$$

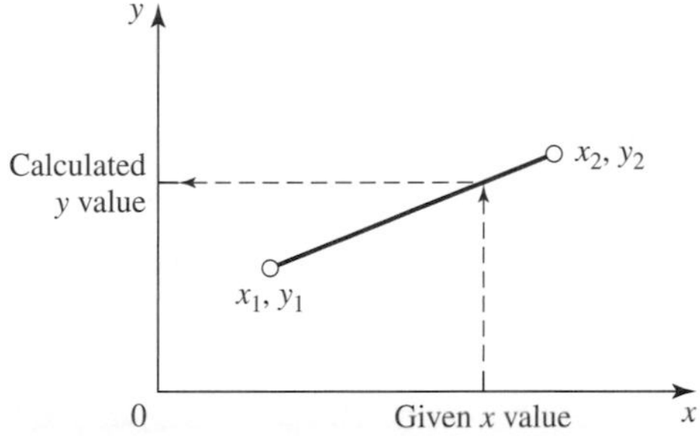

Figure 9.10

Linear interpolation between two points.

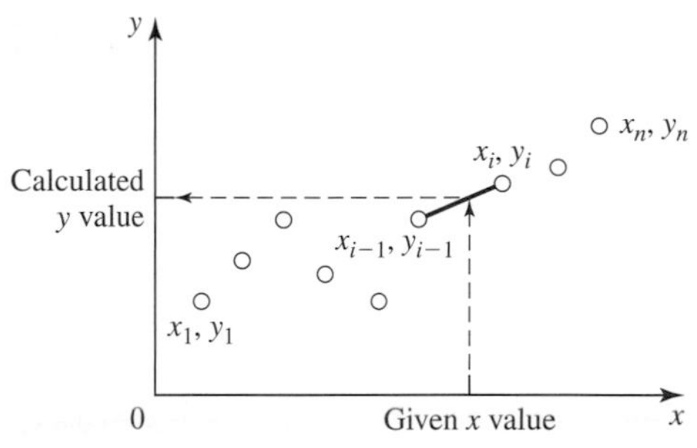

Figure 9.11

Graph of *n* data points with interpolation between points *i* – 1 and *i*.

The x distance from x_1 to the given x value is $(x_{value} - x_1)$. So, the calculated y value is

$$y_{value} = \frac{(y_2 - y_1)}{(x_2 - x_1)}(x_{value} - x_1) + y_1 \tag{9.2}$$

where x_{value} is the given x value and y_{value} is the calculated y value. If we have a set of n data points as shown in Fig. 9.11 and are interested in interpolating between points $(i - 1)$ and i, then the equation becomes

$$y_{value} = \frac{(y_i - y_{i-1})}{(x_i - x_{i-1})}(x_{value} - x_{i-1}) + y_{i-1} \tag{9.3}$$

We will use this equation in our source code.

SPECIFIC EXAMPLE

Suppose we have the measured voltages and times that follow and want to estimate the voltage at 25 milliseconds.

Data point	Time (milliseconds)	Voltage (millivolts)
0	0	23
1	5	78
2	7	89
3	9	−12
4	14	0
5	19	90
6	29	18
7	34	−23
8	37	76
9	45	98

At 25 milliseconds, we realize that we are between data points 5 and 6. Using Eqn. (9.3) with $(i - 1) = 5$ and $i = 6$, we have

$$y_{value} = \frac{(y_6 - y_5)}{(x_6 - x_5)}(x_{value} - x_5) + y_5 = \frac{(18 - 90)}{(29 - 19)}(25 - 19) + 90 = 46.8$$

Therefore, our estimate of the voltage at 25 milliseconds is 46.8 millivolts.

ALGORITHM AND CODE SEGMENTS

We follow these steps:

1. Read all the data point *x* and *y* coordinates.
2. Read the *x* value for which the *y* value is to be calculated.
3. Determine the data point numbers immediately to the left and right of the *x* value specified.
4. Interpolate using Eqn. (9.3).
5. Print the results.

We can generate the source code from this algorithm by breaking down each task and writing each step somewhat individually. Steps 2 and 5 are straightforward. Next we describe steps 1, 3, and 4.

STEP 1. READ ALL DATA POINT x AND y COORDINATES

For instance, using one-dimensional arrays of type `double`, if we call the time `x[]` and the voltage `y[]`, the following loop reads 10 data points from the data file specified by `infile`:

```
for (i = 0; i < 10; i++)     infile >> x[i] >> y[i];
```

Note that using C++'s array data structure, the first data point has an array index of 0, so the preceding loop goes from 0 to 9 (because 9 is the last integer that is less than 10).

STEP 3. DETERMINE DATA POINT NUMBERS IMMEDIATELY TO LEFT AND RIGHT OF x VALUE SPECIFIED

The following loop determines the data point number immediately to the right of the given `x` value.

```
i = 0;
while (x_value > x[i]) i++;
```

After completing this loop, the value of `i` is equal to the index of the `x[]` array value immediately to the right of the given `x_value`. To verify this, we tabulate the values for each step of the loop for the specific example (with `x_value` = 25 and `x[ ]` = 0, 5, 7, 9, 14, 19, 29, 34, 37, 45):

Statement	Test expression and comments	`i`	`x_value`	`x[i]`
Before loop values		0	25	0
`while (x_value > x[i])`	True, 25 > 0, enter loop body			
`i++;`		1		5
`while (x_value > x[i])`	True, 25 > 5, enter loop body			
`i++;`		2		7
`while (x_value > x[i])`	True, 25 > 7, enter loop body			
`i++;`		3		9
`while (x_value > x[i])`	True, 25 > 9, enter loop body			
`i++;`		4		14
`while (x_value > x[i])`	True, 25 > 14, enter loop body			
`i++;`		5		19
`while (x_value > x[i])`	True, 25 > 19, enter loop body			
`i++;`		6		29
`while (x_value > x[i])`	False, 25 < 29, loop exited			

Thus, `i` = 6 at the end of the loop, which means that `(i - 1)` = 5. These two indices give the values of `x[]` to the right and left of the `x_value`. With these indices, the values of `x[ ]` and `y[ ]` for Eqn. 9.3 can be obtained.

STEP 4. INTERPOLATE USING EQN. 9.3

The following line of code applies Eqn. 9.3 using the indices `i` (= 6) and `i - 1` (= 5).

```
y_value = ((x_value - x[i - 1]) / (x[i] - x[i - 1]))
        * (y[i] - y[i - 1]) + y[i - 1];
```

Source Code

The complete source code is shown here.

```
#include <iostream>
#include <fstream>
using namespace std;
const int NUM_PTS=10;
int main ( )
{
      double x[NUM_PTS], y[NUM_PTS], x_value, y_value;
      int i;
      ifstream infile("C:\\INTERP.DAT");

      for (i = 0; i < NUM_PTS; i++) infile >> x[i] >> y[i];   // Reading the input file.

      cout << "Enter a value of time between " << x[0] << " and"
          << x[NUM_PTS-1] << endl;
      cin >> x_value;   // Reading the typed value.

      i=0;
      while (x_value > x[i]) i++;   // Loop that increments the array index until the typed value (x_value) is less than the array value (x[i]).
      y_value = ((x_value-x[i-1])/(x[i]-x[i-1]))*(y[i]-y[i-1])+y[i-1];   // Eqn. 9.3

      cout << "The value of the voltage at time = "
          << x_value << " is " << y_value << endl;
}
```

INPUT DATA FILE

```
0    23
5    78
7    89
9    -12
14   0
19   90
29   18
34   -23
37   76
45   98
```

Output

```
The value of the voltage at time = 25 is 46.8
```

Comments

The `const int` type variable `NUM_PTS` has been used to declare the size of `x[ ]` and `y[ ]` to facilitate a future change in the number of data points collected. The variable `NUM_PTS` has been used in defining the loop used to read the input data file and in printing out the rightmost value in the input data prompt of `x[ ]` because we were explicitly given that each file would have 10 points. Had we not been given this information, we would have made `NUM_PTS` larger than any expected number of points and read the file with a loop using `eof` in the test expression as shown in Lesson 9.3. For this program design, should we want to change the number of points input, we need to change the number 10 in the variable definition. A program design using `eof` is better in most cases.

One can see from this example that with arrays and loops, it takes only a small number of lines of code to create a useful program.

Modification Exercises

1. Replace the `while` loop in the program with a `do-while` loop.
2. Replace the `while` loop in the program with a `for` loop.
3. Modify the program to handle 100 data points instead of 10.
4. Make the program print out the coordinates of the two nearest data points to (`x_value, y_value`).
5. Modify the program to have two functions—one for input and the other for calculations and output.

APPLICATION EXAMPLE 9.2 WAVE HEIGHT ANALYSIS

TOPICS

- 1-D array manipulation
- Mean and median
- Numerical method example

Problem Statement

As part of a study to evaluate the reasons why a particular beach is eroding quickly, a number of wave height (Fig. 9.12) measurements have been made. To calculate the movement of the sand, it is necessary to determine an average wave height from the measurements. Two different types of averages can be computed, the *mean* and the *median*. Write a program that can calculate the mean and median values of measured wave heights (consider an odd number of measured wave heights only). Read the input wave heights from a file and print the results to the screen.

Figure 9.12
Illustration of wave height.

Solution

RELEVANT EQUATIONS

We define the following terms:

x_i = ith value in a list of numbers
n = number of x values in list

Using these terms we have the definition of the mean:

$$\bar{x} = \frac{\sum_{i=1}^{n} x_i}{n} \quad (9.4)$$

where the left symbol is called *x-bar* and is the mean of the set of n values. In other words, the mean is the sum of all the values in a list divided by the number of values.

The median of a set of n data points commonly is described as the value in a list that has an equal number of values greater than and less than the median value. For example, for the five values 10, 13, 24, 9, 1, the median value is 10 because two values (13 and 24) are greater than 10 and two values (1 and 9) are less than 10.

This definition is not quite accurate because it does not account for the possibility of having like values. For instance, for the five values 9, 10, 10, 13, 24, the median is 10. Here, it can be seen that the median is the value for which both the number of values less than or equal to it and greater than or equal to it is greater than half of the total number of values. In this case, the number of values less than or equal to 10 is 3 (values 9, 10, and 10), and the number of values greater than or equal to 10 is 4 (values 10, 10, 13, and 24). Since both 3 and 4 are greater than half the number of values ($5/2 = 2.5$), 10 is the median.

We can write these conditions in equation form:

n_{lower} = number of values less than or equal to x_i
n_{higher} = number of values greater than or equal to x_i

If n_{lower} is greater than or equal to $n/2$ *and* n_{higher} is greater than or equal to $n/2$, then

$$x_{\text{med}} = x_i$$

where x_{med} = median value.

Note that, in this example, we consider only an odd number of values in a list because the definition of median becomes less clear for an even number of values. Another approach in finding the median is to first sort the values (that is, arrange in ascending numerical order) and then select the value at the center of the sort as the median. Because we discuss sorting in other examples, we will not use sorting here to find the median.

SPECIFIC EXAMPLE

Once per day over a period of approximately one month (29 days), wave heights have been measured. The following values have been found for each day (measurements in centimeters):

```
67 87 56 34 05 98 56 67 87 90 45 42 31 97 58 78 12 16
22 42 83 95 53 27 49 85 58 79 79
```

Using Eqn. 9.4, the mean of these is found to be the sum of the values (1778) divided by the number of them (29):

$$x_{\text{mean}} = 1778/29 = 61.3$$

Therefore, the mean wave height is 61.3 cm.

To find the median with the set of equations that we developed, we take each value and compare it to all the others to get the number of lower and higher values. For instance, if we take the first value in the list, 67, and compare it to all the other values, we find that 17 values are less than or equal to 67, and 14 values are greater than or equal to 67. Therefore, 67 is not the median value because the total number of values (29) divided by 2 is 14.5, and although 17 is greater than 14.5, 14 is not greater than 14.5 (and our requirement is that *both* must be greater than 14.5). Next, we list the values, in order, and the number of values above and below that value:

Value x_i	Number of values <= x_i	Number of values >= x_i
67	17	14
87	25	6
56	13	18
34	6	24
85	23	8
98	29	1
56	13	18
67	17	14
87	25	6
90	26	4
45	9	21
42	8	23
31	5	25
97	28	2
58	15	16

Clearly, this is not a complete list. We stopped the list at 58 because *both* the number of values less than or equal to 58 and the number of values greater than or equal to 58 are greater than 14.5 (being 15 and 16, respectively). So, we need to go no further. We have found the median. It is 58.

ALGORITHM AND CODE SEGMENTS

There are three parts to this program:

1. Reading the input data.
2. Calculating the mean.
3. Calculating the median.

READING THE INPUT DATA

The input steps are:

1. Open the data file.
2. Read the input data values of wave heights from the data file.

The code for this is straightforward so we do not develop it here. See Lesson 9.3 for more detail.

CALCULATING THE MEAN

The steps and code for calculating the mean are:

1. Sum all the values in the list. The following loop sums all the values of `x[]`, where `num_pts` is the number of `x[]` values:

   ```
   sum = 0.0;
   for (i = 0; i < num_pts; i++) sum += x[i];
   ```

   Observe the importance of making `sum` = 0.0 before the loop. This assures that only the values of the array elements are summed by `sum += x[i]`. See Lesson 9.3 for a trace of the loop.

2. Divide the sum by the number of values in the list. The following code does this calculation. Note that typically `num_pts` will be specified as an integer whereas `sum` and `mean` are `double`s. This leads to mixed arithmetic, of which you should be careful. Here, we use an implicit conversion (which is done automatically by C++) to a `double` type. With `sum` and `mean` declared to be `double`, this statement assigns `mean` correctly:

   ```
   mean = sum / num_pts;
   ```

CALCULATING THE MEDIAN

The steps and code for calculating the median are:

1. Compare a value in the list to the other values in the list, and
   a. Count the number of values less than or equal to the compared value.
   b. Count the number of values greater than or equal to the compared value.
2. If both 1a and 1b are greater than $n/2$, then we have found the median, and we stop.
3. If either 1a or 1b are not greater than $n/2$, then we repeat step 1 with the next value on the list.

Developing the code for each of the steps follows:

STEP 1

Using `x[j]` as the value being compared to all the others, the loop that follows performs Steps 1a and 1b:

```
count_higher = 0;
count_lower = 0;
for (i = 0; i < num_pts; i++)
         {
         if (x[j] <= x[i]) count_higher++;

         if (x[j] >= x[i]) count_lower++;

         }
```

Initializing the counter variables to be zero. This must be done before the beginning of the loop.

Looping over all the points.

If the compare value is less than or equal to another value, add 1 to the `count_higher` variable.

If the compare value is greater than or equal to another value, add 1 to the `count_lower` variable.

After completing this loop, `count_lower` and `count_higher` are the correct values.

STEPS 2 AND 3

We must use each value in the list as the compared value `x[j]`, so we put the above code into a loop over all the data points. However, we do not necessarily want to loop over all the data points, because we may encounter the median as one of the first points checked. Therefore, we can break out of the loop early. To illustrate different types of loops and the `break` statement, we show two different methods for writing this control structure. First we show a `while` loop with a `break` statement, and then we show a `do-while` loop with no `break` statement.

For the `while` loop, the condition for breaking out of the loop (as described in the algorithm section) is that both `count_lower` and `count_higher` are greater than `num_pts/2.0`. A `break` statement is allowed in a loop body (as well as a `switch` body). A `break` statement in a loop body causes control to transfer out of the nearest enclosing loop as follows:

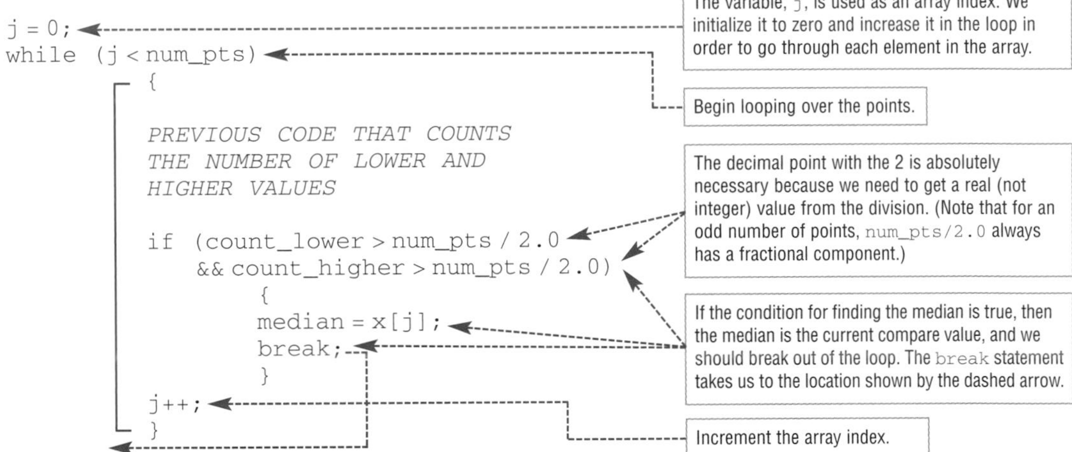

By breaking out of the loop early we have saved computation and found the median value. However, if possible, it is considered to be better programming practice to avoid the use of `break` statements in looping structures. This can be done by putting the `break` condition within the loop's controlling condition. For instance, another way to look at this problem is to realize that looping should continue if either `count_higher` or `count_lower` is less than `num_pts/2.0`. Using a `do-while` loop gives the following code:

```
j = -1;                          ← Initialize the array index variable.
do
{
      j++;                       ← Increment the array index variable each time
                                   through the loop.
      PREVIOUS CODE THAT COUNTS
      THE NUMBER OF LOWER AND
      HIGHER VALUES
}     while (j < num_pts &&
            (count_lower < ((num_pts) / 2.0) ||
            count_higher < ((num_pts) / 2.0)));
                                 ← Continue looping while either count_lower
                                   or count_higher is less than
                                   num_pts/2.0, otherwise stop.
median = x[j];                   ← The median is the compare value at the time
                                   that looping has stopped.
```

Note that the structure of the do-while loop is cleaner than that of the while loop because it does not use the break statement. It is possible to write a while loop for this case without using a break statement. We leave this for you as an exercise.

Source Code

The complete source code (which incorporates the previously described code with the do-while loop) follows:

```
#include <iostream>
#include <fstream>
using namespace std;
const int MAX_NUM_PTS=100;

int main()
{
    int x[MAX_NUM_PTS], num_pts, i, j, count_lower,
      count_higher, median;
    double sum, mean;
    ifstream infile("C:\\DATA\\AVERAGE.DAT");

    infile >> num_pts;                                    ]---- Reading the data file.
    for (i = 0; i < num_pts; i++) infile >> x[i];         ]


    sum = 0.0;                                            ]
    for (i = 0; i < num_pts; i++) sum += x[i];            ]---- Calculating the mean.
    mean = sum / num_pts;                                 ]


    j = -1;
    do
       {
       j++;
       count_lower = 0;
       count_higher = 0;
       for (i=0; i < num_pts; i++)
            {
            if (x[j] <= x[i]) count_higher++;                   Calculating the
            if (x[j] >= x[i]) count_lower++;                    median.
            }
       }      while (j < num_pts && count_lower < (num_pts / 2.0)
                  || count_higher < (num_pts / 2.0));
    median = x[j];

    cout << "The mean of the values is: " << mean << endl
         << "The median value is:       " << median << endl;

}
```

INPUT FILE AVERAGE.DAT

```
29
67 87 56 34 85 98 56 67 87 90 45 42 31 97 58 78 12 16 22 42 83 95 53 27 49
85 58 79 79
```

Output

```
The mean of the values is: 61.310
The median value is:       58
```

Comments

In this program, we defined the maximum number of points as 100 and read in the actual number of data points as the first item in the data file. Should we want to analyze more than 100 points, we would need to change this value.

Because we are very interested in developing efficient code, we are interested in assessing the efficiency of our algorithms. Part of assessing an algorithm that involves comparisons is evaluating how many comparisons are made in executing the algorithm. Determining the number of comparisons is not necessarily straightforward because different situations cause different numbers of comparisons to be made. For instance, for our algorithm to evaluate the median of a list of n numbers, we see that if the median value is the first value in our list (just by chance) we will make only n comparisons (because just one pass through the list gives us the median).

However, should the median be the last value in the list (again by chance) we would make n comparisons for each of the n values; that is, n^2 comparisons to perform a median evaluation. If we had 1000 values in our list, this would mean we would make $1000^2 = 1$ million comparisons. You can see that, for this particular algorithm, the number of comparisons can be quite great. Therefore, developing a more efficient algorithm may be quite beneficial. We will not develop one here; however, we want to make you aware that the search for efficient algorithms is a science. You very well may take courses later in your educational career that focus on algorithm development.

Modification Exercises

1. Replace the `do-while` loop with a `while` loop that needs no `break` statement.
2. Make `x[]` an array of `double` rather than `int`.
3. Modify the program to handle 12 lists of wave height data (one for each month in a year) in the input file. The input data file would be

   ```
   n1
   h1 h2 h3 ... hn1
   ```

```
n2
h1 h2 h3 ... hn3
.
.
.
.
n12
h1 h2 .... hn12
```

4. Remove the decimal point on 2.0. Does the program still work properly? Why or why not?
5. Make three functions for this program—one for input, one for the mean, and one for the median.

APPLICATION EXAMPLE 9.3 DEALING FIVE CARDS EACH TO FOUR PLAYERS

TOPICS

- Using random numbers with arrays
- Swapping
- Arrays and functions
- Working with playing cards

Problem Statement

Write a program that simulates dealing five playing cards each to four players. Make sure that no cards are dealt twice.

Solution

RELEVANT EQUATIONS AND BACKGROUND

Computers are frequently used to simulate card games. This program illustrates a simple method for distributing cards randomly to four players. Fundamental to the method is a size 52 array that contains 52 different integers (0–51). Each integer represents a different card. For instance, in this method the integer 51 represents the ace of hearts. Table 9.4 lists all the integers and card names.

TABLE 9.4 — Correspondence between integer values and card name

Integer	Card	Integer	Card	Integer	Card	Integer	Card
0	2 Spades	13	5 Clubs	26	8 Diamonds	39	Jack Hearts
1	2 Clubs	14	5 Diamonds	27	8 Hearts	40	Queen Spades
2	2 Diamonds	15	5 Hearts	28	9 Spades	41	Queen Clubs
3	2 Hearts	16	6 Spades	29	9 Clubs	42	Queen Diamonds
4	3 Spades	17	6 Clubs	30	9 Diamonds	43	Queen Hearts
5	3 Clubs	18	6 Diamonds	31	9 Hearts	44	King Spades
6	3 Diamonds	19	6 Hearts	32	10 Spades	45	King Clubs
7	3 Hearts	20	7 Spades	33	10 Clubs	46	King Diamonds
8	4 Spades	21	7 Clubs	34	10 Diamonds	47	King Hearts
9	4 Clubs	22	7 Diamonds	35	10 Hearts	48	Ace Spades
10	4 Diamonds	23	7 Hearts	36	Jack Spades	49	Ace Clubs
11	4 Hearts	24	8 Spades	37	Jack Clubs	50	Ace Diamonds
12	5 Spades	25	8 Clubs	38	Jack Diamonds	51	Ace Hearts

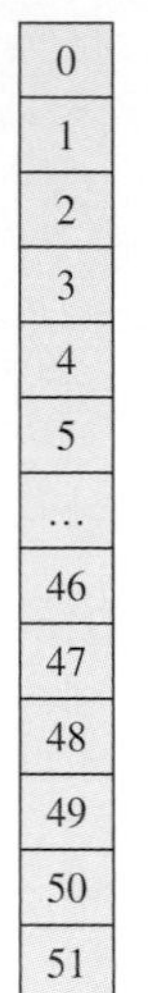

Figure 9.13

Original array of card numbers. We begin by searching for a random number in the range 0–51. This number becomes the index of the card that is dealt.

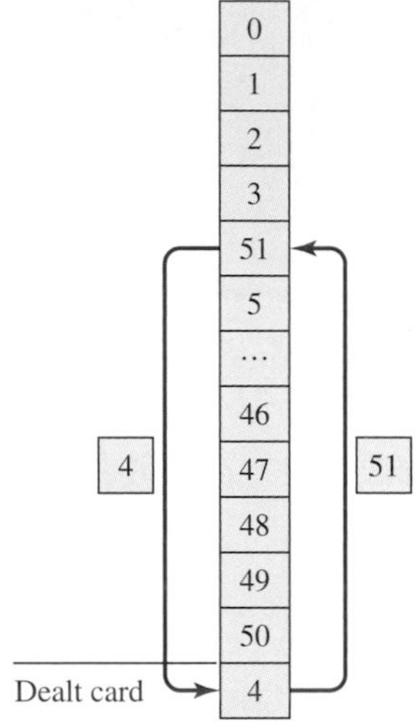

Figure 9.14

Array after one card has been dealt. The random index chosen is 4. Therefore, we move the value in the fourth location to the end (index 51) and move the 51 to the fourth location. Since one card is dealt, we now search for a random index in the range 0–50.

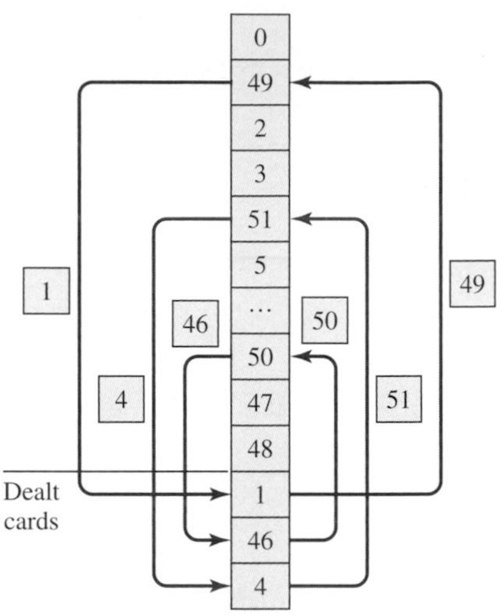

Figure 9.15

Array after three cards have been dealt. The random indices obtained were 4, 46, and 1. Consequently we have moved 51 to space 4, 50 to space 46, and 49 to space 1. To proceed, we search for a random value in the range 0 to 48. Note that if the next random value is again 1, then we move the value 49 into space 48.

For most of the rest of this example, we work with the card numbers and not the card names. The procedure in distributing cards begins with creating an array that contains all the card numbers (Fig. 9.13). We then get a random number in the range 0–51. This selects the index of the array from which the first card is taken. If this random value is 4 (Fig. 9.14), we swap the values in the fourth and last position. This means that we deal card 4 (the 3 of spades). We use the end of the array to hold the dealt cards and the beginning of the array to hold the cards that have not yet been dealt. Since we have dealt just one card, the dealt card region is only one array element at the end.

Now we search for the next card to deal only in the undealt card region (indices 0–50). The card chosen is then swapped with the 50th location. Figure 9.15 shows the array after dealing three cards. Values in the 49th, 50th, and 51st positions have been swapped with the values in the randomly chosen indices (1, 46, and 4, respectively). Each time we deal a card, we search for a random value over a range that is one less than the previous search range. In this program, we deal 20 cards, so this procedure is followed 20 times. After doing this, the array's first 32 elements contain undealt cards, and the last 20 contain the cards that are dealt.

We allocate the dealt cards to the players in rotating fashion: card 51 goes to player 1, card 50 goes to player 2, card 49 goes to player 3, card 48 goes to player 4, and so on until all 20 cards are distributed.

SPECIFIC EXAMPLE

Examine Figs. 9.13, 9.14 and 9.15 to see 3 cards being selected for dealing. The cards are then distributed from the end of the deck to the four players according to Fig. 9.16.

ALGORITHM AND CODE SEGMENTS

The steps for this program are:

1. Declare an array of 52 integers for the card deck and four arrays of five integers for the players' hands.
2. Initialize the array of 52 to be the values 0–51.
3. Select the card values to be dealt by repeating 20 times:
   a. Select a random index in the undealt card range.
   b. Swap the value at the random index with the value at the index of the last undealt card.

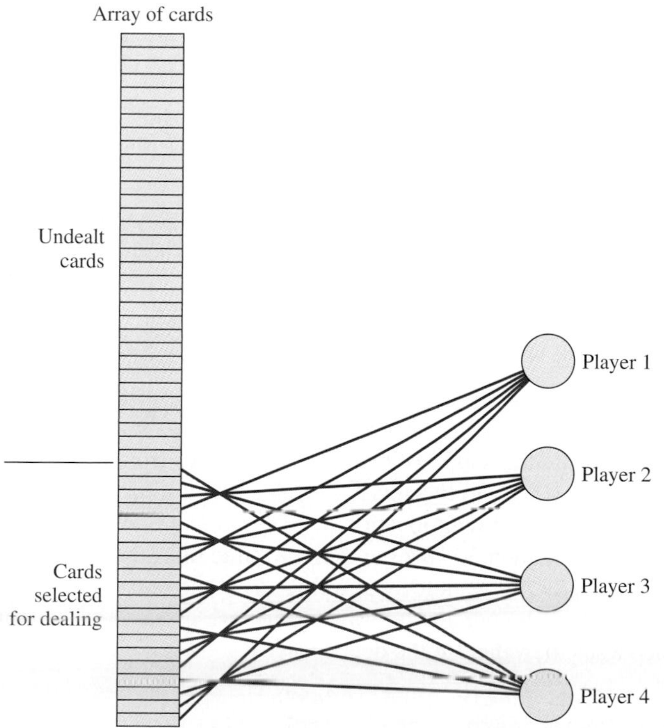

Figure 9.16
Distributing cards from the end of the deck array to the four players.

4. For each hand, copy the value of every fourth element from the end of the card deck array to a hand array.
5. Print the card name from each integer in the hand arrays.

STEPS 1 AND 2

These are straightforward and are shown in the source code. The names of the arrays are:

```
int deck [52];
int hand1 [5], hand2 [5], hand3 [5], hand4 [5];
```

The other steps are described next.

STEP 3—SELECT THE CARD VALUES TO BE DEALT

If we were not concerned about dealing the same card twice, we could simply select a random number in the range 0–51 20 consecutive times. Since this is not acceptable, we need to change the range each time we select a card to deal. That is, the first time the range is 0–51, the second time the range is 0–50, and the third time the range is 0–49. We continue in this manner until the range is 0–32, and then we stop.

To generate a random number in the range 0–51, we use the expression:

```
rand () % (52)
```

To generate a random number in the range 0–50, we use the expression:

```
rand () % (51)
```

And, to generate a random number in the range 0–32, we use the expression:

```
rand () % (33)
```

Therefore, we need to generate a loop that makes the second operand of the `%` operator go from 52 to 33. The following loop accomplishes this:

```
for (i = 51; i > 31; i--)
        {
        dealt_card_index = rand () % (i + 1);
        }
```

Note that this loop last executes when `i` = 32, which makes `i` + 1 = 33, which is what we want. Within this loop, we want to swap values from the random index selected (`dealt_card_index`) to the last undealt card location. The first time through the loop, we want to swap with location 51. The second time through the loop, we want to swap with location 50. We see that the value of `i` in the loop represents the swapping location. So, we want to swap values from the `dealt_card_index` location to the `i` location. Remember, to swap values we use a `temp` variable. The following code swaps the values in the deck array:

```
temp = deck [dealt_card_index];
deck [dealt_card_index] = deck [i];
deck [i] = temp;
```

The entire loop is:

```
for (i = 51; i > 31; i--)
        {
        dealt_card_index = rand () % (i + 1);
        temp = deck [dealt_card_index];
        deck [dealt_card_index] = deck [i];
        deck [i] = temp;
        }
```

STEP 4—PASS THE CARDS TO THE HANDS

We want to pass every fourth card from the end of the deck to each hand (see Fig. 9.16). For the first hand we want `hand1[0]` to `hand1[4]` to get the cards in the deck at locations 51, 47, 43, 39, and 35. The following statements do it:

```
hand1 [0] - deck [51];
hand1 [1] = deck [47];
hand1 [2] = deck [43];
hand1 [3] = deck [39];
hand1 [4] = deck [35];
```

but it is better to use a loop. This loop gives the values to `hand1[]`:

```
for (i = 51, j = 0; i >= 35; i -= 4, j++) hand1 [j] = deck [i];
```

Note that we use both `i` and `j` in the loop control statements with a comma separating the `i` and `j` initializations and the `i` and `j` incrementations. Note also that `i` decreases by 4 each time through the loop. In the loop, `j` goes from 0 to 4 (which is correct), while `i` is 51, 47, 43, 39, and 35 (which is correct). Loops for the other hands are similar. They are:

```
for (i = 50, j = 0; i >= 34; i -= 4, j++) hand2 [j] = deck [i];
for (i = 49, j = 0; i >= 33; i -= 4, j++) hand3 [j] = deck [i];
for (i = 48, j = 0; i >= 32; i -= 4, j++) hand4 [j] = deck [i];
```

STEP 5—DETERMINING THE CARD NAME FROM THE CARD VALUE

From Table 9.4, we see that the card values 35 and less are all number cards (2–10). The values 36 and above are face cards. We can compute the numbers from the card values using the expression

```
card_value / 4 + 2
```

This works because we are using integer division, which truncates the decimal portion of the division. This is an example of using the truncation in integer division to our advantage. For instance, the card value of 35 produces the expression:

```
35 / 4 + 2
```

In real numbers, 35/4 is 8.75, but with integer division the 0.75 is truncated and the result is 8. Therefore $35/4 + 2$ is 10, and this is the correct value as shown in Table 9.4. You can try other values in this expression, and you will see that they all agree with Table 9.4. A statement printing the correct card number is

```
if (card_value < 36) cout << ((card_value / 4) + 2) << " of ";
```

We also note from Table 9.4 that card values 36–39 are Jacks, 40–43 are Queens, 44–47 are Kings, and 48–51 are Aces. The following `if-else-if` structure prints the correct card names from the card values.

```
if      (card_value < 36)                            cout << ((card_value / 4) + 2) << " of ";
else if (36 <= card_value && card_value <= 39)       cout << "Jack of ";
else if (40 <= card_value && card_value <= 43)       cout << "Queen of ";
else if (44 <= card_value && card_value<= 47)        cout << "King of ";
else                                                 cout << "Ace of ";
```

To get the suit printed correctly, we note from Table 9.4 that the order in the list for each suit is spades, clubs, diamonds, and hearts. Using the remainder (`mod`) operator, we note that when `card_value % 4` is 0, the suit is spades, when it is 1 the suit is clubs, when it is 2 the suit is diamonds, and when it is 3 the suit is hearts. The following `if-else-if` structure prints the correct suit:

```
if      (card_value % 4 == 0) cout << "spades, ";
else if (card_value % 4 == 1) cout << "clubs, ";
else if (card_value % 4 == 2) cout << "diamonds, ";
else                          cout << "hearts, ";
```

In the source code, we put all this in a function called `print_card_name()`. This function is passed the card value and prints the correct card name.

OTHER FEATURES OF THE SOURCE CODE

The source code includes all the elements described. It also prints the card values in the deck array and hands after the dealt cards have been selected and swapped. Read the code to see the entire program.

Source Code

```
#include <iostream>
#include <ctime>
#include <cstdlib>
using namespace std;

void print_card_name (int);

int main()
{
        int deck[52];
        int hand1[5], hand2[5], hand3[5], hand4[5];
        int i, j, dealt_card_index, temp;

        srand (time (0));

        for (i = 0; i < 52; i++) deck[i] = i;
```

These are needed to use the `rand()` function seeded with the `time` function.

Declaring the function for printing the card name.

Declaring the arrays.

Seeding the `rand` function with the `time` function.

Initializing the deck array with the values 0–51.

```
    for (i = 51; i > 31; i--)
            {
            dealt_card_index = rand () % (i + 1);
            temp = deck[dealt_card_index];
            deck[dealt_card_index] = deck[i];
            deck[i] = temp;
            }

    for (i = 51, j = 0; i >= 35; i -= 4, j++) hand1[j] = deck[i];
    for (i = 50, j = 0; i >= 34; i -= 4, j++) hand2[j] = deck[i];
    for (i = 49, j = 0; i >= 33; i -= 4, j++) hand3[j] = deck[i];
    for (i = 48, j = 0; i >= 32; i -= 4, j++) hand4[j] = deck[i];

    for (i = 0; i < 52; i++)
            {
            cout << deck[i] << "  ";
            if (i == 12 || i == 25 || i == 38 || i == 51) cout << endl;
            }

    cout << endl;

    for (i = 0; i < 5; i++) cout << hand1[i] << "  ";
    cout << endl;
    for (i = 0; i < 5; i++) cout << hand2[i] << "  ";
    cout << endl;
    for (i = 0; i < 5; i++) cout << hand3[i] << "  ";
    cout << endl;
    for (i = 0; i < 5; i++) cout << hand4[i] << "  ";
    cout << endl << endl;

    cout << "First player's hand:" << endl;
    for (i = 0; i < 5; i++) print_card_name (hand1[i]);
    cout << endl << endl;

    cout << "Second player's hand:" << endl;
    for (i = 0; i < 5; i++) print_card_name (hand2[i]);
    cout << endl << endl;

    cout << "Third player's hand:" << endl;
    for (i = 0; i < 5; i++) print_card_name (hand3[i]);
    cout << endl << endl;

    cout << "Fourth player's hand:" << endl;
    for (i = 0; i < 5; i++) print_card_name (hand4[i]);
    cout << endl << endl;

}
```

Selecting the cards to be dealt and swapping them to the end of the array.

Passing the selected cards to the hands.

Printing out the numeric card values of the deck (with a new line every 13 values).

Printing out the numeric card values for each hand.

Calling the `print_card_name()` function to print the name for each card in each hand.

```
void print_card_name (int card_value)
{

        if      (card_value < 36)                       cout << ((card_value / 4)
                                                         + 2) << " of";
        else if (36 <= card_value && card_value <= 39) cout << "Jack of";
        else if (40 <= card_value && card_value <= 43) cout << "Queen of";
        else if (44 <= card_value && card_value <= 47) cout << "King of";
        else                                            cout << "Ace of";


        if      (card_value % 4 == 0) cout << "spades, ";
        else if (card_value % 4 == 1) cout << "clubs, ";
        else if (card_value % 4 == 2) cout << "diamonds, ";
        else                          cout << "hearts, ";

        return;
}
```

Printing the face name of the card from the card value.

Determining the suit from the card value.

Output

```
0 50 2 46 4 5 32 7 8 9 51 41 12
13 14 39 16 17 48 34 47 21 22 23 24 25
26 27 28 43 30 31 33 6 45 11 10 19 49
15 18 35 42 29 1 38 3 20 40 37 44 36

36 20 29 15 11
44 3 42 49 45
37 38 35 19 6
40 1 18 10 33

First player's hand
Jack of spades, 7 of spades, 9 of clubs, 5 of hearts, 4 of hearts

Second player's hand
King of spades, 2 of hearts, Queen of diamonds, Ace of clubs, King of clubs

Third player's hand
Jack of clubs, Jack of diamonds, 10 of hearts, 6 of hearts, 3 of diamonds

Fourth player's hand
Queen of spades, 2 of clubs, 6 of diamonds, 4 of diamonds, 10 of clubs
```

This is the array with the card numbers 33 and later being the ones dealt. The cards between 0 and 31 are not dealt.

These are the card numbers for the cards dealt to players 1, 2, 3, and 4. Note that they come from the end of the array.

Table 9.4 shows that these card names correspond to the card numbers listed for each player.

Comments

This program shows you how you can begin to simulate a card game. You can extend this program by arriving at a total for each hand, or by allowing the players to play the hand they are dealt. Creating these features can add considerable complexity to the program.

The program can be made more compact if we use a 2-D array (size 4×5) for the hands instead of four 1-D arrays. You will see in Chapter 10 how this can be done.

Modification Exercises

Modify the program to:

1. Deal cards to six players instead of four.
2. Deal seven cards to each player instead of five.
3. Deal all the cards to four players.
4. Deal seven cards to six players.

APPLICATION EXAMPLE 9.4 BUBBLE SORT AND EXCHANGE SORT

TOPICS

- 1-D array manipulation
- Complex looping with arrays

Problem Statement

Write a program that uses the bubble sort and the exchange sort (also called *selection sort*) to sort the array {33, 44, 11, 22}.

Solution

Since the coding for the sorts is fairly standard, we show this example somewhat differently from the others. Instead of describing the thought processes in developing the code, we simply present the code and describe it after giving some background and describing the mechanics of the sorts.

BACKGROUND

A fundamental operation on arrays is sorting them; that is, arranging the elements such that they are in a specified order, usually from minimum value to maximum value.

For instance, suppose we have array `b[]` that has following elements: `b[0]` = 34, `b[1]` = 23, `b[2]` = 64, `b[3]` = 39, `b[4]` = 84, `b[5]` = 91, `b[6]` = 73. This array is considered to be sorted if we rearrange the values of the array elements to be `b[0]` = 23, `b[1]` = 34, `b[2]` = 39, `b[3]` = 64, `b[4]` = 73, `b[5]` = 84, `b[6]` = 91 because the values of the array elements increase with increasing subscript values.

To do this rearrangement, you can see that we need to do a considerable amount of swapping of array element values. For instance, we swap the values of 23 and 34 between elements `b[0]` and `b[1]`. The goal of writing sorting algorithms is to do this type of swapping very efficiently. We do not describe all the possible sorting methods or even all the issues raised in writing sorting algorithms. In fact, entire college courses are devoted to simply the topic of sorting. We lack the space here to fully cover sorting. However, in this example, we introduce you to the most basic sorting techniques: the bubble sort and exchange sort.

MECHANICS OF THE BUBBLE SORT

A bubble sort is called that because the process is similar to a bubble in water rising to the surface. In an array, it means that largest value moves ("bubbles") to the highest array element.

To sort the 1-D array, `b[4]` $= \{33, 44, 11, 22\}$, in ascending order using the bubble sort, we first compare `b[0]` and `b[1]`. If `b[0]` > `b[1]`, then we swap the values of `b[0]` and `b[1]`; otherwise, we do no rearrangement. Similarly, we perform the same actions for `b[1]` and `b[2]`. If `b[1]` > `b[2]`, then we swap the values of `b[1]` and `b[2]`. We continue this with the last pair, `b[2]` and `b[3]`. If `b[2]` > `b[3]`, then we swap the values of `b[2]` and `b[3]`. All these actions cause the greatest value in the array to move into the highest element, `b[3]`. This concludes the first pass through the array.

Figure 9.17 shows the actions of the bubble sort on a larger array for three passes. Each line in the figure represents the contents of the array each time a comparison is made. Each H-like symbol:

⊢⊣

indicates a comparison. A black H-like symbol represents a comparison and a swap. A color H-like symbol represents a comparison with no swap (since the right value is already greater than the left value). The bubble value is circled. It can be seen that for the first pass, initially, 44 is compared and swapped until it encounters 88. Then 88 is continuously compared and swapped until it is properly located at the end of the array. That is, 88 is the bubble value (the maximum of movable values), and it moves to the end of the array. For the second pass, 77 is the bubble value and is continuously compared and swapped until it is properly located next to 88. And, for the third pass, 66 is continuously compared and swapped until it is properly located next to 77. With seven passes, all the array elements can be properly located, and the sort is completed.

MECHANICS OF THE EXCHANGE SORT

The exchange sort could also be called the swap maximum sort, meaning that the maximum value in the list is swapped with the value in the end location. Unlike the bubble sort that takes a large value and continually swaps it up the array, the exchange sort looks for the largest value in the list first. Then it swaps only once per pass through the array. In this program, we perform the following steps for the exchange sort.

To sort the 1-D array, b[4] = {33, 44, 11, 22}, in ascending order using the exchange sort, we first find the maximum value in the array (44). Then we swap the values of 44 and the end value (22). At this point, 44 is in the correct location, and we take it out of consideration. We search the rest of the array for the maximum value and get 33. We then swap 33 and the end value we are considering (11). At this point, both 44 and 33 are in the correct locations, and we continue until only one array element is left to consider.

Figure 9.18 shows the actions of the exchange sort on a larger array. Each line in the figure represents the contents of the array at the beginning and end of each pass. At the end of all seven passes, the array is sorted.

CODE FOR THE BUBBLE SORT

While the bubble sort actions are simple to describe, the code for the bubble sort is not so simple. We show how the code works by going through it line by line for the array used in this lesson's program.

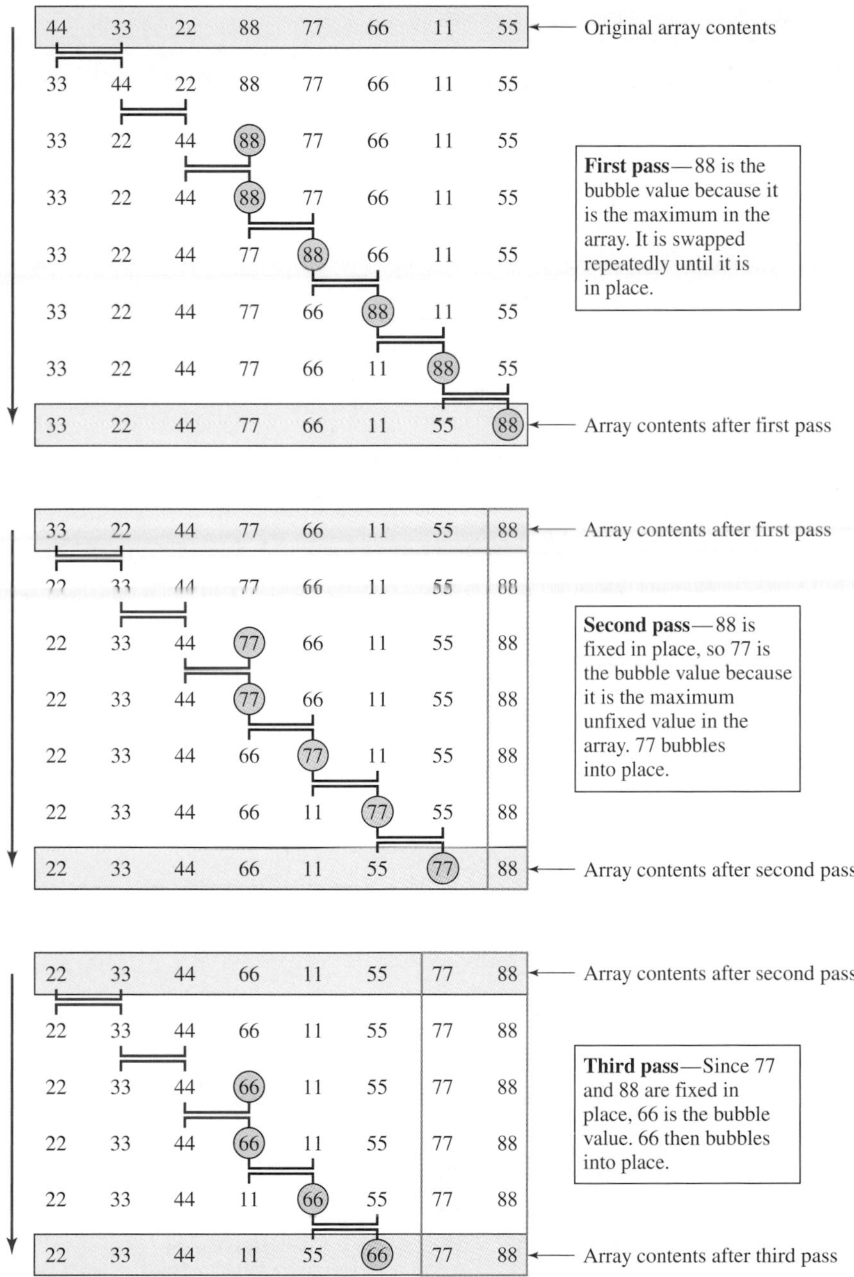

Original array contents
First pass—88 is the bubble value because it is the maximum in the array. It is swapped repeatedly until it is in place.
Array contents after first pass
Array contents after first pass
Second pass—88 is fixed in place, so 77 is the bubble value because it is the maximum unfixed value in the array. 77 bubbles into place.
Array contents after second pass
Array contents after second pass
Third pass—Since 77 and 88 are fixed in place, 66 is the bubble value. 66 then bubbles into place.
Array contents after third pass

Figure 9.17

Three passes of the bubble sort on the array shown at the top of the figure. Each line shows the array contents at each step of the sort. The H-like symbols indicate comparisons and possible swaps. A color H indicates a comparison, but no swap (note that the successive lines are identical, meaning no swap has taken place). A black H indicates a comparison and a swap (note that the successive lines are different, meaning a swap has occurred). The circled value is the bubble value (maximum) for that pass. The rectangle at the right indicates values that are properly arranged and therefore fixed in place and no longer operated upon.

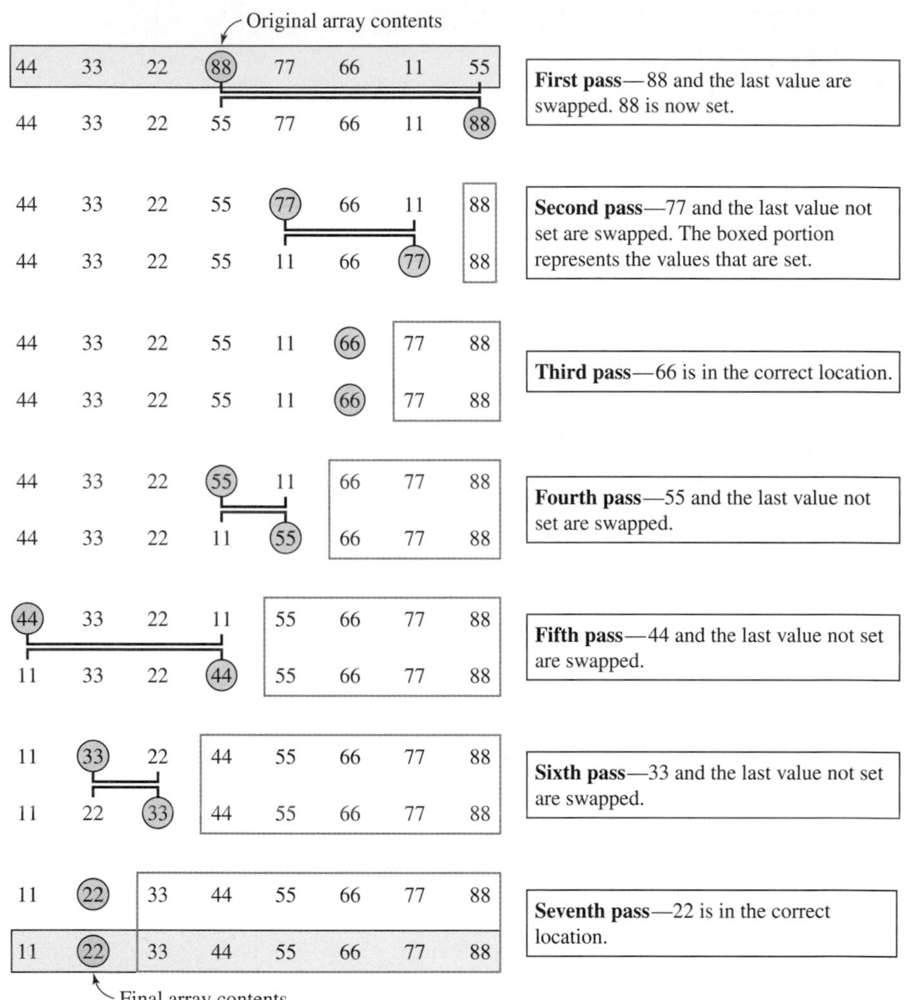

Figure 9.18

All seven passes of the exchange sort on the array shown at the top of the figure. The last array shown is properly sorted.

We present the code for the bubble sort to sort the `b[]` array (size 4) here. It consists of an outer loop and an inner loop. The code is:

```
START = 0;
END = 4;
for (i = START; i < END; i++)
      {
      for (j = START; j < END - i - 1; j++)
            {
            if (b[j] > b[j + 1])
                  {
                  temp = b[j + 1];
                  b[j + 1] = b[j];
                  b[j] = temp;
                  }
            }
      }
```

These three statements swap the values of `b[j]` and `b[j + 1]`.

For the first pass, this loop executes over the entire range (START to END, that is, the greatest `b[j + 1]` is `b[END]`). On the second pass, one element is properly placed, so this loop executes one less than the entire range. On the third pass through the loop, two elements are properly placed, so the loop executes two less than the entire range.

Each time through this loop is one pass through the array values.

A line by line trace of the code for the first pass is given in the following table. Because we have already examined the code for swapping values, it is shown in the table simply as one line. To understand the bubble sort, compare the table statements (column 1) to the bubble sort code, read the table line by line, and think through how the values change with each statement. Because the loop control statements are not simple, we have included them in the table in the order in which they are executed.

Inner loop.

Statement	Test expression and comments	i	j	b[0]	b[1]	b[2]	b[3]
Before loop values	START = 0, END = 4			33	44	11	22
`i = START;`		0					
`i < END;`	0 < 4 is true, outer loop begins						
`j = START;`			0				
`j < END - i - 1;`	0 < 3 is true, inner loop begins						
`if b[j] > b[j + 1];`	`b[0] > b[1]` is false, `if` statement body not executed						
`Swap b[j] and b[j + 1]`	Not executed						
`j++;`			1				
`j < END - i - 1;`	1 < 3 is true, inner loop continues						
`if b[j] > b[j + 1];`	`b[1] > b[2]` is true, `if` statement body executed						
`Swap b[j] and b[j + 1]`	`b[1]` and `b[2]` are swapped				11	44	
`j++;`			2				
`j < END - i - 1;`	2 < 3 is true, inner loop continues						
`if b[j] > b[j + 1];`	`b[2] > b[3]` is true, `if` statement body executed						
`Swap b[j] and b[j + 1]`	`b[2]` and `b[3]` are swapped					22	44
`j++;`			3				
`j < END - i - 1;`	3 < 3 is false, inner loop exited						
`i++;`		1					
	After 3 executions of the inner loop (which is one pass), the array values are the last ones in the columns. Note that 44 has bubbled to the highest array element.			33	11	22	44

Note that each execution of the inner loop makes a single comparison of two values and swaps the values if they are not in ascending order. The inner loop repeats until one pass through all the array elements is completed. The outer loop eliminates the properly placed values and repeats the passes.

Each time the array changes, here are the values

```
33 44 11 22
33 11 44 22
33 11 22 44   <------------  End pass 1 (44 has shifted to the last element).

11 33 22 44
11 22 33 44   <------------  End pass 2 (33 has shifted to the second to last element).
```

No other passes make any changes.

CODE FOR THE EXCHANGE SORT

The code for the exchange sort is more difficult to understand than the figures. Again there is an inner loop and an outer loop. The steps used in the code are:

1. We find the maximum value in the array by first assigning the last array element value to the variable `max`. Then, one by one, we compare `max` with the rest of the array elements; if `max` is smaller than any array element, then we replace `max` with this element and use the variable `wheremax` to remember the location (array index) of the new maximum. We continue the process through all the array elements. When completed, the variable `max` is the maximum value in the array, and `wheremax` is the array index of the element that holds the maximum value.
2. We swap the found maximum value with the value at the last element of the array.
3. Since the largest value of the group is found and stored in the last element, we eliminate the last element from the search group. This completes the first pass.
4. We then repeat steps 1, 2, and 3 until the array is in ascending order.

The source code for the exchange sort to sort the size 4 array called `c[ ]` is:

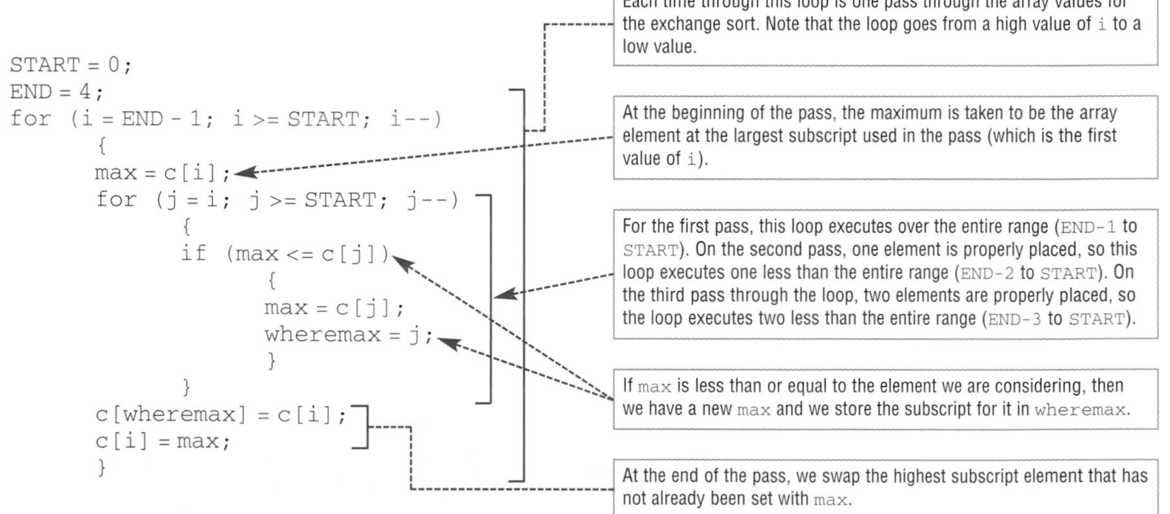

START = 0;
END = 4;
for (i = END - 1; i >= START; i--)
{
max = c[i];
for (j = i; j >= START; j--)
{
if (max <= c[j])
{
max = c[j];
wheremax = j;
}
}
c[wheremax] = c[i];
c[i] = max;
}
Each time through this loop is one pass through the array values for the exchange sort. Note that the loop goes from a high value of i to a low value.
At the beginning of the pass, the maximum is taken to be the array element at the largest subscript used in the pass (which is the first value of i).
For the first pass, this loop executes over the entire range (END-1 to START). On the second pass, one element is properly placed, so this loop executes one less than the entire range (END-2 to START). On the third pass through the loop, two elements are properly placed, so the loop executes two less than the entire range (END-3 to START).
If max is less than or equal to the element we are considering, then we have a new max and we store the subscript for it in wheremax.
At the end of the pass, we swap the highest subscript element that has not already been set with max.

The following table illustrates the actions of one pass of the exchange sort line by line. To understand the exchange sort, compare the table statements (column 1) to the exchange sort code, read the table line by line, and think through how the values change with each statement.

Note that the code consists of a nested loop. The inner loop searches through the array and finds the maximum value. The outer loop makes the swap, eliminates the properly placed elements, and repeats the procedure.

Statement	Test expression and comments	i	j	max	wheremax	c[0]	c[1]	c[2]	c[3]
Before loop values	START = 0, END = 4					33	44	11	22
`for i = END - 1;`		3							
`i >= START;`	3 >= 0 is true, outer loop begins								
`max = c[i];`	`max = c[3]` = 22			22					
`for j = i;`			3						
`j >= START;`	3 >= 0 is true, inner loop begins								
`if max <= c[j];`	22 <= 22 is true, if statement body executed								
`max = c[j];`	`max = c[3]`			22					
`wheremax = j;`					3				
`j--;`			2						
`j >= START;`	2 >= 0 is true, inner loop continues								
`if max <= c[j];`	22 <= 11 is false, if statement body not executed								
`max = c[j];`	Not executed								
`wheremax = j;`	Not executed								
`j--;`			1						
`j >= START;`	1 >= 0 is true, inner loop continues								
`if max <= c[j];`	22 <= 44 is true, if statement body executed								
`max = c[j];`				44					
`wheremax = j;`					1				
`j--;`			0						
`j >= START;`	0 >= 0 is true, inner loop continues								
`if max <= c[j];`	33 <= 44 is false, if statement body not executed								
`max = c[j];`	Not executed								
`wheremax = j;`	Not executed								
`j--;`			–1						
`j >= START;`	–1 >= 0 is false, inner loop terminates								
`c[wheremax] = c[i];`	`c[1] = c[3]` (beginning to swap `c[1]` and `c[3]`)						22		
`c[i] = max;`	`c[3]` = 44 (swapping complete)								44
`i--;`	Outer loop continues	2							
	After four executions of the inner loop, the array values are the last ones in the columns. Note that 44 has been swapped to the end of the array.					33	22	11	44

Inner loop.

The four passes of the exchange maximum sort for this lesson's program are summarized here.

i	j	Action	Comments
3	3	`max = c[3]` = 22	Array initially is 33, 44, 11, 22
	2	if `c[2] > max`	False, no action
	1	if `c[1] > max`	True, `max` = 44, `wheremax` = 1. (44 > 22)
	0	if `c[0] > max`	False, no action
		22 and 44 swap locations	44 goes to [3], 22 goes to [`wheremax`]

i	j	Action	Comments
2	2	`max = c[2]` = 11	Array is now 33, 22, 11, 44
	1	if `c[1] > max`	True, `max` = 22, `wheremax` = 1. (22 > 11)
	0	if `c[0] > max`	True, `max` = 33, `wheremax` = 0. (33 > 22)
		11 and 33 swap locations	33 goes to [2], 11 goes to [`wheremax`]
1	1	`max = c[1]` = 22	Array is now 11, 22, 33, 44
	0	if `c[0] > max`	False, no action.
0		No action	`c[0]` is automatically the smallest

Here are the values each time the array changes:

33 44 11 22
Initial array.
33 22 11 44
End pass 1, 22, and 44 have been swapped.
11 22 33 44
End pass 2, 11, and 33 have been swapped.

No other passes make any changes.

The complete source code is given next.

Source Code

```
#include <cmath>
#include <iostream>
#include <iomanip>
using namespace std;

const int START = 0, END = 4, SIZE = 10;

int main()
{
      int i, j, k, b[SIZE], c[SIZE];
      int temp, max, wheremax=END-1;
      int a[END]={33,44,11,22};

for (i = START; i < END ;i++) b[i] = c[i] = a[i];

    for (i = START; i < END ; i++)
      {
      for (j = START; j < END - i - 1; j++)
            {
            if (b[j] > b[j + 1])
                        {
                  temp = b[j + 1];
                  b[j + 1] = b[j];
                  b[j] = temp;
                        }
            }
      }
```

Maximum size of array to be sorted.

Initializing the `a[]` array.

Making all the arrays the same.

Bubble sort.

```
for (i = END - 1; i >= START; i--)
        {
        max = c[i];
        for(j = i; j >= START; j--)
                  {
                  if (max <= c[j])
                          {
                          max = c[j];
                          wheremax = j;
                          }
                  }
         c[wheremax] = c[i];
         c[i]  = max;
         }

         for (i = START; i < END; i++)
                 cout << "i=" << i << ", a[i]=" << a[i] << ", b[i]=" << b[i]
                       << ", c[i]=" << c[i] << endl;
}
```

Exchange sort.

Output

```
i=0, a[i]=33, b[i]=11, c[i]=11
i=1, a[i]=44, b[i]=22, c[i]=22
i=2, a[i]=11, b[i]=33, c[i]=33
i=3, a[i]=22, b[i]=44, c[i]=44
```

The output shows that the arrays have indeed been sorted.

Comments

Sorting illustrates complex array index manipulation. To manipulate an array in the manner you wish, you must write the loops and `if` control structures carefully.

We could have shown an exchange minimum sort also. It works similar to the exchange sort, but it searches for the minimum value and puts it in the lowest array position. There are numerous other types of sorts. However, we do not have the space here to cover them all.

Modification Exercises

1. Modify the program to sort the array `a[]` = {78, 99, 328, 8, 89, 22}.
2. Modify the program to sort the array `a[]` = {78, 99, 328, 8, 89, 22, 34, 54, 82, 98, 66, 43, 65}.
3. Modify the exchange sort to perform an exchange minimum sort.

LESSON EXERCISES

LESSON 9.1 EXERCISES

1. True or false:

a. All elements of a given array have the same data type.

b. All elements of a given array are placed randomly in computer memory.

c. All elements of a given array may be displayed by simply indicating the array name.

d. The subscript of the first element of a 1-D C++ array is 1.

e. A 1-D array is declared as `a[99]`. This means that in the program body, we can use `a[1]` to `a[100]`.

2. Find the error(s), if any, in each of these statements:

a. `int a, b(2);`

b. `float a23b[99], 1xy[66];`

c. `void city[36], town[45];`

d. `double temperature[-100];`

e. `long phone[200];`

f. The first and last array elements in the array just defined are `phone[0]` and `phone[200]`.

3. Find errors in this program:

```
int main ()
    const double N=2;
    double a[N],b;
    a[1]=N;
    N=99;
    a[2]=N;
    }
```

Solutions

1. a. true
b. false
c. false
d. false
e. false

2. a. `int a, b[2];`
b. `float a23b[99], xy1[66];`
c. An array cannot be of the void type.
d. `double temperature[100];` subscript must be > 0
e. No error
f. The first and the last array elements are `phone[0]` and `phone[199]`.

LESSON 9.2 EXERCISES

1. True or false:

a. There is more than one method for initializing a 1-D array.

b. An array can be initialized using `cout`.

c. The number of initial values of a given array must be less than or equal to the array size.

2. Find error(s), if any, in each of these statements:

a. `int a = {11,22}, b[33];`

b. `float c[3] = {11,22,33,44};`

c. `double d(4) = (11,22,33,44);`

d. `d[4] = {11 22 33 44};`

e. `int a[3]/11,22,33/;`

3. The number of cars crossing a bridge from Monday through Sunday in a given week are 986, 818, 638, 763, 992, 534, and 683. Use these numbers to initialize an array and write a program to generate the following output. The daily average number of cars crossing the bridge is 773. The maximum number of cars crossing the bridge in a day is 992, which occurs on Friday.

Solutions

1. a. true
b. false
c. true

2. a. `int a[2] = {11,22},b[33];`
b. `float c[4] = {11,22,33,44};`
or
`float c[ ] = {11,22,33,44};`
c. `double d[4] = {11,22,33,44};`
d. Must show array data type.
e. `int a[3] = {11,22,33};`

LESSON 9.3 EXERCISES

1. Based on

```
int a[3] = {1,2,3}, b[3] = {4,5,6}, c[3] = {1,2};
ifstream infile ("C:\\L9_3c.dat");
```

determine whether the following statements are true or false:

a. The statement

```
c = a + b;
```

will add the data stored in arrays `a[]` and `b[]` and assign the result to array `c[]`.

b. The statement

```
c[0] = a[1] + b[2];
```

is incorrect because 0, 1, and 2 are different subscript numbers.

c. The statement

```
infile >> a[1] >> a[3] >> a[2];
```

can be used to read three `int` type integers from a file and store them in array `a[]`.

2. Find error(s), if any, in each of these statements (assume `i[]` is an `int` type array with five elements, `f[]` is a `double` type array with six elements, and `infile` is an `ifstream` object):

a. `infile << i[2],i[4];`

b. `infile << i[0];`

c. `infile >> i[5] >> f[6];`

d. `infile >> i[1] >> f[1];`

3. Using the input file with sentinel values given in the Description portion of the lesson, make a variable value table for the following loop. Does the loop work properly?

```
i=0;
while (vehicles_per_day[i++] != -1)
      {
      infile >> vehicles_per_day[i];
      }
```

4. Write a program that uses arrays to read the following input file:

```
1  30.0
2  45.0
3  60.0
4  90.0
```

and then process the data and generate the following output:

```
N    X(degree)    cos(X)
1    30.0         0.8667
2    45.0         0.7071
3    60.0         0.5000
4    90.0         0.0000
```

5. A surveyor's notebook contains a figure like Fig. 9.19. Find the area between the straight fence and the riverbank. Assume all units are in meters, and all lines between the riverbank and the fence line are perpendicular to the fence line. Use the trapezoidal rule as described previously, two `double` type arrays, and `ifstream` objects to solve the problem.

Weather: sunny Location: John McDonald's ranch Date: 2/20/2003

Station (m)	Offset (m)
0	50
100	75
215	98
300	70
375	60

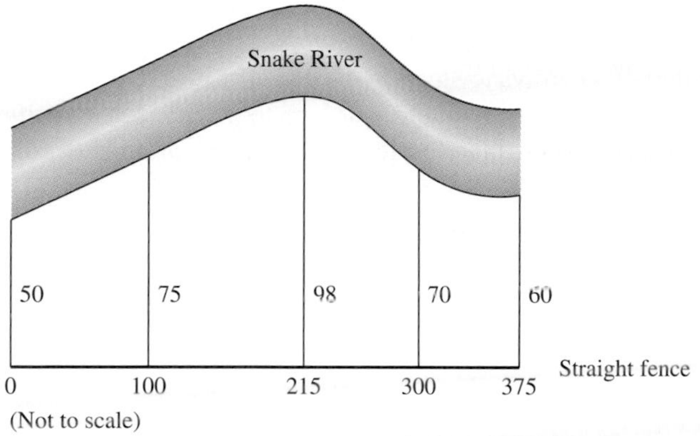

Figure 9.19

Problem 4.

Solutions

1. a. false
   b. false
   c. false
2. a. `infile >> i[2] >> i[4];`
   b. `infile >> i[0];`
   c. `infile >> i[4] >> f[5];`
   d. No error

LESSON 9.4 EXERCISES

1. True or false:

   a. In a function call, if one of the arguments is an array name not followed by brackets, then this passes the entire array to the function by copying each element into the memory region for the function.

   b. If we want to pass the value of a single array element, we need not use & in the argument list of the function call.

   c. It is not possible in C++ to give a function access to all of an array's elements without giving the function the ability to modify those elements.

   d. Pointer notation can be used with numeric arrays.

   e. The name of an array, not followed by brackets, indicates the address of the first element of the array.

   f. If we want to transfer the number of elements in an array to a function, we should use a separate argument in the argument list to do so.

2. The following table shows the length, width, and thickness of a stack of steel plates:

Length (ft)	Width (ft)	Thickness (in)
12.0	6.3	2.2
13.0	7.4	3.3
14.0	8.5	4.4
15.0	9.6	5.5

Use three 1-D arrays to store the length, width, and thickness information; then convert the units from foot or inch to meters, calculate the weights of the steel plates, and save the results in a 1-D array (assume the unit weight of steel is 7800 kg/m^3).

Solutions

1. a. false
b. false
c. false
d. true
e. true
f. true

LESSON 9.5 EXERCISES

1. True or false:

a. We can use global variables to size arrays that are members of classes.

b. Constant type data is shared by objects.

c. We cannot modify `const` type data in programs.

d. Array data members must be passed to member functions through the argument list.

2. Make a table that traces the nested `for` loop in this lesson's program. Verify that it indeed finds the minimum value.

Solutions

1. a. true, but encapsulation is violated.
b. false, static data is shared.
c. true
d. false

LESSON 9.6 EXERCISES

1. True or false:

a. An array of objects is the same as an object containing an array.

b. Engineers have little use for arrays of objects.

c. We can sort elements of an array of objects.

2. Write a program to read a file as shown below using an array of objects.

Display this file neatly on the screen.

```
Initial       Height(ft)       Age       SN
J             5.61             21        123-45-6789
T             6.12             36        987-65-4321
R             5.87             87        111-22-3333
J             3.14             4         444-55-6666
```

Solutions

1. a. false
   b. false
   c. true

APPLICATION EXERCISES

1. The number of millions of gallons of sewage that are disposed of each day for a major city is measured continuously for about one month. The records, saved in a file, EX6_1.DAT, follow:

```
123, 134, 122, 128, 116, 96, 83, 144, 143, 156, 128, 138,
121, 129, 117, 96, 87, 148, 149, 151, 129, 138, 127,
126, 115, 94, 83, 142
```

Write a program to calculate the frequency distribution using an interval of 10 million gallons per day. The input specification is to use the array `sewage_amt[100]` to read the number of millions of gallons from file EX6_1.DAT. The output specification is to display the following data on the screen:

Day no.	Millions of gallons
1	123
2	134
3	122
...	...

Sewage per day	Frequency of occurrence
81–90	3
91–100	3
101–111	0
...	

2. Modify the program so that the input is read by calling a function named `read_data ()`.

3. Modify the program so that the output is displayed by calling a function `display ()`. The declaration of the `display ()` function is:

```
void display (int mil_gal[], int array_size);
```

where `mil_gal` represents an array to be used to pass the information in the array `sewage_amt[100]`, and the `array_size` is the total number of records.

4. A 1-D array has these 10 elements.

```
4.4  3.3  2.2  5.5  1.1  6.6  7.7  10.0  9.9  8.8
```

Write a bubble sort program to sort the array in descending order.

5. The program in file Ae6_14 on the website displays the $y = \sin(x)$ curve on the screen.

Modify the program, so it will plot the curve of the $x[50]$ and $y[50]$ data as follows instead of plotting the $y = \sin(x)$ curve:

```
x[i]     y[i]
0.0       0.4
0.2       0.5
1.5       0.9
2.3       0.7
2.8       0.2
3.3      -0.3
4.4      -0.8
6.1      -0.9
```

6. Modify the program so that the `main ()` function calls a function named `xy_range ()`. The function will find the values of `xmin`, `xmax`, `ymin`, and `ymax` based on the data just given.

7. Write a program that asks a user to roll a single die twice to get a sum value of 7. If the sum is 11, the user loses. If the sum is neither 7 nor 11, the user neither wins nor loses, meaning that there is no decision.

8. Modify the program to allow the user to collect points. Give the user 100 points to begin, and keep track of how many points the user has. Allow the user to choose how many points he or she can win or lose for each decision. The amount of points that the user chooses may not exceed the amount of points that the user currently has. Give the user the option to stop at any time.

9. Write a program to simulate the card game 21 for a single player. Give the user two cards to begin. Ask the user if he or she would like another card, up to a total of five. A user who exceeds 21 loses. A user whose total is greater than or equal to 17 wins. If the user has five cards with the total being less than or equal to 21, the user wins. Otherwise no decision is given. Make sure that no card is dealt twice.

10. Modify the program of Problem 9 by allowing the user to collect points as described in Problem 8.

CHAPTER 10

MULTI-DIMENSIONAL NUMERIC ARRAYS

CHAPTER TOPICS

In this chapter, you will learn how to:

- Manipulate multidimensional arrays
- Use arrays with classes and objects
- Perform calculations with multidimensional arrays

In your algebra courses you encountered the use of matrices in calculations. For instance, you found that you could express the following algebraic equations:

$$3x + 4y + 8z = 15$$
$$2x - 3y + 9z = 8$$
$$4x + 7y - 6z = 5$$

in the form:

$$\begin{bmatrix} 3 & 4 & 8 \\ 2 & -3 & 9 \\ 4 & 7 & -6 \end{bmatrix} \begin{Bmatrix} x \\ y \\ z \end{Bmatrix} = \begin{Bmatrix} 15 \\ 8 \\ 5 \end{Bmatrix}$$

With a slight modification, this form of expressing equations is particularly useful. Instead of representing the variables x, y, and z, we prefer to use x_0, x_1, and x_2 as follows:

$$\begin{bmatrix} 3 & 4 & 8 \\ 2 & -3 & 9 \\ 4 & 7 & -6 \end{bmatrix} \begin{Bmatrix} x_0 \\ x_1 \\ x_2 \end{Bmatrix} = \begin{Bmatrix} 15 \\ 8 \\ 5 \end{Bmatrix}$$

There are two advantages of this form:

1. As matrices get bigger it is simple to include more variables, even up to x_{100} or x_{1000}.
2. Subscripted variables are conveniently represented by array elements in C++ programs.

We could write a computer program to solve this particular set of equations. (Remember, when we say solve this set of equations, we mean find the values of x_0, x_1, and x_2 that make all three equations true.) However, a computer program of this sort would have limited usefulness because it is unlikely that we would need to solve this particular set of equations very frequently. It would be more useful if we could write a computer program to solve a set of three equations with any values in the coefficient matrix and any values in the right-hand side vector. To do this, in our computer program, we need to treat the values in the matrix and right-hand side vector as variables, because we will be allowed to change them as we try to solve different problems. The traditional form of naming of variables in the coefficient matrix and the right-hand side vector is:

$$\begin{bmatrix} a_{00} & a_{01} & a_{02} \\ a_{10} & a_{11} & a_{12} \\ a_{20} & a_{21} & a_{22} \end{bmatrix} \begin{Bmatrix} x_0 \\ x_1 \\ x_2 \end{Bmatrix} = \begin{Bmatrix} b_0 \\ b_1 \\ b_2 \end{Bmatrix}$$

If, in the matrix, we call the first row, row 0, and the first column, column 0, we see that the double subscript naming scheme for a is $a_{\text{row column}}$. In other words, for a_{21} (for instance), the 2 represents the row and the 1 represents the column at which this value is located in the matrix. (Note: sometimes the first row is row 1 and the first column is column 1 but here we choose to begin with 0 since it is more like C++.)

In a program, how do we represent the "a" matrix? Just as single subscripts led us to use one-dimensional arrays, double subscripts leads us to use two-dimensional arrays. In other words, the variable a_{02} would be represented in C++ as `a[0][2]`. We will find that this representation in C++ will make it very simple for us to write programs in matrix arithmetic. In the application examples, we work a problem with matrices, so at this point we will not go through all the details. For now, we just want you to realize that a very common usage of two-dimensional arrays is matrix coefficients.

In this chapter, we illustrate how to use multidimensional arrays.

LESSON 10.1 DECLARING, INITIALIZING, AND PRINTING

TOPICS

- Concept of multidimensional arrays
- Comparing one- and multidimensional arrays
- Initializing multidimensional arrays
- Printing multidimensional arrays

QUESTION YOU SHOULD ATTEMPT TO ANSWER

1. What number of nested loop levels would we need to print the entire contents of the rainfall array?

Matrix coefficients are, of course, not the only use for multidimensional arrays. Suppose that we collect daily rainfall data at a particular airport rain gauge during the years 2000 to 2009 (10 years). At the end of each day, we could obtain the amount of rain (in cm) collected by the rain gauge. After the first year, for instance, we may be interested in performing calculations on this data, determining the average rainfall per day, the month in which the rainfall is heaviest, and other such useful information. We realize that we are going to want to do this computation periodically over the 10-year period. To write a computer program to do these calculations, we would find it convenient to store the rainfall data in an array (all the data being like-type data, rainfall).

For this, a one-dimensional array, `rainfall[]` is not particularly practical. This is because we would need 10 × 365 = 3650 array elements (one for each day), and there is no apparent correspondence between the array index and the date. For instance, it is not obvious to us the date corresponding to array element `rainfall[827]`. Instead, it is easier for us to use a three-dimensional array, `rainfall[][][]`. With this three-dimensional array we could use the year as the first index, the month as the second index, and the day as the third index. Thus, `rainfall[6][11][23]`, would represent the rainfall on November 23, 2006. Also, `rainfall[6][11][1]` to `rainfall[6][11][30]` represents the 30 elements of the array `rainfall[][][]` that contain rainfall data for the month of November 2006. The loop:

determines the total rainfall for the month of November 2006. You need not understand the details of this loop at this time; however, we want you to realize the convenience that multidimensional arrays provide in writing programs.

monthly_rainfall = 0.0;
for (i = 1; i <= 30; i++)
{
monthly_rainfall += rainfall[6][11][i];
}
Initialize the monthly total to be zero.
Loop over all the days in a month.
Add each day's rainfall of the 11th month of year 2006 to the other days in the same month.

In summary, because of the correspondence between the way that engineers and scientists typically group information, we find that multidimensional arrays are a very convenient and useful form for storing and manipulating data. Read this lesson's program to see how to declare, initialize, and perform calculations with 2- and 3-dimensional arrays.

Source Code

```
#include <iostream>
#include <iomanip>
#include <fstream>
using namespace std;
int main ( )
{
       int i, j, year, month, day;
       int b[2][3] = {51,52,53,54,55,56};
       int rainfall[10][13][32];
       ifstream infile ("C:\\L6_4.DAT");

       for (i = 0;  i < 2;  i++)
              {
              for (j = 0;  j < 3;  j++)
                     {
                     cout << "b[" << i << "][" << j << "] = " << b[i][j] << "      ";
                     }
              cout << endl;
              }

       infile >> year >> month;
       for (day = 1;  day <= 31;  day++)
             {
             infile >> rainfall[year][month][day];
             }

       cout << endl << "Rainfall  for Year = " << year
            << ", Month = " << month << endl << endl;
       for (day = 1;  day <= 31;  day++)
             {
             cout << setw(3) << rainfall[year][month][day];
             if  (day == 7 || day == 14 || day == 21 || day == 28)  cout << endl;
             }
             cout << endl;
}
```

Both `b[][]` and `rainfall[][][]` are multidimensional arrays; `b[][]` is a two-dimensional array because it has two sets of brackets, and `rainfall[][][]` is a three-dimensional array because it has three sets of brackets. The array `b[][]` has 2 * 3 = 6 elements; `rainfall[][][]` has 10 * 13 * 32 = 4160 elements.

The maximum values of the loop control variables correspond to the declared array size, `b[2][3]`.

This `cout` statement simply creates a new line. It is needed only to make the output look the way that a two-dimensional array is typically written. It is placed in the outer loop after the inner loop.

A nested loop structure is often used with multidimensional arrays. Here, each element of the `b[][]` array is printed.

This loop reads one month of rainfall data. The loop loops over 31 days. Note that the year and month subscripts do not change each time through the loop.

This loop prints one month of rainfall data. The loop loops over 31 days.

Array output must look neat. This `if` structure creates a new line each seven increments of the variable, `day`. This makes the output look like a calendar.

Input File L8_1.DAT

```
4 12
0 2 0 29  0  1 2
3 0 7 22 11 12 6
0 3 4  2  8  7 5
7 6 0  4  9  7 8
1 9 8
```

Output

```
b[0][0] = 51          b[0][1] = 52          b[0][2] = 53
b[1][0] = 54          b[1][1] = 55          b[1][2] = 56

Rainfall for Year = 4, Month = 12
0  2  0 29  0  1  2
3  0  7 22 11 12  6
0  3  4  2  8  7  5
7  6  0  4  9  7  8
1  9  8
```

The output is in the form of a neat table. A `cout` statement devoted entirely to creating a new line is needed to make such a table.

Description

Representations of multidimensional arrays. A visual image of a one-dimensional array is a list of numbers; a visual image of a two-dimensional array is a matrix or a table (Fig. 10.1); and an image of a three-dimensional array is a block (Fig. 10.2). However, it is difficult to create a visual image of arrays with a greater dimension than three. In many cases it is not worth the effort to try to develop a visual picture even for three-dimensional arrays. For instance, for our array, `rainfall[][][]`, it was not necessary to create a physical image of a three-dimensional array because the division of year/month/day is natural. In fact, we easily could create a four-dimensional array of rainfall by simply breaking the data down into hours instead of just days, giving us `rainfall[year][month][day][hour]`. A five-dimensional array could take us down to the minute. All these are natural divisions with which you can work without developing a complex visual image. In other words, you need not struggle trying to develop a mental picture of a five-dimensional array. When you create large-dimensional arrays in programs, your divisions should be natural. If you make your divisions natural, you will find that it is straightforward to work with multidimensional arrays.

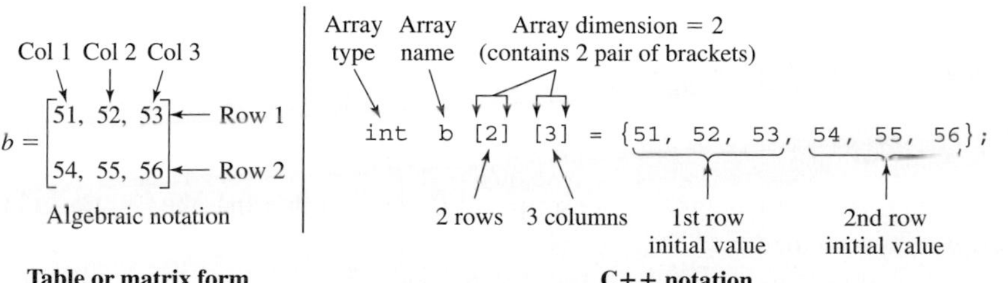

Figure 10.1

Conceptual image of the two-dimensional array, `b[][]`, for Lesson 10.1's program.

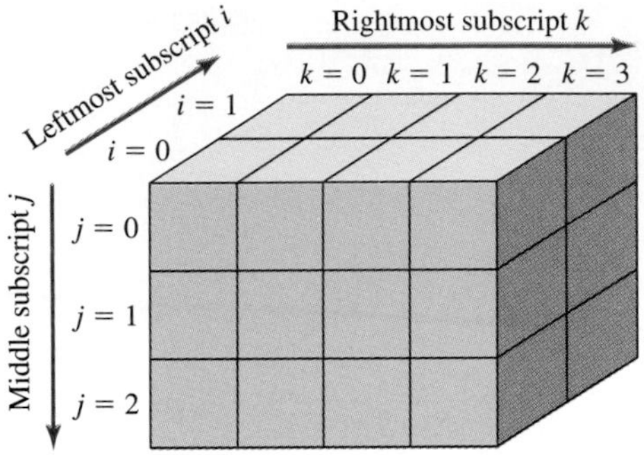

Figure 10.2

Image of 3-D array of size `[2][3][4]`.

Although visual images may be good conceptual tools for working with two or three-dimensional arrays, C++ actually stores the values in a line of adjacent memory cells. An image of a long list of values is equally valid and may be necessary at times when evaluating the contents of particular memory cells with multidimensional arrays.

Declaring multidimensional arrays. Declaring multidimensional arrays is similar to declaring one-dimensional arrays. For example,

```
int b[2][3];
```

declares (see Fig. 10.1) that:

- The name of the array is `b`.
- The type of the array elements is `int`.
- The dimension is 2 (it has two pairs of brackets `[]`).
- The number of elements or size is $2 \times 3 = 6$ (the product of the numbers in brackets).

Although you may have use for a large number of dimensions at some time in your programming career, you probably will find that it is unusual to need more than three dimensions. Therefore, in this text, we will focus on arrays with fewer dimensions. Should you need more dimensions, it is straightforward to extend the concepts described in this text.

Initializing multidimensional arrays in a declaration. Similar to a 1-D array, a multidimensional array can be initialized directly in the declaration. Using this method for a 2-D array, the array elements are initialized by row. For example, array `b[][]` with six elements is initialized in the declaration

```
int b[2][3] = {51, 52, 53, 54, 55, 56};
```

This initializes the elements to be

```
b[0][0] = 51    b[0][1] = 52    b[0][2] = 53
b[1][0] = 54    b[1][1] = 55    b[1][2] = 56
```

Note again that C++ begins its subscripts at 0. Also in this list, the rightmost subscript is incremented first.

We can use braces to separate rows in two-dimensional arrays. We have not shown the following declaration in this lesson's program, but we could have declared a two-dimensional array, `c[][]`. For instance, the declaration and initialization

```
int c[4][3] = {{1, 2, 3},
               {4, 5, 6},
               {7, 8, 9},
               {10,11,12}};
```

has each row contained in a separate set of braces. The advantage of this display is that the subscripts for each array element become more obvious. In addition, if we leave some values out of each row, we implicitly initialize them to 0. For instance,

```
int c[4][3] = {{1, 2},
               {4, 5, 6},
               {7},
               {10,11,12}};
```

initializes `c[0][2]`, `c[2][1]`, and `c[2][2]` to be 0.

We also can declare the far left dimension size (number of rows for a 2-D array) implicitly. For instance, the declaration

```
int c[][3] = {{1, 2, 3},
              {4, 5, 6},
              {7, 8, 9},
              {10,11,12}};
```

implicitly declares the number of rows to be 4.

Multidimensional array storage requirements. The product of the subscripts in the array declaration determines the storage requirements of multidimensional arrays. In this lesson's program, we declared the size of `rainfall[][][]` to be `rainfall[10][13][32]` to represent 10 years of daily rainfall data. Therefore, room for $10 \times 13 \times 32 = 4160$ `double`s is reserved in memory for this array.

For this particular array, we have not made the most efficient use of memory, since there are only 12 months in a year and at most 31 days in a month. We sized our array to be larger than is needed (which is `rainfall[10][12][31]`) because C++ begins its subscripting at 0. Had we sized `rainfall[][][]` for only 12 months, then the month of December would be represented by the subscript 11. Also, had we sized `rainfall[][][]` for only 31 days, then the 22nd day of the month would be represented by the subscript 21. It can be envisioned that this could cause some difficulties at one point in the programming process and could lead to bugs in a program. So, we have chosen to avoid this potential problem by simply adding one to the size of these dimensions.

This may not be the best programming practice because we require the program to reserve more memory than it needs. For small programs, this is not an issue and you are better off having a programming strategy that reduces the likelihood of error than one that saves insignificant amounts of memory. However, for larger programs, it may be important for you to reduce memory consumption. If this is the case, then you must adjust your programming to accommodate the fact that C++ begins at 0.

Remember, because the product of the declaration subscripts determines the size of memory reserved, as you add more dimensions to your arrays, the storage requirements may rise dramatically. It is possible to declare an array that is too big for your system. Should you do so, the computer will indicate an error on execution (not compilation).

Printing multidimensional arrays. Usually, we use a nested loop to print the elements of a multidimensional array. For a two-dimensional array, we use a two-deep nested loop with one variable controlling one subscript and another variable controlling the other. For example, for the array `b[2][3]` from this lesson's program, the following nested loop prints all the elements in the form of a matrix or table:

```
for (i = 0;i < 2;i++)
        {
        for (j = 0;j < 3;j++)
                {
                cout << "b[" << i << "][" << j << "] = " << b[i][j] << "     ";
                }
        cout << endl;
        }
```

Note that the outer loop loops over the number of rows and the inner loop loops over the number of columns. The inner loop (using `j` as the controlling variable) prints all the columns of one row, and the elements appear to be in one row in the output (see the output for this lesson's program). On leaving this loop, we have a single `cout` statement (contained within the outer loop) for the sole purpose of creating a new line. After creating a new line, control goes back to the inner loop to print another row. You should trace the flow of this loop (use a table of `i` and `j` values) to make sure that you understand it. You will use this form frequently in printing the results of your array calculations.

To print the rainfall data to the screen, we began with a short heading for the array and then used a loop to print a single month of data. To make the output appear somewhat like a calendar, an `if` statement with a `cout` statement created a new line every seven days (see this lesson's source code).

LESSON 10.2 READING 2-D ARRAYS FROM A FILE, STORAGE ARRANGEMENT, AND FUNCTIONS

TOPICS

- Reading an entire 2-D array from a file
- Element storage arrangement for multidimensional arrays
- Calling a function with a multidimensional array
- Using a multidimensional array in a function

This lesson's program is broken up into four sections:

1. Reading a 2-D array from a file.
2. Passing 2-D array information to a function.
3. Printing a 2-D array.
4. Using a function that performs operations on a 2-D array.

In working with arrays, it is necessary to remember that in the array declaration, we specify the maximum possible number of elements not the actual number of elements to be occupied.

The declared size should be larger (by a little bit) than the largest expected array to be stored.

We usually initialize array elements by reading them in from a file because a typical practical sized array has many elements. With one-dimensional arrays, it was relatively simple to count the number of elements actually being read in and set the loop control variables that work with the arrays to match the actual number of elements. With two-dimensional arrays, it also is possible to count the total number of elements being read in, but to work with 2-D arrays in loops, it is necessary to know how many rows and columns there are. One way to make this distinction is to have the number of rows and columns as input data in the file. In this lesson's program, we read the number of rows and columns of a 2-D array and the elements of the array. The array is modified in a function and printed to the screen.

Read the program. Note how a 2-D array is indicated in a function declaration.

QUESTION YOU SHOULD ATTEMPT TO ANSWER

1. Is an entire array passed to `function1`?

Source Code

```
#include <iostream>
#include <fstream>
using namespace std;

const int MAX_NUM_ROWS = 8, MAX_NUM_COLS = 10;

void function1(int, int, int[ ][MAX_NUM_COLS]);

int main ( )
{
     int i, j, num_rows, num_cols;
     int a[MAX_NUM_ROWS][MAX_NUM_COLS];
     ifstream infile ("C:\\L7_2.DAT");

//****************************************************************
//    SECTION 1 - READING A 2-D ARRAY FROM A FILE
//****************************************************************

     infile >> num_rows >> num_cols;
     for (i = 0; i < num_rows; i++)
          {
          for (j = 0; j < num_cols; j++)
               {
               infile >> a[i][j];
               }
          }
//************************************************************
// SECTION 2 - PASSING 2-D ARRAY INFORMATION TO A FUNCTION
//************************************************************

     function1(num_rows, num_cols, a);
```

`const int` variables for defining the maximum number of rows and columns of a 2-D array.

In a function declaration a 2-D array argument can have the left set of brackets empty, but the other set of brackets must be filled.

Declaring `a[][]` to be a 2-D array.

The actual number of rows and columns are read from the file and then used to control the loop to read the array elements.

Elements of a 2-D array are read one at a time, therefore a nested loop is required.

Calling `function1`. We pass the number of rows and number of columns along with the array address to the function.

```
//*************************************************************
// SECTION 3 - PRINTING A 2-D ARRAY
//*************************************************************
      for (i = 0; i < num_rows; i++)
             {
             for (j = 0; j < num_cols; j++)
                    {
                    cout << a[i][j] << " ";
                    }
             cout << endl;
             }
}

//*******************************************************************
// SECTION 4 - FUNCTION THAT PERFORMS OPERATIONS ON A 2-D ARRAY
//*******************************************************************

void function1 (int m, int n, int b[ ][MAX_NUM_COLS])
{
      int i,j;

      for (i = 0; i < m; i++)
             {
             for (j = 0; j < n; j++)
                    {
                    b[i][j] += 100;
                    }
             }
}
```

Elements of a 2-D array are printed one at a time using a nested loop.

In a function header a 2-D array argument can have the left set of brackets empty, but the other set of brackets must be filled.

Within a function, we also work with a 2-D array element by element.

Input File L7_2.DAT

```
3 4
1 2 3 4
2 4 6 8
3 5 7 9
```

Output

```
101 102 103 104
102 104 106 108
103 105 107 109
```

Description

Reading a multidimensional array from a file. In this lesson's program, the first line of the input file contained the number of rows and columns of our array, `a[][]`. This information allows us to properly work with the data. For arrays, remember the declared size gives the total number of elements that *can be used* by an array. It does not indicate how many are *actually used* for a particular problem. By reading in the number of rows and columns, we give the program the information needed to limit the number of array elements on which to operate.

Similar to how we print a two-dimensional array, we use a two-deep nested `for` loop to read the elements of a two-dimensional array. The following code first reads the number of rows and columns and uses those values in a nested loop to read the elements of the array `a[][]` from the data file represented by `infile`:

```
infile >> num_rows >> num_cols;
for (i = 0;  i < num_rows;  i++)
        {
        for (j = 0;  j < num_cols;  j++)
                {
                infile >> a[i][j];
                }
        }
```

Note that the outer loop loops over the number of rows and the inner loop loops over the number of columns, and that we read just a single element with each execution of the `infile` statement. Also, because this type of stream input automatically advances to a new line in its search for the next nonwhitespace value, there is no need to tell it to advance to a new line after a complete execution of the inner loop. For a three-dimensional array, a three-deep nested loop would work to read the array values from a file.

You may wonder what needs to be done if the number of rows and columns is not given as input. In this case, as we saw for one-dimensional arrays, it is possible for a program to use a loop to count the number of array elements until the end of file is encountered. However, it is more difficult to implement this system for two-dimensional arrays because we can get only the total number of elements and not the numbers of rows and columns.

Such things as sentinel values (values that are distinct from and cannot be confused with the other data values) can be used in a data file to indicate, for instance, the end of a row of data. Similar to how we handled the end of file, a program can be used to count the number of array elements until the sentinel value is encountered, giving the program the number of columns. The number of times that the sentinel value is encountered gives the number of rows.

Another way would be to put only the number of rows and the values of the array elements in the input file. By counting the number of values until the end of file is encountered, the number of columns can be calculated.

The method you use to determine or indicate the number of rows or columns can be developed based on the requirements of your problem.

Storage of two-dimensional arrays. The data file shows that array `a[][]` has three rows and four columns, meaning that it has a total of 12 elements. However, the declaration for `a[][]` is for eight rows and ten columns, meaning that a total 80 elements is reserved for `a[][]`.

One way to envision such a two-dimensional array is in matrix form, with the occupied rows and columns in the upper left corner and the rest of the array containing

Figure 10.3

Order of storage for the `a[][]` array in Lesson 10.2's program. The symbol * represents a memory location that has not been filled but may contain meaningless bits.

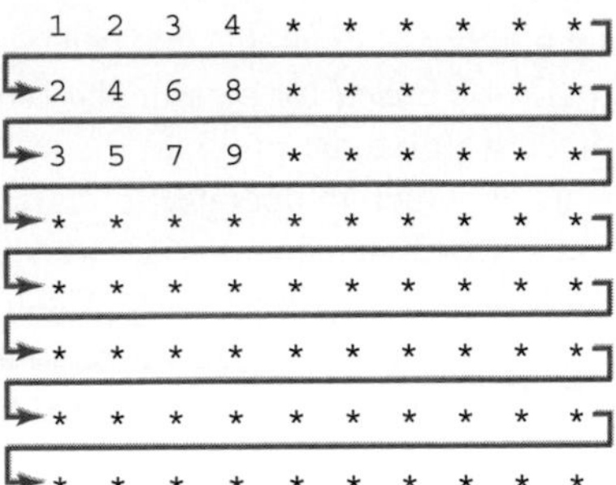

meaningless digits (represented by *):

```
1 2 3 4 * * * * * *
2 4 6 8 * * * * * *
3 5 7 9 * * * * * *
* * * * * * * * * *
* * * * * * * * * *
* * * * * * * * * *
* * * * * * * * * *
* * * * * * * * * *
```

Note that we have shown the entire declared array with eight rows and ten columns but only part of it filled.

Because C++ stores even multidimensional arrays in a linear type of fashion, the actual order of filled memory addresses for this array is in the order shown in Fig. 10.3.

You can see in Fig. 10.3 that the *filled* memory locations are not contiguous. The first four locations are filled, and the next six are not. Then four more are filled, and the following six are not. We describe this because there are times when you may need to access, for instance, the 10th element of a two-dimensional array. In this particular example, the 10th element is empty even though there are 12 initialized array elements. Unless you understand the order of storage, you may cause your program to access an uninitialized element.

Storage of three and greater dimension arrays. For 3-D arrays, the order of storage is that the first element stored has 0 in all its subscripts. The second element stored has all its subscripts 0 except the far right, which has a value of 1. For instance, for a 3-D array `e[][][]` (with a declared size of `e[2][3][4]`, which has a total of $2 \times 3 \times 4 = 24$ elements), the array elements are stored in this order (the space between every fourth element is shown only for visual clarity):

```
e[0][0][0]
e[0][0][1]
e[0][0][2]
e[0][0][3]

e[0][1][0]
e[0][1][1]
e[0][1][2]
e[0][1][3]
```

```
e[0][2][0]
e[0][2][1]
e[0][2][2]
e[0][2][3]

e[1][0][0]
e[1][0][1]
e[1][0][2]
e[1][0][3]

e[1][1][0]
e[1][1][1]
e[1][1][2]
e[1][1][3]

e[1][2][0]
e[1][2][1]
e[1][2][2]
e[1][2][3]
```

As you can see, the far right subscript increments first. The other subscripts increment in order from right to left.

For an array element, `e[x][y][z]` of an array declared with a size `e[I][J][K]`, C++ uses the following type of formula to locate the array element's position in the list and therefore its position in memory:

```
sequence location = x * (J * K) + y * (K) + z + 1
```

For example, for the previous 3-D array, `e[][][]`, we have declared the size to give `I` = 2, `J` = 3, and `K` = 4. The sequence location for element `e[0][1][2]` (`x` = 0, `y` = 1, `z` = 2) is

```
sequence location = 0 * (3 * 4) + 1 * (4) + 2 + 1 = 7
```

Therefore, in computer memory, `e[0][1][2]` is the seventh element stored (as illustrated in the list).

Note that in the formula the variable `I` (the leftmost size in the array declaration) never appears. In fact, one can develop similar formulas for greater numbers of dimensions (we leave this to you to do as an exercise), and it would be found that the declared size of the far left dimension is never needed to find the location in memory of an array element, whereas all the other sizes are required. Knowing this is significant because it plays a role in transferring multidimensional arrays to functions. When transferring multidimensional arrays to functions, we must pass along enough information to the function for it to be able to calculate the location of each array element in memory. Therefore, we must pass to the function the sizes of all the dimensions except the far left one. Should we choose, we can transfer the far left one as well; however, it is not required.

Passing multidimensional arrays to functions. The following function declaration, call, and header were used in this lesson's program:

Declaration `void function1(int, int, int[ ][MAX_NUM_COLS]);`

Call `function1(num_rows, num_cols, a);`

Header `void function1(int m, int n, int b[ ][MAX_NUM_COLS])`

This transfers the filled number of rows to m, the filled number of columns to n, and the address of array a[][] to b. The maximum possible number of columns is given in the declaration of b[][] in the argument list. In this function declaration and header, we must indicate that the third argument refers to a multidimensional array using two pairs of brackets. Like we saw with 1-D arrays, we do *not* pass a copy of the entire array to the function, only a copy of the address. In other words, if we look at the memory cells reserved for main and function1 in this lesson's program, they would be:

Variables in main

Name	Type	Address	Value
i	int	FFC7	0
j	int	FFC5	0
num_rows	int	FFC3	3
num_cols	int	FFC1	4
a	Array of int—size 8 × 10	FFFE	1
			2
			3
			4
			And others (see input file)

Variables in function1

Name	Type	Address	Value
m	int	FFAF	3
n	int	FFAD	4
b	Address of int	FFA1	FFFE

Note that b simply contains an address and not an entire array. This saves memory because all the array elements are not stored twice (once for main and again for function1). However, it also means that function1 accesses the original array directly and can modify the original array values. The programmer writing a function being passed an array address in this manner must realize that when the function modifies the array values, the original array is modified and may not be recoverable.

Recall that for a one-dimensional array, we indicated an array by using one pair of brackets. However, unlike the situation with a one-dimensional array for which the brackets were empty, we need to include the declared size of the second subscript (maximum number of columns) in the brackets. We need to include the maximum number of columns because the value is required in the formula used to calculate the sequence location of an element in a multidimensional array.

We can develop the sequence location formula to represent the location of an element of a two-dimensional array. For an array element, a[x][y] of an array declared with a size a[MAX_NUM_ROWS][MAX_NUM_COLS], the sequence location formula is:

```
sequence location = (x * MAX_NUM_COLS) + y + 1
```

For example, for this lesson's 2-D array a[][], we have MAX_NUM_COLS = 10. The sequence location for element a[1][2] ($x = 1, y = 2$) is

```
sequence location = (1 * 10) + 2 + 1 = 13
```

From the input file it can be seen that a[1][2] = 6, which is the 13th element in the list according to Fig. 10.3.

Note that in this formula and the calculation, MAX_NUM_COLS does appear, but MAX_NUM_ROWS does not. So, to locate an array element's position, only MAX_NUM_COLS needs to be known by a function. This is accomplished in C++ by including it in the second pair of brackets in the function declaration and function header.

If we were using a three- or four-dimensional array, except for the first pair of brackets all the brackets would be filled with their declared sizes. For instance, for a four-dimensional array declared as

```
const int I = 10, J = 5, K = 8, L = 3;
int a[I][J][K][L];
```

a declaration for a function, function1, would be of the form:

```
void function1 (int, int, int, int, int[ ][J][K][L]);
```

Note that the first four int values in this declaration are for passing the actually used size for each dimension. Remember, C++ only uses the values in brackets to calculate a location in memory. We must pass the used amount of each dimension as separate arguments. In this lesson's program, this was the variables m and n.

The const qualifier. If we want to assure that a multidimensional array is not modified in a function, we can use the const qualifier. This would give for the previous function

```
void function1 (int, int, int, int, const int[ ][J][K][L]);
```

Manipulating multidimensional arrays within a function. As with one-dimensional arrays, we use loops in functions to manipulate multidimensional array data. We use the number of rows and columns to control the loops. For instance, in this lesson's program, the body of function1 used m and n (number of rows and columns) to control the printing loop. In the application examples, we show more complex manipulations on multidimensional arrays in functions.

APPLICATION EXAMPLE 10.1 MATRIX-VECTOR MULTIPLICATION

TOPICS

- 2-D array manipulation
- Numerical method example

Problem Statement

Write a program that multiplies a matrix, a[][], and a vector, x[], giving a vector, b[], result (that is [a][x] = [b]). Read the input data from a file that contains the data in the form that looks like a matrix and vector; for example (using traditional subscripting, not C++ subscripting),

$$
\begin{array}{lllllll l}
a_{11} & a_{12} & a_{13} & a_{14} & a_{15} & a_{16} & a_{17} & x_1 \\
a_{21} & a_{22} & a_{23} & a_{24} & a_{25} & a_{26} & a_{27} & x_2 \\
a_{31} & a_{32} & a_{33} & a_{34} & a_{35} & a_{36} & a_{37} & x_3 \\
 & & & & & & & x_4 \\
 & & & & & & & x_5 \\
 & & & & & & & x_6 \\
 & & & & & & & x_7
\end{array}
$$

where the subscripts for the elements of the matrix are $a_{\text{row column}}$. Print the result to the screen. Write the program to handle the case of the number of rows being less than the number of columns.

Solution

First, assemble the relevant equations. Here, we briefly review multiplying a matrix and vector. For the given matrix and vector, the following equations give the components of the `b[]` vector:

$$b_1 = a_{11}x_1 + a_{12}x_2 + a_{13}x_3 + a_{14}x_4 + a_{15}x_5 + a_{16}x_6 + a_{17}x_7$$
$$b_2 = a_{21}x_1 + a_{22}x_2 + a_{23}x_3 + a_{24}x_4 + a_{25}x_5 + a_{26}x_6 + a_{27}x_7$$
$$b_3 = a_{31}x_1 + a_{32}x_2 + a_{33}x_3 + a_{34}x_4 + a_{35}x_5 + a_{36}x_6 + a_{37}x_7$$

We choose to write these equations in summation form because we found in Chapter 6 that, once written in summation form, the equations easily are translated into code with loops. For this case,

$$b_1 = \sum_{j=1}^{7} a_{1j}x_j$$
$$b_2 = \sum_{j=1}^{7} a_{2j}x_j$$
$$b_3 = \sum_{j=1}^{7} a_{3j}x_j$$

If you expand these three summation equations, you will see they are identical to the previous three equations. In general, we find that if we have n columns in our matrix, any value b_i can be represented as

$$b_i = \sum_{j=1}^{n} a_{ij}x_j \tag{10.1}$$

where i is 1, 2, or 3.

If we have m rows in our matrix, then we will have m values of b. Therefore, we should compute b_i from $i = 1$ to $i = m$.

SPECIFIC EXAMPLE

We evaluate the product `[a][x] = [b]` of the following matrix `[a]` (with 4 rows and 5 columns) and vector `[x]` (with 5 elements).

$$\begin{bmatrix} 2 & 4 & 5 & 3 & 6 \\ 9 & 8 & 4 & 1 & 4 \\ 0 & 9 & 1 & 3 & 9 \\ 9 & 8 & 2 & 4 & 1 \end{bmatrix} \begin{bmatrix} 2 \\ 5 \\ 2 \\ 5 \\ 1 \end{bmatrix}$$

We get [b] =

$$\begin{matrix} 2*2+4*5+5*2+3*5+6*1 = \\ 9*2+8*5+4*2+1*5+4*1 = \\ 0*2+9*5+1*2+3*5+9*1 = \\ 9*2+8*5+2*2+4*5+1*1 = \end{matrix} \begin{bmatrix} 55 \\ 75 \\ 71 \\ 83 \end{bmatrix}$$

ALGORITHM AND CODE SEGMENTS

The algorithm is straightforward:

1. Read the input data.
2. Calculate the b vector.
3. Print the b vector result.

The development of the code for steps 1 and 2 are shown next.

READING INPUT DATA

It is worth discussing the reading of the input data because the loops are not simple. The input file takes the shape of the matrix and vector to be multiplied, where the vector has a number of elements equal to the number of columns of the matrix. For instance, the following is a sample data file with the first line being the number of rows and columns in the matrix and the other lines being the matrix and vector:

```
3 8
2 4 6 4 3 6 8 9 4
9 8 7 6 5 8 9 6 3
8 7 6 4 1 0 2 8 6
                3
                4
                6
                0
                3
```

For infile representing the input data file and num_rows and num_cols representing the number of rows and columns of the matrix, the line

```
infile >> num_rows >> num_cols;
```

reads the first line of the data file. We can establish the loops using the values of num_rows and num_cols read with this line. Using the subscript i to represent the column and j to represent the row, the nested loop that follows reads the matrix and part of the vector from the data file. (Note: Because C++ begins at 0 not 1 for its subscripts, we do not follow exactly the subscript numbering shown at the beginning of this application example. Everything is shifted by 1.)

```
for (i = 0; i < num_rows; i++)  <---- Loop i over all the rows of the matrix.
     {
     for (j = 0; j < num_cols; j++)  <---- Loop over all the columns.
          {
          infile >> a[i][j];   ---- This inner loop reads the ith row of the a[][] matrix.
          }
     infile >> x[i];  <---- After having read each row of the matrix, this
                            statement reads the first element of the vector.
     }
```

With this code, we will have read lines 2, 3, and 4 of the sample data file. We now need to read lines 5, 6, 7, 8, and 9, which contain only elements of the vector. Again, because C++ begins at 0 for its subscripts, we do not begin the loop for reading x[] at num_rows + 1, we begin at num_rows. The next loop reads the rest of the x[] values:

```
for (i = num_rows; i < num_cols; i++) infile >> x[i];
```

Remember that the input skips over whitespace when reading numeric data, so shifting the column vector many spaces in the input file to the right has no significance.

CALCULATE THE b VECTOR

We use the right side of Eqn. 10.1 to create the inner loop for calculating an element of the vector `b[]`. The outer loop is used to compute all the `b[]` values. Compare the following code to Eqn. 10.1 to understand how the loop is created:

```
for (i = 0; i < num_rows; i++)
          {
          b[i] = 0;
          for (j = 0; j < num_cols; j++)
                   {
                   b[i] += a[i][j] * x[j];
                   }
          cout << endl << b[i];
          }
```

Outer loop (to compute all values of `b[]`). Note that the number of `b[]` values is the same as the number of rows.

Initializing `b[i]` to zero. This must be located between the inner and outer loops to make `b[]` for each row initially zero and so that the calculation can be performed.

Loop to calculate one element of the `b[]` vector. Compare this to the right side of Eqn. 10.1. Note that the number of multiplications is equal to the number of columns.

Print the `b[]` element calculated.

Note that between the outer and inner loop we have printed the value of each element of the `b[]` vector to the screen.

The entire source code follows.

Source Code

```
#include <iostream>
#include <fstream>
using namespace std;
const int MAX_NUM_ROWS = 20, MAX_NUM_COLS = 20;

int main ( )
{
      int a[MAX_NUM_ROWS][MAX_NUM_COLS], x[MAX_NUM_COLS];
      int b[MAX_NUM_ROWS];
      int i, j, num_rows, num_cols;
      ifstream infile ("C:\\DATA\\MATVECT.DAT");

      infile >> num_rows >> num_cols;

      for (i = 0; i < num_rows; i++)
            {
            for (j = 0; j < num_cols; j++)
                  {
                  infile >> a[i][j];
                  }
            infile >> x[i];
            }
      for (i = num_rows; i < num_cols; i++) infile >> x[i];
```

Reading the input file.

```
        cout << "b vector" << endl;
        for (i = 0; i < num_rows; i++)
            {
            b[i] = 0;
            for (j = 0; j < num_cols; j++)
                {
                b[i] += a[i][j] * x[j];
                }
            cout << b[i] << endl;
            }
}
```

Calculating the b vector.

INPUT DATA FILE

```
4 5
2 4 5 3 6 2
9 8 4 1 4 5
0 9 1 3 9 2
9 8 2 4 1 5
          1
```

Output

```
b vector
55
75
71
83
```

Comment

You will see that as you work with arrays in programming, much of your effort will be in manipulating the subscripts of the components of the arrays.

We also can see that it is relatively straightforward to take equations written in summation form and create loops that perform the calculations. The loops simply manipulate the subscripts used in the summation form. Because of the ease of conversion from equation to code, we recommend you write your equations in summation form whenever possible.

Modification Exercises

1. Make the matrix and both vectors `double` instead of `int`.
2. Modify the program to handle the situation of the number of rows being greater than the number of columns. Why will the current program not work in this situation?
3. Modify the program to have two functions—one for input and the other for calculations and output.

APPLICATION EXAMPLE 10.2 SEARCHING AND FILE COMPRESSION

TOPICS

- 2-D array manipulation
- File operations

Problem Statement

Write a program that compresses a file by creating a new file that can be used to generate it. The new file should be smaller than the original file. Check the result by making the program capable of using the new file to recreate the original file.

Solution

One method for compressing (or encoding) a file is to recognize repeated digits and replace the runs of repetition with a number representing the repetition length. For instance, the line

```
0011110000011111111111
```

can be represented with the line

```
2 4 5 11
```

because there are 2 zeros, 4 ones, 5 zeros, and 11 ones. It must be understood in advance that only zeros and ones appear and that zeros are the first to appear in a line. The new line of code is shorter and requires less memory than the original line. Thus, storing the new line is more efficient than storing the original. To expand (or decode) a compressed line, one need only carry out a reverse implementation. For instance, an encoded line

```
19 23 8 5
```

is decoded to be

```
0000000000000000000111111111111111111111110000000011111
```

SPECIFIC EXAMPLE

For this application example, we will work with a file containing 30 lines with 60 digits in each line as shown in Fig. 10.4. This is a type of bitmap with a treelike shape (traced by the ones).

By counting the numbers of zeros and ones in the file shown in Fig. 10.4, we get the encoded file shown in Fig. 10.5. You can see that the file in Fig. 10.5 is considerably smaller than the file in Fig. 10.4.

We can then use the file in Fig. 10.5 to generate the file in Fig. 10.4 by simply printing zeros and ones the number of times listed for each line.

ALGORITHM AND CODE SEGMENTS

This program consists of the following three basic steps.

1. Read the bitmap type file.
2. Compress (or encode) the file.
3. Expand (or decode) the file.

READ THE BITMAP TYPE FILE

To get the entire process going we need to read from the bitmap type file. This file has ones and zeros but no spaces! Typically, numbers in a file have spaces between them

```
000000000000000000111111111111111000000000000000000000000000
000000000000001111111111111111111111000000000000000000000000
000000000000011111111111111111111111111000000000000000000000
000000000000111111111111100000011111111100000000000000000000
000000000000111111111111000000001111111110000000000000000000
000000000000111111111110000000000111111110000000000000000000
000000000000111111111110000000000111111111000000000000000000
000000000001111111111110000000000111111111000000000000000000
000000000001111111111110000000000111111111000000000000000000
000000000001111111111110000000000111111111100000000000000000
000000000011111111111110000000000111111111100000000000000000
000000000011111111111110000000000111111111100000000000000000
000000000011111111111110000000000111111111100000000000000000
000000000011111111111110000000000111111111100000000000000000
000000000001111111111110000000000111111111100000000000000000
000000000000111111111111100000011111111100000000000000000000
000000000000011111111111111111111111111000000000000000000000
000000000000001111111111111111111111000000000000000000000000
000000000000000000111111111111111000000000000000000000000000
000000000000000000011111111111110000000000000000000000000000
000000000000000000001111111111100000000000000000000000000000
000000000000000000000111111111000000000000000000000000000000
000000000000000000000011111110000000000000000000000000000000
000000000000000000000011111110000000000000000000000000000000
000000000000000000000011111110000000000000000000000000000000
000000000000000000000011111110000000000000000000000000000000
000000000000000000000011111110000000000000000000000000000000
000000000000000000000011111110000000000000000000000000000000
000000000000000000000011111110000000000000000000000000000000
000000000000000000000000000000000000000000000000000000000000
```

Figure 10.4

Bitmap type sequence of zero and one that forms a tree-like figure. This figure serves as the input file for this application program.

to indicate the end of one number and the beginning of another. Without spaces, we could inadvertently make our program treat each line as a single integer with 30 digits. This, clearly, is not what we want. You may recall, though, from Lesson 4.4 that reading character data does not require spaces between the characters. Therefore, if we treat the input data file as a 2-D array `x[][]` of `char` (rather than an array of `int`), C++ will automatically read one digit of input at a time. The following code reads the data file and assigns either zero or one to each element of the `x[][]` array.

```
const int SIZE1 = 30, SIZE2 = 60;
char x[SIZE1][SIZE2];
for (i = 0; i < SIZE1; i++)
      {
      for (j = 0; j < SIZE2; j++)
            {
            infile >> x[i][j];
            }
      }
```

Using `const int` to size an array of `char`.

Loop over all the lines.

Loop over all the digits in one line.

Read one digit at a time into an array of `char`.

```
18 15 27
14 22 24
13 26 21
12 13  6  9 20
12 12  8  9 19
12 11 10  8 19
12 11 10  9 18
11 12 10  9 18
11 12 10  9 18
11 12 10 10 17
10 13 10 10 17
10 13 10 10 17
10 13 10 10 17
10 13 10 10 17
11 12 10 10 17
12 13  6  9 20
13 26 21
14 22 24
18 15 27
19 13 28
20 11 29
21  9 30
22  7 31
22  7 31
22  7 31
22  7 31
22  7 31
22  7 31
22  7 31
60
```

Figure 10.5

Compressed file representing type of bit map shown in Fig. 10.4.

COMPRESS THE FILE

To compress the file, we follow these steps:

1. Search a row for the first value that is different from the previous one. In other words, find the first 1 after a number of 0s or the first 0 after a number of 1s.
2. Count the number of digits passed to get to this value.

Figure 10.6

Illustration of search through a line with the loop shown.

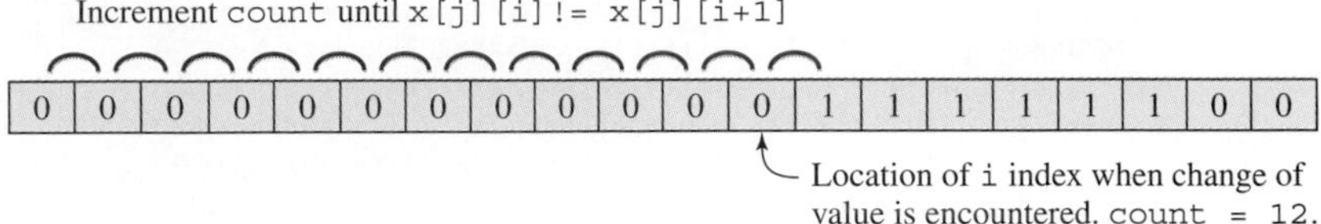
Increment count until x[j][i] != x[j][i+1]
0 0 0 0 0 0 0 0 0 0 0 0 1 1 1 1 1 1 0 0
Location of i index when change of value is encountered. count = 12.

3. Restart the count.
4. Repeat steps 1–3.

Steps 1 and 2 are illustrated in Fig. 10.6. We take the array as being `x[j][i]`, where `j` represents the row number and `i` the column number. We move from the left until `x[j][i]` is not equal to `x[j][i + 1]` (which means we encounter the first 1). In doing so, our array index, `i`, is equal to the index at the last 0 (12), and the count is also equal to 12 since 12 zeros are present.

The following code compresses a single line of the file.

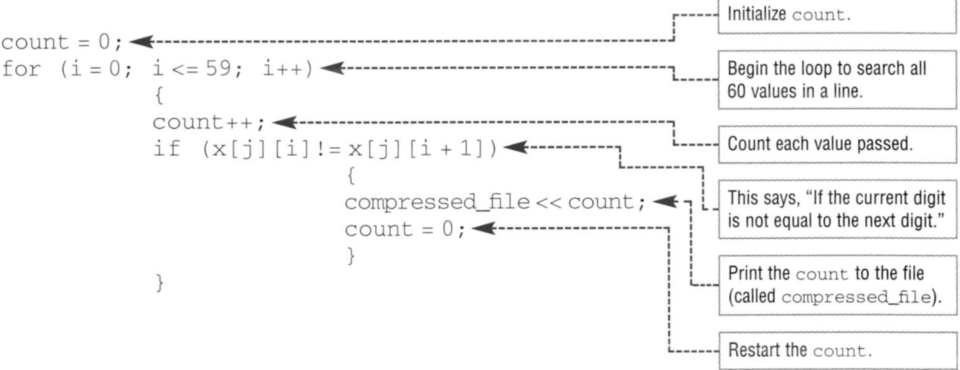
count = 0;
for (i = 0; i <= 59; i++)
{
count++;
if (x[j][i] != x[j][i + 1])
{
compressed_file << count;
count = 0;
}
}
Initialize count.
Begin the loop to search all 60 values in a line.
Count each value passed.
This says, "If the current digit is not equal to the next digit."
Print the count to the file (called compressed_file).
Restart the count.

We need to add three things to this sequence:

1. Compress all 30 lines.
2. Print the count and restart it if we are at the end of a line (`i` equal to 59).
3. Print a blank line after completing the search of one line.

The following code includes these added features:

```
for (j = 0; j <= 29; j++)          // Begin search of each of 30 lines.
    {
    count = 0;
    for (i = 0; i <= 59; i++)
        {
        count++;
        if (i == 59 || x[j][i] != x[j][i + 1])   // If at the end of line, print and restart count.
            {
            compressed_file << count;
            count = 0;
            }
        }
    compressed_file << endl;       // Create new line in file.
    }
```

EXPAND THE FILE

To expand one line of a compressed file, we follow the steps:

1. Set the first value (which we will call `a`) to be printed as 0.
2. Read the `count` from the compressed file.
3. Print the value of `a` (0 or 1) to the screen `count` times.
4. Toggle the value of `a` to be 1 from 0 or 0 from 1.
5. Sum all the `count`s in a line.
6. Repeat steps 2–5 until the sum of the `count`s = 60 (the number of digits in one line).

Using these six steps, the following code prints a single line of the bitmap type figure.

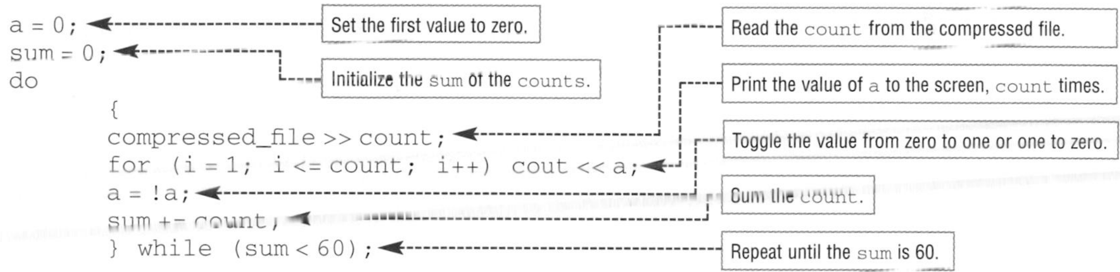
a = 0;
sum = 0;
do
{
compressed_file >> count;
for (i = 1; i <= count; i++) cout << a;
a = !a;
sum += count;
} while (sum < 60);
Set the first value to zero.
Initialize the sum of the counts.
Read the count from the compressed file.
Print the value of a to the screen, count times.
Toggle the value from zero to one or one to zero.
Sum the count.
Repeat until the sum is 60.

We need to perform the previous steps for each of the 30 lines. The process necessitates creating a new line for the output.

```
for (j = 1; j <= 30; j++)
        {
        a = 0;
        sum = 0;
        do
                {
                compressed_file >> count;
                for (i = 1; i <= count; i++) cout << a;
                a = !a;
                sum += count;
                } while (sum < 60);
        cout << endl;
        }
```

Loop over all the lines.

Previous code that prints a line of a decompressed file.

Begin new line on screen.

FILE INPUT AND OUTPUT

In writing this program, a few issues arise regarding reading from and writing to files. First, we need to both write to and read from the compressed file. We write to the file the `count`s from each line, and then we read the `count`s to print the original file. Prior to this, we only opened a file for either reading or writing but not both. To open a file for both reading and writing we create an `fstream` type object (not `ifstream` or `ofstream`). We call the file `compressed_file`. Within the parentheses in the declaration, we give the file name, and we indicate that the file is to be used for both input and output in the following manner:

```
fstream compressed_file ("C:\\DATA\\A6_5.OUT", ios :: in | ios :: out);
```

In this statement, `ios :: in | ios :: out` indicates that the file is to be used for both input and output. At this point, we will not go into the details of how this works; simply remember that adding `ios :: in | ios :: out` after a comma in the parentheses opens the file for both input and output.

Second, although we have not described this previously, it is worth noting now that associated with each file are two *file position indicators*. The file position indicators indicate the locations within a file at which reading or writing is to begin. In other words, at the end of writing to a file, the file position indicators are at the end of the file. This means that should we choose to write further in the file, the material printed would be put at the location of the writing file position indicator—at the end of the file. However, should we want to read from the file after having written to it, we need to reset the reading file position indicator to the beginning of the file. If we were to try to read from the file without having reset the reading file position indicator, we would encounter the end of the file without having read anything.

For instance, after the first 10 lines have been written, the file position indicators are located as shown in Fig. 10.7:

Resetting the reading position indicator to 0 bytes from the beginning of the file causes the indicator to be located at the beginning of the file as shown in Fig. 10.8.

In our program, we need to add a line to the code that resets the reading file position indicator. The C++ library function for doing this is `seekg`, which can be called with an `fstream` object. The call to this function takes the following form:

```
compressed_file.seekg (0, ios :: beg);
```

The arguments (`0` and `ios :: beg`) in the call to the function specify that the file position indicator should be reset to 0 bytes from the beginning of the file. (Note, file position indicators are sometimes called *file pointers* : *put pointer* for writing and

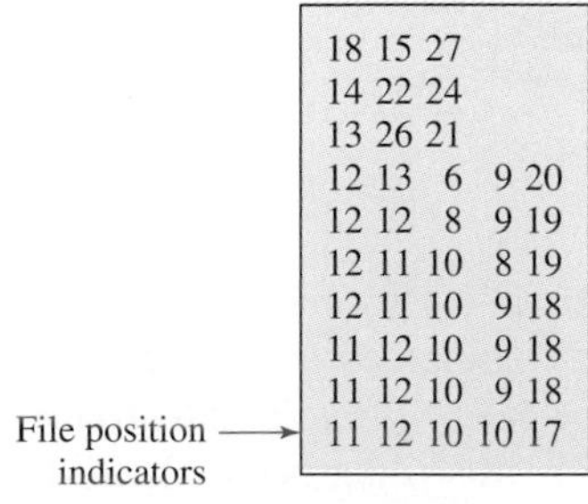

Figure 10.7

File position indicators after 10 lines have been written.

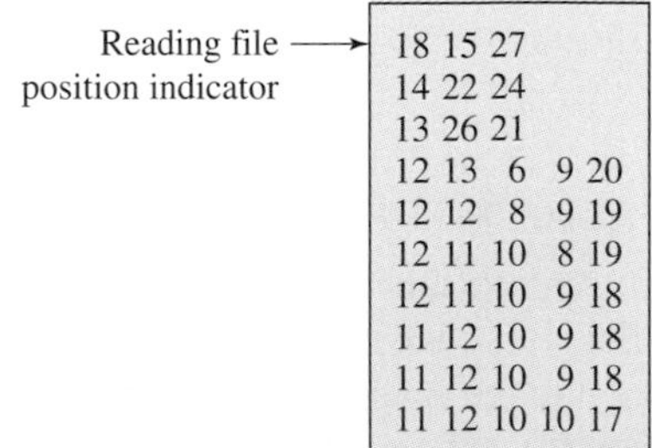

Figure 10.8

Reading file position indicator after the indicator has been reset to the beginning of the file.

get pointer for reading. We will not use these terms to avoid confusion with the term pointer used with pointer variables.) This line must be inserted in the code *after* the compressed file is created and *before* the compressed file is expanded.

Source Code

We have taken the blocks of code and put them in a final program. Only a few annotations are given since the code has already been explained.

```
#include <iostream>
#include <fstream>    <-- Including the fstream header so that we can open a file for both reading and writing.
#include <iomanip>
using namespace std;
const int SIZE1 = 30, SIZE2 = 60;
int main ( )
{
    char x[SIZE1][SIZE2];
    int i,j,a,count,sum;
    ifstream infile ("C:\\DATA\\A6_5.DAT");
    fstream compressed_file ("C:\\DATA\\A6_5.OUT", ios :: in | ios :: out);  <-- Opening a file for both reading and writing.

    for (i = 0; i < SIZE1; i++)
        {
        for (j = 0; j < SIZE2; j++)
            {
            infile >> x[i][j];            <-- Reading the input file.
            }
        }


    count = 0;

    for (j = 0; j < SIZE1; j++)
        {
        for (i = 0; i < SIZE2; i++)
            {
            count++;
            if (i == SIZE2 - 1 || x[j][i] != x[j][i + 1])   <-- Compressing the file.
                {
                compressed_file << count << " ";
                count = 0;
                }
            }
        compressed_file << endl;
        }
```

```
    compressed_file.seekg (0, ios :: beg);    <-- Resetting the reading file position indicator.
    for (j = 1; j <= SIZE1; j++)
            {
            a = 0;
            sum = 0;
            do
                    {
                    compressed_file >> count;
                    for (i = 1; i <= count; i++) cout << a;
                    a = !a;
                    sum += count;
                    } while (sum < SIZE2);
            cout << endl;
            }
}
```

Expanding the file.

INPUT FILE

Identical to Fig. 10.4.

OUTPUT FILE

Identical to Fig. 10.5.

Output

Identical to Fig. 10.4.

Comment

We indeed have created a file that is considerably smaller than the original file, and it can be used to create the original file should we want to do so.

In the complete source code, we have used `const int` type variables to size the arrays and to control all the loops.

Modification Exercises

1. Modify the program and input file to handle bitmaps of size 20 by 40. Is it easy to do?
2. Modify the program to have three functions—one for reading the input file, one for compressing the file, and one for expanding the file.

LESSON EXERCISES

LESSON 10.1 EXERCISES

1. Based on the declarations:

```
int a[3][1] = {1,2,3}, b[3], c[3][2], d[2][3];
```

determine whether each of the following statements is true or false:

a. Array `c[3][2]` contains $3 + 2 = 5$ elements.

b. The 1-D array `b[12]` can be used to store all data saved in the 2-D array `a[3][4]`.

c. Array `d[2][3]` contains six elements: `d[0]`, `d[1]`, `d[2]`, `d[3]`, `d[4]`, and `d[5]`.

d. Array `c[3][2]` contains six elements: `c[1][0]`, `c[1][1]`, `c[1][2]`, `c[0][0]`, `c[0][1]`, and `c[0][2]`.

e. Array `c[3][2]` can be thought of as containing three 1-D subarrays while array `d[2][3]` can be thought of as containing only two 1-D subarrays.

2. Find the error(s), if any, in each of these declarations:

a. `int a[2][0];`

b. `float a23b[99][77], 1xy[66][77];`

c. `double city[36][34], town(12)(34);`

d. `int a(2,3)={11,22,33,44};`

3. Use a nested `for` loop to print array `a[3][2]` and a nested `while` loop to print array `b[2][3]` defined here and print both in matrix form:

```
int a[3][2] = {11,22,33,44,55,66},
  b[2][3] = {111,222,333,444,555,666};
```

4. Array `a[3][4][2]` is initialized as follows:

```
int a[3][4][2] = {1,2,3,4,5,6,7,8,9,10,11,12,13,14,15,16,
  17,18,19,20,21,22,23,24};
```

What are the values of `a[1][1][1]`, `a[2][1][1]`, and `a[2][2][1]`?

5. Array `x[2][3][4][5]` is initialized as follows:

```
int x[2][3][4][5] = {1,2,3, ... through 120};
```

What are the values of `x[1][2][3][4]`, `x[0][1][3][1]`, and `x[1][0][0][4]`?

Solutions

1. a. false
b. true
c. false
d. false
e. true

2. a. The minimum subscript number is 1, not 0.
b. `float a23b[99][77], xy1[66][77],`
c. `long city[36][34], town[12][34];`
d. `int a[2][3]={11,22,33,44};`

LESSON 10.2 EXERCISES

1. True or false:

a. We can pass an array element by element, but it is usually easier to pass the array address.

b. We use pairs of brackets in function headers and declarations to indicate the dimension of the array referred to in the argument list.

c. If we have three pairs of brackets in a declaration, the last two must be filled with constant integers.

d. To efficiently work with a multidimensional array, it is necessary to pass the filled size of the array as separate arguments in a function call.

e. A partially filled multidimensional array has all its filled memory positions together at the beginning of the reserved block of memory.

2. The table below shows the length, width, and thickness of a stack of steel plates:

Length (ft)	Width (ft)	Thickness (in)
12.0	6.3	2.2
13.0	7.4	3.3
14.0	8.5	4.4
15.0	9.6	5.5

Within a function, use a 2-D array to store the length, width, and thickness information. Then convert the units from foot or inch to meter, calculate the weight of the steel plates, and save the results in a 1-D array (assume the unit weight of a steel plate is 7800 kg/m^3).

Solutions

1. a. true
b. true
c. true
d. true
e. false

APPLICATION EXERCISES

1. Construction engineers use concrete to build high-rise buildings. Since concrete nearly is incapable of resisting tension loads, reinforcing steel, known as rebar, is embedded in concrete to resist tension. The bar is available in a number of sizes. The following table shows the ASTM (American Society for Testing and Materials) standard reinforcing bars' size, weight, and diameter:

Size	Weight (lb/ft)	Diameter (in)	Size	Weight (lb/ft)	Diameter (in)
2	0.167	0.250	8	2.670	1.000
3	0.376	0.375	9	3.400	1.128
4	0.668	0.500	10	4.303	1.270
5	1.043	0.625	11	5.313	1.410
6	1.502	0.750	14	7.650	1.693
7	2.044	0.875	18	13.600	2.257

The next table shows the type and length of rebar used for the basement of a parking garage:

Size	Length (ft)
4	5000.0
10	2000.0
14	1200.0
18	900.0

Write a program to calculate the total weight of the rebar used.

The input specifications are these:

Use a 2-D array named `bar_data[20][3]` to read the ASTM standard reinforcing bars' size, weight, and diameter.

Use a 2-D array named `bar_used[10][2]` to read the bar used and length for the basement.

The output specification is to display the following data on the screen:

Size	Diameter (in)	Length (ft)	Weight (lb)
4	0.500	5000.0	3340.0
10	1.270	2000.0	. . .
14	1.693	1200.0	. . .
18	2.257	900.0	. . .
Total		. . .	. . .

2. Modify the program so that the output is generated by calling a function named `output()` from the `main()` function. The declaration of the `output()` function must contain at least the following two formal parameters:

```
void output (double input_bar_data[],
  double input_bar_used[], ...);
```

3. Modify the program to convert the output to metric units. Use the following conversions:

   1 in = 2.54 cm
   1 ft = 12.0 inch
   1 lb = 0.454 kg
   1 m = 100 cm

The output specifications are these: The output shall display the following data on the screen:

Size	**Diameter (cm)**	**Length (m)**	**Weight (kg)**
4	1.27	1524.0	1516.4
10	...	...	...
14	...	...	...
18	...	...	...
Total		...	...

4. Write a program that can calculate the sum of three equally sized matrices, [A], [B], and [C].

The input specifications are these:

Read the input from a file with the first line of the file being the number of rows and columns of each matrix.
The rest of the file has the elements of the matrices.

The output specification is to print the results to a file.

5. Write a program that can multiply two 6×6 matrices. The input specification is to read the matrices line by line from a file. The ouput specification is to print the output matrix to the screen.

6. Write a program that can multiply an $n \times m$ and $m \times n$ matrix together.

The input specifications are these:

Read n and m from the file.
Read the two matrices from a file.

The ouput specification is to print the results to a file.

7. Write a program that can solve a 3×3 set of equations such as

$$\begin{aligned} 3x_1 + 4x_2 - 5x_3 &= 2 \\ 22x_1 + 6x_2 - 12x_3 &= 28 \\ 6x_1 - 3x_2 + 2x_3 &= 5 \end{aligned}$$

Write the algorithm by solving these equations by hand, using the following steps. The input specifications are these:

Read the coefficients of x_1, x_2, and x_3 from a file.
Read the right-hand side of the equations from the same file.

The output specification is to print the solutions to the equations to the screen.

8. A 2-D array has these 20 elements:

```
3  33   333   3333
5  55   555   5555
1  11   111   1111
4  44   444   4444
2  22   222   2222
```

Write an exchange maximum program to do the following:

a. Sort the array so that it will look like this:

```
5    55    555    5555
4    44    444    4444
3    33    333    3333
2    22    222    2222
1    11    111    1111
```

b. Sort the array so that it will look like this:

```
1111    111    11   1
2222    222    22   2
3333    333    33   3
4444    444    44   4
5555    555    55   5
```

9. Use the following method to calculate the determinant of a 2-D $n \times n$ integer array. Assume $n = 3$ and the array `a[3][3]` is as follows:

```
11 12 13
21 22 23
31 32 33
```

The determinant $D = (11 \times 22 \times 33) + (13 \times 21 \times 32) + (12 \times 23 \times 31) - (13 \times 22 \times 31) - (11 \times 23 \times 32) - (12 \times 21 \times 33) = 0$.

The input specifications are these:

Read array `a[3][3]` as shown.

Use a `for` loop to generate eight 2-D arrays `b[n][n]` for which to find the determinants, where $n = 2, 3, 4, 5, 6, 7$, and 8.

The value stored in array element `b[i][j] = IJ` (the syntax `IJ` means placing `J` on the right side of `I`), where

`I` = `i` + 1 and `J` = `j` + 1

For example, when $n = 8$, `B[0][0]` = 11, `B[0][7]` = 18, `B[7][0]` = 81, `B[7][7]` = 88.

The output specification is to display the following data on the screen:

Array `a[3][3]` and its determinants.
Arrays `b[n][n]` and their determinants.

CHAPTER 11

POINTER VARIABLES

CHAPTER TOPICS

In this chapter, you will learn how to:

- Declare and initialize pointer variables
- Pass addresses to functions
- Return an address from a function
- Reserve memory during execution
- Link classes with accessor functions

Pointer variables (also called *pointers*) are variables that are used to store *addresses* rather than integers (like `int`) or real numbers (like `double`).

Being able to work with addresses in a program makes C++ able to perform low-level operations. This gives a programmer considerable control and increases the power of C++. Of course, control does not come without a price. You will see that if you make errors in programming with pointers, you can get some serious program crashes that can even result in freezing your computer!

We will see that pointer variables can be used to efficiently link classes and objects. They work extremely well in creating data structures such as stacks, queues, and linked lists. They are also necessary for using C++'s operators for reserving and unreserving memory during program execution. Although much can be accomplished in programming without pointer variables, you will find your programming skills are considerably enhanced by mastering the use of pointer variables.

Pointers have traditionally been considered a difficult topic to learn. However, if you understand the table of variables that C++ creates in working with pointer variables, you will likely find pointer variables reasonably straightforward to work with. In this chapter, we illustrate the mechanics of working with pointers. In subsequent chapters (12, 14, 15, and 16) we illustrate how they are used in C++ programs.

LESSON 11.1 BASICS OF POINTER VARIABLES AND ADDRESSES

TOPICS

- Pointer variable definition
- Using addresses
- "Address of" operator
- Dereferencing operator

QUESTION YOU SHOULD ATTEMPT TO ANSWER

1. What three different uses does the * symbol have in this program?

We can use addresses in programs in much the same way that we use street addresses in our daily lives. For instance, if there were a package waiting for us at a particular address, what would we do? Of course, we would go to that address and get the package. In our programs, we can do something similar. If we have an address we can get a value that is stored at that address using a special C++ operator (unary `*`).

Or, suppose we wanted to go to a friend's house but did not know his address. We would look up in a directory (using his name) and find his address. Similarly, C++ has an operator (`&`) that means "address of" to get the address of a particular variable.

Carrying the analogy of everyday life further, suppose we are asked to store cargo at a particular address we are given. To plan appropriately, we need to know if the address is for a small apartment, a garage, a warehouse, or whatever. In other words, we need to know the size of the location at the address we want to store something. C++ acts similarly with its addresses. It needs to know whether the memory cells at a particular address are capable of storing an `int`, `double`, or `float`, for instance. A programmer states the size of the value stored at the address in the declaration of the pointer variable.

Table 11.1 summarizes everyday life actions and the actions we can do in a program. Read the table to see examples of the C++ operators that work with addresses. Note that the operators `*` and `&` have been used in this book previously in performing operations that had nothing to do with addresses. We used `*` for multiplication of two variables (making it a binary operator) and `&` in creating references (that we used to transfer information to functions). We will see that we need to use these operators

TABLE 11.1 — Comparison between life actions and program actions

Example in daily life	Similar operation in program	C++ operation	Comment on C++ operation
Fetching a package from a location	Getting a value at an address	`*pointer_variable`	Uses unary `*` operator—not multiplication or binary `*` operator
Looking up a friend's address	Obtaining a variable's address	`&ordinary_variable`	Uses `&` operator in executable statement
Stating that at an address the storage region is large or small (for instance, a warehouse or small garage)	Declaring a pointer variable to have the address of a `double`, `int`, or other.	`double* pointer_variable;`	Uses `*` in a declaration to indicate that `pointer_variable` holds the address of a `double`

properly to assure there is no ambiguity between using them for address operations and ordinary operations.

This lesson's program calculates the volume of a cube using both ordinary variables and pointer variables. Follow the source code, and observe some address and basic pointer variable operations.

Source Code

```
#include <iostream>
using namespace std;

int main ( )
{
        double volume, height = 10.5, width = 5.2, depth = 3.1;

        double* height_address;
        double* width_address;
        double* depth_address;


        height_address = &height;
        width_address  = &width;
        depth_address  = &depth;


        volume = height * width * depth;
        cout << "Volume = " << volume << endl;


        volume = (*height_address) *
          (*width_address) * (*depth_address);
        cout << "Volume = " << volume << endl;
```

Declaring and initializing the dimensions of the cube.

Declaring three pointer variables: `height_address`, `width_address`, and `depth_address`. The `*` is needed to indicate that *addresses* (not ordinary `double`s) are stored in the variables' memory cells.

Assigning addresses to the pointer variables. The `&` operator is used to specify "address of" `height`, "address of" `width`, and "address of" `depth`.

We can calculate the `volume` using the ordinary variables: `height`, `width`, and `depth`.

We can also calculate the volume using the addresses of the ordinary variables. The `*` operator, used just before the pointer variables, means "get the value at." Here, we "get the values" at `height_address`, `width_address`, and `depth_address`.

```
        cout << "&volume = " << &volume << endl
             << "&height = " << &height << endl
             << "&width = " << &width << endl
             << "&depth = " << &depth << endl
             << "height_address = " << height_address << endl
             << "width_address = " << width_address << endl
             << "depth_address = " << depth_address << endl;
             << "&height_address = " << &height_address << endl
             << "&width_address = " << &width_address << endl
             << "&depth_address = " << &depth_address << endl;
}
```

Printing the addresses.

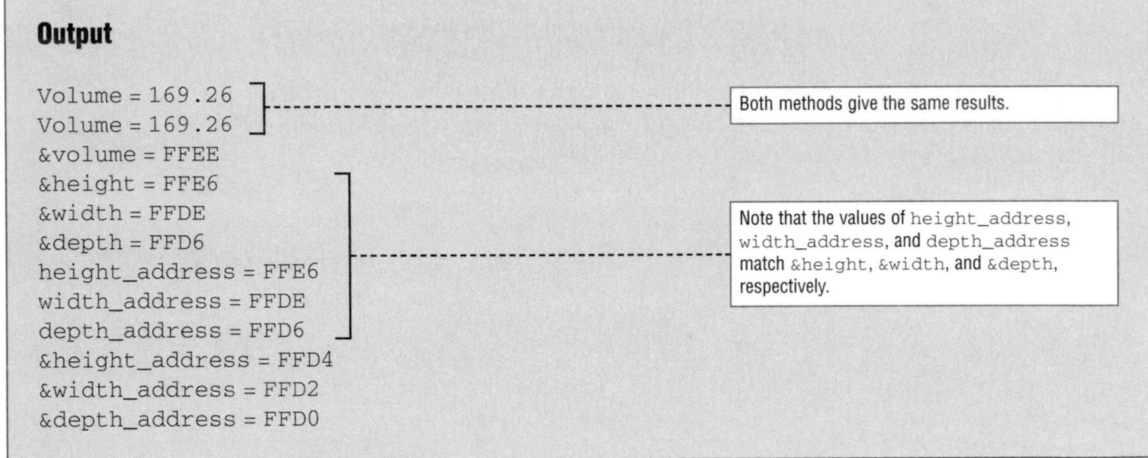

Output

```
Volume = 169.26
Volume = 169.26
&volume = FFEE
&height = FFE6
&width = FFDE
&depth = FFD6
height_address = FFE6
width_address = FFDE
depth_address = FFD6
&height_address = FFD4
&width_address = FFD2
&depth_address = FFD0
```

Both methods give the same results.
Note that the values of height_address, width_address, and depth_address match &height, &width, and &depth, respectively.

Description

Declaring a pointer variable. Pointer variables are declared with a data type, `*`, and identifier, for instance:

```
double* height_address;
```

declares `height_address` to be a pointer variable. This means that `height_address` can store an address rather than an integer or real number. The `double` in the declaration indicates that at the address stored by `height_address` is a `double` value.

In general, we can declare a pointer variable with:

```
type* pointer_variable;
```

where *`type`* is any ordinary data type such as `int` or `double`, and *`pointer_variable`* is a programmer chosen name that conforms to the identifier rules. The `*` is required to follow the data type. Whitespace is allowed between *`type`* and `*`, although in this text, we prefer to use no whitespace. Without whitespace, it is more obvious that the declaration is for *`type*`* and not just *`type`*.

Note that a declaration for a pointer variable is similar to a declaration for an ordinary variable in that the declaration simply reserves space for storage. The declaration does *not* put anything into the storage space. We must initialize or assign an address to a pointer variable to make use of it.

Assigning an address to a pointer variable. We use the "address of" operator (&) to help us assign addresses to pointer variables. For example,

```
height_address = &height;
```

assigns the address of the ordinary variable height to the pointer variable height_address.

In general, we can assign an address to a pointer variable using an assignment statement of the sort:

```
pointer_variable = &ordinary_variable;
```

where *pointer_variable* is the name of the pointer variable, and *ordinary_variable* is the name of the ordinary variable.

Table of variables. In this lesson's program we declare and initialize three pointer variables and four ordinary variables. After executing the program, the table of variables is shown in Table 11.2.

Note that the *values* of the pointer variables (height_address, width_address, and depth_address) are *addresses* not integer or real values! The arrows in the table indicate the correspondence between the ordinary and pointer variables. Because we made the assignment height_address = &height, height_address holds FFE6, which is the address of height. Similarly, the assignment statements in the program:

```
width_address = &width;
depth_address = &depth;
```

cause the other pointer variables, width_address and depth_address to hold addresses in their memory cells. The arrows in Table 11.2 show why these variables are called pointer variables. In effect, the addresses in the value column "point to" addresses of other variables.

Using a pointer variable. A pointer variable can be used to access a value. We simply go to the address that the pointer variable stores and get it. The unary * operator

TABLE 11.2 — Table of variables for this lesson's program

Name	Type	Address	Value
volume	double	FFEE	169.26
height	double	FFE6	10.5
width	double	FFDE	5.2
depth	double	FFD6	3.1
height_address	Address of double	FFD4	FFE6
width_address	Address of double	FFD2	FFDE
depth_address	Address of double	FFD0	FFD6

does it. For instance,

```
*height_address
```

gets the value stored at the location held by height_address. Since the value held by height_address is FFE6, *height_address gets the value at address FFE6, which is 10.5 (as indicated in the Table 11.2). Remember, when we write

```
*pointer_variable
```

in an executable statement (not a declaration), we are indicating a value not an address. Because of this, we can use *pointer_variable on the right side of an assignment statement as we did with

```
volume = (*height_address) * (*width_address)
  * (*depth_address);
```

in this lesson's program. Here:

```
*height_address
*width_address
*depth_address
```

indicate values and therefore can be put into arithmetic expressions.

You should be aware that a common suffix for pointer variables is ptr. In other words, common names for the pointer variables used in this program might be

```
height_ptr
width_ptr
depth_ptr
```

In this text, we sometimes use the suffix address because we believe it to be more descriptive of what the variable stores and, therefore, easier for a learning programmer to understand.

Visual image of & and * actions. The actions of the & ("address of") and * ("get the value at the address") operators are illustrated in the table of values shown in Table 11.3. The & operation is represented by an arrow pointing to the left. The * operation is a zig-zag arrow going to the left and then to the right. This table shows the actions &height and *depth_address. The visual images of the arrows can be

TABLE 11.3 — Actions of & and *. Shown here are &height and *depth_address

Name	Type	Address		Value
volume	double	FFEE	&	169.26
height	double	FFE6	←	10.5
width	double	FFDE		5.2
depth	double	FFD6	→	3.1
height_address	Address of double	FFD4		FFE6
width_address	Address of double	FFD2	*	FFDE
depth_address	Address of double	FFD0		FFD6

used to remember the actions of these operators. If you forget what these operators do, you can think of this visual image.

Uses of *. Note that * has been used in the programs in this book for three different purposes. They are

1. The binary multiplication operator, for example,

```
volume = height * depth * width;
```

2. The declaration specifier indicating that an address is to be stored in a variable's memory cell, for example,

```
double* height_address;
```

3. The unary operator (unary meaning that there is only one operand) indicating to get a value or access the memory cells at the address stored, for example,

```
(*height_address)
```

Note that we are also allowed to use the unary * operator on the *left* side of an assignment statement. We have not shown it in this lesson's program, but we could have assigned a value to the variable height using:

```
*height_address = 10.5;
```

The left side of the assignment statement accesses height's memory cells, and therefore this statement puts the value 10.5 into those memory cells.

We point out these different applications of * because it is important that you not confuse one application with another. Observe that whenever * is used in a declaration or header, the usage corresponds to the second purpose. When * appears in an assignment statement, you will need to look at the expression closely and determine if it is a binary or unary operator to distinguish between the first and third purposes.

Uses of &. The & symbol has been used in the programs in this book for two different purposes. They are

1. In a declaration (typically a function declaration) or function header to indicate a reference.
2. In an executable statement to indicate "address of."

When & is used in a function declaration such as

```
void function1 (double&)
```

it is the first purpose, and it indicates that the argument is a reference (alias) in function1 (see Chapter 7). When & is used in an executable statement such as:

```
height_address - &height;
```

it is the second purpose, and it means the address of height (which is FFE6).

In general, an & used in the argument list of a function declaration or header (not function call) indicates purpose 1 (a reference). (Note that we can create a reference without involving a function, but this is not commonly done.) When & is used in an assignment statement or function call, it usually corresponds to the second purpose ("address of").

Notation. The spacing in a declaration or header using `*` is somewhat flexible depending on a programmer's preference.

Either of these styles is acceptable in declarations with pointer variables.

```
double* height;
double *height;
```

We prefer the first of these because it clearly indicates that `height` is the pointer variable and the type is `double*` (meaning a pointer type). However, this type of spacing becomes clumsy when many pointer variables are used in a normal declaration (as we may find to be useful). For instance, in this lesson's program, to declare pointer variables `height_address`, `depth_address`, and `width_address` all on the same line, C++ does *not* accept this as correct

```
double* height_address, width_address, depth_address;
```

It is a bit of a quirk in the C++ syntax in that if you made this declaration, C++ would interpret this to make `height_address` a pointer variable, but `width_address` and `depth_address` would be ordinary `double` variables! Using the spacing we like requires three declarations

```
double* height_address;
double* width_address;
double* depth_address;
```

as we have used in this lesson's program.

However, this all can be done in one declaration using the other spacing method with

```
double *height_address, *width_address, *depth_address;
```

This declaration is interpreted by C++ to mean that `height_address`, `width_address`, and `depth_address` are all pointer variables. This is probably the most commonly used form, but we find it somewhat confusing for students learning about pointers, and therefore use the separate declaration form. Remember, when you see this type of notation, the variable names are `height_address`, `width_address`, and `depth_address`, not `*height_address`, `*width_address`, and `*depth_address`.

Invalid operations with `&` and `*`.

- We cannot use the statement (for example)

  ```
  &height = FFE6;
  ```

  if we wanted for some reason to make sure to store the variable `height` in the memory cell whose address is FFE6, because we have no control over the address. We do not know, at the time we are writing our program, that the memory cell FFE6 will be open. (There are other problems with this statement, not worth discussing at this time.) C++ determines the addresses itself, so, we cannot have `&` on the left side of an assignment statement!

- While we can use the `&` operator on all the variables in this program (provided it is not on the left side of an assignment statement), we are not allowed to use the unary `*` operator on all the variables. The unary `*` operator must be used only on variables declared with `*` in the declaration—that is, pointer variables. Thus, we cannot use

```
*height = 10.5;
```

in `main` because the variable `height` had no `*` in its declaration (and, so, has no address in its memory cell).

- We also cannot have the statement

```
height_address = 10.5;
```

because the variable `height_address` should hold only an address.

- We can have pointer variables of different types. For instance, in this lesson's program we could have declared a pointer variable `integer_address` with the declaration

```
int* integer_address;
```

Had we done so, we would not have been allowed to write

```
integer_address = &height;
```

because `integer_address` is an integer type pointer variable while `height` is a `double`. Remember, the pointer variable type and the address type must be identical. An exception to this is that C++ allows a `void*` type pointer, such as

```
void* multi_type_address;
```

which allows the assignment:

```
multi_type_address = &height;
```

This pointer variable has some advantages when multiple types are used. However, we will not use such a pointer variable in this text.

Another analogy. Students frequently find pointer variables somewhat abstract, so we offer another analogy that may add some clarification to the previous discussion (see Fig. 11.1). If you feel comfortable with the material already presented in this lesson, you do not need to read this section. The analogy is as follows.

Suppose that:

1. You own a van and are interested in going into the business of renting it out to people that need it for moving.
2. You must keep the van at a remote location.
3. There is a rental support agency that keeps a registry book of vehicles available for rent.

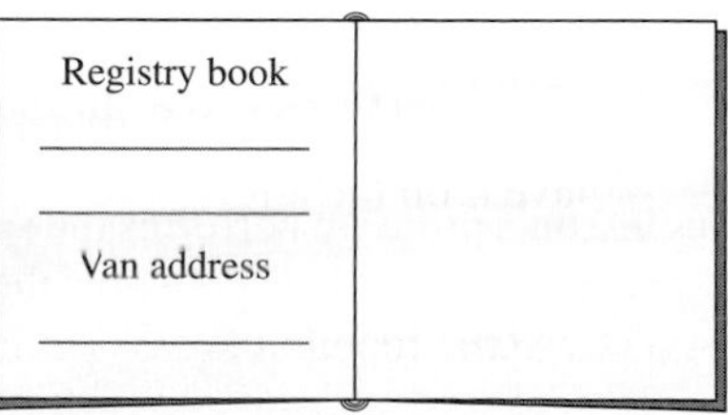

Figure 11.1

A van in a garage is like an initialized ordinary variable. The registry book with the van address is like an initialized pointer variable.

The steps you need to make your business work can be similar to working with pointer variables in a program. The steps are:

1. Ask the rental support agency to reserve a line in their registry book for you to write the address where your van is located. (Like declaring a pointer variable.)
2. Reserve a remote location to store your van. That is, reserve space for your van. (Like declaring an ordinary variable.)
3. Store your van at the location. (Like initializing the ordinary variable.)
4. Write the address of your van in the agency's registry book. (Like using the `&` operator and assigning the address of the ordinary variable to the pointer variable.)
5. People go to the address, get the van, and use it. (Like using the unary `*` operator with a pointer variable.)

Analogies by nature are not perfect, but this one may make you feel more comfortable with the concept of addresses and pointer variables. Figure 11.1 shows the van in a garage. This is similar to an initialized ordinary variable (the variable's memory cell is the garage; the variable's value is the van). The registry book with the van's address is like an initialized pointer variable (the pointer variable's memory cell is the line in the registry; the pointer variable's value is the address written). Using the van address to get the van is like using the `*` operator on a pointer variable.

Comment. The same addresses may or may not be printed out when this lesson's program (or other programs in this chapter) is run on a different computer system such as yours. The actual addresses are not important to the performance of this program. As long as the correspondence of the addresses for the different variables exists, the program will perform properly.

LESSON 11.2 POINTER VARIABLES AND FUNCTIONS

TOPICS

- Transferring an address to a function
- Using an address in a function

QUESTION YOU SHOULD ATTEMPT TO ANSWER

1. The variable height is 10.5 in `main`. Should we desire, can we change this value within function `calc_volume()`?

We saw in Chapters 9 and 10 that we can pass addresses to functions. Passing addresses to functions is valuable in working with arrays because it eliminates the need for storing an entire array's contents in the function's memory region. We will see that there are also other situations when passing addresses to functions is valuable. For instance, we may be interested in passing the address of an object or an ordinary variable to a function.

If we want to transfer the address of an ordinary variable to a function, we need to indicate so in the function declaration, call, and header. In the declaration and header, we use `double*` or `int*` (or *`type*`*) in the argument list to indicate an address is being received. In the function call we use `&variable` in the argument list to pass an address.

This lesson's program performs the same calculations as Lesson 11.1's program. Read the source code and observe how the addresses of `height`, `width`, and `depth` go from `main` to the function `calc_volume()`.

Source Code

```
#include <iostream>
using namespace std;

double calc_volume (double*, double*, double*);

int main ( )
{
        double volume, height = 10.5, width = 5.2, depth = 3.1;

        volume = height * width * depth;
        cout << "Volume = " << volume << endl;

        volume = calc_volume (&height, &width, &depth);
        cout << "Volume = " << volume << endl;
}

double calc_volume(double* height_address,double* width_address,double* depth_address)
{
        double volume;
        volume = (*height_address) * (*width_address) * (*depth_address);
        return (volume);
}
```

Declaring a function with three pointer variables (type `double*`) as arguments. This means these arguments hold addresses. The function returns a `double`.

Declaring and initializing ordinary variables.

Calculating the volume using ordinary variables.

Calling the function to calculate the volume. Here, the `height`, `width`, and `depth` addresses (`&height`, `&width`, and `&depth`) are passed to the pointer variables (`height_address`, `width_address`, and `depth_address`).

Within the function we use `*height_address`, `*width_address`, and `*depth_address`. These represent the values `height`, `width`, and `depth`, respectively.

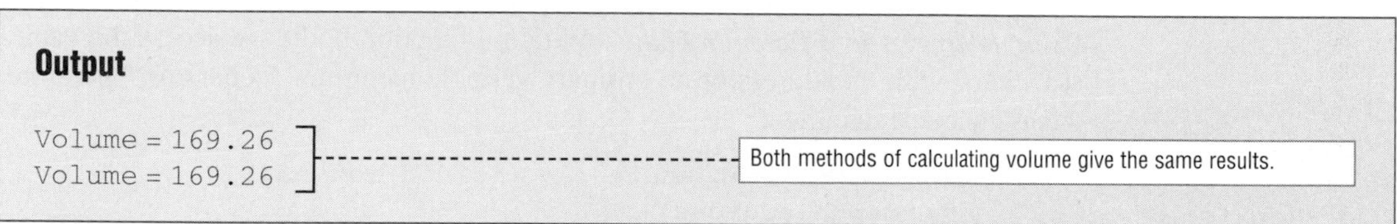
Output
Volume = 169.26
Volume = 169.26
Both methods of calculating volume give the same results.

Description

Transferring addresses to functions. The function declaration, call, and header in this lesson's program illustrate the way addresses are passed to functions. They are:

```
double calc_volume (double*, double*, double*);            <-- Function declaration.

volume = calc_volume (&height, &width, &depth);            <-- Function call.

double calc_volume (double* height_address, double* width_address, double* depth_address)    <-- Function header.
```

TABLE 11.4 — Table of variables for Lesson 11.2's program

Name	Type	Address	Value
In main			
volume	double	FFEE	169.26
height	double	FFE6	10.5
width	double	FFDE	5.2
depth	double	FFD6	3.1
In calc_volume			
height_address	Address of double	FFD4	FFE6
width_address	Address of double	FFD2	FFDE
depth_address	Address of double	FFD0	FFD6
volume	double	FFCD	169.26

It is seen from these that the function declaration has three pointer variables, the function call has three addresses, and the function header has three pointer variables. This means the addresses are passed to the pointer variables. The table of values (Table 11.4) shows that the pointer variables of function calc_volume hold the addresses of the variables in main.

In other words, this transfer of information to a function is equivalent to the statements:

```
height_address = &height;
width_address = &width;
depth_address = &depth;
```

Note that we did not need to use the & operator to transfer the address of an array to a function because the name of the array without brackets means the array address. Remember, to transfer the address of an ordinary variable to a function use the & operator in the function call.

Using addresses in a function body. Within a function body, we access the values associated with an address of an ordinary variable using the * operator. Therefore, the assignment statement

```
volume = (*height_address) * (*width_address)
  * (*depth_address);
```

accesses the values of height, width, and depth in a manner shown in Table 11.5. Because the variables in function calc_volume access main's variables' memory cells, the calc_volume function can modify main's variables. We do not modify them in this lesson's program; however, often the purpose of passing addresses to a function is to have the function modify the values of the variables in the function call.

References vs. pointer variables for information transfer to a function. If we want to modify a variable's value in a function, we can also use the pass by reference form (Lesson 7.3). In most cases, the pass by reference form is preferable to passing addresses because serious errors can be caused if addresses are used improperly. However, we show passing addresses to pointer variables because you may see such actions in programs written by others and because these actions are fundamental.

TABLE 11.5 — The actions of `*height_address`, `*width_address`, and `*depth_address` on the table of variables for Lesson 11.2's program

Name	Type	Address	Value
In main			
volume	double	FFEE	169.26
height	double	FFE6	10.5
width	double	FFDE	5.2
depth	double	FFD6	3.1
In calc_volume			
height_address	Address of double	FFD4	FFE6
width_address	Address of double	FFD2	FFDE
depth_address	Address of double	FFD0	FFD6
volume	double	FFCD	169.26

LESSON 11.3 POINTER VARIABLES WITH ARRAYS AND FUNCTIONS

TOPICS

- Using * notation in passing array information to a function
- Working with a pointer variable in a function

QUESTION YOU SHOULD ATTEMPT TO ANSWER

1. What type of notation is used with the pointer variable `b` in `function2`?

We can use pointer variables to transfer array information to a function. As we discussed in Lesson 9.4 (if you forget this lesson, you should reread it), C++ allows the pointer declaration form (with `*`) to be used in place of the bracket declaration form (with `[]`) to transfer the address of an array to a function. Now we can understand why it works.

Consider a program similar to the one in Lesson 9.4. Read the code and see how `double*` rather than `double[]` appears in the function declaration and header.

Source Code

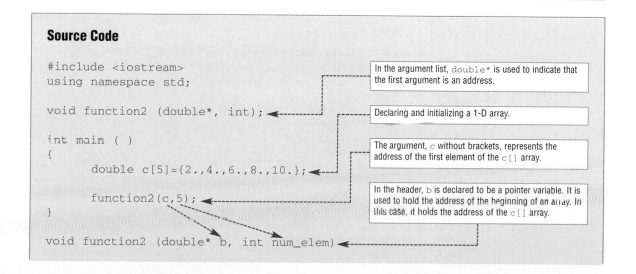

```
#include <iostream>
using namespace std;

void function2 (double*, int);

int main ( )
{
      double c[5]={2.,4.,6.,8.,10.};

      function2(c,5);
}

void function2 (double* b, int num_elem)
```

In the argument list, `double*` is used to indicate that the first argument is an address.

Declaring and initializing a 1-D array.

The argument, `c` without brackets, represents the address of the first element of the `c[]` array.

In the header, `b` is declared to be a pointer variable. It is used to hold the address of the beginning of an array. In this case, it holds the address of the `c[]` array.

```
{
        int i;
        for   (i = 0; i < num_elem; i++)
               {
               b[i] *= 10.;
               cout << b[i] << endl;
               }
}
```

Even though b is a pointer variable, C++ allows the use of array notation (as shown by b[i]) to access memory cells located beyond the one stored by b.

Output

```
2
4
6
8
10
```

Description

Transfer of information to the function. Note that the declaration, call, and header for `function2` are:

Function declaration	**`void function2 (double*, int);`**
Function call	**`function2 (c, 5);`**
Function header	**`void function2 (double* b, int num_elem)`**

The function declaration indicates that the first argument is a pointer variable (meaning it holds an address). The function call has the array name `c`, which you should recall represents the address of the beginning of the `c[]` array. The first argument in the function header indicates that `b` is the name of the pointer variable. The arrows show that the address of the `c[]` array is stored in the `b` variable. Thus, within `function2`, the identifier `b` is used to work with the array elements.

Function body. Within the body of the function

```
for (i = 0; i < num_elem; i++) b[i] *= 10.;
```

C++ allows array type notation with `b` (as in `b[i]`) to move beyond the address stored by the `b` pointer variable. Therefore, within `function2`, `b[0]` represents the value at the memory cell address stored by `b`. And `b[1]` represents the value in the memory cell that is 1 (for a `double`, 4 bytes) past the address stored by `b`. The number enclosed in brackets represents the number of memory cells past the address stored by `b`.

TABLE 11.6 — Passing a value, identifier, and address to a function

Passed to a function	Type in function declaration and header (*type* indicates `int`, `double`, or other)	Argument in function call
Value	*type*	*name* (of ordinary variable)
Identifier	*type&*	*name* (of ordinary variable)
Address	*type** or *type[]*	*name* (of array) or *&name* (of ordinary variable)

In general, an acceptable form for declaring, calling, and defining a function being transferred an array is:

Declaration
```
rtype function (type*, int);
```

Call
```
function (array, num);
```

Definition
```
rtype function (type* b, int num_elem)
{
code using b with brackets (b[i])
}
```

where *rtype* is the function return type, *function* is the function name, *type* is the array data type, *num* and *num_elem* are the number of array elements with which to work, *array* is the array name, and *b* is the name of the pointer variable used to store the address of the array. Using such notation (that is, with the transfer of address information in the argument list being written with * and not brackets [], as used in Chapter 9) still allows the function body to use brackets with the pointer variable. This makes the pointer variable name look like an array name. However, the contents of the array are not stored in the memory region for the function. Only the address of the beginning of the array is stored there.

In summary, we have seen in this text that we can pass to a function a *value*, *identifier*, or *address*. Remember, we pass a value when we want a function to work with an ordinary variable value and *not change* it. We pass an identifier (using a reference) when we want a function to work with an ordinary variable value and *change* it. We pass an address when we want a function to work with an array. Table 11.6 summarizes how we write the type in the function declaration and function call to pass these entities to a function.

LESSON 11.4 OTHER MANIPULATIONS WITH POINTER VARIABLES

TOPICS

- Array notation with pointer variables
- Pointer arithmetic

C++ allows addition and subtraction with pointer variables. However, if we add 1 to a pointer variable, C++ does not interpret this to be adding 1 byte to the address. Instead, C++ is smart enough to look at the type of the pointer variable being added to and adds the proper number of bytes. (For this lesson we assume

QUESTION YOU SHOULD ATTEMPT TO ANSWER

1. In previous programs, we used an array name alone to represent the address of the first element. How has the address of the first element been represented in this program?

that a `double` occupies 8 bytes of memory, which is the minimum required by standard C++.) For instance, if a pointer variable is declared to be `double*`, then adding 1 to that variable adds 8 bytes so that the pointer can advance to the next `double` in memory.

Read the program and observe how `&` can be used with array values and how we can use array notation and pointer arithmetic with pointer variables.

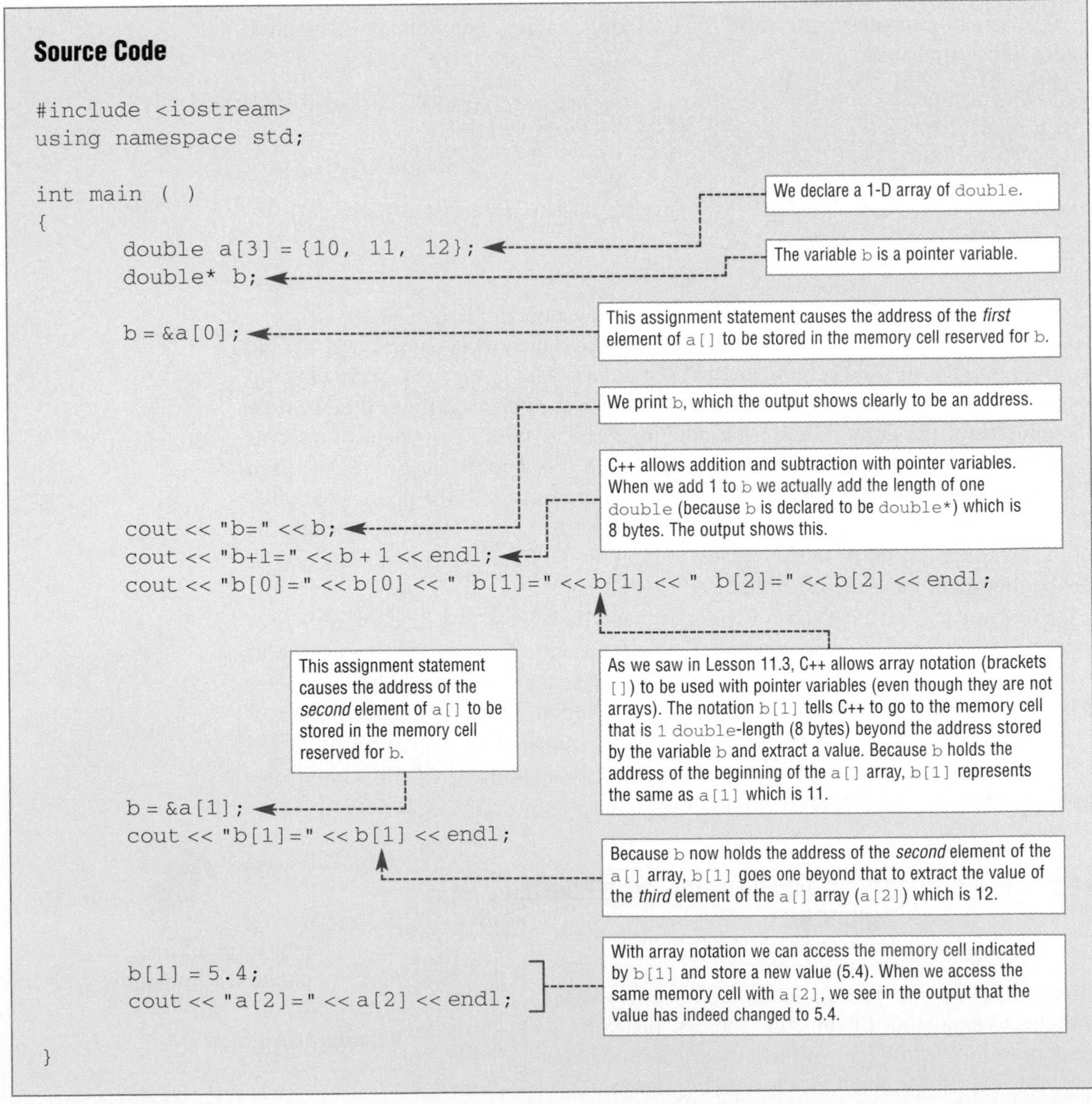

Source Code
#include <iostream>
using namespace std;
int main ( )
{
double a[3] = {10, 11, 12};
double* b;
b = &a[0];
cout << "b=" << b;
cout << "b+1=" << b + 1 << endl;
cout << "b[0]=" << b[0] << " b[1]=" << b[1] << " b[2]=" << b[2] << endl;
b = &a[1];
cout << "b[1]=" << b[1] << endl;
b[1] = 5.4;
cout << "a[2]=" << a[2] << endl;
}
We declare a 1-D array of double.
The variable b is a pointer variable.
This assignment statement causes the address of the first element of a[] to be stored in the memory cell reserved for b.
We print b, which the output shows clearly to be an address.
C++ allows addition and subtraction with pointer variables. When we add 1 to b we actually add the length of one double (because b is declared to be double*) which is 8 bytes. The output shows this.
This assignment statement causes the address of the second element of a[] to be stored in the memory cell reserved for b.
As we saw in Lesson 11.3, C++ allows array notation (brackets []) to be used with pointer variables (even though they are not arrays). The notation b[1] tells C++ to go to the memory cell that is 1 double-length (8 bytes) beyond the address stored by the variable b and extract a value. Because b holds the address of the beginning of the a[] array, b[1] represents the same as a[1] which is 11.
Because b now holds the address of the second element of the a[] array, b[1] goes one beyond that to extract the value of the third element of the a[] array (a[2]) which is 12.
With array notation we can access the memory cell indicated by b[1] and store a new value (5.4). When we access the same memory cell with a[2], we see in the output that the value has indeed changed to 5.4.

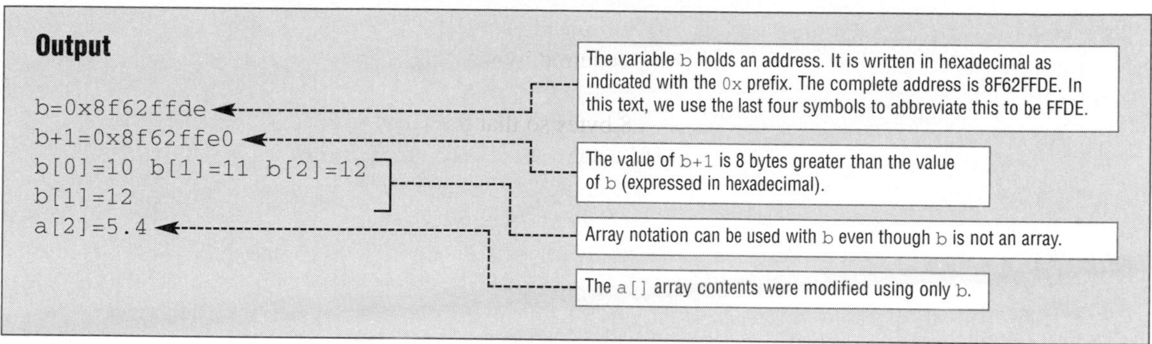
Output
b=0x8f62ffde
b+1=0x8f62ffe0
b[0]=10 b[1]=11 b[2]=12
b[1]=12
a[2]=5.4
The variable b holds an address. It is written in hexadecimal as indicated with the 0x prefix. The complete address is 8F62FFDE. In this text, we use the last four symbols to abbreviate this to be FFDE.
The value of b+1 is 8 bytes greater than the value of b (expressed in hexadecimal).
Array notation can be used with b even though b is not an array.
The a[] array contents were modified using only b.

Description

Variable values. The declaration in this lesson's program:

```
double* b;
```

declares `b` to be a pointer variable. Table 11.7 shows the variables in this lesson's program after executing the first assignment statement `b = &a[0]`. Note that the value of `b` is the address of `a[0]`, FFDE.

Pointer arithmetic. We can perform addition and subtraction with pointer variables. The purpose of performing addition is to advance to a subsequent memory cell. Declaring a pointer to be `double*`, tells C++ that a single memory cell is 8 bytes. Therefore, when we add 1 to a `double*` pointer variable, we add 8 bytes to the address. For instance, with `b` holding the address FFDE, adding 1 to it, using the expression `b+1`, creates the address FFE0 (which is 8 bytes greater than FFDE in hexadecimal). This is shown in the output.

Storing other array addresses in a pointer variable. The following assignment statement and `cout` statement print the values of the `a[]` array because we first assign the address of the beginning of the `a[]` array to `b` (Fig. 11.2, top) and then use array notation with `b`:

```
b = &a[0];
cout << "b[0]=" << b[0] << " b[1]=" << b[1] << " b[2]=" << b[2]
     << endl;
```

We are not restricted to assigning only the address of the beginning of an array to a pointer variable. For instance, we can assign to `b` the address of the second

TABLE 11.7 — Variables in Lesson 11.4's program

Name	Type		Address	Value
a	Array of double			
	a[0]	double	FFDE	10
	a[1]	double	FFE0	11
	a[2]	double	FFEE	12
b	double*		FEC0	FFDE

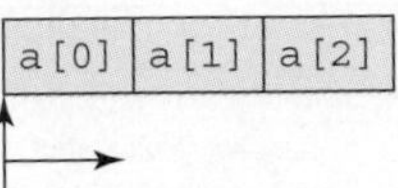

When b = &a[0], b[1] represents a[1] because the pointer advances to one double length past the beginning of the array.

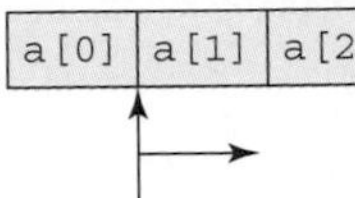

When b = &a[1], b[1] represents a[2] because the pointer advances to one double length past the address of a[1].

Figure 11.2

Action of pointer with array notation.

element (Fig. 11.2, bottom) of a[] and then use array notation with b as given here.

```
b = &a[1];
cout << "b[1]=" << b[1] << endl;
```

With this assignment statement, the value accessed by b[1] is not a[1] but a[2]. Thus, the printed value with this cout statement is 12 not 11.

We can also use b to change the values of a[]. With the following assignment statements

```
b = &a[1];
b[1] = 5.4;
```

we replace the value 12 in a[2] with 5.4.

Comment. Remember, C++ does not do range checking. If you tell it to go to an address that goes well beyond the declared size of an array (for instance, by using b + 9), it will do so without indicating an error message and will likely crash your program.

LESSON 11.5 RETURNING AN ADDRESS FROM A FUNCTION

TOPICS

- Returning addresses from functions
- Using pointer variables like arrays

QUESTION YOU SHOULD ATTEMPT TO ANSWER

1. What is stored in the memory cell reserved for c in the function get_array_address?

We will see that there are times when we want to return the address of an array from a function and work with that address like we work with 1-D arrays (that is, with bracket notation). The return type for a function that returns an address is indicated with *. To return an int address, we use int*. To return a double address, we use double*.

Once an address has been returned from a function, it can be assigned to a pointer variable. Then, using bracket notation ([]) with the pointer variable, we can access memory cells at other addresses.

Read the source code, and observe how we return an address from a function and continue to work with that address using 1-D array notation.

Source Code

```
#include <iostream>
using namespace std;

double* get_array_address(double[]);

int main ( )
{

        double a[3]={10, 11, 12};
        double* b;

        b = get_array_address(a);

        cout << b[0] << "  " << b[1] << "  " << b[2] << endl;

        cout << "b=" << b << "  " << "a=" << a << endl;
}

double* get_array_address(double c[])
{
        return c;
}
```

The function return type is `double*`. This means the function returns the address of a `double`.

We pass the address of the beginning of an array of `double` to the function. Note that brackets also indicate address. We could also use `double*` as the function argument type.

We initialize an array of `double`s.

The variable `b` is a pointer variable. It is declared to hold an address of a `double`.

The `get_array_address()` function is passed the address of the beginning of the `a[]` array. The function returns an address that is assigned to the pointer variable `b`.

When we use `b[2]`, C++ accesses the value located 2 memory cells beyond the address stored by `b`.

Here, we print the address stored in `b`'s memory cells. The output shows that it is the same as the beginning of the `a[]` array.

The variable `c` receives the address of the beginning of the `a[]` array. This function performs the simple task of returning the address stored by `c`.

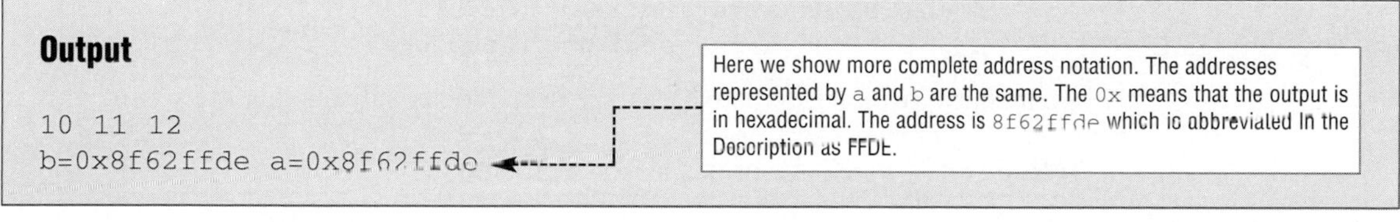
Output

```
10 11 12
b=0x8f62ffde a=0x8f62ffde
```

Here we show more complete address notation. The addresses represented by `a` and `b` are the same. The `0x` means that the output is in hexadecimal. The address is `8f62ffde` which is abbreviated in the Description as FFDE.

Description

Returning an address from a function. To return an address from a function, we need to indicate such in the function declaration and header. For instance, in this lesson's program, the function declaration and header are:

```
double* get_array_address (double[]);
double* get_array_address (double c[])
```

Both these indicate that an address of a `double` is returned from function `get_array_address()` because the return type is `double*`.

In addition, the body of the function must have a return statement with a variable that indicates an address. For this lesson's program, the statement was

```
return c;
```

where `c` is indicated in the function header to be the address of a `double`.

Assigning the address to a pointer variable. In this lesson's program we declared a single pointer variable, `b`, with the declaration

```
double* b;
```

We assigned an address to `b` with the statement

```
b = get_array_address (a);
```

Because of the way the `get_array_address()` function is defined, the outcome of this statement is to assign the address of the `a[]` array to `b`. The result of these statements is in Table 11.8 used by C++ for the variables in `main`.

Working with the pointer variable outside the function. Note that while `a[]` in this lesson's program is clearly an array, `b` is a single variable that stores the address of the first element of `a[]`. As we saw in Lesson 11.4, C++ allows us to use array notation with `b` to access memory cells beyond FFDE. Consequently, we can use `b[0]`, `b[1]`, and `b[2]` in the program body even though `b` does not represent an array. We find this convenient because it allows us to easily access elements of an array. Thus, `b[2]` accesses the same memory cells as `a[2]`.

Indicating addresses. Note that we have also used brackets to indicate an address. As we have seen previously, in the argument list of the function declaration, the type `double[]` means that an address is in that location. We made a brief comment earlier that `double*` can be used to replace `double[]`. In other words, the following function declarations

```
double* get_array_address (double[]);
double* get_array_address (double*);
```

are identical in effect. In both cases, the declarations indicate that the argument is an

TABLE 11.8 — Variables for this lesson's program

Name	Type		Address	Value
a	Array of double			
	a[0]	double	FFDE	10
	a[1]	double	FFE0	11
	a[2]	double	FFEE	12
b	Address of double		FFCD	FFDE

address. The first is more traditional for having numeric arrays in the argument list, but the second is also acceptable.

Summary. We have shown how to return an address from a function. We have also shown how to work with that address outside the function in a form that looks like a 1-D array (which is what we want to do). This works very well when the address is the beginning of a 1-D array. However, all this becomes more complicated with multidimensional arrays. This is covered in Lesson 11.6.

LESSON 11.6 RETURNING THE ADDRESS OF A MULTIDIMENSIONAL ARRAY

TOPICS

- Pointers to arrays
- Returning pointers to arrays
- Using `typedef`

QUESTION YOU SHOULD ATTEMPT TO ANSWER

1. What kind of array notation can be used with a pointer to a 1-D array?

The size of the memory being pointed to (with a pointer to an individual value) is equal to 2, 4, or 8 bytes (for example) depending on the type of variable (`int`, `double`, or other). However, we can make a pointer variable point to much more than just 2, 4, or 8 bytes. We can make a pointer point to an entire array. In this lesson we look at pointers to arrays. Such a pointer holds the address of the beginning of the array (as we illustrated in Lesson 11.5), but the pointer variable declaration indicates that the size of memory pointed to is greater than just a single value.

Despite the fact that the pointer points to an entire array, we ultimately are interested in using that pointer variable to access an individual value of the array. How do we access individual values with a pointer to an array? We use array notation. We have seen (Lesson 11.5) that C++ allows *1-D* array notation (indicated by a single pair of brackets) when using a pointer to a *single* variable (to access memory cells beyond the address stored). In addition, C++ allows *2-D* array notation when using a pointer to a *1-D* array. Also, C++ allows *3-D* array notation when using a pointer to a *2-D* array. In general, C++ allows the dimension of the array notation to be one more than the dimension of the array pointed to.

In the previous lesson, we used a function that worked with a *1-D array,* and hence we returned from the function a pointer to a *single* value. Doing so, allowed us to use 1-D array notation to access the array outside the function (this is the natural way that we want to work with a 1-D array). In this lesson, we use a function that works with a *2-D array,* and we return from the function a pointer to a *1-D array*. Doing so, allows us to use 2-D array notation to access the array outside the function (which is the natural way to work with a 2-D array).

The syntax for creating a pointer to a 1-D array is complex. For instance

```
double (*f)[2];
```

declares `f` to be a pointer to a 1-D array of `double` of size 2. The parentheses around `*f` are required. Similarly

```
double (*h)[3][5];
```

declares `h` to be a pointer to a 2-D array of `double` of size 3×5. It is easiest to simply memorize and accept the logic of the syntax.

C++ allows us to create shorthand for such complex declarations using the keyword `typedef`. For instance

```
typedef double (*array_pointer)[2];
```

creates the shorthand `array_pointer` to represent a pointer to a 1-D array of `double` with a size of 2. Then, we can use the following as a declaration.

```
array_pointer f;
```

This declares `f` to be a pointer to a 1-D array of `double` of size 2 and can be used in place of `double (*f)[2];`. If we want to return such a pointer from a function we can use the following function declaration

```
array_pointer function2 (argument_list);
```

This declaration, together with the previous `typedef` statement, indicates that `function2` returns a pointer to a 1-D array of `double` of size 2. This means that outside the function we can use 2-D array notation with the pointer returned by the function. This is what we want.

Read the source code and observe how the process works.

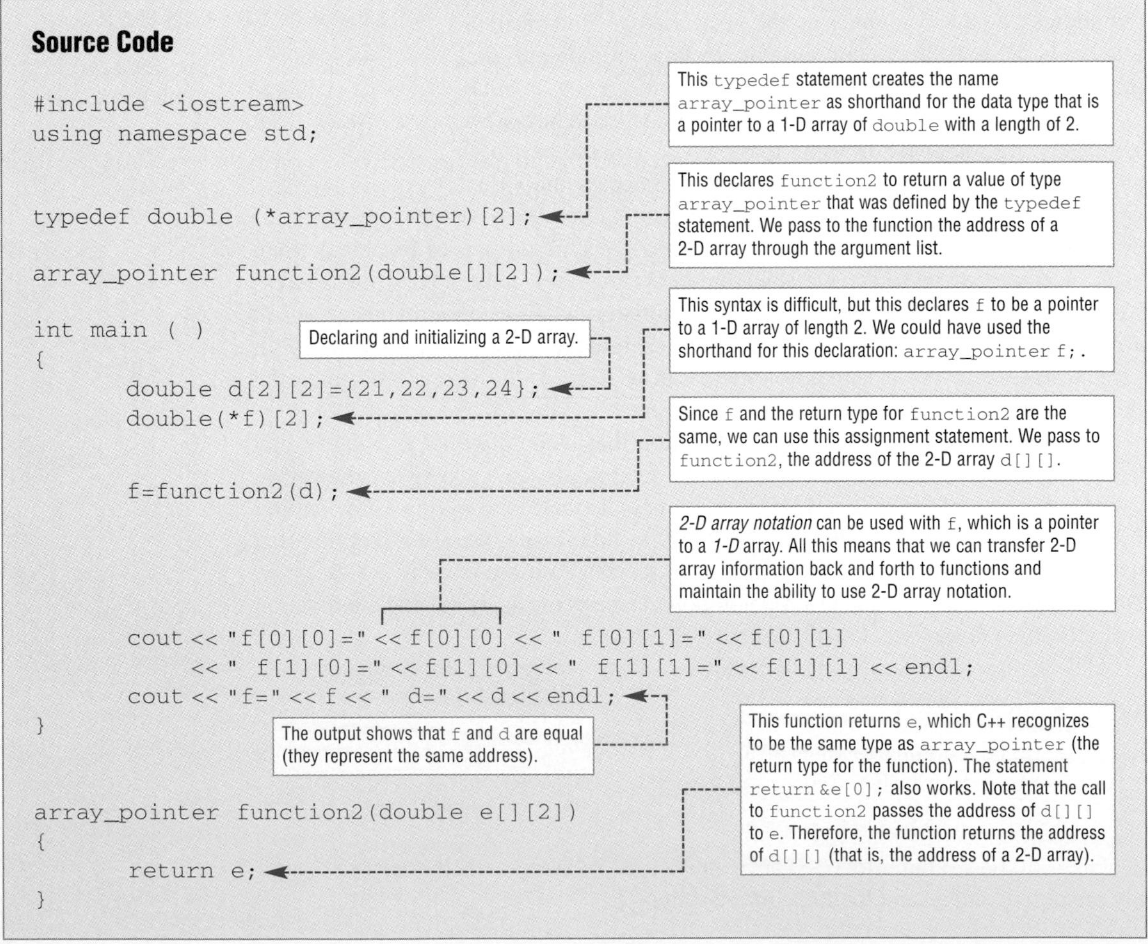

Source Code

```
#include <iostream>
using namespace std;

typedef double (*array_pointer)[2];

array_pointer function2(double[][2]);

int main ( )
{
      double d[2][2]={21,22,23,24};
      double(*f)[2];

      f=function2(d);

      cout << "f[0][0]=" << f[0][0] << "  f[0][1]=" << f[0][1]
          << "  f[1][0]=" << f[1][0] << "  f[1][1]=" << f[1][1] << endl;
      cout << "f=" << f << "  d=" << d << endl;
}

array_pointer function2(double e[][2])
{
      return e;
}
```

This typedef statement creates the name array_pointer as shorthand for the data type that is a pointer to a 1-D array of double with a length of 2.
This declares function2 to return a value of type array_pointer that was defined by the typedef statement. We pass to the function the address of a 2-D array through the argument list.
Declaring and initializing a 2-D array.
This syntax is difficult, but this declares f to be a pointer to a 1-D array of length 2. We could have used the shorthand for this declaration: array_pointer f;.
Since f and the return type for function2 are the same, we can use this assignment statement. We pass to function2, the address of the 2-D array d[][].
2-D array notation can be used with f, which is a pointer to a 1-D array. All this means that we can transfer 2-D array information back and forth to functions and maintain the ability to use 2-D array notation.
The output shows that f and d are equal (they represent the same address).
This function returns e, which C++ recognizes to be the same type as array_pointer (the return type for the function). The statement return &e[0]; also works. Note that the call to function2 passes the address of d[][] to e. Therefore, the function returns the address of d[][] (that is, the address of a 2-D array).

Output

```
f[0][0]=21 f[0][1]=22 f[1][0]=23 f[1][1]=24
f=0x8f62ffcd d=0x8f62ffcd
```

Using f and 2-D array notation, we get the same array values as d[][]. This only works if f and d represent the same address *and* are the same type.

Description

Declaring pointers to arrays. We must use parentheses in the declarations of pointers to arrays. For instance:

```
double (*f)[2];
```

declares f to be a pointer to a one-dimensional array of double of size [2]. This is different from a pointer to an individual double as would have been declared with

```
double *f;
```

Therefore, it is important to use both parentheses and brackets in declaring pointers to arrays. Be aware that the type and size of what a pointer points to are critical in using it properly.

Using pointers to arrays. Without going into the details, we can assign the address of a 2-D array to a pointer variable that is declared to point to a 1-D array. C++ then allows the use of 2-D array notation with the pointer variable. For example, the following declarations and statements are legal.

```
double d[2][2];
double (*f)[2];
f = d;
f[0][0] = 21; f[0][1] = 22; f[1][0] = 23; f[1][1] = 24;
```

Declaring a 2-D array and a pointer to a 1-D array.

Assigning the array address to the pointer variable.

Assigning values to the array using the pointer variable.

These statements initialize the values of the d[][] array using the f pointer variable.

The basic `typedef` statement. The keyword typedef is used to create an alias for a data type (but not a new data type). In its most basic form, it creates an alias or synonym for an ordinary data type. For instance

```
typedef int Integer;
```

makes Integer an alias for int. Its use in a program means the declaration

```
Integer a, b, c;
```

is equivalent to

```
int a,b,c;
```

In general, the basic form for a typedef statement is:

```
typedef type synonym_1, synonym_2, synonym_n;
```

where `type` can be any valid data type including `int`, `float`, or `double`. Also, *synonym_1*, *synonym_2*, and *synonym_n* represent a list of valid identifiers that can be used to represent `type`. Any number of synonyms can be used in the list of synonyms.

***Uses of* `typedef`.** There are a number of reasons for using `typedef`.

- Using a `typedef` to create a descriptive synonym can improve the readability and therefore the understandability of the code.
- A `typedef` can make it easier to modify programs that are implementation dependent. For instance, suppose that you have developed a program that is dependent upon the type, `int`, being two bytes long and that you have used the following `typedef`.

  ```
  typedef int TWOBYTES;
  ```

  This means that in your program, you have declarations of the sort

  ```
  TWOBYTES a, b, c;
  ```

  which declares that `a`, `b`, and `c` are two byte integers. Suppose also that you want to change the program to work in an environment that has `short` as two bytes and `int` as four bytes. Then, the `typedef` statement could be modified to be:

  ```
  typedef short TWOBYTES;
  ```

  to get the program to work in the new environment. Such a technique prevents the need for changing every declaration in the program from `int` to `short`. Thus, `typedef` has made modification of implementation dependent code simple.

***Arrays and* `typedef`.** The syntax of `typedef` with arrays is somewhat different from the basic syntax. For instance

```
typedef int Array[30];
```

creates an alias for declaring integer arrays of size 30. With this `typedef`, the declaration:

```
Array yy, zz;
```

is equivalent to:

```
int yy[30], zz[30];
```

In general, the form of `typedef` with a 1-D array is

```
typedef type name[size];
```

where `type` is the type of values in the array, `name` is the alias to be used as the data type in a declaration, and `size` is the array size.

***Pointers to arrays and* `typedef`.** To create a `typedef` for a pointer to a 1-D array, we combine the forms for declaring a pointer to an array and `typedef` with an array to give the form:

```
typedef type (*name)[size];
```

where *type* is the type of values in the array, *name* is the alias to be used as the data type in a declaration, and *size* is the array size.

In this lesson's program

```
typedef double (*array_pointer)[2];
```

creates the alias `array_pointer` for declarations of pointers to 1-D arrays of `double` with size 2.

Returning a pointer to an array from a function. Using the `typedef` in this lesson's program, the declaration

```
array_pointer function2 (argument);
```

indicates a pointer to a 1-D array is returned from the function. When we assign the return value to a pointer of the same type (as we did with `f` in this lesson's program, then we can work with `f` using 2-D array notation, as in the `cout` statement

```
cout << "f[0][0] = " << f[0][0]<< " f[0][1] = " << f[0][1]
     << " f[1][0] = " << f[1][0]<< " f[1][1] = " << f[1][1]
     << endl;
```

C++ concept of multidimensional arrays. The reason that this works is that C++ regards multidimensional arrays as arrays of arrays. For instance, if we have an array declared as

```
int a[2][3][7];
```

and initialized the array as shown here (shown as two 2-D arrays of size `[3][7]` for simplicity)

```
a[0]
1   2  3  4  5  6  7
8   9 10 11 12 13 14
15 16 17 18 19 20 21

a[1]
22 23 24 25 26 27 28
29 30 31 32 33 34 35
36 37 38 39 40 41 42
```

then C++ can work with this array by treating it as:

1. 2 arrays of size `[3][7]`
2. 6 arrays of size `[7]`
3. 42 integers

Because of the way C++ deals with arrays, we can declare pointers to arrays of these sizes:

```
int (*b)[3][7], (*c)[7], *d;
```

where `b` is a pointer to an array of size `[3][7]`, `c` is a pointer to an array of size `[7]`, and `d` is a pointer to a single value. We can assign addresses to these pointer variables

TABLE 11.9 — Values of pointer variables assigned array addresses

Name	Type	Address	Value
a	3-D Array of int size [2][3][7]	FFCD	1 to 42
b	Pointer to 2-D int array size [3][7]	FFBD	FFCD
c	Pointer to 1-D int array size [7]	FFAD	FFCD
d	Pointer to int	FF9D	FFCD

using the & operator.

```
b = &a[0];
c = &a[0][0];
d = &a[0][0][0];
```

The right sides of these assignment statements differ in the number of subscripts used with a. The meanings of the right sides are the following

&a[0] = the address of the first of two arrays of size [3][7]
&a[0][0] = the address of the first of six arrays of size [7]
&a[0][0][0] = the address of the first integer value

Suppose that on execution of the program, the address FFCD is used for storing the array. After making the assignments, the table of values is as shown in Table 11.9.

Note that the *values* of b, c, and d are all identical (FFCD, the address of the beginning of a[][][]); however their *types* are all different. This is why the right sides of the assignment statements are all different.

With the assignments, we have properly assigned values to the pointer variables. C++ does not allow the following assignments because the right and left sides are not the same type:

```
b = &a[0][0][0];
c = &a[0];
d = &a[0][0];
```

We can, however, use these assignment statements

```
b = &a[1];
c = &a[0][1];
d = &a[0][0][1];
```

The right sides of these statements mean

&a[1] = the address of the second of two arrays of size [3][7]
&a[0][1] = the address of the second of six arrays of size [7]
&a[0][0][1] = the address of the second integer value

In summary, we can use the & operator and the pointer variables to point to various locations in the array. However, the type of pointer variable and the address indicated on the right side of the assignment statement must match for C++ to allow the assignment. At this point, there is no need to memorize the forms. When you need to work with pointers and multidimensional arrays, simply refer back to this lesson.

***Assignments without* `&`.** Without the `&` operator, we can use the following assignments which mean the same as the first ones

```
b = a;
c = a[0];
d = a[0][0];
```

Note that `a` with no `&` and no brackets indicates the address of the first of two arrays of size `[3][7]`. Similarly, `a` with no `&` and fewer than three pairs of brackets indicates an address. The type of pointer variable the address can be assigned to depends on the number of brackets included. Again, there is no need to memorize this.

Pointer arithmetic with pointers to arrays. We have not shown it in this lesson's program, but when we perform addition with a pointer to an array, we add the number of bytes represented by the pointer. For instance, assuming 2 bytes per `int`, adding 1 to `b` causes us to add `[3]` × `[7]` × 2 bytes = 42 bytes (because `b` points to a size `[3][7]` array of `int`). Thus, `b + 1` takes us 42 bytes past FFCD, the value of `b`. Similarly, `c + 1` takes us `[7]` × 2 bytes = 14 bytes past FFCD (because `c` points to a size `[7]` array of `int`), and `d + 1` takes us 2 bytes past FFCD (because `d` points to a single `int`).

Summary. In summary, a pointer's type influences how we work with it. The number of subscripts we use with a pointer variable depends on its type. Also, we must use properly matched types when making assignments with pointer variables.

LESSON 11.7 POINTERS TO OBJECTS

TOPICS

- Creating a pointer to an object
- Using the arrow operator

QUESTION YOU SHOULD ATTEMPT TO ANSWER

1. What are the two operands used with the arrow operator?

A pointer variable can be used to hold the address of an object. C++ allows us to use the address to access data members and call member functions. A special operator called the arrow operator (consisting of a negative and greater than symbol with no space between, `->`) is used to access the members with an object's address.

Pointers to objects help us connect classes together. We will not say more here. Detailed examples are shown in Chapter 14. Read the source code to understand the mechanics of using a pointer to an object.

Source Code

```
#include <iostream>
using namespace std;

class Square
{
        private:
                double side_length, area;
        public:
                Square (double);
                void calc_area ();
};
```

The attributes of a square are `side_length` and `area`.

The class has a constructor and a function to calculate the area.

```
Square :: Square (double side_length_var)
        :side_length (side_length_var)
{
}

void Square :: calc_area ()
{
        area = side_length * side_length;
        cout << "Area = " << area << endl;
}

int main ( )
{
        Square sq1(4.5);
        Square* sq1_address;


        sq1_address = &sq1;
        cout << "&sq1 = " << &sq1 << endl << " sq1_address = " << sq1_address << endl;
        sq1_address -> calc_area();
}
```

The constructor initializes the side length.

Calculating the area.

The `sq1` object is initialized with sides of length 4.5.

This pointer is capable of holding the address of a `Square` object.

The pointer variable is assigned the address of the `sq1` object.

We call the member function using the pointer variable and the arrow operator. This is equivalent to using `sq1.calc_area();`.

Output

```
&sq1 = FFE6
sq1_address = FFE6
Area = 20.25
```

Description

Declaring a pointer to an object. Declaring a pointer to an object is similar to declaring a pointer to an ordinary variable. For instance, in this lesson's program:

```
Square* sq1_address;
```

declares `sq1_address` to be a pointer variable for a `Square` object. In general, the form for declaring a pointer to an object is:

```
Class_name* pointer_name;
```

Where *`Class_name`* is the name of the class and *`pointer_name`* is a programmer chosen name for the pointer variable.

Initializing a pointer to an object. The `&` operator can be used to initialize a pointer to an object. In this lesson's program the assignment statement:

```
sq1_address = &sq1;
```

initializes `sq1_address` to be the address of the `sq1` object.

In general, the form:

pointer_name = &*object_name*;

initializes the *pointer_name* variable to be the address of the object called *object_name*.

Calling a member function with a pointer to an object. We use the arrow operator (->) to call a function with a pointer to an object. In this lesson's program, the statement

sq1_address -> calc_area();

calls the calc_area() function with the sq1_address pointer variable. In doing so, the data members for the object referred to by the pointer variable sq1_address (in this case, sq1) are automatically passed to the calc_area() function.

In general, we call a member function (with two arguments) with the form

pointer_name -> *function_name*(*arg1*, *arg2*)

where *function_name* is the name of the member function, and *arg1* and *arg2* are the names of the variables being passed to the function. The *pointer_name* variable must be initialized to be the address of an object for this form to work correctly.

LESSON 11.8 POINTERS AS DATA MEMBERS

TOPICS

- Defining a pointer data member
- Initializing a pointer data member in a constructor function
- Using a pointer data member in a member function

QUESTION YOU SHOULD ATTEMPT TO ANSWER

1. Is the array initialized before the constructor is called for the Triangle class?

A pointer variable can be a data member for a class. One important use for pointers as data members is in working with arrays. A pointer can hold the address of the beginning of an array. This may eliminate the need for an object of the class to hold an entire array. This can save memory.

In this lesson's program, we create a Triangle class. A data member of the class *could* be an array consisting of the *x* and *y* coordinates of the corners of the triangle. Instead, we create a data member that is a pointer variable. This pointer variable is used to hold the address of the array holding the coordinates of the corner points of the triangle. Read the program and see how a constructor function can initialize a pointer variable, and how another member function can use a pointer variable. Note that we create a Point structure that can hold both the *x* and *y* coordinates of each corner point. The array then is type Point and the pointer variable, therefore, is type Point*.

Source Code

```
#include <iostream>
using namespace std;

struct Point
{
        public:
                double x, y;
};
```

The Point structure holds both x and y coordinates.

```
class Triangle
{
        private:
                Point* corners_address;
        public:
                Triangle (Point*);
                void show_corners ();
};


Triangle :: Triangle (Point* corners_address_var)

        : corners_address (corners_address_var)
{
        cout << "corners_address = " << corners_address << endl;
}


void Triangle :: show_corners ()
{
        cout << "Coordinates of endpoints" << endl
            << "(" << corners_address[0].x << ","
            << corners_address[0].y << ")" << endl
            << "("<< corners_address[1].x << ","
            << corners_address[1].y << ")" << endl
            << "("<< corners_address[2].x << ","
            << corners_address[2].y << ")" << endl;
}


int main ( )
{
          Point corners[3];
          Triangle tr1(corners);

          cout << "corners = " << corners << endl << endl;

          corners[0].x = 5;
          corners[0].y = 7;
          corners[1].x = 10;
          corners[1].y = 3;
          corners[2].x = 8;
          corners[2].y = 12;

          tr1.show_corners ();
}
```

The corners_address variable is type Point*. It can hold the address of an array of Point.

The constructor initializes the pointer variable (type Point*).

The arrows show the transfer of information to the pointer variable corners_address. The function also prints out the value of corners_address.

Printing the actual array contents using the pointer variable corners_address. Note that array notation (with brackets []) is allowed with the pointer variable.

Declaring (reserving memory) for an array of 3 Points.

Declaring an object and initializing it with the address of the array.

Printing the array address.

Initializing the array values.

Printing the array values using the pointer variable (see the body of the show_corners function).

Output

```
corners_address = FFC4
corners = FFC4
```

The value of the pointer variable and the array address are the same.

```
Coordinates of end points
(5,7)
(10,3)
(8,12)
```

The pointer variable has successfully accessed the array.

Description

Defining a class with a pointer data member. A pointer can be a data member like any other type of variable. In this lesson's program, the class definition:

```
class Triangle
{
        private:
                Point* corners_address;
        public:
                Triangle(Point*);
                void show_corners();
};
```

makes the variable `corners_address` a pointer variable of type `Point*`.

In general, the form making a pointer variable a data member is:

```
class Class_name
{
        private:
                type* pointer_name;
        public:
                type function_name();
};
```

Where *`Class_name`* is the name of the class, *`type`* is any valid data type including the name of a `struct` or class, and *`function_name`* is the name of a member function.

Initializing a pointer data member. A private pointer data member must be initialized within a member function. In this lesson's program, we initialize the pointer variable in the constructor function. The value is passed through the argument list in the declaration of the object. The declarations:

```
Point corners[3];
Triangle tr1 (corners);
```

first create an array named `corners[]`. Then the address of the array is passed to the constructor function for the object `tr1`. Note that the elements of the array are uninitialized. This is acceptable because it is only the address of the array, not the values of the data members, that is transferred to the constructor.

The constructor initializes the value of the pointer variable with the address. The transfer of data from the object declaration to the constructor function is:

```
Triangle tr1 (corners);                         Object declaration.

Triangle :: Triangle (Point* corners_address_var)

        :corners_address (corners_address_var)          Constructor
{                                                       function.
        cout << " corners_address = " << corners_address << endl;
}
```

The value of `corners` goes to `corners_address_var` to `corners_address`. Thus, the value of `corners_address` is initialized.

Using the pointer variable to access values. After the array values were initialized in `main` with the statements:

```
corners[0].x = 5;
corners[0].y = 7;
corners[1].x = 10;
corners[1].y = 3;
corners[2].x = 8;
corners[2].y = 12;
```

the values are accessed within the member function `show_corners` with the notation

```
corners_address[0].x
corners_address[0].y
corners_address[1].x
corners_address[1].y
corners_address[2].x
corners_address[2].y
```

Thus, we have successfully accessed all the members of an array within a member function. The class itself, though, does not contain an array data member. It has only a pointer data member.

Usefulness of pointer data members. We will see that pointer data members are particularly useful for accessing nonmember values (both array and ordinary values) from within a member function. Using pointer data members in such a manner is one way that we can connect classes and objects.

LESSON 11.9 DYNAMIC MEMORY ALLOCATION

TOPICS

- The `new` operator
- The `delete` operator

As we have seen, programming with arrays can waste considerable memory because the programmer sets the size of an array, but a user fills it. If a user does not fill an array completely, memory is wasted. Such memory waste may be unacceptable. Also, there may be times when we cannot make a good estimate of the largest possible size for an array while we are writing a program. In such cases, we run the risk of a user crashing a program by trying to put more into an array than space allows.

QUESTION YOU SHOULD ATTEMPT TO ANSWER

1. What might be a disadvantage to using dynamic memory allocation?

To help us optimize the memory space we use, C++ has the `new` and `delete` operators. These operators enable us to reserve and unreserve memory for arrays (and ordinary data) while a program is executing. This is called dynamic memory allocation. In this lesson's program, we ask a *user* to specify the size of an array. Then we use `new` to reserve just enough memory for the array. We fill the memory in a separate `for` loop. When finished with the memory, we unreserve it (or release it) using `delete`. Pointer variables are important in the use of `new` and `delete` because these operators work with the addresses of the memory reserved.

In this program we create an array of pass codes for a class of students (one pass code for each student). The user enters the number of students in the class, and memory is reserved for the pass code array using the `new` operator. The array is filled with random numbers in the range 1000 to 9999. See Lesson 7.8 to review random numbers if you have forgotten them.

If you try running this program yourself, you will see that your output is different from what we show and different each time you run the program. Read the program and annotations; then read the Description to learn how to dynamically reserve memory. Note that there is no explicit declaration for an array in this program! We declare only a pointer variable. (For simplicity, this program does not guarantee a different pass code for each student.)

Source Code

```
#include <iostream>
#include <cstdlib>
#include <ctime>
using namespace std;
int main ( )
{
        int i, num;
        int* pass_codes;

        cout << "Enter the number of students." << endl;
        cin >> num;
        cout << "The pass codes are:" << endl;

        pass_codes = new int[num];
```

The `cstdlib` header is needed for functions `rand()` and `srand()` and operators `new` and `delete`.

The `ctime` header is needed for the `time()` function.

Declaring a pointer variable called `pass_codes`.

The user specifies the number of pass codes needed.

The `new` operator reserves memory for `num` integers. The `new` operator "returns" the address of the beginning of this memory. The address of the memory is assigned to the `pass_codes` pointer variable with the assignment statement.

```
        srand (time (0));

        for (i = 0; i < num; i++)
                {
                pass_codes[i] = rand() % 9000 + 1000;
                cout << pass_codes[i] << " ";
                }
        cout << endl;

        cout << "The array address = " << pass_codes << endl;
        delete [] pass_codes;
}
```

The `time()` function returns the time of day in seconds from midnight. This value serves as input to function `srand()`.

The `srand()` function, through the global variable, "seeds" the `rand()` function (see Lesson 7.8).

The calculation `rand() % 9000` produces a random number in the range 0-8999, and `rand() % 9000 + 1000` creates a random number in the range 1000–9999. Even though `pass_codes` is a pointer variable, we can use 1-D array notation (with a single pair of brackets) to fill and access memory cells beyond the address stored by `pass_codes`.

The `delete` operator releases or unreserves all the memory reserved at the address indicated by `pass_codes`.

Output

```
Enter the number of students
10
The pass codes are:
1668 1632 8485 1035 1596 2093 3984 4306 9974 7670
The array address = 0F7A
```

Description

The* `new` *operator. The form for using the `new` operator to reserve memory for an array is

```
new type [num_elements]
```

where *`type`* is the data type of the elements to be stored in the array such as `int` or `double`, and *`num_elements`* is the number of array elements. In this lesson's program

```
new int [num]
```

reserves memory for an array of `int` with the number of elements being `num` (which is 10 as entered by the user).

Note that the *user* specifies the number of memory cells to be reserved and not the *programmer*. This means that each user reserves only what is needed. A user that has only a few students reserves only a little memory, whereas a user that has many students reserves a lot of memory. Thus, the programmer does not need to worry about declaring an array to be too big or too small.

Although new reserves memory, it does *not* fill the memory with values. To enable the program to fill the memory, new returns the address of the memory it reserves. Typically, this value is assigned to a pointer variable of the same type. In general, the form is

```
type* array_address;
array_address = new type [num];
```

where *type* is any valid C++ data type, *array_address* is any valid identifier for the pointer variable, and *num* is the number of array elements. In this lesson's program, the declaration and assignment statement

```
int* pass_codes;
pass_codes = new int [num];
```

declare the integer pointer variable pass_codes, and assigns the address of the memory reserved with new to pass_codes. Note that there must be a match between the type used with new and the pointer variable type. In other words, pass_codes cannot be type double*. It must be type int* so that it can be assigned the address returned by new.

After the address of the memory has been assigned to the pointer variable, the elements of the memory can be accessed using 1-D array notation. In this lesson's program, the individual elements are accessed using

```
pass_codes[i]
```

because, as we have seen previously, we can use 1-D array notation to access memory cells beyond the location stored by the pointer variable.

You should observe that nowhere in the program is there a declaration of the sort

```
int pass_codes[10];
```

which is ordinary static memory allocation that takes place when a program is *compiled.* The dynamic memory allocation system with new replaces the static form and allocates memory when a program is *executed.* The consequence is that a program using static memory allocation executes more quickly than the same program using dynamic memory allocation. As a result, you may save memory using dynamic allocation, but you may also increase execution time. The needs of your program (whether speed or memory should be optimized) influence whether or not you should use new to size your arrays.

To reserve memory for a single value with new, the form is

```
new type
```

where *type* is any valid C++ data type such as int or double. Also, the cstdlib header file is required for using new.

The* delete *operator. When a program completes execution all memory is automatically released. However, in a program that makes extensive use of dynamic memory allocation, releasing memory prior to the end of execution may be necessary to assure sufficient available memory for other calls to new. Even if this is not the case, it is good programming practice to manually unreserve memory using the delete operator. The form is

```
delete [] array_address;
```

where `array_address` is the pointer variable. In this lesson's program

```
delete [] pass_codes;
```

releases the memory stored at the address indicated by `pass_codes`. C++ is smart enough to know the size of memory reserved by `new` at the `pass_codes` address and releases not just one memory cell but enough for all the array. Note that the memory is not really deleted: it still exists. It is simply eliminated from the list of reserved memory cell locations, and therefore the memory is free to be used for another application.

To delete the memory for a single element we use the form

```
delete address;
```

You must be careful with `delete`. Make sure that you are deleting memory that has been properly reserved. If you try to delete memory using a pointer variable that has not been initialized, you can cause a major problem in your program.

This lesson's program. After seeding the `rand()` function with `srand`, we create a random number in the range of 1000 to 9999 with the expression

```
rand ( ) % 9000 + 1000;
```

The `for` loop in the program fills the `pass_codes[] array`. The end result is that each element of the `pass_codes[]` array is filled with a random number from 1000 to 9999 as shown in the output. These are good 4-digit pass codes.

APPLICATION EXAMPLE 11.1 UNDERGROUND POLLUTION PLUME BOUNDARIES*

Problem Statement

TOPICS

- Returning a pointer from a function
- Using accessor functions to connect two classes
- Determining if a point is in a polygon
- Numerical method example

Write a program that determines whether a particular sampling point is located within an underground pollution plume. The plume of underground pollution is described by the *x-y* coordinates of 10 points on its boundary, all of which are in the first quadrant of an *x-y* plot. Read the coordinates of the 10 points from a data file and the coordinates of the sample point from the keyboard. Write a message to the screen indicating whether the point is located in the plume or not.

Solution

BACKGROUND

A region of underground pollution is called a plume because it is shaped like a plume of smoke. A map of a plume from a leaking storage tank is illustrated in Fig. 11.3.

**Note:* This program illustrates a practical problem using a pointer returned from a function. For more complex pointer manipulations in practical programs, see Chapter 16, Lessons 1–4.

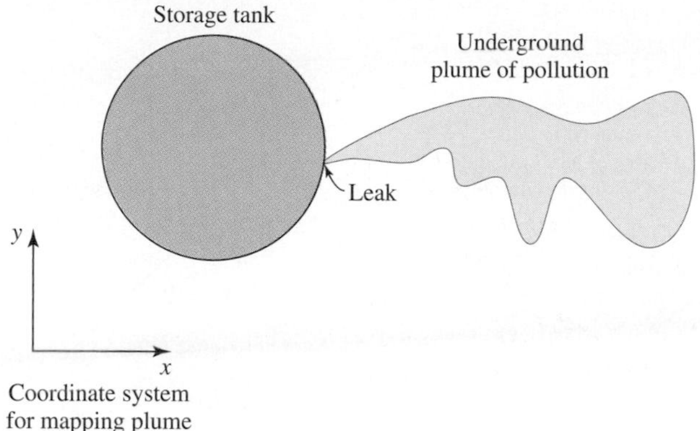

Figure 11.3

Bird's-eye view of a pollution plume from leaking storage tank. The tank is aboveground; the plume is underground.

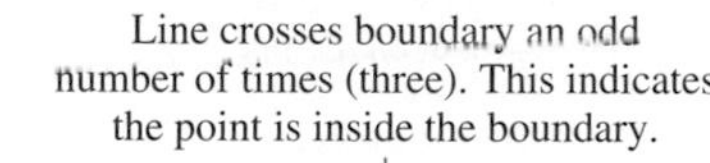

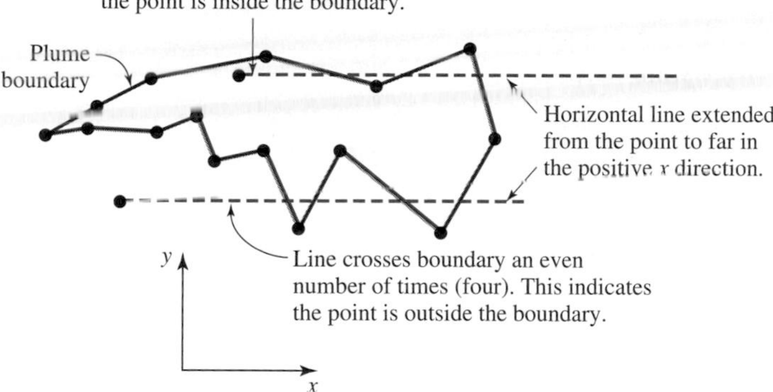

Figure 11.4

Pollution plume delineated by the points on the boundary.

Plumes are mapped to understand their movement and behavior. In this example, we use an *x*-*y* coordinate system for establishing points on the boundary of the plume.

To determine whether a point is inside or outside the plume, draw a horizontal line from the point considered to a very large distance and count the number of times the line crosses the plume boundary (Fig. 11.4). If the horizontal line crosses the boundary an even number of times, then the point is outside the plume. If the horizontal line crosses the boundary an odd number of times, then the point is inside the plume. This program's function is to determine the number of times that the horizontal line crosses the plume boundary.

We will represent the plume boundary with a series of straight line segments as shown in Fig. 11.4. Then we will determine if the line segment represented by the horizontal dashed line in this figure intersects each line segment of the plume boundary.

ASSEMBLE RELEVANT EQUATIONS

Determining the intersection point of two line *segments* is similar to determining the intersection point of two *lines* (see Figs. 11.5 and 11.6). The method that we show

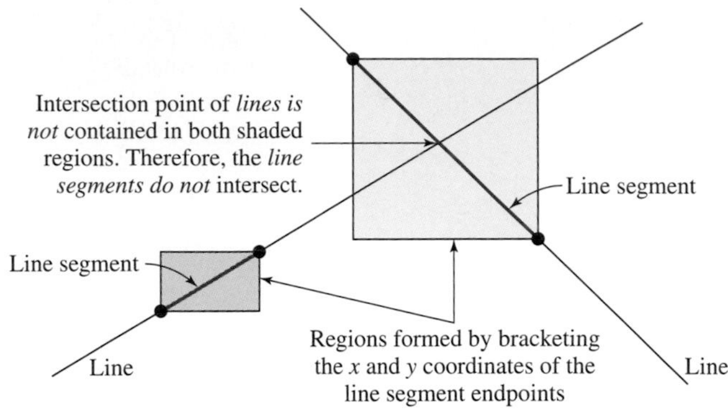

Figure 11.5
Two line segments that do not intersect. Note that the shaded regions are separated from each other.

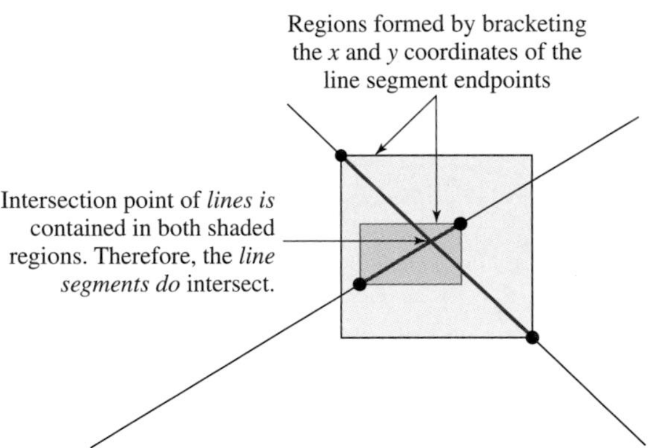

Figure 11.6
Two line segments that do intersect. Note that the shaded areas completely overlap each other.

here consists of first finding the intersection point of the two lines that encompass the line segments and then determining if this point falls on both line segments.

The slope and intercept of a line defined by a line segment are:

$$m = (y_2 - y_1)/(x_2 - x_1) \tag{11.1}$$

$$b = y_2 - mx_2 \tag{11.2}$$

where the endpoints of the line segment are (x_1, y_1) and (x_2, y_2), and where m is the slope and b is the intercept.

We have previously covered the intersection of two lines with the slopes and intercepts given. The equations are:

$$x = (b_2 - b_1)/(m_1 - m_2) \tag{11.3}$$

$$y = m_1 x + b_1 \tag{11.4}$$

where x and y are the coordinates of the intersection point, and m_1, m_2, b_1, and b_2 are the slopes and intercepts of the two lines.

To determine whether the intersection point (x, y) falls onto the line segments, we determine if it falls within the rectangular shaded region outlined by the line segments' endpoints. This is shown in Fig. 11.5. The rectangular shaded region is created by bracketing the line segment endpoints.

In this problem, we must be able to distinguish between the x and y coordinates of the two line segments. Thus, we use $seg1_{x1}$, $seg1_{y1}$, $seg1_{x2}$, and $seg1_{y2}$ to indicate the coordinates of both endpoints of the first line segment, and $seg2_{x1}$, $seg2_{y1}$, $seg2_{x2}$, and $seg2_{y2}$ to indicate the coordinates of both endpoints of the second line segment.

In order to use relational expressions to determine whether a point falls within the shaded region, we determine:

$$\begin{aligned}
x_{low1} &= \text{the lower of segment 1's endpoint } x \text{ coordinates} \\
&\quad (\text{lower of } seg1_{x1} \text{ and } seg1_{x2}) \\
y_{low1} &= \text{the lower of segment 1's endpoint } y \text{ coordinates} \\
&\quad (\text{lower of } seg1_{y1} \text{ and } seg1_{y2}) \\
x_{high1} &= \text{the greater of segment 1's endpoint } x \text{ coordinates} \\
&\quad (\text{greater of } seg1_{x1} \text{ and } seg1_{x2}) \\
y_{high1} &= \text{the greater of segment 1's endpoint } y \text{ coordinates} \\
&\quad (\text{greater of } seg1_{y1} \text{ and } seg1_{y2}) \\
x_{low2} &= \text{the lower of segment 2's endpoint } x \text{ coordinates} \\
&\quad (\text{lower of } seg2_{x1} \text{ and } seg2_{x2}) \\
y_{low2} &= \text{the lower of segment 2's endpoint } y \text{ coordinates} \\
&\quad (\text{lower of } seg2_{y1} \text{ and } seg2_{y2}) \\
x_{high2} &= \text{the greater of segment 2's endpoint } x \text{ coordinates} \\
&\quad (\text{greater of } seg2_{x1} \text{ and } seg2_{x2}) \\
y_{high2} &= \text{the greater of segment 2's endpoint } y \text{ coordinates} \\
&\quad (\text{greater of } seg2_{y1} \text{ and } seg2_{y2})
\end{aligned} \tag{11.5}$$

The line segments intersect (rather than just the lines intersect) when all of the following are true:

$$\begin{aligned}
x_{low1} &<= x <= x_{high1} \\
x_{low2} &<= x <= x_{high2} \\
y_{low1} &<= y <= y_{high1} \\
y_{low2} &<= y <= y_{high2}
\end{aligned} \tag{11.6}$$

This is illustrated in Fig. 11.6 with the shaded regions. If the intersection point (x, y) falls within both shaded regions, then the above four relational expressions are true and the line segments intersect.

SPECIFIC EXAMPLE

We will determine whether the point (12, 27) falls within the plume (Fig. 11.7) defined by the coordinates listed in the following table:

x	*y*	*x*	*y*
0	0	19	44
3	5	20	55
4	16	25	31
7	35	24	4
10	22	10	3

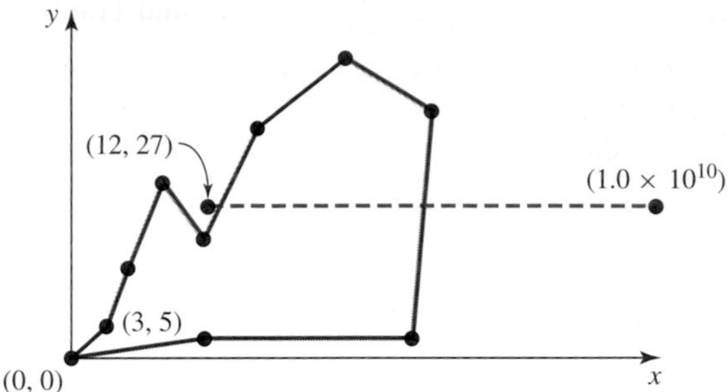

Figure 11.7

Plume defined by endpoints of line segments. A long horizontal line is drawn from the point being considered.

We begin by creating a line segment using the first two points as endpoints. Thus, we have:

Line segment 1:

$$\text{seg1}_{x1} = 0 \qquad \text{seg1}_{y1} = 0$$
$$\text{seg1}_{x2} = 3 \qquad \text{seg1}_{y2} = 5$$

A second line segment is created with the point (12, 27) and (1.0×10^{10}, 27) which makes this a very long line segment meant to intersect all possible plume boundaries. We will call this line segment the probe. This is the dashed line in Fig. 11.7. With this line segment we have:

Line segment 2:

$$\text{seg2}_{x1} = 12 \qquad \text{seg2}_{y1} = 27$$
$$\text{seg2}_{x2} = 1.0 \times 10^{10} \qquad \text{seg2}_{y2} = 27$$

Using Eqns. 11.1 to 11.4 we get:

$$m_1 = (5 - 0)/(3 - 0) = 1.667$$
$$m_2 = (27 - 27)/(1.0 \times 10^{10} - 12) = 0.0$$
$$b_1 = 5 - 1.667(3) = 0.0$$
$$b_2 = 27 - 0.0(1.0 \times 10^{10}) = 27$$
$$x = (27 - 0)/(1.667 - 0) = 16.2$$
$$y = 1.667(16.2) + 0.0 = 27$$

Thus, the intersection point of the two *lines* encompassing the line *segments* is (16.2, 27). To determine whether the two line segments intersect, we use the relational expressions of Eqns. 11.5 and 11.6. By observation we have

Line segment 1:

$$x_{\text{low1}} = 0 \qquad y_{\text{low1}} = 0$$
$$x_{\text{high1}} = 3 \qquad y_{\text{high1}} = 5$$

Line segment 2:

$$x_{\text{low2}} = 12 \qquad y_{\text{low2}} = 27$$
$$x_{\text{high2}} = 1.0 \times 10^{10} \qquad y_{\text{high2}} = 27$$

Applying the relational expressions of Eqns. 11.5 and 11.6:

$$0 <= x <= 3$$
$$12 <= x <= 1.0 \times 10^{10}$$
$$0 <= y <= 5$$
$$27 <= y <= 27$$

with $x = 16.2$ and $y = 27$, we get:

$$0 <= 16.2 <= 3$$
$$12 <= 16.2 <= 1.0 \times 10^{10}$$
$$0 <= 27 <= 5$$
$$27 <= 27 <= 27$$

We see that the first and third of these relational expressions is false, and therefore the intersection point of the *lines* is not contained on the line *segments*. Therefore, the line segments do not intersect.

We continue by finding if each line segment on the plume boundary intersects with the horizontal dashed line. For each of the 10 line segments we have:

Line segment	Intersection with horizontal dashed line?	Line segment	Intersection with horizontal dashed line?
1	No	6	No
2	No	7	No
3	No	8	Yes
4	No	9	No
5	Yes	10	No

The total number of crossings is 2 (line segments 5 and 8). Because this is an even number, the point is not located within the plume boundary.

Note that the 10th line segment connects the 10th and first data points. Therefore, in our program, we need to wrap the plume around to the beginning to completely close the boundary to the plume.

CLASSES AND STRUCTS

- The fundamental geometric entities used in this program are points and line segments, so we create `struct`s for them. As we have seen before, the *x* and *y* coordinates are the primary attributes of a point and are the `Point` data members. A line segment has two endpoints (type `Point`), and a slope and intercept of the encompassing line. Therefore, the definitions of the `struct`s are:

```
struct Point
        {
        public:
                double x, y;
        };

struct Line_seg
        {
        public:
                Point endpt1, endpt2;
                double slope, intercept;
        };
```

The two line segment endpoints are type `Point`.

The `slope` and `intercept` are type `double`.

- We choose to create a class for the map of the plume (called Boundary_map). The plume boundary is defined by 10 points, so an array, size 10, of type Point is the data member. To make use of the map, we need to read the data points (function read_boundary_pts) and wrap the plume boundary around from the last point to the first (function map_wrap_around). We use *accessor* functions to make use of the map data. These *public* functions have the sole purpose of returning *private* data. For the Boundary_map class they are get_boundary_pts() and get_num_boundary_pts(). We add a constructor to initialize data to zero. The class definition is:

```
class Boundary_map
{
        private:
                enum {NUM_MAP_PTS = 10};
                Point boundary_pts[NUM_MAP_PTS + 1];
        public:
                Boundary_map ();
                void read_boundary_pts ();
                void map_wrap_around ();
                Point* get_boundary_pts ();
                int get_num_boundary_pts ();
};
```

We size the array of points using enum.

An array of type Point holds the plume boundary points.

Constructor.

Reading and wrapping the points.

Accessor functions that return private data.

Note that we define the number of map points within the class (10). We add one point to the boundary_pts[] array to make the 11th point be a duplicate of the first point and close the plume boundary. None of the functions has any arguments because this class works strictly with the Boundary_map data. The accessor functions have return types that match the type of data they are accessing. The get_num_boundary_pts() function returns an int (in this case the number 11).

We cannot return an entire array from a function, so the get_boundary_pts() function returns the *address* of the boundary_pts() array. The array is type Point, so the function returns type Point*. This is the method described in Lesson 11.5. Because C++ allows us to use array notation with pointer variables, the function that calls the get_boundary_pts() function can use the data like an ordinary array.

- The other major entity used in this program (besides the plume map) is the probe. Therefore, we choose to create a Probe class. The data members that define a probe are the point at which a water sample is taken (called sample_pt), and the end points of the line segment created by the probe (endpt1 and endpt2). In order to keep the connections between the classes reasonably simple (more complex connections are illustrated in Chapter 14), the Probe class should perform the operations that interact the probe with the map. Therefore, we need a data member that keeps track of the number of intersections between the probe and the map boundary (called num_crosses).

  Actions of the class (performed in member functions) are to read the sample point (called read_sample_pt()) and to test each segment of the map boundary for an intersection (called check_map_boundary()). This last function makes use of the techniques for finding the intersection of two lines (calculated in function `probe_line_intersect()`) and for finding the intersection of two line segments (calculated in function `probe_line_seg_intersect`).

The class definition is:

```
class Probe
{
        private:
                Point sample_pt, endpt1, endpt2;
                int num_crosses;
                Point probe_line_intersect (Line_seg);
                int probe_line_seg_intersect (Point,
                  Line_seg);
        public:
                Probe ();
                void read_sample_pt ();
                void check_map_boundary (Point*, int);
};
```

Sample point and 2 endpoints of the probe.

These are private functions because they are called only from member function `check_map_boundary()`.

Constructor.

This function receives the address of the map points array (type `Point*`).

The function `read_sample_pt()` has no arguments and returns nothing because it simply assigns values to the *x* and *y* coordinates of `sample_pt`. The function `check_map_boundary()` has two arguments. This function is passed the address of the map boundary points array (the first argument, type `Point*`) and the number of array elements (type `int`). The `probe_line_seg_intersect()` function works with two line segments and the line intersection point. One line segment goes through the argument list (type `Line_seg`); the other is the probe, whose data members are automatically passed to the function. The point is passed through the argument list (type `Point`).

Note in this definition, we have two *private* functions. Previously in this text, all our functions had been *public*. We use private functions here because the `probe_line_intersect()` and `probe_line_seg_intersect()` functions are called only by the member function `check_map_boundary()`. The private functions are not meant to be called by functions outside the class. Therefore, it is appropriate to make them private rather than public member functions. In general, you should specify private functions for activities that are meant to be used only within the class itself.

ALGORITHM AND CODE SEGMENTS

The algorithms for the difficult member functions are shown here. The other functions are simply annotated in the source code.

FUNCTION `probe_line_intersect ()`

This function returns the intersection point of two lines (the probe and the line encompassing a map boundary line segment). In addition, it must account for the unusual conditions of the map line segment being vertical or horizontal (Fig. 11.8). If the following declarations are made in the function:

```
Line_seg      map_line_seg;
Point         intersect_pt;
double        probe_slope, probe_intercept;
```

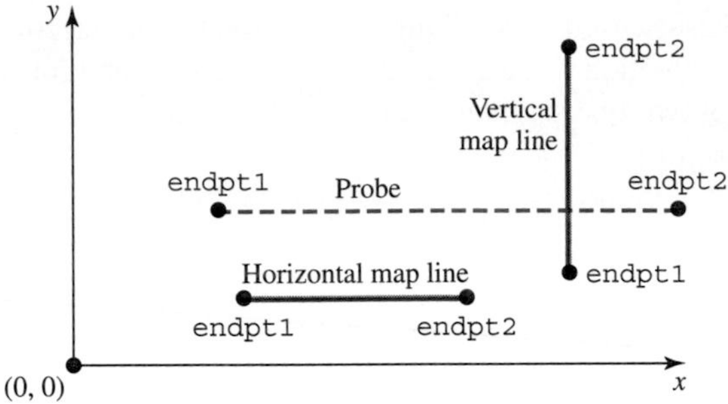

Figure 11.8
Special cases of horizontal and vertical map lines.

then we can check for the map line segment being vertical with the `if` control structure:

> This expression checks if the two map line segment endpoint `x` coordinates are approximately the same. Note that we are comparing real numbers so we cannot use `==`. We must use `fabs(difference)<small_number`.

```
if (fabs (map_line_seg.endpt2.x - map_line_seg.endpt1.x) < 1.0E-20)
        {
        intersect_pt.x = map_line_seg.endpt1.x;
        intersect_pt.y = endpt1.y;
        }
```

> When the map line segment is vertical, the `x` intersection value is at the `x` value of the map line segment (`map_line_seg.endpt1.x`). The `y` intersection value is at the `y` value of the probe (indicated simply by `endpt1.y` because function `probe_line_intersect` is a `Probe` member function).

We can check for the map line segment being horizontal with the `if` control structure:

```
map_line_seg.slope = (map_line_seg.endpt2.y - map_line_seg.endpt1.y) /
                     (map_line_seg.endpt2.x - map_line_seg.endpt1.x);
```

> Calculating the slope using Eqn. 11.1.

```
if (fabs (map_line_seg.slope) < 1.0E-20)
```

> Check if the slope is zero. Note, we cannot use `==0` because the slope is a real number. Instead we check if the slope is very small.

```
        {
        intersect_pt.x = LARGE_NUM;
        intersect_pt.y = endpt2.y;
        }
```

> The intersection point is at the probe `y` coordinate but a long way out in the `x` direction.

We calculate the intersection point of the two lines under ordinary circumstances with Eqns. 11.3 and 11.4:

```
intersect_pt.x = (probe_intercept - map_line_seg.intercept) /
                 (map_line_seg.slope - probe_slope);

intersect_pt.y = map_line_seg.slope * intersect_pt.x
                 + map_line_seg.intercept;
```

We return the intersection point with:

```
return (intersect_pt);
```

FUNCTION `probe_line_seg_intersect ()`

This function first determines which line segment endpoints are lowest and highest. For example, for line segment 1,

```
x_low_1 = (seg1.endpt1.x < seg1.endpt2.x) ? seg1.endpt1.x
        : seg1.endpt2.x;
```

compares which is the least: the x coordinate of endpoint 1 or endpoint 2 (this is the expression in parentheses). The value of the lower of these is assigned to `x_low_1`. This function determines all the high and low values for the purpose of creating the shaded regions of Figs. 11.6 and 11.7. We have a total of eight statements similar to the one shown. These statements determine the lower and higher values of all four endpoints (x and y) as given in Eqns. 11.5.

Then the function uses Eqn. 11.6 to determine if the intersection point falls within both shaded regions of Fig. 11.7. The `if` control structure:

```
if ((x_low_1 <= intersect_pt.x && intersect_pt.x <= x_high_1) &&
    (x_low_2 <= intersect_pt.x && intersect_pt.x <= x_high_2) &&
    (y_low_1 <= intersect_pt.y && intersect_pt.y <= y_high_1) &&
    (y_low_2 <= intersect_pt.y && intersect_pt.y <= y_high_2))
            {
            return (1);
            }
else
            {
            return (0);
            }
```

returns 1 from the function if the intersection point is on the line segments and 0 if it is not.

FUNCTION `check_map_boundary ()`

This function receives through its argument list the address of the beginning of the boundary points array and the number of points in the array. The function header is:

```
void Probe :: check_map_boundary (Point* bnd_pt, int num_pts)
```

This means that within the function, we can use array notation with `bnd_pt` (as in `bnd_pt[i]`) to access the boundary point values. The value of `num_pts` is used to control the function's loops.

The function is:

```
void Probe :: check_map_boundary (Point* bnd_pt, int num_pts)
{
        int i, does_cross, even_odd;  <------ Integer values to control the loop and indicate whether the line
                                              segments cross (does_cross) and the evenness or oddness of
                                              the number of crossings for all the line segments (even_odd).

        Point intersect_pt;     ]------ An intersection point and single line segment variable.
        Line_seg map_line_seg;  ]

        for (i = 0; i < num_pts - 1; i++)  <------ Looping over all the boundary points.
              {
              map_line_seg.endpt1 = bnd_pt[i];      ]--- Two adjacent points form the map line
              map_line_seg.endpt2 = bnd_pt[i + 1];  ]    segment endpoints.
```

The *line* intersection point is returned by the probe_line_intersect() function. This function is passed the map line segment through the argument list.

```
        intersect_pt = probe_line_intersect (map_line_seg);
```

The probe_line_seg_intersect() function is passed the *line* intersection point and the map line segment. It has the probe line segment automatically because it is a Probe member function.

```
        does_cross = probe_line_seg_intersect(intersect_pt,
          map_line_seg);
        num_crosses += does_cross;
        }
```

The value of does_cross (returned from probe_line_seg_intersect()) is 1 if the line segments intersect. The variable num_crosses stores the number of times crossed for the entire map.

```
    even_odd = num_crosses % 2;
    if (even_odd == 0) cout << "The sample point "
        "is outside the plume." << endl;
    if (even_odd == 1) cout << "The sample point "
        "is inside the plume." << endl;
}
```

To determine if a number is odd or even, use %2 and see if the result is 0 or 1. If it is zero, the number is even. If it is one, the number is odd.

FUNCTION main

In main, we declare objects and call public member functions. Since we are working with one probe and one map, we declare a single object of each class:

```
Boundary_map     plume_map;
Probe            probe_from_water_sample;
```

We start by initializing the map, reading the data, and closing the map boundary. We use the plume_map object to call the functions:

```
plume_map . read_boundary_pts();
plume_map . map_wrap_around();
```

Then we read the sample point for the probe:

```
probe_from_water_sample . read_sample_pt();
```

We perform the bulk of the calculations by calling the check_map_boundary() function of the Probe class. This is the key line that connects the two classes. By using the address of the map boundary array returned from the function get_map_boundary_pts() and the number of boundary points from the get_num_boundary_pts() function, we can call the check_map_boundary() function. The function call is:

Probe object plus function name.

```
probe_from_water_sample . check_map_boundary
      (plume_map . get_boundary_pts(), plume_map . get_num_boundary_pts());
```

Boundary_map object plus function name. Boundary_map object plus function name.

Note that the arguments of the Probe class function are calls to Boundary_map class functions (because the Boundary_map functions return the values needed by the Probe class function). This connects the two classes.

The complete source code follows.

Source Code

```
#include <iostream>
#include <cmath>
#include <fstream>
using namespace std;

const int LARGE_NUM = 1.0E10;

struct Point
{
        public:
                double x, y;
};

struct Line_seg
{
        public:
                Point endpt1, endpt2;
                double slope, intercept;
};

class Boundary_map
{
        private:
                enum {NUM_MAP_PTS = 10};
                Point boundary_pts[NUM_MAP_PTS + 1];
        public:
                Boundary_map ();
                void read_boundary_pts ();
                void map_wrap_around ();
                Point* get_boundary_pts ();
                int get_num_boundary_pts ();
};

class Probe
{
        private:
                Point sample_pt, endpt1, endpt2;
                int num_crosses;
                Point probe_line_intersect (Line_seg);
                int probe_line_seg_intersect (Point, Line_seg);
        public:
                Probe ();
                void read_sample_pt ();
                void check_map_boundary (Point*, int);
};
```

Definitions of structs.

Definitions of classes.

```
Boundary_map :: Boundary_map ()
{
        int i;
        for (i = 0; i < NUM_MAP_PTS + 1; i++)
                     {
                     boundary_pts[i].x = 0;
                     boundary_pts[i].y = 0;
                     }
}
```

Constructor function that initializes data.

```
void Boundary_map :: read_boundary_pts ()
{
        int i;
        ifstream infile ("C:\\BNDARY.DAT");
        for (i = 0; i < NUM_MAP_PTS; i++)
                     {
                     infile >> boundary_pts[i].x;
                     infile >> boundary_pts[i].y;
                     }
}
```

Reading the map data.

```
void Boundary_map :: map_wrap_around ()
{
        boundary_pts[NUM_MAP_PTS] = boundary_pts[0];
}
```

Connecting the first and last data points.

```
Point* Boundary_map :: get_boundary_pts ()
{
        return (boundary_pts);
}
```

Accessor function that returns the address of the map boundary point array.

```
int Boundary_map :: get_num_boundary_pts ()
{
        return (NUM_MAP_PTS + 1);
}
```

Accessor function that returns the number of map data points (after connecting the first and last points).

```
Probe :: Probe ()
{
        sample_pt.x = 0;
        sample_pt.y = 0;
        endpt1.x = 0;
        endpt1.y = 0;
        endpt2.x = LARGE_NUM;
        endpt2.y = 0;
        num_crosses = 0;
}
```

Constructor function that initializes data.

```
void Probe :: read_sample_pt ()
{
        cout << "Enter the x and y coordinates of the
          sample point" << endl;
        cin >> sample_pt.x >> sample_pt.y;
        endpt1 = sample_pt;
        endpt2.y = sample_pt.y;
}

Point Probe :: probe_line_intersect (Line_seg map_line_seg)
{
        Point intersect_pt;
        double probe_slope, probe_intercept;
        if (fabs (map_line_seg.endpt2.x - map_line_seg.endpt1.x) < 1.0E-20)
                {
                intersect_pt.x = map_line_seg.endpt1.x;
                intersect_pt.y = endpt1.y;
                }
        else
                {
                map_line_seg.slope = (map_line_seg.endpt2.y
                  - map_line_seg.endpt1.y) / (map_line_seg.endpt2.x
                  - map_line_seg.endpt1.x);

                map_line_seg.intercept = map_line_seg.endpt2.y
                  - map_line_seg.slope * map_line_seg.endpt2.x;

                probe_slope = 0.0;
                probe_intercept = sample_pt.y;

                if (fabs (map_line_seg.slope) < 1.0E-20)
                        {
                        intersect_pt.x = LARGE_NUM;
                        intersect_pt.y = LARGE_NUM;
                        }

                intersect_pt.x = (probe_intercept - map_line_seg.intercept) /
                  (map_line_seg.slope - probe_slope);

                intersect_pt.y = map_line_seg.slope * intersect_pt.x
                  + map_line_seg.intercept;
                }

        return (intersect_pt);
}
```

Reading the sample point.

Calculating the line-probe intersection point.

```
int Probe :: probe_line_seg_intersect (Point intersect_pt, Line_seg seg2)
{
        Line_seg seg1;
        double x_low_1, x_high_1, x_low_2, x_high_2;
        double y_low_1, y_high_1, y_low_2, y_high_2;

        seg1.endpt1 = endpt1;
        seg1.endpt2 = endpt2;

        x_low_1 = (seg1.endpt1.x < seg1.endpt2.x) ?
          seg1.endpt1.x : seg1.endpt2.x;
        x_high_1 = (seg1.endpt1.x > seg1.endpt2.x) ?
          seg1.endpt1.x : seg1.endpt2.x;
        x_low_2 = (seg2.endpt1.x < seg2.endpt2.x) ?
          seg2.endpt1.x : seg2.endpt2.x;
        x_high_2 = (seg2.endpt1.x > seg2.endpt2.x) ?
          seg2.endpt1.x : seg2.endpt2.x;
        y_low_1 = (seg1.endpt1. y < seg1.endpt2.y) ?
          seg1.endpt1.y : seg1.endpt2.y;
        y_high_1 = (seg1.endpt1. y > seg1.endpt2.y) ?
          seg1.endpt1.y : seg1.endpt2.y;
        y_low_2 = (seg2.endpt1. y < seg2.endpt2.y) ?
          seg2.endpt1.y : seg2.endpt2.y;
        y_high_2 = (seg2.endpt1. y > seg2.endpt2.y) ?
          seg2.endpt1.y : seg2.endpt2.y;

        if ((x_low_1 <= intersect_pt.x && intersect_pt.x
          <= x_high_1) && (x_low_2 <= intersect_pt.x &&
          intersect_pt.x <= x_high_2) && (y_low_1
          <= intersect_pt.y && intersect_pt.y <= y_high_1) &&
          (y_low_2 <= intersect_pt.y && intersect_pt.y
          <= y_high_2))

          {
          return (1);
          }

        else

          {
          return (0);
          }

}
```

Determining if the probe and line segment intersect.

```
void Probe :: check_map_boundary (Point* bnd_pt, int num_pts)
{
        int i, does_cross, even_odd;
        Point intersect_pt;
        Line_seg map_line_seg;
        for (i = 0; i < num_pts - 1; i++)
                   {
                   map_line_seg.endpt1 = bnd_pt[i];
                   map_line_seg.endpt2 = bnd_pt[i + 1];
                   intersect_pt = probe_line_intersect
                     (map_line_seg);
                   does_cross = probe_line_seg_intersect
                     (intersect_pt, map_line_seg);
                   num_crosses += does_cross;
                   }
        even_odd = num_crosses % 2;
        if (even_odd == 0) cout << "The sample point is outside the "
           "plume." << endl;
        if (even_odd == 1) cout << "The sample point is inside the "
           "plume." << endl;
}

int main ( )
{
        Boundary_map plume_map;
        Probe        probe_from_water_sample;

        plume_map.read_boundary_pts ();
        plume_map.map_wrap_around ();

        probe_from_water_sample.read_sample_pt ();

        probe_from_water_sample.check_map_boundary
          (plume_map.get_boundary_pts (),
          plume_map.get_num_boundary_pts ());
}
```

Evaluating all the map line segments. Calling the private `Probe` member functions.

Initializing the objects.

Performing all the calculations.

Output

```
                Enter the x and y coordinates of the sample point.
keyboard input  12 27
                The sample point is outside the plume.
```

Comments

The Boundary_map class has a 1-D array as a data member, and therefore we return the address of a 1-D array from the get_boundary_pts() function. If the class had a multidimensional array data member, then we would have had to use the methods shown in Lesson 11.6 to correctly return the array address from the accessor function.

Connecting classes in the manner we have done here can sometimes be clumsy because it involves many calls to accessor functions. In Chapter 14, we show other ways of having classes and objects interact that do not involve the multiple accessor function calls. These methods can be considered somewhat cleaner than the method in this example.

Again, you can see that the main function is reasonably simple. This is somewhat typical for a program involving classes and objects.

To trace the order of execution, begin in main and go to the constructor functions for the objects declared. Then follow the functions as they are called. The order of function execution is:

```
Boundary_map();
Probe();

Boundary_map :: read_boundary_pts ( );
Boundary_map :: map_wrap_around ( );

Probe :: read_sample_pt ( );

Boundary_map :: get_boundary_pts ( );
Boundary_map :: get_num_boundary_pts ( );
Boundary_map :: check_map_boundary ( );

Probe :: probe_line_intersect ( );
Probe :: probe_line_seg_intersect ( );
```

We used the ?: operator to determine the lower and higher of two points. This helps us determine the shaded region. The ?: operator is very convenient for comparing two values and selecting just one of them.

Modification Exercises

1. This program is designed to handle 10 points for defining the plume boundary. Modify the program so that it can use 100 points to define the plume boundary.
2. Modify the program so that it can read 10 sample points and determine which are contained in the plume boundary.
3. In this program we have the probe as a horizontal line going far in the positive x direction. However, the probe can go in any direction. Modify the program so that the probe goes at a 45 degree angle from the sample point.
4. Modify the program to make the function, probe_line_seg_intersect(), a general function for determining whether or not any two line segments intersect.

LESSON EXERCISES

LESSON 11.1 EXERCISES

1. True or false:

a. A pointer variable can be used to store an ordinary integer.

b. No space is allowed between the * operator and the data type in a declaration.

c. The * operator cannot appear on the left side of an assignment statement.

d. Brackets can immediately follow a pointer variable name in an executable statement.

e. We can use & on the left side of an assignment statement.

2. Given the following declarations, find the error(s) if any in the statements given.

```
int circle_id;
int* circle_id_address;
double radius;
double* radius_address;
```

a. `circle_id` = FFF3;

b. `circle_id_address` = FFF3;

c. `circle_id_address = radius_address;`

d. `radius_address = *radius;`

e. `radius = *radius_address;`

Solutions

1. a. false
b. false
c. false
d. true
e. false

2. a. `circle_id` = 2223;
b. `circle_id_address = &circle_id;`
c. `circle_id_address = &circle_id;`
d. `radius_address = &radius;`
e. No compilation error, but `*radius_address` should be initialized before executing this statement.

LESSON 11.2 EXERCISES

1. True or false:

a. When we pass a variable address to a function, we usually want the function to modify the variable.

b. It is more common to use pass by reference than to pass a single variable address.

c. The `*` operator can be used within a function to access the memory cells at the address held by a pointer variable.

d. We cannot use the `&` operator in the argument list of a function call.

2. Given the declarations shown, find the error(s) if any in the following statements.

```
int calc_area (int*, int*);

int main()
{
          int height, width, area;
```

a. `calc_area (width, height);`

b. `calc_area (*width, *height);`

c. `calc_area (&width, &height);`

d. `area = calc_area (width, height);`

e. `area = &height * &width;`

Solutions

1. a. true
b. true
c. true
d. false

2. a. No error, but `calc_area ()` function cannot modify the values of width and height.
b. `calc_area (&width, &height);` or `calc_area (width, height);`
c. No error. The `calc_area ()` function can modify the values of width and height if so desired.
d. No error.
e. `area = height * width;`

LESSON 11.3 EXERCISES

1. True or false:

a. We cannot pass addresses to a function.

b. We should not use the `&` operator in a function call.

c. We can use the unary `*` operator in a function body to access the values at a particular address.

d. The argument type `double*` or `double[]` can be used to transfer an array address to a function.

e. We can use bracket (`[]`) notation with pointer variables.

2. Consider the following beginning of a program. Find the error(s), if any, in the statements a to e if they were to appear in `main`:

```
#include <iostream>
using namespace std;
int function1(int*, double*);
```

```
double function2(double*, int);
int main()
{
     int c[5], d;
     double b[8], e;
```

a. `function1 (&c, &b);`

b. `function2 (b,c);`

c. `c = function1 (c,b);`

d. `e = function2 (b,d);`

e. `d = function1 (c,b);`

Solutions

1. a. false
   b. false
   c. true
   d. true
   e. true
2. a. `function1 (c,b);`
   b. `function2 (c,b);`
   c. `d = function1 (c,b);`
   d. No error.
   e. No error.

LESSON 11.4 EXERCISES

1. True or false:

   a. We cannot use subtraction with a pointer variable.

   b. Array notation can be used with pointer variables.

   c. We do not need to initialize pointer variables before they are used.

2. Given the following declarations

```
int a[5] = {1,2,3,4,5};
int* b;
double* c[3] = {6,7,8};
double* d;
```

   find errors, if any in the following statements.

   a. `b = a[0];`

   b. `cout << b + 1 << endl;`

   c. `b = &c[2];`

   d. `d = FFEE;`

   e. `d = &c[3];`

Solutions

1. a. false
   b. true
   c. false
2. a. `b = &a[0];`
   b. No error, but `b` must be initialized prior to using the statement.
   c. `b = &a[2];`
   d. `d = &c[0];` or other valid use of `&` on right side of assignment statement.
   e. No error will be indicated on compilation, but goes beyond array bounds. Use `d = &c[2]`.

LESSON 11.5 EXERCISES

1. True or false:

   a. We can return an address from a function.

   b. To return an address of an array of `double` from a function, the function return type should be `double#`.

   c. C++ will go to the memory address you tell it without giving an error message.

   d. Array notation cannot be used with a single pointer variable.

2. Write a program that has a function that sums two equally sized 1-D arrays and returns the address of the array that holds the sum.

Solutions

1. a. true
   b. false
   c. true
   d. false

LESSON 11.6 EXERCISES

1. True or false:

   a. A `typedef` statement creates a new data type.

   b. We cannot return a pointer to an array from a function.

   c. Parentheses are required in declaring a pointer to an array.

   d. We use 4-D array notation with a pointer to a 3-D array.

   e. A `typedef` statement can be used to create an alias for an ordinary data type.

2. Find errors, if any, in the following statements.

   a. `int* (d)[3];`

   b. `typedef (double*)[3] array_pointer;`

   c. `double*[4] function1(double*[4]);`

   d. `typedef int Double;`

   e. `double (*)[4][5];`

3. Write a program that passes the address of a 3-D array to a function and returns a pointer to a 2-D array.

Solutions

1. a. false
   b. false
   c. true
   d. true
   e. true
2. a. `int (*d)[3];`
   b. `typedef double (*array_pointer)[3];`
   c. `typedef double (*array_pointer[3];`
      `array_pointer function1 (array_pointer);`
   d. No error, but `Double` would represent `int` in declarations and this is confusing.
   e. `double (*h)[4][5];`

LESSON 11.7 EXERCISES

1. True or false:

   a. Pointers to objects can be used to call member functions.

   b. Pointers to objects can be used to access member data.

   c. The arrow operator is a unary operator.

   d. Space is allowed between the - and > in the arrow operator.

Solutions

1. a. true
   b. True, but data members must be public.
   c. false
   d. false

LESSON 11.8 EXERCISES

1. True or false:

   a. Both `struct` type and class type pointer variables can be used as data members.

   b. We must initialize array values before assigning the array address to a pointer variable.

   c. Data member pointer variables can be used to connect classes.

Solutions

1. a. true
   b. false
   c. true

LESSON 11.9 EXERCISES

1. True or false:

   a. The word `new` is a keyword.

   b. The word `new` calls the `new` function.

c. We cannot reserve memory for a single variable; we can reserve memory only for an array.

d. The `new` operator both reserves memory and fills the memory space.

e. The `delete` operator can be used only after the memory values have been made zero.

2. Find the error(s) if any, in the following statements.

a. `delete array;`

b. `new [8];`

c. `new double[8];`

d. `delete [10] array;`

e. `new[1] = 3;`

Solutions

1. a. true
b. false
c. false
d. false
e. false

2. a. No error, provided array is a pointer to a single variable.
b. `new int[8];`
c. No error.
d. `delete [] array;`
e. `array[1] = 3;`

APPLICATION EXERCISES

Use classes and functions that return pointers to solve the application exercises at the end of Chapters 9 and 10.

CHAPTER 12

CHARACTER ARRAYS

CHAPTER TOPICS

In this chapter, you will learn how to:

- Manipulate text information using C strings
- Read text information from a file and keyboard
- Use text in practical programs

Analyzing and manipulating text is an important programming task. Word processing software, for instance, has text manipulation at its core. Also, scientific programs frequently have text associated with numeric data. Even each digit of numeric data can be treated as text and analyzed for patterns or validity (making sure, for instance, that no letters or other characters appear in the middle of numbers). Overall, all sorts of technical and nontechnical types of programs deal with text. In this chapter and in Chapter 13, we illustrate C++'s text manipulating capabilities.

Character arrays are a fundamental form of storing text. In character arrays, we store what are known as *C strings* (called that because they were developed initially in the C language). When we store C strings in character arrays, we store a single character in each element. C strings are important in C++ because they are basic and are still used widely in C++ programs. C++ has a more advanced style of strings, which are included in the `string` class. We cover the `string` class in Chapter 13.

When working with numeric arrays it made some sense to use element by element manipulations in loops. With strings, we will see that it is often more convenient to use the address of the first element of the string and library functions to perform manipulations. Because we are working with addresses, we will find that pointer variables are important in working with strings.

Lessons 3.3 and 4.4 were devoted to single characters. If you skipped these lessons, or have forgotten how to work with single characters, read Lessons 3.3 and 4.4 now.

LESSON 12.1 DECLARING, INITIALIZING, AND PRINTING

TOPICS

- Declaring C strings
- Initializing C strings
- Printing C strings
- Terminating C strings

QUESTION YOU SHOULD ATTEMPT TO ANSWER

1. What is the difference between using single and double quotes?

In this source code, we declare three character arrays and a single character variable. The first character array `bb[]` is initialized element by element using assignment statements. Each assignment statement fills one element of the `bb[]` array with a single character. This is a tedious way to fill an array, but it illustrates the required last character, which is `\0` (the null character, treated as a single entity as described in Chapter 2). Every character array needs `\0` as the last filled array element to be manipulated by the string library functions.

The other arrays in this program (`cc[]` and `dd[]`) are initialized using the `strcpy()` function. Read the program to see how to initialize and print all the character arrays.

Source Code

```
#include <iostream>
#include <cstring>
using namespace std;
int main ( )
```

The `cstring` header is needed for the C string library functions.

```
{
    char aa;
    char bb[4], cc[100], dd[100];

    aa = 'g';
    bb[0] = 'C';
    bb[1] = 'a';
    bb[2] = 't';
    bb[3] = '\0';

    strcpy(cc," Line 1. \n Line 2.");
    strcpy(dd,cc);

    cout << aa << endl << bb << endl << cc << endl << dd << endl;
}
```

Declaring a single character variable.

Declaring three character arrays.

Using single quotes to assign a single character to aa.

Assigning a character to each of the first three elements of the bb[] array using single quotes.

The fourth character is \0, which C++ regards as a single character. This character is required by C++ to terminate the string.

We can initialize a string using the strcpy library function. This statement puts the text enclosed in double quotes into the cc[] array. Note that \n is contained in the text. The output shows that the \n is treated as the newline character and creates a new line of text.

We can also use the strcpy function to copy the contents of one character array into another. This statement copies the contents of cc[] into dd[].

We can use cout to print all the strings. Only the name of the array is needed in the statement. The output shows that cc[] and dd[] are the same.

Output

```
g
Cat
 Line 1.
 Line 2.
 Line 1.
 Line 2.
```

Description

Character array declarations. We declare arrays of characters to store strings. For instance, the declaration

```
char bb[4], cc[100], dd[100];
```

declares bb[], cc[], and dd[] to be arrays of characters. The maximum number of characters that can be stored in these arrays is one less than the number enclosed in brackets. This means that bb[] can hold 3 characters, and cc[] and dd[] can hold 99 characters. Why one less than the declared number? C++ requires that the last character in a string be the null (\0) character. This leaves the other memory cells free to hold any other characters.

Initializing strings character by character. In this lesson's program, we have stored a string in the `bb[]` array, character by character, with the statements:

```
bb[0] = 'C';
bb[1] = 'a';
bb[2] = 't';
bb[3] = '\0'
```

Single quotes are used to surround a single character. C++ treats `\0` as a single character, and we have manually assigned it to the last element of the string. The null character, written as `\0`, is stored in memory as 1 byte with all the bits set to 0. The contents of this array are therefore:

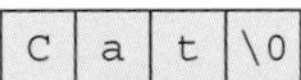

Initializing strings and string storage. Initializing strings character by character with assignment statements is inefficient. Fortunately, C++ has library functions that make it easy for us to initialize strings. The function `strcpy`, whose declaration is in the header `cstring` (which must be included), copies a string into an array. For instance, the statement

```
strcpy (cc, " Line 1. \n Line 2.");
```

causes the string enclosed in double quotes to be copied to the memory cells of the `cc[]` array. The function automatically adds the terminating null character when the string is stored in memory. Therefore, the contents of this array are:

	L	i	n	e		1	.		\n		L	i	n	e		2	.	\0

Even though only 18 characters (including spaces, which are considered characters) are enclosed in double quotes, 19 memory cells are required to store the string. Observe that the `\n` and `\0` occupy only one cell.

The table of variables for this lesson's program is the following (not including the `\0` at the end of each string):

Variable name	Type	Address	Value
aa	char	FFF5	g
bb	array of char	FFF0	Cat
cc	array of char	FF8C	Line 1. \n Line 2.
dd	array of char	FF28	Line 1. \n Line 2.

We can convert the hexadecimal values of the addresses

```
FF28  FF8C  FFF0  FFF5
(dd)  (cc)  (bb)  (aa)
```

to decimal values and work with the decimal values to see how many bytes are between the addresses indicated. Converting these to decimal gives:

```
65320  65420  65520  65525
(dd)   (cc)   (bb)   (aa)
```

Between `dd` and `cc` we have $65420 - 65320 = 100$ bytes; between `cc` and `bb` we have $65520 - 65420 = 100$ bytes; and between `bb` and `aa` we have $65525 - 65520 = 5$ bytes. The arrays, `cc[]` and `dd[]`, were declared to have 100 elements,

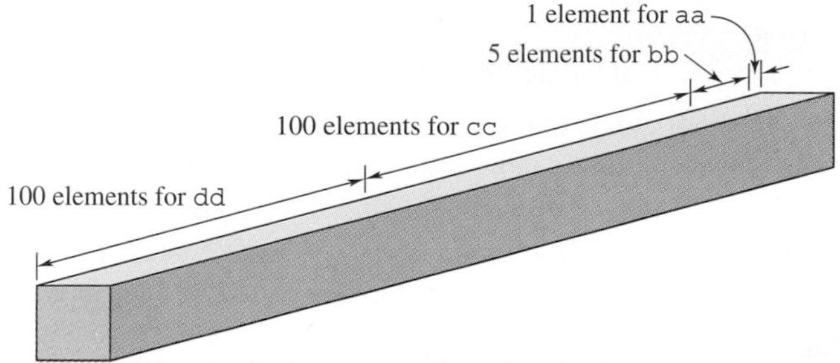

Figure 12.1

Arrangement of memory for Lesson 12.1's program.

bb[] to have four elements, and aa to be just one element. The addresses illustrate that the memory for all of these is closely packed. (Note, that bb[] had only four elements declared, but 5 bytes separate bb[] and aa. The exact memory addresses are said to be implementation dependent, meaning a different C++ compiler may have only 4 bytes between bb[] and aa. We will not concern ourselves with this particular detail in this text.) Thus, for this particular compilation and execution of this program, we have the order of memory shown in Fig. 12.1 illustrated in a linear fashion.

With this illustration of memory, you can see that if we attempt to write a string into dd that covers more than 100 elements, we will extend into cc's memory region. In fact, because C++ does not check whether or not boundaries are exceeded it will indeed write over a portion of cc[] without indicating an error or that it even has occurred! Therefore, it is up to you, the programmer, to make sure that this does not happen. If you accidentally exceed the bounds of an array you will cause unexpected results and will have a difficult time in finding your error.

The memory is *arranged* (meaning the order of the arrays and variables, and the size of the block of memory needed for all declared data structures is set) during compilation. This means that we must make sure that our arrays are sized with the maximum that may be needed in any possible problem. In other words, we cannot enlarge the declared size of our arrays during execution to accommodate extra data without using dynamic data storage techniques. We also cannot, during execution, rearrange these set memory cells. If we try to do this we will crash our program.

The memory is *reserved* during execution. At this time, the program sets aside the block of memory in the arrangement that the C++ compiler has already determined. In other words, a block of memory for the local variables and arrays in a function is not reserved until the function is called. The memory stays reserved for that function until the function has completed execution. Then the memory is released (unless specified to do otherwise) so that the next function being called can utilize this memory.

During execution our program can change a value in a memory cell (like a character or integer), but it is not allowed to change the cell's address. For example, for this lesson's program we cannot assign a new address for the dd[] array. In other words, dd[] is set to be at address FF28. If we attempt to change the address, our program will crash or not compile. We mention this because you may accidentally try to do this. Especially when working with character arrays, it is easy to forget that the name of the array without brackets means an address and to write an assignment statement with the name of the string on the left side. For instance, in this lesson's program, we cannot write:

```
dd = cc;
```

or

```
dd = " Line1. \n Line 2.";
```

because dd is an address and cannot appear on the left side of an assignment statement (also said, dd is not an L-value—L meaning left). Assignment statements of these types try to get us to change a cell's address, which we cannot do.

We will see that in working with strings, we must keep in mind what represents addresses and use these only in their proper locations. As you go through the rest of this chapter, pay close attention and note the many different ways that addresses are represented.

Note that we can use assignment statements only to store characters one at a time as we did with the bb[] array in this lesson's program.

Also in this lesson's program, we have used the statement

```
strcpy (dd, cc);
```

This statement copies all the characters in the cc[] array to the dd[] array memory cells. Since an array name without brackets represents the address of the beginning of the array, we have passed the address of two arrays to function strcpy. With strcpy, a copy of the contents of the second array is stored at the address of the first array given in the argument list. Remember, if we want to copy the string stored in cc[] to the memory cells for dd[] we cannot use dd = cc;. We must use strcpy(dd,cc). Also, we must make sure that the declared size of the first array in the call to strcpy is large enough to hold the second array. If it is not declared large enough, we will overwrite adjacent memory cells, and this is undesirable.

We can initialize a character array in a declaration, however, we will not illustrate this until Lesson 12.5. The reason for the delay is to avoid confusion, because what appear to be illegal assignment statements are legal when used in a declaration. At this point, if you see character arrays that are initialized in their declaration, be aware that things that appear to be illegal are being done, but because they are done within a declaration they are allowed.

String literals. Even though no variable is associated with the string literal

```
" Line 1. \n Line 2."
```

in this lesson's program, C++ stores this string in memory and is aware of what address it is stored at. In fact, when this string is written in the strcpy statement, C++ passes its *address* to the strcpy function. Thus, the statement

```
strcpy (cc, " Line 1. \n Line 2.");
```

passes the address of the cc[] array and the address of the string in double quotes to strcpy. In general, C++ treats a string literal written in a program as the address of that string literal. This treatment is consistent with the statement strcpy(dd,cc);, where, it is clearly seen that both arguments represent addresses. More will be said about this in Lesson 12.5.

Difference between a single character and a string. If we were to write

```
char aa, ee[2];
aa = 'g';
strcpy (ee, "g");
```

the contents of the memory cells for aa and ee[] would not be the same. The memory cell for aa would contain only the single character g. However, the memory cells for ee would contain both g and \0. Because of this difference, we cannot treat aa as a string, but we can treat ee as a string.

Printing strings. A cout statement can be used to print strings. The statement

```
cout << aa << endl << bb << endl << cc << endl << dd << endl;
```

prints all the strings in this lesson's program. Note that had bb[], cc[], and dd[] been declared as numeric rather than character arrays, this cout statement would have printed the addresses of the beginning of the arrays not the contents! C++ is smart enough to recognize bb[], cc[], and dd[] as character arrays and print their contents not their addresses.

LESSON 12.2 SOME CHARACTER AND STRING LIBRARY FUNCTIONS

TOPICS

- String length
- String size
- Individual character operations

QUESTION YOU SHOULD ATTEMPT TO ANSWER

1. Is text[0] made into a lowercase letter?

In this lesson we learn the capabilities of a few character and string functions. Character functions operate on a single character of a string. String functions work on an entire string.

The character functions in the source code work with the case (uppercase or lowercase) of a character. One function determines the case and the other changes the case.

One string function in the source code determines the number of characters stored in a character array and the other determines how many bytes are reserved for a character array. Read the source code to see how a program can work with individual characters and entire strings.

Source Code

```
#include <iostream>
#include <cstring>
#include <ctype>
using namespace std;
int main ( )
{
      char cc, text[70];
      int occupied, reserved;

      strcpy(text,"An incomplete sentence.");

      occupied = strlen(text);

      reserved = sizeof(text)/sizeof(char);
```

- #include <ctype>: The ctype header is needed for the character library functions that check or change the case or kind of a character.
- char cc, text[70];: Declaring a character variable and a character array.
- int occupied, reserved;: Declaring two integers.
- strcpy: Initializing the character array.
- occupied = strlen(text);: The strlen function calculates and returns the number of characters *stored* in the character array.
- reserved = sizeof(text)/sizeof(char);: The sizeof operator determines the number of bytes *declared* or specified for its argument.

```
        cout << "occupied=" << occupied
             << "reserved=" << reserved << endl;

        if (isupper(text[0])) cc = tolower(text[0]);
        cout << text << endl << cc << endl;
}
```

The `isupper` and `tolower` functions operate on a single character not a string. The function `isupper` determines if a character is uppercase, and `tolower` returns the lowercase version of its argument.

Output

```
occupied=23 reserved=70
An incomplete sentence.
a
```

This is the lowercase version of the first character in the string.

Description

The `strlen` function. The function `strlen` is used to determine the number of characters actually *stored* in a particular character array. It uses the address of the first element of the array to begin its search for the null character. The function counts the number of memory cells until it encounters that character. The form to use `strlen` is

```
strlen (address);
```

where the *`address`* tells `strlen` where to begin its search and is often the name of a character array (which indicates the address of the first character of the array). The function returns the number of bytes or memory cells up to but not including the null character in the string. The statement:

```
occupied = strlen (text);
```

assigns to `occupied` the value of the number of characters in the string `text` (excluding the null character).

The `strlen` function is useful because it allows us to know exactly how much memory is needed for a particular string. We can use this to optimize our memory usage using dynamic memory allocation. In addition, it can help us avoid inadvertently overwriting memory by going beyond the bounds that we want to write.

Most other string functions are like `strlen` in that they require that the address of a string be one argument in the argument list.

The `sizeof` operator. The `sizeof` operator computes the number of bytes *reserved* for storage of a specified variable or variable type. That it is an operator rather than a function is of little importance to us, except to note that we need not always put parentheses around the argument. In this text we will use parentheses in all cases to avoid potential problems from not using them.

The form for using `sizeof` is

```
sizeof (name)
```

where *name* can be a variable name or type. For instance, two legitimate applications of `sizeof` are

```
sizeof (char);
sizeof (text);
```

In the first of these, `sizeof` returns the number of bytes used by the system to represent a `char`. In the second, `sizeof` returns the number of bytes reserved for the character array `text`. Note that, in this case, `sizeof` returns a value different from the value returned by `strlen`. This is because `sizeof` returns the number of bytes *reserved* for `text`, which is 70, whereas `strlen` returns the number of characters that are actually *stored,* which is 23.

In this lesson's program we divided `sizeof(text)` by `sizeof(char)` to determine the number of element places reserved for the array. If we want to know the number of elements reserved for an array, it is not sufficient to know only the number of bytes reserved. We must divide that number of bytes by the number of bytes used for the array's element type, because standard C++ does not explicitly set the number of bytes to be used for each type except `char`. For instance, one C++ implementation may use two bytes for an `int` while another may use four bytes. To keep our code portable, we divide by the number of bytes in the element type.

By definition, C++ gives a `char` one byte. Therefore, `sizeof(char)` is always equal to 1, and we really did not need to divide by `sizeof(char)` in this program. However, we did so to emphasize that you should divide by the `sizeof` the element type in the array (for instance, `sizeof(int)` for an integer array or `sizeof(double)` for a `double` array) to determine the number of elements reserved for an array.

In the expression `sizeof(text)`, the array name, `text`, does not have brackets with it. However, this is one time in C++ (and we will not see any others in this book) where an array name without brackets does not mean an address. So, remember this one exception. When using the `sizeof` operator, an array name without brackets does not mean an address; it is simply an identifier. The operator `sizeof` finds the allocated storage associated with that identifier.

The `isupper` function. This function works with a single character, not a string. This function determines whether or not the character used as the argument is uppercase. If it is not, the function returns `0`. If it is, the function returns a nonzero integer. For example, in this lesson's program, `isupper` was used in the expression

```
if (isupper (text[0]))
```

The argument, `text[0]`, is the character A. So the function `isupper` returns the value 1, and the `if` expression is true.

The `tolower` function. This function also works with a single character, not a string. If the argument for `tolower` is an uppercase letter, the function returns the lowercase version of this letter. It does not modify the argument itself. For instance, in this lesson's program, we have used the following statement

```
if (isupper (text[0])) cc = tolower (text[0]);
```

Because `text[0]` is the uppercase letter 'A', `tolower(text[0])` returns the lowercase letter 'a'. The assignment statement assigns 'a' to the variable `cc`. This is verified in the output from the program. However, because the function `tolower` does not modify the argument `text[0]`, the first character of `text[]` remains the uppercase letter A. This is also verified in the output.

The `isdigit` function. Not shown in this lesson's program is the function `isdigit`. This function is commonly used to analyze whether a particular character in a string is one of the 0–9 digits. It is helpful for checking input data. For instance, if we prompt the user to enter a digit from the keyboard, we can use `isdigit` to check that indeed a digit has been typed. If something other than a digit has been typed, an error message can be displayed and the user can be prompted to reenter the data.

Other character and string functions in the C++ library. Table 12.1 lists the character functions available in the C++ library whose declarations are in the `ctype` header. We will not show the use of these functions; however, we believe the descriptions in the table give you sufficient information to use them in your programs. Note that each of the functions takes a single character as an argument, indicated as `int` because C++ treats characters as integers. Figure 12.2 illustrates the naming of C++'s character groups.

Table 12.2 lists other C++ string functions and the tasks they perform. You should read this table to learn the types of operations the string functions can perform. You do not need the details at this time. When you decide that you want to use one of these functions, you should refer to Appendix B. This appendix has a program that illustrates the use of these functions and gives you enough detail to use them.

TABLE 12.1 — Character functions in C++ library

Function	Operation
`isalnum (int)`	Returns a nonzero integer if the argument is any lower- or uppercase letter or 0–9 digit. Otherwise, it returns the integer 0.
`isalpha (int)`	Returns a nonzero integer if the argument is any lower- or uppercase letter. Otherwise, it returns the integer 0.
`iscntrl (int)`	Returns a nonzero integer if the argument is any control character (being new line ('`\n`'), horizontal tab ('`\t`'), carriage return ('`\r`'), form feed ('`\f`'), vertical tab ('`\v`'), backspace ('`\b`'), or alert ('`\a`')). Otherwise, it returns the integer 0.
`isdigit (int)`	Returns a nonzero integer if the argument is any 0–9 digit. Otherwise, it returns the integer 0.
`isgraph (int)`	Returns a nonzero integer if the argument is any printing character except space (' '). Otherwise, it returns the integer 0.
`islower (int)`	Returns a nonzero integer if the argument is a lowercase letter. Otherwise, it returns the integer 0.
`isprint (int)`	Returns a nonzero integer if the argument is any printing character including space (' '). Otherwise, it returns the integer 0.
`ispunct (int)`	Returns a nonzero integer if the argument is any printing character other than space (' '), lower- or uppercase letter, or 0–9 digit. Otherwise, it returns the integer 0.
`isspace (int)`	Returns a nonzero integer if the argument is space (' '), new line ('`\n`'), horizontal tab ('`\t`'), carriage return ('`\r`'), form feed ('`\f`'), or vertical tab ('`\v`'). Otherwise, it returns the integer 0.
`isupper (int)`	Returns a nonzero integer if the argument is an uppercase letter. Otherwise, it returns the integer 0.
`isxdigit (int)`	Returns a nonzero integer if the argument is any 0–9 digit, lowercase letters a–f, or uppercase letters A–F; that is, any hexadecimal digit. Otherwise, it returns the integer 0.
`tolower (int)`	If the argument is an uppercase letter, this function returns the corresponding lowercase letter. Otherwise, the argument is returned unchanged.
`toupper (int)`	If the argument is a lowercase letter, this function returns the corresponding uppercase letter. Otherwise, the argument is returned unchanged.

TABLE 12.2 — Operations of other string functions

Type of operations	Function name	Comment
Conversion from string to numeric value	`atoi`	Finds the first integer in a string. Returns the value of that number (an `int`).
	`atof`	Finds the first real number in a string. Returns the value of that number (a `double`).
	`atol`	Finds the first integer in a string. Returns `long`.
	`strtod`	Finds the first real number in a string. Returns the value of that number (a `double`), passes address of end of numeric portion.
	`strtol`	Finds the first real number in a string. Returns the value of that number (a `long`), passes address of end of numeric portion.
	`strtoul`	Finds the first integer in a string. Returns the value of that number (an unsigned `long`), passes address of end of numeric portion.
Copying one string or a portion of a string into memory cells reserved for another string	`strcat`	Copies second string onto the tail end of first string. Returns address of first string.
	`strcpy`	Copies second string onto the beginning of the first string. Returns address of first string.
	`strncpy`	Copies specified number of characters from second string to beginning of first string. Returns address of first string.
	`strtok`	Copies null character into first string at location of matching character in second string. Returns address of location at which null character placed.
Finding the address or position of a particular character, string or portion of a string in a given string	`strchr` (address)	Finds specified single character in string. Returns address of first occurrence of character.
	`strcspn` (position)	Finds first occurrence in first string of any character in second string. Returns position of character in first string.
	`strpbrk` (address)	Finds first occurrence in first string of any character in second string. Returns address of character in first string.
	`strrchr` (address)	Finds last occurrence in first string of any character in second string. Returns address of character in first string.
	`strspn` (position)	Finds the first character in first string that does not occur in second string. Returns position of character in first string.
	`strstr` (address)	Finds the first occurrence of the second string in the first string. Returns the address of the beginning of the second string in the first string.
Comparing two strings lexicographically	`strcmp`	Compares first string to second string. Returns `int` indicating which string is greater lexicographically (see Appendix B).
	`strncmp`	Compares specified number of characters from first string to second string. Returns `int` indicating which is greater lexicographically (see Appendix B).
Finding the length of a string	`strlen`	Returns number of characters in string excluding null character.
Determining the address of a string describing an error	`strerror`	Returns address of string that describes error.

See Appendix C for more details.

Figure 12.2

Names and groupings of characters.

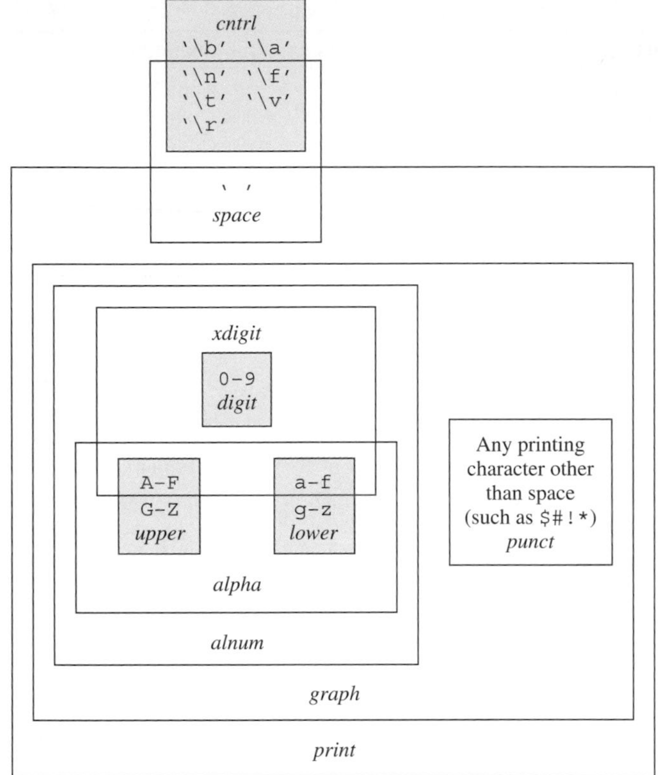

LESSON 12.3 2-D CHARACTER ARRAYS

TOPICS

- Declaring 2-D character arrays
- Initializing 2-D character arrays
- Printing 2-D character arrays

QUESTION YOU SHOULD ATTEMPT TO ANSWER

1. How many characters can we put into each line of `b[][]`?

A common way to store strings is in two-dimensional character arrays. Each row of a 2-D character array can be considered a separate string if it is terminated with the null character, `\0`.

One reason for using two-dimensional character arrays is that we are accustomed to looking at 2-D representations of text, and our image of a 2-D array being rows and columns fits what we commonly see. For instance, if this page of text had 100 lines down and 80 characters across, we could store the entire page in a character array `aa[100][80]`.

We can extend this to three dimensions by thinking of a book. For instance, a 400-page book could be represented by a 3-D array `aa[400][100][80]`. When text is stored in this manner it is easy for us to visualize what we are using.

We must realize, though, that sometimes our row-column image of arrays is not sufficient for us to work with them. In such cases, we must use a linear model of the storage of multidimensional arrays. Read the code to see how to declare, initialize, and print strings with 2-D character arrays.

Source Code

```
#include <iostream>
#include <cstring>
using namespace std;
int main ( )
{
      const int NUM_ROWS = 3, NUM_COLS = 15;
      char bb[NUM_ROWS][NUM_COLS]; <------ Declaring a 2-D character array.
      int i;

      strcpy(bb[0],"The bb array ");
      strcpy(bb[1],"has ");
      strcpy(bb[2],"3 strings.");

      for (i = 0; i < NUM_ROWS; i++) cout << bb[i] << endl;
}
```

Initializing each row of the array using the address of the beginning of each row (`b[0]`, `b[1]`, and `b[2]`) as arguments.

Printing each row using `b[i]` with `cout`.

Output

```
The bb array
has
3 strings.
```

Description

Declaring a 2-D character array. We declare 2-D character arrays with the keyword `char` followed by an identifier with two sets of brackets. The form is

```
char name [num_rows][num_columns];
```

where *name* can be any valid identifier and *num_rows* and *num_columns* must be positive integer constants. For example,

```
const int NUM_ROWS = 3, NUM_COLS = 15;
char bb [NUM_ROWS][NUM_COLS];
```

declares `bb[][]` to be a character array with 45 character-size memory cells. These cells may be thought of as being three rows and 15 columns.

Initializing a 2-D character array. We can use `strcpy` to initialize 2-D character arrays. We pass to `strcpy` the address of the beginning of each row of the array we wish to initialize. Because `bb[][]` is a 2-D array, the address of each row is indicated using just a single set of brackets. For instance, in this lesson's program

```
strcpy (bb[0], "The bb array ");
strcpy (bb[1], "has ");
strcpy (bb[2], "3 strings.");
```

uses `bb[0]`, `bb[1]`, and `bb[2]` (the addresses of the first, second, and third rows, respectively) to initialize the `bb[][]` array to be

T	h	e		b	b		a	r	r	a	y		\0	
h	a	s		\0										
3		s	t	r	i	n	g	s	.	\0				

Note that each row has `\0` and that each double-quote enclosed string is stored in a row. The length of each string in the list must be smaller than the declared size of the second dimension. In this case, the size of the second dimension, 15, is greater than the size of the longest string, `"The bb array \0"`, which contains 14 characters (including the terminating null character).

When you are initializing your strings in this manner, it is important that you not forget about the terminating null character that must be put at the end of each string. The size of your second dimension must include this character.

Printing 2-D character arrays. We can use `cout` to print strings stored in 2-D character arrays using the address of each row. Thus

```
for (i = 0; i < 3; i++) cout << bb[i] << endl;
```

prints each row of the `bb[][]` array.

Using the `sizeof` operator with 2-D character arrays. Depending on what we use as the operand, we can determine the declared size of the entire array, a single row, or a single element. We did not show it in this lesson's program, but for the 2-D array `bb[][]`,

```
sizeof (bb[0]);
```

calculates the declared size (or number of columns) of the first row of `bb[][]`. This is 15, which is the declared number of columns.

If we use `bb` with no brackets as the operand, we can evaluate the size of the entire array. For instance, if we had used

```
sizeof (bb);
```

the operator calculates 45, which is the total number of bytes reserved for the entire `bb[][]` array. If we wanted to calculate the number of rows reserved for `bb[][]`, we could have written the expression

```
sizeof (bb) / sizeof (bb[0]);
```

This evaluates to be 45/15, which is 3, the reserved number of rows.

Using the `strlen` function with 2-D character arrays. We did not show it in this lesson's program, but to use `strlen`, we need to pass to it the address of the beginning of each string, which is the address of the beginning of each row. Therefore, the expression

```
strlen (bb[0]);
```

passes to `strlen` the address of the beginning of the first row of `bb[][]`, and `strlen` returns the number of characters in that row (excluding the terminating null character).

Copying the contents of one 2-D character array into the memory cells reserved for another 2-D character array. We have not shown it in this lesson's program, but we can use the `strcpy` function to copy from one character array to another. For instance, if we had two arrays declared as

```
char cc[4][40], dd[4][40];
```

we can use a loop such as

```
for (i = 0; i < 4; i++) strcpy (cc[i], dd[i]);
```

to copy the `dd[][]` array contents, one row at a time, into `cc[][]`. To successfully copy the string, it is imperative for enough memory to have been reserved for the `cc[][]` array to accommodate each string stored in `dd[][]`.

LESSON 12.4 KEYBOARD AND FILE INPUT

TOPICS

- Reading a single word
- Reading paragraphs

QUESTION YOU SHOULD ATTEMPT TO ANSWER

1. Why is the ignore function needed?

To this point we have covered how to print strings, but not how to read them from the keyboard or a file. In this lesson we describe reading strings typed in by a user and those that are included in a file. Read the program, and pay particular attention to the difference between reading a single word and an entire line of text with spaces. Note that to read more than a single word, we need to use the `cin` object and a member function.

Source Code

```
#include <iostream>
#include <iomanip>
#include <fstream>
using namespace std;
int main ( )
{
      const int WORD_LENGTH = 15, MULTILINES = 800, LINE = 100;
      char aa[WORD_LENGTH], bb[MULTILINES], cc[3][LINE];
      ifstream infile("C:\\L7_4.DAT");
      int i;

      cout << "Enter a single word" << endl;
      cin >> setw (sizeof(aa)) >> aa;
      cin.ignore (1000,'\n');
      cout << aa << endl << endl;
```

Declaring two 1-D and one 2-D character arrays.

Opening an input file.

We use `cin` to read a single *word* entered by the user. Here, the first word of keyboard input is assigned to `aa[]`. The `setw` manipulator, used in the manner shown here, limits the number of characters read to `sizeof(aa)`.

The `ignore` function should be used after reading with `cin`. This processes any extraneous characters typed by the user after the first whitespace in response to the previous `cin` statement. The `1000` indicates the maximum number of characters to be ignored. The `\n` is a sentinel value indicating the last character to be ignored (meaning the last character to be ignored is `"Enter"`).

```
      cout << "Enter a few lines. "
              "Terminate with #." << endl;
      cin.getline (bb, sizeof(bb), '#');
      cin.ignore (1000, '\n');
      cout << bb << endl << endl;

      for(i = 0; i < 3; i++)
              {
              infile.getline (cc[i],
                sizeof(cc[i]));
              cout << cc[i];
              }

}
```

The getline function is used to read entire *lines* of input. Here, keyboard input is assigned to the bb[] array, with the number of characters limited by sizeof(bb). The function checks each character entered by a user. If # (the third argument) is entered, the function stops reading the input. The ignore function is used to process any other characters typed by the user after # (including "Enter").

We can use getline with an ifstream object (here, infile) to read data from a file. The cc[][] array is two-dimensional. The address of the beginning of each row is used as an argument to getline. By using a for loop, we can store the lines of a file into the rows of a 2-D character array.

Input File L7_4.DAT

```
Line 1 of text.
Line 2 of text.
Line 3 of text.
```

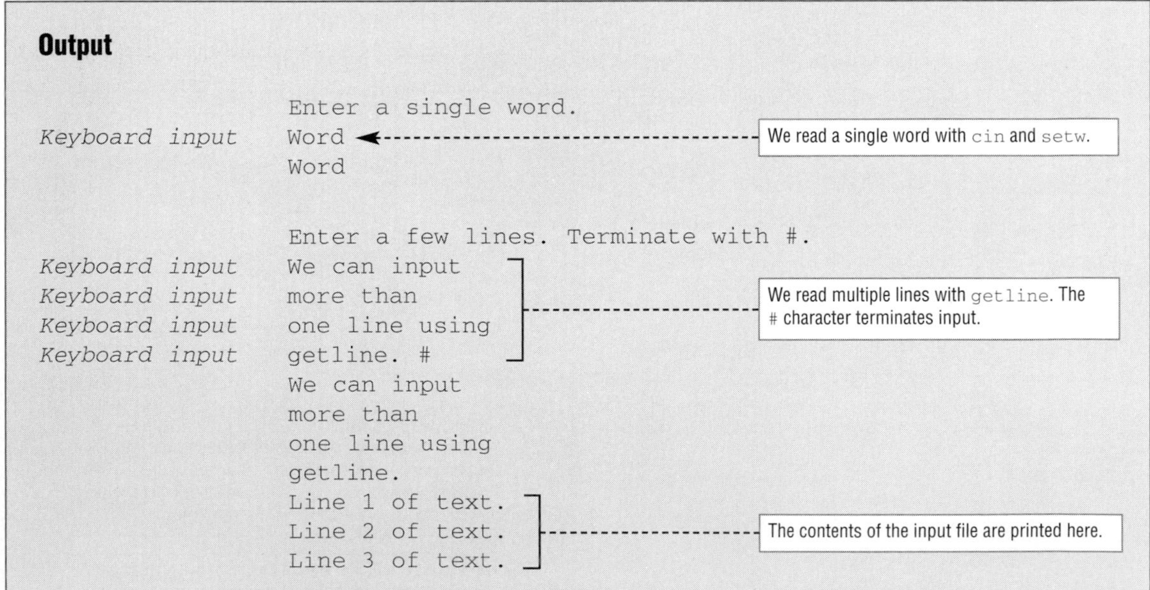
Output
Enter a single word.
Keyboard input Word
We read a single word with cin and setw.
Word
Enter a few lines. Terminate with #.
Keyboard input We can input
Keyboard input more than
Keyboard input one line using
Keyboard input getline. #
We read multiple lines with getline. The # character terminates input.
We can input
more than
one line using
getline.
Line 1 of text.
Line 2 of text.
Line 3 of text.
The contents of the input file are printed here.

Description

Reading a single word (characters with no spaces). We can read a single word from the keyboard using cin with the setw manipulator. The statement

```
cin >> setw (sizeof (aa)) >> aa;
```

reads characters until whitespace (including space and "Enter") is typed, and stores the characters in the `aa[]` array. The maximum number of characters stored into `aa[]` by this statement is limited to the numerical value of `sizeof(aa)`, which is the argument of the `setw` manipulator.

We could use `cin` without `setw`, but this would risk overflowing the array. For instance,

```
cin >> aa;
```

also reads until a whitespace character is encountered. However, if the number of characters exceeds the declared size of `aa[]`, C++ still attempts to store them in `aa[]`. Memory cells adjacent to `aa[]` become overwritten and may cause the program to crash. Therefore, it is recommended to use `setw` with `cin` when reading strings.

The declared size of the array used with `cin` should be at least two greater than the greatest anticipated input. This allows for the terminating whitespace and `\0` characters. For instance, in this lesson's program, with `aa[]` declared to have a size of 15, a user can successfully enter 13 letters of a word and have them all stored in `aa[]`. With the input given in this lesson, `aa[]` is assigned the following.

W	o	r	d	\n	\0									

If a user enters 14 or more letters when executing this lesson's program, no whitespace character will be contained in the string, but the last character stored in `aa[]` will be `\0`. Characters beyond 14 are discarded. Note that it is not necessary to use the manipulator `setw(sizeof(aa) - 1)` to make sure that space remains for an ending null character. Using `cin` with `setw(sizeof(aa))` automatically allows for the ending null character.

Because the terminator for using `cin` with strings is whitespace, `cin` is good for reading a single word, but not for reading entire sentences.

Reading multiple lines (including spaces and "Enter"). We can read multiple lines from the keyboard using the member function `getline`. The statement

```
cin.getline (bb, sizeof (bb), '#');
```

reads characters until a `#` is typed, and stores the characters in the `bb[]` array. The maximum number of characters read by this statement is limited to the numerical value of `sizeof(bb)`. With the `getline` function, any whitespace character typed by the user is included in the string. Therefore, we can read entire paragraphs or pages of text with `getline`. A typical form for the use of this function is

```
cin.getline (name, num_char, 'terminator');
```

where *name* is the name of the array (indicating the address of the first memory cell for the array), *num_char* is the maximum number of characters to be retrieved by `getline` from the keyboard and *terminator* is the terminating character the user should type to indicate the end of input. Using `sizeof(`*name*`)` for the value of *num_char* assures that the characters for the array will not spill over into the adjacent memory cells.

If the *terminator* (rather than the value of *num_char*) stops input, the *terminator* is read, but not inserted into the *name* array. If only one line of input is to be read by the program, the `terminator` can be specified to be `'\n'`. However, doing so is not required as the `getline` function has `'\n'` as a default value for the last argument. Therefore, had we used in this lesson's program

```
cin.getline (bb, sizeof (bb));
```

we would have read a single line of input from the keyboard.

Reading an input file. The entire contents of a file can be read using `getline`. A convenient method uses a 2-D character array. Each line of a file can be read into a different row of an array using a `for` loop. For instance, for the `cc[][]` array with three rows, the loop

```
for (i = 0; i < 3; i++)
         {
         infile.getline (cc[i], sizeof (cc[i]));
         }
```

reads three lines of the file associated with the object `infile` one line at a time (because, for the third argument of the call to `getline`, the default `\n` termination character is used). The first `getline` argument is the address of a row of the `cc[][]` array, and the second argument is the declared size of a row.

In general, if a 2-D array is declared larger in rows and columns than a file is in lines and length of lines, a loop of the sort

```
for (i = 0; i < num_lines; i++)
         {
         infile.getline (row_address, num_char);
         }
```

will read the file and store it in the array. In this loop, `num_lines` is the number of lines in the file, `row_address` is the address of a different row of the array each time through the loop, and `num_char` is the length of the lines of the file.

When sizing the array for file reading, remember to include space for two extra characters per line, the end of line `\n` character, and the string termination character, `\0`.

Extraneous input characters with keyboard input. Program users do not necessarily follow instructions. For instance, if a user enters multiple words (even when instructed not to) for the statement

```
cin >> setw (sizeof (aa)) >> aa;
```

the extra words remain in the input buffer (described in Chapter 3). Subsequent keyboard input statements will read the extra words. This is likely undesirable. Even if no extra words are typed, the "Enter" is left behind in the buffer. To prevent reading it and anything else remaining in the buffer, the `ignore` member function should be called after the `cin` statement. The `ignore` function's purpose is to read and discard characters. The statement

```
cin.ignore (1000, '\n');
```

reads and discards 1000 characters or until `\n` is encountered in the input buffer. Here, 1000 is used simply as an arbitrarily large number. It is most likely a user will type “Enter” (represented by `\n`) long before typing 1000 characters. The general form for the `ignore` function is

```
cin.ignore (num_char, 'terminator');
```

where *num_char* is the maximum number of characters to be discarded, and *terminator* is a character that indicates the end of character discarding. A good terminator is `\n` for many circumstances because typing “Enter” in response to a `cin` statement with strings causes program execution to continue. Therefore, `\n` is nearly always in the input stream.

Also, if we read numeric data using `cin` and follow it with reading a string with `getline`, an error can occur. An error may be caused by the `\n` that is left in the input buffer after the numeric data is read. Therefore, a call to the `ignore` function is appropriate *prior* to the `getline` call to process the `\n`. If the `\n` is not processed by `ignore`, `getline` reads the `\n`, and this may terminate the `getline` input, which is likely an error.

LESSON 12.5 DECLARATIONS AND POINTER VARIABLES

TOPICS

- Initializing C strings in declarations
- Arrays of pointers

QUESTION YOU SHOULD ATTEMPT TO ANSWER

1. Why are the two output statements in loops identical?

In this program, we use 1-D and 2-D character arrays to store strings, and we initialize these strings within the declarations. We have deliberately postponed the discussion of doing this seemingly simple operation because its form leads to considerable confusion. What you will learn with this lesson is that within a *declaration,* an = sign is used to store strings in character arrays. Remember, in an *executable statement,* we cannot use = to assign a string to a character array.

In this lesson, we will assign a double quote enclosed string (that is, a string constant or string literal, which, as we have stated, represents the *address* of the string as it is stored in memory) to a pointer variable. Although this appears to be using = to store a string, it is not. Such an assignment simply stores the address of the string literal in the pointer variable.

We also create an array of pointer variables, size 3. Each element of this array stores an address, and therefore in the array we store three different addresses. Each is the address of a different string literal. We initialize the array of pointers in the declaration by listing three double quote enclosed strings.

In summary, we show four different ways to store or access strings: a 1-D character array, a 2-D character array, a single pointer variable, and an array of pointer variables. All strings stored or accessed in these different ways are printed using `cout`. As we saw with numeric arrays, 1-D character arrays and single pointer variables are treated similarly. We will also see that 2-D character arrays and arrays of pointer variables are treated similarly.

Read the program and observe how the declarations are written and how the strings are printed. Remember, much of what you see in this program appears to be illegal. We will explain how this program contains all legal statements in the Description portion of the lesson.

Source Code

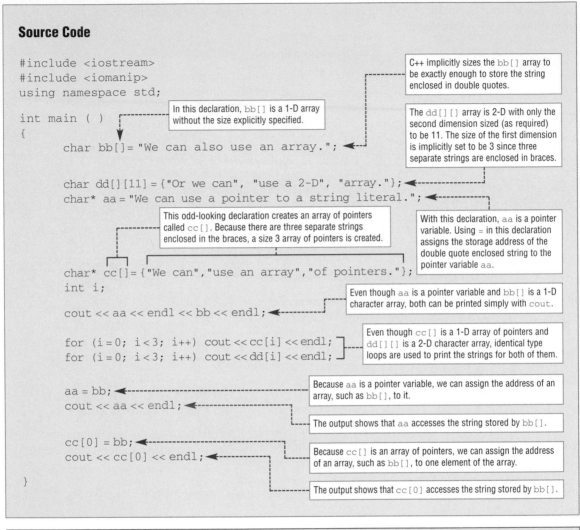

```
#include <iostream>
#include <iomanip>
using namespace std;

int main ( )
{
      char bb[]= "We can also use an array.";

      char dd[][11]={"Or we can", "use a 2-D", "array."};
      char* aa="We can use a pointer to a string literal.";

      char* cc[]={"We can","use an array","of pointers."};
      int i;

      cout << aa << endl << bb << endl;

      for (i=0; i<3; i++) cout << cc[i] << endl;
      for (i=0; i<3; i++) cout << dd[i] << endl;

      aa = bb;
      cout << aa << endl;

      cc[0] = bb;
      cout << cc[0] << endl;
}
```

C++ implicitly sizes the bb[] array to be exactly enough to store the string enclosed in double quotes.

In this declaration, bb[] is a 1-D array without the size explicitly specified.

The dd[][] array is 2-D with only the second dimension sized (as required) to be 11. The size of the first dimension is implicitly set to be 3 since three separate strings are enclosed in braces.

This odd-looking declaration creates an array of pointers called cc[]. Because there are three separate strings enclosed in the braces, a size 3 array of pointers is created.

With this declaration, aa is a pointer variable. Using = in this declaration assigns the storage address of the double quote enclosed string to the pointer variable aa.

Even though aa is a pointer variable and bb[] is a 1-D character array, both can be printed simply with cout.

Even though cc[] is a 1-D array of pointers and dd[][] is a 2-D character array, identical type loops are used to print the strings for both of them.

Because aa is a pointer variable, we can assign the address of an array, such as bb[], to it.

The output shows that aa accesses the string stored by bb[].

Because cc[] is an array of pointers, we can assign the address of an array, such as bb[], to one element of the array.

The output shows that cc[0] accesses the string stored by bb[].

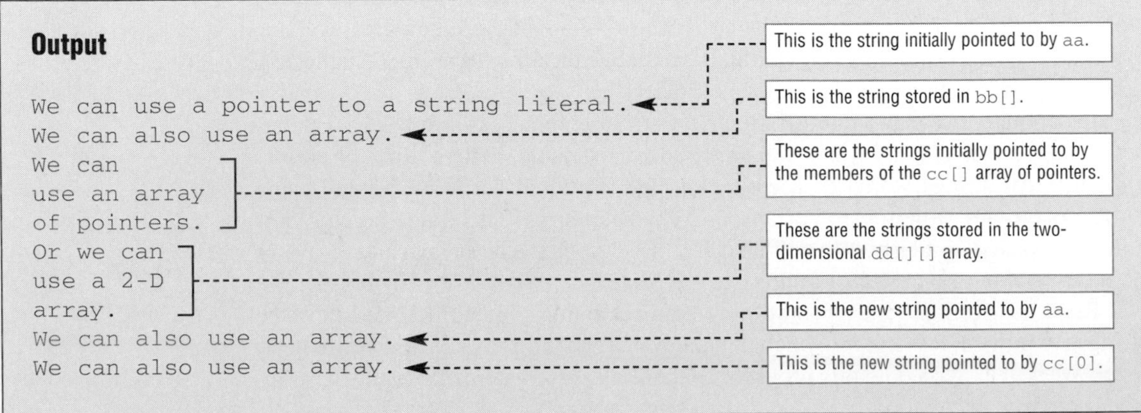

Description

Declaring and initializing 1-D character arrays. Within a declaration, 1-D character arrays can be initialized with an equal sign and a double quote enclosed string. For example

```
char bb[] = "We can also use an array.";
```

implicitly declares the size of `bb[]` to be 26 (for the 25 characters enclosed in double quotes and the `\0` terminating character). This declaration causes each character in the string to be stored in a separate element of the array. C++ allows us to use `=` with strings only in a declaration. When we do so, we are not strictly performing an assignment. C++ simply knows to put the characters enclosed in double quotes into the memory cells reserved for the array.

Note that we *cannot* use the following assignment statement in a program body:

```
bb[] = "We can also use an array.";
```

To put a string into the memory cells reserved for a 1-D character array, we must use `strcpy` in a manner like this

```
strcpy (bb, "We can also use an array");
```

The storage for `bb[]` is illustrated in the table of variables shown in Fig. 12.3. Note that like other variables, `bb[]` has memory reserved for it in the stack, and, therefore, the string is stored in the stack. This means that we can modify the contents of the memory cells holding this string during program execution.

Figure 12.3

Table of variables for the stack and heap region of memory for Lesson 12.5's program.

Stack Region of Memory

Name	Type	Address	Value
aa	pointer (to char)	FFF4	00E9
bb	array of char, size=[26]	FFC8	We can also use an array.\0
cc	array of pointers (to char), size=[3]	FFEE	0114
		FFF0	011B
		FFF2	0128
dd	2-D array of char, size=[3][11]	FFA6	Or we can\0
		FFB1	use a 2-D\0
		FFBC	array.\0

Heap Region of Memory

Type	Address	Value
String literal, size=[42]	00E9	We can use a pointer to a string literal.\0
String literal, size=[7]	0114	We can\0
String literal, size=[13]	011B	use an array\0
String literal, size=[33]	0128	of pointers.\0

Figure 12.4

Contents of each element of the dd[][] array which has the second dimension size 11. Note that some cells remain empty, meaning that some memory is wasted.

Stack—3 strings stored in a 2-D array

O	r		w	e		c	a	n	\0	
u	s	e		a		2	-	D	\0	
a	r	r	a	y	.	\0				

Declaring and initializing 2-D character arrays. We can initialize 2-D character arrays in declarations by enclosing strings in braces. For instance

```
char dd[][11] = {"Or we can", "use a 2-D", "array."};
```

explicitly declares the size of the second dimension of dd[][] to be 11 and implicitly declares the size of the first dimension to be 3 (because there are three strings enclosed in braces). This declaration causes each string to be stored in the stack in a separate row of the dd[][] array as shown in Fig. 12.3. The size of the second dimension (11) is greater than the number of characters in any of the three strings plus 1 (for the \0 terminating character).

An image of the storage is illustrated in Fig. 12.4, which shows that 11 elements are reserved for each row of the array. Only some of the elements are occupied since none of the strings contains the full 11 characters. This wastes memory, although not very much for this case. In general, though, using 2-D arrays for storing strings has the potential for wasting memory, since there is often variability in the lengths of strings stored, and a 2-D array requires that the size of the second dimension be sufficient to store the longest string of the group.

Note that we cannot use = to assign a string to a row of a 2-D character array in a program body. For instance, the following statement is not allowed

```
dd[0] = "Or we can";
```

To assign such a string we need to use strcpy in the manner

```
strcpy (dd[0], "Or we can");
```

***Declaring and initializing a pointer to* `char`.** Another way to work with a string is to declare and initialize a pointer variable to point to a string literal in a declaration. For instance, the declaration

```
char* aa = {"We can use a pointer to a string literal."};
```

declares the pointer variable aa to hold the address of the first character of the string, "We can use a pointer to a string literal.". This string is stored automatically by C++ in the heap region of memory, not the stack (where variables are stored).

This is illustrated in Fig. 12.3 which shows that the variable aa holds an address (00E9) as its value (which is correct since it is a pointer variable). The address is a very low number, which is indicative of the heap. The figure also shows that the actual characters of the string are stored in the heap. In addition, note that there is no "Name" column in the heap table. Therefore, we cannot use an identifier to access these memory cells. The only way to access these memory cells is through the pointer variable aa.

We can also modify the address stored by aa, and, therefore, access a different string with aa. For instance, the statement

```
aa = bb;
```

assigns the address of bb[] (FFC8) to aa. The cout statement following this assignment such as

```
cout << aa << endl;
```

prints out the bb[] string. Note that we cannot have the assignment

```
bb = aa;
```

because bb is not a pointer variable; it simply represents the address of the bb[] array.

Declaring and initializing an array of pointers to char. An array of pointers is simply an array in which each element holds an address. The following declares such an array.

```
char* cc [3];
```

For this declaration, char* is the type, cc is the array name, and three elements are contained in the array (meaning the array holds three addresses).

We can also both declare and initialize such an array. The following declaration also creates a char* type array called cc with three elements.

```
char* cc[] = {"We can", "use an array", "of pointers."};
```

Here, no size is given for the array (the brackets are empty), and we have enclosed three comma separated strings in the braces. This means that this array is implicitly declared to have a size of three, and each element of the array holds an address of one of the strings.

These strings are stored in the heap region of memory. This is shown in Fig. 12.3. From this figure, it can be seen that the variables cc[0], cc[1], and cc[2] hold the addresses 0114, 011B, and 0128, respectively. These addresses are the addresses of the strings in the heap.

An image of the storage is illustrated in Fig. 12.5, which shows that the memory reserved for each string is just the right size. No memory is wasted in this method, in contrast to 2-D character arrays, which do waste some memory.

Should we choose, we *can* modify the addresses stored by the elements of the pointer array. For instance, the statement

```
cc [0] = bb;
```

Heap—3 string literals

W	e		c	a	n	\0						
u	s	e		a	n		a	r	r	a	y	\0
o	f		p	o	i	n	t	e	r	s	.	\0

Figure 12.5

Contents of each element of the strings pointed to by the cc[] array. Because C++ automatically reserves only the exact amount of space for string literals, none of the cells are empty, meaning that no memory is wasted.

assigns the address of bb[] (FFC8) to cc[0]. The cout statement following this assignment

```
cout << cc  [0] << endl;
```

prints out the bb[] string. Note that we cannot have the assignment

```
bb = cc  [0];
```

because bb is not a pointer variable; it simply represents the address of the bb[] array.

You should make sure that you feel comfortable with the concept of an array of pointers (or array of addresses). Review Fig. 12.3 if you do not. We will see that arrays of pointers have uses beyond what we show here.

Summary. We can use 1-D arrays, 2-D arrays, pointer variables, and arrays of pointers to work with strings. Each of these stores strings in a different way. A programmer should be aware of the differences in order to program effectively. Figure 12.3 illustrates the differences and shows the data stored in the stack and heap.

Also, C++ does not allow the use of = in executable statements to assign strings. However, within declarations, C++ does allow the use of = for initializing strings.

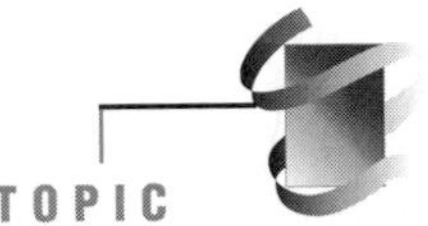

LESSON 12.6 STRINGS AND FUNCTIONS

TOPIC

- Passing strings to functions

QUESTION YOU SHOULD ATTEMPT TO ANSWER

1. What is the value of sizeof(bb)?

In Lesson 12.5, we used four different types of declarations for C strings:

1. One-dimensional character arrays.
2. Two-dimensional character arrays.
3. Pointers to char.
4. Arrays of pointers to char.

In this lesson we illustrate how to use each of these forms with functions.

We learned previously that we could not pass an entire array to a function. Instead, we simply pass the address of the beginning of an array, and the function works with that address to access the array elements. Therefore, to allow a function to work with a C string stored in an array, we put the address of that array in a function call.

Also, we learned that a pointer variable can be used to hold the address of the beginning of a C string. Therefore, to allow a function to work with a C string indicated by a pointer variable, we put the pointer variable in a function call. This pointer variable also indicates an address. When we have an array of pointers to C strings, to allow a function to work with all these strings, we put the address of the array of pointers in a function call.

In summary, to allow a function to work with any of the four forms, we put an address in the function call. The other important elements in getting functions to work with C strings are the function declaration and the function body. Read the program to see how to use C strings with functions.

Source Code

```
#include <iostream>
#include <cstring>
using namespace std;
const int LENGTH = 20;

void function1 (char ee[], char ff[][LENGTH], char* gg,
                char* hh[], int num_rows_ff, int num_elems_hh);

int main ( )
{
          char aa[] = "One-dimensional array.";
          char bb[][LENGTH] = {"Two-","dimensional ",
                               "array."};
          char* cc = "Pointer to string literal.";
          char* dd[] = {"Array ","of pointers ",
                        "to string ","literals."};
          int num_rows_bb, num_elems_dd;

          num_rows_bb = sizeof (bb) / LENGTH;
          num_elems_dd = sizeof (dd) / sizeof (char*);

          function1(aa, bb, cc, dd, num_rows_bb, num_elems_dd);
}
void function1 (char ee[], char ff[][LENGTH], char* gg, char* hh[],
  int num_rows_ff, int num_elems_hh)

{
        int i;

        cout << ee << endl;
        for (i = 0; i < num_rows_ff; i++)
            cout << ff[i];
        cout << endl;

        cout << gg << endl;
        for (i = 0; i < num_elems_hh; i++)
            cout << hh[i];
        cout << endl;
}
```

Function declaration. Addresses representing four forms of C strings (a 1-D array, a 2-D array, a pointer to a single variable, and an array of pointers) are passed to this function.

1-D array.

2-D array.

Pointer to string.

Array of pointers to strings.

Addresses representing all these are passed to the function.

The `sizeof` operator can be used to calculate the number of rows of `bb[][]` and the number of elements of `dd[]`. We pass these to a function to work with the arrays in the function.

All these represent addresses even though they are declared very differently.

These declarations match the corresponding declarations in `main`.

We need to receive the number of rows of a 2-D `char` array and number of elements of an array of pointers to work effectively with the arrays in the function.

Within a function, we work with the variables and arrays according to the way they are indicated in the function header. This means that `ee[]` is a 1-D array, `ff[][]` is a 2-D array, `gg` is a pointer variable, and `hh[]` is an array of pointers.

Output

```
One-dimensional array.
Two-dimensional array.
Pointer to string literal.
Array of pointers to string literals.
```

Description

String declarations, function declarations, and function calls. In this lesson's program, the declarations

```
char  aa[] =           "One-dimensional array.";
char  bb[][LENGTH] = {"Two-","dimensional ","array."};
char* cc =             "Pointer to string literal.";
char* dd[] =           {"Array ","of pointers ","to string ",
                         "literals."};
```

indicate that `aa[]` is a 1-D character array, `bb[][]` is a 2-D character array, `cc` is a pointer to a string literal, and `dd[]` is an array of pointers to string literals. We have initialized each of these in its declaration. This allows some of the brackets to be empty. The 1-D array is given one set of brackets, which are empty. The 2-D array is given two sets of brackets with the first set empty, while the second set is given a size using the constant integer `LENGTH`. The pointer to the string literal is indicated with `*` in the declaration. The array of pointers is indicated with both `*` and empty brackets.

The form of the declarations is important because an identical form should be used in the function declaration (although C++ allows some exceptions to this, which we will not cover here). This allows a transfer to a function to take place between variables of identical form. For instance, the call and header for `function1`

```
    function1(aa, bb, cc, dd, num_rows_bb, num_elems_dd);

void function1 (char ee[], char ff[][LENGTH], char* gg, char* hh[],
                int num_rows_ff, int num_elems_hh)
```

has `ee`, `ff`, `gg`, and `hh` with the same forms as those declared for `aa`, `bb`, `cc`, and `dd`, respectively.

Remember, we can transfer to a function a value or an address. In the function call, `aa`, `bb`, `cc`, and `dd` all represent addresses (even though they all have been declared differently). In order, they mean the following

- The address of the first element of `aa[]`.
- The address of the first element of `bb[][]`.
- The value of `cc`, which is an address since it is a pointer variable.
- The address of the first element of `dd[]`.

Stack—region of memory for `main`

Name	Type	Address	Value
aa	char array, 1-D-size=[23]	FFD0	`One dimensional array.`
bb	char array, 2-D-size =[3][20]	FF94	`Two`
		FFA8	`dimensional`
		FFBC	`array.`
cc	pointer to char	FFF4	0103
dd	array of pointers to char-size=[4]	FFEC	011F, 0126, 0133, 013E
num_rows_bb	int	FFEA	3
num_elems_dd	int	FFE8	4

Stack—region of memory for `function1`

Name	Type	Address	Value
ee	pointer to char	FF88	FFD0
ff	pointer to char 1-D array with size=20	FF8A	FF94
gg	pointer to char	FF8C	0103
hh	pointer to char pointer	FF8E	FFEC
num_rows_ff	int	FF90	3
num_elems_hh	int	FF92	4

Heap—region of memory for string literals

Type	Address	Value
string literal	0103	`Pointer to string literal.`
string literal	011F	`Array`
	0126	`of pointers`
	0133	`to string`
	013E	`literals.`

Figure 12.6

The stack and heap regions of memory for Lesson 12.6's program.

Therefore, in this lesson's program, we are transferring four addresses to `function1`. The transfer is `aa` to `ee`, `bb` to `ff`, `cc` to `gg`, and `dd` to `hh`.

The contents of memory are shown in Fig. 12.6. There are three regions in this figure, the stack holding the `main` variables, the stack region holding the `function1` variables, and the heap holding the string literals. The connections between these regions are indicated with arrows. Note that in the region of memory for `main`, `aa[]` and `bb[][]` hold characters in their values, while `cc` and `dd[]` hold addresses in their values. Note also that in the region of memory for `function1`, the values for `ee`, `ff`, `gg`, and `hh` are all addresses.

The notation, with `[]` and `*` in the function header, simply indicates how the addresses can be used within a function. The meanings are summarized in Fig. 12.7.

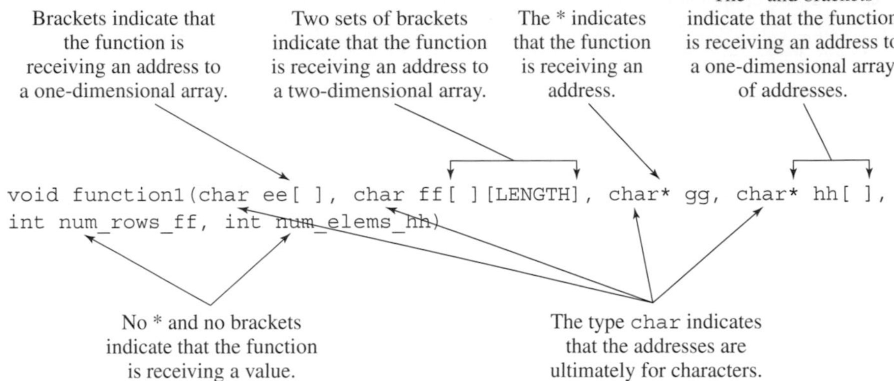

Brackets indicate that the function is receiving an address to a one-dimensional array.
Two sets of brackets indicate that the function is receiving an address to a two-dimensional array.
The * indicates that the function is receiving an address.
The * and brackets indicate that the function is receiving an address to a one-dimensional array of addresses.
void function1(char ee[ ], char ff[ ][LENGTH], char* gg, char* hh[ ],
int num_rows_ff, int num_elems_hh)
No * and no brackets indicate that the function is receiving a value.
The type char indicates that the addresses are ultimately for characters.

Figure 12.7

The header for `function1` with notations of the meanings of each argument.

In many cases, the program will not compile if the way the function call arguments are declared in `main` and the way that the arguments are given in the function declaration do not match. Therefore, if the compiler indicates a type mismatch between the function call and declaration, look at your declarations and make sure that the types match.

Previously, we did not have to pay particularly close attention to a type mismatch because we were working with only one-dimensional or multidimensional arrays of numeric values. It is reasonably straightforward with them to indicate that an address is being received by a function by using brackets in the function header. When working with arrays of pointers, things are more complicated. The `*` and `[]` must be used properly to assure correct data transfer to a function.

Other information to pass to the function. In addition to the addresses related to the strings, we have passed the number of rows of `bb[][]` and the number of elements of `dd[]` to the function. This is necessary to assure that we can work with the arrays in the function body.

To determine the number of rows of `bb[][]` and the number of elements of `dd[]`, we use the `sizeof` operator to get the declared size of each of these. For instance, `sizeof(bb)` and `sizeof(dd)` compute the total number of bytes reserved for `bb[][]` and `dd[]`, respectively. For the 2-D array `bb[][]`, knowing that a character occupies 1 byte, we can get the number of rows by dividing the total size by the length of one row. This statement calculates the number of rows of `bb[][]`:

```
num_rows_bb = sizeof (bb) / LENGTH;
```

Because `dd[]` is a 1-D array, we get the number of elements by dividing the total size by the size of a single element. We realize that this array contains addresses (type `char*`), not integers (type `int`) or real numbers (type `double`). As a result, we divide by `sizeof(char*)`. Although odd looking, `sizeof(char*)` gives us the number of bytes reserved for storing an address of a `char`. The next statement calculates the number of elements of `dd[]`:

```
num_elems_dd = sizeof (dd) / sizeof (char*);
```

A typical size for `char*` is 2 bytes. This is also a common size for `int*`, `double*`, and other addresses.

It was necessary to calculate the number of rows of `bb[][]` and the number of elements of `dd[]` because it often is important to pass the size of an array through the parameter list. By doing this, a function can work efficiently with the array. Unlike numeric arrays, though, we need not pass the size of 1-D character arrays because these often are treated as strings and therefore not used element by element. However, for 2-D character arrays we should pass the number of rows, and for 1-D pointer arrays we should pass the number of elements.

Function body. The statements in the function body must be consistent with the form in the function header. Therefore, `ee` is treated as an array of characters (even though it is not, see Fig. 12.6) and printed out with the statement

```
cout << ee << endl;
```

The variable `ff` is treated as a two-dimensional character array (even though it is not, see Fig. 12.6) and is printed with the loop

```
for (i = 0; i < num_rows_ff; i++) cout << ff[i];
```

The variable `gg` (see Fig. 12.6 for the type), holds the address of a string literal, and the string literal is printed with the statement

```
cout << gg << endl;
```

The variable `hh[]` is treated as a two-dimensional array (even though it is not, see Fig. 12.6). It is used to print three string literals with the loop

```
for (i = 0; i < num_elems_hh; i++) cout << hh[i];
```

We will not go through exactly how this all works as it has to do with pointer arithmetic which will not be covered in detail in this text. Just remember, follow the form of the declarations in writing your program statements.

Reasons for different types. We have shown all these different types (and there are more, as you can imagine, if we use 3-D arrays) because there are times when each type works best for your programming situation and because you will likely encounter these types as you work with the code of others. At this stage in your programming experience, we suggest that you use primarily 1-D and 2-D character arrays since they are the easiest conceptually to work with. Be aware, though, that when passing these to functions, pointer variables are used in the functions to simulate 1-D and 2-D array actions.

APPLICATION EXAMPLE 12.1 CREATION OF A SPREADSHEET TYPE PROGRAM

TOPIC

- Individual character operations

Problem Statement

Write a simple spreadsheet type program capable of reading a table of data from a file and performing addition, subtraction, multiplication, or division on the numbers column by column. The input should consist of a file with a table of eight rows and five columns of numbers. The first column is column A, the second is column B, continuing with the last column being column E. Prompt the user to enter an equation with five operands and four operators from the keyboard involving these columns. For instance, $A + B - C + E \times D$, which indicates the operations to be performed on each column of numbers. The program should be capable of creating a "results" column that represents the result of the user input equation. Print this result to the screen. This program shows how to use individual character input to perform practical calculations.

Solution

RELEVANT EQUATIONS AND BACKGROUND INFORMATION

A spreadsheet program works with tables of data and performs operations column by column (among many other things). An example of such a program is Microsoft Excel. For instance, we may have a table of student grades:

Name	Score, exam 1	Score, exam 2	Score, exam 3
John Doe	68	43	81
Mary Green	87	76	98
Mark White	76	73	83
Sam Brown	92	65	97
Susan Jones	83	56	92

In a spreadsheet program, we can create input data in a tabular form that looks very much like the table just shown. We then write simple equations as input to create new columns containing our desired information. For instance, we could use a spreadsheet program on the table of data to get a fifth column that contains the average of the three exam scores. To get this, we would simply add the scores of exams 1, 2, and 3 (which are in columns 2, 3, and 4) and divide the sum by 3.

In this example, we write a very simple version of a program that can do operations such as these. With the data in a file, we read it into memory. Then, at the keyboard, we write an equation representing what to do with each column and have our program perform the operations written in the equation.

Because we are doing only addition, subtraction, multiplication, and division, the equations are rather trivial. So, we will not dwell on them in this section. Instead we will illustrate the operations with a sample calculation.

SPECIFIC EXAMPLE

For a data file consisting of (the A, B, C, D, and E are not in the file, only the numbers)

A	B	C	D	E
1	3	2	3	4
2	5	4	6	8
3	7	6	9	12
4	9	8	12	16
5	11	10	15	20
6	13	12	18	24
7	15	14	21	28
8	17	16	24	32

we can perform the action of A − C + B × E − D, where the variables A, B, C, D, and E represent their respective columns of numbers. The associativity of the action will be from left to right with no order of precedence of the operators. In other words, the multiplication in this expression will not be carried out prior to the addition or subtraction.

The result of this for the first row would be $1 - 2 + 3 \times 4 - 3 = 5$. Continuing for the rest of the rows gives the following result:

Result of A − C + B × E − D
5
18
39
68
105
150
203
264

DATA STRUCTURES

Now that you have begun to develop experience in programming, you need to draw on the experience to help you make early decisions that will affect the rest of the programming process. Specifically, you need to decide how to store your data (for instance, what dimension of arrays should be used) because this will affect how you work with the data in your programs.

Before you get going, you must make these decisions, then work with the structures. If the structures become too cumbersome to implement, you can change them. However, changing your data structures may mean rewriting a considerable amount of code. Therefore, it is worthwhile to spend time in choosing your data structures as well as you can before going further in the programming process.

In this program, we have two categories of data to consider:

1. The columns of input data.
2. The result column.

We have several data structure options from which to choose:

1. Since we have five columns of input data we could create five 1-D arrays, `a[]`, `b[]`, `c[]`, `d[]`, and `e[]`, that is, one for each column. We could create a sixth array with the results, called `result[]`. All these arrays would have size of 8 because we have eight rows in our table. We would declare these as

```
double a[8], b[8], c[8], d[8], e[8], result[8];
```

2. Since we have eight rows, we could create eight 1-D arrays, `row1[]`, `row2[]`, `row3[]`, . . . , `row8[]`. If we choose this option, we would have a size of 6 for each of these because we have five data columns and a result column. These would be declared

```
double row1[6], row2[6], row3[6], row4[6], row5[6],
  row6[6], row7[6], row8[6];
```

3. Since we have what can be called a table or matrix, we could choose a 2-D array to represent the columns and rows. In addition, we could have a 1-D array represent the result. For the 2-D array, we have eight rows and five columns. Together with the eight rows, for the result column, we have the following declaration:

```
double a[8][5], result[8];
```

4. Last, we could put the result column in as the last column in the 2-D array rather than having it separate. This gives us six columns in our table, leading to the following declaration:

```
double a[8][6];
```

For the particular program specified for this example, any of these options can be used. Given the time and effort, we could write a successful program with any of these data structures. In a sense, then, there is no wrong answer in choosing one of them. However, in most cases, given a choice between a series of 1-D arrays and a 2-D array, the 2-D array will be easier to implement and more flexible for making future changes. Therefore, we can narrow our choices down to numbers 3 and 4. Of these two, we will choose number 3. Number 4 offers flexibility advantages, but we will choose number 3 because the result is clearly separate from the input information. However, number 4 is perfectly acceptable and easily could be used.

We recommend that, with your programs, you make a similar list of options of data structures. Having them listed in front of you allows you to consider all the possibilities. With more experience, you will feel more comfortable choosing one of the options. However, after choosing one, you may realize that you have made a bad decision. This may become obvious if you find that the programming becomes too difficult. If this occurs, consider another structure on the list, because it may solve some of your programming problems. Remember, even after you have written a considerable amount of code, if you see a better way of writing your program, you should start over and try again.

ALGORITHM

The general algorithm can be stated as follows:

1. Read the input data from the data file, which consists of the numbers in the table with eight rows and five columns.
2. Prompt the user to enter an equation in the form of "operand operator operand operator operand operator operand operator operand". For example, "A + B * C − D * E." Read the first operand.
3. Take the first operand from the entered equation and use it to set the first nonzero values in the `result[]` array.
4. Read the remaining four operators and four operands and perform the operations one at a time on the `result[]` array.
5. Print the `result[]` array to the screen.

   We describe the development of the code for each of the steps here.

STEP 1. READ THE INPUT DATA

The first impact of our choice of data structure being a two-dimensional array is in the way that we read the data. Since we have previously covered using a two-deep nested loop to read a 2-D array of data, we will not dwell on it here. We will simply show the loops and note that the outer loop loops over the number of rows (8) and the inner loop loops over the number of columns (5).

```
for (i = 0; i < NUM_ROWS; i++)
            {
            for (j = 0; j < NUM_COLS; j++)
                        {
                        infile >> a[i][j];
                        }
            }
```

After executing this loop all the numeric data in the file is stored in the 2-D array `a[][]`. Each column of `a[][]` (indicated by the second subscript) is a column of the spreadsheet data. Because we work with spreadsheet data column by column, we will need to set the second subscript of `a[][]` appropriately when we work with the data.

STEP 2. PROMPT THE USER TO ENTER AN EQUATION AND READ THE FIRST OPERAND

We first declare the variables `operand` and `operatr` (we cannot use `operator`, spelled properly, because it is a reserved word in C++) to be single characters. Then we prompt the user to enter an equation and read the first character. This code does it.

```
char operand, operatr;
cout << "Enter a command of the sort A+B*C-D*E:" << endl;
cin >> operand;
```

Note that only one character is read by this `cin` statement (even though the user has entered 9 characters), and it is a letter in the range A–E. The other eight characters in the equation entered by the user remain in the input buffer. These eight characters are read later by a different `cin` statement.

STEP 3. INITIALIZE THE `result[]` ARRAY

We determine the column corresponding to the letter (`operand`) read by the `cin` statement in step 2 by converting the letter to its integer value. To do this, we use the integer equivalents of the letters A–E. Recall that for the ASCII code, an integer corresponds to each character. The ASCII codes for A–E and the corresponding second subscript (representing the column because the subscripts are `a[row][column]`) of `a[][]` are

Character	ASCII code	Second subscript of `a[][]` array
A	65	0
B	66	1
C	67	2
D	68	3
E	69	4

For instance, when a user enters the letter C, we need to be able to compute the number 2 to get the correct second subscript of `a[][]`. We note that $67 - 65 = 2$, which can be calculated using

```
static_cast <int> ('C') - static_cast <int> ('A')
```

In general, to get the correct second subscript for `a[][]` we use

```
static_cast <int> (operand) - static_cast <int> ('A')
```

Using this, the following loop initializes the `result[]` array with the correct second subscript of the `a[][]` array:

```
for(j = 0; j < NUM_ROWS; j++) result[j] = a[j][static_cast
  <int> (operand) - static_cast <int> ('A')];
```

STEP 4. READ THE REMAINING FOUR OPERATORS AND FOUR OPERANDS AND PERFORM THE OPERATIONS ONE AT A TIME

This is the heart of the program. We read an operator and an operand, and then switch to the portion of code that performs the correct operations. The form is:

```
for (i = 0; i < NUM_OPERANDS - 1; i++)
         {
         cin >> operatr;
         cin >> operand;
         switch (operatr)
              {
              case '+':
                   addition operations
              case '-':
                   subtraction operations
              case '*':
                   multiplication operations
              case '/':
                   division operations
              default:
              }
```

Loop over the number of operators (4) which is the number of operands – 1.

Read an operator.

Read a letter representing the column with which to work.

Switch control based on the operator read.

Perform addition if operator is +.

Perform subtraction if operator is –.

Perform multiplication if operator is *.

Perform division if operator is /.

Note that the symbols +, –, *, and / are considered to be characters. The `switch` structure is capable of taking a character as an argument, and, thus, it selects the operations based on the character input.

The code for the *addition operations* is shown here. The other operations simply replace += with –=, *=, and /=.

```
for (j = 0; j < NUM_ROWS; j++)
         {
         result[j] += a[j][static_cast <int> (operand) - static_cast <int> ('A')];
         }
break;
```

Loop over number of rows so that each row of the spreadsheet is added.

Add the column to the result.

Break out of the switch structure.

Note that in this code, the value of the second subscript for the `a[][]` array is determined using the method described under step 3. Similar loops can be written for the other operators.

Each of the above steps has been put into the complete source code shown below. Note how the `switch` structure performs the operations specified by the operator entered by the user.

Source Code

```
#include <iostream>
#include <fstream>
using namespace std;

int main ( )
{
    const int NUM_COLS = 5, NUM_ROWS = 8, NUM_OPERANDS = 5;
    char operatr, operand;  <-- Declaring two characters.
    int i, j;
    double a[NUM_ROWS][NUM_COLS], result[NUM_ROWS] = {0.}; <-- Declaring two arrays.
    ifstream infile ("C:\\SPREAD.DAT");

    for (i = 0; i < NUM_ROWS; i++)
            {
            for (j = 0; j < NUM_COLS; j++)
                    {
                    infile >> a[i][j];
                    }
            }
    (Reading the file containing the spreadsheet numbers and storing them in the 2-D numeric array a[][].)

    cout << "Enter a command of the sort A+B*C-D*E:" << endl; <-- Prompting the user to enter an equation.
    cin >> operand; <-- Reading the first letter.

    for (j = 0; j < NUM_ROWS; j++)
          result[j] += a [j][static_cast <int> operand - static_cast <int> ('A')]; <-- Making result[] the first letter column.

    for (i = 0; i < NUM_OPERANDS - 1; i++)
          {
          cin >> operatr;
          cin >> operand;   (Reading the next operator and operand.)

          switch (operatr) <-- Switch based on the operator entered.
            {
            case '+':
                  for (j = 0; j < NUM_ROWS; j++)
                        {
                        result[j] += a[j][static_cast <int> operand -
                        static_cast <int> ('A')];
                        }
                  break;
```

```
                case '-':
                        for(j = 0; j < NUM_ROWS; j++)
                               {
                               result[j] -= a[j][static_cast <int> operand -
                               static_cast <int> ('A')];
                               }
                        break;
                case '*':
                        for (j = 0; j < NUM_ROWS; j++)
                               {
                               result[j] *= a[j][static_cast <int> operand -
                                 static_cast <int> ('A')];
                               }
                        break;
                case '/':
                        for (j = 0; j < NUM_ROWS; j++)
                               {
                               result[j] /= a [j][static_cast <int> operand -
                                 static_cast <int> ('A')];
                               }
                        break;
                default:
                        break;
            }
        }
    cout << "Result " << endl;
    for (i = 0; i < NUM_ROWS; i++) cout << result[i] << endl;
}
```

INPUT FILE SPREAD.DAT

```
1    3    2    3    4
2    5    4    6    8
3    7    6    9    12
4    9    8    12   16
5    11   10   15   20
6    13   12   18   24
7    15   14   21   28
8    17   16   24   32
```

Output

Output to screen	Enter a command of the sort A+B*C-D*E:
Keyboard input	A-C+B*E-D

```
Output to screen      Result
                      5
                      18
                      39
                      68
                      105
                      150
                      203
                      264
```

Comments

To keep this program relatively simple, we deliberately neglected doing any data checking. If the user accidentally types something incorrect, the program will fail.

Modification Exercises

1. Modify the program so that it can handle an equation with 10 operands and nine operators. In other words, an acceptable input equation would be C / D – E + A / C – B / E – B + C + D
2. Modify the program so that it can handle an input table with 10 columns (A–J). Change the input file so that it has 10 columns. Have the program accept 10 operands and nine operators.
3. Modify the program so that it can use a variable number of operands. Have the program automatically determine the number of operands entered.
4. Modify the program so that it prints an error message if an unacceptable operand or operator has been typed. Make sure that the program does not stop executing. Allow the user to type in a new equation. Repeat the process until the user types in an acceptable equation.
5. Modify the program so that it can handle one set of parentheses. In other words, an acceptable equation would be A * (B + C + D – E). Although this sounds simple, it does involve a fair amount of rewriting of the program.

APPLICATION EXAMPLE 12.2 UNITS CONVERSION PROGRAM

TOPIC

- C string operations

Problem Statement

Write a program that converts measurements of length or weight in one set of units to another set of units. Input should be typed in from the keyboard in the form of (for example)

```
5.2 cm to inches
```

Output should be to the screen giving the original measurement and the measurement in the new units. For example,

```
5.2 cm is 2.047 inches
```

Solution

RELEVANT EQUATIONS

We will use the following form to convert units:

$$x_{\text{new}} = x_{\text{old}} c_1 / c_2 \tag{12.1}$$

where x_{new} = value in new units
x_{old} = value in old units
c_1 = number of old units per base unit
c_2 = number of new units per base unit

To obtain values of c_1 and c_2, we need to select a base unit for both length and weight. For length, we choose meters and for weight, we choose newtons. Note that we could have chosen other base units. This leads to the Tables 12.3 and 12.4 of values of c_1 and c_2.

SPECIFIC EXAMPLE

To convert 5.2 cm to inches, using Eqn. 12.1, we get

$$x_{\text{new}} = (5.2)(0.01)/(0.254) = 2.047 \text{ in}$$

where the old units are cm (which gives c_1 from the table) and the new units are inches (which gives c_2 from the table).

Similarly, to convert 5000 lb to kN, we have

$$x_{\text{new}} = (5000)(4.452)/(1000) = 22.26 \text{ kN}$$

ARRAYS

In this program, we work with strings instead of single characters (which we used in Application Example 12.1). With strings, we must use arrays.

TABLE 12.3 — Length

Unit	c_1 or c_2 (number of meters in one unit)
mm (millimeter)	0.001
cm (centimeter)	0.01
m (meter)	1.0
km (kilometer)	1000
inch (inch)	0.0254
ft (feet)	0.3048
yd (yard)	0.9144
miles (English mile)	1609

TABLE 12.4 — Weight

Unit	c_1 or c_2 (number of newtons in one unit)
N (newton)	1.0
kN (kilonewton)	1000
MN (meganewton)	1,000,000
ounces (16 ounces = 1 lb)	0.2782
lb (pound)	4.452
ton (English ton = 2000 lb)	8905

In the program, our strings are single words (the units involved) instead of entire lines or sentences. We have eight different length units to store and six different weight units to store for a total of 14 different units. We choose to put them all in one constant 2-D array called `units[][]`. We make the array constant because it never changes throughout the execution of the program. (Note: we could have put each in a separate 1-D array, but this is unwieldy.) This leads to

```
const char units[14][7] = {"mm", "cm", "m", "km", "inches",
                           "ft", "yd", "miles", "N", "kN",
                           "MN", "ounces", "lb", "ton"};
```

The size of the first subscript (14) is set to contain all the words, and the second subscript (7) is set to accommodate the largest word in the list (which is ounces with six letters and `\0`).

Since we put all the units in one array, we put all of the conversion factors into another array (called `conv_fc[]`) in an order corresponding to the order for the `units[][]` array. This leads to the following:

```
const double conv_fc[14] = {0.001, 0.01, 1.0, 1000., 0.0254,
  0.3048, 0.9144, 1609., 1.0, 1000., 1.0e+06, 0.2782,
  4.452, 8905.};
```

Remember that because this is a numeric array, it is only one dimension. Because of the correspondence between the arrays `units[][]` and `conv_fc[]` they are said to be parallel arrays.

CLASS

We choose to create a units conversion class (not to illustrate object-oriented design, but simply to show how to use a class with the thought that we can use the class in other programs as well). This class would read and store the input data and compute the new units. Therefore, the class members are

```
class Units_conversion
{
    private:
            char from_units[7], to_units[7], word[3];
            int from_index, to_index;
            double from_value, to_value;
    public:
            void read_data();
            void set_indices();
            void calc_new_units();
};
```

In this class, the arrays `from_units[]` and `to_units[]` are the names of the initial and final units, respectively. The member, `word[]` is simply a dummy variable for the word "to." Also, `from_index` is the first subscript for the `units[][]` array representing the original units, and `to_index` is the first subscript for the `units[][]` array representing the new units. The data members `from_value` and `to_value` are the initial and final numeric values. The goal of the program is to compute the value of `to_value`.

The function member read_data() reads the line of input entered by the user, set_indices() finds the correct first indices of the units[][] array that match from_units[] and to_units[], and calc_new_units() calculates the numeric value for the new units and prints the result.

These data and function members represent the set of information and activities needed for performing units conversion in the form specified for this program.

MEMBER FUNCTIONS

FUNCTION read_data()

An example of one line of input is

```
5.2 cm to inches
```

This can be broken down into the following variable names:

```
from_value from_units word to_units
```

The one line input has both double and char values in it. Because a space separates each of the input values, cin works well for reading this information.

This leads to the cin statement in the function:

```
void Units_conversion :: read_data()
{
        cout << "Enter request in the form \"5.2 cm to inches\":\n\n"\
                "\tAllowable units are mm, cm, m, km, inches, ft, yd, miles,\n"
                "\tN, kN, MN, ounces, lb, and ton.\n\n\n";

        cin >> from_value >> from_units >> word >> to_units;
}
```

No arguments or declared variables are needed for the function because only data members are used within it.

FUNCTION set_indices()

We must find a match between the units the user has entered and the list of units in the units[][] array. Because this involves comparing strings, we use the strcmp() function. The user first enters from_units. To compare this string to the list, we need to create a loop. Each cycle through the loop compares from_units to a word in units[][]. The goal is to find a match in units[][] and save the array index that gives the match. The following loop accomplishes this:

```
from_index = 0;
while (strcmp (from_units, units[from_index])) from_index++;
```

In this loop, when a match occurs between from_units and units[from_index], the function strcmp() returns 0 and causes the while loop to terminate. On termination of the loop, the value of from_index is equal to the index that produces a match with the old units. We will use this index in further calculations.

A similar loop can be used for the to_units:

```
to_index = 0;
while (strcmp (to_units, units[to_index])) to_index++;
```

In this loop, when a match occurs between to_units and units[to_index], the function strcmp() returns 0 and causes the while loop to terminate. On termination of this loop, the value of to_index is equal to the index that produces a match with the new units. The entire function is:

```
void Units_conversion :: set_indices()
{
     from_index = 0;
     to_index = 0;
     while (strcmp (from_units, units[from_index])) from_index++;
     while (strcmp (to_units, units[to_index])) to_index++;
}
```

Again, no arguments or declared variables are needed for the function because only data members are used within it.

FUNCTION CALC_NEW_UNITS()

This function uses Eqn. 12.1 to calculate the numeric value of the measurement in the new units. The statement:

```
to_value = from_value * conv_factors[from_index] /
  conv_factors[to_index];
```

uses from_index and to_index calculated in the function set_indices() to reference the correct values in conv_factors[]. The entire function is:

```
void Units_conversion :: calc_new_units()
{
     to_value = from_value * conv_factors[from_index] /
       conv_factors[to_index];

     cout << from_value << "  " << from_units << " is equal to "
          << to_value << "  " << to_units << endl;
}
```

No arguments or declared variables are needed for the function because only data members are used within it.

Source Code

The complete source code includes the main function. In this function are the object declaration and calls to the member functions.

```
#include <iostream>
#include <cstring>
using namespace std;

const double conv_factors[14] = {0.001,0.01,1.0,1000.,0.0254,0.3048,
                                 0.9144,1609.,1.0,1000.,1.0e+06,0.2782,
                                 4.452,8905.};
const char units[14][7] = {"mm","cm","m","km","inches","ft","yd","miles",
                           "N","kN","MN","ounces","lb","ton"};
```

```
class Units_conversion
{
    private:
            char from_units[7], to_units[7], word[3];
            double from_value, to_value;
            int from_index, to_index;
    public:
            void read_data ();
            void set_indices ();
            void calc_new_units ();
};

void Units_conversion :: read_data ()
{
    cout << "Enter request in the form \"5.2 cm to inches\":\n\n"\
           "\tAllowable units are mm, cm, m, km, inches, ft, yd, miles,\n"
           "\tN, kN, MN, ounces, lb, and ton.\n\n\n";

    cin >> from_value >> from_units >> word>>to_units;
}

void Units_conversion :: set_indices ()
{
    from_index = 0;
    to_index = 0;
    while (strcmp (from_units,units[from_index]))      from_index++;
    while (strcmp (to_units,units[to_index]))            to_index++;

}

void Units_conversion :: calc_new_units ()
{
    to_value = from_value / conv_factors[to_index] * conv_factors[from_index];

    cout << from_value << "  " << from_units << " is equal to " << to_value
        << "  " << to_units << endl;
}

int main ( )
{
    Units_conversion units_obj;

    units_obj.read_data ();
    units_obj.set_indices ();
    units_obj.calc_new_units ();
}
```

Declaring an object of the `Units_conversion` class.

Calling each of the member functions.

Output

```
                Enter request in the form "5.2 cm to inches":

                     Allowable units are mm, cm, m, km, inches, ft, yd, miles,
                     N, kN, MN, ounces, lb, and ton.

Keyboard input  5.2 cm to inches
                5.2 cm is equal to 2.047 inches
```

Comments

Note that we have included `<cstring>` because we used `strcmp()` in the program. Again, in the interest of simplicity, we have done no data checking in this program. If the units entered are different from those on the list, the program fails.

Modification Exercises

1. Modify the program so that it can calculate length unit conversions using decimeters and micrometers.
2. Modify the program to handle weight unit conversions using kg-force and kilopounds.
3. Modify the program to calculate pressure unit conversions. Use psi (pounds per square inch), kPa (kilo Pascals), MPa (mega Pascals), psf (pounds per square foot), and ksf (kilopounds per square foot).
4. Modify the program so that it checks the units typed in by the user. If the units are not on the list of possible units, print an error message to the screen.

LESSON EXERCISES

LESSON 12.1 EXERCISES

1. Given these declarations

   ```
   char aa, bb[10], cc[15], dd[15];
   ```

   find errors, if any, in the following statements:

   a. `strcpy(bb,aa);`

   b. `strcpy(bb,"This is 23");`

   c. `aa="f";`

   d. `dd="A string";`

   e. `strcpy(cc,'Many words');`

2. Find the errors in this program:

   ```
   #include <iostream>

   using namespace std;
   ```

```
int main ( )
{
      char dd[20], pp[30], rr[5];

      dd[6] = "D";
      pp = "Panda",
      strcpy ("abcd",rr);
}
```

Solutions

1. a. `strcpy (bb,cc)` (We cannot use a single character as an argument to `strcpy`.)
   b. `strcpy (bb,"This is 2");` (The string "This is 23" has 10 characters showing, and the size of `bb` is declared to be 10. However, there is no room for `\0` that C++ must add.)
   c. `aa = 'f';`
   d. `strcpy (dd,"A string");`
   e. `strcpy (cc,"Many words");`

LESSON 12.2 EXERCISES

1. Find errors, if any, in the following statements:

   a.
   ```
   int b;
   b = sizelen (double);
   ```
   b.
   ```
   int d;
   d = strlen ("1234567890");
   ```
   c.
   ```
   long f;
   f = strlen ('q');
   ```
   d.
   ```
   char g[20];
   int h;
   strcpy (g,"1234567890");
   h = strlen (g[]);
   ```
   e.
   ```
   char aa[30];
   int bb;
   strcpy (aa, "APPLE");
   bb = sizeof (aa[]);
   ```

2. Find errors in this program:

   ```
   #include <stdio.h>
   int main ( )
   {
   char aa[10], bb[50];
   strcpy (aa,'Dragon');
   strcpy (bb, "Apple, pear, peach, plum");
   strcpy (aa,bb);
   }
   ```

3. Write a program to display the following output on the screen. The program should define

   ```
   char date[30], sender[50], status[40], page[10];
   ```

and show this output on the screen:

```
1234567890123456789012345678901234567890123456789901234
Fax Transaction Report  P.01
```

Date	Sender	Status
12/23/2005	Dell, Kevin	OK
12/24/2005	Halton, Bors	Out of paper

Solutions

1. a. `b = sizeof (double);`
   b. No error.
   c. `f = strlen ("q");`
   d. `h = strlen (g);`
   e. `bb = sizeof (aa);`

LESSON 12.3 EXERCISES

1. Find the errors, if any, in the following statements:

a.
```
char aa[2][10]
strcpy (aa[0],"aaa);
strcpy (aa[1],"bbb");
strcpy (aa[2],"ccc");
```

b.
```
char bb[2][3]
strcpy (bb[0],"aaa");
strcpy (bb[1],"bbb");
```

c.
```
char  cc[][25]
strcpy (cc[0],"Good");
strcpy (cc[1] "morning");
```

2. Find errors in the following program:

```
void main void()
{
     char a[][12] ={'aaa', 'bbb', 'ccc'};
     char b[2][2];
     strcpy (a[0],a['aaa']);
     strcpy (a[1],'bbb');
     strcpy (b[0],a[0]);
     a[0][0] = strlen(a);
     strcpy (b[0][1], a[0][1]);
     b[1][0] = a[1][0];
}
```

3. Write a program that contains a 2-D array named `student[5][100]`. The array should be used to store this information:

Name	Age	Math grade
John Kelly	21	3.3
Brian Jason	23	1.8
Mary Fox	19	4.0

The first column should have the student names, the second column should have their ages, and the last column should contain their grades. Display the table on the screen.

Solutions

1. a. `char aa[2][10];`
   `strcpy (aa[0],"aaa");`
   `strcpy (aa[1],"bbb");`
   Maximum of two strings in `aa[]`.
   b. `char bb[2][4];`
   `strcpy (bb[0],"aaa");`
   `strcpy (bb[1],"bbb");`
   c. `char cc[2][25];`
   `strcpy (cc[0],"Good");`
   `strcpy (cc[1], "morning");`

LESSON 12.4 EXERCISES

1. Find errors, if any, in the following statements:

a.
```
char a[10];
cin >> a[10];
```

b.
```
char a[10],b[10];
cin >> a >> b;
```

c.
```
char a[1];
cin >> a;
```

d.
```
char a[30];
cin.getline (30,a);
```

2. Find errors in this program:

```
void main(void)
{
     char name[2][30], number[2][10];
     cout << "Please type your first name, a blank, and last
            name) << endl;
     cin >> name;
     cout << "Name=" << name << endl;

     cout << "Please type a number, press the return key, and
            another number << endl;
     cin >> number[0] >> endl;
     cout << number << endl;
}
```

3. Write a program to read your name and mailing address from the keyboard, and then display them on the screen and store them in a file.

Solutions

1. a. No error, but only a single character is read. Extra characters typed remain in the input buffer.
   b. No error. The first word typed is assigned to `a[]` the second to `b[]`.

c. `char a[20];` The array must be declared larger to accommodate more than the terminating `\0` character.
d. `cin.getline(a,30);`

LESSON 12.5 EXERCISES

1. Find errors, if any, in the following statements:

a. `char *paa = "aa" "bb" "cc";`

b. `char* pbb = "abc[3]";`

c. `char* pcc[3] = {"a","b","c[3]"};`

d. `char* pdd[2] = {"aa" "bb" "cc"};`

2. Find errors in the following program:

```
#include <cstring>
int main ( )
{
    char dd[3][8] = {"Dog", "Donkey", "Dragon"},
      *x[3]={"aa",'bb'};
    x[2] = dd[3];

    for (i = 0; i < 3; i++)
    cout << " x[" << i << ""]" << " = " << x[i] << endl;

}
```

3. In a declaration, use a 2-D `char` array, `name[][30]`, to save the following names: peTer dodge, kEith hill, erIc randy, and lisa freDo. Write a program to change the names to

a. Peter Dodge, Keith Hill, Eric Randy, and Lisa Fredo

b. PETER DODGE, KEITH HILL, ERIC RANDY, and LISA FREDO

Solutions

1. a. No error, `paa` is initialized with the address of the string literal `"aabbcc"`.
b. No error, `pbb` is initialized with the address of the string literal `"abc[3]"`.
c. No error, `pcc[2]` is initialized with the address of the string literal `"c[3]"`.
d. No error. However, only `pdd[0]` is initialized with string `"aabbcc"`.

LESSON 12.6 EXERCISES

1. True or false

a. Entire strings are easily passed to functions.

b. We can pass only an address or a value to a function.

c. Matching types is important in function calls and function declarations.

d. For functions to properly work with strings in 2-D character arrays, we need to pass the number of rows of the array as a separate argument.

e. Arrays of pointers can be used to work with strings and functions.

2. Given the following declarations, find the errors, if any, in the function calls.

```
char aa[]= "A simple string.";
char bb[3][30]={"Three"," different ","strings."};
char* cc= "Another string.";
char* dd[4]={"Addresses ","can be ","stored in ","arrays
  also."};

void function1 (char, char[]);
void function2 (char*, char[][30], int);
void function3 (char [], char* [], int);
```

a. `function1 (cc, aa); function1 ('c', aa);` first argument must be a single character.

b. `function2 (cc, bb, 2); function2 (cc, bb, 3);` third argument should be the number of rows of `bb[][]`.

c. `function3 (aa, dd, 3); function3 (aa, dd, 4);` third argument should be the number of elements of `dd[]`.

d. `function2 (aa, bb, 3); function2 (cc, bb, 3);`

e. `function3 (aa, bb, 3); function3 (aa, dd, 4);`

3. Write a program that uses 2 functions, one that uses 1-D and 2-D character arrays and the other that uses a pointer and an array of pointers. Have the first function read five strings entered at the keyboard. Transfer the information to the other function and have that function print out the entered strings.

Solutions

1. a. false
b. true
c. true
d. true
e. true

2. a. `function1 ('c', aa);` first argument must be a single character.
b. `function2 (cc, bb, 3);` third argument should be the number of rows of `bb[][]`.
c. `function3 (aa, dd, 4);` third argument should be the number of elements of `dd[]`.
d. `function2 (cc, bb, 3);`
e. `function3 (aa, dd, 4);`

APPLICATION EXERCISES

1. You have the following clients for your consulting firm:

Client	Business type
Acme Construction	Machinery design
Johnson Electrical	Switch manufacturing
Brown Heating and Cooling	Boiler design
Smith Switches	Switch manufacturing
Jones Computers	Computer sales
Williams Cleaning Equipment	Machinery sales

To keep track of your clients in an orderly manner, you need a program that can arrange them alphabetically by name or by business type. Write such a program using a bubble sort. The input specifications are to

Read the client and business from a file.

Read the requirement of sorting according to name or business from the keyboard.

The output specification is to put the arranged list into an output file.

2. At times you may be required to show your work to a third party to illustrate your capabilities. However, to protect the privacy of the client for whom the work was done, you need to eliminate some of the details. Write a program that can take a text report and replace all the cost figures (preceded by $) with **** and replace all instances of the client's name with "Client X." The input specifications are to

Read the text report from a file.

Read the client's name from the keyboard.

The output specification is to put the censored report into a file.

3. Write a program that can add equations with variables. For instance, the two equations

$$3a + 9b + 10c - 8d = 6$$
$$9a - 2b + 3c - 4d = 4$$

sum to

$$12a + 7b + 13c - 12d = 10$$

The input specification is to read two equations from the keyboard. The output specification is to print the result to the screen.

4. The kinetic energy, E, of a body of mass, m, moving at a constant velocity, v, is $E = 0.5mv^2$. Write a program that reads the values of m and v with their units from the keyboard in the form $m = 5$ kg. Acceptable units for m are kg, gm, and mg. Acceptable units for v are m/sec, km/hr, cm/sec, and mm/sec. Print the output energy in joules where 1 joule = 1 kg m^2/sec^2.

5. We want to determine the allowable force to be applied to a cable without the cable stretching an excessive amount. The change in length, D, of the cable is found from the equation $D = (PL)/(AE)$, where P = tensile force in the cable, A = crosssectional area of the cable, L = initial cable length, and E = modulus of elasticity of the cable material. The value of E depends on the type of material from which the cable is made. For instance, this table gives some values of E (where 1 MN = 225,000 lb):

Material	E (MN/m^2)
Steel	200,000
Iron	100,000
Aluminum	190,000
Brass	100,000
Bronze	80,000
Copper	120,000

Write a program that computes the change in length of a cable given the input data of

Material type
Cable length
Cross-sectional area
Tension in cable

The input specifications are read in from the keyboard. The user should be prompted for each input value. The output specification is to print the result to the screen.

6. Use either a 2-D `char` array with five rows or an array of five string objects. The contents are the following:

```
cc    c    ccc    cccc
ee    e    eee    eeee
aa    a    aaa    aaaa
dd    d    ddd    dddd
bb    b    bbb    bbbb
```

Write a program to:

a. Sort the array using an exchange sort so that it will look like

```
e    ee    eee    eeee
d    dd    ddd    dddd
c    cc    ccc    cccc
b    bb    bbb    bbbb
a    aa    aaa    aaaa
```

b. Sort the array using a bubble sort and rearrange the elements so that it will look like

```
aaaa    aaa    aa    a
bbbb    bbb    bb    b
cccc    ccc    cc    c
dddd    ddd    dd    d
eeee    eee    ee    e
```

7. Write a text-formatting program that reads a given text file and generates another text file for which the length of each line is specified by the user. The keyboard input specifications are:

The name of the original text file.
The maximum length, L, allowed in each line.
The name of the output file.

The output specifications are to print:

The original text file.
A line to separate the original text file and the new formatted text file. The line should contain a total of L digit characters (0 through 9) starting from 1. For example, if L is 25, then the line should be

```
1234567890123456789012345
```

The new formatted text file.

The program should not break any word and should not combine two paragraphs into one.

8. Modify Problem 7 so that the output aligns the paragraph at the left indent.
9. Modify Problem 7 so that the output aligns the paragraph at the right indent. You may need to add blank characters between words.
10. Modify Problem 7 so that the output centers the paragraph between the left and right indents. You may need to add blank characters between words.
11. Modify Problem 7 so that the output aligns the paragraph at both the right and the left indents. You may need to add blank characters between words.
12. Write a program to find if a file contains a specified word. The keyboard input specifications are:

    The name of the original text file.
    The word to be found.
    The screen output specification is to display the line that contains the specified word. If the file contains more than one specified word, all of them should be displayed on the screen.

13. Write a program to replace a misspelled word with a correct one. The keyboard input specifications are:

    The name of the original text file.
    The misspelled word to be replaced.
    The correct word that replaces the wrong one.
    The name of the new text file.

    The output specifications are to:

    Display the line that contains the misspelled word.
    Display this line after the correction is made.
    Save the file that has been corrected.

14. Write a program that can perform a simple cut and paste operation for a given file. The keyboard input specifications are:

    The name of the original text file.
    The boundary of the cut section, which is represented by the starting word(s) and the ending word(s). Note that the word to be used for the cut and paste boundary must be unique. If the word is not unique, you may need to use more than one word to define the boundary.
    The location to start the paste section, which is represented by a specified word(s).
    The new output file name.

    The program specifications are to:

    Call a function to display the line that contains the starting word(s) for the cut section.
    Call a function to display the line that contains the ending word(s) of the cut section.
    Display the line that contains the word for placing in the pasted section.
    Save the file that has been cut and pasted.

15. Write a program to split a text file into several equal length files. The keyboard input specifications are:

The name of the original text file.
The total number of split files.
The names of each split file.

The output specifications are to:

Display the name of the original text file.
Display the total number of split files.
Display the names of each split file.
Save each split file.

16. Write a program that can correctly sort a file of words with both upper- and lowercase first letters. For instance, suppose the words in the file consist of the words on this page. Use an exchange maximum sort to rearrange the words with no influence from the first letter's case. For instance, the word For should come before the word influence. To do this you will have to temporarily convert the case of the first letter to lowercase, alphabetize it with the other words, then return the case to its original type.

CHAPTER 13

THE C++ STRING CLASS

CHAPTER TOPICS

In this chapter, you will learn how to:

- Create strings with the C++ `string` class
- Use the C++ `string` class in practical programs

A relatively recent addition to C++ is the `string` class. Programmers can use objects of the `string` class to manipulate text as an alternative to using character arrays and C strings. In many ways, `string` objects are superior to C strings. For instance, with `string` objects, we do not need to set a particular array size that may be accidentally exceeded (as can occur with character arrays). Other advantages of `string` objects are described in the rest of this chapter. Overall, for new programs you should use the methods shown in this chapter rather than those shown in Chapter 12.

The lessons in this chapter show the basics of string manipulation, and the application example shows how C++ strings can be used in a practical program. As you read the chapter, note the differences between working with C++ strings and Chapter 12's character arrays.

LESSON 13.1 C++ STRING CLASS (1)—INTRODUCTION

TOPICS

- Declaring C++ strings
- Initializing C++ strings
- Printing C++ strings
- C++ string operators

QUESTION YOU SHOULD ATTEMPT TO ANSWER

1. What does the + sign do?

One advantage of `string` objects is that C++ automatically keeps track of the size of the text stored in them and automatically expands the memory region used to store the text as needed. This means that we do not need to specify the size of a `string` object like we do when we declare a character array. In addition, we will see that it is less likely that we will overwrite adjacent memory cells when we use `string` objects than when we use C strings because C++ *does* do range checking when we use `string` objects in some manners (unlike C strings where no range checking occurs).

Another advantage is that we can use operators to perform some string manipulations. For instance, = can be used for assignment and + can be used to join strings together.

Read the program and see how to initialize `string` objects and use operators with them.

Source Code

```
#include <iostream>
#include <string>
using namespace std;

int main ( )
{
        string s1, s2, s3;

        s1 = "We can ";
        s2 = "use =, +, < and other operators with string objects.";

        s3 = s1 + s2;

        if (s1 < s2) cout << s3 << endl;

}
```

- The `string` header is needed to declare `string` objects. (`#include <string>`)
- Three `string` objects are declared. Note that these are not declared as arrays. (`string s1, s2, s3;`)
- An = can be used to initialize a `string` object. (`s1`, `s2` assignments)
- The + sign can be used to attach one string onto the end of another. Here, `s2` is put onto the end of `s1`. (`s3 = s1 + s2;`)
- The < can be used to compare two strings lexicographically. (`if (s1 < s2)`)

Output

```
We can use =, +, > and other operators with string objects.
```

The `s1` string is less lexicographically than the `s2` string, so `s3` is printed.

Description

Declaring `string` objects. We can declare `string` objects using `string` (the class name) and listing the object names. For instance,

```
string s1, s2, s3;
```

declares `s1`, `s2`, and `s3` to be `string` objects. Note that we do not use brackets to indicate a size as we do when we declare a character array.

Initializing `string` objects. Unlike with character arrays, we can initialize `string` objects using `=`. In this lesson's program, the statements

```
s1 = "We can ";
s2 = "use =, +, > and other operators with string objects.";
```

initialize both `s1` and `s2`. C++ automatically reserves sufficient memory for the string on the right side of the assignment statement. Therefore, the programmer is relieved from the task of choosing the correct array size for all possible strings to be stored in the array. This eliminates a potential source of error.

We will illustrate other ways to initialize `string` objects in Lesson 13.2.

Contents of `string` objects. The null character is not necessarily the last in the `string` object text. In other words, C++ does not require that `s1` contain "`We can \0`". Typically, a data member of the `string` class stores the size of the text in the object, and this data member is used in `string` manipulations.

Operators and `string` objects. C++ has overloaded (or customized) some of the arithmetic and relational operators to work with `string` objects. For instance, the `+` sign is used to concatenate (which means to connect) strings together. For example,

```
s3 = s1 + s2;
```

stores characters consisting of `s1` and `s2` strings in succession, into `s3`.

The `<` operator is used to compare two strings lexicographically. The statement

```
if (s1 < s2) cout << s3 << endl;
```

compares `s1` and `s2`. If `s1` is first lexicographically, then the `cout` statement is executed. When comparing strings that are all lowercase or all uppercase letters with no symbols, a lexicographical comparison is simply an alphabetic comparison. One string is less than the other, lexicographically, if it comes first in the alphabet. When cases are mixed or symbols are present, then the comparison is based on the integer equivalent of each character as described in Chapter 3. Note from the ASCII character set in Appendix D, the uppercase letters have integer equivalents that are less than the lowercase letters. As a result, in this lesson's program, the "W" in `s1` is less than the "u" in `s2`, and therefore is first lexicographically, and the `cout` statement is executed.

TABLE 13.1 — Operators for `string` objects

Type	Operator	Action
Assignment	=	Stores string in `string` object
	+=	Concatenates and stores string in `string` object
Lexicographical comparison	==	Is true if two strings are identical
	!=	Is true if two strings are not identical
	>	Is true if first string is greater lexicographically than second
	<	Is true if first string is less lexicographically than second
	>=	Is true if first string is greater or equal lexicographically than second
	<=	Is true if first string is less or equal lexicographically than second
Input/output	>>	For use with input objects and `string` objects
	<<	For use with output objects and `string` objects
Character access	[]	Can be used like brackets are used with arrays to access individual characters
Concatenation	+	Connects two strings

The list of other string operators and their meanings is shown in Table 13.1. Note that not all the arithmetic operators are used. Using -, * or / with `string` objects will cause a compilation error. Note also that brackets [] can be used to access individual characters in the same manner that they can be used with C strings. However, no range checking is done when character access is performed using brackets with `string` objects. The `at()` member function, described in Lesson 13.2, provides another method for accessing characters that is safer than brackets because the function does perform range checking and does not allow access beyond the end of the string.

We have not shown it in this lesson's program, but C++ allows + to add single characters or C strings to `string` objects. For instance, we could have used

```
s3 = s1 + 'x';
s3 = s1 + "word";
```

to add `'x'` or `"word"` to the end of the `s1` string and store it in `s3`.

C strings vs. `string` objects. A considerable amount of existing C++ code uses C style strings. Therefore you need to be familiar with C strings to work with older programs. Also, because the C strings are more basic, they tend to be faster in execution. So, if speed is of primary concern for your own programs, C strings may be the better choice. However, C++ added the `string` class to improve the ability of programmers to manipulate text in a convenient and safe manner. This means that if you properly use `string` objects, it is more likely that you will create code that can be more easily modified and with fewer errors.

LESSON 13.2 C++ STRING CLASS (2)—SOME MEMBER FUNCTIONS

TOPICS

- Initializing C++ `string` objects in a declaration
- C++ `string` functions

There are many more operations that need to be performed with `string` objects than what can be represented with the operators given in Table 13.1. Actions such as searching for strings within strings, inserting strings into other strings, and erasing portions of strings are performed with member functions of the `string` class.

Remember that calling a member function involves using an object name with the dot operator and function name. When working with two `string` objects, such as is done when inserting one string into another, one object is used with the dot operator (called the invoking object), and the other object is passed through the function's argument list. In the string functions, it is the invoking string object that is modified.

In this lesson, we show how to use the member functions find, replace, erase, and insert. We also show how to initialize string objects in declarations. Read the program to see how to use some string member functions and how to initialize string objects in declarations.

QUESTION YOU SHOULD ATTEMPT TO ANSWER

1. What are the arguments for the erase function?

Source Code

```
#include <iostream>
#include <string>
using namespace std;

int main ( )
{
        string s1 ("String of many words."), s2 = "many";
        int i;

        i = s1.find (s2);

        s1.replace (i, 4, "few");
        cout << s1 << endl;

        s1.erase (10, 4);
        cout << s1 << endl;

        s1.insert (10, "simple ");
        cout << s1 << endl;
}
```

Putting a string in parentheses after the object name initializes the object.

An = can also be used to initialize a string object in a declaration.

This call to find, returns the position of the s2 string within the s1 string. Here, i is set equal to 10 because the beginning of "many" is at location 10 in string s1.

This replaces four characters of s1 with "few". The value of i is the location of "many" from the call to find, and represents where the replacement begins.

This erases four characters of the s1 string beginning at location 10.

This inserts "simple" at the 10th position in the s1 string.

Output

```
String of few words.
String of words.
String of simple words.
```

Description

Initializing a string object in a declaration. In this program, we have shown two ways to initialize a string object in a declaration. The first uses parentheses:

```
string  s1 ("String of many words.");
```

and the second uses =:

```
string  s2 = "many";
```

Both of these declarations call a constructor function for the `string` class. The `string` constructor function assigns the string enclosed in parentheses or after an = sign to the object declared. Thus, `s1` is initialized to `"String of many words."` and `s2` is initialized to `"many"`.

The* `find` *function. The `find` function searches for a string within a string. The most basic form of a call to `find` is

```
ob1. find (ob2);
```

This call attempts to find the first occurrence of the string *ob2* within the `string` object *ob1*. If *ob2* is found within *ob1*, the `find` function returns the position within *ob1* of the beginning of *ob2*. For instance, in this lesson's program, the statement

```
i = s1.find (s2);
```

looks for `s2` (which is `"many"`) within `s1` (which is `"String of many words."`). The return value is 10 because the "m" in `"many"` is at the 10th location in the string. Note that, like C strings in character arrays, the first index for a `string` object is zero. Therefore, `i` is assigned the value 10. Note also that if `find` returns a value that is greater than the greatest allowed `int` value, this assignment will cause an error.

The `find` function is overloaded in the `string` class. Another version of the function has two arguments. The second argument indicates the index at which the search for the string is to begin. Therefore, an equally valid call to `find` would take the form:

```
ob1.find (ob2, index);
```

where *index* represents an integer value for the index at the beginning of the search.

C++ performs automatic type conversion from C strings to `string` objects when C strings are in a `string` function call. Therefore, the first argument of a call to `find` can be a C type string instead of a `string` object. So an equally valid statement that calls `find` in this lesson's program would be

```
i = s1.find ("many");
```

No matter how `find` is called, if the string is not found, the return value is the `public: static const unsigned` value `npos` that is a data member of the `string` class. The value of `npos` is set to be −1 in its declaration, and therefore we can compare the return value to −1 to see if the string is not found. The actual type of the return value of `find` is not `int`. This may cause some problems when comparing the return value to other values. However, we will not go into the details here because for many cases, assigning the return value to an `int` variable works without error.

The* `replace` *function. The `replace` function replaces characters within a `string` object with another string. The most basic form of a call to `replace` is

```
ob1. replace (index, num, ob2);
```

This call replaces *num* characters in *ob1* beginning at *index* with *ob2*. C++ also allows a C string to be used as *ob2*. For instance, in this lesson's program, `s1` is initially

```
"String of many words."
```

The statement

```
s1. replace (i, 4, "few");
```

replaces four characters of `s1` beginning at index `i` (which from the previous assignment statement is 10, indicating the beginning of `"many"`) with `"few"`, and the `s1` object becomes

```
"String of few words."
```

The `replace` function is also overloaded. A second version of `replace` has two more arguments that allow a portion of a string to be the replacement text. The form is

```
ob1. replace (index1, num1, ob2, index2, num2);
```

where *`index1`* and *`num1`* are the index and number of characters in *`ob1`* (indicating the portion of *`ob1`* to be replaced), and *`index2`* and *`num2`* are the index and number of characters in *`ob2`* (indicating the portion of *`ob2`* that is to be inserted into *`ob1`*).

The `replace` function returns a reference to the invoking object.

The `erase` function. The `erase` function eliminates characters within a `string` object. The most basic form of a call to `erase` is

```
ob1. erase (index, num);
```

This call eliminates *`num`* characters in *`ob1`* beginning at *`index`*. For instance, in this lesson's program, the statement

```
s1.erase (10, 4);
```

removes four characters beginning at index 10 from the `s1` object. After executing this statement, the `s1` object becomes

```
"String of words."
```

The `erase` function returns a reference to the invoking object.

The `insert` function. The `insert` function adds characters to a string object. The most basic form of a call to `insert` is

```
ob1. insert (index, ob2);
```

This call inserts *`ob2`* into *`ob1`* beginning at *`index`*. A C type string is allowed in place of *`ob2`*. For instance, in this lesson's program, the statement

```
s1. insert (10, "simple ");
```

inserts `"simple"` into `s1` beginning at index 10. After executing this statement, `s1` becomes

```
"String of simple words."
```

The `insert` function returns a reference to the invoking object.

Note that it is not necessary to be concerned about enough memory being reserved in *`ob1`* for the inserted characters. The `string` class automatically expands the memory region a sufficient amount to accommodate the new characters. Relieving a programmer from worrying about having reserved enough memory is one advantage that `string` objects have over C strings.

Other `string` functions. Space does not permit a detailed discussion of all the versions of the other `string` functions. However, one version of some commonly used functions is summarized in Table 13.2. Read especially the first and last columns of the table to have some understanding of the capabilities of the `string` functions.

TABLE 13.2 — Other `string` functions. In this table, *ob1* is the invoking object, *index* and *num* are integer values, and *ob2* is a second `string` object

Function name	Arguments in a sample call	Return value	Description
Searching within a string			
find	(*ob2*, *index*)	Index of first character of *ob2* in *ob1* (returns npos if *ob2* is not in *ob1*)	Searches for first occurrence of *ob2* within *ob1* beginning at *index* and going forward in *ob1*. The default value for *index* is 0.
rfind	(*ob2*, *index*)	Index of first character of *ob2* in *ob1* (returns npos if *ob2* is not in *ob1*)	Searches for first occurrence of *ob2* within *ob1* beginning at *index* and going backward in *ob1*. The default value for *index* is at the end of *ob1*.
find_first_of	(*ob2*, *index*)	Index of first character in both *ob2* and *ob1* (returns npos if no character of *ob2* is in *ob1*)	Searches for any character that is in both *ob2* and *ob1* beginning at *index*. For instance, if *ob2* contains all the vowels and *index* is zero, then the function returns the index of the first vowel found in *ob1*.
find_first_not_of	(*ob2*, *index*)	Index of first character in *ob1* that is not in *ob2* (returns npos if all characters of *ob1* are in *ob2*)	Searches for any character in *ob1* that is not in *ob2* beginning at *index*. For instance, if *ob2* contains all the vowels, *ob1* is all letters, and *index* is zero, then the function returns the index of the first consonant found in *ob1*.
find_last_of	(*ob2*, *index*)	Index of last character in both *ob2* and *ob1* (returns npos if no character of *ob2* is in *ob1*)	Searches for any character that is in both *ob2* and *ob1*. The search goes backward beginning at *index*. For instance, if *ob1* is all letters, *ob2* contains all the vowels, and *index* is the default value (the last index in the string), then the function returns the index of the last vowel found in *ob1*.

TABLE 13.2 — *(continued)*

Function name	Arguments in a sample call	Return value	Description
find_last_not_of	(*ob2*, *index*)	Index of last character in *ob1* that is not in *ob2* (returns npos if all characters of *ob1* are in *ob2*)	Searches for any character in *ob1* that is not in *ob2*. The search goes backward beginning at index. For instance, if *ob1* is all letters and *ob2* contains all the vowels, and *index* is the default value (the last index in the string), then the function returns the index of the last consonant found in *ob1*.
substr	(*index*, *num*)	String of *num* characters beginning at *index*	Returns a string object that is a substring of *ob1*. It consists of *num* characters beginning at *index*. If *index* and *num* are not used, the entire remaining string is returned.
Modifying a string			
append	(*ob2*, *index*, *num*)	Invoking object	Appends the string of *num* characters of *ob2* beginning at *index* onto the end of *ob1*.
assign	(*ob2*, *index*, *num*)	Invoking object	Assigns *num* characters beginning at *index* of *ob2* to *ob1*.
erase	(*index*, *num*)	Invoking object	Removes *num* characters from *ob1* beginning at *index*.
insert	(*index*, *ob2*)	Invoking object	Inserts *ob2* into *ob1* beginning at *index*.
push_back	(*char*)	No return value	Appends a single character, *char*, to *ob1*.
replace	(*index*, *num*, *ob2*)	Invoking object	Replaces *num* characters in *ob1* beginning at *index* with *ob2*.
resize	(*num*, *char*)		Changes the size of *ob1* to have *num* characters (can make it longer or shorter). If it is made longer, the rest of *ob1* is filled with *char*. If it is made shorter, some characters are lost.
swap	(*ob2*)	No return value	Swaps the contents of *ob1* and *ob2*.
Comparing strings			
compare	(*index*, *num*, *ob2*)	0 if an exact match occurs, >0 if the characters from *ob1* are greater lexicographically than *ob2*, <0 if the characters from *ob1* are less lexicographically than *ob2*	Compares *num* characters beginning at *index* of *ob1* with *ob2*.

(continued)

TABLE 13.2 — *(continued)*

Function name	Arguments in a sample call	Return value	Description
Characteristics of strings			
`capacity`	( )	Capacity of *ob1*	Returns the capacity of *ob1* not requiring reallocation.
`empty`	( )	0 if *ob1* has no characters	Determines if *ob1* is empty or not.
`length`	( )	Number of characters in *ob1*	Determines actual number of characters stored in an object.
`max_size`	( )	Maximum number of characters possible for a string object	Determines the maximum size possible for a string object.
`reserve`	(*num*)	No return value	Reserves *num* characters for *ob1*, but does not reduce the size below the current number of characters.
`size`	( )	Number of characters in *ob1*	Similar to length, returns the actual number of characters stored in an object.
Accessing individual characters			
`at`	(*index*)	Character in *ob1* at *index*	Used for accessing an individual character in a string. Similar to brackets [] for C strings. However, unlike brackets, if access beyond a string's end is attempted, an error is indicated. Therefore, this is safer character access than brackets.
Conversions to other types			
`c_str`	( )	Address of beginning of C string equivalent of invoking object. The null character is automatically appended to the string.	Creates a C string from a `string` object. The return value is a constant, so the string it points to cannot be modified.
`copy`	(*array*, *num*, *index*)	Number of characters copied to *array*.	Copies *num* characters beginning at *index* from *ob1* to the character array, *array*. No null character is added to the end, so *array* is not a valid C string.
`data`	( )	Address of beginning of "character array equivalent" of the invoking object. No null character is appended to the string.	Creates ordinary character array from a `string` object. The return value is a constant and cannot be modified.

LESSON 13.3 C++ STRING CLASS (3)—KEYBOARD AND FILE INPUT

TOPICS

- Reading from the keyboard
- Reading from a file

QUESTION YOU SHOULD ATTEMPT TO ANSWER

1. Why is it prudent to use the ignore function?

In this lesson we describe how to initialize string objects by reading keyboard and file input. Like we did with C strings, we use cin, getline, and ignore. However, the form of using getline is significantly different from its form with C strings. Also, when an array of string objects is declared, we are storing many strings (not many characters, as with character arrays). Read the program and compare it to the program of Lesson 12.4. Observe the differences between working with character arrays and string objects. Also observe how to work with an array of string objects.

Source Code

```
#include <iostream>
#include <fstream>
#include <string>
using namespace std;

int main ( )
{
        string s1, s2, s3[3];
        ifstream infile("C:\\L13_3.DAT");
        int i;

        cout << "Enter a single word" << endl;
        cin >> s1;
        cin.ignore (1000,'\n');
        cout << s1 << endl << endl;

        cout << "Enter a few lines. Terminate with #." << endl;
        getline (cin, s2, '#');
        cin.ignore (1000, '\n');
        cout << s2 << endl << endl;

        for(i = 0; i < 3; i++)
              {
              getline (infile, s3[i]);
              cout << s3[i];
              }

}
```

Declaring two string objects and an array of objects.

Opening an input file.

Using cin alone to read a single word typed by a user. Characters after whitespace is entered are not read. Note that no setw manipulator is needed because we are using string objects not character arrays.

The ignore function discards any characters that may be entered by a user after whitespace.

The getline function has cin, a string object, and a terminator as arguments. This call is used to read entire lines of input. Here, keyboard input is assigned to the s2 object. The function checks each character entered by a user. If # is entered, the function stops reading the input. The ignore function is used to process "Enter" and any other characters typed by the user after #.

We can use an ifstream object (here, infile) as an argument to getline to read data from a file. The other argument is one element of an array of string objects. By using a for loop, we can store one line of a file per array element.

Input File L13_3.DAT

```
Line 1 of text.
Line 2 of text.
Line 3 of text.
```

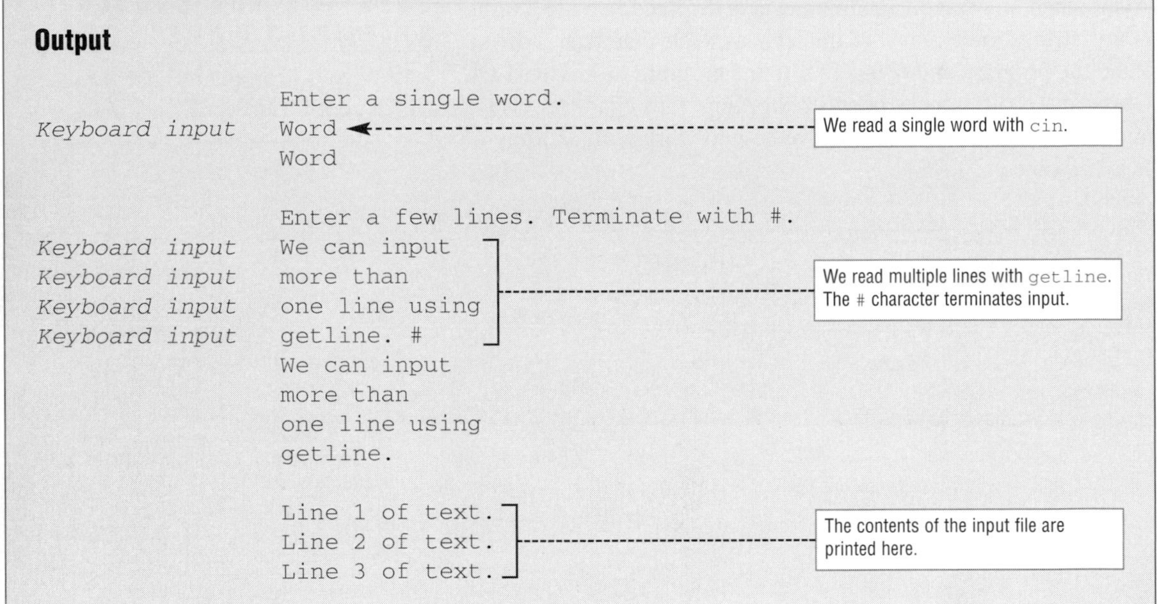
Output
Enter a single word.
Keyboard input Word
Word
We read a single word with cin.
Enter a few lines. Terminate with #.
Keyboard input We can input
Keyboard input more than
Keyboard input one line using
Keyboard input getline. #
We can input
more than
one line using
getline.
We read multiple lines with getline. The # character terminates input.
Line 1 of text.
Line 2 of text.
Line 3 of text.
The contents of the input file are printed here.

Description

Reading a single word (characters with no spaces). We can read a single word from the keyboard using `cin`. The statement

```
cin >> s1;
```

reads characters until whitespace (including space and "`Enter`") is typed, and stores the characters in the `s1` object. The amount of memory reserved for `s1` is automatically made sufficient to store all the characters entered by the user. It is not necessary for a programmer to be concerned about the declared size of an array as one must be when working with C strings.

Because the terminator for using `cin` with strings is whitespace, `cin` is good for reading a single word, but not for reading entire sentences.

Reading multiple lines (including spaces and `"Enter"`). We can read multiple lines from the keyboard using the function `getline` (contained in `<string>`). The statement

```
getline (cin, s2, '#');
```

reads characters until a # is typed and stores the characters in the s2 object. With the getline function, any whitespace character typed by the user is included in the string. Therefore, we can read entire paragraphs or pages of text with getline. The general form for the use of this function with cin is

```
getline (cin, ob1, 'terminator');
```

where *ob1* is the name of the string object, and *terminator* is the terminating character the user should type to indicate the end of input. The *terminator* is read, but not inserted into the *ob1* object. If only one line of input is to be read by the program, the *terminator* can be specified to be '\n'. However, doing so is not required as the getline function has '\n' as a default value for the last argument. Therefore, had we used in this lesson's program

```
getline (cin, ob1);
```

we would have read a single line of input from the keyboard.

Reading an input file. The entire contents of a file can be read using getline. A convenient method uses a 1-D array of string objects. Each line of a file can be read into a different element of the array using a for loop. For instance, for the s3[] array with three elements, the loop

```
for (i = 0;   i < 3;   i++)
          {
          getline (infile, s3[i]);
          }
```

reads three lines of the file associated with the object infile, one line at a time (because, for the third argument of the call to getline, the default \n termination character is used).

In general, for a 1-D array of string objects, a loop of the sort

```
for (i = 0;   i < num_lines;   i++)
          {
          getline (infile, element);
          }
```

will read the file and store each line in a different element of the array. In this loop, *num_lines* is the number of lines in the file; *element* is a different element of the array each time through the loop.

Again, it is not necessary for the programmer to be concerned with reserving enough memory for each line. The string objects automatically size themselves to accommodate the line read.

Extraneous input characters with keyboard input. Because program users do not necessarily follow instructions, the ignore function should be used in a manner similar to that described previously. For details, see Lesson 12.4.

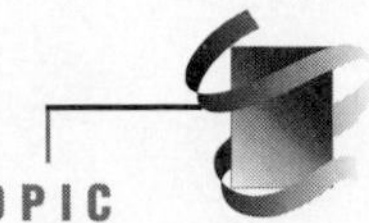

LESSON 13.4 C++ STRING CLASS (4)—STRINGS AND FUNCTIONS

TOPIC

- Passing string objects and string object information to functions

QUESTION YOU SHOULD ATTEMPT TO ANSWER

1. What are the words in the object returned by `function1`?

In this lesson we describe how to work with `string` objects and functions. This is much simpler than working with C strings and functions. However, many different declaration forms can be used with `string` objects. This program shows how to work with a number of forms. The source code also shows how to use the += operator with `string` objects. Read the program, and pay particular attention to the argument list for the function and the way the function is called.

Source Code

```
#include <iostream>
#include <string>
using namespace std;

string function1 (string, const string[], string&, string[]);

int main ( )
{
        string s1 = "String object. ", s2[3] = {"Array of ",
                    "three string ", "objects."}, s3;
        string s4 = "Modifiable string", s5[2] = {"Modifiable array",
                    "Modifiable"};

        s3 = function1 (s1, s2, s4, s5);

        cout << s3 << endl << s4 << endl << s5[0] << endl << s5[1] << endl;
}

string function1 (string ss1, const string ss2[], string& ss4, string ss5[])
{
        ss4 += " modified.";
        ss5[0]+= ", element zero.";
        ss5[1]+= " array, element one.";
        return (ss1 + ss2[0] + ss2[1] + ss2[2]);
}
```

Function declaration that indicates `string` objects in various forms passed to the function. The function also returns a `string` object.

Declaring `string` objects and arrays of objects.

Calling the function with `string` objects in various forms. The function returns a `string` object that is assigned to `s3`.

The types in the header match the types in the call.

These statements modify the `s4` and `s5[] string` objects. This is allowable because `ss4` is a reference for `s4`, and `ss5` is the address of `s5` with no `const` qualifier.

Output

```
String object. Array of three string objects.
Modifiable string modified.
Modifiable array, element zero.
Modifiable array element one.
```

This output shows that `s3` is the sum of `s1` and all three elements of `s2[]`.

This output shows that `s4` and `s5[]` have been modified in `function1`.

Description

Function declaration and call. In the argument list of the following declaration

```
string function1 (string, const string[], string&, string[]);
```

`string`	Indicates that a copy of a `string` object is passed to `function1`.
`const string[]`	Indicates that an address of an array of `string` objects is passed to `function1`. The `const` indicates that `function1` cannot modify the contents of any of the `string` objects in the array.
`string&`	Indicates that an alias for a `string` object is created in `function1`. This means that `function1` can modify the `string` object directly.
`string[]`	Indicates that an address of an array of `string` objects is passed to `function1`. Because no `const` is used, `function1` can modify the contents of the objects in the array.

The return type for the function is `string`, which means it returns a `string` object.

In general, `string` objects are passed like other objects. A copy is passed when the type `string` is used in the argument list. The keyword `const` prevents array elements from being modified. The `&` symbol indicates a reference. When no `const` qualifies an array, the array can be modified. In your own programs, use the form that fits your purpose.

The following correspondence exists in the function call and header for this lesson's program

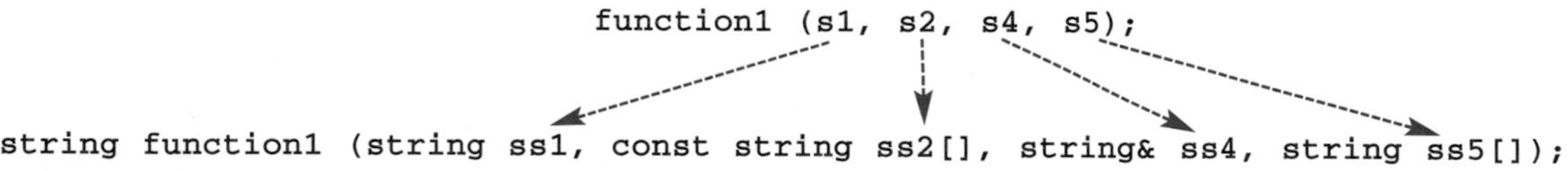

This works because `s1`, `s2`, `s4`, and `s5` have been declared in `main` to be a `string` object, an array of `string` objects, a `string` object, and an array of `string` objects, respectively, meaning that all the types match properly.

Like other types of data, when passing `string` objects to functions, the types must match.

Function body. Within the function body, we can use each argument in a manner that fits its type. However, `ss2[]` cannot be used on the left side of an assignment statement because it is preceded by the `const` qualifier. In addition, when we modify `ss4` and `ss5[]` with the statements

```
ss4 += " modified.";
ss5[0] += ", element zero.";
ss5[1] += " array, element one.";
```

we actually modify `s4` and `s5[]` because of the correspondence in the function call and header and because the header indicates that `ss4` is a reference and `ss5[]`

receives an address without the const qualifier. The return statement

```
return (ss1 + ss2[0] + ss2[1] + ss2[2]);
```

returns a string object that is composed of four strings connected together. In main, the statement

```
s3 = function1 (s1, s2, s4, s5);
```

assigns the string to s3. In general, a return statement can be used to return a string object from a function.

LESSON 13.5 STRINGS, CLASSES, AND OBJECTS

TOPIC

- Using member functions to manipulate string objects

QUESTION YOU SHOULD ATTEMPT TO ANSWER

1. What is the difference between using getline with a string object and using getline with a C string?

In this lesson we describe how to use string objects and C strings as class data members. The data members are private, as they should be to maintain encapsulation. This means that one way to work with the data is with accessor (or "get") functions. In this program, we use a member function (read_data) to initialize all the data members. Then we print the data members using cout and the "get" functions. Read the program and pay particular attention to the way the types are returned from the "get" functions.

Source Code

```
#include <iostream>
#include <string>
using namespace std;

class Class1
{
        private:
                char aa[20];
                string s1;
        public:
                char* get_aa ();
                string get_s1 ();
                void read_data ();
};

char* Class1 :: get_aa()
{
        return aa;
}
```

A C string and a string object are private data members of Class1.

The "get" functions return a private data member.

This function reads both data members.

Returning the address of the aa[] character array. Note that the return type is char*, meaning the address of the first element of the aa[] array.

```
string Class1 :: get_s1 ()
{
        return s1;
}

void Class1 :: read_data ()
{
        cout << "Enter your first name and last name." << endl;
        getline (cin, s1);
        cout << "Enter your telephone number." << endl;
        cin.getline (aa);
}

int main ( )
{
        Class1  ob1;

        ob1.read_data();
        cout << ob1.get_s1 << endl << ob1.get_aa () << endl;
}
```

Returning the `s1` `string` object.

Reading the data.

Declaring an object of the class.

Because `main` is not a member function, we must access the strings using the accessor functions.

Output

```
                Enter your first name and last name.
Keyboard input  Bob Smith
                Enter your telephone number.
Keyboard input  202 555-2345
                Bob Smith
                202 555-2345
```

Description

Class definition. Both C strings and `string` objects can be members of a class. Functions to manipulate the strings are also needed to be members of the class. For instance,

```
class Class1
      {
      private:
            char aa[20];
            string s1;
       public:
            char* get_aa ();
            string get_s1 ();
            void read_data ();
      };
```

has the C string character array `aa[]` and the `string` object `s1` as data members. The functions `get_aa()` and `get_s1()` access the strings. The function `read_data()` reads keyboard input for the strings.

Member functions. To read the data, we simply use the `getline` function in the following manner

```
void Class1 :: read_data ( )
       {
       cout << "Enter your first name and last name."
            << endl;
       getline (cin,  s1);
       cout << "Enter your telephone number." << endl;
       cin.getline (aa);
       }
```

Note that the function does not return a value, so it has type `void`. Note also that when `getline` is used with a string object, `cin` is an argument. When `getline` is used with a C string, `cin` is the invoking object. Also, `s1` and `aa` do not need to be declared in `read_data` because `read_data` is a member function.

The "`get`" functions that access the data members simply return the value of the data member:

```
char* Class1 :: get_aa ( )
      {
      return aa;
      }


string Class1 :: get_s1 ( )
      {
      return s1;
      }
```

It is important that the return type for these functions be consistent with the data member type. Since we cannot return a character array from `get_aa ()`, we must return the address of the array using type `char*`. In Chapter 14, we will describe how to use `const` to assure that the address is not used to modify the contents of the `private` data member `aa[]`. When returning a `string` object with `get_s1`, we simply use type `string`.

Working with the class. To work with the class, an object of the class is declared, which allows the member functions to be called. For instance

```
Class1 ob1;
ob1.read_data ();
cout << ob1.get_s1 << endl << ob1.get_aa () << endl;
```

declares `ob1` to be of type `Class1` and calls `read_data()`, `get_s1()`, and `get_aa()`. Remember, we cannot access `aa[]` and `s1` directly from `main` because `main` is not a member function. This, of course, is fundamental to object-oriented programming because it assures that the class controls how the data can be accessed and manipulated.

APPLICATION EXAMPLE 13.1 EARTHQUAKE ANECDOTAL REPORT ANALYSIS

TOPICS

- Initializing `string` objects
- Searching `string` objects

Problem Statement

Write a program that can help develop a modified Mercalli earthquake intensity map from a moderate earthquake using anecdotal data from people who felt the earthquake.

Available to you are several sentence descriptions from a large number of individuals of what each of them felt during the earthquake shaking. All descriptions are in one file. Each description begins with the individual's location city. This is followed by a description of the shaking they underwent and terminated with a # sign. The last character in the file is &.

The output from your program should consist of a table of cities and intensities. The number of those experiencing each intensity in each city should be listed in the table.

Solution

RELEVANT EQUATIONS AND BACKGROUND INFORMATION

After a major earthquake, information is collected regarding the severity of shaking at different locations. For a given earthquake, the shaking is greater in some locations than others. A map can be drawn indicating the amount of shaking at various locations in the affected region. This map can be used to help predict locations of strong shaking in future earthquakes, and therefore it is a tool that can be used by engineers and city planners.

Because the number of sites with earthquake measuring equipment in an area is small, earthquake analysts rely on anecdotal descriptions by individuals experiencing the motion to help them estimate the level of shaking that took place at sites without instruments. A large volume of information may result because a large number of people experience the shaking in a moderate earthquake in an urban area. A computer evaluation of the anecdotal comments can improve efficiency in evaluating the information.

For this example, we give a simplified version of the actual modified Mercalli intensity scale. It works in the following manner. If someone uses the word *strong* in describing the shaking, then we say that person experienced a modified Mercalli intensity (MMI) of 8. If the person uses *weak,* we give it an MMI = 4. A full table of what we use for descriptive words and MMI follows:

Modified Mercalli intensity	Descriptive words
4	Mild, weak, slow
6	Moderate, medium, tempered
8	Strong, powerful, sharp
10	Violent, destructive, extreme

We solicit data from five cities in the region of a recent moderate earthquake: San Francisco, Berkeley, Palo Alto, Santa Cruz, and San Jose. Realizing that each city may not have just one MMI, we simply tally all the MMIs sent to us from each city.

SPECIFIC EXAMPLE

Suppose we have the following anecdotal descriptions of a particular earthquake. Note that we have the city first, then one or two comments, terminated with a # sign.

```
San Francisco.
I felt a strong shock followed by rolling waves.
It lasted a long time.#
Berkeley.
It was mild shaking, rattling windows.
It frightened my dog.#
Palo Alto.
The shaking was very violent.#
Santa Cruz.
The earthquake was very destructive.
It knocked down the chimney on my house.#
Palo Alto.
The extreme shaking made me feel like I was on a
boat in rough sea.#
San Francisco.
I slept right through it. It was much weaker than our
last earthquake.#&
```

Using our table we can assign an MMI to each of these descriptions. We get

City	Descriptive word used	MMI
San Francisco	Strong	8
Berkeley	Mild	4
Palo Alto	Violent	10
Santa Cruz	Destructive	10
Palo Alto	Extreme	10
San Francisco	Weak	4

We can tally these responses in a grid of MMI vs. City as shown in Table 13.3.

Table 13.3 can help us assess the intensity of shaking in each city. This table is an example of the final product that we expect to have from this program.

APPROACH

We will write this program twice to demonstrate optimizing both memory usage and execution speed:

1. ***Optimizing memory usage.*** In this program, we will read only one anecdotal description at a time, which means not much memory is used. However, this requires numerous executions of reading the file, which is a relatively slow

TABLE 13.3 — Number of responses of each MMI

MMI	San Francisco	Berkeley	Palo Alto	Santa Cruz	San Jose
4	1	1	0	0	0
6	0	0	0	0	0
8	1	0	0	0	0
10	0	0	2	1	0

process. Therefore, this program does not use much memory but executes slowly.

2. ***Optimizing execution speed.*** In this program, we will read the entire file and store it in memory, which means execution is fast because the file is read all at once. However, this uses memory equal to the size of the file, which can be considerable. Therefore, this program is fast in execution but uses a large amount of memory.

Both programs require arrays of `string` objects for the cities and descriptors. Each array element (`string` object) holds a different city name or descriptor. The arrays are made constant and sized with `const int` values to protect the data and allow for easy modification in the future. These are:

```
const int NUM_CITIES = 5,   NUM_DESCRIPTORS = 12;
string city[NUM_CITIES] = {"San Francisco", "Berkeley", "Palo Alto",
                           "Santa Cruz", "San Jose"};
string descriptor[NUM_DESCRIPTORS] = {"mild", "weak", "slow", "moderate",
                                      "medium", "tempered", "strong",
                                      "powerful", "sharp", "violent",
                                      "destructive", "extreme"};
```

We also decided to arrange the descriptor array in such a way as to show a correlation between the order of the descriptors listed and the MMI. For instance, the first three words, `"mild"`, `"weak"`, and `"slow"`, correspond with MMI = 4. The next three words correspond with MMI = 6, the next three for MMI = 8, and the last three for MMI = 10. So, the first subscript for this array is directly related to the MMI that the descriptor represents. We use this correspondence in our program. This is not necessarily the best design, but it is adequate for what we want to illustrate with this program.

Our final result from the program is a table with four rows (one for each MMI) and five columns (one for each city). For our example, the contents of the table (as shown in Table 13.3) are:

```
1    1    0    0    0
0    0    0    0    0
1    0    0    0    0
0    0    2    1    0
```

Because it is a table with four rows, a 2-D array with the size of the first dimension being 4 works well to store it. The name of the array is `tally` and its declaration is:

```
int tally [4][NUM_CITIES];
```

For the program that optimizes memory usage, we need only a single `string` object to store a single anecdotal description:

```
string anecdote;
```

For the program that optimizes execution speed, we need two `string` objects, one to store the entire file and one to store a single anecdotal description:

```
string entire_file, anecdote;
```

ALGORITHM

MEMORY OPTIMIZING PROGRAM

The steps involved in the program that optimizes memory are:

1. Read a single anecdote.
2. Determine which city name is in the anecdote.
3. Determine which descriptive word (which gives the MMI) is in the anecdote.
4. Increase the `tally[][]` by one for the given city and MMI.
5. Read another anecdote and repeat steps 2–4.
6. Print the results in the form of a table.

These are described step by step.

1. *Read a single anecdote.* Assuming we have first opened a file (using the `ifstream` object `infile`), we use `getline` with the sentinel value being `#` (since `#` is located at the end of each anecdote):

   ```
   getline (infile, anecdote, '#');
   ```

   After this `getline` call is executed, the `string` object `anecdote` holds all the lines of a single anecdotal report.

2. *Determine the city name.* The `find` function is used on the `anecdote` string to identify the city. The goal is to determine the matching index (called `city_index`) of the city name in the `city[]` array. This loop does it:

   ```
   while (anecdote.find (city [city_index]) == -1) city_index++;
   ```

   Note that this call to `find` returns a positive integer only when the city name (indicated by `city[city_index]`) is found within the `anecdote` string object. Otherwise it returns -1. Thus, this loop stops executing when `city_index` gives a match between what is contained in the `anecdote` and what is indicated in the `city[]` array. The value of `city_index` at the termination of this loop indicates the city in the `anecdote` and is used later in the program.

3. *Determine the descriptor.* This loop is very similar to the previous one. After it is executed, the value of `descriptor_index` indicates the descriptor given in `anecdote`:

   ```
   while (anecdote.find(descriptor[descriptor_index]) == -1)
     descriptor_index++;
   ```

4. *Increase the* `tally[][]`. The relationship between the value of the `descriptor_index` and the change in the `tally[][]` array is shown in this table:

`descriptor_index`	0–2 (MMI = 4)	3–5 (MMI = 6)	6–8 (MMI = 8)	9–11 (MMI = 10)
	Increase a first row `tally[0][]`	Increase a second row `tally[1][]`	Increase a third row `tally[2][]`	Increase a fourth row `tally[3][]`

Note that the `descriptor_index` is related to the first index of the `tally[][]` array, the row. The `city_index` is related to the second index of `tally[][]`, the column. The following `if-else-if` control structure increments the correct value of `tally[][]` using the `city_index` calculated in step 2.

```
if (0 <= descriptor_index && descriptor_index <= 2)     ← If the descriptor_index is 0–2.
              {
              tally[0][city_index]++;                   ← Increase a first row tally[][].
              }
else if (3 <= descriptor_index && descriptor_index <= 5) ← If the descriptor_index is 3–5.
              {
              tally[1][city_index]++;                   ← Increase a second row tally[][].
              }
else if (6 <= descriptor_index && descriptor_index <= 8) ← If the descriptor_index is 6–8.
              {
              tally[2][city_index]++;                   ← Increase a third row tally[][].
              }
else if (9 <= descriptor_index && descriptor_index <= 11) ← If the descriptor_index is 9–11.
              {
              tally[3][city_index]++;                   ← Increase a fourth row tally[][].
              }
```

5. *Read another anecdote and repeat steps 2–4.* To repeat steps, we need a loop. One way to write the loop is to have steps 2–4 at the beginning of the loop and read another anecdote at the end of the loop, as shown here:

```
while (!infile.eof)
       {
       while (anecdote.find (city[city_index]) == -1) city_index++;
       while (anecdote.find (descriptor[descriptor_index]) == -1)
         descriptor_index++;
       previously described if-else-if control structure
       getline (infile, anecdote, '#');
       }
```

Note that the loop continues until the end of the file is encountered.

SPEED OPTIMIZING PROGRAM

The steps involved in the program that optimizes speed are:

1. Read the entire file.
2. Isolate the anecdote of interest.
3. Determine which city name is in the anecdote.
4. Determine which descriptive word (which gives the MMI) is in the anecdote.
5. Increase the `tally[][]` by one for the given city and MMI.
6. Isolate the next anecdote.
7. Repeat steps 3–6.
8. Print the results in the form of a table.

Steps 1, 2, 6, and 7 are described here. Steps 3, 4, 5, and 8 are identical to steps used in the memory optimizing program.

1. *Read the entire file.* Assuming we have first opened a file (using the ifstream object infile), we use getline with the sentinel value being & (since & is located at the end of the file) and store the information in a string object called entire_file:

```
string entire_file;
getline (infile, entire_file, '&');
```

2. *Isolate the anecdote of interest.* To isolate our anecdote, we step through the entire_file string, one anecdote at a time. This means that we look for each successive #. We also keep track of the index at which we previously stopped, called the current_index. These two lines initialize the first anecdote string object (note: current_index and index_at_pound are integers initialized to 0).

```
index_at_pound = entire_file.find ('#', current_index);
anecdote = entire_file.substr (current_index, index_at_pound
                                  - current_index);
```

The first line finds the first # in the entire_file string (because current_index is 0 and as described in Lesson 13.2; the second argument in a call to find() indicates the index at which the search is to begin). The second line uses the substr() function (also described in Lesson 13.2) to return the string located between current_index and index_at_pound. The first argument of the call to substr() is the beginning index, and the second argument is the length of the string to be extracted, which here is equal to index_at_pound minus the current_index. This substring is put into the anecdote string object with the assignment statement. Figure 13.1 illustrates the relationship between current_index and index_at_pound.

After executing the two lines, anecdote holds a single earthquake description just as it did for the memory optimizing program. This makes steps 3, 4, and 5 for this program equivalent to steps 2, 3, and 4 for the memory optimizing program.

6. *Isolate the next anecdote.* To isolate the next anecdote, we shift both the current_index and the index_at_pound. The current_index goes to one past the previous index_at_pound, and the index_at_pound goes to the next #, as shown in Fig. 13.1. These lines isolate the next anecdote.

```
current_index = index_at_pound + 1;
index_at_pound = entire_file.find ('#', current_index);
anecdote = entire_file.substr (current_index, index_at_pound
                                  - current_index);
```

The first line shifts the current_index. The second line finds the next # after the current_index (which is the second argument in the function call). The third line uses the substr() function as described for step 2.

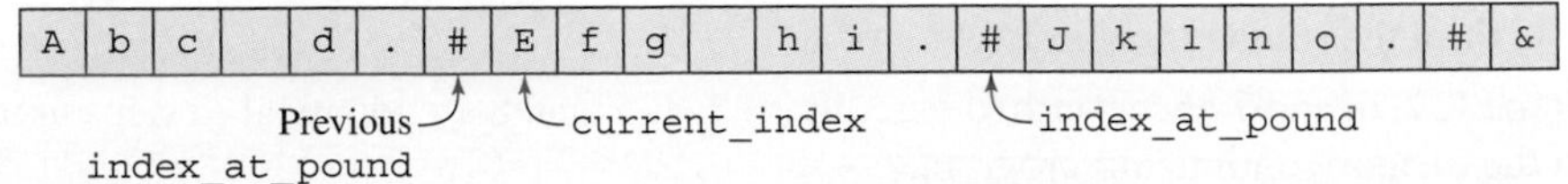

Figure 13.1

Illustration of the indices used in the speed optimizing program. Note that the current_index is one after the previous index_at_pound, and the index_at_pound is at the first # after current_index.

7. *Repeat steps 3–6.* A `while` loop is used, with the test expression checking for the presence of `&` which is the last character in the file. The body of the loop contains statements described earlier. The loop is:

```
while (entire_file.at(index_at_pound + 1) != '&')
        {
        while (anecdote.find (city[city_index]) == -1) city_index++;
        while (anecdote.find (descriptor[descriptor_index]) == -1)
          descriptor_index++;
        previous if-else-if control structure.
        current_index = index_at_pound + 1;
        index_at_pound = entire_file.find ('#', current_index);
        anecdote = entire_file.substr (current_index, index_at_pound
                                      - current_index);
        }
```

Note the use of the `at` function to examine a single character of the `entire_file` string. All the steps are put into the complete source codes shown next with minimal notations since the code has been previously explained.

Source Code for Memory Optimizing Program

```
#include <iostream>
#include <iomanip>
#include <string>
#include <fstream>
using namespace std;

const int NUM_CITIES = 5,  NUM_DESCRIPTORS = 12;
string city[NUM_CITIES] = {"San Francisco", "Berkeley", "Palo Alto",
                          "Santa Cruz", "San Jose"};
string descriptor[NUM_DESCRIPTORS] = {"mild", "weak", "slow", "moderate",
                                     "medium", "tempered", "strong",
                                     "powerful", "sharp", "violent",
                                     "destructive", "extreme"};

int main ( )
{
        int city_index = 0 , descriptor_index = 0, i, j, k;
        string anecdote;
        ifstream infile ("C:\\EQREPT.TXT");

        getline (infile, anecdote, '#');
        while (!infile.eof)
                {
                while (anecdote.find(city[city_index]) == -1) city_index++;
                while (anecdote.find(descriptor[descriptor_index]) == -1)
                  descriptor_index++;
```

```
                    if (0 <= descriptor_index && descriptor_index <= 2)
                                    {
                                    tally[0][city_index]++;
                                    }
                    else if (3 <= descriptor_index && descriptor_index <= 5)
                                    {
                                    tally[1][city_index]++;
                                    }
                    else if (6 <= descriptor_index && descriptor_index <= 8)
                                    {
                                    tally[2][city_index]++;
                                    }
                    else if (9 <= descriptor_index && descriptor_index <= 11)
                                    {
                                    tally[3][city_index]++;
                                    }
                    getline (infile, anecdote, '#');
                    }


         cout << "
Final tally of Modified Mercalli intensities:

Modified
Mercalli
Intensity  San Francisco  Berkeley  Palo Alto  Santa Cruz  San Jose" << endl;

         for (i = 4, j = 0; i <= 10; i += 2, j++)
                   {
                   cout << setw(8) << i;
                   for (k = 0; k < 5; k++)
                             {
                             cout << setw (15) << tally[j][k];
                             }
                   cout << endl;
                   }
}
```

Printing the output table.

Source Code for Speed Optimizing Program

```
#include <iostream>
#include <string>
#include <iomanip>
#include <fstream>
using namespace std;
```

```
const int NUM_CITIES = 5, NUM_DESCRIPTORS = 12;
string city[NUM_CITIES] = {"San Francisco", "Berkeley", "Palo Alto",
                          "Santa Cruz", "San Jose"};
string descriptor[NUM_DESCRIPTORS] = {"mild", "weak","slow", "moderate",
                                      "medium", "tempered", "strong",
                                      "powerful", "sharp", "violent",
                                      "destructive", "extreme"};

int main ( )
{
        int city_index = 0, descriptor_index = 0, index_at_pound = 0,
          current_index = 0, i, j, k;
        string entire_file, anecdote;
        ifstream infile ("C:\\EQREPT.TXT");


        getline (infile, entire_file, '&');

        index_at_pound = entire_file.find ('#', current_index);
        anecdote = entire_file.substr (current_index,
          index_at_pound - current_index);

        while (entire_file.at (index_at_pound + 1) != '&')
               {
               while (anecdote.find (city[city_index]) == -1)
                 city_index++;
               while (anecdote.find (descriptor[descriptor_index]) == -1)
                 descriptor_index++;

                        if (0 <= descriptor_index && descriptor_index <= 2)
                                      {
                                      tally[0][city_index]++;
                                      }
                        else if (3 <= descriptor_index && descriptor_index
                                 <= 5)
                                      {
                                      tally[1][city_index]++;
                                      }
                        else if (6 <= descriptor_index && descriptor_index
                                 <= 8)
                                      {
                                      tally[2][city_index]++;
                                      }
                        else if (9 <= descriptor_index && descriptor_index
                                 <= 11)
                                      {
                                      tally[3][city_index]++;
                                      }
```

```
                    current_index = index_at_pound + 1;
                    index_at_pound = entire_file.find ('#', current_index);
                    anecdote = entire_file.substr (current_index,
                      index_at_pound - current_index);


                    }



          cout << "
Final tally of Modified Mercalli intensities:

Modified
Mercalli
Intensity  San Francisco  Berkeley  Palo Alto  Santa Cruz  San Jose" << endl;

          for (i = 4, j = 0; i <= 10; i += 2, j++)
                      {
                      cout << setw (8) << i;
                      for (k = 0; k < 5; k++)
                                  {
                                  cout << setw (15) << tally[j][k];
                                  }
                      cout << endl;
                      }

}
```

Printing the output table.

INPUT FILE—EQREPT.TXT

```
San Francisco,
I felt a strong shock followed by rolling waves.
It lasted a long time.#
Berkeley.
It was mild shaking, rattling windows.
It frightened my dog.#
Palo Alto.
The shaking was very violent.#
Santa Cruz.
The earthquake was very destructive.
It knocked down the chimney on my house.#
Palo Alto.
The extreme shaking made me feel like I was on a
boat in rough sea.#
San Francisco.
I slept right through it. It was much weaker than our
last earthquake.#
```

Output

```
Final tally of Modified Mercalli intensities:

Modified
Mercalli
intensity    San Francisco    Berkeley    Palo Alto    Santa Cruz    San Jose

 4           1                1           0            0             0
 6           0                0           0            0             0
 8           1                0           0            0             0
10           0                0           2            1             0
```

Comments

This is not the perfect program to do this type of analysis. For instance, if a report were to have "the motions were not strong" we would focus only on the word strong and neglect the word not. Thus, we would misclassify the meaning of the report. Therefore, this program would not work in practice. However, we show it to illustrate working with `string` objects.

Once again, for simplicity, we have done little data checking in this program. As a minimum, we should print error messages or somehow flag reports that lack a correct city or proper descriptor words.

Modification Exercises

1. Add the following descriptors:

MMI	Descriptor
4	Feeble
6	Firm
8	Jolting
10	Devastating

2. Modify the program to print error messages (but continue executing) if no proper cities or descriptors are used in a report.
3. Make the program check for multiple acceptable descriptors in a given report. Print an error message if the descriptors cause conflicting MMIs to be interpreted.

LESSON EXERCISES

LESSON 13.1 EXERCISES

1. True or false:

   a. Objects of the `string` class work just like character arrays.

   b. We can use `strcpy` to assign strings to `string` objects.

   c. The + operator can be used with `string` objects to connect two strings together.

d. The - operator is used to remove characters from a `string` object.

e. The == operator can be used to determine if two `string` objects are identical.

2. Given the declaration

```
string s1, s2, s3, s4;
```

Find errors, if any, in the following statements.

a. `s4 = s1 + s2 + s3;`

b. `s1 = s3 - s2;`

c. `if (s4 > (s2 + s3)) cout << s4;`

d. `s1 = 'Many words';`

e. `s3 = "One sentence " + "and another sentence";`

3. Write a program that uses a different `string` object for the first five sentences of the introduction to this lesson. Arrange the sentences in alphabetical order and print them out.

Solutions

1. a. false
b. false
c. true
d. false
e. true

2. a. No error.
b. `s1 = s3 + s2;`
c. No error.
d. `s1 = "Many words";`
e. No error.

LESSON 13.2 EXERCISES

1. True or false:

a. Some of the `string` functions are overloaded.

b. Some of the `string` functions have default arguments.

c. C strings can be used in the argument lists for `string` function calls.

d. The `replace` function can only replace one entire string with another entire string.

e. The `erase` function can be used to eliminate single characters from a string.

2. Given the following declarations, find errors, if any, in the following statements.

```
string s1 = "This is an example.", s2;
int i;
```

a. `s2.find(s1);`

b. `i = s1.replace(8, 2, "no");`

c. `s1.erase(10, 3);`

d. `s1.insert("a simple", 8);`

e. `s1.find(s);`

3. Assume that you have changed your address sometime in your lifetime. Write a program that uses a single `string` object to print your first and last names, old address, new address, and current phone number. Use the functions `find`, `insert`, and `replace`.

Solutions

1. a. true
b. true
c. true
d. false
e. true

2. a. No error, but meaningless because `s2` is not initialized.
b. `s1.replace(8, 2, "no");`
c. No error.
d. `s1.replace(8, 2, "a simple");`
e. `s1.find("s");`

LESSON 13.3 EXERCISES

1. True or false:

a. The declaration `string s1[20];` reserves memory for a string that can store 20 characters.

b. We can use `cin` without the `setw` manipulator to initialize `string` objects.

c. Whitespace is the terminator when we use `cin >>` to initialize `string` objects.

d. To read whitespace, we use the `getline` function.

e. We can use arrays of `string` objects to read files one line at a time.

2. Given the following declarations, find errors, if any, in statements a to e.

```
string s1, s2, s3[5];
int i;
```

a. `s2.getline(cin);`

b. `cin >> s3;`

c. `cin.ignore(1000);`

d. `getline(s3[0],cin);`

e. `cin.getline(s1);`

3. Write a program that reads a user's full name from the keyboard and then reads a 50 line text file.

Solutions

1. a. false
b. true
c. true

d. true
e. true

2. a. `getline(cin,s2);`
b. `cin >> s3[0];`
c. No error, but without a terminator, 1000 characters will be ignored.
d. `getline(cin, s3[0]);`
e. `getline(cin, s1);`

LESSON 13.4 EXERCISES

1. True or false:

a. In a function header, `string[]` passes a `string` object to a function.

b. In a function header, `const string[]` passes a `string` object to a function that is not allowed to modify it.

c. In a function header, `string&` creates an alias for a `string` object in a function.

d. It is possible to return a `string` object from a function.

e. In passing `string` objects to functions, we must make sure the types match.

2. Write a program that uses two functions. The first function reads four strings from the keyboard: first name, last name, address, and telephone number. Pass the information to another function that returns a single string that has all the information. Print the information out on four separate lines.

Solutions

1. a. false
b. false
c. true
d. frue
e. true

LESSON 13.5 EXERCISES

1. True or false:

a. `String` type objects are the only types of objects that can be members of a class.

b. Accessor functions return the value or address of a data member.

c. We cannot directly access private member data from `main` because it is not a member function.

Solutions

1. a. false
b. true
c. true

APPLICATION EXERCISE

1. Repeat the exercises in Chapter 12 using the C++ string class.

CHAPTER 14

MORE ABOUT CLASSES, OBJECTS, AND OBJECT-ORIENTED DESIGN

CHAPTER TOPICS

In this chapter, you will learn how to:

- Develop classes with more features and capabilities
- Create "has a" and "uses" class relationships

In this chapter, we go beyond the class and object basics we presented in Chapter 8. We begin with a discussion of copy constructors and destructors. Then we show how, using such special qualifiers as `static`, `const`, and `friend`, we can add features to our classes and protect data from inadvertent modification. This is followed by operator overloading, a process of creating definitions for C++ operators. All these are valuable for creating robust individual classes.

However, a major part of program design is in getting classes and objects of different classes to interact. Most complex programs use more than one class. These classes must be able to perform their individual functions and make use of, or be available for use, by another class. In Application Example 9.1, we saw how one class can access another class's data using an accessor function. This type of interaction becomes clumsy when many calls to accessor functions are necessary. As a result, other interaction types are used.

In this text, we cover three more types of interactions that are generically called "has a", "is a", and "uses" relationships. In more formal terms, the "has a" relationship is a form of *composition,* the "is a" relationship is a form of *generalization,* and the "uses" relationship is a form of *association*. In Chapter 15 we cover inheritance (generalization) and the "is a" relationship. In this chapter, we cover "has a" and "uses" relationships.

Read the chapter to learn how to create more complex classes and class interactions.

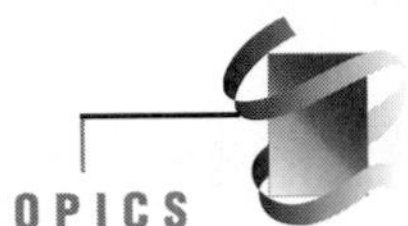

LESSON 14.1 COPY CONSTRUCTORS AND DESTRUCTORS

TOPICS

- Creating your own copy constructor
- Destructor functions
- Reserving and releasing memory for an object

QUESTION YOU SHOULD ATTEMPT TO ANSWER

1. How are destructors named?

You may need to create your own copy constructor rather than use the C++ default copy constructor (Lesson 8.5). This may likely be true if a pointer is a class data member.

Suppose we are developing a program for storm sewer system design. Within such a program, we may have classes that represent parts of the sewer system including pipes, pumps, and inlets. In this lesson's program, we develop a simplified `Sewer_inlet` class (the sewer inlet is the grated part you see on the street where the water enters). With the data members, we want to characterize the grate opening area and connecting inlets (as shown in Fig. 14.1).

Each inlet has an identification number. An array of four integers (maximum) can be used to represent the connecting inlets. For instance, the connector array for inlet 2 shown in Fig. 14.1 would be {3, 5, 6, 8}

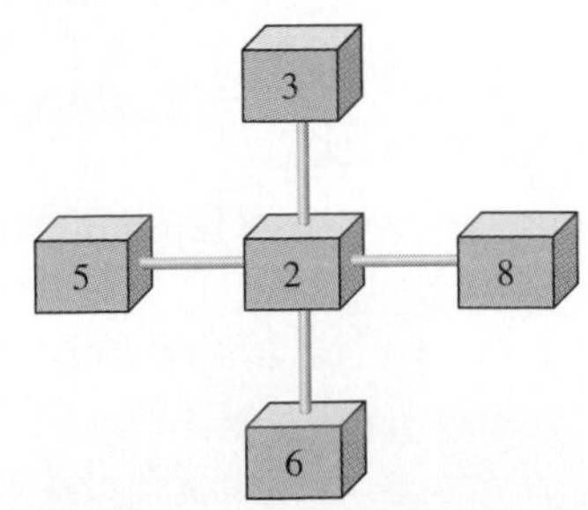

Figure 14.1

Sketch of central inlet connected by pipes to four other inlets. Each inlet is described by an identification number.

because these are the identification numbers of the connecting inlets. For the purposes of illustration, we use dynamic memory allocation to reserve memory for the array. By doing this, we need only a pointer to `int` not an array of `int` as a data member of the `Sewer_inlet` class. The class constructor uses `new` to reserve memory and initialize the pointer value to be the return value from `new`. Because we want each individual inlet to reserve a different region of memory, we cannot use the default copy constructor to initialize new objects. In other words, each inlet should have a different value for its pointer variable. Therefore, the default copy constructor is inappropriate, and we need to create our own copy constructor.

In addition, we create a *destructor* function or destructor. A destructor is a member function that is automatically called when an object goes out of scope. A destructor typically does clean-up work associated with an object. The destructor in this lesson's source code releases the memory saved by an object's constructor.

Read the source code and annotations to see how a copy constructor and a destructor are created. Note that we call our own copy constructor in the same manner as we call the C++ default copy constructor, and that there is no explicit call to the destructor.

Source Code

```
#include <iostream>
#include <cstdlib>
using namespace std;

class Sewer_inlet
{
        private:
                double area;
                int* connector;
        public:
                Sewer_inlet ( );
                Sewer_inlet (Sewer_inlet&);
                ~Sewer_inlet ( );
                void set_connectors ( );
                void show_data ( );
};

Sewer_inlet :: Sewer_inlet ( )
              : area (50)
{
        connector = new int[4];
}

Sewer_inlet :: Sewer_inlet (Sewer_inlet& inlet)
              : area (inlet.area)
{
        connector = new int[4];
}
```

The data member, `connector`, is an integer pointer variable.

A no-argument constructor.

You can identify a copy constructor as the constructor that has a single argument that is a reference to an object of the same class.

A destructor has a name with ~ in front of the class name. It takes no arguments.

No-argument constructor definition. It initializes `area` to 50, and `connector` is given the address of the memory reserved for a size 4 array.

Copy constructor definition. The identifier `inlet` is a dummy representing the object being copied. In the initialization part, the data member `area` is made the same for both objects by making `area` equal to `inlet.area`. However, `connector` is given a completely new value in the body of the function.

```
Sewer_inlet :: ~Sewer_inlet ( )
{
        delete[] connector;
        cout << "Memory released at " << connector << endl;
}

void Sewer_inlet :: set_connectors ( )
{
        cout << "Enter the 4 connecting inlet numbers." << endl;
        cin >> connector[0] >> connector[1] >> connector[2] >> connector[3];
}

void Sewer_inlet :: show_data ( )
{
        cout << "area = " << area << "  connector array address = "
             << connector << endl;
        cout << "connecting inlets = " << connector[0] << "  " << connector[1]
             << "  " << connector[2] << "  " << connector[3] << endl << endl;
}

int main ( )
{
          Sewer_inlet inlet1, inlet2 (inlet1);

          cout << "For inlet 1: ";
          inlet1.set_connectors ( );
          inlet1.show_data ( )

          cout << "For inlet 2: ";
          inlet2.set_connectors ( );
          inlet2.show_data ( );
}
```

Destructor function definition. It releases the memory.

Function for inputting array element values.

Function for printing data member values.

Calls the no-argument constructor.

This calls the copy constructor.

Note that both member functions are called explicitly, but the destructor is never explicitly called.

Output

```
                For inlet 1: Enter the 4 connecting inlet numbers.
Keyboard input  6 2 3 4
                area = 50 connector array address = 0x8f4b120c
                connecting inlets = 6 2 3 4

                For inlet 2: Enter the 4 connecting inlet numbers.
Keyboard input  7 1 8 5
                area = 50 connector array address = 0x8f4b1218
                connecting inlets = 7 1 8 5

                Memory released at 0x8f4b1218
                Memory released at 0x8f4b120c
```

The connector array addresses do not agree. This is the desired result for our copy constructor because `inlet1` connects to inlets 6, 2, 3, and 4 while `inlet2` connects to inlets 7, 1, 8, and 5.

Even though the destructor has not been explicitly called, it clearly has been executed.

Description

Pointer data member. In this lesson's program the class definition includes:

```
int* connector;
```

It is initialized in the no-argument constructor with:

```
{
connector = new int[4];
}
```

which reserves space for an array of four integers in the heap region of memory. The data member `connector` stores the address of the beginning of the array (which is returned by `new`).

Because we can use 1-D array notation with such a pointer, the statement in the `set_connectors()` member function:

```
cin >> connector[0] >> connector[1] >> connector[2]
    >> connector[3];
```

stores values in the memory pointed to by `connector`.

Creating a copy constructor. By definition, a copy constructor is called with an object as an argument. Typically, pass by reference is used. For this lesson's program, the call (which is in a declaration) and function header are

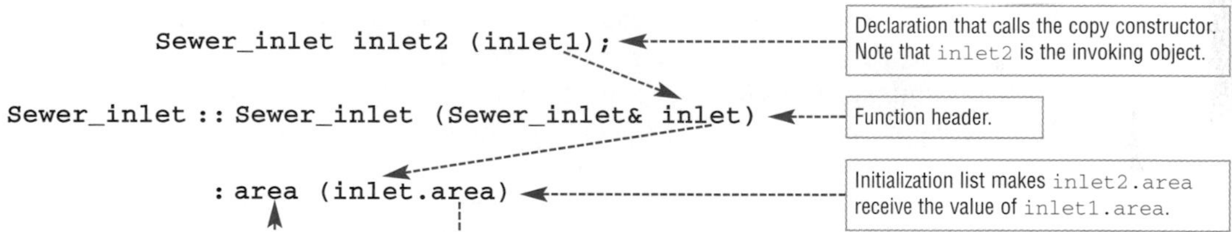

In this declaration, we can see that the object `inlet1` is copied to `inlet2`. The argument `inlet1` is passed to `inlet`. Because `inlet` is a reference, `inlet` becomes an alias for `inlet1`. The initialization part of the function uses the alias and the dot operator to initialize data members.

Here, `inlet.area` refers to `inlet1.area` (because `inlet` is an alias for `inlet1`). Since the constructor function is called with the `inlet2` object, `area` refers to `inlet2.area`. Therefore, the effect of this part is to make `inlet2.area` equal to `inlet1.area`.

In general, the header for a copy constructor is:

```
Class :: Class (Class& alias)
```

where *`Class`* is the class name and *`alias`* is the alias for the object being copied. Values directly copied can be listed in the initialization section as in:

```
: member1 (alias.member1), member2 (alias.member2)
```

where *`member1`* and *`member2`* are data member names. Such a statement copies *`member1`* and *`member2`* from one object to another.

The body of the function is used to initialize other data members and perform whatever other operations are needed. The body in this lesson's program:

```
{
connector = new int[4];
}
```

initializes `connector` for `inlet2`. Note that this means that `inlet1.connector` and `inlet2.connector` are not equal. This is the desired result because we do not want `connector` to point to the same memory for both objects. Had we used the default copy constructor, `inlet2.connector` would have contained the same address as `inlet1.connector`. Then any operations done with `inlet2.connector` would have changed data associated with `inlet1` (which is undesirable).

Note that we could also have called the copy constructor using `=` as illustrated in Lesson 8.5. The form is:

```
Sewer_inlet inlet2 = inlet1;
```

Destructor functions. A destructor function is a member function that is called automatically when an object goes out of scope. For instance, when the function in which an object is declared completes execution, the object goes out of scope and the destructor is called. In this lesson's program, the objects are declared in `main`:

```
Sewer_inlet inlet1, inlet2(inlet1);
```

When `main` completes execution, the objects `inlet1` and `inlet2` go out of scope, and the destructor is called for each object. This is shown in the output with the statements indicating that the destructors have been called.

The name of a destructor function is required to be the class name preceded by a tilde (~). The function cannot return a value, and it cannot contain arguments. For instance the `Sewer_inlet` destructor declaration and header are:

```
~Sewer_inlet ( );  <---------- Declaration given in class definition.
Sewer_inlet :: ~Sewer_inlet ( )  <---------- Header in function definition.
```

In general, the destructor declaration and header take the form

```
~Class ( );  <---------- Declaration given in class definition.
Class :: ~Class ( );  <---------- Header in function definition.
```

where *`Class`* is the class name.

While destructor functions can be programmed to perform most any operation, they commonly perform clean-up work associated with objects. In particular, releasing reserved memory is an important activity for destructors. If a destructor does not release memory, then the possibility of running out of memory for a program increases. You can see from this lesson's program that the primary activity of the destructor is in releasing reserved memory. Although memory will automatically be released by the operating system at the termination of a program, it is good practice to have destructors release memory during execution.

LESSON 14.2 SPECIAL QUALIFIERS (1)—`static`

TOPICS

- Creating `static` data members
- Creating `static` function members

QUESTION YOU SHOULD ATTEMPT TO ANSWER

1. How do we call a member function without an invoking object?

Recall from Lesson 7.5 that the `static` storage class specifier used in a variable declaration gives so-called permanent storage (in the heap) for the variable. This means a value stored in memory for the `static` variable is permitted to persist through the entire execution of the program. However, even though the memory is permanently reserved, the memory is not accessible from anywhere in the program. When `static` is used with a *local variable,* access to the memory is allowed only from the function in which the variable is declared. When `static` is used with a *global variable* or *function,* access to the memory is allowed only from the file with the declaration.

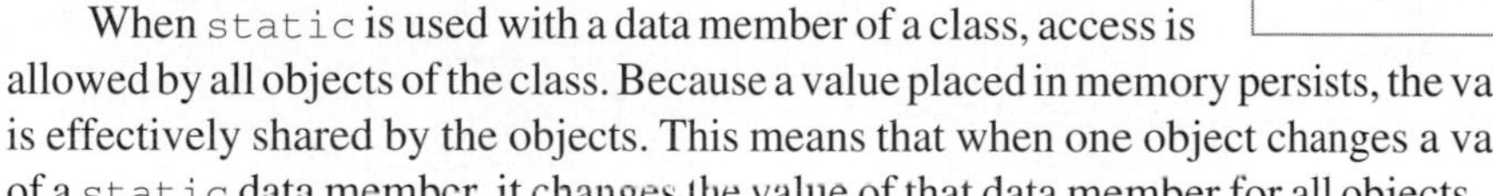

When `static` is used with a data member of a class, access is allowed by all objects of the class. Because a value placed in memory persists, the value is effectively shared by the objects. This means that when one object changes a value of a `static` data member, it changes the value of that data member for all objects.

To illustrate the usefulness of `static`, in this lesson's program we create a simple model of a networked computer using a `Net_computer` class. The `static` data member `number_logged_on`, keeps track of the number of computers logged onto the network. Such a number allows each computer to know if a network is crowded. As each computer logs on, the `static` data member, accessible to all computers, is incremented.

Read the program to see how the `static` data member `number_logged_on` increases each time a computer accesses the network. Note that since a `static` data member is shared by all objects, we can access that data member by calling a function *without* an object associated with it. To do so, we define a `static` member function of the class.

Source Code

```
#include <iostream>
using namespace std;

class Net_computer
{
        private:
                static int number_logged_on;
        public:
                Net_computer ();
                static void show_number ();
                void show_address ();
};

int Net_computer :: number_logged on = 0;
```

You can use the keyword `static` to declare both data and function members.

Printing the address of `number_logged_on`.

A `static` data member is initialized outside any member function. This makes it look like a global variable, but it is not because the scope resolution operator limits its scope to class `Net_computer`. The keyword `static` does not appear.

```
Net_computer :: Net_computer ()
{
      char response;
      cout << "Do you want to log onto the network? Y/N " << endl;
      cin >> response;
      if (response == 'Y') number_logged_on++;
}

void Net_computer :: show_number ()
{
      cout << "Number logged on = " << number_logged_on << endl;
}

void Network :: show_address ()
{
      cout << "Address of number_logged_on = " << &number_logged_on << endl;
}


int main ( )
{
      int i;
      Net_computer computer[4];
      Net_computer :: show_number ();
      for (i = 0; i < 4; i++) computer[i].show_address ();

}
```

The constructor function increases the static data member `number_logged_on` when a computer indicates it wants access to the network.

The `static` keyword does *not* appear in the function header.

Printing the address of `number_logged_on`.

Four objects are created. This calls the constructor four times.

No object is associated with this call to `show_number()`! Instead, the class name and scope resolution operator are used. This is allowed because `show_number()` is a `static` function.

The address of data member `number_logged_on` associated with each object is printed.

Output

```
                  Do you want to log onto the network? Y/N
Keyboard input    Y
                  Do you want to log onto the network? Y/N
Keyboard input    N
                  Do you want to log onto the network? Y/N
Keyboard input    Y
                  Do you want to log onto the network? Y/N
Keyboard input    N
                  Number logged on = 2
                  Address of number_logged_on = 00A8
                  Address of number_logged_on = 00A8
                  Address of number_logged_on = 00A8
                  Address of number_logged_on = 00A8
```

Each constructor prints this line.

The static data member has successfully kept track of the number of positive responses.

This output shows that the address of `number_logged_on` associated with each object is identical.

Description

static data members. static data members are:

1. Shared by all objects of a class.
2. Declared by the keyword static in the class definition.
3. Initialized outside any member function (without the keyword static but with the class name and scope resolution operator).
4. Accessible and modifiable by invoking an ordinary member function on *any* object.
5. Accessible and modifiable by invoking a static member function on the class (not the object).
6. Specified as public or private (or other) in accessibility.

Each of these is described next.

- *Shared by all objects.* An image of the sharing of static data members among three objects is shown in Fig. 14.2. The sharing allows each object to access and modify the same information, which can be very useful.

  In this lesson's program, the address of the static data member number_logged_on is printed four times, once for each object. All the addresses are identical, being 00A8. This indicates that all objects access the same memory cells, and indeed, this data member is effectively shared by all objects of the class. In addition, the low address indicates that the storage is on the heap, which is the permanent storage region of memory.
- *Declared by the keyword static in the class definition.* In this lesson's program the shared data is the integer number_logged_on. It is declared in

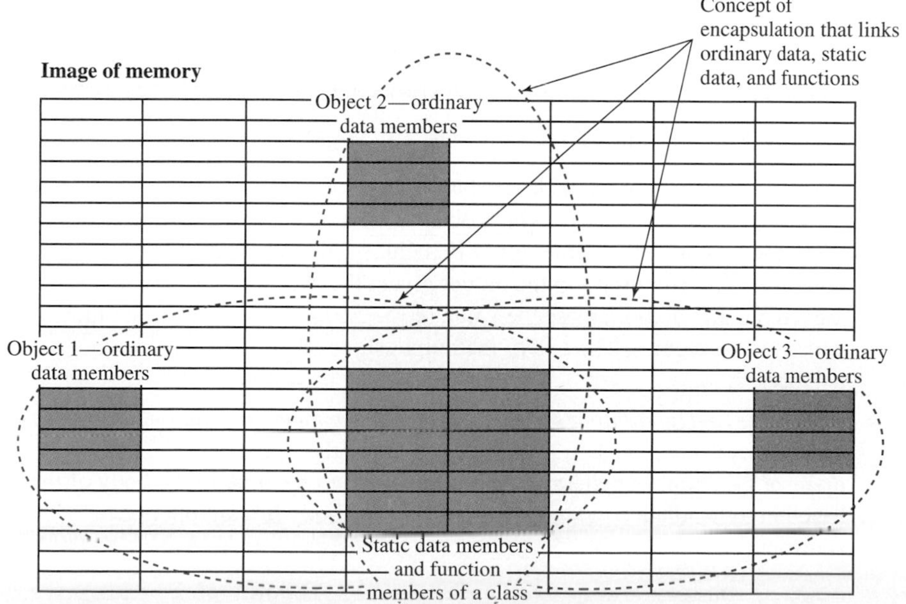

Figure 14.2

An image of memory that illustrates the concept of encapsulating ordinary data, static data, and functions. Here, three objects are shown. The memory for the ordinary data members of each object is separate and unique. However, the memory needed for the static data members (and functions) is shared among the objects in a class.

the class definition with the keyword static at the start of the declaration:

```
static int number_logged_on;
```

In general, static data members are declared in a class definition with the form:

```
static type name;
```

where *type* is the data type such as int or double, and *name* is the data identifier. Such data members can have either public or private access. Those with private access can be modified only within member functions.

- *Initialized outside any member function.* The number_logged_on static data member is initialized in the statement:

  ```
  int Net_computer :: number_logged_on = 0;
  ```

  which is outside any member function. The general form for such initialization is

  ```
  type Class :: variable = value;
  ```

  where *type* is the static variable type such as int or double, *Class* is the class name, *variable* is the static variable name, and *value* is the initial static variable value. Note that the use of the class name and scope resolution operator (double colon) is similar to the use of them in a member function definition. If the class name and double colon are not used in the initialization of a static data member, then *variable* becomes a global variable, which is not the desired result. Remember, initialize your static variables outside the class definition but with the class name and double colon. The static data members not explicitly initialized are initialized to 0 by C++.

- *Accessible and modifiable by invoking an ordinary member function on any object.* In this lesson's program, the static data member is modified in the constructor function (which is a member function). Each time the expression:

  ```
  number_logged_on++;
  ```

  in the constructor is executed, the shared value of number_logged_on increases. It does not matter which object declaration causes the increase. Since there is only one value stored in memory, all objects access the same memory cells. Therefore, in the output given, the first and third computers are logged on, and both increase the value of number_logged_on when their constructor executes. The end of the output shows that number_logged_on is indeed 2.

- *Accessible and modifiable by invoking a static member function on the class.* The value of number_logged_on is printed in the show_number static member function. In general, nothing special need be done in the body of the function to handle a static data member. The body is a simple cout statement:

  ```
  cout << "Number logged on = " << number_logged_on << endl;
  ```

- *Specified as* `public` *or* `private` *(or other) in accessibility.* The `static` data members with `public` access may be modified using an object and dot operator or with the class name and scope resolution operator. For example, if `number_logged_on` were `public` in this lesson's program, either of the following two statements in `main` would increment it:

```
computer[0].number_logged_on++;
Net_computer :: number_logged_on++;
```

  Note that because a `static` member is not directly associated with a particular object, C++ allows the class name alone and not an object to specify the data.

  The `static` data members with `private` access are modifiable by member functions as described previously.

`static` function members. Member functions specified to be `static` are designed to manipulate `static` data. Such functions are:

1. Declared to be `static` by preceding the declaration with the `static` keyword in the class definition.
2. Not necessarily invoked using an object and dot operator (as with ordinary member functions).
3. Without the keyword `static` in the function header.
4. Not allowed access to non`static` data and function members.
5. Allowed to be called even when no class objects exist in a program.

Each of these is described next.

- *Declared to be* `static` *by preceding the declaration with the* `static` *keyword.* For example, in this lesson's program, the function `show_number` is made `static` with:

```
static void show_number ();
```

- *Not necessarily invoked with an object and dot operator.* A static function is typically invoked using the class name and scope resolution operator. For instance, in this lesson's program:

```
Net_computer :: show_number ();
```

  However, the function could have been invoked with an object and dot operator with the same result:

```
computer[0].show_number ();
```

  but it is considered better practice to call a `static` function without an object.

- *Without the keyword* `static` *in the function header.* The function header:

```
void Net_computer :: show_number ()
```

  does *not* use the keyword `static` (and it is a syntax error to do so).

- *Not allowed access to nonstatic data and function members.* The function body

```
{
cout << "Number logged on = " << number_logged_on << endl;
}
```

does not access any nonstatic data or function members. Any attempt to utilize nonstatic data or function members results in a compilation error.

If a function is intended to modify both static and nonstatic data, then the function cannot be specified as static. This means that an ordinary member function is used to modify static data (which is allowed).

- *Can be called even when no class objects exist in a program.* We did not show it in this lesson's program, but we could have called the static member function show_number() before declaring any object! For instance, the beginning of the body of main could have been:

```
Net_computer :: show_number ();
Net_computer computer[4];
```

which calls show_number() before any computer[] object is declared. Because number_logged_on is initialized to 0, the output from these statements is

```
Number logged on = 0
```

Remember, static member functions do not require an object, and, therefore, can be called even when no objects exist.

Scope. Static data members must be initialized in file scope. That is, we cannot initialize a static data member outside the file.

LESSON 14.3 SPECIAL QUALIFIERS (2)—const

TOPICS

- All sorts of members declared const
- Objects declared const
- More about references
- The mutable keyword

QUESTION YOU SHOULD ATTEMPT TO ANSWER

1. Where is the reference data member initialized?

In this lesson we illustrate the use of the keyword const with data members (including ordinary type data members, pointers, and references), function members, and objects. Simply said, data members and objects qualified by const cannot be modified after they have been initialized, and function members qualified with const do not modify the invoking object's data.

In general, you should use const wherever possible in your programs. Using const protects data because it reduces the likelihood of improper modification. It communicates to other programmers that you have restricted modification of certain data members, which frequently simplifies the work of other programmers (because it saves them from searching through code looking for statements that modify data members). Also, if you are modifying code written by others, be aware of the use of const. Its use indicates how the original programmers envisioned the data should be manipulated.

Read this lesson's program, and note the many ways `const` can be used in declarations. Be aware that the location of `const` influences its meaning.

Source Code

```
#include <iostream>
using namespace std;

class Class1
{
       private:
               const int aa;
               const int* bb;
               int* const cc;
               const int* const dd;
               const int& ee;

       public:
               Class1 (const int, const int*, int* const,
                      const int* const, const int&);
               void show_data () const;
};

Class1 :: Class1 (const int aa_var, const int* bb_var, int* const cc_var,
       const int* const dd_var, const int& ee_var)
      : aa (aa_var), bb (bb_var), cc (cc_var), dd (dd_var), ee (ee_var)
{
       cout << "Constructor executed." << endl;
}

void Class1 :: show_data ( ) const
{
       cout << "aa = " << aa << "  bb = " << bb
           << "cc = " << cc << "  dd = " << dd << "  ee = " << ee << endl;
}


int main ( )
{
        int ff = 10, gg = 15, hh = 20, ii = 25;

        const Class1 object1 (5, &ff, &gg, &hh, ii);
        object1.show_data ();
}
```

Callouts:

- `const int aa;` — Ordinary data member with `const`.
- `const int* bb;` — Pointer data member with `const` before `int`.
- `int* const cc;` — Pointer data member with `const` after `int`.
- `const int* const dd;` — Pointer data member with `const` before and after `int`.
- `const int& ee;` — Reference data member with `const`.
- Constructor declaration — The constructor arguments use `const` in the same manner as the data members.
- `void show_data () const;` — In the declaration of a member function, the `const` is given after the function name and argument list.
- Constructor definition and initialization list — All the `const` data members are initialized in the initialization list. This is required.
- `void Class1 :: show_data ( ) const` — In the function definition, the `const` follows the argument list but is before the open brace.
- `const Class1 object1` — Declaring a `const` object.
- `(5, &ff, &gg, &hh, ii)` — The constructor is called with a constant, three addresses, and an ordinary integer variable as arguments.
- `object1.show_data ();` — Calling a constant function with a constant object.

Output

```
aa = 5   bb = FFF4   cc = FFF2   dd = FFF0   ee = 25
```

Description

Ordinary data members with `const`. To indicate an ordinary data member to be constant, the keyword `const` is used at the beginning of the declaration in the class definition. For instance, in this lesson's program:

```
const int aa;
```

indicates that `aa` is a `const` integer data member, which means that after initialization, the value of `aa` cannot be modified. In general, the form to make ordinary data members constant is:

```
const type var1, var2, var3;
```

where *`type`* is a data type, and *`var1`*, *`var2`*, and *`var3`* are variable names.

When an ordinary data member is constant, it must be initialized in the initialization list of the constructor. If you try to initialize it anywhere else, a compilation error occurs. Remember you cannot initialize constant data members in the body of the constructor, you must do it in the initialization list. In addition, you cannot initialize the data member within the class definition. In other words, for this lesson's program, we cannot use

```
const int aa = 5;
```

to initialize `aa` to 5.

In general, all data members (for which you intend no modifications in your program) should be made `const`. In addition to the safety this affords, `const` also tells any programmers working with your code that no functions modify a data member so qualified. This can save a programmer time searching through functions for statements that may change the value of a particular data member.

Pointer data members with `const`. In using `const` with pointer members, three options are available with three different meanings:

1. Using `const` before the data type (like `bb` in this lesson's program).
2. Using `const` after the data type (like `cc` in this lesson's program).
3. Using `const` before and after the data type (like `dd` in this lesson's program).

When `const` is before the data type, the value pointed to cannot be modified. When `const` is after the data type, the address stored by the pointer variable cannot be modified. And, when `const` is before and after the data type, neither the value pointed to nor the address stored by the pointer variable can be modified. A summary of this is given in Table 14.1. The declaration should be read from right to left as shown in the table.

For example, in this lesson's program (see Table 14.2):

1. The variable `bb` points to `ff` (which is initialized to 10) because of the way the constructor is called. The value 10 cannot be changed by `bb`.

TABLE 14.1 — Use of const with pointer variables including examples from Lesson 14.3's program

Placement of const	Example (and text description obtained by reading the declaration from right to left)	Allowed to change (using the pointer variable)	Not allowed to change (using the pointer variable)
Before the data type	const int* bb; (bb is a pointer to an integer constant)	Address stored by bb (FFF4)	Value of the int that bb points to (10)
After the data type	int* const cc; (cc is a constant pointer to an integer)	Value of the int that cc points to (15)	Address stored by cc (FFF2)
Before and after the data type	const int* const dd; (dd is a constant pointer to an integer constant)		Value of the int that dd points to (20) and address stored by dd (FFF0)

Table 14.2 shows the storage for Lesson 14.3's program.

TABLE 14.2 — Table of variables for Lesson 14.3's program

Name	Type	Address	Value
aa	Class1 :: const int	FFE4	5
bb	Class1 :: const int*	FFE6	FFF4
cc	Class1 :: int* const	FFE8	FFF2
dd	Class1 :: const int* const	FFEA	FFF0
ee	Class1 :: const int&	FFEE	25
ff	int	FFF4	10
gg	int	FFF2	15
hh	int	FFF0	20
ii	int	FFEE	25

Note that bb points to ff, cc points to gg, and dd points to hh. Also, ee and ii have the same address.

2. The pointer variable cc stores the address FFF2 (which points to gg) by the actions of the constructor. The value FFF2 cannot be changed for cc.
3. The pointer variable dd stores the address FFF0 (which points to hh) by the actions of the constructor. The value of hh is initialized to 20. The value FFF0 for dd cannot be modified. The value of 20 for hh cannot be modified by dd.

C++ does not allow us to eliminate the constant characteristic of a variable once it has been established as being constant (without using techniques beyond the scope of this book). This means that if we have created a const int, we cannot assign its address to an ordinary int* pointer. This type of assignment requires a const int* pointer. For example, suppose the following is written:

```
const int mm = 30;
int* pp = &mm;
```

A compilation error occurs because pp is not type const int*. If such an assignment were allowed, then one could change the value of mm (to 50, for instance) by writing:

```
*pp = 50;
```

which would violate the desire of making mm constant. Therefore, a pointer to a const int must be const and the following would work:

```
const int mm = 30;
const int* pp = &mm;
```

With such declarations, we cannot change the value of mm with pp.

On the other hand, C++ does allow us to make the pointer constant while the ordinary variable it points to is not. This means that the following declarations and assignments:

```
int mm = 30;
const int* pp = &mm;
```

are allowed. This simply means that mm can change the value 30, but pp cannot. Once such a declaration and assignment for pp has been made, if we only work with pp, we have effectively created the const restriction to mm.

In general, once a const restriction is applied, we cannot eliminate it using a pointer. However, if no const restriction is applied, we can effectively create it by declaring a const pointer, assigning the address to it, and working with the pointer.

References. Previously, we used references only within a function header (see Chapter 7). However, we are allowed to declare references within a function body. For instance:

```
#include <iostream>
using namespace std;
int main ( )
{
      double aa;
      double& rr = aa;
      aa = 3.14;
      cout << "rr = " << rr <<;
      rr = 2.71828;
      cout << "  aa = " << aa << endl;
}
```

Declaring rr to be a reference. A reference must be initialized in its declaration. This declaration indicates that rr is an alias for aa. C++ does not allow us to make rr an alias for any other variable later in the program. The first alias is the only one permitted.

These statements initialize aa to 3.14 and prints rr = 3.14 because rr is an alias for aa.

The assignment statement rr = 2.71828 makes aa = 2.71828, again because rr is an alias for aa.

prints "rr = 3.14 aa = 2.71828" as output because both rr and aa refer to the same memory cells. The initialization for a reference is an unusual type of initialization. In this particular case, you should observe that it is *not* necessary to initialize aa before initializing rr. This is unlike the situation for ordinary variables. In other words, if rr were an ordinary variable and not a reference, the statements

```
double aa;
double rr = aa;
```

would be dangerous because aa has no meaningful value and rr is given that meaningless value. Because a reference only creates an alias, we can initialize a reference with an *uninitialized* variable, because it is only the name of the variable that is important, not its value.

Using const in the declaration of a reference means that the value stored in the memory cells indicated by the reference variable cannot be changed by the reference variable. For instance if the previous program used const with rr:

```
#include <iostream>
using namespace std;
int main ( )
{
        double aa;
        const double& rr = aa;
        aa = 3.14;
        cout << "rr = " << rr <<;
        rr = 2.71828;
        cout << "  aa = " << aa << endl;
}
```

Compilation error: we cannot use rr to change a value because it is declared const.

a compilation error would have occurred because C++ does not allow any modifications with const references.

***Reference data members with* const.** C++ requires that a reference data member (const or not) be initialized in the initialization list of the constructor function. For instance, the data member ee, declared as:

```
const int& ee;
```

is initialized in the constructor initialization list:

```
Class1 :: Class1 (const int aa_var, const int* bb_var,
          int* const cc_var, const int* const dd_var,
          const int& ee_var)
         : aa (aa_var), bb (bb_var), cc (cc_var),
          dd (dd_var), ee (ee_var)
```

ee is initialized with ee_var which is the 5th argument in the argument list.

with the temporary variable ee_var. The call to the constructor:

```
const Class1 object1 (5, &ff, &gg, &hh, ii);
```

which passes the fifth argument (ii) to ee_var, is used to initialize ee. Therefore, ee is an alias for ii. Because ii has the value of 25, printing ee prints 25 as shown in the output. Using const in the declaration for ee means that ee cannot be used to change the value of ii.

In general, to use a const reference data member, the form for the class definition (declaration), constructor, and object declaration, respectively, are:

```
const type& ref;
```

In class definition (declaration of data member).

```
Class :: Class (const type& ref_var)
       : ref (ref_var)
```

Constructor function.

```
Class object (base_variable);
```

Declaration of object.

where *type* is the data type, *ref* is the name of the reference, *Class* is the class name, *ref_var* is a temporary variable name, *object* is the object name, and *base_variable* is the name of the variable being aliased. In this form, *ref* becomes an alias for *base_variable*. It is a safe alias because the const qualifier prevents *ref* from modifying *base_variable*.

There is no

```
const type& const ref;
```

form (with two const) as there is with pointers. The reason is that the second const is somewhat redundant. C++ automatically makes all references const (meaning they are only allowed to take a single alias). Since C++ does not allow us to specify a second alias for a reference, the reference is, in effect, constant.

Constant member functions. Declaring a member function const, makes the C++ compiler check for any statements in the function that may modify data members. A compilation error is produced if a statement is found to attempt to modify a data member. Using const member functions protects data members from being inadvertently modified in an unauthorized manner.

The function show_data() was denoted const in both the function declaration and the function definition with

```
    void show_data ( ) const;          <---- Function declaration.
void Class1 :: show_data ( ) const     <---- Function header.
```

Note that in both cases, the const follows the argument list (which in this example is empty).

To declare a function (with 2 arguments) const, the form is:

```
type function (type, type) const;
```

And, the header for such a const function is:

```
type Class :: function (type arg1a, type arg2a) const
```

where *Class* is the class name, *function* is the function name, *type* represents the types of arguments and return value (not necessarily all the same), and the *arg*s are the argument names.

Constant objects. Declaring an object to be const, effectively makes all its data members const. In other words, none of the data members of a const object can change after being initialized in the initialization list of the constructor. Constant objects can only invoke member functions specified as const.

In this lesson's program, object1 was declared const with the declaration:

```
const Class1 object1 (5, &ff, &gg, &hh, ii);
```

In general, to declare a const object (and call the constructor with 3 arguments), the form is:

```
const Class object (arg1, arg2, arg3);
```

We can use a const object to call a function with:

```
object.function (arg1b, arg2b);
```

where *arg1b* and *arg2b* represent data items being passed to the function. Note that if *function* is not declared *const*, we cannot call *function* with *object*.

***Other uses of* const.** C++ allows us to use const in more ways than we can describe thoroughly in this lesson. For instance:

```
const int function1(int, double);
```

declares function1 to return a constant integer. Note that the const here is given before the function name rather than after the argument list (as given for the function in this lesson's program).

Without going into details, we can create a pointer to a pointer (that is, a variable that holds the address of a pointer variable) using * twice. For instance,

```
int** aa;
```

indicates aa is a pointer to a pointer. C++ allows us to insert const if we desire in the following way:

```
int* const* aa;
```

This makes aa a pointer to a const pointer to an integer (reading from right to left).

We can also mix & and *. For instance

```
int*& aa;
```

declares aa to be a reference to a pointer to an integer. While

```
int* const& aa;
```

makes aa a reference to a const pointer to an integer (also reading from right to left).

Mutable data members. Not shown in this lesson's program is the keyword mutable. It is used with nonconstant data members. A data member specified to be mutable can be modified by a constant member function. For instance, the class definition,

```
class Class1
{
        private:
                mutable int aa;
        public:
                void function1 () const;
};
```

object declaration

```
const Class1 object1;
```

and function definition

```
void Class1 :: function1 () const
{
      aa = 10;
}
```

indicate that `object1` is a constant object and `function1` is a constant function. However, the mutable specification for `aa` overrides the constantness and allows `aa` to be modified by `function1`.

Summary. In writing your own programs, use `const` in the proper manner as described in this lesson. Even if your program works well without using `const`, go back and put `const` wherever it is appropriate. This makes your program more reliable and easier to modify.

LESSON 14.4 SPECIAL QUALIFIERS (3)—`friend` (FUNCTION)

TOPICS

- Declaring, defining and calling `friend` functions
- Passing objects by reference

QUESTION YOU SHOULD ATTEMPT TO ANSWER

1. Do we use an invoking object to call a `friend` function?

The `friend` keyword is used to indicate that a function has a special relationship with a class. Typically, `friend` is specified for a function that is not a member of any class. This specification allows the function to access private data members directly. (Remember, without a `friend` designation, only member functions can access private data members directly.)

Using `friend` is somewhat controversial in the object-oriented design community. It seems to violate the concept of encapsulation and the purpose of using objects and classes (which is to rigidly restrict access to private data). Despite this, you will likely see it in programs written by others, so we present it here. In general, if `friend` is implemented conscientiously, it can be safe and effective for such things as operator overloading (which is discussed later in this chapter). However, be aware that it can be abused, and the overuse of `friend` will often indicate a poorly designed program.

In this lesson's program, we create a `Complex` class for working with complex numbers. The `friend` function `add_complex` adds two complex numbers and returns the result. Read the program to see how a nonmember function can be designated a `friend` of a class.

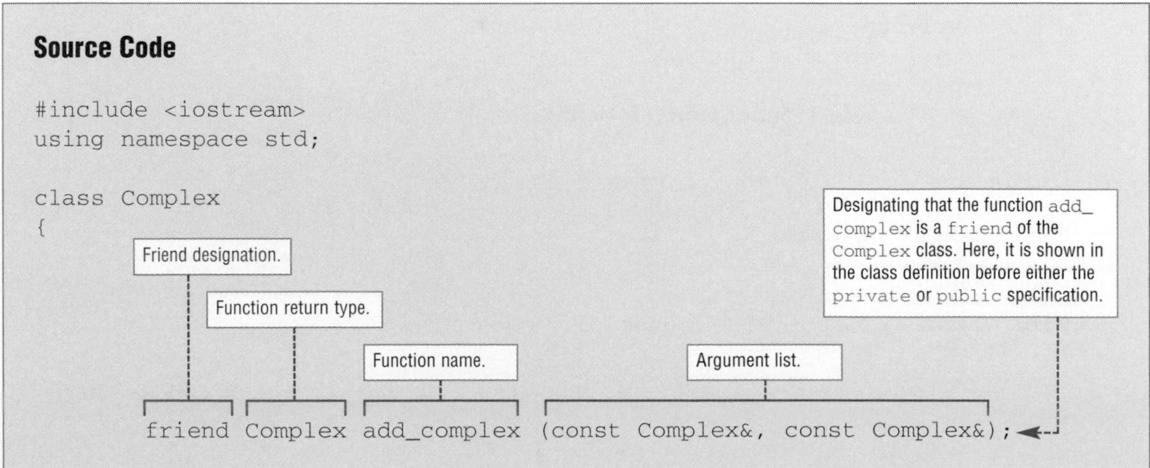
Source Code
#include <iostream>
using namespace std;
class Complex
{
Friend designation.
Function return type.
Function name.
Argument list.
Designating that the function add_complex is a friend of the Complex class. Here, it is shown in the class definition before either the private or public specification.
friend Complex add_complex (const Complex&, const Complex&);

```
        private:
                double imag, real;

        public:
                Complex ();
                Complex (double, double);
                void show_data ();
};

Complex add_complex (const Complex& aa, const Complex& bb)
{
        Complex cc;

        cc.imag = aa.imag + bb.imag;
        cc.real = aa.real + bb.real;

        return(cc);
}

Complex :: Complex ()
        : real (0), imag (0)
{
}

Complex :: Complex (double real_var, double imag_var)
        : real (real_var), imag (imag_var)
{
}

void Complex :: show_data ()
{
        cout << "real = " << real << " imag = " << imag << endl;
}

int main ( )
{
        Complex object1 (10,5), object2 (20,3), object3;
        object3 = add_complex (object1, object2);
        object3.show_data ();
}
```

No-argument constructor.

Two-argument constructor.

The definition of the `friend` function does *not* include the keyword `friend`. This function does not belong to any class. It is a freestanding function (there is no `Complex::` designation). This function returns an object that is the sum of the two objects passed through the argument list.

Function return type.

Function name.

Argument list.

Note that `add_complex` has direct access (using simply the object name and dot operator) to the `private` data members of `Complex` objects even though `add_complex` is not a member function!

The no-argument constructor initializes the data members to zero.

The two-argument constructor initializes the data members to the argument values.

With this call, `object3` becomes the sum of `object1` and `object2`. Note that `add_complex` has been called with no invoking object because `add_complex` is not a member function.

Output

```
real = 30 imag = 8
```

Description

Declaring* `friend` *functions. A `friend` function is declared with the keyword `friend` in the class definition. In other words, the *class* grants friendship to the *function*. You can remember this because it is similar to human interaction where friendship is granted (not taken) from one to another. In this lesson's program,

```
friend Complex add_complex (const Complex&, const Complex&);
```

declares the function `add_complex` to be a `friend` function. This function returns a `Complex` object and is passed two `Complex` objects by reference.

In general, the form for declaring a `friend` function (with two arguments) is:

```
friend type function (type, type);
```

where the *`type`*s are data types (not necessarily all the same) and *`function`* is the function name. Such a declaration makes *`function`* a `friend` of the class in which the declaration appears.

The `friend` function declaration is typically put at the beginning of the class definition prior to the `private` and `public` access qualifiers. However, this is not required, and placing a `friend` function in the `private` or `public` region has no influence on the function's performance (because it is not a member function). When more than one function is to be made a `friend` of the class, the `friend` function declarations become a so-called *friends list*.

Defining* `friend` *functions. The keyword `friend` is not used in the function definition. The definition of the `friend` function in this lesson's program:

```
Complex add_complex (const Complex& aa, const Complex& bb)
{
      Complex cc;

      cc.imag = aa.imag + bb.imag;
      cc.real = aa.real + bb.real;

      return (cc);
}
```

reveals that it is a `friend` function because it directly accesses the private data members (`real` and `imag`) of the `Complex` objects `aa`, `bb`, and `cc`. Without this class having been declared a `friend` in the `Complex` class definition, a compilation error would have occurred because of the attempt to access private data members.

Calling* `friend` *functions. Because a `friend` function is not a member function, no invoking object is used in the function call. For instance:

```
add_complex (object1, object2);
```

calls the `add_complex` function and passes `object1` and `object2`. In general, a call to a `friend` function (with 2 arguments) is made by:

```
function (arg1, arg2);
```

where *`function`* is the function name and *`arg1`* and *`arg2`* are argument names.

Using references for passing objects. We have not previously shown how objects are passed by reference but do so in this lesson. The function call and header in this lesson's program are:

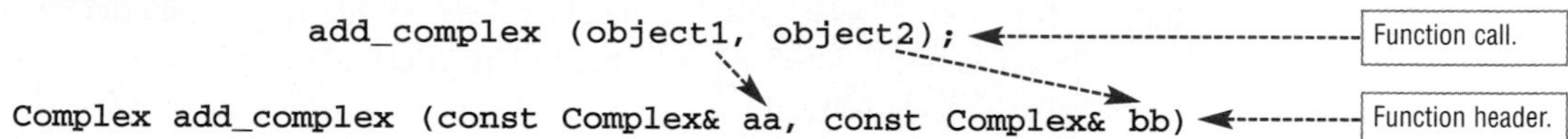

Because `object1` and `object2` are objects of class `Complex`, using `Complex&` in the header for `aa` and `bb` makes `aa` an alias for `object1` and `bb` an alias for `object2`. The `const` qualifier indicates that `aa` and `bb` cannot modify the data members of `object1` and `object2`. Within the body of the function `aa.real`, `aa.imag`, `bb.real`, and `bb.imag` represent `object1.real`, `object1.imag`, `object2.real`, and `object2.imag`, respectively. As you can see, passing objects by reference is very similar to passing standard data types by reference.

Passing objects by reference saves memory because all the data members of each object are not copied to the function region of memory. Consequently, objects are frequently passed by reference.

Implications of `friend` functions. The `friend` function concept is illustrated in Fig. 14.3. From this illustration, it can be seen that the `friend` function has access to the private data members of all objects of a class. This is a modification of the encapsulation shown in Fig. 8.6. Although a `friend` function is not a member of the class, in some cases, we can think of a `friend` function as extending the class by creating what is (effectively) a `public` class member function that is called with no invoking object.

Using `friend` functions can simplify some programming activities especially when it comes to overloading operators (described later in this chapter). Also, without going into the details, the call to a `friend` function can sometimes look more natural than a call to a member function (because there is no object and dot operator needed).

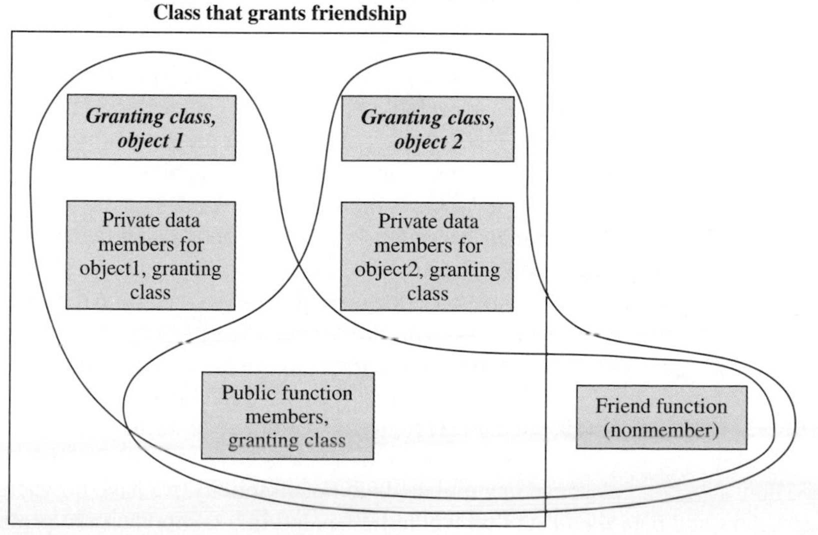

Figure 14.3

Illustration of the relationship between a `friend` function and the objects of a granting class. Note that all objects share the member functions and the `friend` function. The `friend` function is outside the class. For this drawing, all data members are `private` and all function members are `public`.

However, a possible breakdown in an object-oriented design can result from the use or overuse of `friend` functions. One of the fundamental qualities of object-oriented design is the restriction that private data members can be modified only by member functions. This means that the class designer has reasonably tight control on how objects can be modified. Because the `friend` designation gives a function outside the class the ability to directly modify `private` data, the integrity of object data could be compromised by a `friend` function. If a function is a `friend` of more than one class, then it is possible for a single function to modify the `private` data of more than one class's objects. The implementation of such a function must be evaluated carefully by the designers of all classes involved. This adds a level of complexity to a program design that could result in problems, especially to future program modifications.

Member functions as `friends`. A `friend` function does not necessarily need to be a freestanding function. It can be a member function of another class. The form (for a function with 2 arguments) is:

```
class Class1
{
        friend Class2 :: function (type, type);
        ...
};
```

where *`Class1`* is the granting class, *`Class2`* is the class of which the function is a member, *`function`* is the function name, and the *`type`*s are data types (not necessarily the same). More will be said about the implications of using such a `friend` in the next lesson that deals with `friend` classes.

LESSON 14.5 SPECIAL QUALIFIERS (4)—`friend` (CLASS)

TOPICS

- Declaring a `friend` class
- Using a `friend` class
- Dangers of `friend` classes

QUESTION YOU SHOULD ATTEMPT TO ANSWER

1. In which line of code does an object of the `Family` class set the pass codes?

An entire class can be granted `friend`ship by another class. All the member functions of a `friend` class can access all the `private` data and function members of the class granting `friend`ship.

`friend` classes are controversial also. They are sometimes used when it is acceptable for some but not all classes to share access to data. For instance, suppose you are programming a controller for a home burglar alarm system that allows several different codes to be typed at the keypad to deactivate the alarm. One code is permanent for the family members. Other codes are one-time-use codes for workers such as carpet cleaners and painters. After a one-time-use code is used, it is removed from the code list.

Classes involved in such a system might be `Controller`, `Family`, and `Maintenance_worker`. Data members for the `Controller` class would include the codes. Such codes should be available to the `Family` class, but not the `Maintenance_worker` class. One way to do this would be to make class `Family` a `friend` of the `Controller` class (as shown in this lesson's program). Read the code to see how a `friend` class can manipulate data. For simplicity, we have not included constructors and data members that would be needed in a comprehensive program.

Source Code

```
#include <iostream>
using namespace std;

class Family;

class Controller
{
        friend class Family;

        private:
                void set_codes ();
                int code[2];
};

class Family
{
        public:
                void set_data (Controller&);
};

void Controller :: set_codes ()
{
        cout << "Enter two codes to create them." << endl;
        cin >> code[0] >> code[1];
}

void Family :: set_data (Controller& control)
{
        control.set_codes ();
        cout << "Code 1 = " << control.code[0]
            << " Code 2 = " << control.code[1] << endl;
}

int main ( )
{
        Controller the_controller;
        Family the_family;

        the_family.set_data (the_controller);
}
```

This is a forward declaration. It simply tells the compiler that class `Family` exists so that class `Controller` can designate it a `friend`.

Designating class `Family` to be a `friend` of class `Controller`.

Here, we have declared a private function `set_codes()`. This function is private because setting the alarm code is an activity restricted to certain type objects. This is an example of a case where a function is not public.

The `Family` function `set_data()` is passed a `Controller` object by reference.

This private `Controller` function sets the codes.

The `set_data` function needs a `Controller` object to access `Controller` data and function members. This object is passed through the argument list by reference.

The `Family` function `set_data()` is allowed to call the private `Controller` function `set_codes()` and access `code[]` directly because `Family` is a `friend` of `Controller`.

An object of both class types is created.

The `Family` object is the invoking object. The `Controller` object is passed through the argument list.

Output

```
                     Enter two codes to create them.
Keyboard input       1234 6789
                     Code 1 = 1234 Code 2 = 6789
```

Description

Designating a `friend` class. A class is granted friendship within the granting class definition. In this lesson's program, the line

```
friend class Family;
```

within the definition of the `Controller` class designates `Family` to be a friend of `Controller`.

In general the form for declaring a `friend` class is:

```
friend class Name;
```

where *`Name`* is the name of the `friend` class. Both keywords `friend` and `class` are required. Although not required, it is common practice to list `friend` classes before the `public` and `private` access specifiers in the granting class definition, as shown in the definition for class `Controller` in this lesson's program.

Note that if the `friend` class is not defined before the granting class, the compiler will not recognize the `friend` class name and signal a compilation error. In this lesson's program, it was necessary for the `Family` class to have a *forward declaration* of:

```
class Family;
```

before the definition of `Controller`. This line simply indicates to the compiler that this class exists and is defined in another location. When the compiler then encounters `Family` in the `Controller` class, it recognizes it as a class name and does not flag an error. You can use such forward declarations whenever a class name needs to be recognized before it is defined.

Defining a `friend` class. A function of a `friend` class uses an object (or objects) of the granting class. Therefore, an object is passed through the argument list. For instance, the definition

```
class Family
{
        public:
                void set_data (Controller&);
};
```

has a `Controller` object passed by reference to the member function `set_data()`. This means that the `Controller` object can be used in `set_data()` to access private Controller data and functions. The function

```
void Family :: set_data (Controller& control)
{
        control.set_codes ( );
        cout << "Code  1 = " << control.code[0]
             << "  Code  2 = " << control.code[1] << endl;
}
```

makes control an alias for the object being passed. It then uses that object to call the function set_codes() and access the private data code[0] and code[1].

A basic general form for defining a friend class:

```
class Friend
{
        public:
                type functionf (Granting&);
};
```

and a member function is:

```
type Friend :: functionf (Granting& objectga)
{
        objectga . functiong ( );
        objectga . datag = ...;
}
```

where *Friend* is the friend class name, *types* are data types (not necessarily the same), *functionf* is the friend class member function name, *Granting* is the granting class name, *objectga* is an alias for a granting class object, *functiong* is a granting class member function name, and *datag* is a granting class data member name. While you can use these forms as a guide, the actual form for a particular use of a friend class and member function depends on the program.

Calling a function of a friend class. In this lesson's program, the friend class function is called in main with the statements:

```
Controller the_controller;
Family the_family;
the_family . set_data (the_controller);
```

Here, an object of each class is declared. The friend class object (the_family) calls its member function (set_data) and passes the granting class object (the_controller).

A basic form for calling a friend class function is:

```
objectf . functionf (objectg);
```

where *objectf* is the friend class object, *functionf* is the friend class member function name, and *objectg* is the granting class object. The actual form for a particular use of a friend class member function depends on the program.

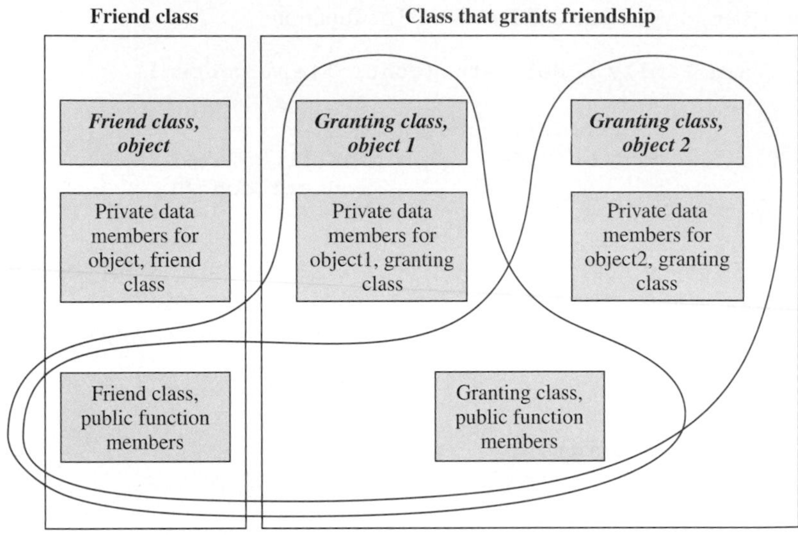

Figure 14.4

Image of connection between granting and `friend` classes. Note that the `friend` functions have access to the private data members of all objects. For this drawing, all data members are private and all function members are public.

Implications of `friend` classes. Fundamentally, granting a class `friend`ship means that `private` member functions and data of the granting class can be accessed from the member functions of the `friend` class. While this sounds relatively benign, the impact on a program can be quite profound. Figure 14.4 illustrates the concept. It can be seen from the figure that the `friend` class functions are extremely powerful. They can access all the `private` data for objects of both the granting and `friend` classes. In effect, a `friend` class adds a new set of functions to the granting class. This may add considerable complexity to a program. If separate designers are used for the classes, communication between them is crucial.

Figure 14.5 shows how the `friend` and granting class objects interacted in this lesson's program (the type of interaction is fairly common). Note how an arrow goes

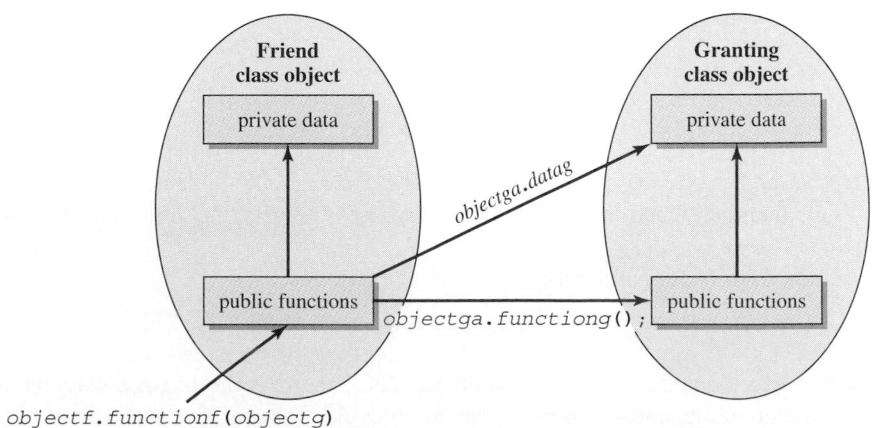

Figure 14.5

Illustration of relationship between `friend` and granting objects for Lesson 14.5's program. Both objects are declared in `main`. The notation next to the arrows (defined in the Description of this lesson) indicates the code needed to perform the access indicated by the arrows. Note that an arrow crossing an object's boundary requires the object name, alias (from a reference), or address (from a pointer). Note also that the `friend` functions access `private` data of the granting class directly.

directly from the friend class function to the granting class data (indicating a direct link between these two). Such a connection would not exist for two objects of different nonfriend classes.

The friend class functions are links between the friend and granting classes. Having many such links may not be desirable. An improved approach may be to use the method shown in Lesson 14.4 to make one member function a friend (or two, as needed) rather than all the member functions (which is the situation when a class is made a friend). We will see in later lessons that there are numerous ways to link objects and classes. Before creating a friend class, other ways to link classes should be explored.

In summary, be careful with friend classes and be aware that they are not allowed by some organizations. With friend classes, the encapsulation concept can be severely compromised, which can result in a poor design. We show friend classes here because they are a feature of C++, they illustrate a manner in which classes can be connected, and because there are supporters of friend classes in the programming community.

LESSON 14.6 OPERATOR OVERLOADING

TOPICS

- Unary operator overloading
- Binary operator overloading
- Overloading with friend functions
- Overloading with member functions

QUESTION YOU SHOULD ATTEMPT TO ANSWER

1. Why do you think it is sometimes beneficial to treat some operator functions as friends rather than members?

Operator overloading creates new definitions of operators for use with objects. For instance, suppose we want the + operator, when used between two objects of a particular class, to do a member-by-member summation. C++ allows us to define such an action for + by using *operator overloading*. The method is to create a function for a class (either a member or friend) called operator+() (which uses the keyword operator, however the name of the function is operator+) in the same manner that we create any other function. Within the body of the function, we simply write the code to perform a member-by-member addition. When a *client* of a class (that is, a function that uses the class's objects) has the expression object1 + object2, the operator+() function is automatically called by C++, and the member-by-member addition is performed. Similarly, we could create an operator-() function for a class. Then, whenever a - sign is used with objects of the class, the operator-() function is called.

You can make your operator functions perform most any operation. For instance, you could make the operator+() function perform multiplication or simply read input. However, doing so is unwise. It is best to have your operator functions perform actions similar to the original operator meaning. In other words, + should do some sort of addition, - subtraction, * multiplication, and / division.

Sometimes applying the original meaning of an operator when used with some classes is open to interpretation. For example, if one of a class's data members is a string, it is not clear what the operator-() function might do to a string. You might make this function take two objects and eliminate matching types of characters from one of the strings. Or you could simply remove a matching number of characters from one of the strings. Both these actions fit the spirit of a minus sign, and both would be a reasonable and acceptable application of the `operator-()` function. The application one should use is simply dependent on the type of problem to be solved. In summary, even though each operator function that you write should reflect the spirit of the operator, many possibilities exist.

As we described earlier, each C++ operator is classified as being unary (taking one operand) or binary (taking two operands). We cannot change this classification when doing operator overloading in our programs. In other words, + is a binary operator (it has two operands). When we use operator overloading, we must do it in a way that exactly two (not one or three) operands are used.

We are allowed to specify an operator function to be a class member or a `friend` of a class. Although C++ allows the body of an operator function to do most anything, it has strict rules that must be followed in creating operator functions. These rules are dependent on the programmer making an operator function a binary `friend`, binary member, or unary member (these are the most commonly used forms).

In this lesson, for the sake of simplicity, we assume all data members to be numeric. We make the operator functions stick closely to their original meaning and perform member-by-member arithmetic manipulations. You should be able to develop your own customized operator functions for your classes from the examples we present in this lesson.

To illustrate a variety of cases, in this source code we show how to overload the

1. Unary operator ++ as a member function.
2. Binary operator = as a member function.
3. Binary operator - as a `friend` function.

To do this, we create a `Point` class that has data members `x` and `y`. Read the code and annotations to see how to define and call operator functions and thereby perform operator overloading.

Note that when we use operator overloading in a class, we make the class more like a data type such as `int` or `double` because operators have defined actions on objects of the class. The name given to such a class is *abstract data type,* abbreviated ADT.

Source Code

```
#include <iostream>
using namespace std;

class Point
{
        friend Point operator- (const Point&, const Point&);
        private:
                double x, y;
```

The `operator-` function is designated as a `friend`. It returns a `Point` object and is passed two `Point` objects by reference.

```
        public:
                Point ();
                Point (double, double);
                Point operator++ ();
                Point operator= (const Point&);
                void show_data ();
};

Point :: Point ()
      : x(0), y(0)
{
}

Point :: Point (double x_var, double y_var)
      : x(x_var), y(y_var)
{
}

Point Point :: operator++ ()
{
        ++x;
        ++y;
        return *this;
}

Point Point :: operator= (const Point& pointb)
{
        x = pointb.x;
        y = pointb.y;
        cout << "Assignment operator function called." << endl;
        return *this;
}

void Point :: show_data ()
{
        cout << "x = " << x << " y = " << y << endl;
}

Point operator- (const Point& pointa, const Point& pointb)
{
        Point difference;
        difference.x = pointa.x - pointb.x;
        difference.y = pointa.y - pointb.y;
        return difference;
}
```

No-argument constructor.

Two-argument constructor.

The `operator++` function is a member function that returns a `Point` object.

The `operator=` function is a member function that returns a `Point` object. It is passed a `Point` object by reference.

The no-argument constructor initializes `x` and `y` to 0.

The two-argument constructor initializes `x` and `y` to the argument values.

Because `operator++` is a member function, `x` and `y` refer to the data members of the invoking object. Thus, this function increments the data members of the invoking object.

The keyword `this` represents a pointer to (or address of) the invoking object. Consequently, the object itself is represented by `*this`. Therefore, the `operator++()` function returns the modified (with the data members incremented) invoking object.

Because `operator=` is a member function, `x` and `y` refer to the data members of the invoking object. However, `pointb.x` and `pointb.y` refer to the data members of the object in the argument list. Thus, this function assigns the argument list object data members to the invoking object data members.

Again, `*this` is used to return the modified invoking object.

The `operator-()` function is a `friend` (which means there is no invoking object). Two objects are passed through the argument list by reference (`pointa` and `pointb`). A temporary object, `difference`, is created and returned. Its data members are the difference in `pointa` and `pointb` data members.

```
int main ( )
{
        Point p1 (10,3), p2 (4,8), p3;
        
        p3 = p1 - p2;
        ++p3;
        p3.show_data ();
}
```

Declaring three objects.

This line illustrates the value of operator overloading. Although it is extremely simple in appearance, it calls both the `operator- ()` and `operator= ()` functions.

This line calls the `operator++ ()` function. The function returns the modified object.

Output

```
Assignment operator function called.
x = 7    y = -4
```

Description

Equivalent function calls. The key to understanding an operator function is in knowing the *equivalent function call* generated by the operator expression. The equivalent function call is generated automatically by C++. In other words, an arithmetic expression such as `p1 - p2` creates a call to the `operator-()` function with `p1` and `p2` as arguments (as used in this lesson's program). Our operator function definition must fit precisely C++'s expectations, or errors will be produced. Here, we show the form C++ expects the function definitions to be. The equivalent function call is dependent upon the classification of the operator function being `friend` or member, binary or unary.

- *Binary* `friend` *functions.* For instance, in this lesson's program, `operator-()` is listed as a binary `friend` function. The expression used in `main` and the automatically generated equivalent function call are:

Here, it is seen that the equivalent function call has two arguments: the first argument is the object before the operator, and the second argument is the object after the operator. C++ creates the equivalent function call from the expression. A programmer has no control over this process.

In general, a binary `friend` function has the following expression and equivalent function call

where `object1` and `object2` are class objects, and + is a placeholder representing any binary operator (such as +, -, *, / or =).

- *Binary member functions.* Binary member functions produce a different type call because member functions have invoking objects. In this lesson's program, the binary operator = was used. The general form of the expression and equivalent function call are:

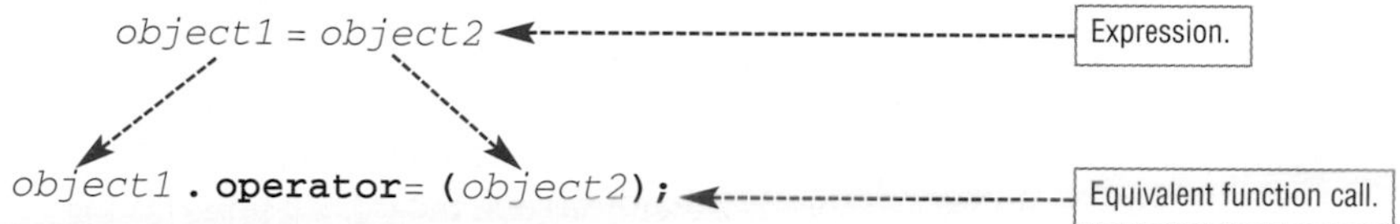

where `object1` and `object2` are class objects, and = is a placeholder representing any binary operator (such as =, +, -, *, or /). Here it can be seen that the object before the operator in the expression is the invoking object, and the object after the operator in the expression is passed through the argument list. The specific example used in this lesson's program is described in detail in the "Function definitions" section.

- *Unary member functions.* Unary operators ++ and -- have the additional complication of being either prefix or postfix. When treated as member operator functions, the prefix ++ and -- have the following form of expression and equivalent function call.

where `object1` is a class object and ++ can be replaced by --. Note that the object following the operator in the expression is the invoking object.

The postfix form for these operators is

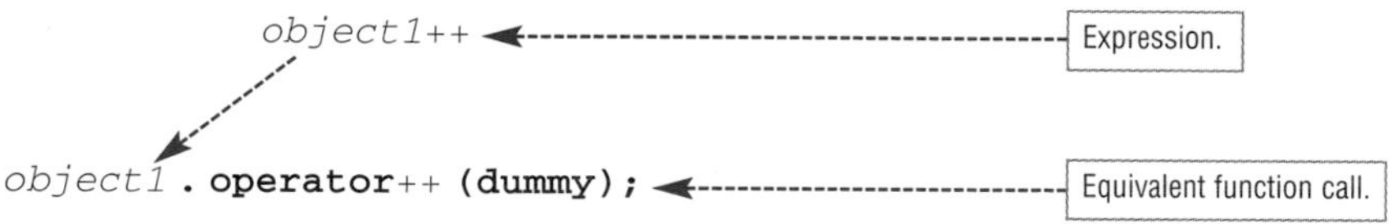

The object preceding the operator in the expression is the invoking object. Note that the function call is not the same as the prefix version. C++ creates a `dummy` variable (type `int`) for the argument list. This `dummy` must be included in the function definition. Therefore, when both the prefix and postfix ++ operator functions are defined for a program, as is typical, the functions are distinct in signature. This distinction allows C++ to determine which operator function to call. The specific example used in this lesson's program is described in detail in the "Function definitions" section.

- *Unary `friend` functions.* Unary `friend` functions are not as commonly used as the others and will not be covered in this text.

Function definitions. It is the responsibility of the programmer to write the function definition. This definition must be consistent with the equivalent function call developed by C++. In other words, C++ determines which object is first in the argument list or which object is the invoking object. The programmer's definition must take this into account.

- *Binary* `friend` *functions.* In this lesson's program, we have chosen to treat the `operator-()` function as a friend with the declaration:

  ```
  friend Point operator- (const Point&, const Point&);
  ```

  Consistent with the equivalent function call for binary `friend` functions, the declaration has two objects in the argument list. We have chosen to pass them by constant reference because the reference means that a copy is not made (which saves memory and speeds execution) and the `const` prevents the original object from being modified in the function body (which is the condition we want). We have chosen to make the function return an object because this is consistent with the original meaning of the - operator. In other words, if we write the expression:

  ```
  object3 = object1 - object2;
  ```

  the right side of the assignment statement is the function call. With our function declaration, an object is returned to this location upon execution of the function, and this object is assigned to `object3`.

  In this lesson's program, the function call (expression), equivalent function call, and function definition are:

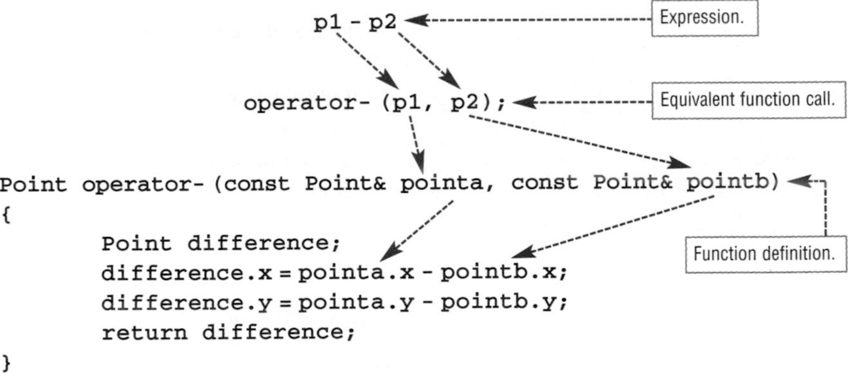

p1 - p2
Expression.
operator- (p1, p2);
Equivalent function call.
Point operator- (const Point& pointa, const Point& pointb)
{
Point difference;
difference.x = pointa.x - pointb.x;
difference.y = pointa.y - pointb.y;
return difference;
}
Function definition.

  From this, one can see how the function arguments are used in the body. The function definition, consistent with the meaning of subtraction, computes the difference for each data member of the objects in the argument list. The result is returned with an object (`difference`) created in the function.

  Note that the order of operation in the statements is important. In other words, we should not write `pointb.x - pointa.x` or `pointb.y - pointa.y` in the body of this function. Doing so would not produce a compilation error, but it would likely introduce a serious logic error. With such statements, client code written as `p1 - p2` would actually calculate `p2 - p1`!

  Your definitions of the `operator-()` function for your programs will likely be quite different from the one shown here. To use your `operator-()` functions successfully, you should determine what is the best meaning of subtraction for your classes, and write your functions to perform these operations.

A general form that you can use as a guide, though, for writing some of your own definitions of binary `friend` functions is

```
Class1 operator- (const Class1& objecta, const Class1& objectb)
{
        Class1 temp;
        temp.member1 = objecta.member1 - objectb.member1;
        temp.member2 = objecta.member2 - objectb.member2;
        return temp;
}
```

where `Class1` is the class name, - is a placeholder for the operator (+, -, *, /, or other), `objecta` and `objectb` are aliases for the two objects in the function call, and `member1` and `member2` are data members of the class. More computation lines can be added to the function body to accommodate more data members.

Table 14.5 shows a general form for a number of binary operator functions that are commonly used as `friends`. We will not discuss them all in detail. When you need to use operator functions, simply refer to the table as a guide.

- *Binary member functions.* In this lesson's program, we have chosen to treat the `operator=()` function as a member function with the declaration:

```
Point operator= (const Point&);
```

Consistent with the equivalent function call for binary member functions, the declaration has one object in the argument list. We have chosen to pass it by constant reference because the reference means that a copy is not made (which saves memory and speeds execution) and the `const` prevents the original object from being modified in the function body (which is the condition we want). We have chosen to make the function return an object because this is consistent with the original meaning of the = operator. Doing so, permits us to write multiple assignment expressions such as:

```
object3 = object2 = object1;
```

because the right = is executed first. An object is returned to this location and assigned to `object3`. The expression, equivalent function call, and function definition for the statements in this lesson's program are:

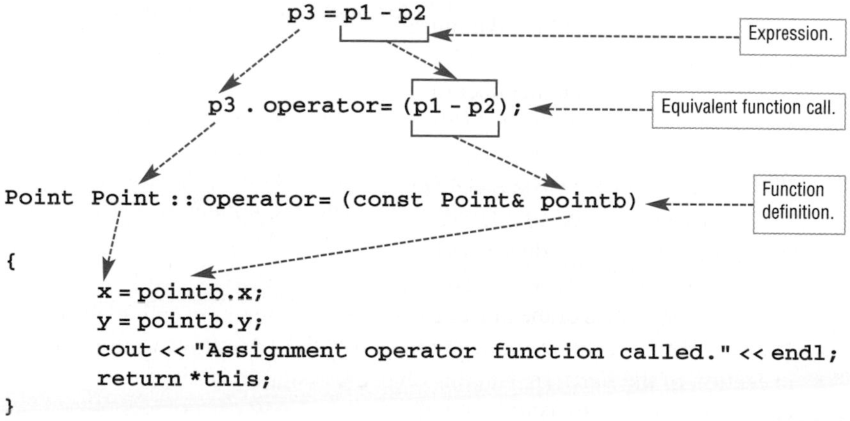

```
                  p3 = p1 - p2                      <---- Expression.

           p3 . operator= (p1 - p2);                <---- Equivalent function call.

Point Point :: operator= (const Point& pointb)      <---- Function definition.
{
        x = pointb.x;
        y = pointb.y;
        cout << "Assignment operator function called." << endl;
        return *this;
}
```

From this, one can see the correspondence between the object in the argument list (point b) and the function body. Also, the invoking object (p3) is represented with its data members only (x and y with no dot operator involved). This, of course, is standard for member functions in general.

In effect, the assignment statements in the body of the operator=() function are equivalent to:

```
p3.x = pointb.x;
p3.y = pointb.y;
```

Using the invoking object properly is important to successfully writing the definitions of binary member functions.

Note that the data members of the invoking object have been modified by the actions of this function, and it is the invoking object that we wish to return to the location of the function call. C++ provides a special keyword to perform this action. It is this, which indicates a pointer to (or address of) the invoking object, and *this indicates the object itself. Therefore, in this function, we return *this because we want the function to return the modified object. Returning *this is common for member operator functions that modify the invoking object.

The function definition we have written for operator=() is consistent with the meaning of =, in that it assigns the value of each data member of the object in the argument list to the corresponding data members of the invoking object. In fact, this is the same action C++ performs by default when the = operator is used with objects. However, if an operator=() function is defined, C++ uses that function rather than the default. This is verified in the output for this lesson's program that shows the "Assignment operator function called" statement.

Note that if a pointer is a member of the class, a member-by-member assignment may not be appropriate. This topic was covered in Lesson 14.1 when we talked about copy constructors.

General forms that you can use as a guide for writing your own definitions of binary member functions are given in Table 14.5.

- *Unary member functions.* In this lesson's program, we have chosen to treat the prefix operator++() function as a member function with the declaration:

```
Point operator++ ();
```

Consistent with the equivalent function call for unary member functions, the declaration has nothing in the argument list. We have chosen to make the function return an object because this is consistent with the original meaning of the ++ operator. Doing so, permits us to write assignment expressions such as:

```
object2 = ++object1;
```

The right side of the assignment statement is the function call (expression). With our function declaration, an object is returned to this location upon execution of the function, and this object is assigned to object2.

In this lesson's program, the function call (expression), equivalent function call, and function definition are:

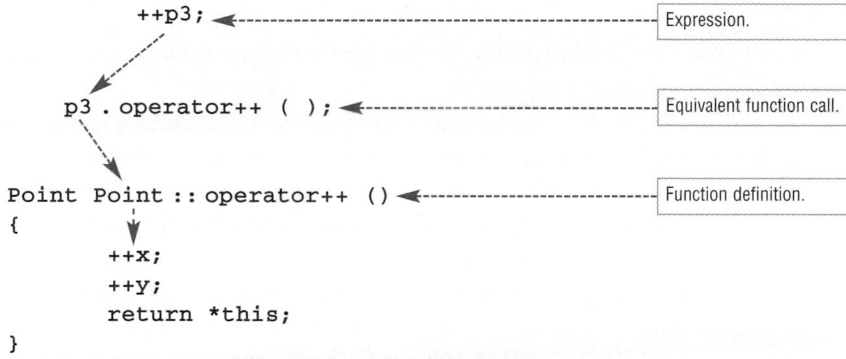
++p3;
Expression.
p3 . operator++ ( );
Equivalent function call.
Point Point :: operator++ ()
Function definition.
{
++x;
++y;
return *this;
}

From this, one can see the invoking object is represented with its data members only (`x` and `y` with no dot operator involved) as is standard for member functions in general. In effect, the statements in the body of the `operator++()` function are equivalent to:

```
++ p3.x;
++ p3.y;
```

Using the invoking object properly is important to successfully writing the definitions of unary member functions.

Again, the data members of the invoking object have been modified by the actions of this function, and it is the invoking object that we wish to return to the location of the function call. Therefore, in this function, we return `*this`, as we did with the binary member function `operator=()`.

The function definition we have written for `operator++()` is consistent with the meaning of `++`, in that it increments the value of each data member of the invoking object. General forms that you can use as a guide for writing your own definitions of unary member functions are given in Table 14.5.

Rules for operator overloading. Now that you know what operator overloading is, you can understand C++'s rules. These are:

1. The set of available and unavailable C++ operators is shown in Tables 14.3 and 14.4. Only the operators in Table 14.3 can be used in defining operator functions.

TABLE 14.3 — Operators that can be overloaded

Previously covered in this text											
`++`	`--`	`+`	`-`	`*`	`/`	`%`	`=`	`+=`	`-=`	`*=`	`/=`
`%=`	`!`	`<`	`>`	`<=`	`>=`	`==`	`!=`	`>>`	`<<`	`()`	`[]`
`&&`	`||`	`new`	`delete`	`new[]`	`delete[]`	`->`	`,`				
Not previously covered in this text											
`~`	`^`	`&`	`|`	`^=`	`&=`	`|=`	`<<=`	`>>=`	`->*`		

TABLE 14.4 — Operators that cannot be overloaded

sizeof	.	.*	::	?:

We are not allowed to make up our own operators. For instance, we cannot use `$` as an operator and create an `operator$()` function.

2. We cannot change the classification of an operator. If an operator is unary, we must use it and define it as a unary operator. If an operator is binary, we must use it and define it as a binary operator. For example, `++` is classified by C++ as a unary operator. We cannot use it and define it as a binary operator.
3. The operator precedence (which operator is executed first) rules described in Chapter 3 still apply, no matter how the operator functions are written. In other words, the binary `+` operator is executed before the binary `=` operator when they apply to objects as well as ordinary data members.
4. Each `friend` or freestanding operator function must take at least one object as an argument. In other words, we cannot make such a function use only C++ standard data types (like `int` or `double`) as arguments. Doing so would attempt to override the built in C++ operator functions for working with standard data, which is not allowed.
5. The equivalent function call for each operator is set by C++ and cannot be modified. For member functions, this means that C++ sets which object is the invoking object. For `friend` and freestanding functions, C++ determines the order of the objects in the argument list.

Member vs. `friend`. In most cases you should choose to make your operator functions class members instead of class `friend`s. However, one advantage of making a binary function a `friend` instead of a member is that one can make some calculations commutative.

For instance, suppose we want to add 5 to each data member of an object of the `Point` class. The expression

```
object1 + 5
```

can be handled with either a `friend` or member function. With a member function, `object1` is the invoking object. However, the expression

```
5 + object1
```

cannot be executed with a member operator function because 5 is not an object. One way to execute such an expression is to create a `friend operator+()` function that takes `(int, Class)` as types of arguments (as well as a second `friend operator+()` function that takes `(Class, int)` as arguments). Then both expressions can be executed.

Another way to handle this problem is with what are called *conversion operator functions*. A function such as `operator int()` can be created. Within this function an equivalent object can be made from an integer. In this text, conversion operator functions will not be covered in any more detail.

C++ requires that overloaded versions of operators `()`, `[]` (both described in Table 14.5), and `->` (overloading not described in this text) be member functions.

TABLE 14.5 — Operator overloading examples

Operator	Operator function (and comments)	Return value or type	Function call (expression)	Equivalent function call
Unary member				
Prefix ++	`Class1 Class1 :: operator++ ( ) {++ member1; return *this;}`	`*this`	`++ object1`	`object1.operator++()`
Postfix ++	`Class1 Class1 :: operator++ (int dummy) {member1++; return *this;}` **(C++ requires the `int` dummy to distinguish prefix and postfix ++. However, the dummy is not used in the function body.)**	`*this`	`object1 ++`	`object1.operator++(0)`
Prefix --	`Class1 Class1 :: operator-- ( ) {-- member1; return *this;}`	`*this`	`-- object1`	`object1.operator--()`
Postfix --	`Class1 Class1 :: operator -- (int dummy) {member1--; return *this;}` **(C++ requires the `int` dummy to distinguish prefix and postfix --. However, the dummy is not used in the function body.)**	`*this`	`object1 --`	`object1.operator--(0)`
!	`bool Class1 :: operator! ( ) const {return !member1;}`	`bool`	`!object1`	`object1.operator!()`
Binary member				
==	`bool Class1 :: operator== (const Class1& objectb) const {return (member1 == objectb.member1);}` **(Could have return `(member1 == objectb.member1 && member2 == objectb.member2);`.)**	`bool`	`object1 == object2`	`object1.operator == (object2)`
!=	`bool Class1 :: operator!= (const Class1& objectb) const {return (member1 != objectb.member1);}` **(Same comment as == comment, but with !=.)**	`bool`	`object1 != object2`	`object1.operator!=(object2)`
<	`bool Class1 :: operator< (const Class1& objectb) const {return (member1 < objectb.member1);}` **(Same comment as == comment, but with <.)**	`bool`	`object1 < object2`	`object1.operator < (object2)`
>	`bool Class1 :: operator> (const Class1& objectb) const {return (member1 > objectb.member1);}` **(Same comment as == comment, but with >.)**	`bool`	`object1 > object2`	`object1.operator > (object2)`
<=	`bool Class1 :: operator<= (const Class1& objectb) const {return (member1 <= objectb.member1);}` **(Same comment as == comment, but with <=.)**	`bool`	`object1 <= object2`	`object1.operator <= (object2)`

(continued)

TABLE 14.5 — *(continued)*

<table>
<tr><th>Operator</th><th>Operator function (and comments)</th><th>Return value or type</th><th>Function call (expression)</th><th>Equivalent function call</th></tr>
<tr><td>>=</td><td>bool Class1 :: operator>= (const Class1& objectb) const
{return (member1 >= objectb.member1);}
(Same comment as == comment, but with >=.)</td><td>bool</td><td>object1 >= object2</td><td>object1.operator >= (object2)</td></tr>
<tr><td>=</td><td>Class1 Class1 :: operator= (const Class1& objectb)
{member1 = objectb.member1; return *this;}
(The return *this is needed to allow multiple assignment such as object1 = object2 = object3;.)</td><td>*this</td><td>object1 = object2</td><td>object1.operator = (object2)</td></tr>
<tr><td>+=</td><td>Class1 Class1 :: operator+= (const Class1& objectb)
{member1 += objectb.member1; return *this;}</td><td>*this</td><td>object1 += object2</td><td>object1.operator += (object2)</td></tr>
<tr><td>-=</td><td>Class1 Class1 :: operator-= (const Class1& objectb)
{member1 -= objectb.member1; return *this;}</td><td>*this</td><td>object1 -= object2</td><td>object1.operator -= (object2)</td></tr>
<tr><td>*=</td><td>Class1 Class1 :: operator*= (const Class1& objectb)
{member1 *= objectb.member1; return *this;}</td><td>*this</td><td>object1 *= object2</td><td>object1.operator *= (object2)</td></tr>
<tr><td>/=</td><td>Class1 Class1 :: operator/= (const Class1& objectb)
{member1 /= objectb.member1; return *this;}</td><td>*this</td><td>object1 /= object2</td><td>object1.operator /= (object2)</td></tr>
<tr><td>%=</td><td>Class1 Class1 :: operator%= (const Class1& objectb)
{member1 %= objectb.member1; return *this;}</td><td>*this</td><td>object1 %= object2</td><td>object1.operator %= (object2)</td></tr>
<tr><td>&&</td><td>bool Class1 :: operator&& (const Class1& objectb) const
{return (member1 && objectb.member1);}
(Difficult to overload in a manner similar to its original meaning.)</td><td>bool</td><td>object1 && object2</td><td>object1.operator&& (object2)</td></tr>
<tr><td>||</td><td>bool Class1 :: operator|| (const Class1& objectb) const
{return (member1 || objectb.member1);}
(Difficult to overload in a manner similar to its original meaning.)</td><td>bool</td><td>object1 || object2</td><td>object1.operator || (object2</td></tr>
<tr><td>[]</td><td>type& Class1 :: operator[] (int i)
{if (i < 0 || i >= MAX) cout << "Array out of bounds error";
return member1[i];}
(In the Class1 definition, member1[] is a type array of size MAX. The simple function here checks for out-of-bounds. Also, object1 is not declared to be an array of objects.)</td><td>type&</td><td>object1[0] or object1[int]</td><td>object1.operator[] (0)</td></tr>
<tr><td>Binary friend</td><td></td><td></td><td></td><td></td></tr>
<tr><td>+</td><td>Class1 operator+ (const Class1& objecta,
const Class1& objectb)
{Class1 temp;
temp.member1 = objecta.member1 + objectb.member1;
return temp;}</td><td>Class1</td><td>object1 + object2</td><td>operator + (object1, object2</td></tr>
</table>

-	*Class1* operator- (const *Class1*& objecta, const *Class1*& *objectb*) {*Class1* temp; temp.*member1* = objecta.*member1*- *objectb.member1*; return temp;}	*Class1*	*object1* - *object2*	operator - (*object1*, *object2*)
*	*Class1* operator* (const *Class1*& objecta, const *Class1*& *objectb*) {*Class1* temp; temp.*member1* = objecta.*member1***objectb. member1*; return temp;}	*Class1*	*object1** *object2*	operator * (*object1*, *object2*)
/	*Class1* operator/ (const *Class1*& objecta, const *Class1*& *objectb*) {*Class1* temp; temp.*member1* = objecta.*member1*/*objectb.member1*; return temp;}	*Class1*	*object1*/ *object2*	operator / (*object1*, *object2*)
%	*Class1* operator% (const *Class1*& objecta, const *Class1*& *objectb*) {*Class1* temp; temp.*member1* = objecta.*member1*% *objectb.member1*; return temp;}	*Class1*	*object1*% *object2*	operator % (*object1*, *object2*)
<<	ostream& operator<< (ostream& *out*, const *Class1*& objecta) {*out* << "*member1*=" << objecta.*member1*;return *out*;} **(return out is required to allow cout << object1 << object2;.)**	ostream&	cout << *object1*;	operator << (cout, *object1*)
>>	istream& operator>> (istream& *in*, const *Class1*& objecta) {*in* >> objecta.*member1*;return *in*;} **(return in is required to allow cin << object1 << object2;. Do not forget to use in.ignore() in the function body where appropriate.)**	istream&	cout << *object1*;	operator << (cout, *object1*)
Unary, binary (or more) member				
( )	*Class1 Class1*::operator() (type aa, type bb, type cc) {*member1* = aa; *member2* = bb; *member3* = cc; return *this;} **(There is no standard body. Overloading () simply creates a shorthand for calling the member function operator(). You can return any type or have any number of arguments.)**	*this or any type	*object1* (a, b, c)	*object1*.operator() (a, b, c)

These examples mimic member-by-member operations in the spirit of the original operator meaning. Use these examples as a guide for developing your own operator functions. *Class1* is the class name. Clients of the class use *object1* and *object2*. Class data members are *member1* and *member2*, and are assumed to be integers. In the operator functions, *objectb* is an alias for *object2* (created by call by reference).

Comments on commonly used operator functions. The following comments can be made about operator overloading (refer to Table 14.5).

1. Only member functions can return `*this`. It is especially important to return `*this` when the invoking object is modified in the function, such as with ++, =, +=, and others.
2. The comparison operators (such as <, >, and ==) return a `bool` (true or false, see Lesson 5.7) when made to simulate their original meaning.
3. The `[]` operator is sometimes overloaded to create safe arrays. Table 14.5 shows a very simple method for doing so.
4. The >> and << operators are commonly overloaded to simplify input and output statements. The operator function prints output or reads input of the data members of the object. The return types `ostream&` and `istream&` are not covered in this text. However, you can use them by simply following the example shown in Table 14.5.
5. The `()` operator is called using an object name followed by an argument list enclosed in parentheses. Consequently, the call looks much like an ordinary function call. However, instead of a function name, an object name is used. It looks much like a call to a constructor function.

LESSON 14.7 UML AND OBJECT-ORIENTED DESIGN

TOPICS

- Programming a composition relationship
- Programming an association relationship
- Using pointers
- Using references

QUESTION YOU SHOULD ATTEMPT TO ANSWER

1. What is the role of the `Composite` constructor?

To this point, we have discussed how to define individual classes. However, a typical program has many classes. Getting the classes and their objects to interact properly is a major part of object-oriented design. In this lesson we show how to connect classes and objects and discuss the *UML* as a tool for developing sound designs.

The UML (*unified modeling language,* originally developed by James Rumbaugh, Grady Booch, and Ivar Jacobson in the mid 1990s) is not what one would normally think of as a language. However, it is one in the sense that it is used to communicate how a program operates (or is to be designed) through a series of diagrams. It can be used with other object-oriented languages such as Java or Smalltalk.

In this book there is not enough room to effectively teach the UML. Many entire textbooks are solely devoted to the subject. Instead, what is presented here is a small (focused, rather than general) subset of the UML. The purpose of the rest of this chapter (including the application examples) is to illustrate how to translate some UML diagrams into working C++ code.

When a programmer uses the UML, he or she creates many diagrams. *Collaboration* diagrams, *use case* diagrams, *state chart* diagrams and *class* diagrams, among others, are all part of the planning and documentation of object-oriented programs developed with the UML. In this text, we will focus on class diagrams because we only want to illustrate some of the issues involved in object-oriented design. Class diagrams show

how classes and objects relate to one another. Terms used to describe the relations include *composition, association, generalization,* and *aggregation,* among others.

The symbols used in UML class diagrams follow a convention. The symbols incorporated in our examples and their uses are:

1. Rectangles—used to enclose classes.
2. Lines—used to connect classes that interact.
3. Arrows and descriptors—used to indicate the type and direction of the interaction.
4. Small filled diamond heads—used to indicate that objects of one class are members of another class.
5. Numbers next to rectangles—used to indicate the number of objects of a class.

A considerable amount of information, such as the class name, data members, and accessibility classification, can be contained within a rectangle used to enclose a class. For example, Fig. 14.6a shows the generic form. It has a rectangle divided into three sections. The top section is the class name in bold letters, the middle section lists the data members, and the bottom section lists the function members. The + indicates public access, and the – indicates private access. Following each member is a colon and the member type (return type for a function) and the initial value (optional).

In Fig. 14.6b, an example of a `Point` class is presented. The two data members, `x` and `y`, are `private`, type `double`, and initialized to 0. Three member functions are `public` and return types `Point` and `void`. The constructor has no return type. As you can see, quite a bit of information is conveyed in such a diagram.

The rectangles for each class are combined in class diagrams to illustrate how they interact. Sometimes the class name alone is used in the rectangles to simplify the look of the diagram. A class diagram illustrating composition and a client-server (or "uses") relationship is shown in Fig. 14.7.

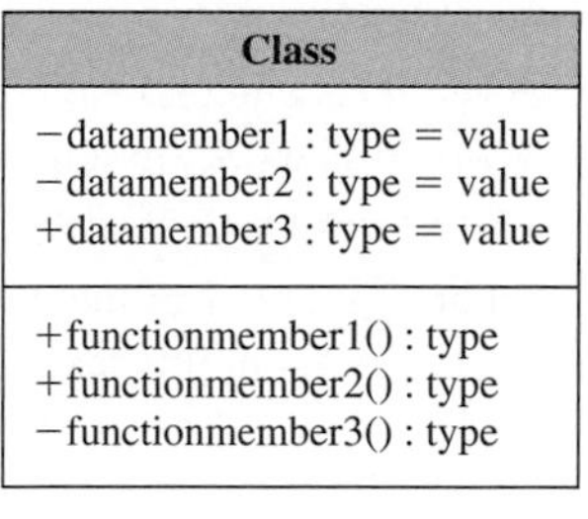

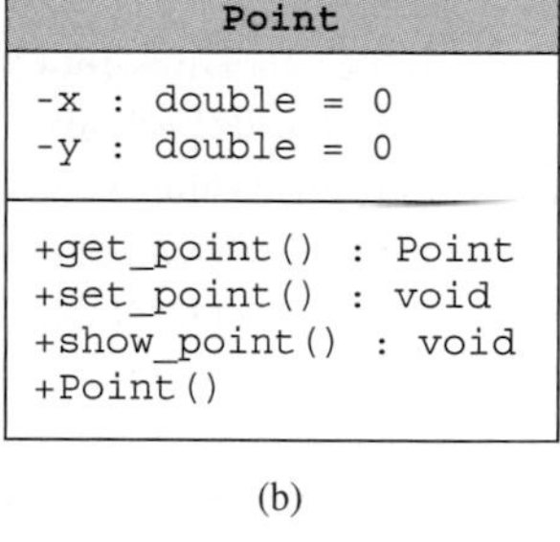

Figure 14.6

UML class representation.
(a) Generic form.
(b) Example of a `Point` class.

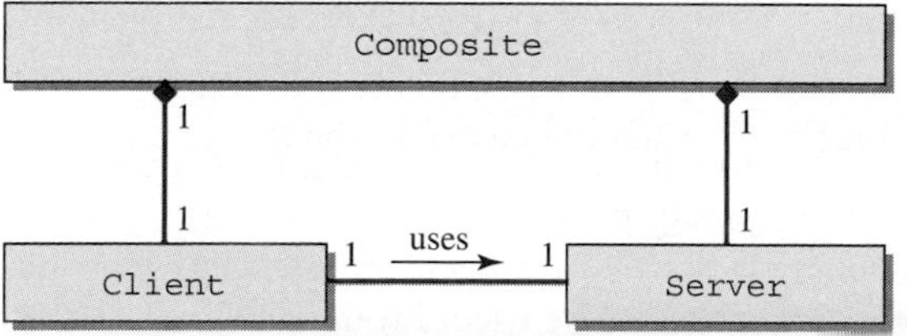

Figure 14.7

Class diagram illustrating composition and a client-server ("uses") relationship.

It has several class diagram elements. The class names are all enclosed in rectangles. The lines with solid diamonds indicate a form of composition. They show that `Client` and `Server` are components of `Composite` (meaning that class `Composite` has data members that are `Client` and `Server` objects). The line between `Client` and `Server` depicts a form of association. In this case the word "uses" above the arrow signifies that the association is "`Client` uses `Server`". `Client` is the client class, and `Server` is the server class. The numbers beside the rectangles reflect the correspondence between the class objects. In this case, all the numbers are 1, which means that one object of `Client` and one object of `Server` are contained in an object of `Composite`. And, one object of `Client` uses one object of `Server`.

In the application examples, we illustrate real classes interacting in a manner similar to that shown in Fig. 14.7, so we will not develop the discussion further at this point. Instead, in this lesson, we illustrate one method for programming this interaction. By learning this lesson and by studying the application examples, you will be able to program the types of interactions shown in Fig. 14.7 in your own programs.

In this lesson's source code, we develop `Composite`, `Client`, and `Server` as shown in Fig. 14.7. `Composite` has `Client` and `Server` objects as data members. This is simply programmed, so we do not discuss programming this relationship further here.

There are several ways to program a "uses" (client-server) relationship:

1. An object of the server class can be declared as a local object in a client class member function. This is easily done, but not appropriate for cases when the server object needs to be accessed by other classes or by other client class member functions.
2. Objects of the client and server classes can be declared in `main` (for instance), and the server object can be passed through argument lists to a client member function. This method can be easily programmed for simple cases (when the path through the argument lists is not too circuitous).
3. Accessor functions can be created in the server class and calls to these can act as arguments to client member functions. While this works, it tends to be quite clumsy. This was illustrated in Application Example 11.1.
4. A pointer to an object of the server class can be a member of the client class. This is a more general method and is the one we show in this lesson's program.

This last method involves the following:

1. The "uses" arrow points from `Client` to `Server`. Therefore, `Client` is made to contain a pointer variable (to a `Server` object). This is type `Server*`.
2. The pointer is initialized in the constructor(s) to hold the address of the `Server` object.
3. The pointer is used to call a `Server` function from a `Client` function. `Client` data member values are passed to the `Server` function through the argument list.

Instead of a pointer to a `Server` object, a reference (which in many ways is less prone to error than a pointer) can be used. From our figure, the reference would be contained in `Client` and be an alias for a `Server` object. The steps are similar to the previous steps. They are:

1. The "uses" arrow points from `Client` to `Server`. Therefore, `Client` is made to contain a reference to a `Server` object. This is type `Server&`.
2. The reference is initialized in the constructor(s) to be an alias for the `Server` object.
3. The reference is used to call a `Server` function from a `Client` function. `Client` data member values are passed to the `Server` function through the argument list.

Two source codes follow. The first works with a pointer, and the second works with a reference. Read the source codes and annotations to see how the class diagram of Fig. 14.7 can be programmed. Pay particular attention to the way the constructors initialize the pointer and reference.

Source Code—Pointer Connection

```
#include <iostream>
using namespace std;

class Server
{
        public:
                Server ();
                void server_function (int);
};

class Client
{
        private:
                int client_data;
                Server* server_ptr;
        public:
                Client (Server*);
                void client_function ();
};

class Composite
{
        private:
                Server server_object;
                Client client_object;
        public:
                Composite ();
                void composite_function ();
};
```

`Server` has a function that accepts an integer through its argument list because `Client` has an `int` data member. This function performs the calculations that `Client` wishes to utilize on its `int` data member.

Client has an `int` (`client_data`) and a pointer (`server_ptr`) to a `Server` object as data members. The `int` represents the data that is passed to `server_function()`. The pointer is used to call `server_function()`.

The `Client` constructor initializes the `Server` pointer to point to the `Server` object contained in `Composite`. This is required.

`Composite` contains a `Client` and `Server` object. When a `Composite` object is declared, space is reserved for all data members. The constructors of contained objects are called according to the initialization line of the `Composite` constructor (if they are present in the line).

```
Composite :: Composite ()
        : client_object (&server_object)
{
        cout << "Composite constructor called."
             << endl;
}

Client :: Client  (Server* server_var)

        : client_data (25), server_ptr (server_var)
{
        cout << "Client  constructor called." << endl;
}

Server :: Server ()
{
        cout << "Server  constructor called." << endl;
}
void Composite :: composite_function ()
{
        client_object.client_function ();
}

void Client :: client_function ()
{
        server_ptr -> server_function (client_data);
}

void Server :: server_function (int data)
{
        cout << "Server  function called. Data = " << data << endl;
}
int main ( )
{
        Composite composite_object;
        composite_object.composite_function ();
}
```

`Composite` constructor. Note that simply declaring a `Composite` object causes all three constructors to be called.

Initialization list for `Composite` constructor. This line calls the `Client` constructor. It passes the address of the `server_object` (`&server_object`) to the `Client` object constructor. This makes `server_ptr` for the `Client` object hold the address of `server_object` (follow the arrows).

`Client` constructor.

`Server` constructor.

A `Client` function is called from a `Composite` function. This is easily done because `client_object` is a data member of class `Composite`.

This statement links `Client` and `Server`. Here, a `Server` function is called using the `Server` pointer (which is a member of the `Client` class). `Client` data (an `int`) is passed through the argument list. All this takes place in a `Client` function. Note that the arrow (`->`) operator is used with a pointer to call a member function.

The `Server` function works with the `Client` data (follow the arrow).

Here, only a `Composite` object is declared, and only a `Composite` function is called.

Source Code—Reference Connection

Note that the missing code is identical to previous source code.

```
class Client
{
        private:
                int client_data;
                Server& server_ref;
```

Client has a `Server` reference as a data member (`server_ref`).

```
        public:
                Client (Server&);
                void client_function ();
};

Composite :: Composite ()
         : client_object (server_object)
{
        cout << "Composite constructor called." << endl;
}

Client :: Client (Server& server_var)

       : client_data (25), server_ref (server_var)
{
        cout << "Client constructor called." << endl;
}

void Client :: client_function ()
{
        server_ref.server_function (client_data);
}
```

The Client constructor initializes the `Server` reference.

The `Client` constructor is passed the `Server` object (`server_object`) by reference. This makes `server_ref` an alias for `server_object` (follow the arrows).

This statement links `Client` and `Server`. The `Server` function is called using the `Server` reference (`server_ref`). `Client` data is passed through the argument list. Note that the dot (`.`) operator is used with a reference to call a member function.

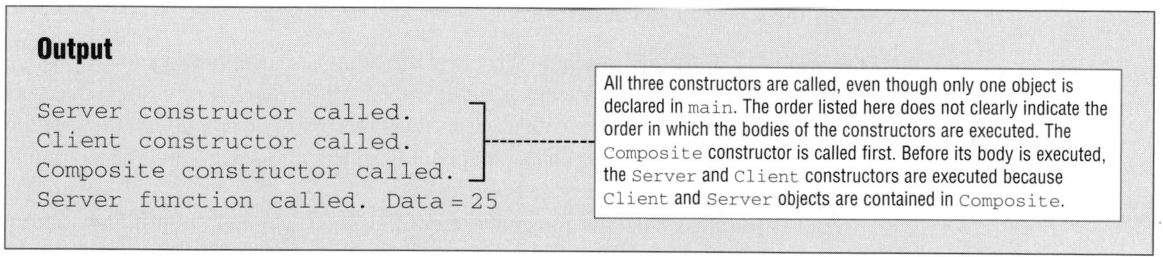
Output
Server constructor called.
Client constructor called.
Composite constructor called.
Server function called. Data = 25
All three constructors are called, even though only one object is declared in main. The order listed here does not clearly indicate the order in which the bodies of the constructors are executed. The Composite constructor is called first. Before its body is executed, the Server and Client constructors are executed because Client and Server objects are contained in Composite.

Description

Composition. Composition represents a "has a" relationship. "Has a" relationships are found quite commonly in object-oriented programming. For instance, if we were writing a program simulating the activities of a car, we would begin by creating a `Car` class. Other classes in the program could be `Wheel` and `Engine`. Objects of these classes would be contained within the `Car` class because a car "has a" wheel and an engine. This particular example is explained in more detail in Application Example 14.2.

The composition relationship in this lesson's program indicates that a `Composite` object "has a" `Client` object and a `Server` object. This relationship is programmed reasonably easily. First, in the `Composite` definition:

```
class Composite
{
        private:
                Server server_object;
                Client client_object;
        public:
                Composite ();
                void composite_function ();
};
```

`server_object` and `client_object` are private data members. Then, the `Composite` constructor initializes the two objects:

```
Composite :: Composite ()
          : client_object (&server_object)
{
      cout << "Composite constructor called." << endl;
}
```

In this code, the `Client` constructor takes an argument and is explicitly called by the initialization line. The `Server` constructor is called implicitly. The constructor for `server_object` is called first because it is listed before `client_object` in the definition of `Composite`. In general, the order of the constructor calls is in the order listed in the class definition. It is not necessary to explicitly call a constructor for all composition relationships. In this case, because we have both composition and a client-server relationship, explicitly calling the client constructor and passing the address of the server object is required.

Association. The "uses" or client-server relationship is a form of association, which is what we describe here. As we noted in the introduction, there is more than one way to program such a relationship. What we show is reasonably complex, but it is effective in that it keeps the server class independent of the client class and has a simple interface (connection) between the two classes.

The server class designer must create both an interface and an implementation. For instance, in the definition of `Server`

```
class Server
{
        public:
                Server ();
                void server_function (int);
};
```

the member function `server_function()` serves as both the interface and implementation. The argument list is the interface because it is through the argument list that data is transferred from a `Client` object to a `Server` object. The implementation is performed within the function body where calculations and other manipulations take place. Depending on the problem being solved, the argument list can be long or short, and the function body can do simple or complex manipulations. Note that a server class defined in this manner can be developed with little regard for the activities of the client class. This is desirable because it allows the server class designer to work reasonably independent from the client class designer.

The programming for the client class is a little more involved. The definition of the class

```
class Client
{
        private:
                int client_data;
                Server* server_ptr;
        public:
                Client (Server*);
                void client_function();
};
```

holds a pointer to a server class object, `server_ptr`. The data members contain sufficient information to make use of the server class through the server class interface. In this case, only an integer (`client_data`) is necessary because the server interface function (`server_function`) has only an integer in its argument list. Note that the `Client` constructor initializes the pointer to the server object (type `Server*` in the constructor argument list). Recall that the `Client` constructor is called in the initialization list of the `Composite` constructor. The process (of making `server_ptr` hold the address of `server_object`) is indicated by the arrows here:

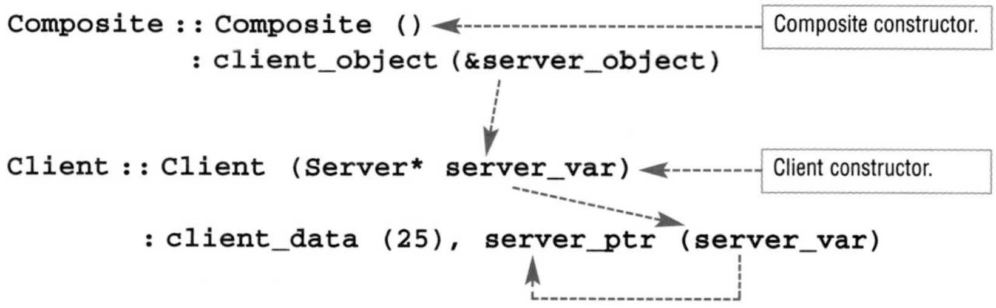

```
Composite :: Composite ()  <---------------- [Composite constructor.]
          : client_object (&server_object)

Client :: Client (Server* server_var)  <---- [Client constructor.]

        : client_data (25), server_ptr (server_var)
```

Note that it is all done within the initialization part of the `Composite` and `Client` constructors.

Figure 14.8 illustrates fundamentally what is done after declaring a single `Composite` object in `main` and calling the constructors (which initializes the `Client` object to hold the address of the `Server` object). The figure shows that the `Client` and `Server` objects are within the `Composite` object. Following the arrows from left to right, a `Composite` function is called in `main`. From the `Composite` function, a `Client` function is called. The `Client` object uses its pointer to the `Server` object to call the `Server` function and pass `Client` data through the argument list. The `Server` function performs the desired actions with the `Client` data and the process is complete.

Note that within the body of the `Client` function we use the address of `server_object` (which is stored in `server_ptr`) to call the `Server` function (`server_function`). Remember, as we saw in Lesson 11.7 when we call a function

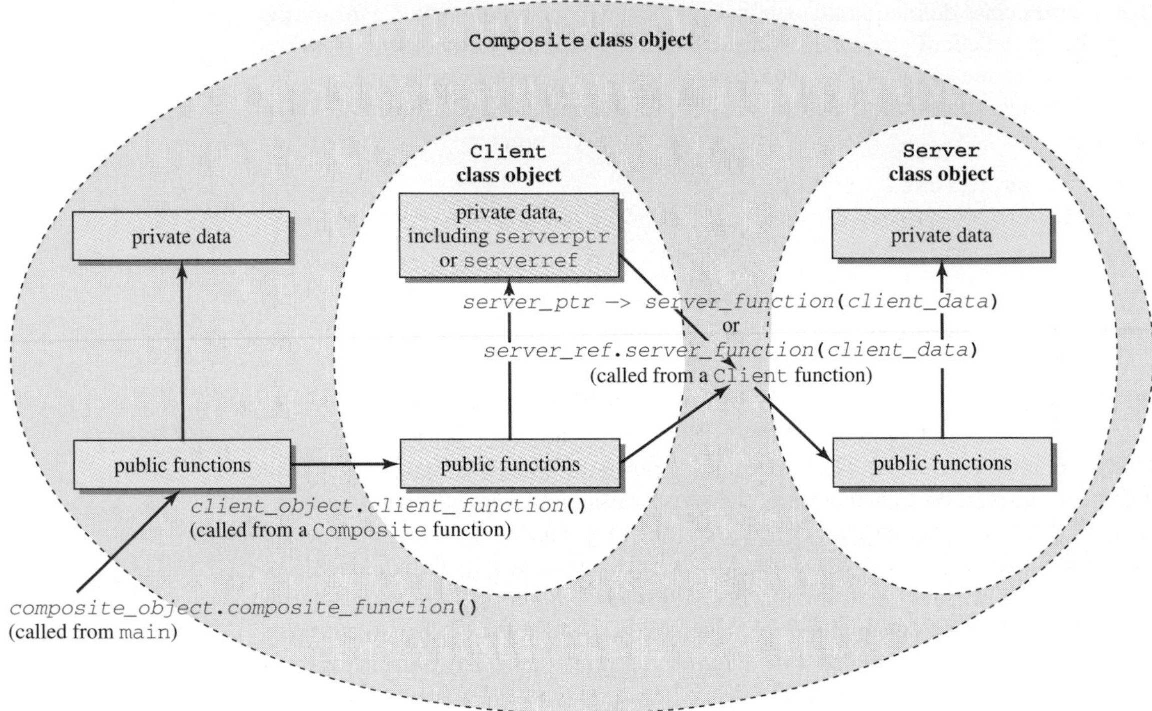

Figure 14.8

Illustration of actions (and access to data) of Lesson 14.7's program. A single composite object is declared in main. The notation next to the arrows (defined in the Description of this lesson) indicates the code needed to perform the access indicated by the arrows. Note that an arrow crossing an object boundary requires use of the object name or address.

with the *address* of an object we use the *arrow* operator. For instance, in the body of client_function(), the line

```
server_ptr -> server_function (client_data);
```

calls server_function with the server_object because server_ptr holds the address of server_object. It is equivalent to the line

```
server_object . server_function (client_data);
```

Note that we cannot use this line because server_object is not a member of Client (while server_ptr is a member). Remember, when using an *object* to call a member function use the *dot* operator, and when using an *address* of an object to call a member function use the *arrow* operator. This is easily remembered because address and arrow both begin with the letter a. Remember that the arrow operator consists of two symbols, - (minus) and > (greater than) with no space between. The arrow operator is designed for working with addresses stored in pointer variables.

Note also from Fig. 14.8 that whenever an action crosses object boundaries, the name (or address) of the object is required to be the invoking object in the code causing the action.

Using references. A reference can be used instead of a pointer in this lesson's program. The process is quite similar to that described for the pointer and will not be covered further. Read the annotations in the second source code for more information. Note, though, that the arrow operator is not used with references. Since a reference is an alias, using it is more like using the original object.

Use of `const`. To simplify the look of the program and focus attention on the creation of the association relationship, we have not specified any data members, functions, or objects as being `const`. However, for your own programs, you should use `const` where appropriate in a manner described in Lesson 14.3. In many cases, using `const` references is safer and less difficult to debug than pointers.

APPLICATION EXAMPLE 14.1 TRAFFIC ACCIDENT ANALYSIS

TOPICS

- Object-oriented design
- "Uses" (client-server) relationship
- Linear regression
- Numerical method example

Problem Statement

For a particular long highway it is believed that there is a correlation between the vehicle density (number of vehicles per 100 m) on the highway and the number of accidents that occur. From casual observation, the number of accidents has been found to increase with an increase in vehicle density up to a certain point. However, once the vehicle density exceeds a certain value, the average vehicle speed is reduced due to congestion, thereby reducing the number of accidents. To predict accident rates and as an aid to produce an improved highway design, we wish to develop equations relating the vehicle density to the number of accidents from observed data.

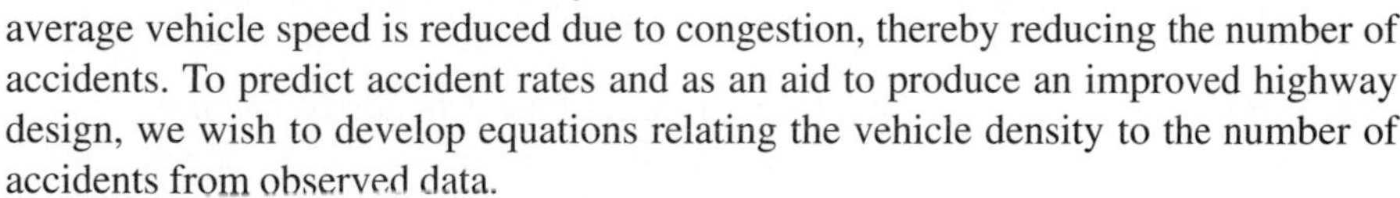

Our goal is to create two straight lines that represent a best fit through the data, one that rises until it reaches the vehicle density at the peak number of accidents and another that decreases from this point. Figure 14.9 illustrates an example of data collected (represented by the circles) and the best fit lines through the data.

The problem is to write a program that can create a best fit straight line through a set of (x, y) data points representing the traffic during the month of December. The points represent observed data with x being the vehicle density and y being the number of accidents. The program should print out a total of four values:

1. Slope of line 1 (m_1).
2. Intercept of line 1 (b_1).
3. Slope of line 2 (m_2).
4. Intercept of line 2 (b_2).

Use an object-oriented design with a reference connecting the classes. Note that the purpose of this example is to illustrate an object-oriented design of a program that performs technical type calculations.

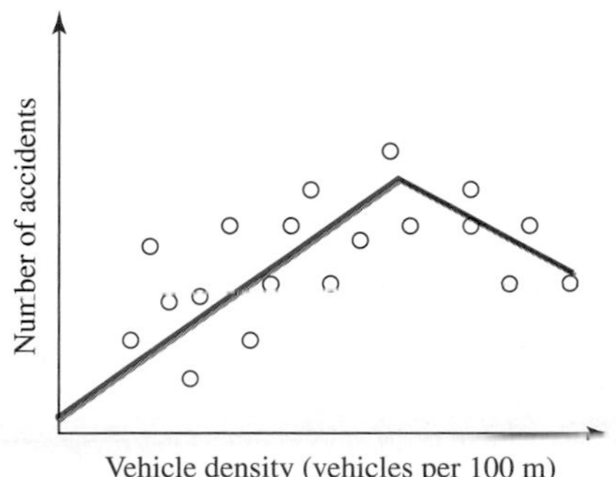

Figure 14.9

Number of accidents related to the vehicle density. Straight lines represent best fit through the data.

Solution

RELEVANT EQUATIONS

We will not go through the derivation (because it goes beyond the scope of this book) but just list the equations representing the slope and intercept of a best fit line. We define the following quantities:

$$\begin{aligned} n &= \text{number of points} \\ c &= \sum_{i=1}^{n} x_i \\ d &= \sum_{i=1}^{n} y_i \\ e &= \sum_{i=1}^{n} x_i^2 \\ f &= \sum_{i=1}^{n} y_i x_i \end{aligned} \tag{14.1}$$

Note that c is simply the sum of all the x values of the data points, and d is the sum of all the y values of the data points. The variable e is the sum of the squares of the x values, and f is the sum of the xy products of the data points. Therefore, these values, despite looking somewhat complicated, can be calculated relatively simply.

The slope (m) and intercept (b) of the best fit line are

$$\begin{aligned} m &= \frac{nf - cd}{ne - c^2} \\ b &= \frac{de - cf}{ne - c^2} \end{aligned} \tag{14.2}$$

SPECIFIC EXAMPLE

We will perform the calculations for the following data representing the month of December:

Data point	Vehicle density (x)	Number of accidents (y)
0	1.4	3
1	2.0	6
2	2.3	4
3	4.5	7
4	6.2	10
5	6.7	15
6	7.0	11
7	8.5	18
8	9.0	13
9	12.7	17
10	13.1	15
11	17.7	16
12	18.5	11
13	20.3	5

We note that the peak accident count is 18 (at point number 7). So, we use points 0–7 to create one line and points 7–13 to create another line. For the first line,

c = sum of the x values $= 1.4 + 2.0 + \cdots + 7.0 + 8.5 = 38.6$
d = sum of the y values $= 3 + 6 + \cdots + 11 + 18 = 74$

To get the value of e, we first square each of the x values and sum them:

$$e = 1.4^2 + 2.0^2 + \cdots + 7.0^2 + 8.5^2 = 236.08$$

To get the value of f, we first get the product of each x, y pair and then sum them.

$$f = 1.4(3) + 2.0(6) + \cdots + 7.0(11) + 8.5(18) = 449.4$$

For the second line:

$$c = 8.5 + 9.0 + \cdots + 18.5 + 20.3 = 99.8$$
$$d = 18 + 13 + \cdots + 11 + 5 = 95$$
$$e = 8.5^2 + 9.0^2 + \cdots + 18.5^2 + 20.3^2 = 1553.78$$
$$f = 8.5(18) + 9.0(13) + \cdots + 18.5(11) + 20.3(5) = 1270.6$$

We can put these values into the equations for m and b giving:

$$m_1 = \frac{8(449.4) - 38.6(74)}{8(236.08) - (38.6)^2} = 1.853$$

$$b_1 = \frac{74(236.08) - 38.6(449.4)}{8(236.08) - (38.6)^2} = 0.3087$$

$$m_2 = \frac{7(1270.6) - 99.8(95)}{7(1553.78) - (99.8)^2} = -0.6403$$

$$b_2 = \frac{95(1553.78) - 99.8(1270.6)}{7(1553.78) - (99.8)^2} = 22.70$$

Thus, the equations of the best fit lines ($y = mx + b$) are:

Line 1	$y = 1.853x + 0.3087$	applies from $x = 1.4$ to $x = 8.5$
Line 2	$y = -0.6403x + 22.70$	applies from $x = 8.5$ to $x = 20.3$

CLASSES AND OBJECTS

We must consider what our classes should be, what they should consist of, and how they should interact. Before you write each program, try to use as much foresight as you can in developing the classes and how they interact. But, be aware that program design is an iterative process. You may need to make repeated modifications to your original plan as you go along.

- First, what should be our classes? Because we are dealing with mathematical concepts and representations of data, the classes and objects that we use are not as obvious as they might be when we are representing tangible objects. One way to help envision the necessary classes is to distinguish between the separate parts of the problem being considered. In our analysis of traffic accidents, we have the accident data evaluation (which involves reading the data file and finding the maximum number of accidents) and the linear regression part (which involves determining the slope and intercept of the best fit line).

Therefore, a good start at developing the classes would be with these two that we call class `Traffic` and class `Linear_regress`.

- Second, of what should the classes consist? The data members should, as a minimum, be capable of defining the class and connecting to other classes. Beyond that, the data members should represent other useful attributes. The function members should be able to work with the data members and interact with other classes as needed.

  For instance, the `Traffic` class consists of its data points. Therefore, as a minimum, the class should have an array of data points as its member. In addition, for this problem, we need the array index that gives the maximum number of accidents and the number of data points. The function members should be able to initialize the data by reading the input file, find the array index at the maximum number of accidents, and interact with the `Linear_regress` class to get the two lines.

  The `Linear_regress` class needs to know the number of points with which it is working, it needs access to the points being evaluated, and it needs the data for a line through those points. Therefore, its data members would be the data points (or rather, the address of the beginning of the array of data points), the number of data points, and slope and intercept of the line created. The `Linear_regress` class, as we use it here, only needs to create the best-fit line from the data, so, to keep it simple, we use only one function member.

  Note that the classes use points and lines. In Application Example 8.1, we described simple `struct`s of type `Point` and `Line` that contain only data members (no function members). In this program we choose to use these as classes, which means that `Point` and `Line` objects can be data members of `Linear_regress` and `Traffic`.

  Using `Point` and `Line` as classes allows us to speak of objects of these classes, which simplifies the discussion. Also, even though `Point` and `Line` have public data members, we do not violate encapsulation because these classes do not have function members.

- Third, how should the classes interact? The relationships between the classes are shown in the diagram in Fig. 14.10. From this, it can be seen that the `Linear_regress` class contains an ordinary data member of type `Line`, and a member function that can be used by `Traffic` to perform the regression. `Traffic` contains an array of type `Point` and a pointer to the `Linear_regress` class. Note that `Linear_regress` is the server class and `Traffic` is the client class. Figure 14.11 shows how objects of the class interact.

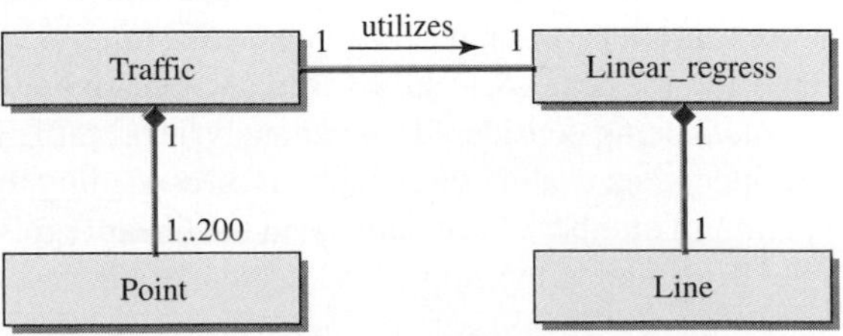

Figure 14.10

Interaction of classes and objects for traffic analysis program.

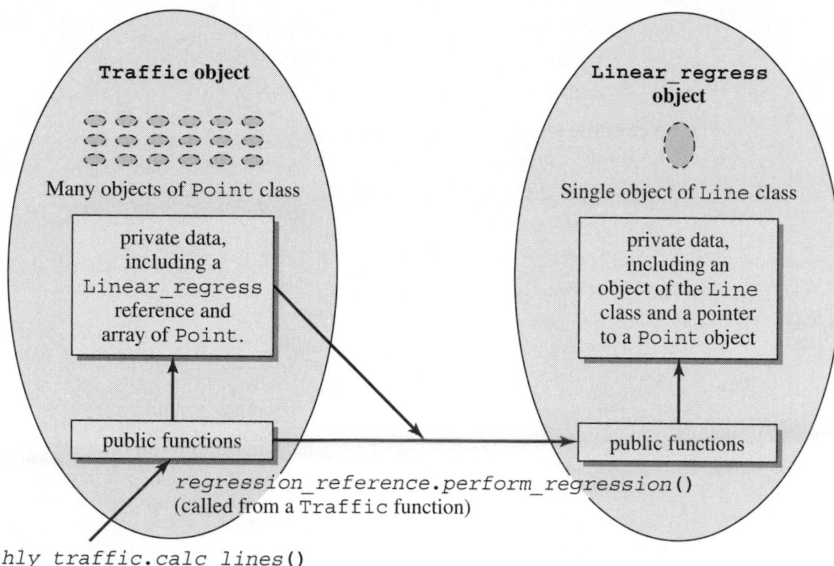

Figure 14.11

Illustration of client-server interaction between Traffic and Linear_regress.

Source Code

To save space, we have described the algorithm and code segments in the source code annotations. Read these annotations to see how to convert the linear regression equations into code. For simplicity, we have put all the regression code into the function perform_regression. Read this function to see how to program a regression analysis. Within this function, observe the use of Eqns. 14.1 and 14.2.

```
#include <iostream>
#include <fstream>
using namespace std;

class Point
{
        public:
                double x, y;
};

class Line
{
        public:
                double m, b;
};

class Linear_regress
{
        private:
                const Point* fit_pts;
                Line fit_line;
                int num_fit_pts;
```

The Point class contains the public data members x and y representing a point's coordinates.

The Line class contains the public data members m and b representing a line's slope and intercept.

The Linear_regress class contains a pointer to hold the address of the array of points being considered. The const qualifier before Point indicates that the contents of the array cannot be changed by the pointer. This data member is not required, because the address of the array is passed through the perform_regression() argument list. It is a data member to simplify programming.

This Line object contains the slope and intercept of the best fit line.

To work with the array, we need to use the number of data points.

```
        public:
                void perform_regression (const Point*, int, int);
};

class Traffic
{
        private:
                enum {MAX_NUM_ACCID_PTS = 200};
                Point accid_pts[MAX_NUM_ACCID_PTS];
                int index_at_max_accid, num_accid_pts;
                const Linear_regress& regression_reference;
        public:
                Traffic (const Linear_regress&);
                void read_data ();
                void find_index_at_max_accid ();
                void calc_lines ();
};
```

This function performs the regression calculations and prints the results.

This is an array with a maximum size of 200 data points.

These data member names are self-explanatory.

The `const regression_reference` is initialized in the constructor and used in the `calc_lines` function to call the `perform_regression` function in a manner shown in Lesson 14.7. This form connects classes `Linear_regress` and `Traffic`.

The pointer variable `array_beginning` receives the address of the beginning of the array of data points.

```
void Linear_regress :: perform_regression (const Point* array_beginning,
                                           int low_subscript, int high_subscript)
```

For the first best-fit line, `low_subscript` is 0 and `high_subscript` is `index_at_max_accid`. For the second best-fit line, `low_subscript` is `index_at_max_accid` and `high_subscript` is `num_accid_pts - 1`.

```
{
        double c, d, e, f, n;
        int i;

        c = d = e = f = 0.0;

        num_fit_pts = high_subscript - low_subscript + 1;
        fit_pts = array_beginning + low_subscript;

        for (i = 0; i < num_fit_pts; i++)
                {
                c += fit_pts[i].x;
                d += fit_pts[i].y;
                e += fit_pts[i].x * fit_pts[i].x;
                f += fit_pts[i].x * fit_pts[i].y;
                }
```

Before the loop, we initialize all the summation variables to 0.0.

The number of points is determined by the difference in the subscripts passed through the argument list.

Using pointer arithmetic, we set the data member `fit_pts` to point to the first element in the range to be fit.

Looping over the range of data points we are considering. Note that `num_fit_pts` is a data member of the `Linear_regress` class and therefore does not need to be declared or passed through the argument list.

Eqns. 14.1 which are in summation form and therefore easily computed using a loop and the `+=` operator. Note that we can use 1-D array notation with the pointer variable `fit_pts`.

```
        n = num_fit_pts;
        fit_line.m = (n * f - c * d)/(n * e - c * c);
        fit_line.b = (d * e - c * f)/(n * e - c * c);
```

Eqns. 14.2. Since `Line` has data members `m` and `b`, we must use the dot operator. So, we use `fit_line.m` and `fit_line.b` for the slope and intercepts of the line, respectively. Also, `fit_line` is a data member of the `Linear_regress` class, so it need not be declared or passed through the argument list.

```
        cout << "The best fit line:" << endl << "   m=" << fit_line.m << endl
             << " b=" << fit_line.b << endl << endl;

}
```

Printing the output.

```
Traffic :: Traffic (const Linear_regress& regress_ref_var)
        : regression_reference (regress_ref_var),
        index_at_max_accid (0), num_accid_pts (0)
{
        int i;
        for (i = 0; i < MAX_NUM_ACCID_PTS; i++)
                    {
                    accid_pts[i].x = 0;
                    accid_pts[i].y = 0;
                    }
}
```

The `regression_reference` is initialized to the argument list variable in the constructor. The other data members are initialized in the constructor also.

```
void Traffic :: read_data ()
{
        int i;

        ifstream infile("C:\\DATA\\BESTLINE.DAT");

        i=0;
        do
                    {
                    infile >> accid_pts[i].x;
                    infile >> accid_pts[i].y;
                    i++;
                    }  while (!infile.eof ());

        num_accid_pts = i - 1;
}
```

Open the input file.

Reading the `x` and `y` values from the data file. Note that `accid_pts[i].x` refers to the `i`th element of the `accid_pts` array. The `x` refers to the `x` data member because `accid_pts[]` is type `Point`.

Continue reading until the end of file has been encountered.

We can use `i` to calculate the number of points in the file.

```
void Traffic :: find_index_at_max_accid ()
{
        int i;
        double max;
```

Function to determine the array index at the maximum number of accidents.

```
        max = accid_pts[0].y;
        for (i = 1; i < num_accid_pts; i++)
                {
                if (accid_pts[i].y >= max)
                        {
                        max = accid_pts[i].y;
                        index_at_max_accid = i;
                        }
                }

}

void Traffic :: calc_lines ()
{
        cout << "Line before maximum accidents." << endl;
        regression_reference . perform_regression(accid_pts, 0,
          index_at_max_accid);

        cout << "Line after maximum accidents." << endl;
        regression_reference.perform_regression (accid_pts, index_at_max_accid,
          num_accid_pts-1);
}

int main ( )
{
        Linear_regress regression_object;
        Traffic        monthly_traffic (regression_object);

        monthly_traffic.read_data ();
        monthly_traffic.find_index_at_max_accid ();
        monthly_traffic.calc_lines ();
}
```

Initially set the maximum to be the first `y` value in the list.

If another `y` value is greater than the maximum, then we create a new maximum and save the index, `i`, of the new maximum value. After executing this function, `index_at_max_accid` has the value we want. This is a data member of class `Traffic`, so we need not return a value from the function.

We pass the address of the beginning of the entire array of data points to the `perform_regression` function.

The reference to the `Linear_regress` object (`regression_reference`) is used to call `perform_regression` from this `Traffic` function. This function connects classes `Traffic` and `Linear_regress`. For the first call, the array indices passed are 0 and `index_at_max_accid`.

For the second call, the array indices passed are `index_at_max_accid` and the index of the last data point (`num_accid_pts-1`).

The `regression_ref` becomes an alias for `regression_object` in the `Traffic` constructor.

The `Traffic` functions are called.

Output (From Program Run with Input Data Given in Specific Example)

```
Line before maximum accidents.
The best fit line:
 m=1.853115
 b=0.308719
```

```
Line after maximum accidents.
The best fit line:
 m=-0.640318
 b=22.70053
```

Comments

Note that there is no class that fills the role of `Composite` in Lesson 14.7. The actions that would take place in a `Composite` function occur in `main`.

Note that we could have made `Linear_regress` a `friend` of `Traffic` and used the `Linear_regress` functions to directly manipulate the `Traffic` data. This design would limit flexibility of the program in allowing for future modifications. We also could have made accessor functions connect the classes to create a simpler form of a "uses" relationship. However, this is quite clumsy. In summary, there are other ways this program could have been written. However, the design shown here has many advantages over the others.

Modification Exercises

1. Modify the program to request a user to type a vehicle density and have the program print the corresponding number of accidents according to the best fit line.
2. Modify the program to request a user to type a number of accidents and have the program print the corresponding vehicle density (two values) from the best fit lines.
3. Modify the program to accept data from five different months (using five objects) and print the results for each.

APPLICATION EXAMPLE 14.2 AUTOMOBILE SIMULATION

TOPICS

- Object-oriented design
- Constructor-functions

Problem Statement

Write a program that roughly simulates the actions of a car using an object-oriented design. Make the car (with an engine, spark plugs, steering wheel, and wheels) inflate its tires, start the engine, and drive to the right. Print a statement indicating that each task has been performed.

Solution

RELEVANT EQUATIONS

No equations are involved. The primary purpose of this example is to illustrate the interaction of objects of different classes.

SPECIFIC EXAMPLE

We will use a car that has 4 wheels and 6 spark plugs. When the tires are inflated, the program will print "Tire inflated" four times. When the engine starts, the program will print "Spark plug ignited" six times. When the steering wheel turns the wheels to the right, the program will print "Wheel turned right" four times.

CLASSES AND OBJECTS

Figure 14.12 shows a class diagram for a program that simulates the actions of a car. The classes, all enclosed in rectangles, are `Car`, `Engine`, `Spark_plug`, `Steering_wheel`, and `Wheel`. Because a car "has a" engine, steering wheel, and wheel, the class `Car` has three solid diamonds with lines connected to classes `Engine`, `Steering_wheel`, and `Wheel`. Because an engine "has a" spark plug, the class `Engine` has one solid diamond with a line leading to class `Spark_plug`. The fact that there is one car with four wheels is indicated with the numbers next to the lines connecting these two. Also, there is one engine with six spark plugs.

The simplest class is `Spark_plug` because it has only one connection to it, and that connection indicates that `Engine` "has a" `Spark_plug` (which means that `Spark_plug` contains no objects or pointers to objects of other classes). The class data members, therefore, are only spark plug attributes, and the function members perform only spark plug activities. The class is:

```
class Spark_plug
{
        private:
                double gap_size;
        public:
                Spark_plug ();
                void ignite ();
};
```

For simplicity, we have included only one spark plug attribute, `gap_size`, and one action, `ignite`. Others could be added for a more thorough simulation. A constructor function, whose purpose is to initialize `gap_size` is included.

Because `Engine` "has a" `Spark_plug`, the `Engine` class has a data member that is type `Spark_plug`. The class is:

```
class Engine
{
        private:
                Spark_plug spark_plug[6];
                int horsepower;
```

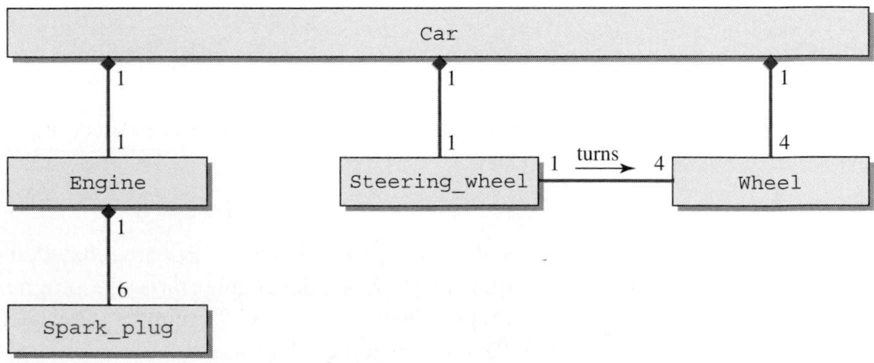

Figure 14.12
Class diagram illustrating the interaction between classes of a car simulation program.

```
        public:
                Engine ();
                void begin_ignition ();
    };
```

Note that because the engine has six spark plugs, the Spark_plug data member is an array of six Spark_plug objects. We will see that the begin_ignition function uses the Spark_plug objects to call the ignite() function of the Spark_plug class. For simplicity, only one data member (horsepower), the constructor function, and the begin_ignition() function member are included. The constructor function initializes horsepower.

The class diagram indicates that the Car class has objects of type Engine, Wheel, and Steering_wheel. The class is:

```
    class Car
    {
        private:
                Wheel wheel[4];
                Engine the_engine;
                Steering_wheel the_steering_wheel;

        public:
                Car ();
                void prepare_tires ();
                void turn_ignition_key ();
                void drive_to_right ();
    };
```

Note that there is an array of four Wheel objects because the car has four wheels. For simplicity, no other attributes of a car, such as color or model are included. We will see that the function members use the objects of the other classes to call functions of the other classes. The function prepare_tires() calls a Wheel function with the Wheel objects, turn_ignition_key() calls an Engine function with the Engine object, and drive_to_right() calls a Steering_wheel function with the Steering_wheel object.

The most complex relationship occurs between classes Steering_wheel and Wheel. The fact that the steering wheel turns the wheels means that classes Steering_wheel and Wheel should interact directly. This is indicated in the class diagram with an arrow from Steering_wheel to Wheel. Above the arrow is the word "turns" that indicates the action that Steering_wheel objects perform on Wheel objects. Our car program can work just like the real world model if Wheel has a public member function (that we name turn_right) that is called from a Steering_Wheel member function (named rotate_clockwise). The relationship between Steering_wheel and Wheel is similar to the "uses" relationship of Lesson 14.7. Here, we program this relationship into our car simulation program. Figure 14.13 has another illustration of the representation of the objects. This figure shows how main calls a Car function, which calls a Steering_wheel function, which calls a Wheel function for each of the four wheels.

Note that a Steering_wheel function cannot simply call a Wheel function. It needs to be able to refer to a particular Wheel object when calling a Wheel function.

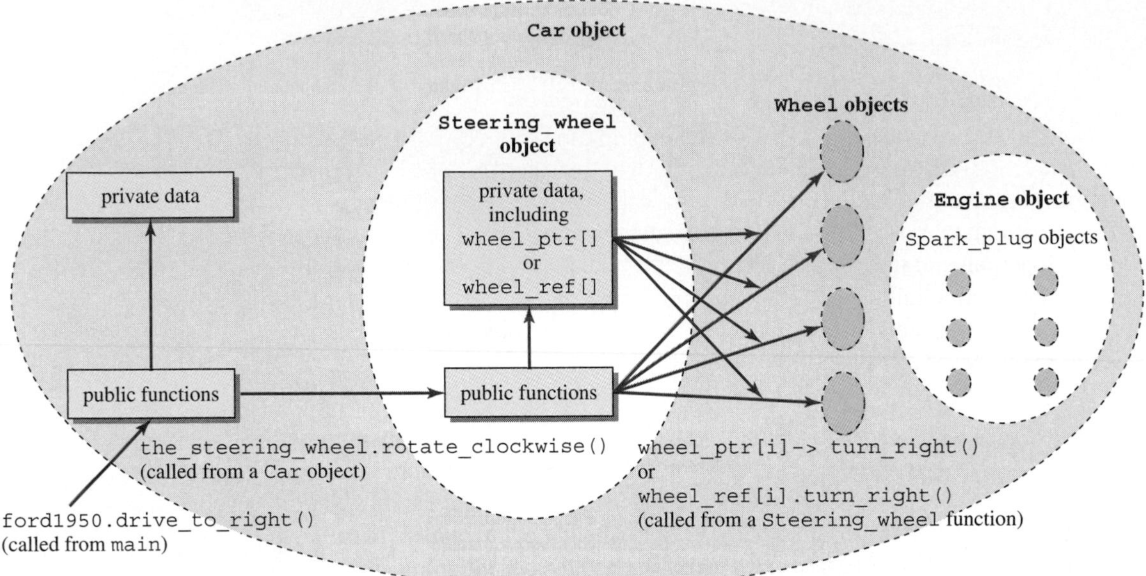

Figure 14.13

Illustration of `Car` object and contained objects. The `Steering_wheel` object turns the `Wheel` objects in a manner similar to the client-server relationship described in Lesson 14.7.

One way for a `Steering_wheel` function to refer to a particular `Wheel` object, is with a `Steering_wheel` data member that is a *pointer* to a `Wheel` object. (Note: We do not want `Steering_wheel` to contain a `Wheel` *object* because a steering wheel does not "have a" wheel; a steering wheel turns a wheel.) Because each wheel needs to be turned, an array of four pointers (type `Wheel*`) is a member of the `Steering_wheel` class. The two class definitions are:

```
class Wheel
{
        private:
                double size;
        public:
                Wheel ();
                void inflate_tires ();
                void turn_right ();
};
```

The `turn_right()` public member function is called from a function of the `Steering_wheel` class. This function serves as a connection between the `Steering_wheel` and `Wheel` classes.

```
class Steering_wheel
{
        private:
                const Wheel* wheel_ptr[4];
                double diameter;
        public:
                Steering_wheel (const Wheel*);
                void rotate_clockwise ();
};
```

For a `Steering_wheel` class function (`rotate_clockwise`) to call a `Wheel` function (`turn_right`) for each wheel, it needs the address of each `Wheel` object stored in the `wheel_ptr[]` array. This is done by passing the address of the beginning of the `wheel_ptr[]` array through the argument list to the `Steering_wheel` constructor. Note that we have used `const Wheel*`. This means that after the constructor has been called, what is pointed to cannot change.

Note that `Steering_wheel` has an array of four pointers called `wheel_ptr[]`.

Also note that `Wheel` has one attribute as a data member (`size`) and a second member function (`inflate_tires`). `Steering_wheel` has one attribute (`diameter`) as a data member. Each class has a constructor function.

ALGORITHM

The problem is not complex in an technical sense. The steps in the analysis are:

1. Prepare the tires.
   a. Inflate the tires.
2. Turn ignition key.
   a. Begin engine ignition.
   b. Ignite the spark plugs.
3. Drive to the right.
   a. Rotate the steering wheel clockwise.
   b. Turn each wheel to the right.

The source code executes the steps. Note that steps 1, 2, and 3 correspond to `Car` functions. Steps 1a and 3b are `Wheel` functions. Step 2a is an `Engine` function. Step 2b is a `Spark_plug` function, and step 3a is a `Steering_wheel` function. Read the source code and pay particular attention to the `drive_to_right()` function of class `Car` and the `Steering_wheel` constructor. This function is important to getting the `Steering_wheel` and `Wheel` classes to work together properly.

Source Code

```
#include <iostream>
using namespace std;
/////////////////////////////////////////////////////////////////////// Classes

class Spark_plug
{
        private:
                double gap_size;
        public:
                Spark_plug ();
                void ignite ();
};



class Engine
{
        private:
                Spark_plug  spark_plug[6];
                int horsepower;
```

Because an engine has six spark plugs, `Engine` contains an array of six spark plug objects.

```
        public:
                Engine ();
                void begin_ignition ();
};


class Wheel
{

        private:
                double size;
        public:
                Wheel ();
                void inflate_tires ();
                void turn_right ();

};


class Steering_wheel
{

        private:
                const Wheel* wheel_ptr[4];
                double diameter;
        public:
                Steering_wheel (const Wheel*);
                void rotate_clockwise ();

};


class Car
{

        private:
                Wheel wheel[4];
                Engine the_engine;
                Steering_wheel the_steering_wheel;


        public:
                Car ();
                void prepare_tires ();
                void turn_ignition_key ();
                void drive_to_right ();

};
```

These are the two classes that interact in a "uses" manner. `Steering_wheel` "turns" `Wheel`.

The function `turn_right()` is called by `rotate_clockwise()` of the `Steering_wheel` class.

The `wheel_ptr[]` array of pointers is used to call `turn_right()` (from class `Wheel`) from `rotate_clockwise()`.

These data members are types of other classes. The `Car` class has a "has a" relationship with these classes.

These functions are the ones that make the car go. These are called to make the simulation.

```
/////////////////////////////////////////////////////////////// Car functions

Car :: Car ()
    : the_steering_wheel (wheel)
{
}


void Car :: prepare_tires ()
{
        int i;
        for (i = 0; i < 4; i++) wheel[i].inflate_tires ();
}


void Car :: turn_ignition_key ()
{
        the_engine.begin_ignition ();
}


void Car :: drive_to_right ()
{
        the_steering_wheel.rotate_clockwise ();
}


/////////////////////////////////////////////// Steering_wheel functions


Steering_wheel :: Steering_wheel (const Wheel* wheel_var)
                : diameter(40)
{
        int i;
        for(i = 0; i < 4; i++) wheel_ptr[i] = wheel_var + i;
}
```

Car constructor.

The `Steering_wheel` constructor is called with the "wheel", address (of the beginning of the `wheel[]` array) as the argument. See Fig. 14.13 and Lesson 14.7 to understand why.

Because the car "has" wheels and an engine (as shown in the class diagram), we call `Wheel` and `Engine` functions directly from `Car` functions (`prepare_tires` and `turn_ignition_key`) using `Wheel` and `Engine` objects. This is allowed because `wheel[]` and `the_engine` are private data members of `Car`.

The `Car` function (`drive_to_right`) calls a `Steering_wheel` function (`rotate_clockwise`), using its `Steering_wheel` object, (`the_steering_wheel`).

The `Steering_wheel` constructor is passed an address to a `Wheel` object. According to the constructor call, `wheel_var` is passed the address of the first member of the `wheel[]` array.

The `Steering_wheel` constructor initializes the `wheel_ptr[]` array. This loop stores `wheel_var` into `wheel_ptr[0]`. Pointer arithmetic is used on the right side of the assignment statement. Remember, adding 1 to an address adds the number of bytes of storage for a single object. Adding 2 adds the number of bytes for two objects. In this manner, we correctly store the addresses into the array of addresses, the `wheel_ptr[]` array which is a member of the `Steering_wheel` class.

```
void Steering_wheel :: rotate_clockwise ( )
{
        int i;
        for (i = 0; i < 4; i++)  wheel_ptr[i] -> turn_right ();
}


//////////////////////////////////////////////////////////  Engine functions

Engine :: Engine ()
      : horsepower (400)
{
}


void Engine :: begin_ignition ()
{
        int i;
        for (i = 0; i < 6; i++) spark_plug[i].ignite ();
}

//////////////////////////////////////////////////////////  Wheel functions
Wheel :: Wheel ()
      : size (15)
{
}

void Wheel :: inflate_tires ()
{
               cout << "Tire inflated." << endl;
}

void Wheel :: turn_right ()
{
               cout << "Wheel turned right." << endl;
}


//////////////////////////////////////////////////////////  Spark_plug functions
Spark_plug :: Spark_plug ()
          : gap_size (1.2)
{
}


void Spark_plug :: ignite ()
{
       cout << "Spark plug ignited." << endl;
}
```

The `Wheel` function (`turn_right`) is called for each wheel using the address of each wheel object (stored in `wheel_ptr[]`).

The engine ignites each of the spark plugs. So, the `Engine` function (`begin_ignition`) calls the `Spark_plug` function (`ignite`) with each of the `spark_plug` objects.

The `cout` statements in these functions simply indicate that the function has been executed.

```
/////////////////////////////////////////////////////////////////////////  main

int main ( )
{
        Car ford1950;
        ford1950.prepare_tires ();
        ford1950.turn_ignition_key ();
        ford1950.drive_to_right ();
}
```

Declaring a car object causes the Steering_wheel, Engine, Spark_plug (6 times), and Wheel (4 times) constructors to be called.

Function prepare_tires calls function inflate_tires.

Function turn_ignition_key calls function begin_ignition which calls function ignite.

Function drive_to_right calls function rotate_clockwise which calls function turn_right.

The main function serves as the driver for our program. It creates a car object and calls the Car functions to simulate the car actions.

Output

```
Tire inflated.
Tire inflated.
Tire inflated.
Tire inflated.
Spark plug ignited.
Spark plug ignited.
Spark plug ignited.
Spark plug ignited.
Spark plug ignited.
Spark plug ignited.
Wheel turned right.
Wheel turned right.
Wheel turned right.
Wheel turned right.
```

Comments

You should try to follow the sequence of operations of the program. Beginning in main, follow the execution with the declaration of the Car object ford1950. This calls the Car constructor, but since Car has Wheel, Engine (which has Spark_plug objects), and Steering_wheel objects as private data members, the constructors for all these classes are also called with the initiation of the Car object.

Then function prepare_tires() is called, and it calls inflate_tires(). Next, turn_ignition_key() calls begin_ignition() which calls ignite(). Lastly, drive_to_right() calls rotate_clockwise() which calls turn_right().

This is a complex program to perform relatively simple tasks. However, it illustrates what is involved in object-oriented design. One advantage is that once the design is set up, it is straightforward to add new objects and have them interact properly with other objects. For instance, we could easily add headlight objects or others to our car object.

TABLE 14.6 — Table of variables for the program. All this data is contained in a single `Car` object

Name	Type		Address	Value
ford1950.the_engine.spark_plug[0].gap_size	Car :: Engine :: Spark_plug ::	double	FFB4	1.2
ford1950.the_engine.spark_plug[1].gap_size			FFBC	1.2
ford1950.the_engine.spark_plug[2].gap_size			FFC4	1.2
ford1950.the_engine.spark_plug[3].gap_size			FFCC	1.2
ford1950.the_engine.spark_plug[4].gap_size			FFD4	1.2
ford1950.the_engine.spark_plug[5].gap_size			FFDC	1.2
ford1950.the_engine.horsepower	Car :: Engine::	int	FFA0	400
ford1950.wheel[0].size	Car :: Wheel::	double	FF94	15
ford1950.wheel[1].size			FF9C	15
ford1950.wheel[2].size			FFA4	15
ford1950.wheel[3].size			FFAC	15
ford1950.the_steering_wheel.wheel_ptr[0]	Car :: Steering_wheel ::	Wheel*	FF86	FF94
ford1950.the_steering_wheel.wheel_ptr[1]			FF88	FF9C
ford1950.the_steering_wheel.wheel_ptr[2]			FF8A	FFA4
ford1950.the_steering_wheel.wheel_ptr[3]			FF8C	FFAC
ford1950.the_steering_wheel.diameter	Car :: Steering_wheel ::	double	FFEE	40

You should also realize that the declaration of the `Car` object (`ford1950`) reserves space for 11 `doubles`, 1 `int`, and 4 pointers! This is because a `car` object includes 6 values of spark plug gap size, 1 value of engine horsepower, 4 values of wheel size, 4 pointers to the wheels, and 1 value of the steering wheel diameter. Had we declared a second car object (like `ford2000`), space for an additional 11 `doubles`, 1 `int`, and 4 pointers would have been reserved.

The data items used in this program are all shown in Table 14.6. Note that we have shown the types (first column) with all the classes (for instance, `Car :: Engine :: Spark_plug` for a `Spark_plug` object) but ending in a basic C++ data type such as `int`, `double`, or pointer (in this case `Wheel*`). In other words, although a class may contain other classes, only a fundamental data type is stored in memory.

Observe from Table 14.6 that the `Steering_wheel` wheel pointers point to the first data members (`size`) of the wheel objects (because these represent the beginnings of the wheel objects). The end result is that this single `Car` object has the information and connections (pointers) to simulate car activities. One can see that if we were to simulate the connection between the brake and the brake lights, that `Car` would have a class `Brake` that contains two pointers to objects of a class `Brake_lights`.

Modification Exercises

1. Create a `Mirror` class and indicate that the mirror has been adjusted properly before starting the car.
2. Add functions so that the car can turn left and go straight.
3. Add an `Odometer` class that connects directly to class `Wheel`. (For inheritance, make two trip odometers and a total mileage odometer.)
4. After having added all the previous classes, have the user of the program direct the car. For instance, give the user the freedom to go straight then turn right. The program should indicate that the instructions have been followed.
5. Add a windshield wiper switch and a `Windshield_wiper` class to the program. Car has a "has a" relationship with both classes. The two new classes should associate with one another.

LESSON EXERCISES

LESSON 14.1 EXERCISES

1. True or false:

   a. A destructor function is called when an object is declared.

   b. A copy constructor is a constructor with an argument that is a reference to an object of the class.

   c. When pointers are used as data members, the default copy constructor will not likely be the correct way to make a copy of an object.

   d. A destructor function has the name of the class followed by ~.

   e. If we do not release memory during execution, we run the risk of running out of memory.

2. Write a program that creates a `Traffic_light` class. Use a pointer data member and `new` to create an array of connecting traffic lights (the ones nearby). Declare four objects and use a copy constructor (not the default copy constructor) to initialize two of the objects. Print the data members.

Solutions

1. a. false
   b. true
   c. true
   d. false
   e. true

LESSON 14.2 EXERCISES

1. True or false:

   a. Static data members can be manipulated by static functions only.

   b. If static data is declared in a class, static functions must also be declared.

   c. Static data members are shared among all objects of a class.

   d. The keyword `static` appears in the function declarator for static member functions.

   e. Static member functions can manipulate member data that is not static.

2. Write a program that has a `Consultant` class. Create 10 consultant objects. Invite each consultant to a meeting. Use a static data member to keep track of the number of consultants participating in the meeting.

Solutions

1. a. false
   b. false
   c. true
   d. false
   e. false

LESSON 14.3 EXERCISES

1. True or false:

   a. Constant ordinary data members must be initialized in the class definition.

   b. Constant pointer data members do not need to be initialized in the constructor function initialization list.

   c. We cannot change the alias for a reference once it has been initialized.

   d. We cannot change the value of the variable aliased using a reference.

   e. A constant object's data members automatically are all constant.

Solutions

1. a. false
   b. false
   c. true
   d. false
   e. true

LESSON 14.4 EXERCISES

1. True or false:

   a. Friendship is granted by a class in the class definition.

   b. The keyword `friend` is included in a `friend` function definition.

   c. A `friend` function can access all data members of the granting class.

   d. Overuse of `friend` functions may indicate a poor program design.

   e. Member functions of one class cannot be friends of another class.

2. Write a program with classes `Fahrenheit` and `Celsius`. Make a function called `add_degrees` a friend of both classes. Have this function return the sum of two temperature measurements in Rankine degrees.

Solutions

1. a. true
   b. false
   c. true
   d. true
   e. false

LESSON 14.5 EXERCISES

1. True or false:

   a. The use of `friend` classes is controversial.

   b. When using friends, it is good practice to have a friend's list at the beginning of the class definition.

   c. A forward declaration of a class means that it will be a `friend` class.

   d. Granting a class friendship means that the granting class's objects can access the private data members of the friend class.

   e. Granting a class friendship means that the friend class's objects can access the private data members of the granting class.

2. Write a program with two classes, `Professor` and `Secretary`. Create an array containing the true/false solutions to an exam with 10 questions. Make class `Secretary` a friend of class `Professor` and allow the `secretary` object to modify the exam solutions.

Solutions

1. a. true
   b. true
   c. false
   d. false
   e. true

LESSON 14.6 EXERCISES

1. True or false:

   a. All overloaded operators must be friends of a class.

   b. There is no difference between overloading a binary and a unary operator.

c. The `++` operator can be overloaded to be a binary operator.

d. All C++ operators can be overloaded.

e. We can make the `+` operator perform subtraction.

2. Modify this lesson's program to include overloading operators `>` and `--`.

Solutions

1. a. false
b. false
c. false
d. false
e. true

LESSON 14.7 EXERCISES

1. True or false:

a. We can write code in the Unified Modeling Language in the same manner that we write code in the C++ language.

b. Composition is the name for an "is a" relationship between classes.

c. There is only one way to write a client-server relationship.

d. Class diagrams help program design.

e. In one type of client-server relationship, the client class contains a pointer to a server object.

2. Write a program that creates a client-server relationship using a local object in a client class member function.

3. Write a program that creates a client-server relationship by passing a server object through the argument list to a client class member function.

4. Write a program that creates a client-server relationship using accessor functions of the server class to pass values to a client class member function.

Solutions

1. a. false
b. false
c. false
d. true
e. true

APPLICATION EXERCISES

1. A warehouse roof is composed of a truss as shown in the figure. Write a program to calculate the self-weight of the roof. Use a `Roof` class that has member `live_load`. Have the `Roof` class use a `Truss` class to get the weight of the truss portion. With the origin of the *x-y* coordinate system at the lower left corner of the truss, use the data point coordinates to get the truss member lengths and therefore the weights.

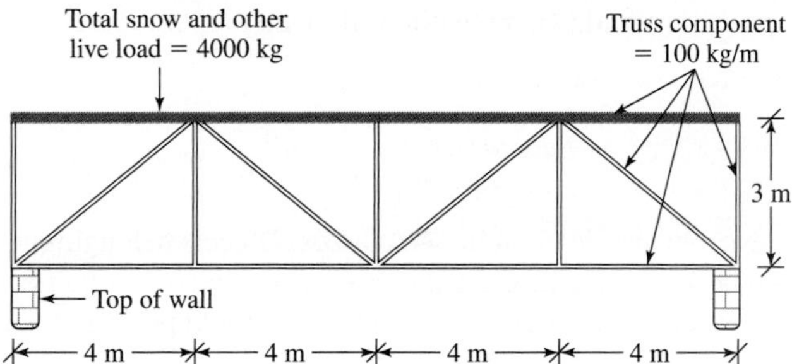

Each line of the data file should have the coordinates of the two endpoints of a truss member. The start of the data file for the shown truss is

```
0 0 0 3
0 0 4 3
0 0 4 0
4 0 4 3
```

Use dynamic storage to make your program capable of handling any number of truss members.

2. The air pollution level of a city on a given day is a function of the time of day (in hours). As an environmental specialist, you have collected carbon dioxide level readings at different times. An example of one day of readings is:

Time	CO_2	Time	CO_2
0:00	58	14:00	78
2:00	51	16:00	86
4:00	47	19:00	82
5:00	51	20:00	86
8:00	55	23:00	65
11:00	67		

Write a program to read 20 days of data, find the time at which the maximum occurs, and determine the average time of day at which the maximum occurs. Create a `Pollution` class with data members `co2`, `h2s`, and `suspended_particles` and member functions to read the data and print the result. Have the `Pollution` class use an `Analysis` class that has function members `maximum()` and `average()`.

3. As a software engineer, you are asked to write a section of a user friendly interface for an application program. The section intends to multiply two numbers based on a user's input string. The numbers can be either real or complex. Use the following four input strings to test your program:

3×4
$5 \times (6 - 7i)$
$(-8 + 9i) \times 10$
$(1 + 2i) \times (-3 - 4i)$

The program should generate the following output:

```
3 x 4 = 12
5 x (6 - 7i) = 30 - 35i
(-8 + 9i) x 10 = -80 + 90i
(1 + 2i) x (-3 - 4i) = 5 - 10i
```

The program should contain two classes. Objects belonging to the first class should be able to decompose the input string to correct numerical operators and operands. Objects of the second class should perform the calculations and display the output on the screen.

4. A trapezoidal-shaped channel contains water as shown in the figure. For an amount of water that flows through a channel in a given amount of time (referred to as Q, which is commonly in ft^3/sec) there is a most likely depth that the water will take (controlled by the energy). This is called the *critical depth*. The energy of flow is $E = y + Q^2/(2gA^2)$, where g is the gravitational constant and A is the cross-sectional area of the water-filled portion of the channel. The critical depth occurs when the energy is a minimum. This makes $dE/dy = 0$, or $1 - (Q^2/(gA^2))(dA/dy) = 0$. Using $dA = T\,dy$, the equation becomes $Q^2T/(gA^3) = 1$. This equation is satisfied when the critical depth is reached. Write a computer program that will determine the critical depth for a trapezoidal channel with the input data being Q, w, and slope of sides. Test the program with the input data $Q = 300$ ft^3/sec, $w = 2,4,6,8,10$ ft, and slopes = 0.5,1,2,3. Note that this will produce 20 values of the critical depth (y_{crit}). Create a class called `Open_channel`. Choose your own data and function members.

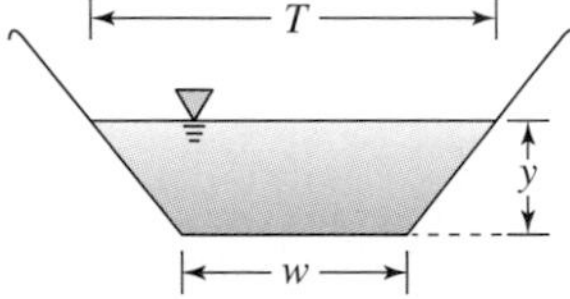

5. Write a program that simulates the actions of a bicycle. Use the classes `bicycle`, `wheel`, `chain`, `front_sprocket`, `rear_sprocket`, `pedal`, and `handle_bars`. Use stubs to create the actions `handle_bars` turning wheel, pedals turning front sprocket, `front_sprocket` pulling chain, chain rotating `rear_sprocket`, `rear_sprocket` turning wheel.

6. Sewage treatment plants discharge treated water (called *effluent*) to waterways. Regulatory agencies require that the quality of the effluent be monitored closely. Average values for suspended solids (ss) and biological oxygen demand (bod) in mg/l are commonly determined. Create an `Average` class that can compute three types of averages (mean, median, and mode). Have a `Discharge` class use the `Average` class. The `Discharge` class should read the data from file disc.dat. Readings every 12 hours for one week (14 values) are given in the file with ss first and bod second. Print the results to the screen.

CHAPTER 15

INHERITANCE AND POLYMORPHISM

CHAPTER TOPICS

In this chapter, you will learn how to:

- Create an inheritance hierarchy
- Use inheritance as a form of class interaction
- Make a virtual class
- Use polymorphism in a practical program

Inheritance is the name of another way in which classes and objects relate. It is a form of generalization. With inheritance between two classes, we speak of one class as the *base* class and the other class as the *derived* class.

Creating an inheritance relationship is another way that correctly working code can be reused and built upon. A base class can be thoroughly tested and debugged by one organization and used by a derived class developed by another organization. Such a practice can result in more complex and reliable software because dependable code is reused. A derived class can add features and capability to a base class. For these reasons, we find that inheritance is a powerful feature of C++.

On a UML class diagram, the inheritance relationship is illustrated with an arrow (with an open triangle arrowhead) from the derived class to the base class as shown in Fig. 15.1. Usually this relationship is drawn with the base class at the top and the derived class below. However as class diagrams become complicated, this may not be possible. Remember, the base class has the touching arrowhead.

When an object of the derived class is declared, an object of the base class is automatically created and contained within the derived class object, Fig. 15.2. In addition, the members of the base class become members of the derived class. This structure is well suited to developing "is a" class relationships.

In this chapter, we will see that a pointer to a derived class object can be automatically converted to a pointer to the contained base class object. This allows us to use a powerful C++ feature called *polymorphism.* Polymorphism originates from the Greek word *polymorphos,* meaning having or assuming various forms or styles. In C++, polymorphism is achieved by creating and using *virtual functions.*

In the first half of this chapter, we cover basic inheritance, and in the second half, we illustrate polymorphism.

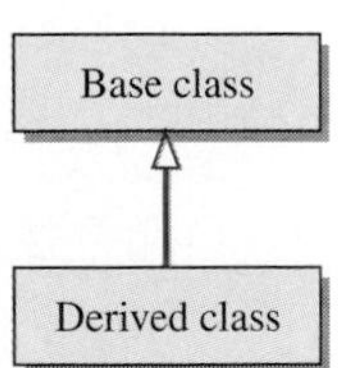

Figure 15.1

UML type class diagram indicating that class `Derived` inherits from class `Base`. Note that the arrowhead is open rather than closed.

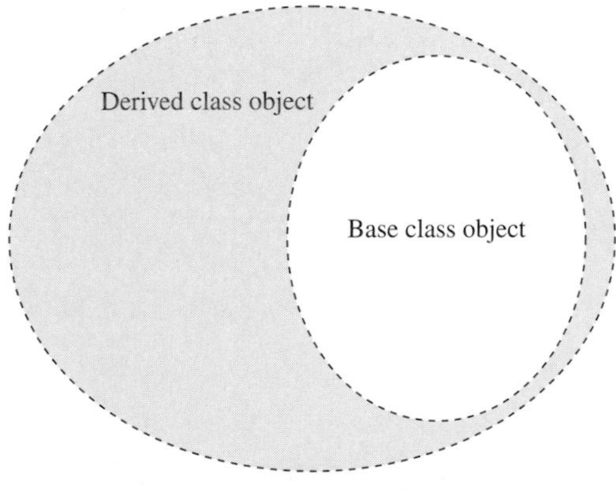

Figure 15.2

Image of the creation of a base class object when a derived class object is declared or instantiated. Note that a base class object is automatically contained within a derived class object.

LESSON 15.1 INHERITANCE (1)—BASICS

In this lesson, we focus on the mechanics of inheritance. We show how a base class (called `Base`) and a derived class (called `Derived`) are defined and how the data and function members of the two classes interact. In Lesson 15.2 we show a more realistic example that illustrates the reasoning behind making one class a base class and another a derived class and the implications of doing so.

Read the source code and annotations. Note that the base class definition does not specify that a class derives from it. It is the derived class that specifies the class it derives from. Also, pay particular attention to the way that the derived class function (`derived_set_show`) uses the base class members.

TOPICS

- Mechanics of inheritance
- Defining base and derived classes
- The `protected` keyword
- Inheritance compared to other class relationships

QUESTION YOU SHOULD ATTEMPT TO ANSWER

1. What do you think the `protected` access specifier means?

Source Code

```
#include <iostream>
using namespace std;

class Base
        {
        private:
                int base_priv_dat;
        protected:
                int base_prot_dat;
        public:
                void base_set_show ();
        };

class Derived : public Base
        {
        private:
                int derived_priv_dat;
        public:
                void derived_set_show ();
        };

void Base :: base_set_show ()
        {
        base_priv_dat = 1;
        base_prot_dat = 2;
        cout << "base_priv_dat = " << base_priv_dat
            << "base_prot dat = " << base_prot_dat << endl;
        }
```

A base class can use `protected`, in addition to `private` and `public`, for access control.

A derived class specifies the name of its base class using a colon and the base class name. The public form of inheritance, specified here, is the form most commonly used.

A base function can manipulate both private and protected base class data.

```
void Derived :: derived_set_show ()
        {
        derived_priv_dat = 3;
        base_prot_dat = 4;
        cout << "derived_priv_dat = " << derived_priv_dat
            << "base_prot_dat = " << base_prot_dat << endl;
        base_set_show ();
        }

int main ( )
{
        Derived d_object;
        d_object.base_set_show ();
        d_object.derived_set_show ();
}
```

A derived function can manipulate protected base class data, but not private base class data.

A derived function can call a public base function without referring to a base object.

We can invoke a *base* function with a *derived* object.

Output

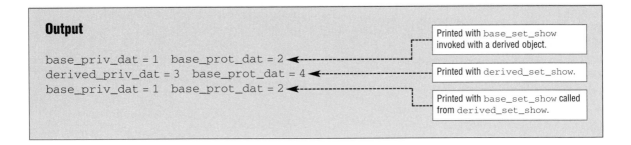

```
base_priv_dat = 1  base_prot_dat = 2
derived_priv_dat = 3  base_prot_dat = 4
base_priv_dat = 1  base_prot_dat = 2
```

Printed with `base_set_show` invoked with a derived object.

Printed with `derived_set_show`.

Printed with `base_set_show` called from `derived_set_show`.

Description

Defining a base class. In theory, a base class can be defined without regard to the fact that it is involved in the inheritance process. Its definition might not indicate in any way that it is a base class for another class. For instance, in this lesson's program, the definition of `Base` is:

```
class Base
        {
        private:
                int base_priv_dat;
        protected:
                int base_prot_dat;
        public:
                void base_set_show ();
        };
```

It in no way uses the name `Derived` to indicate the class that inherits from it. The only indication that it is likely to serve as a base class is through the use of the `protected` access specifier.

In practice, such classes are often specifically designed to be used as base classes for other classes. The intention, however, is that the base class is an independent class that works with and controls access to its data in a manner that is meant to be efficient and safe.

The `protected` access specifier. Base class members specified as `protected` can be accessed directly by functions of both derived classes and the base class (but not other classes). In contrast, base class members specified as `private` can be accessed directly only by functions of the base class.

One comment should be made about the `protected` access specifier: it may give too much access to derived classes. Some programmers prefer to have the base class hold tighter control on data manipulation and therefore use only `private` access. Check with your instructor or employer on the policy you should follow. In this text, we will illustrate the use of `protected` data, with the thought that one should be careful with it.

Defining a derived class. A derived class must denote the class from which it inherits. For instance:

```
class Derived : public Base
        {
        private:
                int derived_priv_dat;
        public:
                void derived_set_show ();
        };
```

indicates that `Base` serves as the base class for `Derived`. The colon follows the derived class name and is required. The keyword `public` characterizes the form of inheritance (`private` or `protected` could have been used, but `public` inheritance is most common, and the other forms will not be covered in detail). The base class name follows the `public`.

The data members should represent data needed by the derived class. The function members, though, work with the members of both the derived and base classes.

Interaction between the base and derived class objects. When `public` inheritance is used, the following access is created between the members of the two classes:

1. `private` base class members are `private` members of the base class only (meaning that only base class member functions can access the `private` base class data members).
2. `protected` base class members are `protected` members of both the derived and base classes (meaning that derived and base class member functions can access the `protected` base class data members, but functions outside either class cannot).
3. `public` base class members are `public` members of the derived and base classes (meaning that `public` members of the base class can be accessed through a derived class object or an address of a derived class object).

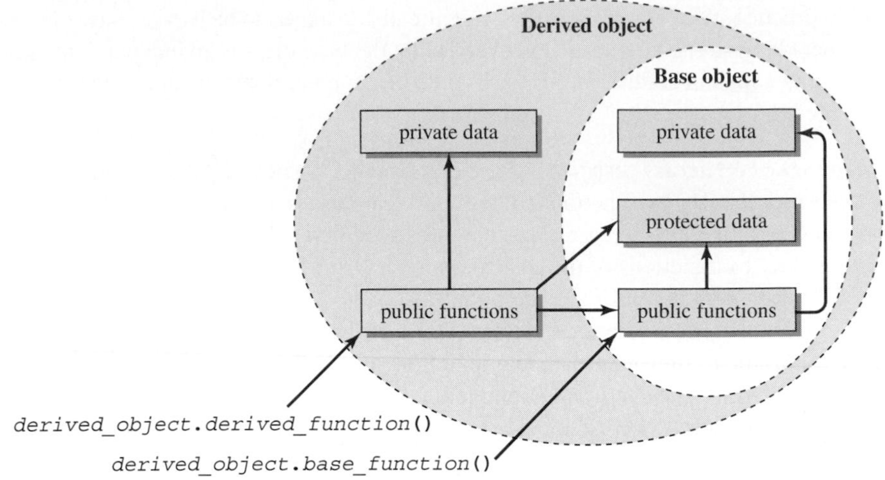

Figure 15.3

Illustration of relationship between base and derived objects. This shows that a derived object contains a base object. The `private` data of a base object cannot be accessed directly by a derived function, but the protected data can. Also, we can invoke a `public` base function with a derived object. Note that these are not all the possibilities for access, but ones that are commonly done.

4. Derived class members convey no special access privileges to base class functions (meaning that we cannot access derived class `private` data from base class functions).
5. The exceptions (to the previous four rules) are that base class constructor functions and overloaded assignment operators do not become members of a derived class.

These relationships are somewhat confusing, so we illustrate them in Fig. 15.3 (assuming that the functions are `public`, and the data is `private` or `protected`). As mentioned, when we declare a derived object (in `main`, for instance), we automatically create both a base and derived class object. These are shown in the figure with the large ellipse representing the derived class object and the enclosed small ellipse representing the base class object. The arrows in this figure show how access to the various members is obtained. For instance, if we want to access the private data of the base class object, we can take one of two approaches (starting in the lower left corner of Fig. 15.3):

1. Call a derived function using the derived object. Have this function then call a base function, which then accesses the private data.
2. Call a base function using the *derived* object. This is possible because, due to inheritance, the base function is considered a member of the derived class. The base function accesses the `private` data.

If we want to access the protected data of the base class, we have three options:

1. Call a derived function using the derived object. Have this function then call a base function, which then accesses the `protected` data.
2. Call a base function using the derived object. The base function accesses the `protected` data.
3. Call a derived function using the derived object. This function then accesses the `protected` data directly. This is possible because, through inheritance, the base `protected` data are `protected` derived members.

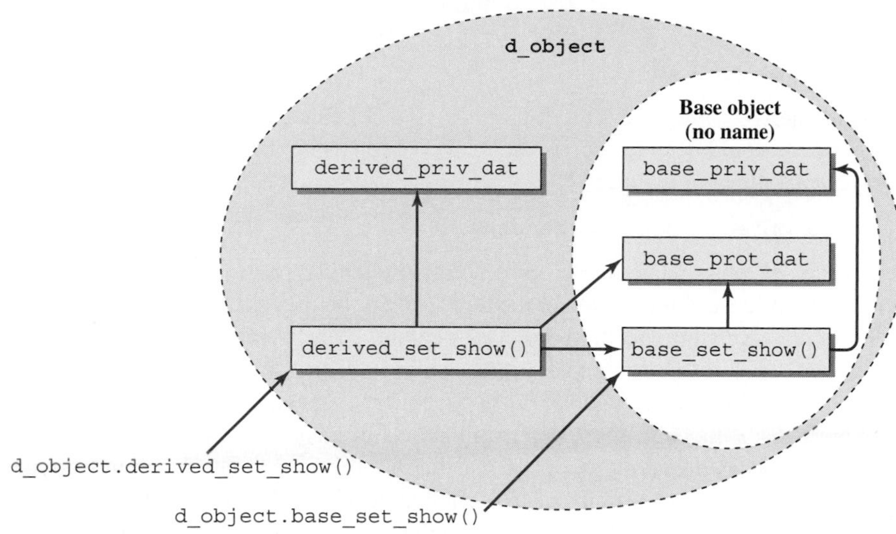

Figure 15.4

Illustration of relationship between base and derived objects for Lesson 15.1's program. Compare this to Fig. 15.3. Observe that this lesson's source code follows the arrows in this figure. Note that the base object has no name. Therefore, we do not use a base object with the dot operator for actions of the arrows that cross object boundaries.

Figure 15.3 shows that the `private` data of the derived class can only be accessed through the functions of the derived class. The allowable access and restrictions on access with inheritance is confusing. Many beginning programmers commit errors by using the access rules improperly. To avoid some of these difficulties, we recommend you use Fig. 15.3 as a guide in writing your own code involving inheritance.

An illustration of the activities of this lesson's program is shown in Fig. 15.4. Note the similarities between this figure and Fig. 15.3. If you trace the source code, you will see that it does follow the arrows and how it accomplishes the access to the data.

Note that because a base class object is contained within a derived class object, memory can be wasted if the base class has considerably more data than what is needed by the derived class. This means that for efficient use of an inheritance relationship between two classes, the base class should not be too much of a generalization of the derived class.

Base class object name. Note also from Fig. 15.4 that the base class object (sometimes called the *sub-object*) has no name! There are a number of implications of this. First, since it has no name, we do not use its name to perform an access that crosses its object boundary (like we have shown for other figures of this type in Chapter 14). You can see that we have used only the derived object name (in the lower left corner of Figs. 15.3 and 15.4) to access both derived and base class functions.

The lack of a base object name raises some questions. For instance, what happens if we create a derived class function that has the identical name and signature of a base class function? Which one is called when we use the expression `derived_object.function()`?

The answer is that the derived class takes precedence, and, hence it is called *overriding* the base class function. In other words, if in this lesson's program we had the member function (for both the base and derived classes):

```
void set_show ();
```

then the call

```
d_object . set_show ();
```

calls the derived object version of the set_show() function. To call the base class version, we would need to specify the Base version using the scope resolution operator in the following manner:

```
d_object . Base :: set_show ();
```

Here, the class name and scope resolution operator (Base ::) explicitly make the call to the base class version of the function. Sometimes a programmer makes the derived class version call the base class version. Even in this case, the base class name and scope resolution operator are required; otherwise the function calls itself (which C++ allows as we will see when we cover recursion).

Note that if the signatures for two functions of identical names in the base and derived classes is different, then C++ may choose the appropriate function from the way it is called. This means that a base function may be called without the scope resolution operator if the function call matches the signature of the base function but not the derived function.

The lack of a base object name also raises the question of what happens if base and derived class data have the same name. For instance, if Base has protected data int ii, and Derived has private data int ii, then what happens if ii is used in a Derived function? The answer is that the Derived ii is used. For example, if a statement such as

```
ii = 5;
```

is in Derived :: set_show () then 5 is assigned to the Derived ii. The statement

```
Base :: ii = 5;
```

in Derived :: set_show () explicitly assigns 5 to the Base ii data member.

However, ii = 5 written in Base :: set_show () assigns 5 to the Base value of ii. We are not allowed to write

```
Derived :: ii = 5;
```

in a base class function because we cannot access derived data from a base class object.

Comparison of types of class and object interactions. We have discussed a number of different types of class and object interactions. They are:

1. Friend and granting class.
2. Client and server class.
3. Composite and component class.
4. Base and derived class.

Miniature versions of the sketches for each of these, illustrating how private data is accessed, are shown in Fig. 15.5. (For the details of these sketches see Figs. 14.6, 14.7, and 15.3.) This figure shows that each of the relationships is different (although it does not show all the differences).

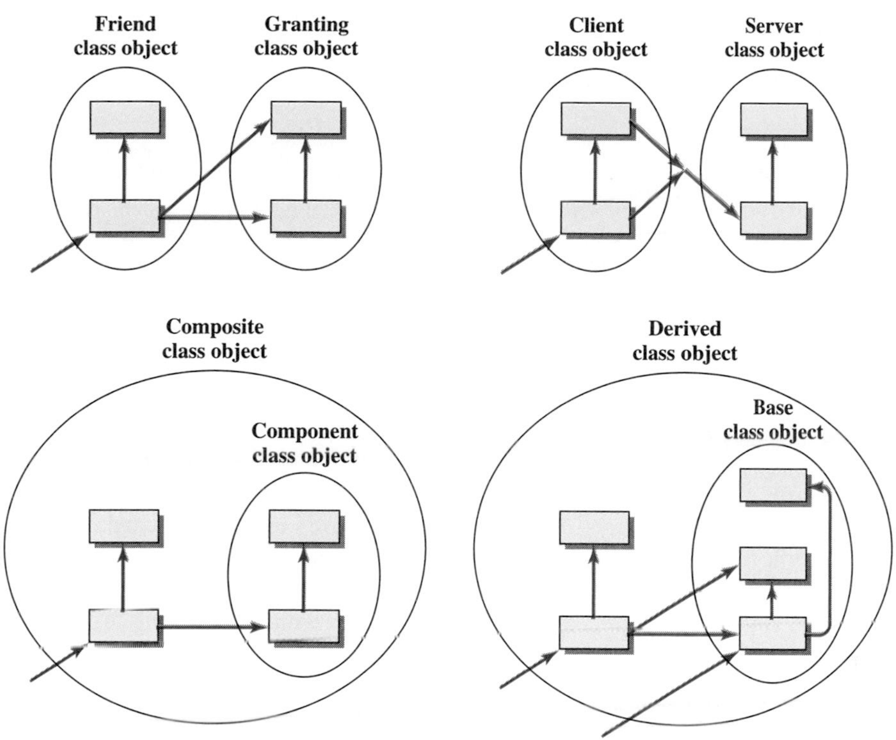

Figure 15.5

Summary sketch of four different types of class relationships. See Figs. 14.6, 14.7, and 15.3 for detailed drawings. Upper boxes represent private data members. Lower boxes represent public member functions. Note the similarities and differences between the four. These sketches do not represent all the possibilities for these class relationships.

Clearly, the method of accessing data is dependent on the relationships established in the programming of the classes. For instance, a friend relationship allows the `friend` class functions to directly access the granting class `private` data. However, a client-server relationship permits access to `private` data only through member functions.

Also, an inheritance relationship permits the derived class object to access some non`public` data of the base class object. However, a composite or composition relationship does not allow the composite class object to access the non`public` data of the component class object.

Not shown in this figure is that a composite relationship may have *many* component objects. However, a basic inheritance relationship permits only *one* base class object. There are also some differences between the way C++ handles pointers for the two relationships. We will describe them later in this chapter.

These are among the many differences between the relationships. In choosing the relationship you want for your programs, consider the "uses" (client-server), "has a" (composition or composite), and "is a" (inheritance, described in Lesson 15.2) as a guide.

`private` and `protected` inheritance. If `private` is used instead of `public` in the inheritance declaration, for instance:

```
class Derived : private Base
```

then `public` and `protected` members of `Base` become `private` members of `Derived`. The `private` members of `Base` remain `private` to `Base` only.

If protected is used, as in

```
class Derived : protected Base
```

then the public and protected members of Base become public and protected members of Derived. The private members of Base remain private to Base only.

Because these forms of inheritance are less common than public inheritance, we will not cover them further. Unless specified otherwise, all comments made in this chapter pertain to public inheritance.

Other uses of inheritance. Inheritance is a class relationship that is well suited to extending or customizing existing code. Independent software vendors sometimes develop base classes from which others can write derived classes. The vendors need to supply primarily object code and information about the base classes. Thus, they are able to protect their source code.

The derived classes can make full use of the base class features and add their own specific features. If a base class has been fully debugged and tested, this form of code reuse cuts software development time and increases reliability.

Also, software vendors can modify base classes without requiring the derived classes to be modified, provided the form of the interfaces between classes remain the same. This allows the base classes to remain up to date without placing an added burden on the developers of the derived classes. It may or may not be necessary to recompile the derived classes after the base classes change.

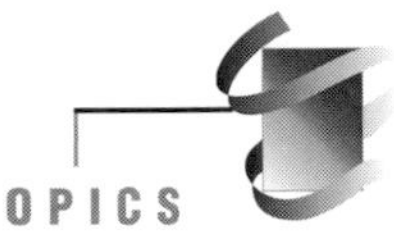

LESSON 15.2 INHERITANCE (2)—CONSTRUCTOR AND DESTRUCTOR FUNCTIONS

TOPICS

- Creating "is a" relationships with inheritance
- Constructors, destructors, and inheritance
- Assignments with inheritance

QUESTION YOU SHOULD ATTEMPT TO ANSWER

1. What would happen if we wrote in main, "triangle1 = polygon1;"?

In this lesson, we describe a situation where inheritance is the appropriate class relationship. For instance, suppose we are performing calculations with triangles and squares. We may wish to write a program with Triangle and Square classes that have members that are exclusively for themselves. We may also want these classes to inherit from a Polygon class (because both triangles and squares are polygons) that has members that are common to all polygons.

Read this lesson's program. Although it is long, it is not particularly complicated. Note that we use constructor and destructor functions with each of the classes. Observe from the output the order in which these functions are called. Pay attention to the type of data that is in Polygon, the base class, and how it differs from the data in the derived classes. Also note that we have used assignment statements with a Polygon object on one side and Square and Triangle objects on the other side.

Source Code

```
#include <iostream>
using namespace std;

class Polygon
      {
      protected:
            int num_sides;
            double area;
            char* name;
      public:
            Polygon ();
            Polygon (char*, int);
            ~Polygon ();
            void show_sides_area ();
      };

class Triangle : public Polygon
      {
      private:
            double base, height;
      public:
            Triangle (double, double);
            ~Triangle ();
            void calc_area ();
      };

class Square : public Polygon
      {
      private:
            double side_length;
      public:
            Square (double);
            ~Square ();
            void calc_area ();
      };


Polygon :: Polygon ()
      {
      cout << "Polygon constructor called." << endl;
      }

Polygon :: Polygon (char* name_var, int num_sides_var)
      : name (name_var), num_sides (num_sides_var), area (0)
      {
      cout << "Polygon constructor called." << endl;
      }
```

The `protected` data is data that is used by `Triangle` and `Square`.

The `Polygon` (base) class has data members that are common to all polygons.

No-argument and two-argument constructors.

This function can be used by any type polygon.

This line indicates that `Triangle` inherits from `Polygon`.

A triangle has a base and height.

This function is made just for triangles.

This line indicates that `Square` inherits from `Polygon`.

A square has a single side length.

This function is made just for squares.

This `Polygon` constructor initializes only `Polygon` data members.

```
Polygon :: ~Polygon ()
        {
        cout << "Polygon destructor called." << endl;
        }

void Polygon :: show_sides_area ()
        {
        cout << name << " " << num_sides << " sides, area = " << area << endl;
        }

Triangle :: Triangle (double base_var, double height_var)
        : base (base_var), height (height_var),
          Polygon ("Triangle", 3)
        {
        cout << "Triangle constructor called." << endl;
        }

Triangle :: ~Triangle ()
        {
        cout << "Triangle destructor called." << endl;
        }

void Triangle :: calc_area ()
        {
        area = 0.5 * base * height;
        }


Square :: Square (double side_length_var)
       : side_length (side_length_var), Polygon ("Square", 4)
        {
        cout << "Square constructor called."<< endl;
        }

Square :: ~Square ()
        {
        cout << "Square destructor called." << endl;
        }

void Square :: calc_area ()
        {
        area = side_length * side_length;
        }

int main ( )
{
        Triangle triangle1 (3.5, 2);
        Square square1 (2.5);
        Polygon polygon1, polygon2;
```

Only `Polygon` data members can be accessed in this `Polygon` function.

Here, in the initialization list, the `Triangle` constructor calls the `Polygon` constructor to initialize the `Polygon` data for a `Triangle` object.

The `Polygon` data member, `area`, is used in a `Triangle` function.

Here, in the initialization list, the `Square` constructor calls the `Polygon` constructor to initialize the `Polygon` data for a `Square` object.

The `Polygon` data member, `area`, is used in a `Square` function.

Declaring a `Triangle`, `Square` and two `Polygon` objects.

```
        triangle1.calc_area ();
        triangle1.show_sides_area ();
        square1.calc_area ();
        square1.show_sides_area ();

        polygon1 = triangle1;
        polygon2 = square1;

        polygon1.show_sides_area ();
        polygon2.show_sides_area ();
}
```

A `Triangle` object (`triangle1`) is used to invoke a `Polygon` function (`show_sides_area`).

A `Square` object (`square1`) is used to invoke a `Polygon` function (`show_sides_area`).

Assigning `Triangle` and `Square` objects to `Polygon` objects.

Printing the sides and areas for the polygons.

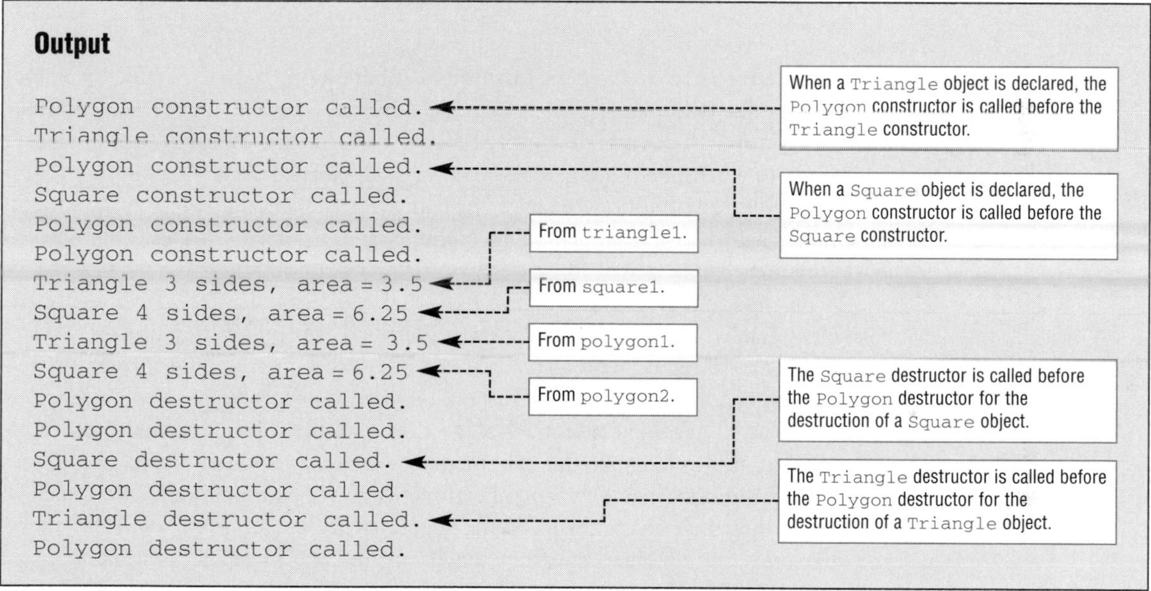
Output
Polygon constructor called.
Triangle constructor called.
Polygon constructor called.
Square constructor called.
Polygon constructor called.
Polygon constructor called.
Triangle 3 sides, area = 3.5
Square 4 sides, area = 6.25
Triangle 3 sides, area = 3.5
Square 4 sides, area = 6.25
Polygon destructor called.
Polygon destructor called.
Square destructor called.
Polygon destructor called.
Triangle destructor called.
Polygon destructor called.
When a Triangle object is declared, the Polygon constructor is called before the Triangle constructor.
When a Square object is declared, the Polygon constructor is called before the Square constructor.
From triangle1.
From square1.
From polygon1.
From polygon2.
The Square destructor is called before the Polygon destructor for the destruction of a Square object.
The Triangle destructor is called before the Polygon destructor for the destruction of a Triangle object.

Description

Base and derived class members. The classes in this lesson's program create an "is a" relationship. A triangle "is a" polygon, and a square "is a" polygon; therefore we create a `Polygon` base class and `Triangle` and `Square` derived classes (see Fig. 15.6). This means that each derived class object automatically has all the properties of a polygon. The `Polygon` data members, `num_sides`, `area`, and `name` are characteristics of all polygons and consequently are appropriate base class data members. The `Triangle` data members, `base` and `height`, are for triangles (not all polygons), and consequently are appropriate derived class data members. The `Square` data member, `side_length`, is for squares (not all polygons), and consequently is an appropriate derived class data member.

Figure 15.6

Sketch of inheritance diagram and objects used in Lesson 15.2's program.

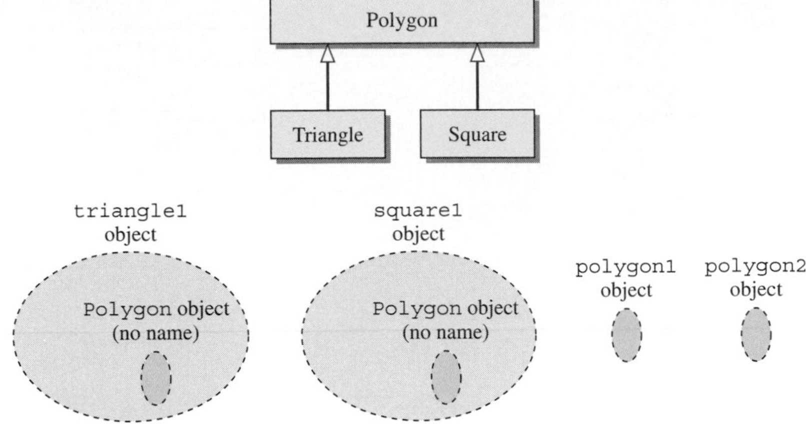

Both derived classes have the function member `calc_area()`. While the names are the same for both classes, the bodies are different (because the area calculations for a triangle and square are, of course, different). This is somewhat typical in that we often want to perform similar calculations for each derived class.

For the design of your own programs using inheritance, put common data members in the base class and specialty data members in the derived classes. Your derived class function members will likely perform similar manipulations.

In this lesson's program, we have used the `protected` access specifier for the base class data (for illustration purposes primarily). This means that derived classes access this data directly, without the base class exhibiting any control over the values allowed for those members. This may cause some problems. For instance, if `area` or `num_sides` is accidentally made negative, the program could crash. One way to avoid this is to make the data members `private`, which means that access only occurs through base class member functions. These functions could check to make sure that the values are positive, rejecting any negative values. Remember, consider the safety of the data when specifying the access of the data members of your base classes. The `protected` specifier may not always be appropriate for shared data.

In addition to derived class objects, `triangle1` and `square1`, we have declared two base class objects, `polygon1` and `polygon2`. An inheritance diagram and an image of all the objects is shown in Fig. 15.6, and the characteristics of all the objects are shown in Table 15.1. Note that the `Triangle` and `Square` objects contain unnamed `Polygon` objects and the `Polygon` objects contain only `Polygon` data members, making them smaller than the derived class objects.

Despite the differences in size, C++ allows us to use the default assignment operator to assign derived class objects to base class objects. An image of the action is shown in Fig. 15.7. It illustrates how C++ takes only the base part of the derived object and assigns it to a base object. Therefore, the statements

```
polygon1 = triangle1;
polygon2 = square1;
```

TABLE 15.1 — Objects for Lesson 15.2's program

Name	Type		Address	Value
square1	Square			
	side_length	double	FFFE	2.5
	num_sides	int (from Polygon)	FFE6	4
	area	double (from Polygon)	FFEE	6.25
	name	char* (from Polygon)	FFDE	Square
triangle1	Triangle			
	base	double	FFCE	3.5
	height	double	FFC6	2
	num_sides	int (from Polygon)	FFBE	3
	area	double (from Polygon)	FFAE	3.5
	name	char* (from Polygon)	FF9E	Triangle
polygon1	Polygon			
	num_sides	int	FF8E	3
	area	double	FF7E	3.5
	name	char*	FF6E	Triangle
polygon2	Polygon			
	num_sides	int	FF56	4
	area	double	FF46	6.25
	name	char*	FF3E	Square

Note that triangle1 and square1 contain Polygon data members as well as their own, and the Polygon objects contain only Polygon data members.

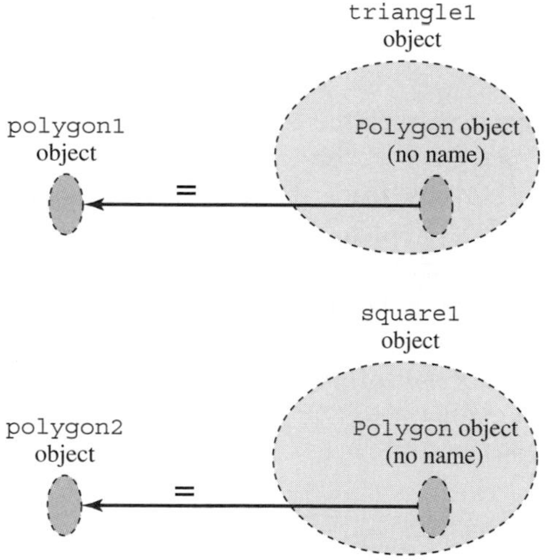

Figure 15.7

When we assign a derived class object to a base class object, only the base class part of the object is copied. This is illustrated schematically here for the objects in Lesson 15.2's program.

assign only Polygon data member (num_sides, area, and name) values of triangle1 and square1 to polygon1 and polygon2, respectively. These values are shown in the output and in Table 15.1. C++ does not allow us to do the opposite. That is, we cannot use the default assignment operator to assign a base class object to a derived class object because a portion of the derived class object would not be

Figure 15.8

The order of execution of constructors and destructors for base and derived classes is similar to the order of construction and destruction of a building. Follow this figure from left to right.

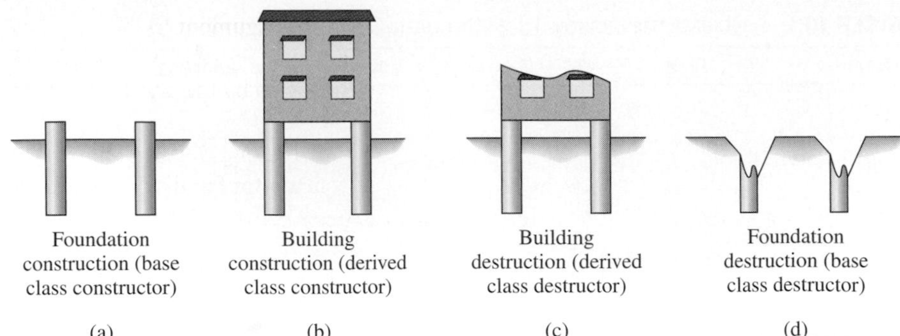

operated upon. We could, however, create our own assignment operator to perform such an operation in the manner we choose.

Order of constructor and destructor function calls. Because a derived class object contains a base class object, both the base and derived constructors are called when a derived class object is instantiated or declared. The base class constructor is called first and the derived class constructor second. When a derived class object is destroyed, the order is reversed. The derived class destructor is called first and the base class destructor second. The order can be remembered if we consider a base class to be similar to a building's foundation and the derived class to be similar to the building (Fig. 15.8). The order of construction is the foundation (base class) first and building (derived class) second. Should we decide to eliminate that structure, we destroy the building (derived class) first and the foundation (base class) second.

The order in which the objects are declared determines the order of constructor calls. In other words, the order for this lesson's program is `triangle1`, `square1`, `polygon1`, `polygon2`, because that is the order in which they are declared. The destructors are called in opposite order: `polygon2`, `polygon1`, `square1`, `triangle1`. In general, objects that go out of scope at the same time have their destructors called in the opposite order of their declarations.

Explicit call to a base class constructor. To pass values to a base class constructor, we can call it explicitly from the derived class constructor. This is done in the initialization list. For instance

```
Triangle :: Triangle (double base_var, double height_var)
          : base (base_var), height (height_var),
            Polygon ("Triangle", 3)
```

calls the `Polygon` constructor with (`"Triangle", 3`) as the argument list. And

```
Square :: Square (double side_length_var)
        : side_length (side_length_var),
          Polygon ("Square", 4)
```

calls the `Polygon` constructor with `("Square", 4)` as the argument list. Doing this initializes the base object within the derived object. Note that because the base object has no name, we use the base class name (`Polygon`) followed by the argument list to call the constructor.

We can also pass values from the derived class constructor call to the base class constructor. In general, to pass values to a base class constructor from a derived class constructor call, the form of the call and initialization list is (with 2 arguments):

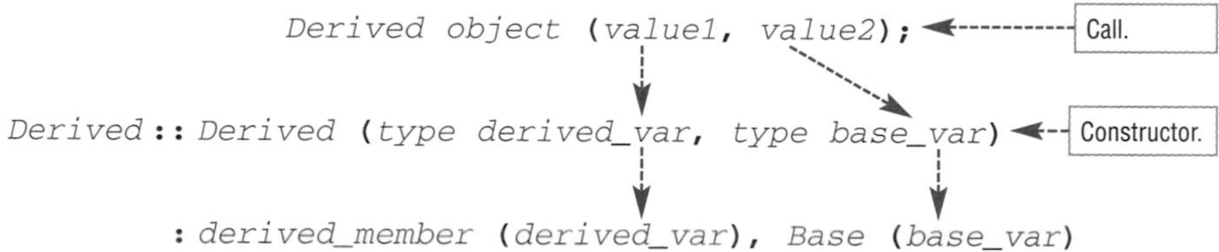

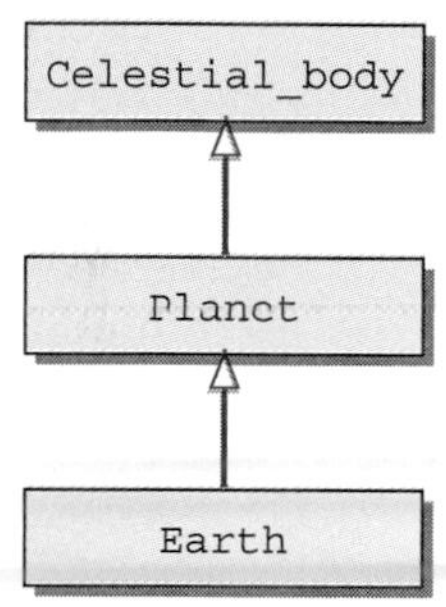

Figure 15.9

Inheritance graph for Lesson 15.3's program.

where *`Derived`* is the derived class name, *`Base`* is the base class name, *`object`* is the derived object name, *`value1`* and *`value2`* are values passed to the derived constructor, *`type`* is a data type (all not necessarily the same), *`derived_var`* and *`base_var`* are temporary variables, and *`derived_member`* is a derived member name. The result of these statements is to pass *`value1`* to *`derived_member`* and *`value2`* to the base class constructor.

One other point should be made. Remember what we said about constructors in Chapter 8. If you define a constructor that takes arguments, C++ will *not* automatically call its no-argument constructor. This applies to base classes as well. In other words, if you define only one base class constructor (with arguments) and declare a derived class object without making an explicit base class constructor call, you will get a compilation error. To correct this, you must make an explicit base class constructor call or define a no-argument base class constructor.

LESSON 15.3 INHERITANCE (3)—LEVELS OF INHERITANCE

TOPICS

- More than one level of inheritance
- Constructors and destructors

QUESTION YOU SHOULD ATTEMPT TO ANSWER

1. What is the order in which functions are called from the declaration in `main`?

It is sometimes desirable to create more than one level of inheritance. In other words, a derived class can serve as a base class for another class creating a three level inheritance hierarchy. In this lesson, we create the classes, `Earth`, `Planet`, and `Celestial_body`. The order of inheritance is shown in Fig. 15.9.

Note that `Earth` is a `Planet` and a `Planet` is a `Celestial_body`. Hence, `Earth` inheriting from `Planet` and `Planet` inheriting from `Celestial_body` is appropriate. In this case, `Planet` is sometimes said to be a direct base class to `Earth`, and `Celestial_body` is an indirect base class to Earth.

Read this lesson's program and note how the `Earth` constructor calls the `Planet` constructor and the `Planet` constructor calls the `Celestial_body` constructor. Also observe how the `Earth` constructor body has access to both `Planet` and `Celestial_body` protected data members.

Source Code

```
#include <iostream.h>
using namespace std;
class Celestial_body
        {
        protected:
                double size;
        public:
                Celestial_body (double);
        };
class Planet : public Celestial_body
        {
        protected:
                double orbit_time;
        public:
                Planet (double, double);
        };
class Earth : public Planet
        {
        private:
                unsigned long int population;
        public:
                Earth ();
        };

Celestial_body :: Celestial_body (double size_var)
            : size (size_var)
        {
        cout << "Celestial_body constructor called." << endl;
        }
Planet :: Planet (double orbit_time_var, double size_var)
       : Celestial_body (size_var), orbit_time (orbit_time_var)
        {
        cout << "Planet constructor called." << endl;
        }
Earth :: Earth ()
      : Planet (1,40000), population (3000000000U)
        {
        cout << "Earth constructor called." << endl;
        cout << "Population = " << population << endl
            << "orbit time = " << orbit_time << endl
            << "size = " << size << endl;
        }
int main ( )
{
        Earth earth;
}
```

The `Celestial_body` class has a data member that is common to all celestial bodies (`size`).

`Planet` inherits from `Celestial_body`.

The `Planet` class has a data member that is common to all planets (`orbit_time`).

`Earth` inherits from `Planet`. Note that there is no mention of `Celestial_body`.

The `Earth` class has a data member that pertains only to `Earth` (population).

The `Planet` constructor calls the `Celestial_body` constructor.

The `Earth` constructor calls the `Planet` constructor, which calls the `Celestial_body` constructor. This process allows `Earth` to initialize the data members of both the `Planet` and `Celestial_body` sub-objects.

This `Earth` function has access to the protected data of both the `Planet` and `Celestial_body` classes.

This calls the `Earth` constructor.

Output

```
Celestial_body constructor called.
Planet constructor called.
Earth constructor called.
Population = 3000000000
Orbit time = 1
Size = 40000
```

The order of calling constructors is from top down in the inheritance graph.

Description

Effect of inheritance levels. When several levels of inheritance are used, an object for the lowest level class contains sub-objects of all the other classes. For instance, for this lesson's program, the `earth` object can be envisioned to be like that shown in Fig. 15.10. Observe from this figure that the `Earth` object (`earth`) contains a `Planet` object, which contains a `Celestial_body` object. Neither the `Planet` object nor the `Celestial_body` object has a name.

The class membership caused by multiple levels of inheritance follows what was written in Lesson 15.1. For this lesson, the public members of the `Celestial_body` and `Planet` objects become public members of the `Earth` object. The protected members of the `Celestial_body` and `Planet` objects become protected members of the `Earth` object. The private members of the `Celestial_body` and `Planet` objects remain private to those classes.

Constructors and destructors. When a derived object is instantiated (or declared), the order of constructor calls follows the same pattern described in Lesson 15.2. With multilevel inheritance, the order can be thought to start from the top in the inheritance diagram and go down. That is, for this lesson's program, the `Celestial_body` constructor is called first, then the `Planet` constructor, and then the `Earth` constructor. The order of destructors (not shown in this lesson's program) is the opposite—`Earth`, `Planet`, and `Celestial_body`.

C++ allows us to call a base class constructor explicitly only one level up on the inheritance graph. For instance, the initialization list for the `Earth` constructor:

```
Earth :: Earth ()
      : Planet (1,40000), population (3000000000U)
```

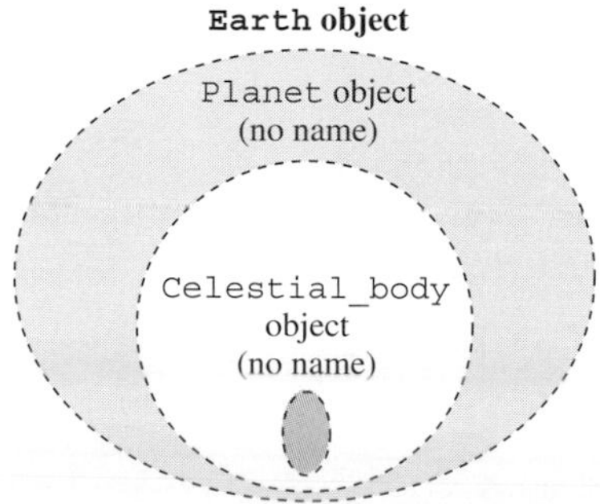

Figure 15.10
Image of objects for Lesson 15.3's program.

has a call to the `Planet` constructor only. From this line, we cannot make an explicit call to the `Celestial_body` constructor. The `Planet` constructor initialization list:

```
Planet :: Planet (double orbit_time_var, double size_var)
       : Celestial_body (size_var), orbit_time (orbit_time_var)
```

contains an explicit call to the `Celestial_body` constructor. Consequently, to pass data from the original object declaration, we must pass it one step at a time up the inheritance graph.

Overriding functions. Although it is not shown in this lesson's program, base class functions can be overridden in any of the classes down the inheritance graph. To call a function from the class lowest on the inheritance graph, simply use the function name and argument list. To call a function that has been overridden, use the class name and scope resolution operator before the function name.

Assignment of objects. As with single level inheritance, we can assign derived class objects to base class objects, but not the reverse. In the assignment, only base class data is copied.

LESSON 15.4 INHERITANCE (4)—MULTIPLE INHERITANCE

TOPICS

- Creating multiple inheritance
- Dealing with name conflicts

QUESTION YOU SHOULD ATTEMPT TO ANSWER

1. What determines the order in which the constructors are called?

A class can inherit from more than one class directly (rather than indirectly as shown in Lesson 15.3). We can use it when one class has an "is a" relationship with more than one class.

For instance, material classification is an important part of environmental assessments. In this lesson's program, we create a `Drinking_liquid` class, a `Cleaning_liquid` class, and a `Water` class. Because water "is a" cleaning liquid *and* a drinking liquid, the `Water` class inherits directly from both `Cleaning_liquid` and `Drinking_liquid`. This is shown in Fig. 15.11.

Multiple inheritance can be quite complex to implement in programs of practical size. Within the OOP community, multiple inheritance has its supporters and detractors. For these two reasons, we simply present an example and describe it. We will not go into further detail about multiple inheritance in this text.

Read the program and annotations to see how `Water` inherits from two classes. Note how the data members of both classes become members of `Water`. Observe that since temperature is a component of both base classes, the `Water` function must indicate to which it is referring.

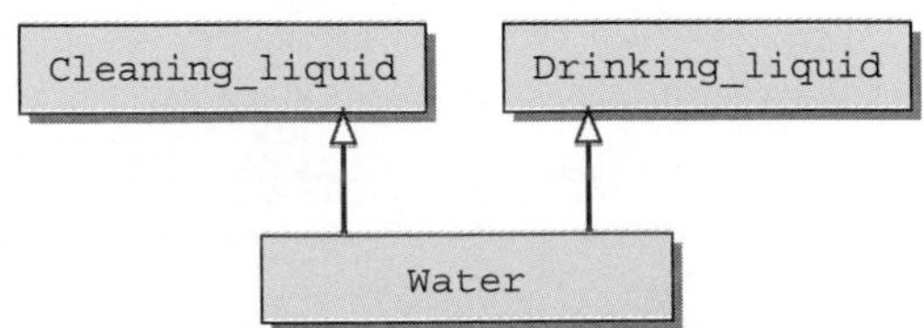

Figure 15.11

Inheritance graph for Lesson 15.4's program.

Source Code

```
#include <iostream>
using namespace std;

class Cleaning_liquid
        {
        protected:
                double ca, mg, temperature;
        public:
                Cleaning_liquid (double, double, double);
        };

class Drinking_liquid
        {
        protected:
                double na, temperature;
        public:
                Drinking_liquid (double, double);
        };

class Water : public Cleaning_liquid, public Drinking_liquid
        {
        public:
                Water ();
        };

Cleaning_liquid :: Cleaning_liquid (double ca_var, double mg_var,
                double temperature_var)
              : ca (ca_var), mg (mg_var), temperature (temperature_var)
        {
        cout << "Cleaning_liquid constructor called." << endl;
        }

Drinking_liquid :: Drinking_liquid (double na_var, double temperature_var)
              : na (na_var), temperature (temperature_var)
        {
        cout << "Drinking_liquid constructor called."<< endl;
        }

Water :: Water ()
      : Drinking_liquid (32, 4), Cleaning_liquid (21, 36, 87)
        {
        cout << "Water constructor called." << endl;
        cout << "Ca = " << ca << "  Mg = " << mg << "  Na = " << na << endl
            << "Cleaning_liquid temperature = "
            << Cleaning_liquid :: temperature << endl
            << "Drinking_liquid temperature = "
            << Drinking_liquid :: temperature << endl;
        }
```

Cleaning liquids have calcium content, magnesium content, and temperature as properties.

Drinking liquids have sodium content and temperature as properties.

Both `Cleaning_liquid` and `Drinking_liquid` are in the inheritance list for `Water`. The order in this list determines the order of the constructor calls (see the output).

`Cleaning_liquid` constructor.

`Drinking_liquid` constructor.

We can make explicit calls to both base class constructors from the derived class constructor initialization list.

We use the class name and `::` to refer to temperature.

```
int main ( )
{
        Water spring_water;
}
```

Output

```
Cleaning_liquid constructor called.
Drinking_liquid constructor called.
Water constructor called.
Ca = 21 Mg = 36 Na = 32
Cleaning_liquid temperature = 87
Drinking_liquid temperature = 4
```

Constructors are called in the order given in the inheritance list.

Description

Effect of multiple inheritance. An image of the objects of this lesson's program is shown in Fig. 15.12. It can be seen that the multiple inheritance makes nameless `Cleaning_liquid` and `Drinking_liquid` objects contained within the `Water` object, `spring_water`. Because the inheritance for both classes is `public`, the `public` and `protected` data members of the base classes become `public` and `protected` members of the derived class, respectively. `private` base class data members remain `private` to their classes. Thus, the properties of cleaning liquids (calcium content, magnesium content, and temperature) and drinking liquids (sodium content and temperature) become data members of `spring_water`.

Name conflicts. Since `temperature` is a member of both `Cleaning_liquid` and `Drinking_liquid`, we cannot simply refer to `temperature` in `Water` functions. We must include the class name and scope resolution operator. Thus, `Cleaning_liquid :: temperature` and `Drinking_liquid :: temperature` appropriately access the temperature data members of the two sub-objects of `spring_water`.

Constructors and destructors. Constructors for both base classes are called when `spring_water` is declared in `main`. Arguments are passed to these constructors

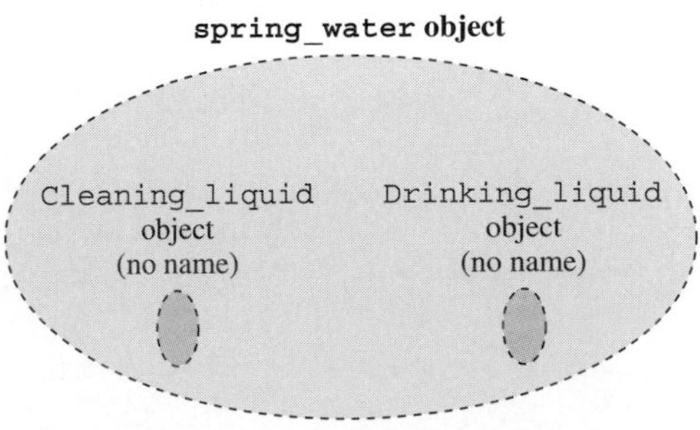

Figure 15.12

Image of objects of Lesson 15.4's program.

using the initialization list in the Water constructor as shown here:

```
Water :: Water ()
       : Drinking_liquid (32, 4), Cleaning_liquid (21, 36, 87)
```

The order in this list determines the order of the constructor calls. The Drinking_liquid constructor is passed two arguments and called first, and the Cleaning_liquid constructor is passed three arguments and called second.

We did not show it in this lesson's program, but the destructor order is the opposite of the constructor order.

Comment. Again, we show only the basics of multiple inheritance here and address only some of the issues. Because it is controversial, we will not use it further in this text.

LESSON 15.5 VIRTUAL FUNCTIONS AND POLYMORPHISM

TOPICS

- Virtual classes
- Pure virtual functions
- Static and dynamic binding
- Mechanism of polymorphism
- Base and derived class pointers

In this lesson, we create polymorphism using inheritance and a pure virtual function. As we mentioned in the introduction to this chapter, polymorphism means taking many forms. In the context of C++, this means that the code making a function call does not explicitly state which function it is calling. As a result, while the program is executing (*not* while it is compiling) C++ must decide which is the correct function to call. Consequently, it can be thought that the program takes many forms because of the run-time actions that can take place.

Previously in this text, we have seen situations where it is not particularly obvious which function is being called when we looked at the source code for a program. For instance, Lesson 7.7, which described function overloading, had many functions with the same name. While it was not obvious which function was being called by a particular statement, a programmer could look at the code alone and determine the function being referred to (by looking at the number and types of arguments). Such a determination is even more difficult when we consider two functions with exactly the same name and signature but for different classes in an inheritance hierarchy (described in Lesson 15.1). However, even in this case, a programmer who knows the rules of C++ can determine the function being called by a particular statement by looking at the code alone.

However, for this lesson's program, no programmer, no matter how knowledgeable, can determine the function being called by looking at only the code! Why? Because the input data influences the function selection. Such a situation is entirely different from anything we have seen previously in this text. The fact that C++ is able to determine the called function on the fly, so to speak, allows programmers to simplify their code in a number of important situations. We will give an illustration in Application Example 15.1. Here, we just show the basic mechanics of how it is done with a simple example. First, a little background.

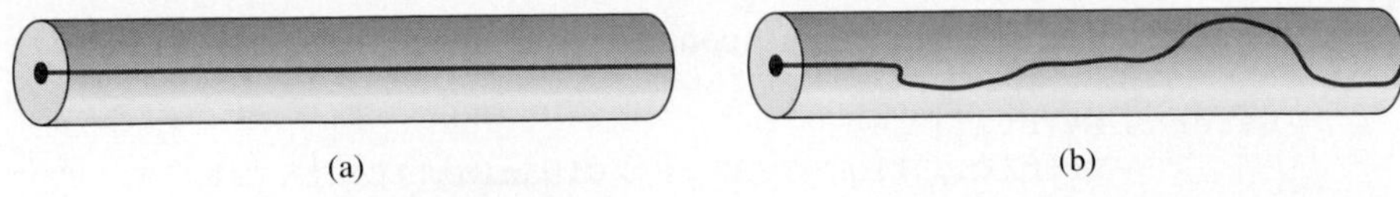

Figure 15.13
Particle path in (a) laminar flow and (b) turbulent flow.

There are two basic types of water flow, laminar and turbulent. The path taken by a particle of water for both types of flow is shown in Fig. 15.13. With laminar flow, the path is straight, and with turbulent flow, the path is circuitous.

One of the primary indicators of the type of flow is velocity. At low velocity, laminar flow occurs, and at high velocity, turbulent flow occurs. Also, as you can imagine, calculations (such as determining water pressure) involving the types of flows are different. In this program, we create the classes `Flow`, `Laminar_flow`, and `Turbulent_flow`. Each class has a function called `calc_pressure` (but as we will see, the one in `Flow` is never used). We ask a user to input a velocity and, based on the value, the program calls the correct `calc_pressure` function.

QUESTION YOU SHOULD ATTEMPT TO ANSWER

1. Why is there no definition for the function `Flow::calc_pressure()` in the program?

Read the source code. Note the use of the keyword `virtual` and the fact that the three `calc_pressure` functions have identical signatures. Also, observe how C++ allows us to assign derived class addresses to base class pointer variables. Observe that it is impossible for you to determine which `calc_pressure` function is called by the expression `ptr -> calc_pressure()` looking at the code alone.

Source Code

```
#include <iostream>
using namespace std;

class Flow
      {
      public:
            virtual void calc_pressure () = 0;
      };

class Laminar_flow : public Flow
      {
      public:
            void calc_pressure ();
      };

class Turbulent_flow : public Flow
      {
      public:
            void calc_pressure ();
      };
```

The keyword `virtual` (which precedes the return type for the function) and `=0` make `calc_pressure` a pure virtual function and `Flow` a virtual class. Note that there is no definition of this function in the code.

Class `Laminar_flow` inherits from `Flow` and has a `calc_pressure` function with the same signature as the `calc_pressure` in `Flow`.

Class `Turbulent_flow` inherits from `Flow` and has a `calc_pressure` function with the same signature as the `calc_pressure` in `Flow`.

```
void Laminar_flow :: calc_pressure ()
        {
        cout << "Laminar flow pressure calculated." << endl;
        }

void Turbulent_flow :: calc_pressure ()
        {
        cout << "Turbulent flow pressure calculated." << endl;
        }

int main ( )
{
        double velocity;
        Flow* ptr;
        Laminar_flow low_flow;
        Turbulent_flow high_flow;

        cout << "Enter velocity." << endl;
        cin >> velocity;

        if (velocity < 5)
                {
                ptr = &low_flow;
                }
        else
                {
                ptr = &high_flow;
                }

        ptr -> calc_pressure ();
}
```

These function bodies are just stubs. They do not perform the calculations; they simply print a message.

Because `Flow` is a virtual class, we cannot declare an object of the class. We can, however, declare a pointer variable of type `Flow*`. The name of that variable is `ptr`.

Declaring objects of type `Laminar_flow` and `Turbulent_flow`.

The velocity is input by the user.

Even though `ptr` is type `Flow*`, C++ allows us to assign addresses of derived class objects to it. This feature is an important tool in creating polymorphism.

This statement calls a `calc_pressure()` function. However, we do not know which one it calls by looking at the code only!

Output

```
                Enter velocity
Keyboard input  8
                Turbulent flow pressure calculated.
```

This velocity determines that the `Turbulent_flow` function is called.

Description

Virtual classes and pure virtual functions. A virtual class is a class for which we are not allowed to create independent objects. It is used as a base class for other classes for which we do want independent objects. C++ automatically makes a class virtual when a pure virtual function is a member of the class.

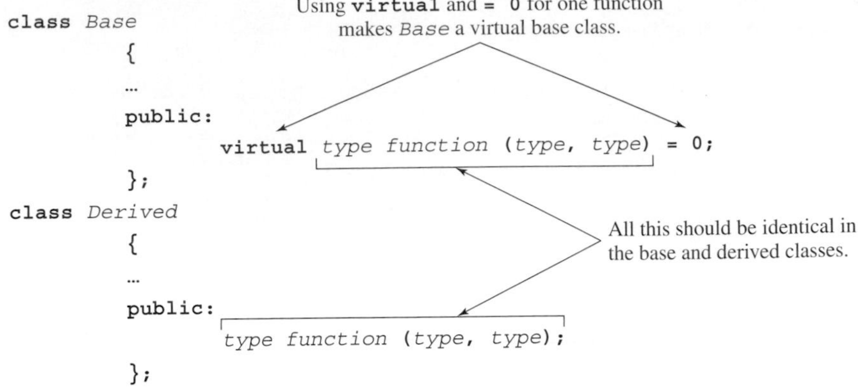

Figure 15.14

Making a virtual base class.

For instance, in this lesson's program, the `Flow` class is made virtual by the line

```
virtual void calc_pressure () = 0;
```

This declares a pure virtual function because it begins with the keyword `virtual` and ends with `= 0`. In general, the form to declare a pure virtual function with two arguments is:

```
virtual type function (type, type) = 0;
```

where *type* is a data type (not necessarily all the same), and *function* is the function name. No definition is needed for this function because it is not actually called. Only functions of derived classes with identical name and signature are called (see Fig. 15.14).

The corresponding functions in the derived classes do not use the keyword `virtual` in their declarations. In this lesson's program, the simple declaration

```
void calc_pressure ();
```

is used in both the `Laminar_flow` and `Turbulent_flow` classes. Definitions are required for these functions because they are not pure virtual.

Note that `Flow` is a virtual class partly because we would never be interested in creating generic flow objects. To actually work with calculations, we need to determine either laminar or turbulent flow.

Pointers and inheritance. We have not yet described how C++ works with pointers to objects in an inheritance hierarchy. Fundamentally, we can declare a base class type pointer variable and assign the address of a derived class object to it. For instance, in this lesson's program, the statements

```
Flow *ptr;
ptr = &low_flow;
ptr = &high_flow;
```

declare `ptr` to be a base class pointer variable; however, they also assign the address of derived class objects (`low_flow` and `high_flow`) to this variable. In general, a base class type pointer variable can be assigned the address of any object down the inheritance graph.

Early and late binding. The fact that C++ allows derived object addresses to be assigned to base class pointer variables means that we must know the contents of the pointer variable to determine which function is called with it. For instance, in using `ptr` to call `calc_pressure()` with the line

```
ptr -> calc_pressure ();
```

the contents of `ptr` (either `&low_flow` or `&high_flow`) must be known to determine if we call the `Laminar_flow` or `Turbulent_flow` version of `calc_pressure()`. Since the contents are dependent on the input data, it is not possible to determine which function this statement calls before the program is executed.

Binding is the association of a function call with a function. Normally it is reasonably simple and done at compile time because the type of object, name of the function, number of arguments, and types of arguments uniquely specify the function called. Binding during compilation is called *early, static,* or *compile-time* binding.

However, with this lesson's program, early binding does not work because the compiler does not know which function to associate with the function call `ptr -> calc_pressure()`. Luckily, C++ supports the mechanism of *late* binding (also called *dynamic* or *run-time* binding). During execution of the program, the *contents* of `ptr` (not the *type,* which is used with early binding) are utilized in creating an association with a particular function. The output shows that the input velocity of 8 indicates turbulent flow, making `ptr` hold the address of the `Turbulent_flow` object, and produce a call to the `Turbulent_flow` version of `calc_pressure()`.

Uses of polymorphism. Clearly, the activities of this lesson's program could have been written in a much simpler manner. However, the power of polymorphism is more evident when many more derived objects and types of objects are used. In such a situation we would like to create an array that contains the addresses of many different types of objects. Then we simply loop through that array and use the addresses to call each object's function. We do not need to create a complex `if` structure to determine the correct function to call. C++ does it automatically using late binding.

A classic example is in graphics programming. Suppose our goal is to draw a picture containing many different types of shapes. To do so, we could create a base class called `Shape` and derived classes of `Circle`, `Triangle`, `Rectangle`, and others. `Shape` would be a virtual class and have a virtual `draw()` function. All the other classes would derive from `Shape` and have their own `draw()` functions. The addresses of each object in a drawing (no matter what type) would be put into an array of `Shape*` (called `shape[]`, for example). Then drawing 20 shapes would be accomplished with this simple loop

```
for (i = 0; i < 20; i++) shape[i] -> draw();
```

Such simplicity of programming is very powerful. In addition, new shapes can be added to the program relatively easily. In Application Example 15.1, another example is given.

APPLICATION EXAMPLE 15.1 CIRCUIT RESISTANCE

Problem Statement

TOPICS

- Inheritance
- Virtual class
- Polymorphism

Write a program to determine the total resistance of a circuit consisting of four subcircuits in parallel. Subcircuits consist of two resistors in series or parallel (Fig. 15.15). Input should be entered from the keyboard and output printed to the screen. Use a virtual class and polymorphism. Calculate the total circuit resistance using a single loop over all the subcircuits.

Solution

RELEVANT EQUATIONS

The equation for series resistance is

$$r_{\text{tot}} = r_1 + r_2 \tag{15.1}$$

and the equation for parallel resistance is

$$r_{\text{tot}} = 1/(1/r_1 + 1/r_2) \tag{15.2}$$

where r_1 and r_2 are the resistances of individual resistors.

SPECIFIC EXAMPLE

For the circuit shown in Fig. 15.15, the resistance of each subcircuit can be found from Eqns. 15.1 and 15.2. Calculating from the top down in the figure, the resistances are

$$r_{\text{sub1}} = 4 + 8 = 12$$
$$r_{\text{sub2}} = 1/(1/9 + 1/7) = 3.94$$
$$r_{\text{sub3}} = 1/(1/3 + 1/6) = 2$$
$$r_{\text{sub4}} = 2 + 1 = 3$$

where the subcircuits are numbered from the top down in Fig. 15.15. Then, using Eqn. 15.2 for the entire circuit

$$r_{\text{tot}} = 1/(1/12 + 1/3.94 + 1/2 + 1/3) = 0.854$$

CLASSES AND DATA STRUCTURES

Since the subcircuits are either in series or parallel, we will create classes for each of them called `Series_resistance` and `Parallel_resistance`. Our goal is to

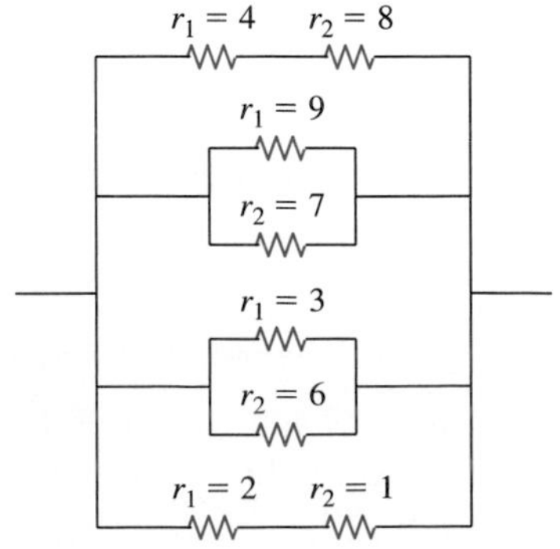

Figure 15.15

Specific example of circuit of resistors. Subcircuits consist of two resistors in series or parallel. The subcircuits are in parallel with each other.

create one object for each subcircuit, put all their addresses (no matter what type) into the same array, then loop over that array to perform resistance calculations. Therefore, to mix types, we need a base class for these that we will call `Resistance`. `Resistance` will be a pure virtual class because each object will be either a series or parallel subcircuit. We will never have the need to create just a plain `Resistance` object.

Because the calculations for series and parallel resistance are different, we choose to make functions `calc_resistance()` members of both the `Series_resistance` and `Parallel_resistance` classes. A pure virtual function of the same name and signature is a member of `Resistance`. The two resistance values for each object and a function for reading the data can also be members of `Resistance`.

ALGORITHM

The calculation of the resistance of the subcircuits is straightforward. For `Series_resistance`, we have a `calc_resistance()` function with the line

```
return (r1 + r2);
```

and for `Parallel_resistance`, we have a `calc_resistance()` function with the line

```
return (1 / (1/r1 + 1/r2));
```

These correspond to Eqns. 15.1 and 15.2, respectively. The more conceptually difficult part of the algorithm is in the calculation of the resistance of the entire circuit. The loop, which performs the calculations of Eqn. 15.2 for four resistors (because there are four subcircuits), is:

```
denominator = 0;
for (i = 0; i < 4; i++)
  denominator += 1 / ptr[i] -> calc_resistance ();
total_resistance = 1 / denominator;
```

The key to its execution is the role of `ptr[]`. Each element of `ptr[]` is an address of either a series subcircuit or parallel subcircuit object. When

```
ptr[i] -> calc_resistance ();
```

is executed, the correct version of `calc_resistance()` is called based on the type of address contained in `ptr[]`. The power of this form is that there is no need to have an `if-else` statement in the loop checking the type of object. For this particular program, one may not see a big advantage, but when there are many objects, many types of objects, and many loops of this sort, the advantages are much greater. Also, the loops do not need to change if different types of objects are added to the system. We simply create another derived class.

Read the source code and annotations to see the entire program.

Source Code

```
#include <iostream>
using namespace std;
```

```
class Resistance
        {
        protected:
                double r1, r2;
        public:
                void read_data ();
                virtual double calc_resistance () = 0;
        };
```

The `Resistance` class is a virtual class because `calc_resistance()` is a pure virtual function. The class contains data (`r1` and `r2`) and function (`read_data`) members that are common to all derived classes.

```
class Series_resistance : public Resistance
        {
        public:
                double calc_resistance ();
        };

class Parallel_resistance : public Resistance
        {
        public:
                double calc_resistance ();
        };
```

Both `Series_resistance` and `Parallel_resistance` inherit from `Resistance`. They have only a `calc_resistance()` member function.

```
void Resistance :: read_data ()
        {
        cout << "Enter 2 resistances." << endl;
        cin >> r1 >> r2;
        }
```

Because the `read_data()` function works for both derived classes, it is a member of `Resistance`. Note that it is not a virtual function, so it needs a definition.

```
double Series_resistance :: calc_resistance ()
        {
        return (r1 + r2);
        }

double Parallel_resistance :: calc_resistance ()
        {
        return (1 / (1 / r1 + 1 / r2));
        }
```

These `calc_resistance()` functions override the virtual `calc_resistance()` function in class `Resistance`. Because the `calc_resistance()` function in class `Resistance` is virtual, it needs no body.

```
int main ( )
{
        Resistance* ptr[4];

        int i;
        char name;
        double denominator, total_resistance;

        for (i = 0; i < 4; i++)
                {
                cout << "Enter type (s or p)" << endl;
                cin >> name;
```

To get the polymorphism to work, we need an array of base class pointers (here, called `ptr[4]`).

The `name` variable, entered by the user, specifies that a subcircuit is either series or parallel.

```
            if (name == 's')
                    {
                    ptr[i] = new Series_resistance;
                    }
            else
                    {
                    ptr[i] = new Parallel_resistance;
                    }

            ptr[i] -> read_data();
            }

        denominator = 0;
        for (i = 0; i < 4; i++) denominator += 1 / ptr[i] -> calc_resistance ();
        total_resistance = 1 / denominator;

        cout << "Total resistance = " << total_resistance << endl;
}
```

For series, we create a new `Series_resistance` object. The `ptr[i]` array element is assigned the address of that object.

For parallel, we create a new `Parallel_resistance` object. The `ptr[i]` array element is assigned the address of that object.

This calls the base class `read_data()` function. We use an address of a derived object to call the function.

Calculating and displaying the total resistance. The `ptr[i]` created in the previous loop determines the `calc_resistance` function called.

Output

```
                Enter type (s or p)
Keyboard input  s
                Enter 2 resistances.
Keyboard input  4 8
                Enter type (s or p)
Keyboard input  p
                Enter 2 resistances.
Keyboard input  9 7
                Enter type (s or p)
Keyboard input  p
                Enter 2 resistances.
Keyboard input  3 6
                Enter type (s or p)
Keyboard input  s
                Enter 2 resistances.
Keyboard input  2 1
                Total resistance = 0.854
```

Comments

For simplicity, we have used only four subcircuits. More can be used with little change to the source code.

Note that we have used `new` to instantiate objects of the derived classes. A total of four objects is instantiated with this method. However, when we program, we do not know the distribution between parallel and series subcircuits. We could have declared four objects each of the `Series_resistance` and `Parallel_resistance` classes, to be safe. But doing so would have reserved memory for eight objects when we need only four. Therefore, using `new` saves memory because it gives the program the flexibility to reserve any distribution of object types.

Modification Exercises

Modify the program so that:

1. Ten subcircuits can be used.

2. The data is read from a file.

3. It can analyze subcircuits that are in series with each other rather than in parallel.

LESSON EXERCISES

LESSON 15.1 EXERCISES

1. True or false:

a. A protected data member can only be accessed by friends of a class.

b. The public form of inheritance is the form most commonly used.

c. All base class data members can be accessed by derived classes.

d. Base and derived class functions must have different signatures.

e. We can use a derived class object to call a base class function.

Solutions

1. a. false
b. true
c. false
d. false
e. true

LESSON 15.2 EXERCISES

1. True or false:

a. In inheritance, members of the derived class are considered to be members of the base class.

b. When we define a base class, we must indicate which classes inherit from it.

c. A base class can have any number of derived classes.

d. Objects of the derived class have sub-objects of the base class.

e. Cyclic diagrams are used to illustrate inheritance.

2. Write a program that creates a `Fluid` base class with derived classes `Gas` and `Liquid`. Create `Gas` objects `oxygen`, `nitrogen`, `helium`, and `hydrogen`, and `Liquid` objects `water`, `oil`, and `alcohol`. Look in your chemistry books for their properties, and create members for each property. Put shared properties in the `Fluid` base class. Print out the values in a neat table.

3. Suppose you were in the following professions. Make a list of base classes, derived classes, and objects you might create if you were to write a program for solving problems in your field.

   a. Agricultural engineer working with plants.

   b. Materials engineer working with metals.

   c. Bioengineer creating mechanical body parts.

   d. Civil engineer constructing public works projects.

Solutions

1. a. false
   b. false
   c. true
   d. true
   e. false

LESSON 15.3 EXERCISES

1. True or false:

   a. We can call a constructor only one level up the inheritance graph.

   b. Constructors are called in the order top down the inheritance graph.

   c. The private members of base classes remain private to themselves.

   d. We cannot assign base class objects to derived class objects.

2. Write a program that creates a `Vehicle`, `Automobile`, `Convertible` class hierarchy. Choose data members that are appropriate for each class. Use constructors in each class. Declare an object of the `Convertible` class.

Solutions

1. a. true
   b. true
   c. true
   d. true

LESSON 15.4 EXERCISES

1. True or false:

   a. Multiple inheritance is quite complicated in programs of practical size.

   b. The private data members of base classes remain private to that class.

   c. Inheriting from two or more base classes is called *multiple inheritance.*

   d. Creating levels of inheritance is also called *multiple inheritance.*

2. List five sets of class names for which multiple inheritance may be appropriate.

Solutions

1. a. true
   b. true
   c. true
   d. false

LESSON 15.5 EXERCISES

1. True or false:
   a. Even a pure virtual function needs a definition.
   b. Virtual objects can be created from virtual classes.
   c. Early binding is the most common form of binding used in programs.
   d. C++ allows us to create base class pointer variables and assign derived class addresses to them.
   e. Dynamic binding takes more execution time than static binding.
2. Consider an air compressor that inflates tires. Below 100 psi, a compressor continues to increase a tire pressure. Above 100 psi the tire bursts, and the pressure is 0. Write a program that creates a virtual class to simulate this behavior.

Solutions

1. a. false
   b. false
   c. true
   d. true
   e. true

APPLICATION EXERCISES

Use inheritance to write the following programs. Write stubs that output a statement indicating a calculation has been performed for the functions instead of the actual calculation when specified to do so.

1. Write a program to analyze a pipe-pump network. Create a network class that has a `calc_pressure` virtual function. For the pipes, the pressure drop is 50 psf per 1000 ft of pipe. For the pumps, the pressure increase is in the input data. Use polymorphism and a single loop to calculate the total pressure change. Read the data from file `pipe_net.dat` (use U for pump and P for pipe). Print the result to the screen. Make your program capable of handling at least 20 pump-pipe combinations. Sample input data indicating a sequence of four pumps and pipes (the number after the letter indicates either the pressure increase for a pump or the length of the pipe):

   U 300 P 800 U 1200 P 1500 U 100 P 3400 U 400 P 6000

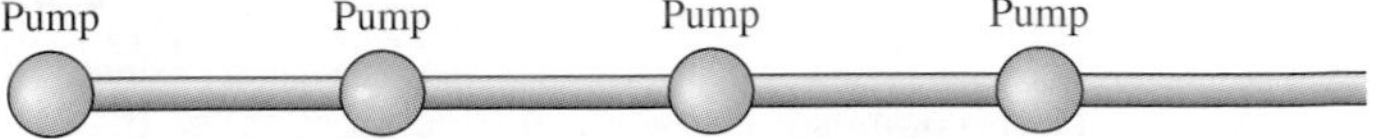

2. Write a program to analyze the deflection of a beam created with many types of beams. Create a beam class that has a `calc_deflection` virtual function. The possible beam types are T beam, I beam, C beam, and pipe beam. The thickness and length of each of the beams is given as input data. The following length/thickness/load/deformation relationships are given for each beam type:

   T beam—0.01 m deflection for 5 kN load, 10 m length, and 0.005 m thickness
   I beam—0.015 m deflection for 8 kN load, 15 m length, and 0.002 m thickness
   C beam—0.02 m deflection for 15 kN load, 20 m length, and 0.007 m thickness
   P beam—0.03 m deflection for 30 kN load, 15 m length, and 0.006 m thickness

   Use linear scaling to calculate deflections for different geometry. Use polymorphism and a single loop to calculate the total deflection. Read the data from `file beam.dat`. Print the result to the screen. Sample input data indicating the load, then a sequence of four beams (the numbers after the letter indicates length and thickness in m, respectively). Make your program capable of handling at least 15 beam sections.

   12.4
   T 1.5 0.03 I 2.3 0.02 T 3.4 0.07 C 1.3 0.03

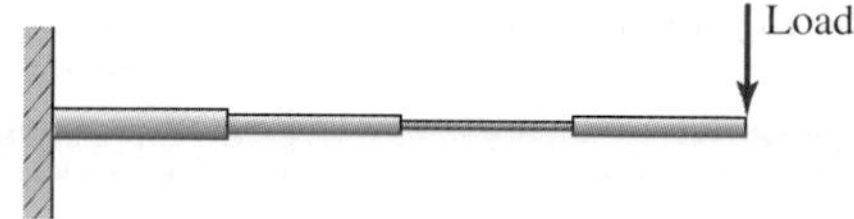

3. A shape consists of combinations of constant (C), linear (L), and parabolic (P) functions. Calculate the area (using negative area for below the x axis) of such a shape using polymorphism and a single loop. Sample input data for three types is

   C 0 3.5 6 L 3.5 6 2.5 −4 P 6 9.3 1 −11 24

   Where the first two numbers after the letters are x coordinates of the beginning and end of the shape. For C, the third number is the constant y value. For L, the third and fourth numbers are m and b, respectively, in $y = mx + b$. For P, the third, fourth, and fifth numbers are a, b, and c, respectively in $y = ax^2 + bx + c$. Make your program capable of handling at least 20 shapes. Use dynamic memory allocation.

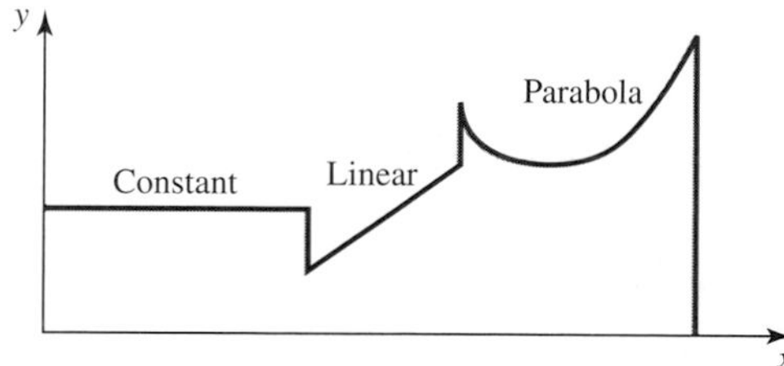

4. Use inheritance and polymorphism to calculate the force required to pull (at a constant velocity) and the weight of material that can be carried by a train

consisting of many different types of cars. The weight (W) and rolling friction coefficient (f) can be used to compute the force ($F = fW$). Consider flat bed (B), box (X), and tank (T) cars. The volume for each type of car is B (10 m^3), X (20 m^3), and T (15 m^3). Read the type of car and density (in kN/m^3) of material being carried. A sample data file (`train.dat`) is

B 5.3 X 6.7 X 5.6 X 7.3 T 9.8 T 8.4 T 10.3 B 3.2 B 4.2

5. Write a program that can find the current in the figure below for any values of the resistances. Assume that many subcircuits with three resistors can be placed in the circuit.

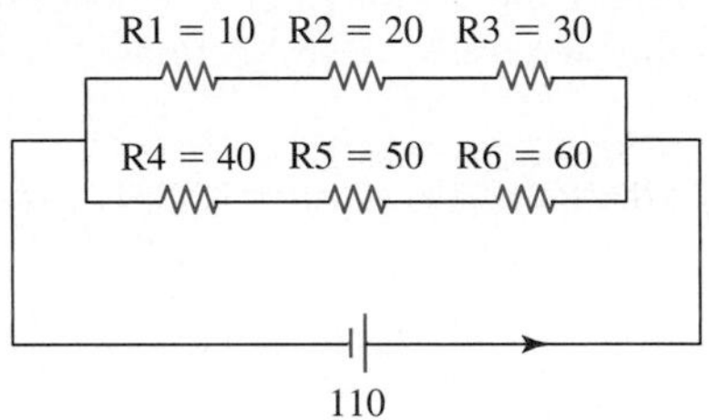

CHAPTER 16

DATA STRUCTURES AND RECURSION

CHAPTER TOPICS

In this chapter, you will learn how to:

- Create list, stack, queue, and tree data structures in C++
- Use recursion

Data structures are used in programming because they enable data to be accessed and modified in a relatively easy manner. By utilizing the advanced data structures taught in this chapter, we will find that we can perform seemingly complex manipulations rather simply. For instance, suppose we had an array of 10,000,000 values, and we wanted to insert a single new value near the beginning of the array and increase the array size to 10,000,001. Doing so would require moving approximately 10,000,000 values to make space for the new value. The effort to do this is considerable and may take significant execution time. However, by using a *linked list* data structure (taught in this chapter) instead of an array to hold the data, we could insert a new value near the beginning and need only two actions to do so! Therefore, we see that the linked list data structure can be quite useful for certain programming projects. In addition to the linked list, in this chapter we illustrate the *stack, queue,* and *tree* data structures. All these are useful for solving certain types of programming problems.

The linked list, stack, queue, and tree are not the only data structures used in programming. In fact, we have already made use of elementary data structures in this text. The first data structure we discussed was an array. We have seen that arrays are valuable for solving many problems (but not all) in programming because they serve to group information that is related. The framework of arrays simulates a number of basic mathematical representations of data and is therefore quite useful to programmers. A `struct` (generically called a *record*) is another data structure we have covered.

We have seen that C++ has array and `struct` data structures automatically built in. That is, C++ has a syntax and format for utilizing arrays and `struct`s. However, the linked list, stack, queue, and tree data structures are not so readily available in C++. Therefore, in this chapter we show how to develop our own versions of them. (Note: in Chapter 17 we show how to use other techniques to access these data structures.)

In this chapter, we create classes (sometimes called *container classes*) of the same names as the data structures. Our goal is to develop a level of *data abstraction* with the classes. If the data abstraction is implemented correctly, the details of the abstraction are invisible to the user of a class, and the abstraction (class) can be utilized by simply knowing the concept. In this book, of course, we show you the details. By knowing the details, you will be able to create a level of data abstraction for your programs.

Also in this chapter, we illustrate the process of *recursion*. Recursion is a form of repetition. In some ways it is similar to the iterative procedures we covered in the chapter on loops (Chapter 6). Some of the drawings we use to illustrate recursion resemble those we used for loops. Recursion is a more specialized application of repetitive actions. We will not say more at this time, and instead leave you to read the details in Lesson 16.5 and in the application examples.

LESSON 16.1 A PROGRAMMER-DEFINED LINKED LIST CLASS

TOPICS

- Defining a linked list class
- Reserving memory for each node
- Initializing each node
- Printing the contents of each node

An object is ideal for creating a linked list because data members (of many different types) are all stored in a contiguous (or nearly contiguous) block of memory. In order to create a linked list, it is necessary for one of the data members to be a pointer variable. The address stored in this pointer variable is the address of the next block of memory (object) included in the linked list and is therefore the link between memory blocks. In this lesson, we first describe the concepts behind a linked list; then we illustrate a program that creates a linked list.

Note: In this and the succeeding lessons of this chapter, we use a number of classes with public data members and no function members. In effect, these classes are `structs`. However, we prefer to use classes here because we want to discuss objects. Although the class has public data members, we do not violate encapsulation because we have no function members.

We call a small block of memory (object) a *node* in a linked list and represent it with a rectangle. Also, we call the address that is stored in the pointer variable in the object a *link* and represent it with a dark square as shown in Fig. 16.1. The arrow that points to the next rectangle illustrates that the address is that of the next object. Within the rectangle, we show text or numeric information that is also stored in the object.

In Fig. 16.1 we show five objects. Each object contains the name of a client company for a consulting firm and the address of the object in which the next company is stored.

Fundamentally, a linked list does not work like an array. We will see that in order to access the 500th node in a linked list we must go node by node from the first to the 500th following the address part of each object (Fig. 16.1). (Note: it is not obvious to you right now why this is necessary.) With arrays, we can go directly to the 500th element by simply using the correct array index. This is an advantage that arrays have over linked lists.

However, because we must go node by node in a linked list, we find that it is easy to delete a node from a list. For instance, if we wanted to delete Hytech Co. from our linked list we could do so by simply changing the address that points to it (currently the one stored in the pointer variable with Natgren Co.'s object). If we make this address point to Mibad Inc., we have effectively deleted Hytech Co. from the list because as we go from node to node in the list, we never reach Hytech Co. (Fig. 16.2). Note that deleting an element in an array takes many more operations because we must shift all of the array elements to close the "empty hole" that may exist when an element is deleted.

Also, we can easily insert a node into a linked list by changing the address stored in the pointer variable for the node preceding the location of the insertion (Fig. 16.3). Here, we have inserted Leyedbak Inc. into the list by changing the address stored in the pointer variable in Zyntex Corp.'s object and having the address stored in the pointer variable for Leyedbak Inc. be the address of Natgren Co. These few operations have caused the new list to appear as shown in Fig. 16.4. Again, inserting an element in an array takes many more operations because we must shift all of the array elements to make space for a new element.

We also find that it is simple to move a node from one location to another in a linked list. For instance, if we wanted to move Natgren Co. to be the last element in the list, we could simply change the pointing of the arrows (or the addresses stored, which indicates changing the locations to which the arrows point) to what is shown in Fig. 16.5. The sketch given in Fig. 16.5 can also be shown as in Fig. 16.6 which clearly illustrates that Natgren Co. has moved to the end of the list. We note that to move Natgren Co. to the end of the list, we changed three addresses, the ones in the pointer variables for the objects for Zyntex Corp, Factell Inc., and Natgren Co. Even if our original list had 1000 nodes and we wanted to move a node to the end of the list, we could still do it by changing just three addresses.

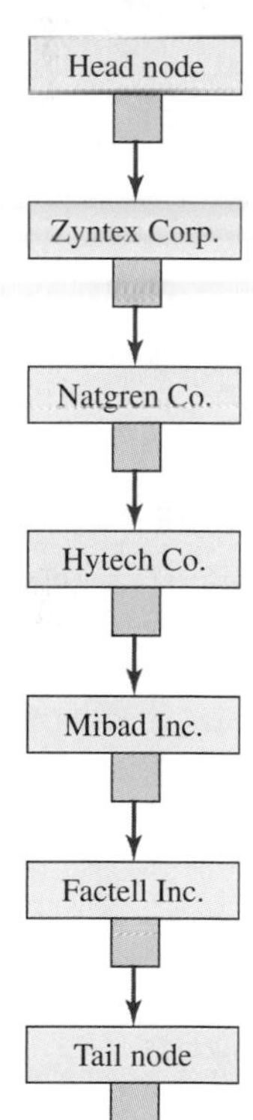

Figure 16.1

Representation of a linked list. Each rectangle square pair represents an object. The shaded portion and arrow represent the address stored in the object's pointer variable.

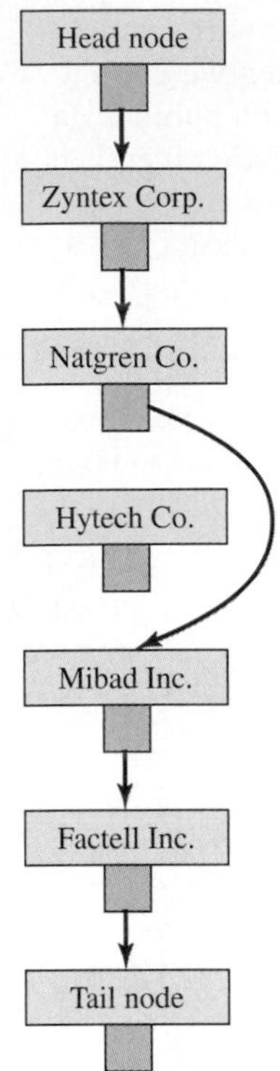

Figure 16.2

By changing the address in object Natgren Co. to Mibad Inc.'s address, we delete Hytech Co. from the linked list. This works because to traverse a linked list, we must go node by node. Although the name Hytech Co. may still exist in memory, we never get to it as we traverse through the linked list.

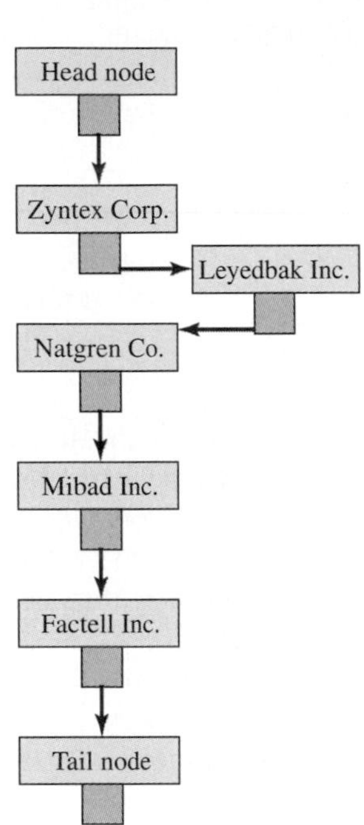

Figure 16.3

We have inserted Leyedbak Inc. into the list by changing the address stored in the pointer variable for Zyntex Corp.'s object and having the address stored in the pointer variable for Leyedbak Inc. be the address of Natgren Co.

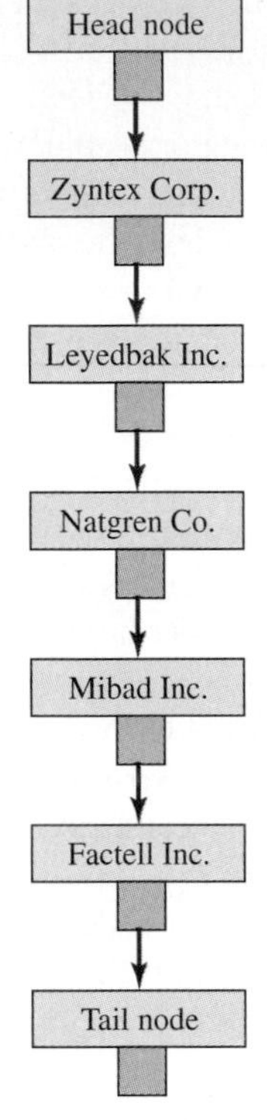

Figure 16.4

This is the list after inserting Leyedbak Inc. The number of operations to do this was very few compared to the number it would take to do this with an array structure.

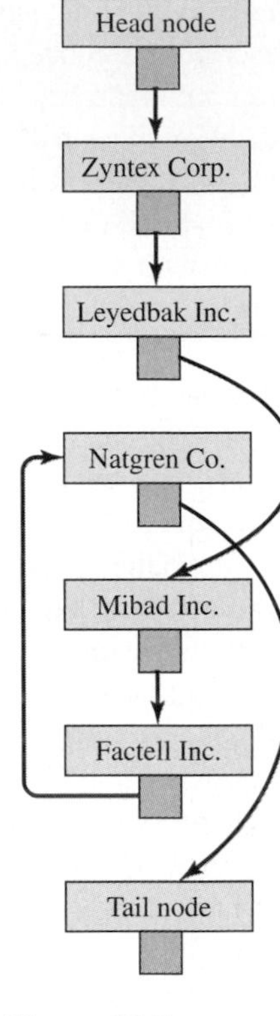

Figure 16.5

By changing the addresses to which the pointer variables point, the order of the list is effectively changed. The list above is the same as that shown in Fig. 16.6.

The few operations that it takes to do this is another advantage that linked lists have over arrays. If we had an array with 1000 elements and wanted to move the 10th element to the end, we would have had to remove the 10th element and move 990 elements forward one place and then put the removed element at the end. Thus, to perform the same task with an array requires many more operations.

Because of some of the advantages that linked lists have over arrays, we find that there are times when linked lists of objects are preferable to arrays of objects. In this lesson we show how to create a linked list class.

The program that we give in this lesson's source code is different from programs that we have used in other lessons in that it illustrates more than just syntax and form. It shows how to create a linked list (it does not show inserting and deleting), and therefore you need to follow the logic and understand the flow in detail to create your own linked lists. In this introduction, we will point out some of the highlights. The

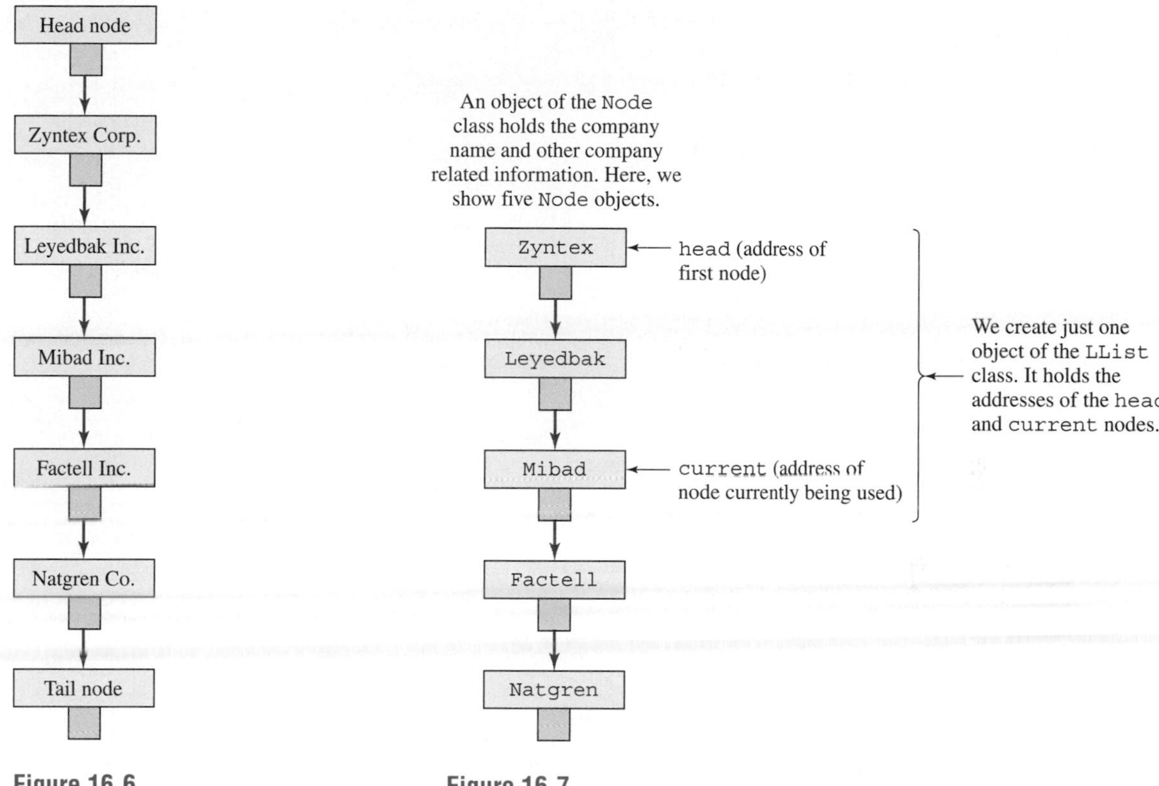

Figure 16.6

This figure is the same as that shown in Fig. 16.5. We have effectively moved Natgren Co. to the end of the list. This has been accomplished by changing just three addresses.

Figure 16.7

`Node` and `LList` objects.

details are given in the explanation following the source code. This program is not a complete application of a linked list. We have deliberately eliminated some details in order to focus on creating nodes and the connections between the nodes.

QUESTION YOU SHOULD ATTEMPT TO ANSWER

1. What is the meaning of `current -> client`?

This program creates a linked list of client names *and* hours billed for a consulting firm. Thus each node of the linked list holds a character array, `client[ ]`, and an integer variable, `hours_billed`.

We use two classes to create the linked list (Fig. 16.7). The first class (called `Node`) holds only data and therefore is like a `struct`. Each object of this class is a node in the list. The other class (called `LList`) holds the member functions that perform operations on the nodes. It also holds the addresses of the head node and "current" node of the list. We create just one object of this class because we are creating only one linked list in our program. In other words, the `LList` object keeps track of which node is the first node and which node is the one we are currently working with.

Read the annotations in the source code and then the description to understand how to create a linked list. Note that because a linked list works with addresses, the arrow operator is used instead of the dot operator to access data members of the nodes.

Source Code

```
#include <iostream>
using namespace std;

class Node
{
        public:
                char client[20];
                int hours_billed;
                Node* next_node;
};

class LList
{
        private:
                Node* head;
                Node* current;
        public:
                void make_list ();
                void show_list ();
};

void LList :: make_list ()
{
        int i;

        head = new Node;

        current = head;
        for (i = 1; i <= 3; i++)
                {
                cout << "Enter client's name and hours billed." << endl;
                cin >> current -> client >> current -> hours_billed;
                current -> next_node = new Node;
                current = current -> next_node;
                }
}

void LList :: show_list ()
{
        int i;
        current = head;
        for (i = 1; i <= 3; i++)
                {
                cout << current -> client << "  " << current -> hours_billed
                    << " hours." << endl;
                current = current -> next_node;
                }
}
```

This is a class with only public data members, no function members. The data are the information contained in a node. A pointer variable of type `Node*` is required for a linked list node. Its name is `next_node` because it holds the address of the subsequent node in the list (this is represented by the darkened square of each node in Figs. 16.1 to 16.7). The other data is simply what is of interest for the particular list being created. In this case, we are interested in keeping track of the client's name and the billing hours.

The linked list class keeps track of the current node being worked on and the head node of the list. It uses the addresses of these nodes to do so. Thus, the types are `Node*`.

The process begins by creating an empty node. The variable, `head`, is assigned the address of this node.

We begin working with the first node, so we set the current node to be the head node.

For this example, we create just three nodes.

A user enters the information asked for. Note that because we are working with addresses, we use `current -> client` not `current.client` and `current-> hours_billed` not `current.hours_billed` to read the client name and number of billed hours. This `cin` statement fills the current object's data members.

This makes the current node hold the address of a new node.

This, in effect, advances us to the next node. This makes the current address equal to the address of the next node (which is the new node).

To begin printing the list, we begin by making the current node the first node.

Looping over all the nodes.

Printing the data for the current node.

Advancing to the next node by making the current node the next node.

```
int main ( )
{
        LList billing;
        billing.make_list ();
        billing.show_list ();
}
```

Declaring a single object of the `LList` class. This list holds the billing information.

Creating and printing the list.

Output

```
                    Enter client's name and hours billed.
Keyboard input      Zyntex 520
                    Enter client's name and hours billed.
Keyboard input      Factell 109
                    Enter client's name and hours billed.
Keyboard input      Natgren 102
                    Zyntex 520 hours.
                    Factell 109 hours.
                    Natgren 102 hours.
```

Description

Visual image of linked list in memory. While Figs. 16.1 to 16.7 were helpful for illustrating some of the basic operations of linked lists, another image is useful for understanding why our program is written with addresses and arrow operators in what appears to be a confusing manner. This image is shown in Fig. 16.8. In this figure, the blocks of memory (representing nodes or objects in the linked list) are randomly distributed in memory. Each block contains the address of the beginning of another block, which allows us to go from one block to another starting at the beginning of the list. In this figure, start at the lower left corner and follow the arrows, block by block, through the list. If we asked you to find the sixth element in the list, the only way for you to do it would be to go block by block, following the arrows until you reached the sixth block. Our program works the same way. It goes block by block because there is no other way to go through the list.

Be aware that each block of memory is identified only by its *address*! There is no variable *name* associated with each block. We can get to the sixth block only because we know its address. Therefore, the program keeps track of the address of the current node we are visiting. This is done with the pointer variable called `current`. Of course, we use a pointer variable because a pointer variable can store an address. Remember, with a name of an object, we use a dot operator to access its public data members, and with the address of an object, we use the arrow operator to access its public data members. This means that if we want to access a data member of the current node, for instance, `client`, we need to use

```
current -> client
```

If we need to get the data member that holds the address of the next node in the list

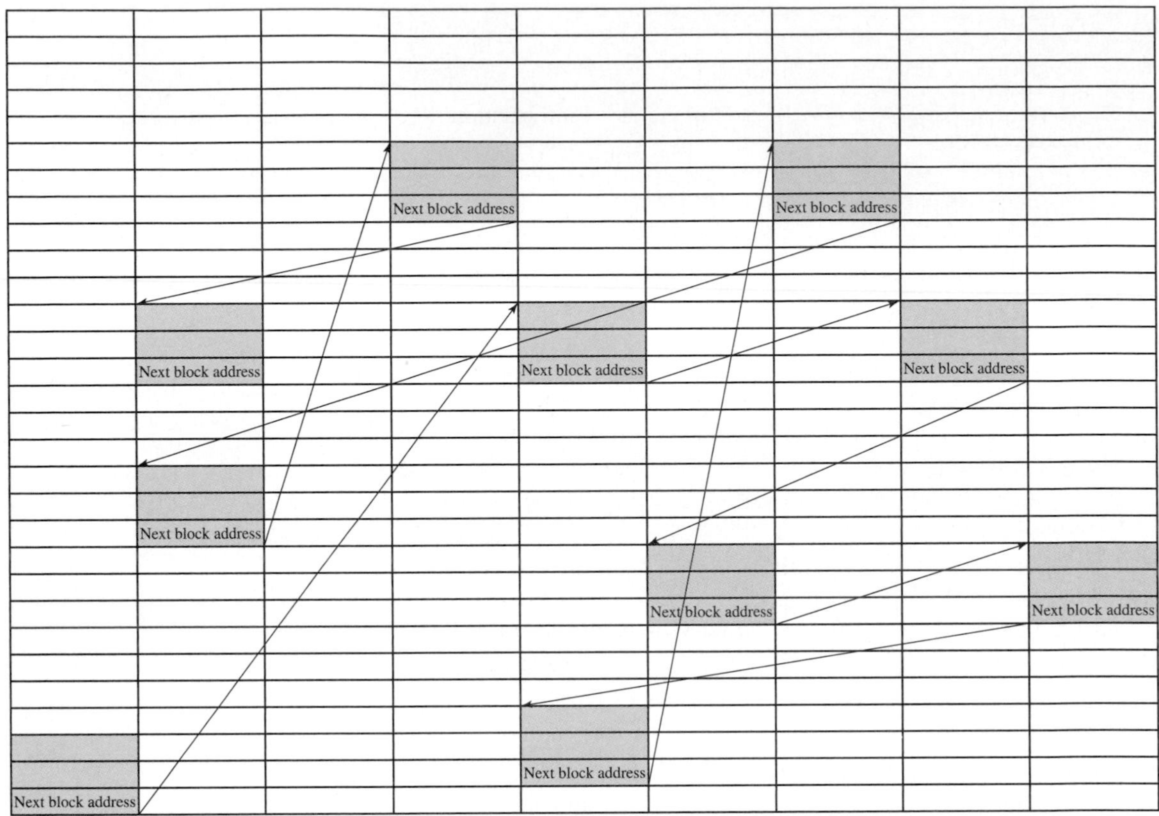

Figure 16.8

An image of a linked list in memory.

(called `next_node`) we use

```
current -> next_node
```

Rather than focusing on the arrow operator, you should simply think of this form as a single variable name. As you follow the code, just think of `current -> client` as the client's name of the current node, and `current -> next_node` as the address of the subsequent node. In other words, although it is confusing looking, simplify the arrow notation in your mind, and you will find it easier to trace the code.

When we use the statement

```
current = current -> next_node
```

we are moving one block down the list. In other words, after executing this statement the new current node is the address held by the old current node (represented by `current -> next_ node`).

Also, not shown in this lesson's program but a later one, is

```
current -> next_node -> next_node
```

This is a single entity meaning the address of the block that is two down the list from the current block. And

```
current = current -> next_node -> next_node
```

advances `current` two blocks down the list.

To add a new node after the current one (that may be at the end of the list), we use

```
current -> next_node = new Node
```

where Node is the name of the class holding the block information. Remember, new returns the address of the block of memory it reserves. Therefore, this statement puts an address into the memory cell represented by current -> next_node (which is the address stored in the current node object).

Note that Fig. 16.8 clearly illustrates that a linked list is very different from an array because array elements are stored in contiguous memory locations, whereas blocks of memory in linked lists are not at all contiguous. With arrays, we know the addresses of all of the elements if we know the address of just one. With a linked list, knowing the address of just one block of memory does not tell us anything about the addresses of any other blocks. With an array, we can move, for instance, from the first element to the twentieth element by simply adding the number of bytes for 20 elements to the address of the first element. To move from the first block to the twentieth block in a linked list, we must read the address of the second block, move to the second block and read the address of the third block, move to the third block and read the address of the fourth block. This must continue block by block until we reach the twentieth block. Thus, it clearly takes more operations to move from node to node in a linked list than it does to go from element to element in an array. However, because of the ease of inserting and deleting nodes, linked lists have advantages over arrays for certain operations.

In addition to keeping track of the current node, we need to keep track of the first node (which we call head) to effectively work with a linked list.

Linked list classes. We use two classes to create a linked list. One holds only the data, which consists of the items of interest and a Node* pointer variable. For this lesson's program, the class is:

```
class Node
{
        public:
                char client[20];
                int hours_billed;
                Node* next_node;
};
```

This class can have any number of members, but one of the members must be a pointer variable to hold an address of a Node object.

In general, a Node class has the form:

```
class Node
{
        public:
                type member1;
                type member2;
                ...
                Node* next_node;
};
```

where *Node* is the class name, *type* are data types (not necessarily all the same), *member1* and *member2* are identifiers representing node data, and *next_node* is the name for storing the address of the next node in the list. The variable *next_node* is represented by the darkened square in Figs. 16.1 to 16.6, and the other data members represent the desired information placed in the light rectangles of these figures. All the data members are public because there are no function members in this class (it is used like a struct, which we covered earlier).

The second class is used to manipulate the nodes. Its data are only pointer variables used to hold addresses of nodes. For this lesson's program, the class is

```
class LList
{
        private:
                Node* head;
                Node* current;
        public:
                void make_list();
                void show_list();
};
```

The head variable is used to store the address of the first object in the list. The current variable is used to hold the address of the node being manipulated. In other words, at any one time in the program, we know only the address of the head node and the address of the current node!

The function members in the LList class create the list and print it; other operations can be added as needed. For simplicity, we have not shown constructors or destructors for this class or any related classes in this chapter. However, they can be used quite effectively for initializing a data structure and deleting memory that is dynamically allocated. Here, we are focusing on the list mechanics and less on creating a robust class. More advanced texts on data structures can be consulted for further details.

Creating a list. In this lesson's program, the function make_list in class LList reserves and fills the memory space for all the nodes of the list. To understand how to create a list, we need to trace the loop in the manner described in Chapter 6. Table 16.1 shows the trace for three iterations through the loop. Follow the statements. Remember, you should think of current -> client and current -> hours_billed as single variable names. Note also that new reserves a block of memory and is used to assign the address of a block to both current and current -> next_node. We do not control what new comes up with for its addresses. It simply gets what is available in the heap. The columns list the variable values *after* execution of the first column statement.

After executing the loop, the memory is filled as shown in Table 16.2, and the linked list has been created. Note that the "Name" column in this table is empty. This illustrates that we cannot access any of the memory blocks by name. We can only get to them using their addresses. That is why the repeated use of the arrow operator is necessary. We must use an address, and the address of one node is stored by the previous node. In this table we have shown arrows to indicate the connections between nodes.

TABLE 16.1 — Trace of loop making the linked list for Lesson 16.1's program

Statements before loop:

```
head = new Node;        (assigns the address 0750 to head)
current = head;         (assigns the address 0750 to current)
```

Statement	current	current -> client	current -> hours_billed	current -> next_node
Before loop	0750	—	—	—
`cin >> current -> client >> current -> hours_billed;`		Zyntex	520	
`current -> next_node = new Node;`				076C
`current = current -> next_node;`	076C			
`cin >> current -> client >> current -> hours_billed;`		Factell	109	
`current -> next_node = new Node;`				0788
`current = current -> next_node;`	0788			
`cin >> current -> client >> current -> hours_billed;`		Natgren	102	
`current -> next_node = new Node;`				07A4
`current = current -> next_node;`	07A4			

TABLE 16.2 — Objects in linked list for Lesson 16.1's program

Name	Type		Address	Value
	Node		0750	
	`char`	`client[20]`		Zyntex
	`int`	`hours_billed`		520
	`Node*`	`next_node`		076C
	Node		076C	
	`char`	`client[20]`		Factell
	`int`	`hours_billed`		109
	`Node*`	`next_node`		0788
	Node		0788	
	`char`	`client[20]`		Natgren
	`int`	`hours_billed`		102
	`Node*`	`next_node`		07A4

Deleting a node. Because we can only access a node through its address, which is stored in the preceding node, we can delete a node by removing its address from the preceding node. For instance, if we wanted to delete the second node in our linked list, we would eliminate the address 076C from the first node (see Table 16.2). After doing this, we would find that no node block has the address 076C. Thus, the second node would be effectively deleted from the list.

However, in order to maintain continuity of the linked list, we must insert another address into the first node block. By inserting the address of the third node, we can complete the list. Table 16.3 illustrates our memory blocks with the second node deleted from the linked list.

In this table, you should observe that nowhere is the address 076C stored. Thus, as we march from node to node, we will never enter the second node and therefore

TABLE 16. 3 — Deleting the second node in the list by changing the value of `next_node` of the first node

Name	Type		Address	Value
	Node		0750	
	char	client[20]		Zyntex
	int	hours_billed		520
	Node*	next_node		0788
	Node		076C	
	char	client[20]		Factell
	int	hours_billed		109
	Node*	next_node		0788
	Node		0788	
	char	client[20]		Natgren
	int	hours_billed		102
	Node*	next_node		07A4

have effectively deleted the second node from our list even if all the information remains stored in its memory block. It is good programming practice to free the memory of a deleted node so that it can be used to store other information.

Inserting and rearranging nodes. We will not describe the code, but to insert or rearrange a linked list, change the addresses according to Figs. 16.3 and 16.5.

Another method for creating a linked list. It is possible to create another type of a linked list that uses arrays. The arrays are parallel, meaning that they correspond element by element. In this form, an array element's subscript is treated in the manner that we have treated an address of a node. One of the parallel arrays is used to hold subscript values. By changing the order of the subscript values stored in this array, we can change the order of the linked list. Space does not permit us to describe this method of creating a linked list.

Comments about linked list creation.

- You may note that all the memory is reserved dynamically one block at a time. Nowhere have we reserved large amounts of space as we often do with arrays when we declare them.
- We make a separate call to `new` to reserve a block of memory for each node of a linked list. If a linked list has 1000 nodes, then we have 1000 calls to `new`. Thus, in a program that uses a linked list, the declarations do *not* reserve blocks of memory for the nodes of the list.
- Note that we do not even declare an ordinary object of type `Node` in class `LList`. We have only pointer variables because we only need to know the address of the object that holds the node's information. With the address of the object, we access the data members of the object. Again, you may notice in

Table 16.2 that the nodes have no name, which means, of course, that we cannot access any of the nodes by name. We must access the nodes by address. Since the address of each node is in the previous node, to traverse the list we must march node by node.

- To change this lesson's program to handle 5000 nodes, we simply change the loop to be from 0 to 5000. None of the declarations, classes, or objects need to change. Class `LList` needs only two pointer variables, and class `Node` simply uses the same data members. In other words, when you write programs with linked lists, you do not need to declare many variables or reserve much memory with your declarations even for very long lists.
- In class `LList`, we generally need only two pointer variables as data members because we work with only one or two nodes at a time. Therefore, we need only to hold the addresses of the blocks of memory for these nodes. As we move from node to node to work with the information at each node, we simply replace the address stored in our pointer variable, `current`, with the address of the next node with which we are working.
- In this lesson's program, we have chosen to hold in the list a character array and an integer, but we could have had many more members and types of members including more character arrays, `doubles`, or numeric arrays.
- Because we go through the loop three times, the last time through the loop we reserve a fourth memory block. This is one more block of memory (at address 07A4) than we need. We could have exited the loop early using a `break` statement, but for simplicity we chose to reserve the memory realizing that it does not occupy much space. Depending on the actions of your program, you may want to exit such a loop early to save memory.
- Observe from Table 16.1 that all the addresses are numerically low. This is because `new` reserves memory in the heap, which has low addresses.

LESSON 16.2 A PROGRAMMER-DEFINED STACK CLASS

TOPICS

- Creating a stack
- Pushing onto a stack
- Popping from a stack

Like the previous lesson, this lesson is unusual in that we describe more than syntax and form. In this lesson we describe a stack, which is a data structure that can be created using the linked list model that we illustrated in Lesson 16.1. In fact, a stack can be considered to be a special case of a linked list. There are other ways to create stacks than what we show in this lesson. However, space does not permit us to describe them.

With a stack we perform only two fundamental operations:

1. Insert a node immediately after the head. This action is called a *push*.
2. Retrieve and delete the node immediately after the head. This action is called a *pop*.

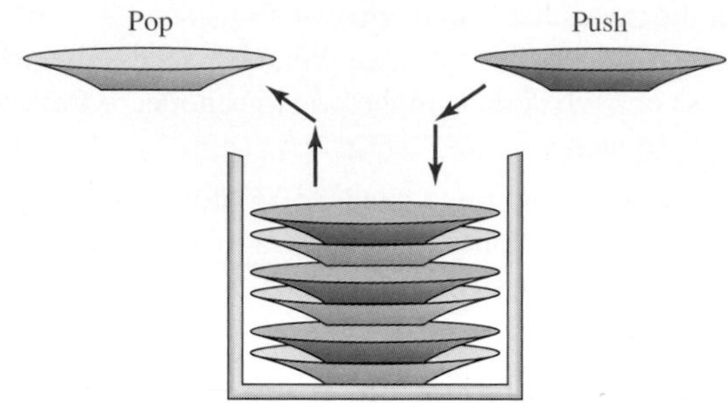

Figure 16.9

Analogy of push and pop using a stack of plates.

Because we only work with nodes at the top of the stack, a commonly used analogy between a stack data structure and something in real life is a stack of plates in a cafeteria line as shown in Fig. 16.9. After the plates have been washed in the kitchen, they are placed at the top of the stack in the cafeteria line. This is similar to a push or many pushes. Each person who eats in the line takes a plate. This is equivalent to a

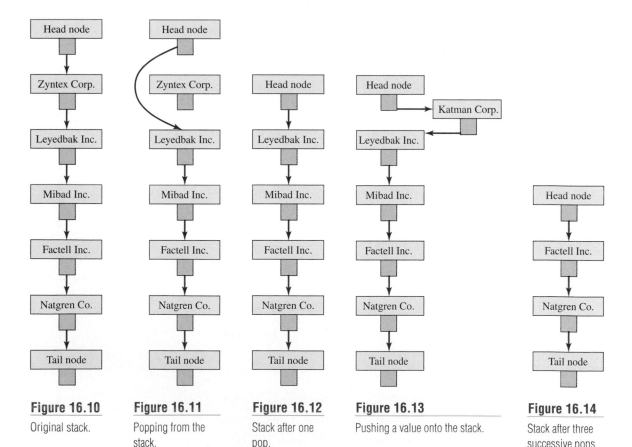

Figure 16.10

Original stack.

Figure 16.11

Popping from the stack.

Figure 16.12

Stack after one pop.

Figure 16.13

Pushing a value onto the stack.

Figure 16.14

Stack after three successive pops after Fig. 16.13.

pop. This is similar to the stack data structure because we are only allowed to place plates at the top of the stack and remove plates from the top of the stack. We do not have access to plates in the middle of the stack without removing the top plates. Similarly, we do not have access to nodes in the middle of a stack data structure without removing nodes at the head.

Using the linked list from the previous lesson we show the actions of push and pop in Figs. 16.10–16.14. Examine these figures before reading the source code.

In creating a stack, we will make use of what can be considered dummy nodes for the head and the tail. These are useful because we know that the node at the top of the stack is pointed to by the head and the node at the bottom of the stack points to the tail. Thus, we know where to find the top of the stack and when we have reached the bottom of the stack.

Why do we create such a data structure? We will find that in addition to simulating some real life actions, a stack is useful for helping us implement more complex data structures such as trees. Read the annotations in the source code and explanation to understand how to create a stack.

QUESTION YOU SHOULD ATTEMPT TO ANSWER

1. Why does function `pop()` have an `int` return type?

Sourec Code

```
#include <iostream>
using namespace std;

class Node
{
        public:
                int key;
                Node* next_node;
};

class Stack
{
        private:
                Node* head;
                Node* tail;

        public:
                Stack ();
                void push (int);
                int pop ();
};
```

`Node` class similar to what we used for the linked list. The data members of a node are an integer (`key`) and an address (`next_node`).

Holding the address of the head and tail nodes.

Function `push( )` for pushing onto the stack.

Function `pop( )` for popping off of the stack.

```
void Stack :: push (int value)
{
        Node* new_node;

        new_node = new Node;
        new_node -> key = value;
        new_node -> next_node = head -> next_node;
        head -> next_node = new_node;
}

int Stack :: pop ()
{
        Node* dummy;
        int value;

        value = head -> next_node -> key;
        dummy = head -> next_node;
        head -> next_node = head -> next_node -> next_node;
        delete (dummy);
        return (value);
}

Stack :: Stack ()
{
        head = new Node;
        tail = new Node;
        head -> next_node = tail;
}

int main ()
{
        Stack inventory;
        int i, value;

        for (i = 1; i <= 3; i++)
                {
                cout << "Enter an integer." << endl;
                cin >> value;
                inventory.push(value);
                }

        cout << endl << "The stack from top to bottom is:" << endl;
        for (i = 1; i <= 3; i++) cout << inventory.pop () << endl;
}
```

The details of this code are given in the Description.

The constructor initializes an empty stack.

Creating two dummy nodes (for the head and tail).

An empty stack has the head node pointing to the tail node.

A stack structure is sometimes used to keep track of inventory items because items are removed and replaced at the top, like a stack.

Pushing a node and making `key = value` on the stack.

The `pop` function returns the value of the key for the top node.

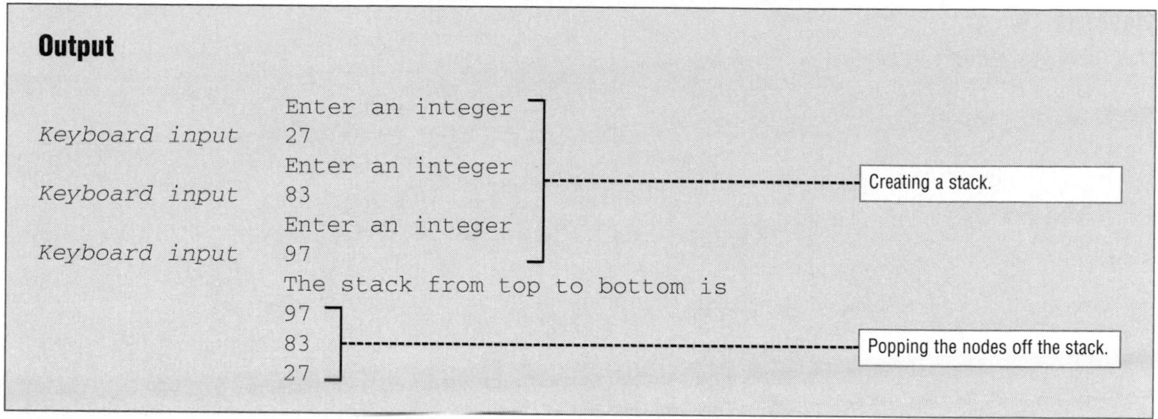
Output
Enter an integer
Keyboard input 27
Enter an integer
Keyboard input 83
Enter an integer
Keyboard input 97
The stack from top to bottom is
97
83
27
Creating a stack.
Popping the nodes off the stack.

Description

Stack classes. We use two classes to create a stack. One class holds only the data and has the same form that we described in Lesson 16.2 for linked lists. For this lesson's program, the class is:

```
class Node
{
        public:
                int key;
                Node* next_node;
};
```

Again, this class can have any number of members, but one of the members must be a pointer variable to hold an address of a `Node` object. The general form for this class is identical to the general linked list form and will not be repeated here.

The second class is used to manipulate the nodes. Its data are only pointer variables used to hold addresses of nodes. The nodes of interest for a stack are the `head` and `tail` (recall they were `head` and `current` for a linked list). For this lesson's program, the class is

```
class Stack
{
        private:
                Node* head;
                Node* tail;
        public:
                Stack ();
                void push (int);
                int pop ();
};
```

The function members here initialize, push, and pop items from the stack. Other operations can be added as needed.

Initializing the stack structure. We create an empty stack by initializing a `head` and a `tail` node. These nodes allow us to find the top (`head`) and bottom (`tail`) of the

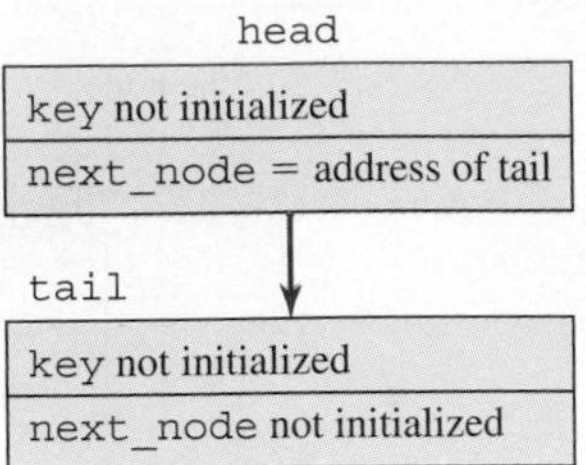

Figure 16.15

The beginning of a stack.

stack when needed. The statements in the `Stack` constructor:

```
head = new Node;
tail = new Node;
head -> next_node = tail;
```

make the head point to the tail with no nodes in between (see Fig. 16.15).

Push. We used the following four statements in `Stack` member function `push` to add a node to the top of the stack:

1. `new_node = new Node;`
2. `new_node -> key = value;`
3. `new_node -> next_node = head -> next_node;`
4. `head -> next_node = new_node`

The actions of each of these statements is described in Fig. 16.16. Follow the figure to understand the actions by statement number.

Pop. We used the following five statements in `Stack` member function `pop()` to remove the top node from the stack and access the key for that node. Note that `head -> next_node` represents the address of the node being popped.

1. `value = head -> next_node -> key;`
2. `dummy = head -> next_node;`
3. `head -> next_node = head -> next_node -> next_node;`
4. `delete(dummy);`
5. `return(value);`

The actions of each of these statements is described in Fig. 16.17.

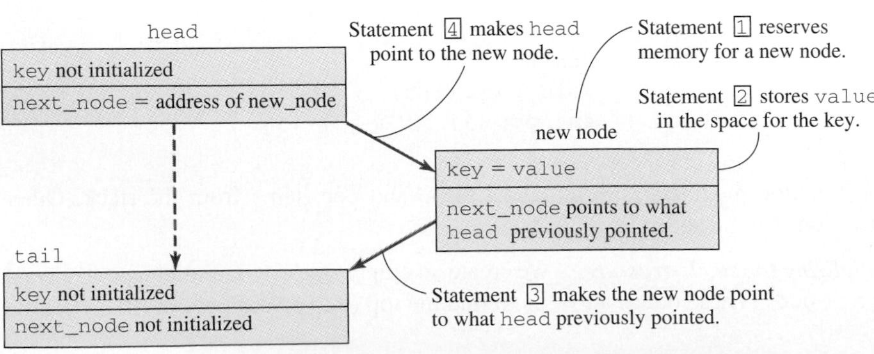

Figure 16.16

The actions of the four statements in `push( )`. The dashed arrow represents what `head` pointed to before `push( )` was called. The actions are similar to those shown in Fig. 16.13.

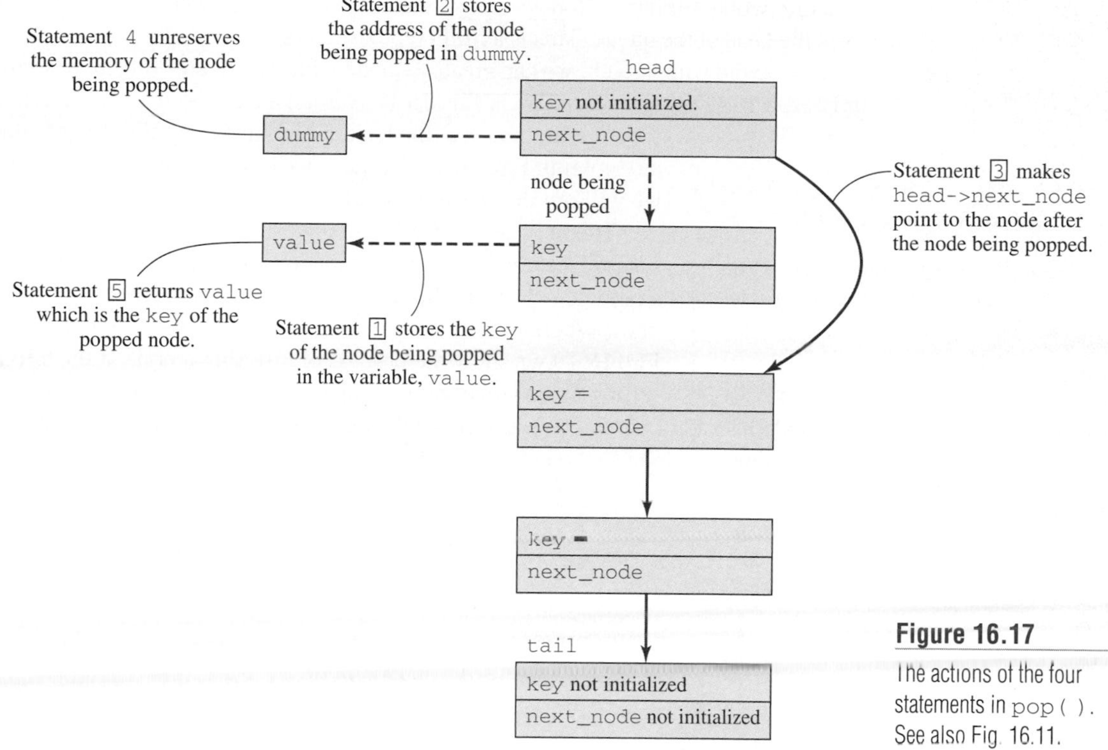
Statement 2 stores the address of the node being popped in dummy.
Statement 4 unreserves the memory of the node being popped.
head
key not initialized.
next_node
dummy
node being popped
Statement 3 makes head->next_node point to the node after the node being popped.
value
key
next_node
Statement 5 returns value which is the key of the popped node.
Statement 1 stores the key of the node being popped in the variable, value.
key =
next_node
key =
next_node
tail
key not initialized
next_node not initialized

Figure 16.17
The actions of the four statements in pop( ). See also Fig. 16.11.

Other stack activities. What we have shown here is a basic stack implementation. A more robust implementation would have done such things as checked to make sure that we did not pop from an empty stack. If we find that the head points to the tail, then we have an empty stack and should not attempt to pop from it. We did not include this check so that we could focus on the creation of the stack. However, in your programs you should check for popping from an empty stack.

LIFO and FIFO. *LIFO* stands for Last In First Out. This describes the stack data structure in that the last node pushed onto the stack is the first node popped off of the stack. LIFO contrasts with *FIFO,* which stands for First In First Out. A *queue* (pronounced "kyoo") is a FIFO type structure in which the first node inserted into the queue is the first node that is removed from the queue. We discuss this data structure in Lesson 16.3.

LESSON 16.3 A PROGRAMMER-DEFINED QUEUE CLASS

TOPICS

- Creating a queue
- Inserting into a queue
- Removing from a queue

We have all experienced queues in our everyday life. When we want to buy groceries we need to wait in a queue. We enter the queue at the end. At the front, people are removed from the queue by having their transactions processed. The queue data structure works similarly. Nodes are inserted at the tail of the queue and are removed from the head of the queue. This is a FIFO type structure.

As we did with a stack, we can create a queue with the linked list form described in Lesson 16.1. We show a queue in Fig. 16.18. We must have both a head and a tail node. The process of removing nodes at the head is similar to popping from a stack as shown in Fig. 16.19. Because we covered this in Lesson 16.2, we will not discuss it in detail here.

The process of inserting a node at the tail means that, unlike a stack, the tail node must point to the node immediately before it as shown in Fig. 16.18. Because the tail points to the last node, we know where to find the last node so we can change its pointer. In Fig. 16.19 we show the process of inserting a node at the tail. Inserting a node involves making the previous last node point to the new node instead of the tail. We also make the new node point to the tail and change the tail pointer to point to the new last node.

QUESTION YOU SHOULD ATTEMPT TO ANSWER

1. How do the data members of the `Queue` class compare to the data members of the `Stack` class of Lesson 16.2?

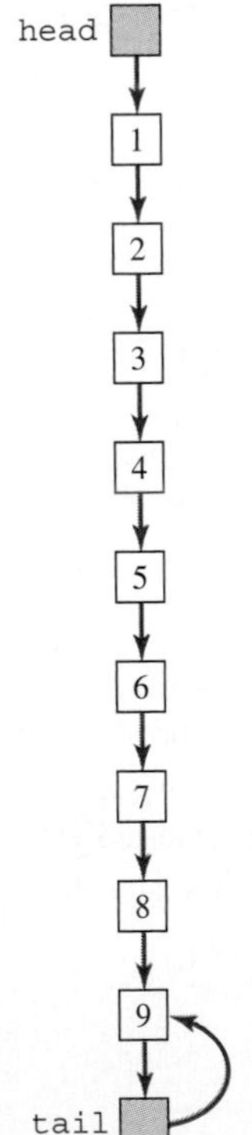
head
1
2
3
4
5
6
7
8
9
tail

Figure 16.18

Original queue. Note that the `tail` node points to the node before it.

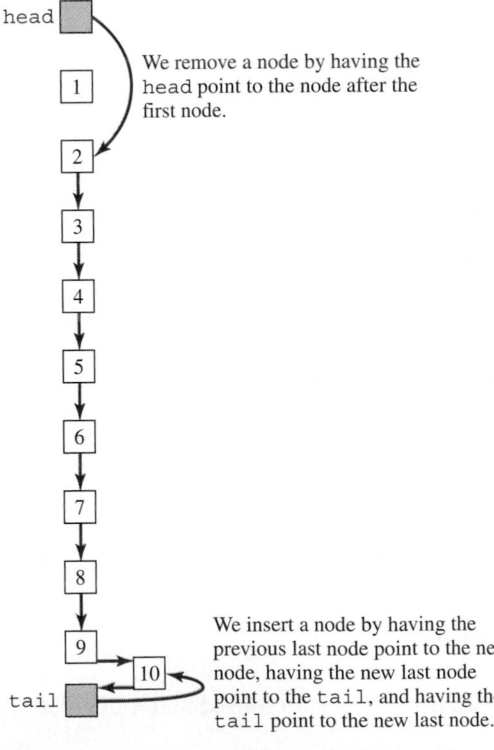
head
We remove a node by having the head point to the node after the first node.
1
2
3
4
5
6
7
8
9
10
tail
We insert a node by having the previous last node point to the new node, having the new last node point to the tail, and having the tail point to the new last node.

Figure 16.19

Removing from a queue at the `head` and inserting into a queue at the `tail`.

This lesson's program illustrates how to perform these operations. Much of the code is very similar to the code for the stack in Lesson 16.2, and, therefore, the annotations focus on the differences between the two codes. Read them and the description.

Source Code

```
#include <iostream.h>
using namespace std;

class Node
{
        public:
                int key;
                Node* next_node;
};

class Queue
{
        private:
                Node* head;
                Node* tail;
        public:
                Queue ();
                void insert (int);
                int remov ();
};

Queue :: Queue ()
{
        head = new Node;
        tail = new Node;
        head -> next_node = tail;
        tail -> next_node = head;
}

void Queue :: insert (int value)
{
        Node* new_node;

        new_node = new Node;
        tail -> next_node -> next_node = new_node;
        tail -> next_node = new_node;
        new_node -> key = value;
        new_node -> next_node = tail;
}
```

This class has the same form as the `Node` class for linked lists and stacks.

Instead of push and pop, we have insert and remove actions.

This constructor body is identical to the `Stack` constructor body.

We insert at the tail (not the head as we do with a stack) This code ic explained in the Description.

```
int Queue :: remov ()
{
        Node* dummy;
        int value;

        value = head -> next_node -> key;
        dummy = head -> next_node;
        head -> next_node = head -> next_node  -> next_node;
        delete  (dummy);
        return  (value);
}

int main ( )
{

        Queue  customers;
        int i,  value;

        for  (i = 1;  i <= 3;  i++)
                  {
                  cout << "Enter  an  integer." << endl;
                  cin >> value;
                  customers.insert  (value);
                  }

        cout << "The  queue  is:" << endl;
        for  (i = 1;  i <= 3;  i++)  cout << customers.remov () << endl;
}
```

We remove at the head, which is the same action as pop. Therefore, this code is identical to pop for `Stack`.

Inserting and removing from the queue.

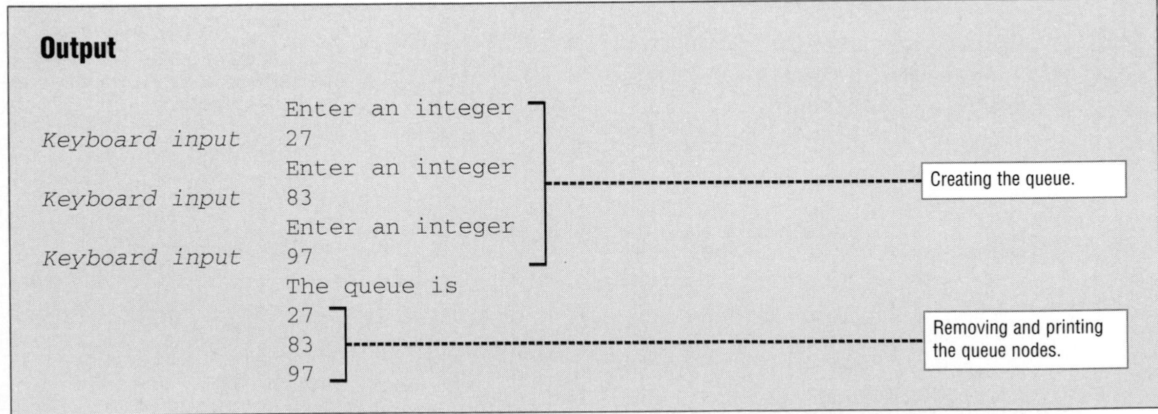

Output

```
                Enter an integer
Keyboard input  27
                Enter an integer
Keyboard input  83
                Enter an integer
Keyboard input  97
                The queue is
                27
                83
                97
```

Creating the queue.
Removing and printing the queue nodes.

Description

Inserting into a queue. First we reserve space for a new node with the statement:

```
new_node = new  Node;
```

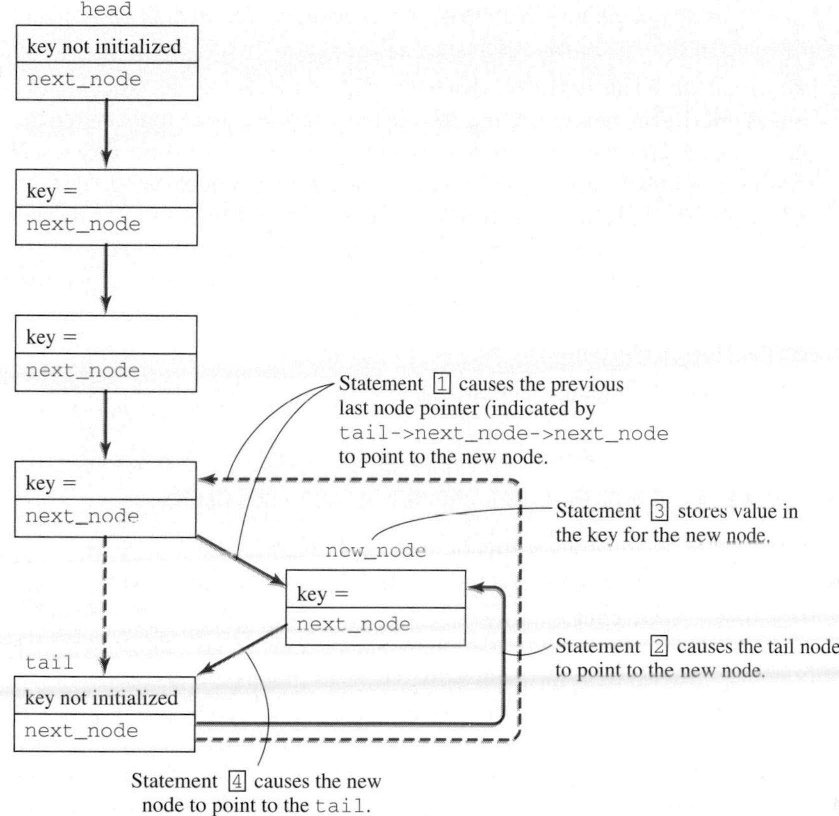

Figure 16.20

The actions of the four statements in `insert()`. The dashed arrows represent pointing before `insert()` is called. Compare this figure to Fig. 16.19.

After this statement, the insert member function of the `Queue` class uses the following four statements.

1. `tail -> next_node -> next_node = new_node;`
2. `tail -> next_node = new_node;`
3. `new_node -> key = value;`
4. `new_node -> next_node = tail;`

The actions of these statements are described in Fig. 16.20. After executing these statements, a new node is inserted at the tail.

Types of queues. Other types of queues are:

1. *Dequeue*—A dequeue is short for "double-ended queue" (pronounced many different ways, among them "dekk," "deek," and "deekyoo"; take your pick). With a dequeue, nodes can be inserted at either end and removed from either end.
2. *Output restricted dequeue*—With this type of dequeue, insertion is allowed at both ends of the queue, but removal is allowed at only one end of the queue.

3. *Input restricted dequeue*—With this type of dequeue, removal is allowed at both ends of the queue, but insertion is allowed at only one end of the queue.
4. *Priority queue*—This is a queue that has a priority for each node. Nodes with highest priority are processed first. Within the priorities, those that entered the queue first are processed first. It works similar to the way that some airlines allow boarding and unboarding of their flights. First-class passengers are given the highest priority and allowed to board and unboard first. Business class is given second priority and allowed to board and unboard second. All other passengers are allowed to board and unboard last. Also, the first first-class passenger in the queue boards first, and the second first-class passenger in the queue boards second. Thus, within equal priorities, the first in the queue is processed first.
5. *Others*—You can imagine that variations of the above can also be created.

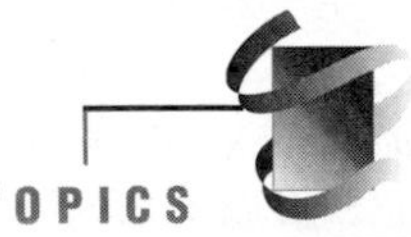

LESSON 16.4 A PROGRAMMER-DEFINED BINARY TREE CLASS

TOPICS

- Creating a binary tree
- Using a stack with a tree

A *tree* is a particular type of a *graph,* and a *binary tree* is a particular type of a tree. In this text we will only develop programs for binary trees and not for general graphs or trees. However, in order to understand how binary trees fit into the bigger picture, we will start with a discussion of graphs.

A graph, as we use it, is not related to what you may have previously called a graph (like an *x-y* plot) in your math classes. In our context, a graph is a data structure that includes nodes similar to what we used in creating linked lists. We have seen how nodes can be connected using linked lists; however, in a linked list, there is only one path to follow from beginning to end. This is because each node has only one pointer, and this pointer points to the next node in the list. If a node can have more than one pointer, then we can create a more general graph. In Fig. 16.21 we show a linked list and a graph.

We will not give formal definitions of graphs but will simply give general descriptions of them. Some terminology is:

1. *Nodes* can also be called *vertices* or *points.*
2. Connections between the nodes are called *edges* or *arcs.*

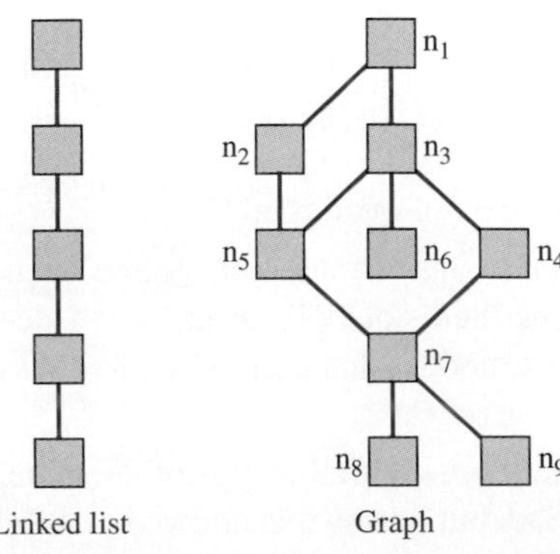

Figure 16.21

Comparing a linked list and a graph.

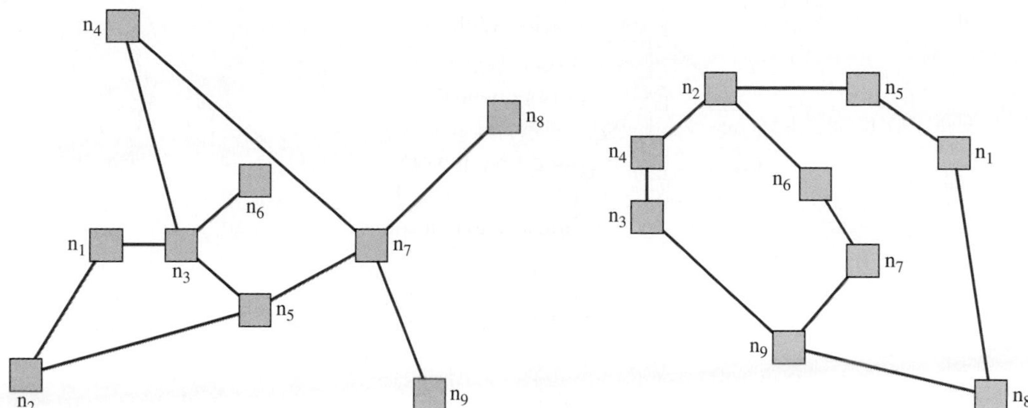

Figure 16.22

Two graphs. Note that the one on the left is the same as the one in Fig. 16.21 because the connections between the nodes are the same.

3. Two nodes are considered to be *adjacent* or *neighbors* if an edge connects them.
4. A *path* between one node and another is indicated by a list of connected nodes between the two.
5. A *simple path* is a path that has no repeated nodes.

Two different graphs are shown in Fig. 16.22. You should observe that the graph on the left part of Fig. 16.22 is the same as the one in Fig. 16.21. Although at first glance they look different, they are the same because the connections between the nodes are the same. For example, for both graphs node 4 is connected to nodes 7 and 3. We can say this about every node in the graphs. Therefore, the graphs are identical.

The most obvious real-life use of graphs is in creating a simulation of a map with the nodes being cities and the edges being roads between the cities (one can visualize this to be similar to the graphs in Fig. 16.22). A *weighted graph* can be created to model the distance between the cities. With a weighted graph, we assign a *length* or *cost* of each edge. By summing the lengths of the edges in a path, we get the distance between two cities.

A *tree* is a graph that has the characteristic that between any two nodes there is only one path, and that path is a simple path. This condition leads to the images shown in Fig. 16.23. A *rooted tree* is a tree that has one node specified to be the root. The root of a tree is traditionally shown at the top of a diagram as shown in

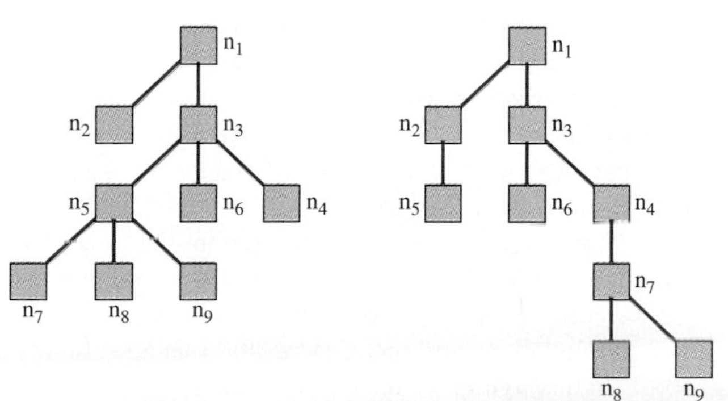

Figure 16.23

Two trees. The one on the right is a binary tree because each node has no more than two children. Observe that there is only one simple path between any two nodes. Contrast this with the graphs of Fig. 16.22 in which more than one simple path can be constructed between two nodes.

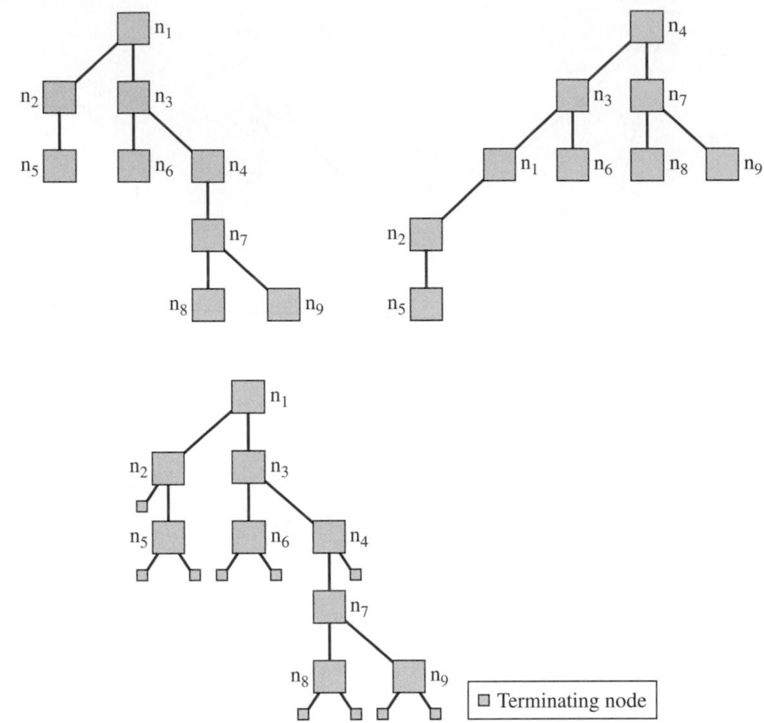

Figure 16.24

Two binary trees that are essentially identical (because the connections for each node are the same) but with different roots.

Figure 16.25

A binary tree for which each regular node has two children. Terminating nodes have been added to assure this. This tree is the same as that shown at the left of Fig. 16.24 but with terminating nodes added.

Fig. 16.24. Any node can be specified as being the root. Once a root is specified, the relationships between the nodes are classified in the following ways, using the tree at the left part of Fig. 16.24 as an example:

1. The root of the tree is n_1.
2. The children of n_3 are n_6 and n_4.
3. The left child of n_3 is n_6, and the right child is n_4.
4. The parent of n_6 and n_4 is n_3.

A binary tree is one in which no node has more than two children. Although not required, to make sure that each regular node of a binary tree has two children, we can add terminating nodes as shown in Fig. 16.25.

This lesson's program illustrates how a binary tree can be created. Binary trees are useful to model the combination of two elements to create another element, which is used with another element to create a new element. For instance, if we were to construct an automobile, we might find that we can illustrate the process using a binary tree such as the one shown in Fig. 16.26. Because we are using two parts to create a third part, which is then used to create another part, we find that a tree can model this process. If we were interested in determining the time schedule of completion, with a tree we clearly see the dependence of the completion of the upper-level elements on the completion of the lower-level elements.

Similarly, we can model an arithmetic calculation using a binary tree. This is shown in Fig. 16.27. In this figure, we have modeled the equation:

$$((5 + 6)/(7 - 9)) * 3 = -16.5$$

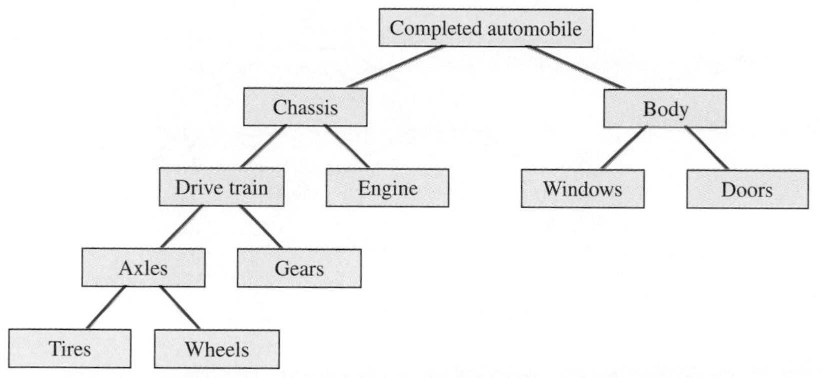

Figure 16.26

A binary tree that illustrates combining different parts to create a final product. This can be used to model the time schedule of completion or the costs of production.

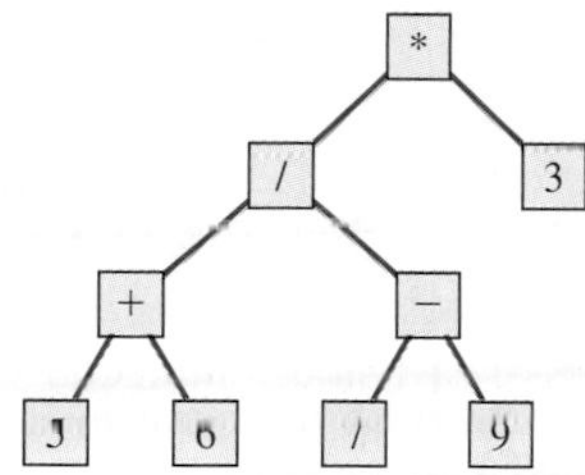

Figure 16.27

A binary tree illustrating the calculation ((5 + 6) / (7 − 9)) * 3.

Binary trees are well-suited to this type of representation because each operator has two operands. More complex equations may not necessarily be capable of being modeled with a binary tree.

In this lesson's program we create the binary tree for this calculation. To create this equation without using parentheses we use what is commonly called "Reverse Polish Notation," which is named after the Polish mathematician who invented it. It can also be called postfix notation. If you have a calculator that operates with this method, then you know that the order of entering the input would be:

$5 \quad 6 + 7 \quad 9 - / \, 3 \, *$

In this lesson's program, we use this input to create the binary tree of Fig. 16.27. We do not solve the equation here, though, but instead solve it in Application Example 16.2.

There are many different ways to create a binary tree. We use a procedure that involves four steps:

1. Reserving memory for the node including space for the values (being numbers or operators for this lesson's program) and the addresses of left and right children.
2. Filling the node's memory cells with the values to be stored in each node.
3. Filling the node's memory cells with the addresses of the left and right children.
4. Assigning the address of the node itself to be the left or right child of another node (unless it is the root).

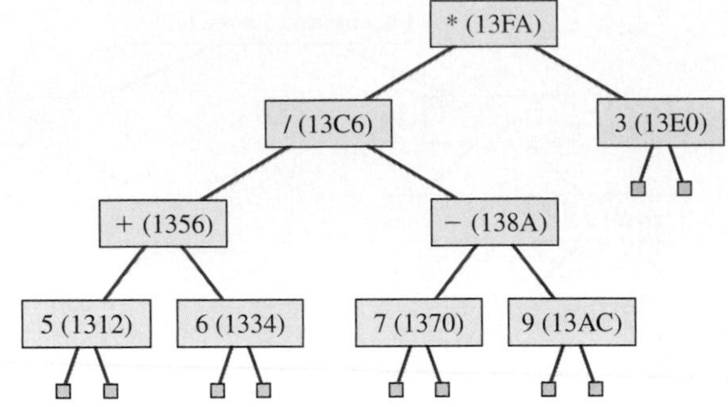

Figure 16.28

Terminating nodes (and addresses of nodes in parentheses) added to the binary tree of Fig. 16.27.

We also utilize a stack to help us perform steps 3 and 4 of the four-step procedure. As a result, we have both a stack and a tree structure (for stack and tree nodes) in our program.

Also, observe from Fig. 16.27 that all the number nodes have no children, whereas the operator nodes each have two children. To make sure that we have a complete binary tree, we put terminating nodes for both the left and right children onto all the number nodes. This is shown in Fig. 16.28 (along with the address of each node obtained from this lesson's program). In this lesson's program, we create terminating nodes for our tree.

Read the program to see how to *create* a binary tree. Read Application Example 16.2 to see how to *use* a binary tree.

QUESTION YOU SHOULD ATTEMPT TO ANSWER

1. How is the "uses" relationship between classes `Tree` and `Stack` created?

Source Code

```
#include <iostream>
using namespace std;

class Tree_node
{
        public:
                char type, operatr;
                double operand;
                Tree_node* left_child;
                Tree_node* right_child;
};

class Tree
{
        private:
                Tree_node* current;
                Tree_node* end;
        public:
                Tree ();
                void make_tree ();
};
```

Data for tree nodes are addresses for left and right children, an operator or operand, and type ('n' or 'o' for number or operator).

For a tree, we keep track of the current node. We also store the terminating node, `end` (that is, all the terminating nodes are taken to be the same node).

In this lesson, we simply create the tree with `make_tree()`. We do not do any manipulations with the tree.

```
class Stack_node
{
        public:
                Tree_node* tree_address;
                Stack_node* next_node;
};
```

A stack node holds the addresses of both a tree node and a stack node as data members. Therefore, we push and pop tree node addresses onto and off of the stack.

```
class Stack
{
        private:
                Stack_node* head;
                Stack_node* tail;
        public:
                Stack ();
                void push (Tree_node*);
                Tree_node* pop ();
};
```

As previously, a stack works with its addresses of the head and tail.

We put tree node addresses onto the stack.

```
Stack :: Stack ()
{
        head = new Stack_node;
        tail = new Stack_node;
        head -> next_node = tail;
}
```

Same stack constructor as previously.

```
void Stack :: push (Tree_node* address)
{
        Stack_node* new_node;

        new_node = new Stack_node;
        new_node -> tree_address = address;
        new_node -> next_node = head -> next_node;
        head -> next_node = new_node;
}

Tree_node* Stack :: pop ()
{
        Stack_node* dummy;
        Tree_node* address;

        address = head -> next_node -> tree_address;
        dummy = head -> next_node;
        head -> next_node = head -> next_node -> next_node;
        delete (dummy);
        return (address);
}
```

The push and pop functions are the same form as used previously. Here, tree node addresses are pushed onto the stack instead of ordinary data. Compare these functions to the push and pop functions of Lesson 16.2's program.

```
Tree :: Tree ()
{
        end = new Tree_node;
        current = end;
}
```

Initializing `current` and `end` in the constructor.

```
Tree_node* Tree :: make_tree ()
{
        Stack the_stack;
        int i;
        cout << "Press enter to begin the program." << endl;
        cout << "Then type the expression (ex. 3 + 4 is n3 n4 o+)." << endl;
        for (i = 1; i <= 9; i++)
                   {
                   current = new Tree_node;
                   cin.ignore ();
                   cin >> current -> type;

                   if (current -> type == 'n')
                            {
                            cin >> current -> operand;
                            current -> left_child = end;
                            current -> right_child = end;
                            cout << current -> operand << "  ";
                            }

                   if (current -> type == 'o')
                            {
                            cin >> current -> operatr;
                            current -> right_child = the_stack.pop ();
                            current -> left_child = the_stack.pop ();
                            cout << current -> operatr << "  ";
                            }
                   the_stack.push (current);
                   cout << "node left = "<< current -> left_child <<"  ";
                   cout << "node right = "<< current -> right_child <<"  ";
                   cout << "node = " << current << endl;
                   }
                   cout << endl;
                   return (current);
}
```

A simple way to use the `Stack` class is to declare a `Stack` object in this `Tree` function. This object goes out of scope after the function executes. This is a "uses" relationship.

Our equation has a total of nine operators/operands.

Reading the character indicating whether the node is a number or operand node.

We assign the number nodes to be operands for the current node. For a number (operand), the left and right children are terminating nodes (`end`, see Fig. 16.28).

We assign the input operator to be the operator for the current node. For an operator, the left and right children come from the stack (see the Description).

We push the node created onto the stack.

We print the addresses of the node, left child, and right child. This allows us to see that we indeed created a tree.

```
int main ( )
{
        Tree arithmetic_expression;
        arithmetic_expression.make_tree ( );
}
```

In this program, we only create the tree. In Application Example 16.4; we perform the calculation that the tree holds.

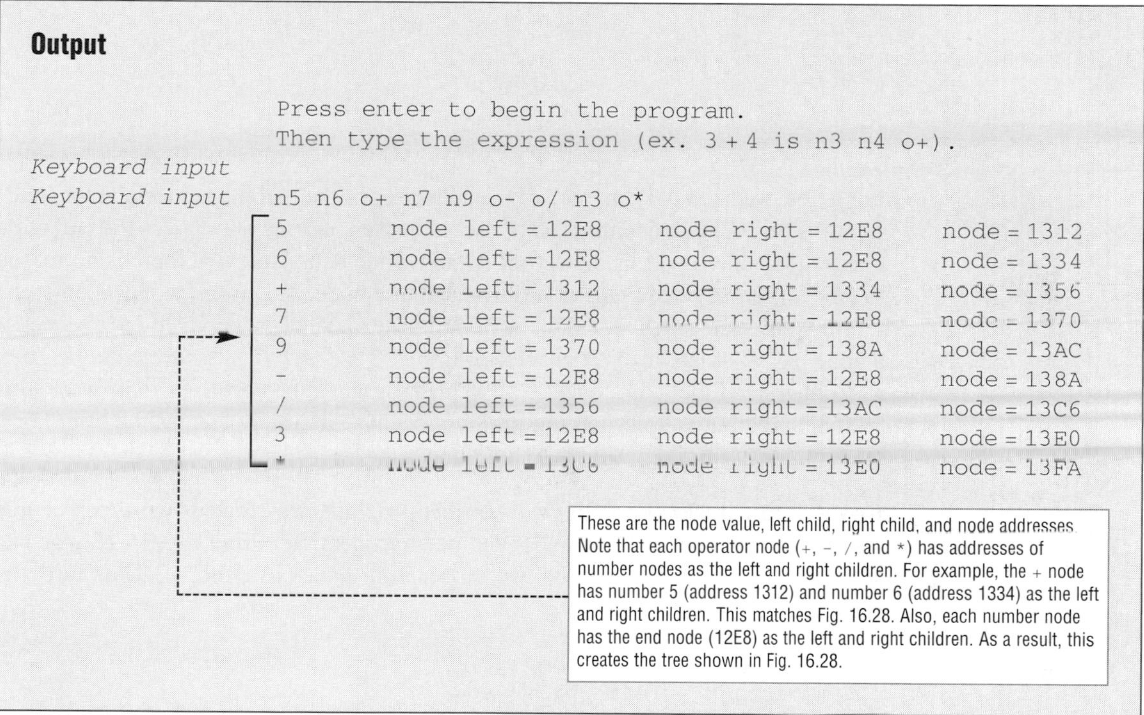

Output

```
                    Press enter to begin the program.
                    Then type the expression (ex. 3 + 4 is n3 n4 o+).
Keyboard input
Keyboard input      n5 n6 o+ n7 n9 o- o/ n3 o*
                    5     node left = 12E8    node right = 12E8    node = 1312
                    6     node left = 12E8    node right = 12E8    node = 1334
                    +     node left = 1312    node right = 1334    node = 1356
                    7     node left = 12E8    node right = 12E8    node = 1370
                    9     node left = 1370    node right = 138A    node = 13AC
                    -     node left = 12E8    node right = 12E8    node = 138A
                    /     node left = 1356    node right = 13AC    node = 13C6
                    3     node left = 12E8    node right = 12E8    node = 13E0
                    *     node left = 13C6    node right = 13E0    node = 13FA
```

These are the node value, left child, right child, and node addresses. Note that each operator node (+, –, /, and *) has addresses of number nodes as the left and right children. For example, the + node has number 5 (address 1312) and number 6 (address 1334) as the left and right children. This matches Fig. 16.28. Also, each number node has the end node (12E8) as the left and right children. As a result, this creates the tree shown in Fig. 16.28.

Description

Tree classes. The two tree classes are similar in form to the linked list and stack classes. One class holds the contents of the nodes, and the other manipulates the nodes. The tree node class for this lesson's program is:

```
class Tree_node
{
        public:
                char type, operatr;
                double operand;
                Tree_node* left_child;
                Tree_node* right_child;
};
```

Two fundamental types of data are in the class, addresses of the children, and data of interest for the problem. In this program, we are working with arithmetic expressions so operators, operands, and types are the data of interest. For a binary tree, the addresses of both the left and right children are required data.

The second tree class for this lesson's program is:

```
class Tree
{
        private:
                Tree_node* current;
                Tree_node* end;
        public:
                Tree ();
                void make_tree ();
};
```

For a tree, we need to keep track of the addresses of the current and terminator (`end`) nodes. The constructor initializes these addresses and the `make_tree()` function creates the nodes and fills them with the tree node data. Note that there is no reason to have different terminating nodes for each tree node. Therefore, we have only one terminating node called `end`. This saves memory and makes it convenient to check if a node has no other values connected to it.

Other tree functions are needed for this program to be useful. In some ways, this lesson's program is a do-nothing program because it simply creates the tree. For a useful tree program see Application Example 16.2.

Creating tree nodes for operands. In this program, we created two types of tree nodes, one for numbers (operands) and one for operators. From Fig. 16.28, you can see that all number nodes have two terminating nodes as children. Therefore, the statements:

```
cin >> current -> operand;
current -> left_child = end;
current -> right_child = end;
```

initialize the operand for the current node to be the input value and the left and right children to be the terminating node.

Creating tree nodes for operators. The tree nodes for the operators are more difficult to create. We use the stack structure to assist us. It works like this: each time we create a node, we push it onto the stack. When we enter an operator node, the top two nodes are popped from the stack to serve as children for the operator. At the end of input, the stack is empty, and each node has its proper children, which means the tree is created.

The steps for this lesson's program are shown in Fig. 16.29. Read this figure beginning at the far left and following the loop structure. Compare the nodes to Fig. 16.28. Observe that each node in Fig. 16.29 has the children shown in Fig. 16.28 (the addresses in the program output and shown in Fig. 16.28 verify this). Therefore, we have created our tree.

Binary search trees. Application Example 6.6 illustrated one form of a binary search tree. Another one is shown in Fig. 16.30, which has each node of the tree having

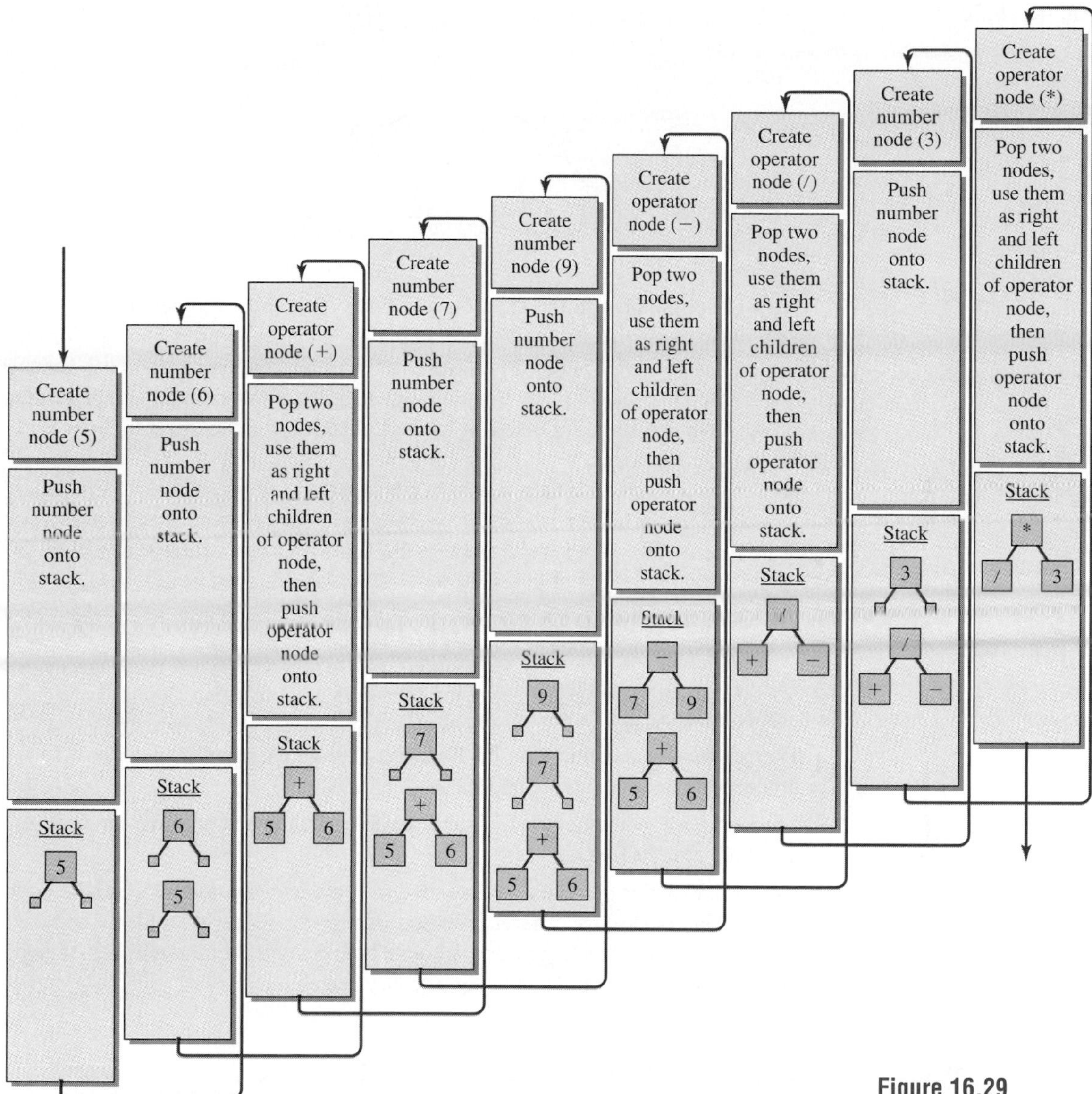

Figure 16.29

Loop creating nodes for the tree for Lesson 16.4's program. Observe how the stack changes each time through the loop. After completion of the loop, each node created has the left and right children corresponding to what is shown in Fig. 16.28.

its key (stored value) being an integer. This tree is in the form of a binary search tree because it has the following property:

> *The value of the key at a particular node is greater than the value of the key of each node in its left subtree but is less than or equal to the value of the key of each node in its right subtree.*

For example, in this tree, 8 is greater than 1, 4, and 6 (its left subtree values) and less than or equal to 9, 10, and 11 (its right subtree values). Such an observation can be made for each node in the tree.

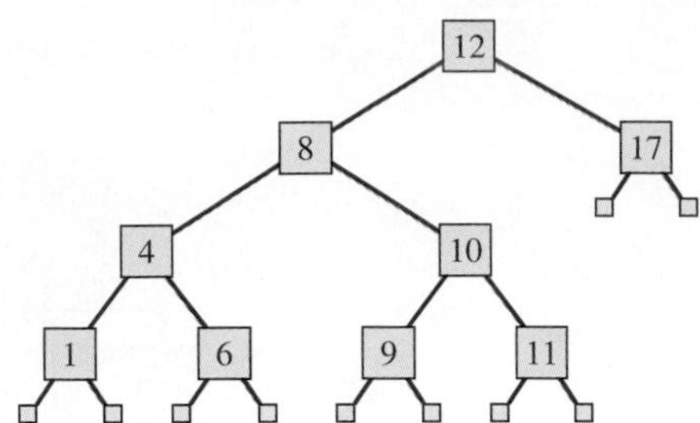

Figure 16.30

Image of a binary search tree with the key for each node being an integer.

We will not go through the creation of a binary search tree in detail in this text. However, we can say that it involves creating a node and comparing the key for that node to the key for other nodes that already exist to find the correct "place" for the new node. Once the correct place is found, by changing pointers in a manner similar to what we have described for inserting into a linked list, we can insert the new node into the binary search tree.

We realize that once a binary search tree is created, it is very simple to find a particular node of interest. For instance, if we wanted to delete the node with the value, 11, in the tree of Fig. 16.30 we could use the following procedure to first find the node (beginning our search at the root):

1. The value at the root is 12. Because 11 is less than 12 we know to continue searching in the left subtree.
2. The next node encountered, then, is 8. Because 11 is greater than 8 we know to proceed to the right subtree of 8.
3. The next node encountered is 10. Because 11 is greater than 10, we know to proceed to the right subtree of 10.
4. The next node encountered is 11, and we have found our node. We can now delete it from the tree.

Note that with this procedure, we needed to visit only four nodes to find the node we wanted. Had we used a different method of visiting nodes, it would have taken more steps to get to it. For large trees, a considerable savings in the number of steps to finding a node can be obtained using a binary search tree.

LESSON 16.5 FUNCTIONS WITH ONE RECURSIVE CALL

TOPICS

- Concept of recursion
- Tracing the flow of a function with one recursive call
- Creating a function with one recursive call

We can use the process of recursion to solve a number of practical problems. For instance, in Application Example 16.1, we show how to compute the value of pi using recursion. In Application Example 16.2, we show how to manipulate a binary tree using recursion. And, in Application Example 16.3 we show a sorting procedure that uses recursion.

In this lesson, though, we show a very simple recursive function. The purpose of this lesson is only to show the flow of control in a program with a function that has just one recursive call. In reviewing this lesson, you should focus on the order of execution of the function statements. If you understand why each statement is executed in succession, you will be prepared for understanding the application examples and the way real problems can be solved using recursion. We begin here by describing the process of recursively calling an ordinary log function.

Suppose that you were interested in finding the log of the log of the log of the log of 5239.7. You could write a single line of code that simply said `x = log (log (log (log (5239.7))));`. Recall that the associativity of operations for evaluating an expression is from left to right. Thus, in evaluating the right side of the assignment statement, the operation denoted by the leftmost log would be performed. This operation is to call the math function, `log`. However, when the math function, `log`, looks at the argument with which it is working it sees the next call to the function, `log`. Thus, it calls the function, `log`, again, at which point the third `log` is seen, and `log` is called a third time, whereupon the fourth `log` is seen, and `log` is called again. At this point, the function, `log`, has been called four times, yet not one logarithm has been calculated. As the function is executed on the fourth call the function realizes that the argument is no longer another call to `log` but the real value of 5239.7.

Now the process goes in reverse. The log of 5239.7 is evaluated to be 8.56402. This value is returned to the third call to `log`, and the log of this value is found to be 2.14757. This value is returned to the second call to `log`, and the log of this value is found to be 0.76434, which is returned to the first `log` call to give −0.26875 as a final result. This value is then assigned to `x` in the assignment statement.

This is a long-winded explanation of a relatively simple calculation, but it introduces an important aspect of the concept of recursion: that there are essentially three phases of operations in recursive calling. The first is the calling phase whereby the function is called repeatedly. During this phase there may or may not (depending on your design) be many calculations or operations performed. This phase ends and the second phase (the reversal) begins when the function encounters the simplest case and actually performs one complete pass through the operations of the function. Then the third (return phase) begins. The values returned allow the earlier function calls to complete their operations and return values back to the very beginning. When the *first* function call has completed its operations, the process is finished.

The `log` function is not considered to be a recursive function in C++ because it does not automatically call itself. In our short example we have used the `log` function in a recursive manner by having it call itself repeatedly to illustrate what happens in recursive calls. In this lesson, though, we illustrate a function that does automatically call itself and thereby is called a recursive function. You can recognize a recursive function in C++ by looking in the function body for a line of code that calls a function by the function's own name and signature. For instance, if the name of the function is `recur` and it is declared as follows:

```
double recur (double, double);
```

Then within the body of function, `recur`, a call to `recur` should occur. For instance:

```
x += recur (c, d);
```

In this lesson's source code, we have the function, `function1`. It is a recursive function because within the `function1` body is a call to `function1`. The purpose of the program is to simply add the values of `i` and `j` a total of five times. We will guide you to observe what statements are executed with each call to the function and what are executed on the returns from the function. This is a simple program designed to demonstrate the flow of programs with a single recursive call (meaning the function has only one statement that calls itself).

When we described calling the `log` function recursively, we determined in advance how many times we were going to call it. We decided to call it four times. A problem with recursive functions though is that since they automatically call themselves it may be possible that they will continue to call themselves forever. In other words, it is necessary for us to build into any recursive function that we write a portion of code that no longer calls the function. Commonly this portion of the function is built within an `if` control structure.

For simplicity, in this lesson's program, we use a global function rather than a member function. We highlight three different regions of the recursive function: the statements before the recursive call, the statements at and after the recursive call but in the true block, and the statements in false block. Note that within the false block, there is no call to `function1()`. Therefore, when the false block is executed, the recursion process reverses. Read the program and annotations, but do not try to follow the flow of the code at this time. The flow is illustrated in the Description.

QUESTION YOU SHOULD ATTEMPT TO ANSWER

1. What are the three sections of a recursive function?

Source Code

```
#include <iostream>
using namespace std;

int function1 (int, int, int);

int main ( )
{
        int a = 10, b = 15, n = 5, sum;
        sum = function1 (a, b, n);
        cout << "The end result is sum = " << sum << endl;
}

int function1 (int i, int j, int k)
{
        int tot;
        k--;
        if(k != 0)
              {
              cout << "Values in phase 1 - calling phase."
                  << endl;
              cout << "i = " << i << " j = " << j << " k = " << k
                  << " tot = " << tot << endl;
```

Declaration of global function, `function1()`.

Call to `function1`.

We change the variable, `k`, with each function call because it is the variable used in the conditional expression of the `if` control structure. It determines whether we enter the true or false block. For this program, we initially enter the true block.

Statements before the call to `function1`. These statements are repeatedly executed during the calling phase.

```
                tot = (i + j) + function1 (i, j, k);

                cout << "Values in phase 2 - "
                        "returning phase." << endl;
                cout << "i = " << i << " j = " << j
                     << " k = " << k << " tot = "
                     << tot << endl;

                return (tot);
                }
        else
                {
                tot = i + j;

                cout << "Values at reversal." << endl;
                cout << "i = " << i << " j = " << j << " k = "
                     << k << " tot = " << tot << endl;

                return (tot);
                }
}
```

Call to `function1` within `function1`. This is the recursive call, and therefore makes `function1` a recursive function.

Statements at and after the call to `function1` in the true block. These statements are repeatedly executed during the returning phase.

Statements in the false block. Note that there is no recursive call in the false block. Thus, if control goes into the false block, these statements are executed once, and the recursive calling phase stops. The process reverses and the return phase of the recursion process begins.

Output

```
Values in phase 1 - calling phase
i = 10 j = 15 k = 4 tot = 0
Values in phase 1 - calling phase
i = 10 j = 15 k = 3 tot = 0
Values in phase 1 - calling phase
i = 10 j = 15 k = 2 tot = 0
Values in phase 1 - calling phase
i = 10 j = 15 k = 1 tot = 0
Values at reversal
i = 10 j = 15 k = 0 tot = 25
Values in phase 2 - returning phase
i = 10 j = 15 k = 1 tot = 50
Values in phase 2 - returning phase
i = 10 j = 15 k = 2 tot = 75
Values in phase 2 - returning phase
i = 10 j = 15 k = 3 tot = 100
Values in phase 2 - returning phase
i = 10 j = 15 k = 4 tot = 125
The end result is sum = 125
```

Statements in the true block (repeatedly executed before the call to `function1`). Note that only the value of `k` changes (going from 4 to 1) each time the statements are printed. This is the calling phase.

Statements executed in the false block. The value of `k` is 0. This shifts control into the false block. At the end of the false block, the first `return` statement is executed. This is the reversal.

Statements in the true block (repeatedly executed after the call to `function1`). Note that the value of `k` goes from 1 to 4. Also, the value of `tot` increases each time it is printed. This is the returning phase.

The final return statement sends control back to `main`, and the result is printed.

Description

Recognizing recursive functions. We know that function1 in this lesson's program is a recursive function because of the statement:

```
tot = (i + j) + function1 (i, j, k);
```

This statement is within function1 and calls function1 itself. This makes function1 a recursive function. In general, to recognize a recursive function, inspect the function body. If the body has a call to a function with an identical name and signature, then it is a recursive function.

For this discussion, we will first describe what is done and then describe why it is done.

Form of a recursive function. As illustrated in this lesson's program, a recursive function has three regions (assuming the use of an if-else control structure with the recursive call in the true block): before the recursive call, the false block, and at and after the recursive call in the true block. For this discussion, we will assume that the true block is entered first because, if it is not entered, there is no recursion.

- *Before the recursive call.* These statements are executed each time the function is called (that is, during the calling phase) until the false block is entered. Using our analogy with x = log (log (log (log (5239.7)))), this is what takes place as we go from left to right: nothing much is being calculated, we are just moving along or counting down to the point where we begin to make a calculation. In this lesson's program, these statements are:

  ```
  k--;
  if (k != 0)
          {
          cout << "Values in phase 1 - calling phase."
               << endl;
          cout << "i = " << i << "  j = "<< j << "  k = " << k
               << " tot = " << tot << endl;
  ```

  Note that k begins at 5 for our data and is immediately decremented by k-- to be 4. Each time the function is called the k-- reduces k by 1. Therefore, these statements are executed for k = 4, 3, 2, and 1. Also, i and j do not change each time through (the output verifies this). When k = 0, we shift to the false block.

- *The false block.* Once k becomes 0, the false block is executed. This is the reversal. These statements are:

  ```
  tot = i + j;
  cout << "Values at reversal." << endl;
  cout << "i = " << i << "  j = " << j << "  k = " << k << "  tot = "
       << tot << endl;
  return (tot);
  ```

  Here, i and j (which are 10 and 15, respectively) are summed, making tot = 25. Then tot is returned. These statements are executed only once.

- *At and after the recursive call in the true block.* These statements are executed repeatedly, as k goes from 1 to 4 for a reason we describe later. This is the returning phase. The statements are:

```
tot = (i + j) + function1 (i, j, k);
cout << "Values in phase 2 - returning phase." << endl;
cout << "i = " << i << " j = " << j << " k = " << k << " tot = "
    << tot << endl;
return (tot);
```

Tracing these statements is difficult. The return value of 25 from the false block is put into the location of "`function1 (i, j, k)`". This makes `tot = (i + j) + 25` which is 50. The `cout` statements are executed, and then the `return` statement sends the 50 to the "`function1 (i, j, k)`" location making `tot = (i + j) + 50` which is 75. Then the `cout` statements are executed, and the `return` statement sends the 75 to the "`function1 (i, j, k)`" location making `tot = (i + j) + 75` which is 100. Again, the `cout` statements are executed, and the `return` statement sends the 100 to the "`function1 (i, j, k)`" location making `tot = (i + j) + 100` which is 125. The `cout` statements are executed and the `return` statement sends the 125 back to `main` (meaning the recursion stops at this point for a reason we describe later).

Illustration of recursion. We know this is confusing so we present a similar discussion that uses a figure to show what occurs. We use our looping type sketch (Fig. 16.31) which has the three regions of the recursive function shown.

Consider the process step by step following the figure. We start immediately after `main` calls `function1` (where it says `i` = 10, `j` = 15, `k` = 5). We enter `function1`, and the statements prior to the `if` control structure are executed. The value of `k` is decremented to be 4 (changing from 5) in these statements. Since the value of `k` is not 0, control goes to the true block of the `if` control structure, and we encounter the assignment statement containing the call to `function1`.

As with all assignment statements, the expression on the right side is first evaluated. Since this expression contains a call to `function1`, the call to `function1` takes place before the entire expression is evaluated. Thus, `function1` is called at this point (that is, prior to the assignment to `tot` and prior to executing any return statement)!

Still following Fig. 16.31, we see that with this function call, control goes to the start of `function1`. In the function, the value of `k` is decremented to be 3. The true block is entered again, and then the call to `function1` is encountered. This is done repeatedly for values of `k` from 4 to 1 as shown by the looping in the top half of the figure.

On the next loop, the value of `k` is again decremented to be 0. With this value of `k`, the false block is entered (following the middle part of the looping figure). The assignment statement `tot = i + j;` is executed and `tot` becomes 25. Next we finally execute our first `return` statement for this function, the recursion process reverses, and the value of `tot` is returned. To where does it return?

The return location is to the statement in the true block of code that includes the function call:

```
tot = (i + j) + function1 (i, j, k);
```

Return location. At this point, this has a value of 25. Therefore, this statement is equivalent to: `tot = (i + j) + 25;`

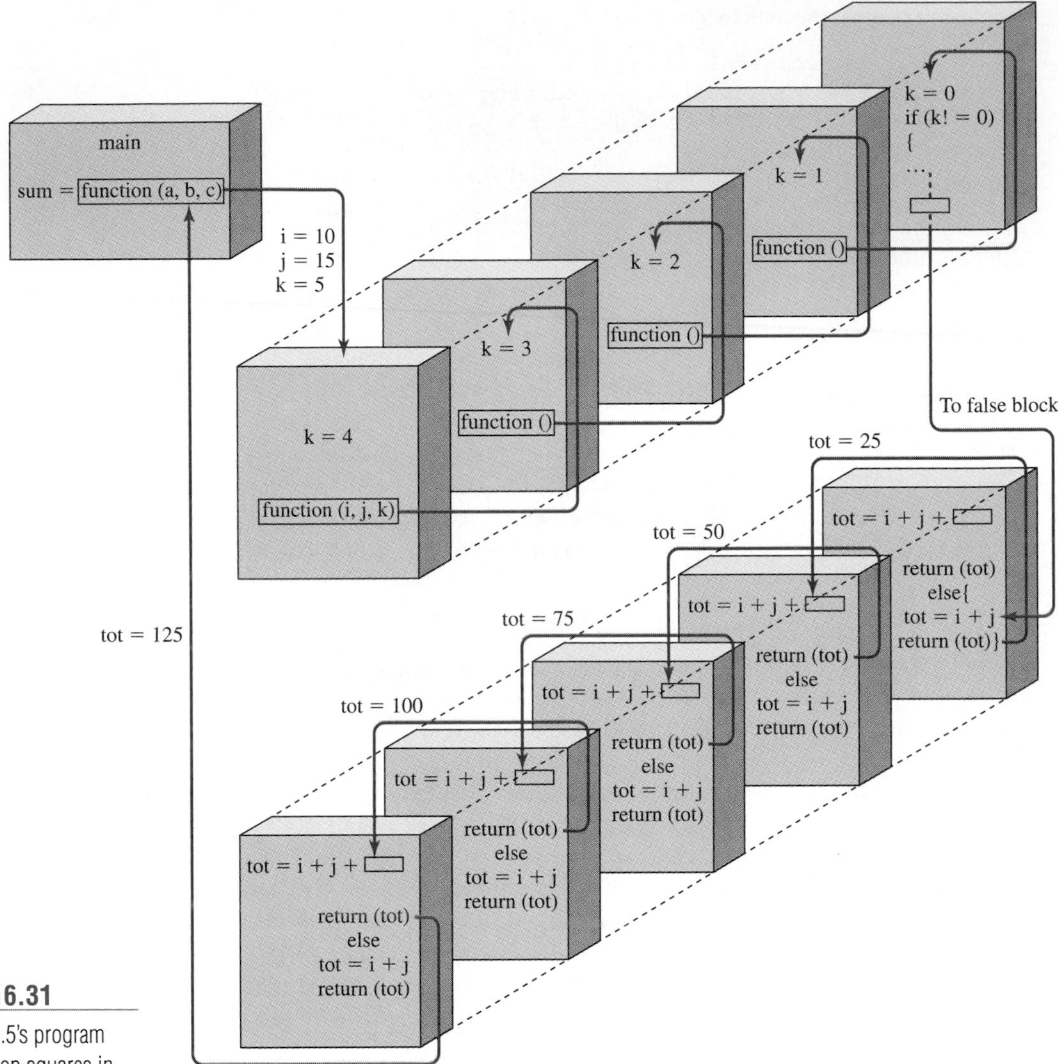

Figure 16.31

Lesson 16.5's program flow. The top squares in the loop are the statements before the function call. The bottom squares are the statements at and after the function call in the true block and the false block. Note that the value of `k` changes each time through the loop. Once the false block is executed, the statements after the function call in the true block are executed.

Now, the assignment statement can be executed. The return value is 25, `i` is 10, and `j` is 15 giving the value of `tot` to be 50. Next the other statements in the true block are executed (that is, the ones after the statement with the function call). The subsequent statement is the `return (tot)` statement. To where does this value of `tot` return? Right back to its call:

```
tot = (i + j) + function1  (i, j, k);
```

Return location. At this point, this has a value of 50. Therefore, this statement is equivalent to: `tot = (i + j) + 50;`

This assignment statement can be completed with the values `i` = 10, `j` = 15, and a return value of 50 making `tot` equal to 75.

The 75 is returned with the `return (tot)` statement. This goes right back into `tot = (i + j) + function1 (i, j, k);` which makes `tot` to be 100 which is returned again to the same assignment statement giving a value of `tot` of 125. This is the last return that needs to be executed, and control goes to the calling statement in `main`, giving sum the value of 125, and the program execution halts.

In other words, recursion stops when all the returns have executed. The number of function calls prior to the reversal determines the number of returns. If we call the function five times before the reversal, then five returns are executed and recursion stops.

In essence, the entire process is that on the sequence of calls, the statements *prior* to the function call in `function1` are repeatedly executed. The reversal is hit and the *false block*—the one without a function call—is executed. Then the statements *at and after* the function call in the true block in `function1` are repeatedly executed.

Mechanics of recursion. We should consider what occurs in memory to understand recursion further. During the calling process for any function, recursive or not, a region of memory is set aside for storing all the function's variables. This memory remains reserved until the function completes execution.

A recursive function is different from an ordinary function in that it calls itself before it finishes executing. In the case of `function1`, it called itself four times without having completed execution once! Adding in the function call from `main`, `function1` was called a total of five times. This means that during execution of this program, five different regions of memory are set aside and kept open for variables `i`, `j`, `k`, and `tot` (`function1`'s local variables) before the reversal of the recursion takes place (see Fig. 16.32).

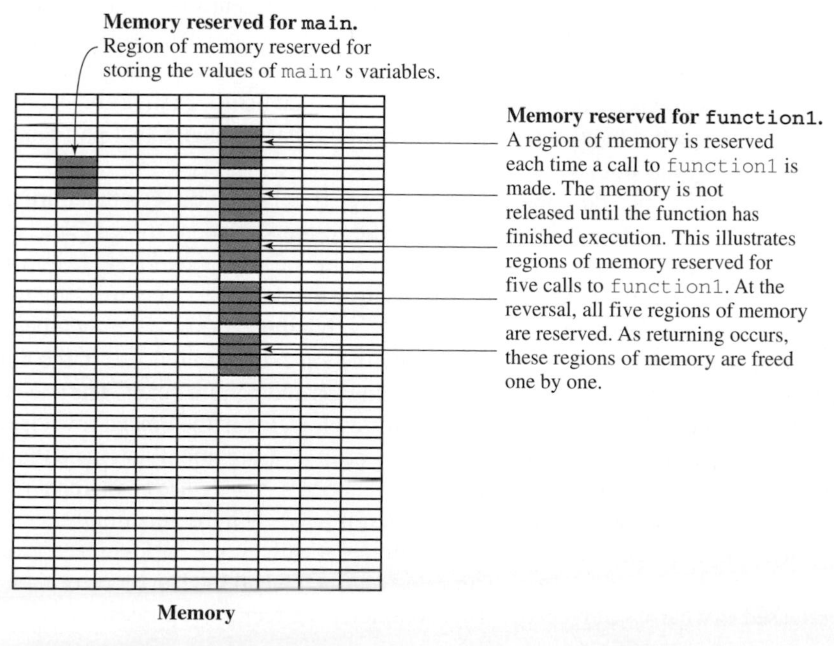

Memory reserved for main.
Region of memory reserved for storing the values of main's variables.
Memory reserved for function1.
A region of memory is reserved each time a call to function1 is made. The memory is not released until the function has finished execution. This illustrates regions of memory reserved for five calls to function1. At the reversal, all five regions of memory are reserved. As returning occurs, these regions of memory are freed one by one.
Memory

Figure 16.32

Reserving regions of memory during calls to `function1`.

Calling—variable values in memory during calling phase

Variable	Variable values in memory region (first call to function1) Value	Variable values in memory region (second call to function1) Value	Variable values in memory region (third call to function1) Value	Variable values in memory region (fourth call to function1) Value	Variable values in memory region (fifth call to function1) Value
i	10	10	10	10	10
j	15	15	15	15	15
k	4	3	2	1	0
tot	0	0	0	0	0

Variable	Variable values in memory region (first call to function1) Value	Variable values in memory region (second call to function1) Value	Variable values in memory region (third call to function1) Value	Variable values in memory region (fourth call to function1) Value	Variable values in memory region (fifth call to function1) Value
i	10	10	10	10	10
j	15	15	15	15	15
k	4	3	2	1	0
tot	125	100	75	50	25

Returning—variable values in memory during returning phase

Figure 16.33

Memory regions and variable values for both the calling and returning phases of Lesson 16.5's program. Note that because `function1` is called five times, five memory regions are reserved.

The values in the memory cells at this time are illustrated in Fig. 16.33 by the top five boxes. The variable values in these five boxes represent the variable values on the calling phase. During the returning phase, these memory regions are returned to. Any values that are changed during the returning phase due to assignment statements being executed are then modified. However, values that do not change are essentially remembered as what they were during the calling phase because that particular region of memory has not changed!

For example, consider the variable `k`. In Fig. 16.33 it can be seen that during the calling phase `k` is changed with each call (due to the statement `k--;`). Thus, each region of memory for each call has a different value of `k`. However, on the returning phase (during which the bottom portion of the true block of the `if` control structure in `function1` is executed) no statements change `k`, but the value of `k` is remembered to be what it was on the calling phase. Compare the top and bottom boxes in the figure. The values of `k` are the same in the corresponding top and bottom boxes. The only variable that has one value in the top box and a different value in the box below it is `tot`. This is because only `tot` appeared on the left side of an assignment statement that was executed on the returning phase. Thus while it appears that we are changing `k` on the return, we are actually just remembering what it was when the function was called.

In essence, because we generate five function calls in the calling phase, we return from the function five times. The value returned when the last block of memory is released is what `main` receives. This completes the recursion process.

Comments. Recursive functions are a very clean way to code some particular repeated processes. In the application examples we show three practical examples of the use of recursive functions. Although, it has been theoretically proven that all recursive structures can be written as iterative structures, we find that for certain problems recursion is cleaner because it does not involve complicated looping and `if` statements.

Recursion is clean, but not without a cost. There are some memory issues with recursion. After some recursive calls, the memory reserved by the function activations is essentially in limbo waiting for the base case or reversal to occur. If there are a large number of recursive calls, the memory capacity of a system may be exceeded.

Also, calling a function has so-called overhead associated with it. The process of reserving and establishing the function in memory takes execution time. Therefore, a program with a recursive function may execute more slowly than an equivalent program with an iterative structure.

APPLICATION EXAMPLE 16.1 CALCULATION OF PI

Problem Statement

Use a global recursive function to estimate the value of π. No input is needed to the program. The output should be the value of π printed to the screen.

TOPICS

- Recursion
- Numerical method example

Solution

RELEVANT EQUATIONS

The French mathematician Vieta (1540–1603) developed the following equation to calculate the value of π:

$$\frac{2\sqrt{2}}{\pi} = \left[\sqrt{\left(\frac{1}{2}+\frac{1}{2}\sqrt{\frac{1}{2}}\right)}\right]\left[\sqrt{\frac{1}{2}+\frac{1}{2}\sqrt{\left(\frac{1}{2}+\frac{1}{2}\sqrt{\frac{1}{2}}\right)}}\right]$$

$$\times\left[\sqrt{\frac{1}{2}+\frac{1}{2}\sqrt{\frac{1}{2}+\frac{1}{2}\sqrt{\left(\frac{1}{2}+\frac{1}{2}\sqrt{\frac{1}{2}}\right)\cdots}}}\right][\ldots etc \ldots]$$

This equation can be used in a recursive function to calculate π.

In order to successfully develop a recursive function, it is necessary to identify the base case. The base case becomes the one evaluated at the reversal, and thus forms the false block of the `if` control structure in the recursive function.

From the above equation, one can see that the base case (or simplest case) is represented by the portion of the equation:

$$\sqrt{\left(\frac{1}{2}+\frac{1}{2}\sqrt{\frac{1}{2}}\right)}$$

With each succeeding term of the equation, the base case gets more deeply embedded within the equation structure. Also, we show three bracketed terms. The first one (far left) is embedded in the second one (middle). And, the second one is embedded in the third one (far right). In other words, each bracketed term is embedded in the term to its right.

In our representation above, we have shown the first three terms of the expression. In our hand calculation, we will calculate the first four terms, and in our computer calculation we will take the first 30 terms.

SPECIFIC CALCULATION

The hand calculation will be done by first calculating an individual term (called `single_term` in the program) and then getting an accumulation (called `accum` in the program) by taking the product of the individual terms previously calculated. If we work from left to right in the equation we get:

First term:

$$\sqrt{\left(\frac{1}{2}+\frac{1}{2}\sqrt{\frac{1}{2}}\right)} = 0.923879532$$

Accumulated value = 0.923879532

Second term:

$$\sqrt{\left(\frac{1}{2}+\frac{1}{2}(0.923879532)\right)} = 0.98078528$$

Accumulated value = 0.98078528 * 0.923879532 = 0.906127445

Third term:

$$\sqrt{\left(\frac{1}{2}+\frac{1}{2}(0.98078528)\right)} = 0.995184726$$

Accumulated value = 0.995184726 * 0.906127445 = 0.901764193

Fourth term:

$$\sqrt{\left(\frac{1}{2}+\frac{1}{2}(0.995184726)\right)} = 0.998795456$$

Accumulated value = 0.998795456 * 0.901764193 = 0.900677978

This is all the terms we will carry, thus:

$$\frac{2\sqrt{2}}{\pi} \approx 0.913612265$$

Solving for π we get:

$$\pi \approx 3.140331165$$

Recall that π is roughly 3.14159. Therefore, the above value is not a very good approximation. We need more terms to get a better result. Note that the purpose of this example is to demonstrate programming recursion. What we show here is not robust enough to perform a true π calculation.

ALGORITHM

A major difference between the recursive function that we will write here and the recursive function that we wrote earlier is that with each recursive call we need to pass not just one but two values on the return. These are:

1. The value of the single term.
2. The accumulated value.

Since we need to return more than one value, we need to make use of the argument list to transfer the information. We could return both values through the argument list. However, for illustration purposes we choose to use a `return` statement to return the value of the single term and the argument list to return the accumulated value.

Keeping this in mind, we can write an algorithm for the recursive function. Our test expression will be the value of *n* being less than or equal to 30 (to carry 30 terms).

Algorithm for recursive pi function:

1. increment *n*
2. `if (n <= 30)`
   a. call recursive function
   b. calculate single term
   c. calculate accumulated value
   d. return single term, pass accumulated value
3. `else`
   a. calculate base case
   b. create accumulated value
   c. return base case, pass accumulated value

Note that the form of this recursive function fits the form we described in Lesson 16.5. The true block has the recursive call, and the false block is the reversal. After repeated calls to the recursive function, the accumulated value can be passed to `main` where the final step of dividing the accumulated value into $2(2)^{0.5}$ can give the value of π. The source code has been written from the algorithm and the specific calculation.

Source Code

```
#include <iostream>
#include <iomanip>      // Needed to print many digits.
#include <cmath>
using namespace std;

double recurs_pi (int, double&);
```

Needed to print many digits.

Declaration of recursive function. The second argument is passed by reference, meaning it can be modified in the function. This is the accumulated value.

```
int main ( )
{

        double pi, grand_total = 0;
        recurs_pi (1, grand_total);
        pi = 2.0 / (sqrt (0.5) * grand_total);
        cout << setprecision(15) << "The value of pi is approximately"
             << pi << endl;
}

double recurs_pi (int n, double& tot)
{
        double z = 0.5, accum, single_term;
        n++;



        if (n <= 30)
                {
                single_term = sqrt(z + z * recurs_pi(n, accum));

                tot = accum * single_term;
                return (single_term);
                }
        else
                {
                single_term = sqrt(z + z * sqrt(z));
                tot = single_term;
                return (single_term);
                }
}
```

Calling the recursive function. The value of `grand_total` is "returned" from the function (because it is passed by reference). The value of 1 begins the count to 30.

Pi is calculated from `grand_total`.

The value of `n` is passed through the argument list. It is incremented before the `if` statement. The true block is entered if we have called the function fewer than 31 times.

Recursive function call. See the specific calculation to understand where the assignment statement comes from.

At the reversal, the value of `tot` goes into `accum` (because `tot` is second in the header argument list, and `accum` is second in the call argument list) and `single_term` is returned to the location shown. This is repeated with every return after the reversal except the values from the true block are used.

Output

```
The value of pi is approximately 3.14159265389793.
```

Comments

- *Flow.* Here, we show a slightly different figure of a recursive function flow than that of Lesson 16.5. Four recursive calls are illustrated schematically in Fig. 16.34. Each panel in this figure represents the function on a different

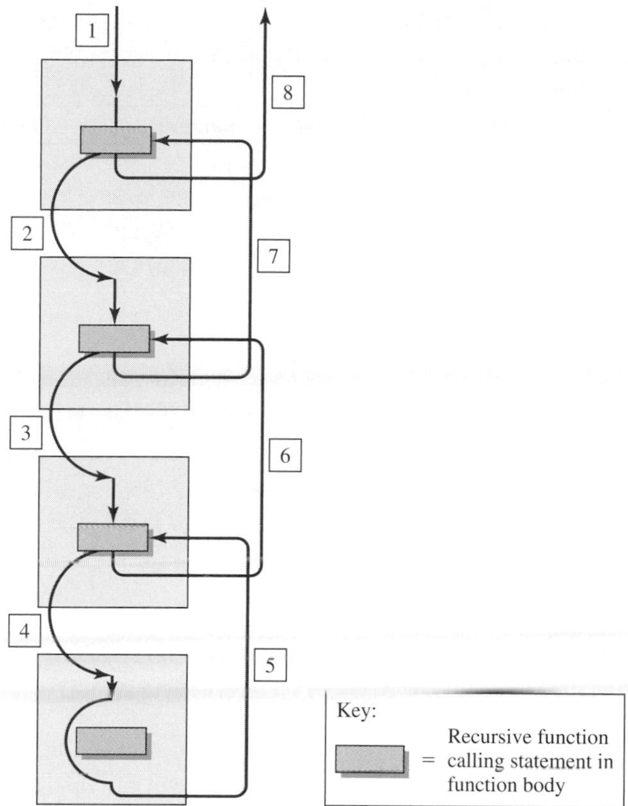

Figure 16.34

Order of operation for four recursive calls for the recursive pi calculation. Note that steps 1, 2, 3, and 4 execute only the part of the function before the function call. Step 5 executes the false block. Steps 6, 7, and 8 execute the last part of the true block.

call. Each embedded small panel represents the function call. You can trace the numbers to see the flow. Following down the figure, the function is called repeatedly until the reversal (the fourth panel), where the call is bypassed and the return sequence begins. On each return, the remainder of the true block is executed.

- *Transfer of data values.* A feature of this program that we have not yet seen for recursive functions is using a reference in the argument list. This causes the effective transfer of a value in the function to an argument in the function call. To understand how this works in this program, we must remember that each function call creates a new memory region for the variables. Table 16.4 shows the values in the memory regions for four function calls. (That is, if we had used `n <= 4` instead of `n <= 30` in the program, the numbers in the table represent the program's calculations. These numbers match the ones shown in the specific example.) Begin by reading this table from the bottom up because the calculations are first performed at the reversal. (Note that we show `tot` in the memory region for simplicity. It is not really in the memory region because it is only an alias or reference.)

TABLE 16.4 — Variable values for each function call. This table is read from the bottom up. Modifying `tot` modifies `accum` on the previous function call

Name	Type	Address	Value	Comment
`n`	`int`		1	Variables in memory region for first call to `recurs_pi`.
`accum`	`double`		0.901764193	
`single_term`	`double`		0.998795456	
`tot`	`double&`		0.900677978	
`n`	`int`		2	Variables in memory region for second call to `recurs_pi`.
`accum`	`double`		0.906127445	
`single_term`	`double`		0.995184726	
`tot`	`double&`		0.901764193	
`n`	`int`		3	Variables in memory region for third call to `recurs_pi`.
`accum`	`double`		0.923879532	
`single_term`	`double`		0.980785280	
`tot`	`double&`		0.906127445	
`n`	`int`		4	Variables in memory region for fourth call to `recurs_pi`.
`accum`	`double`			
`single_term`	`double`		0.923879532	
`tot`	`double&`		0.923879532	

It can be seen from Table 16.4 that the value of `tot` in the fourth call (the base case, which is calculated in the false block of the `if` control structure) is transferred to `accum` on the third call. This occurs because we have used a reference for the second argument in the function declaration, which makes the value of `tot` in the function pass to the second term in the function call. Then the value of `tot` on the third call is transferred to `accum` on the second call, and `tot` on the second call is transferred to `accum` on the first call. Lastly (not shown in the table), `tot` on the first call is transferred to `grand_total` in `main`.

When creating your own recursive functions, it is useful to sketch such a table for just a few recursive calls to illustrate how you want to transfer information from the base case up to the initial function call in `main`.

- *Debugging.* You are also going to need to debug your recursive functions. To do this, note that you can evaluate the performance of a recursive function in a manner similar to that of evaluating the performance of a loop structure. By making a table of the values and how they change with each recursive call it is possible to trace the operations of the function.

  For debugging purposes, set a small limit on `n` in the recursive function. That way you can do a hand calculation of all of the numbers. You can then compare your hand calculation to the values your program gives on each step. Use either `cout` statements or the compiler's debugger to get the values on each step.

In tracing the flow of the program shown in this application example, we first realize that during the calling phase, the only calculation that is done is the increment of `n`. Thus, we do not need to trace any values during the calling phase. We can start at the reversal. This puts us into the false block of the `if` control structure. If you are using `cout` statements, to trace the flow of the program, put them into both the true and false block.

The returning phase begins, and control shifts to the point of the function call in the true block of the `if` control structure. With the value returned the expression containing the function call can be evaluated. The single term and total are the same and easily calculated by hand. The assignment statement gives a new value for the single term. This also can be calculated by hand. The following table results.

Return step from reversal	Value of single term	Accumulated value
Reversal ($n = 4$)	0.923879532	0.923879532
1	0.980785280	0.906127445
2	0.995184726	0.901764193
3	0.998795456	0.900677978

Since this program works correctly, it does not need to be debugged. But the procedure described here can be used to debug similar programs.

- *Developing your own programs with recursive functions.* You will find that developing your own recursive functions is not simple. We recommend that you take the following steps to get going:

1. Recognize the base case or simplest case.
2. Do a simple hand calculation—working backward from the base case. As you are doing the hand calculation, recognize how many values you must return from each call.
3. If you need to return more than one value from each call, you know you must use the argument list to transfer values.
4. Start writing the recursive function with the false block in the `if` control structure. Put the base case into the false block. Put in a return statement.
5. Decide on what your test condition is to be. Put in the test condition and a statement that changes the test condition for each function call. Make sure that the condition is tested and changed for *every* function call. This means that the statement that changes the test condition must appear before the condition is tested. This is important. Without it, your recursive functions could go on forever.
6. Write the true block of the `if` control structure. In it should be a call to the function—the recursive call. You can get this part correct if you think about the transfer of information (what is returned) during the return phase of the recursive process. Begin your logic process by thinking about the reversal. In other words, ask yourself, What is the value returned from the function at the reversal? that is, the base case value. That value will be

returned to the location of the recursive call. Realizing this, write your true block around that value (also use any other values that the recursive function returns).

7. As you are beginning, use just a few recursive calls. You can debug the program by making a table of the values as shown in Table 16.4.

Following these steps will get you on your way to writing a large number of programs with recursive functions.

Modification Exercises

1. Add statements to the program to print a table of the form shown in Table 16.4. Print the table to a file.
2. A factorial computation is somewhat similar to the computation performed for this application program. Recall that the factorial of 5 is 1 * 2 * 3 * 4 * 5. Modify the program so that it performs factorial calculations using a recursive form.

APPLICATION EXAMPLE 16.2 PERFORMING ARITHMETIC OPERATIONS

TOPICS

- Recursion
- Stack
- Tree
- Numerical method example

Problem Statement

Write a program that can perform the operation:

$$((5 + 6)/(7 - 9)) * 3$$

using a binary tree as shown in Fig. 16.35. Enter the operation using postfix notation in the form:

$$5\ 6 + 7\ 9 - /\ 3\ *$$

Use the program in Lesson 16.4 to create the tree. Use a recursive function to traverse the tree. Write the result of the expression to the screen. The program should be general enough to perform similar postfix type operations. Please review Lesson 16.4 if you do not remember it well.

Solution

RELEVANT EQUATIONS

The only equation involved is the arithmetic expression as given in the problem statement.

SPECIFIC EXAMPLE

The result of the expression is:

$$((5 + 6)/(7 - 9)) * 3 = -16.5$$

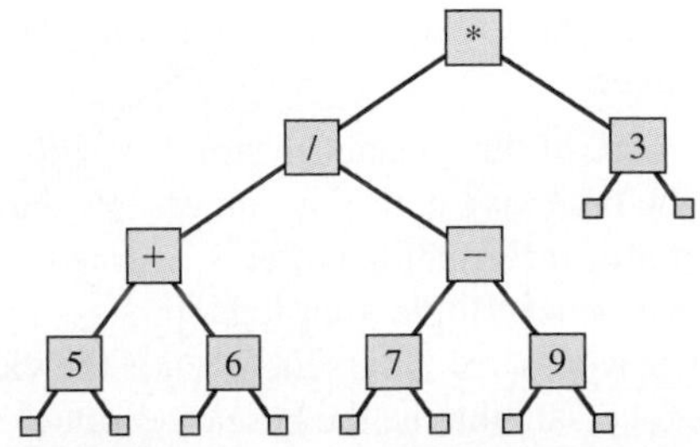

Figure 16.35

Binary tree of arithmetic expression.

DATA STRUCTURES

As described in Lesson 16.4, we use both a tree and a stack structure. However, we find that we need to add to the tree structure a member that can store the result of the operation involving the left and right children. For instance, the tree shown in Fig. 16.35 has a subtree shown in Fig. 16.36. The result of the operation in the subtree is $5 + 6 = 11$. We can store the number, 11, in a member of the "+" tree node. To do this, we create a member of the tree node, `cum`, that we did not have in Lesson 16.4. This gives us the following tree node:

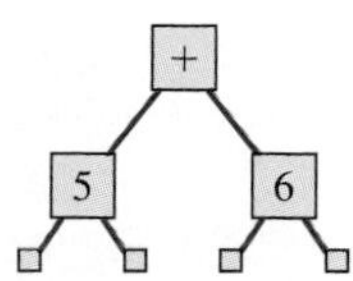

Figure 16.36

Subtree of the larger tree. The result of this expression, 11, can be stored in the block of memory reserved for the '+' node. To do this, we create a member of the tree structure, `cum`, to hold the cumulative result of the operation involving the left and right children of a node.

```
class Tree_node
        {
        public:
                char type, operatr;
                double operand, cum;
                Tree_node* left_child;
                Tree_node* right_child;
        };
```

The member, `cum`, is of type `double` because it will hold the real result of the arithmetic expression. The value of `cum` for the node that is the root is the final result of the expression. In Fig. 16.37 we show the value of `cum` for each node.

ALGORITHM

What we did not show in Lesson 16.4 is performing the operation indicated by the expression. To perform the operation we must traverse the tree. There are three standard ways of traversing a binary tree, called:

1. Preorder
2. Inorder
3. Postorder

Because we created the tree using a postfix expression, we should traverse the tree in postorder. Postorder involves beginning at the root and following the steps in the order listed:

1. Traverse the left subtree of the node in postorder.
2. Traverse the right subtree of the node in postorder.
3. Visit the node.

While this sounds somewhat cryptic, it is simple to program. If we call the recursive function that traverses the tree, `traverse`, then the following form of

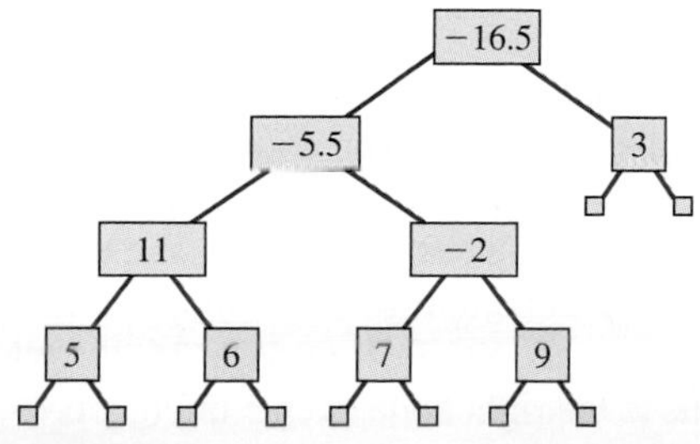

Figure 16.37

The value of `cum` for each node.

statements in the function body perform the three steps (when "visiting" the node means printing the operator):

```
traverse (node -> left_child);
traverse (node -> right_child);
cout << "Operator = " << node -> operatr << endl;
```

In other words, for a postorder traversal of a tree, we have a recursive call with the left child, a recursive call with the right child, and an operation. The above statements are not exact; however, we create our function, `traverse`, with the realization that we need this general form.

You may recall that in creating a recursive function, we need to recognize the base case or simplest case to help us recognize the reversal point. For a tree, the reversal is reached when we encounter a terminating node. For our tree, if either of the children of a node is a terminating node then we have reached a reversal point.

In this book, we create recursive functions using an `if` control structure with the false block being the base case (and thus the reversal) and the true block having the recursive calls. Thus, the form of the function, `traverse`, becomes:

```
void Tree :: traverse (Tree_node* node)
        {
        if (node -> left_child != end)
                {
                traverse (node -> left_child);
                traverse (node -> right_child);
                cout << "Operator = "
                    << node -> operatr << endl;
                }
        else
                {
                node -> cum = node -> operand;
                return;
                }
        }
```

The address of the node with which we are working is passed to traverse().
If we are not at a reversal (that is, not at an operand which has a terminating node) then we are at an operator.
Recursive call with the left_child.
Recursive call with the right_child.
Here, we simply print the operator. In the complete source code, we do other operations.
We return from the false block because the operands are at the end of the tree.
The false block works with the operands, which are at the reversal. This simply says that the cumulative total at an operand node is equal to the value of the operand. See Fig. 16.37.

Note that with the above code, we only enter the true block of the function when the node contains an operator and not a number (or operand). This is because none of the operator nodes have a terminating node as a child.

The flow of such a function for a seven node tree in Fig. 16.38 can be illustrated much like a tree (Fig. 16.39). Follow the numbered lines in Fig. 16.39 and trace along with Fig. 16.38. First there is a call to the left node, and this continues until an end is hit (steps 2 and 3, which correspond to going from + to 3 in Fig. 16.38).

Then returning takes place (step 4 in Fig. 16.39, which is going to * in Fig. 16.38) to allow calls to the right node (step 5 in Fig. 16.39, which is going to + in

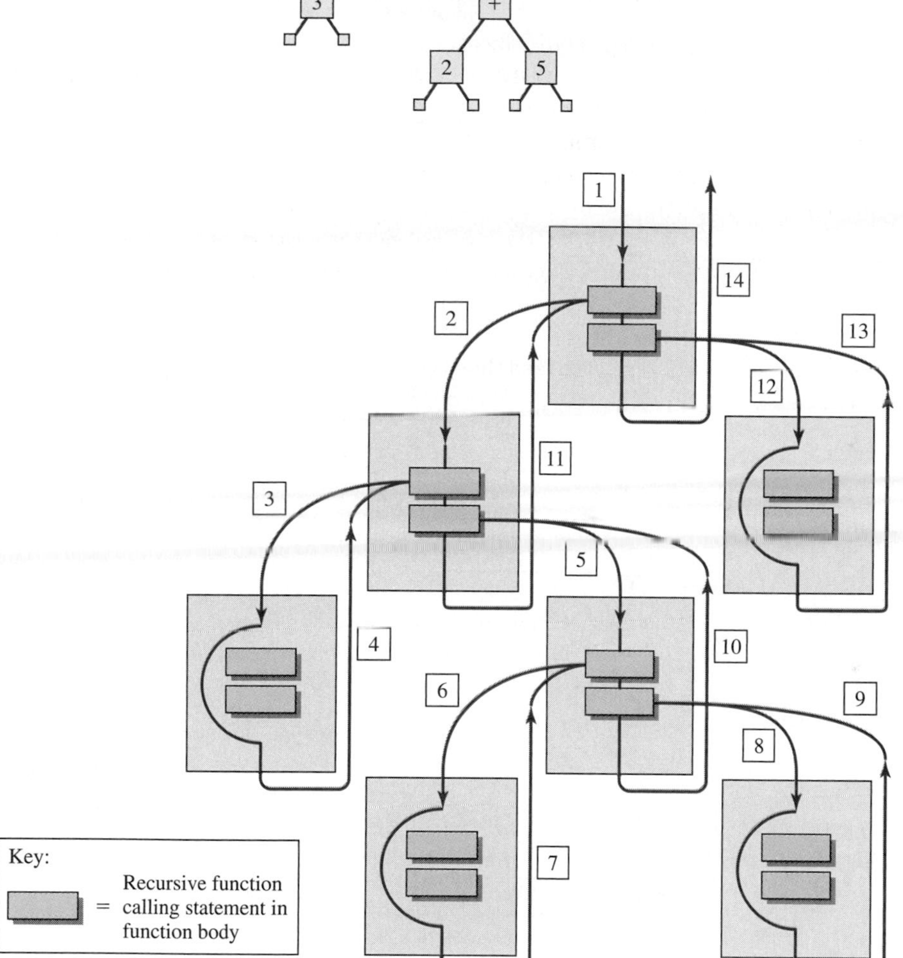

Figure 16.38
Seven node tree corresponding to Fig. 16.39.

Figure 16.39
This figure shows the order of operation for a function that has two recursive calls for the case where there are a small number of calls (Fig. 16.38). Trace the numbered lines to understand how the program flows.

Fig. 16.38). All the steps are shown in Table 16.5. Read this table to understand the program actions.

We show these two figures (Figs. 16.38 and 16.39) because they look like each other. They illustrate how recursion with two calls represents a binary tree. For a larger tree, the order of function calls is shown in Fig. 16.40. Look at this figure and follow the numbered steps. Note how the steps continually follow the left node until all the left nodes of the subtree are traversed. Then the right nodes are traversed.

In the previous code, we simply printed the operator after the left and right children were visited. We really need to perform the operation. The following `if-else` control structure uses the operator and performs the operation on the

TABLE 16.5 — Flow of program with function `traverse` as it operates upon the tree of Fig. 16.38 in the manner shown in Fig. 16.39

Step in Fig. 16.39	Action in Fig. 16.38	Action in program
1	Going to + (the root)	Making the first call to `traverse` in `main`. No calculations are done because we are initially entering an operator node.
2	Going to *	Making the first recursive call to `traverse` (in `traverse`), which is going to the left child. No calculations are done yet because we need to get the left and right child values.
3	Going to 3	Making a recursive call to `traverse`, which is again going to the left child. No calculations are done because we are at an operand.
4	Going back to *	Returning the value of 3 to `traverse` because we execute the false block and `cum` is equal to the `operand`.
5	Going to +	Making a recursive call to `traverse` (with the second call statement in the function, which is equivalent to going to the right node).
6	Going to 2	Making a recursive call to `traverse` (with the first call statement in the function, which is equivalent to going to the left node).
7	Going back to +	Returning the value of 2 to `traverse` because we execute the false block and `cum` is equal to the `operand`.
8	Going to 5	Making a recursive call to `traverse` (with the second call statement in the function, which is equivalent to going to the right node).
9	Going back to +	Returning the value of 5 to `traverse` because we execute the false block and `cum` is equal to the `operand`.
10	Performing the calculation with the left and right children of + and returning the result to *. Going back to *.	At this point we have previously returned twice to + (see column 2), and therefore we perform the calculation with the left and right children of + and return the value of the calculation to *.
11	Performing the calculation with the left and right children of * and returning the result to the root +. Going back to the root +.	At this point we have previously returned twice to * (see column 2), and therefore we perform the calculation with the left and right children of * and return the value of the calculation to the root +.
12	Going to 8.	Making a recursive call to `traverse` (with the second call statement in the function, which is equivalent to going to the right node).
13	Going back to the root +.	Returning the value of 8 to the root + memory region of `traverse` because we execute the false block and `cum` is equal to the `operand`.
14	Performing the calculation with the left and right children of the root + and returning the result to `main`.	At this point we have previously returned twice to the root + (see column 2), and therefore we perform the calculation with the left and right children of root + and return the value of the calculation to `main`.

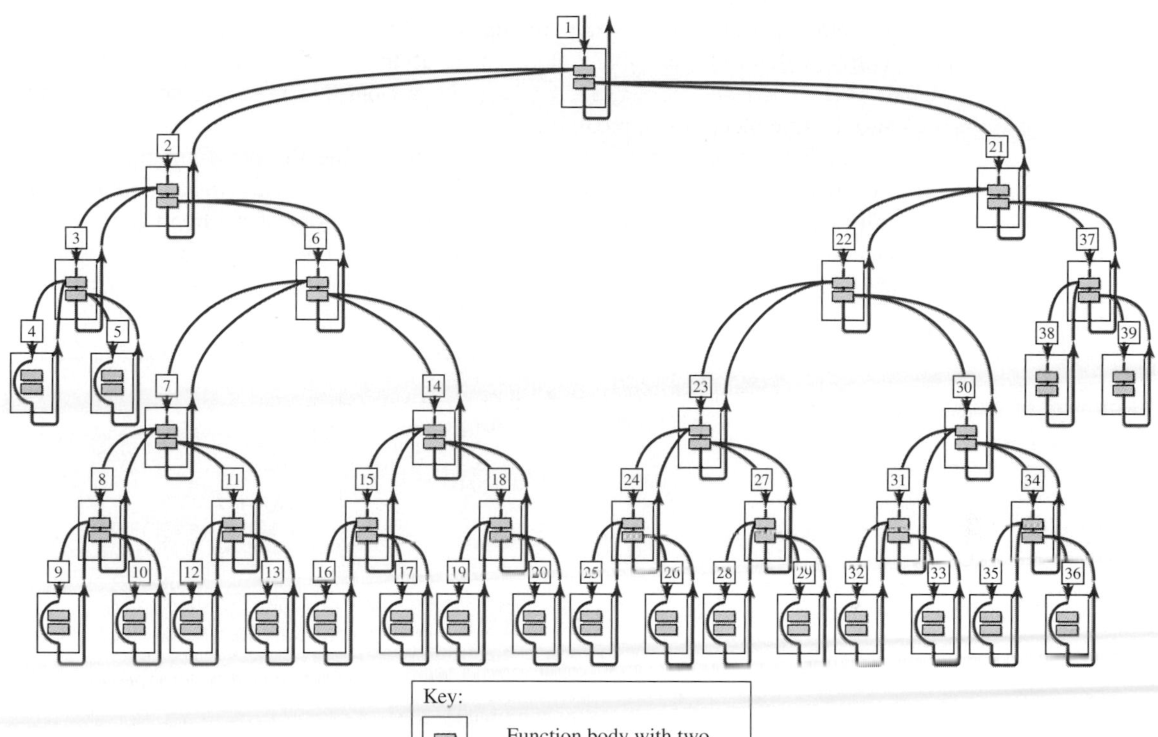

Figure 16.40

Flow of 39 recursive calls. Compare this to Fig. 16.39. Note that in both these figures, the operations are first performed on the left then the right. Note also that this figure looks like a binary tree.

left and right children:

```
if (node -> operatr == '+')
          {
          node -> cum = node -> left_child -> cum + node
               -> right_child -> cum;
          }
else      if (node -> operatr == '*')
          {
          node -> cum = node -> left_child -> cum * node
               -> right_child -> cum;
          }
else      if (node -> operatr == '-')
          {
          node -> cum = node -> left_child -> cum - node
               -> right_child -> cum;
          }
else      if (node -> operatr == '/')
          {
          node -> cum = node -> left_child -> cum / node
               -> right_child -> cum;
          }
cout << "The node cumulative total is: "
     << node -> cum << endl;
```

Performing addition.

Performing multiplication.

Performing subtraction.

Performing division.

Printing the cumulative total for the current node.

Note that in each case the cumulative value stored at the node (`node -> cum`) works with the cumulative value stored at the left and right children (`left_child -> cum` and `right_child -> cum`). We put this `if-else` control structure into the true block of the recursive function.

In the source code, we first create the tree using the program shown in Lesson 16.4 (with the added member, `cum`, of the `Tree_node` class to accumulate the result of the arithmetic operation). Then we return the root of the tree from the `Tree` member function `make_tree()`. This is the starting node for our traverse, which is the code we have discussed in this application example.

Source Code

```
#include <iostream>
using namespace std;

class Tree_node
{
        public:
                char type, operatr;
                double operand, cum;
                Tree_node* left_child;
                Tree_node* right_child;
};

class Tree
{
        private:
                Tree_node* current;
                Tree_node* end;
        public:
                Tree ();
                Tree_node* make_tree ();
                void traverse (Tree_node*);
};

class Stack_node
{
        public:
                Tree_node* tree_address;
                Stack_node* next_node;
};

class Stack
{
        private:
                Stack_node* head;
                Stack_node* tail;
```

The member, `cum`, accumulates the result of the tree calculations. Each node has a `cum`. For a number node, `cum` is equal to the number. For an operator node, `cum` is the result of the operation involving the left and right children.

The function, `traverse`, is a recursive function used to visit each node of the tree. It starts by working with the root of the tree, whose address is returned from the function `make_tree()`.

```
        public:
                Stack ();
                void push (Tree_node*);
                Tree_node* pop ();
};

Stack :: Stack ()
{
        head = new Stack_node;
        tail = new Stack_node;
        head -> next_node = tail;
}

void Stack :: push (Tree_node* address)
{
        Stack_node* new_node;

        new_node = new Stack_node;
        new_node -> tree_address = address;
        new_node -> next_node = head -> next_node;
        head -> next_node = new_node;
}

Tree_node* Stack :: pop ()
{
        Stack_node* dummy;
        Tree_node* address;

        address = head -> next_node -> tree_address;
        dummy = head -> next_node;
        head -> next_node = head -> next_node -> next_node;
        delete (dummy);
        return (address);
}

Tree :: Tree ()
{
        end = new Tree_node;
        current = end;
}

Tree_node* Tree :: make_tree ()
{
        Stack the_stack;
        int i;
        cout << "Press enter to begin the program." << endl;
        cout << "Then type the expression (ex. 3+4 is n3 n4 o+)."
            << endl;
```

Stack class from Lesson 16.4

```
          for (i = 1;  i <= 9;  i++)
                    {
                    current = new Tree_node;
                    cin.ignore ();
                    cin >> current -> type;

                    if (current -> type == 'n')
                              {
                              cin >> current -> operand;
                              current -> left_child = end;
                              current -> right_child = end;
                              }

                    if (current -> type == 'o')
                              {
                              cin >> current -> operatr;
                              current -> right_child = the_stack.pop ();
                              current -> left_child = the_stack.pop ();
                              }
                    the_stack.push (current);
                    }
                    return (current);
}

void Tree :: traverse (Tree_node* node)
{
          if (node -> left_child != end)
                    {
                    traverse(node -> left_child);
                    traverse(node -> right_child);
                    if (node -> operatr == '+')
                              {
                              cout << "Left =" << node -> left_child -> cum
                                   <<"  ";
                              cout << "Right =" << node -> right_child -> cum
                                   <<"  ";
                              cout << "Operator = + " << endl;
                              node -> cum = node -> left_child -> cum + node
                                   -> right_child -> cum;
                              }
                    else      if  (node -> operatr == '*')
                              {
                              cout << "Left = " << node -> left_child -> cum << "  ";
                              cout << "Right = " << node -> right_child -> cum << "  ";
                              cout << "Operator = * " << endl;
                              node -> cum = node -> left_child -> cum * node
                                   -> right_child -> cum;
                              }
```

Creating the tree (Lesson 16.4).

Traversing the tree using postorder.

```
                    else      if (node -> operatr == '-')
                              {
                              cout << "Left =" << node -> left_child -> cum <<" ";
                              cout << "Right  =" << node -> right_child -> cum << "  ";
                              cout << "Operator = -  " << endl;
                              node -> cum = node -> left_child -> cum-node
                                   -> right_child -> cum;
                              }
                    else      if (node -> operatr == '/')
                              {
                              cout << "Left =" << node -> left_child -> cum << "  ";
                              cout << "Right =" << node -> right_child -> cum << "  ";
                              cout << "Operator = /  " << endl;
                              node -> cum = node -> left_child -> cum / node
                                   -> right_child -> cum;
                              }
                    cout << "The node cumulative total is: " << node -> cum << endl;
                    }
          else
                    {
                    node -> cum = node -> operand;
                    return;
                    }
}

int main ( )
{
          Tree arithmetic_expression;
          Tree_node* root;
          root = arithmetic_expression.make_tree ();
          arithmetic_expression . traverse (root);
}
```

Operations done while visiting the node.

If the node has the end node for a child, return.

Creating a single tree object because we are working with a single tree.

We use a variable (`root`) to hold the address of the root of the tree. This is returned from the `make_tree` function.

We traverse the tree by calling traverse and passing the address of the root.

Output

```
Press enter to begin the program.
Then type the expression (ex. 3+4 is n3 n4 o+).

n5 n6 o+ n7 n9 o- o/ n3 o*
Left = 5 Right = 6 operator = +
The node cumulative total is: 11
Left = 7 Right = 9 operator = -
The node cumulative total is: -2
Left = 11 Right = -2 operator = /
The node cumulative total is: -5.5
Left = -5.5 Right = 3 operator = *
The node cumulative total is: -16.5
```

Comments

You should observe the similarity of Figs. 16.39 and 16.40 to the shape of a binary tree. Because of this similarity, we find that a recursive function with two recursive calls models a binary tree quite well.

Although we would not have obtained the correct arithmetic answer, we could have traversed the tree in preorder or inorder. These have the following steps.

Preorder

1. Visit the node.
2. Traverse the node's left subtree in preorder.
3. Traverse the node's right subtree in preorder.

These steps lead to the following true block in the function, `traverse`, if (when we visit the node) we simply print the operator:

```
cout << "Operator = " << current -> operatr << endl;
traverse (current -> left_child, end);
traverse (current -> right_child, end);
```

This would lead to the output being printed in the order:

```
* / + 5 6 - 7 9 3
```

The inorder method of traversal is:

Inorder

1. Traverse the node's left subtree in inorder.
2. Visit the node.
3. Traverse the node's right subtree in inorder.

This leads to the following statements in the true block of the function, `traverse`.

```
traverse (current -> left_child, end);
cout << "Operator = " << current -> operatr << endl;
traverse (current -> right_child, end);
```

This would lead to the output being printed in the order:

```
5 + 6 / 7 - 9 * 3
```

Had we wanted to perform an arithmetic calculation with preorder or inorder traversal, we would have had to have changed the `if-else` control structure in the function, `traverse`.

Modification Exercises

1. Modify the program so that it can handle 21 binary tree nodes.
2. Modify the program so that the user can enter the number of nodes that are to be in the tree.
3. Modify the program to perform the calculation $5 + 6 / 7 - 9 * 3$ without any consideration of parentheses using an inorder traversal of the tree.
4. Modify the program so that the tree is created by entering the data in inorder.

APPLICATION EXAMPLE 16.3 QUICKSORT ALGORITHM

TOPICS

- Recursion
- Sorting

Problem Statement

Write a program that can sort a list of integers using the quicksort algorithm.

Solution

The quicksort algorithm (Hoare, C. A. R., "QuickSort," *Computer Journal,* vol. 5, pp. 10–15, 1962) performs substantially better than the bubble sort algorithm and has been found to be an efficient sorting method for a number of different types of sorting problems. It is used in commercial software.

Quicksort uses a partitioning approach to sorting. It essentially breaks a list into two parts (left and right) where the left part is made to contain only values less than a certain value in the list, and the right part is made to contain only values greater than the value in the list. Between the two parts, the value is inserted. When quicksort has accomplished this partitioning, the value is in the correct sorted location (so it does not need to be worked on further), and quicksort has created two separate lists, which if sorted individually without regard to the other, would result in a completely sorted single list. Quicksort then works with the two separate lists, repeating the process until all individual values are in their proper locations.

SPECIFIC EXAMPLE

An unordered list of numbers is shown here. First, a value from the list is chosen. This value is called the *pivot value*. Our algorithm uses the rightmost value (29) as the pivot to get things going. With this value we begin from both the left and right. Our goal with this pass is to get the number 29 in its proper position. From the right we look for values less than 29 (because any values less than 29 on this portion of the list are out of place), and from the left we look for values greater than 29 (because any values greater than 29 on this portion of the list are out of place). When we encounter an out-of-place value on both sides, we swap them.

From the left we hit 98, and from the right we hit 18.

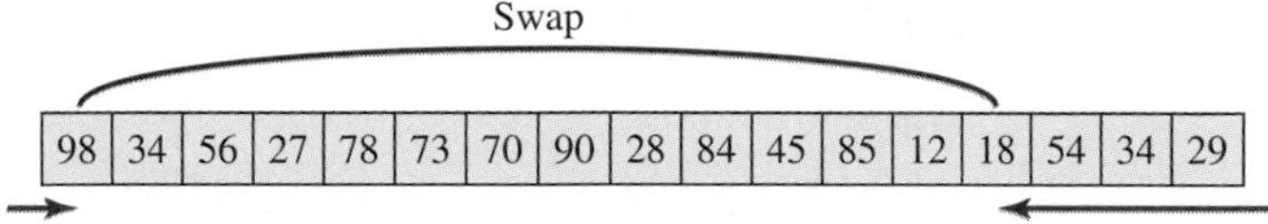

We now swap these two values and proceed from them giving:

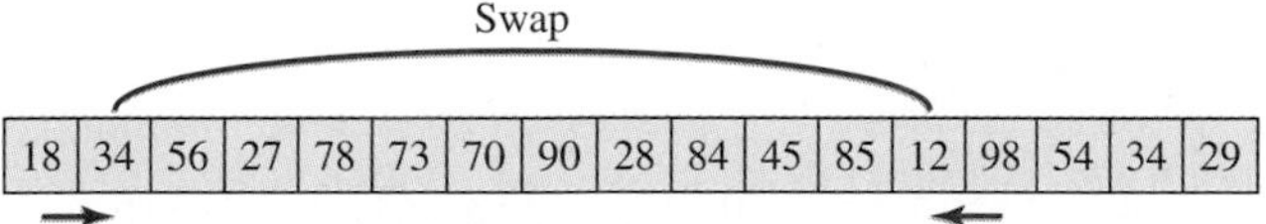

We hit 34 and 12. We swap them and proceed, giving:

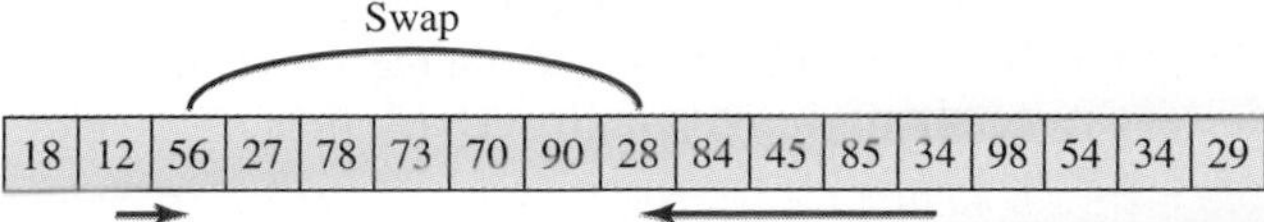

We hit 56 and 28. We swap them and proceed giving:

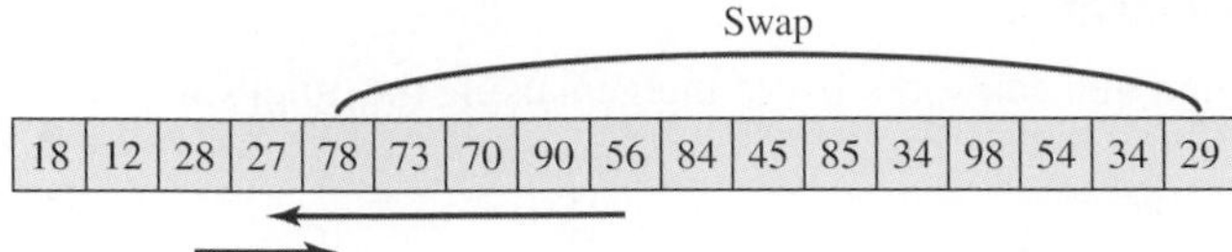

We hit 78 and 27. At this point our left position has gone past our right position making the arrows overlap. This indicates that we stop and swap our pivot (29) with the left position value (78), giving:

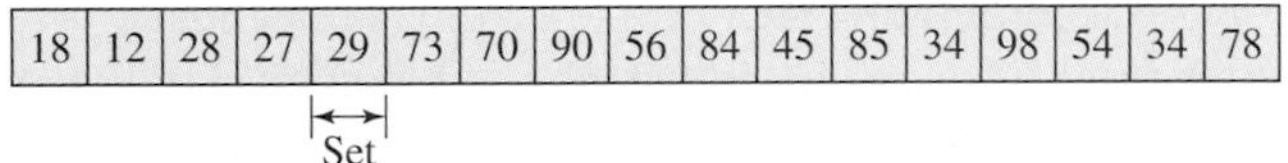

At this point, our pivot value, 29, is in its proper location with all values to the left of it being less than 29, and all values to the right of it being greater than 29. As a result, we do not need to touch the location with 29 in it any more. In addition, we have created two new lists: to the left of 29 and to the right of 29. If we sort these two lists independently, we end up with a single sorted list.

In our algorithm, when given a choice, we will work with the left list; therefore, we now operate on the left list. We set the pivot value as 27 (the rightmost value in the list) and look for numbers less than 27 and greater than 27 as we proceed from the right and left respectively. The arrow on the left goes to 28 and the arrow on the right goes to 12.

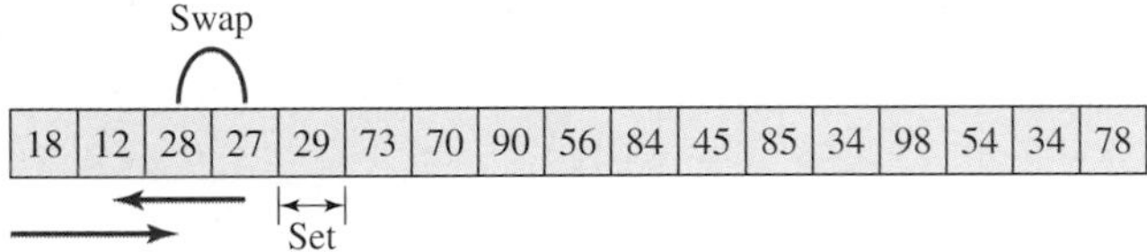

Since the two arrows overlap, we stop and swap the pivot (27) with the value indicated by the left arrow (28), giving:

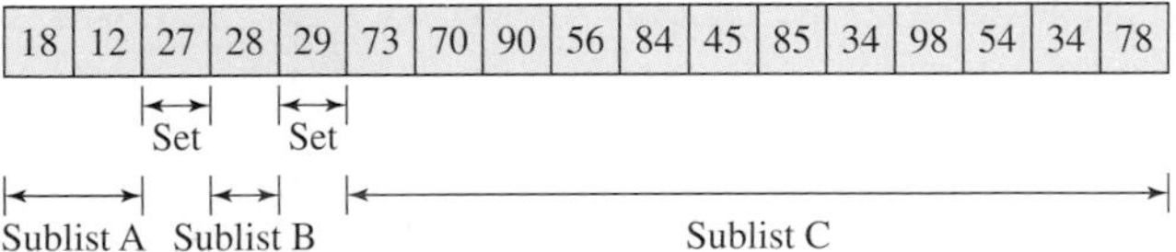

At this point we have the values 27 and 29 in their proper locations and have created three sublists. Since we always choose the left list, we work on sublist A. Without going into the details, we end up switching the 18 and 12, putting both of them in their proper location. Then we work on sublist B. We check to see if the starting locations for the right and left are the same (meaning only one value is present in the sublist), and then we do nothing. Then sublist C is addressed using a pivot of 78.

In abbreviated form, we list the steps in the diagram below.

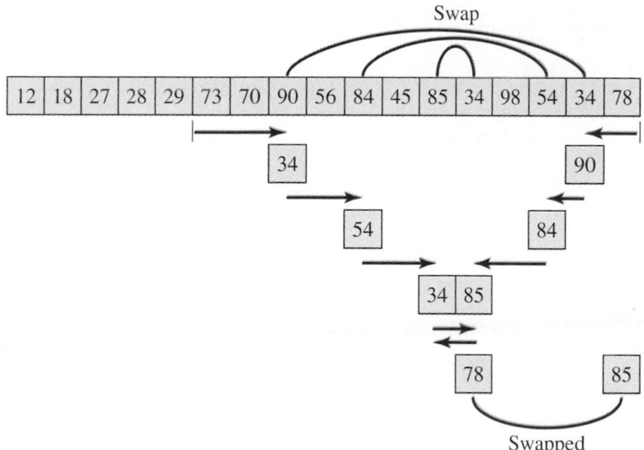

The steps in the diagram are:

1. Find values >78 and <78 (being 90 and 34).
2. Swap 90 and 34.
3. Find values >78 and <78 (being 84 and 54).
4. Swap 84 and 54.
5. Find values >78 and <78 (being 85 and 34).
6. Swap 85 and 34.
7. Find values >78 and <78 (being 85 and 34 again).
8. Since the arrows have crossed, stop and swap the location indicated by the left arrow (85) with the far right value (78).
9. The result of this pass is indicated by the lowest numbers in each column and is shown next.

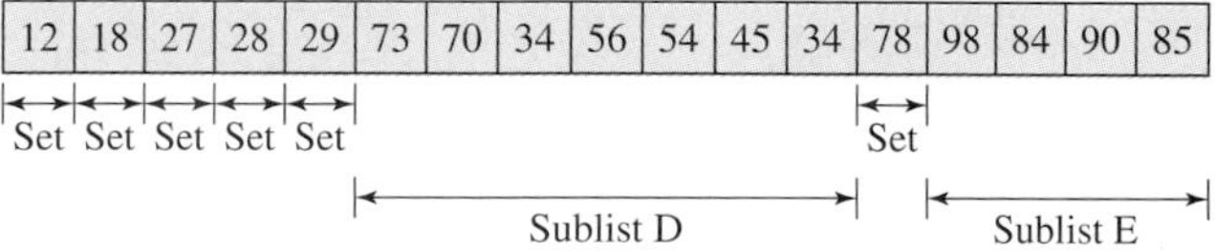

At this point, the value 78 is in its proper location and two sublists are created. Since we always take the left list, we would work with sublist D next. We will not go through the rest of the procedure in detail; however, we encourage you to follow the steps and complete the sort by hand.

A schematic illustration of the operations of a list (that is, breaking a list into sublists) is shown in Fig. 16.41. If we follow down this figure, we see how first the left portion of the list and then the right portion of the list is sorted. A tree-like image of Fig. 16.41 is shown in Fig. 16.42. If you compare the figures, you see

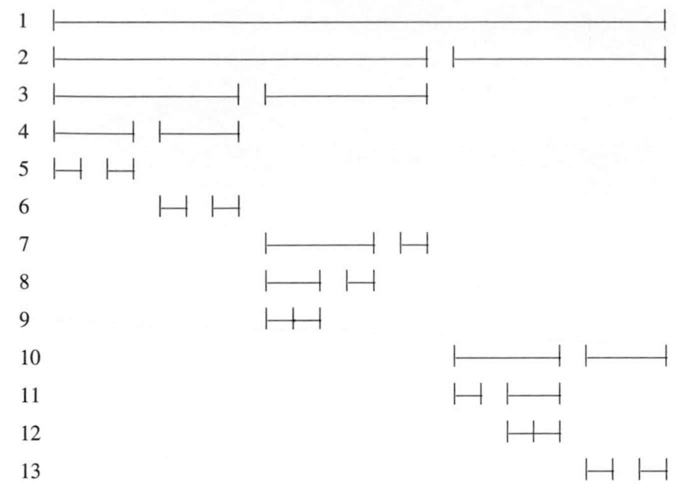

Figure 16.41

Pattern of operation of quicksort on a list. Read this diagram from the top line, and then follow down each succeeding line. Each time a list is broken into sublists, the left sublist is first to be operated upon. This continues until no more left sublists are unsorted. Then the right sublist is evaluated. You can see from this diagram that first the low numbers are sorted and then, as the sort proceeds, the higher numbers are sorted. The last portion of the list to be sorted is the far-right end.

that each of the 13 levels (labeled on the left sides of the figures) is identical. We show the tree-like image because we have previously illustrated how traversing a tree is easily programmed using recursion. Therefore, we will see that recursion is involved in the quicksort process. First, we describe how to program the swapping type operations.

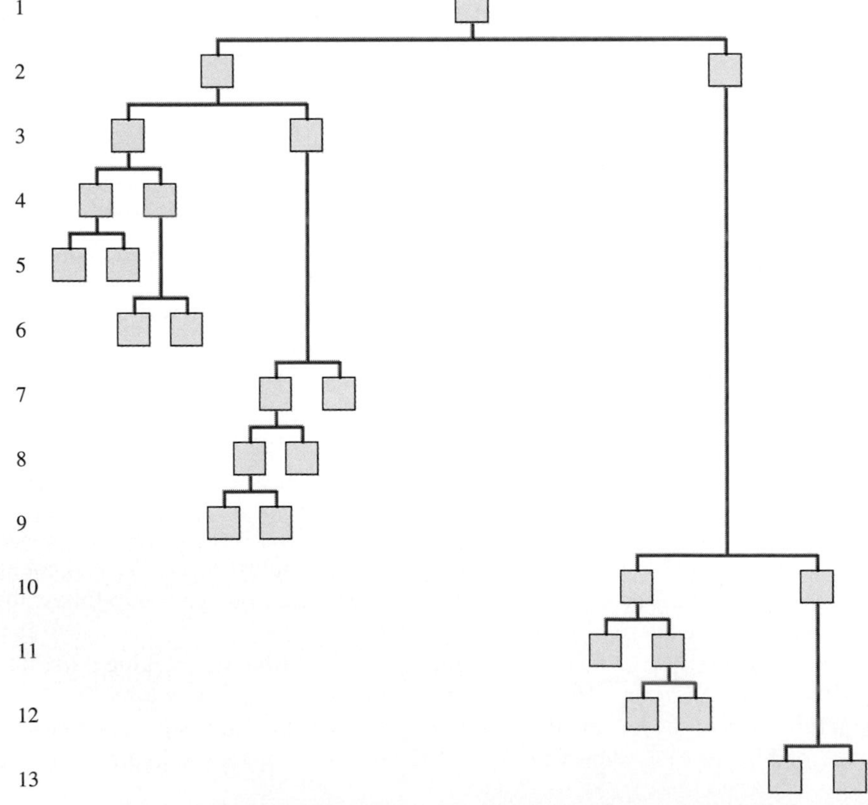

Figure 16.42

Tree-like representation of Fig. 16.41. As we have seen, recursion is well suited for programming a structure of this type.

ALGORITHM AND CODE SEGMENTS

From the hand example and Fig. 16.42, we can see that the overall procedure is the following:

1. Establish the starting points for the left and right arrows.
2. Set the pivot equal to the value at the right starting point.
3. Move from the left to find a value greater than the pivot.
4. Move from the right to find a value less than the pivot.
5. If the arrows do not overlap, swap the values in steps 3 and 4 and repeat steps 3 through 5.
6. If the arrows overlap, stop and swap the pivot and the value indicated by the left arrow.
7. At this point the pivot value has been put into its proper location and two new sublists have been created.

We repeat steps 1–7 for each left sublist created. We use steps 1–7 on a right sublist after the last left sublist has been sorted.

One other step should be done before all of this, and this is to check that the right starting point is indeed to the right of the left starting point. If it is not, then the list has already been sorted and none of the steps need to be done. We will develop the source code step by step from the algorithm.

We will call the list array `a[]`. The variable `i` is the index value that moves from the left, and `j` is the index that moves from the right.

In order to move from the left to a value greater than the pivot we can use a `while` loop. For instance the loop:

```
while (a[++i] < pivot);
```

causes the value of the index, `i`, to be incremented continuously until a value in the array `a[]` is found to be greater than or equal to the pivot. At the end of executing this loop, the value of `i` is equal to the subscript of the first value from the left that is greater than or equal to the pivot. This represents the location of the arrowhead of the left arrow.

Similarly, the loop:

```
while (a[--j] > pivot);
```

causes the value of the index, `j`, to be decremented continuously until a value in the array `a[]` is found to be less than or equal to the pivot. At the end of executing this loop, the value of `j` is equal to the subscript of the first value from the right that is less than or equal to the pivot. This represents the location of the arrowhead of the right arrow.

Note that at the end of this, if the value of `i` is greater than or equal to the value of `j` then the arrowheads overlap, and we should not do any swapping of values. The statement:

```
if (i >= j) break;
```

takes us out of any loop that does the swapping.

In order to swap the values of a[i] and a[j], we use the following code (with the variable temp as a variable that is used for the temporary storage of a value so that the swap can be completed):

```
temp = a[i];
a[i] = a[j];
a[j] = temp;
```

Recall how we swap two values. Since two actions cannot be done simultaneously, an intermediate storage location (here represented by the variable, temp) must always be used. The action of these three statements is (using a[i] = 90 and a[j] = 34):

		a[i]	90
Action of:	temp = a[i];	a[j]	34
		temp	90
		a[i]	34
Action of:	a[i] = a[j];	a[j]	34
		temp	90
		a[i]	34
Action of:	a[j] = temp;	a[j]	90
		temp	90

The end result being that the values of a[i] and a[j] have been swapped.

We can put all these statements together within a loop to form one complete pass through a sublist:

```
while (1)              <-- Create loop that needs a break; to terminate.
      {
      while (a[++i] < pivot);   <-- Increase i (move from left) until a value >= pivot is hit.
      while (a[--j] > pivot);   <-- Decrease j (move from right) until a value <= pivot is hit.
      if (i >= j) break;        <-- Exit loop if arrowheads overlap.
      temp = a[i];  ┐
      a[i] = a[j];  ├-- Swap the values indicated by the left and right arrowheads.
      a[j] = temp;  ┘
      }
```

The loop created by the line while(1) could be an infinite loop since the value 1 is always true. However, the statement if (i >= j) break; causes the loop to terminate. Be careful when you write this type of loop. If i never becomes greater than or equal to j, the loop will not terminate and it will make it appear that your computer (if you are running it on a PC) has locked up.

If the initial indices of the tails of the left and right arrows are the variables left_position and right_position, we can swap the pivot (a[right_position]) and the value at the left arrowhead (a[i]) with the following sequence of statements:

```
temp = a[i];
a[i] = a[right_position];
a[right_position] = temp;
```

Adding this to the previous gives the following:

```
while (1)
          {
          while (a[++i] < pivot);
          while (a[--j] > pivot);
          if (i >= j) break;
          swap = a[i];
          a[i] = a[j];
          a[j] = swap;
          }
swap = a[i];
a[i] = a[right_position];
a[right_position] = swap;
```

Loop to move arrowheads from left and right and swap the values at their arrowheads. Exit the loop when the arrowheads overlap.

Upon exiting the loop, swap the values at the left arrowhead and the far-right position.

Before we get this process going we must check that the left position is not to the right of the right position and that we initialize the values of `i` and `j` and the `pivot`. These statements are:

```
if (right_position > left_position)
          {
          pivot = a[right_position];
          i = left_position - 1;
          j = right_position;
          }
```

If the tail of the right arrow is to the right of the tail of the left arrow, set the pivot to be the tail of the right arrow.

Initialize `i` to be the tail of the left arrow – 1.

Initialize `j` to be the tail of the right arrow.

We can put our previous statements into this conditional giving.

```
if (right_position > left_position)
          {
          pivot = a[right_position];
          i = left_position - 1;
          j = right_position;
                    while (1)
                              {
                              while (a[++i] < pivot);
                              while (a[--j] > pivot);
                              if (i >= j) break;
                              swap = a[i];
                              a[i] = a[j];
                              a[j] = swap;
                              }
                    temp = a[i];
                    a[i] = a[right_position];
                    a[right_position] = temp;
          }
```

If the tail of the right arrow is to the left of (less than) the tail of the left arrow, then there is no need to sort the sublist.

Initialize arrowheads and pivot.

Loop to swap values indicated by arrowheads.

Move pivot into its proper position.

The above statements form one complete pass. At the end of this we have the pivot value in its proper location (`a[i]`), a left sublist that goes from `a[left_position]` to `a[i - 1]`, and a right sublist that goes from `a[i + 1]` to `a[right_position]`.

We repeat this procedure for the left and right sublists. This can be done in different ways, but it lends itself to using recursion (as we saw with the tree-like structure in Fig. 16.42). Because we need to repeat the procedure for both the left and right sublists, we need two recursive calls instead of just one.

For our function, we will first put in the recursive calls, and then we will follow the flow of the program. Calling the function `qksort()`, we show the source code here. Note the two recursive calls in this function. The first call works on the left sublist, and the second call works on the right sublist.

```
int qksort(int a[], int left_position, int right_position)
{
        int pivot, i, j, swap;

        PREVIOUS CODE

             qksort(a, left_position, i - 1);
             qksort(a, i + 1, right_position);
             }
}
```

Parameters are the array and the locations of the tails of the left and right arrows.

Call to `qksort` to sort left sublist.

Call to `qksort` to sort right sublist.

The flow of this function is similar to what is illustrated in Figs. 16.39 and 16.40, so we do not repeat the discussion here. The complete source code, including the `main` function, is shown. It sorts the list given by the array, `list[]`.

Source Code

```
#include <iostream>
using namespace std;

void qksort(int a[], int left_position, int right_position);

int main ()
{
        const int SIZE = 17;
        int list[] = {98,34,56,27,78,73,70,90,28,84,45,85,12,18,54,34,29};
        int i;

        qksort(list, 0, SIZE - 1);

        for (i = 0; i < SIZE; i++)  cout << list[i] <<" ";

        cout << endl;
}

void qksort(int a[], int left_position, int right_position)
{
        int pivot, i, j, swap;
        if (right_position > left_position)
                {
                pivot = a[right_position];
                i = left_position - 1;
                j = right_position;
```

We do not return a value from `qksort`.

We begin by sorting the entire list (from index 0 to the largest index).

In `qksort`, we modify the `list[]` array using `a[]`.

This is the `if` conditional for the recursive `qksort` function.

```
        while (1)
              {
              while (a[++i] < pivot);
              while (a[--j] > pivot);
              if (i >= j) break;
              swap = a[i];
              a[i] = a[j];
              a[j] = swap;
              }

        swap = a[i];
        a[i] = a[right_position];
        a[right_position] = swap;
        qksort(a, left_position, i - 1);
        qksort(a, i + 1, right_position);
        }
}
```

Two recursive calls to qksort.

There is no false block in qksort because qksort does not return a value. We simply perform no operations if the sublist is already sorted.

Output

```
12 18 27 28 29 34 34 45 54 56 70 73 78 84 85 90 98
```

Comments

One method of evaluating the performance of sorting algorithms is to examine the number of comparisons needed to complete a sort. For a given number of items, N, in a list, the number of comparisons needed for a particular method is not necessarily constant because some lists may begin with a favorable order already. For instance, the most favorable initial arrangement for quicksort is one in which each time two sublists are created, they are both of the same size. The analysis goes beyond the scope of this book; however, we can say that the number of comparisons on average for the quicksort is on the order of $N \log_2 N$. For the bubble sort it is on the order of N^2. Thus for 10,000 values in a list, quicksort on average requires on the order of $10000(\log_2 10000) = 132{,}900$ comparisons, whereas the bubble sort requires on the order of $(10{,}000)^2 = 100{,}000{,}000$ comparisons. Clearly, quicksort is far superior to the bubble sort.

A number of suggestions for improving the quicksort algorithm have been made since the method was first developed. A popular one is to use a pivot value that is different from the far right value. If a median of the left, middle, and right values is used, the likelihood of a more even split in the creation of the sublists increases. This improves the efficiency of the method.

Modification Exercise

Modify the program to sort a list of doubles.

LESSON EXERCISES

LESSON 16.1 EXERCISES

1. True or false:

a. With a linked list, we can use only the memory needed.

b. We need to use an array to get a linked list to work.

c. The node class for a linked list must have a pointer variable to an object of the class.

d. The linked list class must have both an ordinary and a pointer variable as members.

e. It is good practice to free the memory of a node deleted from a linked list.

2. Given the following class definitions:

```
class Node
        {
        public:
                int aa;
                double bb;
                Node* next_node;
        };

class LList
        {
        private:
                Node* current;
                Node* head;
                ...
         public:
                functions
         };
```

find the errors, if any, in the following statements for function `make_list()`:

a. `*current = *head;`

b. `head = new Node*;`

c. `current = current.next_node;`

d. `cin >> current -> aa;`

Solutions

1. a. true
b. false
c. true
d. false
e. true

2. a. `current = head;`
b. `head = new Node;`
c. `current = current -> next_node;`
d. No error.

LESSON 16.2 EXERCISES

1. True or false:

a. A stack can only be created by using the method shown in this lesson.

b. A stack is a special case of a linked list.

c. A stack is a FIFO type structure.

d. It is good practice to release the memory of a node popped from a stack.

e. It is good practice to check if the stack has nodes before attempting to pop from it.

2. Given the classes and objects listed for this lesson's program, find the errors, if any, in the following statements:

a. `inventory.push(value,tail);`

b. `int push(int)` *(as a function declaration)*

c. `head -> value = 23.4;`

Solutions

1. a. false
b. true
c. false
d. true
e. true

2. a. `inventory.push(value);`
b. `void push(int)`
c. The head node only points to the top node on the stack, thus no value should be stored in it.

LESSON 16.3 EXERCISES

1. True or false:

a. An ordinary queue is a FIFO type structure.

b. In an ordinary queue, we insert a new node at the head of the queue.

c. In an ordinary queue, we remove a node from the tail.

d. A priority queue is a common type of queue used in determining the order that jobs should be printed on shared printers.

e. The only way that a queue can be implemented is with the method we have shown for this lesson's program.

Solutions

1. a. true
b. false
c. false
d. true
e. false

LESSON 16.4 EXERCISES

1. True or false:

a. We can use a stack to create a binary tree.

b. A tree node can have only two children.

c. A binary tree node can have only two children.

d. A graph is a special instance of a tree.

e. The root of a tree is typically drawn at the bottom of the tree.

Solutions

1. a. true
b. false
c. true
d. false
e. false

LESSON 16.5 EXERCISES

1. True or false:

a. The name of a recursive function must appear at least once in its function body.

b. A recursive function must have a control statement to prevent the program from running indefinitely.

c. There is no `void` type recursive function.

d. A recursive function must return a value to its calling function, otherwise it cannot continue the recursive process.

2. Write a program that calls a function to read a one to six digit octal base number, and then convert it to a decimal base number.

3. Rewrite Problem 2 using a recursive function.

Solutions

1. a. true
b. true
c. false
d. false

APPLICATION EXERCISES

1. In industrial engineering, it is sometimes necessary to simulate manufacturing and service operations for the purpose of improving efficiency and optimizing the system. In this problem you are to model a rapid oil change and lubrication business. The queue data structure can be used to do this. Assume that the station has the following:

a. There are three bays for changing oil.

b. It takes 15 minutes to service each car.

c. One car arrives randomly between every 2 and 20 minutes.

d. At the end of a 12-hour day, all waiting cars are sent away.

Write your program to model 30 days of operation. Determine the average waiting time for the cars and the total amount of idle time for the bays. Run your program 12 times to get an understanding of the variability of the results. Report all of your answers.

2. Have the program automatically execute 50 times and average the results of all 50 runs.

3. Modify the program of Problem 1 to handle five bays. How does this change the answers?

4. The company is thinking of issuing a preferred customer card to minimize the waiting for certain customers. Allow these customers to move to the front of the queue. Have 15 of these customers appear each day. What is the average waiting time for the nonpreferred customers?

5. Change the number of preferred customers in the program of Problem 4 until the waiting time for the other customers increases 10 percent, 30 percent, and 100 percent. How many preferred customers can be created if the other customers are to wait no more than an additional 25 percent if 0.5 percent of all preferred customers arrive each day?

6. A small bicycle manufacturing company is reliant upon its suppliers to deliver crucial parts in a timely manner for it to be able to complete a bicycle. However, its suppliers are not able to deliver parts in a completely predictable manner. Use three different stacks to model the supply and use of chains, wheel rims, and spokes. Each bicycle uses 100 spokes, two wheel rims, and one chain. The suppliers offer the following reliability of delivery:

	Spokes	Wheel rims	Chains
Frequency of delivery	Every 30 to 60 days	Every 30 to 90 days	Every 40 to 150 days
Number delivered	3000 to 5000	400 to 700	180 to 400

Assume that all other parts are on hand and do not affect production. If the parts are delivered randomly in the above ranges, determine how many bicycles can be made in a three-year period. At the end of this time, how many of each type of parts is on hand? Have your program automatically execute 50 times so that you get an understanding of the effects of the randomness.

7. Modify the program of Problem 6 to consider the supply of brakes. Assume that 200 to 900 brakes can be delivered every 20 to 100 days. How many bikes can be manufactured now?

8. Have the program of Problem 6 print a weekly report of the number of parts on hand. Have it compute the number of days for which no bicycle is manufactured.

9. The exact boundaries of a large city are being determined by locating individual points on its boundaries. Each point is given x and y coordinates according to a predetermined coordinate system. As each individual point is located, the boundaries of the city are updated. Initially the city's boundaries are determined with just four points:

x (ft)	*y* (ft)
58	93
3597	198
3498	78965
87	97866

The location of a new point on the list is important because the boundary is formed by connecting the adjacent points on the list. Write a program that creates a list of boundary points that can be continuously updated. Begin with the four listed points. Have points added by first inputting the coordinates of the new boundary point and then the coordinates of the boundary point that it succeeds. Use a linked list structure to do this. Each new data point should be inserted in the linked list. Print the final list of boundary points.

10. Modify the program of Problem 9 so that it calculates the length of the boundary each time a new point is added.

11. On complex construction projects, a sequence of steps must be taken in a particular order to complete the project on schedule and reliably. This is called a *critical path*. The steps in a critical path are sometimes modified as the project progresses because some actions are not forseeable. Write a program that uses a linked list to represent a critical path. Read the description of the activity from the keyboard and the name of the activity that it follows. Add this activity to the critical path, and print out the new critical path. The first activity should follow "head."

12. Transportation engineers coordinate bus traffic in major cities. Consider 10 different bus stops on one particular bus line. Use a queue for each stop. Assume that the patrons arrive randomly at each stop at a rate of one every 3–6 minutes. Each time a passenger boards a bus, the bus is delayed 10 seconds. The time for the bus to drive between stops is four minutes. Write a program that simulates the driving of two buses. The buses begin at evenly spaced intervals along the route. In other words, the buses begin at the first and sixth stops. Determine the average waiting time for the patrons at the stops.

13. Modify the program of Problem 12 to use three buses evenly spaced. What is the average waiting time now?

14. Modify the program of Problem 12 to limit the number of passengers allowed on a bus. Allow no more than 10 passengers at a time. Determine the average waiting time of passengers able to get on a bus and the number of passengers left stranded.

15. Modify the program of Problem 12 to determine the number of buses necessary to assure that only one passenger is stranded.

16. Modify the passenger arrival rates bus programs and the spacing between bus stops to gain an understanding of the effects of these parameters.

17. Products that have limited shelf life are put onto shelves in a supermarket in a manner similar to that of the stack data structure. New products arriving are simply put in front of older products. Customers remove the newer products until the older ones become exposed. Write a program that simulates this behavior for four different products. Assume that new products arrive every day according to the following schedule:

	Bread	Milk	Eggs	Chicken
Supply	8:00 AM, 50 loaves	11:00 AM, 100 liters	2:00 PM, 40 boxes	4:00 PM, 60 chickens
Removal	Random, every 3–15 minutes	Random, every 1–6 minutes	Random, every 4–8 minutes	Random, every 5–10 minutes

At the end of every third day (12-hour day), the leftover product is discarded. If no product exists when a customer wants it, register a complaint with management. Determine the amount of product that is discarded and the number of complaints registered over a 30-day period.

18. Have the program you wrote in Problem 17 select randomly among the following supply and removal rates and compute the amount of product that is discarded and the number of complaints registered:

Supply arrival time	Supply number of units	Removal (minutes)
8:00 AM	200	2–5
9:30 AM	40	10–30
11:00 AM	90	25–60
12:00 PM	350	20–90
1:00 PM	20	4–9
2:00 PM	400	12–20
4:00 PM	700	5–15
6:00 PM	120	8–30

CHAPTER 17

TEMPLATES AND THE C++ STANDARD TEMPLATE LIBRARY

CHAPTER TOPICS

In this chapter, you will learn how to:

- Create template functions and classes
- Use some features of the Standard Template Library

Templates are another feature that C++ offers. As their name implies, templates are frameworks or forms. We can have template functions, which are forms of functions on which real functions can be built. We can also have template classes, which are forms for constructing real classes. C++ allows us to create our own templates, or we can use the templates in the Standard Template Library (STL), which is a library of templates (as the name indicates).

In this chapter, we start with examples of template functions and template classes. Then we go into the STL. In the same way that we have covered the other parts of the C++ language one step at a time, we cover the STL one step at a time. We show one aspect of the STL, use it in some basic manipulations, then show another aspect.

The core of the STL is containers, iterators, and algorithms (which are described in the lessons). If you know these you can use a good bit of the STL (although there is much more). The intent in this book is simply to produce some examples and give some exposure to the STL.

A description of a library tends to be short in concepts and long in lists of vocabulary, parameters, names, and purposes. In Lesson 17.5, after three lessons of exposure to the STL, we give a list of STL features and components. We could present this earlier, but students tend to get lost in the vocabulary and become confused before they try to work with the STL, which is reasonably simple to use. Therefore, we show you how to work with the STL before we show the details.

If you skipped Chapter 16, you should read just the introductions to Lessons 16.1 to 16.4 prior to reading Lesson 17.3.

In these programs, we use `using namespace std;`. This fits the C++ standard, although some compilers may generate warnings or errors when this is done. If you run into these problems, use `std::` to name items directly.

LESSON 17.1 FUNCTION TEMPLATES

TOPICS

- Creating function templates
- Using function templates

We have used function overloading to create functions of the same name to work with different data types. For instance, a function `sum()` may be written to add two integers. Then we could overload `sum()` to add two `double`s. And, we could overload it again to add two long integers. This process works well, but can be clumsy. For instance, if there is a fundamental error, then all the functions must be changed. Also, multiple function definitions lengthen the code, which can make it more difficult to work with.

Function templates can solve some of the problems caused by function overloading and add considerable versatility to programs. Function templates express the general form for a function in much the same way that we illustrate the general form of C++ syntax in this book. For instance, we might say that the general form for the definition of the function `sum` is:

```
type sum (type a, type b)
      {
      return (a + b);
      }
```

where *type* is a valid C++ data type. For a function template, the C++ syntax is quite similar (except for the first line), it is:

```
template <class Type>
Type sum (Type a, Type b)
        {
        return (a + b);
        }
```

After the first line, the code is nearly identical to the general form with `Type` replacing *type*. The first line indicates that `Type` is the identifier that represents a generic data type in the function definition. `Type` is referred to as a *type parameter*. Whether `Type` refers to a `double` or `int`, for instance, is determined by the function call. If both arguments in the function call are `double`, then `sum()` adds two `double`s. If both arguments in the function call are `int`, then sum adds two `int`s.

This lesson's program uses two type parameters instead of just one in the function template. The function `get_val()` returns the greater of two array elements. Read the program and note that the types of arguments in the two function calls are different.

QUESTION YOU SHOULD ATTEMPT TO ANSWER

1. How can we create a template function with three generic types?

Source Code

```
#include <iostream>
using namespace std;

template <class Type1, class Type2>
Type1 get_val (Type1 a[], Type2 i, Type2 j)
        {
        if (a[i] > a[j])  return a[i];
        else              return a[j];
        }

int main ( )
{
        double y[5] = {5.2, 6.4, 7.6, 8.8, 9.0};
        char z[20] = "A character array.";

        cout << get_val (y, 2, 4) << " ";
        cout << get_val (z, 3, 8) << endl;
}
```

Both `Type1` and `Type2` represent generic data types.

The function name is `get_val` with a return type of `Type1`. The argument `a[]` represents an array of `Type1`, and `i` and `j` are type `Type2`.

Returning the greater of two array elements.

The first argument in the function call is the address of an array of type `double`, the second and third arguments are `int`. This call makes `Type1` `double` and `Type2` `int`.

The first argument in the function call is the address of an array of type `char`; the second and third arguments are `int`. This call makes `Type1` `char` and `Type2` `int`.

Output

```
9 t
```

Description

Defining function templates. The first line of a function template begins with the keyword `template`. Within angle brackets (<>) are the keyword `class` and identifiers for the template data types in a comma separated list. The general form for three template data types is:

```
template <class Type1, class Type2, class Type3>
```

where *Type1*, *Type2*, and *Type3* are any valid identifiers of the type parameters that are used to represent data types in the function template definition. The keyword `class` is used because classes may be regarded as abstract data types. The rest of the function template definition has the same form as an ordinary function definition. However, the type parameters are used in place of ordinary data types like `int`, `double`, and `char` in both the header and body.

For instance, the `get_val()` function template

```
template <class Type1, class Type2>
Type1 get_val (Type1 a[], Type2 i, Type2 j)
      {
      if (a[i] > a[j])         return a[i];
      else                     return a[j];
      }
```

uses type parameters `Type1` and `Type2` to indicate the return value type and the argument types. Within the function, the arguments are used as they normally would.

Using function templates. A function template is called in the same manner as an ordinary function. For instance,

```
get_val (y, 2, 4)
```

calls a version of the `get_val` function template. The actual return and argument data types with which the function works are determined by the data types in the argument list of the function call. Because in the function call `y` is type `double` and 2 and 4 are integers, `Type1` for `get_val` is `double` and `Type2` is `int`. Since the function returns `Type1`, it returns a `double`. In the function call:

```
get_val (z, 3, 8)
```

`z` is type `char`, and 3 and 8 are type `int`. Therefore, `Type1` represents type `char` and `Type2` represents type `int` for this function call.

Although not shown in this lesson's program, the `get_val()` function can handle arrays with large numbers of elements. `Type2` would ordinarily represent type `int`. But, for cases where the largest `int` allowed by the system is smaller than the number of array elements we want to include, `Type2` could represent `unsigned long int`. To make it do so, we would call `get_val` with `unsigned long int` as the type for the second and third values. The explicit form of an `unsigned long`, with UL as a suffix on a number (see Chapter 3), may be required for the second and third arguments.

Mixing ordinary and template data types. Had we not wanted to include the feature of being able to work with very long arrays, we could have made the `get_val` function template to be

```
template <class Type1>
Type1 get_val (Type1 x[], int i, int j)
      {
      if (a[i] > a[j])        return a[i];
      else                    return a[j];
      }
```

Note that it is permissible to have both generic data types and ordinary data types together in the function header and body.

It should also be noted that data of the generic data types can be declared in the function template body. For instance, if we wanted to reserve memory in `get_val`, we could have used the lines:

```
Type1* b;
b = new Type1;
```

within the body of `get_val`. These lines declare `b` to be a `Type1` pointer variable, and assign the address of newly reserved memory to `b`. Overall, wherever an ordinary data type is used in a function body, a generic data type can be used.

Mechanics of function templates. C++ treats function templates somewhat like it treats overloaded functions in that it makes a decision, during compilation, regarding the form of the function being called. It looks at the function call, then generates instructions for a function that matches the call. For instance, when the compiler encounters the first call in this lesson's program, it generates instructions for a version of `get_val()` that works with `double` and `int`. When it encounters the second call, it generates another set of instructions that works with `char` and `int`. Therefore, it generates a different set of instructions for each type of function call. If more than one call exists for the same type of function, C++ is smart enough to realize that the instructions for that type of function already exist and does not regenerate the instructions.

This explanation allows us to describe some terminology. *Function templates* are templates (that is, the general form code of the sort we used in this lesson's program). *Template functions* are functions (that is, the instructions put into memory with the data types matching the function calls). We do not use this somewhat confusing terminology extensively, but you should be aware of it.

Errors with function templates. Although it may seem that with function templates, we do not need to worry about the data types in our function calls, we actually do. In fact, we still need to be very careful that the function calls have data types that are compatible with the function bodies. For instance, in this lesson's program, we are not allowed to have `double` values for the second and third arguments. That is, the function call

```
get_val (y, 3.2, 8.5)
```

is not valid because within the function body, the second and third arguments are used as array subscripts which can only be integer types.

If you use objects as arguments in the function calls rather than ordinary data as arguments, make sure that the operators used in the function are defined for the class.

You may need to overload the function's operators within the class to enable the function template to work. Remember to look closely at the operators used in your function template bodies. If the operators are not defined for the argument data types in the function calls, you will produce errors.

Function templates vs. overloaded functions. A function template cannot necessarily be used to replace overloaded functions. Overloaded functions are meant to perform *similar* tasks. Typically, the body of each overloaded function is different. However, function templates perform the *same* operations for each different data type. (Of course, the operations may be defined differently for different data types, possibly using operator overloading, but this is a separate issue.)

Also, with overloaded functions, we can vary the number of arguments. With a single function template, the number of arguments in each function call must be the same. We can, however, overload function templates to overcome this deficiency.

Overloading function templates. Function templates can become more versatile if we overload them. We have not shown it in this lesson's program, but C++ allows us to specify more than one function template with the same name. The number or distribution of the types of arguments can distinguish them. Also, an ordinary function with the same name as a function template is allowed if it is distinguishable in the numbers and types of arguments. When matching a function call to a function, C++ first looks for an ordinary function, then a function template.

Examples of function templates. Function templates are most useful for operations that apply to many data types. A common example is the sorting operation on arrays. The operations are nearly the same whether we have an array of `int`, `double`, or `char`. Rearranging, removing, inserting and other simple manipulation operations are good candidates for making function templates.

Comment. What we show as the first two lines of a function template definition is sometimes coded as a single line. For example, this lesson's function template could start

```
template <class Type1, class Type2> Type1 get_val (Type1 a[], Type2 i, Type2 j)
```

However, in this text, we use the two line form because it looks simpler.

Also, for a single type parameter, many programmers use just `T` instead of `Type` as we have used.

LESSON 17.2 CLASS TEMPLATES

TOPICS

- Creating class templates
- Using class templates

In the same way that a function template is defined like a general form for a function, a class template is defined like a general form for a class. For instance, a general form for a class called `Class1` with a data member `value`, a constructor, a member function set_value(), and a member function get_value() would be:

```
class Class1
{
        private:
                type value;
        public:
                Class1 ();
                void set_value (type);
                type get_value ();
};
```

where *type* is the data type (int, double, or other) of value. The class template for such a class looks quite similar to this (except for the first line). It is:

```
template <class Type>
class Class1
{
        private:
                Type value;
        public:
                Class1 ();
                void set_value (Type);
                Type get_value ();
};
```

The first line indicates a template and the name used to represent the data type. The rest of the class definition is identical to the general form with Type replacing *type*.

Using such a class template allows us to create an object of the class and use the data type of our choice for Type. We need a special syntax to declare an object from a class template because an ordinary syntax, such as

```
Class1 ob;
```

is not capable of indicating the data type being used for Type. In other words, with this declaration, C++ does not know if ob.value is to be an int, double, or other. The correct syntax is

```
Class1 <double> ob;
```

This indicates that double is to be used everywhere Type is in the class definition, and therefore, ob.value is type double. We will see that there are many situations when working with class templates that a bracketed data type (for example, <int>, <double>, or <Type>) is written after the class name.

Read the program and note the syntax needed to define the member functions.

QUESTION YOU SHOULD ATTEMPT TO ANSWER

1. How can we create a template class with two generic types?

Source Code

```
#include <iostream>
using namespace std;

template <class Type>
class Class1
{
        private:
                Type value;
        public:
                Class1 ();
                void set_value (Type);
                Type get_value ();
};

template <class Type>
Class1 <Type> :: Class1 ()
        {
        cout << "Constructor executed." << endl;
        }

template <class Type>
void Class1 <Type> :: set_value (Type bb)
        {
        value = bb;
        }

template <class Type>
Type Class1 <Type> :: get_value ()
        {
        return value;
        }

int main ( )
{
        Class1 <double> ob;
        double x = 3.5
        ob.set_value (x);
        cout << ob.get_value () << endl;

}
```

Class template definition.

Constructor function definition. Note the first line indicates that it belongs to a template class using `Type`. Also, `Class1 <Type> ::` is needed, not just `Class1 ::`.

Member function definition. It starts with `template <class Type>` and `void Class1 <Type> ::` not just `void Class1 ::`.

Member function definition. It starts with `template <class Type>` and `Type Class1 <Type> ::` not just `Type Class1 ::`.

Declaring an object that uses the class template. This notation indicates that `Type` for this object is `double`.

Calling a member function requires no special syntax.

Output

```
Constructor executed.
3.5
```

Description

Defining class templates. The first line of a class template (with a single data type) is similar to that used with a function template. It is:

```
template <class Type>
```

where *Type* is any valid identifier and is used to represent a data type in the class template definition. The class template definition has the same form as an ordinary class definition. However, the template data type *Type* is used in place of ordinary data types like int, double, and char throughout the class. See the definition of Class1 in this lesson's program for an example.

Member function definitions. Member function definitions require the template <class *Type*> line prior to the function header. Also, prior to the double colon, the class name and bracketed Type are required. The form for a function with two arguments is

```
template <class Type>
type Classname <Type> :: functionname (Type x, Type y)
```

where *Type* is the identifier used with the class definition, *type* is the function return type, *Classname* is the class template name, *functionname* is the member function name, and *x* and *y* are names of data used in the function. Remember, it is not good enough to use simply the class template name preceding the double colon. The <*Type*> must be there also. Nothing special need be done with the function bodies, except they are permitted to work with the data type *Type*.

Using class templates. An object is declared with the template class name and data type. For instance, in this lesson's program

```
Class1 <double> ob;
```

reserves memory for an object called ob with data member value being type double, a function member set_value() having a double type argument, and a function member get_value() returning a double. Nothing special need be done with member function calls. The object, dot operator, function name, and arguments are used in the same manner as calls to member functions of objects of ordinary classes. This lesson's source code illustrates the calls.

Mechanics of class templates. During compilation, a declaration for an object using a class template causes memory to be reserved for all the data members and instructions to be generated and stored for all function members. The data type used for these is the type specified in brackets in the declaration. If another object with the same bracketed data type is declared, new memory for data members is reserved, but no new function instructions are generated. Therefore, the compiler, in essence, creates a separate class for each type of object declared. This class is called a template class. Again, do not get confused by the terminology. A *class template* is a template, and a *template class* is a class. A program can generate many template classes from one class template.

Examples of class templates. The classic example of a class template is one that simulates a stack. We will not dwell on the details, so if you skipped Chapter 16, there is no reason to cover it now. Let us just say that a stack is a data structure like an array is a data structure. An array is something that holds data. We can have an array of `double` or an array of `int`. That is, an array can work with many kinds of data. Similarly, a stack is a data structure that holds data. It can hold integers, `double`s, or other data types as we see fit. However, a stack is implemented in the form of a class in C++. Therefore, a class template can work very well with a stack data structure. By using a class template rather than an ordinary class, we can get the stack class to work for most any data type.

A class template works for a stack, partly because a stack's member functions primarily set and access data. Such operations are easily done for many different data types. A class template might not work well if the operations for a class are more complex because some complex operations may not be defined for many data types. Clearly, if the member functions of a class can work on only one or two types of data, there may be little reason to create a class template. Therefore, before you endeavor to create a class template, make sure your operations apply to many data types.

One further comment about stacks. A lack of complex operations means that stacks are primarily ways of containing data not operating on it. Consequently, a stack is known as a container class. For the most part, class templates work very well with container classes. Linked lists, stacks, queues, and trees are all considered to be containers. If you covered Chapter 16, we encourage you to try to make one of the container classes into a class template.

As you will see with the C++ Standard Template Library, there are many situations for which class templates are appropriate.

`static` data members in class templates. Recall that `static` data members are data members that are shared among all the objects of a particular class. C++ allows us to use the keyword `static` to qualify data members listed in a class template. All objects instantiated from a particular template class (not class template) share the `static` data members.

`friends` ***of class templates.*** We can use the `friend` designation for functions, template functions, classes, and template classes in the `friend`s list in class templates. Roughly speaking, the following applies for the four cases (assuming a single type parameter).

- *Ordinary function is designated a* `friend`. Such a function is a `friend` of each template class instantiated from the class template.
- *Ordinary class is designated a* `friend`. Such a class is a `friend` of each template class instantiated from the class template.
- *Template function is* `friend`. Only the matching type function is a `friend` of the class. In other words, if the type parameter for both the function and class is `int`, they are `friend`s.
- *Template class is* `friend`. Only the matching type class is a `friend`. In other words, if the type parameter for both classes is `int`, they are `friend`s.

The syntax for these can be complex. We will not discuss it further in this text.

Default type parameter arguments. C++ allows us to set a default for the data type used for the data type parameter. For instance, in this lesson's program, we could have written the beginning of the class template definition as

```
template <class Type = double>
class Class1
```

to specify `double` as the default data type. The following declaration:

```
Class1<> ob;
```

instantiates an object with `double` as the type parameter. Note that the brackets, although empty, are still required in the declaration. Also, the default can be overridden by enclosing a different data type in brackets in the declaration.

Inheritance to and from class templates. Class templates can be involved in an inheritance hierarchy. The hierarchy can consist of both template classes and ordinary classes. We will not go into further details.

Class template with two type parameters. Not shown in this lesson's program is a template class with more than one generic data type. Had we wanted, we could have created a class template like this:

```
template <class Type1, class Type2>
class Class1
{
        private:
                Type1 value;
                Type2 number;
        public:
                Class1 ();
                void set_value (Type1, Type2);
};
```

The header of the member function definitions would be

```
template <class Type1, class Type2>
Class1 <Type1, Type2> :: Class1 ()
```

and

```
template <class Type1, class Type2>
void Class1 <Type1, Type2> :: set_value (Type1 x, Type2 y)
```

The object declarations would be

```
Class1 <double, int> ob;
```

to make `Type1 double` and `Type2 int`.

Class template with a type parameter and a non-type parameter. You may have noticed that the list enclosed in angle brackets looks much like an argument list for a function. In fact, it acts much like one in that it passes information to the template. C++ does not restrict us to passing only type information (like `double`, `int`, or other). It allows us to pass constant *values* through this list. The constants in the list are called *non-type parameters*. In other words, when we declare an object using a class template, we can list types and values. For example, a declaration may look like

```
Class1 <double, 20> ob;
```

The following class template definition might correspond to this declaration:

```
template <class Type, int num_elems>
class Class1
{
        private:
                Type value[num_elems];
        public:
                Class1 ();
                member functions...
};
```

Note that the second argument in angle brackets is specified to be `int` not `class`. The declaration and definition make `num_elems = 20`, which is used in sizing the array data member `value[]`. In fact, the constant `num_elems` can be used in the bodies of member functions to control loops and perform other functions. It cannot, however, appear on the left side of an assignment statement as it is a constant.

Comment. The subject of templates opens up a whole new world of programming called *generic* programming. We cannot cover the topic sufficiently here. What we have shown gives you the ability to create some simple templates and understand some of the syntax involved in using the Standard Template Library, which we cover next.

LESSON 17.3 STANDARD TEMPLATE LIBRARY (1)—SEQUENCE CONTAINERS

TOPICS

- Vectors
- Deques
- Lists

C++ has a library of class and function templates in the Standard Template Library. You can use STL templates in your own programs. Doing so can simplify your programming effort considerably. For instance, the STL can be used for such things as creating and sorting arrays without the need for writing the sorting code. Also stacks and trees are easily created and manipulated.

The STL is vast and complex. An entirely new vocabulary accompanies the STL. We could spend many pages discussing the background. Since we do not have the space for all this, we focus on using the STL. Along the way, we will introduce and explain the vocabulary we use. One comment about the vocabulary: an STL definition and a common definition may not be the same. For example, you know what a vector is. However, although there are similarities, an STL vector and what we commonly think is a vector are not the same. The STL vector has particular properties and characteristics. To effectively use the STL, you should learn the properties and characteristics that we highlight for the different STL components.

QUESTION YOU SHOULD ATTEMPT TO ANSWER

1. What do you think is the difference between `push_back()` and `push_front()`?

As we mentioned in Lesson 17.2, the data structures we discussed in Chapter 16 can be considered to be container classes or containers. This lesson illustrates initializing and printing the sequence container class templates called `vector`, `deque`, and `list`. Read the program and note the header files included, the instantiation of objects from class templates, and the member functions used with the objects.

Source Code

```
#include <iostream>
#include <vector>
#include <deque>
#include <list>

using namespace std;

int main ( )
{
        vector <int> vector1;
        deque <char> deque1;
        list <double> list1;

        int i;

        vector1.push_back (2);
        vector1.push_back (4);
        vector1.push_back (6);
        vector1.push_back (8);
        vector1.push_back (10);

        deque1.push_back ('a');
        deque1.push_back ('b');
        deque1.push_back ('c');
        deque1.push_back ('d');
        deque1.push_front ('e');

        list1.push_back (1.1);
        list1.push_back (2.2);
        list1.push_back (3.3);
        list1.push_back (4.4);
        list1.push_front (5.5);

        cout << "vector1   list1   deque1" << endl;

        for (i = 0; i < 5; i++)
                        {
                        cout << vector1[i] << "  " << deque1[i]
                            << "  " << list1.front () << endl;
                        list1.pop_front ();
                        }

}
```

Each STL class template has its own header file.

Declaring a `vector` of `int`, a `deque` of `char` and a `list` of `double`.

Only the `push_back()` function is used with `vector`. We cannot use the `push_front()` function. Here, we push five integers onto `vector1`.

Both the `push_back()` and `push_front()` functions can be used with deques and lists. Here, we push five characters onto `deque1` and five doubles onto `list1`.

We can access the individual elements of vectors and deques using array-like notation. We cannot use array-like notation with lists. Here we access the list elements using member functions `front()` and `pop_front()`.

Output

```
vector1   deque1   list1
2         e        5.5
4         a        1.1
6         b        2.2
8         c        3.3
10        d        4.4
```

Description

Sequence containers. Sequence containers are containers designed for a programmer who needs to directly control the position of an element within the container. Commonly, a programmer specifies adding an element at the beginning or end of the container. We may access the first position, last position, or intermediate position in a manner dependent upon which sequence container we use.

The STL sequence containers are `vector`, `deque`, and `list`. The elements of the `vector` and `deque` containers are stored in contiguous memory locations much the same as C++ arrays. (Actually, a `deque` can be partially segmented in memory. However, for the most part, a `deque` performs like all elements are contiguous). The elements of the `list` container are not stored in contiguous memory locations. The `list` structure is more like the linked list described in Lesson 16.1.

The method of storage affects the method of access. Because `vector` and `deque` elements are in contiguous memory locations, we can access the elements using array-like notation. We cannot use such notation to access `list` elements. To access `list` elements, we need to progress from element to element in a manner similar to that described for the linked list.

Dynamic memory allocation is used to reserve memory for all three sequence containers. This means that memory is reserved element by element during execution. This is different from arrays, where a declaration reserves memory for all array elements during compilation. The "`push`" family of functions reserve memory and initialize a single element of the sequence containers. Repeated execution of these functions can create an entire `vector`, `deque`, or `list`. Recall that we used a push type operation to create the stack data structure. Therefore, we see that the sequence containers also have stack-like characteristics.

In summary, the sequence containers all have the characteristic that their elements are accessed by position. They have a combination of characteristics that resemble arrays, stacks, and linked lists. To effectively use the sequence containers, we need to be aware of the characteristics.

Vectors. To use a vector, we need to include the `<vector>` header as shown in this lesson's program. The `vector` declaration follows the form we had in Lesson 17.2 for class templates. For instance,

```
vector <int> vector1;
```

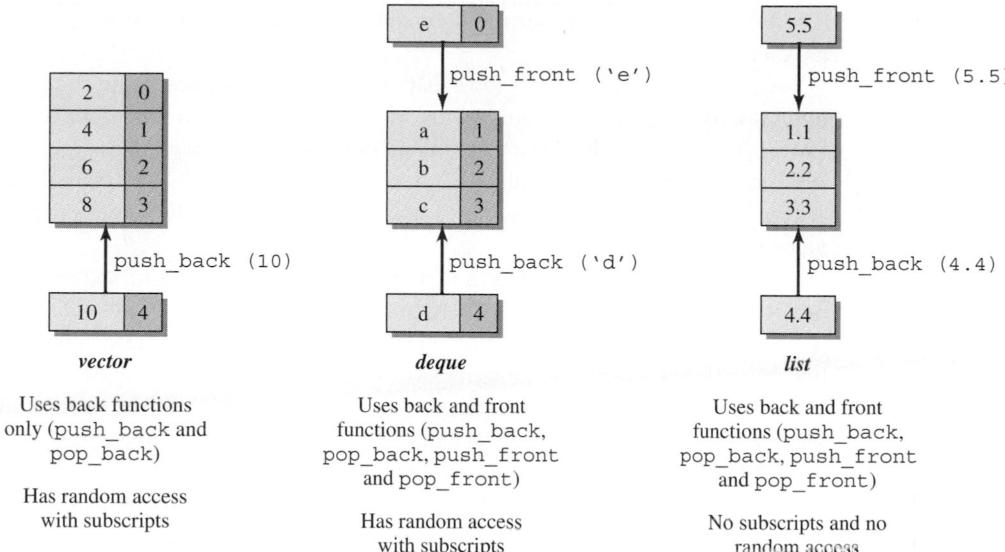

Figure 17.1

Illustration of some characteristics of vectors, deques, and lists. The actions in Lesson 17.3's program are shown. The numbers in the darkly shaded squares in the vector and deque illustrations represent the element indices.

declares `vector1` to be a vector container of `int`. Then, like stacks, vectors are created by pushing. However, for a vector, you need to visualize an upside-down stack of plates (not right-side up as in Fig. 16.9). The `push_back()` member function pushes a value onto the bottom of the `vector` (last member) as shown in the left part of Fig. 17.1. The statement

```
vector1.push_back (2);
```

puts the value 2 at the first location of `vector1` because there is no other value in the `vector`. Then, the statement

```
vector1.push_back (4);
```

puts the value 4 into the second position. Each call to `push_back()` reserves memory and inserts a value into that memory. The five calls to `push_back()` in this lesson's program create a vector with values 2, 4, 6, 8, and 10.

Although we create the vector like a stack, we can access the `vector` like an array. The loop:

```
for (i = 0; i < 5; i++) cout << vector1[i] << endl;
```

prints all five vector values using `vector1[i]`.

We have not shown it in this lesson's program, but once the vector is created, we can modify the values with array notation. For instance, we could have made the first element 100 and the last element 50 with the lines

```
vector1[0] = 100;
vector1[4] = 50;
```

Note that, like arrays, the first element has the subscript 0. Because we can directly access a single element anywhere in the vector, vectors are said to have *random access.* The word random in this context does not mean unpredictable. That is, random access does not mean unpredictable access. It means direct access at any location.

The left part of Fig. 17.1 shows that `push_back()` applies to the end of the vector. Also, the shaded boxes indicate the subscripts, meaning that random access is allowed. Not shown in this lesson's program or the figure is the `pop_back()` function. We can remove the vector values by popping them from the back or bottom of the vector. However, unlike a typical pop, the `pop_back()` function does not return the value of the element.

You may have noticed that the computing community has mixed metaphors in naming data structures and functions. A stack produces a vertical image in one's mind, as does a list. (When writing a grocery list, for example, few people create a horizontal list of words. We all write a vertical list.) However, the names `push_back` and `push_front` do not fit a vertical image unless we think of the back as the bottom and the front as the top. The names `push_bottom` and `push_top` would make more sense but they are not used.

If we attempt to put more into a vector than available contiguous space allows, C++ automatically finds (if possible) greater contiguous space and puts the vector there.

Deques. Note that the STL container `deque` is not spelled dequeue, which is the proper spelling for the double ended queue data structure! Remember to use the simpler spelling in your programs. To use a deque, we need to include the `<deque>` header as shown in this lesson's program. The `deque` declaration

```
deque <char> deque1;
```

declares `deque1` to be a deque container of `char`. Unlike a vector, a deque can be created by pushing onto both the front (top) and back (bottom) using `push_front()` and `push_back()` as shown in the middle of Fig. 17.1. The statement

```
deque1.push_back ('a');
```

puts the character `'a'` at the first location of deque1 because there is no other value in the deque. Then, the statement

```
deque1.push_back ('b');
```

puts the character `'b'` into the second position. The four calls to `push_back()` with `deque1` in this lesson's program create a deque with characters `a`, `b`, `c`, and `d`. Then the `push_front()` member function is used:

```
deque1.push_front ('e');
```

to put the character `'e'` in the first position of the deque.

Again, although we create the deque like a stack, we can access the deque like an array. The loop:

```
for (i = 0; i < 5; i++) cout << deque1[i] << endl;
```

prints all five deque values using `deque1[i]`.

Like vectors, once the deque is created, we can modify the values with array notation. For instance, we could have made the first element `'z'` and the last element 'x' with the lines

```
deque1[0] = 'z';
deque1[4] = 'x';
```

Note that, like arrays, the first element has the subscript 0. This accessibility means that deques also have so-called random access.

Also, not shown in this lesson's program or Fig. 17.1 is that deques have the pop_front() and pop_back() member functions for removing elements. Again, these member functions do not return the values of the elements popped.

Lists. To use a list, we need to include the <list> header as shown in this lesson's program. The list declaration

```
list <double> list1;
```

declares list1 to be a list container of doubles. Like a deque, a list can be created by pushing onto both the front and back using push_front() and push_back() as shown in the right part of Fig. 17.1. The statement

```
list1.push_back (1.1);
```

puts the value 1.1 at the first location of list1 because there is no other value in the list. Then, the statement

```
list1.push_back (2.2);
```

puts the value 2.2 into the second position. The four calls to push_back() with list1 in this lesson's program create a list with values 1.1, 2.2, 3.3, and 4.4. Then the push_front() function is used:

```
list1.push_front (5.5);
```

to put the value 5.5 in the first position of the list.

The container list is called a *doubly linked list.* Each element has two pointer values, one that points to the next element and another that points to the previous element. Therefore, it is possible to move both forward and backward in the list. Figure 17.2 shows an illustration. If you were asked to find the fourth element in the

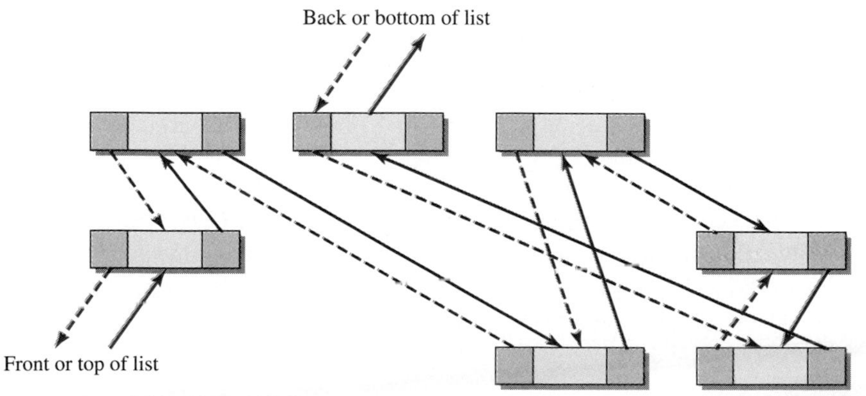

Figure 17.2
Illustration of doubly linked list. The solid arrows indicate pointing to the next element. The dashed arrows indicate pointing to the previous elements. Note that the only way to go through the list is following the arrows element by element. You can follow the solid arrows from the front or the dashed arrows from the back. The shaded parts of the elements represent the pointers contained within the element.

list on this figure, you would need to follow the arrows. You could follow the dashed arrows from the back or the solid arrows from the front. In effect, we do not know where in memory an element of a list will be located, so we cannot access elements using brackets in array notation.

In the next lesson we illustrate how to go element by element through a list. In this lesson we show how to access and print the front or top elements. Two member functions are needed, `front()`, which returns the value of the top element and `pop_front()`, which removes the top element. The statements

```
cout << list1.front () << endl;
list1.pop_front ();
```

print the top element and remove the top element. Putting these statements in a loop, as shown in this lesson's program prints the entire list. This is not the best approach, though, because after the loop has executed, the list is empty. In Lesson 17.4, we show you a better way to print a list.

Note that we cannot use

```
cout << list1.pop_front () << endl;
```

to both print and remove an element because the `pop_front()` function does not return the element's value. Also, like deques, lists have member function `pop_back`.

LESSON 17.4 STANDARD TEMPLATE LIBRARY (2)—ITERATORS

TOPICS

- Using iterators
- Creating `const` iterators

QUESTION YOU SHOULD ATTEMPT TO ANSWER

1. Which operators have been used with the iterator in this program?

The STL has a type of object called an *iterator* to help us move through containers. Iterators work somewhat like pointers. However, they are designed to be user-friendly pointers in that they know the type of container they are working with (in fact, each container has its own type of iterator) and automatically perform actions that might require several lines of code for ordinary pointers.

In Lesson 17.3, we destroyed the list in the process of printing it because we could not access individual elements using bracket notation. In this lesson, we use an iterator to help us access each element and print the items in the list without destroying it. If you read Lesson 16.1 then you know that a somewhat tricky statement involving a pointer is needed to progress from one node to the next in a linked list. A programmer's life is much simpler with an iterator, because to go from one node to the next in a list with an iterator, we simply use the `++` operator. The iterator is smart enough to know to follow the pointer to the next element in a list with `++`.

In addition, we can use an iterator to modify values in a list (which again, we are not able to do with bracket notation). The `*` operator is used in much the same way that it is used with pointers to do this.

Read the program and observe how the keyword `iterator` is used to declare `pp` to be an iterator. Then see how `pp` is used in a loop to print the values in a list.

Source Code

```
#include <iostream>
#include <list>

using namespace std;

int main ( )
{
        list <double> list1;
        list <double> :: iterator pp;
        int i;

        list1.push_back (1.1);
        list1.push_back (2.2);
        list1.push_back (3.3);
        list1.push_back (4.4);
        list1.push_front (5.5);

        for (pp = list1.begin (); pp != list1.end (); ++pp) cout << *pp << " ";

        cout << endl;

        pp = list1.begin ();

        *pp = 6.6;

        for (pp = list1.begin (); pp != list1.end (); ++pp) cout << *pp << " ";

        cout << endl;
}
```

No special header is needed for iterators.

This syntax creates an iterator called pp. This iterator can be used only with lists of double.

Creating a list identical to that of Lesson 17.3.

This loop uses pp to go from the beginning of the list to the end. The *pp represents the value of an element indicated by pp.

Resetting pp to indicate the first element in the list.

Changing the value of the first element using *pp.

Printing the list again. The output shows that the list has changed.

Output

```
5.5 1.1 2.2 3.3 4.4
6.6 1.1 2.2 3.3 4.4
```

Description

Declaring an iterator. An iterator is declared with the type of container on which it operates and the type `iterator`. For instance

```
list <double> :: iterator pp;
```

declares `pp` to be an iterator that operates on a `list` of `double`. The general form for declaring an iterator is

```
container <type> :: iterator name;
```

where *container* is the type of container, such as list, vector, or deque, *type* is the data type in the container, and *name* is any valid identifier for the iterator. The angle brackets and double colon are required as shown.

We need not include a special header file for an ordinary iterator because each container defines its own iterator. Therefore, the container header (like <list> or <vector>) is sufficient for using the iterators of these containers.

Using an iterator. Like a pointer, we need to initialize an iterator to point to a location first, then we can manipulate the iterator. In this lesson's program, we initialize the pp iterator with the statement in the for loop

```
pp = list1.begin ();
```

The begin() member function returns an iterator object that points to the memory location of the first element in the list. Consequently, the iterator pp is assigned to point to the first element. The iterator is modified with the for loop increment expression

```
++pp;
```

This expression automatically advances the iterator to point to the next node in the list. An iterator is smart enough to advance properly even when the next element in the list is *not* adjacent in memory. It automatically follows the list and thereby relieves a programmer from writing code to get a pointer to advance. Here, ++pp is used instead of pp++ because, for some implementations, the prefix ++ performs more efficiently than the postfix ++.

In this lesson's program, after many loop executions, the iterator progresses to past the end of the list. The loop is terminated with the conditional expression

```
pp != list1.end ();
```

The end() member function returns an object that points to one past the last element of the list (which can be considered to be like the tail node described in Lesson 16.1). Therefore, this expression evaluates to false when pp advances past the last element, and this terminates the loop. Figure 17.3 illustrates the returns from begin() and end(). It shows how end() returns a pointer to after the end. Note that the test expression cannot be written

```
pp < list1.end ();
```

because such a comparison is not allowed for list iterators.

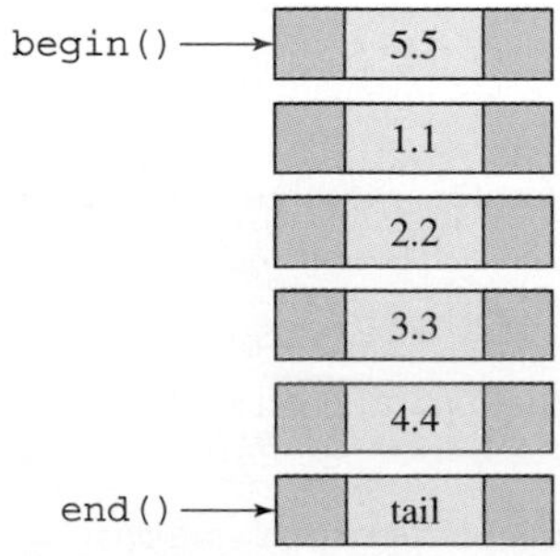

Figure 17.3

Iterators returned by the member functions begin() and end().

We can access the element pointed to by the iterator using the unary `*` operator. We have not used this operator much in this text, so we remind you how it is used with pointers. For a pointer named `ptr`, `ptr` refers to an address, and `*ptr` refers to the value at that address. Similarly, with `pp` as an iterator, `pp` refers to an element of a container, and `*pp` refers to the value of that element. Consequently,

```
cout << *pp << "  ";
```

prints the value of the element referred to by `pp`. This statement in the loop in this lesson's program

```
for (pp = list1.begin (); pp != list1.end (); ++pp)
     cout << *pp << "  ";
```

prints the values of all the list elements.

We can also use the unary `*` operator and an iterator to change the value of an element. The statements

```
pp = list1.begin ();
*pp = 6.6;
```

first make `pp` point to the first element in the list, then the second statement makes 6.6 the value of that element using the `*` operator. Remember, an iterator *name* alone indicates an address or position of an element, and `*`*name* represents the value of the element.

Constant iterators. If an iterator is used only for performing such actions as printing element values and not modifying them, then a constant iterator using the type `const_iterator` can be used. In this lesson's program such a declaration would look like

```
list <double> :: const_iterator pp;
```

In general, the form for declaring a constant iterator is

```
container <type> :: const_iterator name;
```

where *container* is the type of container, such as `list`, `vector`, or `deque`, *type* is the data type in the container, and *name* is any valid identifier for the iterator. The angle brackets and double colon are required as shown.

List iterators and operators. C++ allows us to use both `++` and `--` to move forward and backward in a list with an iterator. Because they can go in both directions, `list` iterators are called *bidirectional* iterators. We cannot, however, advance more than one element at a time. In other words, in this lesson's program, we cannot use

```
pp += 2;
```

to move the iterator two locations forward. We are allowed to perform such actions with `vector` or `deque` iterators. In general, the operators available to us for `list` iterators are the unary `*` operator, `++`, `--`, `=`, `==`, and `!=`.

LESSON 17.5 STANDARD TEMPLATE LIBRARY (3)—ALGORITHMS

TOPICS

- Several algorithms
- More about creating vectors
- Using `ostream` iterators

QUESTION YOU SHOULD ATTEMPT TO ANSWER

1. What are the names of the algorithms used in this program?

We have been using the term algorithm in the dictionary sense in this book, meaning "a step by step procedure for solving a problem." Algorithms in the STL have a different definition. They are global template functions (of the form we illustrated in Lesson 17.1), not member functions. They are designed specifically to work with containers using iterators. A particular algorithm may be capable of working with many different types of containers, ordinary arrays, or even container classes developed by a programmer if certain requirements are met. Algorithms perform such tasks as sorting, finding, merging, and swapping within and between containers.

Since algorithms are not member functions, they are not called with an object and dot operator. They are called simply with the function (algorithm) name and argument list.

The STL has a large number of algorithms and many different forms for each algorithm. We cannot cover all the different algorithms and forms in this program. Instead, in this program, we focus on using algorithms and iterators together in a few different ways. We also show various methods to initialize vectors and how to use ostream iterators. Read the program to see how to work with algorithms, iterators, and vectors.

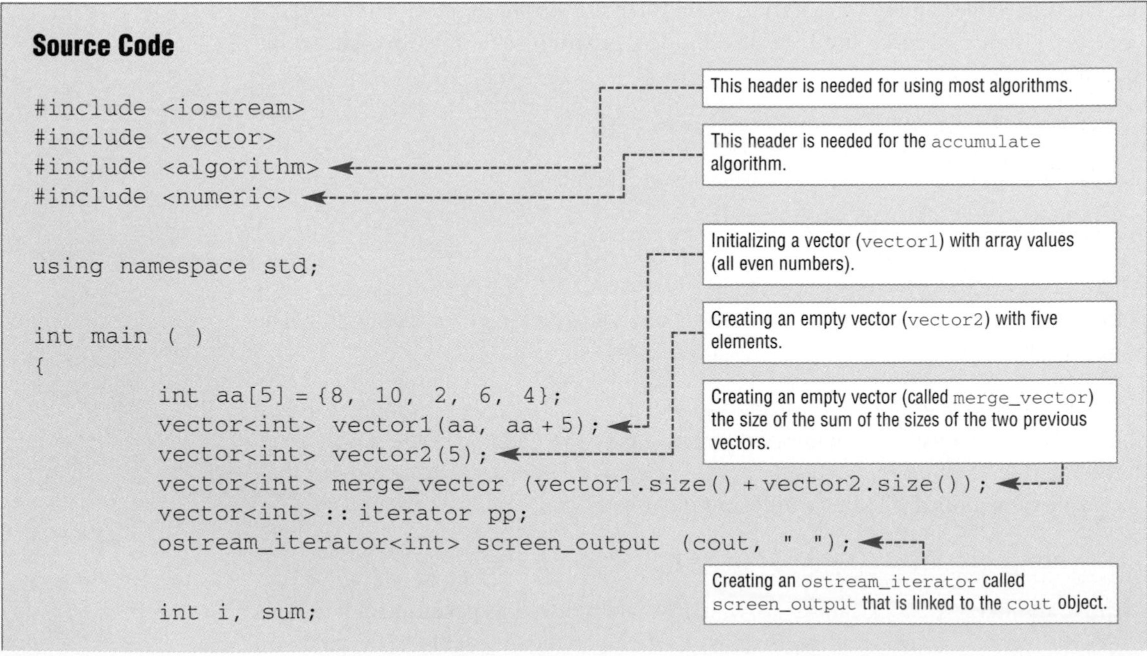

Source Code

```
#include <iostream>
#include <vector>
#include <algorithm>
#include <numeric>

using namespace std;

int main ( )
{
        int aa[5] = {8, 10, 2, 6, 4};
        vector<int> vector1(aa, aa + 5);
        vector<int> vector2(5);
        vector<int> merge_vector (vector1.size() + vector2.size());
        vector<int> :: iterator pp;
        ostream_iterator<int> screen_output (cout, " ");

        int i, sum;
```

This header is needed for using most algorithms.
This header is needed for the accumulate algorithm.
Initializing a vector (vector1) with array values (all even numbers).
Creating an empty vector (vector2) with five elements.
Creating an empty vector (called merge_vector) the size of the sum of the sizes of the two previous vectors.
Creating an ostream_iterator called screen_output that is linked to the cout object.

```
    vector2[0] = 1;
    vector2[1] = 3;
    vector2[2] = 5;
    vector2[3] = 7;
    vector2[4] = 9;

    sort (vector1.begin (), vector1.end ());

    pp = max_element (vector1.begin (), vector1.begin () + 3);
    cout << "The maximum of the first 3 values is " << *pp << endl;

    sum = accumulate (vector1.begin (), vector1.end (), 0);
    cout << "The sum of the vector values is " << sum << endl;

    merge (vector1.begin (), vector1.end (), vector2.begin (),
           vector2.end (), merge_vector.begin ());
    cout << "The merged vector is ";

    copy (merge_vector.begin (), merge_vector.end (), screen_output);
    cout << endl;
}
```

Initializing `vector2` to be all odd values.

Sorting the entire first vector.

Finding the maximum value in the first three elements.

Calculating the sum of all the values in `vector1`.

Merging two vectors and storing the result in a third vector.

Copying the contents of the `merge_vector` to the object linked to the `screen_output` iterator. This prints the vector.

Output

```
The maximum of the first 3 values is 6
The sum of the vector values is 30
The merged vector is 1 2 3 4 5 6 7 8 9 10
```

This is printed using the `ostream` iterator (not a loop).

Description

More about instantiating `vectors`. In this lesson, we show three new ways to instantiate vectors. The first way is to initialize the vector with array values. For instance

```
vector <int> vector1 (aa, aa + 5);
```

initializes `vector1` with the first through fifth values of the `aa[]` array. The constructor takes two addresses as arguments with the first being the beginning of the range and the second being the end of the range. In this lesson's program, since `aa[]` has five elements, the `vector1` values are the same as the `aa[]` values.

We can also instantiate an empty vector (or a vector with noninitialized values) using an integer argument in the constructor. For example

```
vector<int> vector2 (5);
```

makes vector2 a vector of int with five empty elements. These elements can be initialized with assignment statements of the sort

```
vector2 [2] = 8;
```

We can also use the size member function to assist us in sizing a vector. The size member function returns an integer representing the number of elements of a container. For instance

```
vector<int> merge_vector (vector1.size () + vector2.size ());
```

creates an empty vector equal in size to the sum of the sizes of vector1 and vector2.

***Creating an* ostream_iterator.** An ostream_iterator is actually called an *iterator adapter*. It is declared quite differently from an ordinary iterator. An ostream_iterator can be linked to an ostream object such as cout in its declaration. Then an algorithm can use the ostream_iterator to write directly to cout to produce screen output of containers. In this lesson's program, the declaration:

```
ostream_iterator<int> screen_output (cout, "  ");
```

creates an ostream_iterator for printing containers holding int values. The name of the iterator is screen_output, and it is linked to cout. The delimiter in the output is " " (that is, two whitespace characters). This delimiter is used to separate the container values when they are printed. In general, the form of the declaration is

```
ostream_iterator<type> name (out_obj, delimiter);
```

where *type* is a valid data type, *name* is any valid identifier, *out_obj* is cout or other output object (such as for file output), and *delimiter* is a const char pointer, typically a string literal.

Once an ostream_iterator is declared, it can be used in algorithms much the same way as other iterators. We show how to use the copy algorithm with an ostream_iterator later in this lesson.

Using algorithms. Nearly all algorithms require the <algorithm> header. However, a small number require the <numeric> header (as shown in this lesson's program). Unlike with containers and iterators, we do not declare algorithms in our programs. The declarations for the algorithms are in the header files.

As with calling a global function, an algorithm is called with the name and argument list. The arguments are typically iterators. A general form for calling an algorithm with 3 arguments is

```
name (iterator1, iterator2, iterator3);
```

where *name* is the name of the algorithm, and *iterator1*, *iterator2*, and *iterator3* are the names of iterators or return values from member functions that are iterators. Frequently, the iterators in the argument list represent a range of a container's elements to be operated upon by the algorithm.

The* `sort` *algorithm. We can use the `sort` algorithm to sort only containers with random access (`vector`s and `deque`s). Therefore, the iterators used in the `sort` call must be iterators for `vector`s or `deque`s. The basic form is:

```
sort (beginning, end);
```

where *beginning* and *end* are iterators indicating the start and finish of a range of elements of the container being sorted. The result is a rearrangement of the elements within a container. In this lesson's program,

```
sort (vector1.begin (), vector1.end ());
```

sorts the `vector1` container to arrange the element values to be 2, 4, 6, 8, 10.

The* `max_element` *algorithm. The `max_element` algorithm finds the maximum element value within a range indicated by iterators. The basic form is

```
max_element (beginning, end);
```

where *beginning* and *end* are iterators indicating the start and finish of a range of elements of the container being searched. The algorithm returns an iterator pointing to the element holding the maximum value in the range. In this lesson's program,

```
pp = max_element (vector1.begin (), vector1.begin () + 3);
```

finds the maximum value in the first three elements of `vector1`. The location of the maximum is stored in the vector iterator `pp`. The value is printed with

```
cout << "The maximum of the first 3 values is "
     << *pp << endl;
```

using the unary `*` operator with `pp` to obtain the value of the maximum.

The* `accumulate` *algorithm. The `accumulate` algorithm finds the sum of the values within a range indicated by iterators. The basic form is

```
accumulate (beginning, end, initial_value);
```

where *beginning* and *end* are iterators indicating the start and finish of a range of elements being summed, and *initial_value* is the initial value used in the sum process (frequently 0). The algorithm returns the value of the sum of the initial value and the elements in the range. In this lesson's program,

```
sum = accumulate (vector1.begin (), vector1.end (), 0);
```

sums all the elements of `vector1`. The algorithm `accumulate` returns the sum. The `accumulate` algorithm requires `#include <numeric>`.

The* `merge` *algorithm. The `merge` algorithm combines two ranges in sorted order. The basic form is

```
merge (beginning1, end1, beginning2, end2, destination);
```

where *beginning1*, *beginning2*, *end1*, and *end2* are iterators indicating the start and finish of the two sorted ranges being merged, and *destination* is an iterator indicating the location of the beginning of the merged elements. The `merge` algorithm returns an iterator indicating the position after the last element in the destination range. In this lesson's program,

```
merge (vector1.begin (), vector1.end (), vector2.begin (),
       vector2.end (), merge_vector.begin ());
```

merges the full range of `vector1` and `vector2`. The result is stored in `merge_vector`. Note that the source vectors must be sorted prior to using the `merge` algorithm. The result is the sorted combination. For instance, in this lesson's program, `vector1` is 2, 4, 6, 8, 10 and `vector2` is 1, 3, 5, 7, 9. The `merge_vector` is 1, 2, 3, 4, 5, 6, 7, 8, 9, 10. Sufficient size is required for the destination container prior to using `merge`.

The `copy` algorithm. As its name implies, the `copy` algorithm copies values from one location to another. The locations are specified using iterators. The form for calling the algorithm is

```
copy (beginning, end, destination);
```

where *`beginning`* and *`end`* are iterators indicating the start and finish of a range of elements of the container being copied, and *`destination`* is an iterator indicating the start of the location for placing the copied values.

In this lesson's program, the call

```
copy (merge_vector.begin (), merge_vector.end (),
      screen_output);
```

copies the entire `merge_vector` (from `begin()` to `end()`) to the `ostream_iterator screen_output`, which is linked to `cout`. This causes the values of the elements of the `merge_vector` to be printed. Instead of an `ostream_iterator`, we could have used an ordinary iterator representing the beginning of a container to copy from one container to another.

Other `algorithms`. To be able to make thorough use of algorithms, we recommend you consult a text solely devoted to the STL.

Summary. Space did not permit us to give more than a brief introduction to the STL. So, here we give an overview of much of the STL so that you can see how the material you know fits into the big picture. We follow this discussion with an introduction to some new topics. The purpose of both of these is to allow you to more easily pursue further study of the STL.

The basic components of the STL, iterators, algorithms, and containers, fundamentally interact in the manner shown in Fig. 17.4. This figure shows that (as you may have observed from the examples) iterators are used to link the containers and algorithms. Iterators are passed to algorithms, causing the algorithms to work on containers.

- *Iterators.* We learned that the iterator types operate differently. An iterator's declaration specifies the type of container on which it works. Assignments can make an iterator point to particular elements in a container. The STL supports five different basic types of iterators: input, output, forward, bidirectional, and random access. They have a hierarchy such that each level has the capabilities of the lower ones and more. The hierarchy is shown in

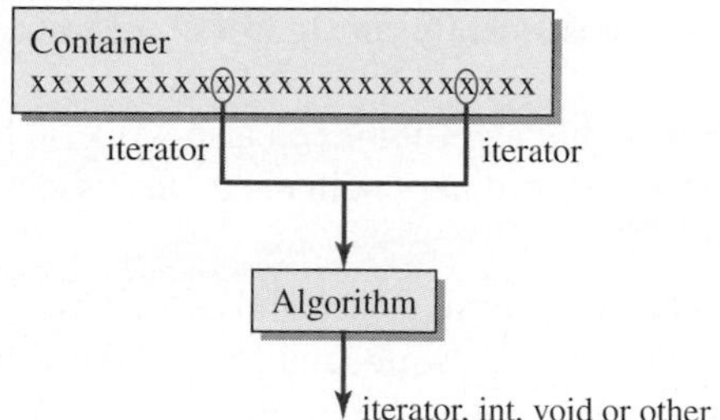

Figure 17.4

Interaction between containers, iterators, and algorithms for an algorithm taking only two iterators.

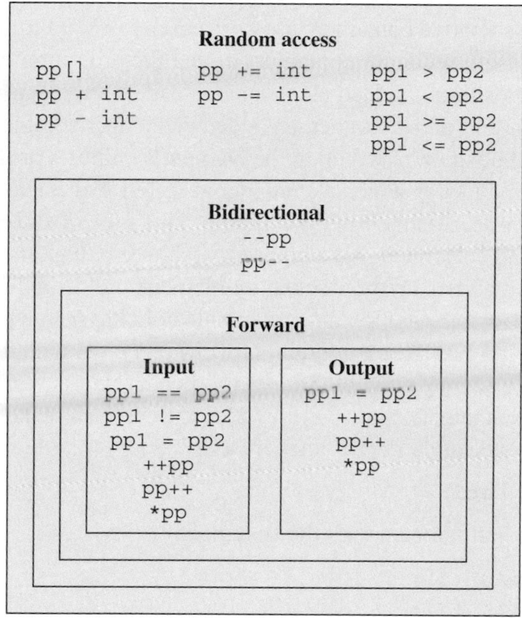

Figure 17.5

Hierarchy of iterator types and their operators. This figure shows that each iterator can use only certain operators. Each iterator type can use all the operators in its box.

Fig. 17.5 using `pp`, `pp1`, and `pp2` as iterators. Each iterator type can use all the operators enclosed in its box. For instance, random access iterators are able to use all the operators of the other iterators and the ones listed for random access.

Also, `istream_iterators` can be declared somewhat like `ostream_iterators` and linked to `cin`. These can be used for input to containers.

- *Algorithms.* As you can imagine, there are many different algorithms. They perform many different types of operations. Some of the operations cause modifications to the original containers (like `sort`), while others leave the original untouched, like `copy`.

  We have only shown one version of each algorithm. However, most of them are overloaded many times and take many different numbers and types of iterators and other data as arguments.

  There must be a type match between an algorithm's operators and iterators for it to work properly. Therefore, an algorithm may not be able to work with all types of iterators. Consequently, an algorithm may not work with all types of containers.

We did not show it, but algorithms can also work on basic data types like arrays. Instead of iterators, ordinary pointers to arrays can be used in the argument lists.

- *Containers.* The STL has both sequence and associative containers. The sequence containers (`vector`, `deque`, and `list`) take either random access or bidirectional iterators. We gave numerous examples of using sequence containers.

  We did not cover associative containers. We will briefly describe them here. The associative containers are `set`, `multiset`, `map`, and `multimap`. They differ from sequence containers in that the programmer does not directly control the position of added elements. Instead of adding an element at the beginning or end of a container, an added element is automatically inserted into a sorted position based upon the element's value. A programmer can control the manner in which a container is sorted. For instance, sorting in increasing or decreasing order is possible. This type of storage simplifies searching and acts much like a binary search tree (Chapter 16).

  The `set` and `multiset` container elements hold single values, whereas the `map` and `multimap` container elements hold key/value pairs. The `multiset` and `multimap` containers allow elements with duplicate values whereas `set` and `map` do not. The `<set>` header works with both `set` and `multiset` containers, and `<map>` works with both `map` and `multimap`.

  We can declare a `set` of integers with

```
set<int> set1;
```

  If we insert integers with the statements

```
set1.insert (5);
set1.insert (3);
set1.insert (7);
```

  the first element is 3, the second is 5, and the last is 7. Note that within the set, they are in sorted order even though they are entered in an unsorted order.

  Lastly, the STL has the containers `complex` and `valarray`. Engineers that work with complex numbers may find `complex` valuable. Also, `valarray` has member functions for manipulating arrays. While they are 1-D in nature, they can be made to simulate 2-D or more arrays (although somewhat inconveniently). Again, should you need these containers, refer to a text devoted to the STL.

LESSON EXERCISES

LESSON 17.1 EXERCISES

1. True or false:

a. The `template` keyword is used to call a template function.

b. A function template is a function.

c. A template function is a template.

d. We can overload function templates.

e. Wherever we use function overloading, we can use a function template.

2. Write a program that uses a function template to return the fifth element of any type of array.

Solutions

1. a. false
   b. false
   c. false
   d. true
   e. false

LESSON 17.2 EXERCISES

1. True or false:

   a. Template classes can use only standard C++ data types.

   b. A class template is a template.

   c. A template class is a class.

   d. The list enclosed in angle brackets works much like a function argument list.

   e. Class templates work well with container type classes.

Solutions

1. a. false
   b. true
   c. true
   d. true
   e. true

LESSON 17.3 EXERCISES

1. True or false:

   a. We can use `pop_back()` with `vector`s.

   b. We can use `pop_front()` with `vector`s and `deque`s.

   c. We can use array notation with `vector`s and `deque`s.

   d. Random access is allowed for `deque`s and `list`s.

   e. The "pop" family of functions return the value popped.

2. Write a program that creates a vector and a deque with 10 elements. Modify the values using assignment statements. Print the final values.

Solutions

1. a. true
   b. false
   c. true
   d. false
   e. false

LESSON 17.4 EXERCISES

1. True or false:

a. `iterators` act somewhat like pointers.

b. We need the `<iterator>` header to use `iterators`.

c. The < operator can be used with `list iterators`.

d. The `*` operator can be used with `list iterators`.

e. A list iterator is a bi-directional `iterator`.

2. Write a program that uses an `iterator` to print the values of a vector.

Solutions

1. a. true
b. false
c. false
d. true
e. true

LESSON 17.5 EXERCISES

1. True or false:

a. `algorithms` are member functions.

b. All `algorithms` need the `<algorithm>` header.

c. The `merge algorithm` works only with sorted containers.

d. `iterators` are commonly passed to `algorithms`.

e. A container's type influences the type of `iterator` that can be used with it.

Solutions

1. a. false
b. false
c. true
d. true
e. true

APPLICATION EXERCISES

1. Use the STL to write the application exercises of Chapter 16.

CHAPTER 18

MISCELLANEOUS TOPICS

CHAPTER TOPICS

In this chapter, you will learn how to:

- Develop programs with multiple files
- Manipulate individual bits
- Write to and read from binary files

There are a few miscellaneous topics that do not fit into any of the other chapters but are important enough to include in the text. The topics are not related. The motivation for learning each of them is provided in the introduction to each lesson.

LESSON 18.1 DEVELOPING MULTIPLE FILE PROGRAMS

TOPICS

- Creating header files
- Preventing double inclusion

QUESTION YOU SHOULD ATTEMPT TO ANSWER

1. What do you think `#ifndef` means?

As programs become large, having different portions of the code in different files is common. Some of the reasons for this are:

1. Using many files makes it possible to accommodate many programmers working on the same project.
2. A large amount of source code is more efficiently managed using multiple files, even with a single programmer.
3. Class libraries in separate files, purchased from independent vendors, may be incorporated into in-house programs.

Separate files can come in two forms: source code and object code. In this lesson's program, we show how to connect three different source code files. In the Description we illustrate the concept of connecting different object code files.

One way to connect source code is with header files. In nearly every program in this text, we have included the standard C++ header file `iostream.h` with the preprocessor directive `#include <iostream>`. (Recall that the preprocessor part of C++ performs actions prior to the translation of source code into object code, see Lesson 2.1.) This header file is a source code file, and you can examine the code if you choose by looking for it among the files contained with your C++ IDE. Figure 2.1 shows, conceptually, how this header file is connected to our own source code. Look at this figure before reading this lesson's program. The figure shows that the source code in the header file is simply inserted into the source code we produce (before the program is compiled, that is, translated into object code).

However, we are not restricted to the C++ library of header files because C++ allows us to create our own header files. This gives us the option of having separate files for class definitions, implementations (member functions), and `main`. This is a commonly used division of code. When these are all in different header files, we simply use the `#include` command to connect them all.

What we show in this lesson is not completely standard, but it works with no special compiler instructions, and it illustrates many of the concepts we want to show. Note that each file in the source code can be independently compiled. This permits correction of syntax errors within a single file. You can use this method easily with the compiler of your choice. In the Description we show other ways to accomplish a similar result.

Read each file's source code. Note the use of any line that begins with # because these are preprocessor directives and not instructions that take place during program execution.

Source Code

File class1.h

```
#ifndef CLASS1_H
#define CLASS1_H

class Class1
{
        private:
                int data;
        public:
                void set_show ();
};

#endif
```

Class definition.

Preprocessor directives that prevent including the file `class1.h` more than once.

File class1im.h

```
#ifndef CLASS1IM_H
#define CLASS1IM_H

#include "class1.h"
#include <iostream>
using namespace std;

void Class1 :: set_show ()
{
        data = 5;
        cout << "data = " << data << endl;
}
#endif
```

Including the class definition file. This allows us to compile this file independently.

Preprocessor directives that prevent including the file `class1im.h` more than once.

Class implementation (member functions).

File L18_1.cpp

```
#include "class1.h"
#include "class1im.h"
#include <iostream>
using namespace std;

int main ( )
{
        Class1 obj;
        obj.set_show ();
}
```

Including the class definition and implementation files.

Using the class.

Output

```
data = 5
```

Description

Creating header files. To create a header file, we create a source code file with the extension `.h`. In this lesson's program, we have created two header files, one with the class definition (`class1.h`) and another with the class implementation (`class1im.h`).

Including header files. To include a header file that we have created, we use the form:

```
#include "name.h"
```

where *name* is the name of the header file. In this lesson's program, we used:

```
#include "class1.h"
#include "class1im.h"
```

in the `L18_1.cpp` source code file. Enclosing the header file name in `" "` rather than <> does not explicitly tell the preprocessor that we have created a new header file, but it tells the preprocessor that the header file is probably not within the library of the standard header files. Thus, the preprocessor searches for the header file elsewhere on disk storage to find it. If you put your header file in the header file library, you can use <> to enclose your header file name. However, we recommend that you use `" "` and put your header file in the directory with the other files of the source code for your program.

Header file contents. Any valid source code can be put into a header file. However, putting each class definition and each class implementation in separate files is a common separation of code. Only three lines need be added to this code, two at the top and one at the bottom. The form is:

```
#ifndef name_h
#define name_h
...
source code
...
#endif
```

where *name_h* can be any name, but typically corresponds to the header file name. We will not go into a lot of detail about the meaning and use of `#ifndef`, `#define`, and `#endif` because it begins a discussion of *conditional inclusion,* which we will not cover in detail in this text (see Table 18.1 for a brief description of preprocessor directives). However, these lines are messages to the preprocessor and are not compiled.

The `#ifndef` is short for "if not defined." The `#define` is a command to define, and the `#endif` ends the sequence. In this lesson's program, the sequence for `class1.h` says "if `class1_h` has not been previously defined, define the code from here to `endif` to be `class1_h`." Like all `if` statements, we can read this in the opposite manner to be "if `class1_h` has been previously defined, do nothing with the code from here to `endif`." It is this second interpretation that is important to us. Why? Because, C++ does not like duplicate code in its source code files, as can occur if `#include "class1.h"` appears in more than one file. As you can imagine, seeing duplicate code messes up all sorts of things such as function calls and class definitions.

TABLE 18.1 — Preprocessor directives

Preprocessor directive	Meaning
`#ifdef`	If the identifier following `#ifdef` is defined in a previous preprocessor directive then this evaluates to true. Otherwise, it evaluates to false. If it is true, the statements in the true block are included. If it is false, the statements in the false block (if a false block is used) are included.
`#if`	If the constant expression following `#if` is true, then the statements in the true block are included. If the constant expression following `#if` is false, then the statements in the false block (if a false block is used) are included.
`#else`	The statements between `#else` and `#endif` form the false block.
`#endif`	This marks the end of the conditional inclusion. One `#endif` must be used for each `#if` or `#ifdef`.
`#ifndef`	If the identifier following `#ifndef` is not defined in a previous preprocessor directive then this evaluates to true. Otherwise it evaluates to false. If it is true, the statements in the true block are included. If it is false, the statements in the false block (if a false block is used) are included.
`#elif`	This works similar to "`else if`" in an `if_else_if` control structure.
`#undef`	This undefines a previously defined identifier.
`defined`	This is a compile time operator that is commonly used with `#elif` to make a conditional dependent upon whether an identifier has been defined. It also can be used as `!defined`, meaning "not defined."

The entire purpose of having the `#ifndef` sequence is to allow multiple files to have `#include "class1.h"` in their code. For instance, in this lesson's program, `#include "class1.h"` is in both `class1im.h` and `L18_1.cpp`. This is permitted because the `#ifndef` sequence prevents two copies of `class1.h` from being included when we compile the `L18_1.cpp` source code.

Although not required for this program, we have the `#ifndef` sequence in file `class1im.h` as well. In general, to be safe, you should include the `#ifndef` sequence in all your header files.

Compiling this lesson's program. With both `class1.h` and `class1im.h` created, we can compile this program simply by asking the compiler to compile `L18_1.cpp`. The preprocessor does the work of finding the header files and putting them together into one source code. We never see it in the process, but the source code compiled for this lesson's program is simply:

```
class Class1
{
        private:
                int data;
        public:
                void set_show ();
};
```

```
using namespace std;
void Class1 :: set_show ()
{
        data = 5;
        cout << "data = " << data << endl;
}
using namespace std;
int main ()
{
        Class1 obj;
        obj.set_show ();
}
```

That is, all the # statements are not compiled, nor are two copies of `class1.h`.

Another method. With the integrated development environment (IDE) we can easily perform more efficient connecting of files than what we have shown here. One problem with the method here is that all the code must be recompiled even if there is only a small change in just one file (although some IDEs may be smarter). This can be time consuming for a developer. A better way is for all correctly working files to be saved as object code files and linked after the changed code has been recompiled (that is, translated into object code). Refer to Fig. 18.1, which illustrates both

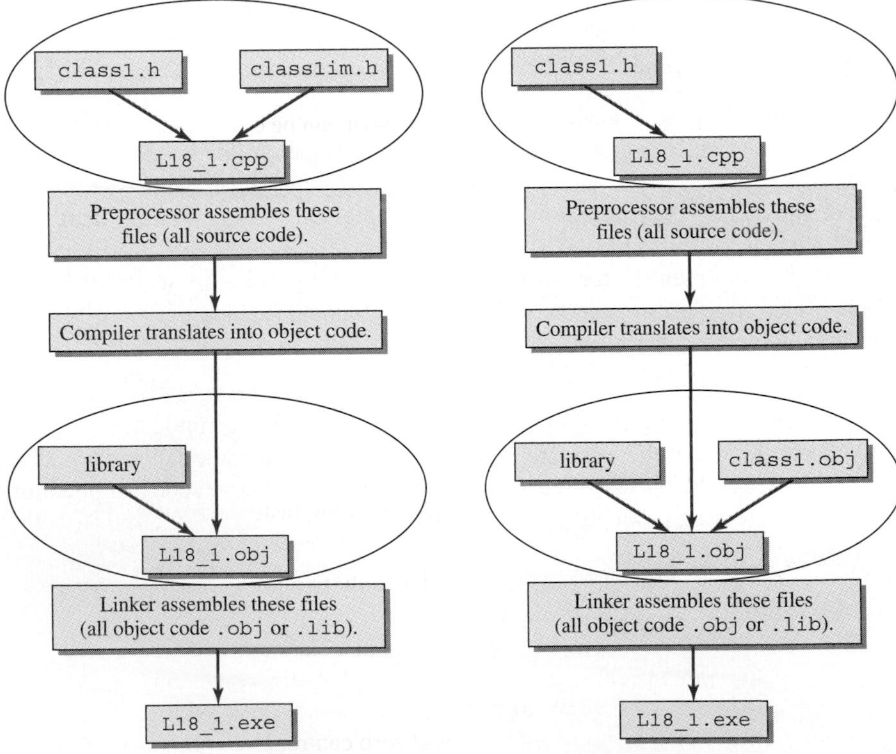

Figure 18.1

Two methods for using multiple files. The left side shows the method used in Lesson 18.1's program. The right side links the class implementation code (`class1.obj`) after it has been compiled.

methods for connecting files. The left side of the figure shows a connection only with (source code) header files as we have done in this lesson's program, while the right side shows both source code header and object code files. Note that the preprocessor assembles all the source code files (`.h` and `.cpp`), and the linker assembles all the object code files (`.obj` and `.lib`).

To manually use the second method with this lesson's source code, remove the `#include "class1im.h"` from `L18_1.cpp`. Rename `class1im.h` to `class1.cpp`. Separately compile `L18_1.cpp` and `class1.cpp`. This creates `L18_1.obj` and `class1.obj` of Fig. 18.1. (Note that if we remove `#include "class1.h"` from `L18_1.cpp`, `L18_1.cpp` will not compile, so the `#include` must remain.) Link `class1.obj` and `L18_1.obj`. This all can be done within the project framework of your IDE. See its documentation for the details.

With this approach, `Class1` need not be developed by you. It can be developed by an independent vendor, who is able to conceal the implementation code for the class from you (because the vendor supplies only object code). As long as the header file with the class definition (interface) does not change, the vendor can modify the implementation and supply you with new object code without you needing to recompile your program. Such a system protects the independent vendor and allows for program improvements.

The role of the independent vendor can also be played by a colleague in your company. This allows both of you to work somewhat independently, yet produce an upgradeable software package that has distinct interfaces.

LESSON 18.2 BITWISE MANIPULATIONS

TOPICS

- Bitwise operators
- Using hexadecimal notation in a C++ program
- Printing individual bits of integers
- Bit fields

C++ is a language that is capable of performing what can be considered very low-level operations such as manipulating individual bits (of 1s and 0s) in memory. C++ provides bitwise operators to perform these manipulations.

There are a number of practical uses of the bitwise operators.

- They can be used in programs that control peripherals such as printers, monitors, disk drives, and modems because in communicating with these devices it is sometimes necessary to control individual bits.
- Instead of using integers or `bool` type values as true or false (1 or 0) flags, we can use individual bits as flags. If we do so, we can pack 16 different flags in one 16-bit integer. This can save memory and allow faster communication. Also, such things as file encryption can be done using the bitwise operators.
- Any array for which each array member has only two possible states can be instead handled with individual bits. For instance, if we are keeping track of the everyday presence or absence of students in a class of 32, we can specify that the first bit represents the first student in alphabetical order, and the other bits represent the other students in alphabetical order. A one can indicate the presence of the student in a given day, and zero can represent absence. Thus,

we need only 32 bits of memory for each day of class to have the entire attendance record. You can imagine that you can create similar representations for other situations in which two states are appropriate.

In order to work with the bitwise operators in a program, we need to consider the status of individual bits in a memory cell (being 1 or 0). In Chapter 1 we described how hexadecimal and octal notation are convenient for representing bit patterns. In this lesson, we use hexadecimal notation in the source code itself and as the form of the output so that we can view and understand the results of the bitwise operators. For convenience, we show again hexadecimal notation and the corresponding bit patterns in Table 18.2.

When a bit has a value of 1 we say that the bit is *set,* and when it is 0 we say that it is *clear*. These words can also be used as verbs so that sometimes we say that we want to set a bit (meaning making it 1) or clear a bit (meaning making it 0).

There are six operators in C++ that allow us to manipulate individual bits in a memory cell. They are `&` (bitwise AND), `|` (bitwise inclusive OR), `^` (bitwise exclusive OR also called XOR), `~` (complement), `>>` (right shift), and `<<` (left shift). The operator, `~`, is a unary operator (meaning it uses only one operand) while all the others are binary operators (meaning that they need two operands).

The first two of these operators, `&` and `|`, work somewhat similarly to their counterparts `&&` and `||` which we used in logical expressions. Recall that in logical expressions, the value of true was represented as 1 or nonzero, and the value of false was represented as 0. We found in Chapter 5 that we had the following for `&&` and `||`:

1 `&&` 1 = 1 (all other situations evaluate to 0, that is: 1 `&&` 0 = 0, 0 `&&` 0 = 0, 0 `&&` 1 = 0)
0 `||` 0 = 0 (all other situations evaluate to 1, that is: 1 `||` 0 = 1, 1 `||` 1 = 1, 0 `||` 1 = 1)

TABLE 18.2 — Hexadecimal notation and bit patterns

Decimal	Hexadecimal	Bit pattern
0	0	0000
1	1	0001
2	2	0010
3	3	0011
4	4	0100
5	5	0101
6	6	0110
7	7	0111
8	8	1000
9	9	1001
10	A	1010
11	B	1011
12	C	1100
13	D	1101
14	E	1110
15	F	1111

The "bitwise and" and "bitwise or" work with single bits but yield the same results:

```
1 & 1 = 1 <-- (all other situations evaluate to 0, that is: 1 & 0 = 0, 0 & 0 = 0, 0 & 1 = 0)

0 | 0 = 0 <-- (all other situations evaluate to 1, that is: 1 | 0 = 1, 1 | 1 = 1, 0 | 1 = 1)
```

With these operators, we go bit by bit to yield the following for a 4-bit example (read down the columns):

Bitwise AND				
(hex A)	1	0	1	0
&				
(hex C)	1	1	0	0
=				
(hex 8)	1	0	0	0

Bitwise OR				
(hex A)	1	0	1	0
|				
(hex C)	1	1	0	0
=				
(hex E)	1	1	1	0

Note that the & and | operations are commutative, meaning 1 & 0 = 0 & 1 and 1 | 0 = 0 | 1.

The complement operator (~) reverses all the bits of its operand. Thus, ~(1010) = 0101.

The "bitwise exclusive or" (^) gives the following results:

```
0 ^ 1 = 1,  1 ^ 0 = 1 <-- (all other situations evaluate to 0, that is: 0 ^ 0 = 0, and 1 ^ 1 = 0)
```

Here is another example. Read down the columns.

Bitwise XOR				
(hex A)	1	0	1	0
^				
(hex C)	1	1	0	0
=				
(hex E)	0	1	1	0

Again, notice that the operation is commutative, meaning that 1 ^ 0 = 0 ^ 1. A summary of the actions of these operators is given in Table 18.3.

The bitwise shift operators (>> and <<) move all the bits in a cell in either the right or left directions and add clear bits in the shift. For instance, if we shift the bit pattern 1011 to the right one place we get 0101. This is illustrated in Fig. 18.2. In this operation, the far right 1 is lost, and a 0 is placed into the leftmost bit location. All other bits are shifted one place to the right. (Note: In some implementations and in certain conditions, a 1 may be placed in the far left location on a right shift. However, we will not consider this possibility in this text.)

TABLE 18.3 — Bitwise operator results

Expression	Result	Expression	Result	Expression	Result	Expression	Result
1 & 1	1	1 | 1	1	1 ^ 1	0	~ 1	0
1 & 0	0	1 | 0	1	1 ^ 0	1	~ 0	1
0 & 1	0	0 | 1	1	0 ^ 1	1		
0 & 0	0	0 | 0	0	0 ^ 0	0		

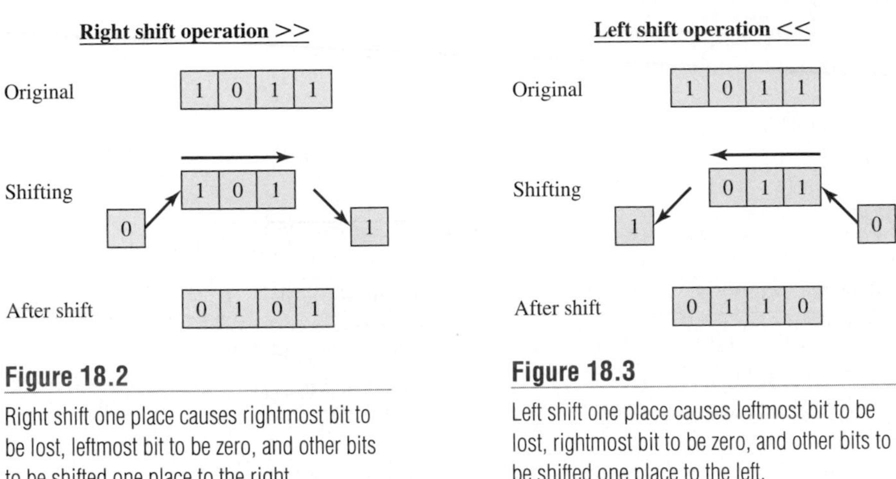

Figure 18.2

Right shift one place causes rightmost bit to be lost, leftmost bit to be zero, and other bits to be shifted one place to the right.

Figure 18.3

Left shift one place causes leftmost bit to be lost, rightmost bit to be zero, and other bits to be shifted one place to the left.

Similarly, if we shift the bit pattern 1011 to the left one place we get 0110. This is illustrated in Fig. 18.3. In this operation, the far left 1 is lost, and a 0 is placed into the rightmost bit location.

More than one place can be shifted in a shift operation. If we shift two places, then two zeros are added, two bits are lost, and the other bits are shifted two places.

There may be times when you want to print the bit representation of your integer type data to the screen. This can be done by creating what is called a *mask* and using it with the bitwise operators to isolate individual bits. After isolating a bit, it can be put into a full sized integer cell and printed using standard `cout` statements. In the Description for this lesson's program, we describe how the `for` loop in the source code performs this operation.

In the program, we illustrate the use of all the bitwise operators. In addition, we show how to print all the bits of a given variable.

QUESTION YOU SHOULD ATTEMPT TO ANSWER

1. How can we set a single bit in the far left storage location?

Source Code

```
#include <iostream>
#include <iomanip>
```

```
using namespace std;

int main ( )
{
        unsigned aa, bb, cc, dd, ee, ff, gg, hh, ii, jj, kk, mm, nn;
        int i;

        aa = 0xDFFF;
        bb = 0x2840;
        cc = 0xFF7F;
        dd = 0x0004;
        ee = 0xA3C5;

        ff = aa & cc;
        gg = bb | dd;
        nn = aa & (~dd);
        hh = aa ^ bb;
        ii = cc >> 1;
        jj = dd << 3;

        cout << hex << "ff=" << ff << "   gg=" << gg << " hh=" << hh << "  ii="
             << ii << " jj=" << jj << " nn=" << nn << endl << endl;

        cout << "The bits for ee (hex A3C5) are:" << endl;

        mm = 0x0000;
        mm = 1 << 15;
        for (i = 16; i >= 1; i--)
             {
             kk = ee & mm;
             kk >>= (i - 1);
             cout << kk << " ";
             mm >>= 1;
             }
        cout << endl;
}
```

We create ordinary unsigned integer type variables for the bitwise manipulations.

Hexadecimal notation begins with 0x. The four hexadecimal symbols after 0x represent 16 bits.

Using bitwise operators, "and," "or," "exclusive or" and "complement."

Shifting the bits of cc one place to the right.

Shifting the bits of dd three places to the left.

The hex stream manipulator causes the values to be printed in hexadecimal.

Setting a bit in the far left location by first making mm's bits all zero, then putting in 1 (shifted 15 places to the left). This makes mm a mask (for initially reading the far left bit).

Printing the individual bits of ee.

Here, using & with a single set bit causes the bit for ee (that is, opposite the bit in the set bit position for mm) to be assigned to kk.

Shifting the bits of kk to the right (i - 1) places. This causes the bit to be shifted to the far right (lowest) bit location with all other bits 0. This means that kk is either 1 or 0 in integer and can be printed with a cout statement.

Shifting the bit in the mask, mm, one to the right.

Output

```
ff=2080, gg=2844, hh=F7BF, ii=7FBF, jj=0020, nn=DFFB

The bits for ee (hex A3C5) are:
1 0 1 0 0 0 1 1 1 1 0 0 0 1 0 1
```

This output is in hexadecimal notation.

The cout statement in the loop is executed 16 times, once for each bit.

Description

Comments. A few comments are necessary before we begin describing this lesson's program.

- Bitwise operators can be used only on integer data types (`char`, `int`, and modifications of these). They cannot be used on `double` or `float` data types.
- Because all systems do not use the same bitwise representations, a given program may not give the same results on all systems. This is an important point of which you should be aware when performing bitwise operations.

To effectively deal with individual bits in a program, it is necessary to be cognizant of the particular implementation that you are using. In other words, you need to know how many bits are used for the data types (`char`, `int`, `double`, or other) and the type of character code being used (ASCII, for example). Also, we have not covered it in detail in Chapter 1, but you may need to know more about the way that negative integers are represented (see Appendix A). In our program, we deal only with unsigned integers, and, thus, do not need to be concerned with negative integers. We also use an implementation that fits C++ minimums where unsigned integers occupy 2 bytes or 16 bits. What we describe here is based on this implementation.

- As we indicated in Chapter 3, in any source code, we represent a hexadecimal number by preceding the notation with 0x or 0X. For example, 0xDFFF represents hexadecimal DFFF and 0xA3C5 represents hexadecimal A3C5. Also, although we did not use octal notation in Lesson 18.2's program, we can represent a number using octal notation using a preceding 0. For example, 0364 represents octal 364 and 0751 represents octal 751.

  To print in hexadecimal or octal, we use `hex` or `oct` as stream manipulators. The source code shows that `cout << hex` causes the items in the stream to print in hexadecimal. To change back to decimal, use the `dec` stream manipulator.
- When we refer to the sixth bit of a value, we are talking about the sixth bit from the right (not the left).

Basic bit operations in this lesson's program. The bit representations of variables in this lesson's program are given in Table 18.4. Note that the values of `aa`, `cc`, and `dd` were deliberately chosen to have all 1s and one 0 or all 0s and one 1. The fundamental manipulations are summarized in Table 18.5 and the details are shown in Table 18.6. The final results are in Table 18.7. Read these tables to see how to set,

TABLE 18.4 — Bit representations of variables in Lesson 18.2's program

Variable name	Hexadecimal representation	Representation in bits
`aa`	DFFF	1101 1111 1111 1111
`bb`	2840	0010 1000 0100 0000
`cc`	FF7F	1111 1111 0111 1111
`dd`	0004	0000 0000 0000 0100
`ee`	A3C5	1010 0011 1100 0101

TABLE 18.5 — Bitwise operator actions

<table>
<tr><th>Operator</th><th>Name</th><th>Type</th><th>Associativity</th><th>Example from program</th><th>Explanation</th></tr>
<tr><td>&</td><td>Bitwise AND</td><td>Binary</td><td>Left to right</td><td>aa & cc</td><td>Clearing bits. This operator sets a one in each bit position where its two operands have ones, and sets zero for other cases. The result has more cleared bits than either of the operands.</td></tr>
<tr><td>|</td><td>Bitwise OR</td><td>Binary</td><td>Left to right</td><td>bb | dd</td><td>Setting bits. This operator sets a zero in each bit position where its two operands have zeros, and sets one for other cases. The result has more set bits than either of the operands.</td></tr>
<tr><td>^</td><td>Bitwise eXclusive OR, or XOR</td><td>Binary</td><td>Left to right</td><td>aa ^ bb</td><td>Reversing some bits. This operator sets a one in each bit position where its two operands have different bits, and sets zeros where they have the same bits.</td></tr>
<tr><td>~</td><td>Bitwise complement</td><td>Unary</td><td>Left to right</td><td>~(bb | dd)</td><td>Reversing all bits. This operator converts a one in each bit position to a zero and a zero in each bit position to a one.</td></tr>
<tr><td><<</td><td>Left shift</td><td>Binary</td><td>Left to right</td><td>dd << 3</td><td>Shifting left. This operator shifts the bits of the left operand to the left by the number of bits specified by the right operand.</td></tr>
<tr><td>>></td><td>Right shift</td><td>Binary</td><td>Left to right</td><td>cc >> 1</td><td>Shifting right. This operator shifts the bits of the left operand to the right by the number of bits specified by the right operand.</td></tr>
</table>

TABLE 18.6 — Bitwise operations in Lesson 18.2's program

<table>
<tr><th>Operation</th><th>Result</th><th>Comment</th></tr>
<tr><td>ff = aa & cc;</td><td>1101 1111 1111 1111 = aa
1111 1111 0111 1111 = cc
1101 1111 0111 1111 = ff</td><td>We have used cc as a mask (with &) to clear the eighth bit of aa. We have stored the result in ff.</td></tr>
<tr><td>gg = bb | dd;</td><td>0010 1000 0100 0000 = bb
0000 0000 0000 0100 = dd
0010 1000 0100 0100 = gg</td><td>We have used dd as a mask (with |) to set the third bit of bb. We have stored the result in gg.</td></tr>
<tr><td>nn = aa & (~dd);</td><td>1101 1111 1111 1111 = aa
1111 1111 1111 1011 = ~dd
1101 1111 1111 1011 = nn</td><td>We have used ~dd as a mask (with &) to clear the third bit of aa. We have stored the result in nn.</td></tr>
<tr><td>hh = aa ^ bb;</td><td>1101 1111 1111 1111 = aa
0010 1000 0100 0000 = bb
1111 0111 1011 1111 = hh</td><td>We have used bb as a mask (with ^) to reverse the seventh, twelfth, and fourteenth bits of aa. We have stored the result in hh.</td></tr>
<tr><td>ii = cc >> 1;</td><td>1111 1111 0111 1111 = cc
0111 1111 1011 1111 = ii</td><td>We have shifted cc to the right one bit location. We have stored the result in ii.</td></tr>
<tr><td>jj = dd << 3;</td><td>0000 0000 0000 0100 = dd
0000 0000 0010 0000 = jj</td><td>We have shifted dd to the left three bit locations. We have stored the result in jj.</td></tr>
</table>

TABLE 18.7 — Hexadecimal representation of the results shown in Table 18.6

Variable name	Representation in bits	Hexadecimal representation
`ff`	1101 1111 0111 1111	DF7F
`gg`	0010 1000 0100 0100	2844
`nn`	1101 1111 1111 1011	DFFB
`hh`	1111 0111 1011 1111	F7BF
`ii`	0111 1111 1011 1111	7FBF
`jj`	0000 0000 0010 0000	0020

clear and perform other manipulations on individual bits. More descriptions follow here.

Masks. As we use it here, a mask is a bit pattern used with the bitwise operators to modify another bit pattern. For instance, in the first two assignment statements in this lesson's program, we use `cc` and `dd` as masks on the variables `aa` and `bb` to create the new bit patterns `ff` and `gg`, respectively.

Frequently, we will use a mask to either clear or set individual bits in a given pattern. Consequently, we must be aware of the methods used to clear and set bits.

Setting a bit. To set a bit, we create a mask with ones in the locations that we want to set bits and zeros in the other locations. Then we use the bitwise OR operator (`|`) with the operands being the mask and the bit pattern we want to modify.

For instance, the bit pattern for `dd` (0000 0000 0000 0100), when used as a mask in this manner, causes the third bit to be set (see Table 18.6). When this mask was used on `bb` (0010 1000 0100 0000) with the bitwise OR operator (`|`) as we did in this lesson's program with the statement `gg = bb | dd`, we created a new bit pattern, gg (0010 1000 0100 0100). Note that the bit pattern for `gg` is the same as `bb` but with the third bit set. Thus, we have successfully used the mask to set a particular bit in a bit pattern.

Clearing a bit. We can use one of two methods to clear a bit:

1. We create a mask with zeros in the locations that we want to clear bits and ones in the other locations. Then we use the bitwise AND operator (`&`) with the operands being the mask and the bit pattern we want to modify.

   For instance, the bit pattern for `cc` (1111 1111 0111 1111), when used as a mask in this manner, causes the eighth bit from the right to be cleared (see Table 18.6). When this mask was used on `aa` (1101 1111 1111 1111) with the bitwise AND operator (`&`) as we did in this lesson's program with the statement `ff = aa & cc`, we created a new bit pattern, `ff` (1101 1111 0111 1111). Note that the bit pattern for `ff` is the same as `aa` but with the eighth bit from the right cleared. Thus, we have successfully used the mask to clear a particular bit in a bit pattern.

2. We create a mask with ones in the locations that we want to clear bits and zeros in the other locations. Then we use the complement operator (`~`) to reverse all the bits of the mask. After doing this, we use the bitwise AND operator (`&`) with the operands being the mask and the bit pattern we want to modify.

   For instance, the bit pattern for `dd` (0000 0000 0000 0100), when used as a mask in this manner, causes the third bit to be cleared (see Table 18.6). The first step is to reverse the bits of this mask with the complement (`~`) operator to give the bit pattern, 1111 1111 1111 1011. When this mask was used on `aa` (1101 1111 1111 1111) with the bitwise AND operator (`&`) as we did in this lesson's program with the statement `nn = aa & (~dd)`, we created a new bit pattern, `nn` (1101 1111 1111 1011). Note that the bit pattern for `nn` is the same as `aa` but with the third bit cleared. Thus, we have successfully used the mask to clear a particular bit in a bit pattern.

In many cases the second method of the two described is more convenient than the first because it is relatively simple to create a bit pattern with a 1 in a particular location.

Creating a bit pattern with a single 1 (the rest 0). To create a bit pattern with a 1 in a particular location and zeros in the other locations, we can use the left shift operator. For instance, the statement:

```
mm = 0x0000;
mm = 1 << 15;
```

causes the bitwise representation of the integer, 1 (0000 0000 0000 0001), to be shifted 15 places to the left giving the bit pattern 1000 0000 0000 0000. Note that shifting 15 places causes a 1 to be in the 16th place from the right.

Similarly, if we used:

```
mm = 1 << 7;
```

we would create the bit pattern 0000 0000 1000 0000 with a 1 in the eighth place.

Thus, because it is easy to create a bit pattern with a 1 in a particular location, we often use the second of the two methods described for clearing a bit.

Compound bitwise operators. We can use compound assignment type operations with the bitwise operators, except the complement (`~`) operator. In other words, `&=`, `|=`, `^=`, `>>=`, and `<<=` are legal operations while `~=` is not.

These operators act in a manner similar to the other compound assignment operations we have used. For instance:

```
kk <<= 7;
```

is the same as:

```
kk = kk << 7;
```

and

```
kk &= aa;
```

is the same as:

```
kk = kk & aa;
```

The reason that we cannot use the complement operator in a compound assignment is that it is a unary operator (meaning it has only one operand). Only binary operators can be used in compound assignment.

Complementing bits. We can complement (reverse) all the bits in a bit pattern using the complement (`~`) operator. However, to complement only some of the bits in a bit pattern, we create a mask with ones in the locations of the bits that we want to complement and zeros in the other locations. Then we use the bitwise eXclusive OR operator (`^`) with the operands being the mask and the bit pattern we want to modify.

For instance, the bit pattern for bb (0010 1000 0100 0000), when used as a mask in this manner, causes the 7th, 12th, and 14th bits to be complemented. When this mask was used on aa (1101 1111 1111 1111) with the bitwise XOR operator (^) as we did in this lesson's program with the statement hh = aa ^ bb, we created a new bit pattern, hh (1111 0111 1011 1111). Note that the bit pattern for hh is the same as aa but with the 7th, 12th, and 14th bits complemented. Thus, we have successfully used the mask to complement particular bits in a bit pattern.

Checking the leftmost bit status. We can check the status (that is, determine whether a bit is set or clear) of the leftmost bit of an integer type variable with the following operations:

1. Create a mask with a 1 in the leftmost position and all other bits 0.
2. Perform a bitwise & operation with the integer and the mask as operands, and store the result in an integer variable. This makes 0 in all but the leftmost bit. The leftmost bit may be 0 or 1 depending on the status of the bit in the leftmost position of the integer.
3. Use the right shift operator to move the leftmost bit to the rightmost location in the integer variable.
4. Determine whether the integer has the value of zero or one (by printing it using cout, for instance).

The following code performs these operations with the mask, mm, being used to determine the status of the leftmost bit of the integer, ee:

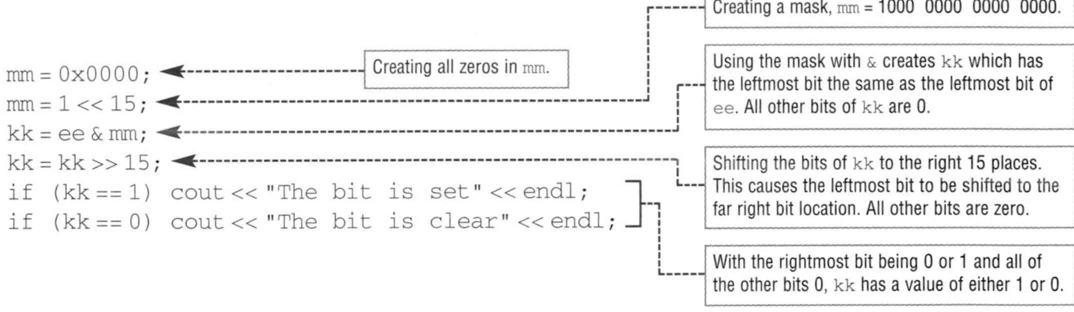

Checking the status of every bit. We can use the method and variables described previously for the leftmost bit with the modification of repeating the operation for each bit (with the mask changing on each repetition). If the mask has the 1 shifting to the right one place each time as shown below:

1000 0000 0000 0000
0100 0000 0000 0000
0010 0000 0000 0000
....
....
0000 0000 0000 0010
0000 0000 0000 0001

then using & with the mask creates a variable, kk, that has zeros everywhere except at the location of the 1 in the mask. At this location, the bit matches the corresponding one in ee. We need only to shift the matching bit in kk to the rightmost location and print it using normal integer printing methods. The following code performs these operations:

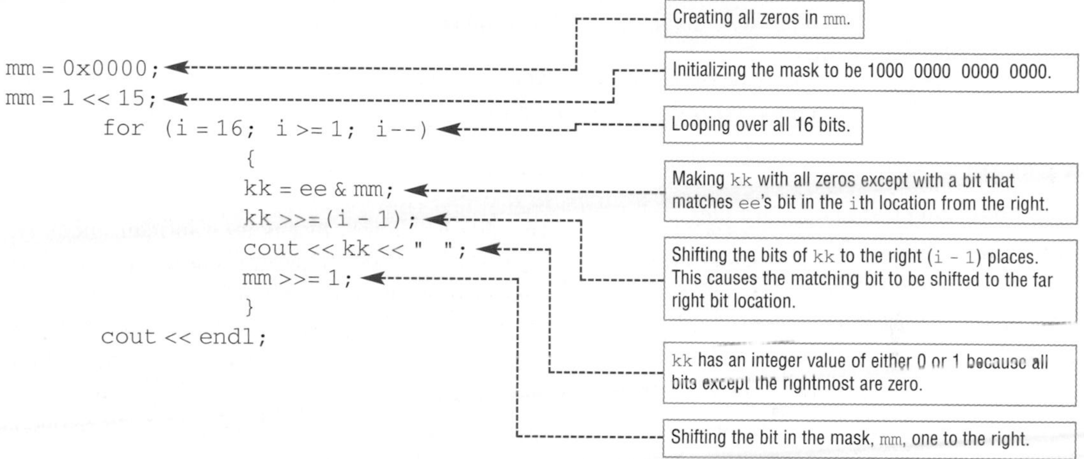
mm = 0x0000;
mm = 1 << 15;
for (i = 16; i >= 1; i--)
{
kk = ee & mm;
kk >>= (i - 1);
cout << kk << " ";
mm >>= 1;
}
cout << endl;
Creating all zeros in mm.
Initializing the mask to be 1000 0000 0000 0000.
Looping over all 16 bits.
Making kk with all zeros except with a bit that matches ee's bit in the ith location from the right.
Shifting the bits of kk to the right (i - 1) places. This causes the matching bit to be shifted to the far right bit location.
kk has an integer value of either 0 or 1 because all bits except the rightmost are zero.
Shifting the bit in the mask, mm, one to the right.

Arithmetic operations with bitwise operators. If we want to multiply or divide an integer by a power of 2, we can use the bitwise shift operators. For instance, the bit pattern 0000 0000 0010 1000 represents the integer, 40. If we shift once to the left, the bit pattern becomes 0000 0000 0101 0000. This represents the integer 80, and we have multiplied by two. If we shift the original bit patten three times to the left, we get 0000 0001 0100 0000, which is 320 which is 2^3 or 8 times our original. Thus, shifting to the left n places is the same as multiplying by 2^n. We can do this provided that we do not shift ones off the left end.

If we shift our original bit pattern to the right one place, we get 0000 0000 0001 0100. This is the integer 20, and we have effectively divided by two. If an integer is an odd number, the result is the same as dividing the integer – 1 by two. For instance, 0000 0000 0010 1001 is 41. Shifting once to the right causes the rightmost 1 to be lost, and the result to be 0000 0000 0001 0100 which is 20. To divide by 8 (2^3) we shift to the right three places. Again, if we lose ones off the right end, we will not get the exact answer.

Bit fields. We have not used them in this lesson's program, but C++ allows us to specify the number of bits to be used to store data members. For instance, the definition:

```
class Bitfield
        {
        public:
                unsigned aa : 3;
                unsigned bb : 4;
                unsigned cc : 2;
        };
```

sets the member, `aa`, to occupy 3 bits, `bb` to occupy 4 bits, and `cc` to occupy 2 bits. Note the colon and number of bits indicated. If in a program we have a declaration:

```
Bitfield mm;
```

then we can access the individual data members using `mm.aa`, `mm.bb`, and `mm.cc`. We will not go through it in detail, but using bit fields the size of just one bit is another way that individual bits can be controlled.

LESSON 18.3 BINARY FILES

TOPICS

- Contrasting text and binary files
- Creating binary files
- Writing to binary files
- Reading from binary files

All the files that we created prior to this lesson have been text files. In text files, the numbers (`int` or `double`) are not stored with the same bit pattern that is used in main memory. For instance, assuming the ASCII system is used (which we will do for this entire lesson), the representation of the integer 25 in main memory and 25 in a text file are shown in Table 18.8. Here, it can be seen that the bit patterns for decimal 25 in main memory and in a text file are not the same.

Because of the difference in bit patterns, it is necessary to perform operations on a number in order to take a value from main memory and copy it into a disk file in text format as shown in Fig. 18.4.

Similarly, when we read a number from a text file we must convert it from the text format to the format used in main memory. This is illustrated in Fig. 18.5.

The operations required to convert between the main memory and text file formats can take considerable time when a significant amount of information is to be transferred. These operations can be eliminated if the same format is used in the disk

TABLE 18.8 — The integer 25 in main memory and in a disk file

Decimal representation	Main memory bit pattern	Text file bit pattern
25	0000 0000 0001 1001 (Standard binary representation for decimal 25.)	0011 0010 (ASCII code for decimal 2.) 0011 0101 (ASCII code for decimal 5.)

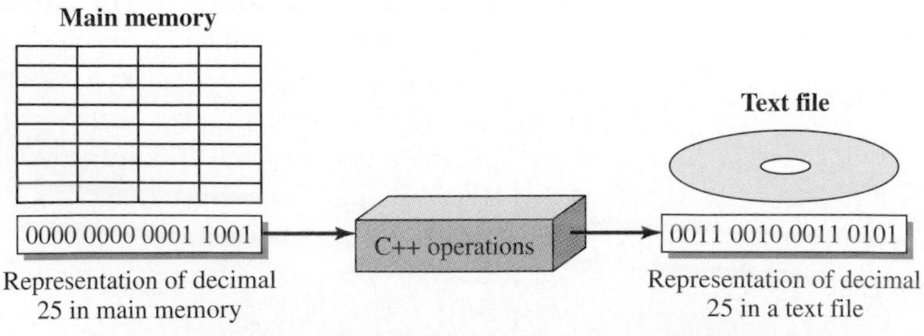

Figure 18.4

Illustration of printing numbers to a text file using C++. Note that the binary representation of the number 25 in main memory is different from its representation in a text file.

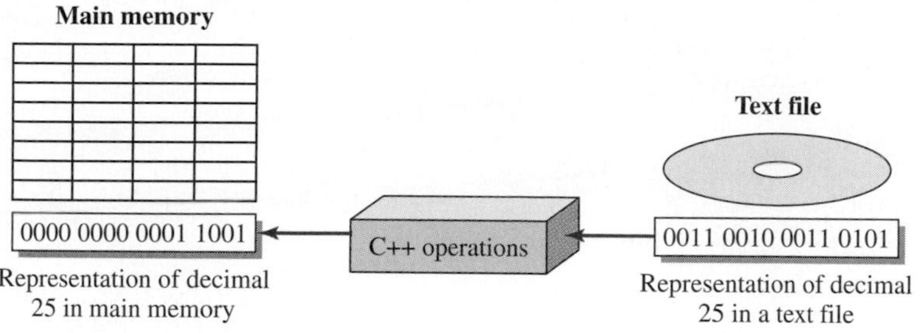

Figure 18.5

Illustration of reading numbers from a text file using C++. Note that the binary representation of the number 25 in main memory is different from its representation in a text file.

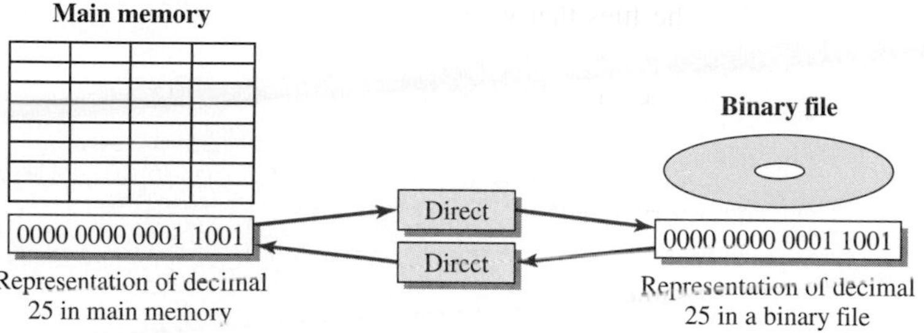

Figure 18.6

Illustration of writing a number to a binary file and reading from a binary file. Observe that the representations of the number, 25, are the same in main memory and in the binary file. Thus, far fewer operations are needed for storing in a binary file than in storing in a text file.

file as is used in main memory, and this is the case for binary files. In Fig. 18.6 we illustrate storing and reading numbers in a binary file.

To write in binary, C++ requires that the process, in essence, go byte by byte and not be concerned with the format or content of the memory or file. Even if we read or write `int` or `double` information (which groups more than one byte memory) we refer to a number of single bytes to read or write (and not a number of `int` or `double` types). This requires us to cast the information we are dealing with to be character type, which is one byte (or more specifically, the address of a character type) so that the C++ functions can simply transfer data from one location to another without regard to content. C++ uses the `reinterpret_cast` operator, which we have not seen before, to do this. In this lesson's program, we use the `reinterpret_cast` operator on an array of integers.

Since binary files are so efficient, you may wonder why we would ever want to use text files. An example can be understood if we consider word processing or editing software. This software needs formatting (grouping of bytes) to properly interpret file information. If you try to read a binary file with editing software, it will show nonsensical symbols in most cases. As a result, a binary file cannot be printed using a printer with a text editor either. Also, a standard text editor can be used to create an input text file, but we cannot use a standard text file to create a binary file for input.

In summary, because writing and reading with binary files is much faster than writing and reading with text files, we can save execution time by using binary files. Text files are convenient for human-created input and human-interpreted output. Binary files are better for computer-created input and computer-interpreted output.

In this lesson, we illustrate a program that creates a binary file, writes to it, and reads from it. Pay particular attention to the way we work with functions `read()` and `write()`.

Source Code

```
#include <iostream>
#include <fstream>
using namespace std;

int main ( )
{

        int value[5] = {2, 4, 6, 8, 10};
        int new_value[5];

        ofstream outfile ("C:\\L18_3.DAT", ios :: out | ios :: binary);

        outfile.write (reinterpret_cast<char*> (value),  5 * sizeof (int));
        outfile.close ();

        ifstream infile ("C:\\L18_3.DAT", ios :: in | ios :: binary);

        infile.read (reinterpret_cast<char*> (new_value), 5*sizeof (int));

        cout << "New value array" << endl;
        cout << new_value[0] << endl << new_value[1] << endl << new_value[2] << endl
             << new_value[3] << endl << new_value[4] << endl << endl;

}
```

Creating one `int` array that is initialized and another `int` array that is not initialized.

Opening an output file for writing in binary format. Note the use of `ios::out | ios:: binary`.

We use the `write` member function to write in binary format.

The array, `value[]`, is an `int` type array. We must cast this as a character array using `reinterpret_cast` to write it in binary.

We must close the file after writing to it because we will reopen the file for reading.

This is the number of bytes that we are writing to the file.

Opening an input file for reading in binary format. Note that the file name `L18_3.DAT` is identical to the file opened for writing. Note also the use of `ios :: in | ios :: binary`.

We use the `read` member function to read in binary format.

The array, `new_value[]`, is an `int` type array. We must cast this as a character array using `reinterpret_cast` to read it in binary.

This is the number of bytes that we are reading from the file.

We print the `new_value` array. The output shows that the `new_value[]` array has successfully received the `value[]` array elements.

Output

```
New value array
2
4
6
8
10
```

The `new_value[]` array is the same as the `value[]` array.

Description

Opening an output file for writing in binary. To open an output file for writing in binary, we use the form:

```
ofstream out_ob ("name", ios :: out | ios :: binary);
```

where `out_ob` is a programmer-chosen output file object name, and `name` is the file name. The second argument in the parentheses:

```
ios :: out | ios :: binary
```

is required to prepare the file for writing in binary. You must type it exactly as shown, with two colons (the scope resolution operator) after `ios` and a "`|`".

Opening an input file for reading in binary. To open an input file for reading in binary, we use the form:

```
ifstream in_ob ("name", ios :: in | ios :: binary);
```

where `in_ob` is a programmer-chosen input file object name, and `name` is the file name. The second argument in the parentheses:

```
ios :: in | ios :: binary
```

is required to prepare the file for reading in binary.

Writing to a file in binary. We use the `write` member function to write to a binary file. The form is

```
out_ob.write (reinterpret_cast<char*> (address), num_bytes);
```

where `out_ob` is as before, `address` is the address of the beginning of the memory cells being written to the file, and `num_bytes` is the number of bytes to be copied from memory to the file. In this lesson's program, the line:

```
outfile . write (reinterpret_cast<char*> (value),
                 5 * sizeof  (int));
```

writes to the file associated with `outfile` (which is `L18_3.DAT`) the elements of the array `value`. The number of bytes to be copied is specified to be five times the number of bytes used for an integer (`5 * sizeof(int)`). The address of the beginning of the `value[]` array (represented by `value`) is the beginning of the memory region being copied to the file. The operator

```
reinterpret_cast<char*>
```

makes C++ interpret the `value` address to represent the beginning of an array of characters, not integers as the array is declared in the program! That is, the declaration:

```
int value[5] = {2, 4, 6, 8, 10};
```

is reinterpreted, in effect, to be an array of characters. This allows C++ to copy bytes without regard to grouping (like `int` or `double` sized groups) from memory to the file. Since the number of bytes is specified to be `5 * sizeof(int)`, the correct number of bytes (going to the end of the array) is copied.

Reading from a binary file. We use the `read` member function to read from a binary file. The form is

```
in_ob . read (reinterpret_cast<char*> (address), num_bytes);
```

where *in_ob* is as before, *address* is the address of the beginning of the memory cells to which the bytes are copied, and *num_bytes* is the number of bytes to be copied from the file to memory. In this lesson's program, the line:

```
infile . read (reinterpret_cast<char*> (value),
               5 * sizeof (int));
```

reads the file associated with `infile` (which is `L18_3.DAT`). The number of bytes read and copied is specified to be five times the number of bytes used for an integer (`5 * sizeof(int)`). The address of the beginning of the `value[]` array (represented by `value`) is the beginning of the memory region to which the file information is copied. The operator

```
reinterpret_cast<char*>
```

makes C++ interpret the `value` address to represent the beginning of an array of characters, not integers in a manner previously explained.

Closing the file. We must close the file after we write to it because we later open it for reading. The line

```
outfile.close ();
```

accomplishes the task.

Value of storing data in a binary file. When dealing with large amounts of data, we may exceed a computer's main memory space. By writing data to a file and later in a program reading the data from that file, we can manipulate large amounts of data using mass storage rather than main memory, thereby reducing the likelihood for exceeding main memory's capabilities. While text files can be used in the same manner, binary files create much faster program execution times.

LESSON EXERCISES

LESSON 18.1 EXERCISES

1. True or false:

a. We cannot combine source codes in different files in C++.

b. With large programs, it is easier to put everything in one file to avoid frequently switching from one file to another.

c. C++ allows us to combine multiple files of the same code.

d. Preprocessor directives are not compiled.

e. #include "class1.h" is the same as #include <class1.h>.

Solutions

1. a. false
b. false
c. false
d. true
e. false

LESSON 18.2 EXERCISES

1. For aa = 0xAD3F, bb = 0xCC43, cc = 0xAC23, dd = 0xFFFB, ee = 0x23F2, find:

a. aa & bb

b. cc | dd

c. dd ^ ee

d. cc

e. aa >> 5

f. dd << 4

Express each of the above in hexadecimal notation according to Table 18.2.

LESSON 18.3 EXERCISES

1. True or false:

a. Writing to a text file is faster than writing to a binary file.

b. When we open a binary file, we need to specify that the file is meant for binary input or output.

c. The write() function writes data from a file to memory.

d. The read() function reads data from memory.

e. After writing to a file, we should close the file so we can read from it.

2. Find the error(s), if any, in the following statements (assuming the declarations in this lesson's program).

a. infile . read (reinterpret_cast (char*) (value), 5 * sizeof (int));

b. outfile . write (reinterpret_cast<char*> (value), 5);

c. ofstream outfile ("C:\\L18_3.DAT", ios::out || ios::binary);

d. outfile.close;

Solutions

1. a. true
   b. true
   c. false
   d. false
   e. true

2. a. `infile . read (reinterpret_cast<char*> (value), 5 * sizeof (int));`
   b. `outfile . write (reinterpret_cast<char*> (value), 5 *sizeof (int));`
   c. `ofstream outfile ("C:\\L18_3.DAT", ios::out | ios :: binary);`
   d. `outfile.close ();`

APPENDIX A

BINARY REPRESENTATION OF NUMBERS

INTEGERS

The problem with the Chapter 1 integer binary scheme is illustrated when the operation of addition is performed on those binary numbers. To add digits in binary the following rules (which are analogous to the decimal rules) apply:

1. $0 + 0 = 0$
2. $1 + 0 = 1$
3. $1 + 1 = 0$ and carry 1 to the column to the left.
4. $1 + 1 +$ carried $1 = 1$ and carry 1 to the column to the left.
5. Any digit to be carried to the left of the leftmost column is to be lost.

EXAMPLE: Perform the following additions using the Chapter 1 signed binary representation:

1. $47 + 58$
2. $23 + (-48)$

Solution: These numbers can be written in the Chapter 1 signed binary scheme in the following way:

$$
\begin{aligned}
47 &= 00101111 \\
58 &= 00111010 \\
23 &= 00010111 \\
-48 &= 10110000
\end{aligned}
$$

Using the rules to add 47 and 58 we get (adding digits starting in the right column):

1 1 1 1 1	Carried ones
0 0 1 0 1 1 1 1	(47)
+ 0 0 1 1 1 0 1 0	(58)
0 1 1 0 1 0 0 1	(105)

The decimal representation of the result is $64 + 32 + 8 + 1 = 105$ (which is correct).

If we use the same procedure to add 23 and −48 we get:

1 1	Carried ones
0 0 0 1 0 1 1 1	(23)
+ 1 0 1 1 0 0 0 0	(−48)
1 1 0 0 0 1 1 1	(−71)

The decimal representation of the result is $-(64 + 4 + 2 + 1) = -71$ (however, the correct answer is -25).

Thus, this particular method does not work for handling negative integer addition. One could create new rules for handling this situation; however, a more efficient way to do it is to create a different way of representing negative numbers, and this is what is done in most computers.

The most popular binary representation for negative integers is called *two's complement*. For the sake of brevity, consider a 4-bit representation (which gives the placeholders, sign $2^2\ 2^1\ 2^0$). The two's complement 4-bit representation for all possible integers is:

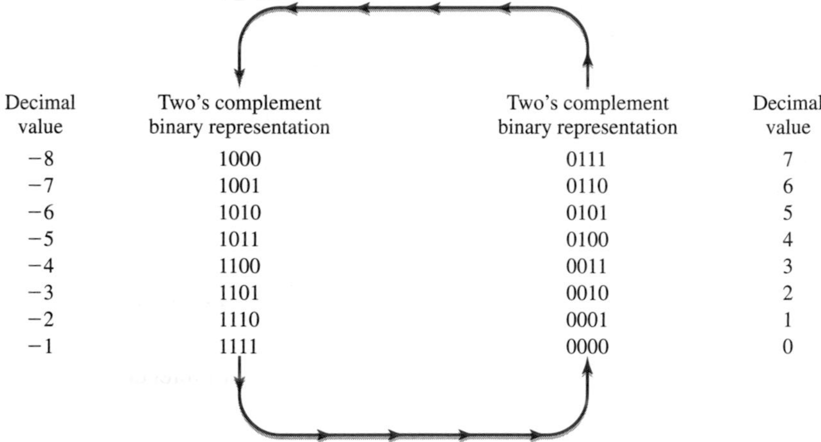

Decimal value	Two's complement binary representation	Two's complement binary representation	Decimal value
−8	1000	0111	7
−7	1001	0110	6
−6	1010	0101	5
−5	1011	0100	4
−4	1100	0011	3
−3	1101	0010	2
−2	1110	0001	1
−1	1111	0000	0

We have deliberately illustrated two's complement with two columns—eight numbers in each column—because it highlights the correspondence of the two binary representations in each row. Note that the two's complement representation of the positive integers is the same as our standard signed binary scheme. However, the negative integers are represented by a completely different system. The negative integers are essentially a "reverse" or complement of the positives—where one has 1s the other has 0s. Consider the two's complement representations of −8 and 7.

−8	1000
7	0111

where −8 has 0s, 7 has 1s, and where −8 has 1, 7 has 0. Similarly, the complement of 0010 is 1101.

The following rules can be discerned from the two's complement representation for converting negative numbers to and from two's complement.

To convert from a negative decimal value to two's complement	To convert from a two's complement (with the leftmost digit being 1) to decimal
1. Temporarily ignore the negative sign and subtract 1 from the positive integer.	1. Reverse all the bits by switching 1s to 0s and 0s to 1s.
2. Determine the binary representation of the positive integer found in step 1.	2. Determine the decimal representation of the binary number found in step 1 using the standard procedure for evaluating decimal values from binary.
3. Reverse all the bits by switching 1s to 0s and 0s to 1s.	3. Add 1 to the decimal value and put in the negative sign.

EXAMPLE: Determine:

1. The eight bit two's complement representation of −48, and
2. The decimal representation of 11011110.

Solution:

1. a. Ignoring the negative sign and subtracting 1 gives 47.
   b. The binary representation of 47 is 00101111.
   c. Reversing the bits gives −48 = 11010000.
2. a. Reversing the bits gives 00100001.
   b. The decimal representation of this is 33.
   c. Adding 1 and putting in a negative sign gives 11011110 = −34.

Note that the leftmost bit in the two's complement representation still acts as a sign bit in that all numbers with zero in that location are positive and all with one are negative. The largest number we can represent with eight bits is 01111111 = 127. The smallest number is 10000000 = −128.

An abbreviated 8-bit two's complement representation of integers is:

Decimal value	Two's complement 8 bit binary representation	Two's complement 8 bit binary representation	Decimal value
−128	10000000	01111111	127
−127	10000001	01111110	126
−126	10000010	01111101	125
−125	10000011	01111100	124
.	.	.	.
.	.	.	.
−4	11111100	00000011	3
−3	11111101	00000010	2
−2	11111110	00000001	1
−1	11111111	00000000	0

The question then becomes does the two's complement method of representation perform addition of negative numbers correctly? The example below demonstrates that it does.

EXAMPLE: Add 23 and −48 using two's complement representation and the rules for addition that were laid out previously.

Solution: The two's complement representation for −48 is 11010000 and for 23 is 00010111. The addition is:

```
   1 1          Carried ones
  00010111      (23)
+ 11010000      (−48)
  --------
  11100111      (−25)
```

Converting 11100111 to decimal gives −25, which is correct.

Thus, it can be seen that the two's complement scheme successfully handles the addition of negative numbers (which is, of course, subtraction). Note that all the bits in the cell are handled by the same addition rules, even the sign bit. In other words, the two's complement representation allows all the bits to be treated alike. This is an advantage because it simplifies the instructions needed for arithmetic operations. Note also that multiplication is simply repeated addition, and division is repeated subtraction. This means that the operations shown in this section represent, in concept, all the fundamental arithmetic operations on integers.

When does this scheme run into problems? Consider the 4-bit two's complement scheme and add 1 to 7. We know the correct answer is 8, but the signed 4-bit binary addition gives:

```
  111      Carried ones
  0001     (1)
+ 0111     (7)
  ----
  1000     (−8)
```

The decimal representation of 1000 is −8, which is, of course, incorrect. It is incorrect because even though the numbers 1 and 7 can be represented with signed 4 bits, the correct answer, 8, cannot. The arrows drawn around the two's complement table indicate how the numbers "wraparound." For instance adding 2 and 7 gives −7 in two's complement, which is again an incorrect answer. Incorrect answers can also occur for 8-bit representations. For instance, in 8 bits $127 + 1 = -128$ and $127 + 2 = -127$, and so on (which can be seen from the wraparound shown in the 8-bit two's complement table).

EXAMPLE: Add 98 and 115 with an 8-bit two's complement integer representation.

Solution:

```
  1  1          Carried ones
  01100010      (98)
+ 01110011      (115)
  --------
  11010101      (−43)
```

The decimal representation of 11010101 is −43, which is incorrect.

The problem of exceeding the largest or smallest number that can be represented is called *overflow* and must be avoided to assure that the computer gives the correct result. Using a greater number of bits is one way to reduce the likelihood of overflow occurring.

For instance the range for 16 bits is:

$$2^{15} - 1 = 32767$$
$$-2^{15} = -32768$$

And for 32 bits is:

$$2^{31} - 1 = 2147483647$$
$$-2^{31} = -2147483648$$

Clearly, using a greater number of bits increases the range substantially; however, no matter how many bits are used overflow is still a possibility. Overflow is a problem that you must be cognizant of when writing your computer programs.

In summary, integers are most commonly stored in memory with a two's complement representation. Arithmetic operations can be readily performed with this scheme. The number of bits controls the size of the integers that can be represented. Overflow is a problem that can occur regardless of the number of bits used.

REAL NUMBERS

Decimal Representation

Before we describe a binary scheme for representing real numbers it is worthwhile to first describe how decimal real numbers are represented.

Real numbers are most commonly written with a decimal point and trailing digits. Consider, for instance, −547.831. Assume for the time being that it is possible to represent the values 0–9, +, −, and decimal point within a single bit. One way of representing the above number in an 8-bit cell would be:

−	5	4	7	.	8	3	1

One can immediately see that this scheme has a distinct limitation in that the largest number that can be represented is:

9	9	9	9	9	9	9	.

which is not a particularly large number. Should we want to store the number 679,934,000 we would need to use more bits. An improved method of storing real numbers would be using scientific notation. In scientific notation it is possible to store much larger numbers without using more than 8 bits.

Recall that with scientific notation, the number −547.831 would be written -5.47831×10^2. In this representation −5.47831 is called the *mantissa,* 2 is called the *exponent,* and 10 is called the *base*. Once the base has been set, only the mantissa and exponent need to be stored. For instance if we were to reserve the two rightmost bits for the exponent and the other 6 bits for the mantissa, the following numbers could be retained in 8-bit cells:

Decimal point (between bit 1 and bit 2)

Value to be stored	Bit values							
679,934,000 = 6.79934 × 10^8	6	7	9	9	3	4	0	8
98766.5767 = 9.87665767 × 10^4	9	8	7	6	6	5	0	4
0.00068453 = 0.68453 × 10^{-3}	0	6	8	4	5	3	−	3
−547.831 = −.547831 × 10^2	−	5	4	7	8	3	0	2
−0.00059321 = −.59321 × 10^{-3}	−	5	9	3	2	1	−	3
	Mantissa						Exponent	

Note the following:

1. The decimal point does not need to be stored because its location is implicitly known to be located after the first bit in the mantissa.
2. Only six digits can be stored for the mantissa. Trailing digits may be lost on storage.
3. For this scheme the largest positive number that can be stored is 9.99999×10^{99}.
4. The smallest positive number that can be stored is 0.00001×10^{-9}.

Just as we saw with integers, the limitation on bits clearly gives us a limitation on the size of numbers we can store. For integers, the smallest positive number possible was not of significant interest to us because we could easily store the smallest positive integer (which is 1). For real numbers, though, the smallest positive number is important because there may be times in computations when we may be interested in storing very small positive numbers.

When we look at the range of numbers for our 8 bit scheme we see an imbalance in the size of the largest and smallest possible numbers. In other words, 9.99999×10^{99} is a very large number, but 0.00001×10^{-9} is not a particularly small number. It would be better if we could somehow store fewer numbers on the "large side" and more numbers on the "small side" with the same number of bits.

This, in fact, can be done if we modify the meaning of our exponents. For instance, we can store 99 in the exponent but interpret it to be 10^{49} which means that we subtract 50 from the stored number to get the true meaning. In reverse, to store our desired number we should add 50 to the exponent. The table below gives examples using two bit exponents:

Desired value to represent	Stored in last two bits
10^{49}	99
10^{28}	78
10^{08}	58
10^{-8}	42
10^{-22}	28
10^{-35}	15
10^{-59}	−9

From this table it can be seen that the largest and smallest positive numbers that can be stored are 9.99999×10^{49} and 0.00001×10^{-59}, respectively. This optimizes the use of our bit storage in that both very large and very small numbers can be stored. The exponent that we have stored is called a biased exponent. In our case the bias is 50.

The table below gives examples using our biased scheme:

Value to be stored	Bit values using biased exponents							
$679{,}934{,}000 = 6.79934 \times 10^8$	6	7	9	9	3	4	5	8
$98766.5767 = 9.87665767 \times 10^4$	9	8	7	6	6	5	5	4
$0.00068453 = 0.68453 \times 10^{-3}$	0	6	8	4	5	3	4	7
$-547.831 = -.547831 \times 10^2$	–	5	4	7	8	3	5	2
$-0.00059321 = -.59321 \times 10^{-3}$	–	5	9	3	2	1	4	7
$0.000000000002754 = 0.2754 \times 10^{-11}$	0	2	7	5	4	0	3	9
$-0.000000007896 = -.7896 \times 10^{-8}$	–	7	8	9	6	0	4	2
	Mantissa						Exponent	

Of course, we cannot store decimal numbers in our bits. However, the described method has many of the concepts used in storing real numbers in a binary scheme.

Binary Representation

We start this discussion by showing a method for converting a decimal real number to a binary real number.

EXAMPLE: Determine the 8-bit binary representation of the decimal number 5.3879.

Solution: This problem can be solved by repeated comparisons of a decimal number to the line of powers of two (in Chapter 1 shown as 4 2 1 0.5 0.25 0.125 0.0625 0.03125).

Follow the table below from left to right, line by line.

	STEP 1—Compare the value in column 1 to the numbers in the line below which are all powers of 2. Put the value 1 into the location for the power of 2, which is just less than or equal to the compare value (put 0 into unfilled places to the left).								**STEP 2**— Find the value of the current binary number.	**STEP 3**— Get the new compare value by subtracting the original decimal number from the current binary number.
	4	**2**	**1**	**0.5**	**0.25**	**0.125**	**0.0625**	**0.03125**		
Compare **5.3879**	1	—	—	—	—	—	—	—	= 4	5.3879 – 4 = 1.3879
Compare **1.3879**	1	0	1	—	—	—	—	—	= 5	5.3879 – 5 = 0.3879
Compare **0.3879**	1	0	1	0	1	—	—	—	= 5.25	5.3879 – 5.25 = 0.1379
Compare **0.1379**	1	0	1	0	1	1	—	—	= 5.375	5.3879 – 5.375 = 0.0129
Compare **0.0129**	1	0	1	0	1	1	0	0	= 5.375	5.3879 – 5.375 = 0.0129

The final result is that decimal 5.3879 is represented in 8-bit binary (not counting the radix point) as 101.01100.

Note that this value does not come out to be exactly 5.3879. If we were to carry more binary digits, we could get closer to the desired value. For instance, binary 101.0110001101 is equal to decimal 5.3876953125, which is still not exactly 5.3879. One can see that it may take very many bits to represent decimal numbers to a high degree of accuracy. In fact, it is not unusual that a number that can be expressed in only a few decimal digits requires many binary digits. Try converting decimal 3.7 to binary to see this. You will sometimes see the effect of this in the programs you write. There may be times when your answers should be zero, but the output may show 0.2345×10^{-80} or some other very small number because precision is lost in the conversion from decimal to binary.

We can also use scientific notation in binary. As with decimal representations of scientific notation, we typically normalize the mantissa—that is, put the radix point to the right of the leftmost digit. For example:

$$101.01100 = 1.0101100 \times 2^2$$

When we store binary real numbers we can utilize many of the same techniques that we illustrated in storing decimal real numbers. These are:

1. Reserve separate portions of the cell for the mantissa and exponent.
2. Avoid using a bit for the radix point since its location is implicitly known.
3. Using a biased exponent optimizes the ability of the storage space to handle large numbers and small fractions.

In addition, we can avoid storing the leftmost digit in a normalized binary number in scientific notation because it is always 1. That is, we need to store only the fractional part of the mantissa since the leftmost 1 and the radix point are known implicitly.

There are numerous methods for storing real numbers. A standard developed by the Institute of Electrical and Electronic Engineers (IEEE) is illustrated in Fig. A.1. It uses 4 bytes (or 32 bits) with:

1. 23 bits for the fractional part of the mantissa.
2. 8 bits for the exponent which is biased by 127 (meaning $00000000 = -127$, $01111111 = 1$, $11111111 = 128$, etc.).
3. 1 bit for the sign of the mantissa with 0 being positive and 1 being negative.

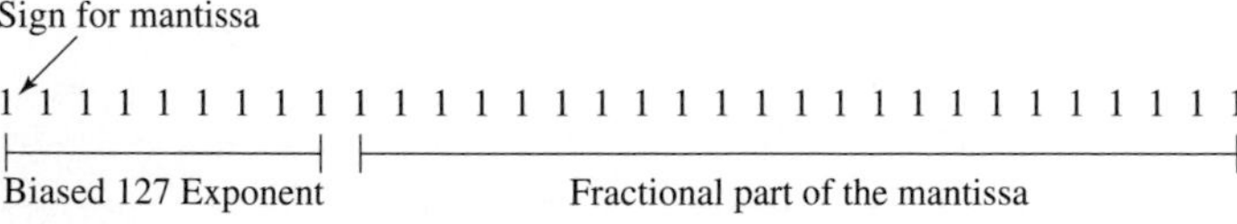

Figure A.1

IEEE format for binary representation of real numbers.

The example below illustrates this format.

EXAMPLE: Determine the decimal meaning for the IEEE 32-bit real number representation shown:

Sign for mantissa

1 1 0 0 0 1 1 0 1 0 1 0 1 1 0 0 0 1 1 0 0 0 0 1 0 1 1 1 0 0 1 0

Biased 127 Exponent — Fractional part of the mantissa

Solution: The exponent before considering the bias is:

Base 2 placeholders	2^7	2^6	2^5	2^4	2^3	2^2	2^1	2^0
Decimal value of placeholders	128	64	32	16	8	4	2	1
Binary digits	1	0	0	0	1	1	0	1
Binary digit times decimal value	128	0	0	0	8	4	0	1

This gives $128 + 8 + 4 + 1 = 141$. The bias is 127, which means this exponent is $141 - 127 = 14$.

Using the sign and fractional part of the mantissa gives that the stored bits represent:

$$-1.01011000110000101110010 \times 2^{14}$$

Moving the radix point 14 places gives the representation:

$$-101011000110000.10111010$$

which is $-(2^{14} + 2^{12} + 2^{10} + 2^9 + 2^5 + 2^4 + 2^{-1} + 2^{-3} + 2^{-4} + 2^{-5} + 2^{-7}) = -22064.72656$

Other formats exist for representing real numbers. One is given here only for the purpose of illustrating some of the concepts.

In summary, like integers, real numbers can be represented in a binary scheme. Scientific notation is used for efficient storage of real numbers. A biased exponent optimizes the ability to store large and small numbers. Even with scientific notation, many numbers that can easily be represented in decimal cannot be exactly represented in binary even with 32 bits.

APPENDIX B

CHARACTER ARRAY FUNCTIONS

The program in this appendix uses most of the character array manipulation functions. The ones in this program are the ones you will most commonly use. You do not need to study or carefully read this program. It is provided primarily as a reference for you so that when you want to use any of these functions you have an example from which to work. However, you should read the rightmost column of the summary table. Doing this will make you aware of the operations that you can perform with these functions.

In looking at the table, you should be aware that the examples in the table follow the code in the program. Thus, to understand the details, you should look at both the table and the source code. We use the character array, `hello[50]`, to hold the contents of the string that we manipulate. This string is initialized to be `"Good"`. With operations of the various functions it progresses to be `"Good morning!"`, `"Good morning! John."`, and `"Good morning! Linda."`.

Many of the string functions require two strings as input arguments. In these examples, we frequently use the string `hello[]` whose address (represented by `hello` without brackets) is an argument in the functions' parameter lists. A second argument is frequently a string constant indicated by a string enclosed in double quotes. Remember that both of these arguments are addresses and that any string in double quotes is an address! Thus, should you want to use these functions in your programs you must use addresses as arguments. This means that where we have shown strings in double quotes or the string indicated by `hello` without brackets, you may use any other form of indicating an address as an argument provided that the address is an address of a character array terminating in a null character (that is, a string).

Again, at this point you do not need to read the source code. You should skip now to the paragraph after the output.

Source Code

```
#include <cstring>
#include <cstdlib>
#include <iostream>
#include <fstream>
using namespace std;
```

```
int main ( )
{
  int pos, len, ia, ib;
  char hello[50] = "Good", token_separator[] = "!,\n \t...";
  char *pa, *pb, *pc;
  double da;
  long la;
  unsigned long ula;
  ofstream outfile("C:\\STRFUNC.OUT");

  outfile << "/****** A - function atoi ********************************/\n";
  ia = atoi("-123.45xyz");
  outfile << "A--- atoi() converts -123.45xyz to ia=" << ia << "\n\n\n";

  outfile << "/****** B - function atof ********************************/\n";
  da = atof("-987.65E+01pqr");
  outfile << "B--- atof() converts -987.65E+01pqr to da=" << da << "\n\n\n";

  outfile << "/****** C - function atol ********************************/\n";
  la = atol("-456.89abc");
  outfile << "C--- atol converts -456.89abc to la=" << la << "\n\n\n";

  outfile << "/****** D - function strcat ******************************/\n";
  pa = strcat(hello," morning!");
  outfile << "D--- hello=" << hello << " $$$ String at pa=" << pa << "\n\n\n";

  outfile << "/****** E - function strchr ******************************/\n";
  pb = strchr(hello,'m');
  pos = pb - hello + 1;
  outfile << "E--- Character 'm' is the " << pos << "th character of string"
        << hello << ",\n         String at pb=" << pb << "\n\n\n";

  outfile << "/****** F - function strcmp ******************************/\n";
  ia = strcmp(hello,"Good xyz");
  if (ia < 0)  outfile << "F--- ia=" << ia << ", " << hello
                  << " is less than   Good xyz!\n\n";
  if (ia == 0) outfile << "F--- ia=" << ia << "2d, " << hello
                  <<" is identical to Good xyz!\n\n";
  if (ia > 0)  outfile << "F--- ia=" << ia << "2d, " << hello
                  <<" is greater than Good xyz!\n\n\n";

  outfile << "/****** H - function strcspn *****************************/\n";
  pos = strcspn(hello, "dog");
  outfile << "H--- The first occurrence of any character in substring, dog,  \n"
          " in string " << hello << " is the " << pos + 1 << "nd character, o\n\n\n";


  outfile << "/****** J - function strlen ******************************/\n";
  len = strlen(hello);
  outfile << "J--- Not including the null character, " << hello
        << " has " << len << " characters\n\n\n";
```

```
outfile << "/****** K - function strncat *******************************/\n";
pb = strncat(hello," John. How are you!",5);
outfile << "K--- hello=" << hello << " $$$ String at pb=" << pb << "\n\n\n";

outfile << "/****** L - function strncmp *******************************/\n";
ib = strncmp(hello,"Good car",15);
if (ib > 0) outfile << "L--- ib=" << ib << ", " << hello
                << " is greater than Good car\n\n\n";

outfile << "/****** M - function strncpy *******************************/\n";
pa = strncpy(hello + 14,"Linda. How are you!", 6);
outfile << "M--- hello=" << hello << " $$$ String at pa=" << pa << "\n\n\n";

outfile << "/****** N - function strpbrk *******************************/\n";
pb = strpbrk(hello,"dear");
outfile << "N--- hello=" << hello << " $$$ String at pb=" << pb << "\n\n\n";

outfile << "/****** O - function strrchr *******************************/\n";
pa = strrchr(hello,'m');
outfile << "O--- hello=" << hello << ", String at pa=" << pa << "\n\n\n\n";

outfile << "/****** P - function strspn ********************************/\n";
ia = strspn("Good year",hello);
outfile << "P--- The " << ia + 1
      << "th character 'y' is the first character in oGdo year\n"
         "    that is not present in " << hello << "\n\n\n";

outfile << "/****** Q - function strstr ********************************/\n";
pa = strstr(hello,"Linda");
ia = pa - hello + 1;
outfile << "Q--- Linda was found at position " << ia << " of " << hello
      << " @@@ \n        String at pa=" << pa << "\n\n\n";

outfile << "/****** R - function strtod ********************************/\n";
da = strtod("123.45abc",&pb);
outfile << "R--- Find double number " << da << " in 123.45abc $$$ String at "
         "pb=" << pb << "\n\n\n";

outfile << "/****** S - function strtol ********************************/\n";
la = strtol("98765xyz",&pa, 10);
outfile << "S--- Find long number " << la << " in 98765xyz $$$ String at "
         "pa=" << pa << "\n\n\n";

outfile << "/****** T - function strtoul *******************************/\n";
ula = strtoul("45678pqr",&pc,10);
outfile << "T--- Find unsigned long " << ula << " in 45678pqr $$$ String at "
         "pc=" << pc << "\n\n\n";

outfile << "/****** U  function strtok ********************************/\n";
outfile << "hello=" << hello << ",      token_separator="
      << token_separator << "\n";
```

```
  pa = strtok(hello,token_separator);
  while (pa != NULL)
      {
      outfile << "U--- String at pa=" << pa << "\n";
      pa = strtok(NULL,token_separator);
      }
}
```

Output

```
/****** A - function atoi **********************************/
A--- atoi() converts -123.45xyz to ia=-123

/****** B - function atof **********************************/
B--- atof() converts -987.65E+01pqr to da=-9876.5

/****** C - function atol **********************************/
C--- atol converts -456.89abc to la=-456

/****** D - function strcat ********************************/
D--- hello=Good morning! $$$ String at pa=Good morning!

/****** E - function strchr ********************************/
E--- Character 'm' is the 6th character of string Good morning!,
        String at pb=morning!

/****** F - function strcmp ********************************/
F--- ia=-11, Good morning! is less than    Good xyz!

/****** H - function strcspn *******************************/
H--- The first occurrence of any character in substring, dog,
     in string Good morning! is the 2nd character, o

/****** J - function strlen ********************************/
J--- Not including the null character, Good morning! has 13 characters

/****** K - function strncat *******************************/
K--- hello=Good morning! John $$$ String at pb=Good morning! John

/****** L - function strncmp *******************************/
L--- ib=10, Good morning! John is greater than Good car

/****** M - function strncpy *******************************/
M--- hello=Good morning! Linda. $$$ String at pa=Linda.
```

```
/****** N - function strpbrk ********************************/
N--- hello=Good morning! Linda. $$$ String at pb=d morning! Linda.

/****** O - function strrchr ********************************/
O--- hello=Good morning! Linda., String at pa=morning! Linda.

/****** P - function strspn *********************************/
P--- The 6th character 'y' is the first character in oGdo year
     that is not present in Good morning! Linda.

/****** Q - function strstr *********************************/
Q--- Linda was found at position 15 of Good morning! Linda. @@@
        String at pa=Linda.

/****** R - function strtod *********************************/
R--- Find double number 123.45 in 123.45abc $$$ String at pb=abc

/****** S - function strtol *********************************/
S--- Find long number 98765 in 98765xyz $$$ String at pa=xyz

/****** T - function strtoul ********************************/
T--- Find unsigned long 45678 in 45678pqr $$$ String at pc=pqr

/****** U - function strtok *********************************/
hello=Good morning! Linda.,      token_separator=!,
      ...
U--- String at pa=Good
U--- String at pa=morning
U--- String at pa=Linda
```

DESCRIPTION

- Table B.1 lists the functions used in this lesson's program and gives a brief explanation of each of them.
- The primary string operated on in this program is `hello[]`. In the table, you should be aware of the progression of the changes in this string as the functions operate on it. Notice that the functions have been used in the program and presented in the table in alphabetical order (except for the last function, `strtok`).
- You do not need to memorize the table. You should, however, read the entire table and get a general understanding of what each function does. You should pay particular attention to the example given for each description. These descriptions give you an idea of what is available for your programming needs.
- When you feel that you want to use one of these functions, you should refer to this table and the implementation of the function in the program. With this information, you should be able to use any of these functions in your programs.

TABLE B.1 — Summary of the string functions

	Function name, example, and required header file	Explanation
1	<u>atoi</u> `ia = atoi("-123.45xyz");` *#include<cstdlib>*	Converts a character string in the form of *whitespace sign digits* to an `int` value. The function returns 0 if the input cannot be converted. In case of overflow, the return value is undefined. The example converts only the characters `'-123'` to `int`. Thus, `ia = -123`. Note: If any character is before *sign digits* other than whitespace, no conversion occurs.
2	<u>atof</u> `da = atof("-987.65E+01pqr");` *#include<cstdlib>*	Converts a character string in the form of *whitespace sign digits .digits d|D|e|E sign digits* to a `double`. The function returns 0.0 if the input cannot be converted. In case of overflow, the return value is undefined. The example converts all characters except `'pqr'` to `double`. Thus, `da = -987.65E+01`. Note: If any character is before *sign digits* other than whitespace, no conversion occurs.
3	<u>atol</u> `la = atol("-456.89abc");` *#include<cstdlib>*	Converts a character string in the form of *whitespace sign digits* to a `long int` value. The function returns 0 if the input cannot be converted. In case of overflow, the return value is undefined. The example converts only the characters `'-456'` to long. Thus, `la = -456`. Note: If any character is before *sign digits* other than whitespace, no conversion occurs.
4	<u>strcat</u> `pa = strcat(hello," morning!");` *Note: prior to executing the above code, the string, hello[ ], is,* `"Good"`. *After executing the above code, the string, hello[ ], is,* `"Good morning!"`. *#include<cstring>*	Appends a copy of the second string, `" morning!"`, to the first string indicated by the address, `hello`, and returns a pointer to the first string to which the second string has been concatenated (which means connected or appended). The first character of `" morning!"` overwrites the null character of hello. The array, `hello[]`, must have declared enough space to accommodate `" morning"`.
5	<u>strchr</u> `pb = strchr(hello,'m');` *The string, hello[ ], is,* `"Good morning!"` *#include<cstring>*	Finds the specified character, `m`, in the string pointed to by `hello`. Returns a pointer, `pb`, to the first occurrence of `'m'` in the string hello. A null pointer is returned if `'m'` is not found in hello. The position of `'m'` within the string hello can be calculated using the statement `pos = pb - hello + 1;` where `pos`, converted to `int`, indicates the position of `'m'` in the `hello` string.
6	<u>strcmp</u> `ia = strcmp(hello,"Good xyz");`	Compares the first string, `hello`, and the second string, `Good xyz`, lexicographically. Returns an

TABLE B.1 — *(continued)*

Function name, example, and required header file	Explanation
The string, hello[ ], is, "Good morning!" #include<cstring>	int value, ia, as follows: ia < 0, first string is less than the 2nd string ia = 0, first string is identical to the 2nd string ia > 0, first string is greater than the 2nd string In this example, the first five characters in both strings are identical, but the sixth characters are different. The characters are 'm' and 'x', which have ASCII values of 109 and 120, respectively. The return value ia is calculated as follows: ia = 'm' - 'x' = 109 - 120 = -11. which indicates that the string hello is less than the string Good xyz!
7 strcpy pa = strcpy(hello,"Good Morning!"); *The string, hello[ ], is,* "Good morning!" *Note: This function was not used in this lesson's program. Please see Lesson 7_3 for its use.* #include<cstring>	Copies the second string into the memory cells reserved for the first string, hello. Returns a pointer, assigned to pa, that points to the first string.
8 strcspn pos = strcspn(hello, "dog"); *The string, hello[ ], is,* "Good morning!" #include<cstring>	Finds the first occurrence of any character in the second string in the first string, hello. Returns the position (meaning the location relative to the first character) of the first character in the first string that also appears in the second string. For example, two characters, d and o, in the second string can be found in the first string. Since the position of character 'o' is in front of the position of character 'd', the return value, pos, is the position of character 'o' in the first string, which is 2. Note that because whitespace is a character, two strings with whitespace may match whitespace and not another character.
9 strlen len = strlen(hello); *The string, hello[ ], is,* "Good morning!" #include<cstring>	Returns the length in bytes of string, hello. The length does not include the string terminating null character, in the example, len = 13
10 strncat pb = strncat(hello," John. How are you!",5); *Note: Before executing the above code the string, hello[ ], is,* "Good morning!" *After executing the above code, the string, hello[ ], is,* "Good morning! John."	Appends the first five characters of the second string to the first string, hello. The first character in the second string overwrites the terminating null character in the first string. A null character from the second string is not copied; however, a null character is added to the end of the concatenated string. This means that the concatenated string will not have two null characters at the end. The first string must have enough

(continued)

TABLE B.1 — *(continued)*

	Function name, example, and required header file	Explanation
	#include<cstring>	declared size to accommodate the second string being added to the end. Returns a pointer, pb, to the new concatenated string, hello.
11	<u>strncmp</u> ib = strncmp(hello, "Good car", 15); *The string, hello[ ], is,* "Good morning! John." *#include<cstring>*	Compares the first 15 characters of string, hello, and the second string, Good car, lexicographically. Returns an int value, ib, as follows: ib < 0, first string is less than the 2nd string ib = 0, first string is identical to the 2nd string ib > 0, first string is greater than the 2nd string See Fig. B.1. In this example, the first five (which is less than 15) characters in both strings are identical, but the sixth characters are different. The characters are 'm' and 'c', which have ASCII values of 109 and 99, respectively. The return value ib is calculated as follows: ib = 'm' − 'c' = 109−99 = 10. which indicates that the string hello is greater than the string Good car.
12	<u>strncpy</u> pa = strncpy(hello + 14, "Linda. How are you!", 6); *Note: Before executing the above code, the string, hello[ ], is,* "Good morning! John." *After executing the above code, the string, hello[ ], is,* "Good morning! Linda." *#include<cstring>*	Copies the first six characters, 'Linda.', from the second string to the first string beginning at the address indicated by hello + 14. The expression, hello + 14, indicates 14 characters past the first character. This sort of addition (with pointers) will be explained in more detail in Chapter 11. This function returns a pointer, assigned to pa, to the first string, hello. In the example, the first string at and after hello + 14 positions is replaced by the string 'Linda.'; after the replacement, a null character is added at the end of the new string hello.
13	<u>strpbrk</u> pb = strpbrk(hello, "dear"); *The string, hello[ ], is,* "Good morning! Linda." *#include<cstring>*	Scans the first string, hello, and determines whether it contains any character of the second string. If it finds a match, the function returns a pointer (which is assigned to pb) to the location of the first occurrence of the matching character in the first string. For example, the second string, dear, contains the character 'd' which is also a component of the first string, "Good morning! Linda."; the pointer, pb, then is assigned the address of the character 'd' in "Good" of the first string. If no match is found, a null pointer is returned.
14	<u>strrchr</u> pa = strrchr(hello, 'o'); *The string, hello[ ], is,* "Good morning! Linda." *#include<cstring>*	Scans the first string, hello, for the last occurrence of the specified character 'o'. If it is found, the function returns a pointer (assigned to pa) to the location of the last occurrence of the matching character in the first string. For example, the first string contains three 'o' characters. The pointer, pa, then is the address of the last character 'o' in the first string (that is, 'o' in "morning". If no match is found, a null pointer is returned.

TABLE B.1 — *(continued)*

	Function name, example, and required header file	Explanation
15	strspn ia = strspn("Good year", hello); *The string, hello[ ], is,* "Good morning! Linda." *#include<cstring>*	Returns the length of the initial portion of the first string that contains only characters that are found in the second string. For example, the first five characters in the first string appear in the second string; however the character 'y' in the first string does not appear in the second string, hello. Therefore, ia = 5.
16	strstr pa = strstr(hello,"Linda"); *The string, hello[ ], is,* "Good morning! Linda." *#include<cstring>*	Finds the second string (excluding the null character) in the first string, hello. Returns a pointer, assigned to pa, to the first occurrence of second string in the first string. In the example, both strings contain 'Linda.'; therefore, pa points to the character 'L' of the first string. If the string is not found, a null pointer is returned.
17	strtod da = strtod("123.45abc",&pb); *#include<cstdlib>*	Converts a character string (that must begin with the first nonwhitespace character being a sign, digits, or decimal point) to a double value. One difference between functions strtod() and atof() is that the strtod() argument list contains the address of a pointer variable, &pb. The value of pb is set by the function, strtod, to be the address of the character in the string where the function stops scanning. The function returns 0 if no conversion can be performed. For example, the function stops scanning at 'abc' because this is after the end of the numeric part of the string. Therefore, pb is equal to the address of 'a' in 'abc'. The value of da is 123.45.
18	strtol la = strtol("98765xyz",&pa, 10); *#include<cstdlib>*	Converts a character string (that must begin with the first nonwhitespace character being a sign, digits, or decimal point) to a long value. One difference between functions strtol() and atol() is that the strtol() function provides a number base for converting the string, 10 for this example. In addition the function has as one of its arguments the address of a pointer variable, &pa. The value of pa is set by the function, strtol, to be the address of the character in the string where the function stops scanning. The function returns 0 if no conversion can be performed. For example, the function stops scanning at 'xyz'. Therefore, pa is equal to the address of 'x' in 'xyz'. The value of la is 98765.
19	strtoul ula = strtoul("45678pqr",&pc, 10);	Converts a character string (that must begin with the first nonwhitespace character being a sign, digits, or decimal point) to an unsigned long value. The function provides a number base for converting the string (10, for this example). In addition, the function has as one of its arguments the address of a pointer variable, &pc, where pc is set by the function to point to a

(continued)

TABLE B.1 — *(continued)*

Function name, example, and required header file	Explanation
	character in the string where the function stops scanning. Returns 0 if no conversion can be performed. For example, the function stops scanning at `'pqr'`; therefore, `*pc` is equal to the address of the `'p'` in `'pqr'`. Note that the declaration and usage of `pc` is slightly different from the usage of `pa` and `pb`, but it fulfills a similar function.
#include<cstdlib>	

20 <u>strtok</u>
`pa = strtok(hello,`
`          token_separator);`
`while (pa!=NULL)`
`    {`
`    printf("%10s\n",pa);`
`    pa = strtok(NULL,`
`             token_separator);`
`    }`
The string, hello[ ], is, `"Good morning! Linda."`
Note: the declaration for token_separator is
token_separator[]="!,\n \t...";
Thus, strtok examines the string, hello, for any character in the above string.
#include<cstdlib> for NULL
#include<cstring> for strtok
	Breaks a string into many strings delimited by the null character. Method: It defines a token in the first string, `hello`, by finding the first character in `hello` that *is not* in the `token_separator` string. This becomes the beginning of the first token. It then searches for the first character that *is* in the `token_separator` string (called `delimiter`). It replaces the delimiter in the string with the null character. It returns a pointer (assigned to `pa`) to the beginning of first token (which is the beginning of the string preceding the first token delimiter found). The function, `strtok`, internally saves a pointer to the character after a delimiter is found. In order to continue replacing each subsequent delimiter with a null character in the string, `hello`, we must make subsequent calls to `strtok` not with our string of interest (`hello`, in this case) but with `NULL` (the null pointer) as an argument. Because the call to `strtok` is with `NULL`, `strtok` uses its internally saved pointer as the beginning of the next search for a delimiter. After executing the statements shown, `hello[]` becomes:
	`Good\0morning\0Linda\0`
	If `strtok` reaches the end of the string, `hello`, without defining a new token, it returns the `NULL` pointer. This is the reason for the "(`pa != NULL`)" test expression.

Figure B.1

Function `strncmp()`.

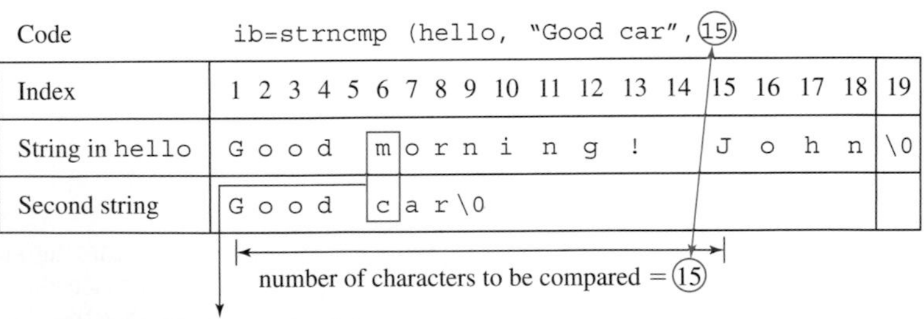

APPENDIX C

OPERATORS

Operator	Name	Associativity	Precedence	Example	Notes
::	Binary scope resolution	Left to right	1	Class1 :: function()	Have function in Class1
()	Parentheses / function	Left to right	2	sin(x)	Call sin function with argument x
[]	Array indexing	Left to right	2	a[5]	Array of five elements
->	Member selection	Left to right	3	ptr -> x	Member named x in a structure that ptr points to
.	Member selection	Left to right	3	str.x	Member x in structure str
static_cast<>	Cast (compile-time, type-checked)	Left to right	3	static_cast<double>x	Creates double value of x
reinterpret_cast<>	Cast (nonstandard)	Left to right	3	reinterpret_cast<int*>ptr	Makes ptr an int* type pointer
++	Post-increment	Left to right	3	x++	Increment x after execution
--	Post-decrement	Left to right	3	x--	Decrement x after execution
*	Pointer indirection	Right to left	4	*ptr	Content of location whose address is stored in ptr
&	Address	Right to left	4	&x	Address of x
!	Logical NOT	Right to left	4	!x	If x is true (1), !x is false (0) and vice versa
~	Bitwise negation	Right to left	4	~x	Toggle 1 bits to 0 and 0 bits to 1

(continued)

Operator	Name	Associativity	Precedence	Example	Notes
-	Negation	Right to left	4	-x	Negate the value of x
+	Plus sign	Right to left	4	+x	Unary plus operator
++	Pre-increment	Right to left	4	++x	Increment x before execution
--	Pre-decrement	Right to left	4	--x	Decrement x before execution
sizeof	Size of data	Right to left	4	sizeof(x)	Return size of x in bytes
new, new[]	Dynamic memory allocation	Right to left	4	ptr = new double[10];	Reserve memory for 10 doubles at address ptr
delete, delete[]	Dynamic memory deallocation	Right to left	4	delete [] ptr;	Unreserve memory reserved by new at ptr
*	Multiply	Left to right	5	x * y	Multiply x and y
/	Divide	Left to right	5	x / y	Divide x by y
%	Modules	Left to right	5	x % y	Find remainder of dividing x by y
+	Addition	Left to right	6	x + y	Add x and y
-	Subtraction	Left to right	6	x - y	Subtract y from x
<<	Left shift	Left to right	7	x << 3	x shifted to left by 3-bit position, which is equal to x = x * 2^3
>>	Right shift	Left to right	7	x >> 3	x shifted to right by 3-bit position, which is equal to x = x / 2^3
<	Less than	Left to right	8	x < y	True (1) if x is less than y, else false (0)
<=	Less than or equal to	Left to right	8	x <= y	True (1) if x is less than or equal to y, else false (0)
>	Greater than	Left to right	8	x > y	True (1) if x is greater than y, else false (0)
>=	Greater than or equal to	Left to right	8	x >= y	True (1) if x is greater than or equal to y, else false (0)

Operator	Name	Associativity	Precedence	Example	Notes
`==`	Equal to	Left to right	9	`x == y`	True (1) if `x` is equal to `y`, else false (0)
`!=`	Not equal to	Left to right	9	`x != y`	True (1) if `x` is not equal to `y`, else false (0)
`&`	Bitwise AND	Left to right	10	`x & y`	Bits become 1s at bits where corresponding bits of `x` and `y` are 1s, else 0s
`^`	Bitwise exclusive OR	Left to right	11	`x ^ y`	Bits become 1s at bits where corresponding bits of `x` and `y` differ, else 0s
`|`	Bitwise OR	Left to right	12	`x | y`	Bits become 1s at bits where corresponding bits of `x` or/and `y` are 1s, 0s if both `x` and `y` are 0
`&&`	Logical AND	Left to right	13	`x && y`	1 if both `x` and `y` are 1, else 0
`||`	Logical OR	Left to right	14	`x || y`	1 if either `x` or/and `y` is 1, 0 if both `x` and `y` are 0
`?:`	Conditional	Right to left	15	`x ? y : z`	If `x` is not 0, `y` is evaluated; else if `x` is 0, `z` is evaluated. For example, `z = (x > y) ? x : y` is equivalent to `z = max(x,y)`.
`=`	Compound assignment	Right to left	16	`x = y`	Assign `x` to `y`
`+=`	Compound assignment	Right to left	16	`x += y`	Equivalent to `x = x + y`
`-=`	Compound assignment	Right to left	16	`x -= y`	Equivalent to `x = x - y`
`*=`	Compound assignment	Right to left	16	`x *= y`	Equivalent to `x = x * y`
`/=`	Compound assignment	Right to left	16	`x /= y`	Equivalent to `x = x / y`
`%=`	Compound assignment	Right to left	16	`x %= y`	Equivalent to `x = x % y`

(continued)

Operator	Name	Associativity	Precedence	Example	Notes
>>=	Compound assignment	Right to left	16	`x >>= y`	Equivalent to `x = x >> y`
<<=	Compound assignment	Right to left	16	`x <<= y`	Equivalent to `x = x << y`
&=	Compound assignment	Right to left	16	`x &= y`	Equivalent to `x = x & y`
|=	Compound assignment	Right to left	16	`x |= y`	Equivalent to `x = x | y`
^=	Compound assignment	Right to left	16	`x ^= y`	Equivalent to `x = x ^ y`
,	Comma/sequential evaluation	Left to right	17	`int x,y;`	First declare `x`, then `y`

APPENDIX D

ASCII TABLE

Decimal	Octal	Hex	Character	Key	Escape sequence
0	0	0	NUL	Ctrl/1	
1	1	1	SOH	Ctrl/A	
2	2	2	STX	Ctrl/B	
3	3	3	ETX	Ctrl/C	
4	4	4	EOT	Ctrl/D	
5	5	5	ENQ	Ctrl/E	
6	6	6	ACK	Ctrl/F	
7	7	7	BEL	Ctrl/G	bell '\a'
8	10	8	BS	Ctrl/H	backspace '\b'
9	11	9	HT	Ctrl/I	horizontal tab '\t'
10	12	A	LF	Ctrl/J	newline '\n'
11	13	B	VT	Ctrl/K	vertical tab '\v'
12	14	C	FF	Ctrl/L	formfeed '\f'
13	15	D	CR	Ctrl/M	carriage return '\r'
14	16	E	SO	Ctrl/N	
15	17	F	SI	Ctrl/O	
16	20	10	DLE	Ctrl/P	
17	21	11	DC1	Ctrl/Q	
18	22	12	DC2	Ctrl/R	
19	23	13	DC3	Ctrl/S	
20	24	14	DC4	Ctrl/T	
21	25	15	NAK	Ctrl/U	
22	26	16	SYN	Ctrl/V	
23	27	17	ETB	Ctrl/W	
24	30	18	CAN	Ctrl/X	
25	31	19	EM	Ctrl/Y	
26	32	1A	SUB	Ctrl/Z	
27	33	1B	ESC	Esc	
28	34	1C	FS	Ctrl/\	
29	35	1D	GS	Ctrl/]	
30	36	1E	RS	Ctrl/=	
31	37	1F	US	Ctrl/-	

(continued)

Decimal	Octal	Hex	Character	Key	Escape sequence
32	40	20	SP	Spacebar	
33	41	21	!		
34	42	22	"		
35	43	23	#		
36	44	24	$		
37	45	25	%		
38	46	26	&		
39	47	27	'		
40	50	28	(		
41	51	29	)		
42	52	2A	*		
43	53	2B	+		
44	54	2C	,		
45	55	2D	-		
46	56	2E	.		
47	57	2F	/		
48	60	30	0		
49	61	31	1		
50	62	32	2		
51	63	33	3		
52	64	34	4		
53	65	35	5		
54	66	36	6		
55	67	37	7		
56	70	38	8		
57	71	39	9		
58	72	3A	:		
59	73	3B	;		
60	74	3C	<		
61	75	3D	=		
62	76	3E	>		
63	77	3F	?		
64	100	40	@		
65	101	41	A		
66	102	42	B		
67	103	43	C		
68	104	44	D		
69	105	45	E		
70	106	46	F		
71	107	47	G		
72	110	48	H		
73	111	49	I		
74	112	4A	J		
75	113	4B	K		

Decimal	Octal	Hex	Character	Key	Escape sequence
76	114	4C	L		
77	115	4D	M		
78	116	4E	N		
79	117	4F	O		
80	120	50	P		
81	121	51	Q		
82	122	52	R		
83	123	53	S		
84	124	54	T		
85	125	55	U		
86	126	56	V		
87	127	57	W		
88	130	58	X		
89	131	59	Y		
90	132	5A	Z		
91	133	5B	[		
92	134	5C	\		
93	135	5D	]		
94	136	5E	^		
95	137	5F	_		
96	140	60	`		
97	141	61	a		
98	142	62	b		
99	143	63	c		
100	144	64	d		
101	145	65	e		
102	146	66	f		
103	147	67	g		
104	150	68	h		
105	151	69	i		
106	152	6A	j		
107	153	6B	k		
108	154	6C	l		
109	155	6D	m		
110	156	6E	n		
111	157	6F	o		
112	160	70	p		
113	161	71	q		
114	162	72	r		
115	163	73	s		
116	164	74	t		
117	165	75	u		
118	166	76	v		
119	167	77	w		

(continued)

Decimal	Octal	Hex	Character	Key	Escape sequence
120	170	78	x		
121	171	79	y		
122	172	7A	z		
123	173	7B	{		
124	174	7C	|		
125	175	7D	}		
126	176	7E	~		
127	177	7F	DEL	Del	

INDEX

SYMBOLS AND NUMBERS

A

D

G

H

I

K

L